CW01305124

The SAGE Handbook of
Coaching

Editorial Board

Dr Anthony Grant
University of Sydney, Australia

Dr Carol Kaufman
Institute of Coaching, USA

Dr Elaine Cox
Oxford Brookes University, UK

Dr Jenny Ferrier-Kerr
University of Waikato, New Zealand

Dr John Bennett
Queen University of Charlotte, USA

Dr Konstantin Korotov
ESMT (European School of Management), Germany

Dr Pansy Lam
University of Hong Kong, Hong Kong

Dr Sunny Stout-Rostron
Sunny Stout-Rostron Associates, South Africa

Professor Andrey Rossohin
Higher School of Economics, Russia

Professor David Clutterbuck
Sheffield Hallam University, UK

Professor Robert Garvey
York St John University, UK

Professor Harald Geissler
Helmut Schmidt University, Germany

The SAGE Handbook of Coaching

Edited by
Tatiana Bachkirova,
Gordon Spence
and David Drake

⑤SAGE reference

Los Angeles | London | New Delhi | Singapore | Washington DC | Melbourne

SAGE

Los Angeles | London | New Delhi
Singapore | Washington DC | Melbourne

SAGE Publications Ltd
1 Oliver's Yard
55 City Road
London EC1Y 1SP

SAGE Publications Inc.
2455 Teller Road
Thousand Oaks, California 91320

SAGE Publications India Pvt Ltd
B 1/I 1 Mohan Cooperative Industrial Area
Mathura Road
New Delhi 110 044

SAGE Publications Asia-Pacific Pte Ltd
3 Church Street
#10-04 Samsung Hub
Singapore 049483

Editor: Susannah Trefgarne
Editorial assistant: Matthew Oldfield
Production editor: Sushant Nailwal
Copyeditor: Jill Birch
Proofreader: Richard Davis
Indexer: Cathryn Pritchard
Marketing manager: Camille Richmond
Cover design: Wendy Scott
Typeset by Cenveo Publisher Services
Printed and bound by CPI Group (UK) Ltd,
Croydon, CR0 4YY

At SAGE we take sustainability seriously. Most of our products are printed in the UK using FSC papers and boards. When we print overseas we ensure sustainable papers are used as measured by the PREPS grading system. We undertake an annual audit to monitor our sustainability.

Introduction & editorial arrangement © Tatiana Bachkirova, Gordon Spence & David Drake, 2017

Chapter 2 © Tatiana Bachkirova 2017
Chapter 3 © Simon Western 2017
Chapter 4 © Anthony M. Grant 2017
Chapter 5 © Trevor Crowe 2017
Chapter 6 © John L. Bennett and Francine Campone 2017
Chapter 7 © Paul Lawrence 2017
Chapter 8 © Konstantin Korotov 2017
Chapter 9 © David Drake and James Pritchard 2017
Chapter 10 © Hany Shoukry 2017
Chapter 11 © Erik de Haan and Judie Gannon 2017
Chapter 12 © David Ashley Clutterbuck and Gordon Spence 2017
Chapter 13 © Sunny Stout-Rostron 2017
Chapter 14 © Peter Jackson 2017
Chapter 15 © Elaine Cox 2017
Chapter 16 © David Drake 2017
Chapter 17 © Alison Maxwell 2017
Chapter 18 © Reinhard Stelter 2017
Chapter 19 © Carmelina Lawton Smith 2017
Chapter 20 © Sophie Francis and Alison Zarecky 2017
Chapter 21 © Travis Kemp 2017
Chapter 22 © Gordon Spence and Stephen Joseph 2017
Chapter 23 © Polly Parker 2017
Chapter 24 © Christian van Nieuwerburgh 2017
Chapter 25 © Geoffrey N. Abbott and Raija Salomaa 2017
Chapter 26 © Andrea D. Ellinger, Robert G. Hamlin and Rona S. Beattie 2017
Chapter 27 © Sean O'Connor and Michael Cavanagh 2017
Chapter 28 © Christian van Nieuwerburgh and Margaret Barr 2017
Chapter 29 © Ruth Q. Wolever, Margaret A. Moore and Meg Jordan 2017
Chapter 30 © Yossi Ives 2017
Chapter 31 © Siegfried Greif 2017
Chapter 32 © Adrian Myers 2017
Chapter 33 © Angela M. Passarelli, Ellen B. Van Oosten and Mark A. Eckert 2017
Chapter 34 © Almuth McDowall 2017
Chapter 35 © David A. Lane 2017
Chapter 36 © David E. Gray 2017
Chapter 37 © Bob Garvey 2017
Chapter 38 © Ioanna Iordanou and Patrick Williams 2017
Chapter 39 © Stella Kanatouri and Harald Geißler 2017
Chapter 40 © Annette Fillery-Travis and Ron Collins 2017

Apart from any fair dealing for the purposes of research or private study, or criticism or review, as permitted under the Copyright, Designs and Patents Act, 1988, this publication may be reproduced, stored or transmitted in any form, or by any means, only with the prior permission in writing of the publishers, or in the case of reprographic reproduction, in accordance with the terms of licences issued by the Copyright Licensing Agency. Enquiries concerning reproduction outside those terms should be sent to the publishers.

Library of Congress Control Number: 2016935241

British Library Cataloguing in Publication data

A catalogue record for this book is available from the British Library

ISBN 978-1-4739-1653-1

Contents

List of Figures ix
List of Tables xi
Notes on the Editors and Contributors xiii

1 Introduction 1
   Tatiana Bachkirova, Gordon Spence and David Drake

PART I POSITIONING COACHING AS A DISCIPLINE

2 Developing a Knowledge Base of Coaching: Questions to Explore 23
   Tatiana Bachkirova

3 The Key Discourses of Coaching 42
   Simon Western

4 Coaching as Evidence-Based Practice: The View Through a Multiple-Perspective Model of Coaching Research 62
   Anthony M. Grant

5 Coaching and Psychotherapy 85
   Trevor Crowe

6 Coaching and Theories of Learning 102
   John L. Bennett and Francine Campone

7 Coaching and Adult Development 121
   Paul Lawrence

8 Coaching for Leadership Development 139
   Konstantin Korotov

9 Coaching for Organisation Development 159
   David Drake and James Pritchard

10 Coaching for Social Change 176
    Hany Shoukry

PART II COACHING AS A PROCESS

11	The Coaching Relationship *Erik de Haan and Judie Gannon*	195
12	Working with Goals in Coaching *David Ashley Clutterbuck and Gordon Spence*	218
13	Working with Diversity in Coaching *Sunny Stout-Rostron*	238
14	Physicality in Coaching: Developing an Embodied Perspective *Peter Jackson*	256
15	Working with Emotions in Coaching *Elaine Cox*	272
16	Working with Narratives in Coaching *David Drake*	291
17	The Use of Feedback for Development in Coaching: Finding the Coach's Stance *Alison Maxwell*	310

PART III COMMON ISSUES IN COACHING

18	Working with Values in Coaching *Reinhard Stelter*	331
19	Coaching for Resilience and Well-being *Carmelina Lawton Smith*	346
20	Working with Strengths in Coaching *Sophie Francis and Alison Zarecky*	363
21	Mindfulness and Coaching: Contemporary Labels for Timeless Practices? *Travis Kemp*	381
22	Coaching for Post-Traumatic Growth: An Appropriate Response to the Devastations of Life? *Gordon Spence and Stephen Joseph*	399
23	Coaching for Role Transitions/Career Change *Polly Parker*	419

PART IV COACHING IN CONTEXTS

24 Interculturally-Sensitive Coaching 439
    Christian van Nieuwerburgh

25 Cross-Cultural Coaching: An Emerging Practice 453
    Geoffrey N. Abbott and Raija Salomaa

26 Coaching in the HRD Context 470
    Andrea D. Ellinger, Robert G. Hamlin and Rona S. Beattie

27 Group and Team Coaching 486
    Sean O'Connor and Michael Cavanagh

28 Coaching in Education 505
    Christian van Nieuwerburgh and Margaret Barr

29 Coaching in Healthcare 521
    Ruth Q. Wolever, Margaret A. Moore and Meg Jordan

30 Coaching in Relationships: Working with Singles, Couples and Parents 544
    Yossi Ives

PART V RESEARCHING COACHING

31 Researching Outcomes of Coaching 569
    Siegfried Greif

32 Researching the Coaching Process 589
    Adrian Myers

33 Neuroscience in Coaching Research and Practice 610
    Angela M. Passarelli, Ellen B. Van Oosten and Mark A. Eckert

34 The Use of Psychological Assessments in Coaching and Coaching Research 627
    Almuth McDowall

PART VI DEVELOPMENT OF COACHES

35 Trends in Development of Coaches (Education and Training):
    Is it Valid, is it Rigorous and is it Relevant? 647
    David A. Lane

36 Towards a Systemic Model of Coaching Supervision 662
    David E. Gray

37	Issues of Assessment and Accreditation of Coaches *Bob Garvey*	680
38	Developing Ethical Capabilities of Coaches *Ioanna Iordanou and Patrick Williams*	696
39	Adapting to Working with New Technologies *Stella Kanatouri and Harald Geißler*	713
40	Discipline, Profession and Industry: How our Choices Shape our Future *Annette Fillery-Travis and Ron Collins*	729

Index   745

List of Figures

2.1	Positioning coaching amongst other disciplines of knowledge	29
2.2	Complexity of factors involved in coaching engagement	30
3.1	The four discourses of coaching	43
3.2	A meta-theory of coaching	57
4.1	Professional expertise, empirical research and evidence-based coaching	64
4.2	The evidence/relevance coaching framework	66
4.3	Growth of coaching publications in business source premier database from 1995 to 2014	68
4.4	The Multiple-Perspective Model of coaching research	70
6.1	Experiential learning cycle	105
6.2	Practical inquiry model	108
6.3	Integrative adult learning approach to coaching	118
9.1	Four ways coaching can contribute to the development of organisations	160
9.2	Degrees of professionalism in coaching	164
12.1	The Agreement–Certainty matrix	228
13.1	Typology of democratic diversity variables	242
13.2	Team strategic capacity: diversity and collective action	244
16.1	An integrative process for working with narratives in coaching	300
17.1	A simple control loop	311
17.2	Feedback at the individual/environmental interface	312
17.3	Feedback as boundary disturbances	322
17.4	A continuum of human motivation related to feedback	323
18.1	Levels of intentional orientation: meanings and values as central in the concept of intentionality – the arrow with the broken line indicates the protreptic ambition in coaching	337
19.1	How coaching helps resilience	356
20.1	Strengths regulation	370
27.1	The hierarchical nature of systems	488
27.2	Three coaching foci for individual coaching	489
27.3	Three coaching foci for team coaching	490
28.1	Global Framework for Coaching in Education	507
33.1	Basic brain anatomy	612
33.2	Levels of analysis in coaching research	614
34.1	The content and reach of psychometric assessments	630
34.2	(Imaginary) neuro-typical profile across a range of ability measures	631
34.3	Neuro-diversive profile: across a range of ability measures	632
34.4	Application of assessments during coaching	632
34.5	Direct relationship between personality and outcomes	634
34.6	Moderated relationship between personality and outcomes	634
34.7	Mediated relationship between personality and outcomes	634

36.1	Interconnected Gestalt fields	666
36.2	TA models: contracts and unconscious processes	668
36.3	The seven foci of supervision	669
36.4	Conceptual framework for coaching supervision	675
40.1	Discipline, profession and industry: key considerations for each concept	741

List of Tables

2.1	An overview of philosophical positions with regard to modernism and postmodernism	26
2.2	Progressive and problematic aspects of modernism and postmodernism	27
2.3	Methods for theory building	34
2.4	Suggestions for knowledge users for differentiating the quality of research, theories and models	36
2.5	Conceptual work and theories of coaching with corresponding philosophical positions	36
2.6	Aspects of coaching practice influenced by the modernist and postmodernist epistemological attitudes	37
3.1	The four discourses of coaching: an overview	45
4.1	Differences between researcher's and practitioner's approach to research	65
6.1	Examples of coaching relationship and process aligned with adult learning	115
7.1	Comparison of six constructive-development frameworks across four broad orders of development	124
7.2	Constructive-developmental measurement tools	127
7.3	Five studies exploring the link between Kegan's orders of consciousness and management effectiveness/motivation	128
7.4	Examples of coaching approaches described by Berger and Fitzgerald (2002) and Berger (2012)	131
7.5	Examples of coaching approaches adopted from Bachkirova (2011)	133
9.1	Five areas where human and organisation development literatures overlap	168
10.1	Four traditions of pedagogies of change	178
11.1	Key recent empirical studies of the coaching relationship	199
11.2	Recent empirical insights on the coach–athlete relationship	204
12.1	Examples of goal dimensions	221
12.2	Varying goal requirements as determined by context	224
12.3	Alternative SMART goal-setting formulations	230
14.1	Contrasting embodied and classical perspectives on physicality	259
15.1	An emotional climate inventory for coaching	285
16.1	How the narrative turn in the social sciences informs coaching	292
17.1	Reasons for using assessments and types of measures used in coaching	315
17.2	Advantages and disadvantages of externally generated feedback	316
17.3	Advantages and disadvantages of internally generated feedback	317
17.4	Summary of feedback perspectives and implications for coaching stance	319
17.5	Comparison of feedback according to learning paradigm	320
17.6	Response to feedback by developmental stage	321
19.1	Six dimensions of psychological well-being	347
19.2	Acceptance and commitment model	354
20.1	Benefits of strengths use	367
20.2	Comparison of formal strengths identification models	369
20.3	Strengths development models	371

22.1	Common outcomes associated with adverse life events	403
22.2	Foundations of the collaborative recovery model	408
23.1	Key theoretical models of change and transition that are commonly used in coaching	424
24.1	Bennett's stages of intercultural sensitivity for coaches	444
24.2	Cultural proficiency	445
24.3	Suggested ideas for best practice in intercultural coaching	448
27.1	Characteristics of working groups and team	492
28.1	Characteristics of working groups and team	507
31.1	Framework of the general evaluation of coaching	573
31.2	Comparison between different taxonomies of outcomes	574
31.3	Classification of post-coaching outcomes	576
31.4	Antecedents of coaching outcome	580
31.5	Coaching process	583
32.1	A review of hypothesis testing coaching process literature	597
32.2	Summary of descriptive studies	601
33.1	Regions of interest involved in coaching-relevant neural systems	616
33.2	Personal discoveries in intentional change theory	620
34.1	Psychometric features	629
34.2	Principles for 360-degree feedback in coaching	637
38.1	The key ethical responsibilities of three professional coaching associations	703
39.1	Examples of purpose-built technologies	716
39.2	Empirical research overview	721

Notes on the Editors and Contributors

THE EDITORS

Tatiana Bachkirova is Professor of Coaching Psychology and Co-Director of the International Centre for Coaching and Mentoring Studies at Oxford Brookes University, UK. Her current research interests are in the area of philosophy and psychology of the development and supervision of coaches. Her publications include *Developmental Coaching: Working with the Self* and the *Complete Handbook of Coaching* (2 editions). Tatiana is a past Co-editor in Chief of *Coaching: An International Journal of Theory, Research and Practice* and currently serves on the editorial boards of three academic journals. She is a member of the Scientific Advisory Council at the Institute of Coaching at Harvard and also Convenor and Chair of the International Conference on Coaching Supervision.

Gordon Spence is Course Director of the Master of Business Coaching at Sydney Business School, University of Wollongong. His current research interests are in the area of employee engagement, workplace wellbeing and the facilitation of autonomous motivation using coaching. Gordon has published numerous journal articles and book chapters on these topics, is co-author of *Management: A Focus on Leaders* and a past section Editor of the *Oxford Handbook of Happiness*. He is a past co-chair of Scientific Advisory Council at the Institute of Coaching at Harvard (2009–2013) and also a current Harnish Scholar, collaborating on coaching research projects with colleagues in the United States and South Africa.

David Drake is founder and Director of the Center for the Narrative Coaching in the USA. His current research interests include integrative development theory as a new paradigm for change and attachment theory (e.g. moments of meeting) as a resource for accelerated rapport and regulation. His publications include *The Philosophy and Practice of Coaching* (editor) and *Narrative Coaching: Bringing Our New Stories to Life*. David has written over fifty publications on narratives, coaching and developing coaches in academic journals and books. David is a Senior Advisory Board member for *Coaching: An International Journal of Theory, Research and Practice*, and he is a Thought Leader for the Institute of Coaching at Harvard.

THE CONTRIBUTORS

Geoffrey N. Abbott is Director of Executive Coaching in the QUT Graduate School of Business in Brisbane, Australia. He facilitates and coaches across programs related to Leadership, including within the Executive MBA, and corporate leadership development programs. Geoff has expertise in global executive coaching. He spent three years coaching with multinational companies and conducting research in Central America and continues to have an interest in the region. Geoff's executive experience is with the Special Broadcasting Service, Australia where he managed strategic planning. He is a Member of the Association for Coaching Global Advisory Board, and co-editor of the *Routledge Companion to International Business Coaching* (Moral and Abbott, 2011).

Margaret Barr is Lead Associate (Scotland) for Growth Coaching International. Her career in schools included teaching business education and economics, head of department, head teacher of a city secondary school, and mentor for aspiring head teachers studying for the Scottish Qualification for Headship, and for new head teachers. She returned to university in 2012 to take an MSc in coaching psychology, and now works with school leaders as a coach and facilitator of coaching training programmes. She is a coach for head teachers on the fellowship programme of the Scottish College for Educational Leadership, and is a certified thinking partner. Voluntary roles include book review editor for the peer-reviewed journal Coaching: An International Journal of Theory, Research and Practice, and communications co-ordinator for supervision with the Association for Coaching.

Rona S. Beattie is a Professor of Human Resource Development (HRD) in the Department of Business Management, Glasgow School for Business and Society, Glasgow Caledonian University, Scotland. She has published widely, presented many papers at international conferences, and is a member of a number of journal editorial boards. While her teaching and research interests are diverse including healthcare management, employee engagement, voluntary sector leadership, and HRM in public service organizations, her first and greatest research passion continues to be coaching, mentoring and the role of line managers as facilitators of learning. She is also a chartered fellow of the Chartered Institute of Personnel and Development (CIPD) and a fellow of the Higher Education Academy (HEA) both in the United Kingdom.

John L. Bennett, PhD, PCC, BCC, is Associate Professor of Business and Behavioral Science and Director of graduate programs at the McColl School of Business, Queens University of Charlotte (USA). He is past-president of the Graduate School Alliance for Educating Coaches (GSAEC) and chaired the 2012 Summit on the Future of Coaching. In 2010, he was named a charter Fellow in The Lewin Center and Founding Fellow of the Institute of Coaching, Harvard Medical School. He is co-author of the book *Coaching for Change* (Routledge, 2013).

Francine Campone, EdD, MCC, is the Director of the Evidence-Based Coaching Program at Fielding Graduate University and coaches leaders through personal and organizational transitions. Her coaching focuses on helping leaders to acquire the skills to clearly articulate vision, generate engagement and commitment, facilitate change within organizations; and to communicate clearly and effectively. Her recent publications include studies on the development of coaches, reflective learning and coaching/psychotherapy boundaries. She is past president of the Graduate School Alliance for Education in Coaching and a contributor to the Academic

Standards for Graduate Coach Education. She is serving on the Academic Standards Committee of GSAEC in developing a peer review process.

Michael Cavanagh is an academic, practitioner and consultant in the field of coaching and leadership development. He is currently the Deputy Director of the Coaching Psychology Unit at the University of Sydney and Visiting Professor at the Institute of work based learning at Middlesex University. Michael's teaching focuses on preparing coaches to work with leaders and teams in complex settings. He is the principal author of the Standards Australia Handbook of Organisational Coaching – one of the world's first ISO aligned National guidelines for the training of coaches and the provision of coaching services. Michael's passion is assisting leaders and organisations to understand and address complex challenges in ways that increase the sustainability of the organisation, its people and the planet.

David Ashley Clutterbuck is Visiting Professor in the coaching and mentoring faculties of Sheffield Hallam, Oxford Brookes and York St John Universities and adjunct faculty at Ashridge. Author or co-author of more than 60 books, he is one of the co-founders of the European Mentoring and Coaching Council. He chaired the EMCC's research committee, in which he still participates, and is now EMCC special ambassador, with a role that includes spreading good practice in coaching and mentoring. His research agenda is driven by helping people and organisations have the quality conversations they need (which may be with themselves) and by seeking to question the evidence base for received wisdom. His co-authored book, *Beyond Goals*, is one example of this.

Ron Collins is an Executive Partner in IBM's Cognitive Solutions Team and he leads large and complex deals world-wide involving Big Data, Analytics and Cognitive Solutions. He specialised in data intensive industries particularly banking but also mobile telecommunications and the Public Sector. He has been involved with large scale data integration, warehousing, analytics and statistical modelling for more than ten years and has worked with major UK banks and with banks worldwide including the Middle East and the Asia-Pacific region. He is currently working on designing and implementing large scale data fabrics for major Banks (retail and investment) including a wide range of open source and propriety software (Hadoop, Spark, Atlas, Cassandra, Titan, etc.) designed to be cloud portable and to run on both pure and hybrid cloud architectures.

Elaine Cox is Principal Lecturer and Co-Director of the International Centre for Coaching and Mentoring Studies at Oxford Brookes University. As well as developing and leading the MA and the Doctor of Coaching and Mentoring programmes at Brookes and authoring many academic articles and books, she is the founding editor of the International Journal of Evidence-Based Coaching and Mentoring. Elaine's research interests include leadership coaching and examining the theoretical underpinnings of coaching and how these impact practice.

Trevor Crowe, PhD, is a Senior Lecturer with the School of Psychology at the University of Wollongong, Australia, where he is currently Director of the Master of Professional Psychology course. He co-coordinates several research projects covering a range of topics including coaching in mental health and substance abuse recovery settings, trauma recovery, sports, and clinical supervision. He has developed several programmes to support recovery and psychological growth including families, people with mental illness and/or substance abuse disorders, and clinicians. Trevor is a Psychologist, Psychotherapist and Certified Addictions Counsellor with over 25 years clinical experience.

Erik de Haan, PhD, is a leadership and organisation development consultant, psychodynamic psychotherapist, executive coach and supervisor. He is the Director of the Ashridge Centre for Coaching and programme leader of the Ashridge Master's (MSc) in Executive Coaching, and the Ashridge Postgraduate Diploma (PG Dip) in Organisational Supervision. Erik is also Professor of Organisation Development & Coaching at the VU University of Amsterdam. He has written more than 150 articles and eleven books in different languages, among which are *Fearless Consulting* (2006), *Coaching with Colleagues* (2004, with Yvonne Burger), *Relational Coaching* (2008), *Supervision in Action* (2011), *Coaching Relationships* (2012, edited with Charlotte Sills), *The Leadership Shadow* (2014, with Anthony Kasozi), *Being Supervised—A Guide for Supervisees* (2015, with Willemine Regouin), and *Management Pocketbook Team Coaching* (2016). He serves on the editorial boards of several peer-reviewed journals, such as the *Journal of Philosophy of Management* and APA's *Consulting Psychology Journal*.

Mark A. Eckert, PhD is an Associate Professor in the Hearing Research Program of the Department of Otolaryngology – Head and Neck Surgery at the Medical University of South Carolina. He is a cognitive neuroscientist whose work focuses on the neurobiology of communication disorders in children with reading disabilities and older adults with speech recognition and hearing impairments. His research includes a focus on neural systems that support perception and optimize task performance.

Andrea D. Ellinger is Professor of Human Resource Development in the College of Business and Technology at The University of Texas at Tyler. She is the former editor of *Human Resource Development Quarterly* and is the recipient of the 2012 Academy of Human Resource Development Outstanding Scholar of the Year Award. She has presented and published her research nationally and internationally. She serves on several editorial boards including *Management Learning*, the *International Journal of Evidence Based Coaching and Mentoring*, the *Journal of Workplace Learning*, *Human Resource Development Quarterly*, and is a Consulting Editor for *Adult Education Quarterly*. Her research interests include informal learning in the workplace, organizational learning, employee engagement, evolving managerial roles, managerial coaching, mentoring, and the learning organization concept.

Annette Fillery-Travis is an Associate Professor at Middlesex University where she is a senior coach educator, researcher and author. After a first career in the natural sciences she has followed her interest in professional development first leading the Professional Development Foundation and more recently the Professional Doctorate at Middlesex University and the EC funded Modern Doctorate Research Consortium. Her main focus here has been the development of doctoral provision for advanced practitioners and it underpinning research pedagogy and the accreditation of coach education within organisations. Her consultancy interests include working with organisations (including Fortune 100 companies and the public sector) on the development of their internal coaches and culture.

Sophie Francis is a Coach who helps business owners, entrepreneurs and leaders shift into new directions, guided by their strengths. She is also a writer and Editorial Director for the Langley Group, specialists in positive psychology, emotional intelligence and neuroscience. An accredited R2 Strengths Profiler practitioner, Sophie supports the professional development of strengths coaches, human capital managers and leaders in R2 practitioner training. Her master's research focussed on how people use their strengths in difficult situations.

Judie Gannon is a Senior Lecturer in the International Centre for Coaching and Mentoring Studies (ICCaMs) at Oxford Brookes University, UK. Originally a manager in the international hotel industry Judie joined academia in 1994 after completing an MA in Industrial Relations (Warwick University). Her PhD (Oxford Brookes University, 2007) explored the resourcing and development of managers in international hotel companies. She also completed a PG Cert in Coaching and Mentoring during this time and has supervised students on the Doctorate in Coaching & Mentoring over the last 7 years. Judie has developed and supported several mentoring schemes across different sectors and has written and presented academic and practitioner papers in the areas of international human resource management, management development, coaching and mentoring. She reviews for several high profile academic journals, is a member of the EMCC and CIPD, and serves on the editorial board of the International Journal of Evidence Based Coaching & Mentoring.

Bob Garvey, PhD, FHEA, FRSA is one of Europe's leading academic practitioners of coaching and mentoring. Bob has extensive experience in working across many sectors of social and economic activity. He writes about coaching and mentoring in various outlets including books and journals. He delivers international Webinars on a variety of coaching and mentoring topics. Bob mentors/coaches a number of people from a variety of organisations and walks of life. He is a member of the European Mentoring and Coaching Council (EMCC) and its special ambassador for mentoring. He is also an honorary member of the International Mentoring Association (IMA) and honorary president of Coaching York. In 2014, the journal, 'Coaching at Work' awarded him a life time achievement award for contributions to mentoring. Also in 2014, Bob received the EMCC's mentor award.

Harald Geißler was Professor for Educational Science at Helmut-Schmidt-University Hamburg/Germany. Since the early 1990s his research is focused on organizational learning and business coaching. In his long years of experience as business coaching practitioner, in 2006 he developed the world's first web-based coaching tool: 'Virtual Coaching (VC) (www.virtual-coaching.net) and started to build up an international e-coaching community. On this topic he published more than 20 articles and two books: 2008 *E-Coaching* and 2012 (with Maren Metz) and *E-Coaching und Online-Beratung* (*E-Coaching and Online-Counselling*). Using his research findings as well as his experience as an e-coaching practitioner he is offering an e-coaching education programme.

Anthony M. Grant PhD MA BA(Hons) is a Coaching Psychologist. He is globally recognised as a key pioneer of Coaching Psychology and evidence-based approaches to coaching. In January 2000, Anthony established the world's first Coaching Psychology Unit at Sydney University where he is the Director of the Coaching Psychology Unit. He has over 100 coaching-related publications. He is a Visiting Professor at Oxford Brookes University; a Senior Fellow at the Melbourne School of Business; and an Associate Fellow at the Säid School of Business, Oxford University. In 2007 Anthony was awarded the British Psychological Society Award for outstanding professional and scientific contribution to Coaching Psychology. In 2009 he was awarded the 'Vision of Excellence Award' from Harvard University for his pioneering work in helping to develop a scientific foundation to coaching. He was a 2014 Scientist in Residence for the ABC - the Australian National Broadcaster and in 2016 he was awarded the Australian Psychological Society 'Workplace Excellence Award for Coaching and Leadership'.

David E. Gray is Professor of Leadership and Organisational Behaviour at the University of Greenwich. His research interests, and publication record, include research methods, management learning (particularly coaching and mentoring), professional identity, action learning, reflective learning, management learning in SMEs and the factors that contribute to SME success. He has published books *Doing Research in the Real World* (Sage, 2014) and *A Critical Introduction to Coaching and Mentoring* (Sage, 2016) and articles on research methods, organizational learning, and coaching and mentoring. David has led a number of EU-funded research programmes including one examining the impact of coaching on the resilience of unemployed managers in their job-searching behaviours and another on how action learning can sustain unemployed managers in starting their own business. David is a member of the International Editorial Board of *Management Learning*.

Siegfried Greif, MSCP, is member of the University of Osnabrueck (Germany) and Head of coaching and change management of a consulting institute (www.ifp.de). He was Professor at the Free University of Berlin and had the chair of Work and Organizational Psychology at the University of Osnabrueck (Germany). Major fields of his research are stress at work, change management and coaching. He is editor of a book series on *Innovative Management* of the German Publisher Hogrefe (Goettingen). Among 16 books he has published one in German on Coaching (2008, Hogrefe), is co-editor of a handbook on key concepts of coaching (2017), many articles in journals and diverse book chapters. He teaches coaching at different Universities and gives courses to practitioners.

Robert G. Hamlin is an Emeritus Professor and Chair of Human Resource Development at the University of Wolverhampton, and an independent management and organization development consultant. His research is mainly focused on managerial and leadership effectiveness, managerial coaching effectiveness, and mentoring effectiveness, and the findings have been published nationally and internationally in a wide range of academic and practitioner journals. He has authored/coedited two books, and has contributed numerous chapters to a range of other HRD-related textbooks.

Ioanna Iordanou is currently a Senior Lecturer in Human Resource Management and Coaching and Mentoring at Oxford Brookes University, UK. She is passionate about researching coaching and mentoring and embedding the study and practice of coaching skills in her pedagogic practice. A historian by trade, she thoroughly enjoys tracing the roots of coaching and mentoring practices in the long-forgotten apprenticeships of the pre-Industrial period. She holds an MA, PhD, a Certificate, and a Diploma in Coaching, all from the University of Warwick, UK. She is the author of Values and Ethics in Coaching (Sage, 2016).

Yossi Ives is a qualified life coach specialising in singles relationship issues and has a PhD in Coaching Psychology. He has written *Relationship Coaching* (Routledge, 2014), a landmark book on coaching for relationship success, and *Goal-Focused Coaching* (Routledge, 2012), on harnessing goals to raise performance. Yossi is the co-founder of JEP (Jewish European Professionals) that organises major events for young professionals from across Europe and beyond (www.jep.eu). He is the founder and chairman of Tag International Development, a humanitarian organisation that shares expertise with developing countries (www.tagdevelopment.org), and Tag Institute for Social Development (www.taginstitute.org), a think tank and research centre that addressed pressing social challenges. He is also the author of Applied Jewish Values in the Social Sciences and Psychology (Springer, 2016) and There Must be a Better Way (Devora, 2008), as well as a Hebrew work on Jewish mysticism. For 15 years Yossi was a practicing rabbi. He lives in London and is married with seven children.

Peter Jackson is a professional coach, supervisor, facilitator and academic. His coaching practice has a particular focus on the challenges of general management and the dynamics of individual change within organisations. At Oxford Brookes University he leads various practice modules and supervises research. His own research into physicality and embodiment looks at individual coaches in action in their natural working environment to explore the many ways in which the coach's practice is inseparable from the experience of 'being-in-the-world'. He has an interest in the intersubjective processes of coaching, reflective learning, professional development and the development of research methods. In particular, how to create robust, useful and applicable knowledge for practitioners.

Meg Jordan PhD, RN, CWP, is Chair of Integrative Health Studies, Somatic Psychology and Human Sexuality at the California Institute of Integral Studies in San Francisco. She is a clinical medical anthropologist, RN specializing in integrative and collaborative practice models, a behavioral health specialist, certified health coach, and grant recipient from Aetna Foundation to explore health coaching for underserved populations. She is author of several books including *How To Be A Health Coach: An Integrative Wellness Approach, The Fitness Instinct*, and founding Editor of *American Fitness* Magazine; Co-President of the National Wellness Institute; and former Director of Integrative Practice at the Health Medicine Institute. She serves on the board of National Consortium for Credentialing Health and Wellness Coaches. In addition to mentoring and teaching graduate students, she has a clinical practice in behavioral medicine, working with guided imagery, cognitive restructuring coaching, and helping people navigate integrative health options.

Stephen Joseph PhD, is interested in the study of human flourishing. Known internationally as a leading expert in positive psychology, he is the editor of the ground breaking book *Positive Psychology in Practice: Promoting human flourishing in work, health, education and everyday life*. He studied at the London School of Economics, before going on to gain his doctorate from Kings College London Institute of Psychiatry, Psychology and Neuroscience for his pioneering work in the field of psychological trauma. He is the author of *What Doesn't Kill Us. The new psychology of posttraumatic growth*. A Professor at the University of Nottingham and a coaching psychologist whose focus is on applying ideas from positive psychology, he helps people overcome challenges and find new directions in their personal and professional lives. His most recent book is *Authentic: How to be yourself and why it matters*.

Stella Kanatouri is currently exploring the state of play in technology-assisted coaching through her doctoral research. Having created an online community with over a 1,000 members dedicated to technology-assisted coaching, Stella is endeavouring to narrow the gap between technology-assisted coaching research and practice. After completing her MSc in Psychology during her career in the Hamburg Ballet, Stella switched her focus towards academic work in adult learning approaches. She is currently working at the Helmut-Schmidt University in Hamburg, where she delivers lectures in coaching, organizational learning and community-based learning.

Travis Kemp, PhD, is an independent Consulting and Coaching Psychologist and Adjunct Associate Professor in the Centre for Business Growth at the University of South Australia. He is a registered Psychologist with practice endorsement in Organisational, Exercise & Sport and Counselling Psychology, a registered Teacher, an accredited Coaching Psychologist, a Certified Professional Manager and Company Director. Travis has held a range of senior executive leadership roles including MBA Director at the University of South Australia. He has published widely in the professional and research literature on leadership, executive performance, education and executive coaching and is co-editor of the international peer-reviewed journal, the *International Coaching Psychology Review* and Honorary Vice President of the International Society of Coaching Psychology.

Konstantin Korotov, PhD, is an Associate Professor and Director of the Center for Leadership Development Research at ESMT – Berlin, in Germany. His research is focused on leadership development, executive education, and coaching. He has authored, co-authored and co-edited six books and dozens of academic and practitioner articles and award-winning case-studies that serve as a foundation for his teaching executives worldwide. He is also the creator of the ESMT Coaching Colloquia series – premier global events for exploring and challenging coaching approaches and practices.

David A. Lane is currently Chair of Association of Professional Executive Coaches and Supervisors (APECS). As well as contributing to research and the professional development of coaching Professor Lane has coached in a wide range of organisations including major consultancies, multinationals, and public sector and government bodies. He also pioneered the international development of work based masters degrees for experienced coaches. His contributions to counselling psychology led to the senior award of the BPS for "Outstanding Scientific Contribution". In 2009 he was honoured by the British Psychological Society for his Distinguished Contribution to Professional Psychology. In 2016 the Royal College of Veterinary Surgeons conferred an Honorary Associateship for his work developing general practice.

Paul Lawrence, PhD, lectures on coaching at the Sydney Business School, University of Wollongong and is a Director at the Centre for Systemic Change (CSC). His research into coaching and change has been published in a number of journals including *Coaching: An International Journal of Theory, Research and Practice* and the *Journal of Change Management*. In 2014 his book *Leading Change: How successful leaders approach change management* was published by Kogan Page. Paul is a practicing coach, working with individuals, teams and groups, and a coaching supervisor. He also consults to organizations, helping them introduce coaching behaviors into the workplace.

Carmelina Lawton Smith is a coaching and development specialist who combines her private consultancy practice with a lecturing role on the MA in Coaching and Mentoring Practice at Oxford Brookes University Business School. In a consultancy role she designs and delivers development workshops for coaches and also offers one-to-one executive coaching. She works internationally with organisations wishing to develop a coaching culture, and has been instrumental in the development of the Spot-Coaching concept. She is a member of the British Psychological Society, and a member of the Oxford Brookes University Supervision Conference Academic Board. In addition she is a member of the Editorial Board of the International Journal of Evidence Based Coaching and a Consulting Editor for the International

Journal of Stress Prevention & Wellbeing. Her recent research interests have focused on resilience in leadership and how coaching can help.

Alison Maxwell is a practicing business and leadership coach, team coach and coach supervisor as well as Associate Lecturer at Oxford Brookes University on the MA in Coaching and Mentoring Practice. Her research interests include the use of feedback in leadership development, coaching self esteem issues and the boundaries between coaching and therapy. She has been published in *Coaching: An International Journal of Theory, Research and Practice, International Coaching Psychology Review* and has a chapter on supervising internal coaches in *Coaching and Mentoring Supervision: Theory and Practice*.

Almuth McDowall is Assistant Dean, Faculty of Business, Economics and Informatics and Head of the Department of Organizational Psychology at Birkbeck, University of London. She oversees a number of funded research projects on a range of work issues, including well being, rewards and career choices, directs an MSc programme, delivers education and supervises the research projects of PhD and MSc and students. Passionate about professional development, Almuth is a past chair of the British Psychological Society's Division of Occupational Psychology, and is both an assessor (where she trains others) and verifier (where she assesses other people's programmes) in psychometric testing.

Margaret A. Moore is a 17-year veteran of the Biotechnology industry in the US, UK, Canada and France. In 2000, Margaret founded Wellcoaches Corporation, in strategic partnership with the American College of Sports Medicine, which has trained more than 10,000 health professionals as health and wellness coaches in 45 countries. Margaret is co-founder and co-director of the Institute of Coaching at McLean Hospital, a Harvard Medical School affiliate, and co-director of the annual Coaching in Leadership & Healthcare conference offered by Harvard Medical School. Margaret teaches a science of coaching psychology program at Harvard University Extension School. She co-founded and co-leads the National Consortium for Credentialing Health & Wellness Coaches, delivering national standards and certification for health and wellness coaches. Margaret co-authored the Coaching Psychology Manual published by Wolters Kluwer (2009, 2015), and two Harvard Health books: *Organize Your Mind, Organize Your Life* (2012), and *Organize Your Emotions, Optimize Your Life* (2016).

Adrian Myers is a Senior Lecturer at Oxford Brookes University where he teaches on the doctoral and masters coaching and mentoring programmes. He is a chartered occupational psychologist and a registered practitioner psychologist with the Health and Care Professions Council. He is an Associate Fellow of the British Psychological Society. He has an MBA (Nottingham Trent University, 2002) and an MSc in Occupational Psychology (London Birkbeck University, 2006). Adrian has an undergraduate degree in Modern Languages (John Moore's University, 1984) and a degree in psychology (Open University, 1992).

Sean O'Connor is a Coaching practitioner, researcher, and academic within the fields of organisational change and development, positive psychology and leadership coaching. Sean holds Masters degree in Coaching Psychology and PhD in Psychology from the University of Sydney. His doctorate research identified the coaching ripple effect, the first ever research assessing the indirect impact of leadership coaching on the wellbeing of others in a system. Dr O'Connor is a Lecturer and Researcher within the Coaching Psychology Unit at the University of Sydney training, supervising a supporting hundreds of early career coaches. In practice,

Sean brings an evidence based analytical, collaborative, and solution-focused approach to helping others to develop, which is embedded in the context of complex systems. He has helped executives, senior leaders, and middle managers to develop and strengthen their leadership skills through individual, group and team coaching and facilitative training approaches.

Angela M. Passarelli, PhD is an Assistant Professor at the College of Charleston, SC. Her research focuses on the psychophysiological dynamics of developmental relationships, particularly in the context of leader development and change. Supported by grants from the Harnisch Foundation at the Harvard Institute of Coaching and the Society for Industrial-Organizational Psychology, her work has been published in outlets such as the *Leadership Quarterly*, *Consulting Psychology Journal*, and the *Academy of Management Learning & Education*. Angela also maintains an executive coaching practice.

Polly Parker is a Professor in Leadership and Director of Education at the University of Queensland's Business School, Australia. She earned her PhD on career communities from the University of Auckland. Her current interests include development, particularly of women, careers and peer coaching. She applies her life-long interest in learning and teaching in academic and corporate settings, particularly in the fields of leadership and careers where she is known as originator and co-developer of the internationally used Intelligent Career Card Sort™. Polly is active in the areas of women's leadership, and executive and career coaching.

James Pritchard is an experienced executive coach, coach supervisor and coaching lead. Over the past four years he has led the Civil Service coaching and mentoring offer in the UK. He has 20 years independent experience as an executive coach and organisational development consultant. His career started in the oil industry, but interest in coaching arose from an earlier background in international sporting competition. He is a qualified Iyengar yoga teacher, and engaged in research at Oxford Brookes University on 'Coaching for Mindful Action', applying yoga philosophy and practice to leadership coaching. He is Director of Mindful Action Coaching Ltd.

Raija Salomaa is one of the coaching pioneers in Finland with experience of coaching across a variety of industries. She has 20 years of professional experience in executive positions within international hotel industry and business travel services. Raija is a founder and ex-board member of International Coach Federation's Finland chapter. Raija also works as a mentor coach for credentialing coaches and as a coaching skills trainer for corporate executives. Currently, she is completing her PhD thesis on coaching of international assignees at the University of Vaasa's Business School, Department of Management.

Hany Shoukry, PhD, is a Researcher/Practitioner in Coaching and Human Development, and is an honorary research associate at Oxford Brookes University. He has worked for over twenty years with individuals and groups living in socially challenging contexts. His research focuses on theories and approaches that link individual development and social change. He developed Coaching for Emancipation in 2011, and currently trains coaches on emancipatory approaches.

Reinhard Stelter holds a PhD in Psychology and is Full Professor of Sport and Coaching Psychology at the University of Copenhagen and Visiting Professor at the Copenhagen Business School (Master of Public Governance). He is Head of the Coaching Psychology Unit at the Department of Nutrition, Exercise and Sports, University of Copenhagen. Reinhard is an accredited member, Associate Fellow and Honorary Vice-President of the International Society of Coaching Psychology (ISCP), and between 2009-2015 he has been a Scientific Advisory Council member of the Institute of Coaching at Harvard Medical School. He is an active researcher and reflective practitioner in the field of coaching psychology. He works as coaching psychologist in his own practice and collaborates with the Copenhagen Coaching Center where he also teaches on a 2-year Master program in Coaching. His major text book *Third Generation Coaching – a Guide to Narrative-Collaborative Theory and Practice* has been published by Springer.

Sunny Stout-Rostron, DProf, is part-time faculty at the University of Stellenbosch, School of Business in Cape Town, and Doctoral Supervisor at the Gordon Institute of Business at the University of Pretoria. Sunny has over 25 years' international experience as an executive coach, and is Founding President of Coaches and Mentors of South Africa (COMENSA). Sunny's books include: *Leadership Coaching for Results: Cutting-edge practices for coach and client* (Knowres, 2014), *Business Coaching International: Transforming individuals and organizations* (Karnac 2009/2013), *Business Coaching Wisdom and Practice: Unlocking the secrets of business coaching* (Knowres, 2009/2012). She is a researcher and contributing author to a range of books and journals.

Christian van Nieuwerburgh, PhD, is Associate Professor of Coaching at Henley Business School, University of Reading. Dr van Nieuwerburgh is Executive Director of the Henley Centre for Coaching and Behavioural Change. He is an active executive coach and highly-regarded academic with a number of publications and an international reputation. Christian is particularly interested in the application of coaching in different contexts and the use of coaching in educational settings. He is currently the Editor in Chief of *Coaching: An International Journal of Theory, Research and Practice*.

Ellen B. Van Oosten, PhD, is Assistant Professor for Organizational Behavior and Faculty Director for Executive Education at Case Western Reserve University. Dr Van Oosten is also Director of the Coaching Research Lab and Master Coach at CWRU. Her research interests include coaching, leadership development, emotional intelligence, and positive relationships at work. Dr. Van Oosten has published scholarly and practitioner articles, which cover topics such as coaching for change, leadership vision and leadership development in organizations. She teaches at the Schools of Management, Engineering and Law at CWRU and regularly delivers workshops for managers and executives.

Simon Western is Adjunct Professor of the University College Dublin, President-Elect of the International Society for the Psychoanalytic Study of Organizations, Chief Executive of Analytic-Network Coaching (www.analyticnetwork.com). Simon has international experience as a leadership coach and strategic consultant and delivers keynote speaking on the topic of 'New leadership for new times'. His current focus is to train executive coaches to support '*leaders to act in good faith to create the good society*'. He is widely published with books including *Leadership a Critical Text*, 2nd edition (Sage, 2013), *Coaching and Mentoring a Critical Text* (Sage, 2012) and *Global Leadership Perspectives Insights and Analysis* (forthcoming Sage, 2016). His previous work roles include Director of Coaching at Lancaster University Management School and Director of Masters in Organizational Consultancy (psychoanalytic approaches) at Tavistock Clinic.

Patrick Williams is a psychologist, author, speaker, and leadership coach, is a pioneer in the field of Life Coaching and founder of the Institute for Life Coach Training, and Coaching the Global Village. Dr Williams has been a developer of leaders for 3 decades. He founded Coaching the Global Village in 2006 to bring the power of the coaching approach to the underserved and resource-poor of the world. CGV associates provide leadership training to grassroots organizations and/or non-profits, NGOS or corporate social change initiatives. Pat's message is that leadership is an activity, not just a position.

Ruth Q. Wolever, PhD, serves as the Director of Vanderbilt Health Coaching through the Osher Center for Integrative Medicine, an Associate Professor of Physical Medicine & Rehabilitation, and Psychiatry & Behavioral Sciences at Vanderbilt University Medical Center and the School of Nursing. As an integrative health coach and clinical health psychologist, Ruth has internationally-recognized expertise in designing, implementing, and evaluating behavior change programs for medical patients and those at risk for chronic disease. She is one of the elected leaders of the National Consortium for Credentialing Health and Wellness Coaches (http://ncchwc.org), a non-profit organization whose mission is to professionalize the field of health and wellness coaching, bringing forth national standards and a uniform job definition that will clarify best practices and allow for rigorous study. Dr. Wolever is also a national leader in the study of mindfulness-based approaches to self-regulation and lifestyle change, and is the Chief Science Officer for eMindful.

Alison Zarecky is a UK-based transition coach, specialising in helping people through periods of change in the workplace and their personal lives. She has worked with a wide range of organizations such as the British Army and Help for Heroes. She is also a volunteer for the European Coaching and Mentoring Council, helping promote high standards of coaching and mentoring in organizations. Her MA dissertation research focussed on the use of strengths coaching with transitioning military and how this can assist with finding career direction. She is an accredited Strengthscope® individual and team coach and a Fireworks™ certified career coach.

Introduction

Tatiana Bachkirova,
Gordon Spence and David Drake

INTENTION FOR THIS VOLUME

Given the steady increase in academic coaching literature over the past two decades, coaching appears to be evolving into a scholarly field in its own right. For example, the field now includes four peer-refereed journals that have published a substantial number of conceptual, theoretical and empirical works, along with many influential scholarly texts. In addition, the field has shown an increasing preparedness to engage in substantial dialogue, with robust debates more frequently seen within both journals and at scholarly meetings around the world (e.g. conferences, symposia). Finally, postgraduate-level coaching education and training is being offered in an increasing number of universities worldwide. This is helpful for two reasons. First, it provides an outlet for the growing body of knowledge mentioned above, which ultimately benefits coaching practice. Second, a growing number of these universities run doctoral programmes that not only help to stimulate on-going research but also raise the quality of this body of knowledge (through the use of rigorous scientific methods).

As such, we think the time is right to present an account of this fast developing discipline, to map out where it is going, and to identify the key debates and issues that are influencing coaching practice and its accompanying research. Accordingly, the intention of this Handbook is to provide graduate students, scholars, and researchers with a premier point of contact with the current theoretical and empirical knowledge base, along with many of the established and emerging debates in the scholarly literature.

The work that follows will provide readers with a retrospective and prospective overview of this literature, along with a clear sense of the multidisciplinary nature of the field. It has been assembled using original chapters prepared by leading and emerging scholars from around the world. Each chapter offers a comprehensive, critical overview of an aspect of coaching, a discussion of the key debates and research, and a review of the emerging issues. Important views are also incorporated from related disciplines and subject areas, in order to acknowledge the systemic and multidisciplinary nature of coaching.

In this Introduction we seek to map the research, theories and conceptual propositions that inform the current state of the coaching discipline. We will also summarise identified problems and conclusions reached within each section of this volume.

SITUATING COACHING

For most of human history, people have drawn support from their immediate social networks to get their physical and psychological needs met. For example, family, friends and other community members (e.g. elders, priests, shamans) have traditionally been the 'helpers' in situations where sense-making was challenged (e.g. after natural disasters), suffering was experienced (e.g. death of loved ones), or life transitions needed to be traversed (e.g. rites of passage). However, more recently, these functions appear to have been handed over to a variety of specialists and professionals that have emerged as part of broader shifts that occurred, particularly in Western industrialised societies. As Naughton (2002) has previously noted:

> ... anxiety, ambition, and the challenges of modern life had combined to create a market for men and women who could provide, for a fee, a service that older generations have once performed for younger generations as a part of the social contract. (p.7)

In this light, it is possible to situate coaching within a chronological sequence of evolving professional practices that emerged to meet changing societal demands. Indeed, a *demand and supply* conceptualisation can be used to reflect upon some of these practices and, in the section that follows, this frame will be used to consider the history of psychotherapy, counselling and, ultimately, coaching. In each case certain *demand* issues can be recognised (e.g. increased social isolation) that were responded to with efforts to create a *supply* to meet such needs (i.e. practitioners with relevant skills). Although not explicitly presented as a demand–supply analysis, Engel (2008) delivers a detailed history of American therapy that accords with such an analytic frame.

As identified by Engel (2008), the emergence of psychoanalysis in the early 20th century constituted the first prototype of a 'talking cure'. Backed by Freud's highly influential works on psychodynamic processes, the psychoanalytic method became dominant in clinical psychiatric treatments for many years. However, the proliferation of this method created an important precedent. That is, it helped to legitimise the use of 'human treatments' or, more specifically, approaches that relied on the power of human relationships to address the psychological concerns of patients. Whilst its popularisation can be seen as a demand-creation factor in itself (as improvements could be seen by others), public demand for other forms of 'helping by talking' had its roots in a variety of other sociocultural and historical factors.

A key demand catalyst for psychotherapy was the need to support military personnel before, during and after the Second World War (WWII). More specifically, the psychological devastation experienced by returned servicemen (and women) created a desperate need for accessible, affordable and practical treatments in the years following WWII (Engel, 2008). As traditional psychoanalysis met few of these criteria, WWII can be seen as a bifurcation point in the history of 'human treatments', with several different forms of psychotherapy developing quickly through this period, along with practitioners who could help meet the needs of traumatised military personnel. It is also during this period that practitioners (e.g. psychotherapists) began to move their treatments away from medication-based formulations (as was characteristic of psychiatry) and towards understanding the psychological nature of human dysfunctions and identifying personal resources for dealing with them.

The growth of psychotherapy since WWII has clearly shown that 'helping by talking' can do much to help alleviate or manage past traumas and acute psychological dysfunction. Indeed, researchers have long noted its general effectiveness (Smith & Glass, 1977) and the continued documentation of its efficacy has led to formal recognition within prominent professional bodies (Campbell, Norcross, Vasquez & Kaslow, 2013) and improvements in public attitudes towards mental illness and support seeking (Schomerus et al., 2012).

The early success of psychotherapy also opened up possibilities for using similar approaches in situations where one's psychological equilibrium is (moderately) impacted by adverse life events. In these cases, which many now associate with 'counselling', it is the desire to cope with challenging situations that primarily motivates clients, with less emphasis placed on exploring psychological root causes or finding cures. The more pragmatic, e.g. solution-focused, orientation of counselling opened up possibilities for utilising 'helping by talking' beyond traditional clinical settings, with counselling services now provided for dealing with issues related to managing general health, drug and alcohol use, career decision-making, workplace challenges, financial affairs, grief reactions, and/or relationship dislocations amongst others. In demand–supply terms, the emergence of counselling (and counsellors) can be seen as creating a supply of practitioners capable of meeting a demand that might best be described as 'latent' (insofar as it relates to more ubiquitous human concerns). Not surprisingly, in the second half of the 20th century an independent professional status for counselling was established in many countries around the world, which helped to distinguish it from psychotherapy and permit a reliable supply of good quality support to those trying to cope with various challenges of life (Corey, 2009; Dryden, 2008; Nelson-Jones, 2010).

We consider the emergence of coaching to be the next step in this trajectory. That is, as individuals recognised that the 'helping by talking' approach need not be limited to healing dysfunction or coping with challenges (as with psychotherapy and counselling), the utility of using such methods for facilitating human growth and development seemed obvious. Indeed, as illustrated by Spence (2007), some of the foundations of coaching can be detected in the activities of the human potential movement (around half a century ago) and its diverse collection of practitioners that sought to help individuals, groups and organisations to become more high functioning and successful. In large part because of its potential to enhance organisational and workplace performance (Kampa-Kokesch & Anderson, 2001), coaching appeared to 'boom' (Naughton, 2002) around the turn of the 21st century.

However, as was noted by many at the time (e.g. Kampa-Kokesch & Anderson, 2001), it was uncertain if coaching would become 'more than the last management or life style fad' (Grant & Cavanagh, 2004, p.12). Notably, almost two decades on, the steady development of the coaching literature could lead one to conclude that coaching is now more than a fad and has matured to a point where it might be legitimately deemed to be an emerging profession. Whatever its status, personal and organisational interest in coaching appears to have remained consistently high, with sponsorship of coaching within private and public-sector organisations continuing to drive demand and, by extension, its supply.

We undertook the job of producing this Handbook because we believe that a new profession of coaching is emerging, one that will be supported by the work presented in the following pages. Of course, as clearly shown in the discussion of psychotherapy, counselling and coaching presented above, humanity's needs continue to develop and diversify over time. With the changing and complex conditions of life it is expected that the needs of individuals and organisations will also change and become more complex. This makes things challenging for practitioners as they seek to internally and externally adapt to the demands they encounter. To make matters worse, substantial bodies of knowledge are being generated about many aspects of human experience, including the requirements for satisfying human needs, stimulating personal and professional growth and how they can all be influenced by meaning-making processes at individual and collective levels. Naturally such knowledge requires significant time to explore and process, with practitioners challenged to gather the skills and experience needed to integrate such learning within their service offerings.

Fortunately for coaching, the evidence shows that public acceptance of professional services is growing (e.g. Schomerus et al., 2012), in lieu of attempts to cope without support. To return to the opening point, this may merely reflect the fundamental importance of supportive social networks for human beings. Even so, the demand for coaching services may continue to be strong for a very long time to come, albeit perhaps within more individualistic, industrialised societies where traditional social structures are less evident. Whatever the case, the ability of practitioners to deliver valued services will rest upon the existence of a rich and textured knowledge base that can provide good and relevant guidance for practitioners. Our hope for this Handbook is that it will stimulate the conceptual discussions, theoretical debates, research questions and empirical work needed to create just such a knowledge base.

OVERVIEW OF CURRENT DEBATES

In reviewing the chapters in this Handbook, we were able to identify a number of debates and contentious issues that seem to concern researchers, educators and academics in the field. These include questions such as:

- Can coaching be defined? Given that it draws from a wide range of knowledge bases and is applied across multiple contexts, is it possible to precisely define what coaching is, even if only for research purposes?
- How are power and value differentials best to be handled in coaching? Given the recognition that coaches often work within contexts that are 'messy' (due to, for instance, cross-cultural factors), is it possible for coaching to be practised value-free? Relatedly, can coaching research be conducted value-free?
- How much additional effort is needed to demonstrate that coaching 'works'? How will we know? Using what evidence? What kind of research is most important for the future of the discipline?
- What constitutes an appropriate approach to goal setting and outcome achievement in coaching? Based on recent additions to the coaching literature (David, Clutterbuck, & Megginson, 2013) and our observations in the field, there seems to be widespread dissatisfaction with traditional approaches to goal setting (e.g. SMART goals) and their suitability to the systemic realities of coaching clients. Indeed, questions are now being asked about the extent to which coaching can be conducted 'goal-free'.
- What are the boundaries of coaching? Whilst coaching scholars and practitioners have long demarcated coaching from other forms of assistance (most notably counselling and psychotherapy), recent applications of coaching are raising questions about whether these boundaries are absolute or arbitrary.

Whilst each debate is substantial and worthy of considerable attention, we will limit ourselves to a brief discussion of the definitional debate that continues to surround coaching (the first of the debates noted above). In doing so, we hope to prime readers for the work that follows, thus preparing the ground for a rich exploration of the field. Of course, it should be noted that the above list is by no means exhaustive and that other debates and contestable issues are to be found in the following chapters.

Defining Coaching

Nearly every text published on coaching begins with an attempt to define the concept and its practice. This is reasonable given that it provides readers (usually practitioners) with an early indication of the author's viewpoint on the fundamental question: What is coaching? Needless to say, these positions differ significantly and, as a result, the definitions influence how the purpose, target market and core processes of coaching are articulated. This is not surprising considering its diverse origins and multidisciplinary nature. However, a number of authors argue that arriving at a common definition of coaching is important if the image of professionalism is to be presented (e.g. Sherman & Freas, 2004).

It should be noted that this book is not primarily focused on advancing the professionalisation of coaching. Rather, its primary aim is to stimulate development of the knowledge base for coaching, thereby making a contribution to further establishing coaching as an applied discipline. As such, this Handbook requires no unified definition of coaching, irrespective of how desirable that might be in principle. Free of the usual preoccupation with defining coaching, the Handbook is able to present an open inquiry into the nature of coaching, along with an examination of whether, and to what extent, such a unified definition might be possible.

Our discussion of this particular debate is organised around the following questions:

1. Is a unified definition of coaching necessary?
2. Why is coaching difficult to define?
3. Is it possible to define coaching using empirical means?
4. What are the implications of not achieving a unified definition?

Question 1: Is a unified definition of coaching necessary?

A number of arguments have been made in relation to the achievement of a unified definition of coaching. Often these are expressed in terms of eliminating problems that stem from its absence. For example, it is quite common to hear concerns about coaching lacking an identity, that it merely blends different approaches and uses theory eclectically, which creates uncertainty, unnecessary mystique and leads to the denigration of coaching as atheoretical (Peltier, 2009; Ellinger, Hamlin & Beattie, 2008). The identity argument is sometimes also associated with being underdeveloped empirically, which makes it difficult to judge the value of coaching (Robson, 2011). Furthermore, an extension of these arguments might be that the absence of a clear definition makes research findings less transferable and, ultimately, less impactful.

Other arguments in favour of a unified definition include the contention that establishing clear boundaries with other disciplines permits more effective training for coaches and clearer guidelines for practice. For others the argument is couched in terms of the need for standards, with the adherence to specific criteria seen as critical for self-regulation within an unregulated industry (Lane, Stelter & Stout-Rostron, 2014). The counter-argument to this is that the establishment of coaching as a discrete area of practice would be problematic and unnecessarily restrictive (Cavanagh, 2009), as the commonalities with counselling and other related professions enrich the practice of coaching.

Question 2: Why is coaching difficult to define?

The starting point for addressing this question is considering what a good definition of practice would entail. According to Bachkirova and Kauffman (2009), two criteria are particularly important for a definition of practice: *universality* and *uniqueness*. The criterion of universality includes an indication of the elements (or features) that are common to all the various types, genres and approaches to coaching. In contrast, the criterion of uniqueness would identify those elements of coaching that would clearly differentiate it from other forms of professional assistance (such as training or counselling). When Bachkirova & Kauffman (2009) applied these criteria to various attempts to define coaching as a professional practice, four types of definition were identified. These included definition focused on purpose (i.e. what coaching is for); process (what coaching involves); context (where it is conducted), and clientele (what population(s) it serves). They concluded that none of the definitions identified could satisfy the universality and uniqueness criteria, as the conceptualisations of coaching under study varied too substantially in terms of coaching types and genres (Bachkirova and Kauffman, 2009).

Theoretical incompatibilities are another factor that may have made precise definitions of coaching hard to come by. As mentioned earlier, some authors have argued for the need to recognise and appreciate the flexibility of coaching rather than aim for 'clear-cut' definitions (e.g. Cavanagh, 2009). This accords with the growing emphasis on the utility of complexity theories in coaching and construal of coaching engagements as complex adaptive systems (Stacey, 2003, 2012; Cavanagh & Lane, 2012; Bachkirova & Lawton Smith, 2015). The difficulty with this construal is that it does not easily marry with the desire to construct a precise definition of coaching. Another source of resistance to universality can be found in the emergence of more pragmatic, postmodern perspectives on coaching. Not only do these perspectives provide tacit advocacy for the existence of diversity in coaching, and recognise the influence of complexity and context, they also provide a substantial critique of the desire to apply fixed rules and regulations to the coaching industry (Garvey, 2011; Western, 2012; Bachkirova and Lawton Smith, 2015).

Question 3: Is it possible to define coaching using empirical means?

One way to approach the task of clarifying a definition of coaching is via the use of scientific methods. In contrast to the traditional approach of reviewing and analysing relevant literature, with the aim of formulating a plausible descriptive statement, the use of empirical means is more complicated, requiring the articulation of a research question, the development of a research design, the collection of data and its subsequent analysis. Within the coaching literature, a precedent for this approach has been provided by Bachkirova, Sibley and Myers (2015). In their study, a specifically designed instrument was used to explore the process aspect of the four criteria outlined earlier. Forty-one coaches from different coaching orientations were asked to describe an imagined coaching session using an instrument based on Q methodology. The findings revealed the existence of a shared perspective in the way that coaching sessions are described, a consensus that was achieved despite the diversity that existed within the sample. As such, a relatively uniform definition of coaching may at least be possible, something that future researchers may wish to explore using other empirical methods such as Delphi methods or grounded theory.

Question 4: What are the implications of not achieving a unified definition?

The implications of not achieving a shared definition of coaching would seem to vary for different stakeholders. For example, current research has revealed that experienced coaching practitioners are aware of the complexity of their field and relatively pragmatic in the way they deal with definitional issues and boundaries with other disciplines (Maxwell, 2009; Baker, 2015). As such, the absence of a unified definition is of less concern to them. For novice coaches, however, this absence is more problematic, as they may struggle to position themselves within an uncertain professional domain. Whilst the unresolved nature of this issue is generally easily accommodated within postgraduate coaching programmes, short-course programmes are likely to find it more unsettling (as their preparation of coaches is more compressed) and is likely to be overlooked through the adoption of a well-cited definition that is easily found in the literature.

Another stakeholder group likely to be troubled by the absence of a widely accepted definition of coaching is potential consumers who lack an experience of being coached. These people will tend to be confused about what coaching is (until they experience it) and are unlikely to be interested in the nuances of the issue. In the case of organisational consumers, many are developing a more sophisticated understanding of the field (and tend to articulate this through the creation of coaching policies, practitioner panels, etc.) and generally seem to find ways of resolving definitional problems through these efforts. However, the lack of clear definitions may well diminish the field in the eyes of members of other professions and so there seem to be good reasons to continuing exploring this basic issue.

A final concern relates to potential obstacles for developing the knowledge base of coaching. Until a reasonable way of conceptualising coaching is proposed, the onus will continue to fall upon researchers to provide clear descriptions of the coaching interventions they study, in order for their findings to be comparable to others. Whilst this transparency would contribute to the pragmatic intention of building on something that is sufficiently explicit, it would also help to create a rich multidimensional picture of the way coaching is conceived and practised in the real world.

OVERVIEW OF THE SECTIONS

Part 1: Positioning Coaching as a Discipline

The aim of this opening section is to position coaching as a developing discipline of knowledge amongst other disciplines: both applied and pure. As such, it could be said that this section focuses on coaching as externally facing rather than on the intricacies of the field. There are at least two reasons for coaching to be externally facing. First, it attracts scholarly work that is required to secure recognition of coaching as a discipline in its own right. Second, it keeps the field connected to bodies of knowledge that are both relevant and critical to high quality practice and research. In some chapters of this section the authors discuss the coaching discipline with a view to negotiating the boundaries with other fields, whilst other chapters focus on how the coaching discipline is profoundly influenced by other fields of knowledge.

Being externally facing also implies appreciation of how coaching is affected by wider discourses in societies as well as social, political and environmental issues. For example, as explained in Chapter 3, whilst the 'psychological expert' and 'managerial coaching' discourses both influence the practice of coaching, the differing assumptions inherent in both create a number of tensions and can be a source of incoherence and confusion. It is also important to note here that chapters in this section demonstrate how coaching can actively contribute to some broad societal concerns and wider areas of inquiry into human nature and practice.

Seen through the lens of the external representation of the coaching discipline in this section, it is possible to recognise the progress being made by coaching scholars in conceptualising the relationship of coaching with other fields and in claiming its place amongst other applied disciplines. At the same time it is possible to identify a number of debates that are of importance to establishing coaching as a field of knowledge. In the brief chapter descriptions that follow, some of these debates are identified and indications are provided about how these debates are addressed by various authors.

The intent to build and expand the knowledge base of coaching requires consideration of questions of the most generic nature, such as 'what is knowledge?' and 'what constitutes valid knowledge?' As such questions reveal significant variations in epistemological positions, their consideration will inevitably give rise to disagreements and tensions. For example, some debates are direct extensions of the 'paradigms war' evident in other disciplines that, as described in Chapter 2 by *Tatiana Bachkirova*, typically divides academic communities into either modernist or postmodernist positions. Although this chapter presents pragmatism as a 'pacifying', alternative perspective, the main message advocates for an appreciation of diversity in research and theory building. It should be noted that this important debate also emerges in other chapters throughout the book and, when it does, the philosophical positions of the authors should be clear to see.

In Chapter 3 *Simon Western* highlights a similar debate about the incompatibility of various approaches to coaching as a function of differences that exist in the professional discourses that underpin them. The focus of the chapter is to illuminate how wider cultural and societal discourses are translated into distinct approaches to coaching, which creates an incoherence in the way that coaching is presented to the wider world, conducted in practice and assessed for its value. Whilst the author defends an attempt to integrate these discourses into a unified model, the real value of the chapter resides in illuminating an important debate on coaching as a discipline.

Coaching as an 'evidence-based practice' is the focus of Chapter 4 by *Anthony Grant*. One of the field's longest standing debates, this chapter focuses on how coaching is presented to a largely modernist external world, with the primary aim to enhance the reputation of the growing discipline. However, the issue of what constitutes 'evidence' remains a subject of much debate, particularly through the lens of competing epistemological attitudes. It is notable that Grant, one of the most recognised advocates of evidence-based coaching, has taken a more inclusive approach to understanding evidence, including highlighting the value of qualitative research, alongside the contribution that can be provided by traditional outcome studies.

Another of the long-standing debates in coaching has concerned the establishment of boundaries between the related disciplines of counselling and psychotherapy. In Chapter 5 *Trevor Crowe* notes that although various stakeholders of coaching seem to require the explicit delineation of coaching from psychotherapy, some specific differentiations (e.g. according to population of users) are largely illusory. He examines the increasing overlap of their characteristics, aims and practices and argues for ways to operationalise inter-professionalism informed by active and ongoing needs assessment and client feedback.

In Chapters 6 and 7 the focus changes to an exploration of the interplay between the emerging discipline of coaching and two established fields of knowledge: theories of learning and theories of adult development. In Chapter 6 *John Bennett* and *Francine Campone* seek to demonstrate a correspondence between the principles of coaching and the tenets of the main theories of learning. They make a case for the inseparability of coaching from this field of knowledge, which is important as it allows coaching to claim a solid theoretical foundation. In Chapter 7 *Paul Lawrence* begins with a similar intention (this time related to theories of adult development), and also provides an overview of the debates surrounding this area of knowledge. Whilst acknowledging the growing popularity of these theories, the author highlights some concerns about this body of knowledge and challenges readers to examine the state of knowledge about coaching in light of the implications that follow from adult development theories.

The last three chapters in this section explore the potential for coaching to positively impact areas of practice such as leadership development and social change. These chapters demonstrate how the coaching literature already contributes to the above disciplines and identify where there are opportunities to advance the synergy. For example, in Chapter 8, *Konstantin Korotov* argues that not only do the disciplines of leadership development and coaching share similar concerns (and inevitable limitations), they also share an opportunity for mutual enrichment.

In Chapter 9 *David Drake* and *James Pritchard* look at coaching through the lens of organisation development. In so doing, they make the case for coaching as a systemic and scalable tool for addressing issues such as learning and development, culture and change in organisations. They argue that coaching is now an essential element in organisation development as an applied field of knowledge. As such, scholars and practitioners in the two disciplines are helping to drive the next generation of scholarship across both disciplines. They close with a look at integrative development theory as an example of the next stage in the evolution of efforts to understand how organisations learn and develop and the role of coaching in the process.

Finally, in Chapter 10, *Hany Shoukry* presents a compelling argument for extending the use of coaching for individual and organisation development to address the issues of importance to societies as a whole. He describes how coaching can contribute to social change when it does not shy away from the needs of the marginalised and oppressed in the world and those who care about more humanised workplaces, essential rights and the environment. In order to coach in this way, practitioners may need to become more socially aware and (rather than adopting a neutral position) be more explicit about where they stand in respect to social issues. Whilst the chapter raises questions that not all in the coaching industry will welcome, they are questions that coaching scholars and researchers should engage if coaching is to become a potent agent of societal level change.

Part 2: Coaching as a Process

A variety of factors influence what occurs in coaching conversations and how those conversations unfold. Taken together these factors represent a set of alternative lenses through which to understand what happens in the coaching relationship, creating backdrops that can help to make sense of the work. This section assembles some of the more prominent process-related themes currently reflected in the coaching literature. These include some well-established topics such as working with the coaching relationship, the role of emotions in coaching, and working with the narratives of the client (and the coach), along with emerging topics, such as working with diversity in coaching, understanding physicality, and recent questioning of the role of goals in coaching.

In the process of presenting these chapters, some debates have been raised that are worthy of mention. One such debate (addressed in Chapter 12) concerns the role of goal-setting in coaching and the extent to which goal-setting is an essential part of the process, or more provocatively, whether it is possible to work 'goal-free' with clients. Another debate (addressed in Chapter 17) concerns the use of feedback in coaching and the role that coaches can or should play. Whilst coaches are often used as 'objective' messengers of feedback, such a role can create a sense of dissonance for coaches as their participation in an evaluative, judgemental process may clash with their humanistic intentions to be non-directive and client-centred.

Given the collaborative and interpersonal nature of coaching, the section commences (appropriately) with an examination of the coaching relationship. In Chapter 11 *Erik de Haan* and *Judie Gannon* review key components of the coaching relationship, along with a summary of past research that has attempted to better understand its essence in workplace, sports and executive contexts. This discussion also focuses on recent developments in attempts to understand the extent to which the historical term 'working alliance' is synonymous with the notion of the coaching relationship.

Two of the most identifiable aspects of coaching – goal setting and goal striving – are addressed in Chapter 12. In this chapter *David Clutterbuck* and *Gordon Spence* begin by acknowledging the existence of an extensive literature on goals, whilst also noting that coaching practitioners and scholars have generally failed to take full advantage of the richness of this literature. More specifically, they challenge the orthodoxy of SMART goal setting in coaching by noting that specific, concrete goals are often an inappropriate response to the challenges of dynamic, complex environments where personal control and predictability are low.

In Chapter 13 *Sunny Stout-Rostron* tackles the multi-faceted topic of working with diversity in coaching. After noting the centrality of 'inclusion' to current perspectives on diversity management, the author illustrates the challenges associated with being inclusive as a consequence of interpersonal variations in gender, race, ethnicity, culture, personality and a variety of other factors (e.g. sexual orientation). As such, there is much for coaches to understand on this topic, yet very little coaching-specific research has been published to date. Nonetheless, some practice-oriented models are identified and discussed, with recommendations made for the benefit of future researchers.

In Chapter 14 *Peter Jackson* presents a compelling overview of the little discussed topic of physicality in coaching. In order to extend the topic beyond a simple understanding of physicality (as mere improvements in one's physical status), a broad and inclusive definition is presented. It encompasses the variety of ways that coaches may notice as their own (or their client's) physiological state and use it for the benefit of the coaching process and/or outcome. By being so inclusive, the author effectively embraces a wide variety of perspectives and embodied practices. These perspectives – which include somatic, integral, existential, behavioural, cognitive-emotional and physical environmental – are organised into an integrative framework designed to act as a reference point for the development of practice and future research (with possible questions presented).

In Chapter 15 *Elaine Cox* provides an account of what is meant by 'working with emotions' in coaching by drawing on sociological, philosophical and psychological theories and emerging research on concepts such as emotional intelligence, emotional regulation, empathy, and emotional labour. Whilst these bodies of work constitute a rich and textured knowledge base, the author notes that relatively little work has been reported on the role of emotions in coaching and, as a stimulus for future research, the chapter concludes with the presentation of an emotional climate inventory for coaching.

In Chapter 16 *David Drake* describes how the telling of stories and the construction of narratives are a natural process that people use to make sense of themselves and the surrounding world. He argues that what emerged from the narrative turn in the social sciences has much to offer coaching practice. Specifically, literary theory, the humanities and psychology offer valuable insights about the structural, socio-cultural and developmental aspects of people's narratives and identities. As such, working with narratives in coaching offers an approach that bridges the personal and the social. He outlines the importance in coaching of working with the client as narrator, utilising the narration process as a resource for change. The author concludes with an integrative process for working with narratives in coaching, which also offers potential for stimulating further research in this area.

In the final chapter of this section *Alison Maxwell* explores literature related to the use of feedback within coaching. In a wide-ranging analysis, it is argued that coaching practice has proceeded with little recognition of feedback theory and research and, as a result, the practice-based literature often lacks coherence. For example, it is pointed out that whilst it is common for coaches to act as conduits for 'external' feedback (e.g. 360-degree feedback), this function can subtly but powerfully undermine the non-directive, non-judgemental stance that many coaches wish to maintain with their clients. As such, the author challenges coaches to find their own stance towards feedback by presenting a review of different types of feedback, along with a range of theoretical perspectives on how coaches can approach this aspect of their work and inform future research.

Part 3: Common Issues in Coaching

In a natural extension of the process-oriented chapters of the previous section, Part 3 focuses on six topics that are getting an increasing amount of attention in the coaching literature. These include chapters on values, resilience, strengths, mindfulness, post-traumatic growth and career transitions. The distinctive characteristic of these topics is not that they are intrinsic to all coaching engagements, but that they often become a focus of coaching conversations by choice of one or both parties. A possible explanation for this is that the topics draw increasing attention because they represent current discourses in societies and coaching communities that emphasise a positive orientation to self and personal growth. The influence of these discourses is evident in the coaching literature and in professional development programmes.

One of the noteworthy aspects of this collection of topics is that they are of equal relevance and importance to coaches as they are to coaching clients. For example, whilst many authors have noted that the exploration and clarification of *values* in coaching is critical if one is to be an authentic leader, it seems equally important for coaches if they are to practise in an authentic way. Similarly, many consider a client's capacity for *mindfulness* to be vital to effective self-regulation and goal attainment, yet a coach will struggle to be helpful if they cannot dispassionately notice a developing desire to be liked by their client or fail to detect their avoidance of a difficult issue. As such, these topics can be thought of as two sides of the same coin. Where practical suggestions are offered or future research directions are proposed, they will often carry potential benefits for both parties. This makes these chapters of considerable potential benefit and, it is hoped, they will provide a catalyst for furthering work in each of these areas.

In Chapter 18 *Reinhard Stelter* argues that values are a central issue in coaching because they provide clients with an implicit foundation for action and assist in navigating the hypercomplexity of modern life. Drawing on a rich body of values-based scholarship, the author presents coaching as the art of *lingering*, the practice of which allows values to naturally emerge from a deeply reflective, collaborative dialogue. The chapter also explores some interesting questions, such as whether values reside as latent resources within people or are socially co-created, and concludes with three value-reflecting coaching approaches (i.e. existential, protrepic and third-generation), along with their various implications for future research.

In Chapter 19 *Carmelina Lawton Smith* notes that coaching is ideal for cultivating resilience because it can help individuals work with their assets (e.g. problem solving skills) and access social support (e.g the coach) as well as encourage a more nuanced analysis of - and sense-making about - the system in which the client is operating. Whilst she notes that recent research suggests that coaching does enhance resilience, it is also noted that considerable fragmentation exists within this literature due to the variety of different conceptual lenses that are used to understand resilience (including perspectives derived from cognitive psychology, mindfulness, and narrative theory). As such, future researchers are encouraged to seek greater conceptual clarity and integration across perspectives, along with empirical testing of models using cross-sectional and longitudinal designs.

In Chapter 20 *Sophie Francis* and *Alison Zarecky* provide a comprehensive overview of the strengths literature as it pertains to coaching. After defining the construct, acknowledging a growing body of empirical work and briefly considering relevant theories, the authors move on to a critique of literature focused on the identification, use, development and integration of strengths (including rare discussions of weaknesses and shadow sides). The chapter concludes with brief descriptions of strengths work within a variety of coaching contexts (e.g. executive coaching, mental health), along with an array of helpful suggestions for strengthening empirical work in the area.

In Chapter 21 *Travis Kemp* provides a stimulating analysis and discussion of mindfulness and coaching. After acknowledging the historical significance of mindfulness and its deep practical importance, the author notes that coaching and mindfulness share a symbiotic connection, oriented as they are towards the creation of healthy and flourishing lives. Whilst noting obvious potential for integration, the author also notes that traditional perspectives on coaching seem to constrain such integration because ownership of the coaching agenda is generally reserved for the coachee, whereas the sustained cultivation of mindfulness seems to require a movement towards 'teaching' and 'education'. As such, the chapter outlines an *anthrogogical* approach to mindfulness and coaching, which provides a flexible approach to learning and permits teaching to be a legitimate component of coaching. Recommendations for future research are based on testing for the effects of an anthrogogical approach to coaching and mindfulness.

In Chapter 22 *Gordon Spence* and *Stephen Joseph* acknowledge the human capacity to find benefit in profoundly challenging circumstances or, stated differently, experience post-traumatic growth (PTG). After delineating different responses to traumatic experience, the authors introduce the concept of PTG and review a variety of literatures to ascertain the extent to which coaching might be an appropriate response to the devastations of life. Despite the existence of little published work in the area, enough relevant research was found to make a case for such a response – provided that the coaching response cultivates a strong sense of hope, focuses on the satisfaction of basic psychological needs and is oriented towards the construction of new personal narratives (that incorporate past traumatic events). The chapter concludes with numerous suggestions for future research.

In Chapter 23 *Polly Parker* considers literature related to coaching for role transitions and career change. This is done against the backdrop of highly volatile, complex contemporary employment markets, where role transitions and career changes can occur quickly and unexpectedly, requiring career actors to be increasingly agile and resilient. The author takes readers on a guided tour of change and transition theories and notes that, while many have relevance to coaching, very little empirical work has been conducted to establish their utility within coaching contexts. Recognising the psychological challenges associated with career transitions, the final sections of the chapter recognise the potential that coaching has to facilitate adult cognitive development, concluding with a call to develop more coaching-specific theories of career change and transition.

Part 4: Coaching in Contexts

Much of the emphasis in coaching and coaching research is on what transpires in and through coaching sessions. Perhaps to distance itself from psychotherapy's focus on understanding the development history of individuals, and organisational development's focus on the future to which people will return, coaching has tended to focus on the individual's development and achievement in the process itself. One of the aims of this section is to advocate for the importance of context in conceptualising and studying coaching. It reflects an increased appreciation of the role that contextual factors play in shaping people's narratives, behaviours and outcomes. It also highlights the need to better understand the different ways that coaching is delivered, as determined by context. Without an appreciation of context, individuals who experience personal change through a coaching process may become dissatisfied if it is not matched by congruent changes in their environment.

The chapters in this section set the stage for a much richer understanding of the role of context for both coaches and coachees. In particular, they raise four important issues. First, they consistently advocate for more definitional clarity of coaching and the development of a taxonomy of coaching that encompasses its different contextual applications. Second, they highlight the need to augment the personal focus in coaching with greater attention given to relational and contextual factors, especially since the coaching literature tends to underestimate the role of context in human learning and development. Third, many of the chapters express concern that traditional ways of conceptualising evidence do not match the nature of coaching and the realities of many contexts in which it is offered. Finally, many of the chapters highlight the importance of developing ways to address the systemic pressures that affect the people they coach. For example, Chapter 29 raises the issue of provider burnout within healthcare. While coaching can be used to modify a range of personal factors (e.g. increase resilience, narrative reframing, new approaches to work), the reality is that burnout is also influenced by a variety of contextual and systemic factors. The complexity and interconnectedness of our world will only make these issues more important in the future. The chapters in this section not only articulate the current landscape for coaching in their context, but they also provide some important new markers to chart a course for the road ahead.

In Chapter 24 *Christian van Nieuwerburgh* introduces us to the need for interculturally-sensitive coaching. He starts by defining culture and focuses on the role of culture in the interplay *between* coaches and coachees. He outlines two classic sets of dimensions for differentiating between cultures and explores more broadly the implications of defining people as 'the Other' and cultures in terms of their differences. He then goes on to advocate for cultural proficiency and intercultural sensitivity as two critical areas of development for coaches and the practice of coaching. He closes with some best practices and challenges for coaches in working this way and, in so doing, provides a useful link between theory and practice.

In Chapter 25 *Geoffrey Abbott* and *Raija Salomaa* address cross-cultural coaching as an emerging practice. They begin by looking at the nature of coaching, particularly its Eastern and Western influences, and the demands on coaches and leaders in working in a volatile, uncertain, complex and ambiguous world. They offer current survey instruments, models and approaches for coaching across cultures. In so doing, they advocate for a holistic approach that highlights the broader cultural influences that are in play in a given situation, more than the details of the specific cultures that are involved. They close with various examples of studies on cultural issues in coaching, many of which offer insights about how it is done well.

In Chapter 26 *Andrea Ellinger*, *Rona Beattie* and *Robert Hamlin* provide an overview of the history and use of coaching in a Human Resource Development (HRD) context. They note that both HRD and coaching have wrestled with issues related to definitional boundaries both within themselves and in relation to one another. They outline different ways in which coaching can be deployed internally and externally within organisations and consider key challenges for each. This represents a contribution to the broader dialogue about what coaching means and how it can be best applied in all of its forms. They note that this is increasingly important for organisations, as coaching is increasingly incorporated within HRD as a capability and a practice. Recommendations for future research focus on the use of coaching in action learning and on requirements for (and drawbacks) of managerial coaching.

In Chapter 27 *Sean O'Connor* and *Michael Cavanagh* offer a solid introduction to groups and teams as a context for coaching. Early on they pose a critical yet under-examined question: Where does change take place in coaching? In other words, what is the fundamental unit of analysis that is relevant to group coaching? In seeking to address this question, the authors identify three sets of relationships across three levels of systems, each of which affects both the process and the outcomes of coaching with groups and teams. In so doing, they propose that individual performance is typically more a function of team dynamics than the other way around. This not only affects how coaching is conducted in this context, but it also has broader implications for how we conceptualise and address people's issues in any coaching context. They offer a good overview of the current research on group and team coaching and the issues faced by leaders who engage in coaching.

In Chapter 28 *Christian van Nieuwerburgh* and *Margaret Barr* outline the critical issues related to coaching in educational contexts. They too acknowledge the challenges posed by the lack of definitional clarity for coaching. One way they address this issue is by providing a chart of the four primary ways in which coaching occurs in education (i.e. leaders, teachers, parents and community, and children and youth). They describe how coaching is typically conducted within each area and how these applications might collectively inform coaching more broadly. They close with a section on ways to further embed coaching in education and offer a global framework as a resource to do so. This chapter, like the one that follows, offers important glimpses into how coaching can be used to advance institutions, those who work in them and those who are served by them.

In Chapter 29 *Ruth Wolever*, *Margaret Moore* and *Meg Jordan* provide a helpful introduction to the current state of coaching in health care and its future opportunities. A notable contribution of this chapter is that it presents a chart of a vast field, something that will be an invaluable guide for those working and researching in this area. Like in Chapter 30, the authors identify three primary applications of coaching: leaders, providers and patients (also known as the Triple Aim). They address the challenges health care faces as it undergoes fundamental, structural shifts – and the implications for coaching as an increasingly important resource. They also identify challenges in determining how qualification decisions are made within health care (and by whom), and what these decisions entitle coaches to do. They close by citing samples of the current research in the area, particularly in respect to health behaviour change, and outline a possible agenda for future research.

In Chapter 30 *Yossi Ives* makes the case for coaching in relationships as a distinct genre. In so doing, he outlines the key issues related to working with singles, couples and parents in coaching. He offers initial thoughts on how to define coaching in relationships, including positioning it as a blend of personal development activity, goal focused work and therapeutic concerns. The author also joins with others in highlighting the relational nature of both coaching and development and the need for greater focus on this perspective to counteract a lingering bias in coaching toward individualist frames. Whilst some practice-based models of coaching in relationships are presented, there was little empirical work to review as the genre is new within coaching. Finally, some useful reflections are offered on the similarities and differences between psychotherapy and coaching as strategies for addressing relational issues and enhancing relational capabilities.

Part 5: Researching Coaching

Although all chapters in this volume engage with relevant research in exploring specific themes and aspects of coaching, there are issues that are pertinent to all researchers of coaching. For example, for anyone engaged in researching the effectiveness of coaching the issue of coaching outcomes is central to their inquiry. On the other hand, qualitative researchers are typically interested in coaching processes and in research methodologies appropriate to those types of investigations. There are also areas of coaching that draw heavily on particular research outputs (e.g. neuroscience and psychological assessment) and are important to recognise for the interest they have to many coaching scholars. Therefore, this section of the book discusses issues and methodologies related to the empirical investigation of coaching outcomes and processes. In addition, recent insights have been gathered from contemporary neuroscience and psychological assessment research, as examples of the emerging dialogue between coaching and relevant fields of research.

The section begins with Chapter 31 and a focus on the research of coaching outcomes. It is presented first as an acknowledgement that this type of research was most needed when coaching was attempting to establish itself as a new discipline. It was a response to the belief that the growth of coaching was contingent upon the confirmation of its effectiveness. In this chapter *Siegfried Greif* highlights a number of issues that exist with coaching outcome research, the most prominent of which is its heterogeneity. Considering that coaching is intangible, complex and co-constructed (with clients), difficulties abound with its evaluation. *Greif* argues that, given these circumstances, it is important to reduce clients' 'informational deficit' when evaluating coaching outcomes and encourage their contribution to the research on coaching effectiveness. This chapter also presents a critique of various research methodologies for outcome studies, along with a set of criteria for evaluating coaching outcomes.

In an extension of the discussion presented in the previous chapter, Chapter 32 moves beyond questions focused on the efficacy of coaching and towards questions more concerned with *how* coaching works (given that coaching outcomes studies seem to suggest that it does). In this chapter *Adrian Myers* starts with a definition of the coaching process and the importance of this focus of inquiry. He draws parallels with the development of process research in psychotherapy, which has made some significant advances of relevance to coaching research. In reviewing recent process research in coaching, the author separates studies into three different categories: hypothesis-testing studies, descriptive studies and theory-building studies. He goes on to suggest that future research into the coaching process could either extend previous work within these categories or develop completely new methodologies. The overarching message of this chapter of relevance to all researchers is the importance of examining their values and beliefs and the role they play in the choices made in the research process.

In Chapter 33 *Angela Passarelli*, *Ellen Van Oosten* and *Mark Eckert* introduce an area of study – neuroscience – that has attracted strong interest from coaching practitioners in recent years. Whilst the availability of (seemingly) relevant findings from a 'hard science' appears attractive to many coaches, very few could claim sufficient understanding and ability to accurately translate such knowledge into coaching practice. In a helpful chapter, the authors provide readers with an overview of the current state of the field and give a fair and balanced representation of what can be realistically claimed from neuroscience at this stage. This overview will also potentially be helpful for researchers in other generic disciplines who are looking to extend the impact of their empirical studies into applied fields such as coaching.

The section concludes with Chapter 34 and *Almuth McDowall*'s examination of the use of psychological assessment in coaching research and practice. In contrast to the very recent explosion of interest in neuroscience, the use of psychological assessment in coaching practice is as old as coaching itself. Similarly, using psychological instruments in coaching research is also not new. Despite its long history, the use of psychological assessment instruments in coaching is an area that is underresearched and their use in research has not been widely examined. The discussion commences with an overview of psychological assessments currently available, moves on to some of the most prevalent debates in the field and then analyses the (surprisingly) limited studies in this area in coaching. The chapter concludes with a number of helpful ideas about advancing coaching research through the use of psychological assessments.

Part 6: Development of Coaches

While there has been a proliferation of programmes to educate and develop coaches over the past two decades, little has been done to assess them or the strategies that are being used. As the field continues to both mature and spread, there seems to be a need to better understand how to develop more mature and masterful professional coaches through university-level programmes or other training providers. There also seems to be a need to better understand how to develop the wide variety of professional and non-professional people who wish to incorporate coaching into their commercial and non-commercial offerings. The challenge, as well articulated in these chapters, is that there is currently no consensus on how best to achieve these aims. In large part this reflects the postprofessional and postmodern nature of work. Even so, the authors in this section make a concerted effort to outline how this area might be advanced by presenting some of the key critiques, important variables and potential frames for future work.

From the work presented in this section, four key issues have emerged. First, coaching is largely an applied discipline that is only just developing its own knowledge base. As such, it draws from other bodies of knowledge to varying degrees, depending on the orientation and/or application. One of the consequences of this is that the potentially conflicting interests of the main stakeholders create a mismatch of intentions (e.g. to practise in an academically informed way, to be commercially viable and to seek to administer coaching as a profession). The challenge ahead will be to find better ways of aligning these areas of interest. Second, addressing this challenge will require new strategies given that the concept of a 'profession' has become increasingly fragile as a result of losing their monopoly on knowledge. Third, the lack of clarity and consensus about what coaching aspires to become can be seen as both a strength (as it has helped the field grow quickly) and a weakness (as it strives to mature). The question then becomes, where can larger questions be raised for the co-development of new pathways forward? Finally, the pace of technological change continues to outstrip our capacity to understand its impact or adapt to its possibilities. As such, it seems that developing more robust and fitting discourses and epistemologies will be essential for addressing these four areas as well as developing and educating coaches.

The section commences with Chapter 35 and a provocative look at the education and training of coaches. In this chapter *David Lane* argues for a reformed approach to education, one that transcends the use of 'competence' (the frame often required by professional coaching bodies) and advocates instead for developing approaches based on capabilities. The author goes on to discuss the value of four theories that could be better utilised for educating and training coaches: developmental, excellence, practice and professional learning. He also considers how three areas of knowledge (i.e. decision sciences, case formulation, and the scientist-practitioner models) could usefully inform coach education. The chapter concludes with an observation that universities and representative bodies continue to lack alignment on matters related to education and training, which (if it continues) may have serious implications for the future of coaching.

In Chapter 36 *David Gray* provides an update on the current state of supervision in coaching. His discussion focuses on two important questions. First, what is the role of supervision in the education of coaches? Second, what are the essential elements of effective supervision? As these questions are explored, the author draws upon developmental, psychotherapeutic and social role models and attempts to fill a gap in the literature by proposing an integrated, systemic model of coaching supervision. The model is accompanied by a description of how it could be used in various supervision settings and the value of situating supervision in a systemic context (within, between and around coaches and coachees). He also calls more broadly for a research agenda that generates a stronger evidence base for supervision in coaching and suggest specific questions that need to be addressed.

A discursive perspective on the assessment and accreditation of coaches is presented by *Bob Garvey* in Chapter 37, with a particular focus on the challenge posed by the psychological and managerial discourses that, according to the author, shape much of coaching. This perspective is influenced by Aristotelian distinctions drawn between *techne*, *episteme* and *phronesis* as forms of knowledge, with the author arguing that the dominant discourse exhibits a strong bias towards the first two epistemologies. He also suggests there is often a significant mismatch between the discourses used in coaching and those used by the coaching bodies, leading to dissatisfaction with policies related to accreditation and assessment processes. The use of adult learning theories – specifically those framed as phases, stages and journeys – is also evaluated to augment the standard conceptualisations of, and approach to, assessment and accreditation. The chapter concludes with an argument for an approach to assessment and accreditation of coaches that is more dynamic, contextual, inclusive and phronetic.

In Chapter 38 *Ioanna Iordanou* and *Patrick Williams* take a historical perspective on developing ethical capabilities in coaches. They observe that because the landscape of ethical standards in coaching is muddled, coaches are left to rely on their own devices regarding the development and maturity of their ethical capabilities. They then go on to explore what that means for practitioners and for the field and what might be done individually and collectively. In so doing they raise the fundamental question of whether a sufficient and unified code of ethics is possible given the pluralistic range of coaches and diverse applications of coaching. As a foundation for these discussions, they trace the development of Western ethics and the ethical frames that have emerged in the process. They use two case studies to illustrate some of the key ethical issues faced by coaches, as well as utilising them as a lens through which to look at the current state of play in coaching. The chapter concludes with the presentation of a framework for making ethical decisions in coaching and developing better ethical capabilities.

Working with new technologies in coaching is the focus of Chapter 39. In this chapter *Stella Kanatouri* and *Harald Geissler* highlight two key technological trends that are affecting coaching: the drive toward more self-directed learning and the presence of more socially-connected learning. The authors cite an array of empirical technological research and explain its relevance to coaching. They makes a strong case that coaching practitioners would benefit from a greater understanding of how different communication media (and supporting tools) potentially affect the coaching intervention from both the client's and coaches' perspective. The chapter also reviews some of the early stage technologies that were purpose-built to enable or support coaching, and highlights what sort of technological innovations might impact coaching in the future. Given the complex and dynamic nature of this area, readers should find the material covered in this chapter to be helpful for informing future decision-making about which technologies to use and for what purpose.

In the final chapter of the section, *Annette Fillery-Travis* and *Ron Collins* provide a thorough historical examination of whether coaching is a discipline, profession or industry (or something else), and how present choices might shape its future status. Similar to the earlier chapters by Lane (Chapter 35) and Garvey (Chapter 37), important points are raised about the larger issues facing coaching and the consequences of choices that the coaching community makes (or does not make) individually and collectively. One of the most interesting propositions they offer is that coaching may not need to keep striving to become a profession, assuming it could ever become one. Instead, the industry may continue to flourish and develop as a service underpinned by a growing discipline. The chapter concludes with some suggestions about possible futures for coaching, including its existence as an independent, eclectic, sub-discipline or new discipline.

FINAL REFLECTIONS

Throughout this Introduction we emphasised that the emerging discipline of coaching is characterised by a range of positions, approaches and different visions of its future. There are also differences in the concerns and priorities of academics and researchers on the one hand, and practitioners and professional bodies on the other. We have drawn attention to the complex relationship that exists between the needs of the industry at its relatively early stage of development and the academic aspirations to create as solid a foundation as possible. These struggles were noticeable in the process of redrafting a substantial number of chapters in this volume. Despite the explicit academic orientation of this book (concerned with mapping the field and critiquing the knowledge base), many authors seemed to be naturally oriented towards addressing the needs of practitioners, through recommendations for practice, rather than stimulating the creation of knowledge through thoughtful analysis of the literature and recommendations for further research.

Indeed, this practice orientation was so strong in some cases that we had to – with huge regret – recommend alternative outlets for publication (as they did not meet the requirements of this Handbook). Whilst this was, on the one hand, disappointing for the purposes of this volume, on the other hand we were encouraged that the field is blessed to have a good number of impressive thinkers who can also write persuasively about matters related to coaching practice. As a result, we feel reassured about the future of the practice-based coaching literature, as the field appears to be well stocked with thoughtful, capable authors.

Our task as editors was made more challenging by the diversity that exists in regards to the multi-disciplinary nature of the field and the different perspectives taken on what constitutes 'knowledge' and 'evidence' (based on different epistemological standpoints). As such, it seems there is no single authority on what is 'right' or 'wrong' when evaluating coaching knowledge. Had we been able to use an agreed framework to review our contributors' chapters, our task would likely have been more straightforward. However, on many occasions we were glad that our own epistemological attitudes were different from each other, as this permitted a 'fair' treatment of the presented material. What we were in general agreement about (and tried to communicate to the contributors) is that each chapter needed to present a comprehensive overview of each topic, along with an attempt to integrate different perspectives (where possible), and proposals for advancing knowledge. We hope that the reader will be able to use this Handbook as a clear, comprehensive and reliable guide for navigating this exciting, evolving, and (at times) confusing body of knowledge.

For us this project was both challenging and rewarding in equal measure. It was a privilege to be involved in the development of such a rich and textured volume. We were aiming for the most comprehensive map of the knowledge on coaching, and sought to cover as many themes and perspectives as were practically possible. In doing so, we also hoped that we might create a 'go-to' academic resource for those who become inspired to undertake empirical investigations in any of the topic areas. When considering a composite of the contributions contained in this Handbook, it was tempting to imagine a bright future for the coaching discipline, to make bold predictions and/or generate ideas to influence its future trajectory. However, we have resisted this temptation. In the spirit of coaching, we will leave these exciting opportunities to the reader and to all those who will participate in making this future happen.

REFERENCES

Bachkirova, T. & Kauffman, C. (2009). The blind men and the elephant: Using criteria of universality and uniqueness in evaluating our attempts to define coaching. *Coaching: An International Journal of Theory, Research and Practice*, 2(2), 95–105.

Bachkirova, T. & Lawton Smith, C. (2015). From competencies to capabilities in the assessment and accreditation of coaches. *International Journal of Evidence Based Coaching and Mentoring*, 13(2), 123–140.

Bachkirova, T., Sibley, J. & Myers, A. (2015). Developing and applying a new instrument for microanalysis of the coaching process: The Coaching Process Q-Set. *Human Resource Development Quarterly*, 26(4), 431–462.

Baker, S. (2015). *Practitioners' perceptions of the boundaries between coaching and counselling.* Unpublished PhD Thesis. University of Bedfordshire.

Campbell, L.F., Norcross, J.C., Vasquez, M.J. & Kaslow, N.J. (2013). Recognition of psychotherapy effectiveness: The APA resolution. *Psychotherapy*, 50(1), 98–101.

Cavanagh, M. (2009). Coaching as a method for joining up the dots: An interview by T. Bachkirova and C. Kauffman. *Coaching: An International Journal of Theory, Research and Practice*, 2(2), 106–116.

Cavanagh, M. & Lane, D. (2012). Coaching Psychology Coming of Age: The challenges we face in the messy world of complexity? *International Coaching Psychology Review*, 7(1), 75–90.

Corey, G. (2009) (8th ed.). *Theory and Practice of Counselling and Psychotherapy*. London: Brookes/Cole.

David, S., Clutterbuck, D. & Megginson, D. (2013). *Beyond Goals: Effective Strategies for Coaching and Mentoring*. Farnham: Govers.

Dryden, W. (2008) (5th ed.) (Ed). *Handbook of Individual Therapy*. London: Sage.

Ellinger, A.D., Hamlin, R.G. & Beattie, R.S. (2008). Behavioural indicators of ineffective managerial coaching: A cross national study. *Journal of European Industrial Training*, 32(4), 240–302.

Engel, J. (2008). *American Therapy: The Rise of Psychotherapy in the United States*. New York: Penguin.

Garvey, B. (2011). *A Very Short, Fairly Interesting and Reasonably Cheap Book about Coaching and Mentoring*. London: Sage.

Grant, A.M. & Cavanagh, M.J. (2004). Toward a profession of coaching, 65 years of progress and challenges for the future. *International Journal of Evidence-Based Coaching and Mentoring*, 2(1), 1–16.

Kampa-Kokesch, S. & Anderson, M.Z. (2001). Executive coaching: A comprehensive review of the literature. *Consulting Psychology Journal: Practice and Research*, 53(4), 205–228.

Lane, D.A., Stelter, R. & Stout-Rostron, S. (2014). The future of coaching as a profession.

In E. Cox, T. Bachkirova & D. Clutterbuck (eds.), *The Complete Handbook of Coaching* (pp. 377–390). London: Sage.

Maxwell, A. (2009). How do business coaches experience the boundary between coaching and therapy/counselling? *Coaching: An International Journal of Theory, Research and Practice*, 2(2), 149–162.

Naughton, J. (2002). The coaching boom: Is it the long-awaited alternative to the medical model? *The Psychotherapy Networker*, 26, 24–33.

Nelson-Jones, R. (2010) (5th ed.). *The Theory and Practice of Counselling*. London: Continuum.

Peltier, B. (2009) (2nd ed.). *The Psychology of Executive Coaching: Theory and Application*. New York: Brunner-Routledge.

Robson, D. (2011). Measuring value in the coaching relationship. *Strategic HR Review*, 10(2), 38–39.

Schomerus, G., Schwahn, C., Holzinger, A., Corrigan, P.W., Grabe, H.J., Carta, M.G. & Angermeyer, M.C. (2012). Evolution of public attitudes about mental illness: A systematic review and meta-analysis. *Acta Psychiatrica Scandinavica*, 125(6), 440–452.

Sherman, S. & Freas, A. (2004). The Wild West of executive coaching. *Harvard Business Review*, 82(11), 82–90.

Smith, M.L. & Glass, G.V. (1977). Meta-analysis of psychotherapy outcome studies. *American Psychologist*, 32(9), 752–760.

Spence, G.B. (2007). Further development of evidence-based coaching: Lessons from the rise and fall of the human potential movement. *Australian Psychologist*, 42(4), 255–265.

Stacey, R.D. (2003). *Strategic Management and Organisational Dynamics: The Challenge of Complexity*. Harlow: Prentice-Hall.

Stacey, R.D. (2012). Comment on debate article: Coaching Psychology Coming of Age: The challenges we face in the messy world of complexity. *International Coaching Psychology Review*, 7(1), 91–95.

Western, S. (2012). *Coaching and Mentoring: A Critical Text*. London: Sage

PART I
Positioning Coaching as a Discipline

Developing a Knowledge Base of Coaching: Questions to Explore

Tatiana Bachkirova

INTRODUCTION

As a developing discipline, coaching is expected to generate a body of knowledge that, although shared in many aspects with other disciplines, also addresses themes and issues that are specific to coaching and includes unique ideas, theories, methodologies and results of research. For the last two decades many researchers, academics, professional bodies and practitioners, each in their own way, have been contributing to the ambition for coaching to be knowledge-based. This Handbook represents their contribution revealing a significant diversity in terms of scope, focus and research methodologies.

This diversity can be explained not only by the multidisciplinary nature of coaching but also by different attitudes the authors may take to the very idea of what knowledge is. Although such diversity creates exceptional opportunities for expanding the breadth and depth of the knowledge base of coaching it might also lead to questions about the validity of such knowledge and criteria for establishing its value. The aim of this chapter is to take as broad a perspective as possible on the knowledge base of applied disciplines in principle in order to consider important questions that need to be asked when a new discipline, such as coaching is being established.

For the purposes of this discussion we can use the following as a working definition and argue that knowledge can be taken as 'a body of information, theories [and] methodologies broadly considered to have passed some tests of validity' (Alvesson, 2001, p. 867). It is important to explore what is meant by 'broad consideration' and 'some tests of validity' if we are to be concerned with the quality of the foundation on which the discipline of coaching is being built. This will help us to address those questions that are pertinent for researchers and the developers of models and theories of coaching, questions that are related to criteria of quality of their projects and propositions. All of the above are also important for coaching practitioners to become clearer about what it is that influences their judgment of the knowledge that constitutes the discipline of coaching and how this knowledge can be productively used. It is an intention in this chapter to demonstrate how an understanding of these complex theoretical issues can only enhance coaching practice at all levels.

In addressing questions of such magnitude, this chapter will position the developing discipline of coaching as a beneficiary not only of other applied disciplines, but also as a subject of influence by wider philosophical perspectives that inevitably shape this area of knowledge. These questions are:

- What is knowledge?
- How is knowledge generated and validated?
- What constitutes a theory for an applied discipline?
- How can theory be developed?
- How can the quality of research and theory be judged?
- How can this knowledge be utilised in practice?

The chapter will address these questions in light of the current debates in the coaching field with the recognition of relevant publications by coaching authors.

WHAT IS KNOWLEDGE?

This question might appear simple at first glance. However, defining knowledge is a task that can be approached in a number of different ways: from the philosophical inquiries into the general principles of knowledge to the knowledge that a practitioner brings to bear on that practice. In the latter sense knowledge is 'what is known' about practice and can reside in the intelligence and competencies of practitioners. In this book, however, 'what is known' is discussed with a purpose of presenting the body of knowledge that can be formally recognised as a foundation of a new discipline. This purpose requires that, in the first place, there is at least some understanding of what the nature of knowledge is in the broadest sense. This inquiry inevitably leads to realisation that from different philosophical positions what is seen as knowledge can be conceived differently. This realisation may give rise to some level of tension and uncertainty in disciplines such as social science, organisational studies, psychology and sociology. To explore the implications of this for coaching in this section we compare two systems of thought that are currently influencing the way researchers and influential thinkers in various fields approach the task of generating knowledge.

It is impossible to acknowledge all of the ongoing debates as to what the nature of knowledge is. Those involved in knowledge production usually start from considering what there is to know, or in other words what the nature of reality is (ontology). Secondly, they then have to decide if what we want to know is 'knowable' in principle and how it is that we come to know it (epistemology). The following question is how this knowledge can be gained (methodology). And finally, it matters how we can verify what we know as valid knowledge, and establish what is true about it. Some actors in the field of coaching may find these questions too abstract and of little practical significance. However, it could be argued that at this stage of the development of coaching as a discipline, those who introduce new theories, begin their scholarship, design educational programmes or create their personal models of coaching practice would all greatly benefit from understanding the principles of the foundation on which they are building.

There are many philosophical positions that have developed as the result of different ways of addressing the above questions (Bem and De Jong, 2013). Consequently, as these positions are at the foundation of any line of inquiry, in all disciplines there are a significant variety of theories and approaches to research and practice. For creating some structure in dealing with this variety, these philosophical positions will be explored under the umbrella of two systems of thought or general worldviews that are currently dominating intellectual and cultural inquiry: modernism and postmodernism. This differentiation is not free from contradictions and inevitably leads to the loss of subtlety and nuances of some specific philosophical positions. However, it also allows for the highlighting of current issues and concerns relevant for the coaching field and is therefore adopted here for pragmatic reasons and in spite of the recognised limitations.

Distinguishing Between Modernism and Postmodernism

A convenient way to understand modernism in the context of this conversation is as the natural-science-centred worldview, a belief system with a commitment to clear, absolute, 'objective' answers to questions about reality. The search for Truth is guided by the ideal of establishing a grand narrative from which all other 'facts' can be explained by linear, deductive logic. Modernism is driven by formal rational methods. It promises increasing social progress based on the rational application of universal laws about human nature that are 'discovered' through social science research. This process was claimed to be the means by which an end could be brought to major ideological differences around the world (Fishman, 1999).

One of the simplest ways to grasp postmodernism is to view it as an epistemological assumption that we are always interpreting our experienced reality through a pair of conceptual glasses based on our goals, past experiences, values, knowledge, language, culture, etc. It is never possible to take the glasses off. There are no superior criteria according to which some particular glasses should be better used or evaluated (Fishman, 1999). As there can be no one grand narrative, only many local ones, the knowledge can only be contingent and partial (Lyotard, 1984). Since there is a plurality of truths, all of which are contextually justified, no over-encompassing Truth is possible. For postmodernists, knowledge is always both relational and positional (Kerruish, 1991). Accordingly, standpoints are always situated in social relations and within ideologies. Power and knowledge are intricately connected and hierarchically arranged (Lyotard, 1984).

In relation to providing an explanation of what is happening in coaching, modernism and postmodernism may suggest different perspectives. Traditional modernism appears mostly in the form of positivist methodologies in search of certainty and predictability. It tends to assume linear cause–effect relationships between established determinants and a proportional increase in their effect. The basic unit of analysis are usually individuals or discrete elements and categories and their contributory effects (e.g. Kochanowski, et al., 2010; Franklin and Franklin, 2012).

Postmodernists see things differently. They stipulate that proportional effects do not necessarily follow some incremental increase of an input; uncertainty and indeterminacy are the name of the game. Rather than aiming for a global theory, postmodernists look for knowledge at the local scale, aiming to consider a significant number of potential influences on the focus of inquiry with appreciation of context and allowing for multiple interpretations of data (Hayles, 1990). Where causation is identified it is often attributed to the dynamic interaction of field rather than to discrete particle effects (Bohm, 1980).

Modernist notions of truth in relation to coaching would generally look like this: that there is an underlying physical reality that is affected as the result of coaching, e.g. that interventions can cause a change in the client's brain and behaviors and can be measured. A specific example of a study that could be aligned with this philosophical position is Jack et al. (2013). Many other research papers published in academic coaching journals would fit in this category particularly those which apply an experimental design (e.g. RCT – randomized control trial) expecting to control for various influences on coaching clients and to isolate an effect of a particular coaching intervention on the behavior of clients in order to measure it. Following established procedures for minimising effect of the researcher and other interfering factors on the findings allows these researchers to claim cause–effect relationship between e.g. specific coaching interventions and outcomes of coaching (e.g. Kochanowski, et al., 2010, or see Grant, 2013, Table 2.1).

Differing from the above, the expression of the postmodernist stance in coaching would be the view that coaching is a process of joint meaning-making – the process in which a coach and client co-create reality while in a dialog, which can in turn affect the state of those involved. Their perspectives on realities would be different but can be agreed on by trying to account for many influencing contexts and theories that both the client and coach hold. An example of the research from this position is a multifaceted analysis of a coaching session by Myers (2014). Researching coaching from this paradigm obviously implies different design from the positivist and postpositivist stance and consequently different criteria of rigour. It offers nevertheless an understanding of the coaching process in a way that is different from the traditional studies.

Although not all qualitative studies are conducted in the postmodernist tradition (e.g. phenomenological or heuristic inquiries), their focus on specific phenomena of coaching with detailed consideration of context and rich description of the psychological background of the study make them more aligned with this paradigm than with the modernist tradition (e.g. Maxwell, 2009; Gyllensten and Palmer, 2006).

Table 2.1 describes the variety of philosophical positions with an attempt to locate these in relation to modernism and postmodernism, acknowledging, of course, that all boundaries between these positions are inevitably permeable and thus open to debates.

Table 2.1 An overview of philosophical positions with regard to modernism and postmodernism

	Modernism	Postmodernism
Philosophical perspectives	Realism (there is reality that is separate from the mind and knowing involves a correspondence between the world and the mind)	Anti-realism (a view of reality as mental, implying that the world is not separate from the mind)
	Objectivism (reality exists outside of the individual and consists of specific entities)	Social constructionism (reality to a large extent is constructed by individuals and groups)
	Empiricism (knowledge comes from experience and through the senses. Scientific methods such as experiments and validated measurement tools can help to establish objective truth)	Critical Theory (is about understanding and theoretical explanation with an aim to reduce entrapment in systems of domination or dependence)
	Positivism (claims to achieve fundamental and objective knowledge about the world through natural sciences methods)	Contextualism (meaning is context-dependent, and contexts are boundless)
	Post-positivism (supports the view that reality exists and retains the idea of objective truth but accepts that it can be known only imperfectly and probabilistically, e.g. specific branches such as subtle realism and critical realism)	Hermeneutics (a method of reconstructing the meaning and experience of cultural products: an interpretation)
		Deconstruction (a process of analysis to reveal contradiction and injustice of conventional concepts and beliefs)
		Post-structuralism (a way of studying how knowledge is produced by analysing an object of study and the system of knowledge that produces it)

It provides a loose but useful set of categorisations which could be particularly informative for researchers at the stage of establishing their position in relation to a new research question. Some of the included positions are more about ontology (e.g. objectivism), others are about epistemology (e.g. empiricism) and some are about both (e.g. realism). The concept of relativism is not included in this table because it is more of a general principle rather than a philosophical perspective. It places the meaning of experiential and physical events in the relationships that exist among them and therefore is often a key criticism that is aimed at postmodernism (Bem and De Jong, 2013).

In distinguishing modernism and postmodernism it is also important to re-emphasise that they are not 'clear-cut' approaches to understanding the world which allow us to separate different philosophical positions. In this chapter they are seen as epistemological attitudes that determine to some extent how knowledge-seeking groups and individuals make sense of what it is that they find out. We also need to remember that the postmodern epistemological attitude is still in its early developmental stages and only provides us with a potential direction as to what comes next. At this stage its priority is to point out the anomalies in the modernist paradigm and it is mainly concerned with asking questions rather than providing answers.

Both, modernism and postmodernism, as epistemological attitudes, have characteristics that can be seen as progressive in relation to knowledge generation and both of them are severely criticised, as it would be expected, from the opposite camp (Table 2.2). This may generate anxiety in those who are new to research and wish for clarity and certainty when designing their projects. It might be also confusing for those who wish to make sense of research data in order to enhance their practice. It is however, a feature of our time and even those who hoped for the end of the 'paradigms war' and wish for some conversion of positions in research, may need to accept that '... there will be no single "conventional paradigm" to which all social scientists may ascribe in some common terms and with mutual understanding. Rather, we stand at the threshold of history marked by multivocality, contested meaning, paradigmatic controversies and new textual forms' (Guba and Lincoln, 2005, p. 212).

Table 2.2 Progressive and problematic aspects of modernism and postmodernism

Aspects	Modernism	Postmodernism
Acknowledgement of progressive contribution	Creating order out of chaos Strong priority of the intellect and rationality over everything traditional, ritualistic, irrational Cultural rise of secularism, science and technology, which are designed to be 'value-free' Opposition to all irrational authority – search for truth and active enhancement of human liberty Development of new techniques for achieving the predictable control of events	Acknowledging disorder Appreciation of diversity – giving voice to relatively powerless Challenging hegemony of rationality – accepting other ways of knowing (e.g. emotions, contemplation) Attempts to uncover power relationship and socio-political agendas Introduction of interpretation – the world is not only a perception but an interpretation
Points of critique	Science becomes scientism – the only source of knowledge Loss of human subjectivity – no depth Dominance of rationality All things have only instrumental value in the overall system	Reality may become nothing but interpretation Denying *depth* in general – no value or perspective is better than any other – flat field Scepticism of all theories At the extreme – anti-everything

Source: based on Fishman, 1999, Cilliers, 2005, Wilber, 2000

Pragmatism: A Helpful Third Way?

All aspects in Table 2.2 illustrate that a search for a 'perfect' perspective could be stimulating and developmental but also a futile exercise. However, for applied fields of knowledge such as coaching it is important to acknowledge the role of pragmatism as a philosophical position that has had a significant role in the modernist/postmodernist divide and is therefore not included in Table 2.1. Although originating earlier in modernism (Dewey, 1910; James, 1955) it has come to be more usually aligned with a postmodern epistemological stance that states that there is no way to know absolutely (Rorty, 2010). It has also been argued (e.g. Fishman, 1999) that pragmatism provides the means of overcoming the dichotomy drawn between epistemological attitudes of modernism and postmodernism by 'transcending the argument'.

Pragmatists do not see the value of stating what reality is like. According to them knowledge is interactive, it is the product of actively exploring the world and establishing what reality is by acting on it (Bem and De Jong, 2013). For example Peirce (1977) argued that the act of knowing includes the object of knowing, the sign of it (e.g. words or methods of studies) and the interpretant of the sign. All three elements are inseparable and therefore it does not make sense to talk about the existence of separate objects or signs as separate representations of independently existing objects. Thus pragmatism does not separate ontology from epistemology and is mainly concerned with the usefulness of knowledge for solving specific problems that we face (Rorty, 2010).

Pragmatism is also influential in challenging the traditional image of science. Science is often identified exclusively with modernistic positivism with consequences for some fields relevant to coaching. For example, according to Ashworth (2000) 'plainly most of psychology … is modernist in its assumptions' (p. 159). However, according to pragmatists, knowledge about the world comes in many varieties: 'science is just more systematic, general, methodical, open, etc. than common sense' (Bem and De Jong, 2013, p. 9). Instead of a fixed and ahistorical tradition of scientific method pragmatists such as Dewey (1910) and James (1955) suggest that there is another meaning of science which is about disciplined, critical, reflective thought that compares and contrasts evidence arguing for alternative interpretations or explanations of a particular phenomenon (Fishman, 1999). This position is being further developed by contemporary pragmatists (e.g. Capps, 2015). Polanyi (1969) also extends this view by emphasising personal responsibility in creative freedom as an ideal to strive for in creating knowledge while recognising constraints created by the judgment of the community of knowers.

Individuals and communities seeking knowledge in applied disciplines are inevitably subject to holding various philosophical positions described in this chapter and their findings and interpretations should be seen in the light of these attitudes. The overall view on the coaching literature demonstrates a significant variety of philosophical positions that are not necessarily acknowledged by the authors. It could be argued that the research on effectiveness of coaching (e.g. Table 2.1 in Grant, 2013) is often driven by the expectations of traditional academia and organisational buyers who are educated in the modernist tradition. The popular, opinion-based literature on coaching (e.g. Whitmore, 2002; Rogers, 2012) is driven by the desire to share experiences, observations and models that represent what worked for these authors in practice. There are also much smaller, but growing categories of publications such as qualitative studies from the social constructivist position (e.g. Maxwell, 2009) and the conceptual work from the critical theory position (e.g. Western, 2012) that have more affinity with postmodern epistemological attitude. In the following sections some criteria for evaluating and using the insights of these will be discussed in further detail.

KNOWLEDGE IN THE MULTIDISCIPLINARY CONTEXT

Coaching has obvious ties to other disciplines such as counselling and psychotherapy, mentoring, leadership development and consultancy, sociology, philosophy, psychology etc. (e.g. Bachkirova, 2007; Garvey, 2014; Day et al., 2009; Kilburg, 2000). Figure 2.1 describes the layers of influence for coaching that start from most generic fields such as philosophy, psychology, biology, but also sociology and the humanities. The next layer depicts more specific disciplines such as ethics, adult development and organisational studies which themselves can be seen as subsections of more generic fields of knowledge. The layer closer to coaching may include therapy, HRD and training and the closest one might be counselling, mentoring and consulting. Within each of these established fields there are various traditions and approaches, each of which might have its own assumptions about human nature and how individuals learn and change. Consequently, coaching practitioners and researchers originally trained in these traditions, may be influenced by theories and discourses dominant in these subject areas.

It is important to notice that the epistemological attitudes of modernism and postmodernism have cross-disciplinary influences on the above fields of knowledge. For example, in a modernist manner a typical professional practice process would look like a step-by-step approach that starts from the laws discovered in basic science, which are then modified in applied research, finalised into a method and finally delivered by a professional as an intervention to a client (Peterson, 1991). However logical, this process would be seen very differently by those who take into account: how an individual client and coach view and experience it (phenomenology of the process); their beliefs, expectations and mutual sense making in interaction (hermeneutics); and many factors of their context and wider environment that are entangled in the coaching process (complexity theories). Figure 2.2 shows that coaching is not a simple intervention and its complexity derives from the combination of the significant number of factors influencing the process and outcomes of coaching. As a complex

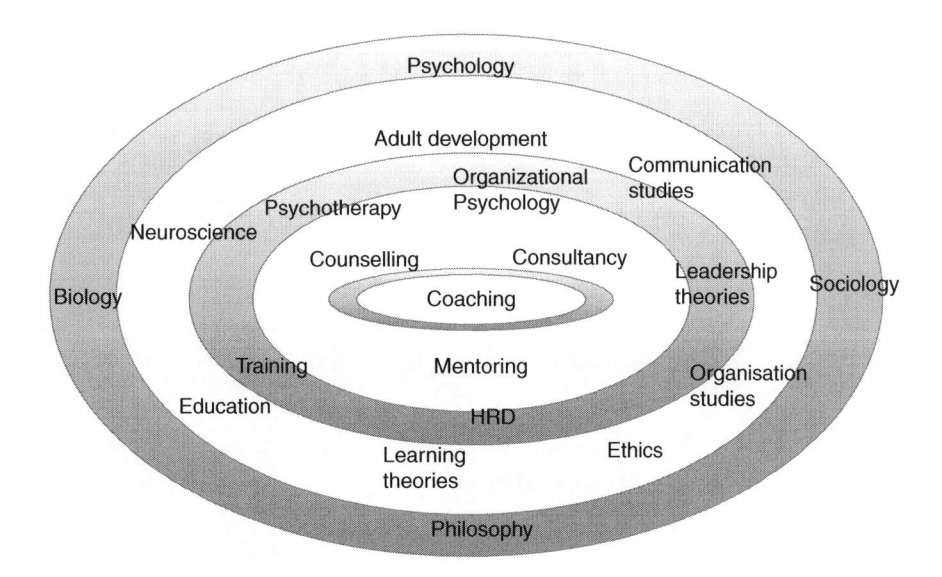

Figure 2.1 Positioning coaching amongst other disciplines of knowledge

interactive process it requires a theoretical/epistemological framework that acknowledges the dynamics of this complexity.

Although complexity theories are not explicitly connected to postmodernism, Cilliers (2005) argued that a postmodern approach is inherently sensitive to complexity as 'it acknowledges the importance of self-organisation whilst denying a conventional theory of representation' (p. 113). The importance of complexity theories for coaching is in providing an alternative perspective on applied practice to the linear cause–effect explanations of reductive positivism.

According to Burnes (2004) we should refer to complexity theories rather than theory, as there are variations on the theme of complexity by different authors (Rescher, 1996; Styhre, 2002; Stacey, 2003). Stacey (2003) argued that other theories seek to construct mathematical models of systems at the macro level, whilst the complex adaptive systems theory (CAS) that he proposed, seeks to formulate rules of interaction for the individual entities that make up a system or population. All complexity theories see natural systems as both non-linear and self-organising. It is not a combination of a number of linear systems but a purposeful system with emerging properties that makes this system adaptive. Adopting a CAS lens to coaching implies that although coaching is an intentional activity of the participants, their relationship and the context of engagement are regarded as being in a state of flux (Stacey, 2003). Consequently, as indicated in Figure 2.2 the quality of coaching engagements is subject to fluctuation in the characteristics of the coach, the characteristics of the client, nuances of the coaching relationship and various contextual factors (Cavanagh and Lane, 2012; Cox et al., 2014). According to this view the process of coaching is seen as 'a conversational, reflexive narrative inquiry ... as an alternative to restrictive rules and procedures' (Stacey, 2012, p. 95). Thus the emergent nature of this process makes its outcomes largely unpredictable (Alvesson, 2001; Cavanagh and

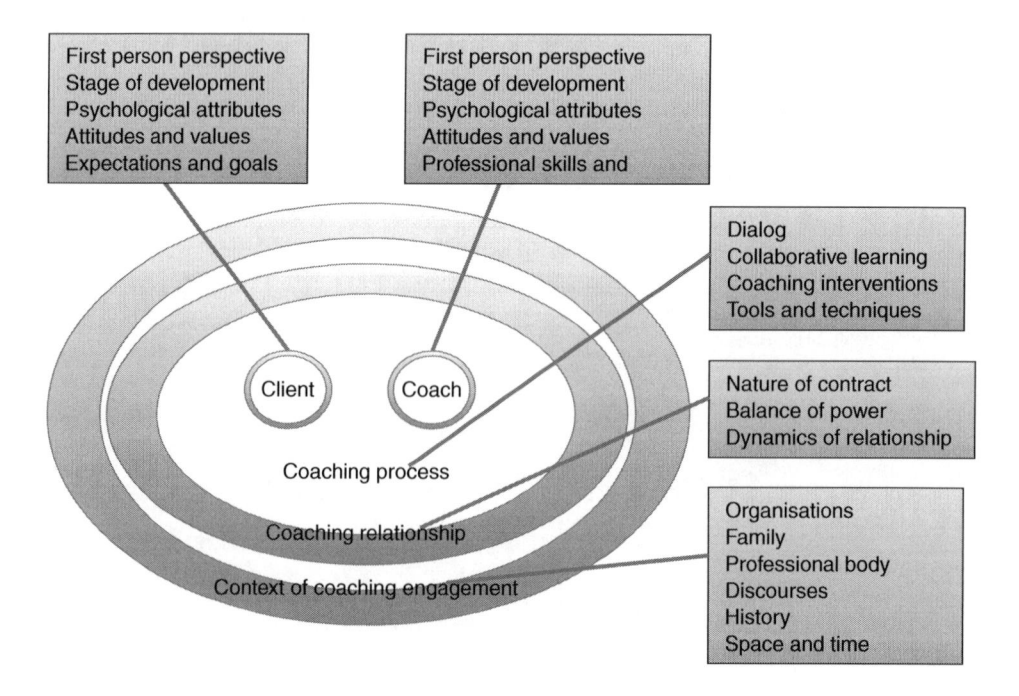

Figure 2.2 Complexity of factors involved in coaching engagement

Lane, 2012; Garvey, 2011; Jones and Corner, 2012; O'Connor and Cavanagh, 2013; Schön, 1983; Stacey, 2003, 2012).

In relation to issues and debates in coaching, this view of the coaching engagement presents a strong challenge, for example, to the assumptions behind competency-based assessments of the coaches. It has been argued (Bachkirova and Lawton Smith, 2015) that approaches to the accreditation of coaches developed by professional bodies are more in line with a modernist view of the world that implies a linear cause–effect relationship between theories, methods and outcomes in applied practice. A more postmodern stance on practice that is in line with complexity theories would question the above causality by introducing the element of joint meaning making of the practitioner and client and the emergent nature of coaching conversations (Stacey, 2003, 2012; Cavanagh and Lane, 2012; Bachkirova and Lawton Smith, 2015; Garvey, 2011; Jones and Corner, 2012). Consequently, Bachkirova and Lawton Smith (2015) argued for a capabilities approach rather than competencies-based frameworks.

If coaching is understood as a process of 'joint meaning making' between coach and client this places it automatically in a hermeneutic context – it is a complex interpretative process and, as such, falls outside of any methodological approaches that seek to limit it to linear-causal relationships. The 'hermeneutic flexibility' of the creative, interpretative dynamic of the coach–client relationship naturally places the theoretical foundations of coaching as a 'knowledge-based discipline' in sympathetic alignment with a postmodern epistemological attitude. However, pragmatism can then rescue it from the obvious pitfalls that postmodernism leaves itself exposed to.

It is important to notice, at the same time, that complexity theories can be also adopted by those researching from the modernist stance (e.g. Boyatzis, 2006; Jack et al., 2013; O'Connor and Cavanagh, 2013). For example, in testing Boyatzis's (2006) Intentional Change Theory (ICT) – an attempt to explain behavioural change, using concepts from complexity theories – some of the studies use approaches that are fairly reductive in relation to the complexity of a coaching conversation. For example, in the study by Jack et al. (2013) the attempt was made to imitate the coaching process by interviewing undergraduate students about their experiences and future goals using a pre-recorded video of the 'coach' who asks specific questions and gives pre-recorded responses. When these pre-recorded questions invited students to contemplate their desired future 'instead of the more typical approach for coaching or advising in which a person is reminded of his/her weaknesses or deficiencies and told how to improve' (p. 374) their brain scans indicated that the former is better than the latter, 'because they activate neural regions and circuits that cause the person to be more cognitively and perceptually open and engage positive motivational processes' (p. 382).

From other theoretical and practical perspectives, these types of experiments may look like an unjustified reduction of the complexity of interaction involved in coaching. It is important nevertheless to build on the advantages provided by the multidisciplinary nature of coaching. Research in neuroscience and epigenetics provides an important additional perspective on the process of coaching that can only add to our understanding of it on the biological level. The insights from this level of analysis are currently available because of the proximity of coaching to other related activities, such as learning and stress management, in relation to which some significant progress has been made. At the same time, it is also important to consider and acknowledge the limitations in the degree of adaptation of such knowledge. For example, it is quite likely that advances in neuroscience will become more relevant for developing the knowledge base of coaching. However, premature promises with far reaching extrapolations of findings (the above study is named 'Visioning in the brain: An fMRI study of inspirational coaching and mentoring') that significantly oversimplify coaching may also create a false image of the profession amongst potential clients, sponsors and those who wish to study coaching.

CREATING A KNOWLEDGE BASE OF COACHING – RESEARCH, THEORIES AND REFLECTIONS ON PRACTICE

In addition to the relevant knowledge from other fields for the last two decades many researchers, academics and practitioners around the world have been working with the aim to advance our understanding of coaching as a unique discipline. Even being educated in various professional fields they are united by the intention to extend the knowledge of coaching. Although this chapter questions the intention to reach certainty in a pursuit for knowledge and instead advocates the 'acceptance of provisional and contingent in everything we do' (Burbules, 1996, p. 46), further understanding of our practice is important and can be advanced by research and theorising. This section will consider what may constitute the knowledge base of coaching and what benchmarks could be considered to ensure a useful contribution.

As in other disciplines, knowledge includes a) the body of rigorous research as well as b) theories, models and conceptual propositions. Both of the above are examined in practice by practitioners through their reflection and analysis. Their systematic reflection and analysis of practice in the form of case studies and action research projects can also contribute to knowledge.

Research and theory building are equally important for the development of the knowledge base. It could be said that research generates evidence of effectiveness and a rich description of coaching practice to allow for the analysis of coaching with various levels of detail. Theories on one hand, provide synthesis of such information in the form of propositions that organise, predict and explain observations by telling how phenomena relate to each other. For example, research studies specific interventions and qualities of the coach that influence the outcome of coaching. Theory, on the other hand, explains why such interventions and behaviours of the coach might be helpful in certain situations.

On Developing Research

So far, there is a clear tendency that the body of research on coaching is growing year by year (Stern and Stout-Rostron, 2013) in comparison to the evident lack of theories specifically developed for coaching. One of the explanations for such a discrepancy is the growing emphasis on the importance of research in postgraduate programmes in coaching, growth of specific research-oriented units in professional bodies, a pressure for large organisational buyers to demonstrate the effectiveness of coaching and limited available funding for research. There are also many publications that provide guidance for running research projects specifically on coaching in the handbooks and academic journals (e.g. Fillary-Travis and Cox, 2014; Saunders and Rojon, 2014).

Although overall awareness about the importance of research in the coaching field is growing, there are differences in the influence of modernist and postmodernist paradigms in the way the research methodologies are chosen, evaluated and disseminated. The dominance of modernism is evident in the preferences of the editors of academic journals and research users for generalisation of findings, large samples and use of statistical packages for analysis. Recognition of this state of affairs is not meant to minimise the value of the modernist types of research. These studies are highly important for the coaching field as they allow testing viable hypotheses, generalisation of findings and provide a meta-perspective on coaching from a number of studies. These studies enrich our understanding of specific and detailed questions about practice and add to the credibility of the field at the stage when it is highly needed. At the same time, the defence of postmodern studies that might seem to be strongly presented in this chapter is intended in order to establish a more balanced stance to what is considered valid knowledge about coaching. The discipline of coaching would equally benefit from the appreciation of rigorous, hypothesis testing research and also contextually grounded studies which provide rich qualitative data and in-depth investigation of specific elements of coaching, giving voice to multiple stakeholders of the coaching engagements (Fillary-Travis and Cox, 2014).

This balanced stance to various methodologies would allow researchers to freely choose the methodology they feel is more suitable to the question they wish to explore, and the epistemological attitude with which they are more philosophically aligned. They should not feel constrained by expectations other than the rigour of the process. In a developing discipline such as coaching, probably more than in the established fields, Feyerabend's (1975) suggestion that knowledge is best obtained 'from a proliferation views rather than from the determined application of a preferred ideology' (p. 52) rings true. He also argued for the need not to destroy, but rather to deprivilege the rules of traditional science and encourage alternative modes of knowledge inquiry.

At the stage of the co-existence of both epistemological attitudes the researchers might well benefit from mutual learning from each other. The writing of postmodernist researchers can be well improved by the standards of clarity and precision usually characteristic of positivist presentation of findings. At the same time, some values advocated by postmodernists would be usefully adopted by traditional researchers. As Mascolo and Dalto (1995) argued, positivist researchers 'would also profit by adding the postmodern value of self-reflexivity to their bag of virtues' (p. 188).

It is important, however, to remember that the appropriate criteria of rigour need to be applied to the studies conducted from different paradigms. For example well known criteria of quality for more traditional research are validity, reliability and generalisability of the findings (Robson, 2001). However, applying the same criteria for evaluating the rigour of qualitative research is inappropriate. This type of research varies in terms of the main philosophical assumptions and therefore needs to be judged according to their relevant principles. For example Lincoln and Guba (1985) described as alternatives to the above criteria of quality three others: confirmability, dependability and transferability – criteria more suitable for qualitative studies. However, even these criteria would vary if different qualitative methodologies were used, such as for example phenomenological study, Grounded Theory or Discourse Analysis (Willig, 2006).

On Developing Theory

As already noted, theory building in coaching is far behind research activity. In order to encourage this process this section includes a discussion of the following aspects:

1. What are the general and specific elements of the theories?
2. What are the methods of theory building?
3. How can a theory be evaluated?

Theory can be described as 'a coherent description, explanation and representation of observed or experienced phenomena' (Gioia and Pitre, 1990, p. 587). Wacker (1998) argued that a theory should have 'four components: definitions, domain, relationships, and predictive claims to answer the natural language questions of who, what, when, where, how, why, should, could and would' (p. 368). It has been argued that any theory of coaching should include the following elements:

- the main concepts and assumptions about human nature
- core distinctive features, such as processes of change and methods and techniques of influencing
- an indication of in what context and with what type of clients this approach would be most or least helpful (Bachkirova et al., 2014).

Theory building is the ongoing process of producing, confirming, applying, and adapting theory (Lynham, 2000). According to Torraco (2002) there are five specific methods for building theory that do not preclude authors from staying aligned with their deep-seated values and assumptions about ontology, epistemology and their other philosophical beliefs. He also argued that some theory-building methods are better suited for the particular purposes of theorising than the others, notwithstanding personal intentions of the theorist. These methods are: Dubin's method, grounded theory, meta-analytic theory building, the social constructionist approach, and theory building from case study research (Torraco, 2002). The adaptation of the description of these for the coaching field is presented in Table 2.3.

It is important to say that not all research projects that use the methods in Table 2.3 lead

Table 2.3 Methods for theory building

Method	Description (adapted from Torraco, 2002)
Dubin's method	Dubin's (1978) method for theory building follows the quantitative research and is used by those who adopt a theory-then-research strategy for theory building. This method is based on the assumptions that knowledge is created to explain, predict, and control the phenomenon of interest and that the discovery of generalisable laws and explanations e.g. of coaching effectiveness is possible and desirable. The method consists of an eight-phase process for theory-building from initial construction and the development of the theory to conducting research for empirical verification.
Grounded Theory	Grounded Theory method is an inductive approach to generating theory. Theory evolves during grounded theory building through continuous interplay between analysis and data collection. During the research process, theory is provisionally verified through continuous matching of theory against data. New theoretical understandings of a particular theme of coaching from the perspective of relevant stakeholders, e.g. coaches or clients, emerge from the data. Theory building using this approach is particularly well suited to generating novel theoretical understandings and tentative hypotheses about under-researched elements and processes of coaching.
Meta-analytic theory	Meta-analytic theory building uses formal statistical techniques to sum up a body of separate but similar empirical studies of, e.g. effectiveness of coaching programmes. The purpose of meta-analysis is to synthesise and organise existing empirical findings on a topic into a coherent pattern. Theory is based on general conclusions drawn from across multiple studies.
The social constructionist approach	Theory building by this method is not undertaken to uncover a theoretical truth or reality but to model an understanding of the sense that people make of e.g. the coaching process. The emphasis is on the specific, the local, and the particular as a means to more closely represent the lived experience of those studied. The researcher remains visible and self-declared during the process of research and theory building, so that it is clear when the voice of the researcher is represented and when the voices of others are put forward. This method seeks to present meaning through carefully crafted narratives of how people make sense of the phenomena in question.
Theory building from case study research	This method focuses on understanding the dynamics present within a single organisation, coaching programme or even one coaching session, by taking advantage of the rich context for empirical observation provided by case settings. It uses qualitative or quantitative methods to explain the dynamics of phenomena occurring within case settings. It is particularly appropriate when little is known about a phenomenon, current perspectives seem inadequate because they have little empirical substantiation, or they conflict with each other or common sense. This method can be consistent with any paradigmatic approaches to knowledge creation.

to a theory. Some of them only provide an element of a theory, some may only develop relevant concepts that could potentially lead to a theory, but others may simply not generate significant findings that allow them to be considered as a theory.

However, it is more difficult to establish the quality of a theory in comparison to the quality of research. In fact, there is no way to prove, in the conventional positivistic sense, that one theory is better than another. This is partly because the methods one would use to make such arguments are based on a set of ontological and epistemological commitments that are different between the authors (Greeno, 1997). However, as Box and Draper said that 'essentially all models are wrong but some are useful' (1987, p. 424), pragmatists would argue that some theories could be more useful than the others for some particular tasks and situations within coaching. Hence, experimentation with theories in practice and theoretical debates are an important part of developing a new discipline and need to be encouraged.

For the purpose of initiating positive approaches to theory development, a theory could be considered useful if it:

- identifies patterns in observations of practice previously unrecognised
- explains relationships between concepts
- extends understanding provided by other theories
- creates building blocks for new theories
- suggests an intervention or a course of action that proves to be useful in coaching practice.

Finally, it is important to highlight that theories of coaching would not be able to establish something absolute about how the coaching engagement functions. They can however, provide dynamic frameworks in which a constructive discourse allows for, or facilitates a creative, pluralistic approach out of which the knowledge base emerges. It is clear that there are no right approaches to practice, or that definitive conclusions can be reached. However, it is important that those producing a theory can rationally justify their approach by reference to empirical data, theoretical discourses and the set of desired aims to be addressed.

HOW KNOWLEDGE IS USED

The knowledge users include coaches, coaching students, researchers, educators of coaching, supervisors, policy makers, organisational sponsors and potentially clients who wish to be informed about the process of coaching. The themes of this chapter can be of concern for all of them as indicators of the quality of practice they are involved with. It is, for example known that industry-funded studies are more likely to report positive outcomes (Killin and Della Sala, 2015). Therefore, one of the first implications of the theme of quality for knowledge users is engagement with a question: What is important for differentiating the quality of sources of knowledge for coaching practice? Table 2.4 describes some ideas that knowledge users can consider in relation to research and theories.

Most of the suggestions in this table were already discussed in previous sections of this chapter. Only the very first suggestion in each column of Table 2.4 may benefit from examples of coaching theories and bodies of work by specific authors and demonstrate how the positioning of these in their philosophical 'home' can help to understand them better. Currently there are only a few fully developed theories that are specifically created for coaching, e.g. a theory of developmental coaching by Bachkirova (2011), a meta-theory of coaching (Western, 2012), and a theory of narrative coaching (Drake, 2015). Although not presented as theory there is also a body of conceptual work by such authors as Garvey (2011), Grant (2013), Hawkins and Smith (2013) which contribute to a conceptual understanding of coaching. The authors are rarely explicit about the philosophical background of their work, but understanding

Table 2.4 Suggestions for knowledge users for differentiating the quality of research, theories and models

What can be useful for evaluating the quality and practical value of:	
Coaching research	Coaching theories and models
Understanding of the paradigm of knowledge (e.g. positivism or constructivism) from which the research is conducted	Understanding a philosophical position at the base of the theory and recognising that social theories are always incomplete and impossible to prove
Understanding of different criteria of quality and rigour according to paradigm	Taking a theory or model as a perspective on practice, one of many possible
Asking questions that can position research findings in relevant contexts	Establishing a specific niche/context where it could be useful
Comparing to the observation of practice and reflection	Evaluating the value of theory and models by experimenting on practice

their epistemological stance can place the purpose and style of their work in an appropriate context. For example, knowing that the work of Garvey (2011) is written from sceptical or critical postmodernism helps to put into context that his purpose is to challenge current discourses in coaching. Similarly, in Table 2.5 the attempt is made to locate a selection of specific conceptual work written on coaching in a potential philosophical orientation, with a caveat the authors may not see it this way.

Knowledge users can also influence the development of the knowledge base of coaching explicitly and implicitly. An explicit part of their contribution may be in taking part in research when there is a call for participants. In a more active way coaches in particular can describe and collect case studies from their own practice with a rich description of processes and contextual details. The bank of such case studies could be invaluable for research purposes.

In terms of a more implicit influence, it is important to recognise that the level of thinking amongst practitioners and other stakeholders also creates dominant discourses that in turn shape the discipline and policies of coaching. For example, some theoretical generalisations and policy decisions are made on the basis of the collected views of coaches when they are participating in various studies or endorse certain policies of professional bodies.

Coaches in particular are interacting with the knowledge base of coaching by making decisions in each particular professional situation. They formulate ways in which to understand and address issues and problems they face (Alvesson and Deetz, 2000). These informed frameworks of knowledge and experience are seen as personal theories-in-use (Argyris and Schon, 1974, 1996) or theories-in-practice (Lynham, 2000, 2002). Some postgraduate programme and accreditation schemes are now asking coaches to make their theories-in-use more explicit and be able

Table 2.5 Conceptual work and theories of coaching with corresponding philosophical positions

Theories and conceptual papers	Influencing philosophical position
Grant (2013), Boyatzis (2006), Palmer (2008)	Post-positivism
Garvey (2011)	Sceptical or critical postmodernism
Bachkirova (2011)	Postmodern pragmatism with developmental structuralism
Hawkins and Smith (2013)	Connectionism and system theories
Western (2012)	Critical theory and contextualism
Drake (2015), Cox (2012)	Social constructionism
Cavanagh and Lane (2012)	Complexity theories

to articulate and defend their position. When the decisions about these positions are made understanding the roots of these positions may help to avoid unexpected surprises. In the words of one insightful secondary school pupil 'nothing I think about are my original thoughts'. What could make them 'mine' is examining their source in light of one's current values and intentions. Using Table 2.6 it is possible to compare potential differences in how modernist and postmodernist epistemological attitudes may be evident in coaching practice.

It is evident that both paradigms are currently present in coaching discourses and all stakeholders are influenced by both of them. This may lead to incompatible beliefs and consequently to incompatible models of practice and policies. For example:

- We believe in the unique self-expression of individuals, but create uniformed competences frameworks.
- We hate hierarchies but develop categories of professionalism, e.g. master–practitioner.
- We advocate evidence-based practices and policies but support gradation of expertise in certification systems without any research supporting that master-coaches demonstrate better results than a novice coach.
- We believe in self-determination of the client but subordinate the needs of the client to the needs of the organisations.

The inconsistent beliefs and policies may need to be examined as we attempt to be more careful and rigorous in our thinking. However, the expectation to be neutral, unbiased, or value-free as coaches is also unrealistic from the postmodernists' point of view. From the position of philosophical hermeneutics and complexity theories Cilliers (2005) suggests that 'to make a responsible judgment – whether it be in law, science or art – would ... involve at least the following components:

- Respecting otherness and difference as values in themselves.
- Gathering as much information on the issue as possible, notwithstanding the fact that it is impossible to gather all the information.
- Considering as many possible consequences of the judgment, notwithstanding the fact that it is impossible to consider all the consequences.
- Making sure that it is possible to revise the judgment as soon as it becomes clear that it has flaws, whether it be under specific circumstances, or in general' (pp. 139–140).

CONCLUSION

This chapter aimed to provide an overview of the influential forces on the process of

Table 2.6 Aspects of coaching practice influenced by the modernist and postmodernist epistemological attitudes

Aspect of coaching	Modernists tendency	Postmodernists tendency
Focus of the coach attention	'Quality': improvement of the client and the client's system	'Equality' and joined meaning making as there is no one 'true' way to see situations or to act
Role of the coach	Expert of the process and facilitator of development	Partner in a dialogue
Coaching relationship	Is a means for successful work (development of trust)	Is a purpose in itself – a model of joined inquiry
Trusted information for development of practice	Results from large projects that use statistical analysis and are published in well-known journals	Findings of qualitative studies with in-depth analysis of data from experienced practitioners in well-described contexts
Evaluation of coaching	Is important as a proof of good work	Is seen as a disruption from learning
Potential problems	Quality and creativity may be compromised by compliance to external expectations	It is difficult to achieve consensus as to where the benchmarks for progress are giving the appearance that 'anything goes'

building a knowledge base for the discipline of coaching and their effect on the current literature on coaching. The literature was reviewed with examples of modernist and postmodernist epistemological attitudes in the way authors conceptualise learning, change and individual development in coaching. Such conceptualisations in turn define what is possible in practice, what theories and methods of practice are relevant and how the outcomes of practices can be evaluated. It is hoped that this chapter can serve as an aid for various stakeholders of coaching in their pursuit for developing as full an awareness as possible about the foundational values of their practice and make informed decisions about research, educational programmes and coaching strategies.

This chapter has focused on questions that have long been of importance to the stakeholders of coaching, and, if coaching is to continue advancing as a discipline, they will not diminish in their importance. As this volume demonstrates, the knowledge base of coaching is growing fast. However, it is vital that the industry develops a more sophisticated understanding about both what knowledge is and how it is best and most appropriately generated. In keeping with the spirit of coaching, the simple process of engaging with such questions is inherently developmental for researchers and practitioners, irrespective of whether the outcomes of future coaching research are satisfying to all it stakeholders.

A strong theme of this chapter is that there is a significant amount of diversity in the philosophical positions, genres and theories currently reflected in the coaching literature. Its key message to readers is that effort should be made to appreciate the diversity of such perspectives, rather than opt for unjustified universality. This message fits well with a core strength of coaching, which aims to work with a unique combination of factors in clients' situations, their self and the whole organism. Thus it attempts to develop unique ways of addressing the challenges that this world presents for them. The uniqueness however is not something completely new. More than often the unique is a creative combination of what is known. In the same way this might be a model for developing a new discipline of coaching.

ACKNOWLEDGMENT

I am grateful to Simon Borrington for insightful comments on the first draft of this chapter. To him I owe the concept of 'epistemological attitude' as an essential one for this chapter.

REFERENCES

Alvesson, M. (2001). Knowledge work: Ambiguity, image and identity. *Human Relations*, 54(7), 863–886.

Alvesson, M. and Deetz, S. (2000). *Doing Critical Management Research*. London: Sage.

Argyris, C. and Schon, D. (1974).*Theory in Practice: Increasing Professional Effectiveness*. San Francisco: Jossey-Bass.

Argyris, C. and Schon, D. (1996). *Organizational Learning II: Theory, Method and Practice*. Reading, Mass.: Addison-Wesley.

Ashworth, P. (2000). *Psychology and 'Human Nature'*. Hove: Taylor & Francis.

Bachkirova, T. (2007) Role of coaching psychology in defining boundaries between counselling and coaching. In S. Palmer & A. Whybrow, (eds.), *Handbook of Coaching Psychology*, London: Routledge, pp. 325–350.

Bachkirova, T. (2011). *Developmental Coaching: Working with the Self*. Maidenhead: Open University Press.

Bachkirova, T., Cox, E. and Clutterbuck, D. (2014). Introduction. In E. Cox, T. Bachkirova and D. Clutterbuck (eds.), *The Complete Handbook of Coaching* (2nd ed.). London: Sage, pp. 1–18.

Bachkirova, T. and Lawton Smith, C. (2015). From competencies to capabilities in the assessment and accreditation of coaches.

International Journal of Evidence Based Coaching and Mentoring, 13(2), 123–140.
Bem, S. and De Jong, H. (2013). *Theoretical Issues in Psychology: An Introduction* (3rd ed.). London: Sage.
Bohm, D. (1980). *Wholeness and the Implicate Order*. London: Routledge.
Box, G. E. P. and Draper, N. R. (1987). *Empirical Model-Building and Response Surfaces*. Hoboken, NJ: John Wiley & Sons.
Boyatzis, R. (2006). An overview of intentional change from a complexity perspective. *Journal of Management Development*, 25 (7), 607–623.
Burbules, N. (1996). Postmodern doubt and philosophy of education. In A. Neiman (ed.), *Philosophy of Education 1995*. Urbana: Philosophy of Education Society, pp. 39–47.
Burnes, B. (2004). From 'Kurt Levin and complexity theories: back to the future'? *Journal of Change Management*, 4(4), 309–325.
Capps, J. (2015). Epistemology, Logic, and Inquiry. In S. Pihlsrom (Ed.), *The Bloomsbury Companion to Pragmatism*. London: Bloomsbury, pp. 81–94.
Cavanagh, M. and Lane, D. (2012). Coaching psychology coming of age: The challenges we face in the messy world of complexity. *International Coaching Psychology Review*, 7(1), 75–90.
Cilliers, P. (2005). *Complexity & Postmodernism: Understanding Complex Systems*, London: Routlege.
Cox, E. (2012). *Coaching Understood*. London: Sage.
Cox, E., Bachkirova, T. and Clutterbuck, D. (2014) Theoretical traditions and coaching genres: Mapping the territory. *Advances in Developing Human Resources*, 16(2), 127–138.
Day, D. V., Harrison, M. M. and Halpin, S. M. (2009). *An Integrative Theory of Leadership Development: Connecting Adult Development, Identity, and Expertise*. New York, NY: Psychology Press.
Dewey, J. (1910). Science as subject-matter and as method. *Science*, 36, 127.
Drake, D. B. (2015). *Narrative Coaching: Bringing Our New Stories to Life*. Petaluma, CA: CNC Press.
Dubin, R. (1978). *Theory Building*, New York: Free Press.
Feyerabend, P. (1975). *Against Method: Outline of an Anarchistic Theory of Knowledge*. London: New Left Books.
Fillary-Travis, A. and Cox, E. (2014). Researching coaching. In E. Cox, T. Bachkirova and D. Clutterbuck (eds.), *The Complete Handbook of Coaching* (2nd ed.). London: Sage.
Fishman, D. (1999). *The Case for Pragmatic Psychology*. New York: New York University Press.
Franklin, J. and Franklin, A. (2012). The long-term independently assessed benefits of coaching: A controlled 18-month follow-up study of two methods. *International Coaching Psychology Review*, 7(1), 33–38.
Garvey, B. (2011). *A Very Short, Fairly Interesting and Reasonably Cheap Book About Coaching and Mentoring*. London: Sage.
Garvey, B. (2014). Mentoring in the coaching world. In E. Cox, T. Bachkirova and D. Clutterbuck (eds.), *The Complete Handbook of Coaching* (2nd ed.). London: Sage, pp. 361–374.
Gioia, D. A. and Pitre, E. (1990). Multiparadigm perspective on theory building. *Academy of Management Review*, 15(4), 584–602.
Grant, A. (2013). The efficacy of coaching. In J. Passmore, D. Peterson and T. Freire (eds.), *The Wiley-Blackwell Handbook of the Psychology of Coaching and Mentoring*. Chichester: Wiley-Blackwell, pp. 15–39.
Greeno, J. G. (1997). On claims and answering the wrong questions. *Educational Research*, 26(1), 5–17.
Guba, E. and Lincoln, Y. (2005). *Handbook of Qualitative Research* (2nd ed.). London: Sage.
Gyllensten, K. and Palmer, S. (2006). Experiences of coaching and stress in the workplace: An interpretative phenomenological analysis. *International Coaching Psychology Review*, 1(1), 86–98.
Hawkins, P. and Smith, N. (2013). *Coaching, Mentoring and Organisational Consultancy: Supervision, Skills and Development* (2nd ed.), Maidenhead: Open University Press.
Hayles, K. (1990). *Chaos Bound: Orderly Disorder in Contemporary Literature and Science*. Ithaca, NY: Cornell University Press.
Jack, A., Boyatzis, R., Khawaja, M, Passarelli, A. and Leckie, R. (2013). Visioning in the brain:

An fMRI study of inspirational coaching and mentoring. *Social Neuroscience*, 8, 369–384.

James, W. (1955). *Pragmatism and four essays from 'The Meaning of Truth'*. New York: Harper Collins.

Jones, R. and Corner, J. (2012). Seeing the forest *and* the trees: A complex adaptive systems lens for mentoring. *Human Relation*, 65(3), 391–411.

Kerruish, V. (1991). *Jurisprudence as Ideology*. New York: Routledge.

Kilburg, R. (2000). *Executive Coaching: Developing Managerial Wisdom in a World of Chaos*. Washington, DC: American Psychological Association.

Killin, L. and Della Sala, S. (2015). Seeing through the double blind. *The Psychologist*, 28(4), 288–291.

Kochanowski, S., Seifert, C. and Yukl, G. (2010). Using coaching to enhance the effects of behavioral feedback to managers. *Journal of Leadership and Organizational Studies*, 17(4), 363–369.

Lincoln, Y. and Guba, E. (1985). *Naturalistic Inquiry*. Newbury Park, CA: Sage Publications.

Lynham, S. (2000). Theory building in the human resource development profession. *Human Resource Development Quarterly*, 11(2), 159–178.

Lynham, S. (2002). The general method of theory-building research in applied disciplines. *Advances in Developing Human Resources*, 4(3), 221–241.

Lyotard, J.-F. (1984). *The Postmodern Condition: A Report on Knowledge* (1979, translation). Manchester: Manchester University Press.

Mascolo, M. F. and Dalto, C. A (1995). Self and modernity on trial: A reply to Gergen's Saturated Self. *Journal of Constructivist Psychology*, 8, 175–191.

Maxwell, A. (2009). How do business coaches experience the boundary between coaching and therapy/counselling? *Coaching: An International Journal of Theory, Research and Practice*, 2(2), 149–162.

Myers, A. (2014). *Multiple Perspective Analysis of a Coaching Session*. Unpublished PhD Thesis, Oxford Brookes University, Oxford.

O'Connor, S. and Cavanagh, M. (2013). The coaching ripple effect: The effects of developmental coaching on wellbeing across organisational networks. *Psychology of Well-Being: Theory, Research and Practice*, 3(2), http://www.psywb.com/content/3/1/2

Palmer, S. (2008). Multimodal coaching and its application to workplace, life and health coaching. *The Coaching Psychologist*, 4(1), 21–29.

Peirce, C. (1977). *Semiotics and Significs*. Ed. Charles Hardwick. Bloomington, IN: Indiana University Press.

Peterson, D. (1991). Connection and disconnection of research and practice in the education of professional psychologists. *American Psychologist*, 46, 422–429.

Polanyi, M. (1969). *Knowing and Being*. Chicago: The University of Chicago Press.

Rescher, N. (1996). *Complexity: a philosophical overview*. New York: Transaction Publishers.

Robson, C. (2001). *Real World Research: A Resource for Social Scientists and Practitioner-Researchers*. Oxford: Blackwell.

Rogers, J. (2012). *Coaching Skills: A Handbook*. Maidenhead: Open University Press.

Rorty, R. (2010). *The Rorty Reader* (eds: C. Voparil and R. Bernstein). Chichester: Wiley-Blackwell.

Saunders, M. and Rojon, C. (2014). There's no madness in my method: Explaining how your coaching research findings are built on firm foundations. *Coaching: An International Journal of Theory, Research and Practice*, 7(1), 74–84.

Schön, A. (1983). *The Reflective Practitioner: How Professionals Think in Action*. London: Temple Smith.

Stacey, R. D. (2003). *Strategic Management and Organisational Dynamics: The Challenge of Complexity*. Harlow: Prentice-Hall.

Stacey, R. D. (2012). Comment on debate article: Coaching psychology coming of age: The challenges we face in the messy world of complexity. *International Coaching Psychology Review*, 7(1), 91–95.

Stern, L. and Stout-Rostron, S. (2013). What progress has been made in coaching research in relation to 16 ICRF focus areas from 2008 to 2012? *Coaching: An International Journal of Theory, Research and Practice*, 6(1), 72–96.

Styhre, A. (2002). Non-linear change in organizations: organization change management informed by complexity theory. *Leadership and Organization Development Journal*, 23(6), 343–351.

Torraco, R. (2002). Research methods for theory building in applied disciplines: A comparative analysis. *Advances in Developing Human Resources*, 4(3), 355–376.

Wacker, J. (1998). A definition of theory: Research guidelines for different theory building research methods in operations managements. *Journal of Operations Management*, 16, 361–385.

Western, S. (2012). *Coaching and Mentoring: A Critical Text*. London: Sage.

Whitmore, J. (2002). *Coaching for Performance: GROWing People, Performance and Purpose*. London: Nicolas Brealey Publishing.

Wilber, K. (2000). *Integral Psychology*. London: Shambhala.

Willig, C. (2006). *Introducing Qualitative Research in Psychology: Adventures in Theory and Method*. Maidenhead: Open University Press.

The Key Discourses of Coaching

Simon Western

INTRODUCTION

This chapter explores the dominant discourses that underpin and shape how coaching is practiced today. The growing body of coaching literature tends to focus on the micro-practices of coaching (how to coach) and traditional coaching theory is based on applied psychotherapeutic models (Bluckert 2006; Garvey et al. 2009; Cox et al. 2014). This creates a gap in the literature leaving out the wider social, theoretical and organizational influences (the discourses) that shape coaching. These wider discourses embrace ideas such as managerialism, religious and spiritual practices, existential philosophy, globalization and the effects of the digital age. The chapter explores the dominant discourses that shape coaching and their impact on its practice. Drawing on previous research and a discourse analysis of coaching (Western 2012) the chapter explores how four key discourses shape coaching today.

WHAT IS DISCOURSE?

The term discourse is used in the Foucauldian tradition (Foucault 1972) that aims to expose how institutionalized patterns of knowledge and power are embedded in our social world, and shape and limit both how we think and our social relations. According to this tradition we are immersed in culture and language that produces and reproduces our subjectivity and identities. Social relations and social norms are shaped by the dominant social discourses that pervade our lives and 'govern our souls' (Rose 1990). As discourses create social norms so they become invisible to us and part of us i.e. 'it's just how things are'.

> We embody the discourses that exist in our culture, our very being is constituted by them, they are part of us, and thus we cannot simply throw them off. (Sullivan, 2003: 41)

Discourse analysis attempts to explore current discourses and how they shape our lives. This chapter draws on critical discourse analysis (Fairclough 1995) to explore the dominant discourses that produce the hidden norms and 'truths' that shape how coaching is practiced. It is also informed by critical theory, organizational and social theory (MacIntyre 1985; Lasch 1979; Parker 2002) and an application of discourse theory (Fairclough 1995; Foucault 1972) to the coaching literature (Bachkirova 2011; De Haan 2008; Garvey et al. 2009; Cox et al. 2014; Western 2012).

The discourses identified in this chapter have been observed through a research methodology (Western 2012) within coaching sessions, in coaching theory and in various sites and texts of coaching such as coaching websites, blogs, training courses and coaching conferences. The chapter identifies four key discourses that shape the mindsets of coaches, coach trainers and coaching institutions, in relation to how they formulate coaching practice. It is argued that they shape how coaches think and work, and also the client's expectations when buying coaching or being coached. Within each discourse there is a variety of coaching approaches underpinned by the assumptions, norms and constraints of each discourse. The position of the author is that there are no right or wrong discourses, and these are not judgments about what coaching should be, rather they are descriptive of what is shaping coaching practice today. Most coaches draw on more than one discourse in their work. Once the discourses are made visible, coaches can think about how the four discourses play out in their coaching approach and why this is. The question is then posed to researchers, coaches, theorists, trainers and professional bodies, as to which discourses are dominating their thinking and practice, and why they are doing so. There is also the related question of how coaches integrate these discourses (when translated into coaching approaches), so they can be complimentary and integrated, rather than be at odds with each other.

The four key discourses identified in this chapter are The Soul Guide discourse, the Psy Expert discourse, the Managerial Discourse and the Network Coach (as shown in Figure 3.1).

Extending the implications of key discourses on coaching practice the chapter includes a discussion of the macro-social influences on coaching, such as the coaching body politic (regulating and professional bodies) and other external influences such as social, economic and technology changes. A meta-theory of coaching is proposed as an integration of the discourses and macro-social influences (Western 2012).

It is hoped this chapter will support the development of the coaching knowledge base in four ways:

1. By providing an account that challenges and contests many mainstream and normative assumptions about coaching.
2. By situating coaching in its wider social context and identifying four dominant discourses that currently shape coaching practice.
3. By providing a heuristic device that allows coaches to become reflective practitioners and ask:

    a) What discourses shape my practice, and why are others marginalized or left out?
    b) Why am I drawn to particular discourses and not others? What purpose does this serve? Is this promoting good coaching or is it an unconscious defence to avoid other difficult work?

Figure 3.1 The four discourses of coaching

Source: Western (2012: 124)

4 By providing a coaching meta-theory that can support the research and development of more effective explanatory and predictive theories of coaching and, in so doing, potentially improve the knowledge base of coaching and its future development.

The chapter will conclude with an outline of some new research questions that emerge from the analysis and discussion.

FOUR DOMINANT DISCOURSES OF COACHING

In this section an overview of the four discourses of coaching is presented (Table 3.1), with a separate discussion included for each.

The Soul Guide Coaching Discourse: A Mirror to the Soul

The Soul Guide Discourse will be familiar to most coaches who work with any emotional depth with clients. Of all the coaching discourses it has the longest continuity, with a genealogy stretching back to pre-modern healers and spiritual guides. This discourse represents the aspect of coaching that has emerged from 'soul-healers' over the centuries, those in socially sanctioned roles who have worked with the interior aspects of the self. This has manifested in different ways (depending on historical and social context) but a pattern can be detected, one that involves an expert helper and a recipient. The helper works in diverse ways to help their 'client' to work with emotions, their spiritual concerns, identity and relationships, the unconscious, the conscience, the human spirit, values and beliefs and our human and existential concerns (e.g. How does one live with meaning? What is the good life and how should it be approached?).

According to Bachkirova (2011), 80% of the world's population have a deep interest in the spiritual. As such, 'Coaching the Soul' is an important, if not easy, subject. Yet this discourse is not limited to spiritual coaching approaches. Rather, it also references a wider discourse that includes the human spirit in any way this can be interpreted. The Soul Guide discourse connects shamanism, spiritual direction, spiritual friendship in monasteries (Aeldred 1977) and the priest and the confessional (Foucault 1978). These traditions have been assimilated and changed over time by the forces of modernity, in particular the secular priesthood of psychoanalysis at the turn of the 20th century and later via psychotherapy and counselling. Bettleheim (1982: 12) argues in *Freud and Man's Soul*, that Freud brought together the word 'psyche' (meaning soul in Greek), with 'analysis' suggesting scientific rigour. Psychoanalysis began as an analysis of the soul in its widest sense (which Bettleheim claims has been lost in the modern quest which privileges science over the soul). Administering to the soul is an act of continuity, and coaches who are influenced by this discourse are continuing a tradition and, at the same time, breaking with it, by bringing a new postmodern twist to the role of today's soul guide.

Soul Guide informed coaching

Coaches working within the Soul Guide discourse hold a 'mirror to the soul' creating a reflective, contemplative space that opens up the realm of wisdom (rather than attaining knowledge), of being (rather than doing), and ultimately human search for truth, meaning, authenticity and love. While the soul space is indefinable, it is accessible through one's personal experience and Soul Guide coaching works in this experiential space. Humanistic, existential and ontological coaching approaches fit within the Soul Guide discourse as the aims are to explore how individuals find meaning and identify how to live more fulfilling lives. Indeed, Soul Guide Coaching is a postmodern version of what previous soul guides were aiming to achieve.

THE KEY DISCOURSES OF COACHING

Table 3.1 The four discourses of coaching: an overview

Discourse	Soul Guide	Psy Expert	Managerial	Network-Coach
Coach Stance	Mirror to the Soul	Technician of the Psyche	Role Coach	Emergent Strategist
Coaching Approach	The coach continues the lineage of 'soul healer', where the coachee reveals their hidden 'inner' selves, desires, inner thoughts and contemporary sins (to be sad, feel weak, anxious – all that need to be hidden at work). To help coachee find their authentic selves: identity, meaning and values.	Applying psychological tools and techniques to help the coachee. Personal performance is the coach's core objective. Psychometric tests, CBT, NLP and other goal- and technique-driven approaches are used.	The coach focuses on the person-in-role and on output. Coach analyses with coachee their multiple roles: e.g. how they lead and motivate their team and individuals to get the best results.	The coach views organizations as networks. They coach to reveal connections and interdependencies. Helps the coachee to think beyond silos where power lies, and how to influence networks. Helps coachee see big picture, look at influences beyond the immediate workplace, and act strategically.
Coach Gaze	Experience	Performance	Productivity	Connectivity
Aim	To create a space for coachee to discover their desire, and to face their inner dilemmas and reflect on the meaning of life and their values. The 'true self' is both discovered and constructed in this redemptive space.	To modify thinking and behaviour to support coachee success. To improve personal performance in both work and 'living'.	To improve role performance and organizational productivity by maximizing efficiency and increasing productivity. Drawing on scientific rationality, and managerial assumptions.	To help coachee take a more connective stance, to see patterns and power in their networks. To develop strategic thinking, to work more emergently across networks, and to be more ethical.
Coachee works on	Inner-Self	Outward-Self	Role-Self	Networked-Self
Coach Expertise	Creating a space for the soul/psyche to speak. Listening and responding with reverence, courage and insight.	To 'coachify' psychological interventions, helping coachee adapt their thinking and behaviour to achieve their goals.	Facilitation of coachee in work-role to achieve greater personal, team and organizational productivity.	The coach facilitates ways to understand and then influence the workplace. Prompts strategic and spatial thinking, and raises ethical questions.

What really makes the Soul Guide Coaching discourse stand apart is that the coach is rarely interested in achieving goals, aims and targets. This coaching is not driven by an instrumental desire to become more productive or efficient, it is the very antithesis of this approach. When coaches do link this soul-work with profit or productivity there is a distortion of the coaching relationship that raises ethical questions. Coaches working in this discourse never try to stay on one linear path but delight in meandering, to be open to new and unexpected insights and to glimpse the future that may come from sharing dreams, associations and fantasies. This coaching approach challenges the dogma of modernity, it celebrates the traditions of the pre-modern alongside the hybrid of the postmodern. As already mentioned, the Soul Guide coach seeks to collaborate with the client to help them discover wisdom rather than knowledge and fulfill desires rather than goals. Bachkirova (2011) offers an example of this coaching discourse, explaining that coaching in relation to the spiritual, in its broadest sense, focuses on three groups:

1. Potential clients who demonstrate capacities beyond those available to individuals with unformed, formed and reformed ego ... this group can include people who are called mystics and sages ... who can bring their organisms on a regular basis to an unusual state of 'no-self'.
2. Clients who have unusual (spiritual/mystical) experiences and wish to integrate these experiences.
3. Clients who have a deep interest in the spiritual ...

Likewise, Sieler (2005) and Rowan (2010) offer examples of working in the Soul Guide discourse. Coaches and clients working in other coaching discourses can be surprised how the Soul Guide discourse can appear unexpectedly in the coaching session. For example, when a coach is working on strategy with a manager, they may (unexpectedly) be confronted with the emotional confessions of that manager. These might include a variety of deep emotions (e.g. hurt, anger or strong desires) and be instructive for the deep secrets or existential angst they might reveal. In such a scenario, Foucault's (1978: 59) claim that 'Western man has become a confessing animal' seems apt, with the alchemy of a soul guided 'talking cure' relationship (which includes coaching) an appropriate response. This is particularly true if the coach doesn't cram the sessions with technique and leaves space for deep listening and reflections, which are the pre-requisite skills of a Soul Guide coach.

The advantages and disadvantages of the Soul Guide coaching

Western (2012) claims that coaching is today's postmodern confessional, where clients find a space to reveal modern-day sins such as deviating from the 'happiness imperative' (Beradi 2009) and challenge the dominant performative expectations of high moral and positive outlooks. Confessing clients not only reveal anxieties and angst but also hopes, dreams and desires. Contemporary workplaces can be very demanding of emotional labour and emotional compliance. The Soul Guide coaching discourse provides a very important 'potential space' for working in more depth with the authentic self rather than with the performative self (which often comes at a big personal cost to the client and any organization they may represent).

However, there are dangers within the Soul Guide discourse, most obviously when the coach flirts with spirituality and depth approaches without being fully experienced or grounded in them. This can lead the coach to open up a client without knowing how to guide the client on a safe journey. Another challenge is that the client can idealize a coach and a collusion can occur between the coaching pair leading to a narcissistic love-in, 'my wonderful coach' and 'my wonderful client'. When this happens the real work ends and a façade takes over. Finally, the Soul Guide coaching approach is more difficult to sell into workplaces, and it is more difficult to train, define and accredit than more technique-based approaches to coaching. Yet 'The Soul Guide opens a liminal space, pauses and hesitates, listening to the heartbeat of the conversation rather than only its content' (Western 2012: 155).

In summary, this discourse creates a coaching space that welcomes disorder, where the unconscious is liberated to speak, where the soul itself finds its voice, where desire is heard and an individual's subjective truth is discovered. Coaching within this discourse offers clients a chance to work on their personal life, focusing on meaning, desire, generosity and authenticity, and then connecting this with their work. The consequences of working within the Soul Guide coaching discourse can be profound, and often in subtle and unexpected ways.

The Psy Expert Coaching Discourse: Technicians of the Psyche

Psy Expert coaching discourse focuses on utilizing psychological tools and techniques that aim to change the client's behaviour, for the purpose of improving their individual performance both at work and in their personal lives. 'Psy' refers to the Psy professions, such as psychiatry, psychology, psychotherapy, and psychiatric social work (Rose 1985, 2011). It is a discourse that draws on the history, knowledge and techniques that have emerged from these professions and been adapted to coaching practice. The coaching profession is under growing pressures to adopt traditional psychology as a core training with some claiming coaches are ill-equipped to do the job without it (Peltier 2001; Linley 2006; Seligman 2007; Zeus & Skiffington 2002).

Psy Expert coaching is fundamentally concerned with working on the outward-self in contrast to the deep inner-self (Soul Guide). These two selves are inextricably connected of course, but the Soul Guide focus is more interested in emotions, identity, spiritual health and deeply human concerns such as the meaning of life. In contrast, the Psy Expert tends to focus on changing behaviour, allaying anxiety to improve performance, influencing others through improved communication skills and is generally about improving workplace performance.

In reflecting on the distinction between coaching and therapy, Ives (2008) argued that 'whilst therapy primarily addresses feelings, coaching is focused on changing actions [changing in feelings are a consequence]' (p.100). This reveals a normative assumption that all coaching works within the Psy Expert discourse, as a Soul Guide Coach (like the therapist) would privilege feelings over actions and not make such a distinction. Indeed, this provides a good example of how faithful adherence to a singular discourse can create a perception about what characterizes 'all of coaching'. However, a coach working in the Soul Guide discourse would make a different distinction between coaching and therapy. This would be that the therapist works on the 'Wounded-Self', trying to deliver healing and reparation through talking about feelings, whereas the Soul Guide focus is on the Celebrated-Self (Western 2012, 2016), and works on wounded-self issues as they arise. Put differently, their main aim is to work with inner-feelings to help the client discover and elaborate their healthy and celebrated self.

In contrast, the outward-self can be observed and is experienced by others. As such, HR professionals and managers like this approach as they can attempt to quantify and reward/punish changes in behaviours using an array of devices (e.g. 360-degree feedback and performance appraisals). Remuneration and career moves are often dependent on such quantifiable soft-data.

Psy Expert informed coaching

Essentially Psy coaches work as 'technicians of the psyche'. Their claims to expertise reside in their technical ability to coach/train executives in new skills and bring about observable and measurable change to cognition/behaviours that inhibit success. They are also focused on facilitating the emergence of resilient behaviours that enhance personal performance. Psy coaching methods vary depending on the coach's specific psychological/coach training, although most coaches use some form of psychometric testing to generate quantifiable 'scientific' data that can be worked with. As may be apparent, this discourse embraces a technocratic and functional ideal of coaching, which operates within an underlying 'clinical paradigm' (with diagnostics to define problems and sets goals, followed by treatments that rely on micro-change psychological approaches). Examples of Psy coaching approaches are Cognitive-Behavioural coaching (Neenan & Dryden 2004; Green Oades & Grant 2006), Neuro-Linguistic-Programming (Grimely 2014, 2007) and

Solution-Focused coaching approaches (Greene & Grant 2003; O'Connell & Palmer 2007).

Psy coaching fits neatly with the scientific-rationalist dominated workplace (Alvesson and Willmott 2012) where the perspective of 'if it can't be measured it doesn't count' dominates thinking (Power 1997; Parker 2002). HR managers are pressured to demonstrate their return on investment in coaching and Psy Expert approaches claim to accommodate this demand. Yet as Mintzberg (2008) says 'learning cannot be measured' and in spite of a convincing body of literature that critiques the 'scientific' validity of the efficacy and particularly of the capability to measure the success of HR soft-interventions such as coaching (Fleetwood & Hesketh, 2006) the Psy discourse speaks the language of the modern workplace and therefore flourishes within it.

For Kilburg (2000) all executive coaching operates within the Psy discourse. He notes, that 'the executive coach uses a wide variety of behavioral techniques and methods to assist the client to achieve a mutually identified set of goals to improve his or her professional performance' (Kilburg, 2000: 65–67). Given that similar observations have also been made by others e.g. Zeus and Skiffington (2002), there appears to be a clear link between coaching and psychology, behaviour change, goals and performance (i.e. the fundamentals of the Psy Expert discourse), which these authors appear to hold as an essential for highly professional coaching practice.

The Psy discourse seems to be growing within coaching for three reasons. Firstly, because of the alignment that exists between the ethos and language of Psy Expert coaching and the dominance of managerial scientific-rationalism in the workplace. Secondly, as coaching moves towards professionalization and regulation, coaching institutions are mimicking psychology and psychotherapy organizational practices (such as supervision, training and accreditation methods). Psy coaching is a comfortable fit within these psychotherapy organizational practices as it emanates from them. This professionalization and regulation of coaching is often described (uncritically) as a good thing, however its lack of critique in the literature is a worrying sign. Not only does it distort coaching, it also limits it practices in other discourses and may reflect the many invested interests (that are not democratically accountable) that are currently trying to claim coaching as their own (for financial and political/power motives).

Thirdly, the popular rise of positive psychology, neuroscience and NLP, support the notion of scientific and technique driven practices to change how people feel and behave. For example Seligman writes:

> Coaching is a practice in search of a backbone, two backbones actually: a scientific, evidence-based backbone and a theoretical backbone. I believe that the new discipline of positive psychology provides both those backbones … (Seligman, 2007: 266)

The theoretical backbone referred to is addressed later in the chapter, whilst the scientific backbone is both a cause and effect of the Psy Discourse. A dominant 'scientific' consensus in workplace environments for 'evidenced-based' coaching leads many to view the Psy Discourse as preferable to other approaches, and renders them unable to see beyond it.

It should be noted that Psy Expert approaches to coaching are not homogeneous. Aaron Beck, one of CBT's founding theorists, differentiates the circumscribed goal approach of CBT from the open-ended 'evocative therapies' of psychoanalysis and client-centred therapy (Beck 1976: 320). This is helpful as it reveals how Psy coaches are not completely dominated by cognitive-behavioural and technique approaches. The 'evocative approach' to Psy coaching used by psychodynamic (Brunning 2006, Newton, Long and Sievers 2006) and person-centred coaching approaches (Joseph 2014) aim to explore the self in a deeper, more open-ended way (which seem to overlap with Soul

Guide coaching). However, in the workplace where 'time is money' and coaching engagements are often compressed, goal-focused and time-limited approaches clearly appeal to managers.

The technique and goal focused Psy approach is heavily critiqued (Laing 1967; Miller 2005). Arnaud writes of CB approaches, 'The client tends therefore to be considered as an object to be modeled rather than as a subject' (Arnaud 2003: 1147–1150). Miller, the Lacanian psychoanalyst, offers a stronger critique of cognitive-behavioural approaches:

> they are training and conditioning techniques .... They only take observable behavior into account .... In times past an eminent mind, the Soviet Pavlov, revealed the efficiency of conditioning, in the dog. To influence humankind using the same means, is horrible ... (Miller, 2005)

Psy Expert coaching has taken a turn recently with the emergence and popularity of positive psychology. Little critiqued in coaching literature, the dangers of positive psychology (PP) are two-fold. First, the scientific and evidence-based claims of PP in coaching have yet to be scrutinized and there is much pseudo-science that goes unchallenged in the field (Western 2012: 223–241). Second, PP is part of social trend that has exploded in the USA around the turn of the century and influences other cultures. This trend is what is variously referred to as the 'happiness imperative' (Beradi 2009) or the 'society of commanded enjoyment' (Stavrakakis, 2007). The implied imperative that one be positive and happy seem ripe to become a cause of deep social trouble. Indeed, coaching as a practice has emerged as part of this social trend (i.e. administering to the Celebrated-Self) and the particular emphasis of positive psychology and solution-focused approaches, seem to negate a more holistic approach to life. Both Furedi (2003) and Beradi (2009) claim that the happiness imperative creates the opposite effect to what is intended, and they support these claims by citing the devastating amounts of depression, anxiety and unhappiness in society. It is worth noting that in the USA (where positive psychology, the happiness imperative and coaching itself is most prevalent), its citizens account for two-thirds of the global market for antidepressants (the most commonly prescribed drugs in the United States (Ehrenreich 2009).

The advantages and disadvantages of Psy Expert coaching

To summarize, the promise of Psy Expert coaching is two-fold. It promises individuals help to change their behaviours and to maximize their performance potential, whilst reducing impediments to that potential. For organizations it aims to align the employee's behaviour with the company's values, leadership competency frameworks and enhance performance. This approach may be good for business, but it also raises ethical questions that are rarely discussed in coaching or managerial circles. It could be argued that the coaching of employees to align their thinking and behaviours to company values and leadership frameworks is a nuanced form of totalitarianism (Tourish & Pinnington 2002). As Casey (1995) points out, employees can become so embedded in normative corporate cultures that they fail to see their own capitulation and entrapment. As such, the challenge that can be presented to Psy Expert coaches is to see beyond the reductionist aims of helping clients achieve performance goals, and to take an ethical stance that appreciates individuality and non-conformity (lest they collude with coercive managerial cultures to produce 'designer employees') (Casey 1995).

The challenges for Psy Expert coaches is that it doesn't enable thinking beyond micro-coaching practices to engage with cultural and systemic questions. Its focus is to transform 'the symptom' rather than discover what the symptom might signify (i.e. what the underlying problem might be and what the context is that gives rise to it). This form of coaching seems not well suited to senior leaders seeking strategic help, as it does not offer an organizational perspective or strategic viewpoint.

At the same time, Psy Expert coaching, being technique driven, can offer short-term interventions that can have an immediate impact on personal behaviour and performance. It offers tangible help that clients can easily access. It is especially helpful for specific challenges (e.g. a skilled leader has specific anxiety issues when public speaking). The Psy coach offers techniques to manage this anxiety, work on the triggers, and can really help to improve performance. Another advantage for coaches is they can learn basic techniques in short time frames (e.g. weekend NLP courses), which lower the barriers to entering the industry. The Psy Expert discourse also aligns well with most workplace mindsets and cultures, which is a strength for the coach when selling and delivering their work, as they share a common language in most workplaces.

The Managerial Coaching Discourse: Role-Coach

The managerial coaching discourse reflects how the culture, practices and assumptions of 'managerialism' have colonized and shaped much of executive coaching practice. The managerial discourse has infiltrated coaching through three routes:

- The managerial discourse that dominates the organizational cultures in which they are coaching.
- The migration of managers into executive and/or internal coaching roles, bring with them their managerial assumptions, skills and knowledge into coaching.
- Management consultancies and university business schools impose onto the executive coaching and coach training they deliver, the 'managerial' mindset bias that dominates their organisational culture. (Western 2012).

Managerialism is a product of modernity and became a dominant social discourse, in the same way as urbanizaiton and industrialization changed economic and social landscapes. Managerialism gains its authority through the same modern ethos driven by science and rationality as the Psy Expert discourse. In addition, the managerial discourse gains a normative authority through a claim of expertise to be able to control/manage the environment (natural, technological and social). This offers a generic blanket of psychological reassurance that 'somebody is in control', which alleviates anxiety and creates an investment in maintaining a managerial culture. MacIntyre (1985) claims the manager as one of the three main characters of the 20th century, alluding to the fact that 'their skills enable them to devise the most efficient means of achieving whatever ends are proposed' (p.74). Parker (2002) illustrates how pervasive this discourse has become, as we find managers everywhere in 'football clubs, hotels, railways, museums: they are universally essential' (p.6).

For MacIntyre (1985) managerial expertise involves maintaining a moral neutrality, having manipulative power, and being expert in achieving the most efficient means to achieve ends. According to this view, the manager's aim is 'the manipulation of human beings into compliant behaviour; and it is by appeal to his own effectiveness in this respect that the manager claims authority within the manipulative mode' (p.74). The managerial discourse has aligned to technological and industrial advances and made huge gains in terms of the mass-production of goods and rising living standards. However, from the earliest days of Taylorism, (Taylor, 1947) there have been questions about the ethics of treating humans like cogs in the wheel of an efficiency driven organisational machine. Yet management today strives to influence employees to achieve its organizational aims in explicit ways (e.g. reward systems) and also implicitly through culture and audit control. Management effectiveness appears to depend on the personality and skills of the manager, the organizational culture and the pressures that can disturb and distort good intentions. Acknowledgement that the ideology of management works in the 'manipulative mode' does not necessarily mean that it is unethical or immoral: many contemporary organizations include checks and balances to avoid such outcomes. However, we must recognize that managerialism has the potential to be inherently coercive. Managers clearly have a task, to drive efficiency and to maximize productivity and performance of the workforce. Working at its best this is done collaboratively with employees, engaging them and offering fair rewards, at its worse there is dehumanizing coercion that takes place.

Managerial discourse informed coaching

Coaching has imported managerial ideas, as many coaches claim expertise in supporting managers to achieve more 'efficient means to achieve their desired ends'. To achieve this coaches also claim what MacIntyre (1985) describes as 'manipulative power' (or the capability to deliver change through coaching and influencing employees' emotions, thoughts and behaviours). To achieve this they draw on both Managerial and Psy Expert skills, rhetoric and technique. Finally, like managers, coaches working in this discourse claim moral neutrality, often referencing a non-directive approach, their neutrality and their role to support the client aims without imposing their own. The question is often raised in coaching circles as to who is the client, as coaches are often serving two masters: 1) the HR team or manager who employs them, and 2) the coachee they work with 'in confidence'. This triangulated position, 'coach, client, coachee' raises very real ethical questions for coaches, when the manager/client who pays the coach wants something very different from what the coachee wants. When all parties are aligned, this arrangement presents few difficulties. However, the tensions of the workplace often become enacted in the relationships between the parties involved. For example, coachee confidentiality can be put under pressure in these circumstances, and the Managerial coaching discourse tends to put pressure on the coach to favour the managerial system and its desires, rather than defend the client.

Coaching in the Managerial discourse shifts the focus from working on the inner-self (Soul Guide) and outward-self (Psy Expert) to focus on coaching the role-self. That is, the coach works with the person-in-role (e.g. Steve the finance director, Mary the CEO) and their coaching task is to improve role performance with the wider aim of improving organizational efficiency and output. The Managerial discourse coach moves towards the position of the coach as an individually-focused organizational consultant (West & Milan 2001), a thinking partner to address how their clients manage human and other resources to improve productivity and success. They rarely work with strategy, however, as the management discourse is constricted to an operational (reductionist) focus (i.e. how to make small incremental gains) rather than re-thinking the big picture. Interestingly, the contemporary focus on 'leadership' and preference for designations like 'Chief Executive Officer' (as opposed to 'Managing Director') seem to reflect a movement away from management control to better reflect the strategic inputs of those working at senior levels (Western 2013; Alvesson & Willmott 2012)

Managerial coaches use goals and targets as their primary tools to raise performance and this has permeated much of executive coaching with the GROW model still widely used (Graham 2010[2006]; Whitmore et al. 2013). In the Managerial coaching discourse goals link personal performance to productivity and output. Whilst goals can be useful for helping to focus the client, they can also be constraining. As Garvey et al (2009) argue, 'coaching goals can limit what is covered and prevent broad development of the person or prevent getting into deep and difficult issues that require a nuanced entry following lengthy dialogue' (p.159). Goals and targets also define how we think about organizational and personal challenges. If we seek happiness and growth via the achievement of one goal after the next, our lives become reduced to the mechanistic, serial pursuit of goals with an unrelenting sense that when one is achieved, the next must be found. This measurable way of living a life may be helpful to some but it is unclear how this offers any holistic understanding or brings deeper meaning to our lives. As such, the client of a Managerial-focused coach seems destined to become condemned to the treadmill of never-ending goal-focused self-improvement. Organizations striving for performance and productivity goals can focus people and offer achievable targets that drive behaviour and offer recognizable achievements. However, if the 'bigger picture' is lost in a manic and relentless striving for targets and goals, there is a very real danger that clients will become accustomed to short-term thinking. A huge contribution to the cause of the 2008 global financial crisis was precisely because of target-orientated behaviour, as each financial institution became obsessed with profit targets, which pleased short-term investors but ignored its implications for the broader financial system. In the UK health sector targets to reduce waiting times in the emergency rooms, seemed sensible and morally right when first conceived. As a result, however, patients started being moved onto trolleys and into dangerous situations as the targets became ends to achieve at any cost (Smith 2013).

The advantages and disadvantages of the Managerial discourse coaching

The rapid rise of coaching has both embraced managerial culture and has also infiltrated the wider management discourse. Coaching has now become a term for many forms of soft-skills. For example, group facilitation becomes team coaching, training individuals becomes coaching your staff, and managers are taught coaching skills and their performance measured against their ability to coach direct reports. Mintzberg (2004) notes that contemporary management is mostly about the 'soft-stuff' and managerialism has shifted from being about overt coercion of employees to managing their subjectivity. To become skilled in working with the 'soft-stuff' managers typically receive personal coaching to manage their own subjectivity and to learn new soft-skills to influence their team (rather than relying on managerial coercion or technical know-how). Having a coach who aligns with the language and ethos of the Managerial discourse is clearly an advantage to managers. To hire, retain and motivate high performing employees managers need to learn to manage differently, and coaches working in the Management discourse are perfectly placed to support this change.

The key benefits of the managerial discourse are the coaching shift from the individual to role focus, which introduces the organization explicitly into the coaching engagement. The managerial coach does not aim for self-actualization (Maslow 1976), but aims for role-actualization (Western 2012). This means the client aims to attain peak performance in their role and it is therefore a highly valued coaching discourse in the workplace.

It should be noted however that the Managerial discourse coaching is not a good fit in more progressive organizations that are attempting to move towards distributed forms of leadership (and away from managerial control as a way of organizing). Many claim this discourse as a 20th century industrial way of working and not fit-for-purpose in the 21st century post-industrial workplace (Laloux 2014). The idea of management-science and managerial control are being re-thought in the light of the knowledge economy and the digital age. New leadership theories and practices of distributed and adaptive leadership (Bolden 2011; Heifetz et al. 2009) and Eco-leadership (Western 2013) are describing how new forms of organization are re-thinking the role of manager. The manager is being usurped by the leader and leadership itself is being redefined. This puts the onus on coaches to question the underpinning ideology of the Management Discourse and to re-think and re-learn their practices if they wish to help managers and leaders move towards the future.

The Network Coaching Discourse: Emergent Strategist

Network Coaching is an emergent coaching discourse that captures the zeitgeist of our times. It is a response to our increasingly networked, global, digitalized and interdependent world (Western 2012). While the industrial landscape in the 20th century was dominated by the manager and 'machine' metaphor, the prevailing metaphor for the 21st century is the 'network', as the post-industrial workplace is dominated by the internet, globalization and the digital economy. This reflects the increasingly interconnected and inter-dependent world where organizations have complex stakeholder relationships, at both local and global levels. The increasingly networked society (Castells 2000) has created new connectivity and inter-dependencies that impact on all social and economic relations. A greater awareness of our fragile environment and of limited natural resources becomes part of this zeitgeist, bringing new eco-system awareness to the workplace. Bill Clinton sums up:

> Our world is more interdependent than ever. Borders have become more like nets than walls, and while this means wealth, ideas, information and talent can move freely around the globe, so can the negative forces shaping our shared fates. The financial crisis that started in the US and swept the globe was further proof that – for better and for worse – we can't escape one another. (Clinton, 2012: 26)

The term network is used to describe the complex web of technology, human/social and natural elements that interact to create the organizational networks we inhabit today. Whether we look at medicine, agriculture, finance, manufacturing, education, social media, global corporations or terrorism, these networks are changing how we work, live and how we relate to each other. Organizational and political leaders are struggling to keep up with the dramatic social changes that are taking place. What seems to be required is a new leadership for the networked age. The Network coaching discourse is the emergent response from coaches who are addressing the question of how to coach leaders to re-imagine their work for the new challenges they face. The major change in this case is to reconfigure the idea of coaching an individual leader, set within a structure of vertical relationships (hierarchy). The vertical gives way to lateral relations, as networks cannot be hierarchical, centrally planned or controlled. It appears that peer-to-peer lateral relationships are now driving change in politics, business, public organizations and in wider society. As a result, the dynamism for change emerges by connecting laterally than through formal vertical organizational structures. The internet and mobile technologies provide new platforms that drive and support these changes. However, the workplace and management training (e.g. MBAs) have been slow to innovate and recognize the new lateral dynamics of change (Mintzberg 2004). Likewise coaching could be seen as reflecting the vertical and traditional ideas of leadership and structure with a few coaches exploring and defining what it means to be working in the Network coaching discourse.

Network Coaching a response to the new Zeitgeist

Network coaches help their clients to develop networked mindsets and let go of 20th century management control mindsets. Network coaching aims to deliver Eco-leaders who are encouraged to see their organizations as 'eco-systems within eco-systems' (Western

2013). Eco-leaders think and act in terms of influencing these eco-systems/networks, seeing patterns and looking at nodes and clusters of informal and formal power to find new ways to influence change. Similarly the coach working within the Network discourse would see leadership everywhere (not confined to the CEO or boardrooms) and would coach leaders to create spaces that enable different types of leadership to flourish. In networks, leaders are seen at nodal points of exchange and at the edges of organizations, close to the customer and to the competitor. These distributed leaders aim for communicating and connections in order to create learning organizations that are adaptive to change.

However, many coaches are trained to coach leaders with ideas that reproduce the old paradigm of thinking such as transformational leadership (Bass 1990). This focuses them on the individual leader they are coaching, rather than the expansive and connected leadership across the network. Although there is a body of coaches working with team coaching and systems theories (Hawkins 2014; Brunning 2006) these approaches have limitations as they do not account for new forms of leadership or new forms of networked organizations and focus on coaching teams in organizational systems with boundaries. Within the network discourse organizations are seen as acting like networked social movements (Castells 2012) and these, so-called, 'leaderless movements' embrace a new kind of Autonomist Leadership (Western 2014) that conceives of leadership as taking place within fluid organizational structures and without the necessity of position of power or hierarchy. Autonomist leadership also takes place in traditional organizations but is typically not seen, rewarded or recognized as leadership. The focus of Network Coaches is to work with these new informal leadership dynamics in ways that influence networks across peer-to-peer relations in lateral dynamics (within both real and virtual networks).

Network Coaching could be seen as an advanced form of systemic coaching. It challenges conventional ideas by expanding the coach's role beyond being a personal adviser focusing on improving performance or living better (Soul Guide/Psy) and it transcends the Managerial discourse that focuses on the person-in-role and improving their operational output. The Network coach works on the premise that there are multiple actors in fluid networks, and that organizations are networks of activity, that operate within other connected networks and eco-systems.

To extend these ideas further Actor-Network theory (Latour 2005; Law 1993) invites network coaches to look both at humans and non-human actors in networks. This brings technology into the foreground and, with it observations that technology changes both how a person works and the person themselves. As Turkle (2011: 2) observes, '[It's] not what computers do for us but what they do to us, to our ways of thinking about ourselves, our relationships, our sense of being human'. How we work across this non-human–human divide, across the virtual and real spaces we now inhabit, is the work of the coach in the Network discourse.

The task of the coach is to locate the client in their networks, to help the client explore the many networks that exist and then create emergent strategies to influence change in these networks. According to Western (2015), the Network coaching task is to help leaders:

- Re-imagine organizations through a networked mindset
- Distribute leadership throughout organizational networks
- Collaborate and connect across virtual and real boundaries
- Create spaces and find nodal points for new leaders/leadership to emerge
- Strive for ethical success
- Discover new opportunities through opening up to emergent strategies
- Create adaptive organizational networks, able to respond quickly to change.

The advantages and disadvantages of Network discourse coaching

The Network discourse is a newcomer in the field of coaching but is becoming increasingly important. In mentoring there is a tradition of working in networks and building on systemic thinking (Higgins & Kram 2001; Chandler & Kram 2005). However, these approaches tend to think of networks in terms of connecting people, without taking the wider network perspectives of actor-network approaches into account. These include technologies (Latour 2005) or the socio-political perspectives (Castells 2000) that broaden our understanding of how new network platforms are transforming social relations and workplaces.

It could be argued that unless coaching becomes more network-informed as a discipline, it could become an outdated and limited profession, restricted to becoming a personalized form of work-based psychology. Without embracing the network discourse it might be difficult for coaches to support progressive senior leaders to deliver ethical and strategic success in the light of tumultuous changes in organizational and social life.

Coaches engaging in the Network discourse are rethinking coaching fundamentals, understanding how the network society changes management, leadership and organizational dynamics, and then finding ways to adapt coaching practice accordingly. The Network discourse also takes coaching into new territory in relation to ethics, shifting the position of coaches from being a neutral sounding board to seeing themselves as an active change agent working with an ethical stance. Focusing on the wider network forces the coaching conversation to address a 'systemic ethics'. This means going beyond the subjective ethics of individuals doing no harm, and looking at the wider network to take responsibility for systemic ethical challenges such as badly treated outsourced workers in Asia, or how the organization impacts on natural environment. The Network discourse imposes this responsibility on all parties, clients and coaches, assuming inter-connectedness and inter-dependence which demands taking responsibility beyond our usual borders.

Network Coaching cannot offer easy or reductionist answers. One cannot capture Network Coaching in an acronym, or teach it through technique approaches. Network Coaching means thinking about connections, seeing patterns, thinking creatively and laterally and being adaptive to the emergence in complex systems. This is counter-intuitive to 'managerial control' and short-term success. It is therefore harder to teach, and harder to sell to conventional thinkers than the other approaches. Having said this, progressive leaders and fast adapting organizations that recognize the challenges of the Network Society, welcome this new approach.

It can be argued that network coaching discourse provides the missing link between coaching and the network society in which we live and work. It tends to be adopted by practitioners who see the world changing fast around them. Coaching from within this discourse encourages the coachee to be more strategic, ethical and take a networked approach to their work.

WORKING ACROSS THE DISCOURSES

A coach or coach training programme may identify with a single discourse, but usually they work within more than one discourse. Hybrid coaching across discourses is not good or bad per se, it can be effective and creative, or confusing and contradictory. Coaches may work from different discourses with intention e.g. utilzing Soul Guide when working with the client on personal issues then switching to Network Coaching when they focus on influencing change at work. Or they may work in a confusing, ad hoc way, beginning their coaching within the Soul Guide tradition, and telling the client they will be non-directive and carefully follow the client's deep inner journey. However, if the coach then becomes anxious that they are not delivering change, or being active enough, they may quickly switch to the Psy Expert discourse and offer expert advice or techniques to help. This discourse change would undermine the coaching process, as the coach switches from being a non-directive listener and following the client's journet, to taking up a technical expert role, in order to allay the coach's anxiety.

As previously highlighted, workplace coaches often operate within a triad (the coach, the coachee and the client employing the coach), which may raise ethical and practical dilemmas. The Network coach is at an advantage here as they would take a 'helicopter view' and work strategically on these issues, whereas coaches working in the other three discourses are more likely to focus on the individual or role and may miss these wider dynamics. Network coaches also go further and place this triad in a broader network context that changes the dynamic once again. Their wider vision and insights can liberate the employee and employer from a blinkered internal view of the company, and bring in new energy, dynamics, challenges and possibilities from the wider networks to which they are connected.

Skilled coaches, when trained to think about these discourses can use them flexibly, adapting to different contexts and client needs. What is important is that coaches are aware of what they are doing and why they are doing it. Otherwise they will be espousing one approach/discourse and practicing another which will confuse both their client or trainee if in a coach training role. Working with these discourses as a backdrop enables the coach to reflect on their practice both during the session and outside of it.

META-THEORY OF COACHING

A meta-theory of coaching is depicted in Figure 3.2 (Western, 2012). In it, the four discourses that allow theorizing about the micro-practices of coaching have been connected to various macro-social influences that also shape coaching. This meta-theory is not an attempt to provide a general and integrated theory of coaching. Its aim is to create a conceptual framework enabling coaches and researchers to explore and critique existing theories, methods and approaches and to develop new explanatory and predictive coaching theories.

As shown, the theory represents the symbiotic connection between the macro-social and micro-practices of coaching, demonstrating how they inform each other. It implies that what coaches do in their practice is influenced by what happens in the macro-social field, which recognizes that coaching does not exist in a vacuum. Despite the fact that scholarly interest in coaching has increased dramatically in recent years, there is still a paucity of specific coaching theory and what theory there is remains largely focused on the micro-practices of coaching, with strong connection to psychotherapy theory (Peltier 2001). For example, in the *Complete Handbook of Coaching* (Cox et al. 2014) nearly all theoretical chapters are drawing from the psychotherapy tradition with chapters including psychodynamic, cognitive behavioural, solution focused, person-centred, gestalt and existential coaching. In this meta-theory the Psy discourse theorizes these psychotherapeutic and psychological aspects of coaching, but does not limit coaching to this discourse and offers other dimensions as well. For example, by making explicit three further discourses, other aspects to coaching are acknowledged and can be employed. In addition to the micro-practices the meta-theory includes the macro-social influences that are absent from many accounts of coaching. A brief overview of these macro-social influences is given in the following section.

Macro-Social Influences

The macro-social influences on coaching can be grouped into three areas:

THE KEY DISCOURSES OF COACHING

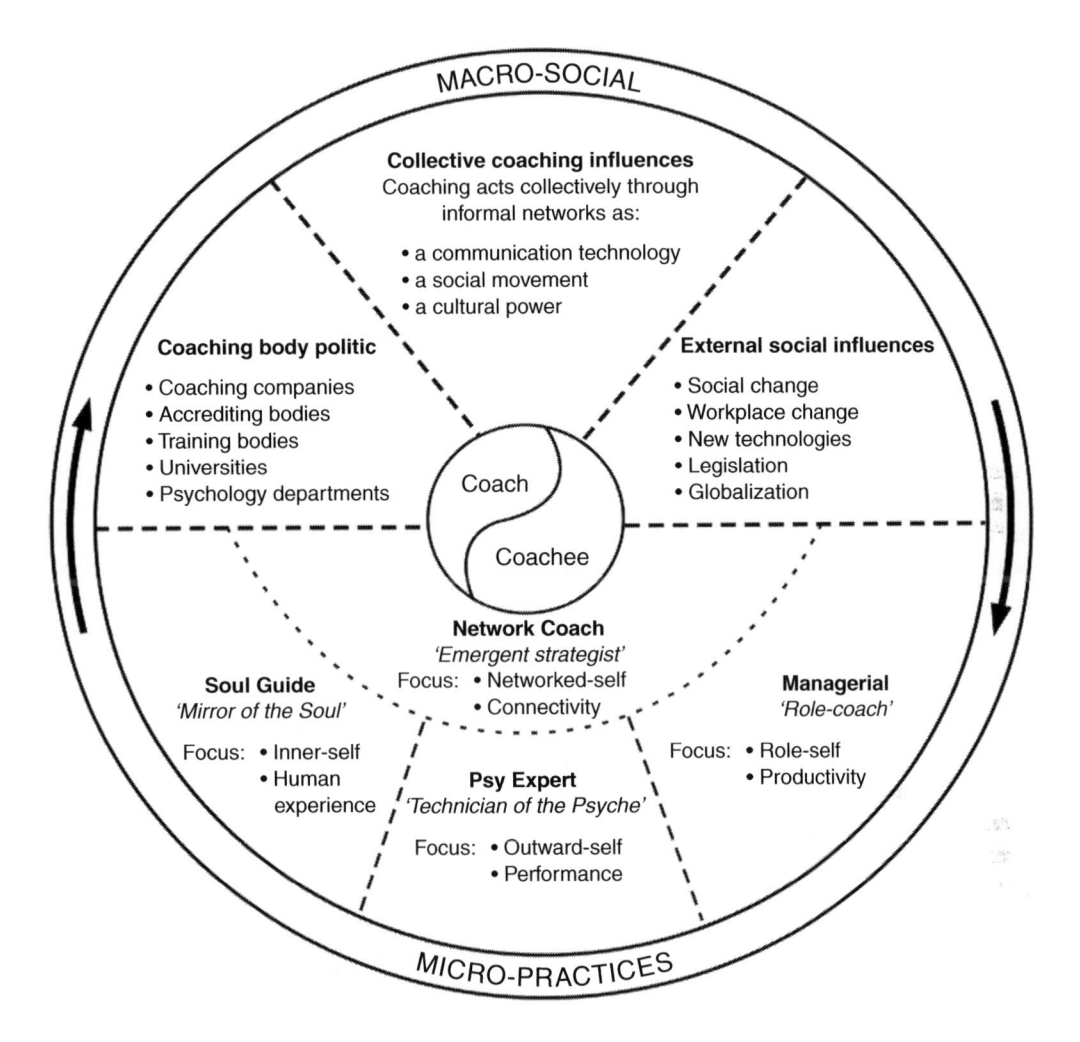

Figure 3.2 A meta-theory of coaching
Source: Western (2012: 242)

1. The Coaching body politic

This examines coaching from an institutional perspective, discussing the relationship between coaching organizations (i.e. coach providers, accrediting and training institutions etc.) and coaching practice. The coaching body politic influence how coaching is practiced, yet there is very little theorizing that makes these links explicit (De Haan 2008). Coaching practice is influenced, and to an extent controlled and regulated, through the implicit cultures and discourses that coaching institutions support. Yet coach-regulating bodies are not accountable to anyone but themselves, and they are working to two agendas; one that is open and one that is unspoken. As Seligman (2007) points out, 'some (coaches) are "accredited" by the self-appointed International Coach Federation and by other rump bodies, but most are not' (p.2). Any meta-theory has to open up these questions. For example, the ICF competency standards all focus on the individual and there is no recognition of the wider context or network. ICF Standard 10 is *Planning and Goal Setting: Planning with the client to develop goals that are (SMART) specific, measurable, attractive, realistic and have target dates.* This immediately forces coaches to work into the Psy Expert and Managerial discourses, excluding the Soul Guide and Network coaching discourses which eschew goals and measuring outcomes as self-limiting and reductionist. When theorizing coaching these institutional actors have to be accounted for, and taking a critical theory approach is helpful as the focus is on explicit and non-explicit power.

2. External social influences

External social influences on coaching may be natural, technological or political-social. For example, coaching may have emerged because the social world in the late 20th century became more individualized and alienating and people simply needed more professional help to deal with this (Giddens 1991). Coaching also changes with new technologies, as can be seen with the widespread use of video coaching that changes a physical encounter to a virtual one. As the natural world impact on workplaces (i.e. climate change, resource shortages), so coaching has to adapt to the difficult questions and its own practice will be emergent, paralleling workplace changes (e.g. adapting to Eco-leadership approaches).

3. Collective coaching influences

Coaches have a collective impact as well as an individual impact. Coaches network with each other both formally (e.g. at training sessions, conferences, company meetings) and also informally (e.g. through relationships with other coaches), both in the physical and virtual realm. Coaches also visit and engage with diverse workplaces and clients and, as such, coaching might reasonably be considered to be an ICT (Information Communication Technology) influencing networks through the cross-fertilization of ideas and the sharing of knowledge and best practice from the different workplaces they visit. Coaches not only communicate to executives within individual sessions, they act as 'memes' communicating in informal networks that shapes both coaching and leadership practice. New and networked social movement theory (Della Porta 1999; Castells 2012) can help to theorize how coaching operates as a ICT without formal leadership or organization.

CONCLUSION

This coaching meta-theory offers a framework for scrutinizing the theories of coaching practice. The four discourses show that coaching engages with and transcends psychotherapeutic influences and becomes a body of knowledge and a unique practice in its own right. Coaching draws on wider resources and influences from the historical and post-modern traditions of Soul Guides, draws on the Psy professions to gain leverage in personal relationships and change, then accesses modernist and direct workplace influences in the Managerial discourse, and finally may utilize the new emergent discourse of the Network Coach to embrace the radical workplace changes taking place in the post-industrial, digital and globalised age. The meta-theory makes the important links to the macro-social influences that also shape coaching.

The four discourses and the meta-theory potentially enable a richer reflection on coaching theory and practice, support an analysis of individual coaching practices, assist with the development of teaching and training practices, and can also inform supervision practices. The meta-theory also provides the tools to look externally at the broader institutional coaching relations and wider social, political and economic influences that impact on coaching in the workplace.

This opens the door for further research in the following areas. Firstly, more empirical studies on how coaches work within these four discourses to discover the strengths, challenges and emergent trends in coaching.

Secondly, research is needed that helps to develop ways in which coaches can work across the four discourses and develop training methods to support this adaptive and holistic approach. Thirdly, as coaching continues to develop and expand, researching the field drawing on critical theory, with a sociological, anthropological lens and using discourse analysis, will help discover other discourses that are emerging and becoming dominant players in the field. Looking at coaching through this broader lens will support the development of new coaching theories and will recognize and support new coaching practices as they emerge.

REFERENCES

Aelred of Rievaulx (1977) *Spiritual Friendship* (Mary Laker, trans.). Kalamazoo, MI: Cistercian Publications.

Alvesson, M. & Willmott, H. (2012) *Making Sense of Management: A Critical Introduction*. London: Sage.

Arnaud, G. (2003) 'A coach or a couch? A Lacanian perspective on executive coaching and consulting', *Human Relations*, 56: 1131.

Bachikrova, T. (2011) *Developmental Coaching Working with the Self*. New York: Open University Press.

Bass, B. (1990) 'From transactional to transformational leadership: Learning to share the vision', *Organizational Dynamics*, 18: 19–31.

Beck, A. (1976) *Cognitive Therapy and the Emotional Disorders*. London: Penguin Books.

Beradi, F. (2009) *The Soul at Work: From Alienation to Autonomy*. Los Angeles, CA: Semiotext(e).

Bettleheim, B. (1982) *Freud and Man's Soul*. New York: Knopf.

Bolden, R. (2011) 'Distributed leadership in organizations: A review of theory and research', *International Journal of Management Reviews*, 13(3): 251–269.

Bluckert, P. (2006) 'The foundations of a psychological approach to executive coaching', *Industrial and Commercial Training*, 37(4): 171–178.

Brunning, H. (2006) *Executive Coaching: Systems-psychodynamic Perspective*. London/New York: Karnac Books.

Casey, C. (1995) *Work Self and Society after Industrialisation*. London: Routledge.

Castells, M. (2000) *The Rise of the Network Society, The Information Age: Economy, Society and Culture Vol. I*. Cambridge, MA/Oxford, UK: Blackwell.

Castells, M. (2012) *Networks of Outrage and Hope*. Chicago, IL: Polity.

Chandler, D.E. and Kram, K.E. (2005) 'Applying an adult development perspective to developmental networks', *Career Developmental International, Special Edition on Mentoring*, 10(6/7): 548–566.

Clinton, B. (2012) 'The case for optimism', *Time Magazine*, 1 October. Clinton's Global Initiative.

Cox, E., Bachkirova, T. & Clutterbuck, D. (eds) (2014) *The Complete Handbook of Coaching*. London: Sage

De Haan, E. (2008) *Relational Coaching*. Sussex: Wiley and Sons.

Della Porta, D. (1999) *Social Movements: An Introduction*. London: Blackwell.

Ehrenreich, B. (2009) *Bright-Sided; How the Relentless Promotion of Positive Thinking has Undermined America*. New York: Henry Holt and Company.

Fairclough, N. (1995) *Critical Discourse Analysis: The Critical Study of Language*. London/New York: Longman.

Fleetwood, S. and Hesketh, A.J. (2006) 'HRM-performance research: Under-theorised and lacking explanatory power', *International Journal of Human Resources Management*, 17(12): 1979–1995.

Foucault, M. (1972) *The Discourse on Language*. New York: Pantheon Books.

Foucault, M. (1978 [French publication, 1976]) *The History of Sexuality, Vol. I: An Introduction* (Robert Hurley, trans.). New York: Pantheon.

Furedi, F. (2003) *Therapy Culture*. London: Routledge.

Garvey, B., Stokes, P. & Megginson, D. (2009) *Coaching and Mentoring: Theory and Practice*. London: Sage.

Giddens, A. (1991) *Modernity and Self Identity: Self and Society in the Late Modern Age*. Cambridge: Polity Press.

Graham, A. (2010 [2006]) 'Behavioural coaching – the GROW model'. In Jonathan Passmore (ed.), *Excellence in Coaching: The Industry Guide* (2nd ed.). London; Philadelphia: Kogan Page. pp. 83–93.

Green, L.S., Oades, L.G. & Grant, A.M. (2006) 'Cognitive-behavioral, solution-focused life coaching: Enhancing goal striving, well-being, and hope', *The Journal of Positive Psychology*, 1(3), 142–149.

Greene, J. & Grant, A.M. (2003) *Solution-Focused Coaching: Managing People in a Complex World*. Pearson Education.

Grimley, B. (2007) 'NLP coaching'. In S. Palmer and S Whybrow (eds) *Handbook of Coaching Psychology: A Guide for Practitioners*. Abingdon, UK: Routledge. pp. 193–210.

Grimely, B. (2014) 'The NLP Approach to Coaching'. In E. Cox., T. Bachkirova & D. Clutterbuck. (eds), *The Complete Handbook of Coaching*. London: Sage. pp. 185–199.

Hawkins, P. (2014) *Leadership Team Coaching: Developing Collective Transformational Leadership*. Kogan Page Publishers.

Heifetz, R.A., Grashow, A. & Linsky, M. (2009). *The Practice of Adaptive Leadership: Tools and Tactics for Changing your Organization and the World*. Harvard Business Press.

Higgins, M.C. and Kram, K.E. (2001) 'Reconceptualizing mentoring at work: a developmental network perspective', *Academy of Management Review*, 26(2): 264–288.

Ives, Y. (2008) 'What is "Coaching"? An exploration of conflicting paradigms', *International Journal of Evidence Based Coaching and Mentoring*, 6(2): 100–109.

Joseph, S. (2014) 'Person-centred coaching'. In E. Cox, T. Bachkirova & D.A. Clutterbuck,. (eds), *The Complete Handbook of Coaching*. London: Sage. pp. 65–77.

Kilburg, R. (2000) *Executive Coaching*. Washington: American Psychological Association.

Laing, R.D. (1967) *The Politics of Experience and the Bird of Paradise*. Penguin, England.

Laloux, F. (2014) *Reinventing Organizations*. Brussels: Nelson Parker.

Lasch, C. (1979) *The Culture of Narcissism: American Life in the Age of Diminishing Expectations*. New York: Warner Books.

Latour, B. (2005) *Reassembling the Social*. Oxford: Oxford University Press.

Law, J. (1993) *Organizing Modernity: Social Ordering and Social Theory*. Oxford: Wiley-Blackwell.

Linley, P.A. (2006) 'Coaching research: Who? what? where? when? why?', *International Journal of Evidence Based Coaching and Mentoring*, 4(2): 1–7.

Maslow, A. (1976) *The Farther Reaches of Human Nature*. New York: Penguin Books.

MacIntyre, A. (1985) *After Virtue: A Study in Moral Theory* (2nd ed.). London: Duckworth.

Miller, J.-A. (2005) 'Response to the anti-Freudians', *Le Point* [Online]. Available at: http://www.lacan.com/antimill.htm (accessed April 2011).

Mintzberg, H. (2004) *Managers Not MBAs: A Hard Look at the Soft Practice of Managing and Management Development*. San Francisco: Barrett Kochler.

Mintzberg, H. (2008) *Mintzberg on Management*. Available at: http://www.forbes.com/sites/stevedenning/2011/04/08/mintzberg-on-management/ retrieved 30 December 2011

Neenan, M. & Dryden, W. (2004) *Cognitive Therapy: 100 Key Points and Techniques*. Hove: Psychology Press.

Newton, J., Long, S.& Sievers, B. (eds) (2006) *Coaching in Depth: The Organizational Role Analysis Approach*. London: Karnac. pp. 127–143.

O'Connell, B. & Palmer, S. (2007) 'Solution-focused coaching'. In S. Palmer and A. Whybrow (eds) *Handbook of Coaching Psychology: A guide for Practitioners*. London: Sage. pp. 278–293.

Parker, M. (2002) *Against Management: Organization in the Age of Managerialism*. Cambridge: Polity Press.

Peltier, B. (2001) *The Psychology of Executive Coaching: Theory and Application*. New York: Brunner Routledge.

Power, M. (1997) *The Audit Society Rituals of Verification*. Oxford: Oxford University Press.

Rose, N. (1985) *The Psychological Complex: Psychology, Politics and Society in England 1869–1939*. London: Routledge.

Rose, N. (1990) *Governing the Soul: The Shaping of the Private Self*. London: Routledge.

Rose, N. (2011) *Power in Therapy: Techne and Ethos* [Online]. Available at: http://www.academyanalyticarts.org/rose2.htm (accessed 28 July 2011).

Rowan, J. (2010) 'The Transpersonal Approach to Coaching'. In E. Cox, T. Bachkirova and D. Clutterbuck (eds), *The Complete Handbook of Coaching*. London: Sage. pp. 145–156.

Sieler, A. (2005) *Coaching to the Human Soul: Ontological Coaching and Deep Change, Vol. 1*. Asia-Pacific: Newfield Institute.

Seligman, M. (2007) 'Coaching and positive psychology', *Australian Psychologist*, 42(4): 266–267.

Smith, R. (2013) http://www.telegraph.co.uk/news/health/news/9824256/Target-culture-that-led-to-Mid-Staffs-still-exists-in-NHS-claims-top-surgeon.html (retrieved January 2016).

Stavrakakis, Y. (2007) *The Lacanian Left*. Edinburgh: Edinburgh University Press.

Sullivan, N. (2003) *A Critical Introduction to Queer Theory*. New York: New York University Press.

Taylor, F.W. (1947) *The Principles of Scientific Management*. New York: Harper and Brothers Publishers.

Tourish, D. & Pinnington, A. (2002) 'Transformational leadership, corporate cultism and the spirituality paradigm: An unholy trinity in the workplace?', *Human Relations*, 55(2): 147–172.

Turkle, S. (2011) *Alone Together; Why We Expect More From Technology and Less From Each Other*. New York: Basic Books.

West, L. & Milan, M. (2001) *The Reflecting Glass*. New York: Palgrave.

Western, S. (2012) *Coaching and Mentoring: A Critical Text*. London: Sage.

Western S. (2013) *Leadership: A Critical Text* (2nd ed.). London: Sage.

Western, S. (2014) 'Autonomist leadership in leaderless movements: anarchists leading the way'. *ephemera: theory & politics in organization*, 14(4), 673–698.

Western, S. (2015) Taken from www.analytic-network.com coaching website (retrieved January 2016)

Western, S. (2016) 'The bridge between two selves', *Coaching Today, Association of Coaching Journal*, forthcoming.

Whitmore, J., Kauffman, C. & Susan, A. (2013) 'GROW grows up: from winning the game to pursuing transpersonal goals'. In S.A. David, D. Clutterbuck & D. Megginson (eds), *Beyond Goals: Effective Strategies for Coaching and Mentoring*. Farnham, Surrey: Gower Publishing Limited. pp. 245–260.

Zeus, P. & Skiffington, S. (2002) *The Coaching at Work Toolkit*. Roseville, NSW: McGraw Hill.

Coaching as Evidence-Based Practice: The View Through a Multiple-Perspective Model of Coaching Research

Anthony M. Grant

INTRODUCTION

We are witnessing the emergence of a significant body of coaching-specific knowledge that draws on and integrates knowledge from a range of disciplines, and this is evident in both theoretical and empirical domains. Indeed, the quantum of published material associated with coaching has increased almost exponentially over the past ten years. Whilst this growth is good for coaching, the increase in and diversity of the knowledge base makes it difficult for practitioners to assimilate and utilise this information in the development of coaching as an evidence-based practice. In this body of literature we see the adoption and utilisation of a broad range of theoretical perspectives from the acutely systemic (e.g., complex adaptive systems or adult developmental), through the biopsychosocial (e.g., cognitive-behavioural theory or learning theory) to biological approaches (e.g., neuroscience).

Similarly, the empirical support for coaching spans a broad range from rigorous coaching-specific research (both qualitative and quantitative), to basic research in disciplines not specifically related to coaching. Further complicating the situation is the fact that coaching research itself is focused on many different facets of coaching, ranging from research focused on the effectiveness of coaching interventions to produce specific outcomes, through to the nature of coach–coachee relationships, to explorations of how the effects of coaching impact on and reverberate through human and organisational systems. The diversity of this data can make it difficult for both researchers and practitioners to grasp specific information from this developing knowledge base and engage in an evidence-based approach in their own personal coaching practice.

This chapter briefly discusses the nature of evidence-based practice as it relates specifically to coaching. Then, following an overview of the current coaching-specific literature, the chapter presents two new frameworks that are useful in understanding and classifying the coaching knowledge base. The first framework delineates the relevance to evidence-based coaching practice of a broad range of research, ranging from coaching-specific research to noncoaching-specific research. The second framework, a multiple-perspective model of coaching research, is used to identify and classify key themes in the coaching literature to date. Informed by such points, the chapter then presents some reflections on the way forward and discusses some implications for evidence-based practice. The aim of this chapter is to help further develop a more nuanced view of evidence-based approaches to coaching practice.

THE DEVELOPMENT OF THE TERM 'EVIDENCE-BASED' COACHING

Adapted from its original use in medical contexts (Sackett, Haynes, Guyatt, & Tugwell, 1996) the term 'evidence-based' coaching was coined at the Coaching Psychology Unit in the University of Sydney in 2003 as a way of distinguishing between coaching that is explicitly grounded in the broader empirical and theoretical knowledge base, and coaching that was developed from the 'pop psychology' personal development genre.

At the time this term was coined the intention was merely to have a flag that indicated that here was an approach to coaching that sought to be grounded on firm and coherent foundations – empirical and theoretical foundations that would allow a discipline of coaching to develop with the same gravitas as other helping modalities such as counselling or clinical psychology. Indeed, at that time the term was more aspirational than actual.

However, the notion of 'evidence-based coaching' seems to have resonated with many people in the coaching industry globally (e.g, Larsen, Kilburn, & Myszak, 2007). There are now peer-reviewed academic journals focusing on evidence-based coaching, university postgraduate degree courses on evidence-based coaching, and many coaching practitioners have incorporated the phrase into their terms of reference.

WHAT DOES EVIDENCE-BASED COACHING REALLY MEAN?

But what does 'evidence-based coaching' really mean? The concept has sparked quite vigorous debate as to the role of 'scientific' evidence in coaching, and what constitutes 'evidence' (e.g., Drake, 2009). Such debate is important and makes a significant contribution to helping coaching as a discipline not to be confined within the rigid boundaries of a medical or reductionist paradigm.

This is important because the term 'evidence-based' within medical contexts is almost synonymous with double-blind randomised-controlled trials and mechanistic manualised treatment protocols. A key underpinning notion in the medical context is that research should dictate practice. However, this is not the case in relation to coaching. Coaching engagements are not medical interventions that follow prescribed regimes. The nonmedical context of coaching means that the medical model may be an unsuitable framework from which to teach, research or practice coaching – although few would argue that applying evidence to practice is not a valuable way of further developing coaching as a discipline.

Hence this chapter takes a broader and less reductionist view than is typically found in medical contexts. This perspective draws on the assumption that translating research into coaching practice (and conversely translating coaching practice into coaching research) can optimise outcomes and lead to more rigorous (and vigorous) coaching research and practice (e.g., Drake, 2009). From this perspective both empirical evidence and professional wisdom (wisdom being comprised of experience, knowledge, and good judgement) have considerable and often equal value. Consequently this chapter employs a more sophisticated understanding of the term 'evidence-based' and refers to the *intelligent and conscientious use of relevant and best current knowledge integrated with professional practitioner expertise in making decisions about how to deliver coaching to coaching clients and in designing and delivering coach training programs* (adapted from Sackett, et al., 1996; Stober & Grant, 2006).

Figure 4.1 illustrates the joint contributions of professional practitioner expertise and empirical evidence. Professional wisdom consists of individual experience about what works in one's coaching practice with one's clients. The individual coach's perspective is important here because coaching is typically an idiosyncratic intervention, not least because the coach–coachee relationship is a major factor in coaching outcomes, and that relationship is by its very nature idiosyncratic.

Although individual views are important, sole reliance on it may result in a myopic perspective. Hence the practitioner group consensus, which allows for multiple perspectives about what works, is also important. This is not to say that practitioner group experience can present an unbiased or objective view on what works. Within any group or subgroup of professionals there are political and social forces at play which will shape the emerging narrative or consensus about what is the 'best' or 'right' way. Nevertheless, regardless of its limitations, it is clear that practitioner wisdom has a vital role in shaping understandings of evidence-based coaching.

The right hand side of Figure 4.1 represents the role of empirical evidence gathered from research. The first issue to be addressed here related to the boundaries between practitioner experience and formal research. There is a sense in which practitioner experience gained as a result of professional coaching practice can be considered to be research. However, following the rationale outlined by a number of eminent authors in the action learning sphere (e.g., Argyris & Schön, 1992; Revans, 1982), I argue that there is an important distinction between information gained in one's professional practice and information gained through formal research initiatives.

In one's professional practice, the primary purpose of practitioner research is the improvement of one's professional practice, where the emphasis is on practical significance, and this information tends to be shared through contacts with one's colleagues, professional or industry associations. In contrast, the aim of formal research is to produce more generalisable knowledge that contributes to the broader knowledge base, the emphasis is often on theoretical significance rather than practical application, and the information tends to be shared primarily through

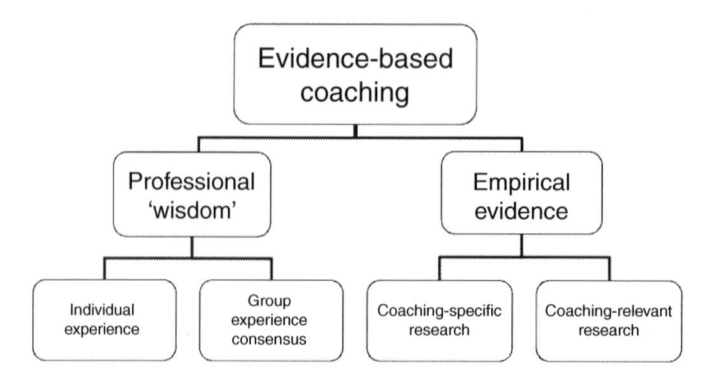

Figure 4.1 Professional expertise, empirical research and evidence-based coaching

peer-reviewed publications, academic conferences, and only then is it disseminated for professional purposes. They are different and they make different contributions to an evidence-based approach to coaching.

The second issue to be addressed relates to what constitutes empirical evidence about coaching. Here I propose two categories: (1) coach-specific research and (2) coaching research that is not specific to coaching but can be considered to be coaching-related research.

Coaching-specific research involves studies that specifically focus on coaching with coaching as the primary focus. These could include, for example, quantitative studies that examine the effectiveness of coaching, the impact of coaching on a range of variables, or qualitative research into, for example, the nature of effective coach–coachee relationships, amongst others. This would also include coaching research using models or techniques from other non-coaching areas or disciplines which can be directly applied in coaching practice – examples here could include cognitive behavioural techniques from clinical psychology, action learning principles or adult learning theory.

Coaching-related research involves studies that are not specifically focused on coaching, but produce data that could be used in coaching practice or might inform coaching practice. These could include, for example, research from economics, management or organisational research, philosophical paradigms, systems theory, neuroscience etc. However, in understanding what constitutes 'empirical evidence' these are not the only categories that count. We also need to consider the rigour of the evidence presented.

Strong evidence can be understood as information and evidence from well-designed and peer-reviewed studies where the methodology is eminently suitable for the research question being addressed, and the results have been replicated in a range of populations where appropriate. It should be emphasised that this is an inclusive position that does not automatically privilege (for example) randomised controlled studies over case studies, as is the case in the medical model. Nor does this position privilege quantitative research over qualitative research. Both approaches have much to offer. Rather this position acknowledges that different research designs

Table 4.1 Differences between researcher's and practitioner's approach to research

	Academic researcher	Practitioner
Primary purpose of conducting research	Production of knowledge	Improvement of one's professional practice
Emphasis on	Contributing to the knowledge base and theoretical significance	Practical significance
Validation of information	Knowledge is deemed 'validated' only after a comprehensive analysis, thorough documentation (typically in rigid discipline-specific writing and presentation style) and peer review	Factors that 'validate' knowledge include face validity, acceptance by clients or stakeholders, public receptivity, marketability, practical applicability
Dissemination of information	Peer-reviewed publication and academic conferences take place before information is presented to public/professional media	Shared through multiple channels including professional associations, industry contacts and clients, and social media
Primary discourse style	Discipline-specific jargon and (often dense) academic language which excludes non-academics	Easily accessible, to-the-point language, designed to reach broad audience

and approaches have utility for addressing different research questions.

In contrast, *weak evidence* is when there are a small number of studies, limited numbers of researchers/sources, limited numbers of research methodologies with limited populations, or poor quality research design, for example with low statistical power or inappropriate analyses. Typically these are not peer reviewed, and this would include opinion articles or anecdotal, unsubstantiated reports.

A useful way to present these concepts is through a two-by-two diagram (see Figure 4.2). This figure is presented as a useful heuristic through which one can categorise and classify different bodies of research. No doubt there would be a myriad of opinions as to which studies or which bodies of knowledge should sit in which quadrant – and it should be noted that this framework is designed to be an aid to those who wish to develop a more sophisticated understanding of evidence-based coaching rather than a definitive typology.

Nevertheless, I would argue that well-designed randomised controlled studies with a range of populations would be situated in the top right hand quadrant (for examples see Theeboom, Beersma, & van Vianen, 2013), along with other methodologies such as well-designed case studies (e.g., Libri & Kemp, 2006; Schnell, 2005), robust mixed method work (Bachkirova, Arthur, & Reading, 2015) or extensive qualitative research (de Haan & Nieß, 2015)

The bottom right hand quadrant encompasses research that is coaching-specific but is not highly rigorous. This is not to say that such researchers set out to purposefully produce research of low rigour. Such research may have been negatively impacted by hard-to-access participant samples, major changes in research context (e.g., redundancies or shifts in economic climate) over the course of the research, or any of the all-to-frequent logistical challenges of conducting field research. Such studies could include quantitative coaching-specific research that has a small size or is exploratory in nature (e.g., Sherlock-Storey, Moss, & Timson, 2013). This section could also include qualitative coaching-specific research that has been poorly designed and superficially analysed, or survey research that has been conducted as a means of promoting a business offering or coaching service (Corbett, 2006).

	Lower Relevance Coach-related Research	Higher Relevance Coach-specific Research
Strong Strength of Evidence **Weak**	**Weaker evidence for coaching** Rigorous coaching-related research	**Stronger evidence for coaching** Rigorous coaching-specific research
	Poorer evidence for coaching Less rigorous coaching-related research	**Weaker evidence for coaching** Less rigorous coaching-specific research

Relevance to Coaching Practice

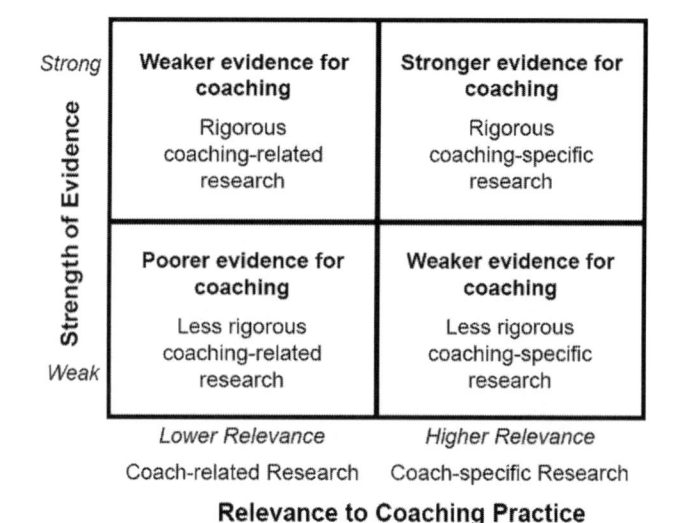

Figure 4.2 The evidence/relevance coaching framework

The top left hand quadrant represents well-designed coaching-related research; that is research that closely aligns with coaching, but is not specifically coaching. Examples here could include empirical studies of the role of self-concordance in goal striving and well-being (Sheldon & Elliot, 1999), review articles on the relationship between goals and performance (Locke, 1996), reports on the impact of positive psychology interventions (Bolier, et al., 2013) or explorations of self-regulation (Baumeister, Vohs, & Tice, 2007) amongst others. Included here also could be coaching-related qualitative research exploring (for example) the lived experience of a person undertaking a programme of positive thinking (Thatcher, 2014)

The bottom right hand quadrant represents the poorest evidence for coaching. Research in this area could include quantitative studies with low statistical power or inappropriate analysis, conceptual incoherency or research with a focus that is only marginally related to coaching. A useful example here is the use of fMRI brain scans and related aspects of neuroscience being put forward as 'proof' that coaching works (Rock & Schwartz, 2006). Despite much marketing material trumpeting the value of neuroscience as a foundation for coaching practice, there are no fMRI studies exploring the direct links between realistic coaching interventions and specific regions of brain activity. Although neuroscience studies may shine an informative light on the dynamics of brain functioning, very little (if any) of this body of research is directly related to observable behavioural change in coaching clients. In addition, much neuroscience research has been heavily criticised for low statistical power and inappropriate analysis (Button, et al., 2013), thus further limiting the direct contribution of neuroscience to an evidenced-based approach to coaching at this point in time.

Other examples in this quadrant could include research on body language and non-verbal communication as applied to coaching (Matsumoto, Hwang, & Frank, 2016), the applicability of learning styles to the coaching relationship (Freedman & Stumpf, 1978; Kolb & Kolb, 2013) or research on the influence of birth order on career progression and responsiveness to career coaching interventions (Leong, Hartung, Goh, & Gaylor, 2001). The main point here is that research in this quadrant is typically indirectly related to actual coaching effectiveness and that such research is either poorly conducted or has attracted significant controversies.

The above examples in all four quadrants have been presented as illustrative examples only. Coaches and researchers will themselves have to determine how they would personally categorise the different types of research that they draw on in their own coaching practice. Nevertheless, the framework presented here gives a useful tool for the refining of one's understanding of the relative relevance of different bodies of research to evidence-based coaching practice.

Having delineated a framework for categorising the relevance of different bodies of both quantitative and qualitative research and their relatedness to an evidence-based approach to coaching, we can now turn our attention to understanding the multi-faceted nature of coaching-specific research.

HOW TO UNDERSTAND COACH-SPECIFIC EVIDENCE? A MULTIPLE-PERSPECTIVE MODEL OF COACHING RESEARCH

The amount of coaching-specific research has grown almost exponentially over the past twenty years. A search of the scholarly literature on the database Business Source Premier in June 2015 using the keyword 'coaching' found a total of 2,103 citations from 1995 to 2015. The distribution of these publications is presented in Figure 4.3 (note: the citations for 2015 are not included in the graph). As can be seen in Figure 4.3 there has been a significant growth in the literature since

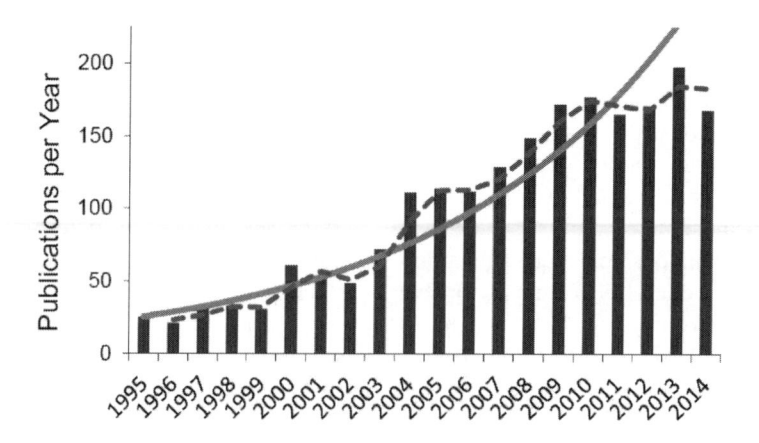

Figure 4.3 Growth of coaching publications in business source premier database from 1995 to 2014

1995. The solid line shows the exponential curve that fits the data, and the dotted line shows the moving average.

It appears that approximately every five years there is a noticeable stepped increase in the number of coaching publications. The escalating quantity of this literature means that it is increasingly difficult for those interested in the development of coaching to maintain a solid understanding of the state of the literature at any point in time. Furthermore, the coaching research has broadened considerably in content. Because of this situation it has become increasingly difficult to keep track of new findings. A common way of thinking about research is by simply making reference to specific studies or authors. However, this way of categorising research is sometimes insufficient to capture the diversity of contemporary coaching research.

To address this issue, following a brief review of the coaching literature, this section presents a model of coaching research that seeks to integrate 10 key perspectives on coaching research. This model provides a visual framework to categorise the findings of various studies, and may prove to be a useful heuristic for those seeking to develop a nuanced view of the contemporary coaching literature.

An overview of coaching research trends

The early coaching research tended to be case studies on the effectiveness of coaching interventions (e.g., Tobias, 1996) or opinion articles on the application of theoretical approaches to specific coaching contexts (e.g., Kilburg, 1997). Other foci included delineating and defining coaching (e.g., Kilburg, 1996), and describing how workplace coaching can be used by managers to improve employees' performance (e.g., Graham, Wedman, & Garvin-Kester, 1994). The 1990s also produced useful reports on how to evaluate executive coaching engagements (e.g, Peterson, 1993, 1996) as well as a number of early quantitative studies on coaching effectiveness (e.g., Miller, 1990; Olivero, Bane, & Kopelman, 1997).

During 2000 to 2010 the nature of the literature began to change with the publication of more within-subject, between-subject and randomised-controlled outcome studies (e.g, Grant, Curtayne, & Burton, 2009; Gyllensten & Palmer, 2005; Miller, Yahne, Moyers, Martinez, & Pirritano, 2004; Spence & Grant, 2007). Coaching outcome research became broader as researchers explored the effectiveness of coaching in a wide variety of applications including life coaching (Grant, 2003), executive coaching (Cerni, Curtis, & Colmar, 2010), coaching with MBA students (Sue-Chan & Latham, 2004), or with medical practitioners (Gattellari, et al., 2005) to name just a few (for a review detailing the changing trends in the coaching literature see Grant, Passmore, Cavanagh, & Parker, 2010).

The Increasing Complexity and Breadth of the Literature

The complexity of the literature has increased even more over time. The current coaching literature includes research into a highly diverse number of areas including research into the coach–coachee relationship (de Haan, Duckworth, Birch, & Jones, 2013; Jowett, Kanakoglou, & Passmore, 2012), psychodynamic theories in coaching (Ward, van de Loo, & ten Have, 2014), cultural and organisational change aspects of coaching (Steed, 2013), the diversity of coachee characteristics (Bozer, Sarros, & Santora, 2013), and the active ingredients of coaching (McKenna & Davis, 2009). Other areas include the impact of coaching on coachee's well-being, resilience or emotional intelligence (Grant, et al., 2009), measurement issues related to coaching outcomes (Smith, 2012), coaches' views on coaching supervision (Grant, 2012), and coaches' personality characteristics (Scoular & Linley, 2006). Workplace examples include factors related to internal organisational coaching (Frisch, 2001), the role of organisational sponsors in organisational coaching (Bond & Seneque, 2012), and the ripple effect of coaching in organisations (O'Connor & Cavanagh, 2013). The above only represent a fraction of the topics that are explored in the coaching literature. It is not surprising then that, in terms of both quantity and breadth of focus, the diverse nature of contemporary coaching research can be confusing and difficult to assimilate, even for experienced observers.

The situation is made more complicated by the fact that many studies report multiple findings. For example, research that focuses on the 'processes' of coaching (e.g., de Haan, 2008; de Haan, et al., 2013), explores a wide range of issues within a single study, often using both quantitative and qualitative methods in a single study.

Other examples include Grant's (2014b) exploration of the efficacy of executive coaching in time of organisational change, finding that coaching facilitated the attainment of coaching-related goals, and also positively impacted on participants' well-being and mental health, as well as finding that positive impacts of coaching generalised to non-work areas such as family life. O'Connor and Cavanagh's (2013) complex systems work in organisations examined the effects of coaching in terms of individual outcomes, inter-personal outcomes and at a systemic organisational level, and these were measured in terms of both behavioural and psychological changes using goal attainment scaling, measures of individual well-being as well as social network analysis. Ladegard and Gjerde (2014) used a two-phase exploratory sequential design and both qualitative and quantitative research methods to assess leadership coaching using both pre-post assessment (and comparison with a control group) and structural equation modelling to explore the relationship between the coach's behaviour and changes in the coachee's self-efficacy and trust in their subordinates as well the relationship between changes in leader's trust in their subordinates and subordinates level of empowerment and turnover intentions. Coaching research is indeed becoming more complex and sophisticated.

A Multiple-Perspective Model of Coaching Research

As yet there has been little recognition of the need to develop a framework or model from which to categorise different research findings. The Multiple-Perspective Model of coaching research (MPM) presented here aims to visually represent a broad range of issues including; outcome research; issues related to coach and coachee; the impact of coaching from individualist, psychological, relational and systemic perspectives; as well as facilitating comparisons between different types of coaching approaches; and the various factors involved in organisational coaching.

This model has ten key areas (see Figure 4.4). Each area represents a potential perspective on the findings of coaching research. This is not meant to be a definitive representation of coaching research but rather aims to be a useful guiding heuristic. (Note: for convenience the descriptions of the 10 areas below discuss these in relation to an individual coachee, but can equally apply to team or group coaching). An example of each area is given as a reference point.

The Ten Areas

- Area A represents attributes of the coachee including how the coachee themselves changes over the course of a coaching engagement; for example, changes in psychopathology, resilience, self-efficacy, leadership style, development, insight or self-reflection, where these are not specific goals of the coaching engagement (e.g., Grant, et al., 2009).
- Area B represents the coachee's goals, that is, the specific goals of the coaching engagement. These could include goal attainment, increased sales, better time management, or other explicitly designated foci for the coaching engagement (e.g., Spence, 2007).
- Area C represents the coachee's immediate personal system. Examples here could include the extent to which the impact of coaching generalises to other areas of the coachee's life in terms of improved self-regulation in general, better relationships with family or work colleagues, or finding greater meaning and purpose in life (e.g., Grant, 2014b).
- Area D represents the attributes of the coach. This could include the coach's personality traits, their

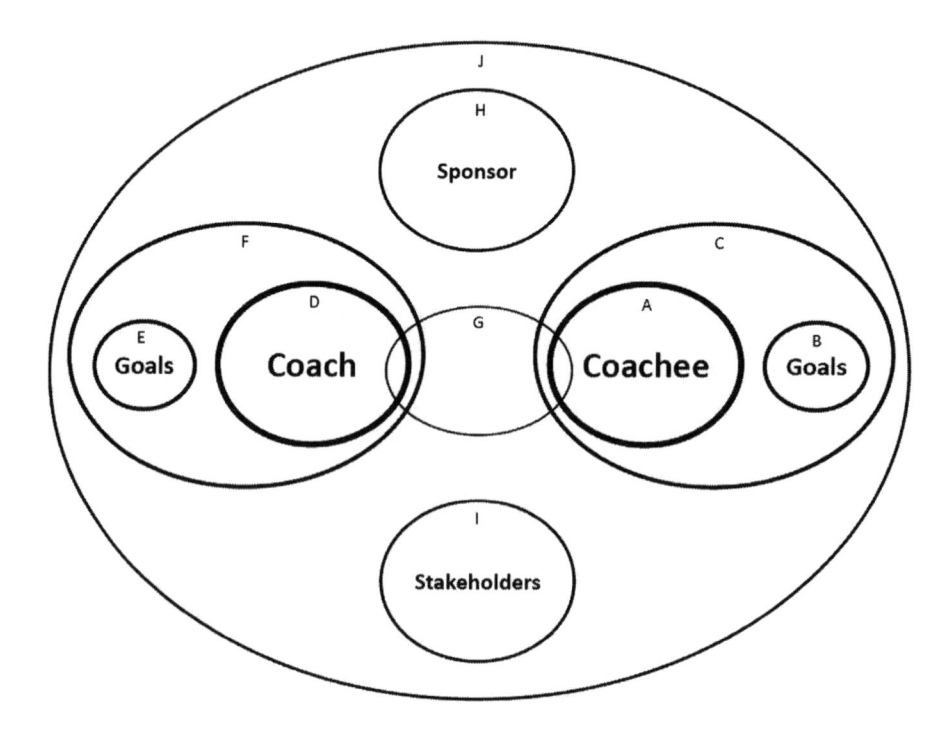

Figure 4.4 The Multiple-Perspective Model of coaching research

prior coaching experience and training, different coaching approaches including preferred methodologies or theoretical frameworks, or changes in the coach themselves over course of the coaching engagement such as increased personal insight (e.g., Sue-Chan, Wood, & Latham, 2012).
- Area E represents the coach's goals for coaching. These could include a range of goal and motivational constructs including the coach's hopes for the coachee's development, the coach's personal criteria for a successful coaching engagement, the coach's fees and remuneration, and the coach's own learning and developmental goals (e.g., David, Clutterbuck, & Megginson, 2014)
- Area F represents the coach's immediate personal system and could include the extent to which the impact of coaching on the coach generalises to other areas of the coach's life, for example, enhanced confidence in dealing with others, shifts in approaches to learning, improvements in personal self-regulation, or general personal development as a result of coaching others (e.g., Peterson, 2011).
- Area G represents the coach–coachee relationship. This could include different aspects of the working alliance and their association with various coaching outcomes, and could involve research that explores the effects of different types of coaching relationships in relation to different coaching engagements (e.g., de Haan, et al., 2013; O'Broin & Palmer, 2010).
- Area H represents, in organisational contexts, the sponsor's influence on and experience of the coaching engagement. For example, the effect of different ways of contracting with the coach, or a manager's participation in setting the agenda for a subordinate's coaching by an external coach, or the utility of a sponsor's feedback during the course of a coaching engagement (e.g., Fillery-Travis, 2015).
- Area I represents the proximal systemic impact of, and influence on, the coaching engagement. This could include stakeholders' personal experience of the coaching engagement (and their influence on it). This could also include the extent to which stakeholders other than the sponsor have direct influence on the coaching processes and on coaching outcomes, or how the stakeholders' perception of the coachee changes over the course of the coaching engagement, or the changes in interactions between individual stakeholders following a coaching intervention with the coachee (e.g., O'Connor & Cavanagh, 2013).
- Area J represents the more distal systemic impact of, and influence on, the coaching engagement. For example, this could include the extent to which the coaching of specific individuals affects the wellbeing and performance of the broader organisation, or conversely how the broader system impacts on the individual being coached, either facilitating or hindering the change process (e.g., Stober, 2008).

It should be noted the precise boundaries between proximal and distal influences and impact are somewhat difficult to define. Suh and Badrinarayanan (2014) define proximal influences as those that impact one's everyday experience, and distal factors as those that are relatively remote to the everyday experience. Although these are somewhat arbitrary delineations, the inclusion in the proposed model of areas I and J allows for a nuanced systemic perspective on the coaching engagement (see Cavanagh and Lane (2012) for a useful discussion on issues related to boundaries in complex systems as they apply to coaching contexts).

TOWARDS THE NEXT GENERATION OF COACHING RESEARCH

Coaching has traditionally been thought of merely as a methodology for enhancing performance and helping people reach goals in their personal and professional lives (Landsberg, 1997). However, the 10 perspectives offered by the MPM Coaching Research Model and the above overview of the literature which demonstrates the multifaceted nature of contemporary coaching-related research, suggest that coaching has terrific potential as a methodology for exploring a wide range of issues related to intentional change on both individual and systemic levels. What might this next generation of coaching research look like in relation to the different areas in the model? The following section of this paper discusses this and presents a few studies that illustrate examples of the research that has been conducted in each area to date, and makes suggestions as to a possible future research agenda.

Area A: Coachee Attributes

Area A relates to the coachee's personal attributes or how the coachee themselves change over the course of a coaching engagement. There have been a number of studies looking at how the coachee's personality, mindset and other personal attributes relate to outcomes (e.g., MacKie, 2015; McCormick & Burch, 2008). Surprisingly, there has been less research into how the impact of coaching someone towards the attainment of specific goals has a generalisation effect in terms of improving psychological functioning (e.g., reduced depression, anxiety or stress), when those issues were not directly addressed in the coaching engagement (e.g., Grant, 2003), even though such generalisation is predicted by a number of well-accepted theoretical propositions (Gregory, Beck, & Carr, 2011). Future research could explore the generalisation effect of coaching, and in doing so potentially develop more sophisticated coaching-related models of self-regulation.

Area B: Coachee's Goals

There is still a need for more outcome studies of coaching that explore the impact of coaching of goal attainment Some commentators have argued that the effectiveness of coaching in terms of facilitating goal attainment can now be assumed (de Haan & Duckworth, 2013). I argue that it is important to continue to build the evidence-base for the effectiveness of coaching as a methodology for facilitating the attainment of specific goals or outcomes. Although there are now enough good quality studies for meta-analyses of the effectiveness of coaching on goal attainment to be conducted (Jones, Woods, & Guillaume, 2015; Theeboom, et al., 2013), and the quantum of coaching outcome studies is increasing, this still is far less than in related fields such as counselling or therapy. We need more well-designed outcome studies, using both quantitative and qualitative approaches.

From a quantitative perspective, one factor that influences the potential of studies to provide solid data on goal attainment is sample size. The average sample size calculated from the Jones, et al. (2015) meta-analysis is 56. Whilst such sample sizes can be informative, there is a tendency to use relatively homogeneous populations. Whilst logistically challenging, future quantitative research should attempt to conduct large scale outcome research with more heterogeneous populations.

There has been some work into how self-determination theory can be used in setting goals in coaching (Spence & Oades, 2011), but as yet there is not yet extensive work exploring the utility of goal theory in actual coaching practice (for an informed discussion see David, Clutterbuck, and Megginson 2013). Other areas of goal research in the quantitative tradition that have had little or no attention to date include the relative impact of different types of goal (e.g., approach and avoidance) on the coaching process, and the effect of different coaching methodologies on goal attainment. Future research could explore the relative impact of approaches to coaching that are not explicitly goal-focused with those that encourage clear goal-setting – seeing which approach was more effective.

From a qualitative perspective future research could explore the idiosyncratic factors that impact on goal attainment. It has been noted by many commentators (e.g., Clutterbuck, 2008) that the goals of coaching often change significantly over the course of a coaching engagement. Such dynamics are hard to track using quantitative methods alone. Qualitative research can bring a powerful lens to bear on the coachee's lived experience and provide valuable insights into the goal-striving process.

Area C: Coachee's Personal System

Area C represents the coachee's immediate personal system. Research here could focus on the generalisation effect and how coaching impacts on the coachee's personal life system. There are many anecdotal reports from coachees mentioning how workplace coaching has helped them be more effective in their personal life, or how coaching has given them the ability to have more meaningful family relationships. Most professional coaches will have heard such reports from their coaching clients at one time or other. Yet there appears to have been very little systematic research into this (Grant, 2014b). Because it is difficult to predict *a prioi* which life domains would be impacted and in what way, and consequently which quantitative measures to use, this is one domain where qualitative research methodologies can prove extremely useful (Bachkirova, Arthur, et al., 2015). Future research could explore how the benefits of workplace coaching generalise to other areas of the coachee's life and the longevity of any changes. Qualitative research in particular would give us better understanding of the impact of coaching in this area, and would provide a compelling rationale for clients to engage with the coaching process.

Area D: Coach's Attributes

A number of studies have examined various attributes of the coach. For example Lewis-Duarte and Bligh (2012) examined coaches' use of a range of influencing tactics during coaching sessions. Spence and Grant (2007) examined whether coach training actually made people become better coaches, finding that whilst peer (untrained coaches) can be effective, professionally trained coaches had superior outcomes with their coaching clients.

Bachkirova and Cox (2007) discuss in some detail how the cognitive-developmental perspective is important for understanding the development of the coach and how that impacts on the coaching process. Dagley (2010) studied 40 exceptional coaches finding that their key personal attributes included credibility, empathy and respect, diagnostic skill and insight, approach flexibility and range. Chinn, Richmond, and Bennett (2015) explored the impact of the coach's prior industry experience on the coachee's goal attainment, finding that industry experience had little impact on goal attainment.

There are a considerable number of possible directions for future research in this area. One issue that has been extensively studied in education is the impact of teachers' expectations of students on students' performance. Research from Rosenthal's classic work (1963) to contemporary studies (Rubie-Davies, 2009) has shown that high expectations on the teacher's part are associated with better educational outcomes for students. This body of research could usefully inform coaching research to determine if the same dynamics are at play – that is, do coaches' expectations of client progress influence actual client progress.

Area E: Coach's Goals and Motivations

There has been very little research in the coaching literature that has examined the influence of the coach's own goals or motivations for coaching. There has been some discussion on this issue in the professional literature. Flaherty (2010) presents a detailed discussion on the issues related to the coach's motivations, and Kemp (2008) argued for the importance of self-management as a primary goal for the coach to hold in order to be an effective practitioner.

Other commentators have made similar observations (e.g., David, et al., 2014; Morgan, Harkins, & Goldsmith, 2011), but as yet there has been no significant in-depth exploration of these issues in the coaching literature. This is somewhat surprising given that there is a significant body of research in relation to sport coaches' goals and motivations for working with athletes (e.g., Jowett, 2008; McLean & Mallett, 2012), much of which has explored the issues from the perspective of self-determination theory (Deci & Ryan, 1980; Rocchi, Pelletier, & Couture, 2013), with its concept of autonomy support are often seen as being central to the coach–coachee relationship in life coaching, workplace and executive coaching (Gabriel, Moran, & Gregory, 2014; Spence & Oades, 2011). Furthermore, there is a significant body of research examining the effect of different goal constructs (e.g., learning vs. performance goals) on performance in a wide range of areas (Gregory & Levy, 2015; Pintrich, 2000).

Future research in this area could explore how the explicit setting of learning goals by the coach before a coaching session impacts coaching outcomes, or the extent to which the findings in the sports coaching literature translate to executive or life coaching.

Area F: Coach's Personal System

To the best of this author's knowledge there have been no empirical studies that have looked at how the experience of being a professional coach impacts on other areas of the coach's life, although there has been some discussion in the professional literature along these lines (e.g., Peterson, 2011).

As coaches frequently play a significant role in facilitating the personal and professional development of their clients it could be reasonably expected there might be a reciprocal impact on the coach's personal or professional life. In the therapeutic literature there is a substantive body of research focused on the potential negative effects of therapy work on therapists' personal lives (e.g., burn out or compassion fatigue) (Negash & Sahin, 2011; Zeeck, et al., 2012), but little is known about the positive effects of being a therapist, although some research has found that the experience of being a family therapist can positively impact on the therapist's own family life (Kaslow & Schultz, 1987).

In relation to coaching, Grant (2008) examined how participation in a professional coach training program impacted on areas of the coaches' lives and found that participation in a 12 week training programme reduced anxiety, increased goal attainment, enhanced cognitive hardiness and was associated with higher levels of personal insight. Drawing on a biological perspective on stress, Boyatzis, Smith, and Blaize (2006) discuss how compassion on the part of the coach can play a significant role in easing the stress related to leaders holding positions of power, and in this way help develop more sustainable leaders.

This area is ripe for future coaching research, which could explore how coaching others helps the coach in terms of having better relationships with family, or better relate to other coaching or consulting clients, or the ability to personally deal more effectively with problems that were specifically addressed by the coachee in coaching.

Area G: The Coach–Coachee Relationship

The coach–coachee relationship has emerged as a new direction in coaching research (McKenna & Davis, 2009), one that echoes much research in the theraputic literature (Lambert & Barley, 2001). As of June 2015 there have been eleven coaching-specific studies which have examined aspects of the coach–coachee relationship.

Scoular and Linley (2006) examined personality similarities or dissimilarities between coach and coachee in terms of Myers-Briggs Type Inventory profiles. Stewart, Palmer, Wilkin, and Kerrin (2008) measured the 'big-five' personality traits (Costa & McCrae, 1992) and general self-efficacy. Passmore

(2007) explored the personal attributes of a coach in the coach–coachee relationship, finding that key coach behaviours included being collaborative, stimulating problem-solving, and focusing on the goals.

Baron and Morin (2009, 2012) studied internal coach–coachee pairs using the Working Alliance Inventory (Horvath & Greenberg, 1986). Boyce, Jackson, and Neal (2010) studied coach–coachee relationships in a US military academy finding that rapport, trust, and commitment positively predicted outcomes. De Haan, Culpin, and Curd (2011) found that the quality of the coach–coachee relationship was a greater factor in outcomes than any specific theoretical approach or coaching intervention technique.

Smith and Brummel (2013) found that the so-called active ingredients of therapy (expectancy, hope and techniques) were significantly related to coaching success, and the setting of clear goals and actions significantly increased outcomes. De Haan, et al. (2013) found that coachee perceptions of the outcome of coaching were significantly related to their perceptions of the working alliance.

Grant (2014a) explored four aspects of the coach–coachee relationship to investigate which was more related to specific measures of coaching success. These were: (1) autonomy support (bonding); (2) the coachee's satisfaction with the actual coach–coachee relationship; (3) the extent to which the relationship was similar to an 'ideal' relationship; and (4) a goal-focused coach–coachee relationship. The best predictor of coaching outcome was the goal-focused relationship.

From a different perspective, Bachkirova, Sibley, and Myers (2015) used a Q-sort methodology to develop an instrument designed for a micro-analysis of the coaching session. Their findings suggest that there may be considerable similarities in the actual practice of coaching in the coach–coachee relationship, despite the existence of a variety of coaching traditions, genres and context in which coaching takes place.

Research in this area is only in its infancy. Studies to date have utilised a broad range of approaches and have produced a range of different findings. The practical implications of the research to date are somewhat unclear. One theme that appears to emerge is the importance of a goal-focus or outcome-focus in the coaching relationship. Whilst rapport within a supportive, collaborative but challenging relationship is an important foundation, the coach's ability to hold the coachee's attention on designated outcomes and goals appears to make a vital contribution to successful coaching.

Area H: Sponsor

This area is most likely to be of relevance to organisational and executive coaching. It is increasingly the norm that organisations that use external executive coaches also use someone in the role of sponsor (Hall, 2014). A sponsor in this context is someone internal to the organisation that provides input in the coach–coachee relationship. The sponsor (or sponsors) can be the coachee's line manager, a HR professional, or a peer, amongst others. By adding an additional perspective it is assumed that an engaged sponsor can bring value by, for example, (1) helping the coach understand the context for coaching; (2) helping clarify how the coaching contract can best be managed; (3) having input into the goals for the coaching engagement; (4) acting as a point of feedback; and (5) helping to wrap-up the coaching engagement in a way that promotes continued development (Masson, Pemberton, & Sparrow, 2006).

Although there has been much discussion in the professional coaching literature on coaching sponsorship in organisational settings (e.g., Hall, Peterson, & Symeon, 2015; Adshead-Grant, 2014), there has been hardly any empirical research conducted on this issue.

A literature search of the database Business Source Premier using the keywords 'coaching' and 'sponsor' resulted in a total of 70 citations. These were almost exclusively opinion articles (e.g., Goodman, 2013), with only one reporting the results of empirical research (de Haan & Nieß, 2015). However combining these two searches only found a total of eight citations, only five of which were related to organisational coaching (Anderson, Williams, & Kramer, 2012; Atkinson, 1980; de Haan & Nieß, 2015; McMahon & Archer, 2010; Page & de Haan, 2014). Of these only one reported on empirical aspects of coaching sponsorship (de Haan & Nieß, 2015).

This is clearly an area where coaching practice is far ahead of research. Because of the complexity of this area in terms of the dynamics of such relationships, this is likely to be a very challenging area to research. Consequently reductionist quantitative approaches are unlikely to produce meaningful data, and this is another area when well-designed qualitative research will shine. There are many questions that future qualitative research could examine. These could include questions such as; under what circumstances (if any) does a sponsor make a difference? Can a sponsor impede coaching progress? To what extent should a sponsor be involved in the actual coaching process? Such research has the potential to give practitioners an important evidence-based framework for practice in this area.

Area I: Stakeholders

This area represents various individual stakeholders' influence on and experience of the coaching engagement. The term 'stakeholder' is frequently used in the executive and organisational coaching literature (Cavanagh & Lane, 2012; Gormley & van Nieuwerburgh, 2014), and 'stakeholders' are widely recognised as being an important facet of the coaching engagement. However the term 'stakeholder' is rarely defined, possibly because its meaning appears intuitive but also because this is such a broad category.

One of the few attempts to define coaching stakeholders comes from Standards Australia (2011) who present one of the most detailed discussions of the roles and responsibilities of various stakeholders in the literature to date. Standards Australia (2011) identify five key stakeholders in a typical organisational coaching engagement; (a) the coachee; (b) the coach; (c) the coachee's manager; (d) Human Resources/Learning and Development professionals; and (e) the sponsoring organisation as a whole. Whilst this is a useful typology, it conflates a number of diverse roles.

In the model presented in the current chapter, stakeholders are defined as individuals or groups of individuals (other than the coachee, coach or designated organisational sponsor) who have a vested interest in the outcomes of the coaching engagement. In organisational contexts these could include peers or other individuals or employees in the organisation, clients or customers of the organisation, and individuals in the organisation's management structure including board directors, or company shareholders.

Whilst there has been much discussion in relation to coaching stakeholders there has been little empirical research in this area. It appears that the majority of work in this area has been in relation to the use of 360-degree feedback used in association with coaching in relation to the perceptions of peers or employees (e.g., MacKie, 2014; Nieminen, Smerek, Kotrba, & Denison, 2013; Thach, 2002).

Some researchers have explored how coaching impacts the relationships between coachees and other stakeholders. In an analysis of 300 business executive coaching cases Wasylyshyn, Shorey, and Chaffin (2012) found that many reported that they formed deeper relationships with key stakeholders – relationships that were more connective versus transactional. This could be a key focus for future research in this area. It would be also informative to explore the expectations of key stakeholders and how these align with actual coaching outcomes. This is particularly poignant when coaching at senior levels in an organisation. Experience indicates that senior management sometimes have unrealistic expectations of the change potential of coaching, particularly with coachees who have challenging personality characteristics (Nelson & Hogan, 2009). Such research has thus the potential to be of great benefit to both coaching practitioners and the organisations they serve. Again, this is an area where well-designed qualitative research has the potential to uncover interesting and useful data in a context that will be challenging to explore.

Area J: The Broader System and the Systemic Impact of Coaching

Area J represents the broader system and the systemic impact of the coaching engagement. As previously mentioned this could include the extent to which the coaching of specific individuals affects the wellbeing and performance of the broader organisation, or the coachee's personal system including distal stakeholders such as the coachee's family, wider industry interests, professional coaching bodies, or the community at large (StandardsAustralia, 2011). Conversely, this perspective could also represent how the broader system impacts on the individual being coached, either facilitating or hindering the change process (e.g., Stober, 2008).

Although there has been a growing body of research exploring the individualistic aspects of coaching, coaching in the larger systemic context has not been well researched as yet. This is partly because the distal effects of a coaching engagement are almost by definition not of primary concern to the purchasers of coaching services and research to date has not focused on such aspects. It is also partly because it is not easy to track the effects of coaching in a large complex adaptive system.

However, the emergence of the relatively new methodology of Social Network Analysis (SNA) can provide researchers with the analytic tools needed to explore the relational components of complex systems by tracking the interconnectivity observed between individuals in a system (Wasserman & Faust, 1994). Such relational data consists of contacts, ties, information flow, influence and communication between individuals.

To date only two studies have used this methodology. Terblanche (2014) conducted a study in which four coachees received six one-hour coaching sessions over a period of four months. The coaching aimed to help coachees identify and change existing patterns of thinking and behaving that they considered limiting. SNA was used to track the changing nature of key relationships in their organisational system, and in doing so Terblanche (2014) concluded that SNA can indeed be a valuable methodology in exploring coaching outcomes from a systemic perspective.

O'Connor and Cavanagh (2013) used SNA to explore the 'coaching ripple effect' – how the impact of coaching affects others in the organisational system. Using data from 20 leaders who received eight coaching sessions it was found that there was a significant increase in goal attainment, transformational leadership and psychological wellbeing measures as well as an increase of the perceived quality of interaction with others in their network. It was found that the closer any member of the network was identified as being connected to those who received coaching, the more likely they were to experience positive increases in wellbeing. This is a new area of research for coaching and one that holds considerable promise for the future.

REFLECTIONS ON THE WAY FORWARD AND IMPLICATIONS FOR EVIDENCE-BASED PRACTICE

If past coaching publication trends continue, we will see a divergent body of coaching knowledge quickly emerge over the next few years. However, this diversity also has implications for those wishing to engage in evidence-based practice.

A good evidence-based coach explicitly draws on best current knowledge in their coaching practice, and most importantly, also knows the limits of such evidence.

They are thus much better prepared to navigate the often ambiguous situations in which they provide their services than a coach who does not have such knowledge to hand – the advantages of using an evidence-based approach seem clear, but this is not necessarily straight-forward.

Given that staying current with emerging knowledge is a key part of good evidence-based practice, the complexity and volume of the data that is starting to emerge means that it is increasingly difficult for individual coaches (particularly those working as a sole trader in private practice) to stay abreast of the current research. The implication here is that coaches may need to devote more time to their professional development and ongoing education, and many will require support from professional coaching associations in order to stay in touch with the scientific research. Such support is already becoming more readily available, for example the International Coach Federation (ICF) now has a Director of Coaching Science, and the ICF now provides access to coaching research through its website (www.coachfederation.org).

As regards to the implications for coach training schools, the increasing demand for well-informed, evidence-based coaches has placed pressure on coach training organisations to deliver coach training that is solidly based on good research. In many ways this is the key to the continued development of an evidence-based coaching industry. Whilst some individuals may transition into being a professional coach without any training whatsoever, the vast majority of professional coaches will undertake some kind of coach training or professional development, even if that is only as a means of establishing professional credibility (George, 2013). Thus, training providers and educational institutions will have a major role to play in delivering evidence-based coach training. For many coach training organisations this means adapting their too-often idiosyncratic proprietary models to incorporate a more substantive theoretical and empirical foundation. Indeed, anecdotal reports suggest that this is already happening, and this is vital if we are to produce the next generation of well-educated coaches: Coaches who are committed to the intelligent and conscientious use of relevant and best current knowledge, and integrating that with solid practitioner expertise when delivering coaching services.

FINAL THOUGHTS

It is clear from the above discussions that coaching research has the potential to encompass a wide range of issues from individualistic, reductionist explorations of the psychological mechanics of change, through to large scale systemic investigations of (for example) how complex systems adapt following coaching for cultural change, and that both quantitative and qualitative methodologies have much to offer. Such diversity makes for a fascinating and potentially fruitful future research agenda as well as a rich and vigorous evidence-based coaching practice. A focus on the further development of coaching in this fashion holds great promise, both for the coaching industry itself and for the purchasers of coaching, whose interests we serve.

ACKNOWLEDGEMENTS

Thanks are due to Dr Sean O'Connor and Dr Michael Cavanagh for their helpful suggestions on earlier versions of this model, and to delegates at the 2015 APA San Diageo conference for their feedback and suggestions. I also wish to acknowledge the inspiration derived from Dr Peter Hawkins's Seven-eyed Model of Coaching Supervision and Dr Michael Cavanagh's Three Reflective Spaces Model. Thanks are also due to Dr Tatiana Bachkirova for very helpful comments on an earlier version of this chapter.

REFERENCES

Adshead-Grant, J. (2014). How to Effectively Engage Coaching Sponsors. *Coaching at Work*, (2), 54–55.

Anderson, S. K., Williams, P., & Kramer, A. L. (2012). Life and Executive Coaching: Some Ethical Issues for Consideration. *APA Handbook of Ethics in Psychology, Vol 2: Practice, Teaching, and Research* (pp. 169–181). Washington, DC: American Psychological Association; US.

Argyris, C., & Schön, D. A. (1992). *On Organizational Learning*. Cambridge, MA: Blackwell.

Atkinson, C. (1980). Management Development Roles: Coach, Sponsor and Mentor. *Personnel Journal*, 59(11), 918–921.

Bachkirova, T., Arthur, L., & Reading, E. (2015). Evaluating a Coaching and Mentoring Programme: Challenges and Solutions. *International Coaching Psychology Review*, 10(2), 175–189.

Bachkirova, T., & Cox, E. (2007). Cognitive-Developmental Approach to the Development of Coaches. In S. Palmer & A. Whybrow (Eds.), *Handbook of Coaching Psychology* (pp. 351–366). London: Routledge.

Bachkirova, T., Sibley, J., & Myers, A. C. (2015). Developing and Applying a New Instrument for Microanalysis of the Coaching Process: The Coaching Process Q-Set. *Human Resource Development Quarterly*, 26(4), 431–462.

Baron, L., & Morin, L. (2009). The Coach–Coachee Relationship in Executive Coaching: A Field Study. *Human Resource Development Quarterly*, 20, 85–106.

Baron, L., & Morin, L. (2012). The Working Alliance in Executive Coaching: Its Impact on Outcomes and How Coaches Can Influence It. In E. de Haan & C. Sills (Eds.), *Coaching Relationships* (pp. 213–226). Faringdon, UK: Libri.

Baumeister, R. F., Vohs, K. D., & Tice, D. M. (2007). The Strength Model of Self-Control. *Current Directions in Psychological Science*, 16, 351–355.

Bolier, L., Haverman, M., Westerhof, G. J., Riper, H., Smit, F., & Bohlmeijer, E. (2013). Positive Psychology Interventions: A Meta-Analysis of Randomized Controlled Studies. *BMC public health*, 13(1), 119.

Bond, C., & Seneque, M. (2012). Conceptualizing Coaching as an Approach to Management and Organizational Development. *Journal of Management Development*, 32(1), 57–72.

Boyatzis, R. E., Smith, M. L., & Blaize, N. (2006). Developing Sustainable Leaders through Coaching and Compassion. *Academy of Management Learning & Education*, 5(1), 8–24.

Boyce, L. A., Jackson, R. J., & Neal, L. J. (2010). Building Successful Leadership Coaching Relationships: Examining Impact of Matching Criteria in a Leadership Coaching Program. *Journal of Management Development [Special Issue on Coaching and the Relationship]*, 29, 914–931.

Bozer, G., Sarros, J. C., & Santora, J. C. (2013). The Role of Coachee Characteristics in Executive Coaching for Effective Sustainability. *Journal of Management Development*, 32(3), 277–294.

Button, K. S., Ioannidis, J. P. A., Mokrysz, C., Nosek, B. A., Flint, J., Robinson, E. S. J., et al. (2013). Power Failure: Why Small Sample Size Undermines the Reliability of Neuroscience. *Nature Reviews Neuroscience*, 14(5), 365–376.

Cavanagh, M., & Lane, D. (2012). Coaching Psychology Coming of Age: The Challenges We Face in the Messy World of Complexity? *International Coaching Psychology Review*, 7(1), 75–90.

Cerni, T., Curtis, G. J., & Colmar, S. H. (2010). Executive Coaching Can Enhance Transformational Leadership. *International Coaching Psychology Review*, 5(1), 81–85.

Chinn, A. T., Richmond, J. P., & Bennett, J. L. (2015). Walking a Mile in an Executive's Shoes: The Influence of Shared Client–Coach Experience on Goal Achievement. *International Coaching Psychology Review*, 10(2), 149–160.

Clutterbuck, D. (2008). Are You a Goal Junkie?. *Training Journal*, May, 43–44.

Corbett, K. (2006). *The Sherpa Report*. Ohio: Sasha Corp.

Costa, P. T., & McCrae, R. R. (1992). *Revised Neo Personality Inventory and Neo Five-Factor Inventory: Professional Manual*. Florida: Psychological Assessment Resources.

Dagley, G. R. (2010). Exceptional Executive Coaches: Practices and Attributes. *International Coaching Psychology Review*, 5(1), 63–80.

David, S., Clutterbuck, D., & Megginson, D. (Eds.). (2013). *Beyond Goals: Effective Strategies for Coaching and Mentoring*. Surrey, UK: Gower.

David, S., Clutterbuck, D., & Megginson, D. (2014). Goal Orientation in Coaching Differs According to Region, Experience, and Education. *International Journal of Evidence Based Coaching and Mentoring*, 12(2), 134–145.

de Haan, E. (2008). Becoming Simultaneously Thicker and Thinner Skinned: The Inherent Conflicts Arising in the Professional Development of Coaches. *Personnel Review*, 37(5), 526–542.

de Haan, E., Culpin, V., & Curd, J. (2011). Executive Coaching in Practice: What Determines Helpfulness for Clients of Coaching? *Personnel Review*, 40(24–44).

de Haan, E., & Duckworth, A. (2013). Signalling a New Trend in Executive Coaching Outcome Research. *International Coaching Psychology Review*, 8(1), 6–19.

de Haan, E., Duckworth, A., Birch, D., & Jones, C. (2013). Executive Coaching Outcome Research: The Contribution of Common Factors Such as Relationship, Personality Match, and Self-Efficacy. *Consulting Psychology Journal: Practice and Research*, 65(1), 40–57.

de Haan, E., & Nieß, C. (2015). Differences between Critical Moments for Clients, Coaches, and Sponsors of Coaching. *International Coaching Psychology Review*, 10(1), 56–61.

Deci, E. L., & Ryan, R. M. (1980). Self-Determination Theory: When Mind Mediates Behavior. *Journal of Mind & Behavior*, 1(1), 33–43.

Drake, D. B. (2009). Evidence Is a Verb: A Relational Approach to Knowledge and Mastery in Coaching. *International Journal of Evidence Based Coaching and Mentoring*, 7(1), 1–12.

Fillery-Travis, A. (2015). *Contracting within the Business Coaching Relationship: A Guide and a Cautionary Tale!* Canada: Worldwide Association of Business Coaches.

Flaherty, J. (2010). *Coaching: Evoking Excellence in Others (3rd Edition)*. New York: Routledge.

Freedman, R. D., & Stumpf, S. A. (1978). What Can One Learn from the Learning Style Inventory? *The Academy of Management Journal*, 21(2), 275–282.

Frisch, M. H. (2001). The Emerging Role of the Internal Coach. *Consulting Psychology Journal: Practice and Research*, 53(4), 240.

Gabriel, A. S., Moran, C. M., & Gregory, J. B. (2014). How Can Humanistic Coaching Affect Employee Well-Being and Performance? An Application of Self-Determination Theory. *Coaching: An International Journal of Theory, Research and Practice*, 7(1), 56–73.

Gattellari, M., Donnelly, N., Taylor, N., Meerkin, M., Hirst, G., & Ward, J. (2005). Does 'Peer Coaching' Increase GP Capacity to Promote Informed Decision Making About PSA Screening? A Cluster Randomised Trial. *Family Practice*, 22(3), 253–265.

George, M. (2013). Seeking Legitimacy: The Professionalization of Life Coaching. *Sociological Inquiry*, 83(2), 179–208.

Goodman, N. (2013). The Personal Touch. *Training*, 50(6), 74.

Gormley, H., & van Nieuwerburgh, C. (2014). Developing Coaching Cultures: A Review of the Literature. *Coaching: An International Journal of Theory, Research and Practice*, 7(2), 90–101.

Graham, S., Wedman, J. F., & Garvin-Kester, B. (1994). Manager Coaching Skills: What Makes a Good Coach? *Performance Improvement Quarterly*, 7(2), 81–94.

Grant, A. M. (2003). The Impact of Life Coaching on Goal Attainment, Metacognition and

Mental Health. *Social Behavior and Personality: An International Journal*, *31*(3), 253–263.

Grant, A. M. (2008). Personal Life Coaching for Coaches-in-Training Enhances Goal Attainment, Insight and Learning. *Coaching: An International Journal of Theory, Research and Practice*, *1*(1), 54–70.

Grant, A. M. (2012). Australian Coaches' Views on Coaching Supervision: A Study with Implications for Australian Coach Education, Training and Practice. *International Journal of Evidence Based Coaching and Mentoring*, *10*(2), 17–33.

Grant, A. M. (2014a). Autonomy Support, Relationship Satisfaction and Goal Focus in the Coach–Coachee Relationship: Which Best Predicts Coaching Success? *Coaching: An International Journal of Theory, Research and Practice*, *7*(1), 18–38.

Grant, A. M. (2014b). The Efficacy of Executive Coaching in Times of Organisational Change. *Journal of Change Management*, *14*(2), 258–280.

Grant, A. M., Curtayne, L., & Burton, G. (2009). Executive Coaching Enhances Goal Attainment, Resilience and Workplace Well-Being: A Randomised Controlled Study. *The Journal of Positive Psychology*, *4*(5), 396–407.

Grant, A. M., Passmore, J., Cavanagh, M. J., & Parker, H. M. (2010). The State of Play in Coaching Today: A Comprehensive Review of the Field. In G. P. Hodgkinson & J. K. Ford (Eds.), *International Review of Industrial and Organizational Psychology 2010* (pp. 125–167). New York: Wiley-Blackwell.

Gregory, J. B., Beck, J. W., & Carr, A. E. (2011). Goals, Feedback, and Self-Regulation: Control Theory as a Natural Framework for Executive Coaching. *Consulting Psychology Journal: Practice and Research*, *63*(1), 26.

Gregory, J. B., & Levy, P. E. (2015). *How Feedback and Goals Drive Behavior: Control Theory*. Washington, DC: American Psychological Association; US.

Gyllensten, K., & Palmer, S. (2005). Can Coaching Reduce Workplace Stress: A Quasi-Experimental Study. *International Journal of Evidence Based Coaching and Mentoring*, *3*(2), 75–85.

Hall, L., Peterson, D., & Symeon, M. (2015). Firms Prefer Coaches Who Do Their Homework. *Coaching at Work*, *10*, 12–12.

Hall, L. I. Z. (2014). Editor's Talking Point. *Coaching at Work*, *9*(6), 3–3.

Horvath, A. O., & Greenberg, L. (1986). The Development of the Working Alliance Inventory: A Research Handbook. In L. Greenberg & W. Pinsoff (Eds.), *Psychotherapeutic Processes: A Research Handbook* (pp. 529–556). New York: Guilford Press.

Jones, R., Woods, S., & Guillaume, Y. (2015). The Effectiveness of Workplace Coaching: A Meta-Analysis of Learning and Performance Outcomes from Coaching. *Journal of Occupational and Organizational Psychology*, ISSN Online: 2044–8325.

Jowett, S. (2008). What Makes Coaches Tick? The Impact of Coaches' Intrinsic and Extrinsic Motives on Their Own Satisfaction and That of Their Athletes. *Scandinavian Journal of Medicine & Science in Sports*, *18*(5), 664–673.

Jowett, S., Kanakoglou, K., & Passmore, J. (2012). The Application of the 3+ 1cs Relationship Model in Executive Coaching. *Consulting Psychology Journal: Practice and Research*, *64*(3), 183–197.

Kaslow, F. W., & Schultz, N. O. (1987). How to Be Sane and Happy as a Family Therapist or the Reciprocal Impact of Family Therapy Teaching and Practice and Therapists' Personal Lives and Mental Health. *Journal of Psychotherapy & the Family*, *3*(2), 79–96.

Kemp, T. (2008). Coach Self-Management: The Foundation of Coaching Effectiveness. In D. Drake, D. Brennan & K. Gørtz (Eds.), *The Philosophy and Practice of Coaching: Insights and Issues for a New Era* (pp. 261–275). San Francisco CA: John Wiley.

Kilburg, R. R. (1996). Toward a Conceptual Understanding and Definition of Executive Coaching. *Consulting Psychology Journal: Practice and Research*, *48*(2), 134–144.

Kilburg, R. R. (1997). Coaching and Executive Character: Core Problems and Basic Approaches. *Consulting Psychology Journal: Practice & Research*, *49*(4), 281–299.

Kolb, A., & Kolb, D. A. (2013). *Kolb Learning Style Inventory: LSI Workbook*. New York: Hay Group.

Ladegard, G., & Gjerde, S. (2014). Leadership Coaching, Leader Role-Efficacy, and Trust in Subordinates. A Mixed Methods Study Assessing Leadership Coaching as a Leadership Development Tool. *The Leadership Quarterly*, 25(4), 631–646.

Lambert, M. J., & Barley, D. E. (2001). Research Summary on the Therapeutic Relationship and Psychotherapy Outcomes. *Psychotherapy: Theory, Research, Practice, Training*, 38(4), 357–361.

Landsberg, M. (1997). *The Tao of Coaching*. London: HarperCollins.

Larsen, J. B., Kilburn, T. R., & Myszak, A. (2007). Developing Evidence-Based Coaching Practices in Denmark. *The Coaching Psychologist*, 3(2), 90–93.

Leong, F. T., Hartung, P. J., Goh, D., & Gaylor, M. (2001). Appraising Birth Order in Career Assessment: Linkages to Holland's and Super's Models. *Journal of Career Assessment*, 9(1), 25–39.

Lewis-Duarte, M., & Bligh, M. C. (2012). Agents of 'Influence': Exploring the Usage, Timing, and Outcomes of Executive Coaching Tactics. *Leadership & Organization Development Journal*, 33(3), 255–281.

Libri, V., & Kemp, T. (2006). Assessing the Efficacy of a Cognitive Behavioural Executive Coaching Programme. *International Coaching Psychology Review*, 1(2), 9–20.

Locke, E. A. (1996). Motivation through Conscious Goal Setting. *Applied & Preventive Psychology*, 5(2), 117–124.

MacKie, D. (2014). The Effectiveness of Strength-Based Executive Coaching in Enhancing Full Range Leadership Development: A Controlled Study. *Consulting Psychology Journal: Practice and Research*, 66(2), 118–137.

MacKie, D. (2015). The Effects of Coachee Readiness and Core Self-Evaluations on Leadership Coaching Outcomes: A Controlled Trial. *Coaching: An International Journal of Theory, Research and Practice*, Published online: 16 Mar 2015, 1–17.

Masson, L., Pemberton, C., & Sparrow, S. (2006). Count to Three for the Magic Coaching Number. *Training & Coaching Today*, 24–24.

Matsumoto, D., Hwang, H. C., & Frank, M. G. (2016). The Body: Postures, Gait, Proxemics, and Haptics. In D. Matsumoto, H. C. Hwang & M. G. Frank (Eds.), *APA Handbook of Nonverbal Communication* (pp. 387–400). Washington, DC, US: American Psychological Association.

McCormick, I., & Burch, G. S. (2008). Personality-Focused Coaching for Leadership Development. *Consulting Psychology Journal: Practice and Research*, 60(3), 267–278.

McKenna, D. D., & Davis, S. L. (2009). Hidden in Plain Sight: The Active Ingredients of Executive Coaching. *Industrial and Organizational Psychology*, 2(3), 244–260.

McLean, K. N., & Mallett, C. J. (2012). What Motivates the Motivators? An Examination of Sports Coaches. *Physical Education & Sport Pedagogy*, 17(1), 21–35.

McMahon, G., & Archer, A. (2010). One Hundred One Coaching Strategies and Techniques *One Hundred One Coaching Strategies and Techniques* (pp. xxi, 302). New York, NY: Routledge/Taylor & Francis Group; US.

Miller, D. J. (1990). The Effect of Managerial Coaching on Transfer of Training. *Dissertation Abstracts International*, 50(8-A), 2435.

Miller, W. R., Yahne, C. E., Moyers, T. B., Martinez, J., & Pirritano, M. (2004). A Randomized Trial of Methods to Help Clinicians Learn Motivational Interviewing. *Journal of Consulting & Clinical Psychology*, 72(6), 1050–1062.

Morgan, H., Harkins, P., & Goldsmith, M. (2011). *The Art and Practice of Leadership Coaching: 50 Top Executive Coaches Reveal Their Secrets*. John Wiley & Sons.

Negash, S., & Sahin, S. (2011). Compassion Fatigue in Marriage and Family Therapy: Implications for Therapists and Clients. *Journal of Marital and Family Therapy*, 37(1), 1–13.

Nelson, E., & Hogan, R. (2009). Coaching on the Dark Side. *International Coaching Psychology Review*, 4(1), 9–21.

Nieminen, L. R. G., Smerek, R., Kotrba, L., & Denison, D. (2013). What Does an Executive Coaching Intervention Add Beyond Facilitated Multisource Feedback? Effects on Leader Self-Ratings and Perceived Effectiveness. *Human Resource Development Quarterly*, 24(2), 145–176.

O'Broin, A., & Palmer, S. (2010). Exploring Key Aspects in the Formation of Coaching

Relationships: Initial Indicators from the Perspective of the Coachee and the Coach. *Coaching: An International Journal of Theory, Research and Practice*, *3*(2), 124–143.

O'Connor, S. A., & Cavanagh, M. J. (2013). The Coaching Ripple Effect: The Effects of Developmental Coaching on Wellbeing across Organisational Networks. *Psychology of Well-Being: Theory, Research and Practice*, *3*(2), 1–23.

Olivero, G., Bane, K., & Kopelman, R. E. (1997). Executive Coaching as a Transfer of Training Tool: Effects on Productivity in a Public Agency. *Public Personnel Management*, *26*(4), 461–469.

Page, N., & de Haan, E. (2014). Does Executive Coaching Work? *The Psychologist*, *27*(8), 582–586.

Passmore, J. (2007). An Integrative Model for Executive Coaching. *Consulting Psychology Journal: Practice and Research*, *59*(1), 68–78.

Peterson, D. B. (1993). Skill Learning and Behavior Change in an Individually Tailored Management Coaching Program. *Unpublished doctoral dissertation*. University of Minnesota, Minneapolis, MN.

Peterson, D. B. (1996). Executive Coaching at Work: The Art of One-on-One Change. *Consulting Psychology Journal: Practice & Research*, *48*(2), 78–86.

Peterson, D. B. (2011). Good to Great Coaching. In G. Hernez-Broome & L. A. Boyce (Eds.), *Advancing Executive Coaching: Setting the Course of Successful Leadership Coaching* (pp. 83–102). San Francisco CA: Jossey-Bass.

Pintrich, P. R. (2000). Multiple Goals, Multiple Pathways: The Role of Goal Orientation in Learning and Achievement. *Journal of Educational Psychology*, *92*(3), 544–555.

Revans, R. W. (1982). What Is Action Learning? *Journal of Management Development*, *1*(3), 64–75.

Rocchi, M. A., Pelletier, L. G., & Couture, A. L. (2013). Determinants of Coach Motivation and Autonomy Supportive Coaching Behaviours. *Psychology of Sport and Exercise*, *14*(6), 852–859.

Rock, D., & Schwartz, J. M. (2006). A Brain-Based Approach to Coaching. *International Journal of Coaching in Organizations*, *4*(2), 32–44.

Rosenthal, R. (1963). The Effect of Experimenter Bias on the Performance of the Albino Rat. *Behavioral Science*, *8*, 183–189.

Rubie-Davies, C. (2009). Teacher Expectations and Labeling. In L. Saha & A. G. Dworkin (Eds.), *International Handbook of Research on Teachers and Teaching* (Vol. 21, pp. 695–707): Springer US.

Sackett, D. L., Haynes, R. B., Guyatt, G. H., & Tugwell, P. (1996). Evidenced Based Medicine: What It Is and What Is Isn't. *British Medical Journal*, *13*, 71–72.

Schnell, E. R. (2005). A Case Study of Executive Coaching as a Support Mechanism During Organizational Growth and Evolution. *Consulting Psychology Journal: Practice & Research*, *57*(1), 41–56.

Scoular, A., & Linley, P. A. (2006). Coaching, Goal-Setting and Personality Type: What Matters?. *The Coaching Psychologist*, *2*, 9–11.

Sheldon, K. M., & Elliot, A. J. (1999). Goal Striving, Need Satisfaction, and Longitudinal Well-Being: The Self-Concordance Model. *Journal of Personality & Social Psychology*, *76*(3), 482–497.

Sherlock-Storey, M., Moss, M., & Timson, S. (2013). Brief Coaching for Resilience During Organisational Change – an Exploratory Study. *The Coaching Psychologist*, *9*(1), 19.

Smith, I. M. (2012). *Understanding Barriers to Measuring the Effectiveness of Executive Coaching: Perspectives from Executive Coaches and Executives*. University of Tulsa, US.

Smith, I. M., & Brummel, B. J. (2013). Investigating the Role of the Active Ingredients in Executive Coaching. *Coaching: An International Journal of Theory, Research and Practice*, *6*(1), 57–71.

Spence, G. B. (2007). Gas Powered Coaching: Goal Attainment Scaling and Its Use in Coaching Research and Practice. *International Coaching Psychology Review*, *2*(2), 155–167.

Spence, G. B., & Grant, A. M. (2007). Professional and Peer Life Coaching and the Enhancement of Goal Striving and Well-Being: An Exploratory Study. *Journal of Positive Psychology*, *2*(3), 185–194.

Spence, G. B., & Oades, L. G. (2011). Coaching with Self-Determination Theory in Mind: Using Theory to Advance Evidence-Based Coaching

Practice. *International Journal of Evidence Based Coaching and Mentoring*, *9*(2), 37–55.

StandardsAustralia. (2011). *Standards Australia: Handbook for Coaching in Organisations Hb 332–2011*. Sydney: Standards Australia.

Steed, J. (2013). Building a Coaching Culture in Your Organisation. In D. Forman, M. Joyce & G. McMahon (Eds.), *Creating a Coaching Culture for Managers in Your Organisation* (pp. 25–33). New York, NY: Routledge/Taylor & Francis Group; US.

Stewart, L. J., Palmer, S., Wilkin, H., & Kerrin, M. (2008). The Influence of Character: Does Personality Impact Coaching Success? *International Journal of Evidence- based Coaching and Mentoring*, *6*, 32–42.

Stober, D. R. (2008). Making It Stick: Coaching as a Tool for Organizational Change. *Coaching: An International Journal of Theory, Research and Practice*, *1*(1), 71–80.

Stober, D. R., & Grant, A. M. (2006). *Evidence Based Coaching Handbook: Putting Best Practices to Work for Your Clients*. Hoboken, NJ: John Wiley.

Sue-Chan, C., & Latham, G. P. (2004). The Relative Effectiveness of External, Peer, and Self-Coaches. *Applied Psychology*, *53*(2), 260–278.

Sue-Chan, C., Wood, R. E., & Latham, G. P. (2012). Effect of a Coach's Regulatory Focus and an Individual's Implicit Person Theory on Individual Performance. *Journal of Management*, *38*(3), 809–835.

Suh, T., & Badrinarayanan, V. (2014). Proximal and Distal Influences on Project Creativity in International Marketing Teams. *International Marketing Review*, *31*(3), 283–307.

Terblanche, N. (2014). Knowledge Sharing in the Organizational Context: Using Social Network Analysis as a Coaching Tool. *International Journal of Evidence Based Coaching and Mentoring*, *12*(2), 146–164.

Thach, L. C. (2002). The Impact of Executive Coaching and 360 Feedback on Leadership Effectiveness. *Leadership and Organization Development Journal*, *23*(4), 205–214.

Thatcher, S. (2014). Making a Habit of Happiness: A Three Week Lived Experience of Positive Thinking. *Mission of the Journal of Excellence*, *16*, 37.

Theeboom, T., Beersma, B., & van Vianen, A. E. M. (2013). Does Coaching Work? A Meta-Analysis on the Effects of Coaching on Individual Level Outcomes in an Organizational Context. *The Journal of Positive Psychology*, *9*(1), 1–18.

Tobias, L. L. (1996). Coaching Executives. *Consulting Psychology Journal: Practice & Research*, *48*(2), 87–95.

Ward, G., van de Loo, E., & ten Have, S. (2014). Psychodynamic Group Executive Coaching: A Literature Review. *International Journal of Evidence Based Coaching and Mentoring*, *12*(1), 63–78.

Wasserman, S., & Faust, K. (1994). *Social Network Analysis: Methods and Applications*. Cambridge: Cambridge University Press.

Wasylyshyn, K. M., Shorey, H. S., & Chaffin, J. S. (2012). Patterns of Leadership Behaviour: Implications for Successful Executive Coaching Outcomes. *The Coaching Psychologist*, *8*(2), 75.

Zeeck, A., Orlinsky, D. E., Hermann, S., Joos, A., Wirsching, M., Weidmann, W., et al. (2012). Stressful Involvement in Psychotherapeutic Work: Therapist, Client and Process Correlates. *Psychotherapy Research*, *22*(5), 543–555.

Coaching and Psychotherapy

Trevor Crowe

INTRODUCTION

Coaching and psychotherapy as fields of knowledge have historically shared much in terms of theory and application in practice, even though there have been efforts to consider them as distinct professions. In this chapter the term psychotherapy is referred more broadly to the work of mental health professionals, which may include counsellors, psychologists and so on, with acknowledgement of the breadth and scope of different mental health roles, and the inadequacy of any term to effectively capture this variation. Whereas psychotherapy rose from a 'healing' tradition to identify, understand and help people satisfy needs, free up blockages and clarify the way ahead, coaching emerged to more directly challenge and support people actively pursue their goals, and to improve performance (Maxwell, 2009; Bachkirova & Cox, 2005). It has been argued that psychotherapy in its more traditional forms is about exploring depth and meaning in service of healing and actualisation (Spinelli, 2008), while coaching is more about focus and specific behaviour change, with clear motivational and behavioural activation function (Cavanagh, Grant, & Kemp, 2005). However, psychotherapy and coaching have continued to evolve and integrate such that the traditional distinctions are less relevant and recognisable in practice (Cox, Bachkirova, & Clutterbuck, 2010).

Although distinctions remain at the extreme ends of the psychotherapy–coaching continuum (Ives, 2008), most attempts to separate coaching from psychotherapy practices have proven to be futile and have potentially restricted coaches from benefiting from the richness of knowledge base and associated skills that are central to interpersonally focused psychotherapy theory, research and practices (Price, 2009; Maxwell, 2009; Spinelli, 2008; Askeland, 2009; Turner, 2010; McKenna & Davis, 2009). Conversely, psychotherapy aimed at exploring and influencing deeper human experiencing, meaning making, healing and identity evolution (Spinelli, 2008), gains much from activating these deeper processes via structured goal striving and behaviour activation strategies (Bachkirova & Cox, 2005; Hart, Blattner, & Leipsic, 2001).

The demarcation of therapy and coaching has also been argued in terms of different client target populations and associated ethical and professional competence issues (Grant, 2006; Maxwell, 2009). This chapter explores this debate in terms of the at times illusionary differentiation of client populations based on need, barriers and opportunity (Cavanagh & Buckley, 2014; Bachkirova & Cox, 2005). Instead it suggests that key areas of cross fertilisation of coaching and psychotherapy should be explored. These may include adopting more client-focused practices (as opposed to discipline-focused approaches – Spinelli, 2008), for example implementing client empowerment models and associated progressive needs/strengths assessment (Roche & Hefferon, 2013), along with a feedback framework to guide the type of support provided for specific and evolving client goals (McKenna & Davis, 2009). It will be argued that a client's goals (rather than symptom constellations or context) should be the determining factor in deciding whether coaching or psychotherapy is required. Clearly, the capacity and competence of the helping professional becomes a critical factor in ensuring that such support is provided ethically (Price, 2009; Bachkirova, 2007; Maxwell, 2009). Much of the latter might be managed by core competency training (Long, 2011; Buckley, 2010; Maxwell, 2009; McKenna & Davis, 2009) combined with targeted supervision for coaches and psychotherapists (Bachkirova, Jackson, & Clutterbuck, 2011; Passmore, 2011; Hawkins, 2010; Armstrong & Geddes, 2009; Maxwell, 2009).

This chapter has four main sections. First, it will explore the apparent increasing overlap of characteristics, aims and practices of coaching and psychotherapy. Second, it will examine the illusion of different client populations for psychotherapy and coaching.

Third, it will elaborate on how the strengths of both approaches can be effectively integrated to overcome the limitations of each, whilst still maintaining ethical and professional boundaries. Finally, it will propose that rather than persisting with the argument about this demarcation, it is more fruitful to guide practice from an inter-professional perspective informed by active and ongoing needs assessment, client feedback, reflective practice, and training and supervision.

OVERLAPPING CHARACTERISTICS, AIMS AND PRACTICES OF COACHING AND PSYCHOTHERAPY

This section explores the frequently occurring themes that continue to emerge regarding the similarities and differences between coaching and psychotherapy. These themes impact the positioning of coaching as an independent discipline, or interdependent pathway in the network of pathways supporting human strivings.

Coaching has been described as being 'essentially about helping individuals regulate and direct their interpersonal and intrapersonal resources to better attain their goals' (Grant, 2006, p. 153). The aim of coaching is typically to assist the client to enhance performance through identifying values aligned goals and translating these goals into actions. Therefore, coaching has clear motivational enhancement and behavioural activation functions (Ives, 2008), as well as providing a reflective, supportive space for the clients to consolidate gains and increase readiness for further change.

The traditional view is that psychotherapy and coaching differ in several ways (Maxwell, 2009). The therapeutic relationship is likely to have a stronger relational focus and emotional bond than the coaching relationship (Ives, 2008). Hart et al. (2001) argued that coaching is more future-oriented, whereas psychotherapy may be more focused on resolving past issues. According to Grant (2006) coaching is more goal and action directed and structured, focused on solutions rather than problems. Others argued that the aim of psychotherapy is to bring the client to a point of stabilisation (i.e., less dominated by symptoms/distress) and help the client to satisfy his/her needs, quench her/his thirst (Slade, 2009; Griffiths & Campbell, 2008). Coaching may be 'de-stabilising', somewhat shaking up the status quo to activate motivation for growth and build change readiness, make the client thirsty (Stober & Grant, 2006). However, although stabilisation/consolidation is an important early stage of most psychotherapeutic approaches, once stable enough the focus is often one of transitioning, challenging the client to move forward (Spinelli, 2008; Slade, Oades, & Jarden, in press).

Increasingly it can be observed that the overlap between coaching and psychotherapy is significant, particularly if a broader range of therapies is considered (e.g. Positive Psychology, Cognitive Behavioural Therapy, Solution Focused Therapy, Acceptance and Commitment Therapy, Gestalt Therapy) and different types of coaching (e.g. Executive, Life, Existential, Transformational coaching (Spinelli, 2008; Cox, Bachkirova, & Clutterbuck, 2010; Ives, 2008). Taking a broad view of these approaches provides recognition that much psychotherapeutic work is future- or growth-oriented, engages goal striving and behaviour activation and motivation enhancement principles. Similarly, many coaching styles (e.g., Existential, Gestalt, Person Centred) engage psychotherapeutic principles and practices (Stober & Grant, 2006; Cox, Bachkirova, & Clutterbuck, 2010). Like therapists, coaches sometimes 'visit' the client's past to make sense of current experiences (Griffiths & Campbell, 2008). In their qualitative study comparing life coaching with counselling from both coach and client perspectives Griffiths and Campbell (2008) found amongst few differences, similarities/common factors dominated, including: listening, questioning, non-judgemental stance, and a process of uncovering (that which sits behind the behaviour). Therefore, supporting clients as they work through their personal processes, resistances and motivation structures reflects core counselling skills regardless of whether the support comes in the form of performance, personal development, or psychotherapeutic interventions (McKenna & Davis, 2009; Hawkins & Smith, 2010).

It is an oversimplification of coaching to suggest that it only aims to help the client to clarify, strive for, and attain goals and associated behaviour change (Spinelli, 2008; Price, 2009). More realistically the aim is to assist the client to vision and grow into the person s/he wants to be. How this occurs may differ across the range of different coaching (and indeed psychotherapy) approaches (for detailed overview, see Ives, 2008; Stober & Grant, 2006; Cox, Bachkirova, & Clutterbuck, 2010). Where the focus is on facilitating the personal growth of the client, Stober, Wildflower and Drake (2006) highlight the increased emphasis on the practitioner–client relationship.

ARE CLIENT POPULATIONS FOR PSYCHOTHERAPY AND COACHING DIFFERENT?

This section will describe the ongoing debate regarding whether coaching and psychotherapy can be differentiated on the basis of the clients served. Although, it is important to recognise that coaching clients often have to negotiate the influence of the organisational context (i.e., additional boundary and accountability factors), this section acknowledges that not all coaching is organisationally defined, and not all psychotherapy is exclusively individually focused. The complexity of client presentations and the coach/psychotherapist responsiveness issues are discussed.

Coaching and psychotherapy clients share a common challenge: their struggles with change (Spinelli, 2008). That is as true for someone striving to break free of the bounds of his/her trauma as it is for someone striving to improve personal performance or improve cohesion in a work team. The main distinguishing factor seems to be the degree to which the struggle/striving is deemed pathological and is stigmatised. Perhaps this is better viewed in terms of the complexity of the struggle rather than diagnostically. Although traditionally psychotherapy has been seen as walking in the world of human suffering (Spinelli, 2008), it is equally about walking with people as they strive to attain meaningful goals as part of shaping and living their preferred identity as part of a fulfilling life (Bachkirova, 2007; Maxwell, 2009). It could also be about helping people open new doors and activating potentials, as well as finding ways to grieve, manage and/or heal old wounds. It has been argued that coaching also encounters a combination of human striving and suffering, albeit in less acute forms (e.g., patterns of thought, emotion and behaviour that hamper personal progress) (Griffiths & Campbell, 2008; Maxwell, 2009). Both coaching and psychotherapy negotiate transitioning and consolidating processes shaped by narratives of hope and fear, strengths and self-doubt, meaning and values, and the reconfiguration of a dynamic identity of multiple selves and potentialities (e.g., Spinelli, 2008). Although the presence of significant suffering adds complexity to the challenges of human striving, it is ultimately human striving that is the essence of psychotherapy and coaching.

Griffiths and Campbell (2008) report evidence that clients tend to move between coaching and therapy rather than sticking to coaching or psychotherapy. They go on to recommend that coaches and psychotherapists prioritise understanding why clients are seeking their services at any particular time to determine whether coaching or psychotherapy is preferable in relation to the client's needs. Furthermore, Askeland (2009) expressed concern related to an overemphasis on continuous improvement striving in coaching leading to potential exhaustion for clients, once again highlighting the need for ongoing assessment and sensitivity to client consolidation needs.

There are several other issues relevant to the discussion regarding the division of coaching and psychotherapy clients along clinical and non-clinical lines. First, it is estimated that over 20% of coaching clients will meet the criteria for a mental disorder at some point in their lives simply by being a member of the human race (Slade, et al., 2009). Although there is limited specific data related to the mental health status of coaching clients, Green, Oades and Grant (2006) reported that more than 23% of life-coaching seekers in Australia (i.e., self selected population) had significant psychological distress and mental disorder symptomatology. Second, in a similar vein, Buckley (2010) suggested that mental health issues are widespread enough within coaching client populations to warrant mental health screening. Furthermore, Buckley insists that if mental health issues are identified in coaching contexts, referral to mental health professionals is warranted whenever the coach lacks a mental health background. However, an encouraging study conducted by Lerner et al. (2015) reported data from a randomised controlled trial examining a telephone-based workforce coaching intervention that indicated significant improvements in work functioning and depression among middle-aged and older adults with these issues ($n=19$ from 5 organisations).

McKelley and Rochlan (2007) discuss the ethical and boundary implications related to coaches' mental health related competence (e.g., only 20% of US coaches have psychological training). They further suggested that psychotherapy by stealth in coaching (even if coaching is used as an adjunct to non-traditional psychotherapy methods such as online therapy), may at least be a starting point to motivate the men in their study to engage in therapy. Finally, Davison and Gasiorowski

(2006) suggested that coaching is a viable method for psychotherapists to reach clients who may not ordinarily attend psychotherapy, and assist these clients to better manage an array of professional and personal issues.

There are a number of key issues when considering the mental health of coaching clients. First, there is little question that a significant proportion of coaching clients, where coaching has been prescribed for performance issues, are vulnerable to burnout (Livni, Crowe, & Gonsalvez, 2012; Veage, et al., 2014). There is evidence that the processes that lead to interpersonal and emotional struggle in clinical samples experiencing mental health problems, also are equally present in the struggles of so called non-clinical samples (Ciarrochi, Bilich, & Godsel, 2010). For example, Veage et al. (2014) suggested that living according to one's personal values has implications for wellbeing, and reported data suggesting that when mental health professionals experience incongruence between personal and workplace values they report higher levels of burnout and reduced wellbeing. Therefore, many of the intervention strategies evidenced to be useful in terms of supporting outcomes for non-clinical populations (e.g., mindfulness, values clarification and alignment, and behavioural activation) appear equally relevant for improving mental health client outcomes (Williams, Ciarrochi, & Deane, 2010). Second, there is a dearth of coaching research regarding the relationship between unhealthy achievement drive and perfectionism, neuroticism or a range of anxiety, depression and personality issues. As mentioned above, Askeland (2009) noted concerns regarding potential exhaustion for clients related to continuous improvement striving, as well as concerns about power imbalances in the coaching relationship and influence of the coach being downplayed. Third, stigma associated with mental and behavioural disorders (e.g., depression, substance abuse) is often implicated in underreporting, denial, and non-treatment of these disorders (Corrigan, 2005). Subsequently, it is possible that specific screening for mental disorders in coaching populations may increase the identification of these disorders. An implication of inadequate understanding of coaching client mental health and broader contextual issues, limits the comprehensiveness of case conceptualisation. This may contribute to a misattribution of slow or minimal coaching progress to client resistance or attitudinal problems, or worse contribute to the exacerbation of underlying client issues. Berglas (2002) astutely posed the question regarding whether coaching should only be considered for problem executives as well as for executive with problems.

Some studies suggest that males are less than half as likely as females to seek help for mental health issues (e.g., Kessler, Demier, & Frank, 2005). However, Gale, Liljenstrand, Pardieu and Nebker (2002) reported the usual female dominance in psychotherapy help-seeking is not reflected in coaching contexts, where more than half of coaching clients are male. Wasylyshyn (2003) reported that 85% of executive coaching clients were male, bearing in mind that such results may perhaps be inflated by gender differences in executive populations. Based on observations like these, McKelley and Rochlen (2007) suggested that coaching may be an alternative to conventional psychotherapy for men, reporting data that suggests a range of personal benefits on par with some psychotherapy outcomes (e.g., improved interpersonal effectiveness, wellbeing and emotional competence, and self knowledge). They suggest that the avoidance of therapy (and the preference for coaching) is based in a strong skills development–achievement orientation/success focus of men along with a preference for stoicism and a keenness to not be perceived as 'weak'. Specifically, they purport coaching may be a method of engaging men in their strengths (e.g., success orientation, goal striving) to revisit mental, emotional and interpersonal health issues as barriers to goal attainment. An implication here is that the avoidance oriented motivation that men may exhibit in relation to help-seeking for typical psychotherapy target issues, might become approach oriented motivation after successful engagement of men in coaching (Elliot, 2006).

Based on these data and observations, it seems reasonable to conclude that a significant proportion of the current and future coaching population are likely to be living with unrecognised mental and behavioural disorders. This lack of recognition (and subsequent intervention) is bound to have an impact, at least in some cases, on progress with the coaching plan. It also renders the argument of the clinical versus non-clinical demarcation of the nature of psychotherapy versus coaching clients as being more spurious than some authors suggest (e.g., Grant & Cavanagh, 2007; Hart, et al., 2001).

From the psychotherapy perspective, maintaining a restricted view of recovery and empowerment for people diagnosed with a mental disorder (to that of medical or rehabilitative conceptualisations) is problematic. The medical view defines recovery as the amelioration or better management of illness symptoms, while the traditional rehabilitative view of recovery is the achievement of improved functioning (Andresen, Oades, & Caputi, 2011). Whilst both of these aspects of recovery are important, at times they are quite restrictive in terms of human development beyond illness experiences. The persistent themes that emerge from the narratives of those who live with or have lived with mental disorders, describing what might be considered as psychological recovery, include the importance of increasing hopefulness, promoting self-determination and ownership of one's own recovery, developing meaningful engagement in life, and positive changes in identity (Andresen, Oades, & Caputi, 2011). Although recovery for most is built upon symptom management and functioning stability, it is clearly more than that (Leamy, et al., 2011; Oades, Deane, & Crowe, in press; Slade, Oades, & Jarden, in press; Slade, 2009). It is a personal journey that reflects the key processes that transformational coaching and existential-humanistic psychotherapy target (Crowe, Oades, Deane, Ciarrochi, & Williams, 2011; Davidson & White, 2007).

The personal journey of recovery in mental illness occurs within a complex interpersonal context (Deane & Crowe, 2007). Mental health professionals need to possess competence in knowledge application and relationship skills to track and manage the many challenges present as part of the interpersonal processes of recovery (Gonsalvez & Crowe, 2014). At a minimum, as Deane and Crowe (2007) suggested, mental health professionals need to be able to establish a safe psychological space to develop and maintain a sufficient working alliance with the client, including the negotiation of recovery goals and tasks. The often complex nature of the interpersonal context of psychotherapy and recovery support means that mental health professionals need to develop and maintain meta-competencies that include reflective practice skills (and engage in effective supervisory support) to avoid interpersonal entanglement that could reinforce/repeat problematic relationship dynamics. All this points to the question – how can coaching support the recovery processes of people living with mental disorders (Deane & Crowe, 2007; Crowe, Oades, Deane, Ciarrochi, & Williams, 2011; Oades, Deane, & Crowe, in press)?

Keyes (2002) purported that people can be working towards wellbeing regardless of whether they are still having mental disorder symptoms or not. His four-quadrant model (flourishing, languishing, floundering, and struggling) suggests that specific mental health interventions aimed at symptom reduction alone at best will move a person from floundering to languishing. However, using strengths and wellbeing coaching to generate positive experiences and emotions increases the likelihood that the person may reach a point of flourishing. If recovery in mental illness is supported by both symptom management and wellbeing enhancement, then there is clearly a place for coaching in recovery support (Oades, Crowe, & Nguyen, 2009; Oades, et al., 2005).

USING STRENGTHS OF BOTH COACHING AND PSYCHOTHERAPY TO OVERCOME THE LIMITATIONS OF EACH WITHIN THE DIFFERENT CONTEXTS

This section will describe some ways in which the strengths of coaching and psychotherapy might be integrated further into the practice of the other to enhance practitioner health, learning and skill, and ultimately client outcomes. In particular it will consider how the behaviour activation competencies of coaching can enhance psychotherapy both in terms of supervision and client work, and how reflective and relationship competencies of psychotherapy can enhance coaching conceptualisation and relationship management. The section will conclude with an example of how coaching practice has been used to enhance mental health recovery support and mental health practitioner training transfer via the purposeful use of parallel processing, which highlights how coaching can be positioned as a discipline in relation to psychotherapy.

The implementation of specific clinical practices is influenced by the interactions between the mental health professionals, clients and a range of contextual factors (Deane, Crowe, King, Kavanagh, & Oades, 2006). Consequently, these interactions often challenge mental health professionals by triggering personal reactions (e.g., burnout, anxiety), as well as clarifying needs and opportunities for professional development (Fixsen, et al., 2005). Many of the same processes that are associated with change for mental health service clients are also in operation for mental health service staff engaged in coaching for their own professional development (Crowe, et al., 2011).

There are high levels of stress, burnout and reduced wellbeing reported in mental health professionals (Kipping, 2000), as well as coaching client populations (e.g., executives), and the coaches themselves. There is evidence that working under these conditions is likely to reduce staff performance and readiness to instigate change in work practices (Hobfoll & Freedy, 1993). Staff retention is decreased, with subsequent loss of corporate memory (e.g., practice and organisational knowledge), where stress and burnout are not adequately managed (Lahaie, 2005). In turn, staff stress may contribute to client distress and organisational instability (Livni, et al., 2012; Deane, et al., 2006).

Although there is a tradition, and in many cases an expectation, that mental health professionals engage in clinical supervision to support their clinical work, it varies considerably across disciplines and in style and frequency. Even though there has been a call for a greater competency focus for clinical supervision (Gonsalvez & Calvert, 2014), including the development of targeted professional development plans, most clinical supervision time traditionally is used discussing the psychotherapist's client work alone (Gonsalvez, 2014). Therefore using a coaching framework (i.e., behaviour activation coaching) to structure clinical supervision sessions around broader competencies management may prove to be a useful way ahead in terms of coaching contributing to psychotherapy practice (Gonsalvez & Crowe, 2014; Crowe, et al., 2011).

Personal and professional coaching for mental health professionals themselves can help with managing their own stress and wellbeing, which in turn may help them to be more present for their clients, as well as provide them with additional coaching strategies to support client recovery journeys (Veage, et al., 2014). Having direct coaching experiences also models good coaching practice, permitting possible transfer from the mental health professional development context to the client support provision context. Further, if managed well and openly, professional development coaching may provide varying degrees of exploration of parallel patterns in interpersonal relationships, which may assist the mental health professional to avoid repeating unhelpful relationship patterns with his/her clients (Crowe, et al., 2011; Turner, 2010).

Coaching literature highlights the importance of the role the coaching relationship plays in facilitating behaviour change (O'Broin & Palmer, 2010). Coaches and coachees have identified coach beliefs, attitudes and characteristics (such as adaptability), bond (i.e., trust, rapport, respect, openness, etc.) and collaboration (i.e., two-way relationship) as important aspects of the coaching relationship (O'Broin & Palmer, 2010). However, similar to the therapeutic relationship, and indeed supervisory relationships, adequate understanding of how power, automatic unconscious processes such as transference and countertransference, and the coach's commitment to being truly present with the other, all affect this two-way processing of the coaching relationship (O'Broin & Palmer, 2010; Crowe, et al., 2011).

Coaches are equally liable to face challenging interpersonal dynamics in similar ways to their clients and extended networks as mental health professionals (Turner, 2010; Askeland, 2009). Parallel processing of interpersonal relationship patterns may be useful if the coach/psychotherapist is experiencing interpersonal difficulties with a client. If a client's relating style is difficult, it is more likely to elicit negative responses from the coach/psychotherapist (Klee, Abeles, & Muller, 1990). However, the coach/psychotherapist relationship style can also elicit positive or negative responses from the client (Mothersole, 1999). How the coach/psychotherapist addresses this is the critical issue here. If s/he is provided with coaching that encourages interpersonal reflection (Safran & Muran, 2000), explores the parallels between this interpersonal dynamic and similar other contexts (e.g., in supervision), and encourages exploration of the interpersonal dynamics and feelings of both the client and the coach/psychotherapist, client outcomes are likely to be better (Foreman & Marmar, 1985).

The management of transference–countertransference dynamics are just as relevant to the coaching and supervisory relationships as they are to the psychotherapeutic relationship (Kemp, 2008). As such, there is a need for coaches, supervisors and therapists alike to engage in self-management of their own cognitions, emotions and behaviours in order to manage their countertransference reactions (Kemp, 2008; O'Broin & Palmer, 2010; Turner, 2010; Askeland, 2009).

The Collaborative Recovery Model

Until recently the possibility of using positive psychology principles and strengths-based coaching for assisting people living with enduring mental disorders was considered unrealistic. However, mental health recovery can be considered as 'optimal functioning under adversity', and The Collaborative Recovery Model (CRM) is now a relatively well-established practice in a variety of mental health contexts in Australia (Oades, et al., 2005; Oades, Deane, & Crowe, 2013). The CRM applies coaching techniques to enhance recovery in mental illness, and parallel processing to enhance mental health practitioner training (Crowe, et al., 2011). The model is a broad systemic framework guiding a range of interventions with consumers, carers, staff and organisational systems. The model is informed significantly by the principles, evidence and practices of positive psychology, recovery and positive organisational scholarship (Oades, Crowe & Nguyen, 2009) and was originally developed to assist clinicians in using evidence based skills with mental health service consumers in a manner consistent with the recovery movement (Oades, et al., 2005; Deane, et al., 2006). There are significant conceptual overlaps with the idea of personal recovery as a journey that involves moving beyond illness, living a meaningful life despite symptoms of illness, and Keyes' (2002) notion of flourishing. The CRM includes assumptions and practices that champion human growth, hope, meaning, self-determination, and collaboration, little of which has been consistently evident in the past in psychiatric practice.

The CRM has been conceptualised as a strength-based (Biswas-Diner, 2009) person-centred coaching model (Oades, Crowe, & Nguyen, 2009). The Life Journey Enhancement Tools (LifeJET) (Oades & Crowe, 2008) have been designed to operationalise key components of the CRM for use in a coaching context. The evidence supporting the utilisation of the CRM in mental health services includes: the link between action planning and improved consumer outcomes (Kelly & Deane, 2009); the relationship between goal type/focus and stage of recovery (Clarke, et al., 2009); and consumer endorsement of CRM practices (Marshall, Oades, & Crowe, 2009).

Despite promising early signs of acceptance of these principles and practices within the mental health system, significant barriers remain to their routine implementation (Deane, et al., 2006). Reflecting upon Grant and Cavanagh's (2007) reporting of studies that describe the additional learning benefits of using staff coaching as a training method, a mental health staff professional development–coaching framework was implemented to improve the transfer of training into practice. The rationale was that if mental health professionals engage in their own transformational coaching experience then they would more likely incorporate this into their recovery support practices with clients. That is, using parallel protocols (i.e., the LifeJET) to enliven the parallels between mental health consumers' and mental health professionals' transformational journeys (i.e., parallel processes), represents a purposeful directing of parallel processing (i.e., the transfer down the line of coaching relationship and behaviour activation experiences from the staff development context into the therapeutic relationship context with clients) (Crowe, et al., 2011).

Drawing on psychotherapy supervision wisdom can enhance directed parallel processing regarding interpersonal relationship dynamics (e.g., transference – repetitive problematic relationship dynamics). Although normally considered an 'unconscious' transference process (Morrissey & Tribe, 2001), a relationally-focused supervisor/coach may be able to step back from the re-enacting with the mental health practitioner the same relationship dynamic within the supervisory relationship as that occurring between the practitioner and the client (Turner, 2010). Consequently, rather than repeating the problematic dynamic (e.g., stuck points or alliance ruptures) (Safran & Muran, 2000), that might be occurring with the client, by directly exploring how the mental health practitioner may be contributing to the stagnation, the supervisor may be able to assist the practitioner to find a way through (Bachkirova, Jackson, & Clutterbuck, 2011). Therefore, their problematic relationship dynamics might be transformed into growth opportunities for both the practitioner and the client (Safran & Muran, 2000), or at least viewed as a learning opportunity (Morrissey & Tribe, 2001). In other words, relationally-focused supervisors/coaches with sufficient alliance rupture management skills can assist with: 1) resolving counter-productive tensions in the relationship (the working alliance and supervisory alliance), 2) understanding how the dynamic might be worked through by the practitioner with the client, and 3) support behaviour change for the practitioner and ultimately with the client.

ADOPTING AN INTER-PROFESSIONAL PERSPECTIVE INFORMED BY ACTIVE AND ONGOING NEEDS ASSESSMENT, CLIENT FEEDBACK, AND COMPETENCY-BASED SUPERVISION

If the debate is to move from the basic demarcation of coaching and psychotherapy to discussions about professionals supporting the growth of individuals, e.g., executive psychotherapy (Sperry, 2008); strengths coaching in mental illness recovery (Oades, et al., 2009), there are several implications to be considered. It is important to have an effective way of managing ethical issues regarding working only within one's competency range (Price, 2009), and transparency regarding this within the working contract between the coach and the client. Mental health disciplines have a history of outlining the bounds of their discipline's competencies range and ethical obligations to refer clients on where the issues they are facing fall beyond these competency limits (e.g., APS Code of Ethics, 2007). When managed well, and with the necessary client motivation and agreement, referrals between professionals from different disciplines can be quite effective. However, the complexity of specific client situations (e.g., co-existing disorders, stigma, conflicting motivations, barriers to accessing other professional services) does not always allow smooth and appropriate referrals to occur. In addition, clients often 'fall between the gaps' when they are shifted between services due to varying needs and the services' perceived capacities to manage complex presentations.

There is a risk that perpetuating the separation of psychotherapy from coaching in an exclusive way will repeat the problems that clients with complex needs have had finding appropriate support when presenting, for example, to specialist mental health or alcohol and other drug treatment services. Complexity of needs (e.g., mental disorders with co-existing substance abuse issues, poor work performance and interpersonal problems) is now recognised as the norm rather than the exception (Davidson & White, 2007). Traditionally this type of complexity has been treated in parallel or sequentially, however this often results in poor treatment outcomes (Grella & Stein, 2006). So there is now greater support for an integrated approach to supporting people with complex needs. There are higher completion rates and lower rates of relapse where integrated support is offered (i.e., simultaneous interventions addressing different needs) (Mueser, Noordsy, Drake, & Fox, 2003).

As mentioned above, organisational coaching clients often have a range of complex needs, even if they don't overtly identify and present them (Buckley, 2010). Some coaching clients (men in particular – McKelley & Rochlen, 2007) report coaching to be more beneficial to them than psychotherapy (Griffiths & Campbell, 2008), often identifying goal striving, behaviour activation and moving in valued life directions as integral to these coaching outcomes. Extending on the complexity of needs issue above into organisational and life coaching contexts, it might be fair to suggest that progress with work and/or life coaching goals may have some positive impact on mental health needs, and vice versa. However, in line with Keyes' four-quadrant flourishing model (Keyes, 2002), wellbeing (health and success) and illness symptoms are only moderately correlated, implying that optimal outcomes are in response to *both* illness management *and* wellbeing enhancement activities. In other words, where both illness and life and/or performance enhancement needs co-exist, progress with both will more likely be achievable when health and success enhancing goals are pursued simultaneously with illness management goals.

IMPLICATIONS FOR THE TRAINING AND FORMAL PREPARATION OF PRACTITIONERS

It is important to ensure that coaches and psychotherapists possess a minimum set of core competencies, and are well supported to manage some complexity of presentation through competency-focused and reflexive supervision (Gonsalvez & Crowe, 2014; Bachkirova, Jackson, & Clutterbuck, 2011). It is also important that coaches have clear pathways to refer to specialists when the level of complexity is clearly beyond their capacity. This then requires: 1) the identification and assessment of core competencies (Gonsalvez & Calvert, 2014; McKenna & Davis, 2009), 2) appropriate supervision resources (preferably inter-professional in nature) (Bachkirova, Jackson, & Clutterbuck, 2011; Maxwell, 2009; Hawkins, 2010; Armstrong & Geddes, 2009; Buckley, 2010), and 3) an assessment process/checklist to determine when referral is required (Turner, 2010; Roche & Hefferon, 2013; Buckley, 2010).

Specific training in mental health issues (e.g., diagnostic criteria, knowledge of evidence-based treatments for specific disorders, risk management skills, etc.) is necessary for providing specific clinical interventions. However, much can be done to support the growth and development of an individual regardless of the mental disorder symptoms they may be experiencing. In fact, as mentioned above, coaching for wellbeing, values aligned living, increasing hope, and self-actualisation has a positive impact on illness symptoms (Slade, 2009). That is not to say that a direct focus on the management of illness symptoms is unnecessary, but rather that an exclusive focus on illness symptom management will unlikely be enough to support the individual to the point of flourishing (Leamy, et al., 2011; Slade, 2009). If as the evidence suggests, wellness or health is not the absence of illness, and vice versa (e.g., Keyes, 2002), then rather than approaching client mental health issues in a demarcated way (i.e., mental illness equals automatic referral), or the coach attempting to manage issues outside of his/her competency range, there needs to be a clear way to determine whether it would be ethical to continue to work with a particular client even with additional supervisory or collegial support (Brennan & Wildflower, 2010).

It might be suggested that core competencies that traverse assessment, intervention and professional issues include: knowledge (including theoretical underpinnings of different interventions or motivation enhancement approaches, identification of mental health issues, etc.); awareness of how to apply knowledge in practice (e.g., using effective case conceptualisation to inform intervention planning); relationship competencies (e.g., alliance and transference management skills); counseling/coaching skills (e.g., active listening, immediacy, goal setting, behaviour activation); attitudes and values (e.g., ethical practice) (Gonsalvez & Calvert, 2014; Maxwell, 2009). These core competencies then would be directed by meta-competencies such as reflective practice and scientist-practitioner principles (Grant & Cavanagh, 2007), which reside with the self of the practitioner (Long, 2011), and can be enlivened in supervision (Passmore, 2011; Hawkins, 2010).

If the coach or psychotherapist lacks competence in any of these domains (e.g., mental health intervention knowledge) then supervision may be able to support this gap to some degree as long as the supervisor has the requisite competencies (Long, 2011; Buckley, 2010; Maxwell, 2009). It would mean that coaches who lack the breadth of competence to manage the complexity of presentation of a particular client would either need to arrange an appropriate referral (and exploration of potential shared care options) or they engage in close, targeted supervision from a suitably qualified supervisor (Bachkirova, Jackson, & Clutterbuck, 2011; Passmore, 2011). The future of coaching then requires a direct focus on developing appropriate supervision resources, which might include a commitment to engaging supervision from disciplines where expertise is consistent with the client's needs configuration (Bachkirova, Jackson, & Clutterbuck, 2011). In other words exploring the use of interdisciplinary or inter-professional supervision (Salter, 2014). An increased use of online and other technology (i.e., e-supervision) allows interdisciplinary or inter-professional supervision or shared care, including peer supervision (Deane, Gonsalvez, Blackman, Saffioti & Andresen, 2015; Bachkirova, Jackson, & Clutterbuck,

2011). However, coaching supervision appears to be underutilised. Hawkins and Schwenk (2006) reported less than half of coaches reporting regular supervision, and where accessed in some form at all (e.g., peer supervision), Grant (2012) found that 30% of coach participants were unsatisfied with their supervision.

There is also the question of what constitutes appropriate core and specialist training for coaches and psychotherapists, and just how that training is delivered. Renshall et al. (2013) highlighted the value of focusing supervision on the person of the practitioner rather than just on technical skills. That way the practitioner is more likely to develop reflection skills and awareness of what s/he brings to the helping context in terms of strengths and unhelpful relationship patterns (Long, 2011; Hawkins, 2010). As with many psychotherapist training pathways working with one's own history is considered important in terms of the therapist being better prepared for therapeutic work, as well as increasing empathy for clients going through their own personal exploration and development processes (Spinelli, 2008; Turner, 2009). As Maxwell (2009, p.160) suggests, the 'tri-partite model of supervision, personal development and theoretical knowledge' used in psychotherapy practice might be consider an 'inevitable' direction to go for coaching, in spite of some resistance (Salter, 2008).

There may be some benefits for coaching supervision from a review of recent developments in psychotherapy supervision (Gonsalvez & Calvert, 2014; Gonsalvez & Crowe, 2014; Crowe, et al., 2011). Although some clinical supervision may appear almost exclusively to focus on the client work itself, psychotherapy supervision has a long practice and research history focusing on the therapeutic relationship between the clinician and the client (including the development and maintenance of the working alliance, the management of the transference relationship, and effective use of the 'real' person-to-person relationship) (Watkins, 2011). The focus of Hawkins' (2010) seven-eyed coaching supervision model on the supervisory relationship can certainly be enhanced by the integration of the additional relationship focused strategies used in psychotherapy supervision, such as parallel processing (Spinelli, 2008; Crowe, et al., 2011) and dialogical reflexivity (Hill, Crowe, & Gonsalvez, 2015). Dialogical reflexivity is here-now, I-Thou engagement with, and conversation about, the relational interactions between the supervisee and supervisor (Hill, et al., 2015, a process only minimally used in coaching relationships currently (Maxwell, 2009).

CLIENT-CENTRED VERSUS DISCIPLINE-CENTRED

Regardless of whether a client shows up in a coaching or psychotherapy context, and considering the above discussion regarding multiple needs, it may be valuable to explore the capacity of coaching to be more client-centred rather than discipline-centred. Maxwell (2009) laments the possibility of coaching activities being restricted and a boundary between coaching and psychotherapy being enforced, calling instead for psychological mindedness to be a core competency in training for coaches. To this end coaches would need to be able to assess psychological problems and associated client needs themselves, or have access to other assessment resources. An appropriate, comprehensive needs (that may include mental health screening – e.g., Mortlock, Deane, & Crowe, 2011), strengths (e.g., Roche & Hefferon, 2013), and quality of life (e.g., Frisch, 2013) assessment would assist with understanding client complexity, and informing conceptualisation and intervention planning. This kind of assessment/conceptualisation allows the possibility of personalised feedback and the collaborative generation of a perhaps broader range of psychological distress/illness management and wellbeing/success oriented goals, and a menu of intervention options. Coupled with an active coaching process and outcome assessment feedback system on par with the feedback-in-treatment psychotherapy practices, the client would remain empowered and self-directing at the centre of her/his intervention plan. Effective feedback-in-treatment from clients and assessment data can inform intervention decisions, as well as identify and reduce risk for poor intervention outcomes (Lambert, et al., 2001).

CONCLUSION

Coaching and psychotherapy have continued to evolve and integrate, rendering previous demarcation attempts irrelevant and restrictive. Key areas of cross fertilisation continue to be explored as strengths of both approaches offer much to the limitations of the other. It has also been argued here that psychotherapy and coaching client populations are not as distinct as previously argued, highlighting the importance of the maintenance of sound ethical practices and professional boundaries to ensure appropriate client care.

In order to effectively respond to the complexity of needs that accompany the client into coaching or psychotherapy four key areas of future developments in practice and research are recommended:

1. The development of a needs assessment that can readily be embedded within case conceptualisation and subsequently inform intervention planning.
2. Structures need to be identified and explored that assist with engaging in interdisciplinary and inter-professional support for the coach/psychotherapist.
3. A coach supervision framework needs to be developed that includes reflexivity training to assist coaches to better respond to clients' complexity of needs.
4. Finally, a research agenda aimed at assisting with these developments and evaluating the impact of these developments is required.

The coaching research agenda would at a minimum need to include: the piloting of various needs assessments; the clarification of current case conceptualisation practices; the clarification of what is considered core coaching competencies; the clarification of the extent and type of mental health issues prevalent in coaching contexts; and the examination of current interdisciplinary practices, opportunities and barriers to increasing use of interdisciplinary supports for coaches and psychotherapists faced with client needs complexity. With these developments we may see the field evolve into one that is client centred rather than discipline centred.

REFERENCES

Andresen, R., Oades, L.G. & Caputi, P. (2011). *Psychological Recovery from Mental Illness: A stage model and method*. Chichester: Wiley Blackwell.

Armstrong, H., & Geddes, M. (2009). Developing coaching supervision practice: An Australian case study. *International Journal of Evidence Based Coaching and Mentoring*, 7(2), 1–15.

Askeland, M.K. (2009). A reflexive inquiry into the ideologies and theoretical assumptions of coaching. *Coaching: An International Journal of Theory, Research and Practice*, 2(1), 65–75.

Australian Psychological Society. (2007). *Code of Ethics*. Melbourne, Victoria: Australia.

Bachkirova, T. (2007). Role of coaching psychology in defining boundaries between counseling and coaching. In S. Palmer and A. Whybrow (eds.), *Handbook of Coaching Psychology: A guide for practitioners* (pp. 351–366). Hove: Routledge.

Bachkirova, T., & Cox, E. (2005). A bridge over troubled water: bringing together coaching and counselling. *Counselling at Work*, 48, 2–9.

Bachkirova, T., Jackson, P., & Clutterbuck, D. (eds.) (2011). *Coaching and Mentoring Supervision*. Open University Press, McGraw-Hill: England.

Berglas S. (2002). The very real dangers of executive coaching. *Harvard Business Review*, 80, 87–92.

Biswas-Diner, R. (2009). Personal coaching as a positive intervention. *Journal of Clinical Psychology: In Session*, 65(5), 544–553.

Brennan, D., & Wildflower, L. (2010). Ethics in coaching. In, E. Cox, T. Bachkirova, & D. Clutterbuck (eds.), *The Complete Handbook of Coaching* (pp. 369–380). London: Sage Publications.

Buckley, A. (2010). Coaching and Mental Health. In E. Cox, T. Bachkirova, & D. Clutterbuck (eds.), *The Complete Handbook of Coaching* (pp.394–404). London: Sage Publications.

Cavanagh, M., & Buckley, A. (2014). Coaching and mental health. In, E. Cox, T. Bachkirova, & D. Clutterbuck, (eds.), *The Complete Handbook of Coaching* (2nd ed.) (pp. 405–417). London: Sage Publications.

Cavanagh, M., Grant, A., & Kemp, T., (eds.) (2005). *Evidence-based Coaching: Volume 1, Theory, Research and Practice from the Behavioural Sciences*. Bowen Hills, Australia: Australian Academic Press.

Ciarrochi, J., Bilich, L., & Godsel, C. (2010). Psychological flexibility as a mechanism of change in Acceptance and Commitment Therapy. In R. Baer (Ed.), *Assessing Mindfulness and Acceptance: Illuminating the Processes of Change*. Oakland, CA: New Harbinger Publications, Inc.

Clarke, S., Oades, L., Crowe, T., Caputi, P. & Deane, F.P. (2009). The role of symptom distress and goal attainment in assisting the psychological recovery in consumers with enduring mental illness. *Journal of Mental Health*, 18, 389–397.

Corrigan, P.W. (Ed.) (2005). *On the Stigma of Mental Iillness: Practical Strategies for Research and Social Change*. Washington, DC, US: American Psychological Association.

Cox, E., Bachkirova, T., & Clutterbuck, D. (eds.) (2010). *The Complete Handbook of Coaching*. London: Sage Publications.

Crowe, T.P., Oades, L.G., Deane, F.P., Ciarrochi, J., & Williams, V. (2011). Parallel processes in clinical supervision: Implications for coaching mental health practitioners. *International Journal of Evidence Based Coaching and Mentoring*, 9(2),56–66.

Davidson, L., & White, W.L. (2007). The concept of recovery as an organizing principle for integrating mental health and addiction services [Electronic Edition]. *Journal of Behavioral Health Services & Research*, 34(2), 109–120.

Davison, M., & Gasiorowski, F. (2006). The trend of coaching: Adler, the literature, and marketplace would agree. *Journal of Individual Psychology*, 62(2), 188–201.

Deane, F. P., & Crowe, T. (2007). Building and maintaining a recovery focused therapeutic relationship. In R. King, C. Lloyd & T. Meehan (eds.), *Psychosocial Rehabilitation: A Practitioner's Handbook* (pp. 57–70). New York: Blackwell.

Deane, F.P., Crowe, T., King, R., Kavanagh, D., & Oades, L.G. (2006). Challenges in implementing evidence-based practice into mental health services. *Australian Health Review*, 30, 305–309.

Deane, F.P., Gonsalvez, C., Blackman, R., Saffioti, D., & Andresen, R. (2015). Issues in the development of e-supervision in professional psychology: a review. *Australian Psychologist*, 50, 241–247.

Elliot, A. (2006). The hierarchical model of approach-avoidance motivation. *Motivation and Emotion*, 30, 111–116.

Fixsen, D.L., Naoom, S.F., Blase, K.A., Friedman, R.M., & Wallace, F. (2005). *Implementation Research: A Synthesis of the Literature*. Tampa, FL: University of South Florida, Louis de la Parte Florida Mental Health Institute, The National Implementation Research Network (FMHI Publications #231).

Foreman, S.A., & Marmar, C.R. (1985). Therapist actions that address initially poor therapeutic alliances in psychotherapy. *American Journal of Psychiatry*, 142, 922–926.

Frisch, M.B. (2013). Evidence-based well-being/positive psychology assessment and intervention with quality of life therapy and coaching and the quality of life inventory (QOLI). *Social Indicators Research*, 114, 193–227.

Gale, J., Liljenstrand, A., Pardieu, J., & Nebeker, D.M. (2002). Executive summary – Coaching: Who, what, when, where, and how. Unpublished manuscript, California School of Organizational Studies at Alliant International University.

Gonsalvez, C.J. (2014). Establishing Supervision Goals and Formalising a Supervision Agreement: A Competency-based Approach. In C. L. Watkins & D.L. Milne (eds.), Wiley Blackwell International Handbook of Clinical Supervision, First Edn., Chapter 12, 282–307. Chicheser: Wiley.

Gonsalvez, C.J., & Calvert, F. (2014). Competency-based models of supervision: Principles and applications, promises and challenges. *Australian Psychologist*, 49, 200–208.

Gonsalvez, C.J., & Crowe, T.P. (2014). Making evaluation more accurate in and meaningful for supervision. *American Journal of Psychotherapy. Special Supervision Issue*, 68(2), 117–193.

Grant, A.M. (2006). An integrative goal-focused approach to executive coaching. In D. Stober, D. & A.M. Grant (eds.), *Evidence-Based Coaching Handbook*. New York: Wiley.

Grant, A.M. (2012). Australian coaches' views on coaching supervision: a study with implications for Australian coach education, training and practice. *International Journal of Evidence Based Coaching and Mentoring*, 10(2), 17–33.

Grant, A.M., & Cavanagh, M. (2007). Evidence-based coaching: Flourishing or languishing? *Australian Psychologist*, 42(4), 239–254.

Green, S., Oades, L.G., & Grant, A.M. (2006). Cognitive behavioural, solution-focused life coaching: Enhancing goal striving, wellbeing and hope. *Journal of Positive Psychology*, 1, 142–149.

Grella, C.E., & Stein, J.A. (2006). Impact of program services on treatment outcomes of patients with comorbid mental and substance use disorders. *Psychiatric Services*, 57, 1007–1015.

Griffiths, K., & Campbell, M.A. (2008). Semantics or substance? Preliminary evidence in the debate between life coaching and counselling. *Coaching: An International Journal of Theory, Research and Practice*, 1(2), 164–175.

Hart, V., Blattner, J., & Leipsic, S. (2001). Coaching versus therapy: a perspective. *Consulting Psychology Journal: Practice and Research*, 53(4), 229–237.

Hawkins, P. (2010). Coaching supervision. In E. Cox, T. Bachkirova, & D. Clutterbuck (eds.), *The Complete Handbook of Coaching* (pp. 381–393). Londin: Sage Publications.

Hawkins, P., & Schwenk, G. (2006). *Coaching Supervision*. London: CIPD Change Agenda.

Hawkins, P., & Smith, N. (2010). Transformational coaching. In E. Cox, T. Bachkirova, & D. Clutterbuck (eds.), *The Complete Handbook of Coaching*. London: Sage Publications.

Hill, H.R., Crowe, T.P., & Gonsalvez, C.J. (2015). Reflective dialogue in clinical supervision: A pilot study involving collaborative review of supervision videos. *Psychotherapy Research*, 6, 1–16. DOI: 10.1080/10503307.2014.996795.

Hobfoll, S.E., & Freedy, J. (1993). Conservation of resources: A general stress theory applied to burnout. In W.B. Schaufeli, C. Maslach, & T. Marek (eds.), *Professional Burnout: Recent Developments in Theory and Research* (pp. 115–129). Washington, DC: Taylor & Francis.

Ives, Y. (2008). What is 'coaching'? An exploration of conflicting paradigms. *International Journal of Evidence Based Coaching and Mentoring*, 6(2), 100–113.

Kelly, P.J., & Deane, F.P. (2009). Relationship between therapeutic homework and clinical outcomes for individuals with severe mental illness. *Australian and New Zealand Journal of Psychiatry*, 43, 968–975.

Kemp, T. (2008). Self-management and the coaching relationship: Exploring coaching impact beyond models and methods. *International Coaching Psychology Review*, 3(1), 32–42.

Kessler, R.C., Demier, O., & Frank, R.G. (2005). Prevalence and treatment of mental disorders, 1990 to 2003. *New England Journal of Medicine*, 352, 2515–2523.

Keyes, C.L. (2002). The mental health continuum: From languishing to flourishing in life. *Journal of Health and Social Behavior*, 43, 207–222.

Kipping, C.J. (2000). Stress in mental health nursing. *International Journal of Nursing Studies*, 37(3), 207–218.

Klee, M.R., Abeles, N., & Muller, R.T. (1990). Therapeutic alliance: Early indicators, course, and outcome. *Psychotherapy*, 27, 166–174.

Lahaie, D. (2005) The impact of corporate memory loss: What happens when a senior executive leaves? *Leadership in Health Services*, 18(3), 35–48.

Lambert, M.J., Whipple, J.L., Smart, D.W., Vermeersch, D.A., Nielsen, S.L., & Hawkins, E.J. (2001). The effects of providing therapists with feedback on patient progress during psychotherapy: Are outcomes enhanced? *Psychotherapy Research*, 11, 49–68.

Leamy, M., Victoria Bird, V., Le Boutillier, C., Williams, J., & Slade, M. (2011). Conceptual framework for personal recovery in mental health: Systematic review and narrative synthesis. *British Journal of Psychiatry*, 199, 445–452. DOI: 10.1192/bjp.bp.110.083733.

Lerner, D., Adler, D.A., Rogers, W.H., Chang, H., Greenhill, A., Cymerman, E., and Azocar, F. (2015). A randomized clinical trial of a telephone depression intervention to reduce employee presenteeism and absenteeism. *Psychiatric Services*, 66(6), 570–577.

Livni, D., Crowe, T.P., & Gonsalvez, C.J. (2012) Effects of supervision modality, intensity and alliance on outcomes for the supervisee. *Rehabilitation Psychology*, 57(2), 178–186.

Long, K. (2011). The self in supervision. In T. Bachkirova, P. Jackson, & D. Clutterbuck, (eds.), *Coaching and Mentoring Supervision* (pp. 78–90). Open University Press, McGraw-Hill: England.

Marshall, S.L., Oades, L.G., & Crowe, T.P. (2009). Mental health consumers' perceptions of receiving recovery-focused services. *Journal of Evaluation in Clinical Practice*, 15, 654–659

Maxwell, A. (2009). How do business coaches experience the boundary between coaching and therapy/counselling? *Coaching: An International Journal of Theory, Research and Practice*, 2(2), 149–162.

McKelley, R., & Rochlen, A.B. (2007). The practice of coaching: Exploring alternatives to therapy for counseling resistant men. *Psychology of Men and Masculinity*, 8(1), 53–65.

McKenna, D.D., & Davis, S.L. (2009). Hidden in plain sight: the active ingredients of executive coaching. *Industrial and Organisational Psychology*, 2, 244–260.

Morrissey, J., & Tribe, R. (2001). Parallel process in supervision. *Counselling Psychology Quarterly*, 14(2), 103–110.

Mortlock, K.S., Deane, F.P., & Crowe, T.P. (2011). Screening for mental disorder comorbidity in Australian alcohol and other drug residential treatment settings. *Journal of Substance Abuse Treatment*, 40, 397–404.

Mothersole, G. (1999). Parallel process: A review. *The Clinical Supervisor*, 18(2), 107–121.

Mueser, K.T., Noordsy, D.L., Drake, R.E., & Fox, L. (2003). *Integrated Treatment for Dual Disorders: A Guide to Effective Practice*. The Guilford Press: New York.

O'Broin, A., & Palmer, S. (2010). Exploring key aspects in the formation of coaching relationships: Initial indicators from the perspective of the coachee and the coach. *Coaching: An International Journal of Theory, Research and Practice*, 3, 124–143.

Oades, L.G. & Crowe, T.P. (2008) *Life Journey Enhancement Tools (Life JET)*. Illawarra Institute for Mental Health, University of Wollongong.

Oades, L.G., Crowe, T.P., & Nguyen, M. (2009). Leadership coaching transforming mental health systems from the inside out: The Collaborative Recovery Model as person-centred strengths based coaching psychology. *International Coaching Psychology Review*, 4(1), 25–36.

Oades, L., Deane, F.P., & Crowe, T. (2013). The Collaborative Recovery Model: Developing positive institutions to facilitate recovery in enduring mental illness. In S.A. David, I. Boniwell, & A.C. Ayers (eds.), *The Oxford Handbook of Happiness* (pp. 1050–1066). Oxford, UK: Oxford University Press.

Oades, L., Deane, F.P., & Crowe, T. (in press). Collaborative Recovery Model: from mental health recovery to wellbeing. In M. Slade, L. Oades, & A. Jarden (eds.), *Wellbeing, Recovery and Mental Health*. Cambridge: Cambridge University Press.

Oades, L., Deane, F., Crowe, T., Lambert, W.G., Kavanagh, D., & Lloyd, C. (2005). Collaborative Recovery: An integrative model for working with individuals who experience chronic and recurring mental illness. *Australasian Psychiatry*, 13, 279–284.

Passmore, J. (Ed.) (2011). *Supervision in Coaching: Supervision, Ethics and Continuous Professional Development*. London: Kogan Page.

Price, J. (2009). The coaching/therapy boundary in organizational coaching. *Coaching: An International Journal of Theory, Research and Practice*, 2(2), 135–148.

Renshall, K., Rhodes, P., Brown, J., Donnelly, M., Donnelly, H., Gosbee, M., Mence, M., Milic, M., Treanor, K., & Wainer, D. (2013). Family of origin coaching for clinicians in a child and adolescent mental health service. *Contemporary Family Therapy*, 35, 684–697.

Roche, B., & Hefferon, K. (2013). The assessment needs to go hand-in-hand with debriefing: the importance of a structured coaching debriefing understanding and applying a positive psychology strengths assessment. *International Coaching Psychology Review*, 8(1), 20–34.

Safran, J.D., & Muran, J.C. (2000). Resolving therapeutic alliance ruptures: Diversity and integration. *Journal of Clinical Psychology*, 56(2), 233–243.

Salter, T. (2008). Exploring current thinking within the field of coaching on the role of supervision. *International Journal of Evidence Based Coaching and Mentoring*, Special Issue (2), 27–39.

Salter, T. (2014), Mentor and Coach: Disciplinary, interdisciplinary and multidisciplinary approaches, *International Journal of Evidence Based Coaching and Mentoring*, Special Issue (8).

Slade, M. (2009). *Personal recovery and mental illness. A guide for mental health professionals*. Cambridge: Cambridge University Press.

Slade, M., Oades, L., & Jarden, A. (in press). Why wellbeing and recovery? In M. Slade, L. Oades, & A. Jarden (eds.), *Wellbeing, Recovery and Mental Health*. Cambridge: Cambridge University Press.

Slade, T., Johnston, A., Teesson, M., Whiteford, H., Burgess, P., Pirkis, J., et al. (2009). *The Mental Health of Australians 2. Report on the 2007 National Survey of Mental Health and Wellbeing*. Canberra: Department of Health and Ageing.

Sperry, L. (2008). Executive coaching: an intervention, role function, or profession. *Consulting Psychology Journal: Practice and Research*, 60(1), 33–37.

Spinelli, E. (2008). Coaching and therapy: similarities and divergences. *International Coaching Psychology Review*, 3(3), 241–249.

Stober, D. and Grant A.M. (eds.) (2006). *Evidence-Based Coaching Handbook*. New York: Wiley.

Stober, D.R., Wildflower, L., & Drake, D. (2006). Evidence-based practice: A potential approach for effective coaching. *International Journal of Evidence Based Coaching and Mentoring*, 4(1), 1–8.

Turner, E. (2010). Coaches' views on the relevance of unconscious dynamics to executive coaching. *Coaching: An International Journal of Theory, Research and Practice*, 3, 12–29.

Veage, S, Ciarrochi, J., Deane, F.P., Andresen, R, Oades, L.G., & Crowe, T.P. (2014). Value congruence, importance and success in the workplace: Links with well-being and burnout amongst mental health practitioners. *Journal of Contextual Behavioral Science*, 3, 258–264.

Wasylyshyn, K.M. (2003). Executive coaching: An outcome study. *Consulting Psychology Journal: Practice and Research*, 55, 94–106.

Watkins, C.E. (2011). Toward a tripartite vision of supervision for psychoanalysis and psychoanalytic psychotherapies: Alliance, transference–countertransference configuration, and real relationship. *Psychoanalytic Review*, 98(4), 557–590.

Williams, V., Ciarrochi, J., & Deane, F. (2010). On being mindful, emotionally aware, and more resilient: A longitudinal pilot study of police recruits. *Australian Psychologist*, 45, 274–282.

Coaching and Theories of Learning

John L. Bennett and Francine Campone

Elaine Cox (2013) defines coaching as a 'facilitated, dialogic learning process' (p. 1). Rogers (2012) defines coaching as a 'partnership of equals whose aim is to achieve speedy, increased and sustainable effectiveness through focused learning in every aspect of the client's life' (p. 7). Both definitions allude to a learning process as an essential element of the coaching experience. Rogers (2012) goes further in suggesting that learning is essential to effecting sustainable change. How, then, can principles of adult learning be integrated into the coaching process?

Learning 'is a tremendously complex phenomenon' (Jarvis, 2012, p. 2) that has been defined variously with respect to behavioral, cognitive and psychological outcomes. Jarvis, Holford, and Griffin (1998) provides the behaviorist's definition of learning as 'any more or less permanent change in behavior, which is the result of experience' (p. 21). The behaviorist's definition focuses on behavior change rather than on knowledge, attitudes, values, or beliefs. The cognitive orientation contends 'learning involves the reorganization of experiences in order to make sense of stimuli from the environment' (Merriam & Caffarella, 1991, p. 129). The social learning theorists posit 'that people learn from observing' (Merriam & Caffarella, 1991, p. 134). The humanist theories consider learning from the perspective of the human potential for growth.

A holistic theory of knowledge and adult learning seeks to integrate three indivisible facets of knowledge (explicit, implicit and emancipatory) and to explore the dynamic interactions of these (Yang, 2003). Explicit knowledge is objective, factual, formal and systematic. Implicit knowledge is personal, context specific, and may be unarticulated. Emancipatory knowledge comprises emotions and affective responses. Within a holistic framework, learning is defined 'as the process whereby knowledge is created, acquired, transformed, converted or utilized in a different context from its origin' (Merriam & Caffarella, 1991, p. 117). Learning is a 'combination of processes whereby the whole-person – body ... and mind ... experiences a social situation the perceived content of which is transformed cognitively, emotively or practically (or through any combination) and integrated into the person's individual biography resulting in a changed (or more experienced) person' (Merriam, Caffarella, and Baumgartner 2007, p. 102). The holistic perspective – integrating body, mind, experience and context – may be applied to the purposes, relationships and processes utilized in coaching.

Cox, Bachkirova, and Clutterbuck (2014) propose that an adult learning foundation to coaching is fundamental to supporting clients to extend and clarify experience and effect changes in behaviors and attitudes. Recent coaching literature positions adult learning as a theoretical basis for coaching interventions to foster self-direction, experiential learning, and knowledge transfer (Cox, 2013); a platform for individual transformation (Gray, 2006); and, a framework for defining coach and client roles and responsibilities (Campone, 2015). Individual coaching may serve as an intervention to support adults to improve their performance, develop capabilities, or transform (Bennett and Bush, 2014).

To position coaching as an opportunity to foster adult learning, we consider the implications of adult learning theories within the framework of coach and client roles, relationship dynamics, and coaching processes. In this chapter, we explore theories and models from foundational disciplines of the coaching field as well as the relatively modest base of empirical studies in coaching that address adult learning principles. Andragogy is discussed as a foundational theory in adult learning, and we examine individual and social learning principles that have evolved from it. Experiential learning is presented as a form of learning, which addresses both the individual's traits and the collaborative aspects of the learner's interactions and learning processes. We complete the review by examining transformative adult learning theories and their implications for sustainable coaching outcomes. We discuss the areas of commonality across theoretical perspectives and models as they inform coaching practice and integrate these into a model for adult learning in coaching which incorporates both individual and collaborative learning within an experiential framework. This model might be framed in a manner similar to the multi-dimensional model studied and presented by Orenstein (2007).

KEY CONCEPTS

Key concepts and frameworks related to learning in the context of coaching, such as andragogy and experiential adult learning, are defined, described and related to coaching. These serve as a foundation for our focus on the individual as a client (or person-being-coached) who is both being coached and learning.

Andragogy

Andragogy is the 'art and science of helping adults learn' and is considered applicable to a variety of adult learning contexts (Knowles, 1984, p. 43). As conceived of by both Cox (2013) and Rogers (2012), coaching may be considered an adult learning context. We begin this section with andragogy to help frame coaching in this way and to provide a set of foundational principles, which are amplified in subsequent adult learning theories and models.

Knowles's (1975, 1984) andragogy is generally acknowledged as foundational in the provision of adult education insofar as his model explicitly differentiates the learning needs of adults from those of children (Baumgartner et al., 2003). Knowles's model proposes four principles: relevance of the learning to the learner, self-direction and control over learning, use of life experience as a learning resource, and the importance of intrinsic motivation. In reviewing and broadening perspectives on adult learning, Merriam, Caffarella, and Baumgartner (2007) position Knowles's learner-centered andragogy as a foundation, supplemented by complementary theories. A three-dimensional view of learning processes incorporates not only the cognitive aspects of learning but acknowledges and connects the learner's emotional experiences and environmental perceptions and experiences. An even more comprehensive perspective on adult learning posits learners as transformed through processing experiences encountered in their social world, which stimulate learning. The literature of individual, collective, and social learning further explores Knowles's (1975) assumptions regarding an adult's natural potential for learning, the relevance of learning focus to the learner, and the role of practice in the learning process.

Principles of andragogy provide guidance into the conditions supporting adult learning. Knowles suggests that a relationship that supports self-direction is one in which adults feel accepted, respected, and supported. Participants engage in a collaborative exploration and learners are full partners in assessing their own needs, planning and implementing actions, and evaluating learning experiences (Merriam, Caffarella, and Baumgartner, 2007). As an educator, Knowles described his shift from being a 'transmitter' to becoming a facilitator – that is, primarily serving as a process manager and content resource with the purpose of 'releasing the creative energies' of others (Knowles, Holton, & Swanson, 2005, p. 256). Cox, Bachkirova, and Clutterbuck (2014) applied the concepts of andragogy to coaching and offer six characteristics for coaching engagements based on Knowles theory:

1. The agenda must be determined by the person-being-coached/client or co-created to support client ownership and direction.
2. Adults are self-directed and feedback must communicate respect for their autonomy.
3. The adult's background and experiences are catalysts for learning and unlearning.
4. The timing and degree of interest in learning activities is driven by need in a current work or life situation.
5. Adult learning is focused on immediacy and potential for application.
6. While external motivators may be relevant, internal needs and values can be more powerful drivers of learning.

In this formulation, the focus on self-direction, experience as a catalyst, and intrinsic motivation address the individual in the coaching engagement. The focus on a co-created agenda, respectful feedback and situationally driven needs address the contextual and social aspects of learning. Effective coach–client engagement rests on the centrality of the client directing and determining the content of the coaching. However, given that centrality, it is also important to engage the client in the co-creation of a relationship, which provides a sense of safety as defined by the client, that acknowledges the client's preferences for partnership roles, and that respects all aspects of the client's life experiences as a resource. The coach's responsibility includes fostering the client's self-efficacy beliefs encouraging persistence, activating the client's resources, and supporting client determination and implementation of action. The coach is also called upon to model persistence, resilience, and alternative perspectives and behaviors. The coach and client both attend to the cognitive and affective dimensions of the interaction.

Experiential Adult Learning

Experiential learning theories situate the individual's in an interactive, real-world context. As in coaching, the learner's personal traits and characteristics inform goals and motivation, as well as engagement in the process, focus, meaning-making, and action. The learner, or client, is embedded in multiple social contexts such as work, family and community as well as the coaching partnership. Coaching and learning are both collaborative processes in which dialogue is directed at stimulating thinking, reflection and change. The principles of experiential learning can be applicable with respect to the clients' actions and reflective learning in their own context, as well as the social and collaborative learning aspects of the coach–client dynamic.

While there are many who practice experiential learning methods, three prominent theorists provide examples of how experiential learning is applied: Schon, Argyris, and Kolb. Schon (1983) argues that our actions are guided by 'theories-in-use,' which are based on assumptions and values. Working together, Argyris and Schon called this Action Science (Argyris & Schon, 1974, 1978; Argyris, Putnam, & Smith, 1985). When people attempt to solve problems, they correct perceived errors in such a way as to maintain the assumptions and values that lie behind their theory-in-use. This process is referred to as 'single-loop learning' or 'Model I.' 'Double-loop learning' or 'Model II,' on the other hand, occurs when one examines the gap between theories-in-use and 'espoused-theories,' which are those theories one refers to in order to explain one's actions. The basic goal of action science is increasing professional effectiveness by helping individuals in small groups shift from using Model I to using Model II in resolving problems.

In collaboration with Argyris, Schon completed works related to learning based on their shared belief that learning involves the detection and correction of error. Their work together produced such books as *Theory in Practice* (Argyris & Schon, 1974) and *Organizational Learning* (Argyris & Schon, 1978). Independently, Schon is perhaps most famous for his work on the concept of the reflective-practitioner (Schon, 1983, 1987).

Kolb is, perhaps, best known for his work in adult learning style theory, that is 'the processes associated with making sense of concrete experiences – and the different styles of learning that may be involved' (Smith, 2001). The learning cycle can begin at any one of the four points (see Figure 6.1). Drawing from the theory of experiential learning, Baker, Jensen, and Kolb (2005) provide a framework based on five process dialectics that serves as the foundational understanding of conversational learning. 'The five dialectics – apprehension and comprehension, reflection and action; epistemological discourse and ontological recourse; individuality and relationality' (p. 411). The learning process often begins with a person carrying out a particular action and then seeing the effect of the action in this situation. Kolb's (1984) experiential learning

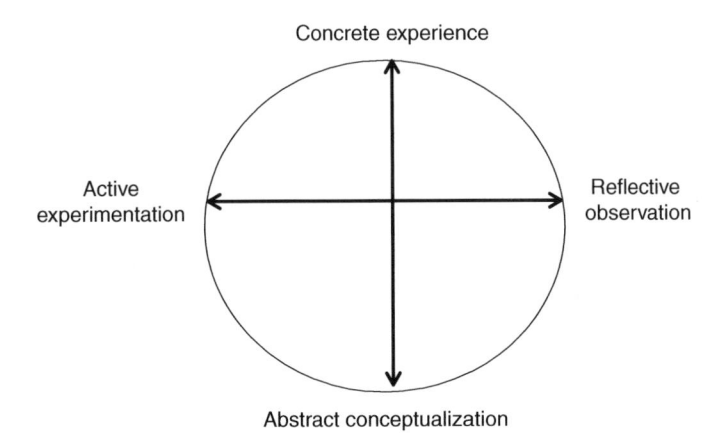

Figure 6.1 Experiential learning cycle
Reproduced with permission
Source: Baker, Jensen, & Kolb, 2005, Figure 1, p. 415

model addresses four stages of the learning cycle: concrete experience, reflective observation, abstract conceptualization, and active experimentation. The cycle can be entered at any point and the learning process is iterative.

We suggest that the concept of learning from experience provides a foundation for several learning methodologies, including problem-based learning and action learning. The term experiential learning has become widely used in a variety of settings – formal as well as informal educational circles. Problem-based learning is that which results from addressing a problem: its understanding and resolution. Action learning stresses the importance of 'doing' in the learning process (Revans, 1982; Marquardt, 1999). A standard component of the coaching process is supporting the client to develop actions following coaching sessions. Both problem-based and action learning entail exploring multiple aspects of the presenting issue, defining desired outcomes, identifying resources and obstacles, formulating and evaluating potential actions, and implementing selected alternatives. Considering action as an experiment allows both coach and client to explore and evaluate outcomes as useful data and to generate or modify change interventions.

INDIVIDUAL LEARNING

The manner and means of engaging in experiential learning are influenced by the qualities, capacities and traits of the learner. The client in a coaching engagement has responsibility for learning both in the context of the coaching interaction and through actions taken in the aftermath of a coaching session to move the coaching agenda forward. The coach cannot act on behalf of the client nor can the coach learn for the client. Therefore, the client's capacity for learning from experience is an essential consideration. When coaches have an understanding of the individual learning capacities and traits of the client, they are better able to support client's growth through experiential learning processes. In this section, we look at the principles of self-direction, self-efficacy, and self-determination and the role these play in the individual learning process. These traits are inextricably linked with learning in collaborative frameworks. However, for purposes of organization, we begin by looking at the individual before moving to the interpersonal aspects of adult learning.

Self-Directed Learning

Self-directed learning emerged from beliefs that adults prefer individualism and autonomy and focuses on such concepts as self-determination, self-actualization, or self-transformation. To illustrate these principles, we examine the work of three theorists: Knowles, Garrison and Houle.

According to Knowles (1975), self-directed learning:

> describes a process in which individuals take the initiative, with or without the help of others, in diagnosing their learning needs, formulating learning goals, identifying human and material resources for learning, choosing and implementing appropriate learning strategies, and evaluating learning outcomes. (p. 18)

Knowles explained that self-directed learners are better learners, adults do not need teachers because they are capable of taking charge of their own learning, and 'the de-institutionalization of education, in the form of open and independent learning systems, is creating a need for learners to develop appropriate skills' (Jarvis, Holford, and Griffin, 1998, p. 81).

Garrison (1997) defines self-directed learning as 'an approach when learners are motivated to assume personal responsibility and collaborative control of the cognitive ... and contextual ... processes in constructing and confirming meaningful and worthwhile learning outcomes' (p. 18). He proposes that the addition of cognitive and metacognitive factors to prevailing self-directed learning theories shifts the focus from self-directed teaching, which emphasizes acquisition of material, to self-directed learning, which is directed at critical evaluation and integration of material.

The three elements of Garrison's (1997) model overlap and are interdependent. Self-management is associated with the external activities of the learning process, such as carrying out learning goals and managing resources. The self-monitoring element of the model encompasses the cognitive and meta-cognitive processes to support the learner's construction of personal meaning. Motivation as 'a pervasive influence' on decisions to enter and persist in learning tasks (Garrison, 1997, p. 26). Task motivation affects determination to diligently sustain intentional effort. As with the other two elements of the model, external conditions and internal states affect motivation to assume responsibility. Garrison associates intrinsic motivation with meaningful and worthwhile learning outcomes.

Houle's (1961) two recurrent themes were that of lifelong learning and of the need to provide suitable supporting structures that coordinate efforts to enable all adults to participate. Houle (1961) identified three broad categories of learner orientations to study: goal-oriented, activity-oriented, and learning-oriented. According to Jarvis, Holford, and Griffin (1998), 'Houle had drawn attention to the fact that many adult learners were self-motivated in their learning. This carried implications for concepts such as personal growth and development' (p. 78). He proposed a 'fundamental system' of educational design and identified components of the system, which he believed were the task of educators to manage (Knowles, Holton, & Swanson, 2005). Houle (1972) proposed seven assumptions before defining the components of the system. The literature related to self-directed learning suggests that facilitators in the learning process, such as coaches, should provide Houle's suitable supporting structure. Borrowing from Knowles suggests that goals and processes are co-created as a contract for learning.

Garrison's (1997) Practical Inquiry Model suggests a framework for coaching in which the coach and client engage in a collaborative exploration through the four quadrants (see Figure 6.2).

The triggering event is initiated in the shared world and consists of a recognized issue, dilemma, or problem that emerges from experience and dialogue to shape or create a goal-oriented focus in the experience. In the second phase, exploration, learning partners move back and forth between private reflection and collaborative discourse to clarify relevant aspects and issues. In the third phase, integration, private reflection and coach–client dialogue help make meaning of ideas emerging from exploration. The fourth phase, resolution, involves taking action. Consistent with principles of adult self-direction, the client selects and enacts the chosen behaviors providing experiential material for further exploration with the coach.

Self-Efficacy

We propose that self-efficacy and self-direction are critical aspects of the adult learning process. Self-efficacy is defined as 'people's judgments of their capabilities to organize and execute courses of action required to attain designated types of performances. It is concerned not with the skills one has but with judgments of what one can do with whatever skills one possesses' (Bandura, 1986, p. 391). Self-efficacy beliefs are considered the 'foundation of human agency' (Bandura, 2001, p. 10). According to Bandura (2001), there are three modes of human agency, defined simply as making things happen on one's own behalf. The first of these is personal agency, an individual taking action to affect a desired outcome. The core features of personal agency are intention, forethought, self-reactiveness, and self-reflectiveness. Intention is grounded in self-motivation and the likelihood of action at a future time. Forethought entails projecting goals and anticipating

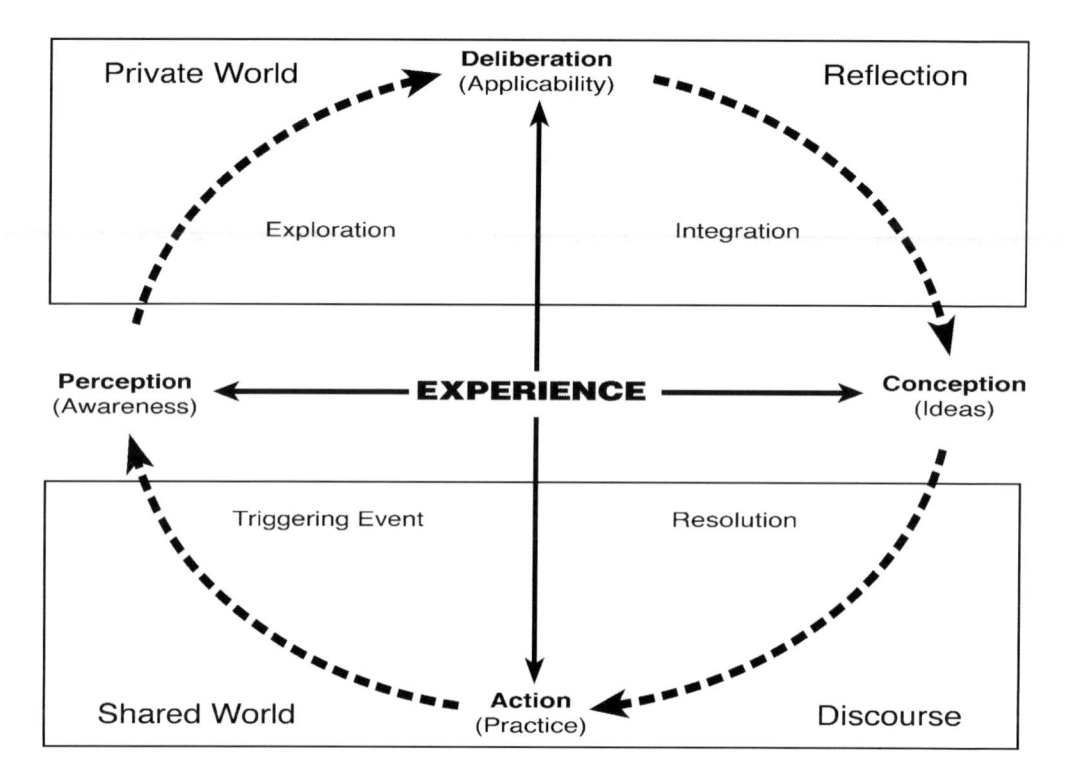

Figure 6.2 Practical inquiry model

Reprinted with permission from the authors, Garrison, Anderson, and Archer, 2009, p. 9

outcomes with personal and social meaning. Self-reactiveness involves setting a course of action to accomplish goals and motivating oneself to implement and sustain. As a meta-cognitive activity, self-reflectiveness is evaluating one's own motivations, values and meaning and calibrating predictions and outcomes in response to actual outcomes. The second mode is proxy agency, which involves accomplishment of goals through another person. Proxy agency may be engaged when an individual lacks requisite knowledge, skills or resources, or perceives another to be better situated to affect the desired outcome. The third mode is collective agency. This mode is predicated on a shared belief in collective power to produce desired outcomes. The collective performance is the result of interactive, coordinated, synergistic dynamics based on the shared intentions, knowledge and skill of the group's members. Bandura (2001) emphasizes that the personal and collective modes are not discrete. Human agency is enacted within and influenced by social (collective) structures.

According to Bandura (1989), the continuation of an effort that has been initiated by goal formulation is impacted by social influences that promote or undermine the strength of personal competencies, values and interests. Learning outcomes may be directed at enhanced technical performance as well as behavioral change. Individuals can influence their own development by choosing and shaping supportive social environments.

Self-efficacy beliefs – acknowledging that one has the power to produce effects by one's own actions – affect whether thoughts are self-enhancing or self-hindering. Strong self-efficacy beliefs are essential to maintaining motivation and persistence in the face of obstacles. These beliefs shape how people respond to social and environmental factors in pursuit of goals. For example, learner participation, facilitated by a learning collaborator such as a coach, is linked to both intrinsic factors such as motivation and external behaviors, including goal selection, active exploration, self- and resource-management and completion of tasks. Self-efficacy beliefs are developed in four ways, as proposed by Bandura (2012). These are mastery experiences in which an individual must exert effort, persevere and overcome obstacles, coming to view failure as a learning opportunity; social modelling of perseverance by similar individuals; social persuasion reinforcing one's self-efficacy; and, developing internal measures of success (that is, self-development) rather than external comparison of the self with others. Social Cognitive Theory recognizes the potential impact of both cognitive and affective processes on self-efficacy beliefs. Cognitive processes may support or hinder an individual's information processing, reasoning, motivation and the ability to construct an effective course of action. Similarly, the synergy between self-efficacy beliefs and affective processes influences the nature of emotional responses to challenging or threatening situations. This influence, in turn, interferes with thinking patterns, motivation, and persistence.

Self-Determination

Along with self-direction and self-efficacy beliefs, self-determination impacts the effectiveness of experiential learning. Deci and Ryan (2000) note that Self-Determination Theory (SDT) 'is part of the adaptive features of the human organism to engage in interesting activities, to exercise capacities, to pursue connectedness in social groups, and to integrate intrapsychic and interpersonal experiences into a relative unity' (p. 229). Hetzner, Heid, and Gruber (2012) conceptualize self-determination as 'the individual's experience of autonomy, competence and social integration' (p. 540). They assert that personal initiative mediates the effects of change readiness and self-determination in reflective learning. In the Hetzner, Heid, and Gruber (2012) version of the learning cycle, an encounter with an experience is followed by reflection for the purpose of developing a strategy for response, enactment of the response, and evaluation of the experience. Reflection may be individual or collaborative and is both retrospective and future oriented. The learner looks back on thoughts or feelings that arose during the experience, critically re-examines, and seeks to generate a new perspective.

Among other factors, Hetzner, Heid and Gruber (2012) evaluated the impact of key aspects of self-determination. These factors included the experience of autonomy in choosing tasks and means of accomplishment, experiences of competence in mastering and accomplishing tasks and learning from experience, and the experience of social integration. Hetzner, Heid and, Gruber (2012) found significant correlation among all three facets of self-determination: autonomy, competence, and social integration. All three were also significantly correlated with reflective learning. They did not find a significant correlation between readiness to change and self-determination. However, they did find significant correlation between personal initiative and all facets of self-determination. Regression analysis showed competence and social integration to have a stronger relationship to reflection than did perceived autonomy. The findings support social integration as an important predictor of quality reflection and reinforce the role of social exchange and social learning in enhancing the quality of reflective learning. Hetzner, Heid and, Gruber (2012) believe the evidence supports the assumption that a supportive team and work environment enhances the individual's perceptions of competence. In turn, the experience of competence provides motivation for individuals to take initiative and solve problems proactively.

According to Ryan, Lynch, Vansteenkiste, and Deci (2011), motivation and personal autonomy are critical issues in facilitating behavioral change because 'positive and lasting results most likely occur when a [coaching] client becomes actively engaged and personally invested in change' (p. 194). This assertion is particularly true in the context of coaching because clients are expected to reach for optimal levels of performance. Therefore, it is critically important for coaches to understand (and know how to work with) the process that impacts personal motivation and readiness to change (Spence & Oades, 2011). According to Spence and Oades (2011), SDT provides a useful guide for coaching by providing a 'nuanced understanding of human motivation' (p. 39) and 'different perspectives for understanding coaching' [italics removed] (p. 40).

COLLABORATIVE AND SOCIAL ADULT LEARNING

The literature linking social constructionism and adult learning explores the role that both the context and the milieu of learning play in coaching and in the adult learning process. From this perspective, 'coaching can be viewed as a type of extended cognition or alliance' that generates a new understanding or extends current understanding and engenders further exploration (Cox, Bachkirova and, Clutterbuck, 2014, p. 105). In this section, we examine three perspectives on the functions of collaboration in adult learning: social cognitive theory, reflective learning, and action learning.

Social Cognitive Theory situates the learning experiences in an interdependent social context. Social learning involves learning by watching others, and learning is an internal process that may or may not change behavior. Further, behavior is directed toward particular goals and eventually becomes self-regulated. Reinforcement and punishment have indirect effects as well as direct ones. Bandura offers a structure he calls triadic codetermination, which emerges from the interplay of intrapersonal influences, behaviors, and environmental forces (Bandura, 2012). The qualities, experiences and behaviors of individuals and the social system within which they function 'operate as interacting determinants that influence one another bi-directionally' (Bandura, 2001, p. 15).

Collective agency is a means of attaining goals through emergent group actions. Because individuals do not exist in isolation, Bandura recognizes collective agency as an equally relevant mode. Group attainments result from shared intentions, knowledge and skills emerging through the 'interactive, coordinated and synergistic dynamics of [participants'] transactions' (Bandura, 2001, p. 14).

Reflective learning is proposed by both Jarvis (2012) and Cox (2005) as an essential step in the experiential learning cycle. Jarvis (2012) argues that both mind and self 'are social constructs so that the person may be regarded as a social construct' (p. 39). Thus, the self at the center of Jarvis' learning model can only emerge through social interaction. As the scope and nature of social interactions broaden, the individual learns about others: attitudes, expectations and other mental content. In responding to these interactions, according to Jarvis, the individual's self-concept and self-identity emerge.

Jarvis's (2012) model of the learning process is initiated by a person in a situation (social context) in which they have an experience, which is incompatible with their theory-in-use or mental model. In this respect, Jarvis' model aligns with Mezirow's (2000) concept of a disorienting dilemma. Jarvis identifies nine possible responses to what he characterizes as a potential learning opportunity. He characterizes three of these as non-learning responses, which ignore, reject or disregard incompatibilities; three non-reflective responses, which apply preconscious or automatic learning, practice or imitation, or rote memorization, and three reflective responses including contemplation, reflective practice, and experimental learning. Jarvis conceives of contemplation as an intellectual and rational approach to reasoning through cognitive discrepancies. In reflective practice, the learner engages not only with the experience and reasoning but assumes responsibility to reflect on reactions and affirm or innovate new responses. In experimental learning, the learner takes action based on contemplation and reflection to create new knowledge based on both cognitive and affective consideration of the experience and the premise on which it was constructed.

Cox's (2005) study integrates an experiential learning approach with a reflection model. She examined the impact of a structured model and tool for reflection on actions directed at transforming perspectives. The model and tool used in the study draws on and amplifies Kolb's experiential learning cycle. Cox (2005) states that the model also acknowledges social constructionism 'by recognizing that actions and responses are influenced by emotions, intentions, values and attitudes as well as external factors' (p. 463). The model used in the study followed Johns (2013) and consisted of four sets of questions with detailed prompts. One question set asked for descriptions of the 'here and now' experience. The second question set invited reflection to explore intentions, interventions, actions taken, outcomes and reactions. The third question set examined internal and external influences on the learner's reactions and consideration of sources. The final set of questions opened consideration of options, alternatives, lessons for future application and implications of learning for practical, aesthetic, ethical and personal ways of learning. The learners in Cox's study worked independently and collectively to debrief their reflections. Overall, the learner response to the tool was positive. Cox (2005) states that her own learning affirmed her position that collaborative and group reflection, combined with individual debriefing with an instructor strengthens individual reflection skills. Her second learning affirmed the importance of ensuring trust to encourage authentic self-disclosure. The reliance on detailed cues may narrow the scope of reflection.

Taken together, social learning theory and critical reflective learning theory offer a coach the role of holding up a mirror and encouraging clients to examine their thoughts, assumptions, beliefs and reactions closely and critically. Fully dialogic coaching incorporates emerging ideas and perspectives to formulate increasingly complex and inclusive frameworks for problem-solving.

Action learning, as presented by Marquardt (1999) integrates experiential and social learning constructs with principles of andragogy. In this framing, action learning comprises parallel processes of problem-solving, experiential learning and transferability of learning to benefit group members and the organization. The model integrates five elements that center on a problem, which is real, important, and meaningful to participants. The action learning group is the core entity in the process and shares a commitment to learning and to taking action. The group engages in iterative cycles of questioning, action, critical reflection and learning. A facilitator helps the group engage in critical reflection as well as filling several managerial functions such as coordinator, catalyst, observer, climate setter, communication enabler, and learning coach.

The action learning process, as framed by O'Neil and Marsick (2014), begins with an action learning consultant and key organizational members co-designing an action learning program. This design addresses the strategic focus, teams, sponsors, projects, learning goals, and developmental needs. The initial design also addresses appropriate learning tools, strategies and length of project. Team or group coaching from an Action Learning perspective fosters the team's ability to engage in on-going learning. This might include cultivating abilities to perceive recurring patterns across contexts, recognize new patterns and generate different responses. Coaches might also foster creative, cross-functional or integrative thinking. While the work of action learning coaches will vary according to the program design, the core task is to create three situations for learning: an environment for learning, specific interventions for learning, and transfer of skills needed for learning. In comparing action learning coaching and executive coaching, O'Neil and Marsick (2014) point to three key differences. When applied in the context of executive, one-to-one professional coaching, action learning coaching involves peer coaching with a team. Executive coaching processes are varied where action learning coaching processes follow a set protocol. Finally, while executive coaching may engage in problem-framing to some degree, the focus is on problem-solving. In action learning coaching, the process entails problem framing and reframing.

TRANSFORMATIVE ADULT LEARNING

Sustainable change emerges from transformative learning. Mezirow (1991) notes, 'the transformative learning process is irreversible once completed. That is, once our understanding is co-clarified and we have committed ourselves fully to taking the action it suggests, we do not regress to levels of less understanding' (p. 152). Transformative learning informs the whole life, requiring an understanding of the epistemological complexities of the current challenge and the ability to shift from the socialized mind to the self-authoring mind. In particular, a cognitive-developmental approach to learning can be useful to adults dealing with the 'hidden curriculum of life' (Kegan, 2000, p. 45). By helping clients critically examine and reconsider their perspectives, coaches can encourage behavioral change in the short term while helping their clients develop more complex, contextually appropriate problem-solving strategies that will serve them in the long term.

The literature of transformative adult learning provides an anchor for the term 'transformation' in coaching. By defining and framing elements of mental models, transformative adult learning theory offers indicators and benchmarks for cognitive shifts effected through coaching. Transformative learning frameworks serve as a complement to behavioral orientations in coaching.

Mezirow (2000) proposes that transformative learning entails objective and subjective reframing of meaning perspectives. Frames of reference or 'meaning perspectives' comprise assumptions, expectations and beliefs, which shape perceptions, cognitions and feelings. Such filters may limit perceptions and interpretations of events and, in turn, inform responses to events. Meaning perspectives are acquired intentionally and unintentionally through individual experiences and implicit or explicit cultural paradigms. Critical reflection on the assumptions of others encountered in a narrative or in task-oriented problem solving constitutes objective reframing. 'Subjective reframing involves critical self-reflection of one's own assumptions about a narrative, a system, an organization, feelings and interpersonal relationships and one's own learning process' (Mezirow, 2000, p. 23).

Personal transformation entails deep structural changes in the way an individual perceives, interprets and responds to events both cognitively and emotionally. Mezirow (2000) describes transformative learning as a 'process by which we transform our taken-for-granted frames of reference (meaning perspectives, habits of mind, mind-sets) to make them more inclusive, discriminating, open, emotionally capable of change and reflective' (p. 7). Kegan (2000) articulates some necessary distinctions to distinguish truly transformative learning from information learning and assimilative processes. According to Kegan (2000), there must be a form to transform – that is, a pre-existing mental model that is transformed as a result of the learning process. Transformative learning changes a way of knowing (an epistemology), not simply behavior.

The epistemological shift includes the whole lifespan and is not limited to formal educational contexts. Kegan (2000) also offers two essentials for adult educators. First, educators must have an understanding of the learner's current epistemologies. Second the educator must understand the epistemological challenges in the learner's current environment. Epistemologies, in Kegan's view, constitute a way of making meaning of inner and outer experiences and a way of re-forming the meaning-making.

Kegan (2000) argues that constructive-developmental theory offers ideas about forms of knowing and the psychological processes of transforming knowing. A 'form of knowing always consists of a temporary equilibrium between the subject and the object in one's knowing' (Kegan, 2000, p. 53). Individuals are subject to thinking and feeling with which they intimately identify. Thinking and feeling which can be viewed, reflected on and controlled becomes 'object.' Constructive-developmental theory looks at the process by which subject becomes object. In the developmental process, what was once 'subject' shifts to 'object,' forming increasingly complex epistemologies. As adults move through the lifespan, they encounter and must cross 'increasingly complex bridges' (Kegan, 2000). Transformative learning can support the required cognitive development by following three principles. First, 'know which bridge we are on' (Kegan, 2000). In Kegan's framework of increasingly complex epistemologies, the least complex adult thinking is situated in what he calls the third order, the socialized mind, which is characterized by a dualistic perspective and discrete categorization. The third order is succeeded by the self-authoring mind, supported by an underlying structure, which is complex and systemic in its view. Kegan's fifth order, the self-transforming mind, has the capacities of trans-system and trans-complex thinking. The first injunction, then, requires being able to determine on which epistemological bridge the learner is standing. The second injunction entails assessing how far along that particular bridge the learner has already progressed. Third, it is essential to ensure the learner is firmly grounded in order to initiate forward momentum.

Two studies provide some insight into the application of Kegan's constructive-developmental approach to coaching. Pinkavova (2010) offers the proposition that Kegan's orders of consciousness can support and inform executive coaching, particularly during organizational transitions. She discusses the stages of consciousness and offers brief anecdotal descriptions of client shift, which she compares to the theoretical framework. Based on her experiences, Pinkavova (2010) concludes that principles of Kegan's orders of consciousness can be useful in fostering clients' understanding of their own preferences and developing capacities to use these effectively.

A more direct application appears in a hypothesis-generating study using the subject–object interview to map cognitive complexity in coaching clients (Garvey-Berger and Atkins, 2009). The working premise of the study was twofold: mapping the client's cognitive complexity would enable the coach to better understand the client, and concomitantly the client might benefit from an understanding of the adult development theories. The researchers specified three goals for the study: to explore participant reactions to the use of adult development theories, to explore the potential for use of the subject–object interview, and to assess potential usefulness and limitations of the interview in a coaching context. The results appear to support the working premise and provide useful data for considering the study goals. The researchers reported a favorable reaction from all participants, citing benefits from the insights gained through the interview process. Participants noted that the process seemed to accelerate access to deeper levels of meaning and material. Some reported that it was helpful to understand the range of complexity of mind and the nature and uses of differing capacities. Garvey-Berger and Atkins (2009) also noted the impact of the process on themselves as coaches. In particular, they report that better understanding their clients' ways of thinking improved their understanding of clients' choices and behaviors and reduced negative judgments. The process also influenced the way they coached, describing the use of adult development theory and the interview process as a form of professional development for themselves.

The subject–object interview protocol may not be applicable or necessary in situations where coaching clients may not need or want more complexity in their way of thinking. Furthermore, learning to use the instrument correctly, administering, and scoring are all time consuming. Nonetheless, Garvey-Berger and Atkins (2009) assert that the use of adult development theory can increase perspective-taking and empathy, and help coaches and clients to better calibrate the coaching agenda and goals to the engagement's potential and limitation. Using the subject–object interview affected the authors' way of asking questions and listening for underlying form and thought structures rather than content.

The subject–object framework may also be applied in the course of reflective learning through a series of dialogic actions. The first of these involves re-engaging with an experience through describing the event using rich description and initial consideration. Re-engagement is followed by holding a dialogue with the description of the event, setting up an objective–subjective tension that considers both rational discernments and feelings. Reflection may involve taking multiple perspectives and considering ethical principles such as autonomy, non-harm and justice. The next stage involves critical reflection: consideration of learned theory, tradition or social norms and the role of each in the meaning making process. A co-created dialogue supports developing and deepening insights leading toward the developing, enacting and evaluating change actions (Johns, 2013).

In coaching, the task of individual transformation involves helping the client learn to articulate, question, and re-evaluate events as defined by others. Through transformative learning, critical thinking and reflection, clients are able to overcome situational, emotional and cognitive constraints and become self-authoring. Both Mezirow (1991) and Johns (2013) consider reflection an 'emancipatory action' that frees an individual from received models and fosters self-authoring. Johns (2013) describes this as movement from 'knowing your place' to being in [the] place 'that grounds desirable and effective practice' (p. 16).

The transformative learning framework includes:

A disorienting dilemma that propels the individual to seek change
A facilitated, critical exploration of interpretations, assumptions, beliefs and values contributing to the disorienting dilemma
An exploration of alternative perspectives and meaning-making
Developing, implementing and evaluating alternative actions
Supported integration and sustainability of new processes. (Mezirow, 2000)

The transformative learning response may arise from contemplation and reflective practice – that is, not only reasoning through the experience, but also reflecting on one's reactions and affirming or innovating an appropriate response. Reflecting on the outcome of experimental actions creates new knowledge based on both cognitive and affective consideration of the experience and the premise on which it was constructed (Jarvis, 2012; Kolb, 1984). In the context of transformative adult learning, deep and critical reflection on experiences entails more than observation; it fosters the emergence of new concepts and meaning-making frameworks that inform the development of further experimentation.

The workplace, in particular, may be considered a prime location for learning through critical reflection on experience with a goal of transforming an individual's mindset (Gray, 2006). Jarvis (2012) suggests there are many processes that may transform knowledge, skills, or attitudes through experience and that the limited term learning 'hides the reality of the complexities of the learning process' (p. 190). Transformative learning occurs in a variety of contexts, which may include coaching. In the complex environment of the workplace, the individual is confronted with a constantly changing set of information, knowledge, requirements, and problems to be resolved. Thus, a function of both adult learning and coaching is to support the individual in gaining contextual understanding, reflect critically on assumptions, and understand the impact of their meaning-making systems on ability to perform responsively. Cognitive maturity entails the ability to reflect on the limits of one's own knowledge and to question the certainty and criteria for that knowledge. Development in adulthood involves cultivating perspectives that are inclusive, differentiated, permeable, and integrated (Mezirow, 1991).

COMMON ELEMENTS IN ADULT LEARNING THEORIES

As the above review suggests, there are a number of frameworks for adult learning. Each addresses some aspect of the interpersonal relationship between learners and their learning facilitators or coaches, as well as defining learning tasks and processes. Some aspects of adult learning theory may be viewed as consistent with the relationship dynamic of coaching as well as suggesting specific coaching tasks and processes. Table 6.1 offers a summary of areas where coaching and adult

Table 6.1 Examples of coaching relationship and process aligned with adult learning

Adult Learning	Quality of Coach/Client Relationship	Power Relationship	Collaborative Learning	Communication	Tools and Techniques
Experiential	• Motivational	• Client self management	• Sense-making • Experience as catalyst • Iterative processes	• Solution oriented	• Styles of learning • Espoused theory • Theory-in-use • Cross-function and integrative thinking
Collaborative and Social	• Extended cognition or alliance • Triadic codetermination	• Learner in a social context • Learner assumes responsibility	• Social learning • Collective agency	• Dialogic	• Reflection • Disorienting dilemmas • Action learning • Learning how to learn • Creative, cross-functional, integrative learning
Transformative	• Co-clarification • Empathetic • Cognitive presence	• Coach–client synergy	• Structural change • Epistemological	• Dialectical	• Objective and subjective reframing • Subject–Object Interview • Critical reflection

learning theories align. 'Attending to this conversational space enables those in the conversation to remain engaged with each other so that differing perspectives can catalyze learning experientially and promote individual learning and organizational learning' (Baker, Jensen, & Kolb, 2005, p. 411).

APPLICATION OF COMMON ELEMENTS TO COACHING

In our view, coaches challenge clients to question assumptions, explore new approaches, and learn from experiences. One of the ways coaches help clients examine and learn in this way is by helping clients consider their mental models and theories-in-action. Clients can gain useful insights by making mental models explicit and considering the frameworks in comparison to a theory-in-use (behaviors). This process of questioning enables clients to develop perspectives, learn from their actions and impacts, and proactively consider possible actions. Ideally, the client develops this 'clinical objectivity,' or, as Kegan (1982, 2003) and Berger (2012) describe it in the context of ego development, a 'subject–object' relationship. In other words, the client develops a capacity to see situations in an objective manner in which defensiveness is lessened, receptivity to experiences is enhanced, and learning occurs.

As the client and coach focus on the client's goals, coaches encourage clients to apply new behaviors and to apply behaviors in new ways. This process of experimentation offers opportunities for reflection by the client and with the coach. From this reflective process, insights can be gained that lead to additional modifications of behaviors and applied in new ways and in different contexts. This process of experimentation, reflection, generalization, and testing illustrates the application of experiential learning through coaching.

The client's role, when aligned with principles of fostering self-efficacy, includes responsibility for determining content, self-assessment of needs, establishment of priorities and determination for actions. The client is encouraged to enact learning through personal agency. Coach and client both engage in an emergent mode of group self-efficacy by responding to each other's learning and to the shifting qualities of the coaching context.

Furthermore, many coaching engagements, particularly executive and organizational coaching are defined in large part by the context in which the client and, often, the coach are embedded. Social cognitive theory introduces a needed degree of complexity in forming these relationships by positioning the coach–client partnership within a larger social framework. While the primary participants themselves constitute a group engaged in a dynamic partnership, Bandura's theoretical framework reinforces the need for coach and client awareness of, and responsiveness to, the broader social context of the engagement.

The adult learning theories that contribute to individual transformation help define the coach–client relationship and support sustainable change. The elements of self-reflection, action and co-learning 'make transformative learning a potentially powerful guide to coaching – and coaching a powerful tool for generating transformative learning' (Gray, 2006, p. 487). The principles of transformative adult learning reinforce the centrality of the adult learner's choice and self-direction. For a client to make meaningful, sustainable change, the coach–client relationship must be grounded in a client-centered partnership. Such relationships are characterized by parity; that is, both partners are viewed as equal contributors, albeit with differing responsibilities.

Transformative adult learning occurs in an environment that is safe, trusting and open, and supports participation, collaboration, exploration, and feedback. The personal and often significant nature of the coaching relationship offers an ideal opportunity for transformative learning (Brookfield, 1995). The coaching partnership may challenge or disrupt the learner's assumptions about self and other.

Coaching aligned with Kolb's experiential learning cycle uses dialogue to explore goals and obstacles, identify actions and apply reflective learning from experience to reformulate change actions. By focusing on key elements of experience, using direct communication and catalytic questions, coaching assist clients to examine experiences critically.

AN INTEGRATIVE ADULT LEARNING APPROACH

Clients arrive at a coaching dialogue with a way of knowing that is based on their prior experiences and learning. Current social contexts such as workplace and community may disrupt existing mental models, which can and should be challenged, as well as supported by, the coach. Coaching helps clients develop new ways of learning, learning how to learn, and learning how to unlearn in order to relearn. We propose a dynamic, multidimensional model for adult learning in coaching that recognizes the dynamics of the client–coach relationship as an individual and social way of learning. Coaching within this framework is characterized by three qualities:

- the coach and client are co-learners
- the purpose is to foster learning from experience in order to generate new ways of perceiving and responding to experience
- the coaching dialogue encompasses both the client's internal experiences and collaborative meaning making.

Andragogy evolved and informed experiential learning. From Baker, Jensen, and Kolb (2005), we see that experiential learning is a dialogic process of client and coach interaction. To support the learning dialogue, the coach and client collaborate to form a learning partnership. Within the partnership, the client assumes the tasks of a self-directed adult learner, identifying objectives, goals, and experiential learning strategies that are meaningful, relevant and immediate for the client. The coach assumes the tasks of reflective learning partner, facilitator, and process-keeper. Together, the coaching dialogue is focused on exploring and extracting insight from the client's past and present experiences as well as from the reflective dynamic of the coaching interaction. As suggested in Garrison's (1997) Practical Inquiry Model, the learning process entails a back and forth exploration between the client's private world, which includes past learning and factors in the present which reinforce existing mental models, and the shared world of discourse and action. New concepts are developed through the interaction of private and shared worlds and these concepts, internalized by the client, result in transformative learning, new and different ways of perceiving and responding to experiences.

PROPOSITIONS FOR FURTHER CONSIDERATION

To highlight the emerging linkage between learning and coaching we have proposed an integrative and dynamic model. However, further exploration is required to fully understand and communicate the potential of focusing coaching as a learning strategy, and the result of doing so. What follows are a few ideas for further consideration in the journey of developing a body of knowledge and evidence to support the practice of coaching as a learning intervention.

Currently, there are numerous studies focused on the behavioral outcomes of coaching (Bozer & Sarros, 2012; Cerni, Curtis, & Colmar, 2010; Moen & Allgood,

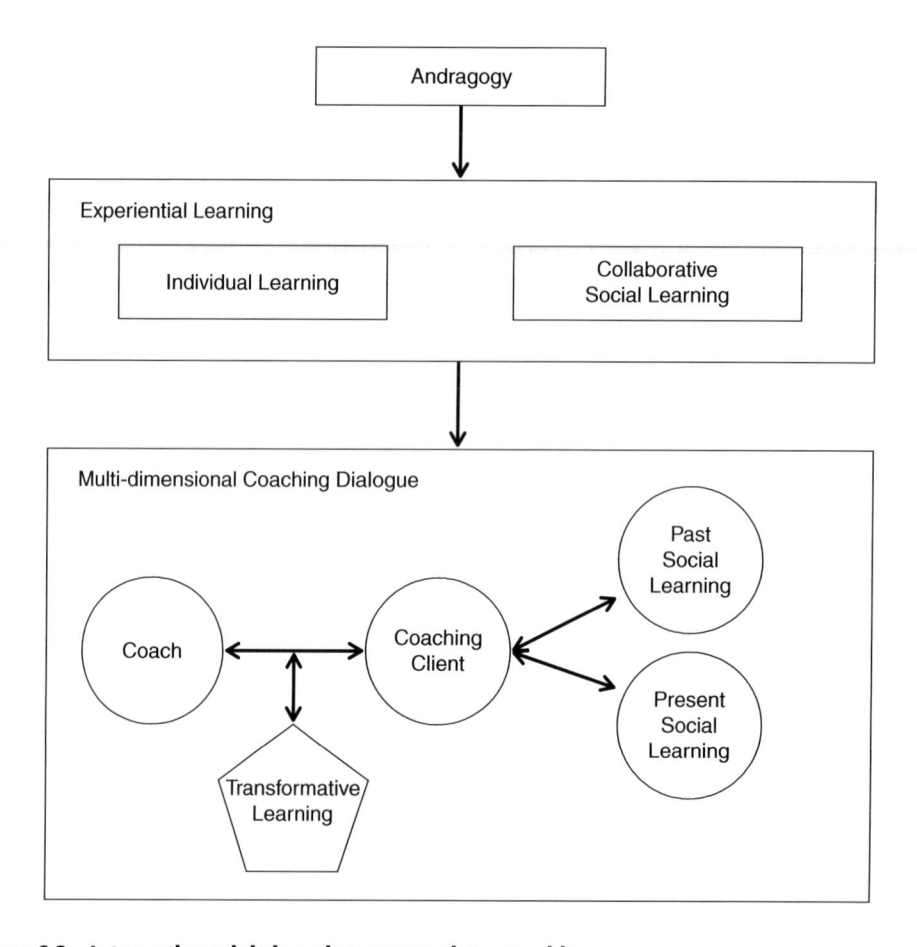

Figure 6.3 Integrative adult learning approach to coaching

2009; Wheeler, 2011). Additional research is needed to understand and document the learning outcomes associated with coaching. Research can be conducted to explore the collaborative and social learning of a coaching engagement through the coach–client relationship, the influence of various social interactions, including the coach and client, as well as the coach, individual client, and organizational client, as applied in the context of work. Notwithstanding Knowles's foundational role in adult learning, recent scholarship suggests that the principles of andragogy originate in an ethnocentric context with a particular emphasis on individualism. Application of the principles of andragogy may require adaptation based on the sociocultural experiences of the learner with respect to autonomy, individual and group identity, relationship to authority, and similar cultural orientations (Baumgartner et al., 2003). As coaching becomes an increasingly global practice, it would be important to further explore the cultural variations of learning theories and their application to coaching. Another potential area of study is to consider the application of each learning approach in the coaching engagement to identify efficacy and impact. Research could be conducted to consider whether and how different learning approaches work in different contexts and with different types of learning agendas, such as coaching focused on performance improvement, development of capabilities, transformation or transition

(Bennett and Bush, 2014). Research should be also conducted to explore an in-depth and broad understanding of learning through the lens of coaching competencies (knowledge, skills and abilities).

REFERENCES

Argyris, C., Putnam, R., & Smith, D. M. (1985). *Action science: Concept, methods, and skills for research and intervention*. San Francisco, CA: Jossey-Bass.

Argyris, C., & Schon, D. A. (1974). *Theory in practice: Increasing professional effectiveness*. San Francisco: Jossey-Bass.

Argyris, C., & Schon, D. A. (1978). *Organizational learning: A theory of action perspective*. Reading, MA: Addison-Wesley.

Baker, A. C., Jensen, P. J., & Kolb, D. A. (2005). Conversation as experiential learning. *Management Learning*, 36(3), 411–427.

Bandura, A. (1986). *Social foundations of thought and action: A social cognitive theory*. Englewood Cliffs, NJ: Prentice-Hall, Inc.

Bandura A. (1989). Human agency in social cognitive theory. *American Psychologist*, 44(9), 1175–1184.

Bandura, A. (2001). Social cognition theory: An agentic perspective. *Annual Review of Psychology*, 52, 1–26.

Bandura A. (2012). On the functional properties of perceived self-efficacy revisited. *Journal of Management*, 38(1), 9–44.

Baumgartner, L. M., Lee, M., Birden, S., & Flowers, F. (2003). Adult learning theory: A primer. Columbus, OH: Center for Education and Training for Employment, Retrieved June 2015 from http://www.cete.org/acve.

Bennett, J. L., & Bush, M. W. (2014). *Coaching for change*. New York, NY: Routledge.

Berger, J. G. (2012). *Changing on the job: Developing leaders for a complex world*. Stanford, CA: Stanford University Press.

Bozer, G., & Sarros, J. C. (2012). Examining the effectiveness of executive coaching on coachees' performance in the Israeli context. *International Journal of Evidence Based Coaching and Mentoring*, 10(1), 14–32.

Brookfield, S. (1995). *Becoming a critically reflective*. San Francisco, CA: Jossey-Bass.

Campone, F. (2015). Executive coaching practices in the adult workplace. In J. Pappas & J. Jerman (eds.), *New Directions for Adult and Continuing Education, no. 148. Transforming adults through coaching* (pp. 59–67). San Francisco, CA: Jossey-Bass.

Cerni, T., Curtis, G. J., & Colmar, S. H. (2010). Executive coaching can enhance transformational leadership. *International Coaching Psychology Review*, 5(1), 81–85.

Cox, E. (2005). Adult learner learning from experience: Using a reflective practice model to support work-based learning. *Reflective Practice*, 6(4), 459–472.

Cox, E. (2013). *Coaching understood: A pragmatic inquiry into the coaching process*. Thousand Oaks, CA: Sage.

Cox, E., Bachkirova, T., & Clutterbuck, D. (2014). Theoretical traditions and coaching genres: Mapping the territory. *Advances in Developing Human Resources*, 16(2), 139–160.

Deci, E. L., & Ryan, R. M. (2000). The 'what' and 'why' of goal pursuits: Human needs and the self-determination of behavior. *Psychological Inquiry*, 11(4), 227–268.

Garrison, D. (1997). Self-directed learning: toward a comprehensive model. *Adult Education Quarterly*, 48(1), 18–33 doi 10.1177/07417169704800103.

Garrison, D. R., Anderson, T., & Archer, W. (2009). Critical thinking, cognitive presence, and computer conferencing in distance education. *American Journal of Distance Education*, 15(1), 7–23.

Garvey-Berger, J., & Atkins, P. W. B. (2009). Mapping complexity of mind: Using the subject–object interview in coaching. *Coaching: An International Journal of Theory, Research & Practice*, 2(1), 23–36.

Gray, D. E. (2006) Executive coaching: Towards a dynamic alliance of psychotherapy and transformative learning process. *Management Learning*, 37(4), 475–497.

Hetzner, S., Heid, H. & Gruber, H. (2012). Change at work and professional learning: How readiness to change, self-determination and personal initiative affect individual learning through reflection. *European Journal of Psychology in Education*, 27, 539–555.

Houle, C. O. (1961). *The inquiring mind.* Madison, WI: The University of Wisconsin Press.

Houle, C. O. (1972) *The design of education.* San Francisco, CA: Jossey Bass.

Jarvis, P. (2012). *Adult learning in the social context.* New York, NY: Routledge.

Jarvis, P., Holford, J., & Griffin, C. (1998). *The theory and practice of learning.* London: Kogan Page Limited.

Johns, C. (2013). *Becoming a reflective practitioner* (4th ed.). Hoboken, NJ: Wiley-Blackwell.

Kegan, R. (1982). *The evolving self: Problem and process in human development.* Cambridge, MA: Harvard University Press.

Kegan, R. (2000). What 'form' transforms? A constructive-developmental approach to transformative learning. In J. Mezirow & Associates (eds.) *Learning as transformation: Critical perspectives on a theory in progress.* (pp. 35–69). San Francisco, CA: Jossey-Bass.

Kegan, R. (2003). *Hidden curriculum of adult life: An adult developmental perspective.* Lecture Series No. 2. Stockholm University, Department of Education. Stockholm.

Knowles, M. (1975). *Self-directed learning: A guide for learners and teachers.* New York, NY: Association Press.

Knowles, M. (1984). *Andragogy in action.* San Francisco, CA: Jossey-Bass.

Knowles, M. S., Holton, E. F., & Swanson, R. A. (2005). *The adult learner: The definitive classic in adult education and human resource development* (6th ed.). Amsterdam: Elsevier.

Kolb, D. A. (1984). *Experiential learning: Experience as the source of learning and development.* Englewood Cliffs, NJ: Prentice-Hall.

Marquardt, M.J. (1999). *Action learning in action: Transforming problems and people for world class organizational learning.* Mountain View, CA: Davies-Black.

Merriam, S. B., & Caffarella, R. S. (1991). *Learning in adulthood: A comprehensive guide.* San Francisco: Jossey-Bass.

Merriam, S. B., Caffarella, R. S., & Baumgartner, L. M. (2007). *Learning in adulthood: A comprehensive guide* (3rd ed.). San Francisco, CA: John Wiley & Sons.

Mezirow, J. (1991). *Transformative adult learning.* San Francisco, CA: Jossey-Bass.

Mezirow, J. (2000). Learning to think like an adult: Core concepts of transformation theory. In J. Mezirow (Ed.), *Learning as Transformation: Critical perspectives on a theory in progress* (pp. 3–33). San Francisco, CA: Jossey-Bass.

Moen, F., & Allgood, E. (2009). Coaching and the effect on self-efficacy. *Organization Development Journal, 27*(4), 69–82.

O'Neil, J., & Marsick, V. J. (2014). Action learning coaching. *Advances in Developing Human Resources, 16*(2) 202–221.

Orenstein, R. L. (2007). *Multidimensional executive coaching.* New York, NY: Springer.

Pinkavova, E. (2010). Keeping our heads above water: Applying Kegan's orders of consciousness theory in coaching. *International Journal of Evidence Based Coaching and Mentoring, 8*(1), 14–21. Retrieved October 2015 from http://ijebcm.brookes.ac.uk/documents/vol08issue1-reflections-02.pdf

Revans, R. W. (1982). *The origin and growth of action learning.* Brickley, UK: Chartwell-Bratt.

Rogers, J. (2012). *Coaching skills: A handbook* (3rd ed.). New York, NY: McGraw-Hill.

Ryan, R. M., Lynch, M. F., Vansteenkiste, M, & Deci, E. L. (2001). Motivation and autonomy in counseling, psychotherapy, and behavior change: A look at theory and practice. *The Counseling Psychologist, 39*(2), 193–260.

Schon, D. A. (1983). *The reflective practitioner: How professionals think in action.* New York, NY: Basic Books.

Schon, D. A. (1987). *Educating the reflective practitioner.* San Francisco, CA: Jossey-Bass.

Smith, M. K. (2001). David A. Kolb on experiential learning. Retrieved from http://www.infed.org/b-explrn.htm

Spence, G. B., & Oades, L. G. (2011). Coaching with self-determination in mind: Using theory to advance evidence-based coaching practice. *International Journal of Evidence Based Coaching & Mentoring, 9*(2), 37–55.

Wheeler, L. (2011). How does the adoption of coaching behaviours by line managers contribute to the achievement of organisational goals? *International Journal of Evidence Based Coaching & Mentoring, 9*(1), 1–15.

Yang, B. (2003). Toward a holistic theory of knowledge and adult learning. *Human Resource Development Review, 2*(2), 106–129.

Coaching and Adult Development

Paul Lawrence

INTRODUCTION

Adult development theories are based on the premise that development is a life-long process, that the ways that people think, feel and make meaning of the world change and evolve over time. There exist many theories as to the nature of this process, most describing a series of stages through which people progress with reference to some dimension of self. If the role of the coach includes being able to identify and facilitate changes in the way that people think and feel, then it behoves coaches to familiarise themselves with adult development theories and to decide how to incorporate that knowledge into their coaching practices. The purpose of this chapter is to provide a high level review of a range of adult development theories and their relevance for academics, researchers and coaching practitioners.

The chapter is divided into four parts; i) a discussion of theory, ii) the presentation and critique of available evidence, iii) contemporary practice challenged through a developmental lens, and iv) issues to consider in integrating adult development theories into coaching practice. In part one a necessarily high level overview of adult development theory is outlined with a particular focus on constructive-developmental theory. Constructive-developmental theory is by no means the only perspective on adult development, but is privileged here since it is the body of work most often referred to in management and leadership literature (McCauley et al., 2006).

In part two the evidence base for adult development theory is reviewed and found to be, as yet, sparse. Despite this lack of evidence advocates of adult development theory argue strongly that coaches should familiarise themselves with the theory and its application. Knowles, Holton and Swanson (2005), for example, suggest that although adult development theories remain largely untested, most people intuitively understand that development continues throughout adult life. They commend anyone working in the adult learning field to develop the capacity to recognise a learner's stage of development and to tailor an intervention accordingly. Kegan (1982) says that to understand anyone in any fundamental way 'you must know where the person is in his or her evolution,' and Laske (1999) claims that the very purpose of coaching is to help people to achieve their full developmental potential. Approaches to coaching based on such strong advocacy of adult development theory have been critiqued not only for lack of evidence, but also for the diagnostic/judgmental role they can imply for the coach, and for the ethical implications that may follow.

In part three adult development theory is positioned as a context against which the limitations of contemporary practice in the fields of coaching, leadership development and the helping professions generally are framed. Finally, in part four, the implications of adult development theory for the practising coach are considered in more detail. Three approaches borne of development theory are reviewed before implications for team/group coaching and professional development are outlined. Part four concludes with suggestions for further research.

ADULT DEVELOPMENT THEORIES DISCUSSED

There are many different types of development theory including psychoanalytic, cognitive, existential, behavioural, ethological and ecological (Santrock, 2006). This chapter focuses on *constructive-developmental* theory because it is the body of work most often referred to in the leadership and coaching literature. Kegan (1980) was the first to coin the phrase 'constructive-developmental', a body of work that has its origins particularly in psychodynamic, existential and cognitive-developmental theories. Kegan (1982) credits Jean Piaget as being the 'central figure' in the evolution of the constructive-developmental tradition. Piaget wrote about 'genetic epistemology', or the development of different ways of knowing in the developing child. He described four stages of cognitive development through which children proceed over the first 11–15 years of life. The process is constructive in that the child is said to actively construct progressively advanced ways of thinking in response to the demands of the environment. Piaget's work was later extended by Kohlberg (1969) who presented a constructive-developmental theory of moral development; by Perry (1970) writing about intellectual development, by King & Kitchener (2004) researching reflective judgment, and of course by Kegan (1982, 1994).

McCauley et al. (2006) listed seven basic propositions of constructive-developmental theory:

1. People actively construct the way they make meaning in the world.
2. People progress through different stages of meaning making and these stages are common to everyone.
3. People progress through these stages in the same invariant order.
4. People don't generally regress to previous ways of meaning making.
5. Later ways of making meaning are more complex than earlier stages.
6. People progress from one way of meaning making to another in response to their environment becoming more complex.
7. The way that people make meaning describes also what they are aware of and therefore what they can describe and act upon.

With reference to the last point, Kegan (1982) articulated constructive-developmental theory in terms of subject–object relations, an ongoing process of differentiation and reintegration. At any stage in a person's development there are aspects of self that they are unaware of that nevertheless shape the way they make meaning of the world. These are the aspects of self to which they are *subject*. There are other aspects of self that the same person is aware of, that they can reflect upon and make choices about. These are the aspects of self that are *object*. Adult development in these terms is an ongoing process in which aspects of self that were previously subject become object. Aspects of self that were previously integral to our sense of self are differentiated and a new sense of self is then re-integrated. This is a dynamic perspective of a developmental process that may continue across the entire life span.

Various developmental theorists describe different aspects of human experience and so cannot be directly compared. McCauley et al. (2006) however, suggested that the theories of Kegan, Torbert and Kohlberg overlap to the extent that three broad successive orders of development may be identified across each; Dependent, Independent and Inter-independent. Table 7.1 builds on their comparison with some additions. First, theories proposed by Loevinger (1976), Cook-Greuter (2005) and Bachkirova (2011) are added. Loevinger (1976) introduced the idea of ego development into the adult development lexicon and her ideas have since been developed further by Torbert (Torbert, Cook-Greuter & Fisher, 2004), Cook-Greuter (2005) and Bachkirova (2011). A particular point of interest in Cook-Greuter's work is her description of counselling styles and how they may differ from stage to stage. Bachkirova's theory is included because of the specific emphasis placed on coaching.

Second, a stage immediately preceding Dependent is included, called here 'Pre-dependent'. Pre-dependent is included because most authors suggest there exists a significant proportion of the adult population that hasn't yet reached the 'Dependent' stage. Colby et al. (1983) suggest that about 15% of adults are still at Kohlberg's Individualism stage at age 20, and that a small proportion of adults still haven't progressed beyond that stage even by the age of 36. Rooke & Torbert (2005) report that 5% of adults are at the Opportunist stage and Kegan (1994) suggests that 13% of the general adult population and 5% of highly educated professionals may not have yet reached the Dependent stage. Whilst the proportion of people at this stage of development may be low, it is important to acknowledge their presence in the workforce. If it is not, then there is a risk that such people end up being labelled, as 'sociopathic' or even 'psychopathic' for example (Kegan 1994), labels that may blind the practitioner to the possibility that such behaviours may in fact be quite 'normal'.

The Pre-dependent stage is called Individualism by Kohlberg (1969), not to be confused with Individualist, the term used by both Torbert and Cook-Greuter to describe a later stage of development. Individualism describes a state in which the individual is able to articulate a personal perspective and to recognise that others have different perspectives. However, the individual may show little interest or capacity for incorporating others' perspectives into his own worldview. The individualist has progressed through dependency to the extent where he is able to disentangle himself once more from an understood sense of others' points of view. The individualist is more empathetic than the Pre-dependent individual, capable of accommodating others' perspectives without becoming enmeshed in them.

As stated earlier, these theories examine different aspects of self, but common themes around dependence, independence and inter-independence may be discerned. The small proportion of adults at the Pre-dependent stage are likely to come across as self-centred, even oblivious to the needs of others. They will likely blame external factors for anything that goes wrong and do not respond well to criticism. Colleagues may become exasperated at their inability to empathise or relate, but this limited capacity to meaningfully engage may not be in any sense pathological. Instead the distance between these people's minds and others' minds is too great for them to experience real empathy. What others think and how they feel is distant, and only relevant if it seems to get in the way of the individual's interests. To ask them to

Table 7.1 Comparison of six constructive-developmental frameworks across four broad orders of development

Framework	Pre-dependent	Dependent			Independent		Inter-independent	
Kohlberg	Individualism	Mutual expectations	Law and order	Social contracts	Universal principles			
Motives for moral action	Concern that others will be nice to me	Anticipation of disapproval from others	Anticipation of failure of duty	Concern to maintain self-respect and respect of the community	Concern about self-condemnation for violating one's own principles			
Definition of 'right'	An equal exchange. Being nice to others means others will be nice to me	Being concerned about other people and their feelings; Being motivated to follow rules and expectations	Upholding social order and maintaining the welfare of the society or group	Upholding the basic rights, values, and legal contracts of society	Guidance by universal ethical principles that all humanity should follow			
Loevinger (1976)	Opportunistic	Conformist	Self aware	Conscientious	Individualistic	Autonomous		Integrated
Theme	Tendency toward self-control	Conforming to social groups and norms	Emergence of self-awareness and self-criticism	Rules internalised. Worried about hurting others rather than breaking rules	Heightened sense of self awareness and concern for emotional independence	Focus on self-fulfilment while recognising emotional interdependence		Fully developed sense of identity and empathy toward others
Relationship to others	Manipulative, protective	Loyal, conforming	Self-aware, deeper interest in relations with others	Responsible, Self-directed	Respectful, tolerant	Interdependent		Broadly empathetic, conciliatory
Kegan	Imperial	Interpersonal/Traditional		Institutional/Modern		Interindividual/Post-modern		
What is object?	Individual points of view	Enduring needs and dispositions		Interpersonal relationships		The autonomous self		
What is subject?	The imperial self	Interpersonal relationships		The autonomous self		The transforming self		

Torbert	Opportunist	Diplomat	Expert	Achiever	Individualist	Strategist	Alchemist
Action logic	Might makes right	Norms rule needs	Craft logic rules norms	System effectiveness rules craft logic	Relativism rules single system	Most valuable principles rule relativism	Deep processes and intersystemic evolution rule principles
Main focus	Winning by whatever means necessary	Socially expected behavior, approval	Expertise, procedure, and efficiency	Delivery of results, effectiveness, success within system	Self in relationship to system; interaction with system	Linking theory and principles with practice, dynamic systems interactions	Interplay of awareness, thought, action, and effects; transforming self and others
Cook-Greuter	Self-defensive	Conformist	Self-conscious	Conscientious	Individualist	Autonomous	Construct-aware
Cognitive style	Concrete and dichotomous	Concrete, aligned with others' expectations	Capable of abstract thought	Starting to appreciate conceptual complexity	More holistic and less linear. Enjoy paradox	Strategic and systemic	Recognition of the limitations of objective, rational thought
Decision making style	This is your problem, not mine	Problems avoided or denied	Listening to others and adding on top	Able to move with conviction. Prepared to take risks and fail	Make room for everyone to express a view	Ability to orchestrate conflicting needs	Adaptable and empowering
Counselling style	–	Advice giving	Fact-finding and advice giving	Greater ability to listen and playback without adding own interpretation	Curious and empathetic	Focus on values and autonomy; becoming the most one can be	Letting others find their own way within their own means and stage of development
Bachkirova		Unformed ego		Formed ego		Reformed ego	
Engagement in action		Reduced sense of control over self and environment. Higher dependency on others for action.		Capacity to take ownership of the past and act independently. 'Mind over body' control of action.		Harmony between mind and body in action. Appreciation of complexity in the relationship between self and environment.	

Sources: McCauley et al. (2006), Loevinger (1976), Kegan (1994), Torbert, Cook-Greuter & Fisher (2004), Cook-Greuter (1985), Bachkirova (2011, 2015), Sandrock (2006)

stand aside from that perspective and to see that perspective alongside others' perspective is to ask them to make meaning of the world differently; it is in effect asking them to *be* something that they are not.

Most adults have progressed at least to the Dependent stage. At this stage people are able to internalize the desires and wishes of others, to which they seek to conform, and are likely to value the structure and safety offered by a group. Group norms are important, and the individual is both sensitive to criticism by others and aware that his own behaviour may trigger anxiety in others, something for which he is likely to feel responsible. People at this stage may appear to lack self-esteem, but to point that out is unlikely to help since they have no independently constructed self. These people are made up of the ideas and beliefs and wishes of those around them. In a corporate environment someone at this stage may present as loyal and compliant, keen to go along with the rules and not let others down. So long as this person is not asked to make an independent decision or to navigate a plethora of mixed beliefs and different opinions, the person may be seen as a content and useful member of the workforce.

Independent adults are no longer as sensitive to the wishes of others; those beliefs and desires are now subject. They are able to analyse others' views and make independent decisions of their own with reference to an internalised set of personal rules and norms. They experience less anxiety at being asked to make a decision that won't please everyone. Like those operating at the Dependent stage, people at this stage can empathise and seek out others views, but they are more likely to show up as autonomous, confident and self-motivated at times of uncertainty and conflict.

A very few adults are 'Inter-independent'. They have learned the limits of their inner system and are curious to explore how others think. People operating at this stage are unlikely to see the world in black and white and are more likely to recognise the commonalities between people and their expressed views. These leaders may be perceived as wise, able to see the 'big picture', and to see connections that others do not. On the other hand, since so few people operate at this level they may be seen as indecisive and overly conceptual by their dependent and independent colleagues, and may ultimately choose to leave the workplace because they find the organizational narrative overly definitive and linear.

These behavioural descriptions could equally be expressed in terms of personality or some other relatively static dimension of self. For example, a tendency to value group norms and expectations might be construed in terms of valuing collaboration, or being risk averse or conflict avoidant. Non-developmental interpretations may lead the coach to advocate strategies that do not make sense to the coachee, strategies based on a way of making meaning that is foreign to the coachee's sense of self. Such approaches may lead to disappointing outcomes and even a breakdown of trust between coach and coachee. Working instead from a developmental perspective the coach is likely to demonstrate more patience with the coachee, recognising the anxieties provoked by the prospect of a transition and the challenging nature of the transition process. The coach may be more likely to balance support and challenge, recognising the significance and sense of assurance proffered by the old way of making meaning.

Having discussed constructive-development theory, as an example of a particular type of adult development theory, the evidence in support of such theories will now be considered.

EVIDENCE AND CRITIQUE

To demonstrate that adults do indeed progress through a series of stages over the course of their lives requires reliable and valid measurement devices. Some of the measurement tools used in the field of leadership and management development are listed in Table 7.2. All of these tools are labour intensive (Bachkirova, 2011, 2014). All require the practitioner to become certified in the tool's use, except the SOI, for which Lahey et al. (2011) have published a user manual. But even the SOI requires 'months of study, practice and conversation' to master (Berger, 2012) and its application requires the transcription and scoring of interviews by multiple raters in order to establish validity and reliability.

The first task of the developmental theorist is to demonstrate that people proceed through a common set of developmental stages over the course of their lifetime with minimal regression. As yet there is scant evidence to definitively support this assertion. Many studies in this area have surveyed a population of people at a particular point in time to illustrate the presence of people operating at the various stages (e.g. Kegan, 1994; Rooke & Torbert, 2005), but such data does not prove that the same people transition through more than one stage. Kegan (1994) reported the results of an incomplete study in which the same people were interviewed on multiple occasions over a nine year period. He suggested that the data provided overwhelming evidence that an increasingly complex way of making meaning unfolds for people over time. Close inspection of the data suggests a less definitive interpretation. In several cases the authors seem unsure how to rate a particular interview, and in six of the 20 cases participant ratings appear to regress from one interview to the next. Furthermore there is as yet limited evidence that the patterns that have emerged apply across different cultures and contexts (e.g. Gilligan, 1992) and some writers have suggested that people may on occasion regress from one stage back to another (Bachkirova, 2011).

There is also as yet a general lack of evidence linking developmental level to managerial effectiveness. Table 7.3 lists the outcomes of several studies conducted using the Subject–Object Interview, most of which use multi-rater survey data as an index of leadership effectiveness. This approach is problematic unless there is some protocol around assessing the level of development of raters as well as those rated. McCauley et al. (2006) report the results of more small scale studies, all completed as part of dissertation work. Those studies provide tantalising evidence that leaders operating at the Dependent level may be less likely to delegate, to make their own decisions, to hold others accountable or to address conflict, than leaders operating at the Independent level, and may be more concerned as to how they are viewed by others. As yet however, few of these

Table 7.2 Constructive-developmental measurement tools

Instrument	Authors	Description
Washington University Sentence Completion Test (WUSCT)	Loevinger & Wessler (1970)	Responses to 36 sentence stems scored by certified raters
Leadership Development Profile (LDP)	Torbert (1987) & Cook-Greuter (2004)	Revised and expanded version of the WUSCT
Reflective Judgment Interview (RJI)	King & Kitchener (2004)	Semi-structured interview scored by certified raters
Subject–Object Interview (SOI)	Lahey et al. (1988)	45–90 minute semi-structured interview
Constructive Developmental Framework (CDF)	Laske (2008a, 2008b)	Three separate assessment tools including the SOI

Table 7.3 Five studies exploring the link between Kegan's orders of consciousness and management effectiveness/motivation

Authors	Study	Tool	Outcome
Harris (2005)	41 executives	SOI + 360 assessment	Superior and peer 360 degree ratings predicted developmental level, subordinate ratings did not.
Eigel & Kuhnert (2005)	21 top executives	SOI	Developmental levels predicted subject matter expert leadership effectiveness ratings and level of seniority.
Bartone et al. (2007)	55 Westpoint cadets over a four year period	SOI + leadership performance indicators	Overall forward trend in psychosocial development over time. Psychosocial development predicted peer, subordinate and supervisor ratings of cadet performance.
Strang & Kuhnert (2009)	67 management executives	SOI + 360 assessment & personality assessment	Subordinate and peer 360 degree ratings predicted developmental level, superior ratings did not.
Bugenhagen & Barbuto (2012)	53 community and educational leaders	SOI + Motivation Sources Inventory	Development linked to instrumental motivation but not to four other sources of motivation.

studies offer compelling evidence. Most include small sample sizes, or focus mainly on the early stages of development.

A Question of Judgment

Aside from a lack of compelling evidence, adult-developmental accounts of coaching have also been criticised on the basis that they appear to be inherently judgmental. Assertions along the lines that all leaders should be operating at least at the Independent stage (Eigel & Kuhnert, 2005) may lead practitioners to assume an expert role, choosing how to intervene on the basis of a judgment as to how developed other people appear to be. This approach is likely to lead to a more directive coaching style in which the coach 'knows best'. Rossiter (1999) suggests that one of the reasons that stage models of development are so popular is that they present practitioners with an easy to follow 'roadmap' to guide their practice and Bachkirova (2014) warns of the seductive properties of such theories. Cox and Jackson (2014) remind us that any developmental model is likely to represent only a partial perspective on adult development and exhort coaches to stay focused on the agenda as defined by the coachee. Kegan (1994) himself advises against becoming too attached to the stages. In his view the first task of the practitioner is not to attempt to shift the individual's way of thinking, but to become a part of that way of thinking in order to understand and support the client. He acknowledges the possibility that an awareness of adult development theory may lead the practitioner to adopt a directive approach, without necessarily being aware of it, and contrasts such an approach with a Rogerian client-centred approach, with its emphasis on listening to understand. People are not the stage, he reminds us, and the stage at which we think a person might be is best regarded only as an indicator. Berger (2012) acknowledges that developmental theory is inherently judgmental, but also points out that everyone holds judgments about many things in life and that those judgments accompany people into every domain of their lives. She argues that the issue is not whether people judge (they do – all the time), but the extent to which the practitioner holds his judgment at arm's length and stays curious.

A Question of Ethics

Other writers have critiqued adult development theories from an ethical standpoint. Rossiter (1999) asks whether it is ethical that the coach enters the coaching room with an intention to assess the coachee's stage of development. Van Diemen Van Thor (2014) carried out Subject–Object Interviews with eight volunteers. Before conducting the interviews she was careful not to provide too much detail as to the 'inner workings' of the instrument. While all eight participants said that they enjoyed the conversation, two of the eight later reported feeling 'taken aback' upon being given more detail as to the nature of the tool and its mechanics. Whilst they had felt the process to be non-directive during the interview itself, upon finding out that the interview was diagnostic they felt quite differently. Van Diemen Van Thor (2014) suggests this is an ethical issue and recommends that the use of tools should be contracted clearly upfront. This issue does not appear to be specific to the use of tools purporting to measure levels of adult development; it applies equally to the use of other instruments, including psychometrics and 360 degree surveys (McCauley & Moxley, 1996).

In summary then, the evidence base for adult development theory is as yet sparse. Such an evidence base is likely to grow only slowly, given the time and resources required to design and implement the kind of longitudinal studies required to test these theories with sufficient rigour. In the meantime there are philosophical and ethical issues arising from a consideration of adult development theories that the coaching community as a whole may be expected to further discuss and debate.

CONTEMPORARY PRACTICE CHALLENGED

Though the evidence base for adult development theories remains underdeveloped, Knowles, Holton and Swanson (2005) suggest that most people intuitively understand that development continues throughout adult life. If this is true then Kegan (1982) may be right in asserting that to understand someone in any fundamental way you must understand their level of development. In this next section contemporary practice in coaching, and the helping professions and leadership development industries generally, are scrutinised through a developmental lens. This analysis raises the possibility that contemporary practice is focused quite narrowly on the transition between Dependent and Independent states and that the needs of other people may be being poorly served, notably those who have not yet reached the Dependent state, and those who have already moved beyond the Independent state.

Words and phrases like 'leading self', 'self awareness' and 'authenticity' feature heavily in both the popular and academic press. The dominant narrative is around the need for leaders to become less reactive and more resilient in the face of ambiguity and conflict. Kouzes and Posner (2002), for example, encourage leaders to clarify their personal values and to explore their 'inner territory'. The discovery of the 'ideal self' is the principal focus of Intentional Change Theory (Boyatzis & McKee, 2005), the ideal self being 'a vision that ignites hope'. Many texts include quotes defining leadership in similar terms. For example:

The privilege of a lifetime is to become who you truly are. – Carl Jung

Only the truth of who you are, if realized, will set you free. – Eckhart Tolle

Seek out that particular mental attribute which makes you feel most deeply and vitally alive, along with which comes the inner voice which says, 'This is the real me,' and when you have found that attitude, follow it. – William James

These kinds of quotes are often cited in leadership programs, many of which are ostensibly about the development of skills required by the autonomous leader seeking to lead change (Stacey, 2012). Some of these writings may reasonably be applied to the transition from Independence to Inter-independence. More often though, the inference appears to be that the goal of the maturing individual is to complete a lifelong journey toward a static and fixed sense of individual self. Less common are explicit accounts of a transition to a more systemic state in which the individual's sense of self is more fluid and transformative, in which the person has come to recognise the significance of interdependency.

The search for authenticity and autonomy may be societal, at least in some western cultures, extending beyond corporate and managerial development. Kegan (1994) illustrates a possible unconscious bias toward Dependent–Independent transition with reference to the work of three famous therapists; Carl Rogers, Fritz Perls and Albert Ellis, all of whom may be seen counselling in the film series *Three Approaches to Psychotherapy*. In the film series each therapist conducts a session with the same client, Gloria, who appears to be Dependent, and each appears to be implicitly or explicitly assuming that their role is to help her to become Independent. For example, Rogers at one point tells Gloria '*It's no damn good to do something that you have not really chosen to do. That is why I am trying to help you find out what your own inner choices are.*' Perls describes his general intention as being to help clients to come to rely on their own resources. Ellis says he wants his client to learn to '*really think for himself.*' Thus framed it might be said that all three therapists took to their sessions a common agenda; helping Gloria transition from Dependence to Independence, regardless of what she may be seeking to gain from counselling. Yalom (2015) tells the story of therapy sessions he conducted with his client Jarod. At one point he confronts Jarod, saying to him; '*I'm struck by your commenting that this is what you think I meant, what I thought. Can you own that yourself? What do you think?*' To which Jarod replies '*Well, it's impossible to answer that is it not, because, if I lack a self, then who or what is the entity that's positing its own nonexistence?*' Yalom is frustrated by this response, but then pleased when Jarod appears to recognize that '... *the centre of one's self-esteem and self-judgement should be within yourself rather than in the mind of another.*'

None of this would matter too much if indeed most adults were functioning somewhere between Dependence and Independence and if their developmental state was directly related to their reason for seeking help. Kegan's (1994) data however suggests that 27% of the population may not yet have attained Dependence, or else may be firmly rooted in Dependence and not yet ready to transition to Independence. His data also suggests that another 40% of people may have already attained Independence or be on their way to Inter-independence. Rooke & Torbert (2005) present a similar picture, categorising just 38% of the population as 'Expert', the action logic immediately preceding Independence. We cannot place too much store on these numbers given that it has been argued previously in this chapter that the evidence base for adult development theory remains underdeveloped. Nevertheless, the analysis alerts us to the possibility that many practitioners may have built their practice models upon a false assumption. This assumption, articulated in the language of constructive-developmental theory, is that all adults are in the process of transitioning from a Dependent state to an Independent state. If such an assumption is widely held then the needs of people operating at other stages of development are unlikely to be met. Furthermore, should such a person express dissatisfaction with their experience of an intervention, they may find themselves labelled as sociopathic, resistant, arrogant or uncooperative, depending on their actual stage of development.

PUTTING THEORY INTO PRACTICE

In this section three aspects of practice are considered: i) the coach working with individuals, ii) the coach working with teams and groups, and iii) the coach working with self. Whilst much of the coaching literature emphasises the dyadic coaching relationship a developmental framework also has implications for the team/group coaching practitioner, some of which are outlined in this section. Adult development theory also has implications for continuing professional development.

Working with Individuals

Adult development theory describes a dynamic ongoing relationship between individuals and their environments. As the demands of these environments change, there come times in people's lives when they find themselves 'in over their heads' (Kegan, 1994). It is at this time particularly that people may present to coaching, framing their predicament in terms that they understand, a narrative that may reveal hidden meaning when viewed through a developmental lens. Helping people transition from one form of meaning making to another may, in such circumstances, be the most valuable contribution a coach can make. This does not imply that the coach must adopt a rigidly diagnostic mindset. Eriksen (2007) reminds us that the notion of a developmental stage remains an idea, as yet an unproven hypothesis, an artifact, a construction. She commends instead a 'soft stage' approach in which coaches remain open to the possibility that meaning making is contextual and in which they hold observations of stage as a 'more or less' tendency to make meaning in certain ways in certain situations. Three such approaches are outlined here.

i) Tailoring the approach to the perceived stage of development

Though Berger (2012) herself says she often uses the SOI she recognises that most coaches do not have time to learn how to use the tool effectively. She suggests instead that coaches practice listening for the meaning making system from which the content of what people say emerges. She suggests that coaches ask questions that help people to 'bump up against' the edges of their understanding and that they listen actively and keep an open mind about the hypotheses that emerge for them. For each of Kegan's transitions Berger and Fitzgerald (2002) and Berger (2012) suggest approaches for the coach to experiment with (Table 7.4).

Table 7.4 Examples of coaching approaches described by Berger and Fitgerald (2002) and Berger (2012)

Transition	Behavioural indicators	Possible approaches
Pre-dependence to Dependence	Aware of own beliefs and feeling, but not yet fully connecting with other's beliefs and feelings. May appear to be motivated solely by own self interest.	Listening without judgement. Inviting the coachee to name the prevailing social norms and consider the consequences of not attending to those norms.
Dependence to Independence	Torn between attending to other's expectations and being guided by a formative self-authored self.	Empathise with a world view in which other's wishes are of paramount importance. Challenging the individual to consider whose voices are most important; external voices or the emerging voice from within.
Independence to Inter-independence	May appear on the one hand certain and autonomous, yet at the same time puzzled that some people are not responding as expected to their strongly held views.	The coachee may appreciate their perspective being validated by a coach, while at the same time being challenged to recognise and question the fallibility of their self-authored system.

This frame is essentially diagnostic and if adhered to rigidly could result in the practitioner persisting dogmatically with an ineffective approach. Used 'loosely' however, the frame may enable the practitioner to be more flexible and adaptable, and to quickly access an approach that works best for the coachee.

ii) Immunity to change

Kegan and Lahey (2001) outlined five steps for helping someone make a transition between orders of consciousness, a methodology they further refined into the 'Immunity to Change' framework (Kegan & Lahey, 2009). Building on the idea that people most often feel stuck when on the brink of transitioning to another stage of development, the Immunity to Change framework enables coach and coachee to reflect upon the nature of the person's 'stuckness'. The coachee may be torn between two commitments, each derived from a different order of thinking. The coach's role is to surface both commitments, only one of which may be immediately apparent, and to help the individual identify some of the implicit assumptions attached to the old commitment that may be holding the person back. Use of the 'Immunity to Change' methodology may help coach and coachee surface new perspectives that the coachee finds useful. The coach isn't required to come up with a judgment as to the coachee's level of development before deciding how to proceed; rather the coachee's possible stage of development emerges from the work. The main limitation of this methodology is that it is not explicitly developmental. Practitioners can work with the framework without acknowledging developmental theory. There is no guidance offered as to how to work with issues once identified.

iii) Coaching according to developmental themes

Bachkirova (2011) argues that developmental theories and measurement tools were never designed with coaching in mind. She writes about the different stages people may progress through in terms of developmental themes; themes that are likely to show up directly in coaching as a consequence of the challenges people experience in their environment. The task of the coach becomes to attend carefully to the presenting theme, which Bachkirova characterizes in terms of ego development, and to adopt whatever approach appears most suited to that challenge (Table 7.5).

This approach is similar to Berger's (2012) approach in that it encourages the practitioner to pay attention to the coachee's likely stage of development and to respond accordingly. For the experienced practitioner, able to access a portfolio of modalities, it goes further in suggesting which modalities may work best in particular circumstances. If verified by future research, such a framework may further enable the coach to work with the coachee in a non-judgmental manner, positioning the choice of modality as the key decision point from which the coach can coach 'as normal'.

What these approaches all have in common is an emphasis on paying attention to the balance between support and challenge. Berger (2012), Kegan (1994), Kegan and Lahey (2001) and Bachkirova (2011, 2012, 2014) all talk of the importance of providing a strong 'holding environment'. From a developmental perspective offering support to someone in their existing way of thinking is as important as challenging the person to change. To leave behind one way of making sense of the world in favour of a new, untested, way of meaning making may be scary. Even small transitions can really 'shake up' the way people see the world (Berger & Fitzgerald, 2002). People may show little inclination to transition unless there is something going on in their life that makes the existing way of doing things uncomfortable. The coachee talking about 'feeling stuck', or 'at their wits end', may be demonstrating a willingness to make a move. Even then a normal response to change is to simultaneously

Table 7.5 Examples of coaching approaches adopted from Bachkirova (2011)

Transition	Challenge	General approach	Particularly useful modalities
Dependence	Learning to stand on one's own two feet. Finding it difficult to disagree with significant people in one's life.	Good parent; providing support and demonstrating patience and trust that the developmental process will happen.	Psychodynamic, cognitive-behavioural, humanist, person-centred.
Independence	Learning to see things from many perspectives. Coming to terms with the realisation that one's way of thinking is not the only way of thinking.	Challenging the coachee not to be satisfied with only one way of thinking. Supporting the coachee in not slipping back.	Cognitive-behavioural, solution-focussed, Gestalt.
Inter-independence	Learning to live with paradox and see through constraints of language. Considering the possibility that there is no such thing as 'self'.	Fellow traveller; helping the coachee explore the existential paradoxes affecting his life.	Existential, narrative, Gestalt.

seek to move on while still clinging on to old ways of doing things.

Working with Groups and Teams

Drath and Palus (1994) question individualistic approaches to leadership development generally, with reference to the social nature of meaning-making. Some change theorists would argue that the meaning-making process is posited squarely as a social process mediated by dialogue, which points to the value of coaching people in a social context (e.g. Weick, Sutcliffe & Obstfeld, 2005; Marshak & Grant, 2008; Thurlow & Mills, 2009; Werkman, 2010). Some writers in the coaching space have similarly questioned whether individual coaching can ever be as impactful as team or group coaching (e.g. Clutterbuck, 2013). At the same time coaching people in groups and teams is recognised to be more complex than coaching individuals and the coach is unlikely to be successful without learning new skills, particularly in learning to identify and work with team dynamics (e.g. Clutterbuck, 2007; Thornton, 2010; Hawkins, 2011).

There exists some preliminary evidence that group work may be a particularly effective means by which to facilitate adult development. Drago-Severson et al. (2001), for example, studied the experience of students in a US community college participating in learning groups. Subjects noticed how participation in these groups not only supported their academic development and provided emotional support, but also how it challenged them to broaden their perspectives. Pre-dependent learners valued the groups as a key informational resource. Dependent learners found a safe and comfortable place to learn from friends and to become more confident. Independent learners enjoyed the sharing of perspectives, which helped them to become more self aware and confident, and to further refine their learning strategies.

The developmental perspective provides a new lens for group coaches to review their practice in the same way that it does individual coaches. Turning once more to the world of therapy, many group therapists structure their practice with reference to the work of Yalom and Leszcz (2005), whose methodologies emphasize providing a space in which people can enhance their understanding of how they are experienced by others.

This kind of approach may function particularly well for people operating in transition from Dependence to Independence but may prove overwhelming for people operating at lower orders (Eriksen, 2007) and disengaging for people operating at the Dependent or higher. To further complicate matters the group/team coach is likely to find himself working with people all operating at different stages of development, further adding to the complexity of managing what happens in the room (Bachkirova, 2014). Adult development theory therefore would seem to have a lot to offer for group/team practitioners as well as those who specialise in individual coaching.

Working with Self

This chapter so far has focussed on the coach looking at the coachee through a developmental lens. However, adult development theories have important implications for coach development and thus for the coaching relationship (e.g. Kuhnert & Lewis, 1987; Laske, 1999, 2008b; Bachkirova, 2011; Berger, 2012). Laske (2008b) writes about the 'black hole' of coaching, a consequence of holding two unexplored assumptions. The first assumption is that the coach and client 'speak the same language', an assumption that may derive from either a Dependent or Independent way of thinking in which it is assumed everyone holds a similar worldview. The second assumption is that coaches are operating from their own values and principles, in other words an assumption that all coaches are operating from at least an Independent way of thinking. Available data on the distribution of stages of development suggest that neither of these assumptions is likely to be true more than 30–50% of the time. The rest of the time coach and coachee will be operating at different developmental stages, and/or the coach may be practising with reference to a model which he does not fully own. This analysis elicits various scenarios: dependent coachees co-creating reactive meaning with dependent coaches; dependent coachees coming to rely on independent coaches; independent coaches labelling pre-dependent coachees sociopathic and resistant to change; independent and inter-independent coaches fostering anxiety in dependent coachees and so on. This presents at least two challenges for the coach. First, being able to recognise his own stage of development and to identify what implications this has in terms of the kinds of approach he/she may be best suited to adapt. Second, creating a psychological distance between oneself and the multitude of coaching institutions, academics, colleagues and clients, all espousing their own rules and norms as to how coaching should be conducted.

The first challenge may be particularly daunting for many coaches. As Jarod put it in Yalom's story – it's hard for a coach to address such a challenge from a more Independent or Inter-independent perspective if he does not have an Independent or Inter-independent perspective to refer from. Furthermore, insofar as coaches may glimpse what their stage of development may be, the prospect that others may believe that this level of development renders them unsuitable to coach may represent a potentially disabling possibility that is most likely to be met with denial. Those comments notwithstanding, Bachkirova (2011) provides suggestions to coaches as to the kinds of skills they may want to focus on and the kind of supervisor they may seek to support them in their development. The onus is on the coach to be developmentally minded and actively engaged in his own developmental process (Bachkirova, 2014). Cook-Greuter (2005) also offers some high level descriptors of counselling styles according to different stages of development, which the coach may use to interpret feedback from coachees, clients and supervisors.

Laske's comments also encourage coaches to reflect upon their coaching models, in particular how they decide what constitutes good practice and how open they are to considering alternative perspectives.

There are many and varied approaches to coaching espoused in the classroom, in books and at standalone presentations and conferences. The Dependent coach may be overly inclined to unquestioningly adopt particular models because of his relationship with the person advocating that approach. So we read occasionally of the concerns of commentators that certain models are faddish and untested, yet very popular. A coach operating from an Independent perspective might be tempted to screen new models against his own beliefs in an attempt to determine which are right, which are wrong, dismissing those that do not fit with his existing beliefs and assumptions. Such an approach may over time lead to clusters and coalitions forming and the erection of artificial boundaries between different coaching models, and indeed between 'coaching' and other forms of intervention. The very notion of the Inter-independent way of thinking may help the industry as whole to become more respectful to itself and to others, more self aware, and less inclined to put walls up between different modalities.

CONCLUSION

Adult development theories present a persuasive argument for the existence of a developmental process that takes place across the entire human lifespan. Though the evidence base is still nascent the general theme underlying many of these theories appears to some to be intuitively sound. The lack of a solid evidence base need not therefore dissuade the interested evidence-based coach from exploring developmental aspects of their coaching practice so long as they do not base their every intervention on an unwavering belief in the sanctity of the model and the diagnostic tools that have grown up around these theories. Such an approach would be presumptuous and, taken to the extreme, does not appear compatible with mainstream definitions of coaching. It appears more akin to consulting models, in which the consultant's role is to diagnose and give advice, or even to a medical model in which the practitioner's role is to diagnose and provide prescription. The most appropriate application of these theories at this time may be to hold them lightly as hypotheses, as points of enquiry. The value of adult development theory in the coaching context is that it offers another perspective, a new point of reference, to further enhance a coach's capacity to develop a deep understanding of his coachees and to initiate interventions that are likely to be both well received and effective. Adult development theory not only challenges coaches to question the mechanics of their practice, but to recognise the significance of their own development and their relationship with their own coaching model and the industry as a whole.

The value of adult development theory should become progressively clear over time as more research is conducted. The existing research base is heavily weighted toward the study of white, wealthy, educated Americans, with just a few studies having been carried out in other cultures/contexts (e.g. Villegas-Reimers, 1996). The list of specific areas for future research in this area is long and may include exploring:

- Connections between different research programs (McCauley et al., 2006) and the core themes that appear common across different theories
- Application of these theories across different cultures, populations and contexts (Strang & Kuhnert, 2009; Bachkirova, 2011)
- What factors trigger the transition process from one stage to another (Eigel & Kuhnert, 2005)
- How to design effective interventions that work best to facilitate that transition (McCauley et al., 2006)
- How to coach teams and groups most effectively from a developmental perspective (Eriksen, 2007)
- The nature of reflection through a developmental lens as practised by people at different levels of development (Merriam, 2004)

- The relationship between leader and follower through a developmental lens (Kuhnert & Lewis, 1987)
- The impact of developmental level on the coach's approach and strategy (Laske, 2008b)
- The development of social systems through an adult developmental lens (McCauley et al., 2006).

REFERENCES

Bachkirova, T. (2011). *Developmental Coaching: Working with the Self*. Open University: Maidenhead, UK.

Bachkirova, T. (2012). Developmental coaching: Developing the Self. In J. Passmore, D. Peterson & T. Ferrer (Eds.), *The Wiley-Blackwell Handbook of the Psychology of Coaching and Mentoring*, pp. 135–154. Wiley-Blackwell: Chichester, UK.

Bachkirova, T. (2014). The Cognitive-Developmental Approach to Coaching. In E. Cox, T. Bachkirova & D. Clutterbuck (Eds.), *The Complete Handbook of Coaching*, 2nd ed., pp. 132–145. Sage: London, UK.

Bachkirova, T. (2015). Developmental coaching: Theory and practice. In R. Wegener, S. Deplazes, M. Hasenbein, H. Künzli, A. Ryter & B. Uebelhardt (Eds.), *Coaching als individuelle Antwort auf gesellschaftliche Herausforderungen*, pp. 224–234. Wiesbaden: Springer VS Research: Wiesbaden.

Bartone, P.T., Snook, S.A., Forsythe, G.B., Lewis, P. & Bullis, R.C. (2007). Psychosocial development and leader performance of military officer cadets, *The Leadership Quarterly*, 18(5), pp. 490–504.

Berger, J.G. (2012). *Changing on the Job: Developing Leaders for a Complex World*. Stanford University Press: Stanford, CA.

Berger, J.G. & Fitzgerald, C. (2002). Leadership and complexity of mind: The role of executive coaching. In C.F. Fitzgerald & J.G. Berger (Eds.), *Executive Coaching: Practices and Perspectives*, pp. 27–58. Davies-Black: Palo Alto, CA.

Boyatzis, R. & McKee, A. (2005). *Resonant Leadership*. Harvard Business School Press: Boston, MA.

Bugenhagen, M.J. & Barbuto, J.E. (2012). Testing the developmental nature of work motivation using Kegan's constructive-development theory. *Journal of Leadership & Organizational Studies*, 19(1), pp. 35–45.

Clutterbuck, D. (2007). *Coaching the Team at Work*. Good News Press: London, UK.

Clutterbuck, D. (2013). Working with emergent goals: A pragmatic approach. In S. David, D. Clutterbuck, & D. Megginson (Eds.), *Beyond Goals: Effective Strategies for Coaching and Mentoring*, pp. 311–326. Aldershot: Gower

Colby, A., Kohlberg, L., Gibbs, J. & Lieberman, M. (1983). A longitudinal study of moral judgment. *Monographs of the Society for Research in Child Development*, 48(1–2, Serial No. 200), pp. 1–96.

Cook-Greuter, S.R. (2004). Making the case for a developmental perspective. *Industrial and Commercial Training*, 36, pp. 275–281.

Cook-Greuter, S.R. (2005). *Ego Development: Nine Levels of Increasing Embrace*. Retrieved from www.cook-greuter.com on 16 October 2015.

Cox, E. & Jackson, P. (2014). Developmental Coaching. In E. Cox, T. Bachkirova & D. Clutterbuck (Eds.), *The Complete Handbook of Coaching*, pp. 217–230. Sage: London, UK.

Drago-Severson, El., Helsing, D., Kegan, R., Popp, N., Broderick, M., & Portnow, K. (2001) The Power of a Cohort and of Collaborative Groups, *Focus on Basics*, 5B, pp. 15–22.

Drath, W. & Palus, C. (1994). *Making Common Sense: Leadership as Meaning-Making in Communities of Practice*. Center for Creative Leadership: Greensboro, NC.

Eigel, K.M. & Kuhnert, K.W. (2005). Authentic development: Leadership development level and executive effectiveness. In W. Gardner, B. Avolio & F. Walumba (Eds.), *Perspectives on Authentic Leadership Development*, pp. 357–385. Elsevier Press: New York.

Eriksen, K. (2007). Counseling the 'imperial' client: Translating Robert Kegan. *Family Journal*, 15(2), pp. 174–182.

Gilligan, C. (1992). *Meeting at the Crossroads: Women's Psychology and Girls' Development*. Harvard University Press: Boston, MA.

Harris, L.S. (2005). *An examination of executive leadership effectiveness using constructive developmental theory*. Unpublished master's thesis, University of Georgia, Athens.

Hawkins, P. (2011). *Leadership Team Coaching*. Routledge: London, UK.

Kegan, R. (1980). Making meaning: The constructive-developmental approach to persons and practice. *The Personnel and Guidance Journal*, 58, pp. 373–380.

Kegan, R. (1982). *The Evolving Self: Problem and Process in Human Development*. Harvard University Press: Cambridge, MA.

Kegan, R. (1994). *In Over Our Heads: The Mental Demands of Modern Life*. Harvard University Press: Cambridge, MA.

Kegan, R. & Lahey, L. (2001). *How the Way We Talk can Change the Way We Work. Seven Languages for Transformation*. Jossey-Bass: San Francisco.

Kegan, R. & Lahey, L. (2009). *Immunity to Change. How to Overcome it and Unlock the Potential in Yourself and Your Organization*. Harvard Business Press: Boston, MA.

King, P.M. & Kitchener, K.S. (2004). Reflective judgment: Theory and research on the development of epistemic assumptions through adulthood. *Educational Psychologist*, 39(1), pp. 5–18.

Knowles, M.S, Holton, E.F. & Swanson, R.A. (2005). *The Adult Learner: The Definitive Classic in Adult Education and Human Resource Development*. Elsevier: Amsterdam.

Kohlberg, L. (1969). *Stages in the Development of Moral Thought and Action*. Holt, Reinhart and Winston: New York.

Kouzes, J.M. & Posner, B.Z. (2002). *The Leadership Challenge*, 3rd ed. Jossey-Bass: California.

Kuhnert, K.W. & Lewis, P. (1987). Transactional and transformational leadership: A constructive/developmental analysis. *Academy of Management Review*, 12, pp. 648–657.

Lahey, L., Souvaine, E., Kegan, R., Goodman, R. & Felix, S. (1988). *A guide to the subject-object interview: Its administration and interpretation*. Harvard University Graduate School of Education Subject–Object Research Group: Cambridge, MA.

Lahey, L., Souvaine, E., Kegan, R., Goodman, R. & Felix, S. (2011). *A Guide to the Subject–Object Interview: Its Administration and Interpretation*. Harvard University Graduate School of Education Subject–Object Research Group: Cambridge, MA.

Laske, O. E. (1999). An integrated model of developmental coaching. *Consulting Psychology Journal: Practice and Research*, 51, pp. 139–159.

Laske, O. (2008a). Mentoring a behavioral coach in thinking developmentally: A dialogue. *International Journal of Evidence Based Coaching and Mentoring*, 6(2), pp. 78–98.

Laske, O.E. (2008b) On the unity of behavioural and developmental perspectives in coaching: A view from the constructive developmental framework. *International Coaching Psychology Review*, 3(2) pp.125–147.

Loevinger, J. (1976) *Ego Development: Conceptions and Theories*. Jossey-Bass: San Francisco, CA.

Loevinger, J. & Wessler, R. (1970). *Measuring Ego Development, vol. 1: Construction of a Sentence Completion Test*. Jossey-Bass: San Francisco, CA.

Marshak, R.M. & Grant, D. (2008) Organizational discourse and new organization development practices. *British Journal of Management*, 19, pp. S7–S19.

McCauley, C.D., Drath, W.H., Palus, C.J., O'Connor, P.M.G. & Baker, B.A., (2006). The use of constructive-developmental theory to advance the understanding of leadership. *The Leadership Quarterly*, 17, pp. 634–653.

McCauley, C.D. & Moxley, R.S. (1996). Developmental 360: How feedback can make managers more effective. *Career Development International*, 1, pp. 15–19.

Merriam, S.B. (2004). The role of cognitive development in Mezirow's transformational learning theory. *Adult Education Quarterly*, 55, pp. 69–70.

Perry, W.G. (1970) *Forms of Intellectual and Ethical Development in the College Years*. Rinehart and Winston: New York.

Rooke, D. & Torbert, W.R. (2005). Seven transformations of leadership. *Harvard Business Review*, 83(4), pp. 66–76.

Rossiter, M. (1999). A narrative approach to development: Implications for adult education. *Adult Education Quarterly*, 50(1), pp. 56–71.

Santrock, J.W. (2006). *Life-Span Development*, 10th ed. McGraw Hill: New York.

Stacey, R. (2012). *Tools and Techniques of Leadership and Management. Meeting the Challenge of Complexity.* Routledge: London and New York.

Strang, S.E. & Kuhnert, K.W. (2009). Personality and Leadership Developmental Levels as predictors of leader performance. *The Leadership Quarterly*, 20(3), pp. 421–433.

Thornton, C. (2010). *Group and Team Coaching*. Routledge: Hove.

Thurlow, A. & Mills, J. (2009). Change, talk and sensemaking. *Journal of Organizational Change Management*, 22(5), pp. 459–479.

Torbert, W.R. (1987). *Managing the Corporate Dream: Restructuring for long-term success*. Dow-Jones-Irwin: Homewood, IL.

Torbert, W., Cook-Greuter, S. & Fisher, D. (2004). *Action Inquiry: The Secret of Timely and Transforming Leadership*. Berret-Koehler: San Francisco, CA.

van Diemen van Thor, F. (2014). Using the 'Autodidact' Subject–Object Interview in coaching: The experience of learning to administer and score the Subject–Object Interview through self-teaching, *International Journal of Evidence Based Coaching & Mentoring*, 8, pp. 9–23.

Villegas-Reimers, E. (1996) Self development of Venezuelan adolescents: A test of Kegan's theory and Subject–Object Interview in another culture. *Journal of Cross-Cultural Psychology*, 27 (1), pp. 25–36.

Weick, K.E, Sutcliffe, K.M. & Obstfeld, D. (2005). Organizing and the process of sensemaking. *Organization Science*, 16(4), pp. 409–421.

Werkman, R (2010) Reinventing organization development: How a sensemaking perspective can enrich OD theories and interventions. *Journal of Change Management*, 10(4), pp. 421–438.

Yalom, I.D. (2015). *Creatures of a Day: And Other Tales of Psychotherapy*. Basic Books: New York.

Yalom, I. D. & Leszcz, M. (2005). *The Theory and Practice of Group Psychotherapy*. Basic Books: New York.

Coaching for Leadership Development

Konstantin Korotov

INTRODUCTION

This chapter discusses the developing discipline of coaching in relation to leadership development in organizations. In the past fifteen years, coaching has been increasingly reported as the type of leadership development intervention that is gaining momentum and popularity (Kampa-Kokesch and Anderson, 2001; Kets de Vries, 2005; Zenger and Stinnet, 2006; Bowles et al. 2007; Schein, 2010; Korotov et al., 2012). At the same time, the academic work on this application of coaching is still in its relatively early stages (Carey et al., 2011), when 'much of the research claims are unsubstantiated by other studies and in this sense may reflect local conditions or populations' (Passmore and Fillery-Travis, 2011: 71). Similarly, although research in various leadership theories has a long history, academic exploration of leadership development has emerged relatively recently, around the turn of the century (Bass, 2008; Day 2000; Day et al., 2014). Leadership development coaching, along with both the fields of coaching and leadership development in general, is clearly one of those areas where the creation of the phenomenon of interest, as well as its proliferation in practice, precede an academic understanding of its dynamics (Argyris, 1969; Hackman and Wageman, 2005).

Building on two still largely separate literatures, coaching and leadership development ones, this chapter aims at outlining the current views on leadership development and leadership development coaching, highlighting important issues in research and practice of coaching, and suggesting opportunities for collaboration between the two fields.

LEADER AND LEADERSHIP DEVELOPMENT

DeRue and Myers (2014: 835) define leadership development as 'the process of preparing individuals and collectives to effectively engage in leading–following interactions.' Leadership development is frequently associated with advancement of managers towards a higher degree of mastery in execution of the leadership roles. Common sense suggests that leadership development should be about helping people be better leaders. However, Boyatzis et al. (2006: 8) state: 'The manner in which we approach the development of leaders is largely dependent on our concept of leadership.' As a result, one of the academic and practical challenges associated with the study and practice of coaching for leadership development is defining what leadership is (or expected to be), and how it should be manifested. The current consensus is that at this stage there are multiple definitions of leadership with which we, both as academics and practitioners, have to live, making sure that we are clear what definition is being used for the purposes of a particular analytic or practical endeavor (Bass, 2008). One of the consequences for the study and practice of leadership development coaching is that due to the possible broad interpretation of the term 'leadership' (Bass, 2008) and a broad taxonomy of theoretical traditions and genres and contexts of coaching (Bachkirova et al., 2010) classification of coaching efforts aimed at leadership development, their comparison, and evaluation of their effectiveness become particularly challenging.

Moreover, evaluation of the plausibility of a particular leadership model and associated methods of helping people develop according to that particular model becomes problematic. Pfeffer (2015: 90) attacks the current leadership development practices (including the work of coaches) by describing them as:

> (1) a well-intentioned, values-laden (2) set of prescriptions – lots of 'should' and 'oughts' – (3) that are mostly not representative of most people in the leadership roles, and (4) are recommendations that are almost certainly not implementable and may be fundamentally misguided.

Although rather extreme in its stance on practical and academic efforts in leadership development, the above evaluation signals to the interested communities the need for more explicit examination of what they do, and acknowledging still existing gaps in practice and research. Reviews of leadership development literatures up to date (Day, 2000; Day et al., 2014; DeRue and Myers, 2014; Kets de Vries and Korotov, 2011) underscore the dualistic nature of organizational efforts to enhance the strength of its leadership cadre: the support provided to individual members of the organization in terms of their capacity to fulfill successfully their leadership roles, and the creation of a well-functioning relationship between those various organizational leaders so that together they can help move their respective organization forward. On the one hand, organizations want to support individuals in their management cadre perform at their best in their leadership functions, taking into account a combination of the specific characteristics of the individual. By supporting a particular person in her or his leadership development they aim at making this individual a better leader. On the other hand, organizations are concerned with making sure that a collection of individual leaders manages to work effectively and efficiently together, leading the organization into the future successfully. In his original discussion of the differences between the two sides of this duality, Day (2000) used two different terms to refer to these organizational efforts: *leader development* (or development of the individual human capital of a particular manager) and *leadership development* (or development of the social capital of the organization, the network of effective links and relationships between managers each carrying her or his own human capital and ready to deploy it within the framework of mutual commitments). While distinguishable in the leadership development academic literature, the terms *leader development* and *leadership development* happen to be used interchangeably by the practitioners, as well as academics beyond the area of leadership development studies.

Dalakoura (2010) explains this insufficient distinction of *leader* and *leadership* development by the fact that most of the published studies looked at leadership as an individual phenomenon. The currently available coaching literature also makes no specific analytic distinction between coaching for *leader* development vs coaching for *leadership* development. Terblanche (2014) raises the point that in general incorporation of relational aspects in an organization into coaching, which, in the opinion of this chapter's author, falls into *leadership* development as opposed to *leader* development, has received little attention in coaching research. It should be noted, however, that the accounts of the practice of coaching are abundant with cases of interventions that are aimed exactly at what leadership literature would classify as *leadership* development. Those are, for example, group/team or individual interventions that help individuals improve working relationships within the management team (Terblanche, 2014), help reach agreement on goals, tasks and mutual expectations (Kets de Vries, 2005), develop support groups (Goldsmith, 2009) or carry out organizational transformation (Oades et al, 2009).

DeRue and Myers (2014) underscore that in modern organizations the advancement of individuals in their leadership capacities and the development of the collective (a group of leaders) are often intertwined and important for effective use of leadership capacity to push the organization forward. Given the strong position leadership development literature takes on the importance of preparation of the 'collectives' for their leadership functions (Day, 2000; Hernez-Broome and Hughes, 2004; Carson et al., 2007; Dalakoura, 2010; Kets de Vries and Korotov, 2011; Day et al., 2014) the voices of authors and practitioners calling for extension of leadership development coaching from helping an individual to helping the collective (e.g. through group coaching) (Kets de Vries, 2005; Kets de Vries et al. 2007; Wageman et.al., 2008; Brown and Grant, 2009; Clutterbuck, 2011) gain visibility. Most of the available leadership coaching literature, however, still focuses on the one-on-one types of interventions, i.e. individual relationships between the executive and the coach within a series of meetings, most likely reflecting on the current reality of prevalence of individual coaching interventions over group ones (Brown and Grant, 2009).

THE PROMISE OF COACHING IN LEADERSHIP DEVELOPMENT

DeRue and Myers (2014) include coaching in their list of elements of leadership development architecture, or 'organizational practices, structures, and cultural factors that influence leadership development process' (p. 845). Frankovelgia and Riddle (2010) write that coaching can be either an intervention in its own right, or an amplifier for other leadership development activities.

While most other leadership development interventions (courses, retreats, readings, experiential learning exercises, etc.) cater to the needs of diverse participants and are largely determined by the provider, leadership development coaching is about individualized treatment of specific issues pertinent to a particular executive in the context of a particular organization (Ely et al., 2010). Coaching potentially offers a higher level of psychological safety than other leadership development practices, and allows for working on an established plan and, if necessary, reacting to the specific developments in the life and work of the coachee. Recent work in leadership development by Day et al. (2009) and Day et al. (2014) posits that leadership development can be explored as unfolding development process starting with parental influence at early age and continuing with acquisition and use of leadership skills. This process is believed to be affected by personality and interpersonal relationships. Should this position be accepted, coaching seems to be particularly suitable for discovery and processing of data about the childhood and youth of the leader, as it provides the necessary boundaries, time, and attention.

Organizations have been involved in various forms of human development activities for a long time, and activities formally targeting leadership growth are a new addition to the repertoire of attempts to make the most of the people at work. Managers are expected to do their job of leading others better, given the increasing complexity of the world organizations have to live and compete in. Hirschhorn (1988) draws attention to the social defense nature of organizational efforts in human development. Since managerial challenges are closely connected with interpersonal issues, they generate anxiety. Traditional management training courses, including those dedicated to the topic of leadership, often shy away from exploration of these deeper-lying and anxiety-provoking issues by offering participants models, instruments, tools, and techniques that offer executives a promise of future control over anxiety-provoking situations. In Hirschhorn's (1988: 107) terms, most of management training 'offers defensive techniques, and it functions itself as a mechanism for containing anxiety by in fact denying it.'

Teaching managers techniques may be viewed as providing them with what Winnicott (1982) calls 'transitional objects', an analogy with a teddy-bear that helps a baby in the process of separation from the mother. Transitional objects help to move gradually from the state of dependency to independence. Hirschhorn (1988) describes the process of using transitional objects (e.g. management techniques and tools) in the process of management development as consisting of four phases. First, authority is attributed to the tool by the management program participant on the basis of identification with the source of the tool. Second, the participant starts using the technique which gives her or him personal authority on the basis of the authority of the method. Third, the manager increases her or his flexibility with using the technique, gradually starting to interact with the world on the basis of her or his own authority. Finally, in the fourth stage, the manager internalizes the method learned in a manner that is most suitable to her or him, and through that she or he achieves differentiation from the initial source of the method (e.g. consultant, trainer, business school professor or coach).

Given the anxiety-provoking nature of leadership development, it is not surprising that organizations and participants expect the providers to offer them acceptable social defense mechanisms (although certainly not under such a label). That may lead to the expectation that the professionals involved in leadership development (faculty, consultants, and coaches) should be able to offer the participants a set of tools that can be applied almost immediately, virtually right after the session. Often this perceived immediate applicability of tools learned during a leadership development intervention serves as a basis for subjective evaluation of the intervention (Korotov, 2007; Florent-Treacy, 2009; Kets de Vries and Korotov, 2011). Coaching, unlike many other formats used in leadership development, is most likely to follow the participant's progression through all of the stages identified by Hirschhorn (1988). This gives the method a potential to expand its legitimacy and power in organizations, but also puts on the practitioners and researchers additional responsibility for further explanation of the mechanisms through which it works, boundary conditions for its effectiveness, and synergy effects with other human development methods.

DEFINING AND DESCRIBING LEADERSHIP DEVELOPMENT COACHING

Leadership development coaching is seen in leadership development literature as a professional intervention where a coach supports a coachee in becoming a more effective leader (Ely et al., 2010). Many authors incorporate leadership development coaching into a broader category of executive coaching, where the latter in general is seen as a leadership development process (Stern, 2004) or simply position it as a helping relationship aiming at improvement of the coachee's performance and satisfaction (Boyce et. al., 2010).

Some authors prefer to describe coaching for leadership development by listing the benefits expected from the use of coaching in leadership development. Thus, Passmore (2015) suggests the following benefits of coaching for the purposes of leadership development: (1) transference of knowledge; (2) skill enhancement; (3) increased self-awareness; (4) enhanced motivation; (5) increase in personal confidence and self-regard; and (6) improvement of well-being. Kombarkaran et al. (2008) suggest that leadership coaching is about helping executives do better with people management, relationships with managers, goal setting and prioritization, engagement and productivity, and dialogue and communication. Practitioners also prefer to describe leadership development coaching as a set of activities or interventions. Thus the Center for Creative Leadership talks about the process of enlisting stakeholders, analyzing assessment results to explore strengths and developmental areas, and creating a personalized coaching plan to help the executive progress (CCL, 2015).

Interestingly, leadership development literature that has been mostly developing apart from the coaching psychology literature (Kemp, 2009), does not provide a specific definition of leadership development coaching either, with the only exception being the above-mentioned Ely et al. (2010). Boyatzis et al. (2006) observe that the title of coach subsumes a variety of types of relationships between the leaders in development and individuals who help them along the way. This observation reflects the current state of the field: everyone seems to accept that the coach helps the coachee become a better leader. It is also widely understood that within the context of organizations, coaching for leadership development is part of the set of methods arranged and paid for by the organization employing the coachee who is involved in a formalized leadership development program.

Coaching activities currently put together under the broad umbrella of coaching for leadership development vary significantly in terms of their foci. Hawkins and Smith (2006) talk about a continuum of coaching types: skills, performance, developmental and transformational. Skills coaching is about developing lacking competencies. In the context of leadership development, examples may be providing feedback to the team, delivering negative news, or managing conflict. Performance coaching helps the coachee apply a variety of competencies to a professional role. Examples include taking over a new department, launching and executing a project involving various people, or carrying out a post-merger integration task. Developmental coaching, which Bachkirova (2013) argues should not be treated distinctly from the transformational coaching, is about helping the coachee expand their capacity and develop as a human being. The developmental genre in coaching (Garvey Berger and Atkins, 2009; Cox and Jackson, 2010; Bachkirova, 2011, 2013; Garvey Berger, 2012) is based on adult development theories, a set of various theories that deal with stages in human development and changes in the individual's view of self and the environment. These theories suggest that there are different levels of psychological development, or guiding structures for understanding self and environment, and those levels build upon one another. The change to the next, more elaborated level happens during the so called developmental movement triggered by changes in the environment or other individuals (McCauley et al., 2006; Bachkirova, 2011, 2013; Day et al., 2014). Interestingly, leadership development literature and coaching literature are starting developing interest in the application of adult development theories to their respective fields independently of one another, and both are still in early stages of progress. Garvey Berger and Atkins (2009), Garvey Berger (2012), and MacKie (2015) are the few examples describing the application of the developmental genre to leadership development.

PERSPECTIVES AND MODELS IN LEADERSHIP DEVELOPMENT COACHING

A recent review of leadership coaching (Passmore, 2015) offers a broad collection of diverse models and perspectives used by coaches in their practice. The chapters in this volume offer a number of frameworks that vary significantly in the degree of their embeddedness in theoretical traditions. Some of them show a clear connection with previous work in the areas of psychology (e.g. psychodynamic tradition, emotional intelligence, positive psychology) or leadership studies (e.g. transformational and transactional leadership, situational leadership). Others draw on anthropological observations or cultural traditions (e.g. African myths and stories), or rethinking of application of historic texts (e.g. military tractates). Still others represent an attempt to build a proprietary model or theory based on reflections about their authors' own practice, or simply describe the coaches' experience of using an existing model from elsewhere (e.g. team roles model by Belbin, 1981).

Stokes and Jolly (2010) write about leadership coaching approaches, which they view as a part of executive coaching, as most commonly based on the psychodynamic, cognitive-behavioural, transactional, and existential approaches. These authors, at the same time, acknowledge a variety of other possible theoretical traditions described in Cox et al. (2010) that can inform leadership coaching practice, such as cognitive-behavioural, solution-focused, person-centred, gestalt, existential, ontological, narrative, cognitive-developmental, transpersonal, positive psychology, and NLP.

Denzin and Lincoln (2000) brought the concept of bricolage into social sciences, and the current practice of leadership development coaching resembles this approach. Bricolage is about looking at the phenomena of interest in an interdisciplinary manner, employing a variety of methodological approaches as those get called for by the unfolding situation (Kincheloe, 2005). An acclaimed coaching guru once mentioned to the author of this chapter: 'I do whatever helps the coachee in the specific situation.' Bricolage as coaching practice embraces the complexity of leadership development, offering the often needed flexibility. However, as a method of inquiry in social sciences it certainly represents significant challenges in terms of academic rigor and acceptance by the academic community (Kincheloe, 2001).

WHAT HAPPENS INSIDE LEADERSHIP COACHING SESSIONS

Whilst much is known about the content of most of the leadership development interventions (e.g. programs, readings, simulations, online learning modules, action learning, etc.) (e.g. Snook et al., 2012), what happens inside coaching is much less known. For example, previous meta-exploration of analytic studies of the management development literature by Collins and Holton (2004) covering the period of 1982–2001 failed to identify sufficient coaching studies to analyze. In addition, a recent review by Carey et al. (2011) suggests that very few of the available published leadership coaching papers allow to identify what actually happens in leadership coaching sessions. Having started with a search that identified over 1,400 papers related to leadership coaching Carey et al. (2011) ended up analyzing only ten papers that possessed enough information about the coaching process to satisfy the inclusion criteria for the study. From this small subset of studies it was concluded that leadership development coaching interventions seem to involve a mixture of relationship building, problem defining, problem solving, and management of the transformation process (e.g. mobilization for action).

Since coaching by definition is a confidential intervention, and, in most cases, an individualized one, it is not surprising that the actual treatment that participants receive in their sessions varies significantly (e.g. Hall et al., 1999; Kets de Vries et al., 2007; Korotov et al., 2012; Korotov, 2013). In fact, attempts to explore the coaches' challenges in running their sessions (Korotov et al., 2012) suggest that there is a great variety of activities coaches engage in, with some of them being far away from the descriptions of traditional coaching genres. For example, coaches may engage in teaching (e.g. sharing with the coachee a theoretical finding or a leadership model), advice giving, sharing other people's practices, or offering their own lessons from non-coaching activities (e.g. from their executive or leadership experience). For example, Bowles et al. (2007) report that in their study coaching involved providing expertise and sharing information. With this variety of activities offered within the intervention, it is difficult to compare the effects of coaching on leadership effectiveness, as it is virtually impossible to guarantee that the treatment received by subjects in the published studies was actually the same. Moreover, a number of the activities happening during coaching interventions would be classified by some authors (e.g. Feldman and Lankau, 2005) as different from what they would call coaching.

A review by Carey et al. (2011) identified three major types of coaching approaches reported in recent literature dealing with leadership or management development in business or healthcare sectors: the consultant approach, the counseling approach, and the organizational input-based approach. The consulting approach is described as being focused on a task, involving structure, and using concrete action plans. The counseling approach is described as a less defined process of exploring behaviors and feelings. The organizational input-based approach is described as the coaching process that is expected to follow organizational requirements regarding leadership factors to be used in the intervention. It should be noted that the accepted definitions of coaching genres (Bachkirova et al., 2010) can easily fit any of Carey et al.'s (2011) coaching approaches. Carey et al. (2011) state that the appropriateness of each of these approaches depends on the needs of the organization and specific executive, however, they stop short of elaborating on the criteria for such matching.

It is not difficult, however, to hypothesize in which instances each of the approaches suggested by Carey et al. (2011) could be best applicable. For example, the consulting approach could be used with practicing of specific models, tools, or behaviors that the coachee needs to add to her or his repertoire or to change. Running effective meetings, delivering bad news, or meeting the needs of the followers in case of organizational uncertainty may be some of the examples where such an approach could be used. Goff et al. (2014) conduct a randomized experiment to explore the impact that coaching has on leadership behaviors of school principals. In a sample of 52, half of the subjects receive followers' feedback on their leadership behavior, while the other half receives both feedback and coaching. While feedback alone is reported to be unlikely to lead to behavioral change, coaching helps make sense of feedback and translate it into behaviors.

What Carey et al. (2011) refer to as the counseling approach might be appropriate for situations where motivation to lead, or employee willingness to engage in leadership development and leadership activities (Chan and Drasgow, 2001; Guillen et al., 2015) is important. The broad category of the counselling approach to leadership development coaching seems compatible with the authentic leader and leadership development stream in leadership literature (Day and Harrison, 2007). This stream talks about development based on gaining self-awareness and establishing trusting relationships with others (Avolio and Gardner, 2005), gaining legitimacy to promote a set of values on behalf of the followers (Eagly, 2005), or considering multiple sides and perspectives on an issue while gathering and processing information in a balanced manner (Ilies et al., 2005).

The organizational-input approach may be applicable when the coach is to help the leader make sense of the organizational leadership practices or specific instruments used within that organization. For example, Anna et al. (2001) studied executive coaching by proxy as leadership development tool. The paper is a case-study of a large, geographically dispersed organization that implemented coaching in helping managers make sense from organization climate surveys, provide feedback to organizational members, plan action based on the results of the survey, and implement the plan. The task of the coaches was not to be consultants or action plan designers to managers but to encourage and support managers in working with the survey results on their own.

Given the bricolage nature of coaching interventions, it is unrealistic to expect a 'pure' version of a particular approach or genre in a leadership coaching intervention. Moreover, with growing trust with the coach and the coaching process, the coachee might start realizing that her or his issues may have deeper roots and additional connections that may need to be explored in order to achieve the best possible resolution of a problem or usage of an opportunity (e.g. Florent-Treacy, 2009; Korotov et al., 2012).

While the processes and developments during the coaching interventions vary and are difficult to compare, we know certain things about their early stages. Most of the leadership coaching interventions reported in literature involve some sort of formal assessment (often using multi-rater tools), with making sense of the assessment data being one of the foundations for the coaching process. Coaches present the assessment feedback provided by followers, peers, and superiors, help the leader objectively interpret the data, evaluate the consequences of reacting or non-reacting to the feedback results, and make plans about possible behavioral changes that, based on the feedback, could support the leader in her or his developmental process (Thach, 2002; Goff et al., 2014). Coaching facilitates the resolution of the dissonance between the picture reflected in the feedback and the self-held beliefs or the expected normative image of a leader in the organization, thus, arguably, supporting leadership development (Goff et al., 2014). In a similar manner, coaching may use results of the coachee's performance during a formalized assessment center to help develop awareness of the discrepancy between the current state of the coachee's leadership competences and the desired future state, for example, organizational expectations of a leader. Analysis of assessment results as a starting point for coaching work allows for a subsequent post-intervention evaluation and comparison of results (e.g. MacKie, 2015). Clearly, an assessment is based on a set of assumptions of what constitutes good leadership within a particular organization or a hypothetically comparable group of individuals (e.g. senior managers or aspiring young leaders). The above-mentioned challenges of picking a 'right' leadership theory apply.

McCormik and Burch (2008) suggest an alternative approach as a starting point for leadership development coaching. The leader's behavioral change and development are expected to start with administration and interpretation of a personality profile of the coachee, for example, the Big Five (Costa and McRae, 1992) or Personality Audit (Kets de Vries et al., 2006). Practitioner accounts of coaching practice suggests broad use of popular and less demanding for the coach psychological instruments, such as MBTI (e.g. Truskie, 2011) or Belbin's (1981) Team Roles Model (Tomlinson and Naughton, 2015). While personality may be one of the least malleable human features, understanding of one's drives and needs is believed to make it easier for an executive to understand the potential hindrances and accelerators on her or his leadership development path.

In some instances, coaching for leadership development purposes may be a part of or a follow-up element in a formal classroom type leadership development program, where the role of the coaching intervention is personalization of the learning taking place in the classroom (Kets de Vries and Korotov, 2007, 2011). The coaching element is included in the overall program design or offered as a follow-up activity and is often based on the agenda inspired by the class-room experience. In line with Hirschhorn (1988), the offer of coaching to a manager participating in a leadership program may in itself play a role of a transitional object in Winnicott's (1982) terms. The outcome of these types of sessions are usually action plans and subjective willingness of the coachee to implement them (Kets de Vries et al., 2007).

Bachkirova (2013) describing developmental coaching (although not specifically referring to coaching for leadership development), an approach grounded in adult development theories, suggests that the coaching engagement starts with the exploration of the coachee's needs, situation, and goals, not unlike with other genres of coaching. While working on issues important to the coachee, the coach, however, gets into the exploration of the developmental theme, eventually aiming at broadening human capacities and supporting the coachee in her or his development as a whole person. The coach might use some of the published instruments for diagnosing the stage of development of the coachee (e.g. Lahey et.al., 1988; Garvey Berger and Atkins, 2009). Bachkirova (2013) and Garvey Berger and Atkins (2009) argue, however, that the use of such instruments requires long training and is labor intensive.

The difference in starting points for coaching interventions and the different degree of complexity of tools used indicates the clear challenge in treating coaching for leadership development as a homogenous process, making comparison between various approaches and evaluation of their effectiveness especially challenging, if not impossible.

THE COACHEE AND THE LEADERSHIP DEVELOPMENT COACHING

While coaching (e.g. Franklin, 2005) and leadership development (e.g. Avolio et al., 2010) literatures acknowledge the need for certain level of readiness for the organization-sponsored developmental efforts to be successful, there seems to be little agreement regarding coachee pre-requisites for effective leadership development through coaching. Thus, the review by Carey et al. (2011) has identified, on the one hand, papers that claim that leadership coaching would be beneficial to everyone, and, on the other hand, papers that suggest that coaching should be recommended only for high functioning individuals, people who are valuable to the organization and motivated enough to progress, or to those who may derail. Goff et al. (2014) specifically underline that leadership coaching in private sector organizations may be provided to individuals who have the necessary motivation and potential, and it is not so clear whether it will be as effective when provided to individuals who struggle with their leadership roles or who are new to them.

Kilburg (2000) and Bowles et al. (2007) underline the importance of the coachee's buy-in for the effectiveness of coaching interventions. Korotov et al. (2012) provide cases of coachee unwillingness to be coached leading to termination of coaching engagement or simple no-shows for appointments. A study by Millard and Korotov (2014) suggests that mental health stigma that is sometimes present in coachee's view of coaching as some form of psychological help, may affect willingness to engage actively in the coaching process.

With the current interest in leadership development literature towards individual trajectories in development (Smith, 2009; Day et al., 2014) and towards developmental approach to coaching in coaching literature (Cox et. al., 2010, Garvey Berger, 2012, Bachkirova, 2013), the question of readiness (for coaching and for leadership development) may be a fruitful area for joining forces between the coaching and leadership development researchers. Developmental theories have attracted the attention of leadership development researchers, although the findings so far are mixed with regard to the higher level of development being a predictor of higher leadership effectiveness (McCauley et al., 2006; Bartone et al., 2007). With the call for exploration of ways of using developmental markers for evaluation of leadership development effects in general (Day et al., 2014), a further look into the coachee and her or his individual developmental progress, possibly with different starting points in terms of readiness for leadership development in general or leadership development coaching in particular is needed.

LEADERSHIP DEVELOPMENT COACHES

The studies that report leadership coaching interventions vary significantly in terms of the types of coaches that deliver the intervention. Surprisingly little is known about the differences among the coaches involved in leadership development. While the review by Carey et al. (2011) mentions that a choice of the wrong coach is one of the obstacles to effective coaching, the current literature offers little in terms of specific coach attributes required for success in leadership interventions. Ely et al. (2010) building on Ting and Hart (2004) claim that for a successful leadership development coaching intervention the relationship between the coachee and the coach needs to be characterized by rapport, collaboration, commitment, trust and confidentiality, the relational qualities that most likely apply to any type of coaching or other type of professional help.

Feldman and Lankau (2005) identified contradicting findings in coaching literature in terms of the credentials and perceptions of executive coaches, in particular with regard to their training in psychology. It should be noted that the leadership development literature also shies away from exploring the prerequisites for providers of leadership development interventions, although some acknowledgment has been made to the fact that helping people grow and change in preparation for higher levels of leadership responsibilities may be different from offering, for example, traditional educational services (Kets de Vries and Korotov, 2007, 2011).

While some of the pros and cons of external and internal coaches for leadership development have been discussed (e.g. Korotov, 2010), little attention is given to potential effect of the differences between the internal and external coaches' training, previous background, or underlying coaching models, genres, or philosophies. For example, Goff et al. (2014) report an intervention where coaches are former school administrators with some coaching training. Hall et al. (1999) explicitly call for training HR managers or other internal organizational members in coaching skills as a response to a cost concern related to use of external coaches. The way such development is implemented in various organizations differs significantly. Thus, Anna et al. (2001) report a two-day training program for managers to act as coaches facilitating leadership development through interpretation of internal survey feedback results.

The study by Bowles et al. (2007) involves coaches who are more experienced senior US military recruitment leaders compared to their respective coachees, who are also military personnel. In this study, the coaches established the goals for their coachees based on their personal experience and later evaluated achievement of those goals. Bowles et al. (2007: 395) claim that the 'coaches had substantial senior leadership experience in recruiting. This experience translated into effective coaching skills, which helped to encourage participant buy-in, convincing participants of the need and benefits of the coaching process.' While as further claimed by the authors the organizational experience of the coaches led to legitimacy of the coaches in the eyes of the coachees, it is not clear how previous practical leadership experience translates into coaching effectiveness. Truijen and Woerkom (2008) mention the risk of internal coaching turning into mentoring. At the same time, McNally and Lukens (2006) provide an account of effective collaboration of an external and internal coach in a leadership development program. It seems that many practitioners (including business leaders) often believe that their experience can relatively easily get translated into coaching abilities (e.g. Kets de Vries et al., 2007, 2010; Korotov et. al., 2012).

Carey et al. (2011) notice that senior leaders, particularly in business settings, prefer to work with external coaches. One of the possible explanations is that the external coaching offers the necessary psychological safety for the respective executive, and helps the internal organizational members avoid the anxiety associated with knowing about the developmental pains experienced by the top executive. Another explanation is that the duality of the role of the internal coach (being the employee of the organization and the top manager's partner in growth) may be contradictory and uncomfortable for the parties involved. The studies of leadership development coaching in the healthcare industry (e.g., Fielden et al., 2009), however, often report the use of internal coaches, which may be explained by the structural constraints (e.g. leadership development funding) in this industry.

Executive coaches have been reported to benefit from having business experience (Feldman and Lankau, 2005). An interesting question arises, to what extent individuals involved in leadership development coaching need to have prior leadership experience themselves. Would it be more attractive to an organization or to a particular coachee to work with a coach who used to be a business leader her- or himself? To what extent would the implicit leadership theories (e.g., Schyns et al., 2011) or schemas held by such a coach about what constitutes good leadership potentially interfere with the process of leadership development coaching? It is not uncommon to meet coaches who, for example, believe that through their work they can and should impart certain values and thus make the world better, or those who believe that their leadership or executive experience is worth sharing. Obviously, an exploration of potential impact of the coach's implicit leadership theories on her or his ability to act as an effective leadership development agent may become an important new investigation opportunity. An additional question arises if there would be a difference if the coach is perceived a successful former leader as opposed to someone who has struggled in her or his leadership practice.

GROUP LEADERSHIP DEVELOPMENT COACHING

While most of the reports on leadership development coaching concern individual coaching interventions, Kets de Vries (2005) has been arguing for the power of group leadership coaching interventions for the purposes of development. In fact, one of the leadership development challenges is the difficulty of transferring the learnings into daily operations, particularly under conditions of resistance on the part of the organization, lack of motivation to question established norms, and fear to apply the cognitive learning from leadership development program. A solution proposed by leadership development literature is designing leadership interventions for groups from the same organization (e.g. DeRue and Myers, 2014). Bilhuber Galli and Müller-Stewens (2012) suggest that for leadership development efforts to translate into development of the social capital in the organizations, managers should be engaged in developmental efforts in the same constellation in which they work or should work together. These authors also acknowledge the potential of leadership development coaching in enhancing managers' self-reflection on business collaboration and, consequently, affecting positively the development of the social capital. While the paper of Bilhuber Galli and Müller-Stewens (2012) doesn't directly consider group leadership development coaching for managers who need to work together, their work resonates well with the call for an increased use of leadership coaching interventions for intact teams (Britton, 2010; Diedrich, 2001; Kets de Vries, 2005; Kets de Vries and Korotov, 2011; Ward, 2008). There may be a good opportunity to explore further the role this coaching approach plays in either serving as a 'triggering effect' (Avolio and Hannah, 2008) for *leader* and/or *leadership* development, or as an enabler for implementation of the leadership learning in daily organizational life. Brown and Grant (2009) suggest that goal-focused group coaching has high underutilized potential for steering organizational change and offer an extension of the GROW model for application to group coaching.

With an increase in interest towards emergence and development of collective leadership structures where group dynamics and interactional processes seem to play a more prominent role than individual leadership attributes of its member (Day et al., 2004; Carson et al., 2007), further attention is warranted to the theorizing and practice of group leadership development coaching.

EVALUATION OF LEADERSHIP COACHING INTERVENTIONS

Both organizations, coachees and coaches, argue Ely et.al. (2010), should benefit strongly from evaluating leadership coaching interventions. Evaluations can serve as support and evidence of effort and progress for the coachee, identification of improvement opportunities and enhancement of the portfolio for the coach, and input for return on investment calculation and leadership development strategy adjustments for organizations. Still, evaluation of any leadership development efforts in organizations has been a challenge (Day, 2014), and so is the assessment of effectiveness of leadership development coaching (Feldman and Lankau, 2005; Joo, 2005; Ely et al., 2010). DeRue and Myers (2014) identified the following categories of outcomes of leadership development interventions in the existing literature: behavioral, affective/motivational, and cognitive. At the same time, Day et al. (2014) claim that the choice of relevant outcome variables for evaluation of leadership development efforts is still an open task for scholars and practitioners. Development by definition takes time, and, therefore, evaluating of outcomes of leadership development efforts, including those of leadership development coaching, needs to reflect the longitudinal nature of the developmental process (Day et al., 2014). Moreover, if the developmental coaching genre is applied for the purposes of leadership development, one can expect that there is never an end to the journey, and all efforts are simply steps towards a fuller development of human potential (Garvey Berger, 2012).

Although measurement of differences in job performance may come up as a logical assessment approach, Day et al. (2014) are adamant that it is a wrong variable for evaluation of effectiveness of leadership development interventions. Their argument goes along the line of the performance being dependent on a variety of factors beyond the leadership competencies of an individual.

Instead, these authors suggest working on identification of developmental markers (signals of one's developmental progress) or proxies for leadership development. One example of such an approach is the work of Vincent et. al. (2015). As a measure of the coaching outcomes the authors explore changes in the consciousness development as measured by the Washington University Sentence Completion Test (Loevinger, 1979). In another example, Garvey Berger and Atkins (2009) report subjective feelings of enjoyment of the coaching process based on the developmental genre and the coachees' self-reported ability to identify their developmental issues quicker than with the other methods.

Unfortunately, most of the published studies on leadership coaching have limited sample sizes, particularly when constrained by the pre-post methodology (Baron and Morin, 2009; Baron et al., 2010). Moreover, the populations that are often convenient for research on leadership coaching (e.g. military cadets) may not be representative of traditional clients in a leadership development context (Cunningham and De La Rosa, 2007; Boyce et.al., 2010). Coaching research often uses non-professional coaches (e.g. trainees or graduates of in-house coaching courses for managers or volunteers acting as coaches in addition to other responsibilities) (Baron et al., 2010; Boyce et al., 2010). Looking at long-term effects of coaching interventions on leadership development outcomes is problematic due to response rate issues (e.g. Thach, 2002) and impossibility of ruling out other factors that may have an impact on a person's leadership behaviors.

Leadership coaching outcomes seem to be most frequently assessed through evaluation of changes in leadership behavior made by the leader her- or himself (Ely et al., 2010). One of the most often mentioned outcomes of the coaching process is increased self-awareness of the coachee (Ely et al., 2010; Schlosser, et al., 2006). Ely et al. (2010) assert that the evaluation of leadership coaching should be done on two dimensions: outcomes and process. MacKie (2007) and Ely et al. (2010) propose using the widely-known Kirpatrick (1994) model from training literature. Ely et al. (2010) also propose using formative evaluation of the coaching intervention. Such an evaluation might include expectations for the intervention, assessment of the coach based on her or his background, and evaluation of the coach–coachee relationships and the coaching process.

Admittedly, evaluation of coaching is as difficult as evaluation of other methods of leadership development. DeRue and Myers (2014) argued that it is currently impossible to discern the effect of a particular leadership development method (on-the-job experience, formal programs, learning from other people). Despite popular beliefs, for example, that most of the leadership learning happens via getting one's hands dirty in real-life work, there is no reported evidence supporting this assumption (DeRue and Myers, 2014). An important question arises: can the same leadership development outcomes be achieved by methods other than coaching? For example, Fielden et al. (2009) report that in a leadership development program for nurses both coaching and mentoring led to the same outcomes. Given the cost of leadership development coaching, this question is certainly important for practitioners. Comparison of the effects of various methods, including coaching, would also be a welcome addition to the academic work on leadership development.

Despite the challenges of leadership development evaluation in general, certain progress has been made. Some established theories from the field of leadership studies allow comparing the effectiveness of coaching as opposed to other leadership development methods. For example, the transformational leadership theory by Bass and Riggio (2006) posits that there are four components in leader behavior that facilitate transformation in followers: (a) idealized influence, (b) inspirational motivation, (c) intellectual stimulation, and (d) individual consideration.

The theory is not difficult to understand, and the face validity of the concept is very high. However, practicing transformational leadership behaviors may be quite a different story, as for many individuals it may require a sizeable reconsideration of what constitutes his or her own leadership identity, and what are the appropriate ways of positioning oneself in the organization. MacKie (2014), for example, undertakes a controlled study whereby he looks at the effect of strengths-based coaching on the transformational behavior of leaders. The application of one and the same coaching genre to the population allows to minimize variance due to different treatment of the subjects, with all the caveats still being there.

Current attempts at establishing evaluation methods for leadership development efforts in general seem to be promising also for the field of leadership development coaching. For example, leadership development literature suggests usage of social network analysis for evaluation of the efforts of *leadership* (organizational social capital) development (Hoppe and Reinelt, 2010; Day et al., 2014). Changes in the structure or relationships among organizational members, types of networks, and other elements of organizational connectivity may help to see if, for example, group leadership coaching efforts affect leadership in the organization.

CONCLUSION

This chapter has identified opportunities for bridging literatures on leadership development and coaching. Both fields have a natural overlap in organizational practice, and both are challenged with common academic issues. Potential research and conceptual work in this shared space can include:

- Defining what leadership is
- Identifying possible leadership models that can serve as foundation for leadership development coaching
- Understanding of how leadership development occurs and how coaching contributes to it
- Exploring how leadership coaching efforts and outcomes can be evaluated
- Examining how different actors involved (e.g. the coachee and the coach) affect the process and results of coachng
- Exploring how leader authentic self is theorized as emerging through her or his interpretation of real-life based self-narrative and its continuous update and reinterpretation.

In addition to the issues and research opportunities identified above, it is possible to suggest the following areas for further academic exploration. Modern leadership development literature starts taking an interest in the developmental processes, aiming at a better understanding how individual leaders progress within a general context of ongoing adult development, and how they develop their ability to collaborate with other leaders and followers (Day et al., 2014). The interest of coaching researchers in how individuals change and develop, and how coaching can support this process (Garvey Berger and Atkins, 2009; Garvey Berger, 2012, Bachkirova, 2011, 2013; MacKie, 2014), seem to be in line with the interest of leadership development scholars applying constructive developmental theories to the field of leadership development. Moreover, both fields seem to have similar challenges in terms of identification of the variables that would allow exploring possible cause–effect relationships between efforts and outcomes in leadership development. Differentiation of leader or leadership development from human development in general will be an important academic task in this case.

In addition to the substantive overlap in interests of leadership development and coaching researchers, the latter can offer methodological solutions to the quest for understanding some leadership development processes. For example, Day et al. (2014), building on literature on expertise and expert performance, posit that people are unlikely to become expert leaders just on the basis of participation in a series of leadership interventions. These authors argue that the 'actual development takes place in the so-called white spaces between such leader development events' (p. 80). According to them, at this stage researchers have no understanding of what may be happening in the leader's ongoing daily practice 'where the crux of development really resides' (p.80). They call therefore for focusing on what goes on in daily lives of executives, which is often the focus of coaching interventions, e.g. the discussions with the coach based on the daily practice of leadership, if recorded or codified with the coachee consent, may provide rich data on practicing leadership that Day et. al. (2014) call for. Moreover, some advanced (and costly) executive coaching methods, such as shadowing the leaders in their daily practice might in addition generate abundant data on daily leadership practice.

In order for leadership coaching to serve as a way to gain data for leadership development research, the field needs to reach an agreement of how data obtained through coaching interventions can be used without jeopardizing the trust between the coach, coachee, and the organization, causing harm to any of the parties involved, and contaminating the data by the coach's direct involvement in the process. Solving this issue, however, may be an important step forward for leadership development coaching, as it can move from being seen as an element of leadership development architecture (DeRue and Myers, 2014) to a complex phenomenon incorporating a variety of interventions at the heart of developmental efforts of the organization.

It is still unlikely, however, for both coaching and leadership development literatures to be able to avoid the question of connection between the efforts and costs incurred by the organization and the effect leadership development coaching (and other leadership development activities) have on the organization. There is a clear interest in the fields of coaching and leadership development to collaborate in order to face this and other challenges. It may be time for the respective academic disciplines also to join efforts.

REFERENCES

Anna, A., Chesley, J., and Davis, K. (2001). Executive coaching by proxy in a large organization: a leadership development tool. *Journal of Leadership & Organizational Studies*, 8(1), 61–68.

Argyris, C. (1969). The incompleteness of the social psychological theory: Examples from small group, cognitive consistency, and attrbution research. *American Psychologist*, 24, 893–908.

Avolio, B. J., Avey, J. B., and Quisenberry, D. (2010). Estimating return on leadership development investment. *The Leadership Quarterly*, 21(4), 633–644.

Avolio, B. J., and Gardner, W. L. (2005). Authentic leadership development: Getting to the root of positive forms of leadership. *The Leadership Quarterly*, 16(3), 315–338.

Avolio, B. J., and Hannah, S. T. (2008). Developmental readiness: Accelerating leader development. *Consulting Psychology Journal: Practice and Research*, 60(4), 331.

Bachkirova, T. (2011). *Developmental Coaching: Working with the Self*. Maidenhead: Open University Press.

Bachkirova, T. (2013). Developmental Coaching – Developing the Self. In J. Passmore (Ed.), *The Wiley-Blackwell Handbook of the Psychology of Coaching and Mentoring* (pp. 135–154). Chichester: John Wiley & Sons.

Bachkirova, T., Cox, E., and Clutterbuck, D. (2010). Introduction. In E. Cox, T. Bachkirova, and D. Clutterbuck (Eds.), *The Complete Handbook of Coaching* (pp. 1–20). London: Sage.

Baron, L., and Morin, L. (2009). The coach–coachee relationship in executive coaching: A field study. *Human Resource Development Quarterly*, 20(1), 85–106. doi: 10.1002/hrdq.20009.

Baron, L., Morin, L., and Morin, D. (2010). Executive coaching: The effect of working alliance discrepancy on the development of coachees' self-efficacy. *Journal of Management Development*, 30(9), 847–864.

Bartone, P. T., Snook, S. A., Forsythe, G. B., Lewis, P., and Bullis, R. C. (2007). Psychosocial development and leader performance of military officer cadets. *The Leadership Quarterly*, 18(5), 490–504.

Bass, B. M. (2008). *The Bass Handbook of Leadership: Theory, Research, & Managerial Practice* (4th ed.). New York, NY: The Free Press.

Bass, B. M., and Riggio, R. E. (2006). *Transformational leadership*. Mahwah, NJ: LEA

Belbin, R. M. (1981). *Management Teams: Why they succeed or fail*. Oxford: Butterworth-Heinemann.

Bilhuber Galli, E., and Müller-Stewens, G. (2012). How to build social capital with leadership development: Lessons from an explorative case study of a multibusiness firm. *The Leadership Quarterly*, 23(1), 176–201. doi: http://dx.doi.org/10.1016/j.leaqua.2011.11.014

Bowles, S., Cunningham, C. J., De La Rosa, G. M., and Picano, J. (2007). Coaching leaders in middle and executive management: Goals, performance, buy-in. *Leadership & Organization Development Journal*, 28(5), 388–408.

Boyatzis, R. E., Smith, M. L., and Blaize, N. (2006). Developing sustainable leaders through coaching and compassion. *Academy of Management Learning & Education*, 5(1), 8–24.

Boyce, L. A., Jackson, J. R., and Neal, J. L. (2010). Building successful leadership coaching relationship: Examining impact of matching criteria in a leadership coaching program. *Journal of Management Development*, 29(10), 914–931.

Britton, J. J. (2010). *Effective Group Coaching: Tried and tested tools and resources for optimum coaching results*. London: John Wiley & Sons.

Brown, S. W., and Grant, A. M. (2009). From GROW to GROUP: theoretical issues and a practical model for group coaching in organizations. *Coaching: An International Journal of Theory, Research and Practice*, 3(1), 30–45.

Carey, W., Philippon, D.J., and Cummings, G.G. (2011). Coaching models for leadesrhip development: An integrative review. *Journal of Leadership Studies*, 5(1), 51–69.

Carson, J. B., Tesluk, P. E., and Marrone, J. A. (2007). Shared leadership in teams: An investigation of antecedent conditions and performance. *Academy of Management Journal*, 50(5), 1217–1234.

CCL. (2015). Leadership Coaching Services: Coaching Individuals, Teams and Organizations for Results that Matter. Retrieved December 22, 2015, from http://www.ccl.org/leadership/pdf/coaching/coachingBrochure.pdf

Chamorro-Premuzic, T. (2016, January 4). Strengths-based coaching can actually weaken you. *Harvard Business Review online*.

Chan, K. Y., and Drasgow, F. (2001). Toward a theory of individual differences and leadership: understanding the motivation to lead. *Journal of Applied Psychology*, 86(3), 481.

Clutterbuck, D. (2011). *Coaching the Team at Work*. London: Nicholas Brealey Publishing.

Collins, D. B., and Holton, E. F. (2004). The effectiveness of managerial leadership development programs: A meta-analysis of studies from 1982 to 2001. *Human Resource Development Quarterly*, 15(2), 217–248. doi: 10.1002/hrdq.1099

Costa, P. T. J., and McRae, R. R. (1992). *Revised NEO Personality Inventory (NEO-PI-R) and NEO Five-Factor Inventory (NEO-FFI) professional manual*. Odessa, Fl: Psychological Assessment Resources, Inc.

Cox, E., Bachkirova, T., and Clutterbuck, D. (Ed.). (2010). *The Complete Handbook of Coaching*. London: Sage.

Cox, E., and Jackson, P. (2010). Developmental Coaching. In E. Cox, T. Bachkirova, and D. Clutterbuck (Eds.), *The Complete Handbook of Coaching* (pp. 217–230). London: Sage.

Cunningham, J. L., and De La Rosa, G. M. (2007). Coaching leaders in middle and executive management: Goals, performance, buy-in. *Leadership & Organization Development Journal*, 28(5), 388–408.

Dalakoura, A. (2010). Differentiating leader and leadership development: A collective framework for leadership development. *Journal of Management Development*, 29(5), 432–441. doi: doi:10.1108/02621711011039204.

Day, D. V. (2000). Leadership Development: A Review in Context. *The Leadership Quarterly*, 11(2), 581–613.

Day, D. V., and Harrison, M. M. (2007). A multi-level, identity-based approach to leadership development. *Human Resource Management Review*, 17(4), 360–373. doi: http://dx.doi.org/10.1016/j.hrmr.2007.08.007

Day, D. V., Harrison, M. M., and Halpin, S. M. (2009). *An Integrative Theory of Leadership Development: Connecting Adult Development, Identity, and Expertise*. New York, NY: Psychology Press.

Day, D. V., Fleenor, J. W., Atwater, L. E., Sturm, R. E., and McKee, R. A. (2014). Advances in leader and leadership development: A review of 25 years of research and theory. *The Leadership Quarterly*, 25(1), 63–82. doi: http://dx.doi.org/10.1016/j.leaqua.2013.11.004

Day, D. V., Gronn, P., and Salas, E. (2004). Leadership capacity in teams. *The Leadership Quarterly*, 15(6), 857–880. doi: http://dx.doi.org/10.1016/j.leaqua.2004.09.001

Denzin, N., and Lincoln, Y. (2000). *Handbook of Qualitative Research*. Thousand Oaks, CA: Sage.

DeRue, D.S., and Myers, C.G. (2014). Leadership development: A review and agenda for future research In D. V. Day (Ed.), The Oxford Handbook of Leadership and Organizations (pp. 832–855). New York, NY: Oxford University Press.

Diedrich, R. C. (2001). Lessons learned in – and guidelines for – coaching executive teams. Consulting Psychology Journal: Practice and Research, 53(4), 238–239. doi: 10.1037/1061-4087.53.4.238

Eagly, A. H. (2005). Achieving relational authenticity in leadership: Does gender matter?. *The Leadership Quarterly*, 16(3), 459–474.

Ely, K., Boyce, L. A., Nelson, J. K., Zaccaro, S. J., Hernez-Broome, G., and Whyman, W. (2010). Evaluating leadership coaching: A review and integrated framework. *Leadership Quarterly*, 21(4), 585–599.

Feldman, D. C., and Lankau, M. J. (2005). Executive coaching: A review and agenda for future research. *Journal of Management*, 31(6), 829–848. doi: Doi 10.1177/0149206305279599

Fielden, S. L., Davidson, M.J., and Sutherland, V.J. (2009). Innovations in Coaching and Mentoring: Implications for Nurse Leadership Development. *Health Services Management Research*, 22, 92–99.

Florent-Treacy, E. (2009). Behind the scenes in the identity laboratory: Participants' narratives of identity transition through group coaching in a leadership development programme. *International Coaching Psychology Review*, 4(1), 71–86.

Franklin, J. (2005). Change readiness in coaching: Potentiating client change. Evidence-Based Coaching Volume 1: Theory, Research and Practice from the Behavioural Sciences, 193.

Frankovelgia, C. C., and Riddle, D. D. (2010). Leadership Coaching. In E. Van Velson, C. D. McCauley, and M. Ruderman (Eds.), *The Center for Creative Leadership Handbook of Leadership Development* (3rd ed., pp. 125–146). San Francisco: Jossey-Bass.

Garvey Berger, J. (2012). *Changing on the Job: Developing Leaders for a Complex World*. Stanford, CA: Stanford University Press.

Garvey Berger, J., and Atkins, P. W. (2009). Mapping complexity of mind: Using the subject–object interview in coaching. *Coaching: An International Journal of Theory, Research and Practice*, 2(1), 23–36.

Goff, P., Guthrie, J.E., Goldring, E., and Bickman, L. (2014). Changing Principals' Leadership through Feedback and Coaching. *Journal of Educational Administration*, 52(5), 682–704.

Goldsmith, M. (2009). Executive coaching: A real world perspective from a real-life coaching practitioner. *International Coaching Psychology Review*, 4(1), 22–24.

Guillén, L., Mayo, M., and Korotov, K. (2015). Is leadership a part of me? A leader identity approach to understanding the motivation to lead. *The Leadership Quarterly*, 26(5), 802–820.

Hackman, J. R., and Wageman, R. (2005). A theory of team coaching. *Academy of Management Review*, 30(2), 269–287. doi: 10.5465/amr.2005.16387885

Hall, D. T., Otazo, K. L., and Hollenbeck, G. P. (1999). Behind closed doors: What really happens in executive coaching. *Organizational dynamics*, 27(3), 39–53.

Hawkins, P., and Smith, N. (2006). *Coaching, Mentoring, and Organizational Consultancy: Supervision and Development*. Maidenhead: Open University Press.

Hernez-Broome, G., and Hughes, R. L. (2004). Leadership development: Past, present, and future. *People and Strategy*, 27(1), 24.

Hirschhorn, L. (1988). *The Workplace Within*. Cambridge, MA: The MIT Press.

Hoppe, B., and Reinelt, C. (2010). Social network analysis and the evaluation of leadership networks. *The Leadership Quarterly*, 21(4), 600–619.

Ilies, R., Morgeson, F. P., and Nahrgang, J. D. (2005). Authentic leadership and eudaemonic well-being: Understanding leader–follower outcomes. *The Leadership Quarterly*, 16(3), 373–394.

Joo, B. (2005). Executive coaching: A conceptual framework from an integrative review of practice and research. *Human Resource Development Review*, 4, 462–488.

Kampa-Kokesch, S., and Anderson, M. Z. (2001). Executive coaching: a comprehensive review of the literature. *Consulting Psychology Journal: Practice and Research*, 53, 205–228.

Kemp, T. (2009). Is coaching an evolved form of leadership? Building a transdisciplinary framework for exploring the coaching alliance. *International Coaching Psychology Review*, 4(1), 105–109.

Kets de Vries, M. (2005). Leadership group coaching in action: The Zen of creating high performance teams. *The Academy of Management Executive*, 19(1), 61–76. doi: 10.5465/ame.2005.15841953

Kets de Vries, M., Guillen-Ramo, L., Korotov, K., and Florent-Treacy, E. (eds.). (2010). *The Coaching Kaleidoscope: Insights from the Inside*. Houndmills: Palgrave.

Kets de Vries, M., and Korotov, K. (2007). Creating Transformational Executive Education Programs. *Academy of Management Learning & Education*, 6(3), 375–387.

Kets de Vries, M.., and Korotov, K. (2011). Transformational leadership development programs: Creating long-term sustainable change. In S. Snook, Nohria, N., and R. Khurana (eds.), *The Handbook for Teaching Leadership: Knowing, Being, and Doing* (pp. 263–282). Los Angeles: Sage.

Kets de Vries, M., Korotov, K., and Florent-Treacy, E. (eds.). (2007). *Coach and Couch: The Psychology of Making Better Leaders*. Houndmills and New York: Palgrave.

Kets de Vries, M.F.R., Vrignaud, P., Korotov, K., Engellau, E., and Florent-Treacy, E. (2006). The development of 'The Personality Audit': A psychodynamic multiple feedback assessment instrument. *International Journal of Human Resource Management*, 17, 898–917.

Kilburg, R. R. (2000). *Executive Coaching: Developing Managerial Wisdom in a World of Chaos*. Washington, DC: American Psychological Association.

Kincheloe, J. L. (2001). Describing the bricolage: Conceptualizing a new rigor in qualitative research. *Qualitative Inquiry*, 7(6), 679–692.

Kincheloe, J. L. (2005). On to the next level: Continuing the coneptualization of bricolage. *Qualitative Inquiry*, 11(2), 323–350.

Kirkpatrick, D. (1994). *Evaluating Training Programs: The Four Levels*. San Francisco: Berrett-Koehler.

Kombarakaran, F., Yang, J, Baker, M N and Fernandes, P B. (2008). Executive coaching: it works. *Consulting Psychology*, 60(1), 78–90.

Korotov, K. (2007). Executive education from the participant's point of view. In M. Kets de Vries, K. Korotov, and E. Florent-Treacy (Eds.), *Coach and Couch: The Psychology of Making Better Leaders*. Houndmills: Palgrave.

Korotov, K. (2010). Executive coaches in organization: insiders from outside. In V. Vaiman (Ed.), *Talent Management of Knowledge Workers* (pp. 180–196). Houndmills: Palgrave McMillan.

Korotov, K. (2013). Behind the closed doors of a coaching session: The issues that keep an execuitve coach up at night. *Training and Management Development Methods*, 27(2), 2.13–12.17.

Korotov, K., Florent-Treacy, E., Kets de Vries, M. F. R., and Bernhardt, A. (2012). *Tricky Coaching: Difficult Cases in Executive Coaching*. Houndmills and New York: Palgrave McMillan.

Lahey, L., Souvaine, E., Kegan, R., Goodman, R., and Felix, S. (1988). *A Guide to the Subject–Object Interview: Its Administration and Interpretation*. Cambridge, MA: Harvard University, Graduate School of Education, Laboratory of Human Development.

Loevinger, J. (1979). Construct validity of the Sentence Completion Test of ego development. *Applied Psychological Measurement*, 3, 281–311.

MacKie, D. (2007). Evaluating the effectiveness of executive coaching: Where we are now and where do we need to be? *Australian Psychologist*, 42, 310–318.

MacKie, D. (2014). The effectiveness of strength-based executive coaching in enhancing full range leadership development: A controlled study. *Consulting Psychology Journal: Practice and Research*, 66, 118–137.

MacKie, D. (2015). Who sees change after leadership coaching? An analysis of impact by rater level and self–other alignment on multi-source feedback. *International Coaching Psychology Review*, 10 (2): 118–130.

McCauley, C. D., Drath W. H., Palus, C. J., O'Connor, P. M., and Baker, B. A. (2006). The use of constructive developmental theory to advance the understanding of leadership. *The Leadership Quarterly*, 17(6), 634–653.

McCormick, I., and Burch, G. S. J. (2008). Personality-focused coaching for leadership development. *Consulting Psychology Journal: Practice and Research*, 60(3), 267.

McNally, K., and Lukens, R. (2006). Leadership Development: An External-Internal Coaching Partnership. *Journal of Nursing Administration*, 36(3), 155–161.

Millard, J. A., and Korotov, K. (2014). Do mental health stigma and gender influence MBAs' willingness to engage in coaching? *International Journal of Mentoring and Coaching in Education*, 3(3), 277–292.

Oades, L. G., Orowe, T. P., and Nguyen, M. (2009). Leadership coaching transforming mental health systems from the inside out: The Collaborative Recovery Model as person-centered strengths based coaching psychology. *International Coaching Psychology Review*, 4(1), 25–36.

Passmore, J. (Ed.) (2015). *Leadership Coaching: Working with Leaders to Develop Elite Performance* (2nd ed.). London: Kogan Page.

Passmore, J., and Fillery-Travis, A. (2011). A critical review of executive coaching research: a decade of progress and what's to come. *Coaching: An International Journal of Theory, Research and Practice*, 4(2), 70–88.

Pfeffer, J. (2015). *Leadership B.S.: Fixing Workplaces and Careers One Truth at a Time*. New York, NY: Harper Collins.

Schein, E. H. (2010). *Organizational culture and leadership* (Vol. 2). John Wiley & Sons.

Schlosser, B., Steinbrenner, D., Kumata, E., and Hunt, J. (2006). The coaching impact study: Measuring the value of executive coaching. *International Journal of Coaching in Organizations*, 4(3), 8–26.

Schyns, B., Kiefer, T., Kerschreiter, R., and Tymon, A. (2011). Teaching Implicit Leadership Theories to Develop Leaders and Leadership: How and Why It Can Make a Difference. *Academy of Management Learning & Education*, 10(3), 397–408. doi: 10.5465/amle.2010.0015

Smith, G. T. (2009). Why do different individuals progress along different life trajectories? *Perspectives on Psychological Science*, 4(4), 415–421.

Snook, S., Nohria, N., and Khurana, R. (ed.) (2012). *The Handbook for Teaching Leadership: Knowing, Doing and Being*. Los Angeles: Sage.

Stern, L. R. (2004). Executive coaching: A working definition. *Consulting Psychology Journal: Practice and Research*, 56(3), 154–162.

Stokes, J., and Jolly, R. (2010). Executive and Leadership Coaching. In E. Cox, T. Bachkirova, and D. Clutterbuck (Ed.), *The Complete Handbook of Coaching*. London: Sage.

Terblanche, N. (2014). Knowledge sharing in the organizational context: Using Social Network Analysis as a coaching tool. *International Journal of Evidence Based Coaching & Mentoring*, 12(2), 146–164.

Thach, E. C. (2002). The impact of executive coaching and 360 feedback on leadership effectiveness. *Leadership & Organization Development Journal*, 23(4), 205–214. doi: doi:10.1108/01437730210429070

Ting, S., and Hart, E. W. (2004). Formal Coaching. In C. D. McCauley and E. Van Velson (Eds.), *The Center for Creative Leadership Handbook of Leadership Development* (2nd ed., pp. 116–150). San Francisco: John Wiley & Sons.

Tomlinson, J., and Naughton, N. (2015). Coaching for team leadership: Using the Belbin 'team roles' model. In J. Passmore (Ed.), *Leadership Coaching: Working with Leaders to Develop Elite Performance* (3rd ed., pp. 297–316). London: Kogan Page.

Truijen, K. J., and van Woerkom, M. (2008). The pitfalls of collegial coaching: An analysis of collegial coaching in medical education and its influence on stimulating reflection and performance of novice clinical teachers. *Journal of Workplace Learning*, 20(5), 316–326.

Truskie, S. (2011). *Coaching transformational leaders with a Myers-Briggs Assessment. CPP White Paper*. Santa Clara, CA: CPP.

Vincent, N., Ward, L., and Denson, L. (2015). Promoting post-conventional consciousness in leaders: Australian community leadership programs. *The Leadership Quarterly*, 26(2), 238–253.

Wageman, R., Nunes, D., Burruss, J. and Hackman, R. (2008). *Senior Leadership Teams*. Boston, MA: Harvard Business School Press.

Ward, G. (2008). Towards executive change: A psychodynamic group coaching model for short executive programmes. *International Journal of Evidence Based Coaching and Mentoring*, 6(1), 67–78.

Winnicott, D. (1982). *Playing and Reality*. New York: Routledge

Zenger, J. H., and Stinnett, K. (2006). Leadership coaching: Developing effective executives. *Chief Learning Officer*, 5(7), 44–47.

Coaching for Organisation Development

David Drake and James Pritchard

INTRODUCTION

This chapter positions coaching as it is used in the development of organisations. It makes the case that coaching can be used as a systemic and scalable tool for enhancing capabilities, culture and change in organisations. Although coaching is increasingly used in conjunction with other related disciplines such as organisation development (OD), there is a gap between their respective literatures and often a disconnection in how they are delivered. We would argue that this is in part a reflection of the fact that psychology and human resource development (HRD) – leadership development in particular – have a stronger presence in the coaching literature. The intention of this chapter is to address this gap by positioning coaching more fully within an organisational context and a systemic perspective. In so doing, it is hoped that it will contribute to the continued evolution of coaching from a process primarily focused on increased functioning of individuals (and teams) to include systemic-level interventions where many forms of coaching are embedded, not just in the learning process but also in how business gets done. This will be increasingly important as the adaptive challenges (Heifetz & Linsky, 2002) faced by organisations – and those who work in them – continue to rise.

The few studies that have been done on the impact of coaching in organisations are largely related to the behaviors of executives who have been coached (e.g. S. Bowles, Cunningham, De La Rosa, & Picano, 2007; Ely et al., 2010; Levenson, 2009). What is less well understood are questions related to if, and how, coaching contributes to broader benefits for organisations as a whole. This chapter is intended to offer a case for conceptually positioning coaching in an organisational context, such that it can provide a stronger platform from which to study its various impacts, including on culture and performance. While such propositions have high face validity, there is a need to better articulate how, why and when this occurs. Accordingly, this chapter starts with a look at coaching from within an organisational frame and then looks at its use in four areas related to the development of organisations, namely (1) culture, (2) capabilities, (3) change, and (4) organisation development itself. These four areas can be seen in Figure 9.1 and are presented according to the level at which issues are addressed (i.e. individual/organisational) and who is served in the process (i.e. people/systems). This frame will be used to organise the work that follows, with the current state of research and practice explored and discussed for each quadrant, along with a final section that will highlight some critical areas for future research.

APPLICATIONS OF COACHING IN ORGANISATIONS

Over the past 20 years, executive coaching has become part of the learning and development portfolio in many organisations. It is built on early definitions of coaching such as, 'unlocking a person's potential to maximize their own performance' (Whitmore, 1992, p. 23) and seen as providing a resource for leaders in supporting personal, instrumental, relational, and contextual competence (Drake, 2007). For the purposes of this chapter, coaching is defined more broadly to include formal and informal uses of coaching methodologies to support learning, development and performance in organisations. A growing list of organisational applications appears later in the chapter, many of which speak to the need to balance psychological perspectives on coaching with more systemic and contextual ones. While the literature on coaching as it relates to the development of organisations (such as through OD) is scarce, there have been some attempts to assess the connections between the two fields (see Bennett & Craig, 2005; Drake, 2007; Hamlin, Ellinger, & Beattie, 2009; Minahan, 2006; Scott, Murrell, Zintz, & Gallagher, 2006; Stout-Rostron, 2010; Swart, 2015). However, in spite of coaching's widespread adoption, evidence for the impact of coaching on the effectiveness of organisations is limited (see Feldman & Lankau, 2005; Joo, 2005; Levenson, 2009; Olivero, Bane, & Kopelman, 1997; Peterson & Luthans, 2003; Smither, London, Flautt, Vargas, & Kucine, 2003).

One challenge has been an inability to isolate the specific contributions of coaching

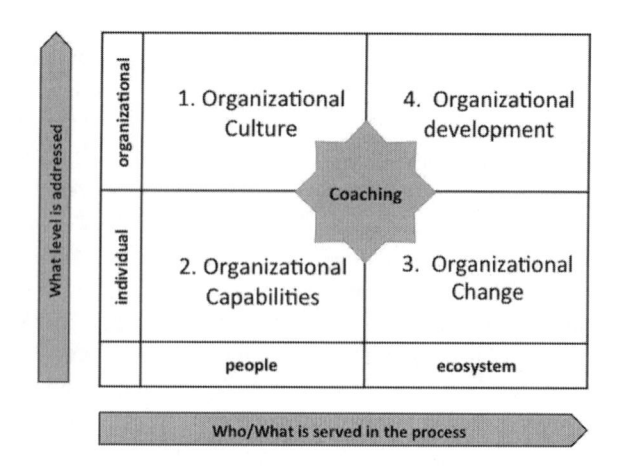

Figure 9.1 Four ways coaching can contribute to the development of organisations

to organisational outcomes, including its utility in comparison to other interventions. One step in this direction has been via efforts to delineate types of coaching, such as Witherspoon and White's (1996) distinctions between skills, development, performance, and organisational results. Other examples include Ellinger and Kim's (2014) analysis of the types of coaching and assessment methods, along with work on the multiple 'faces' of coaching (Joo, Sushko, & McLean, 2012). While most coaching assignments generally address more than one of these areas of focus, the distinctions are helpful in looking at what is required for and expected from different types of coaching. Further delineations are needed if we are to better understand the range of potential contributions coaching can make to organisations and their people (see Hamlin et al., 2009). This would also enable coaching providers to take on a more systemic perspective (and potentially a greater number of roles) when working in organisations.

Questions that emerge when looking at the role of coaching in enhancing organisational effectiveness include:

- Whose agenda is being served by coaching?
- How much of this agenda is explicitly acknowledged?
- How compatible are the agendas of different stakeholders?
- Are these agendas aligned to what it will take to reach the desired objectives?
- Have the 'shadow' elements in these agendas been addressed?

In considering these questions, it seems more apt to consider stakeholder 'agendas' in their dynamic and complex interaction, rather than as fixed, singular perspectives on what is needed from coaching. At the same time, the more coherent and shared their agendas, the more likely they are to have influence on the choices in the coaching space. Issues often arise in organisations when any two sets of agendas related to coaching (between or within stakeholder groups) do not align with one another or when coaching is applied in an ad hoc fashion rather than as part of a strategic deployment (Walker-Fraser, 2011). For example, the coachee seeks coaching for better work-life balance and the organisation expects coaching to deliver better performance from the leader; neither of which may be linked to other talent/development processes in the organisation.

As Kilburg (1996) has previously noted, a coach may feel torn in such cases between loyalty to the individual and responsibility to the organisation. The overarching question, both conceptually and pragmatically is, 'Whenever there is a conflict of objectives, whose needs should take precedence?' The answer is likely to vary according to the nature of the coaching engagement, the stipulations in the contract, the maturity and expectations of the culture, the sponsor and the source of the funds, and even the beliefs and assumptions of the coach. What seems to be called for is the adoption of a multiple stakeholder framework on how to utilise and assess coaching in organisations, along with a more systemic and contextual perspective on the coaching process and its outcomes (e.g. Joo, 2005). Seen this way, coaching can be used as an opportunity – for the professionals involved and those affected in the organisation – for strategic conversations about how to align efforts to develop people and the organisation.

The challenge for coaches is how to address coachees' needs as people, their needs within roles and the needs of multiple stakeholders in regards to what happens before, during and after coaching. These stakeholders include (at a minimum) the coach, the individual being coached and a representative of the organisational agenda (e.g. a manager). Beyond these primary stakeholders, others who have a vested interest in coaching might include a Human Resources representative, an internal coaching specialist and peers or direct reports of the person coached. If the coaching is part of a development program, there will also likely be program directors and/or learning and development (L&D) professionals. The impact of coaching on individual development and on organisational effectiveness will be influenced by whatever and whomever's agenda is seen as uppermost, and the degree to which the existence and needs of multiple agendas is openly discussed and addressed. Ultimately, the aim is to increase our understanding of how successful coaching relationships are formed and successful outcomes are achieved so as to benefit the individual and the organisation.

Organisations can use various means to align coaching to their wider agendas, for example:

- briefing coaches on company vision, corporate strategy, key competency/capability frameworks, job descriptions and success criteria for leaders;
- creating a select pool of coaches (sometimes single-sourced) to maintain a common understanding of the culture, development agendas and expectations of coaching;
- taking a systemic approach to contracting that involves multiple stakeholders and articulates the desired expectations for scope, priorities, communications, etc.;
- utilising common themes from coaching engagements that generate insights about the state of the organisation and issues that warrant attention;
- adopting a multi-faceted approach to evaluating coaching (e.g. assessing the outcomes from coaching engagements and the capacity of the organisation to learn about itself);
- bringing together internal and external coaches for group supervision and on-going development relative to the priorities in the organisation; and
- involving coaches in programmes for a specific audience or purpose (e.g. leadership, talent, diversity) so as to increase the impact for participants and on the organisation.

Each of these represents an opportunity for organisations, the professionals involved and those who study these issues to deepen their understanding on how coaching can best be positioned in an organisational context.

Whatever the parameters set by the organisation in contracting with the coach, what happens in coaching sessions generally remains confidential (Coutu & Kauffman, 2009). Where there is a divergence of interests, the coach may need to tread a fine line to avoid oppressing the coachee as an agent of the organisation (and risk losing rapport and trust with them), or colluding with the client against the organisation (and risk losing rapport and trust with them – not to mention perhaps the role or contract). This speaks to a growing need in coaching to address the ethical issues related to helping coachees navigate the tensions between assimilation and accommodation, authenticity and efficacy, personal vision and organisational realities.

In formulating ethical principles it is important to address both the professional and interpersonal issues as well as those related to the larger systems. This will inform and be informed by similar efforts within related disciplines that deal with issues related to systemic organisational factors. In so doing, we can draw on authors who have explored the opportunities and challenges related to the presence of organisational agendas in coaching (see Giglio, Diamante, & Urban, 1998; Hooijberg & Lane, 2009; Kiel, Rimmer, Williams, & Doyle, 1996; McNally & Lukens, 2006; Saporito, 1996). This will help coaching researchers and practitioners develop more systemic and effective approaches to ethically applying coaching in the following four areas in organisations, as shown in Figure 9.1.

Quadrant 1: Coaching and Organisational Culture

The significant impact of culture and social systems on adult development began to be more fully appreciated in the 1960's as part of the narrative turn in the social sciences (Czarniawska, 2004). As Lerner (1985) noted, 'interest emerged in the bidirectional relations between developing people and the multilevel, interrelated settings within which they live their lives [and do their work]' (p. 155). As a result, a proper understanding of what it requires to develop people individually and collectively increasingly came to include an appreciation for the context in which development occurs – which in turn shapes the context. One of the ways this is often done in the field of OD is to view organisational cultures as systems of patterns of interaction. Authors such as Morgan (1997) identified the *psychic prison*, the *political*, the *machine* and the *organism* as metaphors that described the most common cultural types. Each of these types brings with it a preferred discourse, set of narratives, interactive dynamics, and roles and emphases for coaching. Together, they speak to a broader need to consider the ways that culture and coaching conversations inform and are informed by one another across time (past, present and future) and space (inside and outside, unconscious and conscious).

Many of the issues coaches encounter when working in this way relate to coachees' experience of gaps between the 'espoused values' and 'values in use' that are reflected in organizational culture (Schein, 1992, 1996, 1999). This presents a familiar dilemma for coaches who recognise the dangers of sending a changed person back into an unchanged environment. In positioning coaching within an OD context, coaches have access to tools and concepts that can help them make decisions about how best to address the systemic and organisational issues affecting the individuals or teams that present for coaching. This is an area that seems ripe for further development, particularly in terms of creating frameworks that can help such decision-making. This, in turn, will require coaching and OD to be more fully aligned within the organisation and the initiative, and more sufficient theoretical or practical constructs for an integrative approach to development.

As Drake (2016) notes, achieving greater results from coaching within a given organisation requires a deeper understanding of (1) the conscious and unconscious aspects of its culture and systems; (2) its dynamics and definitions of success and efficacy; and (3) the degree to which an individual's changes will be supported (and how to make shifts to enhance the ecosystem of support). Theorists offer differing views about which leverage points to focus on in terms of organisational issues that impact people's growth and performance. For example, Schein (1988) sees organisational ineffectiveness as a function of inconsistent cultural assumptions and values; Senge (1990) views it more as a function of poorly designed systems and the inevitable result of erroneous perceptions of causality; and Argyris and Schön (1974, 1978) consider it a function of a lack of awareness and interpersonal competence. Again, the challenge for coaches is to determine where there is the most potential leverage in the coachee's environment – and the scope of the agreements – and how to authentically and appropriately adapt their coaching as a result.

At the same time, it is important to recognise that culture is deep, extensive, and stable. As Schein (1999) proposes, an organisation's culture is 'right' as long as it succeeds in its primary task. He also argued that one cannot 'create' a new culture. However, it is possible to stimulate a new way of thinking and to reinforce it at every turn, although people are unlikely to internalise it or volitionally endorse it unless it actually works better over time (Schein, 1999). This is where a more integrative approach is needed to developing people and organisations such that they can help each other work better. Increasingly, organisations are seeking to embed coaching cultures as a part of the means to do so (see Clutterbuck & Megginson, 2005; Hart, 2003; Lloyd, 2005; McComb, 2012; Megginson & Clutterbuck, 2006; Wilson, 2011). According to Hawkins (2012), a coaching culture:

> ... exists in an organisation when a coaching approach is a key aspect of how the leaders, managers and staff engage and develop all their people and engage their stakeholders, in ways that creates increased individual, team and organisational performance and shared value for all stakeholders. (p. 21)

Developing a coaching culture often involves formally and informally incorporating coaching in roles and relationships, and encouraging coaching conversations throughout the organisation. As such, a key requirement for fostering a coaching culture in any organisation would seem to be supporting coaching in all its various forms, both formal or informal (see the coaching spectrum presented in Figure 9.2). It can be argued that for coaching to become part of a culture, all members of an organisation need to accept responsibility for it. This reflects Hunt and Weintraub's (2007) observation that a coaching organisation makes effective and regular use of coaching as a means of promoting both individual development and organisational learning in service of the organisation's larger goals. However, coaching cannot be an isolated activity if it is to have any lasting impact on the organisation and its culture.

In addition, Hawkins (2012) delineates three additional elements that underpin the creation of a coaching culture in organisations: First, a clear and coherent coaching strategy that is linked to the broader mission and strategy of the organisation, whilst allowing for flexible applications of coaching to meet situational and emergent needs. Second, clear connections between coaching and the wider organisational culture changes underway. Third, an integrating and supportive infrastructure, sufficient resources and clear guidance on their use. If any of the three elements are missing or diminished, the overall initiative will suffer accordingly. Of particular interest are the often overlooked sociological, political, contextual and systemic issues related to development.

According to a variety of authors (see Anderson, Frankovelgia, & Hernez-Broome, 2009; Drake, 2016; Hawkins, 2012), the following are markers of a well functioning coaching culture:

- The effective use of internal and external formal coaching resources.
- The centrality of coaching in management and leadership styles.
- The integration of coaching in all HR and performance processes.
- The integration of coaching in all talent and development programs.
- The use of coaching in how teams operate and work gets done.
- The presence of shared resources that are regularly accessed for growth.
- The commitment to personal and collective accountability for the whole.

To the degree that an organisation is not flourishing in this regard, the question becomes how to bring about the necessary changes to the culture and capabilities through individual and collective development efforts.

Quadrant 2: Coaching and Organisational Capabilities

Coaching impacts the development of organisations as a resource for developing skills, attitudes, understanding and aspirations of individuals and teams/groups in service of shared objectives. Initially, as McCauley and Hezlett (2001) have argued, coaching was predominantly seen as an intervention that was designed to assist executives who were in danger of stalling their careers or losing their roles because of a particular derailer in their performance. Over time, it also came to include working with high potential executives, who seemed to warrant additional development to support their progression in the organisation. More recently, there has

colleague with a listening ear → understanding of process, but no formal training → coaching skills training, e.g. manager as coach → trained as internal job plus coach or mentor → experienced internal or external executive coach → acredited and experienced executive coach, with supervision

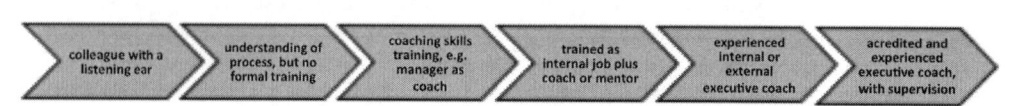

Figure 9.2 Degrees of professionalism in coaching

been interest in more proactive approaches such as efforts to increase the coaching capabilities in leaders, managers and employees to improve staff retention (e.g. Ellinger, Ellinger, & Keller, 2005), teamwork (e.g. McCulloch, Rathbone, & Catchpole, 2011) and service delivery (e.g. Pemberton, 2012). Walker-Fraser (2011) offers a helpful summary of the characteristics and capabilities required for managerial coaching: 'Organizations could benefit from the research implications when developing a strategic approach to leadership development that places executive coaching as an integral part of organizational learning' (p. 75).

However, there still appears to be a need to better understand how coaching could most effectively be used to support larger organisational initiatives and objectives. What are the deeper connections needed between personal and collective capability-building processes and between HRD and OD functions in organisations? For example, Brown and Harvey (2011) estimate that 80% of OD practitioners use Schein's process consulting methodologies, and that process consulting is the most often-used OD skill set. The central emphasis in process consulting is on facilitating the self-directed learning and growth of the client, an emphasis that is echoed in the majority of coaching philosophies (Grant, Passmore, Cavanagh, & Parker, 2010). These similarities were noted in a survey by Anderson (2007), in which over half of the 216 respondents reported that coaching must be integrated with broader leadership development processes and be linked to business objectives and outcomes in order to be successful and sustainable. Yet, only 5% rated their organisations as extremely effective in these two areas, and over one-third of the overall respondents reported no centralised oversight or management of coaching in their organisation (p. 11).

A first step would be to identify all of the potential ways in which coaching could be deployed in an organisation and perhaps even develop a taxonomy by which to assess and develop the coaching capabilities in organisations. This would need to include coaching as a specific role an internal or external person can take (designated or situated) and coaching as an intentional approach to significant conversations. Either way, coaching becomes more embedded in the ways in which work gets done and people get developed. Some of the potential applications include:

- Buddying, e.g. on-boarding new employees
- Coaching as community service
- Coaching as customer/client service
- External professional coaching
- Group coaching
- Peer-to-peer coaching and mentoring
- Internal job plus coaching
- Internal professional coaching
- Managers as coaches for team members
- Mentoring by a more experienced colleague
- Reverse mentoring
- Self-coaching resources
- Team/Board coaching.

Each of these enriches the capabilities of those involved (on all sides) as well as having larger implications for the development and culture of the organisation. While there is certainly a need to further develop our understanding of the coaching process, there is a need as well to understand the indirect benefits and how best to capitalise on them. For example, Hunt and Weintraub (2007) note that,

> peer support is often available 'just in time' to help deal with spontaneously emerging learning needs. Peer coaching can also be viewed as a form of social capital, networks of people who by virtue of their relationships with one another are more capable than they would be without those relationships. The peer network also provides support for the diffusion of knowledge from a coaching conversation to other parts of the organization. (p. 21)

This has been demonstrated by coaching researchers using social network analysis, where the 'ripple effects' of coaching in organisations has been detected using wellbeing variables (O'Connor & Cavanagh, 2013). Significant events in organisations also provide context and boundaries for coaching conversations (Coutu & Kauffman, 2009; Katz & Miller, 1996), for example when people move into new roles, new leadership has come on-board, and external pressures or changes are felt in the environment.

Such examples reflect the need for better integration of coaching within critical change, development and performance initiatives in order to attain greater value from the investment in terms of significant, sustainable progress on key objectives. Whereas, historically, many internal and external coaching professionals were primarily trained in and focused on a person-centered orientation, there appears to be a growing requirement in some organisations that more senior coaches (internal or external) act as 'trusted advisors' (Maister, Green, & Galford, 2000) who can work fluently across the domains of OD, coaching and the business to develop broader solutions that make a difference. The implications of this trend include: (1) a more overt incorporation of organisational and operational needs in designing coaching interventions; (2) the need for a more nuanced understanding of the notion of 'fit' in matching coaches and clients; and (3) increased partnerships across specialisations to be able to meet the systemic needs of organisations and develop the holistic capabilities of those who work in them. Taken together, this could lead to a better understanding of how and when coaching can be used to enrich, evolve or extend the culture in an organisation.

Quadrant 3: Coaching and Organisational Change

The third area where coaching is used to enhance the development of organisations is in the context of leading change (see Beckhard & Pritchard, 1992; Kotter, 1995; Marshak, 1993). Given that change is increasingly continuous, complex and disruptive in nature, there is a need to better understand the role and impact of coaching in supporting both the external and internal processes of change. This requires a shift away from old assumptions that change is an episodic 'event' and can be orchestrated and managed with the right tools and methods. Rather, organisations are likely to be better served by assumptions that change is an emergent stream of interactions that reflect the reality of organisational life, its ongoing and communicative character, and how it deals with the matters of daily practices (Tsoukas & Chia, 2002). Coaching has an important role to play in change initiatives as a resource for dealing with organisational realities in new ways, improving interactions and communications, and fostering new daily practices (both mindsets and behaviors). A good example of this is Malone's (2001) research on improving self-efficacy through coaching in support of organisational change. In this sense, coaching is analogous to a governor gear in that it enables people and organisations to remain generatively attuned with one another, their market and their aspirations.

This is understood to include both the wider, external changes that organisations regularly undertake to remain competitive and healthy, and the personal, internal transitions that people go through as part of that process. Change refers to alternations in the *external* environment, planned or unplanned, such as the promotion to a new position in an organisation. Transitions refer to the *internal* and adaptive processes people go through in relation to changes in the past, present or future. There is a dynamic rather than linear relationship between change and transitions. For example, a client has made some important internal shifts (transition) but is not yet ready to act on them at work (change). Efforts to develop organisations tend to focus on external changes that necessitate internal transitions and coaching tends to focus on internal transitions that produce external changes. The critical question for those wanting to research coaching in this context is how these two processes can be better and more equitably aligned in organisations.

Another area that is ripe for study is how work on personal and systemic resistance can be brought together to provide a more comprehensive framework for change in organisations. One of the reasons change is often difficult in organisations is that cultures and practices are protected by individual and collective defenses, which reinforce one another and act to exclude information that is necessary for change (Argyris, 1980, 1990; Nystrom & Starbuck, 1984). As Brown and Starkey (2000) note, information that threatens an organisation's collective self-concept is ignored, rejected, reinterpreted, hidden, or lost. In this way, the processes by which organisations preserve their identities are, in many ways, analogous to the methods that individuals employ in defense of their own self-concepts.

Working with individual and collective resistance requires a fundamental reframing of the challenge – from its perception as a barrier to change, to seeing it as an opening for acknowledgment and development. Coaching can then be tailored to systemically address the specific developmental needs for each individual (Gardini, Giuliani, & Marricchi, 2011) and at each level in the organisation, or as Oshry (2007) described it, as *Tops*, *Middles*, *Bottoms* and *Customers*. The benefits of such an approach might include (i) a stronger correspondence between what happens in coaching and what happens in the organisation as a result, and (ii) a greater emphasis in coaching on the contextual and systemic nature of change and development. This would seem to necessitate an integration of coaching in many forms throughout the organisation so there are many points of contact through which people and the organisation each increase their capabilities to make the most of openings for change. Because of the action orientation in coaching as a resource for development and performance, there is the potential to shift attention from merely increasing employee engagement to creating 'cultures of contribution' (Drake, 2016). Rather than focusing on overcoming resistance, the focus is on creating the conditions in which people and the organisation help each other be at their best and adapt.

Quadrant 4: Coaching and Organisation Development

Much of the work in this area is based in the organisation development literature. Some scholars consider OD to be within the purview of HRD (McLagan, 1989), which is often seen as the part of HR management that deals with training and developing employees. Others conceive of OD as a complementary but separate field of study (see Weisbord, 1987 for an excellent overview of its early history). Either way, coaching is seen as one tool in the broader array of options to help individuals and organisations meet their developmental needs. It seems important then that coaching be seen as a more holistic approach to development by both OD and HRD leaders and those who coach among others. Even though it is not always easy to draw sharp distinctions given the interdisciplinary nature of coaching, more conceptual and empirical clarification is needed regarding the boundaries between coaching and other forms of organisational and psychological intervention (Grant et al., 2010).

Weick (1977, 1982, 1993, 2001) and Weick and Quinn (1999) was one of the early champions of this systemic approach to helping organisations operate and adapt more effectively. More recently, Beckhard (2006) provided a comprehensive definition of OD as 'an effort (1) planned, (2) organization-wide, and (3) managed from the top, to (4) increase organization effectiveness and health through (5) planned interventions in the organization's "processes," using behavioral-science knowledge' (p. 3). However, the philosophy inherent in much of coaching seems to align more closely with more contemporary perspectives on developing organisations. Such views tend to regard OD efforts as being: (1) emergent within structures, (2) enacted through connected communities and (3) coordinated across the network to (4) increase wellbeing and systemically meaningful outcomes through (5) a robust set of guiding principles and shared knowledge to facilitate the desired changes in mindsets, behaviors and environments in service of the core aspirations (Drake, 2016).

However, little literature exists on how the fields that inform the development of people and the development of organisations can best work together theoretically or practically. For example, each discipline could enrich the other through a shared inquiry into the nature of what Weick (1984) called 'small wins' as a resource for change and transitions. The need for greater integration is heightened by the fact that both disciplines are ripe for disruption, in large part due to the significant complexities and changes in organisations and economies. Table 9.1 cites five areas as examples of where the two domains overlap and could beneficially be brought together in a generative manner.

Integrative development

Research by the CIPD, UK (2008) into coaching trends, using a sample of 729 HR members, found that only 25% of organizations had coaching formally written into a learning and development strategy; coaching was perceived to be a stand-alone process. In the 2010 survey of HR professionals, they identified the major organisational change for organisational learning in the next five years, would be a 'greater integration between coaching, organisational development and performance management to drive organisational change' (CIPD, 2010, p. 2).

Lewin (1952) described a dialectical relationship between changes in perception/cognition and behavior. He asserted that one must know the totality of forces operating in that individual's psychological field in order to understand the behavior of an individual. He had the critical insight that it was the total field – not the elements in isolation – that produces behavior. Almost three decades later, Hanna (1988) developed this theme by proposing that the true competitive advantage is found in the ability to produce real systems change that is enduring. For Hanna this requires two things: (1) 'changing the basic values and assumptions – the core culture – when they are out of sync with

Table 9.1 Five areas where human and organisation development literatures overlap

	Influences on how organizations develop	Implications for coaching
Complexity	(Aldrich, 1997, 1999; Olson & Eoyang, 2001; Stacey, 1996, 2001)	The need to rethink development from an evolutionary and complex adaptive systems perspective in order for them to be effective in a VUCA[1] world
Learning	(Lave, 1996; Marquardt, 2011; Pascale & Miller, 1999; Wenger, 1998)	The need to focus more on learning as situated, connected and enacted; structure coaching processes and agreements to embed what has transformed
Narratives	(Czarniawska, 1997, 1998; Drake, 2015; Drake & Lanahan, 2007)	The need to connect coachee's stories with the narratives from which they came, in which they live and work, and to which they aspire
Shadows	(Bowles, 1990, 1991; Marshak, 2006; Shaw, 1997)	The need to balance gains from positive psychologies with developmental and existential psychologies to address the full spectrum of our humanity
Sustainability	(Hawken, Lovins, & Lovins, 2013; Laloux, 2014; Scharmer, 2007)	The need for coaching to help leaders and teams address the seismic changes related to sustainability and the changing nature of work and need to self-organize

[1] Volatile, Uncertain, Complex and Ambiguous

business requirements; and (2) structurally reinforcing work behaviors through the design of the organisation to be congruent with the desired strategy' (p. 67). Together, they speak to the need to address four core elements that are required for development and change – behavior, environment, aspiration and mindset (BEAM) – which serve as the core elements of integrative development (Drake, 2016).

The integrative nature of this emerging body of work can be seen in the proposition that it transcends and includes three classic approaches to developing organisations (Bushe & Marshak, 2009, 2015; D. Grant & Marshak, 2008). These include the *diagrammatic* (focused on changing environments and how people are organised), the *diagnostic* (focused on changing behaviors and how people act and perform, and the *dialogic* (focused on changing mindsets and how people think and communicate). A more contemporary *integrative* approach focused on changing the dynamic interactions of mindsets, behaviors and environments so that people and organisations co-evolve is called for.

This emerging body of work follows in the footsteps of similar efforts in other disciplines such as medicine and psychotherapy. For the purposes of this discussion, the term *integrative* is taken to mean combining and coordinating diverse elements into a holistic manner. In this case, integrative development brings adult development and organisation development into a unified theory and set of practices. In so doing, it also provides a theory of development and change, and it brings together three disciplines (coaching, training and OD) to enable people and organisations to develop together. It addresses the fact that many practitioners struggle with the same challenge faced by organisations. Namely, just as practitioners work with organisations to break down silos to create more agile and collaborative ways of working, so too must development-oriented practitioners do the same if they are to remain relevant and effective.

In integrative development, behavior is influenced by both mindset (and the identity and stories that support it) and environment (and the culture and stories that support it). As such, the aim is to develop people at all three levels (mindset, environment and behavior) at the same time so that each one enriches the other and the results are more sustainable. This is important because many of the factors that shape performance at work are a result of the environment not the individuals (e.g. inefficient structures or systems, outdated processes, conflicting rewards, role confusion or misalignment, or the culture itself). And yet, efforts to develop people and change are still based in old thinking and frames of reference. A good example of this are schools, where young people are still being prepared for a future that no longer exists. It seems a new approach is needed, one in which people personally and collectively grow in sync with what they are aspiring to do and what that will require. It seems to be about co-creating the future or what can be thought of as a Do-It-Yourself-Together approach (DIYT).

Coaching can be used to support development in any of these three areas as well as connect them together for more sustained results. In terms of the four BEAM elements in this work: Behaviours are key for people seeking to enhance their skills; Environments are key for people seeking new ways of working; Aspirations are a reflection of the motivations and purpose for development and Mindsets are key for people seeking to develop themselves. When taken together, these elements provide a resource that people can use to move themselves toward their objectives. One of the benefits of working this way is that people can envision working a new way and develop themselves in the process so they are more capable of delivering on their vision. The net result is that coaching shifts from being largely a specialised activity and towards being a more holistic way in which work gets done and conversations are held.

As Revans (1980) noted, if the group members are unable to change themselves, they will not be able to change what goes on around them. He argues that 'one cannot change the system ... unless one is also changed in the process, since the logical structure of both changes is in correspondence with each other' (p. 277). An integrative approach enables a movement away from trying to change organisations and instead promotes consideration of how more self-organised criticality and change readiness can be developed (see Franklin, 2005) along with a continuous re-invention. Integrative development is an emerging body of work that can be used to frame research and work within organisations in ways that allow people to develop themselves while also developing the organisation (and vice versa). Coaching would seem to be a natural catalyst and resource for integrative development projects of this type.

IMPLICATIONS FOR COACHING AS A DISCIPLINE

All professional disciplines privilege some bodies of knowledge more than others. In looking at coaching in relation to the development of organisations, it may be useful to use a gestalt frame of figure and ground (Minehan, 2006), in preference to a hierarchical one based on somewhat artificial distinctions. This will alleviate the need to privilege one over the other, as both are essential. Such an approach balances the observations of Scott, Murrell, Zintz and Gallagher (2006) that, 'coaching doesn't require the conceptual and theoretical organisational knowledge or competencies required for the more complex dynamics of group and organisation behavior that are required in OD' (Scott et al., 2006, p. 9). The same could be said about OD not requiring the conceptual and theoretical knowledge or the competencies required for the more complex dynamics of human development and change that are required in coaching. Coaches and organisational consultants are generally hired for different deliverables and outcomes, even as both support change in organisations and are increasingly asked to work across their disciplines in support of larger initiatives.

Rather than implying preferential status to any one discipline or perspective, a higher standard could be set for all coaches who work in organisations. As noted in a recent forum[1] coaching sponsors in large organisations are increasingly expecting coaches to bring a more integrative understanding of development. As such, coaches need to more fully recognise the systemic nature of both individual and organisational change. It is important to recognise, however, that the debate within and across the disciplines is more about the disciplines becoming more sophisticated about their own practice rather than imposing their taxonomies on organisations. As Weick (1996) noted, our clients remain unmoved by our rivalries, meaning that they will view the world and their work with little regard for any arbitrary disciplinary boundaries they may be violating. Instead, they are steadfastly focused on solving their organisational problems. As such, a more fully interdisciplinary approach to coaching can be developed as a 'key factor in achieving organisational renewal through personal transformation' (Mandler, 2005, p. 3). This would also provide a stronger platform for future research in and about coaching.

FUTURE RESEARCH

Writing on trends for utilising coaching in organisations, Anderson, Frankovelgia, and Hernez-Broome (2009) noted that:

> The effective management of coaching as a strategic initiative appears to be lagging as coaching needs to be more fully integrated with talent management and other leadership development initiatives. The expectations for what coaching can deliver still exceed what is being achieved. When

leaders were asked what outcomes they expected from coaching and how effectively these outcomes were being realized, wide gaps emerged. (p. 3)

This points the way toward some of the critical needs for more research and scholarship in supporting the on-going evolution of coaching. As Grant and collegaues (2010) suggest, we should 'go well beyond merely examining the ROI for coaching programs ... to research the impact of coaching interventions not just on the individuals, but on different groups and workplace teams, whole organizations as well as the wider community' (p. 38). The net results may include the delineation of a subset of coaching (similar to executive coaching) in which the focus is on coaching in organisations in service of projects related to culture, capabilities, change and/or development.

To this end, the following are key areas for further study to deepen and advocate for an enhanced understanding of coaching in relation to the development of organisations:

- the key factors and differences in a multi-stakeholder approach to coaching;
- the sources and nature of secondary benefits from coaching for organisations;
- the ethical issues related to tensions between coaching the person versus the role;
- a taxonomy of the uses of formal and informal uses of coaching in organisations;
- the phases organisations move through in creating a coaching culture; and
- theory building and testing for integrative development theory.

CONCLUSION

In a global survey of 1,541 CEOs, IBM (2010) reported that 79% of respondents anticipated a more complex future environment but fewer than half believed their organisations were capable of responding creatively to this increased complexity. For Radjou, Prabhu, and Ahuja (2012), there are five major components of complexity – scarcity, diversity, interconnectivity, velocity, and breakneck globalisation – that sit at the heart of these challenges. This chapter has argued that one way to deal with these levels of complexity, is to seek a connection between the literature related to the development of people with the literature related to the development of organisations. Doing so would enable coaches to take a more systemic and sustainable approach to change.

The personal gains achieved through coaching will have the greatest effect in organisations if they can be tied to larger initiatives and processes in the system, such that the desired behaviors are supported and aligned with organisational objectives. The systemic gains achieved through the development of organisations will have the greatest effect for individuals if they are tied to initiatives in which the required behaviors are supported and aligned with their personal and professional objectives. However, recent studies on the high levels of stress and fatigue in organisations suggest that many people continue to try and 'manage' change as if it were a discrete event through which one needs to endure (until normality is restored). A core proposal of this chapter is that change would be better viewed as an evolutionary *process*, rather than merely a transactional *project*. When perceived in this way, the idea of what is 'normal' becomes decoupled from an image of the past or the future and becomes a state of mind grounded in the present. It has also been argued that the time has come to look more seriously at formalising the integrative and interdisciplinary nature of coaching in organisations by drawing on a richer array of knowledge, approaches and practice domains.

NOTE

1 Collaborating for the Future of Coaching, London, 2015

REFERENCES

Aldrich, Howard. (1979). *Organizations and environments*. Englewood Cliffs, NJ: Prentice-Hall.

Aldrich, Howard. (1999). *Organizations evolving*. Thousand Oaks, CA: Sage.

Anderson, M. (2007). The strategic contribution of corporate universities to leadership coaching. In M. Allen (Ed.), *The next generation of corporate universities: Innovative approaches for developing people and expanding organizational capabilities* (pp. 307–322). San Francisco, CA: Pfeiffer.

Anderson, Merrill C., Frankovelgia, Candice, & Hernez-Broome, Gina. (2009). *Creating coaching cultures: What business leaders expect and strategies to get there*. Greensboro, NC: Center for Creative Leadership.

Argyris, Chris. (1980). Making the undiscussable and its undiscussability discussable. *Public Administration Review*, 40(3), 205–213. doi:10.2307/975372

Argyris, Chris. (1990). *Overcoming organizational defenses: Facilitating organizational learning*. Englewood Cliffs, NJ: Prentice-Hall.

Argyris, Chris, & Schön, Donald A. (1974). *Theory in practice: Increasing professional effectiveness*. San Francisco, CA: Jossey-Bass.

Argyris, Chris, & Schön, Donald A. (1978). *Organizational learning: A theory of action perspective*. Reading, MA: Addison-Wesley.

Beckhard, Richard, & Gallos, J.V. (2006). What is organization development? *Org Dev & Trng, 6E (lae)*, 12.

Beckhard, Richard, & Pritchard, Wendy. (1992). *Changing the essence: The art of creating and leading fundamental change in organizations*. San Francisco, CA: Jossey-Bass.

Bennett, John L, & Craig, Wanda. (2005). Coaching eye for the OD practitioner. *OD Practitioner*, 37(3), 51.

Bowles, Martin L. (1990). Recognizing deep structures in organizations. *Organization Studies*, 11(3), 395–412.

Bowles, Martin L. (1991). The organization shadow. *Organization Studies*, 12(3), 387–404.

Bowles, Stephen, Cunningham, Christopher J.L., De La Rosa, Gabriel M., & Picano, James. (2007). Coaching leaders in middle and executive management: Goals, performance, buy-in. *Leadership & Organization Development Journal*, 28(5), 388–408.

Brown, Andrew D., & Starkey, Ken. (2000). Organizational identity and learning: A psychodynamic perspective. *Academy of Management Review*, 25(1), 102–120.

Brown, Donald R., & Harvey, Don. (2011). *An experiential approach to organization development*. Upper Saddle River, NJ: Prentice Hall.

Bushe, Gervase R., & Marshak, Robert J. (2009). Revisioning organization development: Diagnostic and dialogic premises and patterns of practice. *Journal of Applied Behavioral Science*, 45(3), 348–368.

Bushe, Gervase R., & Marshak, Robert J. (Eds.). (2015). *Dialogic organization development: The theory and practice of transformational change*. San Francisco, CA: Berrett-Koehler.

Chartered Institute of Personnel and Development (CIPD). (2010). Annual survey report: Learning and development. Retrieved from London, UK: http://www.cipd.co.uk/binaries/5215_Learning_talent_development_survey_report.pdf

Clutterbuck, David, & Megginson, David. (2005). *Making coaching work: Creating a coaching culture*. London: Chartered Institute of Personnel and Development.

Coutu, Diane, & Kauffman, Carol. (2009). The realities of executive coaching. *Harvard Business Review* (Research Report), 1–25.

Czarniawska, Barbara. (1997). *Narrating the organization: Dramas of institutional identity*. Chicago: University of Chicago Press.

Czarniawska, Barbara. (1998). *A narrative approach to organization studies*. Thousand Oaks, CA: Sage.

Czarniawska, Barbara. (2004). *Narratives in social science research*. London, UK: Sage.

Drake, David B. (2007). An integrated approach to coaching: The emerging story in a large professional services firm. *International Journal of Coaching in Organizations*, 5(3), 22–35.

Drake, David B. (2016). *Reinventing learning and change: The power of Integrative Development at work*. Petaluma, CA: Center for Narrative Coaching & Design.

Drake, David B., & Lanahan, Brian. (2007). The story-driven organization. *Global Business and Organizational Excellence*, 36–46.

Ellinger, Alexander E., Ellinger, Andrea D., & Keller, Scott B. (2005). Supervisory coaching in a logistics context. *International Journal of Physical Distribution & Logistics Management, 35*(9), 620–636.

Ellinger, Andrea D., & Kim, Sewon. (2014). Coaching and human resource development examining relevant theories, coaching genres, and scales to advance research and practice. *Advances in Developing Human Resources, 16*(2), 127–138.

Ely, Katherine, Boyce, Lisa A., Nelson, Johnathan K., Zaccaro, Stephen J., Hernez-Broome, Gina, & Whyman, Wynne. (2010). Evaluating leadership coaching: A review and integrated framework. *The Leadership Quarterly, 21*(4), 585–599.

Feldman, Daniel C., & Lankau, Melenie J. (2005). Executive coaching: A review and agenda for future research. *Journal of Management, 31*(6), 829–848.

Franklin, John. (2005). Change readiness in coaching: Potentiating client change. *evidence-based coaching, 1*, 193–200.

Gardini, Marco, Giuliani, Giovanni, & Marricchi, Marco. (2011). Finding the right place to start change. *McKinsey Quarterly*, 1–5.

Giglio, Leo, Diamante, Thomas, & Urban, Julie M. (1998). Coaching a leader: leveraging change at the top. *Journal of Management Development, 17*(2), 93–105.

Grant, Anthony M., Passmore, Jonathan, Cavanagh, Michael J., & Parker, Helen M. (2010). The state of play in coaching today: A comprehensive review of the field. *International Review of Industrial and Organizational Psychology, 25*(1), 125–167.

Grant, David, & Marshak, Robert J. (2008). *A discourse-theory of organizational change*. Paper presented at the 8th International Conference on Organizational Discourse: Translations, Transformations and Transgressions, London.

Hamlin, Robert G., Ellinger, Andrea D., & Beattie, R.S. (2009). Toward a profession of coaching? A definitional examination of 'coaching','organization development', and 'human resource development'. *International Journal of Evidence Based Coaching and Mentoring, 7*(1), 13–38.

Hanna, David P. (1988). *Designing organizations for high performance* (Vol. 12693): Ft Press.

Hart, E. Wayne. (2003). Developing a coaching culture. *Center for Creative Leadership, 858*, 638–8053.

Hawken, Paul, Lovins, Amory B., & Lovins, L. Hunter. (2013). *Natural capitalism: The next industrial revolution*: Routledge.

Hawkins, Peter. (2012). *Creating a coaching culture: Developing a coaching strategy for your organization*: McGraw-Hill Education (UK).

Heifetz, Ronald A., & Linsky, Marty. (2002). *Leadership on the line: Staying alive through the dangers of leading*. Boston, MA: Harvard Business School Press.

Hooijberg, Robert, & Lane, Nancy. (2009). Using multisource feedback coaching effectively in executive education. *Academy of Management Learning & Education, 8*(4), 483–493.

Hunt, James M. & Weintraub, Joseph R. (2007) *The Coaching Organization: A Strategy for Developing Leaders*. London, UK: Sage.

IBM. (2010). *Capitalizing on compelxity: Insights from the global Chief Executive Officer study*. Retrieved from https://www.hrbartender.com/images/Capitalizing_on_Complexity.pdf

Joo, Baek-Kyoo Brian. (2005). Executive coaching: A conceptual framework from an integrative review of practice and research. *Human Resource Development Review, 4*(4), 462–488.

Joo, Baek-Kyoo Brian, Sushko, Jerilynn S., & McLean, Gary N. (2012). Multiple faces of coaching: Manager-as-coach, executive coaching, and formal mentoring. *Organization Development Journal, 30*(1), 19.

Katz, Judith H., & Miller, Frederick A. (1996). Coaching leaders through culture change. *Consulting Psychology Journal: Practice and Research, 48*(2), 104–114. doi:10.1037/1061-4087.48.2.104

Kiel, Fred, Rimmer, Eric, Williams, Kathryn, & Doyle, Marilyn. (1996). Coaching at the top. *Consulting Psychology Journal: Practice and Research, 48*(2), 67.

Kilburg, Richard R. (1996). Toward a conceptual understanding and definition of executive coaching. *Consulting Psychology Journal: Practice and Research, 48*(2), 134–144. doi:10.1037/1061-4087.48.2.134

Kotter, John. (1995, March–April). Leading change: Why transformation efforts fail. *Harvard Business Review*, 59–67.

Laloux, Frederic. (2014). *Reinventing organizations: A guide to creating organizations *inspired by the next stage of human consciousness*. Brussels, Belgium: Nelson Parker.

Lave, Jean. (1996). The practice of learning. In Seth Chaiklin & Jean Lave (Eds.), *Understanding practice: Perspectives on activity and context* (pp. 3–32). Cambridge, UK: Cambridge University Press.

Lerner, Richard M. (1985). Individual and context in developmental psychology: Conceptual and theoretical issues *Individual development and social change: Explanatory analysis* (pp. 155–187).

Levenson, Alec. (2009). Measuring and maximizing the business impact of executive coaching. *Consulting Psychology Journal: Practice and Research*, 61(2), 103.

Lewin, Kurt. (1952). *Field theory in social science*. London, UK: Tavistock.

Lloyd, Bruce. (2005). Coaching, culture and leadership. *Team Performance Management: An International Journal*, 11(3/4), 133–138.

Maister, David H., Green, Charles H. & Galford, Robert M. (2000) *The Trusted Advisor*. New York: The Free Press.

Malone, John W. (2001). Shining a new light on organizational change: Improving self-efficacy through coaching. *Organization Development Journal*, 19(2), 27.

Mandler, T. (2005). *The Integration of Context in the Coaching Process*. Melbourne Business School/Mt. Eliza Centre for Executive Education.

Marquardt, Michael J. (2011). *Optimizing the power of action learning* (2nd ed.). Boston, MA: Nicholas Brealey.

Marshak, Robert J. (1993). Managing the metaphors of change. *Organizational Dynamics*, (Summer), 44–56.

Marshak, Robert J. (2006). *Covert processes at work: Managing the five hidden dimensions of organizational change*. San Francisco, CA: Berrett-Koehler.

McCauley, Cynthia D., & Hezlett, Sarah A. (2001). Individual development in the workplace. *Handbook of industrial, work, and organizational psychology*, 2(1), 313–335.

McComb, Christiaan. (2012). Developing coaching culture: Are your coaching relationships healthy? *Industrial and Commercial Training*, 44(4), 232–235.

McCulloch, P., Rathbone, J., & Catchpole, K. (2011). Interventions to improve teamwork and communications among healthcare staff. *British Journal of Surgery*, 98(4), 469–479.

McLagan, Patricia A. (1989). Models for HRD practice. *Training & Development Journal*, 43(9), 49–60.

McNally, Kimberly, & Lukens, Rosemary. (2006). Leadership development: An external–internal coaching partnership. *Journal of Nursing Administration*, 36(3), 155–161.

Megginson, David, & Clutterbuck, David. (2006). Creating a coaching culture. *Industrial and Commercial Training*, 38(5), 232–237.

Minahan, Matt. (2006, Summer). The foundations of coaching. *OD Practitioner*, 38, 4–7.

Morgan, Gareth. (1997). *Images of organizations*. Thousand Oaks, CA: Sage.

Nystrom, Paul C., & Starbuck, William H. (1984). To avoid organizational crises, unlearn. *Organizational Dynamics* (Spring), 53–65.

O'Connor, Sean, & Cavanagh, Michael. (2013). The coaching ripple effect: The effects of developmental coaching on wellbeing across organisational networks. *Psychology of Well-Being: Theory, Research and Practice*, 3(1), 1–23.

Olivero, Gerald, Bane, K. Denise, & Kopelman, Richard E. (1997). Executive coaching as a transfer of training tool: Effects on productivity in a public agency. *Public Personnel Management*, 26(4), 461–469.

Olson, Edwin E., & Eoyang, Glenda H. (2001). *Facilitating organizational change: Lessons from complexity science*. San Francisco, CA: Jossey-Bass/Pfieffer.

Oshry, Barry. (2007). *Seeing systems: Unlocking the mysteries of organizational life*: Berrett-Koehler Publishers.

Pascale, Richard T., & Miller, Anne H. (1999). The Action Lab: Creating a greenhouse for organizational change. http://www.strategy-business.com/article/13809?gko=561ee

Pemberton, Carole. (2012). *Coaching to Solutions*. Routledge.

Peterson, Suzanne J., & Luthans, Fred. (2003). The positive impact and development of hopeful leaders. *Leadership & Organization Development Journal*, 24(1), 26–31.

Radjou, Navi, Prabhu, Jaideep, & Ahuja, Simone. (2012). *Jugaad innovation: Think frugal, be flexible, generate breakthrough growth*. John Wiley & Sons.

Revans, Reg W. (1980). *Action learning: New techniques for management*. London, UK: Blond & Briggs.

Saporito, Thomas J. (1996). Business-linked executive development: Coaching senior executives. *Consulting Psychology Journal: Practice and Research*, 48(2), 96.

Scharmer, C. Otto. (2007). *Theory U: Leading from the future as it emerges*. Boston, MA: Society for Organizational Learning.

Schein, Edgar. (1988). *Process consultation*. Menlo Park: Addison-Wesley.

Schein, Edgar. (1992). *Organizational culture and leadership*. San Francisco, CA: Jossey-Bass.

Schein, Edgar. (1996). Three cultures of management: The key to organizational learning *Sloan Management Review*, 38(1), 9–21.

Schein, Edgar. (1999). *The corporate culture survival guide*. San Francisco, CA: Jossey-Bass.

Scott, Beverly, Murrell, Lisa, Zintz, Andrea, & Gallagher, Denny. (2006, Summer). Is coaching OD? *OD Practitioner*, 38, 8–11.

Senge, Peter M. (1990). *The fifth discipline: The art and practice of the learning organization*. New York, NY: Doubleday.

Shaw, Patricia. (1997). Intervening in the shadow systems of organizations. *Journal of Organizational Change Management*, 10(3), 235–250.

Smither, James W., London, Manuel, Flautt, Raymond, Vargas, Yvette, & Kucine, Ivy. (2003). Can working with an executive coach improve multisource feedback ratings over time? A quasi-experimental field study. *Personnel Psychology*, 56(1), 23–44.

Stacey, Ralph. (1996). *Complexity and creativity in organizations*. San Francisco, CA: Berrett-Koehler.

Stacey, Ralph. (2001). *Complex responsive processes in organizations*. London, UK: Routledge.

Stout-Rostron, Sunny. (2010). How is coaching impacting systemic and cultural change within organizations? *International Journal of Coaching in Organizations*, 8(4), 5–27.

Swart, Chené. (2015). Coaching from a Dialogic OD paradigm. *Dialogic Organization Development*, 349–370.

Tsoukas, Haridimos, & Chia, Robert. (2002). On organizational becoming: Rethinking positional change. *Organization Science*, 13(5), 567–582.

Walker-Fraser, Alison. (2011). An HR perspective on executive coaching for organizational learning. *International Journal of Evidence Based Coaching and Mentoring*, 9(2), 67–79.

Weick, Karl E. (1977). Organization design: Organizations as self-designing systems. *Organizational Dynamics*, 6(2), 31–46.

Weick, Karl E. (1982). Management of organizational change among loosely coupled elements. In P.S. Goodman (Ed.), *Change in organizations* (pp. 375–408). San Francisco, CA: Jossey-Bass.

Weick, Karl E. (1984). Small wins: Redefining the scale of social problems. *American Psychologist*, 39(1), 40–49.

Weick, Karl E. (1993). Organizational redesign as improvisation. In George P. Huber & William H. Glick (Eds.), *Organizational change and redesign: Ideas and insights for improving performance* (pp. 346–379). Oxford, UK: Oxford University Press.

Weick, Karl E. (1996). Speaking to practice: The scholarship of integration. *Journal of Management Inquiry*, 5(3), 251–258.

Weick, Karl E. (2001). *Making sense in organizations*. Malden, MA: Blackwell.

Weick, Karl E., & Quinn, Robert E. (1999). Organizational change and development. *Annual Review of Psychology*, 50, 361–386.

Weisbord, Marvin R. (1987). *Productive workplaces: Organizing and managing for dignity, meaning and community*. San Francisco, CA: Jossey-Bass.

Wenger, Etienne. (1998). *Communities of practice: Learning, meaning, and identity*. New York, NY: Cambridge University Press.

Whitmore, John. (1992). *Coaching for performance* (Third ed.). London, UK: Nicholas Brealey.

Wilson, Carol. (2011). Developing a coaching culture. *Industrial and Commercial Training*, 43(7), 407–414.

Witherspoon, Robert, & White, Randall P. (1996). Executive coaching: A continuum of roles. *Consulting Psychology Journal: Practice and Research*, 48(2), 124.

Coaching for Social Change

Hany Shoukry

INTRODUCTION

Much of the coaching literature has focused on its application in organizational settings, mostly in Western countries, and within an individualistic self-improvement paradigm. This chapter explores coaching as a human development approach that can foster social change. It proposes that, besides the organizational and individual domains, coaching can play an important role in the social domain, and that all three domains are closely interconnected.

Coaching theorists are starting to argue that we should understand how world needs and individual needs are connected, and use coaching as one of the most powerful means of meeting both needs (Outhwaite & Bettridge, 2009). There are several critiques, such as Du Toit (2014) and Western (2012), of how coaching could be used to maintain oppression, and research, such as Shoukry (2014), into how coaching can become emancipatory. However, coaching for social change is still under-researched and under-theorized. Hence, this chapter is an attempt to lay a foundation for this emerging field, drawing on critical theory and postmodernism, sociology, psychology, and pedagogy.

Different sociological theories define social change in different ways. For example, social change may be defined as any alteration in the social system, that may involve a change in the social structure, processes, relations or any other aspects of the society (Sztompka, 1993). Such definition has the risk of being overly neutral, as opposed to other definitions that consider social change as development or progress, with the equally problematic nature of such terms. For the purpose of this chapter, social change is defined as 'change that makes society or workplaces more humanizing, in terms of fostering human rights, and thriving towards what would seem more just, ecologically sustainable, inclusive, empowering and peaceful', while appreciating that all of these normative ideals can be defined in different ways within different cultures and ideologies, and can be sought via different social and economic models.

The chapter starts by discussing the interrelation between individual development and social change; and exploring how this relation inspired the emergence of critical pedagogies and approaches within many disciplines. Coaching is then critically analysed as a potential approach for social change. Next, the different contexts and models of coaching for social change are presented, followed by a discussion of the implications of the social change aspect on the coaching process and the development of coaches. I conclude with a discussion of how the social agenda may impact coaching body politic, coaching theory, and future research.

INDIVIDUAL DEVELOPMENT AND SOCIAL CHANGE

What does social change mean in today's world? And how does it relate to an approach for individual development such as coaching? To answer these questions, we need to understand how the boundaries and interactions between individual and society are changing.

It was not until the 1970s that the significant impact of culture and social systems on adult development began to be adequately discussed (Naumann & Hüfner, 2013). As Lerner (2013) notes: 'Interest emerged in the bidirectional relations between developing people and the multilevel, interrelated settings within which they live their lives (e.g., the family, the community, the physical environment, and the culture, including its system of symbols and values)' (p. 155). A proper understanding of what it means to develop individually needs to incorporate an understanding of the context where this development takes place.

It is not hard to see why coaching has gained such a warm reception in the context of present times. The demands of modern life on individuals' cognitive and emotional development have significantly increased (Kegan, 1994). At a macro level, we are enduring a sustained period of psychosocial fragmentation, where the self has become severed from its traditional points of anchorage. Globalization, new technologies, and transnational corporations have created an environment where the individual is the basic unit for social reproduction, and where socially prescribed biographies are being replaced with self-produced ones (Adams, 2007). A fixed cohesive identity has become a burden, as new careers are emerging, social networks are breaking the barriers of distance and time, and relocation across the globe is becoming more frequent (Bauman, 2004).

Is this rise of individualization emancipatory? Does it signify the triumph of human agency over social structures? Adams (2007) argues that the same inequalities still exist, but are more individualized. The first implication of this is that simple class or race categories are no longer representative of the individual's identity, which makes solidarity over a social cause, and collaboration for social change, more problematic (Putnam, 2001).

The second implication has to do with how oppression works. Oppression defines the experience of significant numbers of people around the world. It acts as a complete system of structural elements that reproduce inequality in everyday practices (Dominelli, 2002). It gets embedded in the unconscious assumptions of people and the normal processes of everyday life (Young, 2000). The most powerful tool for maintaining oppression is its internalization, when oppressive ideologies become embedded in personal beliefs, and socially prescribed roles become part of people's identities. The internalization of oppression means that even when external oppressive conditions change, people aim to recreate them, because they have in them the image of their oppressor (Freire, 1970). Internalized oppression affects individuals with self-hatred, fear, feelings of inferiority, resignation, isolation, and powerlessness

(Pheterson, 1986). Even being a bystander in an oppressive environment results in a long list of psychic wounds (Watkins & Shulman, 2008).

Oppression is therefore experienced at a deeply personal level, with collective political action becoming more challenging. This is where coaching becomes critically relevant for social change. Resisting oppression needs to take place from the inside out. Social change starts by internal steps such as empowerment of the self, dismantling dysfunctional beliefs, and gaining inspiration and authenticity (Harro, 2000). Emancipation becomes a personal project that involves a transformation within the individual that results in social change. Coaching interventions can play a role at the heart of the tension between individual agency and social structure. Coaching can act as an enabler for personal transformation and action, supporting individuals in understanding how society is shaping their experience and their beliefs, and in acting to change their immediate and wider social conditions.

LOCATING COACHING FOR SOCIAL CHANGE

The Critical Pedagogical Tradition

A useful way to locate coaching for social change is to compare it against different pedagogical traditions. I use here the taxonomy suggested by Boud (1989), and discussed in Chappell et al. (2003) and Usher et al. (2004). There are four pedagogical traditions, compared in Table 10.1: (1) The training tradition, focusing on efficient learning to acquire predefined skills and knowledge, assuming that the learner, content and learning process are neutral; (2) The andragogy tradition, focusing on learning from experience, assuming that the learner is self-directed and resourceful, and that subjective experience is the source of real knowledge; (3) The humanistic tradition, focusing on realising an authentic self, assuming that the self possesses innate knowledge and tendencies; and (4) The critical tradition: focusing on emancipation and social change, assuming that knowledge is socially constructed and should be critiqued.

In the first three traditions, objective knowledge, subjective experience and self, respectively, are considered authentic, rather than socially constructed. These traditions have been criticized as being overly individualistic. They portray social problems as largely individual problems with individual solutions, while implicitly accepting the social world as given. On the other hand, the critical tradition acknowledges the social realm, perhaps as the only reality, focusing on liberating individuals from oppression through ideology critique, and social action.

The mainstream of coaching has evolved primarily within the andragogy and humanistic

Table 10.1 Four traditions of pedagogies of change

	Training	Andragogy	Humanistic	Critical
Learner is	Neutral	Unique, Rational meaning-maker	Holistic, Self-knowing consciousness	Social actor, Socially-formed consciousness
Success depends on	Learning efficiency	Self-direction, Reflectiveness	Learner-centricity, Authenticity	Ideology critique, Social action
Knowledge is	Objective, Pre-defined	Subjective, Experiential	Subjective, Innate	Socially constructed
Seeks to	Acquisition of skills and knowledge	Learn from experience	Realise authentic self	Liberate from oppression, Change society

traditions (Western, 2012). Coaching celebrates the self, it assumes a resourceful and self-directed individual, and relies on reflecting on experience and relationships (Rogers, 2008). Some coaching models have common elements with the training tradition, focusing on changing behaviours and acquiring skills. On the other hand, coaching for social change originates within a critical worldview that sees experiences and meanings as socially constructed, and proposes that individual transformation must be linked to social change.

The Rise of Critical Approaches

Another way to understand coaching for social change is to compare it to critical approaches within other disciplines. Many human development and helping disciplines have started to develop critical genres within their practices, even before the early rise of coaching. For example, in education, critical pedagogy has led the way, based on the seminal work of Paulo Freire. Critical pedagogy practitioners try to balance a belief in human agency, and an awareness of social structure. They aim to provide learners with the tools that would allow them to challenge inequalities and injustices, and to collectively change society if they choose to do so (Usher et al., 2004). Other critical approaches within education include the theory of transformative learning (Mezirow, 2000), and feminist pedagogy (MacDonald, 2002).

In the fields of psychiatry and psychotherapy, there have been multiple critiques to how traditional approaches may form part of the oppressive structure. Fanon (1967) called for a new practice that would aim to liberate the oppressed rather than contribute to their oppression. A similar call came from the work of Martín-Baró in Latin America, leading to the creation of liberation psychology (Watkins & Shulman, 2008). Psychologies of liberation give primacy to the attainment of collective liberty, as opposed to the focus on individual narratives, that is, balancing the attention given to alleviating the symptoms of the individual's suffering with the aim to change pathogenic social conditions (Bulhan, 2004). Another approach in that domain is feminist therapy, which is based on the premise that personal problems are created and intensified by structural inequality and societal power imbalances (Magnet & Diamond, 2010).

More recently, a similar trend could be seen in person-centred therapy (PCT). This is particularly relevant, as PCT has been a key inspiration to coaching (Palmer & Whybrow, 2007). In 2005, a network called 'Person-Centred Practitioners for Social Change' was formed, with the following mission: 'We want to voice our opposition to inequalities and oppression in the world. We celebrate diversity and commit ourselves to working towards social justice. We aim to raise public awareness about the political, social and economic causes of distress in society. We aim to promote relationships where people listen to each other and each person has a voice. We believe in acting with honesty, integrity and transparency, whilst aiming to value and understand all others' (Proctor, 2006, p. 2).

It could be argued that coaching for social change is to mainstream coaching what critical approaches in education and psychotherapy are to traditional approaches within those disciplines. It aims to fill the gap in the current coaching theory, while leveraging the potential of coaching as an enabler for change. Like these approaches, coaching for social change emerges from a critique of disconnecting individual development from social change, and an appreciation of the power of coaching in connecting these two domains.

CRITICAL ANALYSIS OF COACHING AS A SOCIAL APPROACH

There is a growing critique to current coaching approaches, theories and culture, in terms of how coaching is too individual, instrumental, and culturally-biased. Meanwhile, there is also a growing hope that coaching can become a social enabler, because it is empowering, reflective and flexible. This section explores both sides of the arguments; the gap in current coaching culture, and the potential of coaching as an approach for social change.

Wildflower (2013) suggests that coaching has roots in the growth of the self-help tradition in the United States in the 1930s and the human potential movement in the 1960s. She argues that the focus on the potential of individuals came partially as a response to a general disbelief in the socioeconomic systems. The growth of coaching is often linked to a growth in individualism (Whitmore, 2007). The individualistic focus has been a key theme for the critique of coaching and the general therapeutic culture of the last few decades (Swan, 2010). Individualizing problems limits the possibility of critically challenging the social beliefs and structures that created these problems in the first place (Du Toit, 2014). Many writers argue that coaching may act as a deflector for organizational tension by individualizing conflicts, so that structural problems are interpreted and narrated as being individual issues (Kühl, 2008; Schultz, 2010; Fatien Diochon and Lovelace, 2015).

Coaching has emerged primarily as a performance improvement approach used in business environments. Coaching theories and research have mainly focused on that context, which have resulted in two issues: First, most coachees are managers at medium to big organizations, a population that is primarily composed of alpha males (Erlandson, 2009). This bias in the experience of coaches may result in a falsely optimistic understanding of how power dynamics, social structures, and organizational culture affect individuals (Lasley et al., 2011). Second, the performance improvement mentality makes coaching less critical. Western (2012) criticizes a domination of the coaching space by 'technocratic functionalist coaches', who apply tools and techniques with instrumental mindsets. Brockbank and McGill (2012) argue that the focus on performance coaching leads to maintaining the status quo, by suppressing challenge and questioning to the existing system. In their view, performance coaching tends to reinforce existing power relations and reproduce social inequalities.

Another critique of coaching is that it stems from a dominant western cultural view (Western, 2012). Within this cultural view there are embedded assumptions about the coachees and their world, such as the belief that coachees are resourceful, and the principles of free will, choice and self-responsibility (Rogers, 2008). These assumptions are questionable in many places in the world, as well as in many communities within western developed countries. Wherever oppressive social structures are present, free will and choice may be prohibited by social coercion, or internally relinquished because of dysfunctional beliefs. In many cases, coachees are bound by socially acquired frames of reference that hinder their resourcefulness.

Some studies respond to the cultural bias in the literature by focusing on coaching in other cultural contexts (For example: Nangalia & Nangalia, 2010; Passmore, 2009). However, a common critique of many of these studies is that they tend to focus on adapting to the local culture and work within its boundaries. The underlying assumption is that the coach needs to accept the social order as a given, regardless of its implications on the individual. Another assumption is that all coachees living within a certain cultural context will prefer to abide by it, thus implicitly denying them the right to resist such an identity and to define their own. Most accounts seem to be missing a critical stance, whereby cultural traits are also questioned and challenged where necessary.

Despite the limitations highlighted above, coaching has a number of strengths that would allow it to be an effective approach for social change. First, coaching is participatory in nature; equality between coach and client is a core principle (Rogers, 2008), coaches are not expected to be more experienced than their coachees (CIPD, 2004), and there is a general consensus that coaching is non-directive (Ives, 2008). Hence, coaching can be seen as a collaborative and facilitative relationship (Grant, 2003). A participatory ethic does not mean that power is not problematic (Welman & Bachkirova, 2010), but it provides an enabling environment for fostering empowerment.

Another important strength of coaching is its capacity to support critical reflection. Cox (2012) argues that 'one of the fundamental, but usually unspoken, aims of coaching is to facilitate clients to become critical' (p. 91). Kristal (2009) suggests that the change happening in coaching is often the result of the process of critical reflection, that may result in either action or a new frame of reference. Critical reflection in coaching helps to transform the client by exposing power relations, challenging what is deemed natural, accepting the reality of conflict, and appreciating the power of language and the prevailing discourse (Brockbank & McGill, 2006). Moreover, coaching provides an environment where such challenge to the coachee's beliefs could be balanced with the needed support and appreciation (Du Toit, 2014).

A third aspect of coaching is flexibility. Coaching is often critiqued for being unregulated and unstandardized, but it is also this fact that makes it open and adaptable to serve different purposes. Western (2012) describes coaching as 'a vital and dynamic space that enables creativity to emerge, whereas other "helping relationships" are often saddled with more restrictive cultures' (p.10). Within this dynamic space, some practitioners have started to explore coaching as an approach for social change, which is the focus of the next section.

CONTEXTS AND MODELS OF COACHING FOR SOCIAL CHANGE

Coaching for social change can take place in various settings; in terms of whether it is supporting leaders, activists or victims; is part of institutional or grassroots efforts, is occurring in culturally-diverse or culturally-specific environments, and is dealing with specific social issues or holistic experiences. Reported studies generally fall into three groups: (1) Coaching business executives to be socially responsible, (2) Coaching leaders and practitioners in the social sector, and (3) Coaching individuals and groups affected by adverse social conditions, to transform their internal and external realities.

Social Change in the Work Domain

Work is identified as a domain for social change from two perspectives: First, corporate executives may be major influencers of the lives of millions of people; through the way they direct their companies in the market. Second, work constitutes a significant part of the individual's experience and identity, organizational systems are similar to public political and social systems, and they have similar tensions between agency and structure. There is also a mutual impact between what happens in an organization, and what happens in the society or societies where this organization exists, so changing the organization becomes a form of social change.

The first group of studies argues that coaching can play a role in making executives act responsibly in their companies and in the world. Eyre (2012), in an interview with Sir John Whitmore, quotes him saying that coaching can save the world, arguing that coaching can help leaders of organizations appreciate the need for a more inclusive and caring capitalism, that balances profit and people. Along the same lines, Outhwaite and Bettridge (2009), and Stern (2011) argue that coaching can help executives to link the social perspective with their organizational and personal goals. Dyer (2002) argues that coaching can help restructure the belief systems of executives to prevent destructive behaviours driven by arrogance and power. This belief is shared by Du Toit and Sim (2010), who argue that critical coaching can help leaders understand their role in establishing corporate social responsibility.

The above accounts do not offer enough detail on how coaches could support leaders to act differently. Meanwhile, Du Toit (2013, 2014) argues that scepticism is one of the key aspects of a coaching approach that would challenge groupthink and the status quo within organizations. The sceptical or critical mindset, associated with critical theory, would enable the coach to challenge the taken for granted values and beliefs in the organization, and help the coachee to act independently, questioning the organizational metanarrative and welcoming new interpretations. Another consideration, by Reissner and Du Toit (2011), is the importance of reflexivity while using narratives, so that stories are not used as tools to influence and distort how reality is perceived within the organization, for example, by reframing unethical market behaviours as bold and daring, or by positioning work overload as a personal achievement.

Focusing on how coaching can help create a reflective learning organization, one that exposes control, inequality and biases rather than perpetuating them, Askew and Carnell (2011) propose a view for transformative coaching, grounded in the theory of transformative learning. They suggest that issues to do with self-identity and power relationships are at the root of many of the concerns that coachees bring to coaching, and argue that a coaching approach that fosters critical consciousness through reflective learning is capable of helping individuals to think differently about themselves, their organization, and their society, as well as empowering them to act as agents of change.

A more detailed coaching approach is provided by Western (2012), who proposes the Analytic-Network coaching process (A-NcP) as a conceptual framework for helping individuals to strive for a collective endeavour to improve workplaces and society. A-NcP includes five frames: (1) Depth analysis, where coachees identify their values, desire, and purpose, (2) Relational analysis, where they understand the dynamics between them and others, (3) Leadership analysis, where they develop their leadership roles, (4) Network analysis, where they understand and build their networks of power and resources, and (5) Strategic analysis, to consolidate the outcomes of the other frames. Western suggests that A-NcP needs to be underpinned by emancipatory ethics: to value the individual, strive for more humane organizations, act responsibly towards the environment, challenge power and injustice, help individuals discover their creativity and autonomy, and to act in good faith to help create the good society.

Coaching in the Social Domain

The second group of studies focuses on a new role for coaching in supporting social entrepreneurs, nonprofit leaders, activists, and social workers. Coaching in the social sector initially focused on leadership development and organizational capacity building, in ways similar to coaching in a business context (Lasley et al., 2011). A good example is the Coaching and Philanthropy project (CAP) in the United States, which provides coaching for nonprofit leaders and teams (Howard, Gislason, & Kellogg, 2010). The CAP project has done surveys and interviews to understand how coaching works in nonprofits. Asking coachees what they hope to get from coaching, 67% chose 'to develop leadership skills/confidence' as a high priority, they also prioritized enhancing management skills, balancing the personal and professional in their lives, and managing organizational change. The CAP project guide lists three key competences for coaches to perform in the nonprofit environment: (1) Understanding of nonprofits, this includes governance structures, fundraising, volunteering, mission, unique nonprofit human resource challenges, cultures and needs across the sector, and the scarcity mindset; (2) Core coaching skills; and (3) Cultural awareness, which transpires in the ability to use coaching in addressing different forms of oppression, and that the coach's work reflects a critical analysis of how power, privilege and difference play out in society.

Coaching is also used to support the implementation of specific social endeavours. For example, de Jager (2011) reports on a programme where 150 executives selected from government, NGOs, business donors and the private sector were offered executive coaching, while working together to develop innovations and change in the sector of orphaned and vulnerable children in South Africa. Similarly, Ngwenya and Hagmann (2007) report on the use of mentoring and coaching to support team leaders in implementing a participatory change programme within a South African community.

More recently, coaching skills started to be used by direct service providers (Lasley et al., 2011). Applications emerged in relation to supporting healthy lifestyle after recovery from substance dependence (LePage & Garcia-Rea, 2012), managing change in gender transition (Grajfoner, 2009), and coaching for wellness and HIV/AIDS awareness (Maitland & Anderson, 2011). The process of coaching and mentoring has also moved into schools, youth and community settings, working with children and adolescents (Qing & Millward, 2014).

Meanwhile, Caspi (2005) examines with some concern the growth of coaching as a mode of practice for social workers. He cites studies on the use of coaching to help people with biopsychosocial challenges, such as eating disorders, grief, family communications, marriages, ADHD, and assisting people with life-threatening illnesses, and comments:

> Because there is no control over who can serve as a coach, how it is practiced, and for what situations, the idea that coaching is being offered for issues that typically fall under the jurisdiction of mental health practitioners should be of great concern. At the same time, coaching may have a lot to offer social work. Currently, we do not know. Empirical examination and discussion about coaching's relationship to social work is needed for the protection of clients and for the benefit of the social work profession. (p. 361)

Coaching research remains somewhat limited in answering those concerns.

Coaching in Oppressive Contexts

The third category for the application of coaching for social change is to coach individuals living in challenging social conditions. For example, the Solidarity Coaching programme offers coaching to individuals with very low income. The programme has been active in France since 2005, and is starting to develop in a number of European countries, under the sponsorship of the European Mentoring and Coaching Council (EMCC, 2015).

Another example is Beyond Emancipation (2015), a programme offering coaching to youths with experience in foster care or probation placements in the United States. It uses a coaching approach called 'CCRW – Creative, Connected, Resourceful and Whole'. The approach is tailored from theories of coaching, permanency, youth development and crisis management, and progresses through six steps: (1) Establishing safety, (2) Getting curious, (3) Supporting awareness, (4) Encouraging exploration, (5) Discovering next steps, and (6) Creating accountability. Similar types of coaching support are provided, through the Coach Network (2015) in the UK, to vulnerable young people, including single parents, ex-offenders and young people disengaged from education.

McGregor (2015) reports on the Coaching Inside and Out (CIAO) programme, supporting women in UK prisons. She describes a model that focuses on visioning and empowerment, by asking coachees what they want to change, and facilitating the process of achieving that change. The coaching process involves the use of a tool to measure improvement across multiple categories. Significant improvement has been reported across all categories, especially in self-reliance and 'social capital' (i.e. supportive networks and relationships).

Beyond these specific communities, there are countless situations where coaching can become either a tool for maintaining the status quo, or an enabler for social change. Consider what is at stake when coaching women in a patriarchal society, working with ethnic or religious minorities, coaching in countries with a history of dictatorship or war, or coaching the poor, illiterate or disabled. In every situation where coachees are part of an oppressive social structure, coaching becomes a political process, even when it takes place under the banners of life, career, or developmental coaching. Acknowledging the significance of the social structure, without denying the coachee's agency, embeds coaching as part of the daily micro-battles of emancipation and social change.

Shoukry (2014, 2016) proposes the Coaching For Emancipation (CFE) framework, as a research-based theoretical and practical framework for the use of coaching in oppressive environments. The CFE framework provides a detailed understanding of how living in oppressive environments affects coaches, coachees, and the coaching process. It suggests that oppression is experienced as a complex web of daily interactions that affects the entire social and psychological experience of the individual, depriving him/her from the concept of choice, and fostering senses of helplessness, unworthiness, self-blame, and grief. When moving through emancipatory journeys, coachees often go through similar cycles: naming oppression, building hope and self-belief, developing critical awareness, facing social resistance, failing and losing hope, finding alternatives, breaking the cycle of oppression through actions of resistance, and transforming their narratives into ones of liberation. The research through which the CFE framework was developed suggests that emotional processes are critical to the emancipatory journey. The framework also points to the negative impact of oppression on the cognitive and emotional development of the coachee.

According to Shoukry (2014), Coaching for emancipation involves a number of processes:

1 **Empowering Dialogue:** A dialogue that balances empathy and appreciation from one side, and confrontation and criticality from the other, with interventions to support the development of self-efficacy, agency, and meaning making, as well as the coachees' emotional fitness and resilience, by dealing with feelings of fear, self-blame, and self-victimisation.
2 **Retelling Narratives:** A process whereby coachees use stories to understand, externalize and re-author their lives, starting from naming oppression in the lived experience, to authoring a narrative of liberation. Narratives help coachees make sense of their fragmented experiences. They provide possibilities for transforming stories of oppression into ones of liberation. As the heroes of their stories, coachees explore how their stories are filled with aspects of resistance, and moments of victory that they can celebrate.
3 **Renewing Beliefs:** A process where coachees understand and challenge the structures leading to their experiences of oppression, be it social structures or deeply held beliefs. Interventions of social analysis and self-reflection are used, allowing the personal and political to re-interpret each other.
4 **Fighting Back:** A process that supports action in three domains; breaking from the reality of daily oppression, experimenting with new ideas and behaviours, and engaging in reflective actions of resistance and change. Given that oppressive environments are often unyielding, supporting action involves careful planning and understanding the implications of social conflict, as well as dealing with the emotional barriers of change.

IMPLICATIONS OF COACHING FOR SOCIAL CHANGE

It is evident from the frameworks presented in the previous section that the use of coaching as a social approach – especially with socially vulnerable individuals – has several implications: The foundation upon which the coaching contract is agreed has to be reviewed, the coaching process needs to incorporate elements to deal with issues of power, internalized oppression and social action, and the development of coaches needs to prepare them to face the unique challenges of that context.

Coaching Contract

In mainstream individual coaching, it is assumed that the coachee owns the agenda, and coaches can claim neutrality, on the basis that coachees have full responsibility for their lives. When coaching takes place within an organizational context, there might be a conflict that has to be negotiated between what the organization and the individual are seeking from coaching. In coaching for social change, the coachee may be a leader or an organization who wants to think differently, a social worker or activist, or an individual affected by social oppression, who either independently seeks coaching or is offered coaching as part of a social initiative. In all of these cases, the first question to ask is who gets to decide what is meant by social change.

There are some naturally unavoidable tensions, between individuals and the organizations they work in, or social initiatives and the individuals they serve. But even if we assume – for simplicity – that the coachee is free to decide the purpose of coaching, the goal of social change is likely to affect many people who are not part of the coaching contract. By supporting the coachee in defining and implementing a social agenda, the coachee is acknowledged as a legitimately subjective narrator and co-creator of the social world. This acknowledgment cannot be value neutral.

A coach, who is choosing to support a social endeavour, is thus acting politically. Whether supporting coachees to find their voice and fight oppression, or challenging leaders to think critically and responsibly, the coach's choices are founded on a specific value-driven worldview; one that includes images of the human being, and the good society. As a result, the social change coach is no longer a neutral technical expert, but an active agent who contributes, implicitly or explicitly, to the definition of what coaching is trying to achieve. Coaches may have to disclose their ethical frameworks and social biases, they may choose proactively which social issues they want to work with, or they may have different models of providing their services (for example, paid or pro bono) based on the client and social issue. The issue of neutrality needs to be considered across the field, as many coaches outside the context of social change may be acting politically, even without being fully aware of it.

Coaching Process

A coaching process that supports social change would need to consider several aspects. First to consider is power, an area where coaching research is still very limited. Socially vulnerable coachees are likely to be more susceptible to the effect of power dynamics. Differences between coach and coachee, in terms of gender, race, class, and other factors may significantly add to the complexity of power in the coaching relationship. Power flows in both directions, as coachees contribute through active consent or resistance (Jones, Armour, & Potrac, 2002). Proctor (2008) suggests that it may be helpful for practitioners to have a checklist of considerations for the dynamics of power. Welman and Bachkirova (2010) argue that power can be used with or without awareness, as a mean of domination or empowerment. Even while aspiring to empower, coaches may end up imposing their own 'liberating' ideas on their coachees, or – on the other extreme – withdrawing from playing their role in guiding the process, for fear of overusing their power. Empowerment is hence a complicated process. For example, Heron (1999) argues that a process that supports empowerment should not avoid the use of power, but needs to manage it, Shoukry (2014) suggests that empowerment in the coaching relationship may detract from focusing on empowerment in the coachee's social context, while Inglis (1997) warns that a focus on empowerment may become part of making people act successfully within the existing system and structures of power, instead of critically analysing, resisting and challenging them.

A second process consideration is the criticality needed to validate the competing worldviews; the subjective reality of the coachee, ideologies and grand narratives used as reference, and the cultural reality of the context where coaching is taking place. There is a danger if any of these realities is uncritically legitimized. The coachee's subjectivity may be reflective of misinterpretation, self-victimization, or internalized oppression, grand narratives are susceptible to become hegemonic, and cultural norms – while important to understand – can often act as ideological devices that validate oppression and injustice. Failing to be critical may mean that coaching becomes part of maintaining the status quo. Meanwhile, the degree of criticality required to analysing these realities is not a small burden on a coaching process that also needs to be emotionally empowering, and practically efficient.

The third consideration in the coaching process is around its scope. From one side, working with social issues requires a holistic approach, where the coachee's experiences are connected across multiple domains (work, family … etc.), the experience of one individual is linked to bigger social structures on many layers (culture, law … etc.), and specific beliefs are linked to broader ideologies. From the other side, coachees are much more engaged when the coaching process is directly linked to their immediate lived experience (Shoukry, 2014). So there is a tension between broadening the scope to help the coachee understand and change the bigger social picture, while keeping it personal and relevant.

Another consideration is about the complexity of social action. Taking action is perhaps the most important and most challenging part of the coaching process. Through action and reflection as praxis, coachees learn about the world they are trying to change, and develop new skills to deal with the challenges of their change projects. Social action is, however, different from actions discussed in other forms of coaching, because social action often takes place in an unwelcoming environment, it challenges the status quo of a system that may have existed for years, it may generate negative reactions even from the coachees' closest circles, it requires lobbying and collaboration with other supporters of the cause, it requires careful planning and assessment of risks, and it may take a very long time before generating outcome. These differences have many implications on the coaching process and the needed skillset of coaches.

Development of Coaches

A change in the coaching context, contract, and process will no doubt require a change in coaches' training and development. Most of current training programmes prepare coaches to work with individuals, to achieve personal goals or improve performance, within a certain cultural and organizational context. Training coaches for social change would involve new requirements in the following areas:

- *Social, cultural and political awareness*: Coaches need to understand the bigger context they are working within, and learn how to help coachees become aware of how social structures and cultural norms affect the way they think and behave. Coaches need to learn about concepts like ideology and social roles, and about mechanisms like socialization and power. Lasley et al. (2011) call this set of skills cultural competence, and argue that coach training programmes

should draw on the vast resources in this area, and should incorporate issues of power, institutional and social inequities, and cultural diversity into coach training curricula.
- **Psychology of the oppressed:** Coaching for social change would often take place in environments that are oppressive in nature, and with people who are often adversely affected by the social system. Because living in these environments affects people deeply, coaches need to use psychological models that incorporate the possible implications of oppression on processes like coachees' self and identity development, motivation, and learning. Coaches also need to consider how internalized oppression may act as an internal barrier to change.
- **Empowerment:** Coaches need to learn how to support the empowerment of their coachees inside and outside the coaching session, how to deal with feelings of powerlessness and self-vicitimization, and how to prepare their coachees emotionally to face the challenge of personal and social change.
- **Critical thinking:** Coaches need to improve their critical thinking skills, and more importantly, their ability to facilitate a critical dialogue, where coachees are supported in critically reflecting on their system of assumptions and beliefs, and in understanding how social structures have been shaping their experiences.
- **Facilitating action:** Taking action in the context of social change may be very different from the types of actions that coaches are used to support. Social action may involve working collaboratively with local or diverse communities, defying power structures, facing social norms and taking risks. Helping coachees to plan, implement and learn from social action is another area that coach training needs to cover.
- **Self-reflectiveness:** Regardless of the context or genre of coaching, coaches are expected to reflect critically on their practice. In the context of social change, this requirement needs to be further emphasized, because the context implies more significant challenges. First to consider is the fact that coaches are often as affected by the social system or oppression as their coachees, sharing some of their struggles, and identifying with their stories. Hence, coaches need to develop awareness of how the social context has affected them, how they are reacting to the coachees' stories, and whether their own doubts and emotions are affecting the coaching process. A second consideration is the importance of reflecting on the impact of power on the coaching relationship, and the awareness of how coaches may be perceived, or may perceive themselves as saviours or defenders of a certain cause, and the impact of such perceptions on their ability to coach.

CONCLUSION

Coaching for social change is a new and growing field that holds a lot of potential. It is increasingly acknowledged that coaching cannot occur in isolation from its social context. Coaching theorists are beginning to argue that coaching has the potential to enable social change, though its current practices are sometimes used in ways that may obstruct change and serve to maintain dysfunctional social and organizational structures.

Social change may take place as part of coaching at work, coaching in the social domain, or coaching individuals living in oppressive environments. In all cases, social change coaches are required to face challenges that are specific to their role: They need to contribute to the coaching agenda rather than act as technical experts; develop cultural competences and critical self-reflectiveness, and support empowerment, criticality, and social action. These challenges are mostly new to the coaching culture. Hence, it is important to consider how the coaching community can support and integrate this new practice, and how coaching theories, and future research, may provide a better foundation for its growth.

Similar to other disciplines, practitioners of coaching do not act independently from the overall culture of their practice. Coaches are socialized into behaving in certain styles, though they retain the ability either to conform or resist such pressures (Jones et al., 2002), both agency and structure shape their experience like they shape the experience of their coachees. Coaches are often under pressure to produce performances that are congruent with the role expectations held by their clients and peers. Using Foucault's concept of governmentality, Usher et al. (2004) argue that practices are governed from within, and maintained through the compliance of practitioners to an identity that is neither their own, nor dictated from above, an ever-moving agenda to which they contribute but do not control. If the fraternity of coaching, as Western (2012) argues, is inclined to a positivistic and individualistic discourse, where critical approaches are not welcomed, then this may create difficulties for the integration of social change into the coaching culture.

It is also important to consider the role of educational institutions, and accrediting professional bodies, in terms of how they could support the growth of a social practice of coaching. Educational and professional bodies often try to be apolitical, but it is through the inclusion of a social perspective into their curriculums, ethical frameworks, initiatives and publications that the language of social change would start to penetrate the coaching discourse. There may also be a need for new models of accreditation and educational funding, in order to make the practice more inclusive for potential coaches who are approaching it as an enabler for social change.

Another dimension is to consider how research institutions encourage the development of coaching theories that study social change. Helping theories include assumptions about the nature of humanness, location of the problem (individual or society), nature of possible solutions (emancipation, change, or adjustment), and the role of the helper (Sanders, 2006). New coaching theories and research needs to examine these assumptions critically, and explore whether they are inadvertently limiting the scope of how coaching can help create a better world. Research methodologies for coaching for social change may also need to reflect a critical, participatory, and emancipatory stance; empowering coachees to impact the way coaching theories are developed.

As a new genre within coaching, there are many aspects of coaching for social change that require further research. I have already discussed some of the key themes for such research, including issues related to the coaching contract, coaching process, coaches' development and overall coaching culture. Other areas for future research may include peer coaching, group coaching, and community coaching, as possible forms of coaching for social change. Most importantly, coaching for social change needs praxis; in the words of Freire (1970), 'reflection and action directed at the structures to be transformed' (p.126). What is needed is research that originates from the true needs and challenges of those whose world is being transformed, one that takes place while being involved in supporting change, as this will expose the real struggles, gaps, and opportunities that coaches need to address.

REFERENCES

Adams, M. (2007). *Self and Social Change*. London: SAGE Publications.
Askew, S., and Carnell, E. (2011). *Transformative Coaching: A Learning Theory for Practice*. London: University of London, Institute of Education.
Bauman, Z. (2004). *Identity: Coversations With Benedetto Vecchi*. Oxford: Wiley-Blackwell.
Beyond Emancipation (2015). Retrieved from http://beyondemancipation.org/coaching/
Boud, D. (1989). Some Competing Traditions in Experiential Learning. In S. W. Weil & I. McGill (eds.), *Making Sense of Experiential Learning: Diversity in Theory and Practice*. Milton Keynes: Society for Research into Higher Education (pp. 38–49). Milton Keynes: Open University Press.
Brockbank, A., and McGill, I. (2006). *Facilitating Reflective Learning Through Mentoring & Coaching*. London: Kogan Page.
Brockbank, A., and McGill, I. (2012). *Facilitating Reflective Learning: Coaching, Mentoring and Supervision* (2nd ed.). London: Kogan Page.

Bulhan, H. A. (2004). *Frantz Fanon and the Psychology of Oppression*. Springer.

Caspi, J. (2005). Coaching and Social Work: Challenges and Concerns. *Social Work*, 50(4), 359–362.

Chappell, C., Rhodes, C., Solomon, N., Tennant, M., and Yates, L. (2003). *Reconstructing the Lifelong Learner: Pedagogy and Identity in Individual, Organisational and Social Change*. London: Taylor & Francis.

CIPD. (2004). *Reorganising for Success: A Survey of HR's Role in Change*. London: CIPD.

Coach Network (2015). Retrieved from http://www.coachnetwork.org/

Cox, E. (2012). *Coaching Understood: A Pragmatic Inquiry Into the Coaching Process*. London: SAGE Publications.

de Jager, W. (2011). *Leadership and Innovation for Social Projects*. In R. Biswas-Diener (Ed.), Positive Psychology as Social Change. Amsterdam: Springer Netherlands.

Dominelli, L. (2002). *Anti-Oppressive Social Work Theory and Practice*. New York: Palgrave Macmillan.

Du Toit, A. (2013). Coaching Vs Groupthink? *Coaching at Work*, 8(2), 57–57.

Du Toit, A. (2014). *Making Sense of Coaching*. London: SAGE Publications.

Du Toit, A., and Sim, S. (2010). *Rethinking Coaching: Critical Theory and the Economic Crisis*. Basingstoke: Palgrave Macmillan.

Dyer, T. J. (2002). Executive Development: Outer Goals and Inner Coaching. *Employment Relations Today (Wiley)*, 29(1), 55–61.

EMCC. (2015). Solidarity Coaching. Retrieved from http://www.solidaritycoaching.org/

Erlandson, E. (2009). Coaching with Men: Alpha Males. In J. Passmore (Ed.), Diversity in Coaching: Working with gender, culture, race and age (pp. 215–236). London: Kogan Page.

Eyre, E. (2012). Can coaching save the world? (cover story). *Training Journal*, 15–18.

Fanon, F. (1967). *The Wretched of the Earth*. Harmondsworth, Middlesex: Penguin Books.

Fatien Diochon, P. and Lovelace, K.J. (2015) The coaching continuum: Power dynamics in the change process. *International Journal of Work Innovation*, 1(3), 305–322.

Freire, P. (1970). *Pedagogy of the Oppressed* (M. Ramos, trans). New York: Herter and Herter.

Grajfoner, D. (2009). Managing Change: Role of coaching psychology in gender transition. *The Coaching Psychologist*, 5(2), 69–75.

Grant, A. M. (2003). The impact of life coaching on goal attainment, metacognition and mental health. *Social Behavior and Personality*, 31(3), 253–264. doi:10.2224/sbp.2003.31.3.253

Harro, B. (2000). The Cycle of Liberation. In M. Adams (Ed.), *Readings for Diversity and Social Justice: An Anthology on Racism, Sexism, Anti-Semitism, Heterosexism, Classism, and Ableism* (pp. 463–469). New York; London: Routledge.

Heron, J. (1999). *The Complete Facilitator's Handbook*. London: Kogan Page.

Howard, K. A., Gislason, M., and Kellogg, V. (2010). Coaching and Philanthropy: An Action Guide for Coaches. https://www.compasspoint.org/sites/default/files/docs/research/1011_capactionguideforcoaches.pdf

Inglis, T. (1997). Empowerment and Emancipation. *Adult Education Quarterly*, 48(1), 3–17. doi:10.1177/074171369704800102

Ives, Y. (2008). What is 'Coaching'? An Exploration of Conflicting Paradigms. *International Journal of Evidence Based Coaching and Mentoring*, 6(2), 100–113.

Jones, R. L., Armour, K. M., and Potrac, P. (2002). Understanding the Coaching Process: A Framework for Social Analysis. *Quest (00336297)*, 54(1), 34–48.

Kegan, R. (1994). *In Over Our Heads: The Mental Demands of Modern Life*. Cambridge, Mass: Harvard University Press.

Kristal, Z. (2009). *Critical Reflection in the Coaching Process*. Paper presented at the Eighth International Transformative Learning Conference, Bermuda.

Kühl, S. (2008). *Coaching und Supervision – Zur personenorientierten Beratung in Organisationen*. Wiesbaden: VS Verlag für Sozialewissenschaften.

Lasley, M., Kellogg, V., Michaels, R., and Brown, S. (2011). *Coaching for Transformation: Pathways to Ignite Personal and Social Change*. USA: Discover Press.

LePage, J. P., and Garcia-Rea, E. A. (2012). Lifestyle coaching's effect on 6-month follow-up in recently homeless substance dependent veterans: A randomized study. *Psychiatric Rehabilitation Journal*, 35(5), 396–402.

Lerner, R. M. (2013). Individual and Context in Developmental Pyschology: Conceptual and Theoretical Issues. In J. R. Nesselroade and A. Von Eye (eds.), *Individual Development and Social Change: Explanatory Analysis* (pp. 155–175). London: Elsevier Science.

MacDonald, A. (2002). Feminist Pedagogy and the Appeal to Epistemic Privilege. In A. MacDonald and S. Sánchez-Casal (eds.), *Twenty-First-Century Feminist Classrooms: Pedagogies of Identity and Difference* (pp. 111–135). Basingstoke: Palgrave Macmillan.

Magnet, S., and Diamond, S. (2010). Feminist Pedagogy Meets Feminist Therapy: Teaching Feminist Therapy in Women's Studies. *Feminist Teacher*, 21(1), 21–35.

Maitland, R., and Anderson, B. (2011). Coaching for Wellness and HIV/AIDS Awareness. In R. Biswas-Diener (Ed.), *Positive Psychology as Social Change*. Amsterdam: Springer Netherlands.

McGregor, C. (2015). *Coaching Behind Bars: Facing Challenges and Creating Hope in a Women's Prison*. Milton Keynes: Open University Press.

Mezirow, J. (Ed.) (2000). *Learning as Transformation: Critical Perspectives on a Theory in Progress*. San Francisco: Jossey-Bass.

Nangalia, L., and Nangalia, A. (2010). The coach in Asian society: Impact of social hierarchy on the coaching relationship. *International Journal of Evidence Based Coaching and Mentoring*, 8(1), 51–66.

Naumann, J., and Hüfner, K. (2013). Evolutionary Aspects of Social and Individual Development: Comments and Illustrations from the World System Perspective. In J. R. Nesselroade & A. Von Eye (Eds.), *Individual Development and Social Change: Explanatory Analysis* (pp. 51–90). London: Elsevier Science.

Ngwenya, H., and Hagmann, J. (2007). Facilitation for change: Triggering emancipation and innovation in rural communities in South Africa. *Farmers First Revisited*. http://www.future-agricultures.org/farmerfirst/files/T2b_Ngwenya.pdf

Outhwaite, A., and Bettridge, N. (2009). From the inside out: Coaching's role in transformation towards a sustainable society. *Coaching Psychologist*, 5(2), 76–89.

Palmer, S., and Whybrow, A. (2007). Coaching Psychology: An Introduction. In S. Palmer and A. Whybrow (eds.), *Handbook of Coaching Psychology* (pp. 1–20). East Sussex: Routledge.

Passmore, J. (2009). *Diversity in Coaching: Working with Gender, Culture, Race and Age*. London: Kogan Page.

Pheterson, G. (1986). Alliances between women: Overcoming internalized oppression and internalized domination. *Signs*, 12(1), 146–160.

Proctor, G. (2006). Opening Remarks. In G. Proctor, M. Cooper, P. Sanders, & B. Malcolm (Eds.), *Politicizing the Person-centred Approach: An Agenda for Social Change* (pp. 1–5). Ross-on-Wye: PCCS Books.

Proctor, G. (2008). Gender dynamics in person-centered therapy: Does gender matter? *Person-Centered and Experiential Psychotherapies*, 7(2), 82–94.

Putnam, R. D. (2001). *Bowling Alone: The Collapse and Revival of American Community*. New York: Simon & Schuster.

Qing, W., & Millward, I. (2014). Developing a unified psychological model of coaching and mentoring in supporting the learning and development of adolescents. *International Journal of Evidence Based Coaching & Mentoring*, 12(2), 91–108.

Reissner, S. C., & Du Toit, A. (2011). Power and the tale: coaching as storyselling. *The Journal of Management Development*, 30(3), 247–259.

Rogers, J. (2008). *Coaching Skills – A Handbook*. Berkshire: Open University Press – McGraw Hill Education.

Sanders, P. (2006). Politics and Therapy: Mapping Areas for Consideration. In G. Proctor, M. Cooper, P. Sanders, & B. Malcolm (Eds.), *Politicizing the Person-centred Approach: An Agenda for Social Change* (pp. 5–16). Ross-on-Wye: PCCS Books.

Schultz, F. (2010). The Politics of Work Coaching – Between Impairing Vision and Creating Visions. Retrieved from University of Surrey website: http://epubs.surrey.ac.uk/2445/1/politics_SCHULZ.pdf

Shoukry, H. (2014). *Coaching for Emancipation: A Framework for Coaching in Oppressive Environments* (PhD). Oxford Brookes University, Oxford.

Shoukry, H. (2016). Coaching for emancipation: A framework for Coaching in oppressive environments. *International Journal of Evidence Based Coaching and Mentoring, 14*(2), 15–30.

Stern, L. (2011). Positively Influencing Leadership for Global Sustainability. In R. Biswas-Diener (Ed.), *Positive Psychology as Social Change* (pp. 248–250). Amsterdam: Springer Netherlands.

Swan, E. (2010). *Worked Up Selves: Personal Development Workers, Self work and Therapeutic Cultures*. Basingstoke: Palgrave Macmillan.

Sztompka, P. (1993). *The Sociology of Social Change*. Oxford: Wiley-Blackwell.

Usher, R., Bryant, I., & Johnston, R. (2004). *Adult Education and the Postmodern Challenge: Learning Beyond the Limits*. London: Taylor & Francis.

Watkins, M., & Shulman, H. (2008). *Toward Psychologies of Liberation*. Basingstoke: Palgrave Macmillan.

Welman, P., & Bachkirova, T. (2010). The Issue of Power in the Coaching Relationship. In S. Palmer & A. McDowall (Eds.), *The Coaching Relationship: Putting People First* (pp. 139–158). New York, NY US: Routledge/Taylor & Francis Group.

Western, S. (2012). *Coaching and Mentoring: A Critical Text*. London: SAGE.

Whitmore, J. (2007). *The Transpersonal: The Inevitable Progression of Coaching*. Paper presented at the 2007 Special Group in Coaching Psychology 3rd Annual Conference, London.

Wildflower, L. (2013). *The Hidden History Of Coaching*. Maidenhead: McGraw-Hill Education.

Young, I. M. (2000). Five Faces of Oppression. In M. Adams, W. J. Blumenfeld, R. Castaneda, H. W. Hackman, M. L. Peters, & X. Zuniga (eds.), *Readings for Diversity and Social Justice* (pp. 35–49). New York: Routledge.

PART II
Coaching as a Process

The Coaching Relationship

Erik de Haan and Judie Gannon

INTRODUCTION

The coaching relationship can be seen to sit centre stage in the practice and research on coaching in accordance with the value we place as human beings on our relationships and need to relate to others (Du Toit, 2014; De Haan & Sills, 2012). Arguably the growing importance of the coaching relationship is particularly apparent where wider societal changes have resulted in less intimacy and stability in personal relationships and the efficacy of the contiguous field of psychotherapy supports the role of professional helping relationships (De Haan & Sills, 2010; Palmer & McDowall, 2010). It is pertinent at this stage to reflect on what might be meant by the term relationship. Jowett, O'Broin and Palmer (2010 p. 20) define a relationship as 'a situation in which two people's feelings, thoughts and behaviours are mutually and causally interdependent.' They also suggest that our concepts of relationships mean they are dynamic, change over time and consist of the actions of both individuals. The quality of relationships is determined by the interrelations and interactions between the two people concerned and the interdependence they experience (Nelson-Jones, 2006).

Compared with other developmental relationships (such as mentor or sponsor), the coaching relationship is argued to be under-researched (Stern & Stout-Rostron, 2013; Rock & Garavan, 2006; Gyllensten & Palmer, 2007). As such the foundation for this chapter is based upon the recognition that the coaching relationship stands alongside other relationships which aim to develop ourselves and others, and include the '"assessment, challenge and support," necessary for development' (Rock & Garavan, 2006 p.331). The 'infinite variability' of developmental relationships, as identified in McCauley and Douglas's (1998) terminology, recognises the possibilities that such relationships may be one-off or long term, formal or informal, initiated by individuals or organisations, or a combination of the two. In addition, they are seen to provide direct or indirect feedback, challenge through the provision of alternative viewpoints, offer provocation to initiate stretch, and support through opportunities to talk and explore. Fundamentally, it is important to acknowledge the variation in features of developmental relationships.

O'Broin and Palmer (2010a, 2010b) explore the coaching relationship from an interpersonal perspective and draw on three areas of helping relationships; counselling, sports psychology and friendship, to identify distinctiveness or 'unique commonalities' of coaching relationships. They deploy Cavanagh and Grant's (2006) argument of the coaching relationship 'as a complex and adaptive system' and suggest that while all forms of relationships will have differentiating features those associated with the coaching relationship centre around the use of the self of the coach and the commitment of the coachee (O'Broin & Palmer, 2010a; 2010b p.12). Ostensibly this recognises that the relationship sits amongst other key variables in the coaching such as the coaching environment, coaches' approaches and training and clients' readiness to engage in coaching.

Following on from this introduction the first part of this chapter will explore some of the key themes which emerge from reviewing the literature surrounding the coaching relationship, namely developing rapport, the role of trust and transparency, commitment, stages of the coaching relationship, as well as attributes of the coach and coachee, which shape the relationship (Gan & Chong, 2015; Reissner & Du Toit, 2011; Gyllensten & Palmer, 2007). These features are all influential in the quality of the coaching relationship and the coaching experience itself but may not lend themselves easily to being researched. By drawing upon empirical studies from the key contexts of executive, employee and sports coaching (Bachkirova, Cox & Clutterbuck, 2014) this chapter will evaluate our existing knowledge of the coaching relationship and the challenges for future research and developing coaching practice. Consolidated tables (see Tables 11.1 and 11.2) have been developed to provide an overview of some of the recent empirical enquiries into coaching across these three contexts.

FEATURES OF THE COACHING RELATIONSHIP

1. Stages in the Coaching Relationship

It is important to recognise that while there are themes which persist across the time a coach and coachee work together some of these themes demand specific attention towards the beginning and end of the relationship, or even at the beginning and end of each coaching session (Cox, 2010; Ianiro et al., 2013). While models with a range of different stages or phases are evident in the literature (Natale & Diamante, 2005; Starr, 2007; Cox, 2013) there is widespread acknowledgement of the importance of focusing upon the coaching relationship early on. As Gyllensten and Palmer (2007 p. 173) argue from their findings 'The relationship was the basis upon which the coaching was built and without a relationship the coaching would not be as effective as it could be.'

Coaching clients report a range of concerns prior to and in early sessions of their coaching relationships, including apprehension, scepticism and fear of their issues being taken seriously (Bluckert, 2005; Gyllensten & Palmer, 2007; Gregory & Levy, 2010; Ianiro et al., 2013). In anticipation of handling such concerns Hardingham (2006) discusses how coaches might handle their clients' fears, specifically in terms of being aware of the potential for coaching to question coachees' competence, real desires and authenticity. A recent study (Ianiro et al., 2013) using an innovative mixed method approach, identified that in the first coaching session the coach's interpersonal behaviour influenced outcome variables as rated by client's ratings of goal attainment. Such insights highlight, the authors argue, the value of the coach displaying confidence and credibility, developing heightened awareness of their verbal and non-verbal behaviours and tackling interactional disruptions specifically in first coaching sessions.

There are, however, also arguments for coaches being aware of these concerns throughout the coaching relationship and indeed within each coaching session (Cox, 2010; Gessnitzer & Kauffeld, 2015), critically at the beginning and end of each session when goals are identified and actions agreed to (Ianiro et al., 2013). Indeed an overall goal focused (and task focused) approach to the coaching relationship was seen to reap coaching success in recent work by Grant (2014). These sections of coaching sessions arguably involve critical bridges between the coaching and the client's and coach's worlds and as such seal the credibility, commitment, trust, transparency and rapport significant for maintaining a quality coaching relationship. Surprisingly there have been few investigations into the issues associated with the concluding of coaching relationships. Cox (2010) draws on the fields of psychotherapy, mentoring and a business-to-business relationship model, as well as mini case studies, to explore the ending of coaching relationships. As part of this analysis she highlights how despite the knowledge that the relationship will come to an end, as typically established in initial or revised contracting, both coachee and coach may experience relatively intense feelings. The value of implementing a review stage in the coaching may at least mediate the potential for negative feelings, such as self-blame or sadness where the relationship has to be ended prematurely. As Cox (2010 p.179) argues 'If the ending is not discussed, planned and celebrated and the relationship is left to fade or to end abruptly without closure, then the potential for marking achievement and fully integrating changes may be lost.' The impact for coachee and coach of such lost opportunities could clearly impact on subsequent development activities and coaching relationships.

2. Bonds and Rapport

As shown in Tables 11.1 and 11.2 the bonds or rapport between coachees and coaches are key features of coaching relationship research, though there may be preferences for different terms depending on context. For example, the athlete–coach relationship in the sports coaching literature, has widely adopted 'closeness' as a representation of this affective aspect of the coaching relationship. Boyce et al. (2010 p.917) define rapport as 'about reducing the differences between the coach and client and building on similarities.' Coach and coachee attributes may have a role to play here, and are certainly topical within the empirical literature, as discussed in a later section of this chapter. However, rapport behaviours are typically identified as being at ease with the other person, showing warmth, genuine interest, mutual attentiveness, and positivity. Overall enhanced rapport means better outcomes satisfaction, compliance, greater self-disclosure and retention within the coaching relationship (Boyce et al., 2010; Gyllensten & Palmer, 2007).

Similarly, Gan and Chong (2015, p.479) summarise rapport as 'mutual understanding, liking and agreement between coach and coachee that tend to reduce the differences between them and allow them to recognize, appreciate and respect each other.' Supporting the arguments of Ianiro et al. (2013) that where coaches are aware of how to ameliorate differences between themselves and their coaches, without compromising their own authenticity and credibility, good connections can emerge from cool beginnings. Specific behavioural features of rapport and bonds are said to include trust, listening, rapport and openness and management of disruptions (O'Broin & Palmer, 2010a, 2010b; Gyllensten & Palmer, 2007). However, bonds in the coaching relationship have been recognised as being viewed differently by participants (De Haan et al., 2011; Gyllensten & Palmer, 2007). In their qualitative study O'Broin and Palmer (2010c) identified that there were a variety of approaches to achieving the quality and types of bond in the coaching relationship, but that these differences were not accountable just to coach and coachee respondents. They also highlighted how different types of coaching require different coaching relationship depths and qualities (Sun et al., 2013; O'Broin & Palmer, 2010c; Ives, 2008) and perhaps most importantly of all that each coachee requires a unique tailoring of the bond in their coaching relationship.

Another aspect of this theme of rapport is that it can be seen to be developing or diminishing all the time and needs reflection and ongoing investment to maintain it (Hardingham, 2006; Ianiro et al., 2013; Sun et al., 2013). As such many have reflected upon the interdependent nature of the coaching relationship where collaboration and reciprocity are evident in this two-way process of respect and support. The transient nature of this connection between coach and coachee occurs at emotional, cognitive and behavioural levels providing researchers with a challenging dynamic to explore and understand (Jowett, Kanakoglu & Passmore, 2012; O'Broin & Palmer, 2010c).

No discussion of the bond in the coaching relationship can pass without recognition of the intellectual and empirical debt owed to the psychotherapeutic literature where the bond is one of the key constructs in the working alliance (Bordin, 1979; de Haan, 2008a; O'Broin & Palmer, 2010a, 2010b, 2010c; Gessnitzer & Kauffeld, 2015). A more detailed discussion on the working alliance and its role in enhancing our investigation and understanding of the coaching relationship, or coaching alliance, is explored later in this chapter.

3. Trust and Transparency

There is widespread support and evidence for the argument that trust forms a critical element in the quality of the coaching relationship (Du Toit, 2014; Cox, 2012; De Haan, 2008b). Boyce et al. (2010 p. 918) argue that trust is the 'mutual confidence that supports the client's willingness to be open, honest and vulnerable and allows the coach to be supportive, non-judgemental and challenging.' Boyce et al. (2010) identified trust, along with rapport, as one of the significant predictors of satisfaction and utility of the coaching relationship in relation to leadership coaching. They argue the presence of trust allows sharing of sensitive, personal information and means coach and client are more likely to engage in risk taking behaviours to facilitate the change desired. Gyllensten and Palmer (2007) highlighted trust as a vital part of the relationship, assuring confidentiality which allows the coachee to let their guard down and engage fully in the developmental experience. Likewise O'Broin and Palmer (2010b) recognise that trust affords safety and security, helps establish and manage boundaries and facilitate open and honest dialogue.

The origins of trust in the coaching relationship emerge from the empathetic understanding condition associated with 'the person-centred approach of Carl Rogers (1967), who argued trust is a vital component in such a relationship' (Du Toit, 2014 p. 70). Trust is fundamental to achieving the desired levels of openness and transparency (O'Broin & Palmer, 2010c). De Haan (2008a) and De Haan & Nieß (2012) indicate openness is crucial when dealing with critical moments in coaching and successful coaching is dependent on a strong trusting relationship rather than the tools and techniques of the coach.

Gyllensten and Palmer (2007 p.174) emphasise the role of transparency alongside trust in their study of the coaching relationship or as they argue the 'relationship was dependent on trust and improved by transparency.' The value of the coach being transparent and explaining the coaching process assisted coachees settle into the relationship from the beginning and work towards their desired outcomes. Transparency also helps reduce uncertainty (Gyllensten & Palmer, 2007; Gan and Chong, 2015). However, Gan and Chong's (2015) study also emphasises the damage which can be done when there are violations of trust and transparency in the coaching relationship, which can typically result in resistance to change and lower satisfaction. This study of executive coaching in Malaysia did, however, question the role of trust suggesting it was not significantly associated with coaching effectiveness.

Table 11.1 Key recent empirical studies of the coaching relationship

Authors, year Outline	Research Method	Overview of study	Key Findings on the coaching relationship	Key observations
Gyllensten & Palmer, 2007 An analysis of the coaching relationship	Interpretative Phenomenological analysis approach 9 participants from two organisations – UK and Scandinavian	• Four themes emerged: stress, confidence, the coaching relationship and coaching as staff investment • Coaching relationship – value of trust and transparency	• Trust as a foundation for the coaching relationship • Transparency – explaining process and theory: 'The relationship was the basis upon which the coaching was built'	
Baron & Morin, 2009 Coach's skills and the coaching relationship	31 coach–coachee dyads Surveys before, during and after intervention using scales from coachee self-efficacy, Working Alliance Inventory, Learning Transfer System Inventory & HR dept data on sessions – North American organisation	• Explores coaching relationship and self-efficacy of coachee in relation to: Coach's relational skills (empathy, respect and trust); Coach's communication skills (questioning, reformulation, reinforcement) and their ability to facilitate learning and results	• Relationship plays a mediating role between coaching received and development of coachees' self-efficacy • Quality of relationship correlates with client self-efficacy • Only coach's ability to facilitate learning and results explained variance in coaching relationship	• Number of sessions influences development of coachee. • Highlights the value of a coach's ability to facilitate a good working relationship.
Boyce, Jackson & Neal, 2010 Matching criteria and relationship processes (rapport, trust and commitment) impact on coaching outcomes	74 coach–client pairs in US military academy leadership coaching program Leadership questionnaire plus items on commonality, credibility, rapport, trust and commitment	• Aspects of coaching relationship may mediate match factors (such as credibility, commonality and compatibility) • Explores links between match, relationship and outcomes	• More effective relationships between coaches and clients with complementary learning styles • Rapport, trust, commitment and collaboration as key processes in coaching relationship • Higher commitment leads to performance improvements	• Successful coaching relationship is critical to coaching success. • Value of matching based on not-similar or complementary learning styles. • Advocates training to support rapport, trust and commitment development where compatibility cannot be achieved.
Gregory & Levy, 2010 Employee coaching relationships; construct clarity and measurement	Developed and deployed PQECR after feedback from 25 subject experts. 2 phases of refinement – 158 useable responses. Plus online survey of 556 employees in multinational manufacturing organisation	• Clarifies the employee coaching relationship construct • Develops a measure for the Perceived Quality of the Employee Coaching Relationship (PQECR)	• Initially based upon 5 dimensions: distinctiveness of the relationship, genuineness, effective communication, comfort with the relationship and facilitating development. Distinctiveness as a dimension is later removed	• Highlights issues of managing accurate feedback from employee coaches. • Advocates further research exploring variables(supervisor characteristics and behaviours, subordinate characteristics and contextual features), which impact relationship quality.

(Continued)

Table 11.1 Continued

Authors, year Outline	Research Method	Overview of study	Key Findings on the coaching relationship	Key observations
O'Broin & Palmer, 2010c Coaching relationship formation – coach and coachee perspectives	12 interviews (6 coaches and 6 coachees). Repertory grid interview method used and content analysis undertaken UK setting	• Qualities which coaches and coachees prioritise in the formation of coaching relationships • How these qualities contribute to the relationship • Views on adaptation of coach to individual coachee	Three main themes emerged of: • Coach attitudes and characteristics • Bond and engagement – linked to engagement and disengagement/disruptions • Collaboration – reciprocity and respect in line with co-creation	Coach's attitudes and self-awareness as well as ability to adapt to client seen as crucial. Value of trust, openness and transparency. Differing perceptions of collaboration and bonding.
Machin, 2010 The internal coaching relationship	6 coach and coachee in-depth interviews during mid phase of programme. Used Interpretative Phenomenological Analysis	• Nature of the internal coaching relationship as experienced by coaches and coaches	• Highlights characteristics of the coach and the client as critical for trust • Trust facilitates ability to work at psychological level and use of challenge	Approaching the coaching relationship on an equal footing is suggested.
De Haan, Culpin & Curd, 2011 Helpfulness for executive coaching clients	Online survey 71 responses from executive coaching clients from initial session and six months later. Items included demographics, coaching information, Coaching Behaviours questionnaire items, Learning styles inventory and open ended questions	• Explores what executive coaching clients find helpful in terms of their coaching experiences	• Highlights value clients place upon the relationship with the coach and coach's qualities • Listening, understanding and encouragement • Limited distinction between specific interventions of the same coach	Broad range of techniques is identified as being helpful. Therefore ability of coaches to deploy many techniques alongside and the development of empathic listening skills are emphasised.
Gregory & Levy, 2011 Variables influencing employee coaching relationships	155 supervisors and 729 direct reports completed survey – part of global manufacturing organisation. Survey included items from Multifactor leadership questionnaire, emotional intelligence, implicit theory, feedback environment scale and PQECR	• Explores the Perceived Quality of Employee Coaching relationship against four supervisor/coach variables: transformational leadership, trust, interactive empathy, emotional intelligence, implicit person theory and organisational feedback environment	• Employee coaching relationships associated with individual consideration, positive feedback environment, building trust and empathy	Highlights importance of developing coaches' skills in developing trust, demonstrating empathy and creating positive feedback environment specifically in employee coaching relationships.
Gregory & Levy, 2012 Employee feedback orientation: implications for effective coaching relationships	479 professional grade employees in global manufacturing company completed online survey which included items of feedback orientation, PQECR and coaching behaviours	• Examines link between feedback orientation and coaching relationship quality as perceived by employee coaches. • Examines impact of supervisor/coaches' actual coaching behaviours on quality of employee coaching relationships	• Subordinates' feedback orientation had a small but significant impact on perceptions of their coaching relationship quality • As expected high-quality employee coaching relationships predict employee coachee ratings of supervisor/coach behaviours	Frequency of interaction linked to perceptions of coaching relationship quality. Advocates HR professionals consider engaging employees with the development of their feedback orientation and further support supervisors in developing genuine coaching relationships.

Jowett, Kanakoglu & Passmore, 2012 Application of the 3+1Cs relationship model to executive coaching	Semi-structured interviews with five coach–coachee dyads (10 participants) using open-ended questions based on the 3+1Cs model	• Attempts to explore how the 3+1Cs model from sports coaching maps onto an understanding of the quality of the executive coaching relationship	• The model appears to work for the coaching dyads explored emphasising the interdependence between the 4 constructs of closeness, commitment, complementarity and co-orientation • Clear evidence of reciprocity and role changes between coach and coachee accounts • No neat mapping of components onto coaching alliance constructs	• Value of understanding the dyadic relationship in executive coaching using the 3+1Cs model. • Opportunity to deploy as a diagnostic tool in coaching relationships.
De Haan, Duckworth, Birch & Jones, 2013 Executive coaching outcome research – the contribution of common factors	156 coaching relationships Networks of experienced and qualified executive coaches Surveys included demographic, MBTI, credential, intervention style, coach techniques and Working Alliance inventory items	• Examines 'common factors' influence on coaching outcome study • Common factors – relationship, the setting, expectations, coach and client personalities and coaching approach/technique	• Working alliance/coaching relationship as rated by the coachee correlates to client rated coaching outcomes • No clear impact of client personality, client-coach personality matching on coaching outcomes	• Questions how in tune coaches are with their clients' views of the coaching relationship. • Ability of individual coaches and clients to co-create their relationship/alliance.
Sun et al., 2013 The working alliance and real relationship in two coaching approaches	40 coachees and 23 coaches Surveyed using Coaching Alliance scale, Supervisory working alliance inventory and Real Relationship Inventory Australian mental health services using coaching to deliver new service delivery model	• Explores the coaching relationship in transformational and skills coaching through the working alliance and 'real relationship' constructs • Working alliance – quality and strength of relationship based on: goals, tasks and bond • Real relationship – personal relationship perspective: genuineness (willingness and authenticity) and realism (realistic, undistorted perceptions)	• Moderate to strong relationship between coachee ratings of real relationship and working alliance • Stronger coaching relationships in Transformational coaching – as rated by both partners • Transformational coaching coachees reported stronger working alliance but only for realism, not for genuineness in 'real relationship' results	• Transformational coaching associated with stronger and deeper coaching relationship compared to skills coaching – value of recognising which coaching approaches are closer to the therapeutic end of the spectrum. • Advocate wider adoption of real relationship over time in coaching context. • Need to develop validated measures of the coaching alliance.
Ianiro, Schermuly & Kauffeld, 2013 Interaction analysis of the coaching relationship: the role of interpersonal dominance and affiliation	Uses the Discussion coding system to analyse video-ed first coaching sessions of students at two German universities Survey included aspects of similarity quality of coaching relationship and goal attainment undertaken at end	• Explores role of interpersonal affiliation and dominance behaviour, and coach–client compatibility on clients' views of the relationship and goal attainment • Takes perspective from interpersonal dynamics from social psychology field	• Coach's mean dominance behaviour in first coaching session is related to client's ratings of goal attainment at the end of the coaching process • Similarity on both interpersonal dynamics for coach and client results in higher ratings of relationship quality and client's end of programme goal attainment ratings	• Highlights how coach might tackle interactional disruptions and the value of coach being confident and aware of verbal and non-verbal dominant behaviours. • Identifies the importance of the first coaching session and understanding of impact of non-verbal behaviours. • Indicates link between relationship quality and goal attainment.

(*Continued*)

Table 11.1 Continued

Authors, year Outline	Research Method	Overview of study	Key Findings on the coaching relationship	Key observations
Grant, 2014 Autonomy support, relationship satisfaction and goal focus in the coaching relationship	49 participants undertaking postgraduate degree programme in coaching in Australia Survey using items from psychological well-being, depression, anxiety and stress, goal attainment and self-insight	• Examines which of the following aspects is most positively correlated to specific coaching outcomes: autonomy support, coachee satisfaction with the actual relationship, similarity of the coaching relationship to an ideal coaching relationship and goal focused coaching relationship	• Goal-focused coaching relationship has significantly more impact on successful coachin • Humanistic supportive coaching relationship has impact on coaching success but not as evident • Association between coachees' experience of coaching as close to ideal relationship and coaching success	Study focused on solution-focused, cognitive behavioural coaching approach to explore these factors. Highlights the role of goals and goal attainment with the coaching relationship as the instrument to facilitate this process.
Gan & Chong, 2015 Coaching relationship in executive coaching in Malaysia	Survey of manager coachees using certified coaches in Malaysia 172 respondents	• Explores relationship between coaching relationship factors of rapport, trust and commitment, and match with coaching effectiveness	• Rapport and commitment significantly influence coaching effectiveness • Trust and matching based on similarities had no effect on coaching effectiveness	Highlight the potential role of Asian culture on results - in relation to deference to coaches which may influence trust and matching factors. Rapport and commitment identified as critical for foundation for successful coaching relationships and outcomes.
Gessnitzer & Kauffeld, 2015 The working alliance in coaching: exploring relationship relevant behaviours	Interaction analysis of videos of 31 coaching dyads Questionnaires using adapted Working Alliance Inventory Germany	• No correlation between client or coach WAI and working alliance behaviour • Coaching success was 'agreement of goals/tasks' but only if client led • Bonding behaviour had no effect at all on goal attainment • Only coaches' perception of the relationship was positively related to coaching success	• Working alliance behaviours strongly dependent on who initiates them • Shorter coaching relationships emphasise work-focused and goal aspects rather than bonding	Innovative methodology. Highlights importance of activeness of client. Value of active listening, paraphrasing and open questions emphasised for supporting change in clients.

Gan and Chong (2015) subsequently argue this is probably because of cultural issues in the Asian context where respect and trust are commonplace and not a priority just for the coaching experience (Gan & Chong, 2015; Daouk-Öyry & Rosinski, 2010; Nangalia & Nangalia, 2010). This cultural dimension highlights again the importance of tailoring the coaching relationship in relation to the client and their background and expectations.

Gan and Chong's (2015) findings also underscore the potential role of power in the coaching relationship where traditional views and behaviours confer in individuals with specific roles, such as coaches, the opportunity to wield power over others (Welman & Bachkirova, 2010; Reissner & Du Toit, 2011). Clients may also exercise excessive power within the relationship, to an extent that the work to be done is unachievable and Welman and Bachkirova (2010) recommend coaches explore their own personal predispositions to exercising power as well as developing the knowledge and skills to deal with power when they experience it inappropriately in the coaching relationship. The study by Gessnitzer and Kauffeld (2015) highlights some of the issues which can arise from dominance in the coaching relationship where agreement of tasks and goals had a strong association with coaching success, but only when the agreement was initiated by the client. Dominance by the coach in the agreement of tasks and goals had a negative effect on goal attainment further accentuating the need for self-awareness and facilitative behaviour by the coach and activeness of the client, early on in the relationship.

4. Commitment, Collaboration and Co-creation

Commitment by both participants in any of the relationships, which fall within the range of helping relationships, is considered a priority (O'Broin & Palmer, 2010b, 2010c; Boyce et al., 2010; Jowett, Kanakoglu & Palmer, 2012). Boyce et al. (2010) argue that commitment can be seen as the allegiance to the work of the coaching experience by both the coach and the client. Gan and Chong (2015 p. 480) refer to commitment as the 'mutual assurance to fulfil responsibilities in the relationship that includes both task and social emotional behaviour.' It is possible to discern two components of commitment here, those referring to the task elements (time-keeping, attendance, preparation) and social-emotional behaviours (expressing energy, perseverance, identifying weaknesses and limitations, identifying and engaging with goals) (Gan & Chong, 2015; Boyce et al., 2010). Gan and Chong (2015) found commitment had a significant association with the coaching relationship, with clients' dedication and engagement to undertake the work associated with achieving change as critical. In the case of employee coaching and executive coaching evidence suggests that a coachee's attachment to the organisation would influence their willingness to invest and commit to the coaching process (McCarthy & Milner, 2013; Gan & Chong, 2015).

Where coach and coachee are committed to discharging their responsibilities associated with their relationship there is acknowledgement of the need for cooperation between the participants (Boyce, et al., 2010; Ianiro et al., 2013; Gessnitzer & Kauffeld, 2015). O'Broin and Palmer (2010c) identified that while coaches and coachees might describe collaboration differently the opportunity to do so was valued and could be achieved where each values the others' contributions and share responsibility for goal achievement. Again this aspect of the coaching relationship is seen to be closely allied to the working alliance as outlined in the psychotherapeutic literature (O'Broin & Palmer, 2010a, 2010c; Jowett, O'Broin & Palmer, 2010; Sun et al., 2013). Commitment and collaboration are also distinct within the sports coaching relationship field too where one of the key dimensions of the 3+1Cs model is commitment (3 + 1Cs represents

Table 11.2 Recent empirical insights on the coach-athlete relationship

Authors, year Outline	Methods and sample	Themes in the relationship	Positive features of the relationship	Negative features of the relationship	Key insights
Jowett & Cockerill, 2003 Olympic medallists' perspectives of the athlete–coach relationship	12 Olympic medallists interviewed	• Three Cs – Closeness, Co-orientation and Complementarity plus associations between these constructs	• Mutual respect, trust, care, concern, support, open communication, shared knowledge and understanding • Clear corresponding roles and tasks	• Betrayal of trust and respect • Focus on the physical performance	Not just a performer also a person. Value of social skills in coach education programmes.
LaVoi, 2007 Exploring closeness in the coach–athlete relationship	Survey of 431 college athletes in USA	• Based on the three Cs explores closeness specifically	• Gender dimension to closeness was expressed • Value of relational expertise of coaches is recognised • Recognises affective, cognitive and behavioural aspects of closeness	Athletes recognise value of closeness but place more responsibility of relationship development on coach	Closeness as a more differentiated construct. Communication is the most factor in a close relationship.
Trzaskoma-Biscerdy, Bognar, Revesz & Geczi, 2007 Coach–athlete relationship in Hungary	Interviews with successful Hungarian coaches and athletes across three sports	• Explore relationship constructs of closeness, complementarity and co-orientation	• Need to establish respect, esteem and love as basis for coaching relationship		Personalise relationship based on needs of the athlete.
Jackson, Grove & Beauchamp, 2010 Examines efficacy beliefs in predicting relationship quality	Survey of 63 youth athletes and their coaches	• Focuses upon self, other and 'relation-inferred self-efficacy' (RISE) beliefs and quality of coach–athlete relationship perceptions	• Suggests that self and other efficacy beliefs may denote cognitive mechanisms which enable the 3Cs		All three efficacy beliefs shape the quality of relationship processes.
Jowett & Nezlek, 2011 Relationship interdependent and satisfaction in coach–athlete dyads	Survey of 138 coach–athlete dyads in individual sports	• Examined link between relationship, interdependence and sport-related satisfaction across gender dyads, competition level and relationship length	• Higher levels of interdependence and satisfaction found at higher levels of competition and in longer relationships	Female coach and male athlete dyads experienced weaker associations between relationship interdependence and satisfaction	Highlights factors (gender, duration and competitiveness) which impact upon interdependence and relationship satisfaction.

Lafreniere, Jowett, Vallerand & Carbonneau, 2011 Passion for coaching and quality of coach–athlete relationship	Survey 103 coach–athlete dyads across gymnastic, volleyball and soccer	• Differentiated harmonious and obsessive passion of coaches • Identified coaches' harmonious passion indirectly predicted high quality relationships • Autonomy supported behaviours beneficial for quality relationships • High quality coach–athlete relationships lead to higher athlete happiness	• Obsessive passion of coaches has negative implications for athletes • Obsessive coaches tend to be defensive and close-minded	Role of harmonious passion in other people's subjective well-being.
Kristiansen, Tomten, Hanstad & Roberts, 2012 Elite Norwegian female athletes' coaching experience	Interview and focus group interviews – case study of two athletes	• Issues of over-training and lack of personalisation of training plans • Training and coaching regimes based on males, unsuitable for female athletes	• Coach mis-communication • Inexperienced coaches • Number of coaches • Autonomy and social support of other athletes discouraged	Raises issues of coach education, lack of coordination between coaches and success not clearly defined
Felton & Jowett, 2013 What do coaches do and how do they relate?	Survey of 300 athletes competing at a variety of levels	• Explores athletes' basic need satisfaction via effects of social environment (coach behaviours) and quality of relationships • Explores athletes' psychological needs satisfaction within the relationship on well- and ill-being	• Psychological needs are fulfilled by supportive autonomous coaching behaviour and quality relationships • Satisfying the competence need may support athletes' well-being and limit ill-being	Athletes' well-being is promoted by coaches' approaches and behaviours associated with positively relating and satisfying psychological needs.

Closeness, Commitment, Complementarity plus Co-orientation – see later for a more detailed discussion (Jowett & Cockerill, 2003; Jowett, O'Broin & Palmer, 2010)). As such the prevalence of the theme of commitment and collaboration is captured in O'Broin & Palmer's (2010c p.140) closing comments that mastery and skills of coaches are needed to be able to manage 'the complex interaction of coachee and coach interpersonal and intrapersonal processes at work in co-creating the coaching relationship'.

5. Coach and Coachee Attributes and Issues of Compatibility

Another prevalent theme within the coaching relationship literature is the area of coach and client characteristics, and relatedly issues of compatibility and matching within the relationship. Unsurprisingly most of the literature focuses on the impact and effect of coach attitudes, attributes and skills on the coaching relationship, as the authors cited in Table 11.1 testify. Gyllensten and Palmer (2007) highlighted the need for coaches to form strong connections and demonstrate professionalism following on from their empirical study of the coaching relationship. Likewise O'Broin and Palmer (2010a, 2010b, 2010c) suggested that the coach's characteristics and attitudes towards adapting to the coachee were critical and that this should include warm friendly behaviour, which would help develop the relationship over time and lead to the generation of new ideas. Coaches' attitudes they argued are based on self-awareness and self-reflection, the coach's belief in coaching, their approach to coaching ethics and professionalism. O'Broin and Palmer's (2010a, 2010b, 2010c) repertory grid interview method study also identified that coach self-awareness was visible to the coachee as well as the coach and as such this prioritised supporting coaches' self-management and self-development.

Evidence from de Haan (2008a; de Haan, et al., 2011; de Haan et al., 2012) indicate that coaches arrive at improved coaching outcomes results if they are viewed by their coachees as friendly and attentive. Coach behaviours, such as displaying listening, understanding and encouragement in conjunction 'with non-verbal affectionate cues like eye contact, smiling, the display of facial expressiveness and head nodding' are associated with better quality coaching relationships (Ianiro et al., 2013 p.28).

In terms of coachee characteristics deemed important for efficacious coaching relationships, motivation, commitment and readiness have been mentioned within the literature but have not featured prominently in coaching relationship studies (Joo, 2005; Bluckert, 2005; Gan & Chong, 2015). Gessnitzer and Kauffeld (2015) also stress the importance of coachee activeness in determining their coaching goals and tasks as do Grant (2014) and de Haan et al. (2016) in more recent studies. In employee coaching Gregory and Levy (2012) identified that employees' feedback orientations have a small but significant effect on their perceptions of the coaching relationship and as such engaging workers with this orientation could support the development of a positive feedback environment and increase receptivity to coaching for a learning organisation.

The impact and issues of managing coach and coachee compatibility have provided particular challenges and a range of results in the area of coaching relationship. Boyce et al. (2010 p. 915) identified that three characteristics for matching seemed evident. These characteristics include 'commonality in personal characteristics or experiences, compatibility in behavioural preferences and credibility with coaching abilities meeting client needs', however, their final results indicated no variation between those 'systematically matched and randomly assigned client–coach pairs … in coaching outcomes' (p.922). Gan and Chong (2015) also found coach and coachee match had no significant association with coaching effectiveness in their study of the executive coaching relationship in Malaysia.

However, they underlined the potential role culture might play here on the perceptions of coaches (mentors or teachers) as highly respected individuals who clients would not attempt to identify similarities with. Sampling issues also led them to suggest that matching was not an evident component of coachee ratings of their coaching relationship experiences.

There is some evidence from the psychotherapy setting where complementarity in dyads leads to more verbal interaction, less physical distance and better outcomes in cooperative tasks. Ianiro, Schermuly and Kauffeld (2013) explored affiliation and dominance based on interpersonal dynamics from social psychological theories. Affiliation, which is seen as crucial for the healthy formation and continuation of most forms of interpersonal relationships, was used as one dimension and dominance, where dominance is captured as self-confident behaviour, was identified as the other dimension. Ianiro et al. (2013) then used affect control theory to understand the impact of similarity and complementarity between coaches and clients. Similarity is based on the premise that social interactions are positive where 'actors have similar needs on both interpersonal dimensions (affiliation and dominance) and thus show similar interpersonal behaviour' (Ianiro et al., 2013 p. 30). Social interactions adhering to the complementarity model, however, exist if the participants show similar needs for affiliation but opposite needs for dominance. The researchers found that the 'Interpersonal compatibility of coach and client seems to be beneficial to the client's ratings of the relationship quality and goal attainment' (Ianiro et al., 2013 p. 37).

Mixed results of the impact of coach–coachee matching on coaching outcome were also evident from the studies of Scoular and Linley (2006) who found that contradictory matches in personality profiles (as determined by the MBTI) was associated with effective coaching outcomes. Conversely, De Haan et al. (2013; 2016) and Wycherley and Cox (2008) found that matching on the basis of demographics or the personality differences of coachee and coach showed no correlation with effectiveness, and cautioned practitioners to be wary of matching on such parameters. Further evidence of the limits of coach–coachee match was identified by Bozer, Joo and Santora (2015) where gender and perceived similarity on coaching outcomes were not significant. However, aspects of self-awareness were seen to be enhanced by same gender coaching and features of actual and perceived similarity were seen to contribute to coach and client 'fit'. As such many authors caution practitioners (coaches, human resource and organisational development professionals) against an emphasis on matching and instead argue for the value of coach–coachee selection based on the coach's accreditation, qualifications and supervision reports (Bozer et al., 2015; De Haan et al., 2016; 2013; Wycherley & Cox, 2008).

This section of the chapter has highlighted five themes which encompass the coaching relationship, namely; the stages of the coaching relationship, rapport and the bonds, trust and transparency, commitment and coach and coachee characteristics. Further insights are now presented in the last two sections of the chapter by drawing upon empirical studies from across the key contexts of executive, employee and sports coaching (Bachkirova, Cox & Clutterbuck, 2014) and then exploring the connections between the coaching relationship and the working alliance construct from the therapeutic relationship field.

COACHING RELATIONSHIPS ACROSS KEY CONTEXTS: SPORTS, EXECUTIVE AND EMPLOYEE COACHING

Three coaching contexts distinguish themselves as presenting particular issues when considering the coaching relationship. The second half of this chapter summarises some of the key studies pertaining to sports, executive and employee coaching before we turn our attention to the role psychotherapy has played in shaping our understanding and approaches to researching the coaching relationship.

Sports Coaching

Sports coaching has a long heritage and the coaching relationship, or more specifically the coach–athlete relationship, has engaged researchers' exploration of the interpersonal dynamics between competitors and their coaches (Ellinger & Kim, 2014; Lafreniere et al., 2011; Jowett & Cockerill, 2003). Attempts to characterise sports coaching suggest these relationships exhibit high levels of social interdependence, are performance oriented and volitional (Jackson, Grove & Beauchamp, 2010). As such effective and healthy coach–athlete relationships are seen to be based upon the interpersonal factors of coaches' and athletes' mutual trust, respect and communication (Trzaskoma-Biscerdy et al., 2007; Jowett & Neziek, 2011). Table 11.2 provides a brief summary of some of the most recent empirical studies on sports coaching. This area has adopted a range of methodologies though perhaps in accordance with the performance dimension to sports quantitative methodologies have become particularly evident. There is, however, a dilemma for sports coaching researchers in that at the non-elite level surveys requiring large sample sizes are attainable; however, at the elite sports level smaller sample sizes are more evident and appropriate. The format for Table 11.2 is also distinctive as the empirical studies were much more likely to capture negative aspects of, and a gender dimension to, the coach–athlete relationship than either of the other two contexts explored in this chapter. This reignites the previous debate on issues of coach–coachee gender match and similarity which as Bozer et al. (2015) highlight is rife in the mentoring literature (O'Brien, Biga, Kessler & Allen, 2010; Allen & Eby, 2003; Scandura & Williams, 2001). However, it may be that where features of specific coaching and mentoring disciplines are similar the impact of gender (and potentially other aspects) on the coach–coachee/mentor–mentee relationship become more evident (Salter & Gannon, 2015).

A prominent feature in the sports coaching relationship research area is the 3+1Cs model, which is described as providing 'a view into the ties that bind the coach and the coachee as it assesses the quality (content) and quantity (intensity) of the coaching relationship, through a wide range of relational components and dimensions that ebb and flow in social interaction' (Jowett, Kanakoglu & Passmore, 2012 p.195). This model is built around Closeness, Commitment and Complementarity as the first 3Cs and the +1 refers to Co-orientation. Closeness represents the emotional ties and comprises interpersonal features such as trust, respect, liking and gratefulness. Commitment denotes the potentially long-term nature of the cognitive connections between the members of the relationship. Finally, Complementarity captures the aspect of cooperation in the relationship where members' interactions are seen to be correspondent and reciprocal (Jowett, O'Broin & Palmer, 2010). The final element of Co-orientation reflects interdependency between the members in the coach–athlete relationship; however, this element operates at several levels as outlined below; 'Co-orientation is capable of assessing the interdependence of two people's 3Cs at three levels: (a) the level at which dyadic members are *actually similar* in the ways they view their relationship; (b) the level at which dyadic members *assume similarity* in terms of how they view their relationship; and (c) the level at which each dyadic member *accurately understands* the other's view regarding the quality of the relationship' (Jowett, O'Broin & Palmer, 2010 p.21 emphasis in the original).

The Closeness, Commitment and Complementarity features of this model have been developed into a questionnaire, the

Coach–Athlete Relationship Questionnaire (CART-Q) with validated items, with a version for coaches and another for athletes, which can be responded to directly or through the levels outlined above (Jowett & Nezlek, 2011). There have been attempts to build bridges between the expertise in sports coaching and specifically executive coaching, and the working alliance (Jowett, O'Broin & Palmer, 2010; Jowett, Kanakoglu & Passmore, 2012). However, there is no clear mapping across the constructs associated with these frameworks, even if, as discussed in the section on the working alliance (later in this chapter), links can be identified.

Executive Coaching

Certainly the predominant context evident in the coaching literature has been that of executive coaching (Stern & Stout-Rostron, 2013). Executive coaching has been defined as 'a form of leadership development which takes place through a series of one-to-one conversations with a qualified "coach"' (de Haan et al., 2013 p.2). Baron and Morin (2009) explored the determinants of the executive coaching relationship and their impact on coaching outcomes and found the coaching relationship has a mediating role in the link between the number of coaching sessions and executives' self-efficacy development. The work of de Haan and colleagues (2008a; 2011; 2012; 2016) has been particularly pivotal in this area and highlights the explanatory value of the working alliance literature in framing the executive coaching relationship as well as challenging some of the evidence from the psychotherapeutic field. For example, the evidence that while coaches' specific interventions may not be directly recognised and valued by clients their relational skills (such as empathic listening, supportive feedback) are valued.

Jowett, Kanakoglu and Passmore (2012) building on previous literature (Jowett et al., 2010; Jowett & Nezlek, 2011) apply an adapted interview schedule version of the 3+1Cs model from sports coaching to the executive coaching context and suggest, 'The analysis of the data uncovered that the participants recognised the importance of the relationship as a medium for identifying needs and satisfying goals on one hand, and on the other hand they reported that their relationship contained such important relational components as trust, respect, liking, support, responsiveness, cooperation and openness' (Jowett, Kanakoglu & Passmore, 2012 p. 192). They suggest that this model offers executive coaches a valuable way of assessing the quality of their coaching relationships and highlight some relationship enhancement strategies which emerge from this adopted model.

Finally, Gan and Chong's (2015) study not only provides a valuable international and cultural dimension to our knowledge of the executive coaching relationship but reiterates the role of rapport and commitment in terms of the relationship and successful outcomes, as assessed by clients. The focus on coaching outcomes, as part of empirical investigations of the executive coaching relationship, is particularly apparent within Table 11.2 and this is perhaps due to the expense and demands for efficacy associated with results in this context (de Haan & Sills, 2012).

Employee Coaching

The rise of managerial or employee coaching has received more limited coverage with some notable exceptions (McCarthy & Milner, 2013; Beattie et al., 2014; Ellinger, Beattie & Hamlin, 2014; Gregory & Levy, 2010; 2011; 2012) to name a few (See Table 11.1). There are clearly challenges and benefits experienced by managerial coaches and employee coaches. For example, familiarity with organisational conventions, context and performance means that managerial coaches may have credibility with their coaches, however where this is not present they will have to work hard to effectively gain rapport and trust. There are also suggestions that employee coaching can augment the relationship between managers and their staff (McCarthy & Milner, 2013). However, as Machin (2010) points out it can be a challenge to achieve coaching on an equal footing in employee coaching relationships. Gregory and Levy (2010; 2011) highlight the employee coaching relationship may be more complex given the prior history of the subordinate and line manager/supervisor. Their employee coaching relationship research pursued the development of a measure of 'the perceived quality of the employee coaching relationship' (PQECR) (Gregory & Levy, 2010). This instrument focuses upon four key features; genuineness within the relationship, effective communication, comfort within the relationship and facilitating development. Using this measure greater evidence has emerged of the importance of trust, the coach's empathy skills, and the frequency and consistency of coaching interactions. However, this coaching context also raises the profile of coaching from the organisational agenda and the impact of the wider organisational environment in terms of ensuring a positive feedback environment, and support for supervisors and line managers coaching skills and employees' engagement with their own feedback orientations (Gregory & Levy, 2011; 2012).

THE WORKING ALLIANCE, COACHING ALLIANCE AND COACHING RELATIONSHIP

It is widely accepted that the development of coaching owes a huge intellectual and professional debt to other helping relationships and discourses, in particular therapy, counselling and psychology (Du Toit, 2014; de Haan, 2008a; de Haan & Sills, 2012). Drawing on Wampold's (2001) arguments for 'common factors' where the relationship is seen as a key feature of professional and personal helping approaches, the arguments pertaining to how coaches may benefit from engaging with the relational perspective in psychology and psychotherapy, deserve examination. As the balance of attention in much of the extant literature has firmly rested on the side of the coach, insights from the fields of therapy and counselling emphasise the relational dynamic between client and therapist/counsellor. It is therefore valuable to consider the ways in which coaching relationships and therapeutic relationships are alike and the ways in which they differ in relation to the coaching relationship, exploring where and how mutually beneficial understanding and expertise can be shared.

Wampold's (2001) 'great psychotherapy debate' provided decisive confirmation that therapeutic interventions are effective to the same level as psychiatric medicine and that there is no one psychotherapeutic approach which shows greater success than others (de Haan, 2008a; de Haan & Sills, 2012). Indeed the evidence suggests that all professional psychotherapy approaches offer active ingredients common across the range of approaches. De Haan and Sills (2012 p.5) summarise these as follows: 'Common factors have to do with the setting (meeting at regular intervals, providing an expectation that things may get better), with a client's desire to be helped (the client's expectations preferences and support networks), with the coach (warmth, quality of listening) and finally with the relationship (quality of communication, trust, agreement about the shared endeavour).'

Within the psychotherapy literature the relationship dimension is typically operationalised as the working alliance, as many of the studies identified in Table 11.1 or mentioned previously (Baron & Morin, 2009; Gessnitzer & Kauffeld, 2015; Kemp, 2011; O'Broin & Palmer, 2010a, 2010b, 2010c; de Haan, 2008a) identify. Building upon Greenson's (1967) arguments, Bordin (1979) further articulated the working alliance concept, which can be defined as collaboration between the client and the therapist built on the development of an attachment bond alongside a mutual commitment to the goals and tasks. Collaboration is fundamental to the working alliance and is a crucial feature of the active participation of both the client and therapist. The mutuality of the relationship is based upon the key features of goals, tasks and bonds (Bordin, 1979; O'Broin & Palmer, 2010b, 2010c; Gessnitzer & Kauffeld, 2015) where 'goals' are the desired results, 'tasks' are the processes required to reach the goals and 'bonds' are the personal relationship features of trust, confidence and acceptance (Sun et al., 2013; Baron & Morin, 2009; O'Broin & Palmer, 2010b). It is, in particular, the mutual agreement of goals and tasks which may arguably create the state for clarity and transparency in the coaching session and accordingly the precursors to trust and respect (O'Broin & Palmer, 2010c) though empirical evidence in this area remains elusive.

Studying the working alliance in coaching settings has typically been undertaken using the Working Alliance Inventory (WAI) (Horvath & Greenberg, 1989; Baron & Morin, 2009; Gessnitzer & Kauffeld, 2015) but with varying degrees of similarity in relation to the results from the therapeutic setting. Baron and Morin (2009 p.87) identified similarities between executive coaching and psychotherapy – particularly in relation to the 'structure of the process' suggesting 'these two forms of personalized relationships both attempt to help individuals understand how their cognitive and emotional reactions interfere with their self-efficacy' (Hodgetts, 2002 cited in Baron & Morin, 2009 p. 87). Using the WAI they found that the coach–coachee relationship played 'a mediating role in the association between the number of sessions received and the development of a manager's self-efficacy.' Baron and Morin (2009 p. 98). These results indicate that the development of the coachee depends upon the amount of coaching undertaken and the coach's ability to facilitate learning and results. While the coach's relational and communication skills have no direct impact.

While some perspectives on the coaching relationship literature identify the coach and coachee have relational facets in common much of the literature identifies the collaborative dimension to the relationship. De Haan et al. (2012 p. 15) highlight from their study that 'the relationship between coach and client only exists in their respective minds (and in the minds of outside observers), causing them to present an "it" in a completely independent way and moreover evaluate "it" completely independently and according to highly personal criteria and expectations.' Yet empirical evidence from the therapeutic literature suggests there is no one version of the helping relationship with therapists, clients and observers perceiving and evaluating 'relationships' independently (Ianiro et al., 2013; Gessnitzer & Kauffeld, 2015). It is also relevant to identify the work of Clarkson (1995) on the limitations of the working alliance and the other relationship variations in the psychotherapeutic relationship at this juncture. Adopting a systemic integrative perspective to psychotherapy Clarkson (1995) identified five modes of relationship, which could be used depending upon the features of clients and their phase in therapy. The working alliance features as part of these five modes alongside the transferential/countertransferential relationship, the reparative developmentally-needed relationship, the person-to-person relationship and the transpersonal relationship. While an adapted version of this model has been deployed in work settings to identify the influence of various relationships by organisational consultants there is limited evidence of its deployment in relation to investigating the coaching relationship (O'Broin & Palmer, 2007).

O'Broin and Palmer (2010c, p. 37) also warn against the conflation of the coaching alliance and the coaching relationship and suggest that the working or coaching alliance is seen as 'The mutual, collaborative process of agreeing the tasks and goals of coaching and reviewing these on an on-going basis … [which] acts as a helpful framework for the coach.' As such the alliance is then a standpoint from which to gauge the extent and form of collaboration and purposiveness of the coaching work that is required, and which is occurring. It is interesting to note though that many studies seem to take the coaching alliance as a proxy for the coaching relationship with their widespread use of WAI as central to their investigations.

A useful departure from this predominant use of the working alliance is evidenced in the work of Sun et al. (2013) who used the 'real relationship' construct alongside the working alliance in their exploration of the coaching relationship and coaching outcomes. This construct views the helping relationship from the personal relationship perspective and highlights two components; realism and genuineness (Sun et al., 2013; Gelso & Hayes, 1998). Realism 'refers to the realistic, undistorted perceptions that one person holds of another', while genuineness is concerned with 'a person's ability and willingness to be authentic, open and honest in their relationship' (Sun et al., 2013 pp.7–8). Two coaching approaches, transformational and skills coaching, were deployed in this study and there was seen to be a moderate to strong relationship between coachees' work alliance and 'real relationship' ratings (Sun et al., 2013). However, transformational coaching occasioned a stronger coaching relationship than skills coaching, as rated by both coaches and coachees. With specific reference to the 'real relationship' results greater realism was reported by the coaches experiencing transformational coaching though genuineness was not significantly higher in this coaching approach. Sun et al. (2013 p. 16) state, 'Transformational coaching resulted in stronger and deeper coaching relationships than skills coaching, supporting the notion that coaching models closer to the therapeutic end of the spectrum require relationships more akin to therapeutic relationships.'

This study clearly supports the arguments of Kauffman and Bachkirova (2009) that different coaching approaches will demand different intensities or traits and brings a rarely seen dimension of the 'real relationship' to our understanding of the coaching relationship.

In the literature there is considerable debate concerning the boundaries of counselling/therapy and coaching (Bluckert, 2005; Gessnitzer & Kauffeld, 2015). These can typically be distilled down to coaching's aim to develop professional skills for the work setting rather than day-to-day functioning (Baron & Morin, 2009; Bluckert, 2005), and coaching's focus on the present and future as opposed to the tendency for therapy to place relatively more emphasis on the past (Baron & Morin, 2009). It has also been argued that coaching tends to be more directive and action-oriented (Baron & Morin, 2009; Ellinger & Kim, 2014). De Haan and colleagues (2016 p. xx) provide further clarity in the distinction between coaching from therapeutic encounters in a study that shows 'evidence that a focus on 'tasks' and 'goals' are more important than the strength of the 'bonds'.' Other discrepancies are apparent when the (employer) organisation is financing the coaching, in particular in executive coaching. This creates a connection between the coach and the organisation, which is not typically seen in psychotherapeutic relationships (Smith & Brummel, 2013). Finally the psychotherapeutic relationship tends to go much deeper and as such requires clinical expertise (Baron & Morin, 2009).

CONCLUSIONS

This chapter has outlined the territory of the coaching relationship literature, highlighting the key themes which have emerged and remain apparent. Rapport and bonds, trust and transparency, commitment, collaboration and co-creation appear as evident in the literature now as the very earliest studies in the field. As part of this chapter we have provided summaries of recent empirical studies which depict the influences, methods and approaches deployed to explore coaching relationship in recent years. There are clear roots and foundations for our subject knowledge but at this stage it is also vital to question whether we should now be exploring further connections and hybrids as coaching emerges as a fully-fledged profession.

Using the knowledge from different coaching contexts, such as employee/managerial, sports and executive coaching, helps us identify the nuances and challenges of coaching relationships and their investigation. However, this across coaching contexts approach also facilitates opportunities for acknowledging and adopting different methodologies and research instruments and viewing the coaching relationship from different perspectives. Introducing the model from sports coaching into executive coaching research assists in challenging our reliance on the coaching alliance model, for example. Likewise the prospect of approaching the sports coaching context with an adapted version of perceived quality of employee coaching relationship (PQECR) instrument from employee coaching with its focus on genuineness, effective communication, comfort with the relationship and facilitates development (Sun et al., 2013) offers the chance to further challenge knowledge boundaries. There are already clear connections between the 'real relationship' and the PQECR in terms of genuineness. Similarly there are comparisons between aspects of the working alliance construct in relation to bonds with the closeness dimension with the 3+1C model. These potential links only tell part of the story though and the coaching relationship research agenda in coming years will hopefully be formed from the established roots and knowledge bases plus the cross-fertilisation of models, constructs and frameworks.

We do have to recognise that exploring the coaching relationship is no easy undertaking as Sun et al. (2013) argue issues of cross-sectional research make it difficult to understand the quality of the coaching relationship over time. Innovative methodologies encouraging methodologies with interaction analysis and longitudinal dimensions will assist in clarifying further our understanding of the stages of development in the coaching relationship. This sets high hurdles for coaching researchers to surpass but as the coaching relationship plays such a crucial role in the effectiveness of coaching we need to share our expertise and collaborate creatively to meet these challenges.

REFERENCES

Allen, T. D., & Eby, L. T. (2003). Relationship effectiveness for mentors: Factors associated with learning and quality. *Journal of Management*, 29(4), 469–486.

Bachkirova, T., Cox, E. & Clutterbuck, D. (2014) Introduction, in Cox, E., Bachkirova, T. & Clutterbuck, D. (eds.) (2014), *The Complete Handbook of Coaching*, 2nd edition, London, Sage Publications.

Bachkirova, T., & Kauffman, C. (2009). The blind men and the elephant: using criteria of universality and uniqueness in evaluating our attempts to define coaching. *Coaching: An International Journal of Theory, Research and Practice*, 2 (2), 95–105.

Baron, L. & Morin, L. (2009) The coach–coachee relationship in executive coaching: a field study, *Human Resource Development Quarterly*, 20(1, Spring), 85–106.

Beattie, R. S., Kim, S., Hagen, M. S., Egan, T. M., Ellinger, A. D., & Hamlin, R. G. (2014). Managerial coaching: a review of the empirical literature and development of a model to guide future practice. *Advances in Developing Human Resources*, 16(2), 184–201.

Bluckert, P. (2005). Critical factors in executive coaching – the coaching relationship. *Industrial and Commercial Training*, 37(7), 336–340.

Bordin, E. S. (1979). The generalizability of the psychoanalytic concept of the working alliance. *Psychotherapy: Theory, Research & Practice*, 16(3), 252.

Boyce, L. A., Jackson, R. J., & Neal, L. J. (2010). Building successful leadership coaching relationships: Examining impact of matching criteria in a leadership coaching program. *Journal of Management Development*, 29(10), pp. 914–931.

Bozer, G., Joo, B. K. & Santora, J. C. (2015). Executive coaching: does coach–coachee matching based on similarity matter? *Consulting Psychology Journal: Practice and Research*, 67(3), 218–233.

Cavanagh, M. J., & Grant, A. M. (2006). Coaching psychology and the scientist–practitioner model. *The Modern Scientist-Practitioner. A Guide to Practice in Psychology*, 146–157.

Clarkson, P. (1996). Researching the 'therapeutic relationship' in psychoanalysis, counselling psychology and psychotherapy–a qualitative inquiry. *Counselling Psychology Quarterly*, 9(2), 143–162.

Cox, E. (2010). Last things first: ending well in the coaching relationship, in Palmer, S. & McDowell, A. (eds.), *The coaching relationship: Putting people First: The Interactional Aspects of Coaching*, London, Routledge, pp. 159–181.

Cox, E. (2012). Individual and organizational trust in a reciprocal peer coaching context, *Mentoring & Tutoring: Partnership in Learning*, 20(3), 427–443.

Cox, E. (2013). *Coaching Understood: A pragmatic inquiry into the coaching process*, London, Sage.

Daouk-Öyry, L., & Rosinski, P. (2010). Coaching across cultures. In Palmer, S. & McDowall, A. (eds.), *The Coaching Relationship: Putting People First*, London, Routledge, pp. 121–138.

De Haan, E. (2008a). Relational Coaching: Journeys Towards Mastering One-to-One Learning. Chichester: Wiley.

De Haan, E. (2008b). Becoming simultaneously thicker and thinner skinned: the inherent conflicts arising in the professional development of coaches. *Personnel Review*, 37(5), 526–542.

De Haan, E., Bertie, C., Day, A. & Sills, C. (2010). Critical Moments of Clients and Coaches: A Direct-Comparison Study. *International Coaching Psychology Review*, 5, 2, 109–128.

De Haan, E., Culpin, V., & Curd, J., (2011). Executive coaching in practice: what determines helpfulness for clients of coaching? *Personnel Review*, 40(1), 24–44.

De Haan, E., Duckworth, A., Birch, D., & Jones, C., (2013). Executive coaching outcome research: the contribution of common factors such as relationship, personality match, and self-efficacy. *Consulting Psychology Journal: Practice and Research*, 65(1), 40–57.

De Haan, E., Grant, A. M., Burger, Y. & Eriksson, P. (2016). A large-scale study of executive and workplace coaching: the relative contributions of relationship, personality match, and self-efficacy, *Consulting Psychology Journal: Practice & Research*, 68(3), 189–207.

De Haan, E., & Nieß, C. (2012). Critical moments in a coaching case study: illustration of a process research model. *Consulting Psychology Journal: Practice and Research*, 64(3), 198.

De Haan, E. & Sills, C. (2010). The relational turn in executive coaching, Guest editorial in *The Journal of Management Development*, 29(10): 845–851.

De Haan, E. & Sills, C. (eds.) (2012). Introduction in *Coaching Relationships: The Relational Coaching Field Book*. Faringdon: Libri Publishing.

Du Toit, A. (2014). *Making Sense of Coaching*, London, Sage.

Ellinger, A., Beattie, R., & Hamlin, R. G. (2014). The manager as coach, Chapter 18 in Cox, E., Bachkirova, T., & Clutterbuck, D. (eds.), *The Complete Handbook of Coaching*, 2nd edition, London, Sage Publications.

Ellinger, A. D., & Kim, S. (2014). Coaching and human resource development examining relevant theories, coaching genres, and scales to advance research and practice. *Advances in Developing Human Resources*, 16(2), 127–138.

Felton, L., & Jowett, S. (2013). 'What do coaches do' and 'how do they relate': Their effects on athletes' psychological needs and functioning. *Scandinavian Journal of Medicine & Science in Sports*, 23(2), 130–139.

Gan, G.C., & Chong, C.W. (2015). Coaching relationship in executive coaching: a Malaysian study. *Journal of Management Development*, 34(4), 476–493

Gelso, C. J., & Hayes, J. A. (1998), *The Psychotherapy Relationship: Theory, research and practice*, New York, Wiley.

Gessnitzer, S., & Kauffeld, S. (2015). The working alliance in coaching: why behavior is the key to success. *The Journal of Applied Behavioral Science*, 51(2), 177–197.

Grant, A. M. (2014). Autonomy support, relationship satisfaction and goal focus in the coach–coachee relationship: which best predicts coaching success? *Coaching: An International Journal of Theory, Research and Practice*, 7(1), 18–38.

Greenson, R. R. (1967). The technique and practice of psycho. *Analysis*, 1, 53.

Gregory, J. B., & Levy, P. E. (2010). Employee coaching relationships: enhancing construct clarity and measurement. *Coaching: An International Journal of Theory, Research and Practice*, 3(2), 109–123.

Gregory, J. B., & Levy, P. E. (2011). It's not me, it's you: a multilevel examination of variables that impact employee coaching relationships. *Consulting Psychology Journal: Practice and Research*, 63(2), 67.

Gregory, J. B., & Levy, P. E. (2012). Employee feedback orientation: implications for effective coaching relationships. *Coaching: An International Journal of Theory, Research and Practice*, 5(2), 86–99.

Gyllensten, K., & Palmer, S. (2007) The coaching relationship: an interpretative phenomenological analysis. *International Coaching Psychology Review*, 2(2), 168–177.

Hardingham, A. (2006) *The Coach's Coach: Personal development for personal developers*, London, CIPD.

Horvath, A. O., & Greenberg, L. S. (1989). Development and validation of the Working Alliance Inventory. *Journal of counseling psychology*, 36(2), 223–233.

Ianiro, P. M., Schermuly, C. C., & Kauffeld, S. (2013) Why interpersonal dominance and affiliation matter: an interaction analysis of the coach-client relationship, *Coaching: An International Journal of Theory, Research and Practice*, 6(1), 25–46,

Ives, Y. (2008). What is 'coaching'? An exploration of conflicting paradigms. *International Journal of Evidence Based Coaching and Mentoring*, 6(2), 100–113.

Jackson, B., Grove, J. R., & Beauchamp, M. R. (2010). Relational efficacy beliefs and relationship quality within coach–athlete dyads. *Journal of Social and Personal Relationships*, 27(8), 1035–1050.

Joo, B. K. B. (2005). Executive coaching: a conceptual framework from an integrative review of practice and research. *Human Resource Development Review*, 4(4), 462–488.

Jowett, S., & Cockerill, I. M. (2003). Olympic medallists' perspective of the athlete–coach relationship. *Psychology of Ssport and Exercise*, 4(4), 313–331.

Jowett, S., Kanakoglou, K., & Passmore, J. (2012). The application of the 3+1Cs relationship model in executive coaching. *Consulting Psychology Journal: Practice and Research*, 64, 183–197.

Jowett, S., & Nezlek, J. (2011). Relationship interdependence and satisfaction with important outcomes in coach–athlete dyads. *Journal of Social and Personal Relationships*, 0265407511420980.

Jowett, S., O'Broin, A., & Palmer, S. (2010). On understanding the role and significance of a key two-person relationship in sport and executive coaching. *Sport & Exercise Psychology Review*, 6(2), 19–30

Kauffman, C., & Bachkirova, T. (2009). Spinning order from chaos: how do we know what to study in coaching research and use it for self-reflective practice? *Coaching: An International Journal of Theory, Research and Practice*, 2(1), 1–9.

Kemp, T. (2011) Building the coaching alliance: illuminating the phenomenon of relationship in coaching, Chapter 7 in Hernez-Broome, G., & Boyce, L. A. (eds.), *Advancing Executive Coaching: Setting the course for successful leadership coaching*, San Francisco, John Wiley & Sons.

Kristiansen, E., Tomten, S. E., Hanstad, D. V., & Roberts, G. C. (2012). Coaching communication issues with elite female athletes: Two Norwegian case studies. *Scandinavian journal of medicine & science in sports*, 22(6), 156–167.

Lafrenière, M. A. K., Jowett, S., Vallerand, R. J., & Carbonneau, N. (2011). Passion for coaching and the quality of the coach–athlete relationship: The mediating role of coaching behaviors. *Psychology of Sport and Exercise*, 12(2), 144–152.

LaVoi, N. M. (2007). Expanding the interpersonal dimension: closeness in the coach-athlete relationship. *International Journal of Sports Science & Coaching*, 2(4), 497–512.

Machin, S. (2010). The nature of the internal coaching relationship. *International Journal of Evidence Based Coaching and Mentoring*, 4, 37–52.

McCarthy, G., & Milner, J. (2013). Managerial coaching: challenges, opportunities and training. *Journal of Management Development*, 32(7), 768–779.

McCauley, C. D., & Douglas, C. A. (1998). Developmental relationships. In C.D. McCauley, R. S. Moxley, & E. Van Velsor (eds.), *The Center for Creative Leadership Handbook of Leadership Development* (pp. 160–193). San Francisco: Jossey-Bass.

Nangalia, L., & Nangalia, A. (2010). The coach in Asian society: impact of social hierarchy on the coaching relationship. *International Journal of Evidence Based Coaching & Mentoring*, 8(1), 51–66.

Natale, S. M., & Diamante, T. (2005). The five stages of executive coaching: better process makes better practice. *Journal of Business Ethics*, 59(4), 361–374.

Nelson-Jones, R. (2006). *Human Relationship Skills: Coaching and self-coaching*, London, Routledge.

O'Brien, K.E., Biga, A., Kessler, S.R. & Allen, T.D. (2010). A meta-analytic investigation of gender differences in mentoring. *Journal of Management*, 36(2), 537–554.

O'Broin, A., & Palmer, S. (2007) Reappraising the coach–client relationship: the unassuming change agent in coaching, Chapter 16 in Palmer, S., & Whybrow, A. (eds.), *Handbook of Coaching Psychology: A Guide for Practitioners*. Routledge.

O'Broin, A., & Palmer, S. (2010a). Introducing an interpersonal perspective on the coaching relationship, Chapter 2 in Palmer, S. & McDowall, A. (eds.), *The Coaching Relationship: Putting People First*, London, Routledge.

O'Broin, A., & Palmer, S. (2010b). Building on an interpersonal perspective on the coaching relationship, Chapter 3 in Palmer, S. & McDowall, A. (eds.), *The Coaching Relationship: Putting People First*, London, Routledge.

O'Broin, A., & Palmer, S. (2010c). Exploring key aspects in the formation of coaching relationships: initial indicators from the perspective of the coachee and the coach. *Coaching: An International Journal of Theory, Research and Practice*, 3(2), 124–143.

Palmer, S., & McDowall, A. (eds.) (2010) *The Coaching Relationship: Putting People First*, London, Routledge.

Reissner, S. C., & Du Toit, A. (2011). Power and the tale: coaching as storytelling. *Journal of Management Development*, 30(3), 247–259.

Rock, A. D., & Garavan, T. N. (2006). Reconceptualizing developmental relationships. *Human Resource Development Review*, 5(3), 330–354.

Rogers, C. R. (1967). The Therapeutic Relationship and its Impact: A Study of Psychotherapy with Schizophrenics. University of Wisconsin Press.

Salter, T., & Gannon, J. M. (2015). Exploring shared and distinctive aspects of coaching and mentoring approaches through six disciplines. *European Journal of Training and Development*, 39(5), 373–392.

Scandura, T. A., & Williams, E. A. (2001). An investigation of the moderating effects of gender on the relationships between mentorship initiation and protégé perceptions of mentoring functions. *Journal of Vocational Behavior*, 59(3), 342–363.

Scoular, A., & Linley, P. A. (2006). Coaching, goal-setting and personality type: what matters?. *The Coaching Psychologist*, 2(1), 9–11.

Smith, I. M., & Brummel, B. J. (2013). Investigating the role of the active ingredients in executive coaching. *Coaching: An International Journal of Theory, Research and Practice*, 6(1), 57–71.

Starr, J. (2007). *The Coaching Manual: The definitive guide to the process, principles and skills of personal coaching*. Pearson Education.

Stern, L., & Stout-Rostron, S. (2013). What progress has been made in coaching research in relation to 16 ICRF focus areas from 2008 to 2012? *Coaching: An International Journal of Theory, Research and Practice*, 6(1), 72–96.

Sun, B. J., Deane, F. P., Crowe, T. P., Andersen, R., Oades, L., & Ciarrochi, J. (2013). A preliminary exploration of the working alliance and the 'real relationship' in two coaching approaches with mental health workers. *International Coaching Psychology Review*, 8(2, September), 6–17

Trzaskoma-Bicsérdy, G., Bognár, J., Révész, L., & Géczi, G. (2007). The coach-athlete relationship in successful Hungarian individual sports.*International Journal of Sports Science & Coaching*, 2(4), 485–495.

Wampold, B. (2001) *The Great Psychotherapy Debate*, Mahwah, NJ, Lawrence Erlbaum.

Welman, P., & Bachkirova, T. (2010). The issue of power in the coaching relationship. Chapter 8 in Palmer, S. & McDowall, A. (eds.), *The Coaching Relationship: Putting People First*, London, Routledge, pp. 139–158.

Wycherley, I. M., & Cox, E. (2008). Factors in the selection and matching of executive coaches in organisations. *Coaching: An International Journal of Theory, Research and Practice*, 1(1), 39–53.

Working with Goals in Coaching

David Ashley Clutterbuck and Gordon Spence

Goals and goal constructs have been a central feature of the coaching literature for almost all its scholarly history. Indeed, evidence of a focus on goals can be detected as far back as Parkes (1955), when goal-setting was recommended as an essential practice for executive development. Since that time numerous scholars have made goals a primary focus of theoretical (e.g. Grant, 2012), methodological (e.g. Spence, 2007) and empirical work (Burke & Linley, 2007; Grant, 2014; O'Connor & Cavanagh, 2012; Spence & Grant, 2007). Whilst goals have generally been considered a fundamental part of behavioural change processes, they tend to have been viewed in two distinct ways.

The first is the linear view, which considers change to be a sequence of relatively discrete events. This view underpins much of the practitioner-based literature (e.g. Downey, 2011; Whitmore, 1996) and assumes that coaching should help people to: (i) identify what they want (goal clarification), (ii) make plans about how they will get there (goal path determination), (iii) take steps to strive towards the goal (goal pursuit), and (iv) maintain motivation and momentum (goal management). Furthermore, this view assumes that some form of measurable change should be detectable from this process, with relatively high predictability at each stage. The second view is a more systemic view (e.g. Clutterbuck, 2013; M. Hall & Gambardella, 2012; Ordóñez, Schweitzer, Galinsky, & Bazerman, 2009; Pryor & Bright, 2011) and considers goals to be highly unstable (due to the complexity of an individual's environment) and requiring considerable flexibility (i.e. an ability to adapt to internal and external change). Goals from this perspective can be seen as *temporary responses* to a set of needs generated by an understanding of internal and external contexts. As this understanding deepens, individuals become more able to formulate goals that will be intrinsically satisfying.

In this chapter, we explore the literature that surrounds the use of goals in coaching. This will be done via a five-part discussion. First, the breadth and depth of the extant goals literature will be acknowledged, with specific attention given to the variety of ways that goals have been defined and conceptualised. Second, we will turn our attention towards two goal theories that have been widely cited in the coaching literature. Our aim is to ascertain – via a brief exploration of goal-setting theory (Locke & Latham, 2002) and self-determination theory (Deci & Ryan, 1985) – how established theory can influence the understanding of goals in coaching, and what perspectives might not currently be well represented. Third, we will summarise some of the criticisms that have been directed towards goal-focused theories and models. Fourth, an overview of the coaching literature focused on goals will be provided, along with the presentation of an alternative perspective to help coaches develop a more nuanced conceptualisation of working with goals in coaching. In the final section, several suggestions are made for the guidance of researchers who are interested in progressing work in this important aspect of coaching.

DEFINITIONS AND DIMENSIONS OF GOALS

The theoretical and empirical goals literature is voluminous, with the bulk of it situated within psychological science. Goal researchers have compiled an incredibly diverse body of work, including investigations into 'the theoretical development of the structure and properties of goals, goal establishment and striving processes, and goal-content taxonomies' (Austin & Vancouver, 1996, p. 338). Indeed, in a comprehensive review of the goal psychology literature, Austin and Vancouver (1996) outlined a total of 31 goal-related theories that have been used to study goals throughout almost all of the twentieth century. Examples include perceptual control theory (Wiener, 1948), industrial goal setting (Locke & Latham, 1990) and the theory of reasoned action (Fishbein & Ajzen, 1977). After noting the presence of 'a large body of facts, an excess of vocabulary, and numerous microtheories' (p. 338), the authors noted the need for a perspective that could coherently encompass the diversity of findings related to the content, processes and structure of goals. Whilst attempts have been made to answer this call over the years (e.g. Karoly, 1999), the field remains highly complex and, from a reflective-practitioner perspective, is not one easily navigated.

The Nature of Goals

As demonstrated by past reviews (e.g. Karoly, 1999), goal constructs are ubiquitous in psychological research, and particularly so in the study of motivated behaviour. Given that human lives can only be lived in the 'direction' of the future, the prominence of goal constructs seems unsurprising. Accordingly, goals have generally been defined as future-focused, mental constructions, or as 'internal representations of desired states, where states are broadly defined as outcomes, events, or processes' (p. 338). Whilst a wide review of goal definitions is not important to the present discussion, it is worth acknowledging that goals have traditionally been closely tied to the concept of self-regulation and feedback control systems (Carver & Scheier, 1998). This is based on early work conducted within cybernetic systems theory and basic self-regulatory models such as Test-Operate, Test-Exit (TOTE; Miller, Galanter, & Pribram, 1960). As Karoly (1999) summarises, such models consider self-regulation to involve an individual's efforts to monitor, activate, inhibit, selectively sequence or otherwise use important specific mechanisms or metaskills in the service of attaining (or avoiding) a personal goal or goals.

Recognising these origins is important to the current discussion because such models were founded on behaviourist stimulus–response principles and, over the course of the last two decades, seem to have strongly influenced the scholarly coaching literature. For example, cybernetic systems form the basis of cognitive-behavioural, solution-focused (CB-SF) coaching models and have been used to shape coaching practice (Grant & Greene, 2003) and research (e.g. Green, Oades, & Grant, 2006; Spence & Grant, 2007). We will return to this point later.

Dimensions of Goals

Whilst many in the coaching industry may understand goals as being a relatively straightforward concept (i.e. a goal is something we want to achieve), researchers have employed several different units of analysis to help guide their investigations over the last four decades. These constructs have included current concerns (Klinger, 1977), personal projects (Little, 1989), life tasks (Cantor & Kihlstrom, 1987) and personal strivings (Emmons, 1992). Although these constructs differ in terms of their level of abstraction and temporal range, all consider people to be future-oriented, self-motivated beings, capable of determining their own futures (Brunstein, Schultheiss, & Maier, 1999). In the context of the current discussion, however, the dimension of goal abstraction is of particular importance and will now be briefly outlined.

Goal abstraction

Simply put, the articulation of goals can occur along a continuum ranging from the more concrete (i.e. highly specific) to the more abstract (i.e. very general). Situated along this continuum is the *personal strivings* construct (mentioned above), which is considered a 'middle-level' unit of analysis (Buss & Cantor, 1989). According to Emmons (1992) personal strivings exist at an intermediate level of abstraction and have been thought to reveal much about the texture of an individual's life. For example, a personal striving to 'avoid maliciously gossiping about others' might be reflective of a person who is *typically* trying to be more tolerant of others and seeking to foster more positive interpersonal relationships. As such, personal strivings are seen to reflect more enduring goals and general intentions that are 'relatively stable over time and consistently expressed in a variety of situations' (Emmons, 1992, p. 315). Research has revealed that personal strivings have important implications for physical and psychological well-being (Emmons, 1992).

As should be apparent, this way of understanding a 'goal' is quite different to the more highly specific, concrete approach to goal setting widely used in coaching. This approach, first outlined by Doran (1981), recommends that goals be expressed in *specific, measureable, assignable, realistic* and *time-related* ways (or SMART goals). As will be argued later, whilst this concrete approach to goal setting appears to have some serious limitations within highly complex, unpredictable environments, many coaches continue to advocate for such methods, seemingly unaware of their limitations.

Goal difficulty and other dimensions

Another dimension of goals that has received considerable attention relates to goal difficulty. Most commonly associated with goal-setting theory (Locke & Latham, 2002), this dimension relates to the observation that goals can vary in the extent to which they challenge an individual's existing physical, intellectual, emotional or behavioural capacities. A widely cited finding from research into this aspect of goals indicates that goal attainment is maximised when goals are both specific (the abstraction dimension) and of optimal *difficulty* (Locke, 1996; Locke & Latham, 2002), provided that they are also accompanied by a requisite level of *goal commitment* (a further dimension of goals).

Table 12.1 Examples of goal dimensions

Dimension	Goal types	Description	Examples
Abstraction	Concrete–Abstract (Emmons, 1992)	The framing of goals at different levels of generality, from the highly specific to the highly expansive.	Concrete: 'Say 10 Hail Marys' Abstract: 'Get closer to God'
Orientation	Approach–Avoidance (Elliot & Thrash, 2002)	Reflect goal behaviours that are instigated by desirable possibilities as opposed to undesirable possibilities.	Approach: 'To stay strong and fit' Avoidance: 'To avoid heart disease'
Outcome	Performance–Learning (Dweck & Leggett, 1988)	Goals adopted in order to win positive judgements about one's competence, as opposed to goals designed to increase competence.	Performance: 'I will sell 10 widgets' Learning: 'I will understand the sales process'
Temporal range	Proximal–Distal (Latham & Seijts, 1999)	Goals with varying time horizons, from the very short term to the very long term.	Proximal: 'Write 1,000 words today' Distal: 'Finish my book this year'
Regulation	Controlled–Autonomous (Sheldon & Elliot, 1998)	Reflects differences in the reasons that underpin goals, either because of some extrinsic inducement, or some intrinsic desire.	Controlled: 'Striving because I should do it' Autonomous: 'Striving because I love to do it'

Whilst the coaching literature appears to have paid scant attention to the richness of the goal literature (possibly because it is so large and complex), Grant (2006) has at least noted that goals can be very different in nature and intent. Beyond dimensions like abstraction, difficulty and commitment, goals can also vary in terms of their orientation, outcome, temporal range and regulation (as shown in Table 12.1).

From Understanding 'How' to Understanding 'Why'

Whilst early goal research was focused on understanding the 'how' of goal setting and goal attainment (using constructs described above), more recent research has focused on investigating the 'why' of goal setting. This stream of research has been more concerned with the underpinning reasons why people do what they do (Deci & Ryan, 2000). More specifically, this has involved investigating the extent to which goals are motivated more by core values and developing interests (i.e. *autonomous* reasons) or more by external inducements or internal compulsions (i.e. *controlled* reasons). Several decades of research

have suggested that these dimensions influence the quantity, duration and success of goal-directed effort, and have important implications for well-being (Niemiec & Ryan, 2013).

GOAL THEORIES IN COACHING

It should be noted that most goal research has occurred independently of the coaching literature and, consequently, theorists and researchers have needed to fit goal theory to coaching practice (e.g. Grant, 2012; Spence & Deci, 2013). In the next section, two such theories will receive closer attention, goal-setting theory (Locke & Latham, 2002) and self-determination theory (Deci & Ryan, 2000). Each will be briefly explored to gain some understanding of how they have informed the practice and research of coaching, and to help determine what perspectives might not currently be well represented.

Goal-setting Theory

There is a history of research into goal setting and goal management going back over 100 years. In their seminal work, Locke and

Latham (1990) built on studies of unconscious goals (Ryan, 1970) and established motivational theory (Bandura, 1986; Fishbein & Ajzen, 1977; Maslow, 1954) to report a positive relationship between goal difficulty (or complexity) and task performance. More specifically, they found that specific (clear) and difficult goals (when supported by unambiguous feedback) have a tendency to reliably motivate people towards the achievement of such goals. Furthermore, they also reported that the process of working toward a goal is (in itself) a major source of motivation. As a result, Locke and Latham (1990) went on to emphasise the importance of two key goal-setting factors: specificity (i.e. the goal's precision, clarity and measurability) and difficulty (i.e. the quantity and intensity of effort needed to achieve the goal). They maintained that specific goals focus attention and encourage planning (about how the desired outcome will be achieved), whilst an appropriate level of challenge (difficulty) provides the motivation needed to pursue the goal. Following two decades of research (that generally confirmed this core proposition), they concluded, 'so long as a person is committed to the goal, has the requisite ability to attain it, and does not have conflicting goals, there is a positive, linear relationship between goal difficulty and task performance' (Locke & Latham, 2006, p. 265).

Influence of goal-setting theory on coaching

Given how widely cited goal-setting theory is within the coaching literature, it is reasonable to conclude that it has also had an influence on the development of coaching research and practice. There would seem to be several reasons for this. First, given the future-focused nature of coaching and the future-focused nature of goals, the theory is highly relevant. Second, the empirical literature that supports its key propositions is quite substantial (Locke, 1996; Locke & Latham, 2002) and, therefore, is apt to be considered (by practitioners) reliable and worthy of attention. Finally, many of the key findings from goal-setting theory (such as the 14 key findings summarised by Locke, 1996), can be readily used to substantiate well-used and widely promoted coaching models, such as SMART (Doran, 1981). Indeed, in many ways, goal-setting theory (despite the authors' own caveats; Locke & Latham, 2006) appears to have had a bright story to tell in respect of the virtues of goal setting and goal striving. However, alternative viewpoints have been expressed that note both the inappropriateness of specific, concrete goal setting in many contexts and the negative effects of unfettered goal striving (e.g. increased risk taking and unethical behaviour). These viewpoints will be explored later in the chapter.

Self-determination Theory

Self-determination theory (SDT) takes a broader perspective on goals. It proposes that people are optimally motivated when sociocultural conditions are created that satisfy their basic psychological needs for autonomy, competence and relatedness (Deci & Ryan, 1985). Whilst SDT is comprised of six sub-theories (see Spence & Deci, 2013 for a summary), only its most relevant features are described here. SDT conceptualises motivation (for goals) as existing on a continuum that varies from controlled to autonomous regulation. Controlled regulation refers to self-regulation that occurs either for external or introjected reasons. External reasons can include either direct pressure or more subtle coercion, when behaviour is energised by either the promise of (material or social) rewards or punishments, whilst introjection represents the partial internalisation of external expectations, usually held as internal sanctions ('should' or 'musts') that act to moderate behaviour. Autonomous regulation refers to self-regulation that occurs when people feel a full sense of choice and self-initiation about their goal pursuits. According to SDT, autonomous motivation is associated with identified and integrated reasons for action. With identified self-regulation, a task or goal (that may originally have been taken on for others) is wholeheartedly endorsed and accepted as being congruent with one's own goals and needs, whilst integrated self-regulation relates to taking action because doing so represents one's identity and infuses life with meaning.

As such, from a self-regulatory standpoint, SDT is more interested in what underpins the goals an individual might adopt (the 'why' of goals), rather than elucidating what the 'mechanics' of such goals should be (the 'how' of goals). Relatedly, SDT is also interested in the content of goals and has highlighted how different types of goals lead to qualitatively different outcomes, by noting difference between extrinsic or intrinsic aspirations or goals (e.g. Kasser & Ryan, 1993). Put simply, extrinsic motivations tend to be associated with becoming rich, famous (or infamous) or trendy, whilst intrinsic motivations tend to be associated with personal growth and contributing to the community. Extensive research has shown that the former tend to have lower levels of overall well-being, less autonomy and less social connectedness, along with less success on learning and performance tasks (Vansteenkiste et al., 2004)

Influence of self-determination theory on coaching

As outlined by Spence and Deci (2013), SDT offers considerable guidance for practising coaches via the theoretical account it gives of the socio-cultural factors that shape human motivation and can influence it over time. As they observe:

> SDT recognizes that the socio-cultural conditions of a person's life often stifle human development and growth. Based on this observation, the presence of a coach can be understood as representing a general improvement in these conditions, provided the coach relates to coachees in a way that supports autonomy, relatedness and competence. (pp. 100–101)

It specifically proposes that the regulation of personal or professional goals (whether they be SMART goals or personal strivings) can be qualitatively altered in coaching by creating supportive conditions that permit the greater levels of subjective goal ownership (i.e. autonomous motivation). In a sense its mini-theories give coaches a basis for understanding how they should *be* in coaching, such that coaches might become more self-determining.

Other Theoretical Influences

Over the past decade the coaching literature has become noticeably more textured by the application of adult developmental theories (e.g. Cook-Greuter, 2000; Kegan, 1994) into coaching contexts, most notably as a foundation for leadership coaching (Garvey Berger, 2012). In an important enhancement of this work, Bachkirova (2013) has reformulated key developmental precepts and proposed a developmental theory specifically for coaching. Whilst an encouraging development, in the context of this discussion, it is sufficient to point out that – from an adult or cognitive developmental perspective – goals selection is strongly influenced by the client's current developmental stage (Kegan, Congleton, & David, 2013). For example, according to Kegan's (1994) theory, a client with a 'socialised mind' would select goals that satisfy their need to gain the esteem of other people, whereas a more 'self-authored' individual will select goals that accord with internal reference points like personal values. In this example, the socialised and self-authored forms of minds are analogous to controlled and autonomous forms of regulation in SDT.

Intentional change theory has also attracted some attention in the coaching literature (ICT; Boyatzis & McKee, 2013) and been accompanied by practical guidance for practitioners (Boyatzis, Smith, Van Oosten, & Woolford, 2013). One of the key propositions of ICT is that goal setting is most effective when it is supported by mindful reflection on what matters most to the individual. That is, when goals are linked to the *ideal self*, the change process becomes grounded in 'intrinsic motivation, personal passion, resonant meaning and belief in possibility – this enables people to be more resilient and robust during work on development and change' (Boyatzis & Howard, 2013, p. 215). In this way ICT also overlaps conceptually with SDT, as goal setting is considered to be sub-optimal when goals emerge from the 'ought self' or are inconsistent with the individual's learning or planning style.

An under Represented View: Goals in Complex Systems

A general criticism of goal research is that there is a high reliance on laboratory studies, which are not replicable in the messy, more complex environment of the outside world (Tubbs, 1986). Indeed, until recently the utility of goals and goal setting in complex systems has received very little attention. Where the role of context has been acknowledged it has only been seen as significant insofar as it helps to resolve immediate problems and assist clients to construct or enact solutions (Tomaschek & Pärsch, 2006). Yet there is a growing literature that suggests long-term change can only be realised by addressing the systems – both internal and external – that influence assumptions and behaviours (Cavanagh, 2006; Hawkins & Smith, 2006; Kahn, 2011; Tomaschek & Pärsch, 2006). As Pryor and Bright (2011) point out, while both linear and systemic processes involve feedback, in linear systems the focus is on the goal itself, and in complex adaptive systems the focus is on responding to feedback and amending goals. Success may be defined in terms of the wider system rather than a specific achievement. They propose that the nature of goals and goal setting needs to be adjusted to take into account the speed of change of the environment. According to Pryor and Bright (2011), there are at least

Table 12.2 Varying goal requirements as determined by context

	Slow changing	Fast changing
Simple problems	SMART performance goals	Flexible performance goals
Complex problems	Learning goals	Fuzzy goals

four scenarios that can influence the types of goals that people may set (see Table 12.2).

First, simple problems in a slowly changing environment seem best tackled through the use of SMART performance goals, as the relative stability of the environment provide a degree of predictability. Second, simple problems in a rapidly changing environment seem to require performance goals that are flexible and can accommodate adjustments that the system requires. Third, complex problems in a slowly changing environment seem to require the adoption of learning goals (rather than performance goals), such that the person can – in the absence of being able to predict outcomes – at least develop a more nuanced appreciation of the operating context. Finally, complex problems in a rapidly changing environment are best served by the adoption of fuzzy goals (or broad intentions) that can guide action, as such environments make it hard to predict outcomes or acquire generalisable learning.

THE CRITICAL CONSIDERATION OF GOAL-FOCUSED THEORIES AND MODELS

Whilst the conventional understanding of goals, goal dynamics and the outcomes of goal pursuit have been widely critiqued, Locke and Latham (2009) have strongly argued that many of the concerns expressed (about their dangerous or damaging effects) have already been addressed. In this section, we outline some examples of goal critiques that have particular relevance to coaching. Attending to such debates is useful because it helps to develop a more sophisticated understanding of goals and how they are best worked with in a variety of coaching contexts.

Stretch Goals

Stretch goals are goals that are perceived by people to exist on the fringes of possibility. Commonly used in organisations of all types, stretch goals are used to galvanise people into new and creative ways of thinking about goal attainment. However, the reality seems to be that they often do not result in successful outcomes but, more often, lead to disappointment and derailment (Sitkin et al., 2011). It seems that the optimal conditions for stretch goals in organisations include recent past success and enough resource flexibility to allow workers to invest in pursuing unconventional ideas. Without these conditions, the likely outcome is failure and reduced motivation to innovate. Drawing on data from Gallup employee surveys, Brim and Liebnau (2011) argue that stretch goals can be harmful if they do not align with individual self-identity, and that a 'slight shift' (rather than a stretch) approach to goal setting is both more productive and engaging for employees.

Other research suggests that people have limitations in respect of how many stretch goals they can pursue at one time and will either pursue a few narrow goals at the expense of others (Shah et al., 2002), or sacrifice quality for quantity (Gilliland & Landis, 1992). Task complexity also creates challenges for individuals and, in such circumstances, learning goals are often more effective than performance goals (Midgley et al., 2001) and associated with greater intrinsic motivation (Sarrazin, et al 2002), task engagement (Deci & Ryan, 2000) and collaboration within teams (Kristof-Brown & Stevens 2001).

SMART Goals

The implication that goals should be SMART has also been challenged from studies of corporate behaviour. For example, Abrahamson and Freedman (2013) found no evidence that companies that engage in extensive strategic planning and SMART goal setting are any more successful than those that do not. In addition, McKee's (1991) study of SMART goals revealed that only 25% of people were motivated by them, whilst 25% preferred to work with the image of a desired state, 25% liked to focus on incremental steps towards the goal (rather than the goal itself) and 25% preferred not to explicitly plan at all. Tellingly, in all but the first group, SMART goals induced stress and reduced motivation, creativity and resilience. Such findings sit noticeably at odds with the popular messaging that surrounds SMART goal use.

'Goals Gone Wild'

In recent years, goal setting theory has been criticised as being overly simplistic. Most notably, Ordóñez et al., (2009) identified a number of problems with goal setting in general and noted that the use of goal setting 'can degrade employee performance by narrowing focus to neglect important but non-specified goals, motivating risky and unethical behaviors, inhibiting learning, corroding organizational culture, and reducing intrinsic motivation ... and] ... in many situations, the damaging effects of goal setting outweigh its benefits' (Ordóñez et al., 2009, p. 6). As will now be shown, based on work published in a variety of domains, these claims appear to carry some weight.

Narrow focus of attention and mindlessness

Focusing on specific, narrow goals appears to induce 'inattentional blindness', which is the tendency to miss important information or opportunities because they are not registered in consciousness. This can manifest itself in numerous different ways, including limiting the detection of opportunities for career advancement (Ibarra & Lineback,

2005) or creating a preoccupation with individual goals at the expense of collective performance (Mitchell and Silver, 1990). The narrow focus induced by goal-setting is also thought to inhibit one's propensity to experiment with alternative methods of task accomplishment, thereby inducing a form of *mindlessness* that is known to constrain creative problem solving and potential learning (Langer, 1989).

Risk taking

Support for the claim that goal setting distorts risk preferences can be found in the negotiation literature, which note that negotiators with goals are more likely to reach an impasse (i.e. failure to reach a reasonable agreement) compared to negotiators who lack goals (Galinsky et al., 2002). This observation closely aligns with prospect theory (Kahneman & Tversky, 1979), which says that decision makers become more risk-seeking in the domain of losses, and has been confirmed by experiments conducted by Larrick et al., (2009) where participants in goal conditions consistently increased risky behaviour in both negotiation and decision making tasks. Finally, Kayes (2006) has also reported on 'goal blindness' in mountaineering, when climbers attempting to summit Mount Everest have engaged in fatal risk-taking (events that can emanate from a mindlessness to context; Langer, 1989).

Unethical behaviour

This objection emerges from research showing that an over-focus on goals has a tendency to lead to cheating, especially in 'near-miss' situations (Schweitzer et al., 2004). Reflecting on the broader implications of such work, Ordóñez and colleagues concluded that 'aggressive goal setting within an organization increases the likelihood of creating an organizational climate ripe for unethical behaviour' (p10). Embedded in this observation is the real possibility that goal setting can trigger (what legal scholars refer to as) *willful ignorance* or *willful blindness* (Luban, 1998) Whilst these concepts denote behavioural constraints similar to the narrowed focus of attention outlined above, they differ in that a willfully ignorant person uses goals as a reason to purposefully overlook more ethical courses of action.

The Value of a Critical Perspective

Past debates in the goals literature (for an interesting example see Ordóñez et al., 2009 and Locke & Latham, 2009) are advantageous for coaches as they develop awareness and deepen understanding about goal setting and goal management. For example, there is evidence that both proximal and distal goals are important, with the former supporting the latter (Latham and Locke, 2007). Furthermore, studies have confirmed that goals produce dysfunctional effects when they stimulate individual competition (Mitchell & Silver, 1990) but enhance group performance when individual and group goals are aligned (Seijts & Latham, 2000). Goals have also been found to negatively impact motivation when people are faced with a complex task, but positively impact motivation for simple tasks (Mossholder, 1980). Finally, goal orientation researchers have noted the influence of implicit theories that Dweck (2012) labels 'fixed' and 'growth' mindsets) on goal selection and found that *learning goals* (compared to *performance goals*) are associated with a range of beneficial intellectual and emotional effects (Yeager & Dweck, 2012).

As such, it is difficult to conclude goal setting is uniformly beneficial nor consistently harmful, as personal characteristics and context always appears to play an important role. Although a detailed set of general principles is beyond the scope of this chapter, we would argue that decisions about goal setting in coaching should emerge from a comprehensive understanding of the client – including their natural inclinations (e.g. towards goals, learning, personal growth) and developmental status (e.g. more 'socialised' or 'self-authored') – and the contexts in which they are required to function (e.g. at work, at home, in the community). It is only through such multi-faceted consideration that the coach and client can make decisions about goal setting. When coaching is orientated in this way it removes goal setting as an imperative of coaching, thereby liberating coaches to work more genuinely with their clients' unique perspectives. As such, the discussion will now turn towards how goals have typically been presented in the coaching literature, including some critique of that work and the presentation of different ways of conceptualising the place of goals in coaching.

GOALS IN THE COACHING LITERATURE

As mentioned, goals have long occupied a central place in the coaching literature. Indeed, the centrality of goals is most obviously reflected in the numerous definitions of coaching that make explicit reference to goals as a core concern of the coaching process (e.g. Grant, 2006; Passmore et al., 2013; Kilburg, 2000). Not surprisingly, this focus on goals is also reflected in many coaching process models.

Coaching Models

This emphasis on goals extends into popular process models of coaching, such as the GROW model (Goal, Reality, Options, Will; Whitmore, 1996). Based on anecdotal reports and our experience, many coaching programmes teach the GROW model (or other variants of it) and, thereby, fundamentally organise their coach training around a primary focus on goals, whether that be related to setting a goal for individual coaching sessions and/or, more broadly, the setting of SMART goals with individuals or groups. Interestingly, whilst little specific research has been conducted on the GROW model, it appears there might be some resistance amongst authors to evidence that contradicts the general view that goal-focused models constitute part of best practice in coaching. For example, Scoular and Linley (2006) observed a series of 120 coaching sessions, between previously unintroduced coaches and coachees, with half of the coaches being instructed to use the GROW model and the other half not. Whilst the analysis revealed no difference in outcome quality across the two groups, rather than question the utility of the GROW model, the authors argued that goal setting 'should still be regarded as best practice in business coaching' (p. 11).

In contrast to formulations (like GROW) that preference the setting of goals at the beginning of the session or coaching engagement, Kilburg (2000) has argued that goal setting is not a critical component of the early stages of coaching. Instead, he advocates for the establishment of goals part way through an engagement, after the coachee has time to cogitate on their current circumstances and more clearly glimpse what they would like to change. Similarly Pemberton (2006) points out that, although the standard view of coaching envisages a clearly articulated goal(s) in the early stages, meaningful goals tend to emerge from skilled conversations and often late in coaching engagements. Relatedly, in a survey of 200 coaches in the United States, Kauffman and Coutu (2009) reported that 96% of coaches indicated that their clients' goals usually changed during the course of a coaching assignment, tending to become more congruent with client insights about what was most important to them.

Finally, the measurement of goals has also been the subject of critique. For example, Spence (2007) argued that the use of goals in coaching research and practice was dominated by relatively simplistic, post-hoc evaluations of goal progress. In an attempt to provide a more rigorous alternative, it was recommended that core *goal attainment scaling* (GAS) procedures would provide more valid method for assessing goal outcomes. Notably, these procedures are a simple extension of SMART goal setting, organised using ladders of attainment and collaborative client–coach goal conversations. At least two studies have been undertaken to test the utility of GAS methods in coaching (Prywes, 2012; Spence, Cavanagh, & Grant, 2008), with positive outcomes reported.

Role in the Coaching Process

Differing perspectives have also emerged about the various roles that goals play in the coaching process. For example, in presenting an integrative goal-focused coaching (GFC) model, Grant (2006) firmly places goal setting and action planning as central to the coaching process. In a critique of the same model, Ives and Cox (2012) conclude that GFC is essentially about raising performance (through small, incremental improvements), rather than psychological transformations (through deep, interpersonal reflection). According to this analysis the GFC model is focused primarily on operational change and small, incremental performance improvements (Jackson & McKergow, 2008), rather than forms of psychological restructuring that can trigger client growth and development (Hall & Duval, 2004).

It is difficult to dispute the logic behind the GFC sequence, in circumstances where goals are relatively straightforward and fixed. However, in dynamic, fluid environments it is unclear how tightly prescribed self-regulation models can be applied. Rather, in these contexts (as outlined earlier in Table 12.2), it seems that clients may best be served by goals that are 'fuzzy' and evolving (Cavanagh, 2006). A model that captures differences in

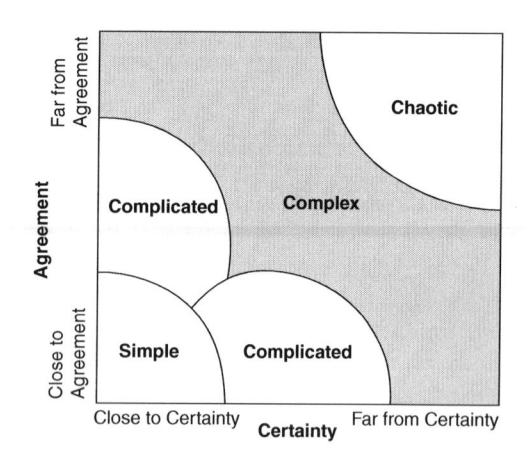

Figure 12.1 The Agreement–Certainty matrix
Source: Stacey (2007)

system dynamics is Stacey's (2007) agreement–certainty matrix (see Figure 12.1). Whilst typically used as a strategic management tool, the model is useful to the present discussion because it reflects how human systems can fluctuate widely from relatively stable (simple) states to complicated, complex and chaotic states. Distinguishing each is the extent to which cause and effect relationships are discernible, which has an impact on how one is best to act.

For example, in simple states (i.e. close to certainty and agreement) cause and effect relationship are relatively evident and linear approaches (like SMART) are justifiable because an action and its outcome(s) can be accurately predicted. However, cause and effect relationships are typically much harder to discern and can often only be perceived in retrospect (e.g. complex states), or not at all (e.g. chaotic states). In such circumstances, much more flexible, non-linear approaches are needed, with linear goal setting generally rendered ineffective (Cavanagh, 2013). An alternative it seems, is to orient oneself towards learning 'about the system and liv[ing] into your evolving vision' (Garvey Berger & Johnston, 2015). For Garvey Berger and Johnston (2015), the recommendation is not to adopt goals but, rather, to create safe-to-fail experiments that can permit one to '[learn] like mad from what happens next' (p. 107).

Other considerations beyond complexity

Of course, system complexity is not the only factor to influence whether SMART goal setting is appropriate. As observed by Drake (2015), it is often the case that clients are unsure of what they truly want, or do not have access to the (material or social) resources they need, or are unsure what actions will be associated with success, or have been demoralised by past attempts to reach goals. In such situations, advocating for specific goal setting is unlikely to be greeted with enthusiasm or energise action.

Despite these client and contextual realities, it is a misnomer to suggest that coaching can be conducted 'goal-free'. This is because (as argued earlier) clients can only live their lives in the direction of the future and it is natural to move towards agreeable future circumstances. As such, many people seem to understand the term 'goal' in a concrete, specific way, despite the existence of a literature that has explored a variety of other goal constructs, like personal strivings (Emmons, 1992). As outlined earlier, a personal striving is a mid-level construct (sitting somewhere between SMART and fuzzy goals) that captures what people are typically trying to do. As such, they seem to reflect what Drake (2015) refers to as intentions, which 'involve setting a clear direction and the resolve to take an action or achieve an outcome – without the necessity of an ultimate goal or a defined path' (p. 194). Given the changing nature of human lives, mid-level goal constructions (such as intentions or personal strivings) would seem to be a better starting point for coaching, as they are broad enough to capture the short- and long-term objectives of a person, and clear enough to permit more specific SMART goal setting where this appears to be useful.

Cultural Differences

There is also some evidence of cultural differences in goal orientation amongst coaches. In a survey of European and North American coaches ($n = 184$), David, Clutterbuck and Megginson (2014) used a nine-item questionnaire to measure goal orientation from the first meeting of a coaching engagement, to its final evaluation. The findings revealed that while goal orientation and experience levels were not correlated for North American coaches, European coaches became less goal oriented as they grew in experience. The authors concluded this difference might be related to differences in the coaching traditions between the two continents, with North America drawing more deeply on behavioural traditions and, with it, a greater focus on goals. Whilst the scholarly coaching literature appears to be silent on this issue, goal researchers have noticed differences in goal orientation (i.e. approach versus avoidance) using samples drawn from individualistic and collectivist cultures. For example, Elliot et al., (2001) found that Asian-Americans (collectivist) set more avoidance goals than non-Asian Americans (individualistic). To the extent that European and North American coaches can be differentiated along collectivist and individual lines, the conclusions of David et al. (2014) seem plausible, given that collectivist cultures are less preoccupied with personal accomplishment and 'standing out'. As no research has been conducted on this question, such a proposition is highly speculative.

FROM PRACTICAL QUESTIONS TO FUTURE RESEARCH DIRECTIONS

Practising coaches could be forgiven for feeling confused about what constitutes evidence-based good practice in relation to goals in coaching. When should they encourage clients to set goals? How specific should these goals be? When is it appropriate to strive assiduously for goals and when might it be better to withhold or suspend effort? As this review of the literature shows, the answers to these questions are not as straightforward as they once may have appeared to be. However, better understanding the complexity surrounding goals should have a positive impact on coaching practice by influencing the way that coaches are trained in working with goals and its recognition through the industry's professional bodies. In particular, coach training would seem to be enhanced by a movement away from simple questions, such as whether or not to set goals, and towards more nuanced perspectives, such as how to work within different goal contexts.

Challenging Preconceptions About Goals

Due to the relatively simplistic way that goals have been presented in the popular press (e.g. Buckingham, 2001), coaching clients are likely to be relatively naïve about goal dynamics in the coaching process. As such, it seems worthwhile to use the initial contracting stage to discuss the possibilities surrounding goal setting and begin the process of ascertaining their potential relevance to clients. This might include:

- Briefly explaining the nature of goals and how they emerge.
- Outlining some dimensions of goals, which can include noting their tendency to evolve and change over time, along with some understanding about how coaches typically deal with such changes.
- Introducing the concept of goal ownership and other motivational aspects of goals.
- Describing challenges in evaluating outcomes, including determining the degree of goal attainment and its value to the individual or collective.

A consequence of such discussion is that both coach and coachee will have a basis for critically challenging and reviewing the value of goals. A useful extension of this more critical approach to working with goals in coaching could include reference to modified goal setting models, which offer an alternative perspective to the more linear approaches that are ubiquitous in the literature. An example of such a model is presented in Table 12.3, which outlines an alternative set of considerations using the SMART formulation.

Table 12.3 Alternative SMART goal-setting formulations

	S – Specific	M – Measureable	A – Actionable	R – Realistic	T – Time-bound
Standard view	Specific goals provide clarity, focus and a motivating expectation of certainty.	Measureable goals enable detailed planning and monitoring of progress.	Once goals are set, persistence is important, as changing goals reduces performance.	Manageable goals lower perceptions of risk and increase chances of success.	Deadlines are motivational and help to reduce procrastination.
	Situational	*Multi-faceted*	*Adaptable*	*Risk-taking*	*Transformational*
Non-linear view	Goals are formed within particular contexts and are always subject to change.	In complex conditions having alternative goals and pathways increases chances of success.	Dynamic environments will create the need for goals to change and evolve.	Changing conditions are risky and require the courage to either modify goals or open new goal pathways.	Widening the boundaries within which goals are contained, opens up potential for change at deeper levels.

Source: Adapted from Winter (2010)
Note: The 'standard' SMART formulation shown above is one of the many variations that currently exist. It has been chosen because these components are more generic and widely cited than Doran's (1981) workplace formulation.

Due to the predominance of the 'standard' way of conceptualising goals, rethinking the nature, origins and dynamics of goals is likely to be unfamiliar for many clients, and potentially disconcerting for some depending on their developmental stage. For example, clients at socialised stages of cognitive development (e.g. stage 3 of Kegan's model) are likely to be troubled by a perspective that removes a clear set of goal setting rules and requirements. However, for clients in later stages of development (i.e. Kegan's stages 4 or 5), this is likely to be less aversive as the removal of these structures are not likely to challenge the way they think about the world.

AREAS FOR FUTURE RESEARCH

The complexity of goal setting and goal striving offer many opportunities for deeper understanding through research. There are open questions relating to the influence of context, personal maturity, the coach–client relationship, the nature of the goal and the relative supportiveness of the client's environment. In addition, relatively little is known about how goals evolve over time and research could explore how goals change in the general course of events, and/or as a consequence of culture, and/or as a function of personal maturation (i.e. socio-emotional and cognitive). Conceivably an array of quantitative and qualitative methods could be employed to investigate these questions and, should this happen, the findings from such studies will greatly enrich the coaching industry's understanding of goal setting and goal management. Some possibilities include:

- Exploring what (if any) scenarios are inappropriate for an immediate focus on goals. For example, what is the value of explicit goal setting to clients who come to coaching feeling confused or uncertain about their most salient issues? Similarly, is it useful to employ goal setting when a client seeks out a coach to act as a soundboard, robustly challenge their thinking and/or help them identify any blind spots in their thinking? Finally, is goal setting needed when the intention of the client is only to explore values, rather than pursue a specific outcome?
- How are coaches best to work with clients whose salient goals have been imposed upon them by a significant third party (such as a manager)? From an SDT perspective, such goals represent a form of controlled regulation that may energise behaviour for some time but never be fully 'owned' if their self-initiation is not adequately supported. However, as has been widely reported in the SDT research literature (Baard et al., 2004; Stone et al., 2009), goal ownership can be facilitated by autonomy supportive actions, such as genuinely seeking to understand the person's perspective (about the goal), providing a meaningful rationale, minimising controlling language, and providing choice about how to attain the goal (where real choice exists). Future research could investigate how effective autonomy supportive coaching practices are for internalising and integrating motivation for imposed goals.
- Given, as claimed by Ibarra (2013), that most leaders do not know precisely what they want to accomplish, what can be learnt about the goal clarification process? Researchers might look to investigate which aspects of the coaching process seem most closely associated with the emergence of goal clarity. For example, as hypothesised by Cavanagh and Spence (2013) does the development of mindfulness in coaching support values clarification and assist a coachee to set more congruent (values-based) goals? What other practices or techniques are especially helpful in this regard?
- Other questions can be posed about the processes involved with goal striving. For instance, what factors make goals more or less achievable (e.g. social support, time pressure)? What types of feedback are especially helpful for creating and sustaining momentum towards goals? To what extent is it useful to relate goal progression to changes in self-understanding and notions of purpose?
- Finally, as argued earlier, there are times when an explicit focus on specific goals and concrete actions seems warranted, and other times when the client is better served by a focus on learning and self-reflection. However, as yet, this issue has not been addressed empirically and future researchers may wish to examine how shifting

between an explicit and implicit focus on goals impact clients. This issue could also be addressed using experimental methods. For example, using a pre-post between-subjects design, participants could be placed into a SMART goal condition (explicit focus) or a personal strivings condition (implicit focus) for the duration of a coaching programme. As personal strivings are a more abstract goal form, representing what people are typically trying to do, the coaching in this condition would be more akin to coaching towards a client's general intentions, rather than coaching towards a concrete SMART goal. Dependent variables for such a study could include goal progression (or attainment), goal commitment, self-efficacy, motivation and well-being measures such as life satisfaction, vitality and/or psychological well-being.

CONCLUSION

Much of the confusion that surrounds goal setting and goal management in coaching stems from failure to appreciate the multifaceted nature of how people establish and pursue desired change. As we have argued in this chapter, developing a nuanced understanding of goals is critically important for coaches if they are to render an optimal form of support for their clients. A substantial portion of this chapter has been devoted to critiquing the 'standard' approach to goal setting in coaching, namely the use of the ubiquitous SMART goal-setting model. It is our view that this model has become something of a default model for goal setting in coaching, despite the existence of a growing body of work that strongly suggests a need for more non-linear approaches.

Whilst it would be difficult to argue that goal setting could ever truly be 'goal-free', it can (and has) been argued that the utilisation of concrete, specific goal setting should at least become a secondary option; only activated once coach and client have determined that it is agreeable to the client and warranted by their operating environment. It has also been noted that the concept of a 'goal' appears to be held in a one-dimensional way by many within the industry, and paying attention to the broader goals literature could help to develop more nuanced understandings. In this regard, personal strivings were suggested as a better starting point in coaching, by virtue of the fact that they are a mid-level construct capable of capturing a person's broader intentions and aspirations.

It is our hope that this chapter will act as a stimulus for developing a more contemporary view of working with goals in coaching. Whilst several suggestions have been made for future research, this was by no means an exhaustive list. Many other possibilities can be brought to mind and, indeed, the opportunity exists to create a body of knowledge that will be specifically relevant to the practice of coaching.

REFERENCES

Abrahamson, E., & Freedman, D. H. (2013). *A Perfect Mess: The Hidden Benefits of Disorder*. London: Hachette.

Austin, J. T., & Vancouver, J. B. (1996). Goal constructs in psychology: Structure, process and content. *Psychological Bulletin*, *120*(3), 338–375.

Baard, P. P., Deci, E. L., & Ryan, R. M. (2004). Intrinsic need satisfaction: A motivational basis of performance and well-being in two work settings. *Journal of Applied Social Psychology*, *34*(10), 2045–2068.

Bachkirova, T. (2013). Developmental coaching: Developing the self. In J. Passmore, D. B. Peterson, & T. Freire (Eds.), *The Wiley-Blackwell Handbook of the Psychology of Coaching and Mentoring* (pp. 135–154). Chichester: Wiley & Sons.

Bandura, A. (1986). *Social Foundations of Thought and Action: A Social-Cognitive View*. Englewood Cliffs, NJ: Prentice Hall.

Boyatzis, R., & McKee, A. (2013). *Resonant Leadership: Renewing Yourself and Connecting with Others Through Mindfulness, Hope and Compassion*. Harvard Business Press.

Boyatzis, R. E., & Howard, A. (2013). When goal setting helps and hinders sustained, desired change. In S. David, D. Clutterbuck, & D. Megginson (Eds.), *Beyond Goals: Effective Strategies for Coaching and Mentoring* (pp. 211–228). Aldershot: Gower.

Boyatzis, R. E., Smith, M. L., Van Oosten, E., & Woolford, L. (2013). Developing resonant leaders through emotional intelligence, vision and coaching. *Organizational Dynamics*, *42*(1), 17–24.

Brim, J. B., & Liebnau, D. (2011). Does setting major development goals work? *Gallup Business Journal*. Retrieved on 19th January 2016 from http://www.gallup.com/businessjournal/150485/setting-major-development-goals-work.aspx

Brunstein, J. C., Schultheiss, O. C., & Maier, G. W. (1999). The pursuit of personal goals: A motivational approach to well-being and life adjustment. In J. Brandstadter & R. M. Lerner (Eds.), *Action and Self-Development: Theory and Research through the Life-Span* (pp. 169-196). California: Sage.

Buckingham, W. (2001). *Ready, Set, Goal!: Choose Your Goals, Stay Motivated, Celebrate Your Success*. Harlow: Longman.

Burke, D., & Linley, P. A. (2007). Enhancing goal self-concordance through coaching. *International Coaching Psychology Review*, *2*(1), 62–69.

Buss, D. M., & Cantor, N. (1989). *Personality Psychology: Recent Trends and Emerging Directions*. New York: Springer.

Cantor, N., & Kihlstrom, J. F. (1987). *Personality and social intelligence*. New Jersey: Prentice Hall.

Carver, C. S., & Scheier, M. F. (1998). *On the Self-Regulation of Behaviour*. New York: Cambridge University Press.

Cavanagh, M. J. (2006). Coaching from a systemic perspective: A complex adaptive conversation. In D. R. Stober & A. M. Grant (Eds.), *Evidence-based Coaching Practice: Putting Best Practices to Work for Your Clients*. Hoboken: Wiley & Sons.

Cavanagh, M. J. (2013). The coaching engagement in the twenty-first century: New paradigms for complex times. In S. A. David, D. Clutterbuck, & D. Megginson (Eds.), *Beyond Goals: Effective Strategies for Coaching and Mentoring*. Aldershot: Gower.

Cavanagh, M., & Spence, G. B. (2013). Mindfulness in coaching: Philosophy, psychology, or just a useful skill? In J. Passmore, D. Peterson, & T. Freire (Eds.), *The Wiley-Blackwell Handbook of the Psychology of Coaching and Mentoring* (pp. 112–134). New York: Wiley-Blackwell.

Clutterbuck, D. (2013). Working with emergent goals: A pragmatic approach. In S. David, D. Clutterbuck, & D. Megginson (Eds.), *Beyond Goals: Effective Strategies for Coaching and Mentoring* (pp. 311–326). Aldershot: Gower.

Cook-Greuter, S. R. (2000). Mature ego development: A gateway to ego transcendence? *Journal of Adult Development*, *7*(4), 227–240.

David, S., Clutterbuck, D., & Megginson, D. (2014). Goal orientation in coaching differs according to region, experience and education. *International Journal of Evidence-Based Coaching*, *12*(2), 134–145.

Deci, E. L., & Ryan, R. M. (1985). *Intrinsic Motivation and Self-determination in Human Behavior*. New York: Plenum Press.

Deci, E. L., & Ryan, R. M. (2000). The 'what' and 'why' of goal pursuits: Human needs and the self-determination of behavior. *Psychological Inquiry*, *11*(4), 227–268.

Doran, G. T. (1981). There's a SMART way to write management's goals and objectives. *Management Review*, *70*(11), 35–36.

Downey, M. (2011). *Effective Coaching: Lessons from the Coach's Coach*. London: Orion.

Drake, D. B. (2015). *Narrative Coaching: Bringing Our New Stories to Life*. Petaluma, CA: CNC Press.

Dweck, C. (2012). *Mindset: How You can Fulfil Your Potential*. London: Hachette.

Dweck, C. S., & Leggett, E. L. (1988). A social-cognitive approach to motivation and personality. *Psychological Review*, *95*(2), 256–273.

Elliot, A. J., & Thrash, T. M. (2002). Approach-avoidance motivation in personality: approach and avoidance temperaments and goals. *Journal of Personality and Social Psychology*, *82*(5), 804–818.

Elliot, A. J., Chirkov, V. I., Kim, Y., & Sheldon, K. M. (2001). A cross-cultural analysis of avoidance (relative to approach) personal goals. *Psychological Science*, *12*(6), 505–510.

Emmons, R. A. (1992). Abstract versus concrete goals: personal striving level, physical illness, and psychological well-being. *Journal of Personality and Social Psychology*, *62*(2), 292–300.

Fishbein, M., & Ajzen, I. (1977). *Belief, Attitude, Intention, and Behavior: An Introduction to Theory and Research*. Reading, MA: Addison-Wesley.

Galinsky, A. D., Mussweiler, T., & Medvec, V. H. (2002). Disconnecting outcomes and evaluations: the role of negotiator focus. *Journal of personality and social psychology*, *83*(5), 1131–1140.

Garvey Berger, J. (2012). *Changing on the Job: Developing Leaders for a Complex World*. Stanford, CA: Stanford University Press.

Garvey Berger, J., & Johnston, K. (2015). *Simple Habits for Complex Times*. Stanford: Stanford Business Books.

Gilliland, S. W., & Landis, R. S. (1992). Quality and quantity goals in a complex decision task: Strategies and outcomes. *Journal of Applied Psychology*, *77*(5), 672–681.

Grant, A. M. (2006). An integrative goal-focused approach to executive coaching. In D. R. Stober & A. M. Grant (Eds.), *Evidence-based Coaching Handbook: Putting Best Practices to Work for your Clients* (pp. 153–192). New York: Wiley & Sons.

Grant, A. M. (2012). An integrated model of goal-focused coaching: An evidence-based framework for teaching and practice. *International Coaching Psychology Review*, *7*(2), 146–165.

Grant, A. M. (2014). Autonomy support, relationship satisfaction and goal focus in the coach–coachee relationship: which best predicts coaching success? *Coaching: An International Journal of Theory, Research and Practice*, *7*(1), 18–38.

Grant, A. M., & Greene, J. (2003). *Coach Yourself: Make Real Changes in Your Life*: Da Capo Press.

Grant, A. M. (2006). An integrative goal-focused approach to executive coaching. In D. R. Stober & A. M. Grant (Eds.), *Evidence-based coaching handbook: Putting best practices to work for your clients* (pp. 153–192). New York: Wiley & Sons.

Green, L. S., Oades, L. G., & Grant, A. M. (2006). Cognitive-behavioral, solution-focused life coaching: Enhancing goal striving, well-being, and hope. *The Journal of Positive Psychology*, *1*(3), 142–149.

Hall, L. M., & Duval, M. (2004). *Meta-Coaching: Coaching Change*. Clifton, CO: Neurosemantic Publications.

Hall, M., & Gambardella, P. (2012). *Systemic Coaching: Coaching With the Whole Person with Meta-Coaching*. Clifton, CO: Neurosemantic Publications.

Hawkins, P., & Smith, N. (2006). *Coaching, Mentoring and Organizational Consultancy*. Maidenhead: Open University Press.

Ibarra, H. (2013). "What else might I do?" Focusing on past success may stand in the way of your potential. *The Focus Magazine*. Retrieved from http://www.egonzehnder.com/the-focus-magazine/topics/the-focus-on-potential/keynote/what-else-might-i-do.html

Ibarra, H., & Lineback, K. (2005). What's your story? *Harvard Business Review*, *83*(1), 64–71.

Ives, Y., & Cox, E. (2012). *Goal-Focused Coaching: Theory and Practice*. London: Routledge.

Jackson, P. Z., & McKergow, M. (2008). *The Solutions Focus: Making Coaching and Change Simple*. London: Nicholas Brealey.

Kahn, M. S. (2011). Coaching on the axis: An integrative and systemic approach to business coaching. *International Coaching Psychology Review*, *6*(2), 194–210.

Kahneman, D., & Tversky, A. (1979). Prospect Theory: An analysis of decision under risk. *Econometrica: Journal of the Econometric Society*, *47*(2), 263–291.

Karoly, P. (1999). A goal systems–self-regulatory perspective on personality, psychopathology, and change. *Review of General Psychology*, *3*(4), 264–291.

Kasser, T., & Ryan, R. M. (1993). A dark side of the American dream: Correlates of financial success as a central life aspiration. *Journal of personality and social psychology*, *65*, 410–422.

Kauffman, C., & Coutu, D. (2009). The realities of executive coaching. *Harvard Business Review: HBR Research Report*, 1–25.

Kayes, D. C. (2006). *Destructive Goal Pursuit: The Mount Everest Disaster*. Basingstoke: Palgrave Macmillan.

Kegan, R. (1994). *In Over Our heads: The Mental Demands of Modern Life*: Harvard University Press.

Kegan, R., Congleton, C., & David, S. A. (2013). The goals behind the goals: Pursuing adult development in the coaching enterprise. In S. A. David, D. Clutterbuck, & D. Megginson (Eds.), *Beyond Goals: Effective Strategies for Coaching and Mentoring*. Aldershot: Gower.

Kilburg, R. R. (2000). *Executive Coaching: Developing Managerial Wisdom in a World of Chaos*. Washignton, DC: American Psychological Association.

Klinger, E. (1977). *Meaning and Void: Inner Experience and the Incentive in People's Lives*. Minneapolis: University of Minnesota Press.

Kristof-Brown, A. L., & Stevens, C. K. (2001). Goal congruence in project teams: Does the fit between members' personal mastery and performance goals matter? *Journal of Applied Psychology*, 86(6), 1083–1095.

Langer, E. J. (1989). *Mindfulness*. Reading, MA: Addison-Wesley.

Larrick, R. P., Heath, C., & Wu, G. (2009). Goal-induced risk taking in negotiation and decision-making. *Social Cognition*, 27(3), 342–364.

Latham, G. P., & Locke, E. A. (2007). New developments in and directions for goal-setting research. *European Psychologist*, 12(4), 290–300.

Latham, G. P., & Seijts, G. H. (1999). The effects of proximal and distal goals on performance on a moderately complex task. *Journal of Organizational Behavior*, 20(4), 421–429.

Little, B. R. (1989). Personal projects analysis: Trivial pursuits, magnificent obsessions, and the search for coherence. In D. M. Buss & N. Cantor (Eds.), *Personality Psychology: Recent Trends and Emerging Directions* (pp. 15–31). New York: Springer.

Locke, E. A. (1996). Motivation through conscious goal setting. *Applied and Preventive Psychology*, 5(2), 117–124.

Locke, E. A., & Latham, G. P. (1990). *A Theory of Goal Setting and Task Performance*: Prentice-Hall.

Locke, E. A., & Latham, G. P. (2002). Building a practically useful theory of goal setting and task motivation: A 35-year odyssey. *American Psychologist*, 57, 9.

Locke, E. A., & Latham, G. P. (2006). New directions in goal-setting theory. *Current Directions in Psychological Science*, 15(5), 265–268.

Locke, E. A., & Latham, G. P. (2009). Has goal setting gone wild or have its attackers abandoned good scholarship? *Academy of Management Perspectives*, 23(1), 17–23.

Luban, D. (1998). Contrived ignorance. *Georgetown Law Journal*, 87(4), 957–980.

Maslow, A. (1954). *Motivation and Personality*. New York: Harper.

McKee, A. (1991). *Individual Differences in Planning for the Future* (Unpublished PhD Dissertation), Case Western Reserve University.

Midgley, C., Kaplan, A., & Middleton, M. (2001). Performance-approach goals: Good for what, for whom, under what circumstances, and at what cost? *Journal of Educational Psychology*, 93(1), 77–86.

Miller, G. A., Galanter, E., & Pribram, K. H. (1960). *Plans and the Structure of Behavior* (Vol. 19). New York: Holt, Rinehart and Winston.

Mitchell, T. R., & Silver, W. S. (1990). Individual and group goals when workers are interdependent: Effects on task strategies and performance. *Journal of Applied Psychology*, 75(2), 185–193.

Mossholder, K. W. (1980). Effects of externally mediated goal-setting on intrinsic motivation: A laboratory experiment. *Journal of Applied Psychology*, 65(2), 202–210.

Niemiec, C. P., & Ryan, R. M. (2013). What makes for a life well lived? Autonomy and its relation to full functioning and organismic wellness. In S. David, I. Boniwell, & A. C. Ayers (Eds.), *Oxford Handbook of Happiness* (pp. 214–226). Oxford: Oxford University Press.

O'Connor, S., & Cavanagh, M. (2012). *The Coaching Ripple Effect: The Individual and Systemic Level Influence of Leadership Development.*

Ordóñez, L. D., Schweitzer, M. E., Galinsky, A. D., & Bazerman, M. H. (2009). Goals gone wild: The systematic side effects of overprescribing goal setting. *The Academy of Management Perspectives*, 23(1), 6–16.

Parkes, R. C. (1955). We use seven guides to help executives develop. *Personnel Journal*, 33, 326–328.

Passmore, J., Petersen, G., & Friere, T. (Eds.). (2013). *The Wiley-Blackwell Handbook of the Psychology of Coaching and Mentoring.* Chichester: Wiley & Sons.

Pemberton, C. (2006). *Coaching to Solutions.* Abingdon: Routledge.

Pryor, R. G. L., & Bright, J. E. H. (2011). *The Chaos Theory of Careers: A New Perspective on Working in the Twenty-First Century.* New York: Routledge.

Prywes, Y. (2012). *Examining the Influence of Goal Attainment Scaling on Changes in Goal Attainment in a Coaching Versus Non-Coaching Context* (PhD). Columbia University, New York.

Ryan, T. A. (1970). *Intentional Behaviour.* New York: Ronald Press.

Sarrazin, P., Vallerand, R., Guillet, E., Pelletier, L., & Cury, F. (2002). Motivation and dropout in female handballers. *Journal of Social Psychology*, 32(3), 395–418.

Schweitzer, M. E., Ordóñez, L., & Douma, B. (2004). Goal setting as a motivator of unethical behaviour. *Academy of Management Journal*, 47(3), 422–432.

Scoular, A., & Linley, A. (2006). Coaching, goal setting and personality type: What matters? *The Coaching Psychologist*, 2(1), 9–11.

Seijts, G. H., & Latham, G. P. (2000). The effects of goal setting and group size on performance in a social dilemma. *Journal of Organizational Behavior*, 32, 104–116.

Shah, Y. J., Friedman, R., & Kruglanski, A. W. (2002). Forgetting all else: On the antecedents and consequences of goal shielding. *Journal of Personality and Social Psychology*, 83(6), 1261–1280.

Sheldon, K. M., & Elliot, A. J. (1998). Not all personal goals are personal: Comparing autonomous and controlled reasons for goals as predictors of effort and attainment. *Personality and Social Psychology Bulletin*, 24(5), 546–557.

Sitkin, B. S., See, K. E., Miller, C. C., Lawless, M. W., & Carton, A. M. (2011). The paradox of stretch goals: Organizations in pursuit of the seemingly impossible. *Academy of Management Review*, 36(3), 544–566.

Spence, G. B. (2007). GAS powered coaching: Goal Attainment Scaling and its use in coaching research and practice. *International Coaching Psychology Review*, 2(2), 155–167.

Spence, G. B., & Deci, E. L. (2013). Self-determination with coaching contexts: Supporting motives and goals that prmote optimal functioning and well-being. In S. David, D. Clutterbuck, & D. Megginson (Eds.), *Beyond Goals: Effective Strategies for Coaching and Mentoring* (pp. 85–108). Padstow, UK: Gower.

Spence, G. B., Cavanagh, M. J., & Grant, A. M. (2008). The integration of mindfulness training and health coaching: An exploratory study. *Coaching: An International Journal of Theory, Research and Practice*, 1(2), 145–163.

Spence, G. B., & Grant, A. M. (2007). Professional and peer life coaching and the enhancement of goal striving and wellbeing: An exploratory study. *The Journal of Positive Psychology*, 3(3), 185–194.

Stacey, R. D. (2007). *Strategic Management and Organisational Dynamics: The Challenge of Complexity to Ways of Thinking about Organisations.* Pearson Education.

Stone, D. N., Deci, E. L., & Ryan, R. M. (2009). Beyond talk: Creating autonomous motivation through self-determination theory. *Journal of General Management*, 34, 75–91.

Tomaschek, N., & Pärsch, S. (2006). *Systemic Coaching: A Target-oriented Approach to Consulting*: Carl-Auer.

Tubbs, M. (1986). Goal setting: A meta-analytic examination of the empirical evidence.

Journal of Applied Psychology, *71*(3), 474–483.

Vansteenkiste, M., Simons, J., Lens, W., Sheldon, K. M., & Deci, E. L. (2004). Motivating learning, performance, and persistence: The synergistic role of intrinsic goals and autonomy-support. *Journal of personality and social psychology*, *87*, 246–260.

Whitmore, J. (1996). *Coaching for Performance* (2nd ed.). London: Nicholas Brearly.

Wiener, N. (1948). *Cybernetics: Control and Communication in the Animal and the Machine*. New York: Wiley & Sons.

Winter, D. A. (2010). How smart is SMART? Retrieved from http://careersintheory.wordpress.com/how-smart-is-smart/

Yeager, D. S., & Dweck, C. S. (2012). Mindsets that promote resilience: When students believe that personal characteristics can be developed. *Educational Psychologist*, *47*(4), 302–314.

Working with Diversity in Coaching

Sunny Stout-Rostron

INTRODUCTION

A major challenge for organizations and institutions today is to manage an increasingly diverse workforce. Individuals must learn to adapt to multicultural diversity, and hence to differences in race, ethnicity, gender, sexual identity, education and language – in addition to a fast-paced, continually changing corporate environment. They must also confront power issues within the hierarchical nature of organizational systems, as well as major economic and life transitions in the workplace. As such, it has become critically important for business coaches to understand the impact of diversity on team performance, co-operation and conflict, particularly as organizations work more and more in team-based and highly competitive environments. Increasingly, contemporary organizations are opting for team coaching as a more effective way to improve team capability and performance, while at the same time saving on costs. In this context, a key question is how diversity within groups can be developed as a 'productive asset rather than becoming a source of conflict and prejudice' (Christian et al., 2006: 459).

This chapter includes a brief overview of recent psychological, social science, human resources and management literature on diversity, with regard to the leadership and management of organizations and workgroups within those organizations. This will include a discussion of the various implications of diversity in the workplace, and suggestions about how coaches can work amid the challenges that diversity brings to individual, team and organizational clients (and to themselves). Although some relevant research will be reviewed, few coaching-specific studies have been reported as 'the evidence-base for coaching can be described as disparate, largely atheoretical and composed of "one-off" findings' (Spence and Oades, 2011: 38). This has also been confirmed by Gray and Goregaokar (2010), who experienced a general difficulty finding past coaching research, and particularly so for executive coaching. More relevant to the current chapter, Motsoaledi and Cilliers (2012) could trace no relevant research on diversity coaching with which to compare their findings. As such, literature has been reviewed from a variety of other fields. While it is unrealistic for coaches to have a comprehensive understanding of all cultural backgrounds, it is possible to develop a broad understanding of the contemporary literature, such that coaches can work effectively and consciously in a diverse environment.

The chapter is organized into a five-part discussion. First, diversity will be defined and then situated within both an historical and contemporary context. Second, the business case for diversity will then be discussed, focusing on the controversy about whether diversity actually enhances performance (which is a matter of some relevance to coaching). Third, a variety of 'lessons' from diversity research will be reviewed, with particular focus given to gender diversity, coaching the alpha executive, along with a deeper understanding of cultural diversity (including race and ethnicity). Fourth, a small selection of models and techniques will be considered for the value they may provide to coaches who are working with diversity. Finally, a number of possibilities for future research are outlined for the benefit of readers who are considering empirical work in this area.

DEFINING DIVERSITY

The Historical and Contemporary Positioning of Diversity

There have been three distinct phases in diversity legislation. The *first* stage began in the 1960s, and lasted three decades, during which time the United States launched the Civil Rights Act (1964), the United Kingdom passed the Sex Discrimination Act (1975), and Australia passed the Human Rights and Equal Opportunity Commission Act (1986). All three pieces of legislation were focused on human rights and equal opportunity (Qin et al., 2014: 137). The *second* stage commenced during the 1980s, when greater attention was paid to initiatives aimed at retaining workforce heterogeneity in organizations. The focus was initially on inclusion and integration programmes, although there were also studies into the effects of social differences in race, gender, age, and physical disability. The *third* stage commenced in the 1990s (and continues to the present day) and involves strong advocacy for the diversity 'business case', which argues that 'increasing diversity would enable organizations to utilize the talents and abilities of all employees, which may be critical for success in an increasingly complex and dynamic business environment' (Qin et al., 2014: 138).

Dimensions of Diversity

There is little agreement amongst social and organizational psychology scholars about how diversity should be defined. However, researchers have suggested working with a comprehensive definition that encompasses 'demographics, skills, abilities, cognitive styles, perceptual orientations, personality dimensions, values, attitudes and beliefs that are germane to group functioning given a specific research context and theoretical orientation toward teams' (King et al., 2009: 263). Nonetheless, debate still exists on the issue of whether diversity refers to 'differences between individuals on any attribute that may lead to the perception that another person is different from the self' (Van Knippenberg et al., 2004: 1008).

Diversity research has focused primarily on six attributes: race, age, gender, education, functional background and tenure (Qin et al., 2014). Within the social sciences, research has generally focused on issues of race, ethnicity, gender, and age. Whilst a variety of other individual characteristics (e.g. educational background, personality traits, learning styles) have also been identified as part of diversity, such categorizations are prone to subvert any meaningful discussion on diversity issues. Some authors have distinguished between 'surface-level' and 'deep-level' differences (Harrison et al., 2002; Chatman and Flynn, 2001), while others have emphasized distinctions between 'low-visibility' and 'high-visibility' diversity variables and either 'low job-relatedness' or 'high job-relatedness' (Pelled, 1996: 617).

Demographic diversity refers to variables such as gender, age and race. A key question raised by researchers is whether demographics provide accurate reflections of differences between people. A CEO may have different information, experiences and perspectives to bring to a strategic issue than a middle manager, whilst those of different ethnic backgrounds will bring different values and perspectives to the formulation of strategy. However, research shows that over time, team members begin to gain familiarity with each other and the demographic measures are then no longer sufficient indicators of 'true diversity' (Jarzabkowski and Searle, 2004: 400).

Informational diversity is related to the 'different functional, educational and industry experience backgrounds that constitute information and knowledge resources upon which the team draws' (Jarzabkowski and Searle, 2004: 400). Team members might have administrative, financial, marketing, technological, logistical, research and development, HR/OD or operational backgrounds and, as experts in their fields, collectively they should be able to envision a strategy for the company, lead a merger, negotiate a major client deal and manage people.

Psychological or *behavioural* diversity involves the different personality styles within a team (Jarzabkowski and Searle, 2004), which give a stronger measure of diversity. Personality is the sum total of ways in which an individual reacts to and interacts with others over time. It is most often described in terms of measurable traits that a person exhibits (Robbins, 2001).

Rethinking Diversity – Inclusion vs Exclusion

The lexicon of this broad field appears to have changed in recent times, with the word 'diversity' being replaced with the term 'inclusion'. Organizations can no longer ignore the fact that diversity management has become a critical factor in maintaining marketplace competitiveness and managing talent. Some organizations are moving away from the standard focus on 'recruitment initiatives, education and training, career development, and mentoring programmes to increase and retain workforce heterogeneity' (Roberson, 2006: 213) and are, instead, focusing on inclusion in the management of diversity.

The concept of inclusion means removing barriers that prevent employees from using their full range of skills and competencies at work. According to Roberson (2006), inclusion is defined as 'the extent to which individuals can access information and resources, are involved in workgroups, and have the ability to influence decision-making processes' (p.213). For some organizations a focus on inclusion has resulted in the development of programmes and initiatives that include employee participation, communication strategies, and community relations (Roberson, 2006).

Roberson (2006) suggests that focusing on the advantages of employing different identity groups in organizations may actually ignore the dynamics and consequences of exclusion from organizational networks of information and opportunity. It is important for coach practitioners to understand their catalytic role in helping clients to comprehend the negative feelings others may experience through unconscious exclusion, and to appreciate the benefits of inclusive behaviour. More research is needed to distinguish between these two concepts of inclusion and exclusion, to identify their specific attributes and practices, and to understand where coaching interventions may play a part.

THE BUSINESS CASE: DOES DIVERSITY ENHANCE PERFORMANCE?

A major objective of research into diversity management has been to 'increase our understanding of the effects that workgroup diversity has on cohesion and performance' (Christian et al., 2006: 460). As defined by Guzzo and Dickson (1996), workgroups are made up of individuals who see themselves and are seen by others as a social entity, yet are interdependent, performing tasks to achieve organizational goals while distinguishing themselves from other workgroups.

Research into workgroup performance since the mid-1980s has suggested that 'mixed-composition workgroups can improve group performance by providing a wider range of perspectives and a broader skills base – but simultaneously it can be detrimental to group cohesion and performance because the diversity in personal backgrounds has the potential to exert a negative influence' (Christian et al., 2006: 460). While highly diverse teams are seemingly more effective in developing productive solutions, social conflict resulting from diversity can be associated with lower performance (Jarzabkowski and Searle, 2004). According to Christian et al. (2006), the desire to understand the effects of diversity on group cohesion and performance has led researchers to classify diversity attributes in the following ways:

- readily detectable vs less observable;
- surface-level vs deep-level;
- highly job-related vs less job-related;
- task-related vs relations-oriented;
- role-related vs inherent.

Notable omissions from this list are cognitive and demographic diversity, which are important if coaches are to grasp the depth of diversity issues when working with individuals and teams in organizations. From the perspective of a coach working with diversity within organizations, the dimensions of most interest are the surface-level, deep-level, cognitive and demographic diversity dimensions.

Surface-level diversity is defined as 'the extent to which a unit is heterogeneous on characteristics such as age, gender, ethnicity, functional background, and organizational tenure' (Mohammed and Angell, 2004: 1015). It has been linked primarily to relationship conflict, and relationship conflict focuses on personality differences, tension, animosity, and annoyance among individuals. *Deep-level* diversity is defined as differences in regards to attitudes, personality, and values (Mohammed and Angell, 2004). Although empirical research 'suggests that both surface- and deep-level diversity make a difference for group outcomes and significantly affect the experiences of the individuals within a team ... results are far from conclusive' (Mohammed and Angell, 2004: 1016). Mohmmed and Angell (2004) have also found that the longer that groups continue to interact, surface-level differences (i.e. gender and ethnicity) become less important, while deep-level diversity becomes more important (Mohammed and Angell, 2004: 1017).

According to Miller, Burke and Glick (1998), *cognitive* diversity is defined in terms of differences in beliefs and preferences held by executives concerning various organizational goals, with the variation in beliefs and preferences often a source of disagreement. Social psychological debates related to interpersonal attraction suggest that cognitive diversity negatively influences cohesion, with research showing that it can become very problematic, something that many organizations struggle to manage (Miller et al., 1998). The implication is that 'cognitive diversity rather than demographic diversity may be the most fruitful arena for research', due to the problems that high levels of cognitive diversity can cause in regards to communication, integration, and political behaviour (Miller et al., 1998).

Demographic diversity refers to the variables of age, gender, race, group tenure, organization tenure, education, or functional

```
            High
                  ┌─────────────────┬─────────────────┐
                  │                 │                 │
                  │      Age        │                 │
                  │     Gender      │   Group tenure  │
                  │      Race       │                 │
                  │                 │                 │
      Visibility  ├─────────────────┼─────────────────┤
                  │                 │                 │
                  │                 │ Organizational  │
                  │                 │     tenure      │
                  │                 │   Education     │
                  │                 │   Functional    │
                  │                 │   background    │
                  └─────────────────┴─────────────────┘
            Low         Job-relatedness         High
```

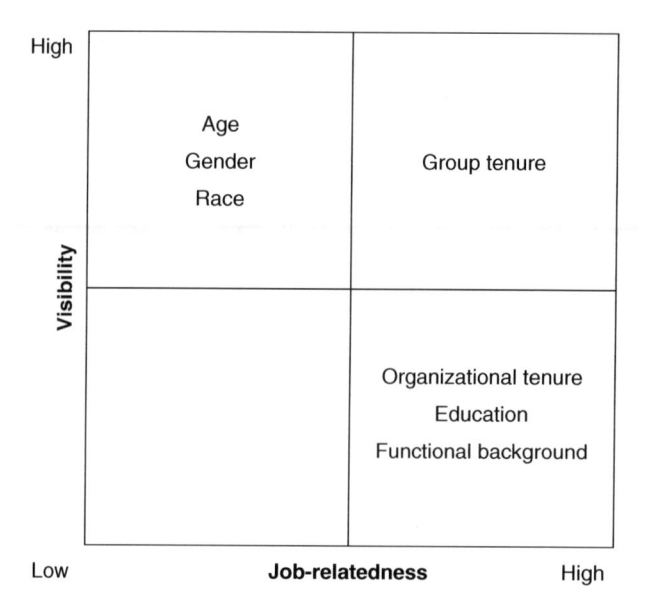

Figure 13.1 Typology of democratic diversity variables
Source: Pelled, 1996

background. According to Pelled (1996), each variable can be classified according to its level of visibility and its level of job-relatedness. Visibility refers to how easily the variable can be observed by members of the group, and job-relatedness refers to the extent that the variable actually shapes perspectives and skills related to cognitive tasks (Pelled, 1996). It is also important to also note that demographic diversity is associated with cognitive diversity, which is useful collectively as a broader range of cognitive perspectives will influence a team's access to information, along with its capacity to solve problems and recognize strategic opportunities (Roberson, 2006).

Dimensions of Workgroup Diversity

Pelled (1996) proposes a model to examine the processes by which workgroup diversity predicts individual and group outcomes. Influenced by a multitude of studies on workgroup diversity, this model focuses specifically on demographic diversity (e.g. employee occupational backgrounds, the presence of women and minorities in the workplace). Each variable in the model is classified according to dimensions of job-relatedness and visibility (see Figure 13.1). Whilst diversity may have a positive impact on turnover, it may have mixed effects for the group's cognitive task performance. In short, the model explores how each demographic diversity variable (i.e. age, gender, race, group tenure, organizational tenure, education, or functional background) can be classified according to its visibility and level of job-relatedness, and how both the latter two dimensions can affect turnover and performance (Pelled, 1996).

Pelled's objective in developing the model was to further define the role of conflict, which she argues is a robust mediator of diversity between demography and organizational outcomes. The two-dimensional model includes a variable with a substantive component (i.e. task-related conflicts) and an affective component (i.e. non-task conflicts). The model suggests that demographic diversity variables have 'positive effects on the affective and substantive dimensions of conflict in groups' (Pelled, 1996: 621). Substantive conflict generated by diversity is more likely to increase cognitive task performance, as it enables the group to critically test their ideas – and earlier social psychological studies have shown that better solutions are generated when opinions are conflicting (Pelled, 1996).

According to Pelled (1996), 'the more job-related a particular type of diversity is, the stronger is its relationship with substantive conflict' (p. 617). For example, organizational tenure diversity will be a stronger predictor of substantive conflict than age diversity. The more visible a particular type of diversity is, the stronger its relationship to affective conflict. For example, age diversity will be a stronger predictor of affective conflict than organizational tenure diversity (Pelled, 1996: 617).

The vertical axis in Figure 13.1 shows 'low' versus 'high' visibility, while the horizontal axis shows 'low' versus 'high' job-relatedness. The model classifies age, gender and race as high in visibility and low in job-relatedness. These attributes are high in visibility as they are easily observable, but they are low in job-relatedness as they do not reflect task perspectives and technical skills. In contrast, organizational tenure, education and functional background are high in job-relatedness, as they directly shape task perspectives and technical skills – but they are less easily observed, and therefore low in visibility (Pelled, 1996).

Some of Pelled's (1996) recommendations include further discussion on how diversity across multiple dimensions influences conflict, and studying how diversity variables act in combination. With regard to coaching diversity, a useful future study would be to explore how coaching might positively impact the negotiation of conflict in workgroups, and to examine if that has any effect on the mixed consequences that diversity has on cognitive task performance. For example, given the fraught political history of South Africa, diversity can present tremendous potential for conflict within the workplace.

Sometimes the problem is not isolated to one aspect of diversity, but can cover a spectrum. Even in organizations with fairly uniform ethnic or cultural homogeneity, there can be latent issues of gender, race, ethnicity, patriarchy and language.

Workgroup Diversity, Conflict and Collective Action

Organizational and social psychological theory provide helpful perspectives for understanding the impact of group heterogeneity on conflict and co-operation processes (King et al., 2009). Diverse work teams comprise members belonging to distinct groups, and have been found to function very differently from homogeneous teams. In terms of *self-identity* and *self-categorization* theories, people define and differentiate themselves through group memberships. Self-categorization relates to how individuals become unified into a group and become capable of collective behaviour. As members are motivated to maintain their social identities, they tend to demonstrate a bias towards those who appear to have similar characteristics, and conflict is a common outcome when members of different groups interact (Mohammed and Angell, 2004).

According to the *similarity–attraction* paradigm, people prefer similarity in their interactions and identify easily with others who have similar values and beliefs. Interestingly, social identity, self-categorization and similarity–attraction theories all seem to lead to the same prediction, which is that members of high-diversity teams will tend to have less positive attitudes towards each other, which may lead to conflict (Mohammed and Angell, 2004). On the other hand, there seems to be 'no direct empirical evidence to support the assumption that maintaining ethnic identity facilitates peaceful inter-group relations' (Perreault, 1997: 113).

Jarzabkowski and Searle (2004) argue that high-diversity teams enter into conflict due to their different perceptions of the strategic environment and the range of possible strategic options. In other words, diverse teams are more likely to engage in conflict due to their differing perspectives. At the same time, teams with low diversity tend to generate fewer options and are less likely to challenge the assumptions of other team members. The difficulty is that more diverse teams are harder to manage, due to the conflict generated among individuals who do not easily understand each other. This can produce social conflict when challenges are perceived to be an attack on a person's values, which can result in defensive and political behaviours. Conflict has been found to be a key intervening variable between diversity and group outcomes, with three main types of conflict identified: relationship, task and process conflict (Ayub and Jehn, 2006). However, the debate about whether conflict is beneficial or detrimental in diverse workgroups continues unabated, and future research should attempt to identify how to maximize the benefits of conflict in workgroups and where coaching can play a role.

Amid the complexity of modern organizations, collected success seems to require balancing diversity in the senior management team with collective action, thereby enhancing the capacity for the team to act as a collective unit (Jarzabkowski and Searle, 2004). According to Jarzabkowski and Searle (2004), there are four 'ideal-type' teams: dysfunctional, consensual, conflictual and effective – and that what is needed are practical ways to enable collective action within those top teams.

As shown in Figure 13.2, teams with low diversity and low collective action will tend to be *dysfunctional* in respect of its strategic capacity (which should, in turn, inhibit company performance). It also predicts that strategic capacity will be compromised for *consensual* teams that have low diversity but high collective action, as they will be prone to unchallenged, poor-quality decision making. In contrast, teams with high diversity but low collective action (a *conflictual* team) will be good at generating a variety of strategic options, but will struggle to convert them

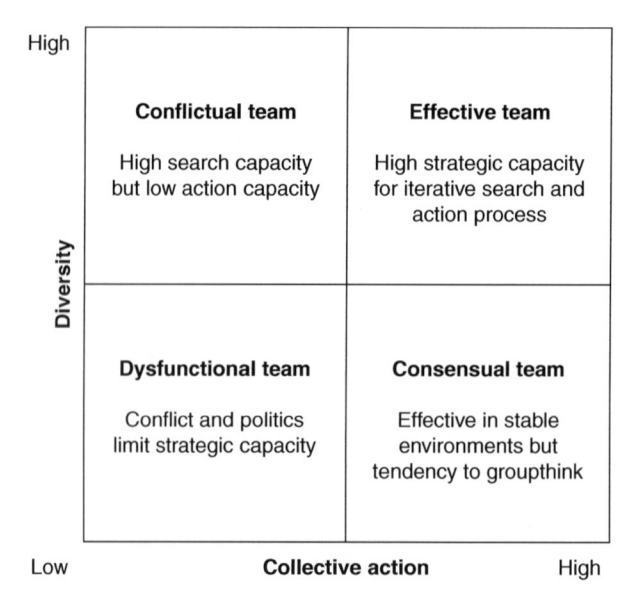

	Diversity High	
	Conflictual team High search capacity but low action capacity	**Effective team** High strategic capacity for iterative search and action process
	Dysfunctional team Conflict and politics limit strategic capacity	**Consensual team** Effective in stable environments but tendency to groupthink
	Low — Collective action — High	

Figure 13.2 Team strategic capacity: diversity and collective action

Source: Jarzabkowski and Searle (2014: 407)

into action. Finally, an *effective* team is one that can leverage the benefits of diversity to generate multiple strategic options (presumably by understanding and accepting other's perspectives), and then maximize this potential by taking effective collective action (Jarzabkowski and Searle, 2004).

Value-in-Diversity vs Diversity-as-Process-Loss

Herring's (2009) research examines the impact of racial and gender diversity on business performance from two competing perspectives. The first is the value-in-diversity perspective, which makes the business case for diversity, whilst the second is the diversity-as-process-loss perspective, which is sceptical of the benefits of diversity. According to Herring, the 'value-in-diversity' perspective is advantageous as 'a diverse workforce, relative to a homogeneous one, is generally beneficial for business, including but not limited to corporate profits and earnings. This is in contradiction to other accounts that view diversity as either non-consequential to business success or actually detrimental by creating conflict, undermining cohesion, and thus decreasing productivity' (Herring, 2009: 208). It is further argued that diversity drives business success because it allows companies to think 'outside the box' by embracing the perspectives of groups that were previously excluded. Similarly, Gatrell and Swan (2008) emphasize that the business case for diversity presumes that a diverse workforce brings material benefits to an organization in the form of increased innovation, customer care and profits.

In contrast, the diversity-as-process-loss perspective emphasizes that diversity introduces conflict and other problems which detract from an organization's efficacy and profitability, thus constraining business performance. Proponents of this perspective argue that diversity brings significant potential costs, and that racial and ethnic diversity are linked with conflict, especially emotional conflict among co-workers (Herring, 2009).

Herring (2009) also proposes a third view. This is the idea that diversity is associated with more group conflict but better business performance, and that conflict forces groups to contest different ideas, be more creative and produce superior solutions to problems. The implication of Herring's research is that homogeneity leads to greater group cohesion but less adaptability and innovation, in keeping with the conclusions of Jarzabkowski and Searle (2004). Further research is evidently needed to explore how diversity can enhance an organization's creativity, problem solving and performance, and that practitioners need to be aware of the cultural and systemic dynamics playing out in organizational teams and workgroups.

WHAT LESSONS FROM DIVERSITY RESEARCH CAN HELP US AS COACHES?

Gender Diversity

For most social theorists, gender is a social construction. This means that 'as for other social categories such as race, sexuality and disability – gender is the result of human social processes, actions, language, thought and practices' (Gatrell and Swan, 2008). Formal workplace activism started in the 1960s and 1970s, and the theories of Marxist feminism, radical feminism and patriarchy from that time have been influential in our understanding of discrimination against women (Stout-Rostron, 2014). The distinction between sex and gender was recognized in the 1960s, and Oakley (1985) was one of the first to distinguish biological 'sex' differences from 'gender' as a set of socio-cultural constructions, identifying how what was often thought of as natural and biological was also social, cultural, political and historical. By the late 1970s and 1980s, most relevant work was on gender divisions of labour, authority and hierarchy, and sexuality in management and organizations (Hearn and Parkin, 1983), and there was a move away from 'women in management' to 'gender in management'.

Further trends from the 1990s onwards have included the recognition of the specific gendering of men in organizations, and gender management in terms of 'visibility' and 'invisibility' in the workplace. Simpson and Lewis (2007) explore the concept that men are constructed to be representative of the norm and to represent humanity, where men are viewed as 'genderless' in organizations, and women are seen to be 'what men are not'. This concept of men as 'gender-free' has been increasingly questioned since the early 1990s, with gender difference being viewed today as an active social construction, 'rather than a natural biological category' (Simpson and Lewis, 2007: 54).

Contemporary research shows a significant number of barriers to women's career development, such as lack of mentoring and role models for women at the highest levels, exclusion from informal networks and channels of communication, stereotyping of women's roles and abilities, sexual harassment, and unfriendly corporate culture (Čurdová, 2005). However, the proportion of women in 'executive, managerial, and administrative roles nearly tripled during the last three decades of the 20th century', with another clear trend being the number of women moving into global political leadership positions (Vecchio, 2002: 643–644). Today a more collaborative approach is bringing women into leadership roles in developed and emerging markets, and we are seeing greater gender inclusivity and empowerment for women as they step into more significant leadership roles.

Implications for Practice

Peltier (2001, 2010) suggests that coaches need to understand how women function within an organization – the reverse of the standard approach to coaching women, which suggests that they need help in finding a way to fit into organizational culture. He also suggests assessing clients and seeing how they view gender and the role it plays (Peltier, 2010). Peltier points out that in the male-dominated world of corporate life there is a need to understand gender politics and differential gender communication patterns, values and tendencies (Peltier, 2010). He mentions the 'glass ceiling' that still prevents women from progressing too high in the organization; and the 'glass walls' that keep women in the new 'pink collar' jobs (Peltier, 2001: 193) such as human resources, organizational development and marketing. What Peltier calls 'erroneous assumptions' about women in the workplace (e.g. that a woman's highest priority is the family), we now identify as 'limiting assumptions' that deliberately exclude women from long-term career development.

It is important not to assume that women represent the only gender concerns, but to broaden the discussion to include men. Men also suffer from negative self-images on an individual and collective level – depending on the culture and country within which they live and work. Generally, masculinity is associated with the 'world of work and with power', although 'working-class men' often have little power and may 'adopt a macho identity to counterbalance the powerlessness in their jobs' (Simpson and Lewis, 2007: 69). This is an important consideration, depending on the organizational culture within which the coach is working. Future research is needed to identify the barriers still preventing women from stepping into more senior and executive roles. This research would need to consider and quantify what cultural and linguistic obstacles are present in different countries and societies. In addition, invaluable research would investigate if, and how, coaching could help women to break through the glass ceilings still present in most multinational corporations.

Coaching the Alpha Executive

Research does not yet demonstrate that men or women are more advantaged in terms of leadership or management competence. From the mid-1980s through to the late 1990s a broad range of studies tried to determine whether female and male leaders differed. The feminine advantage perspective contends that women are 'inclined to a co-operative leadership style that includes team structure, while males are inclined to a competitive leadership style that includes hierarchical structure' (Vecchio, 2002: 647). Other versions of the feminine advantage perspective argue that males prefer an 'alpha style' of leadership based on command-and-control, whereas females prefer a 'beta style' of leadership based on social interaction (Vecchio, 2002: 648).

Ludeman and Erlandson (2004) defined the 'alpha male' as 'highly intelligent, confident, and successful', claiming that they represent 'about 70 per cent of all senior executives'. They depicted alpha males as 'people who aren't happy unless they're the top dogs'. In their research, they claimed to have rarely found successful female leaders with equally strong personalities, or to find women who matched the 'complete alpha profile' (Ludeman and Erlandson, 2004: 58). When asked why so many alpha males need executive coaches, the researchers explained that their 'quintessential strengths are also what make them so challenging, and often frustrating, to work with. Independent and action-oriented, alphas take extraordinarily high levels of performance for granted, both in themselves and in others.' On the other hand, alpha males have 'little or no natural curiosity about people or feelings'; they rely on exhaustive data to reach business conclusions, but often make snap judgements about other people, and are 'surprisingly oblivious to the effect they have on others' (Ludeman and Erlandson, 2004: 58–59). The authors suggest that alphas make perfect mid-level managers overseeing processes, but as they approach CEO level they are expected to become inspirational people managers, which is often beyond their capabilities.

Implications for Practice

According to Erlandson (2009), gender should be approached as a key to working with men and women senior executives. When dealing with a dominant, confident, results-driven male individual, the coach may uncover evidence of 'wreckage caused by boys behaving badly' (Erlandson, 2009: 219). After proposing the existence of four different alpha male types, Erlandson suggests a coaching approach that is ultimately shared with the leader's team. In contrast, Ludeman (2009) details the 'micro-inequities' faced by women leaders in the workplace and explains the characteristics of alpha and beta women (Ludeman, 2009), whilst advocating the need for the importance of understanding an array of different ways to work with women leaders.

In a rare study, Skinner (2014) investigated the developmental factors involved in executive coaching for women in Australia. Her research found a need for a gender perspective in coaching women. The data suggested that executive coaching played an important role in supporting the formation of a professional identity for senior women, along with providing vital support for basic psychological needs and motivation. The importance of role models, and indeed the coach as a role model, was also highlighted by the participants, as well as the 'pivotal role that executive coaching played in exploring ways to be authentic in their leadership role, particularly in relating to male traits of leadership' (Skinner, 2014: 109). Stated differently, the research highlighted that executive coaching was valuable for women leaders because it enabled them to define their own personalized approach to leadership, rather than internalizing the prevailing male norms (Skinner, 2014). In line with social identity theory, the coaching process provided contextual support for identity formation, via engagement in regular dialogue and reflection. As a result the senior women became more able to authentically identify themselves as leaders, developing a deep sense of self, being clear about personal values and beliefs, and finding ways to sustain their leadership roles in the long term (Skinner, 2014).

The implications for coaching are to suggest a more gender-sensitive approach, reinforcing the role of executive coaching in mediating the impact of the all-too-often male leadership environment, the need to develop a unique identity as a leader which differs from accepted male norms, and the need for coaches to understand the gendered work environment of executives (Skinner, 2014). Taking this a step further, the fundamental issue which still needs to be addressed is how women leaders can be defined without referring to the masculine norm of leadership? How can women find their own self-definition and self-assertion, which can be positioned as integral and equal to that of men? In this context, what could be the role and responsibility of the executive coach? Such questions would all be useful focal points for future research.

Gender and Coach Matching

Whilst there has been little empirical work reported on gender and coach matching, Gray and Goregaokar (2010) have examined the issue using the literature on mentoring relationships and matching as a proxy. In the mentoring literature, there is a focus on the issue of gender, with evidence suggesting that 'same-gender matching for women may circumvent some of the potential sexual overtones of cross-gender mentoring' (Gray and Goregaokar, 2010: 528). This study highlighted that cross-gender mentoring relationships may be of limited value, because men are unlikely to provide adequate role models or because they lack empathy for the complexities that women face.

Initial qualitative results suggested that female executives favoured the choice of female coaches, partly as a role model of business success, while male executives tended to justify the selection of a female coach as more approachable for the discussion of personal issues (Gray and Goregaokar, 2010: 527). However, quantitative analysis showed that gender is not a significant factor in the coach selection process, and that executive coaching programmes need to provide both male and female coaches for selection (Gray and Goregaokar, 2010). It seems that coaching and mentoring may share similar dilemmas when it comes to cross-gender matching, even though mentoring tends to be based on a longer-term relationship, and coaching on a shorter-term relationship.

An interesting finding was that executive coaches need to be alerted to the potential for negative psychosocial intimacy in coaching, which is the potential for sexist attitudes and even sexual harassment from male executives (Gray and Goregaokar, 2010). This is the first study to highlight the potential for such inappropriate behaviour in either a coaching or mentoring intervention. It highlights the need for further detailed research and statistical findings – specifically within the discipline of coaching.

Race and Ethnicity

The issues of racism, discrimination and prejudice are often denied in the corporate workplace. Yet these factors present massive challenges in the socio-political sphere, and can have a huge impact on confidence and self-esteem. For coaches there is a need to think practically about issues of race and ethnicity in the workplace, examining cultural understandings of power, rank, privilege and other cultural assumptions. Questions may also arise concerning the differences between the practitioner's and the client's ethnicity and culture, with practitioners able to maintain awareness of assumptions that may limit or empower both coach and client. As observed by Marques (2014), people are 'in different ways and in varying degrees, shaped by our cultural background – therefore our way of making sense of the world is culturally determined' (p. 154).

In South Africa, for example, the majority of coaches are predominantly white males, with a pronounced western and Eurocentric outlook. However, they may be coaching a black African, mixed-race or Indian female – all of whom will have extremely different social and cultural backgrounds and traditions. If not examined, subtle differences could lead to misunderstandings and a lack of success in the coaching process. Faced with diversity, it is the coach's role to be self-aware and guide the process for both coach and client – the outcome could be either very negative or extremely enriching.

According to Motsoaledi and Cilliers (2012), workplace diversity research has increased over the last few years with a focus on multiculturalism, cultural intelligence, and cross-cultural diversity – showing that an awareness of diversity improves performance and relationships at work. The researchers agree with contemporary research which suggests that effective diversity management as a business strategy is geared to increase organizational competitiveness, and that an awareness of diversity improves performance and relationships at work. The purpose of this research was to describe the application of systems psychodynamic role analysis to assist executives to work effectively with both conscious and unconscious diversity dynamics in their organizations. A systems psychodynamic approach was used to create awareness of below-the-surface diversity dynamics, as well as the need for executives to address diversity challenges more effectively. The coaching sessions were found to provide a space for reflection and a place to contain anxieties. At the end of the coaching the executives had begun to display more 'executive wisdom', with a stronger sense of self and a greater understanding of how to manage relationships more effectively (Motsoaledi and Cilliers, 2012).

These findings highlight four diversity challenges: gender, race, ethnicity and authority. Of these, three specific gender findings are worthy of mention. These include that women leaders discarded their femininity to engage with traditional masculine leadership roles; shifting power relations between black men and black women evoked deep anxiety in the black men; and white executives still held significant power in the workplace and in transformation structures. It was concluded that 'executive coaching from a systems psychodynamic perspective displays trustworthiness in improving participants' diversity awareness, especially with regard to gender, race, ethnicity and authorization' (Motsoaledi and Cilliers, 2012).

In addressing important diversity challenges in the context of transforming South African organizations, the study found that ethnic affiliation fostered support, and increased access to resources and to networks of power. What was clear was the strong need for affiliation, survival and domination, including the use of the English language as a tool of power against those who could not speak the language proficiently (Motsoaledi and Cilliers, 2012). The researchers' recommendations for future research in executive coaching would be to focus further on a systems psychodynamic perspective, with a focus on ethnicity, disability, age, language and sexual orientation. As they argued, it would be important to include all diverse groups in South Africa and the study could also be replicated in other countries with a high degree of diversity (such as India and Brazil).

It is important to note that this study was strongly psychotherapy-oriented and, as such, its conclusions may be applicable only to approaches to coaching that focus on deep personal transformation and change. However, the study is valuable because it focuses on diversity issues in public sector organizations (including gender), and studies systemic dysfunctionality within government institutions, which is often exacerbated by diversity issues.

Cultural Diversity

According to Coultas et al. (2011), executive coaching and the cultural diversification of the workplace are two emerging trends that have improved the performance of middle- and top-level leaders. Two interesting questions emerge from this observation. First, how do organizational cultural values affect the coaching of these executives? Second, what is the cultural adaptability of the coach to the coachee and to the organization? Thus far, coaching research has had little to say on these questions.

It is important to consider how culture is defined, particularly within a business context, including classifications and dimensions of culture, and how these may be applied to business coaching (Janse van Rensburg, 2014). Rosinski (2003) advocates understanding different cultures as necessary for a coach to broaden their understanding and be better equipped to assist the client. He distinguishes between professional or organizational cultures and national cultures, and indicates various groupings of diversity such as geography and nationality (including region, religion and ethnicity), discipline, profession and education, organization (including industry, corporation, union and function), social life (including family, friends, social class and clubs), and gender and sexual orientation. What is particularly relevant for coaches is the finding that management effectiveness is independent of culture and race, and that ethnically diverse management will not inhibit corporate competitive performance (Thomas & Bendixen, 2000). Worldwide research is needed to help coaches and organizations understand the cultural implications of their work with senior managers and executives.

Coultas et al. (2011) suggest that 'culturally uninformed coaching techniques are ineffective at best and damaging and costly at worst, and that coaches today need not only to have a deeper understanding of cultures (i.e. acknowledging individual differences) but also be able to adapt (i.e. individualize) coaching strategies for maximum effect when dealing with culturally different others' (p. 150).

One of the clear functions of the coach is to understand the culture, values and relationship systems within the workplace, and to know what are the accepted standards of diverse cultural influences. Recent research suggests the need to develop a theoretical framework to provide guidelines in culturally diverse contexts. In developing their own integrative approaches to diversity coaching, coaches should consider their own experience and training, and choose theoretical models that will suit a wide range of clients.

TECHNIQUES FOR THE PRACTITIONER WORKING WITH DIVERSITY

Corey and Corey Co-Leadership Model

Facilitation is most often used within organizations when people come together to work in teams. This style of management has become more prevalent in organizations today, hence many team coaches require skills as facilitators. In essence, the role of the team coach is to let the group become responsible for their aims and outcomes, and to manage that group process. As such, models like Corey and Corey's (2010) Co-Leadership Model become relevant for coaches who facilitate groups or teams. The advantage is that team members learn from two perspectives, and co-leaders converse and learn together.

The DELTA Model

The DELTA model addresses executive coaching from a values-sensitive, motivational approach. It suggests that, due to the globalization and diversity of executives, we need to develop culturally competent executive coaches by:

1 *Determining* cultural values (i.e. determining the cultural values of coachees through a survey on attitudes);
2 *Employing* typical coaching techniques (i.e. feedback interventions and goal setting in a way that is culturally appropriate);

3 *Looking and listening* for motivational needs and deficiencies (i.e. considering executive coaching through a motivational lens such as the Pritchard-Ashwood motivational framework to assess motivational levels and needs);
4 *Tailoring* coaching techniques to motivational needs and cultural values (i.e. understanding psychological and personalogical differences and cultural dimensions, and adapting accordingly); and
5 *Assessing* the effectiveness of the approaches used (i.e. tailoring coaching interventions to individual motivational deficiencies, and addressing those needs).

The DELTA model claims to be a flexible, paradigmatic approach with five elements to help coaches motivate and develop culturally diverse executives (Coultas et al., 2011). Although the model emphasizes the 'cultural fit' of coach to coachee, it should also consider the individual client's fit within the organizational culture. Coach practitioners need to develop an awareness and sensitivity to client cultural values, and at the same time help executives to be flexible and adaptable within their own organizational culture.

Deep Democracy Model

The Deep Democracy Model (Mindell, 2002) is useful when coaching diverse teams and emerging conflict needs to be resolved. Drawing from psychotherapeutic origins, this model of group facilitation emphasizes the critical importance of acknowledging each voice and every feeling, if a group or team is to come to know itself and resolve its issues. It is important to note that although all voices need to be heard, this does not necessarily mean that everyone has equal power. The work aims to support all the people in the group or team, and all the issues. The approach is 'democratic' because it validates every voice and holds that decisions are wisest when majority and minority voices are both valued. It is 'deep' because it goes far beyond the conventional methods of facilitating the exchange of ideas and instead surfaces emotions, values, beliefs, and personalities to inform and enrich the group's process (Mindell, 2002). Instead of focusing on majority rule, Deep Democracy suggests that all voices, states of awareness, and frameworks of reality are important, and that decisions are wisest when majority and minority voices are both valued.

As a technique, Deep Democracy is a highly effective way to facilitate group decisions and begin to manage group conflict. Briefly, the specific intention is inclusion, even of dissenting voices. The approach includes the dissenting voice because it recognizes that it contains a wisdom for the group, viewing dissenters as emissaries of a submerged (secondary) issue that needs to be brought into the open. The basic premise is that the team will be stronger if everyone's voice is heard. This means hearing and including the wisdom of the minority.

Deep Democracy looks at issues and roles rather than individuals and the facilitator ensures that the individual is protected and not scapegoated. Rather than an individual creating difficulty or tension, it is seen that they are playing a role, and voicing something that is in the group. Working with roles means that individuals can step into and try on roles that are usually uncomfortable for them. Role types include: leader, manager, employee, customer, stakeholder, community, activist, saboteur, or ghost role (someone who has recently left the team). For example, a normally silent member can be empowered to take on the role of 'activist' – and safely voice dissenting, critical views. In this way, empathy and understanding of other points of view develops within the team. However, at the end of a Deep Democracy process, it is important to put the team into pairs to share what they have learned and ask what action they plan to take. In the plenary, the coach then facilitates an open discussion to plan how the team and individual team members are to go forward.

FUTURE RESEARCH

As modern companies remove the barriers that formerly separated workers of different backgrounds, leaders and academics are finding that diversity is a topic they can no longer ignore. Managing diversity has become a critical factor to maintain marketplace competitiveness and to effectively manage talent. However, the main conclusion is that diversity is a complex matter that involves demographic, informational and psychological/behavioural differences which may prove difficult to manage productively.

Over the past 20 years research studies show mixed results as to how diversity impacts the strategic capacity of a business. A broad conclusion is that 'mixed-composition workgroups can improve group performance by providing a wider range of perspectives and a broader skills base – but simultaneously it can be detrimental to group cohesion and performance because the diversity in personal backgrounds has the potential to exert a negative influence' (Christian et al., 2006, p. 460).

Research has shown that there can be negative outcomes of team diversity within organizations, and that conflict is common when members of different groups interact. The other side of the argument is that diversity, if embraced and managed, can also be closely linked to business success. By including those previously excluded, 'outside-the-box thinking' is generated which produces more creative and innovative business performance.

Barak (2014) distinguishes between the 'exclusion workplace' and the 'inclusive workplace', highlighting the importance for organizations of moving towards a globally inclusive workplace. Contemporary research indicates that leaders need acquired diversity (i.e. traits gained from experience) to establish an 'inclusive' culture in which all employees feel free to contribute ideas.

In terms of gender diversity, research does not yet demonstrate that men or women are more advantaged in terms of leadership or management competence. It seems that the search for differences in leadership and management styles on the part of men and women has yielded ambiguous results. In terms of coaching men or women, what is important to understand is the context within which the leader works, and what range of behaviours they are able to integrate and balance to be competent in their position. It is also critically important to understand the culture of the society – and the underlying values and culture of the business – in which they work.

Future research is needed to understand how coaching can contribute to building 'inclusive' organizational cultures, managing conflict in diverse teams, and understanding how to work with the differing styles of management between men and women. Research is also required to understand the contribution that coaching makes to organizational strategic capacity and culture. Two key questions that arise are: First, how do organizational cultural values affect the coaching of executives? Second, what is the cultural adaptability of the coach to the coachee and to the organization? Another step would be an increase in case study research to discern what level of contribution coaching makes within organizations, particularly with regard to all the various manifestations of diversity and the increasing requirements of 'diversity' legislation.

CONCLUSION

This chapter has shown that diversity takes many different forms and can be extraordinarily subtle and complex. As such, it can sometimes take coaches by surprise, even when they think they know the field. What is critically needed for coach practitioners is a broader understanding of the various arguments around the issue of diversity, and an understanding of diversity dynamics in the organizational cultures to which they consult. Managers and academics are finding that even in organizations with fairly uniform ethnic or cultural homogeneity, there can be underlying issues of gender, patriarchy and hierarchy. Also, the problem is not always confined to one aspect of diversity, such as race, gender, culture or religion, but can cover more subtle, yet less visible factors, such as attitudes, personality and values, all of which need more research.

To operate within an organizational context, coach practitioners need to develop an awareness of their own responses to diversity. It is vital that coach practitioners understand their own prejudices, biases, limiting thinking and life conditioning. This means being able to 'see' through a multiplicity of lenses. In other words, to see not just through their own individual perspective as coaches, but through the lenses of clients whose background, culture, education, experience, hopes and fears may be very different from their own. Also, because the circuits of discrimination are complex, part of understanding organizational culture for the coach is to clarify the cultural knowledge and social processes that operate within a client organization on a daily basis. Only then will coaches be able to work with their clients in the coaching conversation, helping clients to identify and liberate themselves from the limiting assumptions they hold about themselves, others and the systems in which they live and work.

It is essential for diversity practitioners to develop an appreciation of the socio-political factors of all their clients, understanding their cultural, educational, ethnic and racial backgrounds. Each practitioner has a responsibility to integrate cultural knowledge into their own education and practice – and most importantly culturally evaluating themselves to understand their own worldview. Only in this way can practitioners increase their competence and empower their clients with their interventions. This level of self-awareness and self-reflection must begin with the coach, and greater diversity education for coach practitioners would be an appropriate place to start.

REFERENCES

Ayub, N. and Jehn, K.A. (2006). National diversity and conflict in multinational workgroups: The moderating effect of nationalism. *International Journal of Conflict Management*, 17(3): 181–202.

Barak, M.E. (2014). *Managing Diversity: Toward a globally inclusive workplace*. Third Edition. London: Sage.

Chatman, J.A. and Flynn, F.J. (2001). The influence of demographic heterogeneity on the emergence and consequences of co-operative norms in work teams. *Academy of Management Journal*, 44(5): 956–974.

Christian, J., Porter, L.W. and Moffitt, G. (2006). Workplace diversity and group relations: An overview. *Group Processes and Intergroup Relations*, 9(4): 459–466.

Corey, M.S. and Corey, G. (2010). *Groups Process and Practice*. Eighth Edition. Belmont, CA: Brooks/Cole.

Coultas, C.W, Bedwell, W.L., Burke, C.S. and Salas, E. (2011). Values-sensitive coaching: The DELTA approach to coaching culturally diverse executives. *Consulting Psychology Journal: Practice and Research*, 63: 149–161.

Čurdová, A. (2005). *Discrimination Against Women in the Workforce and the Workplace*. Report of the Committee on Equal Opportunities for Women and Men, Document 10484. Strasbourg: Parliamentary Assembly of the Council of Europe.

Erlandson, E. (2009). Coaching with men: Alpha males. In Passmore, J. (ed.), *Diversity in Coaching: Working with gender, culture, race and age*. London: Association for Coaching; Philadelphia, PA: Kogan Page. pp. 216–236.

Gatrell, C. and Swan, E. (2008). *Gender and Diversity in Management: An Introduction*. London: Sage.

Gray, D.E. and Goregaokar, H. (2010). Choosing an executive coach: The influence of gender on the coach–coachee matching process. *Management Learning*, 41(5): 525–544.

Guzzo, R.A. and Dickson, M.W. (1996). Teams in organizations: Recent research on performance and effectiveness. *Annual Review of Psychology*, 47: 307–338.

Harrison, D.A., Price, K.H., Gavin, J.H. and Florey, A. (2002). Time, teams, and task performance: Changing effects of surface- and deep-level diversity on group functioning. *Academy of Management Journal*, 45(5): 1029–1045.

Hearn, J. and Parkin, W. (1983). Gender and organizations: A selective review and a critique of a neglected area. *Organization Studies*, 4: 219–242.

Herring, C. (2009). Does diversity pay? Race, gender, and the business case for diversity. *American Sociological Review*, 74: 208–224.

Janse van Rensburg, M. (2014). Diversity, culture and gender. In Stout-Rostron, S. (ed) *Business Coaching International: Transforming individuals and organizations*. Second Edition. London: Karnac. pp. 208–229.

Jarzabkowski, P. and Searle, R.H. (2004). Harnessing diversity and collective action in the top management team. *Long Range Planning*, 37: 399–419.

King, E.B., Hebi, M.R. and Beal, D.J. (2009). Conflict and co-operation in diverse workgroups. *Journal of Social Issues*, 65(2): 261–283.

Ludeman, K. (2009). Coaching with women. In Passmore, J. (ed.), *Diversity in Coaching: Working with gender, culture, race and age*. London: Association for Coaching; Philadelphia, PA: Kogan Page. pp. 237–254.

Ludeman, K. and Erlandson, E. (2004). Coaching the alpha male. *Harvard Business Review*, 82(5): 58–67.

Marques, D. (2014). Diversity, culture and gender. In Stout-Rostron, S (ed). *Business Coaching International: Transforming individuals and organizations*. Second Edition. London: Karnac. pp. 190–208.

Miller, C.C., Burke, L.M. and Glick, W.H. (1998). Cognitive diversity among upper-echelon executives: Implications for strategic decision processes. *Strategic Management Journal*, 19: 39–58.

Mindell, A. (2002). *The Deep Democracy of Open Forums: Practical steps to conflict prevention, and resolution for the family, workplace and world*. Charlottesville, VA: Hampton Roads.

Mohammed, S. and Angell, L.C. (2004). Surface- and deep-level diversity in workgroups: Examining the moderating effects of team orientation and team process on relationship conflict. *Journal of Organizational Behaviour*, 25: 1015–1039.

Motsoaledi, L. and Cilliers, F. (2012). Executive coaching in diversity from the systems psychodynamic perspective. *South African Journal of Industrial Psychology*, 38(2): 32–43.

Oakley, A. (1985). *Sex, Gender and Society*. Revised Edition. Aldershot: Gower.

Pelled, L.H. (1996). Demographic diversity, conflict, and workgroup outcomes: An intervening process theory. *Organization Science*, 7(6): 615–631.

Peltier, B. (2001). *The Psychology of Executive Coaching: Theory and application*. New York, NY: Brunner-Routledge.

Peltier, B. (2010). *The Psychology of Executive Coaching: Theory and application*. Revised Edition. New York, NY: Brunner-Routledge.

Perreault, S. (1997). Similarity and attraction among majority and minority groups in a multicultural context. *International Journal of Intercultural Relationships*, 21(1): 113–123.

Qin, J., Muenjohn, N. and Chhetri, P. (2014). A review of diversity conceptualizations: Variety, trends, and a framework. *Human Resource Development Review*, 13(2): 133–157.

Robbins, S.P. (2001). *Organizational Behaviour*. Englewood Cliffs, NJ: Prentice-Hall.

Roberson, Q.M. (2006). Disentangling the meanings of diversity and inclusion in organizations. *Group and Organization Management*, 31(2): 212–236.

Rosinski, P. (2003). *Coaching Across Cultures: New tools for leveraging national, corporate and professional differences*. London: Nicholas Brealey.

Simpson, R. and Lewis, P. (2007). *Voice, Visibility and the Gendering of Organizations: Management, work and organizations*. Hampshire: Palgrave Macmillan.

Skinner, S. (2014). Understanding the importance of gender and leader identity formation in executive coaching for senior women. *Coaching: An International Journal of Theory, Research and Practice*, 7(2): 102–114.

Spence, G.B. and Oades, L.G. (2011). Coaching with self-determination theory in mind: Using theory to advance evidence-based coaching practice. *International Journal of Evidence-Based Coaching and Mentoring*, 9(2): 37–55.

Stout-Rostron, S. (2014). *Business Coaching International: Transforming individuals and organizations*. Second Edition. London: Karnac.

Thomas, A. and Bendixen, M. (2000). The management implication of ethnicity in South Africa. *Journal of International Business Studies*, 31(3): 507–519.

Van Knippenberg, D., De Dreu, D.K.W. and Homan, A.C. (2004). Work group diversity and group performance: An integrative model and research agenda. *Journal of Applied Psychology*, 89: 1008–1022.

Vecchio, R.P. (2002). Leadership and gender advantage. *The Leadership Quarterly*, 13: 643–671.

14

Physicality in Coaching: Developing an Embodied Perspective

Peter Jackson

Many students of coaching would be excused for conceptualising coaching as a practice embedded primarily in language. Much of the rapidly expanding practitioner literature has focused on different formulations of skills, techniques and methodologies through which a client's issues can be discussed and explored. Concepts such as the body, embodiment and physicality have been largely absent. For example, within two generally excellent reviews of the field none of the eighteen chapters dealing with 'theoretical approaches' (Cox, Bachkirova and Clutterbuck, 2014) or 'single theory perspectives' (Stober and Grant, 2006) directly approached the topic of the coach's or the client's physicality. Yet physicality is not absent from practitioners' thinking or the practice itself (Matthews, 2013). There are also empirical and theoretical contributions from other fields (such as psychotherapy, outdoor education, phenomenology and cognition) that would contribute to an understanding of the physicality of coaching. However, in this area, as in other aspects of coaching, 'coaching practice has been largely disconnected from the peer reviewed literature' (Grant, Cavanagh and Parker, 2010, p. 158).

This chapter is intended to help re-establish a connection between coaching practice, its peer-reviewed literature in coaching and allied fields of knowledge. It commences by providing a working definition of physicality in coaching. This is followed by the presentation of a suggested conceptual framework that draws from philosophy and some emerging perspectives from cognitive science and other disciplines. A review of physicality in the coaching practitioner and peer-reviewed literature is then presented and related to this conceptual framework. Finally, implications for practice and for future directions in research are explored.

DEFINITIONS

In the context of this discussion, the definitions of physicality and coaching overlap and are to some extent interdependent. Beginning with an everyday understanding of the concept, physicality can mean everything pertaining to the body. This can include concepts at many different levels of analysis, from mechanical skills, appearance, behaviours and exercise to disease, or the endocrine and nervous systems. This comprehensive formulation, however, provides too little focus for debate and discussion. Conversely, it is possible to take too narrow a view of physicality, which is limited to that which is externally evident such as gross bodily movement, actions and aspects of appearance. This, as the review will demonstrate, would exclude opportunities to develop an understanding of some subtle practices, such as those based on felt experience (Gendlin, 1962, 1996, 2003). In order to present a pragmatic middle way, this chapter will define physicality in coaching as:

> The various ways in which the coach may notice his/her own physiological state, or that of the client, and draw attention to them in pursuit of the coaching process or outcome. This can include the coach choosing to actively manage the coaching locale, or their own positional relationships within it, as a way of affecting physiological state.

For the following discussion, a definition of coaching is also needed. After reviewing numerous definitions in the literature, the following general description of coaching was adopted, as proposed by Cox et al. (2014):

> Coaching is a human development process that involves structured, focused interaction and the use of appropriate strategies, tools and techniques to promote desirable and sustainable change for the benefit of the coachee and potentially for other stakeholders. (p. 1)

In order to focus specifically on physicality as defined above, the following boundaries are added to Cox et al.'s definition:

- coaching constitutes some form of discursive, dialogic process in addition to the physical; and,
- the coaching dynamic may include some unconscious aspects of the coach's behaviours, of the coaching situation (in terms of its locale), and of the coachee's experience.

Hence interventions primarily focused on feeling better, relieving physical symptoms, or physiological conditioning for their own sake (for example, massage, physiotherapy, physical training) are removed from the scope of the discussion, while actions that may be below full consciousness or are unintentional are permitted.

A CONCEPTUAL FRAMEWORK: FROM DUALISM TO EMBODIED PHENOMENOLOGY

As already noted, there has been a relative neglect of the body, the bodily, or the physical in the general corpus of coaching literature. While it is by no means a total absence (indeed this chapter will highlight several examples of relevant work), the neglect sits in stark contrast to some allied fields, such as body psychotherapy. It is proposed here that some of that neglect is because there is no ready framework within which to conceptualise where the body appears either in practice or in the literature. By looking at perspectives on the interaction from phenomenology, linguistics and psychotherapy, this section will suggest such a framework.

The typical starting point for thinking about the body in cognition and change involves a rejection of Descartes. As Strozzi-Heckler notes, 'when Descartes declared, "I think therefore I am," he removed the body from Western philosophy in one clean cut' (Strozzi-Heckler, 2014, p. 17). This view of Descartes, however, conflates Descartes with the European Enlightenment as a whole, whilst also arguing that his formulation elevated thinking over feeling (thereby relegating the importance of the body). Both positions are contentious. In the first instance, Descartes represented only one voice amongst a diversity of Enlightenment positions, and indeed, many of his more applied theories (such as the circulation of the blood) were very quickly countered. In the second instance, Descartes' basic argument was only that the act of thinking confirmed his existence (rather than made it important). So while it is fair that Descartes' dualism represents an 'abyssal separation between body and mind' (Damasio, 1994, p. 249), it would be wrong to use this as an excuse to reject other aspects of the Enlightenment such as rational science and therefore retreat into the esoteric.

While practitioner literature may simplify the issue of dualism, more theoretical work elsewhere may help in problematising the issues of mind–body in order to achieve a better understanding of its complexity. For example, recent discussions about the body in psychology (Sampson, 1998), sociology (Waskul and Vannini, 2006a) and philosophy (Clark, 2008) explicitly recognise the interaction and interdependence of meaning between the body-self and other internal (brain) and external entities (environment). Indeed many see meaning as residing as much in the body as in the brain. As Waskul and Vannini describe it, 'the body is … an enormous vessel of meaning of utmost significance to both personhood and society' (Waskul and Vannini, 2006b, p.3).

This more fluid ontological position enables a more integrative framework within which the discussion of 'physical' practices can take place. Many of these authors refer for their foundation to the philosophy of Merleau-Ponty, whose phenomenology described the sense of self and of the world emerging from an embodied interaction with that world:

> One's own body is in the world just as the heart is in the organism: it continuously breathes life into the visible spectacle, animates it and nourishes it from within, and forms a system with it. (Merleau-Ponty, 2012, p. 207)

For Merleau-Ponty the world is not observed from nowhere, but something continuous with the perceiver. This position predicts a number of elaborations. For example, scholars in the field of linguistics (Johnson, 1990; Lakoff and Johnson, 1999) have developed the idea that language emerges from embodied experience, with much of it a metaphorical reference to key dimensions in which we experience the world ('up-ness' vs 'down-ness'; 'in-ness' vs 'out-ness'). In addition, Röhricht et al. (2014) have argued for a radical enactive phenomenology, within which they conceptualise embodied cognition to be an experience in its own right, rather than an information processing mechanism. Relating it to the field of psychotherapy, they argue that 'an intersubjective embodied interaction that involves proprioception and kinaesthesia […] forms part of the clinical reasoning and assessment processes, whether the therapist or the patient are reflectively aware of it or not' (Röhricht et al., 2014, p. 14). The work of Merleau-Ponty, along with later elaborations of his embodied phenomenology, therefore represent a valuable lens through which to attempt to understand the potential for physicality in coaching.

Developing from a similar perspective, but with a more applied focus, Reich's theories lie behind many of the models that formulate the body as storing and expressing the memory of earlier experience. Reich first describes 'armor' as a defence against external stimuli, including analysis, as a threat to the patient's neurosis: 'a psychic defense apparatus' (Reich, 1972, p. 52). Through the tensing of different parts of the musculature, depending on the individual's issue, these characters are detectable by general demeanour, and Reich comes to the conclusion that, 'Psychic and somatic rigidity […] are not analogous manifestations, they are functionally identical' (p. 346). Reich's leap from traditional psychoanalysis was to see physical intervention for neurosis as inevitable: 'if we are really serious about the unitary concept of the organism […] then it is altogether out of the question to break up a living organism into character traits here, muscles there, and plasma functions elsewhere' (p. 357). Interest in body psychotherapy is growing after some period of decline since Reich (Totton, 2003) though Soth (2010) warns against adoption of bodywork as a 'technique', thereby swinging from one side of Damasio's (1994) 'abyssal separation' to the other.

From these foundations can be derived aspects of an 'embodied paradigm', consisting of ontological, epistemological and practice considerations. Ontologically, it recognises the continuity of *being-in-the-world* first conceptualised by Heidegger (1927) and further developed into an embodied phenomenology by Merleau-Ponty. Phenomenology and particularly embodied phenomenology emphasises what is knowable as experiential and situated. Consequently there is logic to body practices that facilitate an embodied experiencing that may be beyond the reach of external observation or expression through language. Table 14.1 shows this perspective on physicality by contrast with a 'classical' or conventional viewpoint. This presentation is not, however, intended as dogma. There is no obligation to embrace Merleau-Ponty before going for a walk with a client simply because it is useful. Neither is it intended to represent an either/or choice. Rather, it is intended to be used as a framework for discussing literature, one that may continue to develop with the contribution of practitioners and academics. It may also prove to be a useful point of reference for the development of practice and evidence, including the constructive flow of knowledge and understanding between paradigms.

Table 14.1 Contrasting embodied and classical perspectives on physicality

An embodied perspective	A classical perspective
ONTOLOGY	
Holistic, continuous, 'being-in-the-world'	Dualistic
EPISTEMOLOGY	
Phenomenological, relative, personal	Objective, scientific, explicit
PRAXIS	
Experiential, personalised, narrative, fluid.	Expert, didactic

PHYSICALITY IN THE COACHING LITERATURE

The practices discussed here are linked by the current conceptualisation of physicality and coaching as described above. They are presented in five themes that highlight conceptual linkages between practices. In the first section (*Somatic awareness and integrative practice*) different propositions are presented to explain how coaches and their clients might gain a better awareness of their own physicality, and how that awareness might help them. This section is assigned the largest portion of the discussion because integrative practice is the foundation from which many of the other themes emerge. Second, *Physicality as expressive of emotional and psychological state* deals with aspects of practices where physical self-presentation (whether conscious or unconscious) are considered symptomatic of underlying psychological conditions or patterns. Third, *Experiencing the client* explores the phenomenon of a practitioner's intuitive feel for their client. Fourth, *Rehearsal and enactment* are treated together as they both concern the physical demonstration of states or intentions – either in a safe, practice space, or in the real world. Finally, some researchers have also explored how the *Physical environment* can play a part in how they work with clients' behaviour and thinking. Although the impact on the individual's body is indirect in this case, it is very much a part of their experience of being in the world and is included for this reason.

Somatic Awareness and Integrative Practice

Integral Coaching
Developed by Hunt (2009) and grounded in integral theory (Wilber, 2000), integral coaching proposes the existence of a 'somatic line' as one of six 'lines of development',

which includes 'the capacity to access, include, and skilfully draw upon the energies of the gross, subtle, and causal realms' (Divine, 2009, p.47). Whilst a full discussion of integral theory is complex and beyond the scope of this chapter, a brief description of key concepts is necessary. In brief, Wilber (2000, 2006) describes energies as part of the outward (physical world) manifestation of the development from inert through consciousness to transpersonal spirituality. Within this system the *gross realm* refers to the non-living and the correlate forces studied in physics (strong nuclear, weak nuclear, electromagnetic, gravity). The *subtle realm* refers to living beings ranging through brain-active to conscious and the correlate energies (emotional, sexual, psychic). Finally, the *causal realm* refers to 'a vast, almost infinite overmental consciousness' (Wilber, 2000, p.38) that is experienced in deep, dreamless sleep. What Divine (2009) is describing is a sensitivity, through the body, to the nature of interaction in the world. In this context, the so-called 'subtle' realm overlaps with the current definition of physicality for the purposes of coaching. In an illustrative case study Divine describes a client somewhat out of touch with his physical and emotional state, an inability to access what those states might represent or what impact they might have on the people he interacts with on a daily basis (Divine, 2009, p49).

Divine is brief on actual methods, though she may have been directing her work at an integral theory audience rather than a coaching audience, and outcome research is scarce. Psycinfo returned two thesis abstracts for the search term 'integral coaching'. In a comparative case study, Stoneham (2009) used integral coaching as part of an intervention to help health leaders to develop leadership styles more attuned to the complex environments in which they work. Kennedy (2013) investigated self-assessed development of the 'use of self' of fifteen graduates of the Integral Coaching programme. The outcome measure in this study, however, was a proprietary instrument specifically measuring integral theory's concept of 'way of being' of the coach.

Somatic Coaching

Using the label 'somatic coaching', Strozzi-Heckler (2014) presents a complete coaching approach focused specifically on the integration of physical and psychological experience, conceptualising 'the human form as the unified space in which humans act, perceive, think, feel, sense, express emotions and moods and live their spiritual longing' (Strozzi-Heckler, 2014, p. 33). From this foundational rejection of substance dualism, the practice then acknowledges Reich's theory that trauma is held in the body (Reich, 1972; see also Rothschild, 2000). Strozzi-Heckler also acknowledges phenomenology as facilitating the development of 'somatics'. Strozzi-Heckler's methodology consists of three interlocking foci:

- Somatic Awareness: becoming aware of sensations
- Somatic Opening: breaking down habitual embodiments of experience, in particular the desire for 'belonging … acknowledgement, legitimization, connection, worth, dignity, and love' (p. 64)
- Somatic Practice: the commitments that are carried physically (and therefore can be changed).

Strean and Strozzi-Heckler (2009) provide fuller illustrations of how somatic 'practices' can help athletes in competition. They point out the non-explicit nature of understanding that is gained from such practices. 'In the same way that structures keep ideas in place, practices are crucial to clients shifting who they are' (Strean and Strozzi-Heckler, 2009, p. 93). Whilst developed from different theoretical foundations, somatic coaching appears to share considerable common ground with integral coaching. What little empirical evidence there is to support these approaches, however, appears to focus on internal dimensions and on the coaching process operating as intended rather than client outcomes.

Ontological Coaching

According to Sieler (2014) there are four interlocking theoretical components underpinning 'Ontological Coaching', one of which is 'philosophical investigations of the body, in particular the writings of Merleau-Ponty and Dewey' (Sieler, 2014, p. 104). From these foundations, seven 'premises' emerge that include 'the dynamic interplay between the three existential domains of language, emotions and body shapes perception and behaviour, and can be equated to the structure of the nervous system ... [such that] ... change occurs through the domains of language, emotions and body being perturbed to generate new meaning' (Sieler, 2014, p. 105). Applied in practice, ontological coaching would involve eliciting a statement from a client (which may relate to an issue they have) and encouraging them to observe their posture and feelings. The congruence between the three foci would then be investigated by coach and client jointly and attempt to be brought closer together with further practice (for a case illustration see Sieler, 2014, p. 111). No empirical investigations of ontological coaching could be found in the scholarly coaching literature.

Existential-Experimental (Embodied) Coaching

Madison (2012) proposes an existential-experiential approach that draws on a process called 'focusing'. According to Gendlin (2003) focusing involves making contact with a special kind of internal bodily awareness or *felt sense*, which is not an emotion per se (that can be readily identified) but a vaguer sense of meaning. When focusing is successful, Gendlin proposes, 'there is a physical change in the body, a felt shift. Then the problem seems different' (Gendlin, 2003, p. 11). Hence Madison describes his practice as *embodied coaching*, as it 'prioritises implicit experience over explicit technique or predictable outcomes' (Madison, 2012, p. 118). He argues that it is constructive to both identify and 'stay with' unresolved bodily experiences associated with strong emotions or emotional experiences. Given the human tendency to avoid such feelings, an embodied coach would seek to draw attention to these feelings and encourage clients to grant themselves permission to experience them from which different understandings should emerge. Although research into embodied coaching is not available, Gendlin's concept of focusing has been thoroughly explored. In the last five years alone, research has explored the use of focusing in working with trauma (Rappaport, 2010, 2015), in developing a sense of connectedness in the natural environment (Harris, 2013), the professional development of counselling psychologists (Siddiqui, 2012), and in the development of creative writing (Tobin and Tisdell, 2015).

Neuro-Linguistic Programming (NLP)

Widely used by many coaches, a technique from NLP called 'six step reframing' (Bandler and Grinder, 1990) considers felt experience in parts of the body as representing unconscious aspects of self. Clients who are attempting to change a habitual behaviour pattern or relate differently to a task (e.g. weight loss, performance anxiety) are encouraged to consult with parts of their unconscious. In response to a series of questions they are asked to gauge their physiological responses as indicative of their unconscious response. Throughout the process they are not encouraged to understand the *content* of the unconscious, rather the unconscious is enrolled in the creative process of finding more helpful behaviours. Whilst Bandler and Grindler give little explanation for how or why this works, the belief appears to be that it bypasses the conscious sense-making part of the mind that has not succeeded in achieving the desired change. Notably, Linder-Pelz and Hall (2007) have offered an Ericksonian perspective by suggesting that 'perceptions, behaviours and states can be [rapidly] changed when the conscious mind is bypassed, especially with the highly skilled use of language' (Linder-Pelz and Hall, 2007, p. 14).

The evidence-base for NLP as a whole is widely discussed and contentious (see Tosey and Mathison, 2007; Sturt et al., 2012). Whilst no empirical, peer-reviewed research could be found addressing the six step reframing technique in the literature, Sterman (1990) has described casework where it has been adapted for use in the therapeutic treatment of alcoholism.

Presence Based Coaching

Silsbee (2008) argues that the development of 'presence' is at the heart of learning and change and, therefore, also at the heart of coaching and leadership as 'presence evokes change in others' (p. 5). He states as a 'core assertion' that 'there are three doorways into presence: mind, body, and heart' (p. 3). With specific reference to the body (and reflecting the ideas of Merleau-Ponty and Heidegger), Silsbee (2008, p. 155) presents the following integration of embodiment concepts:

- Our shape perfectly reflects our history
- Our body determines our experience
- A wealth of sensation is available through our bodies
- Sensation provides an early warning system for our habits
- Practice through the body allows us to build, and stabilise, new competencies
- Joy and fulfillment are body experiences

In response to these principles Silsbee suggests five main strategies. First, the practice of *centering*, or engaging with an awareness of the body sensation. Second, the importance of *building somatic awareness* is emphasised in order to focus on sensation and delay moving to interpretation of what it seems to mean either socially or emotionally. For this, body-scan exercises are recommended. Third, *somatic self-observation* extends on this by seeking to develop awareness of sensations in response to others. Fourth, the somatic expression of urges are addressed through *working with urges*, which focuses attention on using somatic awareness to 'catch' conditioned responses. Finally, *taking up a body practice* (such as pilates, yoga, rock climbing) is recommended 'to build a body able to work in partnership' (Silsbee, 2008, p. 162). Silsbee's practice is closely related to Mindfulness. For a full discussion of Mindfulness and coaching, see Kemp (Chapter 21, this volume).

The six styles of practice explored in this section demonstrate various ways in which a reconnection with the bodily and one's own sense of the body is thought to facilitate progress in coaching. As noted, the theoretical influences vary and include more practice-oriented theories (e.g. Gendlin and Reich) and more philosophical theories (e.g. Wilber and Merleau-Ponty). In addition, little formalised empirical evidence exists to support the efficacy of these approaches and, of the case studies that do exist, most are carried out by practitioners who have some vested interest in the approach they are reporting on. Directions for future research in this area will be considered in the last section of this chapter.

Physicality as Expressive of Emotional and Psychological State

The concepts underlying the practices described in this section are also based on a model of mind–body interconnectedness. Here they concern the outward manifestation of the linkage rather than the body–mind experience in its own right. The client may or may not be aware of these manifestations, though they may be visible to the coach and others.

Whitworth et al. (2007) express a position that meaning is developed through deeply embedded habits of mind conditioned by language, culture and roles. Furthermore they argue that 'there will also be a posture to that perspective, sometimes quite literally, because people embody the perspective they are in and portray it physically, in their bodies' (Whitworth et al., 2007, p. 134).

Examples illustrate how mood is reflected in posture, for example, when talking about a topic in a positive (uplifting, optimistic) light compared with talking about the same topic more negatively (in terms of risk, unpleasantness). Although this position echoes Silsbee's (and earlier Reich's) claim that experience is carried in the body, the operation of the concept for Whitworth et al. is more narrowly situated in the moment, or the particular perspective being expressed at the time.

Cotter's (1996) description of the use of 'bioenergetics' to support personal development of managers attending courses at Cranfield University in the UK represents a step further towards typing. Bioenergetic analysis is Alexander Lowen's development of Reich's concept that the unity of mind and body means that emotional and psychological traits are equally expressed and retained in the body (Lowen, 1994). Lowen's development of this concept as bioenergetics relates particular physical features to sub-optimal developmental experiences at specific stages of an individual's childhood, resulting in five body–mind types. Cotter's use of bioenergetics with managers with generally normal functioning therefore departs from Lowen's original therapeutic objective. The body–mind types are seen much like personality types rather than pathologies, albeit reflecting areas for development as well as strengths. Embodiment is seen as essential in bioenergetics to bring about enduring change. Participants are encouraged to release the tensions typically associated with particular traits or patterns of behaviour, for example, a propensity for anger can be helped through physical activity to release tension in the upper back, shoulders and face. Physical activity will release emotion that must also be discussed in order to integrate learning and change. The resultant integration is described as exhilarating.

The well-known NLP technique of observing eye-movement can be seen in a similar way. Here eye movements are considered to indicate both the preferred representational system (PRS) and the cognitive mode of thinking at the time (memory or imagination). Bandler and Grinder (1990) claim that one of the key skills they modeled from the practice of Virginia Satir was the ability to match the client's use of language according to whether they predominantly used visual, auditory or kinaesthetic references. Eye movement is used as a cue to which system the client is using. Bandler and Grinder (1990) point out that the pattern of cues may be individualised, though there is a common pattern for right-handed individuals (commonly reversed for left-handed people). They therefore recommend that the practitioner determine experimentally the pattern in use by an individual client by using questions which are expected to activate different systems: 'What colour are the carpets in your car' (visual/remembered); 'What does cat fur feel like?' (kinaesthetic). It is noted that the concept of a stable PRS and its expression through eye movement are contested (Sharpley, 1987; Heap, 1988).

The various positions founded on the external expression of internal processing each have their own evidence base. The general concept may also gain support from the concept of embodied cognition – the extent to which 'conceptual content is reductively constituted by information that is represented within the sensory and motor systems' (Mahon and Caramazza, 2008, p. 59). Of particular interest in this area of coaching is the phenomenon of 'power posing', where Carney et al. (2010) have shown that adopting expansive 'power' poses as opposed to closed, contractive, 'low-power' poses produces short-term changes in testosterone and cortisol levels.

Experiencing the Client

A number of coaching practitioner texts suggest various ways in which coaches can use the immediate physical experience of being with their client to explore dynamics within the relationship. The idea of the 'self as tool' (Bluckert, 2006) is sometimes expressed as an advanced form of listening (Whitworth et al., 2007; Rogers, 2012) or by reference to the concept of counter-transference (de Haan, 2011; Sandler, 2011; Lee, 2014). Indeed Orenstein (2002) makes a clear argument that the counter-transferential experience is central to the 'use of the self'.

Empirical research investigating the nature of the unconscious dynamics in coaching is scarce. Nonetheless, assertions that practitioners should take heed of such dynamics appear to be received and taken up. In a survey of 235 practitioners in the UK, Turner (2010) found that between 83% of respondents considered transference when they reviewed their coaching sessions and 77% counter-transference; 90% answered that coach training should include training in how to handle unconscious processes. The survey had significant limitations as regards methods, though it does successfully demonstrate that the idea of a personal, felt response is at least recognised as an agenda in the coaching field.

In a smaller qualitative study of nine coaches' engagement with emotion Cremona (2010) found that as part of their repertoire of strategies to handle emotion in the coaching session, participants both checked their own physical responses and reflected back the client's physical (especially postural) appearance.

Looking more closely at the physical manifestation of such processes, Shaw (2004) summarises a qualitative study involving over 90 participating psychotherapists. He reports specific physiological responses, and that psychotherapists tended to explain these as aspects of a sympathetic or transferential process. Examples included feelings of tension across the shoulders as a client approached a topic about which they were anxious; feeling hungry or sick after seeing clients with bulimia or anorexia.

As part of the widely used 'seven-eyed model' of supervision which is applied both in coaching and psychotherapy, Hawkins and Smith propose that insights into a case become available to coaching supervisors when the coaching client is imaginatively brought 'into the room' through detailed and accurate description by the coach (Hawkins and Smith, 2013). Rather than providing factual data, it is argued that this detailed description offers the supervisor an immediate sense of the coaching client through their experience of the coach. They warn of the supervisee's tendency to offer interpretations rather than their own immediate experience and the tendency to edit the fine detail of the client's physical expression out of their account. The emphasis of the technique is on deferring diagnosis or theorising. The process of gleaning meaning from this vicarious encounter is not made explicit, though it is embedded in their discussion of the parallel process, transference and counter-transference within the seven-eyed model of supervision.

The role of experiencing the client is also evident in Gestalt-influenced coaching literature. The Gestalt approach adopts an intentional focus on awareness of the self and experience as it presents in the moment and away from solutions, goal-setting or performance criteria (Bluckert, 2006, 2014; Leary-Joyce, 2014). Bluckert describes how the coach's feedback to the client on physical aspects of their encounter in the here and now forms part of the 'awareness' stage of the Gestalt 'cycle of experience' (Bluckert, 2006, p. 139).

A number of the practices that acknowledge an integrated body–mind also pay attention to the possibility of an embodied nature of the coach–client interaction. Hence, Hunt outlines specific body awareness as part of the practitioner's training in Integral Coaching, in order to 'hold the full complexity of another human being with somatic patience, presence, and courage' (2009, p. 19). Silsbee (2008) emphasises the role of the coach's own presence in managing the 'relational field' between coach and client and Madison's (2012) account of Experiential–Existential coaching is also imbued with the calls for the coach to access their own felt sense as a tool in the coaching process.

The phenomenon of embodied counter-transference is widely recognised in psychotherapy. Rowan (1998) describes how it appears in different psychotherapeutic modalities and Totton (2003) outlines the range of writers providing accounts of the phenomenon. A qualitative study by Kennedy (2013) exploring the relationship between integral development and coaches' use of the self argued that students of an integral coaching programme reported enhanced presence and authenticity as well as use of self as an instrument.

There is a notable interest in the practitioner community that mirror neuron theory provides an explanation and mechanism for such phenomena as empathy and embodied counter-transference. As a product of what to many practitioners appears as 'hard' science it is appealing, but needs to be treated with caution. As Carramazza et al. (2014) have outlined, mirror neuron theory and research to investigate it are at an early stage. Research to date has largely looked at the phenomenon in primates, focuses primarily on the restricted scope of action gestures (not emotional mirroring) and that assumptions that mirror neurons are necessarily motor neurons based on their location are unsubstantiated.

Rehearsal and Enactment

The previous sections have illustrated how various practitioners conceptualise the body–mind and the impact this conceptualisation is thought to have on the intersubjective experience. Rehearsal and enactment represent two ways in which somatic experience might be used not only to facilitate insight, but to enable action. The terms rehearsal and enactment are used here, respectively, to refer to the physical acting out of possible behaviours in the coaching room, and to the transfer of those behaviours into the real world of the client's lifespace. In some practices, these two domains are not differentiated.

Hawkins and Smith urge a form of rehearsal to encourage coaches to 'create the shift in the room'. They argue that a cognitive resolution is insufficient and a desired change for the client must be somehow enacted during the session (Hawkins and Smith, 2013, p. 264). Rehearsal also appears in Peterson's (2006) description of behavioural coaching which identifies 'real world practice' and 'the opportunity for feedback' as key stages in the 'developmental pipeline' (Peterson, 2006, p. 54). Peterson's emphasis is slightly more on enactment than on rehearsal, emphasising change in work and life settings over the coaching session.

Reflecting the behavioural mechanisms of Hawkins and Smith (2013) and Peterson (2006), Strozzi-Heckler (2014) states, 'we are an anthology of the practices we've been engaged in over a lifetime' (p. 74). Again, insight is not enough, but for Strozzi-Heckler practice is more about new attitudes: 'Practices help develop a "new shape" that allows us to be more present, open, and connected' (Strozzi-Heckler, 2014, p. 76). Further, Hunt talks not only about making new patterns habitual – here referred to as 'New Way of Being' (NWOB) as opposed to the 'Current Way of Being' (CWOB) – but also as a new perspective on the previous construction of self: 'As the NWOB becomes embodied over time, the client is able to work with their CWOB aspects through the capacities of their NWOB' (Hunt, 2009, p. 15). Hamill (2011) provides a specific example. In this case, an individual's tendency for deference in conflict situations is not only identified (creating insight for the individual) but also linked to her habitual physical behaviours (posture, gesture, facial communication). She is then encouraged to practice – in the safety of the training/consulting relationship – the physical behaviours that would be associated with a more assertive response to conflict, that is, 'to take a stand for her dignity' (Hamill, 2011, p. 9).

In systemic coaching (Whittington, 2012) the constellation method is borrowed from family systems therapy (Manné, 2012) and applied in a coaching context. In a constellation the facilitator positions individuals from a group of participants (who are not involved directly in the client's issue) to represent aspects of the client's problem system. They may represent colleagues, family members, organisations or even abstract concepts. They may be asked to express their feelings, or to take actions under the direction of the facilitator, but they do not need to 'role play'. Constellations are intended to rely on the non-explicit subjectivity triggered through spatial enactment of a systemic scenario. 'Representatives' are able to feel and say things pertinent to the issue holder – or at least things which the issue holder can make sense of – without knowledge of the scenario that they are 'sculpting'. Hence there is a melding of felt experience, embodied emotion and metaphor. It is thought that in general the issue holder does not feel the need to understand the mechanism (Whittington, 2012).

Rehearsal appears to be a popular technique in practice. Cremona (2010) found that coaches widely used rehearsal, the Gestalt 'empty chair' technique and visualisation from alternative perspectives in responding to clients' presentation of emotional content. Also participants in an action research project to explore the use Gardiner's multiple intelligences in coach/mentor relationships reported by Harding (2006) used self-observation via video and imaginative perspective-taking on a goal supported by moving to different parts of the room.

Physical Environment

The physical environment may be used in different ways to facilitate change through coaching. The following examples show the potential effect on individual defences, the intersubjective experience and the metaphor of perspective-taking.

Kemp (2006) explores the potential for the use of techniques and concepts from adventure programming in coaching practice. Kemp identifies the key aspects of such an approach in the following attributes: an experience of uncertainty, risk or (possibly emotional) discomfort; with an element of problem solving; in a situation to some extent contained by the coach; who also takes a role in the setting up and drawing out of learning. The *nature* of the adventure is not pre-specified, indeed the experience of uncertainty and risk are subjective and individual, and by extension adventure does not even need to imply physical effort. It is the novelty of the environment that is thought to be significant, as it is in a novel environment that clients can break out of patterned ways of thinking about their own capability. At the same time, the focus of attention on the detail of problem solving allows clients to forget or ignore their usual defensive routines. The coach may frame the experience in order to underline the potential learning points for clients to carry into their work-life.

Corazon et al. (2011) attempt to theorise the use of metaphor for learning in outdoor therapy, referring to the embodied nature of metaphor (Johnson, 1990). They argue that the engagement with parallel physical experience may 'strengthen the consolidation of the explicit learning entailed in the metaphor' (Corazon et al., 2011, p. 166). Examples of paths, seeds, growth, change, orientation are suggested.

Russell and Farnham (2004) review evidence supporting arguments that the experience of the wilderness is psychologically restorative, that physical activity is an outlet for negative emotions, and that graded physical activity has positive impact on self-esteem and self-efficacy. Each of these effects could be seen to enhance the coaching process and outcomes. An explanation of one restorative effect is attempted in Kaplan's (1995) proposition of directed attention fatigue (Attention Restoration Theory – ART). Kaplan argues that sustained attention on topics of little intrinsic interest may require active inhibition of distractions. As this is an active process it is subject to fatigue. Kaplan goes on to argue that attention to intrinsically interesting topics ('fascination') should allow the individual respite from this effort. So natural settings are restorative because they offer both a 'soft fascination' and the experience of simply being away from usual concerns. The experience of 'being away' is further dependent on the extent of the environment (sufficient for a degree of immersion) and its compatibility (to the extent that it does not become a challenge in itself, unrelated to the individual's purpose). Empirical evidence cited by Kaplan appears to support at least the notion of the restorative effect of natural settings on attention, if not the process hypothesised. In a later experimental design, Kaplan and colleagues (Berman, Jonides and Kaplan, 2008) demonstrate the specific enhancements of cognitive tasks in line with predictions from ART. In addition, Berto (2005) shows experimentally that viewing photographs of restorative environments improved performance in subsequent sustained attention tests.

PROGRESSING THE FIELD: PRACTICE AND RESEARCH

The starting point of this chapter was the apparent neglect of physicality in the coaching practitioner literature. Indeed, the body and physicality are largely absent from the majority of practitioner and professional texts, and coaching-specific research into physicality is largely limited to descriptions of practitioners' own idiosyncratic practices. However, the previous sections exploring the five themes of physicality demonstrate the following points. First, that various implications of various aspects of physicality are embedded in many practices. Second, that these considerations may be important in fully understanding the coaching process. Third, that some historical precedents can be traced through more mature disciplines such as body psychotherapy and adventure programming. Finally, that cognitive and social psychology offer theory and evidence to help understand some of these phenomena. In summary, physicality has a very real place in coaching practice, with some theory to guide it and some evidence to indicate its significance. Consequently, from a practice perspective, there may be a great deal to be added to professional education and development. Some of this is already available, though to some extent, this has to be dependent on a stronger evidence base.

We must therefore look at the ways in which research can help to extend current knowledge on the value and importance of the 'embodied perspective' in coaching. Key research questions might address:

- What embodied practices are currently being utilised by practising coaches?
- In what ways are embodied practices introduced to clients and then delivered?
- What is the impact of different embodied practices on clients?
- To what extent are these practices perceived (by coaches and clients) as being relevant to different coaching challenges?
- Can aspects of the intersubjective be effectively operationalised in order to enhance their empirical investigation?

Naturally these questions raise methodological issues. From a positivist perspective, the constructs at play are poorly defined. For example, how would embodied counter-transference be measured? How do we observe a coach's intuition? There may be a tendency to borrow from harder sciences, and indeed, in earlier sections there are examples of where this is helpful. This is not a complete answer, however, as there is a risk of producing findings that are too abstract, too divorced from the context of practice, to be useful. They may be relevant only in their original contexts.

Whilst the embodied perspective does seem to lend itself well to phenomenological, interpretivist research methods (as constructs like self and the world become difficult to separate), it is recognised that quantitative methods have a great contribution to the continued development of coaching knowledge. It is suggested that there is a key role for exploratory research in establishing useful hypotheses as this potentially gives rise qualitative or quantitative projects. Whatever may occur, new methodological solutions to tap into the more context-dependent aspects of physicality in coaching may need to be embraced.

CONCLUSION

This chapter was motivated to some extent by the absence of the body from the professional discourse. To read the main bulk of the practitioner and peer-reviewed literature, as well as training courses and professional forums, it is as if the body does not play a part in coaching practice. For a number of reasons, the body and the physicality of the participants in the coaching interaction have not been extensively explored in the coaching practice or research literatures. Seeing the field from an embodied perspective, however, it is hard *not* to see both their presence, and the value of understanding them better. Accepting and engaging with this embodied perspective is the first step to developing a more coherent professional knowledge base.

REFERENCES

Bandler, R. and Grinder, J. (1990) *Frogs into princes: Introduction to Neurolinguistic Programming*. Revised edition. Enfield: Eden Grove Editions.

Berman, M. G., Jonides, J. and Kaplan, S. (2008) 'The cognitive benefits of interacting with nature', *Psychological Science*, 19(12), pp. 1207–1212.

Berto, R. (2005) 'Exposure to restorative environments helps restore attentional capacity', *Journal of Environmental Psychology*, 25(3), pp. 249–259.

Bluckert, P. (2006) *Psychological dimensions of executive coaching*. Maidenhead: Open University Press.

Bluckert, P. (2014) 'The Gestalt approach to coaching', in Cox, E., Bachkirova, T., and Clutterbuck, D. (eds) *The complete handbook of coaching*. 2nd edn. London: Sage, pp. 77–90.

Caramazza, A., Anzellotti, S., Strand, L. and Lingnau, A. (2014) 'Embodied cognition and mirror neurons: A critical assessment', *Annual Review of Neuroscience*, 37, pp. 1–15.

Carney, D. R., Cuddy, A. J. C. and Yap, A. J. (2010) 'Power posing: Brief nonverbal displays affect neuroendocrine levels and risk tolerance', *Psychological Science*, 21(10), pp. 1363–1368.

Clark, A. (2008) *Supersizing the mind: Embodiment, action, and cognitive extension*. Oxford: Oxford University Press.

Corazon, S., Schilhab, T. and Stigsdotter, U. (2011) 'Developing the therapeutic potential of embodied cognition and metaphors in nature-based therapy: Lessons from theory to practice', *Journal of Adventure Education & Outdoor Learning*, 11(2), pp. 161–171.

Cotter, S. (1996) 'Using bioenergetics to develop managers: Ten years of practical application of body–mind psychology with over a thousand managers at Cranfield University', *Journal of Management Development*, 15, pp. 8–16.

Cox, E., Bachkirova, T. and Clutterbuck, D. (eds) (2014) *The complete handbook of coaching*. 2nd edn. London: Sage.

Cremona, K. (2010) 'Coaching and emotions: An exploration of how coaches engage and think about emotion', *Coaching: An International Journal of Theory, Research & Practice*, 3(1), pp. 46–59.

Damasio, A. R. (1994) *Descartes' error: Emotion, rationality and the human brain*. New York: Putnam.

Divine, L. (2009) 'A Unique View into You', *Journal of Integral Theory and Practice, V4. 1*, 4(1), pp. 41–67.

Gendlin, E. T. (1962) *Experiencing and the creation of meaning: A philosophical and psychological approach to the subjective*. Evanston, IL: Northwestern University Press.

Gendlin, E. T. (1996) *Focusing-oriented psychotherapy: A manual of the experiential method*. New York: Guilford Press.

Gendlin, E. T. (2003) *Focusing*. London: Random House.

Grant, A. M., Cavanagh, M. J. and Parker, H. M. (2010) 'The state of play in coaching today: A comprehensive review of the field', *International Review of Industrial and Organizational Psychology 2010*, 25, pp. 125–167.

de Haan, E. (2011) *Relational coaching: Journeys towards mastering one-to-one learning*. Chichester: John Wiley & Sons.

Hamill, P. (2011) 'Embodied leadership: Towards a new way of developing leaders', *Strategic HR Review*, 10(5), pp. 5–10.

Harding, C. (2006) 'Using the multiple intelligences as a learning intervention: A model for coaching and mentoring', *International Journal of Evidence Based Coaching and Mentoring*, 4(2), pp. 19–41.

Harris, A. (2013) 'Gendlin and ecopsychology: Focusing in nature', *Person-Centered and Experiential Psychotherapies*, 12(4), pp. 330–343.

Hawkins, P. and Smith, N. (2013) *Coaching, mentoring and organizational consultancy: Supervision, skills and development*. 2nd edn. Maidenhead: Open University Press.

Heap, M. (1988) 'Neurolinguistic Programming: An interim verdict', in Heap, M. (ed.) *Hypnosis: Current clinical, experimental and forensic practices*. London: Croom Helm, pp. 268–280.

Heidegger, M. (1927) *Being and time: A translation of 'Sein und Zeit'*. Translated by J. Stambaugh. Albany: State University of New York Press.

Hunt, J. (2009) 'Transcending and including our Current Way of Being', *Journal of Integral Theory and Practice*, 4(1), pp. 1–20.

Johnson, M. (1990) *The body in the mind: The bodily basis of meaning, imagination and reason*. 2nd edn. Chicago: University of Chicago Press.

Kaplan, S. (1995) 'The restorative benefits of nature: Toward an integrative framework', *Journal of Environmental Psychology*, 15(3), pp. 169–182.

Kemp, T. (2006) 'An adventure-based framework for coaching', in Stober, D. R. and Grant, A. M. (eds) *Evidence based coaching handbook: Putting best practices to work for your clients*. Hoboken, NJ: Wiley.

Kennedy, D. L. (2013) *The impact of development on coaches' use of self as instrument*. PhD thesis. Fielding Graduate University.

Lakoff, G. and Johnson, M. (1999) *Philosophy in the flesh: The embodied mind and its challenge to Western thought*. New York: Basic Books.

Leary-Joyce, J. (2014) *The fertile void: Gestalt coaching at work*. St Albans: AoEC Press.

Lee, G. (2014) 'The psychodynamic approach to coaching', in Cox, E., Bachkirova, T., and Clutterbuck, D. (eds) *The complete handbook of coaching*. 2nd edn. London: Sage, pp. 21–33.

Linder-Pelz, S. and Hall, L. M. (2007) 'The theoretical roots of NLP-based coaching', *The Coaching Psychologist*, 3(1), pp. 12–15.

Lowen, A. (1994) *Bioenergetics: The revolutionary therapy that uses the language of the body to heal the problems of the mind*. New York: Arkana.

Madison, G. (2012) 'Let your body be your coach: An experiential–existential perspective on embodied coaching', in Van Deurzen, E. and Hanaway, M. (eds) *Existential perspectives on coaching*. Basingstoke: Palgrave Macmillan, pp. 117–127.

Mahon, B. Z. and Caramazza, A. (2008) 'A critical look at the embodied cognition hypothesis and a new proposal for grounding conceptual content', *Journal of Physiology-Paris*, 102(1–3), pp. 59–70.

Manné, J. (2012) *Family constellations: A practical guide to uncovering the origins of family conflict*. Berkeley, CA: North Atlantic Books.

Matthews, T. (2013) 'More than a brain on legs: An exploration of working with the body in coaching', *International Journal of Evidence Based Coaching & Mentoring*, Special Issue (7), pp. 26–38.

Merleau-Ponty, M. (2012) *Phenomenology of Perception*. Translated by D. A. Landes. Abingdon: Routledge.

Orenstein, R. L. (2002) 'Executive coaching – it's not just about the executive', *The Journal of Applied Behavioral Science*, 38(3), pp. 355–374.

Peterson, D. B. (2006) 'People are complex and the world is messy: A behavior-based approach to executive coaching', in Stober, D. R. and Grant, A. M. (eds) *Evidence based coaching handbook: Putting best practices to work for your clients*. Hoboken, NJ: Wiley, pp. 51–76.

Rappaport, L. (2010) 'Focusing-oriented art therapy: Working with trauma', *Person-Centered and Experiential Psychotherapies*, 9(2), pp. 128–142.

Rappaport, L. (2015) 'Focusing-oriented expressive arts therapy and mindfulness with children and adolescents experiencing trauma', in Malchiodi, C. A. (ed.) *Creative interventions with traumatized children*. 2nd edn. New York, NY, US: Guilford Press, pp. 301–323.

Reich, W. (1972) *Character Analysis*. 3rd edn. Translated by V. Carfagno. New York: Farrar, Straus and Giroux.

Rogers, J. (2012) *Coaching skills: A handbook*. 3rd edn. Maidenhead: Open University Press.

Röhricht, F., Gallagher, S., Geuter, U. and Hutto, D. D. (2014) 'Embodied cognition and body psychotherapy: The construction of new therapeutic environments', *Sensoria: A Journal of Mind, Brain & Culture*, 10(1), pp. 11–20.

Rothschild, B. (2000) *The body remembers: The psychophysiology of trauma and trauma treatment*. London: WW Norton & Company.

Rowan, J. (1998) 'Linking: Its place in therapy', *International Journal of Psychotherapy*, 3(3), pp. 245–254.

Russell, K. and Farnham, J. (2004) 'A concurrent model of the wilderness therapy process', *Journal of Adventure Education & Outdoor Learning*, 4(1), pp. 39–55.

Sampson, E. (1998) 'Establishing embodiment in psychology', in Stam, H. (ed.) *The body and psychology*. London: Sage.

Sandler, C. (2011) *Executive coaching*. Maidenhead: Open University Press.

Sharpley, C. F. (1987) 'Research findings on neurolinguistic programming: Nonsupportive data or an untestable theory?', *Journal of Counseling Psychology*, 34(1), pp. 103–107.

Shaw, R. (2004) 'Psychotherapist embodiment', *Counselling & Psychotherapy Journal*, 15(4), pp. 14–17.

Siddiqui, N. I. (2012) 'How does a second-wave cognitive behavioural practitioner manage a transition to third-wave practice?', *Counselling Psychology Review*, 27(2), pp. 36–51.

Sieler, A. (2014) 'Ontological coaching', in Cox, E., Bachkirova, T., and Clutterbuck, D. (eds) *The complete handbook of coaching*. 2nd edn. London: Sage.

Silsbee, D. (2008) *Presence-based coaching: Cultivating self-generative leaders through mind, body, and heart*. San Franscisco: Jossey Bass.

Soth, M. (2010) 'The return of the repressed body: Not a smooth affair', *The Psychotherapist*, (47), pp. 19–21.

Sterman, C. M. (1990) 'A specific neuro-linguistic programming technique effective in the treatment of alcoholism', in Sterman, C. M. (ed.) *Neuro-linguistic programming in alcoholism treatment*. Binghamton, NY: The Haworth Press, pp. 91–103.

Stober, D. R. and Grant, A. (2006) *Evidence based coaching handbook: Putting best practices to work for your clients*. Hoboken, NJ: John Wiley & Sons.

Stoneham, D. (2009) *Changing practices, transforming paradigms: An appreciative approach to developing integral leaders*. PhD thesis. California Institute of Integral Studies.

Strean, W. B. and Strozzi-Heckler, R. (2009) '(The) body (of) knowledge: Somatic contributions to the practice of sport psychology', *Journal of Applied Sport Psychology*, 21(1), pp. 91–98.

Strozzi-Heckler, R. (2014) *The art of somatic coaching: Embodying skillful action, wisdom, and compassion*. Berkeley, California: North Atlantic Books.

Sturt, J., Ali, S., Robertson, W., Metcalfe, D., Grove, A., Bourne, C. and Bridle, C. (2012) 'Neurolinguistic programming: A systematic review of the effects on health outcomes', *British Journal of General Practice*, 62(604), pp. e757–e764.

Tobin, J. A. and Tisdell, E. J. (2015) 'I know down to my ribs: A narrative research study on the embodied adult learning of creative writers', *Adult Education Quarterly*, 65(3), pp. 215–231.

Tosey, P. and Mathison, J. (2007) 'Fabulous creatures of HRD: A critical natural history of neuro-linguistic programming', in. *8th International Conference on Human Resource Development Research & Practice across Europe*, Oxford Brookes University.

Totton, N. (2003) *Body psychotherapy: An introduction*. Maidenhead: Open University Press.

Turner, E. (2010) 'Coaches' views on the relevance of unconscious dynamics to executive coaching', *Coaching: An International Journal of Theory, Research and Practice*, 3(1), pp. 12–29.

Waskul, D. and Vannini, P. (eds) (2006a) *Body/embodiment: Symbolic interaction and the sociology of the body*. Aldershot: Ashgate Publishing Limited.

Waskul, D. and Vannini, P. (2006b) 'The body in symbolic interaction', in Waskul, D. and Vannini, P. (eds) *Body/embodiment: Symbolic interaction and the sociology of the body*. Aldershot: Ashgate Publishing Limited.

Whittington, J. (2012) *Systemic coaching and constellations: An introduction to the principles, practices and application*. London: Kogan Page.

Whitworth, L., Kimsey-House, K., Kimsey-House, H. and Sandahl, P. (2007) *Co-active coaching: New skills for coaching people toward success in work and life*. Mountain View, CA: Davies-Black Publishing.

Wilber, K. (2000) *Integral psychology: Consciousness, spirit, psychology, therapy*. Boston: Shambhala Publications.

Wilber, K. (2006) *Excerpt G: Toward a comprehensive theory of subtle energies*. Available at: http://www.kenwilber.com/Writings/PDF/ExcerptG_KOSMOS_2004.pdf (Accessed: 7 July 2015).

15

Working with Emotions in Coaching

Elaine Cox

INTRODUCTION

The part emotions play in coaching is an area that is largely under theorised, despite recognition that emotions have a fundamental part to play in the reasoning process and memory formation (Taylor, 2001) and that both of these functions are vital to the coaching process. From a coaching perspective very few researchers have examined any aspects of emotion and the motivations and drivers associated with them. Hefferon (2013) for example only positions her discussion of the role of emotions in coaching within the field of positive psychology, appearing to link emotions entirely with the quest for happiness and wellbeing. This is indicative of the lack of attention paid to the role of emotions in a coaching setting. On the other hand, researchers in other fields explain emotions as having an important role in formulating ethical judgments (Nussbaum, 2004), as creating meaning (Dirkx, 2008; Greenberg 2004), and more recently as playing a role in organisational behaviour (Ashkanasy and Humphrey, 2011) and organisational compassion (Simpson, Clegg and Pitsis, 2014). In this chapter therefore, it is necessary to bring together a range of theories and research from other disciplines that have a bearing on the meaning and use of emotions in coaching.

In order to define and discuss what is meant by working with emotion in coaching, the chapter begins by examining ways in which emotion can be apparent in coaching. It then moves, in the second section, to investigate the nature and function of emotions in general. Then, drawing on theories of emotion from key disciplines including sociology and psychology, the third section examines the perception and role of emotions specifically in organisations where the majority of coaching takes place. In this section the concepts of emotional intelligence, emotion regulation and emotional labour emerge as significant.

The fourth section returns to working with emotion in a coaching context and this leads into a conclusion presenting an emotional climate inventory that explicitly relates the findings of the chapter with gaps in current coaching and emotion research.

WAYS EMOTION IS EVIDENT IN COACHING

Working with emotion in the helping disciplines, whether in therapy, counselling or coaching, is usually understood to mean the recognition and interception of clients' feelings, such that they are brought into consciousness in order to work with them in some way. This work might involve some form of transformation of the emotion, attempts at regulation or just encouraging acceptance so that the client can move forward.

Emotions play a significant role in everyone's lives. It is inevitable therefore that coaches and clients experience emotions during coaching sessions. In 2007, Bachkirova and Cox examined the personal theories of emotion that organisational coaches hold, suggesting that 'complex actions of individuals are affected by personal theories even when they are not conscious and/or articulated' (2007: 601). Their findings offer examples of what they term the 'emotionality of coaching' (603) and pinpoint where in the coaching process emotion might be detected:

- A client could arrive in a state of emotional turmoil, and this may undermine previously organised thoughts or behaviour.
- During the coaching some feelings related to events in the client's life may intrude on their goal-directed focus and may interrupt it. The intrusion may persist over time and override other plans.
- The client seems to be influenced by some seemingly insignificant details such as a tone of the coach's voice, facial expression or small details of the environment.
- Some expressions of emotion by the coach, such as smiling, laughter or even expression of some negative emotions, may impact the working relationship with a client further, adding to rapport and mutual understanding.
- The coach could experience a strong feeling, e.g. that something in the process is not right even when there are no rational indications.

Bachkirova and Cox (2007: 605) also reported three different ways in which emotions are perceived by coaches. The first perception is that emotions signify a client problem that needs extra intervention from the coach – one which it would be better to have under control, or to shape in order to resolve the issue. The second view is that emotions are 'normal and inevitable': they need attention in order to make sense of what is indicated as much any other behavioural phenomenon, but it is unnecessary to control them. The third perception recognises that emotions are good signs, indicating important developments in the coaching process: the coach facilitates exploration, staying with the emotion to allow full expression. Thus emotions might be successfully used in coaching for motivating clients.

Bachkirova and Cox's findings reveal that the coaches' attitudes to emotions at work followed a similar ambiguous pattern to that identified by Fineman (2000). They were polarised around perceiving emotions as either very helpful and a useful source of motivation, or as contributing to difficulties in the workplace.

In a parallel paper, Cox and Bachkirova (2007) reported that coaches often experienced considerable uneasiness when faced with overt displays of emotion by clients. They highlighted how coaches deal with the difficult emotions they encounter in their practice, defining difficult emotional situations as 'those that give the coach a 'bad feeling', i.e. those that tend make the coach feel uncomfortable in some way' (Cox and Bachkirova, 2007: 180). A range of client emotions was identified as being more difficult to work with, especially anger, apathy and resignation, lack of drive, despair, hopelessness. This list supports the view that some emotions are more difficult than others to empathise and work with. Tiedens (2001) similarly suggests that depression and fear elicited negative emotions by evoking uncertainty and pessimism. Cox and Bachkirova further acknowledged that 'what is termed a difficult emotion may vary from coach to coach and be dependent upon a number of internal and external factors' (2007: 180).

The coaches in Cox and Bachkirova's study expressed uncertainty in how to handle emotions that they perceived as difficult: there seemed to be a range of emotions presented by clients that affected a coach's own emotions and so created difficult situations in the coaching process. It was also found that coaches may yet be influenced by the traditional ideas identified by Fineman (2000) and Pizarro (2000): they cling to the notion that 'emotions should only be explored within a counselling setting and, as in many organisations, the traditional view that emotion interferes with rationality may still influence thinking' (2007: 178). Cox and Bachkirova reported on how coaches tackle these perceived difficulties by dealing with emotional situations in one of three ways:

1 Analysing and reflecting on the emotion, viewing it either as their own issue which they may take to supervision, or viewing it as belonging to the client.
2 Exploring an emotion with the client in the coaching session and actively using the energy they perceive as captured within it.
3 Referring the client to another professional or terminating the process.

These findings showed most coaches view emotions as needing to be managed or regulated, while some coaches suggested they work with emotion by helping clients to express emotion more fully, to name it and use it productively.

Cox and Bachkirova (2007) also proposed that 'since "transformational" and "empowering" are terms that epitomise the coaching relationship it would seem that there is a role for coaching here in helping clients to reduce problems such as stress at work – not through control and regulation of their emotions, but by acknowledging and understanding them as normal' (p.183). This finding supports Patrick's (2004) and Cox and Patrick's (2012) research that found that in the workplace coaching clients who are supported to understand their emotions rather than control them are more likely to experience significant growth.

In recent years support for understanding emotions through coaching has emerged in other settings such as the health and wellness domain (Kenworthy, Passarelli and Van Oosten, 2014) and in the field of parental emotion coaching where the approach to coaching involves acknowledging and validating a child's emotions and guiding them on how to manage their feelings. This has been identified as important for their emotional development and growth (Ellis, Alisic, et al., 2014; Wilson, Havighurst and Harley, 2014).

DEFINITION AND NATURE OF EMOTION

Views about the nature of emotion differ widely, not only practically in the coaching setting, but also theoretically. Some theorists view emotion as evolutionary, as the development of an inherent reflex (Griffiths, 2004; Damasio, 2000), and suggest that emotions are physical responses to events. Other authors take a more cognitive perspective, suggesting that although emotions are physical responses to external stimuli, these responses are always mediated through cognitive appraisal (Lazarus, 2013; Nussbaum 2001). A third perspective views emotion as socially constructed (Hess, 2001).

Evolutionary

Evolutionary theorists have a positive view of emotion and stress the importance of emotions as motivators and initiators of action. Emotions are also perceived to play a significant role in self-regulation (Nicholson and De Waal-Andrews, 2005). They are seen as expressions of the subconscious that facilitate the setting of priorities and the ability to prioritise problems (Frijda, 1986). In this conceptualisation, the fear, for example, that a mottephobe feels when a large moth enters the room would be completely involuntary – an innate emotional arousal.

Damasio (2000) also believes emotion is primary and independent of cognition. He described emotions as complex patterns of response that operate outside our consciousness, which subsequently lead to feelings that are the sensory patterns that signal pain and pleasure to our conscious mind. Consciousness, Damasio suggests, occurs at a conjunction between feelings and reason, so that becoming conscious of feelings prompts a rational process resulting in interpretation and subsequent regulation. Interestingly, since in Damasio's model emotions are more like impulses and can only be mediated through feelings, instead of using the word emotion we should perhaps be talking about 'working with feelings', to avoid assuming that we can have any direct impact on emotions. Greenberg (2004) also acknowledges how emotion precedes cognition. The fact that amygdala form emotional memories is the basis of therapy and is what therapists believe makes emotions difficult to change. However, it is also argued that both the automatic and conscious cognitive processes involved in self-regulation can be enhanced through coaching (Ives and Cox, 2012). A key aspect of goal focused coaching is the fostering of balance between automatic processes, such as emotions, and more conscious regulatory activity, such as monitoring and feedback, in order to address client goals, including change goals.

Cognitive

Cognitive theories suggest that the emotion process relies on cognitive manipulation and personal meaning arrived at using cognition. Nussbuam reinforces this view, suggesting emotions are always 'about something' (2001: 28). She argues that the way in which we perceive things and the beliefs we consequently hold about them are what distinguish one emotion from another, not their existence as impulses. Emotions thus involve complex beliefs about what we see: 'they insist on the real importance of their object, but they also embody the person's own commitment to the object' (p. 33). In this analysis each individual values what the object represents for them. This cognitive approach to evaluation is evident in the transactional model of stress and coping, for example, where primary appraisal of objects or events precedes further evaluation of coping resources and strategies (Lazarus and Folkman, 1984).

Greenberg (2004) suggests that people live in a constant process of making sense of their emotion and some forms of therapy work directly with the emotions to first diagnose and then manipulate them cognitively to achieve client well-being or success. One example is described by Neenan and Dryden (2002) who claim avoidance behaviour is the result of an emotional problem and the way to 'release' the emotion is to identify the beliefs and thoughts involved in maintaining the avoidance. They advocate the use of the ABC model, which is similar to Ellis et al.'s (1997) five stage rational emotive therapy model (ABCDE) involving identifying thoughts and beliefs that are currently influencing specific attitudes and expectations. According to Neenan and Dryden the self-acceptance engendered through the process reduces the 'duration, frequency and intensity' (2002: 160) of troublesome emotions because the client stops attacking him/herself and acknowledges something needs to change.

A cognitive view of emotion would imply that a fear of moths is felt, but the fear is not inherent in the experience of the moth itself: instead the fear can be moderated by rational admonishments such as 'this is a comparatively small moth', or by recognising that it may be a rare moth and should not be harmed. Thus behavioural responses to the fear can be mediated by cognitive activity.

The cognitive view of emotions is also responsible for references in the psychological literature to how, traditionally, some emotions are held to negatively affect our ability to think logically, while others have a more positive influence (Fredrickson, 2001; Greenberg, 2004). Greenberg claimed that emotions can be separated into four types: healthy core feelings (adaptive primary emotions); chronic bad feelings (maladaptive primary emotions); reactive or defensive emotions that can obscure primary feelings (secondary emotions); influencing or manipulative emotions used by people to get what they want (instrumental emotions). He suggested that positive emotions have links with improving problem solving, motivating people to learn and helping them build resilience 'by undoing the effects of negative emotion' (p.4). However, he also points out that negative emotions such as anxiety, anger, sorrow or regret are useful to us or they would not exist. These disagreeable feelings draw our attention to situations that may be crucial to our well-being and indeed survival. In fact, researchers such as Greenberg have attempted to explain how primary emotions, such as fear, are in essence positive. In Greenberg's (2004) view all emotions are normal and only become maladaptive, secondary or instrumental as a result of events or cognition. This echoes Fineman's (2005) view. He queries what sense it makes to 'bracket off' positive emotions, because that would assume they are separate states and deny that they are intrinsically linked to negative emotions.

For therapy to progress, it is usual to distinguish between different types of emotional experiences and link them with 'different types of in-session intervention' (Greenberg, 2004: 7). Definitions of primary and secondary emotions are important in this assessment and emotions are labelled positive or negative and considered maladaptive if they will not change. These distinctions provide therapists with a map to guide intervention. It could be argued however, that in coaching, although clients need to take account of their feelings, they do not need to *re-feel* the emotion, or change the emotion, since the objective is not normally adaptation, but rather mindfulness and acceptance (Cox, 2013). Alado, Nolen-Hoeksema and Schweizer explain how mindfulness is conceptualised as 'non-elaborative, non-judgemental, present-centred awareness in which thoughts, feelings, and sensations are accepted as they are' (2010: 219).

Socially Constructed

Fineman (2005) has also argued that the 'same' emotion can be felt and responded to differently according to cultural and social factors. Indeed, some research suggests there are differences in emotion eliciting events as well as emotional reactions in different cultures. Suh et al. (1998) for example, report that collectivistic cultures focus on external socially shared elements of an emotion stimulus whereas individualistic cultures pay more attention to the internal signals. Hess also considers that although the basic emotion process may be biologically grounded, 'the type of events attended to, the appraisal of these events, and the relevant norms for behavior may vary as a function of culture, gender, relative power status' (2001: 390).

Similarly, Lupton argues that emotions are 'experienced, understood and named via social and cultural processes' (1998: 15). Thus the social constructionist perspective would suggest that mottephobia is the result of a learned response: perhaps mother was afraid of moths and her response was imitated. Dirkx points out how 'scholars representing this perspective are particularly interested in the implications that emotional experiences and expression hold for one's sense of self and one's relationships with others and the broader world' (2008:. 12), which in turn suggests links with developmental coaching (Bachkirova, 2011).

Advances in neuroscientific research are poised to add to our understanding of how the brain processes emotional signals and in particular the complex nature of social construction and interaction at work. However, Grant (2015: 31) argues that currently the link between neuroscientific findings and coaching practice 'are tenuous at best'. Boyatzis (2014) similarly confirms that the main contribution of neuroscience, particularly in relation to understanding emotion, is to confirm our previous assumptions about the benefit of engaging emotions through the practice of coaching. In research by Jack, Boyatzis et al. (2013) two types of coaching were used as a methodology to examine the activation of a positive emotional attractor (PEA) and a negative emotional attractor (NEA) in a target group of 31 undergraduate students. The results of the study appear to give credence to a future focused coaching approach that produced more positive and beneficial results in the brain versus a problem focused approach that produced feelings of guilt and self-consciousness. This is an area where further research would be valuable.

The Role of Emotions in Motivation

Most research looking at the role of emotions in motivation occurs mainly in the sports coaching domain. Hill and Davis (2014) for example identify how the way in which coaches regulate their emotions has implications for performance and wellbeing. They argue that effective emotion regulation is 'critical for coaches in order to maintain harmonious relationships with others (e.g., athletes and other coaches) and safeguard their own well-being' (2014: 2) and suggest that the way coaches regulate their own emotions also has implications for the athletes they work with, influencing how they manage their emotions and determining subsequent emotional experiences and performances.

The absence of research in the area of emotion and motivation may be related to a more general point that Goldie makes about the status of feelings: Goldie (2000) acknowledges that because it is so hard to describe the place of feelings in emotion, we have tended to explore the cognitive, thinking aspects and treat feelings as a separate add-on or appendage. This he believes is wrong. He argues for the intentionality of feelings to be placed 'centre stage' (p. 52) and explains the concept of 'feeling towards' which involves recognising the emotional relevance or salience of a feeling. The theory contends that emotions can be superseded by other emotions when the second emotion becomes more salient for us. Once this happens, as Goldie suggests, no amount of intellectual explanation can intervene. The salience of things we value is thus an integral part of emotion and impacts our motivation.

Drawing on this theory of 'feeling towards', what Greenberg (2004) considers the most fundamental principle in therapeutic emotion processing is the transformation of emotions through displacement. This principle, he argues is unlike the rational emotive model since it involves by-passing cognitive reasoning and instead transforming a maladaptive emotional state by replacing it with a different emotion. Similarly, in research by Tugade and Frederickson (2000) and Frederickson (2001) positive emotions were found to 'undo' lingering negative emotions. The basic observation was that key components of positive emotions are not compatible with negative emotions and so the negative emotions are displaced.

Greenberg further confirms how emotions are important for providing information about important needs, values, or goals. They are, he argues, 'biologically-based relational action tendencies that result from the appraisal of the situation' (2004: 3) and so are involved in goal setting and motivation. In motivational systems theory, Ford (1992) explains that emotions serve as signals of what is happening or may happen in the current situation, describing emotions as '… an empowering source of information about how to influence motivational patterns' (p. 145). Although, a number of theories have been developed to explain the way in which individuals regulate or control emotions and how that affects motivation, Mayer and Turner (2006) have called for future research to focus on the integration of emotion, motivation, and cognition as equal elements of the social process of learning. Coaching would seem an ideal context for such exploration.

The Role of Emotion in Transformational Learning

Emotion also has a key part to play in the transformative learning that occurs during or as a result of coaching when, for example, clients are making significant changes in their lives. Transformative learning is described as: '… *the process of learning through critical self-reflection, which results in the reformulation of a "meaning perspective" to allow a more inclusive, discriminating and integrative understanding of experience*' (Mezirow, 1990: xii).

Mezirow acknowledged that the transformative learning process is 'threatening, emotionally charged, and extremely difficult' (1995: 48). Others have stressed even further the affective nature of transformative learning, arguing that transformation carries with it a degree of emotionality (Dirkx, 2008); a period of vulnerability, discomfort, neutrality (Bridges, 2009) or 'bounded instability' (Stacey, 1995). Indeed, it is many people's experience that the point of recognition and acceptance of a shift in meaning perspective that leads to transformation is accompanied by affective responses in the form of tears of elation or relief. The initial 'disorienting dilemma' is also often accompanied by a range of complex emotions including grief, denial, anger, guilt and resentment (Adams, Hayes and Hopson, 1976). Thus many theorists have questioned whether the rationality of Mezirow's process is the only way to achieve perspective transformation, citing the existence of 'other ways of knowing' including affective learning, extra-rational influences and intuition (Taylor, 2001). Furthermore, Rimé, Corsini and Herbette (2002) conducted empirical research that showed that the sharing of emotion is linked to a need to complete 'emotion-related cognitive business' (2002: 205) and that the need to share is seen as all-encompassing and an important part of making meaning. Many have even suggested that complex transformative learning happens *only when* an affective change occurs (Hooper, 2007; Dirkx, 2008). Such authors place feelings and emotions at the centre of transformative learning, listing grieving or coping with an emotional crisis as integral to the process.

PERCEPTIONS OF EMOTION IN ORGANISATIONS

With the recognition that much coaching takes place within an organisational context (Susing, Green and Grant, 2011), it is important to examine research that focuses on how emotionality is perceived in organisations. The literature reveals there is acknowledgment that emotions affect behaviour in the workplace, but that they are usually negatively perceived. The customary response to emotional display within organisations is to make arrangements to deal with emotions since they are deemed to adversely impact rationality (Fineman, 2000) and constrain productivity (Speedy, 2005).

Fineman's (2000) arguments regarding the tensions between rationality and emotion in workplace included three possible positions that people could hold: emotions interfere with rationality; emotions serve rationality; or emotions and rationality entwine. In the first position, reason and rationality are privileged over emotion: emotions are irrational and where they impact on interrelations in organisations they create difficulties. This traditional way of perceiving emotion has a long philosophical history said to trace back to Plato, Kant and Weber. Plato suggested that emotions 'pervert reason and should be tightly controlled' (Hess, 2001: 387); Kant considered emotions to be antagonistic to the reasoning process (Pizarro, 2000) and in Weber's words 'bureaucracy develops more perfectly, the more it is dehumanised, the more completely it succeeds in eliminating from official business love, hatred, and all purely personal, irrational and emotional elements which escape calculation' (Weber, 1978: 975). Weber's claim became attractive to rationalists and grew in strength despite it being part of his critique of bureaucracy!

Fineman's second position suggests that rationality is served by emotions: feelings can inform our thinking, so that rationality appears to be enhanced through recognition of emotions. According to Ashforth and Humphrey (1995: 120) management research and practice has emphasised 'rationality at the expense of emotionality'. Rather than seeing emotion as the converse of rationality, they argue that there needs to be recognition of the 'functional complementarity of emotionality and rationality' (1995: 120) supporting Fineman's (2000) challenge to the effectiveness of favouring rationality and suppressing emotion in organisations: he suggests instead that we acknowledge that emotional processes serve rationality in important ways.

The third position proposes that rationality and emotions are fundamentally linked. Fineman confirms that thinking is never separate from feeling: since the two constantly interpenetrate 'much of what we describe as rational is in fact emotional' (2000: 11) Buck's (1991: 136) explanation captures this third position: 'Everything that is real is emotional; the rational is our subsequent linguistically structured elaboration of that reality.'

In the coaching field, Harvey has recently reinforced the traditional position, proposing that emotions can interfere with reasoning, and giving the oft cited example of how stress distorts judgment. He argues that 'it is not uncommon for a coachee who is under pressure or facing a crisis to seem to lose his (sic) ability to make simple decisions' (2014: 29) explaining that 'anger, inflaming the amygdale area in the brain, can have the same mind-altering effect'. Yet, he also suggests, emotions are crucial to human decision making.

Emotion and Gender

In Cox and Bachkirova's research, gender was identified in a variety of responses from coaches, with some stating they made no gender distinction when working with emotion: others however admitted they 'may be more tolerant with females and experience more discomfort when males displayed their feelings' (2007: 187). Cox and Bachkirova believe this is an example of how unexamined assumptions about emotions are absorbed from the dominant culture and impede the coaching process and that this difference in approach to displayed emotion reflects the situation in the workplace.

According to Shields (2013) beliefs about emotions are highly gendered and Sachs and Blackmore (1998) report that female executives were expected to control their emotions, since displays of feeling were frequently perceived as weak or irrational. Rationality was privileged because of its seeming male connection, with a consequent devaluing and marginalisation of emotions in organisations (Lupton, 1998): femininity was linked with the emotional and the private, whilst masculinity was more often associated with the rational and public. 'Ideal' femininity, according to Speedy (2005) includes such attributes as gentleness, empathy, sensitivity, a caring disposition and heightened awareness to others' feelings, but women are also viewed as having negative emotions that include envy, jealousy, rage, irrationality and aggressiveness. Men, on the other hand, are constructed as 'rational, tough, direct, self-controlled, logical, strong and unemotional' (Speedy, 2005: 7).

There is little empirical research that focuses specifically on coaching and the emotional differences displayed by men and women. However, Ludeman and Erlandson (2004) have attacked the stereotypical male qualities by making a direct assertion that males in the workplace need a different type of coaching to remodel their highly rational 'alpha' profile. They suggest that it is the male alpha that needs to change through coaching in order to avoid problems caused through an excess of authority and rationality, whereas women already 'place more value on interpersonal relationships and pay closer attention to people's feelings' (2004: 3).

Changes in Emotional Climate

Articles such as Ludeman and Erlandson's indicate that a shift in workplace culture may be occurring. Cox and Bachkirova note how reservations are being expressed in relation to 'the extreme rationality that has tended to govern bureaucratic organisational structures in the past' (2007. p.180). They suggest a view of emotion as a resource is emerging and cite a range of factors: 'the growth of emotion work, the impact of globalisation and the influx of more women and people from different cultures into organisations' (p.180). Speedy (2005) also confirms that most theorists no longer question whether emotionality should play an integral part in the workplace, believing that, 'emotions create the meaning of work' (2005: 2) and are pivotal in understanding organisational life.

Part of this shift in perspective can be related to an increased emphasis on employee wellbeing and the recognition that improved emotional climate contributes to this. Black's (2008) review suggested that employers have a key role in the promotion of adult health and wellbeing. She argued that employers who invest in developing emotional resilience in their workers play an important role in tackling wider health problems.

The benefits of improved emotional climate in the workplace were also studied by Vallen (1993) with the suggestion that the creation of a more supportive and participative work climate may increase both retention and productivity. According to Hodson (1997) and Hartel, Gough and Hartel (2008), workers who have good relationships with each other are more likely to have good peer communications, greater job satisfaction, and better relations with management.

Emotional Intelligence (EI)

The popularisation of emotional intelligence (EI) is another factor that is claimed as bringing emotion 'out of the organizational closet' (Fineman, 2000: 17). Cartwright and Pappas (2008: 149) confirm how it has become linked to a range of outcomes such as career success, life satisfaction and health and EI is considered vital in a number of areas including '… self-awareness, motivation, self-regulation, empathy and adeptness in relationships' (Goleman, 1998: 28).

However, the concept of EI, and its associated methods, has generated considerable debate since its popularisation by Goleman in the 1990s. The majority of research has focused on the measurement of EI for selection of personnel or the enhancement of leadership and management capability and this is one of the major criticisms. Cartwright and Pappas (2008) described how EI and its link with increased performance has become attractive to recruiters in organisations, but that research into its validity and efficacy has been restricted to test construction and exploration of psychometric properties.

Fineman (2000) further warns that Goleman's assertions have driven a whole EI industry without a solid research foundation, while more recently Roberts, MacCann, Matthews and Zeidner (2010) also confirm how its popularisation appears to have driven the industry with 'potential for great confusion among scientists and practitioners' (p.823).

Fineman's concern is that in identifying EI, a 'moral order' of emotions may be created which could lead to the valuing of 'emotionally intelligent' people over the seemingly less emotionally intelligent. Such categorisation also assumes that emotions can be easily identified as traits and that some are more desirable than others. Fineman (2000) suggests our psychological processes, that include defensive, displacement and screening processes, all contribute to making it impossible to know what emotions are in fact impacting on behaviours.

Fineman and others (e.g. Roberts et al., 2010) therefore champion the original work of Mayer and colleagues (Mayer and Salovey, 1997; Mayer, Salovey anad Caruso, 2004) who researched EI as a multi-dimensional construct of four factors: verbal and non-verbal appraisal and expression of emotion; using emotions to assist in problem-solving; regulating one's own, and others' emotions; and promoting intellectual and emotional growth using emotional knowledge. Mayer et al. (2004) themselves point out that conceptualisations made by Goleman (1998) or Bar-On (1997), for example, are based on a mixed model defined as 'an array of non-cognitive capabilities, competencies and skills' which 'often have little or nothing specifically to do with emotion or intelligence and, consequently, fail to map onto the term emotional intelligence' (Mayer et al., 2004: 197). Fineman (2000) also pointed out how misleading the Goleman conceptualisation is in relation to emotion. He argues that when methods of developing EI are discussed it is apparent that it is more about intelligence than about emotion.

Despite these debates, for the purpose of this chapter it is useful to link the early definition of EI from Salovey and Mayer with the concept of emotion regulation. Salovey and Mayer define EI as 'the ability to monitor one's own and others' feelings and emotions, to discriminate among them, and to use this information to guide one's thinking and actions' (1990: 189). This ability model describes a set of cognitive abilities that involve perceiving and reasoning, with information that emerges from feelings and is closely related to self-regulation (Mayer and Salovey, 1997, Lawrence et al., 2011). In coach training EI is thought to be a beneficial attribute, not only for the aspiring coach, but also for the clients that the coach will support. This is mainly because of its inherent links with emotion regulation (Ives and Cox, 2012; Bachkirova, 2011).

Regulation of Emotion

As suggested above, emotional intelligence is closely linked with the regulation of our own, and others' emotions (Mayer and Salovey, 1997). According to Mayer and colleagues knowledge is at the heart of emotion regulation and emotion regulation skills are partly influenced by mental ability and the capacity to learn, solve problems and process complex information (Mayer et al., 2008).

Pizarro also argued that because emotions are linked to our values and beliefs, emotions actually help reasoning by focusing attention on the problem and 'allowing us to pay attention to features of the situation that may escape us otherwise' (2000: 358). They therefore permit some regulation through cognitive attention. Gross, Richards and John (2006) also supported this argument, claiming that 'successful emotion regulation is a pre-requisite for adaptive functioning: to get along with others we must be able to regulate which emotions we have and how we experience and express these emotions' (p. 2).

According to Gross (1998), emotion regulation strategies can be categorised as either (a) antecedent-focused (i.e., they are initiated before the emotion occurs) or (b) response-focused (i.e., initiated after the emotion occurs). Individuals are considered to show different preferences for implementing these strategies. Ashkanasy's (2003) model falls into the second category. He explained how people regulate their emotional responses at four different points in the emotion experiencing process:

i) externally, at the problem level, by removing themselves from the emotional situation;
ii) internally, by cognitive regulation that changes their appraisal of the situation;
iii) internally, by responding differently to the emotional stimulation itself (for example by taking time out);
iv) externally, by modifying their response (e.g. ignoring someone instead of hitting them).

One of the main principles of emotion focused therapy is the regulation of emotions that are deemed 'under-regulated'. Greenberg explains emotion regulation skills as: 'identifying and labelling emotions, allowing and tolerating emotions, establishing a working distance, increasing positive emotions, reducing vulnerability to negative emotions, self-soothing, breathing, and distraction' (2004: 10). Emotion regulation in therapy involves helping the client create distance from distressing emotions and 'developing self-soothing capacities to calm and comfort core anxieties and humiliation' (p. 10).

It can be noted how different this idea of emotion focused therapy is from definitions of coaching. Greenberg (2004) explains how therapy involves changing 'both emotional experience and the narratives in which they are embedded' (p.5). In coaching it could be argued that it is just the narrative that gets changed: just as it is not necessary to shovel out the darkness before we can switch on a light, so in order to achieve results or support changes to happen through coaching it is not necessary to unpack or change the emotions that underpin previous behaviours (Ives and Cox, 2014). Acceptance is the key, rather than change.

However, effective emotion regulation is seen as important for coaches as a part of preserving their relationships with clients and others and crucially as important for safeguarding their own well-being (Jowett, Lafrenière and Vallerand, 2013). It has also been suggested that coaches have choices about how to regulate their emotions. They have a choice between (a) minimising the attention paid to client emotions and (b) working with them to achieve results (Bachkirova and Cox, 2007). It can be seen how such decisions could link with the choices about regulation suggested by Ashkanasy.

Some of the ways in which emotion is regulated in the workplace are often conceptualised as deep acting and surface acting (Haver et al., 2013). These include; surface acting as in emotional labour; deep acting through the use of empathy for example; or the awareness and use of naturally felt emotions. Both, Haver et al. argue, involve regulating observable facial and bodily reactions in order to align with another individual's emotional displays. In the case of empathy, it is almost always for the benefit of the client in a therapy setting. In the case of emotional labour, such regulation can be as much for the benefit of the organisation as the individual customer. These two concepts are discussed below, as examples of emotion regulation.

Empathy

One of the ways in which therapists and coaches work with emotion is through the use of empathy. Empathy involves being in the client's place moment by moment and 'feeling as if' (Schmid, 2001: 2–3). Adler and Towne describe it as 'the ability to project oneself into another person's point of view, so as to experience the other's thoughts and feelings' (1990: 400). Carl Rogers explained it as follows:

> Empathy, or being empathic, is to receive the internal frame of reference of another with accuracy and with the emotional components and meanings which pertain thereto as if one were the person, but without ever losing the *'as if'* condition. Thus it means to sense the hurt or the pleasure of another as he senses it and to perceive the causes thereof as he perceives them, but without ever losing the recognition that it is as if I were hurt or pleased and so forth. If this *'as if'* quality is lost, then the state is one of identification. (Rogers, 1959: 210–211, emphasis added)

Rogers suggested that through empathy the counsellor becomes a 'confident companion to the person in his/her inner world', and that by being in what he called 'the flow of his/her experiencing' the counsellor helps the client to understand more fully and 'to move forward' (1959: 210–211). He argues that for counsellors to be with another in this way means that they lay aside their own views and values in order to enter the client's world without prejudice. Thus they do not avoid particular emotions just because they find them uncomfortable to work with, as this could be seen as a lack of empathy.

However, as Cox (2013) has argued the function of empathy in coaching may be more limited. Therapeutic work generally assumes that the client's condition is hidden and needs to be determined using empathy, and other forms of therapy: 'it is almost as though the client is an object with static points of view that the therapist must try to understand' (2013: 50). In a therapeutic setting the implied objectivity of the empathic approach (the '*as if*' nature of it) is helpful since it enables the medical model of therapy to be applied: 'the therapist empathises with clients enough to gain trust and gather information about their state of mind, and is then equipped to make a diagnosis' (2013: 50). However, in coaching, Cox suggests, 'even such benign hypothesis testing is not generally acceptable' (2013: 50).

Cox suggests, therefore, that empathy plays a different, more restricted role in coaching, one where there is 'less emphasis on the moment to moment psychological state of the client, and more on what is being constructed or produced between coach and client in the coaching room' (2013: 51). Empathic listening is useful especially during initial exploration, but as Cox argues 'it cannot assist hypothesis formulation, since coaching does not follow a medical model' (2013: 50). Coaches remain non-judgmental in relation to the client throughout the process in order to engender a sense of the clients' ownership of their coaching issues.

Emotional Labour

Many organisations utilise what is termed 'emotional labour' as part of everyday interaction with customers and clients. Hochschild (1983) first used the concept to explain the roles of workers who need to produce appropriate emotional responses as part of their job. Health, sales and service work all involve 'emotional labour', where the objective is to 'provide predictability and maintain harmony in the workplace, while enhancing competitive productivity' (Speedy, 2005: 4). The process requires effort and regulation to maintain emotional balance and accord: ordinary feelings and emotions are modified or offset in some way so that the workers can influence customers, handle complaints or resolve problems.

It is argued however that the surface acting involved in emotional labour can result in emotional dissonance which can be damaging, causing stress and burnout (Hochschild, 1983). Richards and Gross (2005) also suggested that control of emotions can come at a 'cognitive price' since it could impair the memory of emotional events and Bono et al. (2005) reported that people required to manage their emotions at work experience more stress and lower job satisfaction. Hartel, Gough and Hartel (2008) have further explained that emotional labour involves separation of the experience of emotion from the actual actions that generated it and that such regulation of emotions may affect the entire process of emotional experience and expression.

Bolton (2003) finds an uncomfortable emphasis on negative outcomes in theories of emotional labour suggesting that attention is too often 'directed to an employee's inability to match feeling with face and the resultant emotional burn-out, dissonance and low job satisfaction' (2003: 3). Whilst Bolton acknowledges that the service sector relies on employees' abilities to manage emotions in a variety of ways, she considers that explanations that present it as one-dimensional, with the focus on 'frustrated managers, emotionally exhausted workers and dissatisfied customers' (p.4), are limited. She questions why there are no accounts of the sense of satisfaction or reward that can come from involvement with emotion work.

Interestingly, Hochschild includes coaching in her list of examples of emotional outsourcing and commodification (2005) and indeed some organisations may see coaching as a form of emotional labour. George (2008) similarly argues that coaching is a highly personalised, intangible activity which combines elements of Hochschild's emotional labour (1983), aspects of interactive service work and certain characteristics of paid and unpaid care work (England, 2005). Thus, even though the occupation of coaching is frequently reported as very enjoyable and worthwhile (De Haan and Burger, 2013), coaches might begin to suffer from the kinds of problems that affect other emotion workers: emotional exhaustion, feelings of burnout, or of depersonalisation and detachment. Emotion work is dependent on feeling and display rules prescribed covertly or overtly by an organisation or a profession to ensure staff or members demonstrate appropriate characteristics: caring, objectivity, rationality etc. and there are certainly significant feeling rules governing the practice of coaching, such as remaining non-judgmental in face of the client (Cox and Bachkirova, 2007). This in turn could lead to distress and burnout.

In the area of coach supervision there is some recognition of the effect of working with emotion on the coach and attention is paid to the area of self-care (Bachkirova et al, 2011). Keep (2013) has researched this area empirically and developed a 'self-care at work' framework, which involves monitoring emotions and feelings, as well as other factors. Keep suggests the framework may be used as a checklist or for setting up an individual self development programme. It could also be used by coaches when working with clients on their own self-care.

WORKING WITH EMOTION IN COACHING

In some conceptualisations of coaching, authors considered working with emotion to be primarily the domain of therapists (Hart, Blattner and Leipsic, 2001; Gray, 2006) and that emotions if they arose during coaching should be managed in some way. Bossons et al. (2015) for example suggest there are things a coach can do to reduce emotional arousal in clients. These include reducing emotional arousal through the use of paraphrasing, which has been demonstrated to create positive feelings. However, other coaching texts such as Rogers (2012) and Cox (2013) have acknowledged that exploring feelings is a core coaching skill of all coaching practitioners which has impact on motivation and regulatory functions. Lee (2003: 28) also incorporated emotions as a key element of his ACE FIRST coaching model, suggesting that it is an important part of self-awareness to be able to identify 'What did you feel? To what extent were your feelings hidden? To what extent were you aware of your feelings?' He argues that encouraging managers 'to notice, name, accept and understand their emotions is a key aspect of leadership coaching, since emotions – and particularly unconscious emotions – are an important potential block to change' (2003: 31).

Sekerka's research into personal moral courage (2010: 5) found that the emotions that managers most frequently expressed were 'worry, loneliness, fear, shock or surprise, and feelings of "hurt" (often stemming from a sense of betrayal)'. She explains how managers 'initially experience a sense of confusion, agitation, or helplessness' but that when these emotions were felt, they were not ignored or repressed, rather, those with moral courage used information from their emotions as cues. They were 'enabled by their emotional awareness rather than being blocked or thwarted by it' (2010: 5). It seems then that being aware of emotions may give clients a head start for coping with them.

As well as being used to raise awareness that can lead to increased performance, coaches might use emotion in a number of different ways with their clients: as a form of intuition in decision making (McLaughlin and Cox, 2016) for example or they may translate it into energy or motivation when anger or other feelings overwhelm (Linger, 2014). Haver et al. (2013) further stress that emotion regulation is a key aspect of effective leadership and is vital to how people handle negative emotions. They suggest that leaders who use emotion regulation in an effective way 'may be able to improve their affect, the quality of their relationships and organisational outcomes' (2013: 287).

Cremona's (2010) qualitative study also identified a number of ways in which coaches work with emotion including acknowledging or playing back the emotion verbally, linking the emotion to thoughts and subsequent action, or asking explicitly what clients are feeling during a session. Some coaches even used therapeutic techniques, such as Gestalt interventions. Cremona (2010: 57) concludes by highlighting the differences between therapy and coaching in relation to emotion. Conventionally, therapy works with past issues and the sharing of personal issues and emotions is encouraged. However, as Cremona points out learning processes are not made explicit in therapy, whereas in coaching they are explicit and one of the defining features. Also in coaching the present and the future are the main focus and expression of emotions, although not discouraged, is not actively encouraged.

FUTURE RESEARCH

Throughout this chapter it can be noted how different therapeutic interventions are explicitly built on various theories of emotion, but it is less clear to what extent they are appropriate in coaching: thus further research is needed. Stimulated by Lipchik's (2014) model of emotional climate in a therapeutic setting, I therefore introduce an emotional climate inventory for coaching (Table 15.1). This inventory is drawn from discussions earlier in the chapter and as well as giving a summary of climate, provides an indication of possible areas for future research.

The first two rows of the inventory show where clients' and coaches' foci lie in relation to coaching, with clients focusing on their own view of emotional reality and their perceptions of current/future possibilities and concerns, while the coach remains client centred and strengths focused. Future research could usefully explore in what ways the client's emotional focus is identified and worked with by the coach. There may be too much emphasis on weaknesses and some black and white thinking on the part of the client which could impact motivation. The coach by contrast will be seeking to build on strengths and to expand perspectives. It would be interesting to study how coaches work with these more negative emotions. There is little research on how coaches achieve such shifts in focus.

Table 15.1 An emotional climate inventory for coaching

Client focus	Coach focus
• His/her own view of reality • The present and future • Capacity to address current concerns • Overcoming weaknesses • Maybe an either/or perspective	• Client-centred view of reality • The present and future • Solutions to current concerns • Building Strengths • Developing both/and perspective
Client needs	*Coach needs*
• To share emotions • Emotional awareness and emotional intelligence • Mutual understanding • Self-regulation and motivation • Transformative learning	• Empathic listening • Awareness of own and others' emotional sensitivities • Understanding of cultural variation • Understanding of emotional intelligence and emotional labour • Self-care and supervision

The inventory in Table 15.1 also suggests that coaches use a future oriented approach with emphasis on solutions. In the neuroscientific research reported earlier beneficial client results were seen from this approach (Jack, Boyatzis, et al., 2013). Additional research in this area could move us towards a physiological theory of coaching in different settings and with different client groups.

The needs of the client, including the need to share and be understood, are shown alongside the corresponding skills needs of the coach in the second part of the inventory. The inventory implies that more research is required in areas such as how coaches use their skills to meet specific client needs, for example: empathic listening during the emotion sharing process, understanding of cultural differences, emotional intelligence and self-regulation theories and the impact of such knowledge on the coaching process and client outcomes. There is also a need to examine coaches' own needs for self-care and supervision in relation to working with emotion.

CONCLUSION

In this chapter the way in which coaches work with emotion was explored. Recent research was examined that considered the nature of emotion and its more general functions. Theories of emotion from the disciplines of sociology and psychology were analysed and related to the role and perception of emotions in workplace coaching. The often contentious concepts of emotional intelligence, emotion regulation and emotional labour were also discussed in some detail.

Later in the chapter I then drew on the theory and research into how coaches use emotion in their practice to create an emotional climate inventory that connects the findings of the chapter with gaps in current coaching and emotion research. As highlighted early in the chapter there is a need for research that integrates emotion, motivation and cognitive elements particularly as they relate to coaching. To that end a number of suggestions for future research were made. In particular, qualitative research is needed that explores how clients' emotional needs are met through the application of specific coaching skills. It may be that neuroscience can also be useful as a strand of research endeavour, not least in convincing sceptics that something important is happening emotionally during coaching.

REFERENCES

Adams, J. D., Hayes, J., & Hopson, B. (1976). Transition: Understanding and. *Managing Personal Change*, London: Robinson.

Adler, R.B. & Towne, N. (1990) *Looking Out, Looking In*. Fort Worth: Holt, Rinehart and Winston.

Aldao, A., Nolen-Hoeksema, S., & Schweizer, S. (2010). Emotion-regulation strategies across psychopathology: A meta-analytic review. *Clinical psychology review*, 30(2), 217–237.

Ashforth, B. & Humphrey, R. (1995) Emotion in the workplace: a reappraisal. *Human Relations*, 48(2): 97–125.

Ashkanasy, N.M. (2003) Emotions in organizations: a multilevel perspective. *Research in Multi-level Issues*, 2: 9–54.

Ashkanasy, N.M. & Humphrey, R.H. (2011) Current research on emotion in organizations. *Emotion Review*, 3: 214–224.

Bachkirova, T. (2011) *Developmental Coaching: Working with the Self*, Maidenhead: McGraw-Hill.

Bachkirova, T. & Cox, E. (2007) Coaching with emotion in organisations: investigation of personal theories. *Leadership and Organization Development*, 28(7): 600–612.

Bachkirova, T., Jackson, P. & Clutterbuck, D. (2011) *Coaching and Mentoring Supervision: Theory and Practice*. Maidenhead: McGraw-Hill Education.

Bar-On, R. (1997) *The Emotional Quotient Inventory (EQ-i): A Test of Emotional Intelligence*. Toronto: Multi-Health Systems.

Black, C. (2008) *Working for a Healthier Tomorrow*. London: TSO. Accessed 31/7/15 from: https://www.gov.uk/government/uploads/system/uploads/attachment_data/file/209782/hwwb-working-for-a-healthier-tomorrow.pdf

Bolton, S. (2003) *Introducing a Typology of Workplace Emotion*. Working Paper. The Department of Organisation, Work and Technology, Lancaster University.

Bossons, P., Riddell, P. & Sartain, D. (2015) *The Neuroscience of Leadership Coaching: Why the Tools and Techniques of Leadership Coaching Work*. Bloomsbury Publishing.

Boyatzis, R.E. (2014) Possible contributions to leadership and management development from neuroscience. *Academy of Management Learning & Education*, 13(2): 300–303.

Bridges, W. (2009) *Managing Transitions: Making the Most of Change*. Boston, MA: Da Capo Press.

Buck, R. (1991) Motivation, emotion and cognition: a developmental-interactionist view. In K.T. Strongman (ed.) *International Review of Studies in Emotion*, Vol. 1. Chichester, UK: John Wiley and Sons. pp. 101–142.

Cartwright, S. & Pappas, C. (2008) Emotional intelligence, its measurement and implications for the workplace. *International Journal of Management Reviews*, 10(2): 149–171.

Cox, E. (2013) *Coaching Understood*. London: Sage.

Cox, E. & Bachkirova, T. (2007) Coaching with emotion: how coaches deal with difficult emotional situations. *International Coaching Psychology Review*, 2(2): 178–189.

Cox, E. & Patrick, C. (2012) Managing emotions at work: how coaching affects retail support workers' performance and motivation. *International Journal of Evidence Based Coaching & Mentoring*, 10(2): 34–51.

Cremona, K. (2010) Coaching and emotions: an exploration of how coaches engage and think about emotion. *Coaching: An International Journal of Theory, Research and Practice*, 3(1): 46–59.

Damasio, A. (2000) *The Feeling of What Happens: Body, Emotion and the Making of Consciousness*. London: Vintage.

De Haan, E. & Burger, Y. (2013) *Coaching with Colleagues 2nd Edition: An Action Guide for One-to-One Learning*. Basingstoke: Palgrave Macmillan.

Dirkx, J.M. (2008) The meaning and role of emotions in adult learning. *New Directions for Adult and Continuing Education*, 120: 7–18.

Ellis, A., Gordon, J., Neenan, M. & Palmer, S. (1997) *Stress Counselling: A Rational Emotive Behaviour Approach*. London: Cassell.

Ellis, B.H., Alisic, E., Reiss, A., Dishion, T. & Fisher, P.A. (2014) Emotion regulation among preschoolers on a continuum of risk: the role of maternal emotion coaching. *Journal of Child and Family Studies*, 23(6): 965–974.

England, P. (2005) Emerging theories of care work. *Annual Review of Sociology*, 31: 381–399.

Fineman, S. (ed.) (2000) *Emotion in Organizations*. 2nd edn. London: Sage.

Fineman, S. (2005) Appreciating emotion at work: paradigm tensions. *International Journal of Work Organisation and Emotion*, 1(1): 4–19.

Ford, M.E. (1992) *Motivating Humans: Goals, Emotions, and Personal Agency Beliefs*. Newbury Park, CA: Sage.

Fredrickson, B. (2001). The role of positive emotions in positive psychology: The broaden-and-build theory of positive emotions. *American Psychologist*, 56: 218–226.

Frijda, N. (1986) *The Emotions: Studies in Emotion and Social Interaction*. Cambridge: Cambridge University Press.

George, M. (2008) Interactions in expert service work: demonstrating professionalism in personal training. *Journal of Contemporary Ethnography*, 37(1): 108–131.

Goldie, P. (2000) *The Emotions: A Philosophical Exploration*. Oxford: Oxford University Press.

Goleman, D. (1998) *Working with Emotional Intelligence*. New York: Bantam Books.

Grant, A.M. (2015) Coaching the brain: neuroscience or neuro-nonsense? *The Coaching Psychologist*, 11(1): 31.

Gray, D.E. (2006) Executive coaching: towards a dynamic alliance of psychsotherapy and transformative learning processes. *Management Learning*, 37(4): 475–497.

Greenberg, L.S. (2004) Emotion–focused therapy. *Clinical Psychology & Psychotherapy*, 11(1): 3–16.

Griffiths, E. (2004) Is emotion a natural kind? In R. C. Solomon (Ed.), *Thinking About Feeling: Contemporary Philosophers on Emotions* (pp. 233–249). New York: Oxford University Press.

Gross, J.J. (1998) Antecedent- and response-focused emotion regulation: divergent consequences for experience, expression, and physiology. *Journal of Personality and Social Psychology*, 74: 224–237.

Gross, J., Richards, J. & John, O. (2006) Emotion regulation in everyday life. In D. Snyder, J. Simpson & J. Hughes (Eds.), *Emotion Regulation in Couples and Families: Pathways to Dysfunction and Health* (pp. 13–35). Washington DC: American Psychological Association.

Hart, V., Blattner, J. & Leipsic, S. (2001) Coaching versus therapy: a perspective. *Consulting Psychology Journal: Practice and Research*, 53(4): 229–237.

Hartel, C., Gough, H. & Hartel, G. (2008) Work-group emotional climate, emotion management skills and service attitudes and performance. *Asia Pacific Journal of Human Resources*, 26(1): 21–37.

Harvey, M. (2014). *Interactional Leadership and how to Coach it: The Art of the Choice-focused Leader*. London: Routledge.

Hatfield, E., Cacioppo, J. & Rapson, R. (1994) *Emotional Contagion*. New York: Cambridge University Press.

Haver, A., Akerjordet, K. & Furunes, T. (2013) Emotion regulation and its implications for leadership: an integrative review and future research agenda. *Journal of Leadership & Organizational Studies*, 20(3): 287–303.

Hefferon, K. (2013) The role of emotions in coaching and mentoring. In J. Passmore, D. Peterson, T. Freire, (Eds), *The Wiley-Blackwell Handbook of the Psychology of Coaching and Mentoring* (pp. 471–482). Oxford: Wiley-Blackwell.

Hess, U. (2001) The experience of emotion: situational influences on the elicitation and experience of emotions. In A. Kaszniak (Ed.), *Emotions, Qualia, and Consciousness* (pp. 386–396). Singapore: World Scientific Publishing.

Hill, A.P. & Davis, P.A. (2014) Perfectionism and emotion regulation in coaches: a test of the 2× 2 model of dispositional perfectionism. *Motivation and Emotion*, 38(5): 715–726.

Hochschild, A. (1983). *The Managed Heart*. Berkeley and Los Angeles: University of California.

Hochschild, A.R. (2005) 'Rent a mom' and other services: markets, meanings and emotions. *International Journal of Work, Organisation and Emotion*, 1(1): 74–86.

Hodson, R. (1997) Group relations at work: solidarity, conflict, and relations with Management. *Work and Occupation*, 24(4): 426–445.

Hooper, B. (2007) Shortening the distance between the 'I' and the 'It': a transformative approach to improving teaching. *Occupational Therapy in Health Care*, 21(1–2): 199–215.

Ives, Y. & Cox, E. (2012) *Goal-focused Coaching*. New York: Routledge.

Ives, Y. & Cox, E. (2014) *Relationship Coaching*. Hove: Routledge.

Jack, A. I., Boyatzis, R. E., Khawaja, M. S., Passarelli, A. M., & Leckie, R. L. (2013). Visioning in the brain: an fMRI study of inspirational coaching and mentoring. *Social neuroscience*, 8(4), 369–384.

Jowett, S., Lafrenière, M.A.K. & Vallerand, R.J. (2013) Passion for activities and relationship quality: a dyadic approach. *Journal of Social and Personal Relationships*, 30(6): 734–749.

Keep, J.A. (2013) *Developing self-care at work*. PhD, University of the West of England. Accessed 31/7/15 from: http://eprints.uwe.ac.uk/21799/

Kenworthy, A.L., Passarelli, A. & Van Oosten, E. (2014) Introduction: Coaching and positive emotions – exploring a collection of resources in the health and wellness domain. *Academy of Management Learning & Education*, 13(2): 290–292.

Lawrence, A.S., Troth, C.A., Jordan, J.P. & Collins, L.A. (2011) A review of emotion regulation and development of a framework for emotion regulation in the workplace. In P.L. Perrewé & D.C. Ganster (Eds.), *Research in Occupational Stress and Well-being: Vol. 9. The Role of Individual Differences in Occupational Stress and Well Being* (pp. 197–263). Bingley, England: Emerald.

Lazarus, R.S. (2013) *Fifty Years of the Research and Theory of RS Lazarus: An Analysis of Historical and Perennial Issues*. Psychology Press.

Lazarus, R. S. & Folkman, S. (1984) *Stress, Appraisal, and Coping*. New York: Springer Publishing Company.

Lee, G. (2003) *Leadership Coaching: From Personal Insight to Organisational Performance*. CIPD Publishing.

Linger, R.A. (2014) *A Qualitative Study of a Mindfulness-based Coaching Intervention* for Perception Shifts and Emotional Rregulation around Workplace Stressors and Quality of Worklife* (Doctoral dissertation, Saybrook University).

Lipchik, E. (2014) The development of my personal solution-focused working model: from 1978 and continuing. *International Journal of Solution-Focused Practices*, 2(2): 63–73.

Ludeman, K. & Erlandson, E. (2004) Coaching the alpha male. *Harvard Business Review*, 82(5): 58–67.

Lupton, D. (1998) *The Emotional Self: A Sociocultural Exploration*. London: Sage.

Mayer, J.D., Roberts, R.D. & Barsade, S.G. (2008) Human abilities: emotional intelligence. *Annual Review of Psychology*, 59: 507–536.

Mayer, J.D. & Salovey, P. (1997) What is emotional intelligence? In P. Salovey and D. Sluyter (Eds.), *Emotional Development and Emotional Intelligence: Educational Implications* (pp. 3–31). New York: Basic Books.

Mayer, J.D., Salovey, P. & Caruso, D.R. (2004) Emotional intelligence: theory, findings, and implications. *Psychological Inquiry*, 197–215.

Mayer, D.K. & Turner, J.C. (2006) Re-conceptualizing emotion and motivation to learn in classroom contexts. *Educational Psychology Review*, 18(4): 377–390.

McLaughlin, M. & Cox, E. (2016) *Leadership Coaching*. New York: Routledge.

Mezirow, J. (1990) *Fostering Critical Reflection in Adulthood: A Guide to Transformative and Emancipatory Learning*. San Francisco: Jossey-Bass.

Mezirow, J. (1995) Transformation theory of adult learning. In M. Welton (Ed.), *In Defense of the Lifeworld: Critical Perspectives on Adult Learning* (pp. 39–70). New York: State University of New York Press.

Neenan, M. & Dryden, W. (2002) *Life Coaching: A Cognitive-Behavioural Approach*. Hove: Brunner-Routledge.

Nicholson, N. & De Waal-Andrews, W. (2005) Playing to win: biological imperatives, self-regulation, and trade-offs in the game of career success. *Journal of Organizational Behavior*, 26: 137–154.

Nussbaum Martha, C. (2001). *Upheavals of Thought: The Intelligence of Emotions*. Cambridge: Cambridge University.

Nussbaum, M.C. (2004) *Emotions as Judgments of Value and Importance*. Oxford: Oxford University Press.

Patrick, C. (2004) *Coaching: Should we Enquire into Emotional Aspects of the Client's Experience?* Oxford Brookes University: MA Thesis.

Pizarro, D. (2000) Nothing more than feelings? The role of emotions in moral judgment. *Journal for the Theory of Social Behaviour*, 30(4): 355–375.

Richards, J.M. & Gross, J.J. (2005) Personality and emotional memory: how regulating emotion impairs memory for emotional events. *Journal of Research in Personality*, 40(5): 631–651.

Rimé, B., Corsini, S. & Herbette, G. (2002) Emotion, verbal expression, and the social sharing of emotion. In S.R. Fussell (Ed.). *The Verbal Communication of Emotions: Interdisciplinary Perspectives* (pp. 185–208). Mahwah, NJ, US: Lawrence Erlbaum Associates Publishers.

Roberts, R.D., MacCann, C., Matthews, G. & Zeidner, M. (2010) Emotional Intelligence: toward a consensus of models and measures. *Social and Personality Psychology Compass*, 4: 821–840.

Rogers. C.R. (1959) A theory of therapy, personality and interpersonal relationships as developed in the client-centered framework. In S. Koch (Ed.) *Psychology: A Study of a Science, Vol. III. Formulations of the person and the social context* (pp. 184–256). New York: McGraw Hill.

Rogers, J. (2012) *Coaching Skills: A Handbook*. McGraw-Hill Education (UK).

Sachs, J. & Blackmore, J. (1998) You never show you can't cope: women in school leadership roles managing their emotions. *Gender and Education*, 10(3): 265–279.

Salovey, P & Mayer, J.D. (1990) Emotional intelligence. *Imagination, Cognition and Personality*, 9(3): 185–211.

Schmid, P.F. (2001) Comprehension: ihe art of not knowing. Dialogical and ethical perspectives on empathy as dialogue in personal and person centred relationships. In S. Haugh & T. Merry (Eds.), *Empathy*. Llongarron, Ross-on-Wye: PCCS Books.

Sekerka, L. (2010) Preserving integrity in the face of corruption: exercising moral courage in the path to right action, *Journal of Moral Philosophy*, 1(3): pp. 1–14.

Shields, S.A. (2013) Gender and emotion: what we think we know, what we need to know, and why it matters. *Psychology of Women Quarterly*, 37(4): 423–435.

Simpson, A.V., Clegg, S. & Pitsis, T. (2014) 'I used to care but things have changed'. A genealogy of compassion in organizational theory. *Journal of Management Inquiry*, 23(4): 347–359.

Speedy, S. (2005) Emotions and emotionality in organisations. *Australian Journal of Business and Social Inquiry*, 3. Available at: www.scu.edu.au/schools/socialsciences/ajbsi/papers/Vol3/speedy.pdf. Accessed 18 April 2006.

Stacey, R.D. (1995) The science of complexity: an alternative perspective for strategic change processes. *Strategic Management Journal*, 16(6): 477–495.

Suh, E., Diener, E., Oishi, S., & Triandis, H. C. (1998). The shifting basis of life satisfaction judgments across cultures: Emotions versus norms. Journal of Personality and Social Psychology, 74(2): 482.

Susing, I., Green, S. & Grant, A. M. (2011) The potential use of the Authenticity Scale as an outcome measure in executive coaching. *The Coaching Psychologist*, 7(1): 16–25.

Taylor, E.W. (2001) Transformative learning theory: a neurobiological perspective of the role of emotions and unconscious ways of knowing. *International Journal of Lifelong Education*, 20(3): 218–236.

Tiedens, L.Z. (2001) The effect of anger on the hostile inferences of aggressive and nonaggressive people: specific emotions, cognitive processing, and chronic accessibility. *Motivation and Emotion*, 25(3): 233–251.

Tugade, M. & Frederickson, B. (2000) Resilient individuals use positive emotions to bounce back from negative emotional arousal. Paper presented at International Society for Research in Emotion, August 2000, Quebec City, Canada.

Vallen, G. (1993) Organizational climate and burnout. *Cornell Hotel and Restaurant Administration* Quarterly, 34(1): 54–60.

Weber, M. (1978) *Economy and Society: An Outline of Interpretive Sociology*. Berkeley: University of California Press.

Wilson, K.R., Havighurst, S.S., & Harley, A.E. (2014) Dads tuning into kids: piloting a new parenting program targeting fathers' emotion coaching skills. *Journal of Community Psychology*, 42(2): 162–168.

Working with Narratives in Coaching

David Drake

INTRODUCTION

While a narrative frame is relatively new in the field of coaching, stories have been an essential component of cultures and communities since the dawn of time. They are at the core of what defines us as humans in terms of our identities, our interactions and our inspirations. This chapter will focus on the process of working with people's narratives and stories in coaching. It draws in part from the field of narrative coaching itself as an example of a third-generation practice in which the main focus is on 'collaborative and co-creative dialogues between a coach and a client(s) who are in a mutual relationship as reflective fellow human beings characterized by varying degrees of symmetry over time' (Stelter, 2014a). It also draws from other narrative processes, which tend to be imbued with these types of values regardless of the coaching methodology in which they are used. They reflect a concern for the people who are narrating their experience, the stories they are sharing and the underlying narratives that inform who they are and how they act.

This chapter provides an overview of the knowledge that is critical for understanding and working with narratives in coaching. First, the narrative turn in the social sciences will be explored in terms of its influence on narrative processes in coaching. This will include descriptions of literary theory (particularly the function and structure of stories), the humanities (particularly social constructionism, phenomenology and anthropology), and psychology (particularly our minds, identities, and needs for learning and development). Second, a narrative-based theory and process of change will be explored. Third, an analysis of the current state of research and recommendations for future research will be offered. Fourth, the conclusion will include some of the implications of a narrative approach for the wider field of coaching.

THE FOUNDATIONS FOR WORKING WITH NARRATIVES IN COACHING

Czarniawska (2004) makes the case that literary theory, the humanities and psychology fed into what became narrative studies as part of the broader 'narrative turn' in the social sciences over the past fifty years. Each of these three domains are central to understanding the role of narratives for people and their value in coaching, as seen in Table 16.1 below.

Literary Theory

Literary theory is a form of literary criticism in which texts are analyzed in a systemic fashion. In the context of coaching, it involves a focus on the analysis and exploration of people's stories through a narrative lens. As Hyvärinen (2008) notes:

> the metaphoric discourse was [intended] to revolutionize the way human action, identity, and life were understood, and here narrative provided an important combination of temporal change and continuity…. [Unfortunately,] the metaphoric discourse was not primarily interested in the study of narratives as such, but rather in their use as a perspective and analytic models for the study of lives. (p. 262)

Coaching would benefit from incorporating applied literary theory so that clients' stories could be seen and leveraged as resources in their own right, not just as psychological expressions.

Literary theorists suggest that there is a deep structure to narrative, and well-formed stories are particular realizations of it (Bruner, 1986b). However, coaching is not about the hunt for 'good' stories, but rather about working with the relevant narrative material in whatever stories are presented. Of course, the better the coaching process, the more of the deeper narrative structure and patterns will be revealed. This involves listening for the explicit stories and implicit narratives as people describe their experiences and aspirations. While stories provide the material and vocabulary in coaching, this chapter focuses on working with the underlying narratives because they are the true driver of change. The term *narrative* is used here to refer to broader patterns and the word *story* is used here to refer to specific instances. For example, stories about a person's issues with her boss could be seen as an expression of her narrative about relationships with authority figures and/or larger cultural narratives about authority as a construct. Drake (2015) defines these two terms more fully as follows:

> A narrative can be seen as a socially- and contextually-constructed communication *structure* marked by temporality and causality, plot and purpose, that enables meaning- and sense-making for those involved. A story is an episodic *form* of communication within oneself or with others that has both conscious and unconscious elements. (p. 108)

Stories are often framed in terms of a three-act structure that reflects people's efforts to: (1) respond to inciting incidents that throw their life out of balance or equilibrium;

Table 16.1 How the narrative turn in the social sciences informs coaching

Field	Conceptualization of narrative	Examples	Focus in coaching
Literary theory	As speech act	(Searle, 1965: Barthes, 1975: Labov and Waletsky, 1967)	How stories are formed
Humanities	As social discourse	(Madigan, 1996: Berger and Luckmann, 1966: Foucault, 1972)	How stories are framed
Psychology	As cognitive schema	(Mandler, 1984: Russell and van Den Broek, 1992: Schank, 1990)	Why stories are told
Source	(cited in Tammi, 2005)		(Drake, 2009a)

(2) identify the object of their desire that they believe will restore the balance; and (3) overcome a series of barriers in pursuit of that object until there is a resolution (Boje, 1998). Without an incident that thwarts the character's status quo and intention, there would not be a story. It is the clash between what the character values and expected to happen *and* what actually happened that sets the character in motion in search of restoration and resolution (Bruner and Luciarello, 1989). As McKee (1997) notes, the energy of the protagonist's desire (function) forms the *Spine* of a story (structure) as its primary unifying force.

Stein and Glenn's (1979) grammatical structure for stories and Burke's (1969) work on dramatism are useful here, particularly the latter with its emphasis on motive as the driver of narratives. His Pentad was composed of five questions that serve as the basis for narrative structure: 'what was done (act), when and where it was done (scene), who did it (agent), how he did it (agency), and why (purpose)' (p. xv). Drake (2003) incorporated the coda (Bruner, 2002) as a sixth element and added a fourth act to acknowledge what happens as a result of the first three acts as described above. Finally, Campbell's (1968, 1973) work on mythological narratives provides a deeper context for the interpretation and transformation of people's stories. The result is a more complete narrative cycle and one that corresponds better to what happens for the teller of a story as it unfolds within the context of coaching.

The stories people tell in coaching are profoundly shaped by the narratives from which they begin and to which they will return. Change can be seen as the journey between one and the other, with both endpoints changed in the process as well. For example, coaches would do well to see people's stories as attempts to resolve what Bruner (1990) calls 'breaches of the commonplace', what McKee (1997) calls 'inciting incidents' and what Mezirow (1991) calls 'disorienting dilemmas.' It is these reversals in circumstances – what Aristotle saw as a *peripeteia* – which spark stories and force tellers to conceive of what they believe will put the situation back into balance (the object of desire). The deeper the desire the more it involves facing their greatest fear or challenge, answering their most essential question, and/or making their hardest choice. While working with narratives in coaching is a deeply relational process, developing a better understanding of literary theory enables coaches to engage with and advocate for the stories themselves as a resource for change.

Humanities

Through the humanities (e.g., political science, sociology and anthropology) we have gained a broader understanding of stories as central to the very fabric of life. In particular, they share an interest in the social discourse that shapes, and is shaped by, the narratives people form to identify and express themselves. This is important because people define themselves by the referent points they and others deem significant. This can be seen, for example, in their *available narratives* (Drake, 2007), which are largely defined by the vocabulary and grammar, the beliefs and norms, of their socio-cultural systems. They are instrumental in the formation of the potential stories people construct as frames for what is possible (Freedman and Combs, 1996). As people begin to recognize the limitations inherent in their available narratives through coaching, they can create more distance from these narratives, see them more clearly, and surface other selves. As alternative potential stories become available, other sympathetic and previously neglected aspects of the person's experience (and related discourse) can be expressed and embodied (White and Epston, 1990; Drake, 2015).

The influence of the humanities can also be seen in the post-structuralist shift from 'stories-as-objects' to 'stories-in-context' (Boje, 1998). As a result, coaches can attend to narrative as content *and* narrative as context, stories as text *and* stories as performance. This frees coaches up to move fluidly in working with people and their narration in service of the process and the objectives. In so doing, clients can be addressed as both narrator and protagonist and the narratives can be addressed at both personal and collective levels. It could be argued that this contextual and systemic perspective is often insufficiently addressed in coaching, with its historical preference for individualistic and atomistic perspectives. A narrative stance is becoming increasingly important as coaching operates more cross-culturally in a hyper-connected and complex world. The anthropological frames found in Campbell's (1973) work on the heroic journey, van Gennep's (1960) and Turner's (1969) work on rites of passage can be quite useful here given their integrative nature.

In many ways, social constructionism was the most influential force in making the narrative turn as it shifted the paradigm through which we saw reality itself. Its roots can be seen in Berger and Luckmann's (1966) treatises on the sociology of knowledge and the social construction of reality and in Gergen's (1973) work, which called for the inclusion of contextual, social, political, and economic phenomena in understanding people. Identity came to be seen not as something that was 'given' but as something bestowed in acts of social recognition (Berger, 1963). This perspective can also be seen, for example, in the work by Anzaldua (1987) on *borderlands identities*, Geertz (1978) on culture from an indigenous view, Sorrell and Montgomery (2001) on *feminist perspectives* on identity formation, and McLaren (1993) on *critical pedagogy*. Social constructionism offered a challenge to the notion of universal truths (Kvale, 1992) and, in so doing, provided a stronger foundation for the notion of 'authorship' (and the potential for 're-authorship') that are central to narrative practices. It supports a view of people as intersubjectively narrated beings who cannot be seen independent of their context and of stories as embedded in networks of reciprocally influencing narratives (Sluzki, 1992).

Phenomenology was also important with its emphasis on people's perception and experience of a phenomenon and, as a result, how they attribute meaning to the world in which they are a part (Husserl, 1971[1927]; Ihde, 1977). One of its central practices is epoché, a method for openly approaching phenomena through attention to the here-and-now and bracketing immediate judgment and interpretation of a situation in the process. Depraz, Varela, and Vermersch (2000) describe the three phases of this process as: (1) suspending one's habitual thoughts; (2) converting or reorienting attention from the external to the internal; and (3) letting go in order to respond to the immediate experience and the knowledge found there. This describes quite well what it takes to work with narratives in coaching. Using a phenomenological approach enables coaches to avoid three common pitfalls: (1) attending to the external symptoms and overlooking the internal dynamics; (2) rigidly adhering to their own habitual thoughts and models; and (3) shaping the experience in terms of their own knowledge

A phenomenological approach to working with narratives enables people to experience the emotions of an event and its meaning in the same moment (McKee, 2004). It enables them to stay present to what is being experienced while exploring what is being experienced, thus providing access to more material that can be used to form a new narrative. It does so by working across what Bruner (1986, 1990) called the 'landscape of action', which answers the epistemic question of what happened, and the 'landscape of consciousness' that addresses the deontic question of what it means. By integrating material from both landscapes, people can construct a full narrative. Working across and within both landscapes also enables people to examine their situation's existential nature and complexity (Spinelli, 2010), verbalize issues that are often rooted in habits and action routines (Drake & Stelter, 2014) and become more accountable for their narrative choices. People can then critically examine their taken-for-granted understandings of themselves and others; the social discourse through which their experiences are framed and narrated; and the systemic and existential issues that affect them. The humanities have profoundly enriched our understanding of how people create and re-create their narratives.

Psychology

Psychology is the third field that contributed to the narrative turn and the one most readily associated with coaching. It informs our understanding of why people tell their stories and what it takes to tell a new story. As we have seen, it relates to the function, energy and motives that drive their stories and inform their lives. It leads to questions such as, 'What are they hoping to accomplish with the stories they tell – and for whom and for what purpose?' 'What value is at stake in their life at this moment?' As McKee (2004) asks, 'What does the person want that, if you gave it to her, would stop the story?' Drake (2015) argues that psychology offers insights on people's narratives at four levels:

- *intentions* (conscious and otherwise) for sharing this story this way in this moment;
- *identities* (as constructed, lived and imagined) of the person telling the story;
- *impacts* (on self and others, intended and unintended) of telling this story;
- *interpretations* (spoken and unspoken) of the telling and impact of this story.

The more coaches can understand about why people tell their stories, the more they will be able to help them reconfigure their narratives in accordance with their hopes for the future. To that end, this section focuses on three areas: (i) how the mind works, (ii) how identities are formed, and (iii) how learning and development can be supported. To bring about changes requires people to renegotiate the nature of and relationships between the narratives in their mind, their lives and their environments.

How our Minds Work

Narratives and neural processes are both structured as volitional movement through time and space. This is one reason why narratives serve as such a natural and rich resource in coaching. People use stories to structure their experience as 'events' in space and seek to join them together in a sensible and causal timeline as part of an ongoing process of meaning- and sense-making (Schank, 1990). Our minds form narratives not only to construe what happened in the past or is happening in the present but, like all complex adaptive systems, also build models that allow them to anticipate the world and the future (Holland, 1995). The stories people most often tell themselves and others – and manifest in their lives – are testament to their most well-worn neural paths. The issues they bring to coaching often reflect bumps along that path and gaps in their narration (e.g., between inner narratives and outer stories, current narratives and desired narratives). People are able to reconfigure their narratives because the brain has access to diverse neural networks (Cozolino, 2006, 2010) and a capacity for emotional and neural plasticity. Development can be seen as a process of acting our way to new stories and narrating our way to new actions.

Many of the narrative patterns adults seek to address in coaching have roots in their pre-verbal experiences as children. The introduction of attachment theory into the coaching literature (Drake, 2009b) brought with it an extensive body of research and practice that can be used – within the bounds of one's capabilities and agreements – in working with people's pre-verbal and verbal narratives. The notions of safe haven, secure base and working models (Bowlby, 1969, 1988; Ainsworth and Bowlby, 1991) as outcomes of the attachment process offer an important frame for understanding what people want from coaching. They, along with the four types of attachment preference, can be used in listening to and working with people's narratives to enhance their sense of security. They also remind us of the need for both resonance and dissonance in coaching so that people can develop the trust to tell their story *and* change their story. To support these efforts, we need to learn more about how the coaching relationship and experience can be used to help people mature their working models (Fonagy et al., 2008) as meta-narratives.

Narrative Identities

While coaching is often focused on helping people make new choices at the episodic and behavioral levels, deeper changes are more likely when their narrative patterns and identities are also addressed (Mattingly, 1998) – particularly those related to self-defining memories (Singer, 2005). A narrative pattern can be seen as the habitual way of framing one's experience that reinforces a set of expectations, actions and anticipated rewards. These patterns and the identities they support largely operate at non-conscious and somatic levels, but they can be made conscious and malleable through working with people's stories. Stories give us access to what Mead (1967[1934]) described as our inner world, as a 'field, a sort of inner forum, in which we are both a spectator and the actor' (p. 401).

Stories enable people to see themselves in new ways as the author of and an actor in their narratives and their lives (Siegel, 1999: Wallin, 2007). James (1927[1892]) spoke about it as the distinction between the *I* (the subject) and the *Me* (the object). Others have described it as the distinction between the *self-as-knower* and the *self-as-known* (Hermans, 2004) and between the *author* (self-as-teller), and the *actor* (self-as-tale-told) (Mancuso and Sarbin, 1983; Sarbin, 1986a, 1986b). Kegan (1994) and Mahony (2003) describe it as the difference between the *I* as the subjective self who is observing and the *Me* as the objective self who is being observed. Scholars such as Gilligan (1982) and McLaren (1993) extended this dialectic by highlighting, respectively, the relational and liminal nature of identity formation.

Other authors have used Piaget's (1962) distinction between imitation/accommodation *and* play/assimilation as another way to understand narrative tensions between safety *and* self-expression, inclusion *and* uniqueness (Brewer and Pickett, 1999), and integration *and* differentiation (Kreiner et al., 2006). These tensions reflect the human striving for (1) stability, consistency, continuity and coherence as the basis for safety and security; and (2) agility, novelty, discontinuity and change as the basis for exploration and growth (Drake, 2008). Identities are shaped by these two often-competing orientations, often resulting in tensions for people between presenting identities that are socially acceptable and functional and embodying identities that are authentic and consistent with how they see themselves (Drake, 2009a). It is important to note that these tensions do not reflect a fixed duality but rather a view of identities as a prism (Stevens-Long, 2000) in which elements move between foreground and background based on the narrative desires and demands in the moment. Identities can thus be seen as performances (Mishler, 1992, 1999) through which people try to keep a particular narrative going (Giddens, 1991) – or adapt it when they cannot.

Identities and narratives can thus be seen as 'psychosocial' (McAdams et al., 1997) processes based in a both/and approach as advocated by Rossiter (1999) and others. As Singer (1996) noted, 'Theorists who embrace a personalogical orientation ... emphasize the individual's processes of storying and meaning making within a cultural context, whereas social constructionist theorists ... are interested in how culture wrote the story of our lives' (p. 452). Identities, then, can be seen as moving feasts, as traveling repertory companies (Singer and Rexhaj, 2006), through which 'people continually calibrate their internal landscapes and external environments in ways they believe will enable them to achieve what is important to them. They do this by deconstructing, constructing and re-constructing selves based on the stories told by, around and about them' (Drake, 2015, p. 58).

Working with narratives helps make visible people's otherwise invisible identity processes, their 'theory of events' (Foucault, 1965). Their stories act as windows into what is true for people, the narrative logic that makes it so for them and the narrative identities that have formed around what is deemed true. They also can act as openings to imagine what else may be possible, what they would gain and who they could become as a result. These openings offer people the space to reflect on, experience and test new aspects of themselves – and the new narratives that go with them. In the process, they may temporarily adopt what Ibarra (1999) calls a 'provisional self' as part of a transition. These vital in-between phases and strategies seem under-explored in coaching even though they are critical to our understanding of how people change and develop. For example, what roles do the 'possible selves' that beckon people from the future play in their development (Markus and Nurius, 1986)? Coaching helps people to retain a sense of a coherent whole with a center that holds, while increasing their capacity to flourish as they push out from the center (Drake, 2015). To make the most from coaching, people need an identity that is stable enough to act and open enough to adapt.

Learning and Development

Coaching can be seen as a semi-structured learning and development process. Its aim is to assist people to become more critically aware of how their presuppositions have come to constrain the way they perceive, understand, and feel about their world; reformulate these assumptions to permit a perspective that is more inclusive *and* permeable, more discriminating *and* integrative; and make decisions or otherwise act upon these new understandings (Mezirow, 1991). How people narrate their experience often yields important clues as to what they need to learn and how they will need to develop in order to achieve what they are seeking. Coaches can draw on situated and social views of learning (Lave and Wenger, 1991), transformative learning theories (Illeris, 2004) and integrative development theory (Drake, 2016) to support them in their role and their work. In large part it is about creating a 'holding environment' (Winnicott, 1965) in which people feel safe enough to tell the whole story and, in the process, can develop themselves in order to bring it to life.

Vygotsky's (1978b) work is useful in this regard in that he was less interested in 'fossilized' forms of learning and development (e.g., capabilities already obtained) and more interested in experiential processes through which new forms or levels of development emerge (e.g., potential for growth). He saw learning and development as social and participatory in nature with an aim toward increased self-regulation. Vygotsky (1978a) saw the importance of what he called 'zones of proximal development,' which he defined as 'the distance between the actual developmental level as determined by independent problem-solving and the level of potential development as determined through problem-solving under adult supervision or in collaboration with more capable peers' (p. 86). These zones are based in a symbiotic relationship between development and learning in which development as an individually internalized process always lags behind learning as a culturally mediated process. As such, coaches can use people's narratives as openings to learn about the issue at hand (e.g., where do you most notice the stress you have described in your body?) before exploring how they can develop themselves (e.g., what are you telling yourself in those moments when you are feeling overly stressed and what would you need to do differently to be more at peace?).

To successfully learn in these zones of proximal development requires sufficient 'scaffolding,' a term introduced by Wood, Bruner and Ross (1976). Bruner (1978) described scaffolding as 'the steps taken to reduce the degrees of freedom taken in carrying out some task so that the child can concentrate on the difficult skill she is in the process of acquiring' (p. 19). Wells (1999) identified three features of scaffolding: '(1) the essentially dialogical nature of the discourse in which knowledge is co-constructed; (2) the significance of the kind of activity in which knowing is embedded and (3) the role of artifacts that mediate knowing' (p. 127). Scaffolding enables people to step from the 'known and familiar' of their problem experience into the 'not yet known, but possible to know' territory of their preferred experience (Carey et al., 2009). It needs to incorporate the structural, objective 'pull' from the environment (its demands, resources and possibilities) and the unique, subjective 'push' from the individual (his capabilities, needs and desires) (Drake, 2015). Scaffolding strengthens the space held in coaching so people can learn what is theirs to learn in a given zone, embody it and apply it. It is often most powerful to work experientially with narratives because it brings client's learning opportunities front and center. The strongest scaffolding is often formed from elements in people's own stories (Drake, 2003; Gergen and Gergen, 2006) as these features are more likely to be recognized and accessed.

If people feel they have sufficient scaffolding they are more willing to engage in 'serious play' in order to explore and experiment with new narratives and identities. The purpose of doing so is to help them decouple their habituated associations between means and ends (Mainemelis and Ronson, 2006). It bypasses their ego defenses and normative scripts while still respecting their humanity and their stories. The result is a safe space in which they can more freely experiment with releasing old identities, behaviors and narratives and then rehearsing new and untested ones to meet their current or anticipated needs (Drake, 2015; Ibarra, 1999; Kolb and Kolb, 2010). As a result, they will be more able to: (1) re-align identity and role expectations (Hall, 1971); (2) negotiate between 'identities claimed' and 'identities granted' (Bartel and Dutton, 2001); (3) navigate the threshold between fantasy and reality (Ibarra and Petriglieri, 2010); (4) circumscribe activities within boundaries and limits in time and space (Mainemelis and Ronson, 2006); and (5) integrate body, spirit and mind at a higher level yet in a non-threatening way (Erikson, 1950).

Another resource for people's development can be found in aspects of themselves and their narratives associated with what Jung (1972) described as their Shadow (see Bly, 1988, Kolodziejski, 2004). Many of the issues that arise in coaching are first seen in people's projections of their Shadow, a means by which they can distance themselves from the challenge to their ego before (hopefully) retrieving it as part of themselves. As Drake (2015) noted, 'What if the characters in the stories we tell represent parts of ourselves projected onto the "other" as a means to work through our own development or identity issues?' (p. 94). Moreover, these traits and energies are often what the person most needs for their development. For example, a person's complaints about a team member who dominates meetings can be used to explore what it would be like to tap into his Shadow about power. The key question here is, 'What is being asked of him through his own story?'

Working with Shadow elements in narratives also opens up a more systemic way of thinking about and addressing strengths in coaching. This starts with an important distinction between intrinsic and extrinsic strengths and proposes that learning and development involve maturing strengths through the incorporation of their Shadow side (see Drake, 2015). The result is a third way that brings forth the best from both. For example: A person's strength in creativity is tempered by the fire of aggression (Shadow) to yield a new story as one who is more decisive about what to create. Coaches can use people's narratives to ascertain their current level of learning and development as well as find opportunities for growth. In keeping with

Vygotsky, it is based in the proposition that what people can do with their coach today, they can more independently and capably do on their own tomorrow.

A NARRATIVE THEORY AND PROCESS OF CHANGE

To work effectively with narratives in coaching requires a suitable theory and process of change. The focus in this section is on four aspects which are central to the process: (1) the authoring and emplotment of stories as a way to understand how people form and frame their stories; (2) a framework as a way to understand the phases of their narration; (3) the significance of positioning as a way to understand the relationships and movements of characters in their stories (including themselves); and (4) the connections between narration and growth as a way to understand how to facilitate change. A narrative-based theory of change augments the dominant psychological frames with those from literary theory and the humanities. It also balances what often seems like a bias toward cognitive dimensions by including other dimensions that are crucial for making and sustaining change. For example, coaches can use somatic practices and embodied experiences to help clients create stronger anchors for change (Drake, 2015; Heller, 1991). Narratives can be viewed through two lenses in terms of change: *authoring*, how and why people tell their stories (function) and *emplotment*, how people form and frame their stories (structure). Working narratively involves helping people to examine their assumptions about reality through a deeper engagement with their stories.

Charon (2006) writes about this distinction in terms of the 'autobiographical gap' between the narrator-who-speaks (the *I* who authors) and the protagonist-who-acts (the *Me* who is emplotted). Bakan's (1966) describes it as the distinction between agency (how we act and express ourselves) and communion (how and why we are in relation to others). People use *emplotment strategies* (Hermans and Kempen, 1993, Mattingly, 1994) to make sense of and choices about their experience using the material and discourse at hand. Change often requires a shift in which events are included, which themes they are organized around, which characters are portrayed as significant, and which voices are privileged in the telling (Botella and Herrero, 2000). Any one of these can be used in coaching to bring about and bolster change. It is particularly useful to listen for what is absent but implicit in narratives (Carey et al., 2009; Derrida, 1978; White, 2007) and for thresholds (Drake, 2007), where typical emplotment strategies are no longer working. It is in these liminal, in-between spaces where growth most often occurs. This is important because experiences that are not consistent with people's preferred self-stories are generally not deemed significant and are often invisible (Schank, 1990; White, 1988). Coaches can help individuals notice exceptions to their current self-descriptions and free themselves to explore alternative territories and possibilities in and for their life.

Drake (2015) has suggested that, 'the changes people are going through [are often] evident in the changes as seen in the characters and relationships in the stories they choose to tell' (p. 94). Narratives shared in coaching can take on special therapeutic powers because they are being addressed through ritual actions (Mattingly, 1998). To make the most of these opportunities requires a structure for change through which to parse the current narratives and formulate new ones. A rite of passage framework offers one such structure for change that is well suited for working with narratives because it incorporates the personal and collective needs for structure *and* anti-structure, elevation *and* subversion, transition *and* continuity in transitions. White and Epston (White and Epston, 1990; Epston and White, 1995; White, 2002) used this framework to depict people's movement through psychotherapy, with a particular emphasis on how social constructs and dominant narratives affected them. Drake (2003, 2015) enhanced the original rites of passage framework through the addition of the vertical axis to demarcate the movement through time and crossing across four thresholds not one. He proposed that the four acts of a narrative aligned with the four phases of transitions and change, as well as the four phases of development that occurs as a result (see Figure 16.1). As a result, the three fields that enabled the narrative turn (literary theory, the humanities and psychology) are integrated into a unified process for researching and working with narratives to bring about change.

Act 1 *situates* the person in her story, the world as she sees it and lives in it now, and the coaching session. Act 2 is about the separation from the original state and the *search* that is underway in the story, and for the person, to find what will restore what has been lost and gain what is sought. Act 3 builds on the individuation that occurs in the process and focuses on what is *shifting* in the person and the story based on what was discovered in the search. Act 4 is about the reincorporation of the person and the new story back into the world and *sustaining* and integrating what has changed. Each of the four phases is separated from the one that follows by a threshold, a doorway that marks a shift in attention in terms of what is happening (and required).

The model offers a way to track and facilitate people's narration in coaching, and it offers insights on the developmental and practical needs and opportunities that are present for the client at each point in the process. There is a lot of attention in coaching to the 'aha' moments that often occurs in the second phase as people make new discoveries. However, research would suggest that more attention should be given to the last two phases in people's narrative process when people are implementing and integrating what they discovered (Goldsmith and Morgan, 2004). The fourth act is critical, in part, because not everyone will embrace the new person and/or the new narrative and not everything within the person will be solidly aligned yet.

As noted earlier, one of the reasons why narratives are useful in supporting change is the strong correspondences between our minds and our stories – both of which operate using temporal and spatial coordinates. Building on this symmetry and his initial research, Drake (2003) proposed that narratives could be viewed as trialogic given their hermeneutic nature. In so doing, he identified the trialogue as being between the *declarative space* of the narrator who is telling the story, the *narrative space* of the story as it is being told, and the *projective space* of the narrative elements that emerge in the process. All three are systematically related to one another in ways that are useful to explore in order to understand what is happening as people tell their stories in coaching. Tillich's (1965) notion of a third area where one can stand outside a duality, Schwartz-Salant's (1998) notion of an imaginal vessel in psychoanalysis, Bhabha's (1990) work on third spaces, and Clandinin and Connelly's (2000) definition of a three-dimensional narrative

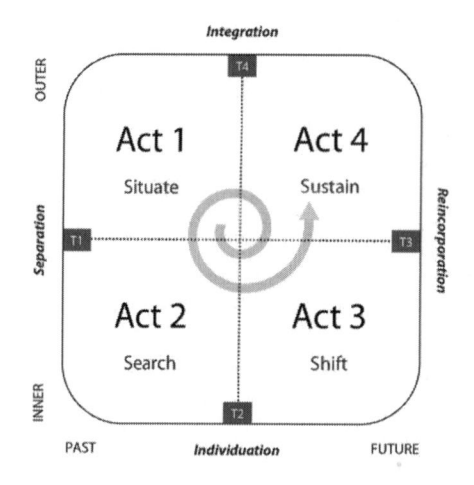

Figure 16.1 An integrative process for working with narratives in coaching

inquiry space were all instrumental in developing this trialogic approach.

The meaning of a story can be interpreted from a variety of perspectives because 'each narrative movement offers the possibility for construing alternatives in the interpersonal configuration of the characters' (Anderson, 2004, p. 318). It is therefore of vital interest to understand how people position themselves and others in their stories and in the coaching conversation. Davies and Harré (1990) suggest that people attempt to clarify, claim and convince others of their identity through positioning themselves in both their internal and external narration. As Anderson (2004) observed, 'Each story serves as a new stage in which the narrator repositions the characters in his or her life within a constantly moving interpersonal field' (p. 317). Riessman (2002) asks a similar question as a narrative researcher, 'How does she locate characters in relation to one another and in relation to herself?' Narratives can thus be reconfigured through a variety of coaching methods so as to provide a stronger and more aligned foundation for what the person is seeking. This involves working with people to increase the range and repertoire of their narrative responses by establishing new relationships between existing story parts or introducing new ones (Hermans, 2004).

One of the benefits of this more inclusive approach is a richer understanding of how people 're-story' (Kenyon and Randall, 1997) or 're-author' (White and Epston, 1990) new narratives that are less beholden to dominant narratives and more supportive of desired new ways of being in the world. Drake (2015) defined it as a process of 'reconfiguration' to highlight the integrative nature of the process that transcends and includes the story and the author as noted above. It utilizes externalization processes to help people when there is a need for greater awareness and acceptance and internalization processes when there is a need for greater accountability and action.

Externalization in this context involves inviting people to situate issues outside themselves such that they can be seen as separate from who they are and addressed more freely as a result. Internalization in this context involves inviting people to bring issues back into themselves, albeit transformed, so they can be seen as part of who they are and enacted more fully as a result. Both of these processes has a role to play in addressing the conflict often inherent in the development process as people re-negotiate their positional preferences and narrative patterns.

Conflict is the axis on which stories turn, the key to the energy that propels them forward, and the crucible for their resolution. The aim in coaching is to help people step into the heart of their conflict in order to clarify what they truly want and what that will require. This can be done a number of ways through the narratives themselves. For example, they can be invited to: (1) move between narrator and protagonist to deepen their insight into what is going on for them; (2) move between positions in their own stories to increase their empathic understanding; (3) step inside their experiences to get a deeper felt-sense of their narrative patterns; or (4) step outside their experiences to gain a larger perspective and experiment with new ways of being and doing. Change seems to require people to loosen the grip of an existing narrative in order to make more space for replacing, reframing or reconfiguring certain aspects to form a new narrative. The unlearning and 'un-narrating' that are required to get to that place are often as difficult as the rest of the change process (Prochaska et al., 1994).

As such, there is a need for a better understanding of how to gauge and enhance change readiness in coaching (see Franklin, 2005) and how narrative positioning over the course of a coaching conversation relates to the ability to change (Cox, 2013). It would also be valuable to increase this knowledge in relation to coaches so as to enhance their training and development. As Corrie and Lane (2010) caution, 'If coaches are not careful they end up serving their own formulations more than those befitting their clients or what is actually happening in the session' (p. 242). In the end, people are most successful in bringing about change if they move well through all four acts (refer to Figure 16.1) and their related phases. To the degree they are successful, they will have made shifts in 'who and how they are as *author* of their stories, as *actor* in their stories, and as *agent* in the narratives around them' (Drake, 2015, p. 180).

A word of caution is needed about some of the challenges that can arise in working with narratives. Strawson (2004) cautions coaches about working narratively with people who may not be inclined towards this approach. One example would be people that function almost exclusively in the paradigmatic (logico-scientific) mode as opposed to the narrative mode (Bruner, 1986). Another example would be people who have experienced trauma that has not been sufficiently addressed. He also cautions coaches to not always accept a client's narrative at face value. This is due to our human bias toward 'narrative smoothing,' by which we gloss over details that challenge the coherence of our narratives and our preferred identities. One strategy that is useful in this regard is to distinguish factual truth (e.g., my boss arrived 15 minutes after the meeting was scheduled to start) from felt truth (e.g., my boss is disrespectful of my time – and, by extension, me). Not everything clients tell us in their stories is factually true. However, rather than argue this point, coaches would do well to explore with people how they came to believe that was true. More broadly, while reflecting on Strawson's concerns, Cox (2013) noted:

> If the construction of the narrative is seen as an ongoing and contingent activity and stories are used as indicators by the coach that there is work to be done, the frozen scripts Strawson feared are continually forestalled or modernised. This enables people to distinguish between the self they knew in the past and the self they are perceiving in the moment. This is probably one of the most important tasks of the coach. (p. 38)

PAST RESEARCH ON WORKING WITH NARRATIVES IN COACHING

Given the values at the heart of narrative work – the direct experience of human phenomena, the advocacy for alternate discourses, the recognition of collective and non-conscious forces affecting our narration, and the commitment to a non-reductionist orientation – it is not surprising that most research related to this process is descriptive and qualitative in nature. Scholars such as Abma (1999), Mattingly (1991), Mishler (1992), Pals (2006) and Rappaport (1993) have laid down a strong foundation of narrative analysis in related disciplines from which coaching could benefit. More opportunities are needed for narrative researchers and narrative practitioners to share their respective bodies of evidence with one another in order to leverage their respective insights and advance their respective practices. This would also strengthen the bridge between research and practice in the field more broadly. Coaching would also do well to learn from researchers in fields such as narrative medicine (see Charon, 2006; Kleinman, 1988; Frank, 1995) where work has been done not only to study the use of narratives in delivering services but also to reframe the meta-narratives upon which our definitions of medicine and health are constructed.

Hewson (1991) provided an exemplary example of how to use classical research – in this case, laboratory findings in cognitive psychology experiments (e.g., Ross and Conway, 1986) (Sherman et al., 1981) – as a guide for practice. For example, the studies she cites found that people selectively recall their past behaviors to make them consistent with their current attitudes. She offered the following advice based on the data, 'Induce your audience to recall attitudinally relevant past behaviors. This should increase commitment to new acquired attitudes' (p. 6). Examples of qualitative research on narratives in coaching include: Blanc-Sahnoun (2009) on using narrative coaching in a professional community after a suicide; Royston (2011) on using narrative coaching with executives in South Africa; Stelter (see Stelter and Law, 2012; Stelter et al.; 2010, Stelter, 2014b) on using narratives in coaching as a collaborative values-based process. Swart (2015) on using narrative coaching in dialogic OD interventions; and Vogel (2012) on comparing approaches to working with narratives in coaching.

There are very few randomized controlled studies in this area, in large part because they largely operate from within a different agenda and frame. However, there are exceptions such as Stelter's (2014a, 2011) research that examined the influence of narrative collaborative group coaching on the career development, self-reflection and general wellbeing of young athletes. The study was based on a randomized, controlled design ($n = 77$) with 31 assigned to a group coaching condition and 46 assigned to a control group. All the participants filled out a validated questionnaire prior to the study, at the midway point, immediately after the final intervention session and five months after the end of the intervention. The findings showed meaningful improvements among the subjects who participated in group coaching.

FUTURE RESEARCH ON WORKING WITH NARRATIVES IN COACHING

The need now is for more research to significantly advance our understanding of the transformative potential of narratives in coaching. In particular, there is need is to better understand the impact of factors such as gender, culture and age on the narratives addressed in coaching. For example, we could learn from researchers such as Nicolopoulou (2008) who noted how children's spontaneous storytelling divided systematically along gender lines. There is also a fundamental need to better understand the relationships between changing narratives and changing behaviors in terms of how each one affects the other. This will require practitioners and researchers to take a deeper look at the social and transpersonal factors at play in people's narratives and stories. Equipped with such knowledge, coaches would be more able to support people's growth through coaching. Other areas of narrative research that would benefit coaching as a whole include:

- Using ethnographic research to support the development of more contemporary rites of passage – for example, the call for more feminine, non-Western and ecological frames (Bynum, 1984);
- Using phenomenological and existential inquiries to enrich our understanding of how to develop people fit for a time of increasing complexity and uncertainty, such as using social analysis to understand the coaching process (Jones et al., 2002);
- Using participatory methods to study the ethical frames for working with people's narratives in coaching and in research on coaching, such as developing a client bill of rights (Drake, 2015);
- Using narrative analysis to study what coaches hear in client stories in order to develop a more nuanced understanding of levels of listening and how to develop these capabilities. This could include, perhaps through developing a guide that delineates different types of listening (Woodcock, 2010);
- Using discourse analysis to unpack the stories coaches tell themselves before, during and after sessions about what they want to do, are doing and have done. For example, the links between coaches' identity and their behavior could be the subject of an investigation (Butcher, 2012);
- Using case studies to critically assess the cognitive, discursive, and dispositional aspects (Gergen and Gergen, 2006) of people's narratives in coaching, like crafting and analyzing stories of leadership practices (Danzig, 1999);
- Using meta-analysis to study the impact of environmental, sociological, political and cultural narratives on people's growth and performance (and vice versa) (see Noer, 2005).

CONCLUSION

Brockbank and McGill (2006) argue that a story is an 'authentic self-disclosure – an attempt to reveal the self as a person and to reach the listener' (p. 156). Coaching takes this further through its interest in what the story is seeking to accomplish. Coaching is a hermeneutic process with a keen interest in the narrator, the narrative material, and the process of narration. Coaches can work with people's stories to help them move towards their desired results. In so doing, they can draw on the flow and processes identified in the four acts framework (Figure 16.1), which integrates the three fields that shaped the narrative turn (literary theory, the humanities and psychology). This enables coaches to better understand how people form their stories, how people frame their stories, why people tell their stories and, importantly, how to help people develop new narratives and tell new stories.

The stories people share in coaching offer a window into:

- the way they *situate* themselves in, construe and navigate their world,
- the cultural and contextual resources that are available as they *search*,
- the openings to reconfigure and reformulate their narratives in order to *shift*, and
- the points of leverage to accelerate and *sustain* their growth.

In the end, people often come to realize through coaching that the stories they tell are both the source of much of their suffering and a path to their liberation. The call now is to deepen our understanding of the connections between narratives and change and between narrative research and narrative practice so that we can evolve the field and its contribution to people's lives.

REFERENCES

Abma, T. A. 1999. Powerful stories: The role of stories in sustaining and transforming professional practice within a mental hospital. In: Josselson, R. & Lieblich, A. (eds.) *Making meaning of narratives*. Thousand Oaks, CA: Sage.

Ainsworth, M. & Bowlby, J. J. 1991. An ethological approach to personality development. *American Psychologist*, 46, 331–341.

Anderson, T. 2004. 'To tell my story': Configuring interpersonal relations within narrative process. In: Angus, L. E. & McLeod, J. (eds.) *Handbook of narrative and psychotherapy: Practice, theory, and research*. Thousand Oaks, CA: Sage.

Anzaldua, G. 1987. *Borderlands | La frontera: The new Mestiza*, San Francisco, CA, Aunt Lute Books.

Bakan, D. 1966. *The duality of human existence: Isolation and communion in Western man*. Boston, Beacon.

Bartel, C. & Dutton, J. E. 2001. Ambiguous organizational memberships: Constructing organizational identities in interactions with others. In: Hogg, M. A. & Terry, D. J. (eds.) *Social identity processes in organizational contexts*. Philadelphia, PA: Psychology Press.

Barthes, R. 1975. An introduction to the structural analysis of narratives. *New Literary History*, 6, 237–272.

Berger, P. L. 1963. *Invitation to sociology*. New York, NY, Doubleday.

Berger, P. L. & Luckmann, T. 1966. *The social construction of reality*. New York, NY, Doubleday.

Bhabha, H. 1990. The third space: Interview with Homi Bhabha. In: Rutherford, J. (ed.) *Identity: Community, culture and difference*. London, UK: Lawrence & Wishart.

Blanc-Sahnoun, P. 2009. Narrative coaching in a professional community after a suicide. *Explorations: An E-Journal of Narrative Practice*, 1, 35–45.

Bly, R. 1988. *A little book on the human shadow*. New York, NY, HarperCollins Publishers.

Boje, D. M. 1998. *The postmodern turn from stories-as-objects to stories-in-context methods* [Online]. Academy of Management. Available: http://www.aom.pace.edu/rmd/1998_forum_postmodern_stories.html [Accessed January 7 2006].

Botella, L. & Herrero, L. 2000. A relational constructivist approach to narrative therapy. *European Journal of Psychotherapy, Counselling & Health*, 3, 407–418.

Bowlby, J. 1969. *Attachment*. New York, NY, Basic Books.

Bowlby, J. 1988. *A secure base: Clinical applications of attachment theory*. London, UK, Routledge.

Brewer, M. B. & Pickett, C. L. 1999. Distinctiveness motives as a source of the social self. In: Tyler, T. R. & Kramer, R. M. (eds.) *The psychology of the social self: Applied social research* (pp. 71–87). Mahweh, NJ: Erlbaum.

Brockbank, A. & McGill, I. 2006. *Facilitating reflective learning through mentoring and coaching*. London, UK, Kogan Page.

Bruner, J. 1978. The role of dialogue in language acquisition. *The child's conception of language*, 2, 241–256.

Bruner, J. 1986. *Actual minds, possible worlds*. Cambridge, MA, Harvard University Press.

Bruner, J. 1990. *Acts of meaning*, Cambridge, MA, Harvard University Press.

Bruner, J. 2002. *Making stories: Law, literature, life*. Cambridge, MA, Harvard University Press.

Bruner, J. & Luciarello, J. 1989. Monologue as narrative recreation of the world. In: Nelson, K. (ed.) *Narratives from the crib*. Cambridge, MA: Harvard University Press.

Burke, K. 1969. *A grammar of motives*. Berkeley, CA, University of California Press.

Butcher, J. 2012. Exploring the link between Identity and Coaching Practice. *International Journal of Evidence Based Coaching and Mentoring*, 6, 119–129.

Bynum, C. W. 1984. Women's stories, women's symbols: A critique of Victor Turner's theory of liminality. In: Moore, R. L. & Reynolds, F. E. (eds.) *Anthropology and the study of religion*. Chicago: Center for the Scientific Study of Religion.

Campbell, J. 1968. *The masks of God: Creative mythology*. New York, NY, Viking.

Campbell, J. 1973. *The hero with a thousand faces*. Princeton, Princeton University Press.

Carey, M., Walther, S. & Russell, S. 2009. The absent but implicit: A map to support therapeutic enquiry. *Family Process*, 48, 319–331.

Charon, R. 2006. *Narrative medicine: Honoring the stories of illness*. New York, Oxford University Press.

Clandinin, D. J., & Connelly, F. M. (2000). *Narrative inquiry: Experience and story in qualitative research*. San Francisco, CA: Jossey-Bass.

Corrie, S. & Lane, D. A. 2010. *Constructing stories, telling tales: A guide to formulation in applied psychology*. London, UK, Karnac.

Cox, E. 2013. *Coaching understood*. London, UK, Sage.

Cozolino, L. 2006. *The neuroscience of human relationships: Attachment and the developing brain*. New York, NY, W.W. Norton.

Cozolino, L. 2010. *The neuroscience of psychotherapy: Healing the social brain*. New York, NY, W.W. Norton.

Czarniawska, B. 2004. *Narratives in social science research*. London, UK, Sage

Danzig, A. 1999. How might leadership be taught? The use of story and narrative to teach leadership. *International Journal of Leadership in Education*. 2, 117–131.

Davies, B. & Harré, R. 1990. Positioning: The discursive production of selves. *Journal for the Theory of Social Behavior*, 20, 43–63.

Depraz, N., Varela, F. J. & Vermersch, P. 2000. The gesture of awareness: An account of structural dynamics. In: Velmans, M. (ed.) *Investigating phenomenal consciousness: New methodologies and maps*. Amsterdam, The Netherlands: John Benjamins.

Derrida, J. 1978. *Writing and difference*. Chicago, University of Chicago Press.

Drake, D. B. 2003. *How stories change: A narrative analysis of liminal experiences and transitions in identity*. Dissertation, Fielding Graduate Institute.

Drake, D. B. 2007. The art of thinking narratively: Implications for coaching psychology and practice. *Australian Psychologist*, 42, 283–294.

Drake, D. B. 2008. Thrice upon a time: Narrative structure and psychology as a platform for coaching. In: Drake, D. B., Brennan, D. & Gørtz, K. (eds.) *The philosophy and practice of coaching: Issues and insights for a new era*. San Francisco, CA: Jossey-Bass.

Drake, D. B. 2009a. Narrative coaching. In: Cox, E., Bachkirova, T. & Clutterbuck, D. (eds.) *The complete handbook of coaching*. London, UK: Sage.

Drake, D. B. 2009b. Using attachment theory in coaching leaders: The search for a coherent narrative *International Coaching Psychology Review*, 4, 49–58.

Drake, D. B. 2015. *Narrative coaching: Bringing our new stories to life*. Petaluma, CA, CNC Press.

Drake, D. B. (2016). *Integrative development: Rethinking how people and organizations change*. Petaluma, CA: CNC Press.

Drake, D. B., & Stelter, R. (2014). Narrative coaching. In J. Passmore (Ed.), *Mastery in coaching: A complete psychological toolkit for advanced coaching* (pp. 65–96). London, UK: Kogan Page.

Epston, D. & White, M. 1995. Constructivism in psychotherapy. In: Neimeyer, R. A. & Mahony, M. J. (eds.) *Constructivism in psychotherapy.* Washington DC: American Psychological Association.

Erikson, E. H. 1950. *Childhood and society*. New York, NY, W.W. Norton.

Fonagy, P., Gergely, G. & Target, M. 2008. Pyschoanalytic constructs and attachment theory and research. In: Cassidy, J. & Shaver, P. R. (eds.) *Handbook of attachment: Theory, research and clinical applications.* Second ed. New York, NY: Guilford Press.

Foucault, M. (1965) *Madness and civilization: A history of insanity in the age of reason*. New York, NY: Random House.

Foucault, M. 1972. *The Archeology of Knowledge*, trans. A. Sheridan. London, Tavistock.

Frank, A. W. 1995. *The wounded storyteller: Body, illness, and ethics*. Chicago, University of Chicago Press.

Franklin, J. 2005. Change readiness in coaching: Potentiating client change. *Evidence-Based Coaching*, 1, 193–200.

Freedman, J. & Combs, G. 1996. *Narrative therapy: The social construction of preferred realities*. New York, NY, W.W. Norton.

Geertz, C. 1978. *The interpretation of cultures*. New York, NY, Basic Books.

Gergen, K. J. 1973. Social psychology as history. *Journal of Personality and Social Psychology*. 26, 309–320.

Gergen, M. M. & Gergen, K. J. 2006. Narratives in action. *Narrative Inquiry*, 16, 112–121.

Giddens, A. 1991. *Modernity and self-identity: Self and society in the late modern age*. Stanford, Stanford University Press.

Gilligan, C. 1982. *In a different voice: Psychological theory and women's development*. Cambridge, MA, Harvard Business School Press.

Goldsmith, M. & Morgan, H. 2004. Leadership is a contact sport: The 'follow-up factor' in management development. *Strategy + Business* [Online]. Available: http://www.strategy-business.com/article/04307?pg=all [Accessed April 22, 2014].

Hall, D. T. 1971. A theoretical model of career subidentity development in organizational settings. *Organizational Behavior and Human Performance*, 6, 50–76.

Heller, S. 1991. *The dance of becoming: Living life as a martial art*. Berkeley, North Atlantic Books.

Hermans, H. J. M. 2004. The innovation of self-narratives: A dialogical approach. In: Angus, L. E. & McLeod, J. (eds.) *Handbook of narrative and psychotherapy: Practice, theory, and research.* Thousand Oaks, CA: Sage.

Hermans, H. J. M. & Kempen, H. J. G. 1993. *The dialogical self: Meaning as movement*. San Diego, CA, Academic Press.

Hewson, D. (1991). From laboratory to therapy room: Prediction questions for reconstructing the 'new-old' story. *Dulwich Centre Newsletter*, 3, 5–12.

Holland, J. H. 1995. *Hidden order*. Reading, MA, Addison-Wesley.

Husserl, E. 1971[1927]. Phenomenology. *The Journal of the British Society for Phenomenology*. 2, 77–90.

Hyvärinen, M. 2008. 'Life as narrative' revisited. *Partial Answers*, 6, 261–277.

Ibarra, H. 1999. Provisional selves: Experimenting with image and identity in professional adaptation. *Administrative Science Quarterly*, 44, 764–791.

Ibarra, H., & Petriglieri, J. L. (2010). Identity work and play. *Journal of Organizational Change Management*, 23(1), 10–25.

Ihde, D. 1977. *Experimental phenomenology: An introduction*. New York, Putnam.

Illeris, K. 2004. *Adult education and adult learning*. Malabar, FL, Krieger Publishing Company.

James, W. 1892[1927]. *Psychology: Briefer course*. New York, NY, Henry Holt.

Jones, R. L., Armour, K. M. & Potrac, P. 2002. Understanding the coaching process: A framework for social analysis. *Quest*, 54, 34–48.

Jung, C. G. 1972. *Two essays on analytical psychology*. Princeton, NJ, Princeton University Press.

Kegan, R. 1994. *In over our heads: The mental demands of modern life*. Cambridge, MA, Harvard University Press.

Kenyon, G. M. & Randall, W. L. 1997. *Restorying our lives: Personal growth through autobiographical reflection*. Westport, CT, Praeger.

Kleinman, A. 1988. *The illness narratives: Suffering, healing and the human condition*. New York, NY, Basic Books.

Kolb, A. Y. & Kolb, D. A. 2010. Learning to play, playing to learn: A case study of a ludic learning space. *Journal of Organizational Change Management*, 32, 26–50.

Kolodziejski, K. 2004. The organization shadow: Exploring the untapped, trapped potential in organizational setting. *Dissertation Abstracts International*, 66, DAI-B, (UMI No. AAT-3166383).

Kreiner, G. E., Hollensbe, E. C. & Sheep, M. L. 2006. Where is the 'me' among the 'we': Identity work and the search for the optimal balance. *Academy of Management Journal*, 49, 1031–1057.

Kvale, S. 1992. Postmodern psychology: A contradiction in terms? In: Kvale, S. (ed.) *Psychology and postmodernism*. Newbury Park, CA: Sage.

Labov, W. & Waletsky, J. 1967. Narrative analysis. In: Helms, J. (ed.) *Essays on the verbal and visual arts*. Seattle, University of Washington.

Lave, J. & Wenger, E. 1991. *Situated learning: Legitimate peripheral participation*. Cambridge, Cambridge University Press.

Madigan, S. 1996. The politics of identity: Considering community discourse in the externalizing of internalized problem conversations. *Journal of Systematic Therapies*, 15, 47–62.

Mahony, M. J. 2003. *Constructive pyschotherapy: A practical guide*. New York, NY, Guilford Press.

Mainemelis, C. & Ronson, S. 2006. Ideas are born in fields of play: Towards a theory of play and creativity in organizational settings. *Research in Organizational Behavior*, 27, 69–81.

Mancuso, J. C. & Sarbin, T. R. 1983. The self-narrative in the enactment of roles. In: Sarbin, T. R. & Scheibe, K. E. (eds.) *Studies in social identity*. Westport, CT: Praeger.

Mandler, J. 1984. *Stories, scripts, and scenes: Aspects of schema theory*. Hillsdale, NJ, Lawrence Erlbaum.

Markus, H. & Nurius, P. 1986. Possible selves. *American Psychologist*, 41, 954–969.

Mattingly, C. 1991. Narrative reflections on practical actions: Two learning experiments in reflective storytelling. In: Schön, D. A. (ed.) *The reflective turn: Case studies in and on educational practice*. New York: Teachers College Press.

Mattingly, C. 1994. The concept of therapeutic 'emplotment'. *Social Science Medicine*, 38, 811–822.

Mattingly, C. 1998. *Healing dramas and clinical plots: The narrative structure of experience*. New York, Cambridge University Press.

McAdams, D. P., Diamond, A., de St. Aubin, E. & Mansfield, E. 1997. Stories of commitment: The psychosocial construction of generative lives. *Journal of Personality and Social Psychology*, 72, 678–694.

McKee, R. 1997. *Story: Substance, structure, style and the principles of screenwriting*. New York, NY, HarperCollins.

McKee, R. (2004, September 10–12). [Story seminar].

McLaren, P. 1993. Border disputes: Multicultural narrative, identity formation, and critical pedagogy in postmodern America. In: McLaughlin, D. & Tierney, W. G. (eds.) *Naming silenced lives: Personal narratives and processes of educational change*. New York, NY: Routledge.

Mead, G. H. 1967[1934]. *Mind, self, and society*. Chicago, University of Chicago Press.

Mezirow, J. 1991. *Transformative dimensions of adult learning*. San Francisco, CA, Jossey-Bass.

Mishler, E. G. 1992. Work, identity, and narrative: An artist-craftsman's story. In: Rosenwald, G. C. & Ochberg, R. L. (eds.) *Storied lives: The cultural politics of self-understanding*. New Haven, CT: Yale University Press.

Mishler, E. G. 1999. *Storylines: Craftartist's narratives of identity*. Cambridge, MA, Harvard University Press.

Nicolopoulou, A. 2008. The elementary forms of narrative coherence in young children's storytellling. *Narrative Inquiry*, 18, 299–325.

Noer, D. 2005. Behaviorally based coaching: A cross-cultural case study. *International Journal of Coaching in organizations*, 3, 14–23.

Pals, J. L. 2006. Narrative identity processing of difficult life experiences: Pathways of personality development and positive self-transformation in adulthood. *Journal of Personality*, 74, 1079–1109.

Piaget, J. 1962. *Play, dreams and imitation in childhood*. New York, NY, W.W. Norton.

Prochaska, J. O., Norcross, J. C. & Diclemente, C. C. 1994. *Changing for good: A revolutionary six-stage program for overcoming bad habits and moving your life positively forward*. New York, NY, HarperCollins.

Rappaport, J. 1993. Narrative studies, personal stories, and identity transformation in the mutual help context. *Journal of Applied Behavioral Science*, 29, 239–256.

Riessman, C. K. 2002. Analysis of personal narrative. In: Gubrium, J. F. & Holstein, J. A. (eds.) *Handbook of interview research*. Thousand Oaks, CA: Sage.

Ross, M. & Conway, M. 1986. Remembering one's own past: the construction of personal histories. In: Sorrentino, R. & Higgins, E. (eds.) *Handbook of motivation and cognition*. New York, NY: Guilford Press.

Rossiter, M. 1999. A narrative approach to development: Implications for adult education. *Adult Education Quarterly*, 50, 56–71.

Royston, V. The opportunities and challenges of applying a narrative coaching methodology to an executive population within South Africa. 1st International Congress for Coaching Psychology Southern Hemisphere, Pretoria, 2011.

Russell, R. L. & van den Broek, P. 1992. Changing narrative schemas in psychotherapy. *Psychotherapy*, 29, 344–354.

Sarbin, T. R. 1986a. The narrative as a root metaphor for psychology. In: Sarbin, T. R. (ed.) *Narrative psychology: The storied nature of human conduct*. Wellesley, MA: Praeger.

Sarbin, T. R. (ed.) 1986b. *Narrative psychology: The storied nature of human conduct*. Westport, CT: Praeger.

Schank, R. 1990. *Tell me a story: A new look at real and artificial memory*. New York, NY, Scribner.

Schwartz-Salant, N. 1998. *The mystery of human relationship: Alchemy and the transformation of the self*. New York, NY, Routledge.

Searle, J. 1965. What is a speech act? In: Black, M. (ed.) *Philosophy in America*. London, UK: Allen and Unwin.

Sherman, S. J., Skov, R. B., Hervitz, E. F. & Stock, C. B. 1981. The effects of explaining hypothetical future events: from possibilty to probability to actuality and beyond. *Journal of Experimental Social Psychology*, 17, 142–158.

Siegel, D. J. 1999. *The developing mind*. New York, NY, Guilford Press.

Singer, J. A. 1996. The story of your life: A process perspective on narrative and emotion in adult development. In: Magai, C. & McFadden, S. H. (eds.) *Handbook of emotion, adult development, and aging*. San Diego, CA: Academic Press.

Singer, J. A. 2005. *Memories that matter: How to use self-defining memories to understand & change your life*. Oakland, CA, New Harbinger

Singer, J. A. & Rexhaj, B. 2006. Narrative coherence and psychotherapy: A commentary. *Journal of Constructivst Psychology*, 19, 209–217.

Sluzki, C. E. 1992. Transformations: A blueprint for narrative changes in therapy. *Family Process*, 31, 217–230.

Sorell, G. T. & Montgomery, M. J. 2001. Feminist perspectives on Erikson's theory: Their relevance for contemporary identity development research. *Identity*. 1, 97–128.

Spinelli, E. 2010. Existential coaching. In: Cox, E., Bachkirova, T. & Clutterbuck, D. (eds.) *The complete handbook of coaching*. London, UK: Sage.

Stein, N. L. & Glenn, C. G. 1979. An analysis of story comprehension in elementary school children. In: Freedle, R. O. (ed.) *New directions in discourse processing*. Greenwich, CT: Ablex.

Stelter, R. 2011. Narrative-collaborative group coaching develops social capital – a randomised control trial and further implications of the social impact of the intervention. *Coaching: An International Journal of Theory, Research and Practice*, 4, 123–137.

Stelter, R. 2014a. *A guide to third generation coaching: Narrative-collaborative theory and practice*. New York, NY, Springer.

Stelter, R. 2014b. Reconstructing dialogues through collaborative practice and a focus on values. *International Coaching Psychology Review*, 9, 51–66.

Stelter, R. & Law, H. 2012. Narrative coaching. *2012: Handbook of the Psychology of Coaching and Mentoring*. Baltimore, 273–301.

Stelter, R., Law, H., Allé, N., Campus, S. & Lane, W. 2010. Coaching-narrative-collaborative practice. *International Coaching Psychology Review*, 5, 152–164.

Stevens-Long, J. 2000. The prism self: Multiplicity on the path to transcendence. In: Young-Eisendrath, P. & Miller, M. E. (eds.) *The psychology of mature spirituality: Integrity, wisdom, transcendence.* Philadelphia, PA: Routledge.

Strawson, G. 2004. Against narrativity. *Ratio*, 17, 428–452.

Swart, C. 2015. Coaching from a Dialogic OD paradigm. *Dialogic Organization Development*, 349–370.

Tillich, P. 1965. Frontiers. *Journal of the American Academy of Religion*, XXXIII, 17–23.

Turner, V. 1969. *The ritual process: Structure and anti-structure.* New York, Aldine Publishing Co.

van Gennep, A. (1960). *The rites of passage* (M. B. Vizedom & G. L. Caffee, Trans.). Chicago: The University of Chicago Press.

Vogel, M. 2012. Story matters: An inquiry into the role of narrative in coaching. *International Journal of Evidence Based Coaching and Mentoring*, 10, 1–11.

Vygotsky, L. S. 1978a. Interaction between learning and development. *Mind in society: The development of higher psychological processes.* Cambridge, MA: Harvard University Press.

Vygotsky, L. S. 1978b. *Mind in society: The development of higher psychological processes.* Cambridge, MA, Harvard University Press.

Wallin, D. J. 2007. *Attachment in psychotherapy.* New York, NY, The Guilford Press.

Wells, G. 1999. *Dialogic inquiry: Towards a socio-cultural practice and theory of education.* Cambridge, Cambridge University Press.

White, M. 1988. The process of questioning: A therapy of literary merit? In: White, M. (ed.) *Collected papers.* Adelaide, South Australia: Dulwich Centre Publications.

White, M. 2002. Journey metaphors. *International Journal of Narrative Therapy & Community Work*, 2002, 12.

White, M. 2007. *Maps of narrative practice.* New York, NY, W.W. Norton.

White, M. & Epston, D. 1990. *Narrative means to therapeutic ends.* New York, NY, W.W. Norton.

Winnicott, D. W. 1965. *The maturational processes and the facilitating environment.* New York, NY, International Universities Press.

Wood, D., Bruner, J. S. & Ross, G. 1976. The role of tutoring in problem solving. *Journal of child psychology and psychiatry*, 17, 89–100.

Woodcock, C. 2010. The listening guide for coaching: exploring qualitative, relational, voice-centered, evidence based methodology for coaches. *Coaching: An International Journal of Theory, Research and Practice*, 3, 144–154.

17

The Use of Feedback for Development in Coaching: Finding the Coach's Stance

Alison Maxwell

INTRODUCTION

Feedback comes in many guises and from many sources, be it the reflection in the mirror first thing in the morning, ad hoc comments from friends or colleagues, to more planned and formal interventions such as the annual performance appraisal or 360/multi-rater assessments as used in many organisations. Feedback is therefore a common way of learning about ourselves in relation to our environment and a potentially powerful intervention for coaches to employ in the service of client performance, personal development and growth.

Whilst feedback is a common entry point to the work (McDowall and Smewing, 2009) and an important component of the coaching process, relatively little has been written to date that critically examines the use of feedback by coaches and the theoretical underpinnings of this type of intervention. This chapter introduces the concept of feedback as typically defined, with a brief overview of the empirical, theoretical and practitioner feedback and 'feedback in coaching' literature. Challenges to the dominant discourse are highlighted, before critiquing some common forms of feedback used in coaching relationships.

The second half of the chapter debates the taken for granted 'behaviourist/objectivist' assumptions surrounding feedback and offers a range of alternate theoretical perspectives that might inform different stances for coaches to take in relation to feedback, with their implications for practice. The chapter concludes with a summary of the issues and challenges raised, and reflects on potential future directions for research.

Feedback Defined

Feedback, as a concept, has it is roots in mechanics, cybernetics and engineering (Weiner, 1954). Drawing on Control Theory, feedback is typically seen as an essential part of a process of self-regulation whereby systems (living and non-living) compare an aspect of current performance or behaviour to a referent level or goal. When discrepancies are detected adjustments are made in the functioning of the system in order that the discrepancy is eliminated or minimised (see Figure 17.1). Feedback, so described, is therefore essentially 'neutral' information from the external environment that may precipitate changes in system behaviour or functioning (Carver and Scheier, 1998; Carver and Scheier, 2002; Gregory et al., 2011).

In human systems, feedback sits at the juncture between the individual and their environment, mediating and regulating the relationship and 'fit' with the environment (see Figure 17.2). From feedback, individuals develop a sense of themselves, particularly in relation to others, as well as learning how to influence and shape their environment. Feedback can therefore signal both the degree to which we have adapted to our external circumstances as well as our relative success in attempts to influence our environment. However feedback, more broadly, can also include the results of our own self-reflections and self-appraisals ('internal' feedback), which can be ignored, rejected or assimilated much as 'external' feedback.

Evaluative Feedback Versus Developmental Feedback

While there are many ways of categorising feedback, for the purposes of this chapter, two types of feedback are distinguished in organisational settings – evaluative and developmental feedback. Typically, performance feedback in organisations is related to an individual's delivery on specific tasks or objectives, often to a predefined standard or criteria. Such feedback can come from many sources, including superiors, peers, reports and customers, as well as task accomplishment. Feedback in this context constitutes more than neutral 'information' from

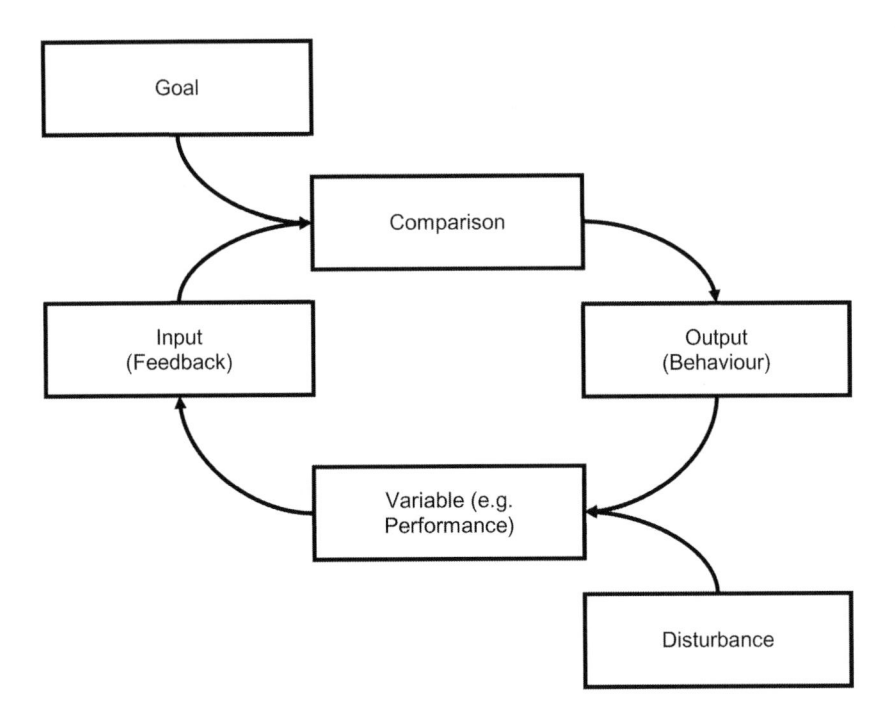

Figure 17.1 A simple control loop

Source: Adapted from Gregory et al. (2011)

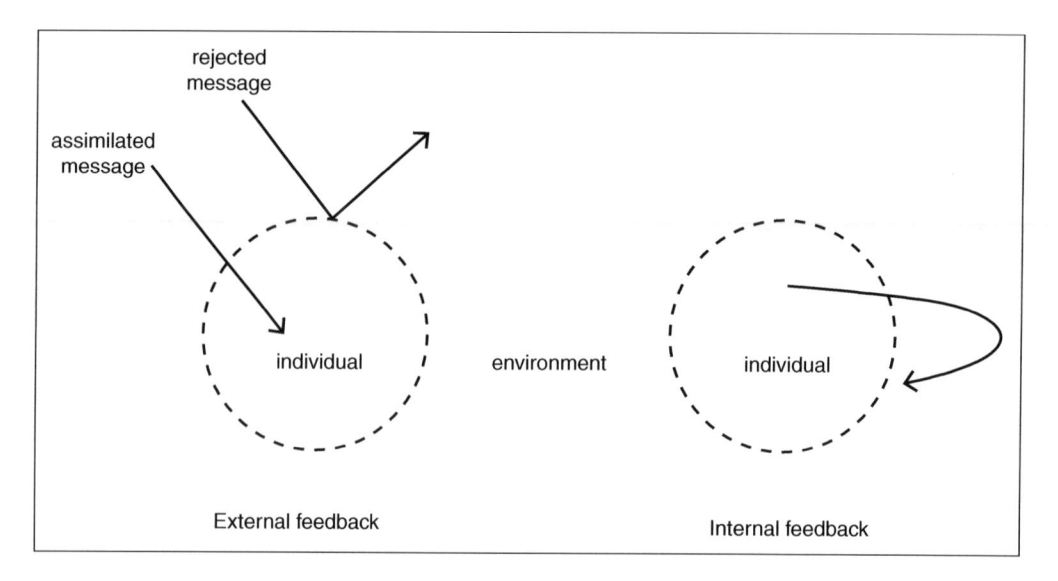

Figure 17.2 Feedback at the individual/environmental interface

the environment, and represents an external objective evaluation or judgement of relative success or failure, which is often linked, directly or indirectly, to remuneration and reward.

In contrast, developmental feedback is offered with the intention of growing the capabilities and capacities of an individual. This includes feedback on behaviours, personal or leadership style, interpersonal impact and relationships with others at work, and is therefore altogether more personally directed and potentially more subjective in nature. While such feedback is often given within existing line management relationships, third parties such as Human Resource (HR) professionals or coaches may deliver developmental feedback on behalf of the organisation. These individuals may have specialist training in feedback instruments as well as feedback techniques.

OVERVIEW OF 'FEEDBACK IN COACHING' LITERATURE

Feedback Literature

Feedback research dates back almost 100 years (Kluger and DeNisi, 1996) and is extensive and multi-disciplinary. Empirical research tends to be largely quantitative in nature and predominantly from the perspective of feedback giving rather than receiving. Studies of feedback interventions and effects can be seen in a wide range of contexts, including education (Hattie and Timperley, 2007; Hattie, 2012), sports (Turman, 2008), psychology (Markus, 1977), health education (Klatt and Kinney, 2012), cultural studies (Piff and Medoza-Denton, 2012), family and parenting studies (Shanley and Niec, 2010; Sanders et al., 2012) as well as the fields of organisational behaviour (Levy and Thompson, 2012), performance enhancement (Hillman et al., 1990; Balcazar et al., 1985) and leadership development (Alimo-Metcalfe, 1998; DeRue and Wellman, 2009). It is only relatively recently that cross-disciplinary perspectives have been developed (Sutton et al., 2012). Feedback research has also covered a multitude of facets, including, for example the effects of feedback valence (Brown, 1986), frequency (Fedor and Buckley, 1987), conditions of acceptance or rejection (Igen et al., 1979), feedback seeking or avoidance (De Stobbeleir and Ashford, 2012), individual feedback orientation and organisational feedback culture (Smither and London, 2002), impact on motivation (Harackiewicz, 1979) and organisational relationships (Geddes and Baron, 1997), goal setting (Harackiewicz, 1979) and subsequent engagement with development activity (Woo et al., 2008) and, of course, links to task performance improvements. Much of the research assumes a causal link between feedback giving and (task) performance, however this has been comprehensively challenged by Kluger and DeNisi (1996) and others.

As with the empirical literature on feedback, the theoretical debate is multi-disciplinary. Attempts have been made to develop theories of feedback (Kluger and DeNisi, 1996; London and Smithers, 2002; Hattie and Timperley, 2007; De Villiers, 2013), however, a cross-disciplinary perspective has yet to emerge. As with much of the literature, the concerns of these theorists are largely with task performance rather than developmental effects.

Feedback in Coaching Literature

In broad terms, the coaching literature makes relatively little reference to or use of the substantial body of empirical and theoretical literature in the wider field. In the empirical coaching literature, the combined effectiveness of coaching and 360-degree/multi-rater feedback is a central concern in many studies (Thach, 2002; Jarzebowski et al., 2012; Kochanowski et al., 2010; Olivero et al., 1997). Other research has looked at the use of psychometrics in coaching, mostly from the perspective of perceived value of particular instruments to coaches (Scoular and Campbell, 2007; Harper, 2008; McDowall and Kurz, 2008; McDowall and Kurz, 2007; Nelson and Hogan, 2009). There appears to be much more limited research beyond these two areas, and little from the perspective of the feedback recipient.

While feedback is an implied element in much of the theoretical literature, it is unusual to find feedback as an explicit focus.

A notable exception is the work of Gregory and colleagues (Gregory et al., 2008; Gregory et al., 2011), which provides a rare example of theory developed specifically for a coaching context. This model identifies client 'feedback orientation' as well the organisational 'feedback culture' as potential determinants of feedback effects.

In the coaching practitioner literature, feedback is usually positioned as one of many skills at a coach's disposal, often as a deceptively simple and 'taken for granted' concept (McDowall, 2012). Multi-rater or 360-degree feedback tools are seen as a common entry point to the work, providing useful diagnostic information, as well as a way of measuring and demonstrating the value of coaching interventions to the organisational client (McDowall and Smewing, 2009). A prime concern revolves around how to deliver perceived 'negative' or 'difficult feedback' to clients' and there are multiple formulations of feedback best practice (e.g. Blakey and Day (2012), Downey (2003), Starr (2008), Rogers (2004), Van Nieuwerburgh (2014), Whitmore (2002)). A theme in the practitioner literature is that of the 'unaware self'. This is informed by popular models such as the Johari window (Luft, 1961) and Goleman's work on Emotional Intelligence (2002). This sort of discussion legitimises the role of coach as feedback giver and positions 'awareness' as external to the client.

Challenges to the Dominant Discourse

Whilst still a minority debate, a number of challenges and questions have been raised in the literature. These include:

- *Challenge to universal benefit.* With a few notable exceptions (e.g. McDowall (2012); Western (2012)), giving feedback is almost universally described in the practitioner literature as a beneficial and positive intervention. This therefore underplays empirical evidence suggesting that feedback giving is a considerably more complex and potentially less benign intervention. For example in a large scale meta-study of feedback interventions, Kluger and DeNisi (1996) found only a modest link between feedback giving and subsequent improvements, with as much as one-third of feedback interventions detrimentally impacting (task) performance, particularly when feedback was directed toward the 'self'. Similar findings have also been reported by Smither et al. (2005).

- *Challenge to the 'non-directive' stance.* While much of the coaching literature espouses a non-directive style of working (Rogers, 2004), this stance potentially sits awkwardly with the practice of giving feedback. For example, Downey (2003) sees feedback as incompatible with a non-directive stance:

> If the session has been run in a non-directive fashion and, suddenly and uninvited, the coach comes out with some feedback, it can be very disruptive to the session and can damage the relationship. (Downey, 2003: 85)

A further challenge has been advanced by Blakey and Day (2012: 54) who suggest that feedback could be conflated with advice giving, preventing the client from having the opportunity to learn and seek feedback for themselves.

- *Challenge to the equal power relationship.* Questions have also been raised about the extent to which judgement and evaluation can be excluded from feedback giving (Downey, 2003). For example, Ladyshewsky (2010: 289) suggests that evaluation, or at least the perception of it, fundamentally shifts the power balance in the coaching relationship, prejudicing the effectiveness of the endeavour. This perspective does not sit comfortably with the use of some tools, particularly when judgement on the behaviour, personality or self is implied or articulated. Rogers (2004: 101) suggests that the use of psychometric tools endows the coach with expert knowledge and status, potentially disempowering the client.
- *Challenge of surrogacy.* Another challenge involves the appropriateness of coaches giving feedback to their clients, when such messages should be, more appropriately, delivered by the client's line manager. Western (2012: 260), for example, suggests that this sort of 'outsourcing' is both common and potentially undermining of the line management relationship. If constrained to such a role the coach, potentially, becomes a surrogate for third party voices, unable to defend or explain feedback data if challenged by the client. The coach therefore becomes an (unwitting) agent of the organisation, prejudicing the working alliance.

TYPES OF FEEDBACK USED BY COACHES

In broad terms, coaches work with two forms of feedback; feedback that is generated *externally* to the client, and feedback that is generated *internally* when clients engage in self-reflection and self-appraisal. In this section both types of feedback are explored, with a critique of some specific tools and methods (see Table 17.2 and Table 17.3).

Coaching with Externally Generated Feedback

At the coach's disposal is an ever-expanding battery of tools, instruments and assessments, ranging from sophisticated psychometrics, to more informal and 'in the moment' techniques (based on the coach's own perceptions and experiences of the client). While the actual extent of feedback in use by coaches is unknown, McDowall and Smewing (2009: 100) suggest that the use of psychometrics and personality assessments is extensive. For example, they found that some 88% of a sample of 90 UK practising professional coaches used personality assessments, 60% stating they used them regularly with at least 70% of their clients. Indeed, this study found that it was unusual not to use some form of personality assessment, with only 4% of the sample feeling that they did not add much value and/or were incompatible with their approach to coaching. This study highlighted a variety of reasons for using such tools, and indicated their utility particularly at the start of a coaching relationship in opening up the conversation (Table 17.1).

In the following section a description of some common forms of 'external' feedback will be provided, along with summaries of their potential advantages and disadvantages (see Table 17.2) and some commentary on the extant empirical literature.

360/Multi-rater assessments

A common entry point to coaching relationships is the use of some form of multi-rater appraisal or 360-degree feedback tool. Typically, in such appraisals, multiple individuals (e.g. self, line manager, peers, customers, reports) are invited to anonymously rate and comment on individuals, often using an organisational competency model as the underpinning framework. The role of the coach is often extended to include debriefing the resulting (confidential) reports, which often (but not always) feed into a follow-up coaching or development programme.

As shown in Table 17.2, there are a number of advantages and disadvantages associated with these tools. For coaches the practical advantages include the presence of other 'voices' (from the client's wider system) in the coaching relationship, avoidance of over-dependence on the coachee's self-story (with others' perspectives acting as a 'reality check' of the client's self-perceptions), and the availability of a means by which client self-awareness can be expanded (thus illuminating potential blind spots).

In general, empirical studies have supported the general effectiveness of mutli-rater feedback in coaching contexts, particularly when such feedback is paired with coaching programmes (McDowall and Kurz, 2008; Cooper, 2010; Smither et al., 2005; Thach, 2002). However, some researchers have reported more mixed results (Luthans and Peterson, 2003), as it is difficult to disentangle the relative contribution of such feedback to coaching. More broadly, multi-rater feedback has several disadvantages (see Table 17.2) and is not without its critics (Jarzebowski et al., 2012). For example, Maurer et al. (2002) suggest that the link between 360-degree feedback and follow-up development activity may be weak. Brett and Atwater (2001) found evidence to suggest that individuals ignore or challenge less favourable 360-degree ratings. McDowall (2012) also questions the psychometric properties of some assessments. Critics of 360-degree feedback also point to the tendency of these tools to focus on development gaps (rather than strengths) and, consequentially, more positively-oriented feedback tools are beginning to attract more attention, such as the 'reflected best' self (Roberts et al., 2005).

Psychometrics/Personality assessments

As with multi-rater feedback, the use of psychometric instruments are another popular entry point to coaching and seen as useful for diagnostic purposes (Western, 2012; McDowall and Kurz, 2007). As shown in Table 17.2, psychometrics are useful because they save time, offer the coach and client a useful shared vocabulary (Rogers, 2004), and give clients enlightening insights (Buckle, 2012).

Table 17.1 Reasons for using assessments and types of measures used in coaching

Reasons given for using assessments	Type of measure used
• Open up areas for discussion (96.3%)	• Personality measures (86.3%)
• Provide a useful source of data (79.3%)	• 360-degree feedback (56.3%)
• Seen as useful to clients (73.2%)	• Learning styles (35%)
• Enable more effective coaching (48.8%)	• Emotional intelligence (31.3%)
• Provide structure to the coaching session (41.5%)	• Interest questionnaires (31.3%)
	• Performance data (26.3%)
	• Intelligence/aptitude tests (20.0%)
	• Competency measures (20.0%)

Source: Adapted from McDowall & Smewing (2009)

Table 17.2 Advantages and disadvantages of externally generated feedback

Form of feedback	Advantages	Disadvantages
360-degree/ multi-rater assessments	• Articulates external perceptions in comparison to self perception • May point out blind spots (i.e. reduce self-delusion) • Avoids over dependence on client's self-story • Provides diagnostic and benchmark information • Used to establish coaching ROI • Potential entry point to the work	• May put coach in the role of message carrier for the organisation • Utility dependent on client's willingness to accept results • May have deficit bias • May create defensiveness and disrupt work relationships • Bias and distortions in results and instruments used • Selective reading of results • Conflicting messages within results
Psychometrics and personality assessments	• Provides 'fast track' information on the client • Provides insights not otherwise available • Potential entry point to the work • Diagnostic information • Legitimises the role of the coach	• Dependent on client's willingness to accept results – may create defensiveness or suspicion • Appropriateness of instrument to client's situation • Inadequate psychometric properties (in some cases) • Coach inadequately trained leading to inappropriate interpretation of reports • Boilerplate reports and risk of 'labelling' • Puts coach in position of expert • Potential 'prop' for inexperienced coaches • Agenda becomes instrument-led
'Immediacy'	• Based on direct 'here and now' experience of the coach of the client • Provides client tangible example of their impact on others	• Introduction of biases and distortions by coach • Assumed link with real world behaviours • Potential to disrupt the coaching relations

However, Rogers (2004: 99) also suggests that inexperienced coaches may be overly attracted to the use of psychometrics for self-serving reasons:

> Working with new coaches I often observe undue interest in questionnaires such as the MBTI. We can all be attracted to these and other tools and techniques out of anxiety … When this is your motive, recognise it for what it is: a way of exerting control over the client and over your own fear of incompetence.

There are also suggestions that psychometrics may be inappropriately or poorly selected, without a rigorous understanding of the theories and limitations underpinning such tools. McDowall (2012: 71), for example, argues that coaches should be more aware of the quality and robustness of feedback instruments and suggests that poor quality instruments 'may at best be misleading and at worst could be seriously damaging, particularly if the content is negative' (p. 71). A further concern is for the appropriate debriefing and interpretation of output (Driver, 2011; McDowall, 2012). These sorts of concern are reflected in more recent publications on the use of psychometrics in coaching (e.g. Association of Coaching (2008); Bourne (2007), which call for coaches to be appropriately qualified in the use of psychometric instruments.

Immediacy

'Immediacy' has its origins in the therapeutic world and involves the skill of offering a coach 'here and now' reactions to the client, as a way of helping the client to understand how they impact others (O'Neill, 2000; Driver, 2011; Pemberton, 2006). Immediacy employs the coach's direct (subjective) experience of the client and assumes that the coach's experience of the client (in coaching sessions) accurately reflects their real-world behaviours. As O'Neill (2000) observes:

> The use of immediacy is the real gold of any coaching moment. Your own interaction with the executive is a window into his characteristic patterns. Particularly in the contracting phase, it is important to feedback your own experience, here and now, of our client, that is, what is happening between you. Again, you act on the belief that what happens in the immediacy of this moment happens 'out there' in the executive's work world. (O'Neill, 2000: 98)

However, as Driver (2011) points out, there is a risk of contamination or bias in the coaches' perceptions. While research on immediacy is limited, there is some evidence linking it to positive outcomes in sports coaching (Turman, 2008) and of its effective use via 'bug-in-ear' technology for teacher development (Rock et al., 2009; Scheeler et al., 2010).

Coaching with Internally Generated Feedback

In contrast to externally derived feedback, 'internal' feedback depends on the client's own self-awareness and self-analysis. Consequently, these forms of feedback are likely to have greater acceptability but with the greater risk of perpetuating fixed self-perceptions (see Table 17.3). With this type of feedback, the role of the coach is one of facilitator rather than of diagnostician or messenger.

Mirroring and paraphrasing

Mirroring is a feedback technique that involves restating the client's words as a way of the client 'seeing' their own thought processes and circumstances more clearly. According to Cox (2013):

> Reflecting back clients' words communicates to them not only that their coach has heard them, but offers up a mirror to those words so that clients can listen to what they have said. (Cox, 2013: 61)

As with 'immediate' feedback, mirroring and paraphrasing occurs in the 'here and now'. However, as a form of 'clean language', mirroring attempts to avoid any subjective bias, judgments or distortions that a coach might introduce by staying closely to the clients' words. Cox (2013) highlights the difficulty of avoiding such interpretations and biases, whilst McDowall and Millward (2010: 61) suggest that non-recognition of feedback may be due to poor 'mirroring' technique as much as the client's lack of self-awareness. This appears to be an under researched area; however studies of the effects of 'clean language' do offer some insights (Lawley et al., 2010).

Table 17.3 Advantages and disadvantages of internally generated feedback

Form of feedback	Strengths	Limitations
'Mirroring' and paraphrasing	• Replay of the coach's words in the 'here and now' • High acceptability to client • Clarification of client's thought processes	• Introduction of biases and distortions • May not extend/challenge client's thought processes
Feed forward	• Use of coachee's past experiences to solve present dilemmas • High acceptability to client	• Relevance of past experiences to present dilemmas
Self-feedback and self appraisal	• High acceptability to client • Grows client's capacities to learn from experiences	• Potential for self-delusion/self-inflation • Limited by client's ability to reflect

Feed forward

Feed forward is the consideration of past solutions and best practices as a way of informing action in the present. This form of positive feedback is focused on bringing back into awareness any previous answers, solutions or psychological states that have proven to be effective for the client. As such, this form of feedback therefore does not depend on external evaluations or descriptors of the client, but on their prior experiences, with the role of the coach to help the client apply past successes to current problems.

Feed forward is gaining increased attention amongst coaches as an effective way to work with clients (McDowall, 2012; McDowall and Millward, 2010) mostly likely because it avoids creating defensiveness and enhances the client's sense of self-efficacy. Some empirical research (e.g. Kluger and Nir (2010); McDowall et al. (2014)) suggests feed forward may be a more effective intervention than feedback interventions, however there is scope for more work in this area, particularly in looking at the combined effects of feed forward and feedback.

Self-feedback

An overlooked form of feedback in the coaching literature is self-feedback or self-assessment. This can include suppressed or withheld information (Bachkirova, 2011; Haidt, 2001) which can be brought into conscious awareness through reflection or discussion with another. In a coaching context, Whitmore (2002) argues that client's self assessment is the most effective form of feedback, avoiding defensiveness and most effectively facilitates learning:

> Generating high quality relevant feedback, as far as possible from within rather than from experts, is essential for continuous improvement, at work, in sport and in all aspects of life. (Whitmore, 2002: 111)

Whitmore and others argue that the role of the coach is therefore not to deliver feedback messages from the external environment, so much as to facilitate reflection and enhance the client's capacity to dispassionately self-observe. Developing the client's reflective and reflexive capability, without self-delusion, therefore becomes a central concern for a coach and the means of developing the client's own self-awareness. To date there has been limited discussion of self-deception in coaching (Bachkirova and Shannon, 2013) and this is an area open for further study.

ALTERNATE THEORETICAL PERSPECTIVES – CHOOSING A STANCE FOR PRACTICE

While coaching theories draw from a wide field of theoretical perspectives, feedback theory, at least in the coaching literature, tends to draw from a narrower range of standpoints. Most obviously it appears to lean heavily on Behaviourist/Objectivist assumptions, which (as outlined above) are highly contestable. To help balance this discussion of feedback, this section will briefly outline a number of theoretical stances in order to illustrate how they might inform the coaches' role and stance, and role of feedback in learning and development (see Table 17.4).

Objectivism

The Objectivist's stance on feedback suggests an external goal that the individual must attempt to match by modifying discrepant behaviours. This stance can be seen throughout the theoretical coaching literature. For example Gregory et al. (2011: 26–27) see Control theory as 'a natural fit as an organizing framework for the role of goals and feedback in executive coaching' and suggest that 'a primary purpose of effective coaching is to help coachees learn to better regulate their behaviour [in] order to. achieve desired outcomes'. A similar perspective is depicted by Grant (2003: 255) with a generic model of self-regulation for goal attainment.

Table 17.4 Summary of feedback perspectives and implications for coaching stance

Perspective	Key theories/authors	Meaning/purpose of feedback	Coach's role	Learning and development	Coaches stance
Adult Learning theory – Objectivism	• Behaviourism (Thorndike, 1927; Atkinson et al., 1983; Skinner, 1968) • Control Theory (Carver and Scheier, 2002) • Goal Setting Theory (Locke and Latham, 1990) • Feedback Intervention Theory (Kluger and DeNisi, 1996))	Discrepancy reduction against an external standard or goal	Ensure client fit with demands of environment	Assimilation of external messages Replication of socially preferred norms and behaviours	Agent of the external environment
Adult Learning theory – Constructivism	• Intentional Change Theory (Boyatzis and Akrivou, 2006) • Social cultural theory (Thurling et al., 2013) • Social constructionism (Mory, 2003)	Individualised/contextual meaning making	Assist in clarification and construction of feedback meaning	Integration of feedback into the self	Agent of client meaning making
	• Cognitive-developmental theories (Bachkirova, 2012; Berger and Fitzgerald, 2002; Kegan, 1982; Cook-Greuter, 2004)	Feedback as indicator of developmental stage	Dependent on developmental stage	Growth within and between development stages	Bridge between development of self concept and fit with external environment
Psychology – 'Self' theories	• Self-enhancement and self-consistency theories (Swann, 1987) • Implicit theories of self (Dweck, 1999)	Feedback response as indicator of self concept	Work with client self-deceptions. Encourage feedback seeking	Toleration of difficult feedback (positive or negative)	Voice for excluded feedback
	• Gestalt psychology (Perls, 1976; Clarkson, 1999)	Feedback response as indicator of boundary conditions/health	Developing discrimination to feedback	Development of a 'semi-permeable membrane'	Guardian of client boundary health
	• Self-determination theory (Ryan and Deci, 2000) • Intentional Change Theory (Boyatzis and Akrivou, 2006))	Conditions of feedback acceptance	Provide support for basic psychological needs (autonomy, competence and relatedness)	Integration of congruent feedback	Facilitate client autonomous motivation

This perspective suggests that the use of feedback in coaching is to point out lack of 'fit' between the client and the demands of the external environment. For example, by using a 360-degree assessment, discrepancies between a desired social standard (e.g. a leadership competency model) and self-perceptions are identified and actions created to close any gap. Development of the individual in this context represents the extent the individual can assimilate the feedback and successfully replicate preferred behaviours and norms.

This perspective has implications for the nature of the coaching relationship and the underlying contract. From this perspective, the coach becomes an agent of the environment, upholding the desired standards and goals rather than necessarily helping individuals question or explore them. The role of the coach is to ensure discrepancies from standards are clear to the client and accepted as valid directions for change. Once accepted, the coach can then help the client find routes to change and create ways of self-monitoring progress. The coach must therefore work to overcome any resistance to unpalatable feedback and reluctance to change.

Constructivism

While conceptually appealing, the Objectivist paradigm has been criticised as being overly simplistic, failing to explain the complexities of human motivation, ignoring prior knowledge, experience and opinion, and privileging an external reality. In contrast, Constructivist perspectives suggest that 'reality' is internally created by the individual, and cannot be separated from the context of their prior knowledge and experiences (see Table 17.5).

The Constructivist perspective has the virtue of recognising that feedback recipients are not 'blank slates', with the meaning of feedback being subjective and inter-subjective. Development from this perspective therefore represents the ability to clarify and construct personal meaning, particularly with ambiguous or conflicting information from multiple sources. Integration of feedback therefore becomes the goal rather than simply assimilation.

Operating under the Constructivist paradigm, the role of the coach shifts from 'agent of the environment' to partnering the client to make sense of feedback received, scaffolding from their prior experiences to new understandings and knowledge. Thus the coach might work with *how* the client constructs meaning from feedback, as much as the content or valence of the message. Translation of feedback into action and behavioural changes is in comparison to personal (internal) goals. For example, in 'Intentional Change Theory' (ICT) (Boyatzis and Akrivou, 2006) the self-conceived 'ideal self' provides the fundamental driver for intended change rather than an external reference or standard.

Cognitive-Developmental Theories

Building on constructivist ideas, cognitive-developmental theorists suggest that a person's response to feedback may be a by-product of his or her developmental stage

Table 17.5 Comparison of feedback according to learning paradigm

Objectivism	Constructivism
Feedback is based upon response match to external reality	Feedback is to guide the learner toward internal reality; facilitates knowledge construction
Feedback contains symbols for learner to process	Feedback aids learner in building symbols
Feedback not related to human experience; reflects external reality	Feedback in the context of human experience
Meaning within feedback information corresponds to categories in the world	Meaning within feedback information determined by internal understanding
Feedback contains symbols that represent external reality	Feedback provides generative, mental 'toolkits'

Source: Adapted from Mory (2003)

(as opposed to an input into it). According to this view, feedback responses are substantially influenced by cognitive-developmental stage, and can have little to do with the content of feedback, its valence or the skill of the provider. For example, Cook-Greuter (2004) notes that:

> No matter how skilfully a superior tries to critique an Opportunist employee, any such attempt will be reacted to as a personal affront or threat to their sense of self and power. The aggressive Opportunist will fight back, argue, and blame something (bad luck) or others (so and so screwed up) for the failure, but never admit to having made a mistake or needing correction. (Cook-Greuter, 2004: 7).

Whilst numerous developmental models exist in the literature (such as Cook-Greuter, 2004), few focus explicitly on coaching. One notable exception is Bachkirova (2011), who uses a four-stage model of adult cognitive development to predict how 360-degree feedback recipients are likely to respond based on their particular stage, and what the consequences of this might be for a coaching relationship (see Table 17.6).

According to this perspective, the role of the coach changes according to stage of client development. At the unformed ego stage, the coach focuses on helping the client to develop a stronger sense of self by attending to 'internal' feedback. At the formed ego stage, the work of the coach is to privilege the external message, thus learning towards the objectivist view. At the reformed ego stage, the coach privileges neither the internal or external perspective, but rather helps the client to explore potential meanings (Bachkirova, 2011).

Self-Theories – Self-Consistency Versus Self-Enhancement

As mentioned earlier, a central concern in the (practitioner) literature is what constitutes best practice in delivering negative feedback. However, for social psychologists (e.g., Swann, 1987) the conflation of negative feedback with 'difficult' feedback may be an over-simplification. They argue that a more complex combination of competing factors

Table 17.6 Response to feedback by developmental stage

Developmental stage	Characteristics	Potential response to feedback
Unformed ego/conformist	• Influenced by others • View of self as an internalisation of how others see them • Dependence on other people	Potentially overly influenced by the views of others and not open to challenge. Confirmatory feedback not seen as adding value and therefore little for coach to work with Feedback that is worse than expectation is potentially overwhelming or traumatising. Coach's role morphs to help dealing with potential trauma rather than development
Formed ego/achievement	• Confident in own view of themselves • Independence from other people	Feedback may be seen as incongruent if they hold a rigid self-conception/limited interest in development Feedback may be seen as very useful if open to development
Reformed ego/authentic	• Able to hold multiple perspectives on self • Tolerance of ambiguity • Interdependence	Curious about feedback but importance will depend on what role it plays in other strategic areas of their life
Ego with a Soul/transcendent	• Broader and more holistic, including spiritual perspectives	Difficult to predict role of feedback

Source: Adapted from Bachkirova (2011: 121–122)

determines whether feedback is accepted or rejected, including:

- Existing Self concept – the tendency to see oneself as negative or positive;
- Self-consistency motivation – the need to preserve a stable self-view (Swann and Read, 1981a; 1981b; Swann, 1997);
- Self-enhancement motivation – the need to increase a sense of self-worth (Brown, 1986; Tesser, 1985).

This suggests that rejected feedback is not always 'negative' feedback and that feedback may be used to confirm self-concept rather than challenge it. For example, Maxwell and Bachkirova (2010) suggest that despite the apparently objective nature of multi-rater feedback, such assessments may at times perpetuate rather than challenge the existing self-image. So conceived, the role of the coach is to ensure that the part of the feedback message that is most likely to be excluded is fully heard and integrated.

Self-Theories – Gestalt 'Boundary Conditions'

In a similar vein, Gestalt psychology has much to say about how individuals respond to feedback, with a focus on the processes of deflection or introjection. Chronic or habitual deflection of external feedback is seen as leaving an individual out of touch with their environment, resulting in individuals meeting their environment with fixed ways of relating and responding. As Clarkson (1999) observes:

> A person who habitually deflects does not use his or her energy in an effective way to get feedback from self, others or the environment. Perhaps no criticism can 'get through' but neither can appreciation or love. (Clarkson, 1999: 57)

In contrast introjection represents acceptance of information from the environment in an indiscriminate and unexamined way, with chronic introjection a barrier to the formation of a healthy sense of self (Clarkson, 1999; Clarkson and Mackewn, 1993), as it privileges the views of others over our own. Accordingly, a 'healthy' adaptive relationship to feedback can be seen where feedback is neither automatically rejected nor accepted, but where discrimination and discernment is applied. Development in this context therefore represents the ability to develop such discrimination, neither privileging the internal view of self or the external messages of the environment. According to this view, the coach works with the client's ability to discriminate feedback, challenging them to develop a 'semi-permeable' boundary between themselves and their environment.

Feedback from environment	Feedback from environment	Feedback from environment
Self	Self	Self
Deflection: Impenmeable boundary, indiscriminate rejection of feedback	Introjection: Weak boundary, indiscriminate acceptance of feedback	Permeable boundary, discriminant acceptance of feedback

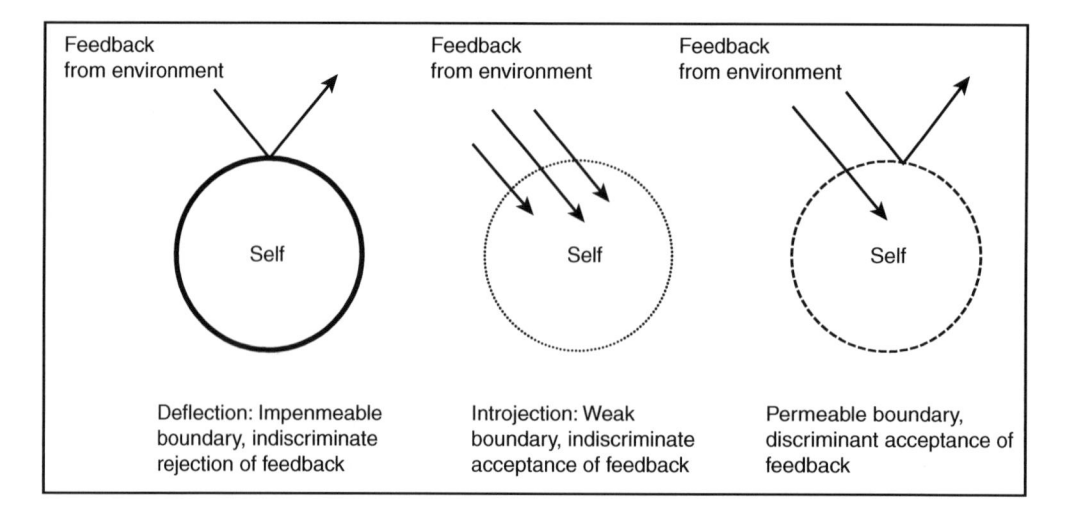

Figure 17.3 Feedback as boundary disturbances

It could be argued that this perspective maps on to cognitive-developmental perspectives, with an unformed ego seen has having an overly porous boundary, the formed ego as having an overly impermeable boundary, and the reformed ego as having found a healthier balance of deflection and introjection.

Self- Theories – Extrinsic vs. Intrinsic Motivation

While the above theories give various constructions on feedback, little has been written on the general conditions between coach and client that might lead to feedback acceptance or rejection. In their work on self-determination theory, Ryan and Deci (2000)propose a range of possible responses to feedback, based on a theoretical continuum of intrinsic and extrinsic motivations (see Figure 17.4). They suggest that while external feedback must be by definition an extrinsic motivator, this does not necessarily imply low acceptance. Rather they suggest that a spectrum of extrinsic motivation exists, ranging from low subjective endorsement (e.g. compliance to external regulation), to higher levels of subjective endorsement (where feedback is easily integrated into one's sense of self).

Ryan and Deci (2000) suggest that higher levels of endorsement can be achieved when socio-cultural conditions are created that support and help satisfy basic psychological needs for autonomy, competence and relatedness. More specifically, Spence and Deci (2013) have suggested that – in situations where feedback is involved – coaches can act as facilitators of autonomous motivation and subjective endorsement by acknowledging the client's perspective, encouraging self-initiation and minimising controlling language.

DIRECTIONS FOR FUTURE RESEARCH

Given the lack of coaching-specific research, the use of feedback in coaching contexts represents a potentially rich seam for future researchers to explore. Potential research questions include:

- Extent of use – what tools are coaches using and in which situations. What contexts or client issues lend themselves to the use of particular types of tools/methods?
- Methods of use – how do coaches use feedback with clients? What is the relative balance between using 'external' and 'internal' feedback?
- Conditions of acceptance – under what circumstances are clients more likely to accept feedback from a coach? What methods of feedback result in acceptance rather than rejection?
- Outcomes of use/ROI – under what conditions does feedback translate into changed behaviour

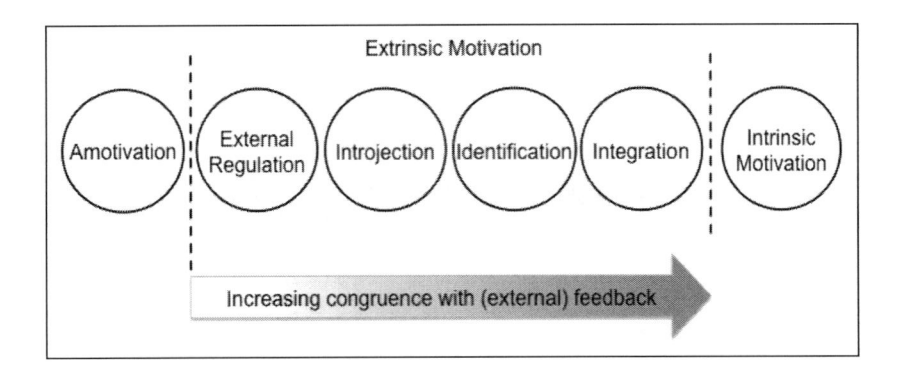

Figure 17.4 A continuum of human motivation related to feedback

Source: Adapted from Ryan and Deci (2000)

or performance? What outcomes is a coach hoping to achieve by using feedback?
- Comparisons of effectiveness – are any particular feedback methods more effective than others? How is effectiveness judged?
- Experiences of feedback – how do coach and client experience giving and receiving feedback. How does receiving feedback from a coach differ for clients from receiving feedback from others (e.g. HR professionals, line manager etc.)? How do clients experience feedback for developmental purposes rather than evaluative purposes?
- Conceptions of use – what theoretical stances inform a coach's use of feedback? Under what circumstances would coaches see the use of feedback as incompatible with their own model of coaching?

It is to be hoped that such studies would help to illuminate this often 'taken for granted' but powerful form of coaching intervention, both informing practice and enhancing our theoretical understanding.

CONCLUSION

As reviewed in this chapter, the use of feedback in coaching has progressed with little reference to the considerable body of theoretical and empirical literature that exists on feedback. The dominant discourse in the coaching literature appears to rest on an assumption of an 'unaware' client, and that greater self-awareness can be provided by external feedback from others. This quasi-objectivist discourse provides a compelling rationale to turn coach into feedback-deliverer, and legitimises much of the current practice. However by leaning toward the objectivist stance, coaches overly privilege external reality as the 'truth' over the experience of the client. Feedback tools then risk being used to diagnose, label and judge, rather than enlighten, strengthen or enable. The coach's work then becomes focused on overcoming client resistances and defences, and finding artful and palatable ways for them to assimilate the external message. Conversely, operating from a purely constructivist stance also presents challenges, in that this risks overly privileging the 'internal' truth, and assumes clients have an accurate understanding of their external context as well as themselves.

Beyond the objectivist/constructivist debate, the theoretical literature on feedback also suggests a number of alternative perspectives, each informing different assumptions about the nature of the 'self', the nature of 'development' and by inference, the appropriate role and stance of the coaching practitioner. These suggest that responses to feedback may be a potential indicator of self-concept, developmental stage and/or psychological 'health'. This requires the coach to be able to understand feedback reactions as indicative of the client's development needs, rather than necessarily getting entangled with feedback veracity, valence or content. Such information may therefore guide the coach to a more nuanced way of operating which both develops the client's sense of self and their ability to remain open to new information from their environment.

REFERENCES

Alimo-Metcalfe B. (1998) 360 Degree Feedback and Leadership Develpment. *International Journal of Selection and Assessment* 6: 35–44.

Association of Coaching. (2008) Psychometrics in coaching: using psychological and psychometric tools for development, London: Kogan Page.

Atkinson RL, Atkinson RC and Hilgard RE. (1983) *Introduction to psychology*, San Diego: Harcourt, Brace & Jovanovich.

Bachkirova T. (2011) *Developmental Coaching: working with the self*, Maidenhead: Open University Press.

Bachkirova T. (2012) Developmental coaching: a new theory and framework for practice. In: Peterson D and Freire T (eds.) *Wiley-Blackwell Handbook of the Psychology of Coaching and Mentoring*. London: Wiley-Blackwell.

Bachkirova T and Shannon N. (2013) Self-deception in leadership from a developmental perspective. *Integral Leadership Review* 13: 21–33.

Balcazar FE, Hopkins B and Suarez Y. (1985) A critical, objective review of performance feedback. *Journal of Organizational Behaviour Management* 7: 65–89.

Blakey I and Day I. (2012) *Challenging coaching: Going beyone traditional coaching to face the FACTS*, London: Nicholas Brearley Publishing.

Berger JG and Fitzgerald, C. (2002) Leadership and complexity of mind. In: Fitzgerald C and Berger JG (eds.), *Executive coaching: Practices and perspectives*. Palo Alto, CA: Davies-Black, 27–58.

Bourne A. (2007) Using psychometrics in coaching. In: Palmer S and Whybrow A (eds.) *Handbook of coaching psychology: a guide for practitioners*. Hove: Routledge, 385–403.

Boyatzis RE and Akrivou K. (2006) The ideal self as the driver of intentional change. *Journal of Management Development* 25: 624–642.

Brett JF and Atwater LE. (2001) 360-degree feedback: Perceptions of accuracy, reactions and perceptions of usefulness. *Journal of Applied Psychology* 86: 930–942.

Brown JD. (1986) Evaluations of self and others: Self-enhancement biases in social judgements. *Social Cognition* 4: 353–376.

Buckle T. (2012) "It can be Life-Changing"; an Interpretative Phenomenological Analysis of the Coach and Coachee's Experience of Psychometrics in Coaching. *International Journal of Evidence Based Coaching and Mentoring*: 102–118.

Carver CS and Scheier MF. (1998) *On the self-regulation of behavior*, Cambridge: Cambridge University Press.

Carver CS and Scheier MF. (2002) Control processes and self-organization as complementary principles underlying behaviour. *Personality and Social Psychology Review* 6: 304–315.

Clarkson P. (1999) *Gestalt counselling in action*. 2nd. ed. London: Sage Publications Ltd.

Clarkson P and Mackewn J. (1993) *Fritz Perls*, London: Sage Publications Ltd.

Cook-Greuter SR. (2004) Making the case for a developmental perspective. *Industrial and Commercial Training* 36: 1–10.

Cooper H. (2010) Raising awareness at the start of a coaching relationship - using 360-degree feedback. In: McMahon G and Archer A (eds.) *101 Coaching strategies and techniques*. Hove: Routledge, 242–243.

Cox E. (2013) *Coaching understood: A pragmatic inquiry into the coaching prcess*, London: Sage Publications Ltd.

De Stobbeleir K and Ashford S. (2012) Feedback-seeking behavior in organizations: Research, theory and implications. In: Sutton RM, Hornsey MJ and Douglas KM (eds.) *Feedback: The communication of praise, criticism, and advice*. New York: Peter Lang Publishing Inc, 247–261.

De Villiers R. (2013) 7 Principles of highly effecgtive managerial feedback: Theory and practice in managerial development interventions. *The International Journal of Management Education* 11: 66–74.

DeRue DS and Wellman N. (2009) Developing leaders via experience: the role of developmental challenge, learning orientation and feedback availability. *Journal of Applied Psychology* 94: 859–875.

Downey M. (2003) *Effective Coaching: Lesson's from the coach's coach*, New York, NY: Texere.

Driver M. (2011) *Coaching positively: Lessons for coaches from positive psychology*, Maidenhead: Open University Press.

Dweck CS. (1999) *Self-theories: Their role in motivation, personality and development*, Philadelphia: Psychology Press.

Fedor DB and Buckley MR. (1987) Providing feedback to organizational members: a reconsideration. *Journal of Business and Psychology* 2: 171–181.

Geddes D and Baron R. (1997) Workplace aggression as a consequence of negative performance feedback. *Management Communication Quaterly* 10: 433–454.

Goleman D, Boyatzis RE and McKee A. (2002) *Primal leadership: learning to lead with emotional intelligence*, Boston, MA: Harvard Business School Press.

Grant AM. (2003) The impact of life coaching on goal attainment, metacognition and mental health. *Social Behavior and Personality* 31: 253–264.

Gregory JB, Beck JW and Carr AE. (2011) Goals, feedback and self-regulation: control theory as a natural framework for executive coaching. *Consulting Psychology Journal: Practice and Research* 63: 26–38.

Gregory JB, Levy PE and Jefferes M. (2008) Development of a model of the feedback process within executive coaching. *Consulting Psychology Journal: Practice and Research* 60: 42–56.

Haidt J. (2001) The emotional dog and its rational tail: a social intuitionist approach to moral judgement. *Psychological Review* 108: 814–834.

Harackiewicz JM. (1979) The effects of reward contingency and performance feedback on instrinsic motivation. *Journal of Personality and Social Psychology* 37: 1352–1363.

Harper A. (2008) Psychometric tests are now a multi-million-pound business: what lies behind a coach's decision to use them? *International Journal of Evidence Based Coaching and Mentoring, Special Issue* 2: 40–51.

Hattie J. (2012) Feedback in schools. In: Sutton RM, Hornsey MJ and Douglas KM (eds.) *Feedback: The communication of prasie, critcism and advice.* New York: Peter Lang Publishing Ltd, 265–278.

Hattie J and Timperley H. (2007) The power of feedback. *Review of Educational Research* 77: 81–112.

Hillman LW, Schwandt DR and Bartz DE. (1990) Enhancing staff members' performance through feedback and coaching. *Journal of Management* 9: 20–27.

Igen DR, Fisher CD and Taylor MS. (1979) Consequences of indiviual feedback on behaviour in organisations. *Journal of Applied Psychology* 64: 349–371.

Jarzebowski A, Palermo J and Van de Berg R. (2012) When feedback is not enough - The impact of regulatory fit on motivation after positive feedback. *International Coaching Psychology Review* 7: 14–32.

Kegan R. (1982) *The evolving self: Problem and process in human development*, London: Harvard University Press.

Klatt CM and Kinney TA. (2012) Using feedback to prepare people for health behavior. In: Sutton RM, Hornsey MJ and Douglas KM (eds.) *Feedback: The communication of praise, ciritcism and advice.* New York: Peter Lang, 291–304.

Kluger AN and DeNisi A. (1996) The effects of feedback interventions on performance: a historical review, a meta-analysis and a preliminary feedback intervention theory. *Psychological Bulletin* 119: 254–284.

Kluger AN and Nir D. (2010) The feedforward interview. *Human Resource Management Review* 20: 235–246.

Kochanowski S, Seifert CF and Yukl G. (2010) Using coaching to enhance the effects of behavioral feedback for managers. *Journal of Leadership & Organizational Studies* 17.

Ladyshewsky R. (2010) Peer coaching. In: Cox E, Bachkirova T and Clutterbuck D (eds.) *The complete handbook of coaching.* London: Sage Publications Ltd, 284–297.

Lawley J, Meyer M, Meese R, et al. (2010) More than a balancing act? 'Clean Language' as an innovative method for exploring work-life balance. (accessed 5/1/16).

Levy PE and Thompson DJ. (2012) Feedback in organizations: Individuaal differences and the social context. In: Sutton RM, Hornsey MJ and Douglas KM (eds.) *Feedback: The communication of praise, criticism, and advice.* New York: Peter Lang Publishing Inc, 217–232.

Locke EA and Latham GP. (1990) *A theory of goal setting and task performance*, Englewood Cliffs, NJ: Prentice Hall.

London M and Smithers JW. (2002) Feedback orientation, feedback culture, and the longitudinal performance management process. *Human Resource Management Review* 12: 81–100.

Luft J. (1961) The Johari window: a graphic model of awarenesss in interpersonal relations. Human Relations Training News, 5. (accessed 1/10/13).

Luthans F and Peterson DJ. (2003) 360-degree feedback with systematic coaching: empirical analysis suggests a winning combination. *Human Resource Management* 42: 243–256.

Markus H. (1977) Self-schemata and processing information about the self. *Journal of Personality and Social Psychology* 35: 83–78.

Maurer TJ, Mitchell DRD and Barbeite FG. (2002) Predictors of attitudes toward a 360-degree feedback system and involvement in post-feedback management development activity. *Journal of Occupational and Organizational Psychology* 75: 87–107.

Maxwell AJ and Bachkirova T. (2010) Applyig psychological theory of self-esteem in coaching practice. *International Coaching Psychology Review* 5: 16–26.

McDowall A. (2012) Using feedback in coaching. In: Passmore J (ed) *Psychometrics in coacihng: using psychological and psychometric tools for development*. 2nd ed. London: Kogan Page Ltd., 59–76.

McDowall A, Freeman K and Marshall S. (2014) Is feedforward the way forward? A comparison of the effects of feedforward coaching and feedback. *International Coaching Psychology Review* 9: 135–146.

McDowall A and Kurz R. (2007) Making the most of psychometric profiles - effective integration into the coaching process. *International Coaching Psychology Review* 2: 299–309.

McDowall A and Kurz R. (2008) Effective integration of 360 degree feedback into the coaching process. *The Coaching Psychologist* 4: 7–19.

McDowall A and Millward L. (2010) Feeding back, feeding forward, and setting goals. In: Palmer S and McDowall A (eds.) *The Coaching Relationship: Putting people first*. Hove: Routledge, 55–78.

McDowall A and Smewing C. (2009) What assessments do coaches use in their practice and why? The Coaching Psychologist 5: 98–103.

Mory EH. (2003) Feedback research revisited. In: Jonassen DH (ed.) *Handbook of research for educational communications and technology*. New York: MacMillan Library Reference, 745–783.

Nelson E and Hogan R. (2009) Coaching on the dark side. *International Coaching Psychology Review* 4: 9–21.

O'Neill MB. (2000) *Executive Coaching with backbone and heart: A systems approach to engaging leaders with their challenges*, San Francisco, CA: Jossey-Bass Inc.

Olivero G, Bane K and Kopelman R. (1997) Executive coaching as a transfer of training tool: effects on productivity in a public agency. *Public Personnel Management* 26: 461–469.

Pemberton C. (2006) *Coaching to solutions: A managers toolkit for performance delivery.*, Oxford: Elsevier Ltd.

Perls FS. (1976) *The Gestalt approach and eye witness to therapy*, New York: Bantam.

Piff PK and Medoza-Denton R. (2012) *Mixed signals: Culture and construal in the provision of feedback across group boundaries,* New York: Peter Lang.

Roberts LM, Spreitzer G, Dutton J, et al. (2005) How to play to your strengths. Harvard Business Review: 75–80.

Rock ML, Gregg M, Howrd PW, et al. (2009) See me, hear me, coach me. Journal fo Staff Development 30: 24–31.

Rogers J. (2004) *Coaching skills: a handbook*, Maidenhead: Open University Press.

Ryan RM and Deci EL. (2000) Intrinsic and extrinsic motivations: Classic definitions and new directions. *Contemporary Educational Psychology* 25: 54–67.

Sanders MR, Mazzucchell TG and Ralph A. (2012) Promoting parienting competence through a self-regulation approach to feedback. In: Sutton RM, Hornsey MJ and Douglas KM (eds.) *Feedback: The communication of praise, ciritcism and advice.* New York: Peter Lang, 305–324.

Scheeler MC, Congdon M and Stansbery S. (2010) Providing immdieate feedback to co-teachers through bug-in-ear technology: An effective method of peer coaching in inclusion classrooms. *Teacher Education and Special Education: the Journal of the Teacher Education Division of the Council for Exceptional Children* 33: 83–96.

Scoular A and Campbell M. (2007) What value do psychometrics bring to business coaching? *Training Journal Magazine* 53 (March).

Shanley JR and Niec LN. (2010) Coaching parent to change: The impact of in vivo feedback on parents' acquisition of skills. *Journal of clinical child and adolescent psychology* 39: 282–287.

Skinner BF. (1968) *The technology of teaching*, Englewood-Cliffs: NJ: Prentice-Hall.

Smither JW and London M. (2002) Feedback orientation, feedback culture, and the longitudinal performance management process. *Human Resource Management Review* 12: 81–100.

Smither JW, London M and Reilly RR. (2005) Does performance improve following multi-source feedback? A theoretical model, meta-analysis and reveiw of empirical findings. *Personnel Psychology,* 58: 33–66.

Spence GB and Deci EL. (2013) Self-determination theory within coaching contexts: supporting motives and golas that promote optimal functioning and well-being. In:

David S, Clutterbuck D and Megginson D (eds.) Beyond goals: Effective strategies for coaching and mentoring. Farnham: Gower Publishing Ltd., 85–108.

Starr J. (2008) Brilliant coaching: how to be a brilliant coach in your workplace, Harlow: Pearson Education Ltd.

Sutton RM, Hornsey MJ and Douglas KM. (2012) Feedback: The communication of praise, criticism, and advice, New York: Peter Lang Publishing Inc.

Swann WB. (1987) Identity negotiation: when two roads meet. Journal of Personality and Social Psychology 53: 1038–1051.

Swann WB. (1997) The trouble with change: self-verification and allegiance to the self. Psychological Science 8 177–180.

Swann WB and Read SJ. (1981a) Self-verification processes: How we sustain our self-conceptions. Journal of Experimental Social Psycologu 17: 351–372.

Swann WB and Read SJ. (1981b) Acquiring self-knowledge: The search for feedback that fits. Journal of Personality and Social Psychology 41: 1119–1128.

Tesser A. (1985) Toward a self-evaluation maintenance model of social behavior. American Psychological Association. Los Angeles.

Thach EC. (2002) The impact of executive coaching and 360 feedback on leadership effectiveness. Leadership & Organization Development Journal 23: 205–214.

Thorndike EL. (1927) The law of effect. American Journal of Psychology 39(1/4): 212–222.

Thurling M, Vermeulen M, Bastiaens T and Stijnen, S. (2013) Understanding feedback: a learning theory perspective. Education Research Review 9: 1–15.

Turman PD. (2008) Coaches' immediacy behaviours as predictors of athletes' perceptions of satisfaction and team cohesion. Western Journal of Communication 72: 162–179.

Van Nieuwerburgh C. (2014) An introduction to coaching skills: A practical guide, London: Sage Publications Ltd.

Weiner N. (1954) The human use of human beings: cybernetics and society, Boston: Da Capo Press.

Western SB. (2012) Coaching and Mentoring: A Critical Text, London: Sage Publications Ltd.

Whitmore J. (2002) Coaching for performance: The new edition of the practical guide, London: Nicholas Brealey.

Woo SE, Sims CS, Rupp DE, and Gibbons AM. (2008) Developmental engagement within and following developmental assessment centers: considering feedback favorability and self-assessor agreement. Personnel Psychology 61: 727–759.

PART III
Common Issues in Coaching

# 18

Working with Values in Coaching

Reinhard Stelter

This chapter deals with the concept of values as an essential point of reference for coaching, mentoring and professional developmental dialogues. Values give individuals a fundamental orientation for their work and their life in general. In that sense, values may be seen as a central issue in coaching. To argue for the importance of this focus on values, a brief analysis of our current society and of today's rapid societal changes will be presented. Value reflections can be seen as a fundamental basis for human meaning making and a general orientation in life, which is especially important in the hyper-complexity of modern life and the challenges it presents for individuals. Values are the entry point to our lived knowledge and practical wisdom. According to Flyvbjerg (2001), instrumental rationality needs to be balanced by value rationality, a balance that 'is crucial to the sustained happiness of the citizens in any society' (p. 4). Values are the implicit foundation for action and social-psychological resilience.

This value rationality shall be developed by presenting coaching as an art of lingering (or the process of slowing down to think and reflect). To provide a foundation for this understanding, the chapter will introduce the reader to values-based scholarship. The importance of values and their creative inclusion in the coaching process will be presented in the light of three different approaches to coaching. These will include *Existential Coaching*; *Protreptic Coaching* (a philosophically-inspired approach), and *Third-Generation Coaching* (a narrative-collaborative approach). This chapter has three primary aims. First, to present and discuss the state of knowledge about values as a central aspect of the coaching process. Second, to show that values can be included in coaching regardless of preferred models or techniques. Third, to suggest some possible future research in regard to the issue of working with values in coaching.

SOCIETAL LEGITIMACY AS THE BASIS FOR THE VALUE ORIENTATION IN COACHING

Social change has helped create a widespread need for coaching and other dialogical processes (e.g. mentoring, counselling, process management), with coaching especially valuable given the central place that it assigns to values in the (self-) reflective process that defines coaching. Four main aspects will be mentioned here as key dimensions of these societal challenges: (1) globalization, (2) hypercomplexity, (3) self-reflexivity and (4) burnout and exhaustion.

The Globalized World

The increasingly global interconnectedness of our world can be seen as the first aspect influencing the role and development of coaching and coaching psychology today. Globality can be defined as the end point of the globalization process and may be seen as a condition that frames our mutual interactions today (including its negative aspects such as terrorism and the inequality between developed and underdeveloped countries). Beck (2000) notes, 'globality means that we have been living for a long time in a world society, in the sense that the notion of closed spaces has become illusory. No country or group can shut itself off from others' (p. 10).

Some of our everyday challenges, in both our private lives and our working lives, can be understood in the light of globality. That is, the change processes people are embedded in are characterized by growing diversity and multiple perspectives on how to interpret change processes and develop possible action strategies. Furthermore, there seems to be a need to recognize that individuals are less able to control certain factors locally. In fact, the very notion of control has been devalued as a result of the impact of globality on individual lives.

The Hypercomplex Society

In our late modern or postmodern society, individuals confront growing diversity in the social world where organizations, institutions and cultures all have their own autonomous 'developmental logic'. Various social contexts are characterized by specific cultures and organizations, and the members in the specific contexts develop their own unique form of communication that both matches, and is shaped by, the local culture. As a consequence of this development, society is losing its internal coherence and cohesion. According to Luhmann (1998), 'the system tends towards "hypercomplexity", towards a multitude of opinions and interpretations about its own complexity' (p. 876; translated by R.S.). This argument holds that it becomes impossible to achieve a uniform and concordant understanding and interpretation of specific societal phenomena or of society at large (see Qvortrup, 2001). Particular observer perspectives determine how the world is perceived. As members of a society, we are increasingly confronted with the question of how to manage differences in perception and how to communicate effectively amid a variety of social environments and cultures, all of which speak different 'languages' and interpret the world in different ways.

In this light, it becomes essential for the coach to include and examine relevant contexts and positions. The basic position for the coach should be that the concept of 'truth' depends on the context and on social agreements in the local culture. As such, 'truth' is an issue of power or social negotiations (Gergen, 2009). This carries an important implication for coaches and consultants, as their ability to be effective will be influenced by their cultural sensitivity and how able they are to work with clients on values clarification at both the personal and organizational levels (e.g. work-life balance).

Self-Reflexivity

Acknowledging the special challenges faced by individuals during periods of profound social change, Giddens (1991) speculated on the importance of reflexivity, which he describes as the ongoing revision of new information that is a characteristic (and necessity) of late modern societies. For Giddens (1991) the development of self-identity is an individual's permanently ongoing reflexive project, while Gergen (2009, 2011) enlarges this line of thought by understanding the self as a product of relational processes where people co-create their reality and themselves.

Burnout and Exhaustion

Arguing along similar lines, Han (2015) critiques the current societal situation and notes the dramatic consequences it has for self-reflexivity. Han argues that our competitive societies are dominated by the *supremacy of positivity*. According to Han, 'Yes, we can' becomes the energizing motto to live by (with the consequence of satiation, overcapacity, communication overload, hyperactivity and multitasking), which generally leads to a state of shallow attention. However, the individual is left with severe psychosocial consequences ranging from tiredness, exhaustion, burnout, depression and attention deficit disorder to borderline personality disorder. Inconveniently people can no longer identify and target an external enemy, rather the enemy is the individual him- or herself. Individuals become focused on their own performance, and control is based on *surveillance of one's own performance*. We live in a control society where self-disciplining has become increasingly intensified during the last decade, a trend that is resulting in disempowerment. Han (2009) argues that we have been moving from a 'marching age' (where we organized our lives in a common rhythm with a clear direction) toward a 'buzzing age' (where we whirr around nervously and hectically without any clear orientation). We have lost the narrative that helped us choose and differentiate.

PROMOTING THE '*VITA CONTEMPLATIVA*': COACHING AS THE ART OF LINGERING

On the basis of this related societal analyses (e.g. Beck, 2000; Qvortrup, 2003; Han, 2015), the concept of *vita contemplativa* (Han, 2009) may be presented as an alternative to the more conventional goal focus in coaching (e.g. Ives & Cox, 2012; Grant, 2012). In some respects, stringent goal-focused coaching can be seen as a form of self-surveillance and exploitive self-control. It is argued that lasting empowerment cannot be achieved by following short-term goals, which often change rapidly and are difficult to manage. However, empowerment tends to unfold slowly, as individuals, groups or teams seek to establish a foundation based on specific values as their implicit frame of reference for action. Although coaching based on value reflection is not the only answer to this problem, it may be a small step in a new direction where individuals working together can develop strategies that offer a path toward reduced satiation, overcapacity and communication overload. Coaching can be a way to unfold contemplation by cultivating the *art of lingering* (Han, 2009).

A consequence of living in a world of hypercomplexity is that it can be difficult to find time to think and reflect. Yet, human growth and development requires us to take our time, take detours and engage in contemplation. Drawing on Heidegger's 'Besinnung' (contemplation), Han (2009) notes that, 'contemplation begins when thinking pauses in its work' (p. 109; translated by R.S.) or when people stop striving for a quick solution and start lingering. The notion of lingering will be explored through a reflection on values, aspirations, dreams and hopes.

What are Values, and What do Values do to Us?

Values can be considered a central part of our identity and, as such, are an essential point of reference for coaching and other developmental dialogues. They connect our actions to our convictions. A value implies the capacity to act and grasps our implicit readiness to do things in a way that is in concordance with our experience, knowledge and beliefs. Kirkeby (2009) describes a value as a perceived sense of '"I can" based on knowledge, and a knowledge of what we have done, and will be able to do, and guided by ethical imagination by both deliberate and intuitive judgment' (p. 156). Deliberate judgment can be related to and unfolded in a coaching conversation where coaching partners are invited to explore an important and perhaps challenging situation in depth, and where they can find key elements of what may be most important for them. In our daily life, these value judgements are often pre-reflective, embodied and intuitively anchored in a specific situation. We have a sense of the event or situation and act on the basis of earlier experience, a *phronetic capacity*. Phronesis is a central concept in Greek philosophy (often translated as practical knowledge) and was described by Aristotle (1999, book 6) as a virtue and set of states. On this he wrote that, 'practical wisdom [phronesis], then, must be a reasoned and true state of capacity to act with regard to human good' (p. 95). As such, phronesis can be considered a specific attitude to things, an attitude grounded in virtues and ultimately in specific values. It can also be established through reflective processes by highlighting or focussing on values. It is 'the capacity to transform the given, normative values into action' (Kirkeby, 2009, p. 161).

In narrative-collaborative practice (Stelter, 2014a; 2014b) the exploration of values is part of the unfolding of the *landscapes of identity*, which supports coachees in their efforts to make sense of their life and work. Here, value reflection and meaning making take place in a process of both social negotiation and individual reflections. It is this reflective process that needs to be unfolded in coaching, where a dialogue on specific values, convictions, ambitions or dreams play an essential role in developing a firm personal foundation and driving force for action. Integrating reflection on central values as a pivotal part of the dialogue means working toward a coaching format that can do two things. First, have a sustainable and long-lasting impact on the coaching partner. Second, enable a new dimension in the coach–coachee relationship, a dimension that includes moments of symmetry between coach and coaching partner, where they can meet as fellow human companions (Stelter, 2016) and are thus able to engage as value-reflecting partners.

In the current literature (e.g., de Gennaro, 2012) values are becoming *en vogue*, receiving growing attention in the literature on leadership, coaching and other forms of organizational and dialogue practice (Brinker et al., 2000; Holmes et al., 2011; Kaiser & Overfield, 2010; Lønning, 2015; Sharpiro & Gross, 2007; Sagiv et al., 2004). A reason for this contemporary focus on value-driven processes may stem from a growing recognition that our life and work risk becoming superficial if they are not anchored in core aspects of the self (e.g. values), which infuse individual and collective action with significance and importance.

A growing number of management theorists are convinced that values and meaning-making can provide just such an anchor, guiding managerial and employee actions and, thus, helping to keep organizations 'on course' (Stacy, 2012; Weick, 1995). For Pohlman, Gardiner and Heffes (2000), *value-driven management* represents a value-based concept to help executives, managers and employees counteract the possibility of making short-term decisions that result in long-term commercial damage. The authors refer to eight value drivers that impact organizational and individual decision-making, including external cultural values, organizational cultural values, individual employee values, customer values, supplier values, third-party values, owner values and competitor values. The framework is intended to promote the understanding that economic value is not the sole objective on the path to economic success.

Within the positive psychology movement, there is a strong awareness of values and their ability to provide a foundation for one's actions that ultimately leads to satisfaction, resilience, well-being and happiness. The Values-In-Action inventory of strengths (VIA-IS) is a well-known inventory based on twenty-four character strengths grouped into six virtue clusters: wisdom and knowledge, courage, humanity, justice, temperance and transcendence (Peterson & Seligman, 2004). The VIA-IS was developed to help people recognize and build upon their strengths and preferred values, and in that sense emphasize what people can and might be willing to do instead of focusing on possible dysfunctions. Based on its online accessibility (www.viacharacter.org), VIA-IS is a widely used instrument that offers anyone easy access to getting to know themselves better.

Within coaching psychology, Williams and Whybrow (2013) have highlighted the importance of organizational values, stating that 'core values are traits or qualities that represent deeply held beliefs. They reflect what is important to us, and what motivates us. ... Values act as guiding principles – as a behavioural and decision-making compass' (p. 31). They propose thirty-one practices to enable organizations and their members to 'reconnect with what is the core, and live these core values on a daily basis' (p. 38).

A Brief Introduction to the Philosophical Foundation of Values

The quest to understand values as core drivers of human existence and action can be traced back to ancient Greek philosophy. In his *Nicomachean Ethics*, Aristotle states *eudaimonia* as the highest good for humans and, in that sense, also the highest aim of all human practical thinking and a crucial influence on the human way of being in action. Therefore, Aristotle's position could be described as represented a situational ethics. Eudaimonia is normally translated from Greek as well-being or happiness, a concept that is highlighted in a renewed form in Positive Psychology (Seligman, 2009) and a state that can be unfolded by the constant striving toward virtuous living (which implies ongoing ethical reflection). Aristotle describes the path toward eudaimonia as being based on good character and education (ēthos in Greek) achieved by striving toward good habits (both of which are reflected in the Greek words éthos). For Aristotle good character could be developed in collaboration with a teacher (like a coach) and by making deliberate choices. The path is always guided by ethical decision-making, which is based on being self-sufficient and not driven by external benefits. In Aristotle's words: 'Now such a thing happiness, above all else, is held to be; for this we choose always for self and never for the sake of something else, but honour, pleasure, reason, and every virtue we choose indeed for themselves ...' (Aristotle, 1999, Book 1, 7; p. 10). From this perspective, striving toward happiness would be seen as intrinsically good, with values assigned a central place and providing a clear orientation (as the individual will prefer the good). An action is right insofar as it is a manifestation of the individual's virtues, and virtues are of good when they are present in the fully flourishing human being. Coaching for compassion (Boyatzis et al., 2012) could be seen as an example for a flourishing approach to coaching by focusing on the need of others and by acting to enhance others' well-being (in contrast to coaching for compliance and a deficiency-based coaching).

In some contrast to the Aristotelian-inspired position we find *consequentialism* or *utilitarianism*. Here, norms and values depend on consequences or usefulness. Ultimately, the consequences determine whether an action is morally right or wrong. John Stuart Mill (1806–1873) was one of the central figures in this tradition. He argued for the *Greatest Happiness Principle*, that actions are judged as right to the degree that they tend to promote happiness to those being affected and as wrong to the degree that they tend to produce the reverse of happiness. This principle supports the motto, 'The aim sanctifies the means' – the aim being happiness. Unlike the ethical stance of the Aristotelian tradition, this perspective is much more closely linked to the usefulness of one's actions. Based on an understanding of impartiality and agent neutrality, the happiness of all counts the same and the good of no one person is preferred to another. Although this utilitarian approach is modified in modern times, it continues to impact political philosophy and social policy today.

The third position is the deontological position, with the German Enlightenment philosopher Immanuel Kant as the central historical figure. Kant did not accept the consequences of actions as criteria for the actions being right or wrong. Rather he placed the emphasis on the motives of the person who performs the action. Kant (1993[1785]) states three significant formulations, the so-called *categorical imperative*, which can be defined as a way of evaluating motivations for action:

- Act only according to that maxim by which you can also will that it would become a universal law.
- Act in such a way that you always treat humanity, whether in your own person or in the person of any other, never simply as a means, but always at the same time as an end.
- Every rational being must so act as if he were through his maxim always a legislating member in a universal kingdom of ends.

In Kant's understanding, human will is assigned to a general and inherent legality, limited only by the inability of the individual to live up to his or her duty. In the second formulation, Kant puts emphasis on *Würde*, personal dignity, which Schallow (2012) describes as 'the capacity of self-governance and autonomy' (p. 137) and as the 'intrinsic worth of the person' (p. 138). As a central figure of the Age of Enlightenment, Kant sees *duty* as a core human ability that everybody has to possess for the sake of the common good. Everyone has the *duty* to work for humanity, and in that sense it is different from Aristotle, since Kant only accepted an act as morally sound if it excluded eudaimonía under any form.

When this discourse on ethics is related to the possible objectives of coaching or similar reflective and developmental dialogues, it becomes clear that there can be much more to coaching than merely supporting and facilitating the coachee's journey from point A to point B. Coach and coachee can become partners and fellow philosophers in a collaborative dialogue. As coaches, we should support, share, deepen and expand on the reflections of our dialogue partner. Values and ethical reflections are the core of human motivation – and hence, the supreme objects of and guidelines for reflection. As outlined above, these fundamental ethical reflections unfold intrinsic values in contrast to the instrumental values (e.g. 'I would like to have a better job') that are the focus of many coaching approaches.

Values as an Ethical and Action-Oriented Foundation of Coaching

Values, as opposed to goals and purpose, can be understood as constituting the highest level of the concept of intentionality (see Figure 18.1). Intentionality is understood as an individual's continuing aims towards the world. These intentions are expressed in relation to specific 'others', tasks or situations, with individuals always able to relate them to their social and physical environment (see Stelter, 2014a).

In this understanding, values have a meaning that is closely related to thinking and action. They reflect our ethical-interpersonal foundation, and give purpose and legitimacy to our goal-directed actions (Stelter, 2009; 2014a). Values are akin to a set of personal 'bearings'. They generate agency, allow individuals to manoeuvre themselves towards expressions of their personal authority, and give decision-making an ethical and authentic foundation. In the domain of leadership, Kirkeby[1] (2000) refers to norms and values as 'the explanatory setting of our actions'

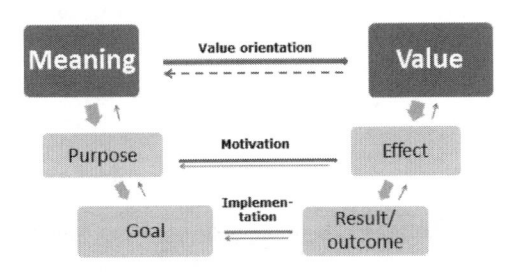

Figure 18.1 Levels of intentional orientation: meanings and values as central in the concept of intentionality – the arrow with the broken line indicates the protreptic ambition in coaching

Source: Adapted from Nitsch, 1986; Stelter, 2014a

(p. 72) and concludes with the observation that 'leadership is the name of the movement whose fixed point is the right moment and the right mood' (p. 74). Values often reflect the implicit aspects of our actions and are thus not always clearly articulated. For Kirkeby (2000) leadership is grounded in our understanding of social competences – competences that concern organizations (i.e. the ability to encourage and engage employees), its customers (by creating a coupling between customer need and the company's technical reality), and the rest of the network (including suppliers, consultants, trade unions and shareholders). In his understanding, the leader's value-based actions are rooted in certain virtues, which are not easily 'operationalizable' but unfold in the individual as a mood or a form of 'attunement' capable of defining the person as an individual who stands for something special (Kirkeby, 2000). A value basis unfolded through virtues implies an *implicit and situational readiness*, already described by the term phronesis. Both leaders and coachees will be prepared for striving for the common good in the events they are involved in. In the later section on protreptic coaching, further insights will be presented into how this type of value-based coaching can support leaders and other coachees in realizing specific ambitions by opening themselves to the event.

It is important to note here that acting on the basis of values is thus not the same as *value-based leadership*, where the point of departure lies in motivating employees by creating a connection to organizational goals (Kraemer, 2011). From this perspective, value activities become more of an ethically anchored developmental project for the individual manager/coachee than a project that concerns the entire organization.

Given the diverse social and organizational values now present in many societies, there seems good reason to encourage coachees to reflect on values as a way of creating a basis for organizing their private and professional lives. Values are not necessarily eternal and universal but are often rooted in practices and events in local communities. Whilst it seems reasonable to claim some values (such as freedom, love or justice) as being universal, there are other values that seem highly contextualized amid the events of everyday life, including interactions and cooperation with others. The ultimate goal is to facilitate and improve leadership, communication and cooperation by reflecting on key values as a fundamental condition and quality in human endeavours and behaviour that will continue to provide a sense of direction in relation to specific goals.

REFLECTING ON VALUES, ASPIRATIONS, HOPES AND DREAMS

Any specific action and its intentions are always meaningful to a coachee and likely to be anchored in values and convictions that are the source of the coachee's aspirations, hopes or dreams. However, as described, a coachee is often not fully aware of their values and, as such, they will usually lie dormant under the surface of action. Whenever a coach asks questions about the values-basis of their actions, these values are brought to the surface, activating them and initiating a process of reflection and development. This will often feel very satisfying to a coachee, as the reflection helps to anchor personal goals in the coachee's sense of identity and long-term aspirations, hopes and dreams. Such conversations in coaching often reveal that certain values and convictions have a very long history, connecting with persons, situations and cultural contexts that the coachee was a part of, and that carry great importance for the coachee. This link to the past and connection to future actions can constitute an essential working perspective in (narrative) coaching. Specific contemporary events and acts are associated more clearly with previous life contexts and events as well as with aspirations and possible action in the future. Sieler (2003+2007]) unfolds a similar agenda in his ontological coaching approach by asking: *What is at stake for you here? What is missing that is important for you? What really matters for you?* These sorts of questions enrich the coachee's story about a particular topic and make it more important and valuable. This expanded life perspective gives coachees a better basis for understanding themselves and their actions.

Are Values Individually Anchored or Developed in Collaboration?

When we introduce values as an issue in the practice of coaching, it is important to closely reflect on the question of whether values are an inherent aspect of being human or a cultural and social phenomenon developed in collaboration with others. Put differently, is coaching a dialogue that generates the coachee's internally latent resources, or a process of co-creation? In the following, a case will be made for both possibilities.

Aristotle uses the term *eudaimonia* to describe the highest human good, not least because it establishes (in his view) a delicate *balance between individual and community ideals*. From this perspective, core values such as the good, the just, the true and the beautiful and, their mutual condition, freedom may be seen as ideals or virtues and the basis for human conduct (see Kirkeby, 2009). Extending this line of reasoning, core values can be considered a basic orientation for the establishment and maintenance of any coaching dialogue.

At the same time, values may vary across contexts, cultures and history. This is the perspective of social constructionists, who are inclined to see all values as having their genesis in human relationships. This perspective is relevant in the sense that people have to negotiate and understand how actions in specific contexts are based on and shaped by particular values. Constructionists appreciate multiple perspectives in their effort to ensure that individual perspectives do not dominate, suppress or silence others' perspectives. From this point of view, it is important to explore and understand how specific values, beliefs, aspirations, dreams and hopes may form the basis for the actions of a given person or group of people. From a constructionist perspective, everything that has meaning in life (everything that is valued and viewed as knowledge, reason and right) has its origins within a set of social relationships. From this epistemological position, values are not absolute but the result of a process of negotiation between parties in specific groups, teams, organizations and society in general. This balance between the individual and socially constructed is one of the main challenges in coaching. The implication for coaches is that they must help the coachee to become aware of the significance of personal values and the negotiation of value positions in specific communities of practice the coachee is part of in work and life.

Two Possible Ways to Work with Values in Coaching Dialogues

In coaching an attention to values, as the basis for an implicit readiness to act in an ethical and reflected way (phronesis), can be unfolded from two perspectives:

1 *Taking one's point of departure in a specific situation, event or task.* The first perspective is what Stelter (2014a) labels the situation-specific perspective and what Rogers (2012) describes as a 'walk through an issue instead of just talking about it' (p. 190). In collaboration with the coach, the coachee can take a closer look at the particulars of a situation or event, re-experiencing and reflecting on it and gradually getting into contact with his or her motives, attitudes, convictions, capacities, beliefs, values and aspirations (which form the basis of the coachee's action). In this way, the coachee comes closer to his or her *landscape of identity* – central issues in regards to his or her self. Values help the individuals (re-)establish their own way of acting.

2 *Dialogue initiated by looking at a specific value or term* (e.g. courage). The second perspective involves reflecting on a central value as a vital aspect of the coachee's life. A *deliberate reflection* on specific values helps us become clearer about who we are, who we would like to be and how things are meaningful to us (depicted as a broken line arrow in Figure 18.1). In that sense, values represent 'a possible mode of certainty' (Kirkeby, 2009, p. 155) and a guide for our lived knowledge and practical wisdom. In the coaching literature comparable approaches might be found in spiritual, ontological, humanistic, person-centered or existential coaching. In narrative coaching, a value orientation might come into focus when the coach asks the coachee, 'If you were to give your story a name, what would you call it?' This question brings an essential perspective into focus.

VALUE REFLECTION IN COACHING PRACTICE

This section presents some selected examples of coaching approaches that focus strongly on values in one way or another. However, working with and including values as an essential part of coaching should not be reduced to these prototypical approaches. Whilst value can be a useful focus within any coaching approach, three unique perspectives have been chosen for this investigation; Existential and Protreptic coaching (as examples of philosophically-inspired approaches), and third-generation coaching (as an example of a narrative-collaborative approach), which also can be understood as an umbrella term for value-reflecting approaches.

Existential Coaching

Existential coaching can be understood as a phenomenological, experience-based and predominantly descriptively focused investigation of the coachee's worldview, which includes 'the whole range of beliefs, values, attitudes, assumptions, affects and behaviours that make up, maintain and identify their "way of being"' (Spinelli, 2010, p. 94). For van Deurzen (2013) a core aim of existential coaching is to teach people to think for themselves about life. In the context of this discussion, 'thinking about life' seems to place an emphasis on values, beliefs, aspirations and core assumptions about one's life and what is really important to it. Based on these central objectives of the existential approach, the task of the coach is to support the clarification of what is essential for the coachee and his or her *life project* (Sartre, 1956). The coach helps to generate and highlight *meaningfulness* as the coachee's fundamental endeavour. This process should lead to a strengthening of existential certainty, security and predictability and thus help fortify the coachee's identity. In a process of being-with and being-for the client as the coach, Spinelli (2010) sees a dual aim for existential coaching:

> First to disclose, together with their client, the underlying, often implicit and inadequately acknowledged, values, beliefs, assumptions, attitudinal stances and their accompanying affective and behavioural components which infuse and maintain the client's worldview. And second, through such explorations, they attempt to illuminate the presenting concerns and issues within the context of that worldview so that whatever it may be of or within that worldview that is being challenged can be clarified and considered. (p. 100)

With its focus on values and beliefs the *existential enquiry* becomes the central objective of this coaching approach, which aims to help coachees achieve ownership of the essentials of their life project. As also mentioned by Spinelli (2010), a leading practitioner and researcher in the field of existential coaching, there is very little published in the area. Future research should increase its focus on this aspect.

Protreptic Coaching

Like existential coaching, protreptic coaching is inspired by phenomenological philosophy, which is primarily interested in the direct investigation and description of phenomena as they are consciously experienced, devoid of preconceptions, presuppositions or theoretical constructions. The word *protreptic* comes from Greek and implies the *turn of individuals to what is most essential in their lives*. Protreptic coaching then aims to direct the coachee and/or organization toward that which is essential for the individual and for the collective. This is often associated with key specific terms that help to uncover the coachee's values-base. In this form of coaching, the coach and the coachee together focus on reflecting on some of the fundamental values that guide individual action. The revitalization of an ancient Greek tradition for leadership development and ethically anchored dialogue is presented as the New Protreptics (Kirkeby, 2009). Protreptic dialogues are not primarily concerned with the understanding of one's motives, or projections but, rather, to the meaning of specific words (e.g., courage) as values, criteria or ontological conditions and consequences.

In effect protreptics is concerned with questions about 'why' and how it establishes a basis for the coachee's being in the world, which can be reconstructed and experienced by reflecting about values. The exceptional and unique characteristic of this approach is that a coaching conversation does not take its starting point in a specific challenging situation, problem or ambition of achievement. Protreptic coaching helps to *prepare* the coachee for a future event through an *anonymizing* procedure, by reflecting on a specific term (such as courage). By reflecting on this term, the coachee prepares for a possible future event, where s/he would benefit from whatever qualities it possesses (e.g. proactivity). The reflective process in protreptic coaching involves an in-depth exploration of the term and what lies behind it, what meaning it holds for the person and why that is personally important. The goal of the protreptic coach is to support others in their striving to understand themselves, and in that sense, to act as the other's servant (Kirkeby, 2009). Because of the general, anonymized and abstract nature of this reflective process, the relationship between coach and coachee often tends to be much more symmetrical than is generally accepted in traditional forms of coaching. The coach is a co-reflecting and collaborative partner in the dialogue.

Third-Generation Coaching

Third-generation coaching can be seen as an umbrella term for all forms of value and meaning-oriented approaches to coaching (including those just presented). According to Stelter (2014a), first-generation coaching aims to solve problems by helping the coachee to move from a troublesome position (A) to a desirable goal (B). In contrast, second-generation coaching positions possible solutions and future possibilities as the path to change. Third-generation coaching is concerned with creating a space for (self-)reflection through collaborative practice, where the coach acts as a (self-)reflecting partner (Stelter, 2014a, 2014b). The simple argument for the promotion of third-generation coaching is the acknowledgement of hypercomplexity in society, which makes it increasingly difficult to move a person forward while having a clear goal or specific solutions in mind.

The aim of third-generation coaching is to invite coachees to engage in a further exploration of their *worldview* by drawing their attention to what is *most essential in their lives*. This focus on *the essential, on values*, makes similarities with existential and protreptic coaching obvious. Stelter's (2014a, 2014b) approach to third-generation coaching includes reflective processes that are based on a narrative-collaborative practice. Here, the coach functions as a dialogue partner who supports the reflective process by resonating the coachee's reflection on the basis of his or her own premises, thus acting as a co-author of new stories that are co-created in the dialogue. In the narrative tradition, this may be unfolded through *outsider witnessing* (White, 2007). This is a particularly effective way of sharing experiences and social realities with each other, an effect that is especially pronounced when the narrative approach is used in a group context. Outsider witnesses (either the coach or a member of a coaching group) reflect on their own thoughts upon hearing the coachee's story, sharing their thoughts on the narrator's aspirations (wishes or dreams) and identity and describing how the story affects them and their own aspirations in relation to life, work, relationships etc. Essential aspects of third-generation coaching include:

1 *Value focus*: The ultimate goal is to facilitate and prepare for leadership, communication and cooperation, not by focusing on specific goals but by reflecting on key values as important landmarks for navigating in life. The protreptic perspective may offer an inspiration here. By reflecting on values, the dialogue essentially strives toward moments of symmetry: The coach and the coachee have a shared interest in examining specific values, because these values are of general relevance to all human beings.
2 *Opportunities for meaning-making*: Meaning-making is one of the most important means of facilitating the coaching dialogue (Stelter, 2007, 2014a, 2014b). Meaning is fundamental because we attribute particular values to our experiences, acts, interactions with others and our personal and professional lives. Things become meaningful when we understand how we feel, think and act, for example by telling stories about ourselves and the world we live in. Meaning-making is based on previous experiences and expectations for the future and is a holistic way of integrating past and present experiences as well as ideas about what the future might bring.
3 *The narrative-collaborative perspective*: Narratives structure life events and order them into a timeline. More specifically, they give stories temporal coherence, help to shape perceptions of events, acts, others, and oneself, whilst also infusing life

with meaning. The plot in any story frames the development of an inner structure and drama (Sarbin, 1986). By telling and listening to stories we make our lives meaningful. In coaching, the aim is to highlight plots and storylines that (in a process of re-membering) need to be renewed and highlighted more clearly. In collaboration with the coach the coachee thickens the story that was nearly forgotten, but which holds significance in regard to fortifying the coachee's identity.

DIRECTIONS FOR FUTURE RESEARCH

Value issues have strong roots in existential and phenomenological thinking, going back to Kierkegaard (1992), Husserl (1970) and Heidegger (1968, 2002), and have played a central role in existential psychology (Frankl, 2006; Yalom, 1980). Within the coaching literature this tradition has been continued by Spinelli (2010) and van Deurzen (2013), while other philosophically informed approaches all exist (e.g., Sieler, 2003+2007). Most of the research done in the area is theoretical and based almost exclusively on case-studies. Stelter was one of the first to conduct research using experimental methods (Stelter, 2014a; Stelter et al., 2011).

As mentioned, coaching-specific research in this area is relatively small and more is needed. Areas for future research could include the following. First, scientist-practitioners (see: Lane & Corrie, 2006, 2012) could investigate how existential, phenomenological, narrative and value-based thinking can be an inspiration to the coaches' practice and decision making in the coaching process. As such, a question for practitioners becomes, how can new integrative, values-based, self-reflective approaches be incorporated into existing practice? As an example, Langdridge (2006, 2012) argues for a combination of existential and solution-focused coaching.

Second, it would be important to investigate how value-reflections as a central element of the coaching dialogue will affect the relationship between coach and coachee. By taking the dialogue to a more general inter-human level, coach and coachee might experience a well-matched collaboration, which may appear in moments of symmetry and relational attunement in the dialogue (Stelter, 2014a). A valuable research perspective would be to take a close look at the relationship as an indicator for the quality of the working alliance between coach and coachee. Third, it would be interesting to investigate how value-oriented executive coaching could influence leader or manager decision-making and personal leadership. Further organizational research might explore whether values-based executive coaching helps to initiate change and to what extent those effects radiate (or ripple) through working teams and whole organizations. It is important to investigate the impact of value-oriented coaching as a key aspect of organizational development.

Finally, an interesting research question relates to how value-oriented coaching might be integrated with value-based leadership on the organizational level (Kraemer, 2011), with the aim of developing employees' individual capacity to act in accordance with their own central values. This type of study could be performed as an action research project in an organization, including an assessment of work satisfaction, well-being, efficiency and productivity.

CONCLUSION

The aim of this chapter was to highlight the importance of values in coaching, asserting that values are fundamental to human identity and everyday personal strivings. A benefit of values is that they establish a form of certainty within individual and/or groups of people with regard to why and how they want to act. Furthermore, the chapter has stressed that the values perspective in coaching is not limited to the three approaches briefly highlighted above. Rather, there has been an encouragement for readers to consider how a values perspective might be integrated within his or her own coaching practice, thus improving and strengthening the impact of coaching for their clients.

NOTE

1 In this chapter, especially in regard to value-based protreptic coaching, I frequently refer to my good colleague Ole Fogh Kirkeby, professor of leadership philosophy, with whom I have the pleasure of teaching the course 'Personal leadership and dialogical coaching' at Copenhagen Business School as part of a Master of Public Governance. Thanks also to Ole for his comments on an earlier draft of this chapter.

REFERENCES

Aristotle (1999). *Nicomachean Ethics* (translated by W. D. Ross). Kitchener: Batoche Books (download http://socserv.socsci.mcmaster.ca/~econ/ugcm/3ll3/aristotle/Ethics.pdf, 10 July 2015).

Beck, U. (2000). *What is globalisation?* Oxford: Policy.

Boyatzis, R. E., Smith, M. L. & Beveridge, A. J. (2013). Coaching with compassion: Inspiring health, well-being and development in organizations. *Journal of Applied Behavioral Science*, 49, 2, 153–178.

Brinker, S., Gunn, B. & Nakai, P. (2000). Leadership from within. *Journal of Human Values*, 6, 1, 65–72.

de Gennaro, I. (ed.) (2012). *Value Sources and Readings on a Key Concept of the Globalized World*. Leiden: BRILL.

Flyvbjerg, B. (2001). *Making social science matter: why social inquiry fails and how it can succeed again*. Cambridge: Cambridge University Press.

Frankl, V. E. (2006). *Man's search for meaning*. New York: Mass Market Paperback.

Gergen, K. J. (2009). *Relational being*. New York: Oxford University Press.

Gergen, K. J. (2011). The delight of continuing the conversation. *Journal of Constructivist Psychology*, 24, 4, 340–344.

Giddens, A. (1991). *Modernity and self-identity: Self and society in the late modern age*. Stanford, CA: Stanford University.

Grant, A. M. (2012). An integrated model of goal-focused coaching: an evidence-based framework for teaching and practice. *International Coaching Psychology Review*, 7, 2, 146–165.

Han, B.-C. (2009). *Duft der Zeit – Ein philosophischer Essay zur Kunst des Verweilen [The smell of time – A philosophical essay on the art of lingering]*. Bielefeld: transcript.

Han, B.-C. (2015). *The burnout society*. Stanford, CA: Stanford University Press (German original from 2010).

Heidegger, M. (1968). *What is called thinking?* New York: Harper & Row.

Heidegger, M. (2002). *Being and time*. London: Routledge.

Holmes, T., Blackmore, E., Hawkins, R. & Wakeford, T. (2011). *The common cause handbook*. UK: Public Interest Research Centre.

Husserl, E. (1970). *The crisis of European sciences and transcentental phenomenology*. Evanston: Northwestern University Press.

Ives, Y. & Cox, E. (2012). *Goal-focused coaching: theory and practice*. London: Routledge.

Kant, I. (1993[1785]). *Grounding for the Metaphysics of Morals* (translated by James W. Ellington; 3rd ed.). Indianapolis: Hackett.

Kaiser, R. & Overfield, D. (2010). The leadership value chain. *The Psychologist-Manager Journal*, 13(3), 164–183.

Kierkegaard, S. (1992). *Either/Or: A fragment of life* (translated by Alastair Hannay; original from 1843). New York: Penguin.

Kirkeby, O. F. (2000). *Management philosophy. a radical-normative perspective*. Heidelberg and New York: Springer.

Kirkeby, O. F. (2009). *The new protreptic – The concept and the art*. Copenhagen: Copenhagen Business School Press.

Kraemer, H. (2011). *From values to action: the four principles of values-based leadership*. San Francisco: Jossey-Bass.

Lane, D. A. & Corrie, S. (2006). *The modern scientist-practitioner – A guide to practice in psychology*. London: Routledge.

Lane, D. A. & Corrie, S. (2012). *Making successful decisions in counselling and psychotherapy – a practical guide*. Berkshire: Open University Press.

Langdridge, D. (2006). Solution focused therapy: a way forward for brief existential therapy? *Existential Analysis*, 17, 2, 359–370.

Langdridge, D. (2012). Existential coaching psychology – developing a model for effective practice. *The Danish Journal of Coaching Psychology*, 2, 1, 83–89 (free download: http://journals.aau.dk/index.php/CP/article/view/239/175).

Lønning, D. J. (2015). Permanence or change: What makes the world tick? *Journal of Human Values*, 21, 1, 37–47.

Luhmann, N. (1998). *Die Gesellschaft der Gesellschaft*. Frankfurt/M.: Suhrkamp.

Mill, J. S. (1998). *Utilitarianism*. Oxford: Oxford University Press.

Nitsch, J.R. (1986). Zur handlungstheoretischen Grundlegung der Sportpsychologie. In H. Gabler, R. Singer & J.R. Nitsch (eds.), *Einführung in die Sportpsychologie, Teil 1*. (pp. 188–270). Schorndorf: Hofmann

Peterson, C. & Seligman, M. (2004). *Character strengths and virtues: A handbook and classification*. New York: Oxford University Press.

Pohlman, R. A. & Gardiner, G. S. with Heffes, E. M. (2000). *Value driven management – How to create and maximize value over time for organizational success*. New York: American Management Association.

Qvortrup, L. (2003). *The hypercomplex society*. New York: Peter Lang.

Rogers, J. (2012). *Coaching skills*. Berkshire: Open University Press.

Sagiv, L., Roccas, S. & Hazan, O. (2004). Value pathways to well-being: Healthy values, valued goal attainment, and environmental congruence. In P. A. Linley & S. Joseph (eds.), *Positive psychology in practice* (pp. 68–85). Chichester: Wiley.

Sarbin, T. R. (ed.) (1986). *Narrative psychology: the storied nature of human conduct*. New York: Praeger.

Sartre, J. P. (1956). *Being and nothingness: an essay on phenomenological ontology*. (trans. H. Barnes). London: Routledge.

Schallow, F. (2012). Kant and the question of values. In I. de Gennaro (ed.). *Value sources and readings on a key concept of the globalized world* (pp. 132–147). Leiden: BRILL.

Seligman, M. E. P. (2009). *Authentic happiness*. New York: Free Press.

Sieler, A. (2003+2007]). *Coaching to the human soul. Ontological coaching and deep change. Vol I + II*. Melbourne: Newfield.

Shapiro, J. P. & Gross, S. J. (2007). *Ethical educational leadership in turbulent times: (Re) solving moral dilemmas*. Mahwah, NJ: Lawrence Erlbaum Associates.

Spinelli, E. (2010). Existential coaching. In E. Cox, T. Bachkirova & D. Clutterbuck (eds.), *The complete handbook of coaching* (pp. 94–106). London: Sage.

Stacy, R. D. (2012). *The tools and techniques of leadership and management: meeting the challenge of complexity*. London: Routledge.

Stelter, R. (2007). Coaching: a process of personal and social meaning making. *International Coaching Psychology Review*, 2, 2, 191–201.

Stelter, R. (2009). Coaching as a reflective space in a society of growing diversity – towards a narrative, postmodern paradigm. *International Coaching Psychology Review*, 4, 2, 207–217.

Stelter, R. (2014a). *A guide to third generation coaching. Narrative-collaborative theory and practice*. Dordrecht: Springer Science+Business Media (also available as e-book).

Stelter, R. (2014b). Third-generation coaching – striving towards value-oriented and collaborative dialogues. *International Coaching Psychology Review*, 9, 1, 33–48.

Stelter, R. (2016). The coach as a fellow human companion. In L. Van Zyl, A. Odendaal & M. Stander (eds.), *Coaching psychology: meta-theoretical perspectives and applications in multi-cultural contexts* (pp.47–66). Switzerland: Springer International Publishing.

Stelter, R., Nielsen, G. & Wikman, J. (2011). Narrative-collaborative group coaching develops social capital – A randomized control trial and further implications of the social impact of the intervention. *Coaching: Theory, Research and Practice*, 4, 2, 123–137.

van Deurzen, E. (2013). The existential ideology and framework for coaching. In E. van Deurzen & M. Hanaway, (eds.), *Existential perspectives on coaching* (pp. 3–20). Basingstoke: Palgrave Macmillan.

Weick, K. E. (1995). *Sensemaking in organisations*. Thousand Oaks: Sage.

White, M. (2007). *Maps of narrative practice*. New York: Norton.

Williams, A. & Whybrow, A. (2013). *The 31 practices – Release the power of your organization's values every day*. London: LID Publishing.

Yalom, I. (1980). *Existential psychotherapy*. New York: Basic Books.

Coaching for Resilience and Well-being

Carmelina Lawton Smith

Personal resilience has been described as the capacity to maintain or recover high levels of well-being in the face of life adversity (Ryff et al., 1998). Recent research suggests that coaching can support resilience, with Grant et al. (2009) finding that a solution-focused coaching programme enhanced manager resilience, despite this not being the aim of the intervention. It appears, therefore, that coaching may already be having an effect on resilience, even when this is not the stated aim. As such, it is important that coaches appreciate the possible impact of their current work, and how they might effectively enhance resilience or well-being when required. A number of texts have emerged to support coaches that draw from a number of alternative philosophical approaches (Pemberton, 2015; Green & Humphrey, 2012; Cooper et al., 2013) but despite the numerous models covered, many issues remain in relation to resilience and well-being in the coaching context. This chapter will summarise a selection of the existing approaches, whilst highlighting some of the remaining gaps in the literature. The discussion will be organised into four parts. First, the terms resilience and well-being will be defined. Second, a conceptualisation of resilience will be presented and discussed. Third, a selection of models will be explored that can help to inform coaching for resilience and well-being. Finally, some recommendations for future research will be made for the purpose of advancing the field.

DEFINING RESILIENCE AND WELL-BEING

While coaching interventions are often aimed at individuals dealing with challenges and stress (Gyllensten & Palmer, 2006), the common coaching paradigm adopted is to treat resilience as a pro-active capability. This is preventative rather than curative, to help individuals buffer the effects of adversity and challenge, so they can remain flexible and sustain performance. Coaching for resilience can therefore be relevant to many contexts such as those dealing with organisational change or personal health issues. Yet there is potential confusion about what is meant by resilience and well-being. This is important for two reasons. Firstly, contracting with clients to deliver an outcome requires a clear agreement on precisely what that outcome should be. Secondly, an individual who is felt to be lacking resilience or well-being might be more likely to need referral to other services. Much has been written about the need for coaches to be aware of the mental health boundary (Bachkirova & Cox, 2005). As such, the lack of clear and agreed definitions of resilience and well-being may make referral decisions more difficult for coaches.

Definitions have generally evolved from research based in the clinical or developmental field and emanated from a curative paradigm. It was this focus on the 'disease model' that led Ryff (1989) to highlight the lack of work being done on psychological well-being and optimal human functioning. She argued that the absence of illness did not equate to the presence of wellness and that a new approach was required. The resulting multifactor model was an attempt to define the core dimensions of well-being (see Table 19.1).

Table 19.1   Six dimensions of psychological well-being

Dimension	Indicators of high functioning	Indicators of low functioning
Self-Acceptance	Possesses a positive attitude towards the self; acknowledges and accepts multiple aspects of self including good and bad qualities; feels positive about past life.	Feels dissatisfied with self; is disappointed with what has occurred in past life, is troubled about certain personal qualities; wishes to be different than what he or she is.
Positive relations with others	Has warm, satisfying, trusting relationships with others; is concerned about the welfare of others; capable of strong empathy, affection, intimacy; understands give and take of human relationships.	Has few close, trusting relationships with others; finds it hard to be warm, open and concerned about others; is isolated and frustrated in interpersonal relationships; not willing to make compromises to sustain important ties with others.
Autonomy	Is self-determined and independent; able to resist social pressures to think and act in certain ways; regulates behaviour from within; evaluates self by personal standards.	Is concerned about the expectations and evaluations of others; relies on judgements of others to make important decisions; conforms to social pressures to think and act in certain ways.
Environmental mastery	Has a sense of mastery and competency in managing their environment; controls complex array of external activities; makes effective use of surrounding opportunities; able to choose or create contexts suitable to personal needs and values.	Has difficulty managing everyday affairs; feels unable to change or improve surrounding context; is unaware of surrounding opportunities; lack sense of control over external world.
Purpose in life	Has goals in life and a sense of directness; feels there is meaning to present and past life; holds belief that give life purpose; has aims and objectives for living.	Lacks a sense of meaning in life; has few goals or aims, lacks sense of direction; does not see purpose of past life; has no outlook or beliefs that give life meaning.
Personal growth	Has a feeling of continued development; sees self as growing and expanding; is open to new experiences; has sense of realising his or her own potential; sees improvement in self and behaviour overtime; is changing in ways that reflect more self-knowledge and effectiveness	Has a sense of personal stagnation; lacks sense of improvement or expansion over time; feels bored and uninterested with life; feels unable to develop new attitudes or behaviours.

Source: Adapted from Ryff (1989)

The ability to maintain well-being through difficult times has been partly attributed to the capacity to remain resilient (Fava & Tomba, 2009) but there has been more debate on how to define resilience. Many authors note ambiguities in how researchers approach the concept of resilience (Zautra et al., 2008; Luthar et al., 2000), highlighting that research is sometimes focused on processes and sometimes on outcomes. For example, Smith et al. (2008) included questionnaire items that asked about outcomes (e.g. 'I tend to bounce back quickly from hard times'), whilst others measure the processes that might increase the chances of such an outcome (e.g. 'I feel that I am optimistic and concentrate on the positives in most situations') (Baruth & Carroll, 2002). This led Zautra et al. (2008) to call for resilient 'outcomes' to be clearly differentiated from the 'processes' that are likely to increase the 'likelihood of those outcomes' (p. 45). They also highlight two potential definitions of resilience, the first being 'recovery' and the second being 'sustainability'. They argue that while recovery ensures survival it may not be enough to support well-being and that sustainability, with a focus on the continued positive pursuit of goals, is essential to resilience. Such an approach would more clearly align with Bonnano (2004: 20), who argues that 'resilience reflects the ability to maintain a stable equilibrium' and should be distinguished from the idea of recovery. Indeed, it might be argued that coaching would be better concerned with sustaining performance (than with recovery) and in helping clients to learn and grow from adversity, otherwise known as *thriving* (Carver, 1998).

Researchers also frequently claim an increase in resilience despite using very different conceptions of the construct. Orzech et al. (2009) used the Self-Compassion Scale (Neff, 2003) 'to measure a form of psychological resilience' (p. 216). By contrast, Wanberg and Banas (2000) measured personal resilience using four items from the Self-Esteem Scale (Rosenberg, 1965). Similar issues arise in coaching, where many studies demonstrate an increase in 'resilience' following coaching, yet use different measures to evidence the effect. For example, Franklin and Doran (2009) used the Resilience Scale for Adults (RSA) (Friborg et al. 2005), Sherlock-Storey et al. (2013) used the Psychological Capital Questionnaire (PsyCap) (Luthans et al., 2007), and Grant et al. (2009) employed the Cognitive Hardiness Scale (Nowack,1990). Each of these scales reflects a very different conception of resilience as the RSA has a strong focus on social aspects while the PsyCap (Luthans et al. 2007) addresses the internal factors of confidence (self-efficacy), optimism, hope and resilience.

This disparity means that it is hard to draw conclusions from empirical research to inform practice. Whilst many studies have claimed 'increases in resilience', it usually takes a close inspection of the methodology section before it is clear 'what' aspect of resilience has been measured. The coaching field would therefore benefit from more clarity in relation to the definitions used in practice and the variables used in research. It may be that in the coaching context it is more appropriate to aim for thriving and sustainable performance based on a process definition of resilience, rather than a recovery outcome focus. This would be more in keeping with the definition of coaching as a developmental process rather than a remedial intervention (Bachkirova, 2011).

CONCEPTUALISATION OF RESILIENCE

The definitional debate in this area is further confused by the alternative conceptualisations of how to approach the topic of resilience. These appear to fall broadly into three categories: asset, systemic and developmental. The *asset* approach involves attempts to identify the personal attributes within the individual that support resilience. However, resilience is known to be affected by factors that exist outside the individual, such as positive relationships (Masten & Reed, 2005). A consideration of these factors is the focus of *systemic* approaches, with the dynamic interaction between elements the primary concern. While both the *asset* and *systemic* approaches attempt to sub-divide resilience into discrete elements, *developmental* approaches take a more holistic perspective. The following section expands on each of these alternative conceptualisations.

Asset Approaches

Asset approaches are based on the premise that a set of attributes within the individual can be defined and (usually) measured to determine resilience. Whether these attributes are nature or nurture is the topic of some debate. For example, Block and Kremen (1996) proposed a trait theory of resilience (termed Ego-Resiliency) that defined resilience as a stable personality characteristic that can develop without exposure to adversity. Scores on the Ego-resilience scale (Block & Kremen, 1996), show positive correlations with Extraversion and Openness and negative correlations with Neuroticism (Fredrickson et al., 2003). Of course, conceiving resilience in this way raises questions about the degree to which coaching may be able to influence resilience, as its trait-like qualities would suggest certain genetic determinants. Whilst some authors suggest that Serotonin levels may be the genetic mechanism linked to resilience (Pemberton, 2015), another mediating variable has been proposed by Schäfer et al., (2015) who reported that high trait resilience was positively correlated with the ability to control attention.

In a study conducted by Schäfer et al. (2015) it was hypothesised that those with high attentional control would use that ability to focus on the positive as an adaptive emotional response to adversity. Yet the high attentional control group attended to both positive and threat stimuli. It was the low control attention group, who tended to focus on the positive stimuli. According to the researchers:

> more trait resilience might be characterized by confronting themselves with threat and being afterwards able to attend to other tasks at hand (due to high attentional control abilities). In contrast, for those with low attentional control it may be more adaptive to avoid threat possibly because they have difficulties in disengaging their attention from threat and engaging in other tasks at hand. (p. 138)

This finding aligns with the work of Coutu (2002), who proposes that resilient leaders attend to reality without a 'rose tinted' perspective, and also display ingenuity and the ability to make meaning from difficult situations. This might suggest that helping clients control their focus of attention can support resilience and may explain why mindfulness training has proved effective (Spence et al., 2008).

A wide variety of asset factors have been identified by researchers, including constructs such as cognitive flexibility, optimism, positive future orientation, hardiness, self-understanding, interpersonal understanding, internal locus of control, high self-esteem, emotional control, sociability, active coping, spirituality and many more (Skodol, 2010; Kent & Davis, 2010). For Reivich and Shatté (2002) self-efficacy, emotion regulation, impulse control, causal analysis, realistic optimism, empathy and 'reaching out' are the seven critical factors making up resilience. Alternatively, Clarke and Nicholson (2010) identified five overarching themes important for leadership resilience, these were optimism, freedom from stress and anxiety, individual accountability, openness and flexibility and problem orientation. Cooper at al. (2013: 43–46) list a number of measures appropriate for the working context and a selection of commercial on-line resilience measures are also now available that can be used in coaching (e.g. i-resilience report,

Resilience quotient, the Resilience Scale), although published empirical support for their validity remains limited.

Some academic work does exist that proposes more empirically validated strategies that can help direct the work of the coach. For example, a review by Jackson et al. (2007) proposed that individual resilience could be developed by: (i) building positive professional relationships and networks, (ii) maintaining positivity, (iii) developing emotional insight, (iv) achieving life-balance and spirituality, and (v) becoming more reflective.

In addition, Sherlock-Storey et al. (2013) implemented a coaching programme to educate and develop resilience across seven key areas: goal setting; explanatory style; strengths use; social support; self-care; self-efficacy; and attaining perspective. The programme used a workbook, reflective activities, a learning log and included three 90 minutes coaching sessions over six-weeks. This more structured approach led to increases in reported resilience post coaching.

When reviewing the literature, the high number of attributes listed generates questions about the scope of the construct and how to make sense of it since such lists often include attitudes, skills, traits, some that might be considered states and even virtues (Richardson, 2002). By contrast, this breadth also suggests that coaches can work with resilience in many different ways and that perhaps a meta-model would be more appropriate to guide the work of the coach.

Systemic Approaches

Despite the extensive work on individual characteristics, many have argued for a more dynamic approach as evidence suggests that resilience involves the integration and interaction of not only internal psychological and biological indicators but also external factors such as social support (Kent & Davis, 2010). One approach that seeks to explain the dynamic interrelationships is the 'conservation of resources model' (Hobfoll, 2002). In proposing a theory to explain diverse reactions to stress, Hobfoll (1989) argued that individuals act to build and to conserve 'resources' that are important to them that include such things as mastery, self-esteem or socio-economic status. If the environment threatens the depletion of such resources then it is experienced as stress. This more dynamic model therefore treats resilience as part of the wider process of maintaining well-being and could explain how normally resilient individuals might experience depletion of resources due to inadequate recovery or replenishment time.

Such a perspective aligns well with complex adaptive systems (CAS) theory that provides a 'useful non-linear approach to thinking about organisational change and the wellbeing of individuals embedded in these systems' (O'Connor & Cavanagh, 2013, p. 1). In a study conducted by O'Connor and Cavanagh (2013), CAS was used to evaluate a leadership coaching programme where well-being, goal attainment and transformational leadership behaviours all saw improvements after coaching. The evaluation showed evidence of a 'ripple effect', where secondary gains were evident in those who were not actually coached (O'Connor & Cavanagh, 2013). Such effects suggest that simple linear relationships of cause and effect are inadequate when addressing well-being and resilience. This might imply that trying to deconstruct, list and measure a set of attributes is an inappropriate way to address resilience.

While seeing resilience as a dynamic process helps represent some of the complex interactions, the challenge becomes how to synthesise and simplify such a perspective in order to make it useful to practitioners. However, this lens could explain why apparently resilient individuals can still face issues. If resilience is simply a set of assets, once learnt these should always be available, but if resilience relies on a dynamic system then assets alone might not ensure resilience in all circumstances. This might suggest that resilience is more transient, which questions the value and use of measures to identify the presence or absence of resilience at a particular point in time.

Developmental Approaches

A more holistic approach is advanced from a developmental perspective. Resilience is seen as 'relative, emerging and changing in transaction with specific circumstances and challenges' (Sutcliffe & Vogus, 2003). According to this view the person or system does not just adapt to new circumstances and add new skills, they learn to become more adaptable when confronted by new challenges. The process of re-construction itself becomes easier with experience, as the system becomes more malleable.

Richardson (2002) describes this holistic view of resilience as a self-actualising force grounded in transpersonal psychology, where an integration of the body, the mind and the spirit can best be characterised as a self-organising system. Such approaches see development as transformational, not as an additive affair (Henning, 2011) and are aligned with the cognitive-developmental approach to coaching (Bachkirova, 2011).

Henning (2011) refers to disruptions as moments of 'disequilibrium' that signify transitions between adult developmental stages. From this perspective, resilience is the ability to weather these transitions, which are generally uncomfortable as they involve a breaking down of existing meaning making structures. For Henning (2011) there are four ways to support the development of resilience: (i) acknowledging the current developmental stage, (ii) healing the past, (iii) maintaining helpful relationships, and (iv) learning about oneself and the surrounding world.

The lack of a shared understanding about resilience is potentially confusing for both coaches and clients. This is partly due to the very different contexts and paradigms from which this research emanates, but may indicate that resilience research needs to be clearly contextualised. Such contextualisation would minimise misunderstandings and bring some coherence when working with resilience. However, at present coaches are working from many different philosophical standpoints and some of the most common models used are summarised in the next section.

MODELS INFORMING COACHING FOR RESILIENCE AND WELL-BEING

Cognitive Approaches

Cognitive Behavioural approaches propose that the attitudes and beliefs individuals hold are simply habitual ways of thinking and behaving, so are rarely examined or questioned. From this perspective:

> Resilience comprises a set of flexible cognitive, behavioural and emotional responses to acute or chronic adversities ... While many factors affect the development of resilience, the most important one is the attitude you adopt to deal with adversity. (Neenan, 2009: 17)

The cognitive approach advises the coach to work with the client to 'dispute' and question the validity of these attitudes and beliefs. The objective is to help the client out of their habitual 'pessimistic automatic thoughts' to consider alternatives and thus choose an interpretation that generates a more helpful consequence, referred to as 'performance enhancing thoughts'. The aim is to establish a more balanced or objective evaluation of the adversity, and to create thoughts that will help move the client forward, promoting flexible thinking, self-acceptance and high frustration tolerance. One suggested tool to achieve this in coaching is 'Resilience Enhancing Imagery' to promote 'Resilience Enhancing

Thinking' (Palmer, 2013). However, empirical research assessing the value of such cognitive techniques remains limited outside the therapeutic setting. While ideas have been extrapolated to coaching, little research has been conducted to specifically evaluate the value of these principles in a coaching context to address resilience and well-being. One notable exception is Grant et al. (2010) who applied a cognitive-behavioural solution-focused approach in a randomised controlled trial with teachers and found increases in resilience. The programme delivered 10 coaching sessions over a 20 week period, focused on goal attainment, leadership style, stress, resilience and well-being.

Many models promoted in practitioner literature adopt cognitive elements and positive psychology in particular builds on these principles to advocate that a change in the focus of thinking can result in greater well-being.

Positive Psychology Models

Positive Psychology is defined as 'the study of the conditions and processes that contribute to the flourishing or optimal functioning of people' (Gable & Haidt, 2005). Researchers within this field are exploring an array of constructs that are of potential value to coaches working with resilience and well-being. One prominent example is the concept of *flourishing*, which Seligman (2011) has proposed has five elements captured by the acronym PERMA: positive emotions (P), engagement (E), relationships (R), meaning (M), and accomplishment (A). The PERMA framework has been the basis of well-being programmes in schools (Kern et al., 2015) together with the Penn Resilience Programme (PRP) (Brunwasser et al., 2009). The PRP has shown significant success in reducing occurrences of depression in schools (Gillham et al., 2007) and in military contexts (Reivich et al., 2011) using cognitive behavioural principles to teach the 'skills' of resilience. The programme includes; problem solving, self-efficacy, self-regulation, emotional awareness, flexibility, empathy, strong relationships and an optimistic explanatory style.

The principle underlying this approach is that positive emotion can activate resources that contribute to well-being and resilience (Folkman, 2008). According to the broaden and build theory (Fredrickson, 2009) there are three consequences of experiencing positive emotion that can create an upward spiral that supports well-being. First, we become more creative and are able to see a broader perspective on situations. Second, we are more able to build intellectual, physical, psychological and social resources, as we become more open to learning and are more likely to form relationships. Third, positive emotion can 'undo' the effects of stressful experience by counteracting the cardiovascular activation caused by negative emotion. It is important to note that resilient individuals are not more resilient than others because of an absence of negative emotions. Rather, they do experience negative emotions but seem able to offset the impact of those emotions by reframing and creating positive interpretations of their experience. Many interventions have been shown to help generate positive emotion (Lyubomirsky, 2011) and theories of hope (Lopez et al., 2004) and optimism (Seligman, 2003) provide other useful tools for the coach to consider.

While, there will be times when a positive focus might be inappropriate, this work does suggest that conversations about positive experiences can be valuable. Extensive literature is available on using strengths as a basis for positive coaching conversations (Linley et al., 2009) and other techniques like 'Feedforward' have been shown to be effective (McDowall et al., 2014). There is additional support for the value of asking clients to describe positive success stories from the concept of *capitalization*. Gable et al. (2004) found that 'communicating personal positive events with others was associated with increased daily positive affect and well-being, above and beyond the impact of the positive event itself' (p. 228). This effect was enhanced when others were perceived to respond actively and constructively. Since coaches will generally respond 'actively and constructively' this has clear implications for the value of eliciting positive stories or discussing strengths in coaching.

Another model with strong links to positive psychology is the Collaborative Recovery Model (CRM; Oades & Anderson, 2012), which has been described as a 'person-centred strengths based' coaching approach (Oades et al., 2009: 25). This emphasises working with strengths and values but the strong focus on collaboration, autonomy and developing a 'growth-mindset' fits well with a coaching approach. The two guiding principles are that recovery is an individual process so it encourages personal responsibility for well-being, and that collaboration should support the growth of autonomy. This autonomous and self-managed approach is consistent with coaching principles so could prove valuable for coaches wishing to work with resilience.

Self-Determination Theory

The importance of promoting autonomy gains further support from self-determination theory (SDT; Deci & Ryan, 2000) which can also contribute to resilience and well-being coaching. As outlined by Spence and Deci (2013), SDT proposes that 'human beings have a set of universal, fundamental psychological needs, the satisfaction of which are essential for healthy development, vital engagement, effective behaving, and psychological well-being' (p. 90). The three basic psychological needs include:

- Autonomy – the need to feel one's behaviour is freely chosen
- Competence – the need to feel one is capable of operating effectively in their environment
- Relatedness – the need to feel well connected to others

One consequence of basic need satisfaction is a feeling of personal well-being (Bernard et al., 2014). As such, SDT has been proposed as a guiding framework for enhancing well-being in coaching (Gabriel et al., 2014) and for highlighting the importance of values enactment (Sheldon & Krieger, 2014) to support intrinsic motivations. Spence and Deci (2013) also detail ways the coach can support autonomy, competence and relatedness in clients, whilst noting that the need for autonomy is considered primary because it helps people act in ways that lead to satisfying psychological outcomes. In contrast, Bernard et al. (2014) found that competence showed the largest impact when measuring mindfulness and subjective vitality as indicators of well-being. There would therefore seem to be much to learn about how to make best use of SDT in coaching for resilience and well-being since both autonomy and competence may play an important role. The third basic need – relatedness – seems less controversial as social support has been identified as key to enhancing resilience in a variety of contexts (Wilson & Ferch, 2005; Jackson et al., 2007). Coaching may also be able to provide the most appropriate type of relationship necessary to support the development of resilience, which needs to encourage freedom and not compromise the sense of autonomy (Flach, 1988). A problem identified by Wilson and Ferch (2005) as the paradox of 'autonomy-community' which they explain as:

> The deeper our involvement in creative and transformative relationships, the more likely we are to grow and gain a stronger sense of self-empowerment and self-cultivation. (p. 51)

Resilience enhancing relationships must therefore support autonomy and build self-esteem, rather than rescue and sympathise. This could indicate that the coaching relationship has a unique role to play in the development of resilience and more research is needed to establish key mechanisms.

Acceptance and Commitment Therapy/Training

Acceptance and Commitment Training (ACT) offers an alternative to the cognitive model by focusing not on changing thoughts, but on learning to accept them. The idea is that when we focus on and try to fight thoughts and feelings we create the very tension we seek to eliminate. This approach argues that by observing the mind and the language it uses we can learn to treat thoughts and feelings as 'passing through'. ACT means accepting thoughts and feeling, choosing a valued direction and taking action (Harris, 2009). This action orientation is in line with the approach many coaches feel is necessary. The central focus of *psychological flexibility*, often highlighted in resilience, makes ACT a potential model that coaches could adopt by working in six domains, shown in Table 19.2.

Moran (2011) suggests that the solid evidence base for ACT and the strong focus on contextualisation makes it an appropriate framework for executive coaching in stressful situations. There are still few outcome studies for non-clinical populations but there is evidence that ACT interventions can reduce levels of stress and burnout (Brinkborg et al., 2011). Despite the limited evidence currently available (Hayes et al., 2006), some authors recommend it as a potential resilience coaching intervention (Pemberton, 2015).

Mindfulness

Mindfulness has been defined as 'the awareness that emerges through paying attention on purpose, in the present moment, and non-judgementally to the unfolding of experience moment to moment' (Kabat-Zinn, 2003: 145).

Mindfulness therefore shares a number of commonalities with ACT by focusing on awareness and the acceptance of feelings and thoughts. Mindfulness-Based Stress Reduction (MBSR) programmes include training on mindfulness practices and cover topics such as stress reactivity, communication skills and self-acceptance. A comprehensive review of mindfulness-based coaching was completed by Virgili (2013), and specific texts related to coaching practice are available (Hall, 2013). Numerous studies show that even brief mindfulness programmes can reduce perceived stress (Klatt et al., 2009), improve burnout symptoms and life satisfaction (Mackenzie et al., 2006) although this requires significant personal practice that is not always completed by participants (Foureur et al., 2013).

Data from the coaching context is more limited although in a group health coaching context the integration of mindfulness training has yielded positive results on goal attainment (Spence et al., 2008). Spence et al. (2008) were able to combine mindfulness

Table 19.2 Acceptance and Commitment Model

Contacting the present moment	Being psychologically present to the physical world and to our own internal world. Being in the here and now to avoid automatic reactions.
Defusion	Learning to 'step back' and observe thinking rather than becoming 'fused' with it. Observing what the mind is doing and telling us, as if thoughts were on leaves floating down a stream.
Acceptance	Making room for painful feelings and emotions to exist. Without fighting or running away from them, sitting with the pain that can be created.
Observing self	Activating the observing self as distinct from the thinking self. Being able to engage pure awareness to observe as an outsider events and thoughts.
Values	Clarifying values is an important step in creating a meaningful life.
Committed Action	Once values are clear action can be taken in line with those values. This may not be easy but the aim is to achieve 'valued living' rather than trying to avoid unpleasant experience.

Source: Harris (2009)

training (MT) with coaching and established that mindfulness training had more impact when delivered before, rather than after coaching. Participants who received MT before coaching also reported decreases in depression and anxiety as measured by the Depression Anxiety and Stress Scale (Lovibond & Lovibond, 1995) although measures of well-being did not reach significance levels.

The health setting has been a common testing ground for mindfulness practice and has shown promising results in promoting resilience in first year paediatric students (Olson et al., 2015). More extensive research with children and youths suggests a role in 'improving cognitive performance and resilience to stress' although the wide range of instruments and the diversity of samples in studies means that data should be treated with caution (Zenner et al. 2014).

Narrative Approach

In times of difficulty the power of narrative has been shown to confer unique benefits. Lawton Smith (2015) completed a qualitative study with eight leaders who had been coached by seven different coaches to identify to what degree they felt coaching had helped their resilience, despite resilience not being the stated aim of the coaching engagement. The leaders interviewed explained that coaching had helped their resilience in five ways. First, it helped them re-claim their self-belief, constant issues tended to undermine their inner confidence, leading to self-doubt and a loss of self-belief. Second, whilst they reported learning about ideas and techniques, they also reported learning about themselves. Third, they valued the ability of the coach to widen their perspective and help them see things in new or different ways. Fourth, coaching was identified as a valuable supportive relationship, for leaders who often did not feel that they could share thoughts and feelings at work (and did not wish to burden friends and family). Finally, leaders expressed the value of simply having space to think. They commented on the value of focused reflective time and the importance of being able to vocalise concerns, emotions or ideas. Coaching seemed to give leaders permission to engage in a type of self-focus that was unacceptable in the organisational setting, where discussions are primarily work-related. All five areas showed overlap and interactions represented in Figure 19.1.

More recent support for these findings come from Timson (2015) who evaluated a coaching programme focused on the resilience of managers in the public sector. The thematic analysis of the qualitative data identified themes that were consistent with Lawton Smith (2015), including the learning of *tools and techniques*, the value of the *time and space* that the coaching sessions gave them, and how important the *independent supportive relationship* with the coaches had been.

Both these studies highlight the importance of having someone who can provide dedicated time and space and act as a 'sounding board'. In trying to define why this process can be so valuable, Niederhoffer and Pennebaker (2005) suggested that 'not talking about emotional upheaval was ultimately unhealthy' (p. 575) because suppression of thoughts or emotions, required physiological work, reflected in central nervous system activity. However, expressing emotion in verbal form seems to confer two benefits. Firstly, in order to construct a coherent narrative that can be conveyed to another person the individual needs to order events that give a sense of control. Secondly, once formed, this narrative can be 'summarized, stored and ultimately forgotten' (p. 576). These cognitive processes give a sense of meaning and closure to potentially difficult events. In order to tell the story to a coach the client is engaged in cognitive meaning making that is, in itself, a valuable process to reduce the emotional impact, but telling the story may reduce the physiological strain caused by inhibition.

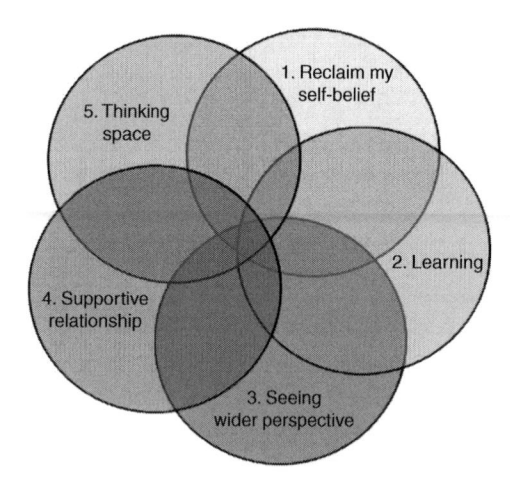

Figure 19.1   How coaching helps resilience

Source: Lawton Smith (2015)

Once the story is told, this brings a secondary benefit by minimising the potential isolation that can result from secrecy. Therefore, the actual process of coaching is likely to help individual resilience by supporting meaning making and by creating a social connection that reduces the physiological strain caused by suppression.

Hardiness

Hardiness is a construct often discussed in tandem with resilience and frequently considered a subset of it. It has been defined by Maddi (2006) as consisting of three hardy attitudes, which include *commitment* (i.e. the belief it is better to stay involved with people and events during tough times), *control* (i.e. the belief that one will be able to influence the outcomes), and *challenge* (i.e. the belief that stress is normal and represents a natural opportunity to grow).

Hardiness has been described as a pathway to resilience and found to be an indicator of mental health (Maddi et al., 2002). Hardy and less hardy individuals seem to experience events in a similar way but those high in hardiness demonstrate higher confidence and self efficacy (Westman, 1990), appraise events as less stressful and engage in more task-focused coping (Delahaij et al., 2010). Despite consistent correlations with numerous positive outcomes, the hardiness construct has been criticised on the validity of merging the three subscales into a single hardiness score (Funk & Houston, 1987) and the lack of causal relationships identified. One suggestion is that since hardy individuals believe in their ability to resolve issues they use less energy in dealing with the internal emotions aroused and can therefore focus personal resources on task-focused strategies and as a result perform better (Westman, 1990).

Closely related to the hardiness construct is mental toughness (MT), which adds *confidence* to the three hardy attitudes outlined above (Clough at al., 2002) and can be measured using the Mental Toughness Questionnaire (MTQ48) (Perry et al., 2013).

Mental Toughness scores have been found to correlate with higher personal well-being and academic performance (Stamp et al., 2015) and in adolescents mental toughness was also found to mitigate high stress and depressive symptoms (Gerber, 2013). Mental Toughness has been successfully enhanced using a strengths-based coaching approach in the sporting context (Gordon, 2012) and some suggest the MTQ48 can form the basis for a coaching discussion (van Nieuwerburgh, 2012) to increase self-awareness and personal responsibility.

FUTURE RESEARCH DIRECTIONS

A number of directions for future research can be proposed. First, work is needed on developing greater conceptual clarity. As coaching research has generally adapted measures and approaches from other disciplines it seems worthwhile to develop a definition and conceptualisation of resilience that clearly fits the coaching context.

Since coaching is a joint meaning-making endeavour, an interesting research direction would be investigating how coaches and clients make meaning of resilience, as a counterpoint to established psychological definitions that may not reflect the felt experience of resilience for individuals. Creating a shared understanding in the coaching interaction is important to gain engagement from clients and stakeholders, and definitions that focus on sustainability and thriving could help minimise the chances of disengagement due to coaching for resilience being seen as a sign of deficit.

Second, given the number of models currently available and their limited empirical validation, more research is needed to establish which non-coaching models are most effective or appropriate for coaching. As many factors have been identified as relevant, it is important to gain an understanding of the respective influence of each, and how they might interact. The coaching relationship also adds another variable. It might be that *any* coaching demonstrates a positive impact, not by virtue of the tools or model used, but simply due to the power of the relationship (de Haan, 2008) and the time and space made available. Further research on the critical mechanisms seems essential to moving forward.

Third, as argued earlier, coaching may have a unique contribution to make to resilience and well-being by providing an integrated approach. The coach may work with individual assets such as problem solving skills or reframing, they can provide the social support required and can encourage analysis of the system within which the individual is operating. In addition, the relationship and opportunity for personal meaning making can encourage the more holistic development proposed by the developmental approach. Yet all personal change occurs in a context so there needs to be a clearer understanding of the potential impact of the system. There may be times when the systemic factors mean that a coaching approach is inappropriate or inadequate to generate the desired effect. Well-being and resilience will be partly dependent on the system and coaching alone is unlikely to be able to resolve all issues.

Finally, the focus on the broader organisational perspective raises two further potential areas for learning. Firstly, if the system can have an impact on the individual it will be important to understand more about how the coached individual can impact the system around them. As such, further work on the radiation (or ripple) effects of coaching on resilience and well-being would be valuable. Secondly, there has been little longitudinal work to establish how the respective approaches work long term. There is a suggestion that resilience may be a resource that fluctuates so research into long-term outcomes is important. With previous research so focused on the individual at a specific point in time, it is now time to take the long and the wide view.

CONCLUSION

Coaching for resilience and well-being draws from many alternative strands of thought and this breadth is creating fragmentation but certain themes are now emerging to guide the work of the coach in this area. While there may be a genetic element, it is clear that coaching can have an impact by helping clients to manage their attention and observe their thought processes. Some thoughts can be questioned for alternative perspectives, while others can be managed and controlled through acceptance. The key is to raise awareness of how the mind is dealing with the information it receives and promote more conscious decision-making. It has also been proposed that broader systemic factors (such as social support) are important. This means coaches can help clients to marshal these resources and start developing the autonomy and control that has been shown to be so vital in promoting resilience. The coaching relationship does seem to confer a space to allow for the personal developmental sense-making that is needed to process challenging events by giving the time and space for a non-judgemental conversation. Because coaching conversations provide opportunities to evaluate alternative perspectives, draw on positive experiences (to counteract negative experiences) and formulate constructive responses, it is able to enhance resilience and well-being. Whilst the coaching literature is still relatively small and more work is needed to understand resilience mechanisms and practical implications, the findings from research conducted to date suggests that coaching has a significant role to play in enhancing resilience and well-being.

REFERENCES

Bachkirova, T. (2011). *Developmental Coaching*, Maidenhead: Open University Press.
Bachkirova, T. and Cox, E. (2005), A Bridge Over Troubled Water, *Counselling at Work*, Spring.
Baruth, K. and Carroll, J. (2002). A Formal Assessment of Resilience: The Baruth Protective Factors Inventory, *The Journal of Individual Psychology*, 58(3): pp. 235–243.
Bernard, D., Martin, J. and Kulik, N. (2014). Self-Determination Theory and Well-Being in the Health Care Profession, *Journal of Applied Biobehavioral Research*, 19(3): pp.157–170.
Block, J. and Kremen, A.M. (1996). IQ and Ego-resiliency: Conceptual and Empirical Connections and Separateness, *Journal of Personality and Social Psychology*, 70(2): pp. 349–361.
Bonanno, G.A. (2004). Loss, Trauma, and Human Resilience: Have we underestimated the Human Capacity to Thrive After Extremely Aversive Events? *American Psychologist*, 59(1): pp. 20–28.
Brinkborg, H., Michanek, J., Hesser, H. and Berglund, G. (2011). Acceptance and Commitment Therapy for the Treatment of Stress Among Social Workers: A Randomized Controlled Trial, *Behaviour Research and Therapy*, 49: pp. 389–398.
Brunwasser, S., Gillham, J. and Kim, E. (2009). A Meta-analytic Review of the Penn Resiliency Program's Effect on Depressive Symptoms, *Journal of Consulting and Clinical psychology*, 77(6): pp. 1042–1054.
Carver, C.S. (1998). Resilience and Thriving: Issues, Models, and Linkages, *Journal of Social Issues*, 54(2): pp. 245–266.
Clarke, J. and Nicholson, J. (2010). *Resilience: Bounce Back from Whatever Life Throws at You*, Richmond: Crimson.
Clough, P., Earle, K. and Sewell, D. (2002). Mental Toughness: The Concept and its Measurement, in Cockerill, I. (Ed.). *Solutions in Sports Psychology*, Padstow: Wadsworth.
Cooper, C., Flint-Taylor, J. and Pearn, M. (2013). *Building Resilience for Success: A Resource for Managers and Organisations*, Basingstoke: Palgrave Macmillan.
Coutu, D. (2002). How Resilience Works, *Harvard Business Review*, 80(5): pp. 46–5.
Deci, E. and Ryan, R. (2000). The 'What' and 'Why' of Goal Pursuits: Human Needs and the Self-determination of Behaviour, *Psychological Inquiry*, 11(4), pp. 227–268
De Haan, E. (2008). *Relational Coaching*, Chichester: Wiley.
Delahaij, R., Gaillard, A. and van Dam, K. (2010). Hardiness and the Response to Stressful Situations: Investigating Mediating Processes, *Personality and Individual Differences*, 49: pp. 386–390.
Fava, G. and Tomba, E. (2009). Increasing Psychological Well-Being and Resilience by Psychotherapeutic Methods, *Journal of Personality*, 77(6): pp. 1904–1934.
Flach, F. (1988). *Resilience: Discovering a New Strength at Times of Stress*, New York: Fawcett Columbine.
Folkman, S. (2008). The Case for Positive Emotion in the Stress Process, *Anxiety, Stress and Coping*, 21(1): pp. 3–14.
Foureur, M., Besley, K., Burton, G., Yu, N. and Crisp, J. (2013). Enhancing the Resilience of Nurses and Midwives: Pilot of a Mindfulness-based Program for Increased Health, Sense of Coherence and Decreased Depression, Anxiety and Stress, *Contemporary Nurse*, 45(1): pp. 114–125.

Franklin, J. and Doran, J. (2009). Does All Coaching Enhance Objective Performance Independently Evaluated by Blind Assessors? The Importance of the Coaching Model and Content, *International Coaching Psychology Review*, 4(2): pp. 128–144.

Fredrickson, B. (2009). *Positivity*, New York: Crown.

Fredrickson, B., Tugade, M., Waugh, C. and Larkin, R. (2003). What Good are Positive Emotions in a Crisis? *Journal of Personality and Social Psychology*, 84(2): pp. 365–376.

Friborg, O., Barlaug, D., Martinussen, M., Rosenvinge, J.H. and Hjemdal, O. (2005). Resilience in Relation to Personality and Intelligence, *International Journal of Methods in Psychiatric Research*, 14(1): pp. 29–42.

Funk, S. and Houston, B. (1987). A Critical Analysis of the Hardiness Scale's Validity and Utility, *Journal of Personality and Social Psychology*, 53(3): pp. 572–578.

Gable, S. and Haidt, J. (2005), What (and Why) Is Positive Psychology, *Review of General Psychology*, 9(2): pp. 103–110.

Gable, R., Reis, H., Impett, E. and Asher, E. (2004). What Do You Do When Things Go Right? The Intrapersonal Benefits of Sharing Positive Events, *Journal of Personality and Social Psychology*, 87(2): pp. 228–245.

Gabriel, A., Moran, C. and Gregory, J. (2014). How Can Humanistic Coaching Affect Employee Well-being and Performance? An Application of Self-determination Theory, *Coaching: An International Journal of Theory and Practice*, 7(1): pp. 56–73.

Gerber, M., Kalak, N., Lemola, S., Clough, P., Perry, J., Pühse, U., Elliot, C., Holsboer-Trachsler, E. and Brand, S. (2013). Are Adolescents With High Mental Toughness Levels More Resilient Against Stress? *Stress and Health*, 29: pp. 164–171.

Gillham, J., Reivich, K. Freres, D., Chaplin T.M., Shatté A.J., ... and Seligman, M.E. (2007). School-based Prevention of Depressive Symptoms: A Randomized Controlled Study of the Effectiveness and Specificity of the Penn Resiliency Programme, *Journal of Consulting and Clinical Psychology*, 75(1): pp. 9–19.

Gordon, S. (2012). Strengths-based Approaches to Developing Mental Toughness: Team and Individual, *International Coaching Psychology Review*, 7(2): pp. 210–222.

Grant, A., Curtayne, L. and Burton, G. (2009). Executive Coaching Enhances Goal Attainment, Resilience and Workplace Well-being: A Randomised Controlled Study, *The Journal of Positive Psychology*, 4(5): pp. 396–407.

Grant, A., Green, L. and Rynsaardt, G. (2010). Developmental Coaching for High School Teachers: Executive Coaching Goes to School, *Consulting Psychology Journal*, 62(3): pp. 151–168.

Green, A. and Humphrey, J. (2012). *Coaching for Resilience: A Practical Guide to Using Positive Psychology*, London: Kogan Page.

Gyllensten, K. and Palmer, S. (2006). Experiences of Coaching and Stress in the Workplace: An Interpretative Phenomenological Analysis, *International Coaching Psychology Review*, 1(1): pp. 86–98.

Hall, L. (2013). *Mindful Coaching*, London: Kogan Page.

Harris, R. (2009). *ACT made simple*, Oakland: New Harbinger.

Hayes, S., Luoma, J., Bond, F., Masuda, A. and Lillis, J. (2006). Acceptance and Commitment Therapy: Model, Processes and Outcomes, *Behaviour Research and Therapy*, 44: pp. 1–25.

Henning, P. (2011). Disequilibrium, Development and Resilience Through Adult Life, *Systems Research and Behavioral Science*, 28: pp. 443–454.

Hobfoll, S. (1989). Conservation of Resources, *American Psychologist*, 44(3): pp. 513–524.

Hobfoll, S. (2002). Social and Psychological Resource Adaptation, *Review of General Psychology*, 6: pp. 307–324.

Jackson, D., Firtko, A. and Edenborough, M. (2007). Personal Resilience as a Strategy for Surviving and Thriving in the Face of Workplace Adversity: A Literature Review, *Journal of Advanced Nursing*, 60(1): pp. 1–9.

Kabat-Zinn, J. (2003). Mindfulness-based Interventions in Context: Past, Present, and Future. *Clinical Psychology: Science and Practice*, 10: pp. 144–156.

Kent, M. and Davis, M. (2010). The Emergence of Capacity-Building Programs and Models of Resilience, in Reich, J., Zautra, A. and Hall, J. (eds.), *Handbook of Adult Resilience*, New York: The Guilford Press.

Kern, M., Waters, L., Adler, A. and White, M. (2015). A Multidimensional Approach to Measuring Well-being in Students: Application of the PERMA Framework, *Journal of Positive Psychology*, 10(3): pp. 262–271.

Klatt, M., Buckworth, J. and Malarkey, W. (2009). Effects of Low-Dose Mindfulness-Based Stress Reduction(MBSR-ld) on Working Adults, *Health Education and Behavior*, 36(3): pp. 601–614.

Lawton Smith, C. (2015). How Coaching Helps Leadership Resilience: The Leadership Perspective, *International Coaching Psychology Review*, 10(1): pp.6–19.

Linley, A., Woolston, L. and Biswas-Diener, R. (2009). Strengths Coaching with Leaders, *International Coaching Psychology Review*, 4(1): pp. 37–48.

Lopez, S.J. et al. (2004). Chapter 24, Strategies for Accentuating Hope, in Linley P. A. and Joseph S (Eds.), *Positive Psychology in Practice*, Hoboken, NJ: John Wiley & Sons.

Lovibond, P. and Lovibond, S. (1995). The Structure of Negative Emotional States: Comparison of the Depression Anxiety Stress scales (DASS) with Beck Depression and Anxiety Inventories, *Behaviour Research and Therapy*, 33(3), pp.335–343.

Luthans, F., Youssef, C. and Avolio, B. (2007). *Psychological Capital*, Oxford: Oxford University Press.

Luthar, S.S., Cicchetti, D. and Becker, B. (2000). The Construct of Resilience: A Critical Evaluation and Guidelines for Future Work, *Child Development*, 71(3): pp.543–562.

Lyubomirsky, S. (2011). *The How of Happiness*, Piatkus.

Mackenzie, C., Poulin, P. and Seidman-Carlson, R. (2006). A Brief Mindfulness-based Stress Reduction Intervention for Nurses and Nurse Aids, *Applied Nursing Research*, 19 (2): pp. 105–109.

Maddi, S. (2006). Hardiness: The Courage to Grow from Stresses, *Journal of Positive Psychology*, 1(3): pp. 160–168.

Maddi, S., Khoshaba, M., Persico, M., Lu, J., Harvey, R. and Bleecker, F. (2002). The Personality Construct of Hardiness, *Journal of Research in Personality*, 36, pp.72–85.

Masten, A. and Reed, M. (2005). Resilience in Development, in Snyder, C. and Lopez, S. (Eds.), *Handbook of Positive Psychology*, Oxford: Oxford University Press.

McDowall, A., Freeman, K. and Marshall, S. (2014). Is FeedForward the way forward? A Comparison of the Effects of Feedforward Coaching and Feedback, *International Coaching Psychology Review*, 9(2): pp. 135–146.

Moran, D. (2011). ACT for Leadership: Using Acceptance and Commitment Training to Develop Crisis-Resilient Change Managers, *The International Journal of Behavioral Consultation and Therapy*, 7(1): pp. 66–75.

Neenan, M. (2009). *Developing Resilience: A Cognitive-Behavioural Approach*, New York: Routledge.

Neff, K. (2003). Development and Validation of a Scale to Measure Self-compassion. *Self and Identity*, 2: pp. 223–250.

Niederhoffer, K. and Pennebaker, J. (2005). Sharing One's Story: On the Benefits of Writing or Talking About Emotional Experience, in Snyder, C. and Lopez, S. (Eds.), *Handbook of Positive Psychology*, Oxford: Oxford University Press.

Nowack, K. (1990). Initial Development of an Inventory to Assess Stress and Health Risk, *Stress Management*, 4(3): pp. 173–180.

Oades, L. and Anderson, J. (2012). Recovery in Austrailia: Marshalling Strengths and Living Values, *International Review of Psychiatry*, 24(1): pp.5–10.

Oades, L., Crowe, T. and Nguyen, M. (2009). Leadership Coaching – Transforming Mental Health Systems from the Inside Out: The Collaborative Recovery Model as Person-centred Strengths-based Coaching Psychology, *International Coaching Psychology Review*, 4(1): pp. 25–36.

O'Connor, S. and Cavanagh, M. (2013). The Coaching Ripple Effect: The Effects of Developmental Coaching on Wellbeing across Organisational Networks, *Psychology of Well-Being*, 3(2): pp.1–23.

Olson, K., Kemper, K. and Mahan, J. (2015). What Factors Promote Resilience and Protect Against Burnout in First-Year Pediatric and Medicine-Pediatric Residents?, *Journal of Evidence-Based Complementary & Alternative Medicine*, 20(3): pp. 192–198.

Orzech, K., Shapirob, S., Warren, K. and McKaya, M. (2009). Intensive Mindfulness Training-related Changes in Cognitive and

Emotional Experience, *The Journal of Positive Psychology*, 4(3): pp. 212–222.

Palmer, S. (2013). Resilience Enhancing Imagery: A Cognitive Behavioural Technique which includes Resilience Undermining Thinking and Resilience Enhancing Thinking, *The Coaching Psychologist*, 9(1): pp. 48–50.

Pemberton, C. (2015). *Resilience: A Practical Guide for Coaches*, Maidenhead: McGraw Hill.

Perry, J.L., Clough, P.J., Crust, L., Earle, K. and Nicholls, A.R. (2013). Factorial Validity of the Mental Toughness Questionnaire-48, *Personality and Individual Differences*, 54: pp. 587–592.

Reivich, K., Seligman, M. and McBride, C. (2011). Master Resilience Training in the US Army, *American Psychologist*, 66(1): pp. 25–34.

Reivich, K. and Shatté, A. (2002). *The Resilience Factor: 7 Keys to Finding Your Inner Strength and Overcoming Life's Hurdles*, New York: Broadway Books.

Richardson, G. (2002). The Metatheory of Resilience and Resiliency, *Journal of Clinical Psychology*, 58(3): pp. 307–321.

Rosenberg, M. (1965). *Society and the Adolescent Self-image*. Princeton, NJ: Princeton University Press.

Ryff, C. (1989). Happiness is Everything, or Is It? Explorations on the Meaning of Psychological Well-Being, *Journal of Personality and Social Psychology*, 57(6): pp.1069–1081.

Ryff, C., Singer, B., Dienberg Love, G. and Essex, M. (1998). Resilience in Adulthood and Later Life, in Lomranz, J. (Ed.), *Handbook of Aaging and Mental Health*, New York: Plenum.

Schäfer, J., Wittchen, H., Höfler, M. and Heinrich, A. (2015). Is Trait Resilience Characterized by Specific Patterns of Attentional Bias to Emotional Stimuli and Attentional Control? *Journal of Behavior Therapy and Experimental Psychiatry*, 48: pp.133–139

Seligman, M. (2003). *Authentic Happiness*, New York: The Free Press.

Seligman, M. (2011). *Flourish*, New York: Simon & Schuster.

Sheldon, K. and Krieger, L. (2014). Walking the Talk: Value Importance, Value Enactment, and Well-being, *Motivation and Emotion*, 38: pp. 609–619.

Sherlock-Storey, M., Moss, M. and Timson, S. (2013). Brief Coaching for Resilience During Organisational Change – An Exploratory Study, *The Coaching Psychologist*, 9(1): pp. 19–26.

Skodol, A. (2010). The Resilient Personality, in Reich, J., Zautra, A. and Hall, J. (eds), *Handbook of Adult Resilience*, New York: The Guilford Press.

Smith, B.W., Dalen, J., Wiggins, K., Tooley, E., Christopher, P. and Bernard, J. (2008). The Brief Resilience Scale: Assessing the Ability to Bounce Back, *International Journal of Behavioural Medicine*, 15: pp. 194–200.

Spence, G., Cavanagh, M. and Grant, A. (2008). The Integration of Mindfulness Training and Health Coaching: An Exploratory Study, *Coaching: An International Journal of Theory, Research & Practice*, 1(2): pp. 145–163.

Spence, G. and Deci, E. (2013). Self-Determination Theory Within Coaching Contexts: Supporting Motives and Goals that Promote Optimal Functioning and Well-being, Ch. 5 in David, S., Clutterbuck, D. and Megginson, D. (Eds.), *Beyond Goals*, Surrey: Gower.

Stamp, E., Crust, L., Swann, C., Perry, J., Clough, P. and Marchant, D. (2015). Relationships Between Mental Toughness and Psychological Wellbeing in Undergraduate Students, *Personality and Individual Differences*, 75: pp. 170–174.

Sutcliffe, K.M. and Vogus, T. (2003). Organising for Resilience, Ch. 7 in Cameron, K.S., Dutton, J. and Quinn, R. (eds.), *Positive Organizational Scholarship*, San Francisco: Berrett-Koehler.

Timson, S. (2015). Exploring What Clients Find Helpful in a Brief Resilience Coaching Programme: A Qualitative Study, *The Coaching Psychologist*, 11(2), pp. 81–88.

van Nieuwerburgh, C. (2012). Coaching for Mental Toughness, in Clough, P. and Strycharczyk, D. (eds.), *Developing Mental Toughness*, London: Kogan Page.

Virgili, M. (2013). Mindfulness-based Coaching: Conceptualisation, Supporting Evidence and Emerging Applications, *International Coaching Psychology Review*, 8(2): pp. 40–57.

Wanberg, C. and Banas, J. (2000). Predictors and Outcomes of Openness to Changes in a

Reorganizing Workplace, *Journal of Applied Psychology*, 85(1): pp. 132–142.

Westman, M. (1990). The Relationship Between Stress and Performance: The Moderating Effect of Hardiness, *Human Performance*, 3(3): pp. 141–155.

Wilson, S.M. and Ferch, S.R. (2005). Enhancing Resilience in the Workplace Through the Practice of Caring Relationships, *Organizational Development Journal*, 23(4): pp. 45–60.

Zautra, A., Hall, J. and Murray, K. (2008). Resilience: A New Integrative Approach to Health and Mental Health Research, *Health Psychology Review*, 2(1): pp. 41–64.

Zenner, C., Herrnleben-Kurz, S. and Walach, H. (2014). Mindfulness-based Interventions in school – A Systematic Review and Meta-analysis, *Frontiers in Psychology*, 5: pp. 1–20.

Working with Strengths in Coaching

Sophie Francis and Alison Zarecky

Strengths seem central to the work coaches do in helping clients' maximize their potential and perform at their best (Whitmore, 2002; Biswas-Diener, 2010). Strengths coaching can be defined as a potential-guided, person-centered approach for enhancing optimal functioning and wellbeing by engaging what people do well (Linley and Harrington, 2006). It is informed by the fundamental assumption that people are naturally inclined to want to discover, grow and develop their potential and that this inner capacity can be 'facilitated and harnessed through the coaching relationship' (p. 37).

With roots in eudemonic philosophy (Aristotle, trans. 2000) and humanistic psychology (Maslow, 1954), strengths were promoted by early management thinkers (e.g. Drucker, 1967), emerging as a core of positive psychology alongside coaching psychology and its solution-focused, abundance-orientated approach (Linley and Harrington, 2006). By focusing on how humans can flourish, positive psychology sought to balance the study of psychology, which had disproportionately focused on human illness, deficit and dysfunction for most of the 20th century (Seligman and Csikszentmihalyi, 2000). Focusing on what is working and strong was seen as important to offset the brain's 'negativity bias', our evolutionary tendency to weigh negative events, emotions and perceptions more strongly than positive (Baumeister et al., 2001; Rozin and Royzman, 2001). Early research then sought to establish theoretical and empirical foundations. Strengths are now an integral part of approaches designed to promote human flourishing and performance, associated with significant benefits such as increased wellbeing (Proctor et al., 2010), goal attainment (Linley et al., 2010a), performance (Clifton and Harter, 2003) and engagement (Harter et al., 2002). This chapter sets out to review the literature on strengths, explore key concepts, signpost major studies and outline current thinking. Because the evidence base is still growing, the chapter takes a broader view, examining literature from positive psychology, humanistic psychology, counseling psychology, organizational psychology and education.

We intend to provide a comprehensive overview of strengths applications in coaching by taking readers through prominent strengths models and tools such as the Values-In-Action Inventory (Peterson and Seligman, 2004), StrengthsFinder® (Buckingham and Clifton, 2001) and R2 Strengths Profiler (Linley, 2010), as well as emerging approaches. Moving past the 'identify and use more' method advocated by earlier researchers and employed by many coaches, this chapter looks at strengths development, along with the underuse and overuse of strengths (Linley, 2008; Kaiser and Overfield, 2011), weaknesses (Linley, 2008), shadow sides (Drake, 2015) and blind spots (Biswas-Diener et al., 2011). We progress to a brief discussion about applying strengths in coaching contexts such as leadership, organizational practice and career transitions.

In line with calls for a more balanced, nuanced approach to strengths (Biswas-Diener et al., 2011; Quinlan et al., 2012), we aim to integrate these perspectives and provide critiques to help coaching practitioners and researchers build on this abundant area of potential for coaching.

WHAT ARE STRENGTHS?

Strengths can be broadly understood as capabilities, skills, talents, values, beliefs and resources (Crowe et al., 2012) that can be drawn upon to achieve valued outcomes (Linley and Harrington, 2006). More specifically they can be seen as 'characteristics that allow a person to perform well or at their personal best' (Wood et al., 2011, p.16), a definition which encompasses personal, physical and psychological strengths.

For Buckingham and Clifton (2001), strengths are 'the ability to produce consistent, near-perfect performance in an activity' (p. 25), the result of natural talents refined by knowledge and skill. This conceptualization arose from empirically based interviews to identify recurring patterns of thought, feeling and behavior associated with work and academic success (Buckingham and Clifton, 2001; Clifton and Anderson, 2002). In contrast, Peterson and Seligman (2004) conceptualize strengths as 'psychological ingredients – processes or mechanisms – that define morally valued virtues' (p. 13). In their taxonomy, strengths of character were classified according to what was found to be universally valued across cultures and history.

Peterson and Seligman (2004) observed that 'signature' or 'top five' strengths convey a sense of ownership, authenticity, vitality and invigoration that engage a powerful yearning and intrinsic motivation to act in accordance with these strengths. For Linley and Harrington (2006) strengths are linked to self-realization (Horney, 1950), self-actualization (Maslow, 1954) and the actualizing tendency (Rogers, 1963). They observed that 'when we use our strengths, we feel good about ourselves, we are better able to achieve things, and we are working toward fulfilling our potential' (p. 41).

Building on these concepts and research, Linley offers the following definition of strengths: 'a pre-existing capacity for a particular way of behaving, thinking, or feeling that is authentic and energizing to the user, and enables optimal functioning, development and performance' (2008: p. 9). He conceives that strengths evolved to help us survive and thrive, the result of adaptive solutions shaped by nature and nurture, enabled by the organismic valuing process (actualizing tendency) and neural learning.

The Nature of Strengths

Biswas-Diener et al. (2011) argue that these definitions of strengths are rooted in trait personality theory. Strengths are generally considered to have a genetic or evolutionary aspect, an assertion that is supported by findings from twin studies (Steger et al., 2007) and strong correlations with personality factors (Linley, 2010). However, these scholars advocate a more dynamic lens, positing that strengths are highly contextual and can be developed. Rather than thinking of strengths as static and/or existing across time and situation, they urge practitioners and researchers to consider how strengths vary within people and might be amenable to learning.

Peterson and Seligman (2004) acknowledge that while character strengths are relatively stable, environmental factors may make them malleable. Personality may be less fixed than previously thought (e.g. Boyce et al., 2013) and there is some evidence certain strengths are more prevalent and may emerge at different life stages (Martinez-Marti and Ruch, 2014). This supports the view of strengths as contextual, unfolding over a lifetime (Smith, 2006; Drake, 2015).

A developmental lens appears particularly important in coaching. For example Drake (2015) states, 'one of the first steps in coaching someone around their strength using a narrative approach is to determine its nature. The key is to identify if the strength is more intrinsically motivated (innate or acquired) or extrinsically motivated (normative or compensatory)' (p.96). Linley et al. (2009) distinguish things we do well that are energizing from those that are de-energizing (calling the latter 'learned behavior'). These may have been extrinsically rewarded yet lack the critical energy component that makes them more intrinsic and sustaining. Strengths can also become draining through overuse, leading to disengagement. Both perspectives highlight the importance of understanding subtle developmental, motivational and situational factors.

It is often noted that people do not always recognize their strengths (Hill, 2001), and that strengths can lie dormant waiting for opportunities or situations to activate them (Lyons and Linley, 2008). Linley et al. (2009) differentiate realized strengths from unrealized strengths, which represent areas of untapped or growth potential or those displayed only in certain situations. Both are performed well and feel energizing; the difference is how frequently these are used. Thus, a strength may be defined in terms of performance, energy and use (Linley, 2008), providing a more context-sensitive and dynamic lens to understand, deploy and develop strengths.

STRENGTHS BENEFITS AND OUTCOMES

Strengths are associated with a wide range of benefits for individuals and their workplaces, each valued in coaching. This section looks at psychological, behavioral and organizational outcomes associated with having, using and developing strengths.

Personal Wellbeing

Character strengths have consistently been shown to predict wellbeing outcomes such as life satisfaction and positive affect (Park et al., 2004; Park et al., 2009), indicating that identifying and using them may positively influence happiness and fulfillment in coachees. Studies show that people who use their strengths have significantly higher levels of psychological and subjective wellbeing, energy and vitality (Proctor et al., 2010; Minhas, 2010; Govindji and Linley, 2007), self-efficacy (Govindji and Linley, 2007) and self-esteem (Wood et al., 2011; Minhas, 2010). Furthermore, strengths use has shown to lead to greater wellbeing and less stress over time (Wood et al., 2011), inferring that strengths interventions supported by coaching may be valuable to build long term resilience in clients.

In a recent meta-analysis of positive psychology interventions (PPIs), Donaldson et al.

(2015) found that strengths-based interventions involving identifying and practicing strengths are effective in increasing life satisfaction (e.g. Proctor et al., 2011); however, others (e.g. Bolier et al., 2013) have concluded that outcomes are weak. Repeated randomized control trials of one common intervention, encouraging people to use their signature strengths in new ways, has demonstrated increased happiness (e.g. Proyer et al., 2015; Seligman et al., 2005). In most of these studies depressive symptoms were also reduced, although replication has produced mixed results (Mongrain and Anselmo-Matthews, 2012) and small effect sizes (Woodworth et al., 2015). However, a follow-up study 3.5 years after a mixed PPI intervention indicates that how a person uses the intervention can explain variance in life satisfaction (6%) and depression (10%) outcomes (Proyer et al., 2014). A similar intervention adapted for work was effective in increasing both signature strengths and wellbeing (Forest et al., 2012), while a longitudinal study of high school students indicated sustained wellbeing benefits one year later (Gillham et al., 2011).

Goal Attainment and Personal Growth

People who use their strengths are more likely to achieve goals (Linley et al., 2010a), a key raison d'etre and outcome of coaching (e.g. Burke and Linley, 2007). Research indicates that certain strengths (curiosity and grit) may predict goal striving and attainment (Sheldon et al., 2015). Personal growth initiative and psychological capital (self-efficacy, hope and optimism) are also emerging outcomes and ingredients (Meyers et al., 2015) that can be stimulated by meaningful goal setting around strength development. Leaders who develop themselves and their teams using strengths have demonstrated strategic goal progress and alignment (Smedley, 2007; Garcea, et al., 2012). In addition, a grounded theory study in a leadership coaching context found strengths use and development enabled a virtuous circle of positive emotion, authenticity and sense of achievement (Elston and Boniwell, 2011). Coaching seems an ideal vehicle to facilitate this.

Performance and Work Engagement

There is increasing evidence that strengths can be harnessed to improve performance and organizational results, with recent empirical studies (e.g. Kong and Ho, 2015; van Woerkom and Meyers, 2015; Botha and Mostert, 2014) building on early research linking strengths with workplace and academic performance (Clifton and Harter, 2003) and work engagement (Harter et al., 2002).

A global study by the Corporate Leadership Council (2002) across organizations and industries ($n = 19,187$) found that self-rated performance rose by 36.4 per cent when managers encouraged staff to focus on strengths (and fell by 26.8 per cent when weaknesses were emphasized). More recently Kong and Ho (2015) established that individuals who used their strengths more at work delivered better performance (both task performance and discretionary helping) based on supervisor ratings. Character strength levels have also been linked to creative task performance (Avey et al., 2012), healthy work behavior (Gander et al., 2012;) and reduced burnout (Harzer and Ruch, 2015). The opportunity to do your best everyday (use your strengths) has also been found to be a predictor of work engagement (Harter et al., 2002; Botha and Mostert, 2014), which in turn can enhance business outcomes such as productivity, profitability, commitment, customer satisfaction and less turnover (Harter et al., 2002).

Only a few coaching studies demonstrate the impact of a strengths approach on performance and engagement. In one study, MacKie (2014) found that a strengths assessment and coaching intervention with executives/senior managers was highly effective in promoting transformational leadership. Within the domain of professional sport, a strengths-based coaching intervention was found to enhance mental toughness in athletes, compared to those exposed to a weakness-focused, coach-led alternative (Gordon and Gucciardi, 2011). Finally, within education, strengths coaching with primary students has been found to generate engagement and hope (Madden et al., 2011).

Assessing Outcome Studies

Based on this review, Table 20.1 summarizes published benefits found to accrue from strengths use.

While empirical investigation of strengths (like coaching) is growing, it has struggled to keep pace with the growth in its related practices. Of the research that does exist, it has been noted that many studies are self-selecting, have relatively small sample sizes, and may be educationally or culturally biased (Donaldson et al., 2015; Meyers et al., 2013). It may be premature to extrapolate outcomes found with college or school students to mature working adults, many of whom are at their career peak. A critique lobbied at strengths studies and assessments in particular is reliance on self-report, although this is disputed by Buschor et al. (2013), who found self-rated character strengths converged with peer-ratings. Nonetheless more objective measures are needed along with a greater understanding of the factors that may influence outcomes or reduce intervention effectiveness. For example, while strengths-based group coaching with graduating university students (McDowall and Butterworth, 2014) produced significant increases in self-efficacy and confidence in goal attainment, these differences were not statistically significant compared to controls.

RELATED THEORIES

A number of theoretical positions can be adopted to better understand strengths and draw out implications for coaching. As an illustration, two perspectives are briefly outlined: self-determination theory (Ryan and Deci, 2000; Sheldon and Elliot, 1999) and broaden and build theory (Fredrickson, 2001). Developing a nuanced understanding of possible process mechanisms can help coaches working with strengths design and evaluate effective interventions.

Table 20.1 Benefits of strengths use

For individuals	For organizations
Happiness and wellbeing	Performance
Less stress and depression	Work engagement
Energy and vitality	Work satisfaction
Resilience	Less burnout
Self-esteem	Healthy work behavior
Self-efficacy	Collaboration
Goal attainment	Transformational leadership behavior
Personal growth	
Intrinsic motivation	*Indirectly:*
Engagement	Productivity
Psychological capital	Profit
Authenticity	Lower turnover
Work as calling	Customer satisfaction
Mental toughness	

Self-Determination Theory

Self-determination theory (SDT) (Ryan and Deci, 2000) shows that people experience high quality, enduring motivation when three psychological needs are satisfied: autonomy, competence and relatedness. In a study of strengths use at work, Kong and Ho (2015) found that strengths use predicted workplace performance and discretionary helping. More specifically, they found that leader autonomy support predicted strengths use and that this relationship was strongest when individuals had strong independent self-construal. This finding is consistent with many SDT studies (see Ryan and Deci, 2000) that confirm a range of beneficial outcomes from the satisfaction of basic needs.

An extension of SDT, self-concordance theory (Sheldon and Elliot, 1999) holds that people tend to move toward intrinsically motivated and beneficial goals over time, as a consequence of an innate organismic valuing process (OVP). Govindji and Linley (2007) established that people who know and use their strengths and are in touch with their own needs and values (i.e. the OVP) tend to be are happier. Linley et al. (2010a) further found strengths use supports self-concordant goal progress, leading to greater psychological need satisfaction and wellbeing, which indicates that linking strengths to self-concordant goals can be beneficial in coaching (Roche and Hefferon, 2013; Burke and Linley, 2007).

Relatedly, strengths may interact with interests, passions and environment in a variety of ways. For example, harmonious passion is the result of engaging in an activity that is loved, freely chosen and an important part of identity, which motivates someone to dedicate time and energy to it (Vallerand et al., 2003). Given that harmonious passion is associated with strengths use, wellbeing and performance (Dubreuil et al., 2014; Forest et al., 2012), fostering this quality by enhancing strengths would seem a worthwhile focus point for coaches when working with clients.

Positive Emotion

The emotional aspect of strengths seems a major motivator for people experimenting with and developing their strengths (Biswas-Diener et al., 2011). Recent research suggests the link between character strengths and positive emotions might be reciprocal; not only do strengths foster positive emotional experiences, repeated positive emotion may nurture strengths (Güsewell and Ruch, 2012). This aligns with the key propositions of broaden and build theory (Fredrickson, 2001) that positive emotions broaden thought-action repertoires and build durable resources, leading to a positive 'upward spiral' toward greater flourishing. Positive affect has also been identified as the mediating factor in organizational strengths use. That is, a strengths climate seems able to elevate employee mood (potentially translating into a more positive and satisfied workplace) and performance (van Woerkom and Meyers, 2015).

STRENGTHS IDENTIFICATION

Strength literature proposes a number of formal and informal methods of identifying strengths.

Formal Strengths Assessment

Table 20.2 outlines four major strengths assessment tools used in coaching. Clifton StrengthsFinder 2.0® (Rath, 2007) was developed in 2001 and is the most widely used in global organizations. Values-in-Action Inventory (VIA; Peterson and Seligman, 2004) is the most rigorously researched and culturally broad model, designed for general use and are freely available online. The R2 Strength Profiler (formerly Realise2; Linley, 2010) is a holistic, context-sensitive tool showing performance and areas of potential growth, burnout and weakness. Strengthscope® (Brook and Brewerton, 2006) draws on similar research about the energizing nature of strengths and is the only major 360-degree strengths profiling tool.

Formal assessment methods are relatively comprehensive, provide a common language and allow data to be easily quantified and compared. While there is some evidence that simply knowing your strengths profile is beneficial (Seligman et al., 2005), research

Table 20.2 Comparison of formal strengths identification models

	Strengths-Finder 2.0®	VIA	R2 Strengths Profiler	Strengthscope®
Orientation	Talent themes	Universal paths to virtues	Strengths, energy, use	Strengths, energy, potential
Domain	Work	Life, work, school	Work, life	Work
Key questions	What's best about what you do at work?	What's best about who you are?	What do you do best? What energizes you most? How often do you do it?	What energizes you most at work? When do your strengths go too far?
Strengths identified	Talents and skills	Core character	Realized and unrealized strengths, learned behaviors, weaknesses	Energizing qualities you are (and potentially can become) great at
Number	34	24	60	24
Focus	Top 5 only	Top 5 signature strengths, but all 24 matter	Top attributes in all 4 quadrants, and others can matter	Top 7 significant strengths, 'bubbling under' strengths, visibility/effectiveness of strengths
Report level	Individual	Individual, children	Individual, team	Individual, 360 degree feedback, team, leadership, organizational
Basis for validity	Polling and surveys	Historical research, specific strengths criteria, reliability & validity studies	Interviews, reliability and validity studies	Reliability and validity studies
Scientific scrutiny	Not peer reviewed	Peer reviewed	Peer reviewed	Independently validated
Practitioner certification	Required	Optional	Recommended	Required

Sources: Adapted from Niemiec (2013a), Rath (2007), Peterson and Seligman (2004), Linley (2010), Brook and Brewerton (2006)

points to the added value of a structured coaching-style debrief (Roche and Hefferon, 2013) to deepen self-awareness, instill self-efficacy and facilitate action, goal attainment and development.

Informal Strengths Assessment

Strengths can be identified through observation and open-ended questioning, a technique known as 'strengthspotting' (Linley, 2008; Linley and Minhas, 2011). Coaches and clients may find this useful to develop a wide strengths vocabulary and ability to recognize strengths in themselves and others. It is also possible to create individual strengths assessments (ISAs), semi-structured yet free-flowing sets of questions to elicit strengths and weaknesses (Linley, 2008). Other informal approaches include the use of stories (Drake, 2015), future-self exercises and strengths cards (Biswas-Diener, 2010), along with the 'reflected best-self exercise' (Quinn et al., 2003), which is a feedback intervention involving surveying others about personal strengths, constructing a profile of strengths, then planning how to use them. While popular literature in this area is plentiful, there is a paucity of peer-reviewed research.

STRENGTHS USE

Early strengths researchers concluded that the consistent association of strengths with wellbeing and performance indicates we should always strive to use them more (Park et al., 2004; Buckingham and Clifton, 2001). However, it has also been noted that strengths can be over-played (Kaiser and Overfield, 2011; Grant and Schwartz, 2011). Linley (2008) suggests two reasons for this. First, people continue to use a strength because it worked well in the past, even though the context and their own development needs may have changed. Second, they may believe using that particular strength is the only strategy available. This may be why overuse rather than underuse of strengths is linked to executive derailment (e.g. Welch et al., 2014; Kaiser and Overfield, 2011). In light of this, Biswas-Diener et al. (2011) have urged practitioners to move beyond the dominant 'identify and use more' strengths intervention paradigm (where individuals identify strengths, receive feedback and change behavior in order to use them more) to adopt a more nuanced approach.

Strengths Regulation

Linley et al. (2009) advocate using the right strength, in the right amount, in the right way, at the right time. They conceive this as a 'golden mean' or optimal performance ratio – for best effect, 'dial up' or 'dial down' the strength to meet situational demands. For example, a leader may need to dial up the strength of candor to create transparency and trust within a team facing uncertainty, and dial it down where tact or confidentiality is required. A leader who achieved technical excellence by being strong on detail may need to dial this down considerably to succeed at a more senior level, while amplifying relationship strengths and leveraging them to develop strategic awareness.

Coaches can use this strengths regulation model (Figure 20.1) to help leaders and others develop agility and the practical wisdom (Schwartz and Sharpe, 2006) to use strengths mindfully (Niemiec, 2013b). This is particularly important considering leadership versatility predicts more than 42 per cent of the variance in overall leadership effectiveness (Kaiser et al., 2007). It may also help address critiques of focusing solely on strengths to the detriment of developing complementary behaviors (Kaiser and Overfield, 2011).

Grant and Schwartz (2011) present evidence that strengths can reach an inflection point, known as an 'inverted U', where positive effects become negative, although this varies across individuals and context (Niemiec, 2013b). For example, a strength or virtue of love promotes empathy and prosocial behavior; when this is overdone, 'empathic arousal' can be experienced as distress and manifest in self-sacrificing behavior and poor task performance. These scholars draw on character strength's ethical origins (Aristotle, trans. 2000), assigning the optimal mean as half way between polarities of virtue and vice, whereas Linley's strengths

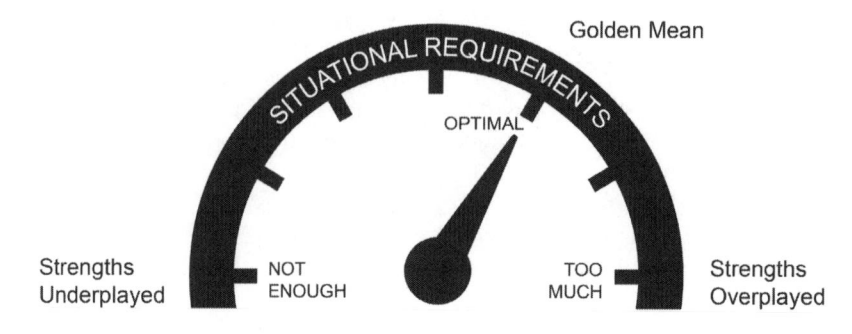

Figure 20.1 Strengths regulation
Source: Adapted from Linley (2008)

regulation model (2008) indicates greater emphasis on the positive.

Niemiec (2015) points out that both overuse and underuse can result in intrapersonal or interpersonal imbalance, observing that signature strengths are more likely to be overused, but can be mitigated by bringing other strengths forward. The concept of overuse can help coaches reframe problems gently and accurately, enabling clients to identify points at which strength use becomes non-optimal. Both Linley (2008) and Niemiec (2015) caution against erring too far toward deficits when applying this approach. Encouraging clients to leverage strengths in the service of more helpful goals or valued outcomes can maintain a positive focus.

STRENGTHS DEVELOPMENT

Individuals can benefit from believing their strengths can be grown and are not static. Dweck and colleagues (Hong et al., 1999) showed that the way people approach their goals directly relates to theories they hold about themselves. If they have a fixed mindset, they believe personal traits or strengths are fixed, therefore not affected by change or effort. In contrast, people with a growth mindset believe traits or strengths are malleable and can be grown by effort. Fixed mindset poses a risk, making people less likely to put effort into developing their strengths and blinkering them to opportunities to use them better, resulting in underperformance (Dweck, 2008). Biswas-Diener et al. (2011) suggest this may explain why some people, after an initial period of excitement about identifying their strengths, stagnate, as they believe nothing more can be done with strengths or their development opportunities lie in improving weaknesses. In one study, talent identification without a strengths development focus showed a shift toward more fixed mindsets (Louis, 2011). Exploring growth mindset with clients seems important for coaches, as it is possible to mature self-theories (Drake, 2015; Dweck, 2008).

Table 20.3 lists several strengths development models that may be useful when working with clients to cultivate strengths and expand growth mindset.

Some authors have noted that strengths can be easily applied using the GROW coaching model (Niemiec, 2013b; Kauffman et al., 2010) to build resources, set goals aligned

Table 20.3 Strengths development models

Model	Summary	Source
R2 Strengths 4M Model	Marshal realized strengths, moderate learned behaviors, minimize weaknesses and maximize unrealized strengths	Linley, Willars & Biswas-Diener (2010)
Strengths Development Stages	Identification, integration into self-concept, behavior change	Clifton & Harter (2003)
Strength Maturation Process	Move through four phases: reactive, inquisitive, transformative, generative	Drake (2015)
Aware–Explore–Apply	Increase awareness, explore benefits of past strengths use, develop action plan for developing specific strengths	Niemiec (2013b)
3S-P Model	Performance at the intersection of strengths, situation and strategy	Linley & Garcea (2012)
Appreciative Inquiry	Strengths-based questioning in coaching and organizations	Cooperrider & Sekerka (2003); Gordon (2008)
Strength-based Counseling Model	Strengths identification occurs after establishing the alliance	Smith (2006)
Strengths-centered Therapy Model	Strengths integrated throughout the engagement	Wong (2006)

with strengths, and support the way forward. Coaches can draw on knowledge of a client's strengths during the options phase by asking which may help or hinder in this situation. They can also adopt an Appreciative Inquiry approach (Gordon and Gucciardi, 2011; Gordon, 2008), crafting coaching questions about past successes, ideal self, dreams for a positive future and optimal strength use (Biswas-Diener, 2010). Narrative coaching (Drake, 2015) can be used to help clients become aware how habitual strengths may be perpetuating old stories, and explore what keeps them from fulfilling aspirations so they can use strengths proactively to develop new stories.

STRENGTHS INTEGRATION

A number of themes have emerged that may guide coaches and researchers in designing more nuanced and effective strengths interventions.

Strengths Balance

Historically, interventions and research have focused on helping people identify their top five strengths, using these to increase wellbeing or performance. However, this appears an artificial and simplistic boundary, as other or lesser strengths may be valuable, and in combination. Biswas-Diener et al. (2011) point out that strengths do not exist in isolation and 'strengths constellations' made up of two or more strengths can work dynamically together, with one providing a foundation for another (Smith, 2006). A preliminary study by Young et al. (2015) found that a balance of strengths was beneficial, supporting growth of less-developed strengths alongside signature strength development and novel use. Proyer et al. (2015) found participants with higher levels of strengths benefitted more from working on lesser rather than signature strengths, while those with comparatively lower strengths levels tended to benefit more from working on signature strengths.

However, Linley et al., (2009) warn that not all behaviors endorsed as high performing are pathways to flourishing. By distinguishing between de-energizing behaviors and strengths, and the context in which they occur, coaches can help clients explore what energizes them and moderate activities they find draining. One strategy clients can use is 'buffering', where a de-energizing activity is sandwiched between two energizing ones. Drake (2015) advises coaches working with extrinsically motivated strengths to 'help the person tap into an underlying intrinsic motivation that can serve as a more sustainable and valued driver' for development (p.96).

Weaknesses

There is little in the strengths and coaching literature on weaknesses or, more specifically, what weaknesses are and what to do about them.

Lesser strengths are often conceived as weaknesses, however Linley et al. (2009) assert that weaknesses can and should be differentiated from strengths by lack of energy as well as poor performance and low endorsement. They argue that a focus on fixing weakness has diminishing returns and is unlikely to convert it into a strength, even though strategies can be developed to mitigate, learn from and improve it. As such, they recommend making weaknesses irrelevant by minimizing them, and while it could be argued that minimizing weaknesses is neither possible nor desirable, the aim is to minimize their negative impact and use where possible. It can be helpful to identify risk relative to a person's current role and to consider whether weaknesses are 'exposed' (causing problems) or 'unexposed' (currently irrelevant yet potentially risky if the situation changes).

Similarly Brewerton (2011) distinguishes between 'limiting' and 'allowable' weakness, genuine blockers from those we can live with or manage with successful strategies. A key strategy in either case is complementary partnering, where a person's weaknesses can be compensated by another's strengths or strengths combined for an uplifting or multiplier effect (Linley et al., 2009; Rath, 2007). Coaches can also help clients get around weaknesses and achieve similar outcomes by drawing on energizing strengths (Linley, 2010b; Brewerton, 2011).

Distinctions have emerged in the empirical literature since the oft-quoted Corporate Leadership Council study (2002), which found a significant performance gap between a strengths and weakness focus. A preliminary study (Rust et al., 2009) found equal success between working on signature strengths compared to a combination of strengths and relative weaknesses, casting doubt on the value of concentrating exclusively on strengths at the expense of weaknesses. Students in a strengths and deficit development intervention both increased personal growth initiative, though gains were greater when focusing on strengths (Meyers et al., 2015). This underscores the importance of coaching with both strengths and weaknesses in mind.

Shadow Sides

Accepting human frailties and flaws as well as strengths is critical in the journey toward greater wholeness, particularly through crisis and transformation (Hall, 2015). De Haan and Kasozi (2015) suggests we balance these by finding the strengths or challenges in our weaknesses. Likewise Drake (2015) notes that the critical role of the shadow in strength development is often neglected. These hidden parts of ourselves, and the archetypal energies they represent, can be used to mature strengths. In many cases people's most potent strengths and development opportunities lie where these weaker points appear to be. Coaching with a narrative or developmental lens can be used to surface unconscious patterns, invite people to examine defenses, release energy suppressing shadow sides, and shift how they project and frame them to harness and integrate potential.

Strengths Blindness

It is common for people to be 'blind' to certain strengths, which Biswas-Diener et al. (2011) suggest may be because of consensus bias, or the tendency to overestimate one's similarity to others. Another possibility is that strengths are so closely interwoven with values, a link explicitly acknowledged in the VIA approach, that they are not necessarily viewed as unique behavior patterns. Conversely, some people overestimate their strengths and contribution to group success while underestimating those of others (i.e. egocentric bias) (Dunning et al., 2004), which can lead to social discord. Others may find their strengths undervalued by their team or organization. This could result in people molding themselves to conform to a group identity, perhaps quashing strengths that do not fit; for example, creativity in some military environments (Zarecky, 2014) or courage in communities that emphasize conformity (Niemiec, 2015). Coaches can help people find a balance between being authentic and true to their strengths and how they fit within the group identity, while appreciating complementary or diverse strengths in others (Welch et al., 2014).

Strengths Sensitivity

Occasionally when people encounter setbacks as a result of using their strengths, it can have a negative impact (Biswas-Diener et al., 2011). It could be that as strengths are a key part of our identity, any criticism from others in an area of strength, or failure to achieve goals through applying our strengths can be disappointing, especially when success is anticipated. Anecdotal evidence indicates people tend to be particularly hard on themselves in these situations, suggesting care and an emphasis on learning over performance goals is needed when giving feedback and coaching around overplayed strengths (Grant and Dweck, 2003).

STRENGTHS IN COACHING CONTEXTS

A strengths perspective is applicable in a wide range of coaching contexts. This section looks briefly at practices in executive coaching, managerial coaching, organizational development, career coaching, mental health and education.

- *Executive Coaching.* Coaches can help leaders act as climate engineers within their organizations by realizing strengths in themselves and others, and using this learning to unlock potential of their teams, leading to higher levels of organizational performance (Linley et al., 2009). According to Welch et al. (2014), expert strengths-based coaches help leaders to develop their strengths in relationship contexts by illuminating strengths in others, revealing blind spots, addressing weaknesses and shadow sides, and also by doing similar developmental work themselves.
- *Manager-as-Coach.* Coaching managers are ideally placed to promote and embed a positive, strengths-based culture within teams and organizations. Trenier et al. (2012) recommend managers use strengthspotting to discover strengths in themselves and team members and develop this knowledge through shared conversations. Useful strategies include complementary partnering, strengths-based delegation, strengths-based teamwork and role shaping (Linley et al., 2009).
- *Organizational Coaching.* Coaches can help organizations enhance performance by shifting the focus from fixing problems and weaknesses to building strengths and identifying opportunities to leverage them (Linley, 2008; Buckingham and Clifton, 2001). Appreciative Inquiry is one well-documented and widely used approach to developing strengths-based organizations (Cooperrider and Sekerka, 2003).
- *Career Coaching.* Working with strengths in career coaching can provide greater clarity about future career pathways than traditional skills-only approaches, by tapping into areas of energy and passion, building self-awareness, confidence, and a sense of authenticity (Trenier, 2010; Zarecky, 2014). It is important that career coaches help clients distinguish between energizing strengths and learned behaviors, to avoid the trap of job roles that may not sustain long-term engagement and development (Linley et al., 2013).
- *Coaching in Mental Health.* Strengths coaching approaches are transforming psychotherapeutic and mental health settings (Crowe et al., 2012). The Collaborative Recovery Model (Oades et al., 2009) embodies a strength lens and guides clinicians, mental health workers, leaders and staff to build a collaborative coaching culture and increase empowerment, self-direction and affirmative mindset in themselves and their clients. A qualitative study by Scheel et al. (2012) found counselors who used a strengths approach identified, amplified and encouraged strengths; understood barriers, individual differences and contexts; facilitated strengths-oriented goals, and reinforced resiliency and meaning by reframing deficit as strength.
- *Coaching in Schools.* Strengths-based coaching programs have been embedded in schools and threaded through student and staff initiatives to create a strengths-based culture (White and Waters, 2015). Others have been effective in increasing students' wellbeing (Quinlan, 2012) and generating engagement and hope (Madden, 2011). Specific interventions include the Strengths Gym (Proctor et al., 2011).

RESEARCH DIRECTIONS

To design and evaluate effective strengths interventions, it is necessary to continue building a better understanding of how strengths work. To this end, key psychological theories (e.g. SDT, broaden and build) should prove useful for identifying specific variables or processes that play a key role in strengths dynamics (Quinlan et al., 2012). Exploring growth mindset and self-theories (Louis, 2011), strengths maturation and shadow sides (Drake, 2015) may also deepen knowledge of strengths development.

The role of context is crucial to understanding the complex, dynamic interplay between individuals and their environments. Specific areas could be the intervention environment, coach's knowledge and attitude to strengths, effect of strength-based interventions on group morale (Quinlan et al., 2012), perceived organizational support (Botha and Mostert, 2014) and the influence of microcultures (Biswas-Diener and Lyubchik, 2013). Culture is increasingly important, demonstrated by recent translation of the VIA into several languages (e.g. Chinese, Israeli and German).

More knowledge about specific strengths coaching interventions would help coaches design effective, evidence-based approaches. For instance, future researchers could investigate issues like: the optimum frequency and length of strengths-based coaching interventions (MacKie, 2014); how strengths interventions are best fitted to individuals (Proyer et al., 2014); how strengths combine with each other (and with weaknesses), and how individual differences influence outcomes (e.g. Proyer et al., 2015).

As evidence grows that a happy workforce is a productive workforce (van Woerkom and Meyers, 2015), further understanding of how strengths facilitate positive emotions and wellbeing in organizations may also be fruitful. Emerging studies on harmonious passion and calling (e.g. Forest et al., 2012; Allan and Duffy, 2014) may further support this. As more coaches adopt strengths-based approaches, studies focusing on coaching in organizations (Welch et al., 2014) will become more important, as will investigations that consider system-level impacts, such as radiation (or ripple) effects (O'Connor and Cavanagh, 2013).

CONCLUSION

The emerging field of strengths and growing evidence base offers a wealth of opportunities for coaches and clients to focus on what is working, what is energizing, and what can grow. The discovery, deployment and development of people's strengths can be seen as a pathway to optimal functioning and a way of surfacing human potential. Strengths can be wellsprings of energy, motivation and potential that can be tapped to achieve valued outcomes and learning, and contribute to teams, organizations and communities.

In this chapter we have argued for a balanced, abundant approach, where weaknesses or shadow sides are not ignored, vulnerability is supported, and strengths are leveraged within an integrated view of human experience and thriving (Bachkirova, 2015; Wong, 2011). This more holistic coaching lens can help individuals mature their strengths and use them, not simply more, but wisely.

REFERENCES

Allan, B.A., & Duffy, R.D. (2014) 'Examining moderators of signature strengths use and well-being: Calling and signature strengths level', *Journal of Happiness Studies*, 15: 323–37.

Aristotle (2000) *The Nicomachean Ethics* (R. Crisp, Trans.). Cambridge: Cambridge University Press.

Avey, J.B., Luthans, F., Hannah, S.T., Sweetman, D., & Peterson, C. (2012) 'Impact of employees' character strengths of wisdom on stress and creative performance', *Human Resource Management Journal*, 22: 165–81.

Bachkirova, T. (2015) 'Foreword', in L. Hall (ed), *Coaching in Times of Crisis and Transformation*. London: Kogan Page.

Baumeister, R.F., Bratslavsky, E., Finkenauer, C. & Vohs, K.D. (2001) 'Bad is stronger than good', *Review of General Psychology*, 5: 323–70.

Biswas-Diener, R. (2010) 'Using your best to make you better', in *Practicing Positive*

Psychology Coaching: Assessment and Strategies for Success. Hoboken, NJ: Wiley, pp. 19–38.

Biswas-Diener, R., Kashdan, T.B., & Minhas, G. (2011) 'A dynamic approach to psychological strength development and intervention', *The Journal of Positive Psychology*, 6: 106–18.

Biswas-Diener, R., & Lyubchik, N. (2013) 'Microculture as a contextual positive psychology intervention', in T.B. Kashdan & J. Ciarrochi (eds.), *Bridging Acceptance and Positive Psychology: A Practitioner's Guide to a Unifying Framework*. Oakland, CA: New Harbinger, pp. 194–214.

Bolier, L., Haverman, M., Westerhof, G.J., Riper, H., Smit, F., & Bohlmeijer, E. (2013) 'Positive psychology interventions: A meta-analysis of randomized controlled studies', *BMC Public Health*, 13: 119.

Botha, C., & Mostert, K. (2014) 'A structural model of job resources, organisational and individual strengths use and work engagement', *SA Journal of Industrial Psychology*, 40: 1–11.

Boyce, C.J., Wood, A.M., & Powdthavee, N. (2013) 'Is personality fixed? Personality changes as much as "variable" economic factors and more strongly predicts changes to life satisfaction', *Social Indicators Research*, 111: 287–305.

Brewerton, P. (2011) 'Using strengths to drive career success', *Strategic HR Review*, 10: 5–10.

Brook, J., & Brewerton, P. (2006) *Strengthscope Technical Manual*. London: Strengths Partnership.

Buckingham, M. & Clifton, D.O. (2001) *Now, Discover Your Strengths*. New York: Free Press.

Burke, D., & Linley, P.A. (2007) 'Enhancing goal self-concordance through coaching', *International Coaching Psychology Review*, 2: 62–9.

Buschor, C., Proyer, R.T., & Ruch, W. (2013) 'Self- and peer-rated character strengths: How do they relate to satisfaction with life and orientations to happiness?' *The Journal of Positive Psychology*, 8: 116–27.

Clifton, D.O., & Anderson, E. (2002) *StrengthsQuest: Discover and Develop Your Strengths, in Academics, Career, and Beyond*. Washington, DC: The Gallup Organization.

Clifton, D., & Harter, J.K. (2003) 'Investing in strengths', in K. Cameron, J. Dutton & R. Quinn (eds.), *Positive Organizational Scholarship: Foundations of a New Discipline*. San Francisco: Barrett-Koehler, pp. 111–21.

Cooperrider, D.L., & Sekerka, L.E. (2003) 'Toward a theory of positive organizational change', in K. Cameron, J. Dutton, & R. Quinn (eds.), *Positive Organizational Scholarship: Foundations of a New Discipline*. San Francisco: Berrett-Koehler, pp. 225–40.

Corporate Leadership Council (2002) *Performance Management Survey*. Washington, DC: Author.

Crowe, T., Deane, F.P., & Oades, L. (2012) 'Individual recovery planning: Aligning values, strengths and goals', in R. King, C. Lloyd, T. Meehan, F.P. Deane, & D.J. Kavanagh (eds.), *Manual of Psychosocial Rehabilitation*. Somerset, NJ: John Wiley & Sons, pp. 81–94.

de Haan, E., & Kasozi, A. (2015) 'Leaders in crisis: Attending to the shadow side', in L. Hall (ed.), *Coaching in Times of Crisis and Transformation*. London: Kogan Page, pp. 144–71.

Donaldson, S.I., Dollwet, M., & Rao, M.A. (2015) 'Happiness, excellence, and optimal human functioning revisited: Examining the peer-reviewed literature linked to positive psychology', *The Journal of Positive Psychology*, 10: 185–95.

Drake, D.B. (2015) *Narrative Coaching: Bringing Our New Stories to Life*. Petaluma, CA: CNC Press.

Drucker, P.F. (1967) *The Effective Executive*. London, UK: Heinemann.

Dubreuil, P., Forest, J., & Courcy, F. (2014) 'From strengths use to work performance: The role of harmonious passion, subjective vitality, and concentration', *The Journal of Positive Psychology*, 9: 335–49.

Dunning, D., Heath, C., & Suls, J. (2004) 'Flawed self-assessment: Implications for health, education, and the workplace', *Psychological Science in the Public Interest*, 5: 69–106.

Dweck, C. (2008) 'Can personality be changed? The role of beliefs in personality and change', *Current Directions in Psychological Science*, 17: 391–4

Elston, F., & Boniwell, I. (2011) 'A grounded theory study of the value derived by women in financial services through a coaching intervention to help them identify their strengths and practise using them in the workplace', *International Coaching Psychology Review*, 6: 16–32.

Forest, J., Mageau, G.A., Crevier-Braud, L., Bergeron, E., Dubreuil, P., & Lavigne, G.L. (2012) 'Harmonious passion as an explanation of the relation between signature strengths' use and well-being at work: Test of an intervention program', *Human Relations*, 65: 1233–52.

Fredrickson, B.L. (2001) 'The role of positive emotions in positive psychology: The broaden-and-build theory of positive emotions', *American Psychologist*, 56: 218–26.

Gander, F., Proyer, R.T., Ruch, W., & Wyss, T. (2012) 'The good character at work: An initial study on the contribution of character strengths in identifying healthy and unhealthy work-related behavior and experience patterns', *International Archives of Occupational and Environmental Health*, 85: 895–904.

Garcea, N., Linley, A., Mazurkiewicz, K., & Bailey, T. (2012) 'Future female talent development', *Strategic HR Review*, 11: 199–204.

Gillham, J., Adams-Deutsch, Z., Werner, J., Reivich, K., Coulter-Heindl, V., Linkins, M. ... Seligman, M.E.P. (2011) 'Character strengths predict subjective well-being during adolescence', *The Journal of Positive Psychology*, 6: 31–44.

Gordon, S. (2008) 'Appreciative inquiry coaching', *International Coaching Psychology Review*, 3: 19–31.

Gordon, S., & Gucciardi, D.F. (2011) 'A strengths-based approach to coaching mental toughness', *Journal of Sport Psychology in Action*, 2: 143–55.

Govindji, R. & Linley, A. (2007) 'Strengths use, self-concordance and well-being: Implications for strengths coaching and coaching psychologists', *International Coaching Psychology Review*, 2: 143–53.

Grant, A.M., & Schwartz, B. (2011) 'Too much of a good thing: The challenge and opportunity of the inverted U', *Perspectives on Psychological Science*, 6: 61–76.

Grant, H., & Dweck, C.S. (2003) 'Clarifying achievement goals and their impact', *Journal of Personality and Social Psychology*, 85: 541–53.

Güsewell, A., & Ruch, W. (2012) 'Are only emotional strengths emotional? Character strengths and disposition to positive emotions', *Applied Psychology: Health and Well-Being*, 4: 218–39.

Hall, L. (2015) 'No mud, no lotus? Crisis as a catalyst for transformation,' in L. Hall (ed.), *Coaching in Times of Crisis and Transformation*. London: Kogan Page, pp. 50–69.

Harter, J.K., Schmidt, F.L., & Hayes, T.L. (2002) 'Business-unit-level relationship between employee satisfaction, employee engagement, and business outcomes: A meta-analysis', *Journal of Applied Psychology*, 87: 268–79.

Harzer, C., & Ruch, W. (2015) 'The relationships of character strengths with coping, work-related stress, and job satisfaction', *Frontiers in Psychology*, 6: 1–12.

Hill, J. (2001). How well do we know our strengths? Paper presented at the British Psychological Society Centenary Conference, Glasgow, April.

Hong, Y.Y., Chiu, C., Dweck, C.S., Lin, D., & Wan, W. (1999) 'Implicit theories, attributions, and coping: A meaning system approach', *Journal of Personality and Social Psychology*, 77: 588–99.

Horney, K. (1950) *Neurosis and Human Growth: The Struggle Toward Self-realisation*. New York: Norton.

Kaiser, R.B., Lindberg, J.T. & Craig, S.B. (2007) 'Assessing the flexibility of managers: A comparison of methods', *International Journal of Selection and Assessment*, 16: 40–55.

Kaiser, R.B., & Overfield, D.V. (2011) 'Strengths, strengths overused, and lopsided leadership', *Consulting Psychology Journal: Practice and Research*, 63: 89–109.

Kauffman, C., Boniwell, I., & Silberman, J. (2010) 'The positive psychology approach to coaching,' in E. Cox, T. Bachkirova, & D. Clutterbuck (eds.), *The Complete Handbook of Coaching*. London: SAGE, pp. 158–71.

Kong, D.T., & Ho, V.T. (2015) 'A self-determination perspective of strengths use at work: Examining its determinant and performance implications', *The Journal of Positive Psychology*, 1–11.

Linley, P.A. (2008) *Average to A+: Realising Strengths in Yourself and Others*. Coventry, UK: CAPP Press.

Linley, P.A. (2010) *Realise2: Technical Report*. Coventry, UK: CAPP Press.

Linley, P.A., Biswas-Diener, R., & Trenier, E. (2013) 'Positive psychology and strengths coaching through transition', in S. Palmer & S. Panchal (eds.), *Developmental Coaching: Life Transitions and Generational Perspectives*. Hove, UK: Routledge, pp. 161–81.

Linley, P.A. & Garcea, N. (2012) 'Three types of Hi-Po and the Realise2 4M Model: Coaching at the intersection of strengths, strategy and situation', in M. Goldsmith, L.S. Lyons & S. McArthur (eds.), *Coaching for Leadership: Writings on leadership from the world's greatest coaches*, 3rd ed. San Francisco: Wiley, pp. 270–78.

Linley, P.A., & Harrington, S. (2006) 'Strengths coaching: A potential guided approach to coaching psychology', *International Coaching Psychology Review*, 1: 37–46.

Linley, P.A., & Minhas, G. (2011) 'The strengths of the strengthspotter: Individual characteristics associated with the identification of strengths in others', *International Coaching Psychology Review*, 6: 6–16.

Linley, P.A., Nielsen, K.M., Gillett, R., & Biswas-Diener, R. (2010a) 'Using signature strengths in pursuit of goals: Effects on goal progress, need satisfaction, and well-being, and implications for coaching psychologists', *International Coaching Psychology Review*, 5: 6–15.

Linley, P.A., Willars, J., & Biswas-Diener, R. (2010b) *The Strengths Book: Be Confident, Be Successful, and Enjoy Better Relationships by Realising the Best of You*. Coventry, UK: Capp Press.

Linley, P.A., Woolston, L., & Biswas-Diener, R. (2009) 'Strengths coaching with leaders', *International Coaching Psychology Review*, 4: 20–31.

Louis, M.C. (2011) 'Strengths interventions in higher education: The effect of identification versus development approaches on implicit self-theory', *The Journal of Positive Psychology*, 6: 204–15.

Lyons, L.S., & Linley, P.A. (2008) 'Situational strengths: A strategic approach linking personal capability to corporate success' *Organisations and People*, 15: 4–11.

MacKie, D. (2014) 'The effectiveness of strength-based executive coaching in enhancing full range leadership development: A controlled study', *Consulting Psychology Journal: Practice and Research*, 66: 118–37.

Madden, W., Green, S., & Grant, A.M. (2011) 'A pilot study evaluating strengths-based coaching for primary school students: Enhancing engagement and hope', *International Coaching Psychology Review*, 6: 71–83.

Martinez-Marti, M.L., & Ruch, W. (2014) 'Character strengths and well-being across the life span: Data from a representative sample of German-speaking adults living in Switzerland', *Frontiers in Psychology*, 5: 1–10.

Maslow, A.H. (1954) *Motivation and Personality*. New York: Harper.

McDowall, A., & Butterworth, L. (2014) 'How does a brief strengths-based group coaching intervention work?' *Coaching: An International Journal of Theory, Research and Practice*, 7: 152–63.

Meyers, M.C., van Woerkom, M., De Reuver, R.S.M., Bakk, Z., & Oberski, D.L. (2015) 'Enhancing psychological capital and personal growth initiative: Working on strengths or deficiencies', *Journal of Counseling Psychology*, 62: 50–62.

Meyers, M.C., van Woerkom, M., & Bakker, A.B. (2013) 'The added value of the positive: A literature review of positive psychology interventions in organizations', *European Journal of Work and Organizational Psychology*, 22: 618–32.

Minhas, G. (2010) 'Developing realised and unrealised strengths: Implications for engagement, self-esteem, life satisfaction and well-being', *Assessment & Development Matters*, 2: 12–6.

Mongrain, M., & Anselmo-Matthews, T. (2012) 'Do positive psychology exercises work? A replication of Seligman et al. (2005)', *Journal of Clinical Psychology*, 68: 382–9.

Niemiec, R.M. (2013a) 'VIA Survey or Strengths-Finder?' *Psychology Today*, December 17.

Niemiec, R.M. (2013b) *Mindfulness and Character Strengths: A Practical Guide to Flourishing*. Cincinnati, OH: VIA Institute on Character.

Niemiec, R.M. (2015) 'The overuse of strengths: 10 principles', *Psyccritiques*, 59(33).

Oades, L.G., Crowe, T.P., & Nguyen, M. (2009) 'Leadership coaching transforming mental health systems from the inside out: Person-centred strengths based coaching psychology', *International Coaching Psychology Review*, 4: 25–36.

O'Connor, S., & Cavanagh, M. (2013) 'The coaching ripple effect: The effects of developmental coaching on wellbeing across organisational networks', *Psychology of Well-Being*, 3: 1–23.

Park, N., Peterson, C., & Ruch, W. (2009) 'Orientations to happiness and life satisfaction in twenty-seven nations', *The Journal of Positive Psychology*, 4: 273–9.

Park, N., Peterson, C., & Seligman, M.E.P. (2004) 'Strengths of character and well-being', *Journal of Social and Clinical Psychology*, 23: 603–19.

Peterson, C., & Seligman, M.E.P. (2004) *Character Strengths and Virtues: A Handbook and Classification*. Washington, DC: American Psychological Association Press.

Proctor, C., Maltby, J. & Linley, P.A. (2010) 'Strengths use as a predictor of well-being and health-related quality of life', *Journal of Happiness Studies*, 12(1): 153–69.

Proctor, C., Tsukayama, E., Wood, A.M., Maltby, J., Eades, J.F., & Linley, P.A. (2011) 'Strengths Gym: The impact of a character strengths-based intervention on the life satisfaction and well-being of adolescents', *The Journal of Positive Psychology*, 6: 377–88.

Proyer, R.T., Gander, F., Wellenzohn, S., & Ruch, W. (2015) 'Strengths-based positive psychology interventions: A randomized placebo-controlled online trial on long-term effects for a signature strengths vs. a lesser strengths-intervention', *Frontiers in Psychology*, 6: 1–14.

Proyer, R.T., Wellenzohn, S., Gander, F., & Ruch, W. (2014) 'Toward a better understanding of what makes positive psychology interventions work: Predicting happiness and depression from the person × intervention fit in a follow-up after 3.5 years', *Applied Psychology: Health and Well-Being*, 7: 108–28.

Quinlan, D., Swain, N., & Vella-Brodrick, D.A. (2012) 'Character strengths interventions: Building on what we know for improved outcomes', *Journal of Happiness Studies*, 13: 1145–63.

Quinn, R.E., Dutton, J.E., Spreitzer, G.M., & Roberts, L.M. (2003) *Reflected Best Self Exercise*. Center for Positive Organizational Scholarship, University of Michigan.

Rath, T. (2007) *StrengthsFinder 2.0*. New York: Gallup Press.

Roche, B., & Hefferon, K. (2013) 'The assessment needs to go hand-in-hand with the debriefing: The importance of a structured coaching debriefing in understanding and applying a positive psychology strengths assessment', *International Coaching Psychology Review*, 8: 20–34.

Rogers, C.R. (1963) 'The actualizing tendency in relation to "motives" and to consciousness', in M.R. Jones (ed.), *Nebraska Symposium on Motivation*. Lincoln, NE: University of Nebraska Press, pp. 1–24.

Rozin, P. & Royzman, E.B. (2001) 'Negativity bias, negativity dominance, and contagion', *Personality and Social Psychology Review*, 5: 296–320.

Rust, T., Diessner, R., & Reade, L. (2009) 'Strengths only or strengths and relative weaknesses? A preliminary study', *The Journal of Psychology*, 143: 465–76.

Ryan, R. & Deci, E. (2000) 'Self-determination theory and the facilitation of intrinsic motivation, social development, and well-being', *American Psychologist*, 55: 68–78.

Scheel, M.J., Davis, C.K., & Henderson, J.D. (2012) 'Therapist use of client strengths: A qualitative study of positive processes', *The Counseling Psychologist*, 41: 392–427.

Schwartz, B. & Sharpe, K.E. (2006) 'Practical wisdom: Aristotle meets positive psychology', *Journal of Happiness Studies,* 7: 377–95.

Seligman, M., Steen, T., Park, N., & Peterson, C. (2005) 'Positive psychology progress: Empirical validation of interventions', *American Psychologist*, 60: 410–21.

Seligman, M.E.P., & Csikszentmihalyi, M. (2000) 'Positive psychology: An introduction', *American Psychologist*, 55: 5–14.

Sheldon, K.M., & Elliot, A.J. (1999) 'Goal striving, need satisfaction, and longitudinal well-being: The self-concordance model', *Journal of Personality and Social Psychology*, 76: 482–97.

Sheldon, K.M., Jose, P.E., Kashdan, T.B., & Jarden, A. (2015) 'Personality, effective goal-striving, and enhanced well-being: Comparing

10 candidate personality strengths' *Personality and Social Psychology Bulletin*, 41: 575–85.

Smedley, T. (2007) 'The powers that BAE', *People Management*, 13: 40–3.

Smith, E.J. (2006) 'The strength-based counseling model', *The Counseling Psychologist*, 34: 13–79.

Steger, M.F., Hicks, B.M., Kashdan, T.B., Krueger, R.F., & Bouchard, T.J. Jr (2007) 'Genetic and environmental influences on the positive traits of the Values in Action classification, and biometric covariance with normal personality', *Journal of Research in Personality*, 41: 524–39.

Trenier, E. (2010) 'Using strengths to guide career transition', *Assessment & Development Matters*, 2: 5–7.

Trenier, E., Harrington, S., & Jamnadas, R. (2012) *Performance Manager: Managing Strengths to Deliver Better Performance Through Your People*. Coventry, UK: CAPP.

Vallerand, R.J., Blanchard, C.M., Mageau, G.A., Koestner, R., Ratelle, C.F., Léonard M., ... Marsolais, J. (2003) 'Les passions de l'âme: On obsessive and harmonious passion', *Journal of Personality and Social Psychology*, 85: 756–67.

van Woerkom, M., & Meyers, M.C. (2015) 'My strengths count! Effects of a strength based psychological climate on positive affect and job performance', *Human Resource Management*, 54: 81–103.

Welch, D., Grossaint, K., Reid, K., & Walker, C. (2014) 'Strengths-based leadership development: Insights from expert coaches', *Consulting Psychology Journal: Practice and Research*, 66: 20–37.

White, M.A., & Waters, L. (2015) 'A case study of "The Good School:" Examples of the use of Peterson's strengths-based approach with students', *The Journal of Positive Psychology*, 10: 69–76.

Whitmore, Sir J. (2002) *Coaching for Performance* (3rd ed.). London: Nicholas Brealey.

Wood, A.M., Linley, P.A., Maltby, J., Kashdan, T.B., & Hurling, R. (2011) 'Using personal and psychological strengths leads to increases in well-being over time: A longitudinal study and the development of the strengths use questionnaire', *Personality and Individual Differences*, 50: 15–19.

Woodworth, R.J., O'Brien-Malone, A., Diamond, M.R., & Schüz, B. (2015) 'Happy Days: Positive Psychology interventions effects on affect in an N-of-1 trial', *International Journal of Clinical and Health Psychology*, 16: 22–9.

Wong, P.T.P. (2011) 'Positive psychology 2.0: Towards a balanced interactive model of the good life', *Canadian Psychology/Psychologie Canadienne*, 52: 69–81.

Wong, Y. (2006) 'Strength-centered therapy: A social constructionist, virtues-based psychotherapy', *Psychotherapy: Theory, Research, Practice, Training*, 43: 133–46.

Young, K.C., Kashdan, T.B., & Macatee, R. (2015) 'Strength balance and implicit strength measurement: New considerations for research on strengths of character', *The Journal of Positive Psychology*, 10: 17–24.

Zarecky, A. (2014) 'How strengths-focussed coaching can help military personnel in their transition to "civvy street"', *International Journal of Evidence Based Coaching and Mentoring*, 8: 54–66.

Mindfulness and Coaching: Contemporary Labels for Timeless Practices?

Travis Kemp

Coaching has been described previously as an applied positive psychology (e.g. Kemp, 2004; Grant, 2009) and similarly, mindfulness has also come to find a comfortable philosophical and contextual home within the broader field of positive psychology (Langer, 2009). The exploration of mindfulness and coaching as a methodological partnership has attracted burgeoning theoretical and research interest in recent years. Whilst empirical investigations relating to the topic remain sparse, embryonic findings have yielded promising support for the efficacy of mindfulness techniques and practices when applied to a coaching context (Spence, Cavanagh & Grant, 2008).

It was Jon Kabat-Zinn (1990) who highlighted that mindfulness lay at the heart of Buddhist meditation, a practice that has itself flourished for more than 2,500 years. As a result, the related fields of mindfulness and meditation boast an extensive foundation of experiential knowledge derived from eastern enquiry and practice that predates Western psychology itself by more than 2,000 years. Given the extent of the intrigue these two practice approaches now attract, it appears timely that an exploration of their structure, relatedness and methodology for facilitating growth and learning is discussed. Hence, the current chapter has three main intentions. The first intention is to provide a broad positioning of contemporary coaching and mindfulness in relation to their status as applied positive psychology practices.

Next, it seeks to highlight and illustrate the inextricably symbiotic connection that exists between mindfulness and coaching, the complementarity of their theoretical underpinnings and how these can be brought together effectively, simply and logically within an integrated framework.

Finally, the chapter will call for a reconceptualisation of the current definitions and practices associated with each of the these two methods in consideration of the extensive emergent and historical bodies of knowledge that inform their core practices and processes, now labelled 'coaching' and 'mindfulness', but which have been practised under their more common headings of 'education' and 'meditation' for millennia. By reinstating these terms to the discourse, it is hoped to further the creation of an integrated framework for contextual understanding that simplifies both practice and research within the broader context of human growth and development.

MEDITATION AND MINDFULNESS: AN OVERVIEW

So widespread has the application of mindfulness become that it is now commonly prescribed for a vast array of conditions including stress, anxiety, depression, addiction, pain, weight management, heart disease, cancer, dementia, sleep, education, workplace performance, leadership and even self-actualisation and enlightenment (McKenzie & Hassed, 2012). In introducing the first issue of the international peer-reviewed scientific journal *Mindfulness*, Singh (2010) highlighted the extensive contemporary proliferation of mindfulness research as the driver behind the creation of this new peer-reviewed publication vehicle to further understanding and practice within the field.

In the subsequent years since Kabat-Zinn's then 'radical' treatment methods utilising *meditation* and *yoga practice* to treat terminally ill patients were trialed (Kabat-Zinn, 1982), mindfulness and meditation have become mainstream terms within the western wellness movement and the broader social vernacular. The applications of mindfulness have also broadened beyond those outlined in the Mindfulness-Based Stress Reduction programs Kabat-Zinn pioneered to, more recently, the achievement of peak performance in highly stressful environments such as combat pilots (Meland et al., 2015), maximising cognitive function and academic performance (e.g. Mrazek et al., 2013) and peak performance athletics (e.g. Gardner & Moore, 2004; Thienot et al., 2014). More broadly, mindfulness practice has been demonstrated to positively impact wellbeing and reduce stress, anxiety and rumination (Shapiro et al., 2008) and significantly increase goal attainment (Spence 2006; Spence, Cavanagh & Grant, 2008).

Of interest to many is the ascension of mindfulness practice in the workplace, despite the dearth of empirical research in this domain (Dane & Brummel, 2013). These researchers conducted a study utilising the Mindful Attention and Awareness Scale (MAAS; Brown & Ryan, 2003) in their exploration of turnover intention, engagement and job performance in restaurant waiting staff. In the conduct of their study, the authors proposed a valuable contextual definition for workplace mindfulness, defining it as; '… the degree to which individuals are mindful in a given work context' (p. 119). Their results indicated a positive directional relationship between workplace mindfulness and job performance; Results that strengthened earlier findings by Reb et al. (2012) of the positive effects of leaders' mindfulness on job performance of subordinates.

Despite the recent widespread reporting across most popular genres of media and literature, mindfulness practice is far from new. The foundations of mindfulness are firmly rooted in Buddhist philosophies and practices, and have been for more than 3,000 years. Indeed, meditation, the *crucible* in which mindfulness resides, has for millennia, served practitioners in their pursuit of deeper awareness and understanding of self, others, environment and existence. In the Buddhist context, this practice has focussed on three distinct areas; *keeping the Buddha in mind*, *being present* and *noticing habit-patterns* (Brazier, 2003). It is the latter two that have translated most readily to contemporary western practices of mindfulness and are terms that have become common in the mindfulness literature.

Meditation, in its most reductionist and simplistic form, can be considered concentration (Henepola Gunaratana, 2002) whilst some western researchers such as Walsh (1983) have described it as:

> ... a family of practices that train attention in order to heighten awareness and bring mental processes under greater voluntary control. The ultimate aims of these practices are the development of deep insight into the nature of mental processes, consciousness, identity, and reality, and the development of optimal states of psychological well-being and consciousness. (p. 19)

Walsh elaborates by identifying mindfulness as the first of seven Buddhist meditators' 'factors of enlightenment' and defines it as; '... *the quality of being aware of the nature of the object of consciousness*' (p. 28). Similarly, Levine (2009) highlights in succinct and simple terms the links between mindfulness and Buddhist meditation. The nine Buddhist practices for attaining Liberation cluster into three main headings; Wisdom, Ethics and Inner Practice. This last cluster encompasses the core of mindfulness practice.

Whilst the notion of introspective, innerpractice appears central to meditation, authors including Littman-Ovadia, Zilcha-Mano and Langer (2014) make explicit the challenges inherent in developing a connection and understanding between the contemplative and experientially focussed eastern approaches that are central to Buddhist practice, and the more contemporary Western scientific approaches utilised to establish empirical knowledge. Whilst most researchers and practitioners in the field clearly acknowledge that a connection appears to exist, the challenges of investigating this phenomenon utilising a scientific paradigm necessitate the creation and validation of a repeatedly and consistently measureable construct. It is here that the challenges of bringing these two divergent philosophies together as a focus point for investigation begin to surface.

THE CHALLENGES OF DEFINING MINDFULNESS

When the curious student of mindfulness is first introduced to the field, she quickly realises that what appears to be a relatively simple construct and approach to practice, remains deceptively difficult to pin-down. Kabat-Zinn (1990), arguably the founder of mindfulness in western therapy (Singh, 2010), offered a definition that has strongly influenced the field's development to date:

> Simply put, mindfulness is moment-to-moment awareness. It is cultivated by purposefully paying attention to things we ordinarily never give a moment's thought to. It is a systematic approach to developing new kinds of control and wisdom in our lives, based on our inner capacities for relaxation, paying attention, awareness, and insight. (p. 2)

However since that point, there have been a plethora of contributions made by scholars in search of an elusive and succinct description of what remains a paradoxical conundrum. Whilst some researchers suggest that mindfulness has been reduced to a contemporary buzzword (Sun, 2014), others have persisted with the formidable task of blending the intangibility of an eastern spiritual practice with the quantitative reductionism of a western scientific paradigm. Authors such as Cavanagh & Spence (2013) have highlighted this 'fuzziness' and described it as a 'confused' construct. In their effort to reduce this confusion, these authors identified four core domains that occupy the current research literature on mindfulness, namely, *state*, *trait*, *process* and *philosophy*. Their exploration yields a succinct definition of the construct: 'A motivated state of decentered awareness brought about by receptive attending to present moment experience' (p. 117).

Ellen Langer, an acknowledged early pioneer within mindfulness research, describes mindfulness as 'the process of actively noticing new things' (Beard, 2014, p.68). Her early research (Langer & Abelson, 1972) highlighted the phenomenon of our inherent *mindlessness* in common communications and interactions with others. It is in exploring mindfulness from the juxtaposition of *mindlessness* that distinguishes Langer's valuable contribution to the literature. In approaching the exploration of mindfulness in this way, Langer (2014) asserts that amongst the many benefits of practising mindfulness is the creation of an inherent awareness of *doubt* and *uncertainty* that subsequently allows for *choice*. With *certainty* of events and phenomena, Langer argued, came mindlessness, automatic and habitual responding which was antithetical to mindful awareness.

However, for some, the problems in arriving at a consensual agreement on the term lie in the conceptual approach taken to understanding the phenomenon itself, rather than articulating the subjective experience and practice of it. Sternberg (2000) addressed this challenge by approaching the issue of definition with a broader question in mind; *How should mindfulness be understood?* Sternberg suggests that the way we choose to approach this broader question fundamentally influences our conceptualisation of the construct and hence the way in which we engage with the practice and investigation of it. To elaborate on his point, he proposes three distinct conceptualisations of mindfulness to be explored, namely, mindfulness as a *cognitive ability*, as a *personality trait* and as a *cognitive style*.

Whilst these attempts at definitional clarity contribute accretively to our breadth of understanding, Carmody (2014) argues that continuing attempts to arrive at a universally agreed upon definition of mindfulness only serve to detract from the underlying practice itself. All mindfulness programs, he argues, focus on the unique *experiencing* and *attending-to* of the individual practitioner that leads to improvements in well-being. According to Carmody, whilst the traditional eastern conceptualisation of mindfulness focuses on personal introspection to reduce mental suffering, western approaches have emphasised the focus firstly on one's attention to environmental cues, then actively manipulating these experiences and responses to achieve a more desirable cognitive-emotional outcome. Thus, the western approach becomes one of challenging one's *intellect* to create new perspectives and meaning from experience in order to subsequently counteract and challenge one's habitual tendency towards mindlessness and prejudice. This strongly self-directed approach to learning mindfulness supports the utilisation of a more explicit teaching and learning model within the coaching engagement.

Recent research presented by Kiken et al. (2015) is of particular significance to these conceptual distinctions. Their study utilised a prospective, observational design with repeated measures of *trait* and *state* mindfulness during the course of a mindfulness-based intervention modelled on Kabat-Zinn's Mindfulness Based Stress Reduction program (Kabat-Zinn, 1990). Their results indicated an increase in *trait* mindfulness consistent with increased *state* mindfulness, facilitated through meditation practice, and associated reductions in stress reduction. These findings suggest embryonic support for the notion of 'practice makes permanent' and highlight the role of learning and skill development in mindfulness practice. Further, if one considers mindfulness as a 'learnable skill' in addition to be a 'state of being', the potential for its integration as both a *method* and an *outcome* within the context of coaching becomes conceivable.

Arguably one of the more perplexing issues facing mindfulness researchers and practitioners lies in the delineation between *personal* practice and *client* practice. The question of whether or not *personal* mindfulness practice by the *practitioner*, in this case, the coach, is a prerequisite for the effective facilitation of mindfulness remains unclear. Many, including Kabat-Zinn (2003) himself suggest that personal practice is essential for those who are researching or teaching mindfulness in therapeutic settings. Further, Singh (2010) suggests that without this personal practice, it is difficult for a therapist to relate to, and provide feedback on, the client's unique experience of mindfulness practice. Whilst the similarities and differences between coaching and therapy continue to attract spirited debate within the literature, the proposition that the coaching alliance (Kemp, 2008, 2011) may be strengthened and made efficacious as a result of the coach's own mindfulness and meditation practice, the expectation that the 'teacher' is also the 'student' would appear vital.

BRINGING COACHING AND MINDFULNESS TOGETHER

Clearly, there is a potentially valuable contribution that both coaching and mindfulness bring to creating a healthy and flourishing life. The challenge remains as to how to practically and effectively bring these two methods together into an integrated intervention that enables the coachee to achieve their growth and development goals most effectively, efficiently and sustainably. Virgili (2013) highlighted that, at that point, very few scholarly articles existed linking mindfulness and coaching; an apparently persistent condition reaffirmed later by Hall (2014, 2015). However, as Virgili justifiably articulates, the importance of *present-moment attention* and *non-judgemental awareness*, and the self-awareness that these practices nurture, are far from foreign to the *practice* of coaching.

To this point, earlier work by Passmore & Marianetti (2007) proposed a number of theoretical applications of mindfulness within coaching practice that included; *preparing for coaching, maintaining focus during the session, remaining emotionally detached, and teaching mindfulness to coachees*. Of note is that the primary focus of the application of mindfulness was the *coach*, rather than the *coachee* however even at this early stage, the coach as *teacher*. Via a reference to Segal, Williams and Teasdale's (2002) earlier work with mindfulness and depression in therapeutic settings, Passmore and Marianetti were amongst the first to formally propose that the specific skills of mindfulness could be beneficially *taught* as an integral part of the coaching process. Providing more substantial empirical evidence for this efficacy, Collard & Walsh (2008) examined the impact of participation in mindfulness coaching groups by non-clinical populations, similar to those found in many coaching cohorts. Their treatment yielded a significant reduction in coachee stress following participation in two mindfulness training sessions over an eight week period.

Broader explorations of the relationship between education and mindfulness were presented by Davis (2012). It was here that the potential of mindfulness practices in educational psychology began to be highlighted with Davis concluding that sufficient evidence to justify the incorporation of mindfulness based approaches into educational practice settings now existed within the mindfulness and education literatures.

Emerging research addressing the more specific application of mindfulness as an effective coaching tool for building physical and mental health (Robins, Kiken, Holt & McCain, 2014) and authentic leadership (Kinsler, 2014) are two examples of the now rapid is the broadening interest in the use of coaching and mindfulness in the field of human development.

Mindfulness and Different Reflective Conversations in Coaching

Of particular pertinence presently is the theoretical construct originally articulated by Cavanagh (2006) and further elaborated upon by Cavanagh and Spence (2013) outlining the five key reflective conversations within the coaching engagement. These conversations include:

- The internal conversation of the coachee
- The conversation between the coachee and their world
- The internal conversation of the coach
- The coach's conversation with his/her world
- The shared conversation of coach and coachee

This theoretical framework highlights the multiple domains within the coaching engagement that lend themselves to mindfulness-based intervention. Whilst some authors, such as Kets de Vries (2014) highlight the criticality of personal reflection on their own internal dialogue and hence, the application of mindfulness to across these multiple coaching conversations appears warranted.

By way of example, the pathway outlined by Cavanagh and Spence highlights the core coach attitude, and behavioural input, of 'acceptance'. This internalised state will likely fluctuate from moment to moment and conversation to conversation within the coach. The argument in support of developing elevated levels of state mindfulness as a coach therefore is that the coach becomes better able to manage her emotional reactivity, and subsequently, behave more flexibly through improved self-regulation. By achieving this aim, the coach can better support her client's goal attainment and self-management as there is greater 'self vs other' clarity in the espoused goal. Of course, phenomenologically, each of these effects represent a dynamic continuum upon which the coach may deviate inconsistently and unpredictably. Likewise, the coachee himself fluctuates in 'mind and mood' perpetually.

The benefits and opportunities that are presented in the blending of coaching with mindfulness are exciting. Both methods are fundamentally geared towards growth, development and flourishing, demonstrate a deeply embedded component of introspection and personal reflection inherent in their practices and apply the insights gained through this process to the outside world. However a functional model for bringing these two practices together is required.

WHERE TO FROM HERE? INTEGRATING COACHING AND MINDFULNESS

A major challenge that we have identified previously in this chapter is establishing a universally validated definition of any new field of enquiry and the subsequent construction of a unique body of knowledge. Whilst increasing effort is currently being applied to these tasks, we have potentially overlooked, at least partially, the deep foundations of practice and understanding that are held within the related bodies of knowledge in *education and learning*; foundations upon which coaching was born. Whilst the topic of *positive education* has stimulated a greater volume of interest and research in the application of positive psychology within educational settings (Gilman, Huebner & Furlong, 2009; Van Nieuwerburgh, 2012), an extensive existing body of knowledge from the broader field of education is still yet to be fully discovered, acknowledged and applied to practice.

Bachkirova et al. (2014) were amongst the first to acknowledge the significance of the role that *education and learning* occupies in underpinning *all* coaching practice. Specifically, they proposed that Knowles' (1970) construct of adult education (androgogy), Kolb's (1984) construct of experiential learning and Mezirow's (2000) construct of transformative learning effectively combined to form a collective body of informing knowledge and practice principles that are now arguably 'relabelled' as coaching in our contemporary discourse. In an attempt to draw these methods together, experiential education provides both a theoretical and functional framework within which coaching and mindfulness can be readily integrated. In exploring the foundations of education most broadly, and by surfacing its deep and extensive knowledge base, the broader field of education becomes an obvious conceptual integrator of these two practice methods.

Experiential Learning

It was Kolb (1984) who first presented his four-stage model of experiential learning formally in the literature. This model, informed by the philosophies of Dewey (1884), amongst others, consisted of an engaging in an *experience*, processing that experience through *reflection*, capturing and synthesising the *learning* from the experience and finally *experimentation* through the direct application of that learning to a new experience. In spite of an ever increasing litany of 'proprietary' coaching models in the popular literature, Kolb's (1984) experiential learning cycle remains the only evidence-based and validated model for facilitated, learner-driven, integrated development activities, of which, coaching is one.

Joplin (1995) provided an eloquent overview of the guiding philosophy underlying experiential education as a discipline. Far from being a contemporary developmental fad, the foundation of experiential education as a unique methodology for achieving significant individual and personal development is firmly grounded in the metaphysical and epistemological teachings of Plato and Socrates. Indeed, experiential education can be seen as closely aligned to the fundamental Socratic philosophies of learning (Crosby, 1995). Whilst consensual agreement as to a single definition of experiential education amongst practitioners remains elusive, several elements common to most descriptions of the construct can be identified (Joplin, 1995).

Two key elements appear most fundamental to the experiential program. Firstly, the learner must engage in an *experience or an activity* and secondly, and equally importantly, there must a *guided or facilitated reflection* following this experience which, in-turn, is translated to meaning and learning. It is this active and guided reflection process which transforms simply *any* experience into experiential education. Joplin outlines nine core characteristics common to effective of experiential programs. The experience must be *learner directed* as opposed to facilitator driven and it must be *personal and affective in nature*. The *process* of achieving an outcome is equally as important as the outcome itself and *self evaluation* in the context of the experience is both an internal and external process. Evaluation of the effectiveness of the experiential program must be conducted through the gathering of a diverse range of data including subjective reports and narrative discourse that captures the participants' unique experience. The experience itself must be central to the learning program as opposed to the experience being secondary to the objective of transferring a body of knowledge or fact didactically to the learner. Unlike alternate pedagogical methodologies, experiential education is based on the participants' *subjective* perception of the event rather than the didactic transfer of a theoretical body of knowledge. The effective articulation of participants' direct experience as knowledge is central to the learning process.

From these descriptions, it can be seen that the coaching process, by any current definition, is clearly experiential learning in its purest form. Hence, there is a simple and ready-made framework for integrating mindfulness practice into this model, whilst at the same time maintaining the flexibility to incorporate the nuanced language of coaching in its application and utilisation.

The Foundations of Andragogy

Experiential education, being a learner-centred model of learning, lends itself seamlessly to the preferred styles of learning expressed by many mature age learners. It was Knowles (1970) however who was the first author to articulate a theoretical construct that identified the specific needs of adult learners and as a distinct form of learning (androgogy) that differed from children's learning styles (or *pedagogy*). Specifically, Knowles argued that:

- Adults need to know the purpose for learning something. (As distinct from children learning for learnings' sake and a less 'critical' need for meaning.)
- Greater breadth and depth of experience (including mistakes) provides the basis for learning activities. (As distinct from children's relative paucity of experience.)
- Adults need to be responsible for and involved in their decisions on education; involvement in the planning and evaluation of their instruction. They are, in effect, collaborators in the process. (As distinct from children who are passive recipients of the process.)
- Adults are most interested in learning content that has immediate relevance to their work and/or personal lives. (As distinct from children who are content to be taught the curriculum as it is mandated and legislated.)
- Adult learning is problem-centered in that in must have a clear purpose and outcome rather than being content of general interest and use. (As distinct from children who appreciate less structured and rigid.)
- Adults respond better to internal motivators rather than external rewards (with children preferring the opposite).

Recent efforts have provided strong validation for both the unique construct of androgogy and its empirical measurement using the Androgogical Practices Inventory (Holton, Wilson & Bates, 2009). The authors reported strong scale reliability and coefficients for *motivation, experience, need to know, readiness, self-directedness, setting of learning objectives, climate setting, evaluation, prepare the learner, designing the learning experience and learning activities*. On reflection, these scales demonstrate remarkable similarities with the coaching process and its intended outcomes and in addition, many of the antecedents that lead to beneficial outcomes from mindfulness practice. Clearly, the theoretical alignment and similarity of method, approach and outcomes could easily classify coaching as an *applied androgogical method* in addition to its status as an applied positive psychology.

Whilst the wholesale adoption of coaching as an androgogical method would be justified, the basic validity of the construct itself remains contentious. Authors such as Kerka (1994), have rightfully drawn attention to the unfounded assumptions perpetuated in self-directed learning, identifying and dispelling three key myths in this regard. The first myth is that adults are naturally self-directed, when, in reality, their capability for self-directed learning varies widely. The second myth is that self-direction is an all-or-nothing concept. In fact, adults have varying degrees of willingness, motivation or ability to assume personal responsibility for learning and the application of these is situationally variable. These may include the degree of choice over goals, objectives, type of participation, content, method, and assessment. The third myth is that self-directed learning means learning in isolation. In truth, the essential ingredient within self-directed learning may be the psychological control that a learner exerts in any setting, be it solitary, informal, or traditional. In addition to these criticisms, other studies such as those presented by Friestad (1998) highlight that both children and adults prefer to learn in an 'androgogical fashion'. Given a conducive environment and efficacious facilitation, even children prefer to be self-directed and experiential in the way they learn.

Proactivity and Self-Determination

Consistent with these assumptions of adult learning (Knowles, Deci and Vansteenkiste, 2004) later contributed three additional observations central to Deci and Ryan's (1980) self-determination theory. Firstly, humans tend to demonstrate inherent *proactivity* and associated desire and effort towards mastering their internal cognitions, perceptions, drivers and emotions. A potentially obscure term to translate, Crant (2000) defined proactive behaviour as: 'taking initiative in improving current circumstances or creating new ones; it involves challenging the status quo rather than passively adapting to present conditions' (p. 436).

Further, Siebert, Kraimer & Crant (2001) distinguished between proactive *behaviour* and proactive *personality* describing the latter as a more stable and endearing disposition to demonstrate personal initiative across a range of situations and contexts. These findings support the important place that *self-direction* plays in the experiential learning process.

Whilst there remains contention regarding the distinctions between pedagogy and androgogy, learning styles appear to be less related to age than first thought. Hence, the potential benefits of establishing an inclusive *education and learning* focussed framework for coaching and mindfulness can be succinctly articulated:

- Coaching is an educational experience.
- Mindfulness is an educational experience.
- Education methodology incorporates both learner-centered and teacher-centered approaches to learning.
- The utilisation and application of each family of approaches is situationally dependent upon the following factors:
    o the skill being taught/learnt
    o the experience and competence of the learner and teacher in the skill itself
    o the context in which the learning and teaching are occurring
    o the timeframe in which the learning and teaching are occurring
    o the shared goals and objectives of the teacher and learner.

One of the arguably contentious consequences of adopting an anthrogogically informed model of human development in the context of coaching is the unique place that many approaches and processes that have been actively excluded from the coaching method to date are arguably both central and critical to a client realising effective learning outcomes. Techniques including *expert advice, technical and corrective feedback, didactic teaching, skills training* and *directive action setting* are all vitally important and implicit techniques that when delivered in the appropriate context and form and at the appropriate time to the appropriate coachee, are invaluable elements of the experiential learning process.

Whilst there have been some theorists courageous enough to argue on behalf of the place of expert knowledge in coaching, they are few and far between and have been largely confined to the executive coaching context and leadership (Elliot, 2005) or business (Boyce et al., 2010). The current discourse therefore argues strongly *against* the popular belief that didactic delivery of expert knowledge detracts from facilitating successful coaching outcomes (Ives, 2008) and, to the contrary, that coaching practitioners are compelled to increase their technical expertise as *educators* and *mindfulness meditators* if they are to be truly effective in supporting their coachees' learning.

An Evolving Convergence of Approaches

As the evolution towards learner-centred teaching progresses, we are witnessing a rapid integration of *experiential, facilitated* and *learner-driven* education and a widespread convergence of coaching with traditional teaching approaches (e.g. van Nieuwerburgh, 2012). Simply stated, the science of learning is deepening and the boundaries between traditional pedagogical and androgogical practices appear to be merging towards a more situationally determined, learner-driven and methodologically flexible style of learning that applies elements of a range of approaches at varying times. Whilst there is no accepted term for this merged method, the adoption of a new term, *anthrogogy*, from the Greek *anthropos* meaning '*human*' may provide a more apt working framework.

By adopting an experiential educational approach to coaching and mindfulness practice, the potential positive impact of the coaching intervention is dramatically expanded. By drawing on the broader informing bodies of knowledge, practice methods and protocols across education, learning and mindfulness, the parameters of coaching practice can be expanded to include 'teaching' as a legitimate component of the coaching method, thus legitimising the formal instruction of mindfulness skills and approaches within the coaching intervention. By broadening the definition of coaching practice to that of an *anthrogogical science*, client process, experience and outcomes can be strengthened through the formal teaching of skillsets that equip them to sustain their own independent wellbeing whilst synchronously, coaching practitioners themselves are better able to broaden and deepen their own capabilities as educators and growth agents.

Positive Psychoeducation

Building on the adoption of an anthrogogical frame to integrate coaching practice with mindfulness, 'positive psychoeducation' also provides a valuable addition. Applied as a facilitative teaching and enrichment method to deepen the coachee's understanding of the *psychology* of mindfulness, positive psychoeducation provides an additional educative component to the coaching engagement.

Traditional psychoeducation has been predominantly utilised as a mental-illness treatment approach that combines psychotherapeutic and educational interventions within a more holistic and competence-based modality that focuses on client wellness, coping and empowerment (Lukens & McFarlane, 2004). The earliest explicit use of the term in the psychiatric literature was by Anderson et al. (1980) but it was the later work by Bäuml et al. (2006) that provided valuable insights into the critical elements central to achieving efficacious patient outcomes. The authors suggest that the goals of psychoeducation include; ensuring basic client competence, facilitating self-responsibility, deepening patients' role as expert, strengthening the role of relatives (others), combining techniques with client empowerment, improving insight into the conditions which restrict the desired state, promoting relapse prevention, supporting broader health and economising educational activities.

Whilst much of the literature has focussed heavily on the clinical and therapeutic applications of psychoeducation to the treatment of psychological disorders, some practitioners within these disciplines have consistently argued for a more empowering, positive and self-efficacious growth-centered approach to the treatment of mental illness (e.g. Egan, 1975, 2013). Indeed, Authier (1977) and earlier, Guerney, Guerney and Stollak (1971) and Guerney, Stollak and Guerney (1970) had highlighted and advocated for the positive, growth-focussed opportunities inherent in the method.

Hence, to effectively integrate mindfulness and coaching practices, the adoption of a broader, experiential and anthrogogical model that outlines a process for effectively teaching the skills and practice of mindfulness may be of benefit. Further, the application of positive psychoeducation techniques to strengthen and consolidate the learning outcomes achieved through the coaching engagement, and to ensure the sustainability of these learned skills, provides a meta-cognitive context to the symbiotic relationship that exists between mindfulness and coaching. Hence, through the purposeful and deliberate application of the methods and techniques of anthrogogical science to the process of coaching, it is proposed that clients will strengthen their mastery of mindfulness whilst concurrently maximising their goal striving and attainment successes.

APPLYING THE NEW FRAMEWORK TO OLD PRACTICES: A TEMPLATE FOR ANTHROGOGICAL ENGAGEMENT

From the outset, a model of anthrogogical coaching may be seen to directly contravene what many consider to be the central tenet of coaching itself. To elaborate, most coaching theorists and researchers to date have argued strongly for the immutable ownership of the coaching agenda residing with the client herself rather than the coach. Hence, the locus of creation and control of goal setting, action planning, problem solving and reflective analysis is owned, by definition, by the client. However, by introducing an anthropological paradigm to the coaching construct, the role of the coach becomes one of cocreator and teacher within the context of a learning experience. By applying the wealth of evidence based education to coaching, clear stages, phases and cycles that are repeated and common to all styles of facilitated anthrogogical learning become evident. By firstly identifying these empirically robust learning stages, then applying these stages to the coaching process, mindfulness can be effectively taught, practised and refined as an integral and concurrent function of the coaching intervention itself and hence, enable mindfulness skill acquisition to be achieved simultaneously with coaching-focussed goal attainment. Further empirical evidence supports the assertion that effective teaching and learning outcomes are achieved largely as a result of high levels of engagement between the teacher and learner across four key stages of the learning process. This *learning alliance* is largely reflective of the phenomenon of the *coaching alliance* (Stober & Grant, 2006; Horvath, 2001; Kemp, 2008, 2011; O'Broin & Palmer, 2010) and hence, warrants an isomorphic transfer from the coaching context to the current anthropological framework being proposed, the four phases of which are presented below.

Stage 1: Level of the Learner

The primary task in this first stage involves the coach establishing an optimal learning experience and environment for the coachee, or learner. This involves identifying and evaluating the level of *competence* and *experience* of the learner in the skill or domain they have elected to focus on. Whilst in the current context, this may be the level of exposure to, and past practice of, meditation or mindfulness, the foundations of this phase apply to all areas in which the coachee is intentionally setting specific objectives and goals. This phase is particularly important in order to match the appropriate learning activities and sequence of those activities to the current *experience and capability* level of the learner, her *demonstrable aptitude* in relation to that skill and her current *motivational set* to learn this skill. In the coaching context, clients' experience of mindfulness meditation practice (MMP) may fall into one of three broad categories; no or minimal exposure, moderate exposure or extensive/deep exposure. For clients in the 'no or minimal' category, appropriate activities such as attendance at an introductory meditation workshop, a mindful awareness exercise within a coaching session, an internet search for beginners' meditation exercises, or a basic practice schedule of breathing and relaxation exercises may be appropriate options as the first progression in their skill acquisition sequence. For those more advanced learners, referral to an experienced meditation teacher or the design of a more disciplined and consistent practice schedule may be most appropriate. As the coach however, the primary focus is to facilitate an effective learning experience for the coachee within the coaching process. If an external expert is required to be engaged in the learning process at this point, then it is the ethical responsibility of the coach to ensure that this resource is sourced appropriately and effectively deployed. Regardless of the current level of the learner, of primary concern to the experiential educator is enabling the coachee to experience early success in her practices and a sense of achievement and competence that nurtures her motivation to continue to practise and refine her performance and maintain a positive sense of agency.

Stage 2: Practice and Participation

The importance of *motivation* and *agency* in achieving states of positive wellbeing have been highlighted by Deci and Ryan (1995). Further, Spence (2006) has previously identified the central importance of Deci and Ryan's self-determination theory (SDT) in achieving efficacious outcomes in coaching. The central tenet of SDT is that at the core of human motivation is an inherently positive drive that seeks to enact effort through one's sense of agency, commitment and striving for personal growth and discovery. These inherent drives serve to meet the innate human needs of *competence*, *relatedness* and *autonomy*.

In addition, Shapiro et al. (2006) highlight three axioms of mindfulness practice; *intention*, *attitude* and *attention*, highlighting that these occur simultaneously and this moment-to-moment process defines mindfulness itself. The first of these, *intention*, is arguably a foundation of not only effective mindfulness practice, but can be considered central to the process of learning, goal setting and goal striving within the coaching engagement. Kabat-Zinn (1994) describes this intention in mindfulness terms as *'on purpose'* (p. 4) meaning that the individual actively engages with mindfulness practice with an expectation that a positively valued outcome will be achieved as a result of her participation. For many would-be mindfulness practitioners within the coaching context, the likelihood of these intended outcomes being achieved significantly influences their motivation and agency to *practice*. However, in the context of executive coaching for example, the drive for *immediacy*, *impact* and *results*, often within a pure business context, may serve to hinder or truncate any mindfulness practice and impede the positive benefits such as improved job performance (Dane & Brummel, 2013) or leadership (Kinsler, 2014) that result from persistent practice.

Extrapolating from Launder's (2001) 'P's of Perfect Pedagogy', effective learning outcomes are significantly aided by 'plenty of pertinent, progressive practice'. Simply, mindfulness needs to be persistently practised. For mindfulness to be of value to those who practice it, the practice must be consistent, disciplined, paced, sequenced and processed in an experiential context to provide meaning, understanding and corrective feedback. If the novice mindfulness practitioner has an expectation of 'blissful calm' from the moment she takes her first soft-stomach breath, she may be sadly disappointed and disheartened after her first mindfulness exercise. It is the coach who can play an active and directive role here, by redirecting the coachee's focus and mindset, using psychoeducative methods to teach the coachee the process of change and mastery and provide specific corrective feedback at their own level of competency and experience.

Stage 3: Consolidation and Consistency

During the third phase of the coaching engagement, both the coach and coachee are compelled to develop, apply or exhibit a deeper set of mindfulness and learning skills. It is at this point in the learning process where continuous practice may become repetitive and boring. The coach may begin to lose their focus or commitment to the coachee. Likewise, the coachee may find that she is slipping into a 'comfortable' mode of engagement with the coach. Recognisable patterns begin to emerge in behaviour and engagement style facilitating the emergence and influence of one or more cognitive biases. It is at this point in the alliance that through a collective focus on mindfulness and processing of experience that motivation can be reengaged through progressively more challenging practices, a change in activity focus or through the creativity of the coach in designing novel or innovative learning tasks. By utilising the anthrogogical approach to coaching, the coach has new freedoms to more proactively engage in the design of the coachee's learning environment and be a more directly active facilitator in the learning journey

Stage 4: Refinement and Mastery

This phase captures the process of continued practice, feedback provision, refinement of performance and engagement. The methodological importance of *progressive sequencing* is of particular importance during this phase as the learner must continue to be challenged with increasingly more complex and challenging practices to extend and refine her repertoire of skills. In the context of mindfulness, the coachee may now be seeking out progressively more demanding practice exercises and in addition, she may also be seeking progressively more challenging environments, relationships or contexts in which she can apply these skills. Whilst maintaining a central point of focused attention in the confines of a quiet and controlled meditation room with a supportive and caring coach is of vital importance to skill acquisition in its early stages, the application of these skills in the 'real' world is the ultimate objective and at the appropriate point, the coach plays an important role in designing, facilitating and processing these 'real' world practices.

Stage 5: Closure and Maintenance

An often-overlooked stage in the learning process is the closure phase. In particular, educators and coaches may overlook the importance of reviewing, capturing the narrative of the experiential journey, anchoring progress and current abilities and celebrating successes. Equally, developing self-directed and managed strategies for continuing progression and mastery establishes a plan for future growth that is of critical importance in the perpetually iterative process of lifelong learning. It is here that coach and coachee stand to gain significant retrospective insight and awareness through a review of not only the content covered in the coaching engagement but the unique subjective experiences of each in the laboratory that is created through the coaching alliance. Personal reflection, introspection and supervision each play an important role in maximising the experiential learning outcomes from the unique coaching engagement.

WHERE TO FROM HERE?

The current chapter has provided a strong justification and validation for the continuation of the use of coaching practice and mindfulness practice as effective methods for supporting human growth, learning and flourishing. In addition, the chapter has drawn attention to their interdependence and their relativity to a long and well established body of knowledge from the field of education, specifically, experiential education. Most importantly, it has proposed the adoption of an integrative experiential education approach to coaching and mindfulness and the opportunity that this integrative framework promises for bringing mindfulness practice together with coaching practice within a rich and rewarding learning environment.

Future research in the field to investigate the unique effects of implementing an *athrogogical* approach to coaching and mindfulness is recommended. By adopting a randomised, treatment-control group trial approach to investigating the comparative impacts of unique coaching methods and protocols, valuable insights into both the phenomenology of the coaching engagement and the relative efficacies of methodological approaches will serve to rigorously investigate these theoretical frameworks and inform their development. Likewise, continuing to turn our research attention to the broader outcomes achieved by adopting a structured and consistent practice of mindfulness will further serve to illuminate our understanding of human learning, growth and development.

CONCLUSION

The chapter has deliberately and overtly issued a challenge to those researchers and practitioners working in the coaching field and with mindfulness. Such is the impact and value that these methods appear to offer, practitioners must be compelled and committed to pursuing their own development and mastery both of athrogical methods and mindfulness. To do this, we must extend and build our knowledge, understanding, competency and capability as teachers, educators and mindfulness practitioners. Indeed, so important is this process of self-reflection and development as a coach to achieving similarly efficacious outcomes for the client, that authors such as Silsbee (2008) have designed integrative coaching models and coaching practices for effectively achieving this. By utilising and applying models such as these, practitioners of coaching and mindfulness will be better positioned to support their client's development.

As a theoretical construct, much effort is needed to experiment with and surface the impact and efficacy of adopting a model of coaching derived from anthrogogy. However, we have presented neither a radical nor unfounded approach to this integrative challenge in this chapter. Rather, we have illuminated the lost opportunity of overlooking a broad suite of models, methods and research that fall within the discipline of education and highlight experiential and anthrogogical education as the historical foundation of coaching and mindfulness practice.

By approaching coaching as an anthrogogical enterprise, and subsequently drawing on the rich and extensive bodies of knowledge that exist across education and teaching, future research with an interdisciplinary approach may illuminate more fully both coaching practice itself and the application of mindfulness as an integral tool to this practice. Likewise, and arguably juxtaposed, the investigation of coaching as an anthrogogical method may well surface insights currently clouded by definitional rigidity within a future integrated and blended field of practice. A theoretical and conceptual loosening of the boundaries defining coaching, teaching and mindfulness may yet yield valuable methodological and phenomenological insights that can strengthen the potency of these efficacious developmental methods.

REFERENCES

Anderson, C.M., Gerard, E., Hogarty, G.E., Reiss, D.J. (1980). Family treatment of adult schizophrenic patients: A psychoeducational approach. *Schizophrenia Bulletin*, 6(3):490–505.

Authier, J. (1977). The Psychoeducation Model: Definition, contemporary roots and context. *Canadian Journal of Counseling and Psychotherapy*, 12(1), 15–22.

Bachkirova, T., Cox, E. & Clutterbuck, D. (2014). Introduction in E. Cox, T. Bachkirova & D. Clutterbuck (Eds.) (2014). *The Complete Handbook of Coaching* (2nd ed.), Los Angeles; London: Sage.

Bäuml, J., Froböse, T., Kraemer, S., Rentrop, M., & Pitschel-Walz, G. (2006). Psychoeducation: A basic psychotherapeutic intervention for patients with schizophrenia and their families. *Schizophrenia Bulletin*, 32(Suppl 1), S1–S9.

Beard, A. (2014). Spotlight: Mindfulness in the Age of Complexity. Interview with Ellen Langer. *Harvard Business Review*, 92(3), 68–73.

Boyce, L.A., Jackson, R.J., & Neal, L. (2010). Building Successful Leadership Coaching Relationships: Examining impact of matching criteria in a leadership coaching programme. *The Journal of Management Development*, 29(10), 914–931.

Brazier, C. (2003). *Buddhist Psychology: Liberate your mind, embrace life*. Constable & Robinson; London.

Brown, K.W. & Ryan, R.M. (2003). The benefits of being present: Mindfulness and its role in psychological well-being. *Journal of Personality and Social Psychology*, 84, 822–848.

Carmody (2014) Eastern and Western approaches to mindfulness: Similarities, differences, and clinical implications. In A. le, C. T. Ngnoumen, E. J. Langer (Eds.), *The Wiley Blackwell Handbook of Mindfulness*. Chichester, UK: Wiley-Blackwell

Cavanagh, M.J. (2006). Coaching from a systemic perspective: A complex adaptive conversation. In D.R. Stober & A.M. Grant (Eds.), *Evidence Based Coaching Handbook: Putting Best Practices to Work for your Clients*. Hoboken, NJ: Wiley & Sons.

Cavanagh, M.J., & Spence, G.B. (2013). Mindfulness in Coaching: Philosophy, psychology or just a useful skill? In J. Passmore, D.B. Peterson & T. Freire (Eds.), *The Wiley-Blackwell Handbook of the Psychology of Coaching and Mentoring*. West Sussex, UK: John Wiley & Sons Ltd.

Collard, P., & Walsh, J. (2008). Sensory Awareness Mindfulness Training in Coaching: Accepting life's challenges. *Journal of Rational Emotive Cognitive Behavioural Therapy*, 26, 30–37.

Crant, J.M. (2000). Proactive behavior in organizations. *Journal of Management*, 26, 435–462.

Crosby, A. (1995). A Critical Look: The philosphical foundations of experiential education, in K. Warren, M. Sakofs, & J.S. Hunt Jr. (Eds.), *The Theory of Experiential Education* (3rd Ed.). Dubuque, Iowa: Kendall Hunt.

Dane, E., & Brummel, B.J. (2013). Examining workplace mindfulness and its relations to job performance and turnover intention. *Human Relations*, 67(1), 105–128.

Davis, T.S. (2012). Mindfulness-Based Approaches and their potential for educational psychology practice. *Educational Psychology in Practice*, 28(1), 31–46.

Deci, E.L., & Ryan, R.M. (1980). Self-determination theory: When mind mediates behaviour. *The Journal of Mind and Behaviour*, 1, 33–43.

Deci, E.L., & Ryan, R.M. (1995). Human autonomy: The basis for true self-esteem. In M. Kernis (Ed.), *Efficacy, agency, and self-esteem* (pp. 31–49). New York: Plenum.

Deci, E.L., & Vansteenkiste, M. (2004). Self-determination Theory and Basic Need Satisfaction: Understanding Human Development in Positive Psychology. *Ricerche di Psicologia*, 27, 17–34.

Dewey, J. (1884). The New Psychology. *Andover Review*, 2, 278–289.

Elliot, R.H. (2005). The parameters of specialist professional leadership coaching. In M. Cavanagh, A.M. Grant & T. Kemp (Eds.), *Evidence-based coaching Volume 1: Theory, research and practice from the behavioural sciences*. Samford Valley, Queensland: Australian Academic Press.

Friestad, J.M. (1998). Andragogy vs. Pedagogy: Comparing Adult and Childen's Learning Preferences. Unpublished Thesis. Drake University, US.

Gardner, F.L., & Moore, Z.E. (2004). A Mindfulness-Acceptance-Commitment-Based Approach to Athletic Performance Enhancement: Theoretical Considerations. *Behavior Therapy*, 35, 707–723.

Gilman, R., Huebner, E.S., & Furlong, M.J. (eds.) (2009). *Handbook of Positive Psychology in Schools*. New York, NY: Routledge.

Grant, A.M. (2009). Coaching Psychology, in S.J. Lopez (Ed.) (2009), *The Encyclopedia of Positive Psychology*. Sussex, UK: Blackwell Publishing Ltd.

Guerney, B., Stollak, G., & Guerney, L. (1970). A Format for a New Mode of Psychological Practice: Or how to escape a zombie. *The Counselling Psychologist*, 2(2), 97–104.

Guerney, B., Guerney, L., & Stollak, G. (1971). The Potential Advantages of Changing from a Medical to an Educational Model. *Interpersonal Development*, 72(2), 238–246.

Hall, L. (2014). Mindful Coaching, in J. Passmore (Ed.), *Mastery in Coaching: A Complete Psychological Toolkit for Advanced Coaching*. London, UK: Association for Coaching/Kogan Page Ltd.

Hall, L. (2015). Mindfulness in Coaching, in J. Reb & P.W.B. Atkins (Eds.), *Mindfulness in Organizations: Foundations, Research, and Applications*. Cambridge: Cambridge University Press.

Henepola Gunaratana, B. (2002). *Mindfulness in Plain English*. Boston: Wisdom.

Holton, E.F., Wilson, L., & Bates, R. (2009). Toward Development of a Generalized Instrument to Measure Androgogy. *Human Resource Development Quarterly*, 20(2) 169–193.

Horvath, A.O. (2001). The Alliance. *Psychotherapy*, 38(4), 365–372.

Ives, J. (2008). What is 'Coaching'? An Exploration of Conflicting Paradigms. *International Journal of Evidence Based Coaching and Mentoring*. 6, 2, 100–113.

Joplin, L. (1995). On Defining Experiential Education, In K. Warren, M. Sakofs, & J.S. Hunt Jr. (Eds.), *The Theory of Experiential Education* (3rd Ed.). Dubuque, Iowa: Kendall Hunt.

Kabat-Zinn, J. (1982). An outpatient program in behavioral medicine for chronic pain patients based on the practice of mindfulness meditation: Theoretical considerations and preliminary results. *General Hospital Psychiatry*, 4, 33–47.

Kabat-Zinn, J. (1990). *Full Catastrophe Living: Using the wisdom of your body and mind to face stress, pain, and illness*. New York: Delacorte.

Kabat-Zinn, J. (1994). *Wherever you go, there you are: Mindfulness meditation in everyday life*. New York: Hyperion.

Kabat-Zinn, J. (2005). *Coming To Our Senses*. Piatkus: London.

Kemp, T. (2004). Executive and Leadership Coaching: A unique application of Positive Psychology to Individual Development. *Second European Conference on Positive Psychology*, Verbania, Pallanza, Italy, July.

Kemp, T.J. (2008). Coach Self-Management: The foundation of coaching effectiveness. In D.B. Drake, D. Brennan & K. Gortz (Eds.), *The Philosophy and Practice of Coaching: Insights and issues for a new era*. Chichester, West Sussex, UK: John Wiley & Sons Ltd.

Kemp T.J. (2011). Building the Coaching Alliance: Constructing a lens for understanding the phenomenon of relationship in coaching. In G. Hernez-Broome & L. A. Boyce (Eds), *Advancing Executive Coaching: Setting the Course for Successful Leadership Coaching* (Chapter 7). San Francisco: Jossey-Bass.

Kerka, S. (1994). *Self-directed learning: Myths and realities* (Report). Washington, DC: Office of Educational Research and Improvement. (ERIC Document Reproduction Service No. ED 365 818).

Kets de Vries, M.F.R. (2014). *Mindful Leadership Coaching: Journeys into the Interior*. New York: Palgrave Macmillan.

Kiken, L.G., Garland, E.L., Bluth, K., Palsson, O.S., & Gaylord, S.A. (2015). From a State to a Trait: Trajectories of State Mindfulness in meditation during intervention predict changes in trait mindfulness. *Personality and Individual Differences*, 81, 41–46.

Kinsler, L. (2014). Born to be me … Who am I again? The development of Authentic Leadership using Evidence-Based Leadership Coaching and Mindfulness. *International Coaching Psychology Review*, 9 (1) 92–105.

Knowles, M.S. (1970). *The Modern Practice of Adult Education: Anrogogy Versus Pedagogy*. New York: Association Press.

Kolb, D.A. (1984). *Experiential Learning: Experience as the Source of Learning and Development*. Englewood Cliffs, NJ: Prentice-Hall.

Langer, E.J. (2009). Mindfulness, in S.J. Lopez (Ed.), *The Encyclopedia of Positive Psychology*. Sussex, UK: Blackwell Publishing Ltd.

Langer, E.J. (2014). Mindfulness Forward and Back, in A. Ie, C.T. Ngnoumen, & E.J. Langer (Eds.), *The Wiley Handbook of Mindfulness* (1st Ed.). New York: John Wiley & Sons, 7–20.

Langer, E.J. & Abelson, R.P. (1972). The semantics of asking a favour: How to succeed in getting help without really dying. *Journal of Personality and Social Psychology*, 24, 1, 26–32.

Launder, A.G. (2001). *Play Practice: The Games Approach to Teaching and Coaching Sports*. Champagne, IL: Human Kinetics.

Levine, M. (2009). Buddhism, in S.J. Lopez (Ed.), *The Encyclopedia of Positive Psychology*. Chichester, West Sussex, England: John Wiley & Sons.

Littman-Ovadia, H., Zilcha-Mano, S., & Langer, E. (2014). Vocational personalities and mindfulness. *Journal of Employment Counseling*, 51, 170–179.

Lukens, E.P., & McFarlane, W.R. (2004). Psychoeducation as Evidence-Based Practice: Considerations for practice, research, and policy. *Brief Treatment and Crisis Intervention*, 4(3), 205–225.

McKenzie, S., & Hassed, C. (2012). *Mindfulness for Life*. New Zealand: Exisle Publishing.

Meland, A., Fonne, V., Wagstaff, A., & Pensgaard, A.M. (2015). Mindfulness-Based Mental Training in a High Performance Combat Aviation Population: A one year intervention study and two year follow-up. *The International Journal of Aviation Psychology*, 25(1), 48–61.

Mezirow, J. (2000). How critical reflection triggers transformative learning. In J. Mezirow & Associates (Eds.), *Learning as Transformation*. San Francisco, CA: Jossey-Bass.

Mrazek, M.D., Franklin, M.S., Phillips, D.T., Baird, B., & Schooler, J.W. (2013). Mindfulness Training Improves Working Memory Capacity and GRE Performance While Reducing Mind Wandering. *Psychological Science*, 24(5), 776–781.

O'Broin, A., & Palmer, S. (2010). The Coaching Alliance as a universal concept spanning conceptual approaches. *Coaching Psychology International*, 3, 1, 3–6.

Passmore, J., & Marianetti, O. (2007). The Role of Mindfulness in Coaching. *The Coaching Psychologist*, 3 (3), 130–136.

Reb, J., Narayanan, J., & Chaturvedi, S. (2012). Leading Mindfully: Two studies on the influence of supervisor trait mindfulness on employee well-being and performance. *Mindfulness*, 5, 36–45.

Robins, J.L.W., Kiken, L., Holt, M., & McCain, N.L. (2014). Mindfulness: An effective coaching tool for improving physical and mental health. *Journal of the American Association of Nurse Practitioners*, 26, 511–518.

Segal, Z.V., Williams, J.M.G., & Teasdale, J.D. (2002). *Mindfulness-based Cognitive Therapy for Depression: A new approach to preventing relapse*. New York: Guilford.

Shapiro, S.L., & Carlson, L.E. (2009). *The Art and Science of Mindfulness*. Washington, DC: American Psychological Association.

Shapiro, S.L., Carlson, L.E., Astin, J.A., & Freedman, B. (2006). Mechanisms of Mindfulness. *Journal of Clinical Psychology*, 62(3), 373–386.

Shapiro, S.L., Oman, D., Thoresen, C.E., Plante, T.G., & Flinders, T. (2008). Cultivating Mindfulness: Effects on well-being. *Journal of Clinical Psychology*, 64(7), 840–862.

Siebert, S.E., Kraimer, M.L., & Crant, M. (2001). What Do Proactive People Do? A longitudinal model linking proactive personality and career success. *Personnel Psychology*, 54, 845–874.

Silsbee, D. (2008). *Presence-Based Coaching: Cultivating self-generative leaders through mind, body, and heart*. San Francisco, CA: Jossey-Bass/Wiley

Singh. N.N. (2010). Mindfulness: A finger pointing to the moon. *Mindfulness*, 1, 1–9.

Spence, G.B. (2006). New Directions in the Psychology of Coaching: The Integration of Mindfulness Training into Evidence-Based Coaching Practice. (Unpublished Doctoral thesis) School of Psychology, University of Sydney, Sydney, Australia.

Spence, G.B., Cavanagh, M.J., & Grant, A.M. (2008). The Integration of Mindfulness Training and Health Coaching: An exploratory study. *Coaching: An International Journal of Theory, Research and Practice*, 1(2), 145–163.

Sternberg, R.J. (2000). Images of Mindfulness. *Journal of Social Issues*, 56(1), 11–26.

Stober, D.R., & Grant, A.M. (Eds.) (2006). *The Handbook of Evidence Based Coaching*. New York: Wiley & Sons.

Sun, J. (2014) Mindfulness in Context: A Historical Discourse Analysis, *Contemporary Buddhism: An Interdisciplinary Journal*, 15(2), 394–415

Thienot, E., Jackson, B., Dimmock, J., Grove, J.R., Bernier. M., & Fournier, J.F. (2014). Development and Preliminary Validation of the Mindfulness Inventory for Sport. *Psychology of Sport and Exercise*, 15, 72–80.

Van Nieuwerburgh, C. (Ed.) (2012). *Coaching in Education: Getting better results for students, educators and parents*. London; Karnac Books.

Virgili, M. (2013). Mindfulness-based Coaching: Conceptualisation, supporting evidence and emerging applications. *International Coaching Psychology Review*, 8, 2, 40–57.

Walsh, R. (1983). Meditation practice and research. *Journal of Humanistic Psychology*, 3, 18–50.

Coaching for Post-Traumatic Growth: An Appropriate Response to the Devastations of Life?

Gordon Spence and Stephen Joseph

INTRODUCTION

Healing stories can touch our hearts and help us understand that life is a series of challenges – not all good, not all bad. Healing stories can help us expand our consciousness so that we can see our lives and the world in new ways. Yes, telling and hearing stories can be powerful medicine. (Carol, 2004, p.16)

This chapter acknowledges the human capacity to deal well with, and benefit from, profoundly challenging circumstances. More specifically, it focuses on the suitability of using coaching to help people grow through traumatic experiences. The pairing of such topics is highly unusual in the coaching literature for two main reasons. First, traumatic experiences are by definition emotionally demanding and are likely to cause people (at least temporarily) to feel disoriented, emote regularly (e.g. express anger, cry), become demotivated or otherwise present themselves in ways that many might consider 'uncoachable'.

Second, for almost 20 years, with some exceptions (e.g. Joseph, 2006), a succession of authors (e.g. Bluckert, 2005; Hart, Blattner, & Leipsic, 2001; Price, 2009; Williams, 2003) have attempted to establish sharp lines of demarcation between coaching and other forms of professional assistance, most notably psychotherapy and counseling. This has resulted in a long and widely-held view within the industry that 'coaching is not therapy' and, a more specific extension of this belief, that personal struggles with depression, anxiety and other types of emotional disequilibrium are not the purview of coaching (Williams, 2003). Whilst more nuanced analyses on this general issue have been presented from time to time (e.g. Bachkirova & Cox, 2005), some recent published work suggests that the binary views of the past may be changing (Campone, 2014; Oades, Crowe, & Nguyen, 2009) and that recognition may be developing that coaching has an important role to play during some of the most difficult periods of a person's life

(Hall, 2015b). Should this precipitate a shift in the way coaching applications are understood, further scholarly work in the area is likely to be assisted by detailed psychological (Joseph, 2011; Levine, 2010) and sociological (Watters, 2010) perspectives that exist on traumatic experiences and their potential to be beneficial.

We seek to elucidate several key issues surrounding this application of coaching via a five-part discussion. In the first part, we will seek to define trauma and describe some of its biopsychosocial effects. Second, as people respond quite differently to adversity, the heterogeneity of such responses will be acknowledged and explored. These will include distinguishing severe trauma outcomes (e.g. posttraumatic stress disorder; PTSD) from other known responses such as *resilience*, *recovery* or a type of benefit-finding referred to as *post-traumatic growth* (PTG; Calhoun & Tedeschi, 2014). Third, we will review literature on the use of coaching as a response to adverse life events, with specific attention given to work reported in the mental health and organisational domains. Fourth, the validity of coaching as a response to the traumatic experiences of clients will be examined, with particular attention given to how coaching might facilitate PTG. Lastly, we will conclude by drawing out the practical implications of this analysis, along with laying out recommendations for researchers who are interested in examining questions that arise from it.

WHAT IS TRAUMA?

Traditionally 'trauma' has been a label used within medical contexts to describe life or limb-threatening physical injuries (Stiell et al., 2008). However, recognition of the presence and importance of *psychological trauma* has grown steadily since the 19th century French physician, Jean Martin Charcot, began studying hysteria in female patients (Ringel & Brandell, 2012). Our interest is in the growth that occurs after the sustainment of psychological wounds or injuries, which occur when the events or circumstances of people's life damage, distort or (partially or completely) challenge their sense of self and understanding of how they fit into the wider world (Thompson & Walsh, 2010).

The causes of psychological trauma are many and varied and can include (but are not limited to) the death of a loved one, physical disablement, medical diagnosis, bullying, homelessness, childhood abuse, wartime experiences, marriage separation, social abandonment and encounters with violence or accidents (Joseph, 2011; Thompson & Walsh, 2010; Whitfield, 2010). It should be noted here that, whilst contemporary perspectives on the aetiology and management of trauma are dominated by Western psychological science, some authors (e.g. Watters, 2010) have drawn attention to the influence of sociological factors on the global prevalence of trauma.

Posttraumatic Stress Disorder (PTSD)

In the *Diagnostic and Statistical Manual of Mental Disorders* (5th edition; DSM-5), PTSD is a condition characterised by four clusters of symptoms; 1. intrusion, 2. avoidance, 3. negative alterations in cognitions and mood, and 4. alterations in arousal and reactivity (American Psychiatric Association, 2013). It is recognised that most people experience such reactions in the days and weeks following events like those described above. As such, a diagnosis of PTSD is generally only made after one month has passed and the reactions are still present. Problems recognised as resulting from PTSD have a severe impact on social and occupational functioning. Whilst not everyone will develop the full syndrome of PTSD, the majority of people who experience a traumatic event will experience at least some of the psychological problems at some frequency and for some duration.

Biological Reactions

In traumatic situations a variety of biological processes are activated. Pupils of the eyes dilate, the heart beats faster, the rate of breathing increases, blood flow increases and is redirected to the muscles for quick movement. These are the reactions of the sympathetic nervous system (SNS) which prepares people for action – flight or fight. But when it is not possible to fight or to flee, the other response is submission. In this instance, the reactions of the parasympathetic nervous system (PNS) are to decrease heart rate and respiration, lower blood pressure, and so on, such that in extreme situations individuals go into a state of stupor called tonic immobility. When in this state conscious recognition of events is maintained, along with associated sensations and emotions. It is thought that this is an instinctive survival mechanism that evolved to protect us in times of danger (Konner, 2007), as tonic immobility may fool predators into not taking further action or (in a more contemporary scenario) it may convince a gunman to walk on.

These reactions are controlled by the brain's limbic system or, more specifically, the amygdala (the brain's 'gatekeeper' for incoming emotional information). In normal circumstances information is passed from the amygdala to the frontal cortex, such that people can process what is happening and create memories. In threatening situations, however, it is thought the amygdala passes information directly to the hypothalamus (the cortical memory centre), releasing chemicals that stimulate the fight or flight response (or tonic immobility) but that circumvent the normal route to learning and the storage of memories. As such, one's memory for events that occur during trauma can be impaired, yet the trauma-related information remains in an active state, awaiting processing. PTSD is therefore seen as a disorder of information processing.

Traumatic Survival

People who survive traumatic events are likely to remain in a high state of alert, experiencing vivid intrusive but unprocessed images and thoughts, until the body's fear system is deactivated and they are able to engage again in normal processing (Joseph, 2011). For most survivors of traumatic events this return to normal processing takes place fairly quickly such that on average, only 8–12% of people exposed to traumatic events – and around a fifth to a quarter of people involved in profoundly traumatic experiences – ever reach the diagnostic threshold for PTSD (Bonanno, Brewin, Kaniasty, & La Greca, 2010). But even for those who do go on to develop PTSD, only a minority will experience a long lasting form of the disorder. Most will be relatively symptom free within six months to a year. With those for whom PTSD remains a problem, around fifty percent will respond well to psychological treatment (Bradley, Greene, Russ, Dutra, & Westen, 2005).

A typical reaction amongst trauma survivors is avoidance. That is, people will often attempt to stay away from reminders, not talk about what happened, and so on. This typically prolongs PTSD as such behaviours prevent the person from processing upsetting memories. As such psychological treatments that have been shown to be most effective in helping those with severe and chronic PTSD typically involve some form of exposure-based training to help the person engage with their memories (Foa, Keane, Friedman, & Cohen, 2008).

Acute and Sub-Acute Forms of Trauma

Trauma is not a monolithic experience. According to Whitfield (2010), even at its extremes (i.e. post-traumatic stress disorder; PTSD), trauma has several variants insofar as individuals fulfill criteria outlined in the DSM-5. Whilst detailing the various forms of acute (severe) trauma (such as Classical PTSD and Complex PTSD) is beyond the scope of this chapter, most are typified by profound disorientation (often to the point of losing a sense of self) and are accompanied by a mixture of dissociation, relationship difficulties, somatisation, re-victimisation, and extreme affective disruption (Briere, 2002; Saakvitne, Tennen, & Affleck, 1998; Thompson & Walsh, 2010; Whitfield, 2010). A factor that most obviously mediates the relationship between devastating life experiences and traumatic reactions is the strength and clarity of one's memories. That is, the more vividly one recalls traumatic past events (and remains aware of them), the more accutely traumatised they will be and the more DSM-5 criteria they will meet.

Given the context of this discussion (i.e. coaching), it seems useful to consider what might be thought of as sub-acute forms of trauma. By this we mean types of distressing, uncomfortable experiences that have significance for people, whilst not necessarily pushing them to the extremes usually encountered by those diagnosed with PTSD. Such experiences might include (but not be limited to) job loss or redundancy, social exclusion and disadvantage, denial of justice, organisational change, prolonged unemployment, breeches of trust or any other intensely troubling experience that may lead to an insidious degradation of psychological health over time. Notably, some attention has recently been drawn towards such experiences, albeit within the context of organisational life (Hall, 2015b).

At this point it is pertinent to note that trauma does not reside *in* adverse events per se. Rather, as proposed by transactional models of stress and coping (e.g. Lazarus & Folkman, 1984), human responses to stressful events are mediated by two subjective appraisals; one related to the level of threat and the other to one's perceived ability to deal successfully with that threat. Restated in terms relevant to the current discussion, the degree to which one experiences trauma will emerge from a *transaction* between a potential trauma event (PTE; e.g. death of a spouse) and how the person appraises that event (Garland, 2007; Garland, Gaylord, & Fredrickson, 2011). According to existentialists like Frankl (1985), how one ascribes meaning to such events is critical to how well one will cope. When understood this way, people are never consigned to their fate because they possess the (greatest) freedom to choose what things will mean to them (Frankl, 1985).

LIVING IN THE AFTERMATH OF ADVERSITY: THE HETEROGENUITY OF RESPONSES

Bonanno and Mancini (2012) note that not everyone reacts the same way when confronted by periods of great hardship and adversity (such as sexual abuse, torture or the death of a child). Whilst one might easily imagine that survivors of terrorist attacks (such as the September 11th attacks) would develop acute PTSD in the aftermath of such experiences, it appears this is not inevitable. For example, DiGrande et al. (2011) reported that PTSD prevalence rates were greater among 9/11 survivors (36%) than the general population within 6 months of the attacks (and only 17% after 12 months). Even though these rates are notably lower than for other terrorist attacks (which, the authors suggest, may possibly be because 9/11 survivors did not fully understand the extreme danger), this data still suggests that around 64% of suvivors were able to deal with their experiences in ways that were not profoundly debilitating.

According to Bonanno (2008), PTSD (or chronic dysfunction) receives a disproportionate amount of scholarly attention, despite it only being one potential reaction to trauma. Other potential reactions, with distinct functional trajectories, include *delayed reactions*, *recovery* and *resilience* (Bonanno & Mancini, 2012), each of which is briefly described below. To this a fourth trajectory can be added; *posttraumatic growth* (Calhoun & Tedeschi, 2014) as this describes a process whereby the person is positively transformed by their encounter with adversity. See Table 22.1 for summary descriptions.

Delayed Reactions

The defining feature of this response is that – in the post-PTE period – the person initially displays only moderate disruption to normal functioning (i.e. subthreshold PTSD) that tends to worsen over time. According to Bonanno and Mancini (2012), this trajectory is part of a gradual decline in functioning, not something that emerges suddenly simply because (according to the traditional view) the person is no longer actively denying their circumstances.

Recovery

At first glance the notion of recovery seems relatively straightforward, implying a normalising period for people (post-PTE), whereby past losses in cogntive, emotional and behavioural functioning are gradually restored. Whilst intuitively satisfying, some construe 'recovery' from trauma and/or mental illness to be more than merely regaining what has previously been lost. One such perspective makes a distinction between clinical recovery and personal recovery (see Oades et al., 2009; Slade, 2009). In line with traditional views, *clinical recovery* refers to the gradual decline in caseness or average symptom levels (Bonanno & Mancini, 2012) or sustained remission, where the reduction of symptomology is accompanied by functional improvement (Slade et al., 2008).

In contrast, *personal recovery* refers to an individual process, whereby the person purposefully moves towards the construction of a preferred identity and a meaningful life (Oades et al., 2009). Notably, this conceptualisation of recovery is framed in terms of

Table 22.1 Common outcomes associated with adverse life events

Outcome	Description
Chronic dysfunction	The development of elevated and long-lasting pathological reactions to an adverse life event. Treatments often formulated based on DSM diagnostic criteria and are usually aimed at helping the person to stablise functioning by dealing with intrusive memories, negative cognitions and mood states, behavioural avoidance and variations in arousal and reactivity.
Delayed reactions	Involves the late onset of elevated pathological reactions. Whilst individuals may only experience mild to moderate reactions immediately post-PTE (due to denial or inhibition), these increase in severity over time and become more chronic in nature. The impact on the person are as for chronic dysfucntion, with late onset being the primary difference.
Recovery	Normal functioning temporarily gives way to threshold or subthreshold psychopathology (e.g. depression) before gradual improvement occurs towards pre-event levels. Recovery can be of two types. *Clinical recovery* involves the gradual decline in symptoms, or sustained remission. *Personal recovery* involves the process of moving towards a preferred identity and meaningful living.
Resilience	The ability to withstand an isolated, potentially highly disruptive event and maintain relatively stable, healthy levels of psychological and physical functioning. Whilst the event will be psychologically challenging, coping generally occurs without needing to change one's existing network of beliefs and assumptions.
Posttraumatic growth	A form of positive psychological change that results from 'finding' personal benefit in the aftermath of an adverse event(s). Cannot occur without first experiencing damage to one's assumptive world, as the 'growth' emanates from shifts one makes in making meaning of the world.

Sources: Bonanno (2008); Bonanno & Mancini (2012); Calhoun & Tedeschi (2014); Oades, Crowe & Ngayen (2009).

psychological growth and (contrary to more medicialised views of recovery) it assumes that mental health consumers are capable of actively participating in creating flourishing mental health. Proponents of this view argue (based on what mental health consumers report about recovery) that parallel recovery processes are possible and that 'growth and development is possible, despite symptoms of illness' (p. 27). As this notion of recovery is central to a coaching-oriented model of collaborative recovery (Oades et al., 2005), these themes will be further explored shortly.

Resilience

Whilst resilient and recovering individuals have often been considered to be the same (McFarlane & Yehuda, 1996), their experiences reflect quite different trajectories (Bonanno, 2008). Unlike recovery trajectories, which involve a movement *back toward* adaptive functioning (in the ways outlined above), resilience involves no such movement. Rather, resilient individuals are able to pass through highly disruptive events and maintain stable, healthy levels of psychological and physical functioning (Bonanno, 2008). Whilst they may initially experience some negative effects (e.g. restless sleep), over time resilient individuals tend to display a functional stability that requires no recapturing of loss functioning (as is the case with recovery).

According to Bonanno (2008) resilience to PTEs is much more common that many believe. He suggests that there has been a general underestimation of the human capacity for resilience and argues that trauma interventions (like critical incident stress de-briefing) in some circumstances might inadvertently pathologise normal reactions and interfere with a person's natural resilience processes (Schank, 1990). According to this line of reasoning, coaches may be best to focus on helping clients access natural reserves of resilience (through supportive gestures like normalising and de-stigmatising client reactions), rather than pursuing planned, structured psychological interventions. Whilst coaching continues to be identified as a means of promoting resilience (e.g. Lawton Smith, 2015), within a PTG coaching context, it is vitally important that coaches remain acutely aware of their ethical responsibilities and practice conscientiously within the boundaries of their competence and contractual obligations.

Posttraumatic Growth

An additional trajectory in the aftermath of trauma is posttraumatic growth (PTG), which refers to the long observed phenomenon of people experiencing positive changes following adversity (Tedeschi & Calhoun, 2004). Also studied under a number of alternative labels, such as adversarial growth (Joseph & Linley, 2005), perceived benefits (McMillen, 1999), stress-related growth (Park, 1998) and thriving (Saakvitne, Tennen & Affleck, 1998), PTG is generally considered a form of personality change (Joseph & Williams, 2005; Jayawickreme & Blackie, 2014) that occurs when:

> [An] individual [has] not only survived, but has experienced changes that are viewed as important, and that go beyond what was the previous status quo. Posttraumatic growth is not simply a return to baseline – it is an experience of improvement that for some persons is deeply profound. (Tedeschi & Calhoun, 2004, p.4)

Whilst the concept is intuitively appealing, the empirical evidence supporting PTG is somewhat mixed. For example, an early review of the PTG literature offered a tentative conclusion that PTG may be facilitated by a mixture of positive reinterpretation, acceptance coping, optimism, intrinsic religiosity and positive affect (Linley & Joseph, 2004). However, most PTG research has been conducted using self-report measures that ask respondents to recall how they have changed over a period of time since an event. This has led to calls for research that can distinguish between people's perception of growth (using measures such as the Posttraumatic Growth Inventory; Tedeschi & Calhoun, 1996) and their actual growth (using well-being based measures; Joseph & Linley, 2008). As a result, it is not clear that the extant body of literature on PTG applies to actual growth. Jayawickreme and Blackie (2014) raise similar methodological limitations, also noting that it is difficult to predict what promotes PTG and how interventions should be designed to cultivate it.

In sum, there does not yet appear to be a universally accepted method or approach to facilitating PTG and, as such, the methods outlined later in this chapter should be considered in the light of this conflicting empirical evidence. From a practice perspective this means that coaching for PTG should proceed somewhat cautiously and, at a minimum, be guided by a coherent theoretical foundation. As will be reviewed in the next section, the coaching literature does contain some guidance on this front, appearing to advocate for an approach that honours the autonomy of the client, validates their abilities, engenders a strong sense of hope and provides the space and time needed to bring new meaning of their experience.

COACHING THROUGH TROUBLING TIMES: SCHOLARLY LITERATURE

Although there is little theoretical or empirical work published on the topic of coaching through and beyond adversity, some useful contributions can be found in the scholarly coaching literature. What has been published can be clustered roughly into two categories. The first relates to the adversity associated with mental illness and how coaching may be used as part of either a treatment strategy (e.g. Campone, 2014), a prevention strategy (e.g. Ellis & Alisic, 2013), or within an approach that addresses both treatment and prevention. In regards to the latter, the Collaborative Recovery Model (CRM; Oades et al., 2005) is of some interest to the present discussion and will shortly be overviewed.

The second category situates coaching more within the domain of work and organisations and includes a recent edited volume on how coaching can be used during times of crisis and transformation (Hall, 2015b). Whilst this collection of work is not empirical in nature, it draws on practice-based reflection to argue that coaching has an important role to play in managing some of the most difficult issues faced by working adults. In the foreword of Hall (2015b), Bachkirova (2015) points out that 'existentialists say that crisis is inevitable and expecting life to be of the same shade all the time is naïve. Therefore, helping clients to live with and to learn from crisis would be a reasonable intention of a coach' (p. xi). Whilst empirical work within this category is much harder to find, we note the existence of work that is tangentially related, specifically the use of coaching for managing emotions at work (Cox & Patrick, 2012; Grant, 2007; Lawton Smith, 2015).

A) Coaching and the Treatment of Mental Illness

The use of coaching to augment health enhancement programs is now relatively widespread (see Wolver & Moore, this volume) with coaching utilised for issues such as the promotion of lifestyle change (e.g. Sahlen, Johansson, Nyström, & Lindholm, 2013) and for managing the challenges of chronic (physical) illnesses (McGonagle, Beatty, & Joffe, 2014). Whilst less widespread, coaching is also beginning to find its way into mental illness treatment protocols, both as a way of managing health issues that emerge from the presence of severe mental illnesses (e.g. obesity; Aschbrenner et al., 2015) and as a means of improving treatment plan adherence rates (Pomerantz, Toney, & Hill, 2010). Whilst the results from these studies generally find coaching to be efficacious in these contexts, a notable feature of these studies is that coaching tends to be relatively brief and delivered via telephone or other technology assisted means.

In a highly unusual case study reported by Campone (2014), a detailed account is provided (over 18 months) of the use of life coaching in the treatment of Jennifer; a 54-year old social worker living with dissociative identity disorder (DID). Commonly associated with severe physical or sexual childhood abuse, DID is extremely tricky to treat and is complicated by the fact that it is difficult to establish and maintain a working alliance due to the presence of deep distrust of others (Campone, 2014). Nonetheless, as part of a multi-component treatment plan (including psychotherapy and psychiatric medications), Jennifer participated in weekly coaching sessions for the initial purpose of improving interpersonal skills and stress management. Overall the inclusion of coaching support was reported to be highly successful, with the following factors seemingly important:

- The life coach (Paul) was a highly experienced practitioner (12 years in coaching) and licensed professional counsellor.
- Clear boundaries were established and maintained, with trauma work specifically ruled 'out of bounds' (p. 5) and left for psychotherapy sessions.
- The coach framed his role as Jennifer's thought partner and supporter for acquiring identified life skills.
- The coaching 'intervention' remained relatively straightforward throughout the process and much appeared to be gained from Paul being stable and consistent throughout, such that Jennifer had the regular experience of 'ordinary social experiences' (p. 7).
- As trust slowly built over time, the focus of coaching expanded to include the desire to write a book and speak publically about her early childhood traumas.

In this case, the inclusion of life coaching appeared to provide Jennifer with a valuable opportunity for switching her focus and considering a brighter possible future for herself. Backed by Paul's belief in her ability to attain her stated goals, Jennifer was able to make significant progress towards her goals, plus reported some softening of her beliefs about the danger posed by the men who came into her life. Campone (2014) concluded the case by stating, 'the presence of a disorder ... need not preclude an individual from coaching or the benefits of coaching. As with all coaching clients, those with a clinical disorder have unique needs as well as unique capabilities. Rather than an exclusionary principle, a more nuanced model for considering the suitability of a client for coaching may emerge as more data are gathered' (p. 12).

B) Coaching and the Enhancement of Emotional Capacities

As adversity draws heavily on a person's ability to understand and regulate their emotions, some acknowledgement should be given to the recent work reported on the use of 'emotion coaching'. This is relevant because the development of emotional skills is known to build resilience, which can, in turn, help to prevent future incidence of mental illness (see Lawton Smith, this volume). Examples of recent work in this area include the increasing use of *maternal emotion coaching* (MEC; Ellis & Alisic, 2013). This simply involves talking with children about emotions in ways that allow them to identify feelings and process emotions in relational settings, such that they gain clarity and understanding

(Havighurst et al., 2013). Pilot MEC data suggests that teaching parents basic skills in how to acknowledge and validate a child's emotions, plus offer guidance on how to manage intense negative emotions, is highly beneficial. For example, MEC has been found to be strongly related to better emotion regulation for traumatised children (Ellis & Alisic, 2013), and better emotional knowledge and skills have been reported for both parents and children in MEC trials using samples of both mothers (Havighurst et al, 2013) and fathers (Wilson, Havighurst, & Harley, 2014).

Emotion-focused coaching programs have also been studied in the work domain, with a focus more on emotional skills as they relate to work performance. For example, one early study by Grant (2007) reported that a 13-week coaching skills training program significantly increased goal-focused coaching skills but not emotional intelligence, leading to the conclusion that 'longer term and repeated interventions may be required to improve emotional intelligence'. In another study focused on the emotional skills of workers, Cox and Patrick (2012) used a combination of individual and group coaching (over a 12-month period) and reported that workers became better able to remain calm in emotional situations, with positive impacts on individual motivation and work performance.

As such, the purposeful use of coaching to enhance emotional management appears to be an area of some promise. Whilst these studies do not directly address the facilitation of PTG, they are tangentially related insofar as the self-awareness and self-knowledge they foster is likely to benefit adults and children when confronted with future PTEs.

C) Coaching and the Collaborative Recovery Model

The CRM has several features that suggest it might be the sort of 'more nuanced' coaching model called for by Campone (2014). First, the CRM is conceptualised as 'a form of person-centred strengths coaching' (Oades, Crowe & Nguyen, 2009, p.26). Second, it is substantially unlike most coaching models insofar as it focuses on the recovery experience of people living with enduring mental illness (such as schizophrenia). Finally, it explicitly identifies personal growth as a component of psychological recovery, by (as outlined earlier) making a distinction between clinical recovery and personal recovery. A brief overview of the philosopical and practical foundations of the CRM is presented in Table 22.2 below.

As mentioned, the CRM sits noticeably at odds with conventional views of coaching, which have tended to see coaching as an intervention for individuals residing at the non-clinical end of the mental health continuum (e.g. Williams, 2003; Bluckert, 2005). The reasoning behind this view tends to be that people who are living with clinical conditions (e.g. depression, anxiety disorders, etc) need clinical interventions, and coaching might inadvertently lead to a worsening of symptoms, particularly in circumstances where naïve, well-intentioned coaches might attempt to work beyond the boundaries of their knowledge and experience (Spence, Cavanagh, & Grant, 2006).

Such views also seem to carry an assumption that the functioning of someone with a mental health condition is so fundamentally compromised that coaching can be of little value (either because their cognitive capacity is impaired, or their motivation is inadequate). The CRM rejects any such assumption. Rather, it draws on arguments made within the recovery movement (Slade, 2009), which emphasise that personal growth and development can be achieved when living with mental illness, despite the presence of symptoms. Recognising the powerful effect that beliefs can have on action, Oades, Crowe and Nguyen (2009) noted that 'the challenge remains ... to change the mindset of staff and patients who have developed fixed mindsets about the abilities of patients. The existence

Table 22.2 Foundations of the Collaborative Recovery Model

Outcome	Description
Guiding Principle 1	*Recovery as an individual process* Stipulates that hope, meaning, identity and responsibility are integral to the process of psychological recovery, and that recovering individuals are capable of setting, pursuing and attaining personal goals that facilitate recovery.
Guiding Principle 2	*Collaboration and autonomy support* Stipulates the creation of conditions that optimise collaboration through the development of a solid working alliance that is autonomy supportive in all interactions and across all recovery protocols.
Component 1	*Change enhancement* Focuses on developing readiness for change by jointly working on: i) clarifying its importance, ii) exploring any ambivalence towards change, and iii) building confidence by identifying strengths, resources and what is manageable.
Component 2	*Collaborative strengths and values clarification* Focuses on developing greater awareness of personal values and strengths using the 'Camera', which asks them to list their values and strengths and then indicate how effectively they have recently been using them.
Component 3	*Collaborative visioning and goal striving* Focuses on development of an integrated, meaningful personal recovery vision using the 'Compass', which encourages people to set SMART goals (consistent with values identified via the Camera) at three alternative levels of attainment.
Component 4	*Collaborative action planning and monitoring* Focuses on systematically working through and agreeing (using the My Action Plan or 'MAP' tool) all key tasks, actions and system of monitoring progress. A documented trail of completed actions is retained to enhance self-efficacy.

Sources: Oades, Deane, Crowe, Lambert, Kavanagh & Lloyd (2005); Oades, Crowe & Nguyen (2009).

of a medical condition is not being questioned here, rather the assumptions around the person's abilities with the medical condition' (p. 27).

Collaborative Goal Technology

As indicated in Table 22.2, central to any application of the CRM are a set of tools designed to build hope, meaning, identity and responsibility. Referred to as Life Journey Enhancement Tools (LifeJET; Oades & Crowe, 2008), each tool seeks to aid collaboration at every step, in the firm belief that the mental health consumer will be able to participate fully in exercises designed to identify personal values and strengths (the *Camera*), set goals and encourage goal striving (the *Compass*), and form action plans and monitor progress (the *MAP*). As these processes are generic to most coaching programs (Grant & Greene, 2003), the LifeJET tools strongly identify the CRM as a coaching model.

Research into the CRM

A notable feature of the CRM is that it permits the development of both individual and systemic level interventions. Whilst some research has been reported on its use with individual mental health consumers (e.g. Clarke, Oades, Crowe, Caputi, & Deane, 2009), much of the research has been focused at the level of health systems. This approach has been based on the assumption that training mental health providers in the CRM should increase empathy for consumers undergoing a recovery process, whilst helping to explicitly transfer recovery training into routine practice (Crowe, this volume). Whilst the use of CRM training has been found to improve mental health workers' knowledge and attitudes towards recovery (Crowe, Deane, Oades, Caputi, & Morland, 2006) and the quality of post-training goal and action planning (Clarke, Crowe, Oades, & Deane, 2009), CRM implementation has been found to be inhibited by a variety of organisational constraints, lack of client responsiveness and poor clinician self-management (Uppal, Oades, Crowe, & Deane, 2010). Encouragingly, when training in the coaching-based CRM was supported by 12 monthly coaching sessions (designed to address implementation problems), significant improvements in the quality of care planning in accordance with the model (Deane et al., 2014).

D) Coaching and Times of Crisis for Working Adults

In an edited volume dedicated to the use of coaching during times of crisis and transformation, Hall (2015a) uses the lotus flower as a metaphor for introducing the topic of post-crisis growth. She notes, 'without the mud, the lotus flower can't exist – the mud provides the nourishment for the lotus plant to grow and bloom' (p. 50). Whilst the author is quick to acknowledge that the idea behind the metaphor is not new (as it is widely recognised within an array of scholarly disciplines, cultures and faith communities), it is unusual to see the idea paired with coaching in such a substantial way.

Coaching is commonly described by authors as being an important source of support and encouragement to clients during difficult and challenging times (Hall, 2015b). However, relatively few attempts have been made to understand the precise nature of these 'negative' experiences and how coaching can help to maximise the benefits that may accrue from them. Whilst the book does not necessarily make substantial theoretical or empirical contributions (constructed, as it is, around an array of themed chapters, case studies and practitioner interviews), it does raise many interesting questions that may become catalysts for future theory and research. There are, for example, questions that can be posed about the transformative experiences of coachees. What types of crises produce the greatest growth and transformation in coaching? What relational conditions are most suitable for facilitating growth and transformation? In addition, questions can also be posed about the transformative experiences of coaches. For example, what (if any) forms of vicarious posttraumatic growth do coaches gain from supporting clients in crisis? What negative effects may there be?

The preceding sections have shown that coaching is currently being used (in a limited way) to supplement efforts to manage mental ill-health (Campone, 2014; Oades et al, 2005), enhance emotional capacities (Cox & Patrick, 2012; Ellis & Alisic, 2013), and support adults through times of crisis and transition (Hall, 2015b). In the final section of this chapter, two further questions will be explored. First, is coaching an appropriate intervention for people who are experiencing trauma? If so, when is it appropriate and for whom? Second, assuming that PTG is a genuine psychological phenomena, how is coaching best configured in order for PTG to occur? We will conclude with some suggestions for further research.

IS COACHING AN APPROPRIATE INTERVENTION FOR PEOPLE EXPERIENCING TRAUMA?

For many in the coaching industry, the notion that coaching might be an appropriate response for facilitating recovery from trauma would be most unacceptable. According to many authors, clients dealing with trauma fall at the 'clinical' (or unhealthy) end of the mental health continuum, rendering them unsuitable for coaching. Simply put, 'coaching is not therapy' (Bluckert, 2005; Williams,

2003). This statement has become something of a mantra within the coaching literature over the past two decades and has been expressed in many different ways. For example, whilst drawing a distinction between skills, performance and developmental forms of coaching, Grant (2005) states:

> Developmental coaching is rather like 'therapy for people who do not need therapy' and often involves the creation of a personal reflective space where the client can explore issues and options and formulate action plans in a confidential, supportive environment. (p.4)

The question of how much coaching is 'rather like' therapy (or counselling) has been regularly explored in the past. Indeed, many attempts have been made to clarify and maintain a clear separation between coaching and its more clinical counterparts. A host of authors have lent their voice to this effort, and included reviews that summarise their convergences and divergences (e.g. Spinelli, 2010; Blucket, 2005), with occasional 'boundary' studies that have sought to build clarity from data collected from practicing coaches (e.g. Price, 2009; Maxwell, 2009; Hart, Blattner & Leipsic, 2001). Whilst authors have repeatedly identified similar lists of distinguishing characteristics, and some have made forceful claims about 'vast differences' and 'solid delineations' (Williams, 2003), many continue to point to the existence of a 'fuzzy space' (Jopling, 2007). The view of several authors in this literature is that the formal preparation of coaches should include a psychologically-oriented syllabus and/or therapeutic training (Maxwell, 2009; Price, 2009; Spence et al., 2006). Bachirova and Cox (2005) go one step further by proposing a process model that bridges the fields, via a coaching process model that takes account of counseling theories. In so doing, they address the 'forced estrangement' of one from the other, which appears to have been promoted mainly by those who do not have formal psychological training, and resisted by those who do.

The Acutualising Tendency and the Client-Centred Approach

Indeed, at the meta-theoretical level coaching and counselling are very similar, insofar as both are based on the goal of maximising the potential of the client. As Stober and Grant (2006) note, whilst contemporary coaching practice has drawn from many different disciplines and traditions, the work of humanistic psychologists like Carl Rogers have been particularly prevalent (for a discussion see Stober, 2006). A prominent example is his notion of an actualising tendency (AT; Rogers, 1942). A common metaphor used to describe the AT is the acorn, a nut that contains within it all the potential to become a magnificent oak tree. As an acorn requires nourishment to release the 'oaktreeness' that is already within, human beings require the support of their basic needs if they are to realise their potential (Joseph, 2015).

The notion of the actualising tendency seems to be, in some form or other, at the core of many approaches to coaching (Kauffman, Joseph, & Scoular, 2015). More specifically, the notion of developmental coaching (Grant, 2005) seems to be synonymous with what Rogers was referring to as counselling. For Rogers, counselling was best to be non-directive, with the therapist's task to follow the client's lead, rather than directing the course of therapy by using interpretative methods or reinforcement schedules. He focused on the reflection of feelings in such a way as to shift the direction of sessions, with the therapist following the client and helping them to uncover their own solutions. In this way, therapists were able to help clients understand for themselves what they needed and how to move forward in life – a very similar idea to what we now refer to as coaching (see Stober, 2006).

Whilst many coaches may not be familiar with the basics of Rogerian theory, they may be aware of Self-Determination theory (SDT: Deci & Ryan, 2008), which is a more recent theory founded on Rogerian ideas (Patterson &

Joseph, 2007) and has been proposed as a useful theoretical foundation for coaching (see Spence & Deci, 2013). In brief, SDT proposes that the support and satisfaction of three basic psychological needs (autonomy, relatedness and competence) are critical to optimising human functioning. In SDT, it is hypothesised that when these basic needs are satisfied people's intrinsic motivation towards growth and positive change is promoted. One of the most prominent theories of posttraumatic growth – the organismic valuing theory (OVP) is a synthesis of Rogers' theory and SDT (Joseph & Linley, 2005). OVP theory posits three things. First, that people are intrinsically motivated towards PTG. Second, that posttraumatic stress is a normal and natural process that can trigger growth. Third, that growth will be facilitated by the satisfaction of basic psychological needs (Joseph & Linley, 2005, p. 269).

HOW IS COACHING BEST CONFIGURED IN ORDER FOR PTG TO OCCUR?

The vast majority of trauma theories and models seek to help individuals cope better with their trauma symptoms and return, as closely as possible, to a pre-trauma level of functioning. For example, the self-trauma model (Briere, 2002) uses exposure techniques to desensitise clients to traumatic material and build upon coping techniques they are already having success with. In contrast, somatic trauma theory (Rothschild, 2003) is more eclectic and its therapies use an array of psychophysiological techniques to reduce the frequency and intensity of flashbacks and improve regulation of hyperarousal. A client who is suffering from intense PTSD will find it difficult to engage in talking therapies or coaching until they are able to process their memories, which can be helped with behavioural techniques and exposure therapy. However, once they are able to talk about their experiences without becoming blocked by avoidance or overwhelmed by intrusions, then coaching for PTG may be considered.

The Importance of 'Telling and Hearing Stories'

Very few trauma theories appear to consider what lies beyond client stabilisation and the recovery of baseline functioning. One exception is constructivist self-development theory (CDST; Saakvitne et al., 1998). CDST focuses on the resumption of personality development in the aftermath of trauma, proposing that growth and pain are not mutually exclusive, but rather 'inextricably linked in recovery from trauma and loss' (p.295). As such, the goals of this insight-oriented therapy are then to facilitate: i) the creation of meaning through the construction of expanded personal narratives (that include traumatic events), and ii) the development of intrapersonal capacities (such as mindfulness) that permit the person to persist with this developmental process. Notably, CDST and the CRM (reviewed earlier) share a similar assumption about client capability (i.e. that they are able to engage in a parallel 'recovery' processes), and CDST also shares conceptual overlap with other theories of PTG (e.g. Tedeschi, Park, & Calhoun, 1998).

As indicated in CSDT, the importance of personal narratives appears to be particularly important in facilitating PTG. According to Joseph (2011), the process of *re-authoring* (White & Epston, 1990) is a critical stage on the path to PTG. He proposes the importance of 'listen[ing] to the stories you tell yourself and open[ing] up to new ways of looking at things. It is here that you begin to move from thinking of yourself as a victim to thinking of yourself as a survivor, and then a thriver' (pp. 175–176). Thus, glimpsing the opportunity to grow is the first step in cultivating the growth mindset. Once established, Joseph (2011) recommends that methods such as metaphor use and expressive writing (along with verbal story telling) be used to facilitate re-authoring.

Fortunately, narrative methods and techniques are not foreign to coaching (Drake, 2007), with well developed articulations of the approach available in the literature (Drake, 2015). Whilst the re-authoring, or reconfiguration (Drake, 2015), of personal narratives is not the only ingredient deemed necessary for PTG to occur (Joseph, 2011), it does appear to be a vital component for moving beyond the psychological shattering of trauma and developing a new assumptive world (that includes the traumatic experience). For this work a relevant theoretical perspective is extremely useful and, in our view, Rogers' (1951) person-centred theory and SDT (Deci & Ryan, 1985) are highly instructive. Both share an orientation towards understanding of how people become fully functioning, which includes being well psychologically adjusted, authentic, and open to experience (Rogers, 1951).

Organismic Valuing and Facilitating Posttraumatic Growth

As mentioned, OVP theory (Joseph & Linley, 2005) synthesises ideas from both Rogers and SDT to suggest that people are intrinsically motivated towards PTG, that posttraumatic stress is a normal and natural process that can trigger growth, and that whilst growth is not inevitable, it can be facilitated by the satisfaction of basic psychological needs. As such, coaches can promote PTG insofar as they are able to support the coachees needs for autonomy, competence and relatedness. In terms of the skills necessary to do this, it is important that the coach is first and foremost able to successfully convey an attitude of unconditional acceptance as only then will the coachee feel sufficiently supported by the coach to change in whatever way is most appropriate to them. If the coachee perceives that they are not accepted unconditionally by the coach their sense of autonomy and their ability to talk openly with the coach will be restricted. Once such a relationship with the coachee exists, the coach may find it useful to share ideas and information on some of the exercises that can be growth promoting, such as how to harvest hope, and identify and value change (Joseph, 2011).

Whilst the use of these non-directive, client-centred, developmental coaching techniques may not be the natural choice of all coaches (e.g. skills coaches), they appear to have particular relevance for clients who are emerging from periods of crisis and trauma (Hall, 2015a). This is because, by definition, PTG must come from within the client so attempts to steer the client towards growth can be self-defeating as each person's trajectory for growth will have its own idiosyncratic pace and direction. Helping clients to re-author their experiences (Drake, 2015; Joseph, 2011) is, in effective, an active search for meaning (Frankl, 1985). When fully engaged, the coaching relationship can assist people to seek and find their own solutions and, with it, the facilitation of PTG.

Should Coaches Attempt to Facilitate PTG?

It is almost certain that coaches already participate in the facilitation of PTG, although this may not be always be known (Lawton Smith, 2015). The mere act of talking to a skilled practitioner about difficult and challenging personal issues is likely to be inherently therapeutic for most people and, as clearly indicated in Hall (2015b), is common place in coaching.

Of course, more acute forms of trauma present coaches with a number of challenges, which invoke predictable questions about boundaries and level of professional competence. Clearly those with Complex PTSD or other variants need specialised assistance, not merely to manage symptoms but also to navigate the cognitive challenges that trauma presents (Joseph, 2011). However, the mere presence of distress should not be viewed as a reason not to engage a coaching client. After all, most people would agree that *depressing* is part of a normal, adaptive response to a devastating life event (like the death of a loved one). Given its 'normality', why should coaches treat this as something that sits outside of coaching? Leaving aside boundaries of competence (which should inform all decisions about when and with whom one coaches), why should a natural reaction to extraordinary circumstances be excluded from the remit of a coach?

Fortunately models now exist to guide such work, such as Joseph's (2011) 6-step THRIVE model. Designed as a self-help tool, THRIVE has potential application within coaching contexts as it details a number of 'signposts' that seem important for the emergence of PTG. These include:

1. *Taking Stock*. Involves tuning in to one's psychological, physical and social realities, and gathering and utilising resources that serve the person well and help to stabilise functioning. In extreme situations, this may involve counselling or therapy (as described earlier).
2. *Harvesting Hope*. Involves developing habits of mind that help to glimpse opportunities for growth.
3. *Re-authoring*. Involves the construction of new personal narratives, that include past traumatic events, and build new networks of beliefs about self, others and the world.
4. *Identifying change*. Involves spotting moments where desired changes are present (e.g. using a diary) or strengths are being displayed.
5. *Valuing change*. Involves placing some personal significance to the change being pursued (i.e. why it matters), which can also help to evoke the new narrative.
6. *Expressing change in action*. Involves the articulation of actions into concrete terms, which can help to make the growth real.

Whilst many of the THRIVE steps outlined above are reflected in other recovery-oriented coaching models (such as the CRM; Oades et al., 2005), and many generic coaching models (e.g. Grant & Greene, 2003), it represents a useful starting position for coaching as it uniquely addresses the aftermath of trauma and adversity.

RESEARCH DIRECTIONS

Whilst people are remarkably resilient in the face of adversity (Bonanno, 2008), most people will experience at least one traumatic event during their lifetime (if not more). As such, this is a strong likelihood that coaches will (or have) work(ed) with traumatised people but be unaware that they are doing so. We believe that a sound understanding of PTG has the potential to enhance coaching practice across the industry. Like many areas in coaching, research into this topic is sorely needed. Possible questions for guiding future research include:

- How prevalent is trauma in coaching clients?
- To what extent do coaches understand trauma, its psychological dimensions and the functional trajectories described earlier in this chapter?
- What do coaches currently do when they encounter clients experiencing emotional difficulties? To what extent do they feel a professional obligation to work towards facilitating PTG?
- Does coaching help facilitate PTG? If so, what forms of coaching work best?
- Can the THRIVE model be used as a useful model for facilitating PTG?
- What psychological processes are particularly important for facilitating PTG? For example, as suggested by OVP theory, is it the support and satisfaction of basic needs (e.g. autonomy, belongingness) that leads to positive outcomes?

Given the paucity of research related to this topic, a variety of different research designs and methods could be envisaged (in response to specific research questions). These might include qualitative projects for assessing coach and coachee experiences in coaching, quantitative projects for assessing the efficacy of specific PTG coaching formulations (e.g. THRIVE), or case studies or other mixed methods projects that enable the assembly of rich, textured data sets.

CONCLUSION

In this chapter we have explored the concept of post-traumatic growth and examined whether it is an appropriate focus for coaching. Whilst the review has shown that people have an extraordinary capacity to be resilient in the most difficult of circumstances, it has also shown that people appear capable of enormous growth as they pass through traumatic experiences. As noted, the coaching literature is showing some signs of accommodating PTG within coaching practice (e.g. Campone, 2014; Oades et al., 2005). Indeed, it is our conclusion that the presence of traumatic aftereffects (e.g. depression, sadness, anxiety) are not, in itself, an impediment to coaching, provided that the coach has the requisite knowledge and experience to appropriately support the client's needs. However, if coaches are to better understand and facilitate PTG, there is a need for researchers to explore questions related to its prevalence in coaching, its psychological dimensions, and its facilitating factors. We hope that researchers interested in this area will benefit from the ideas that have been explored.

REFERENCES

American Psychiatric Association. (2013). *Diagnostic and Statistical Manual of Mental Disorders (DSM-5)*. Washington, DC: APA.

Aschbrenner, K. A., Naslund, J. A., Barre, L. K., Mueser, K. T., Kinney, A., & Bartels, S. J. (2015). Peer health coaching for overweight and obese individuals with serious mental illness: intervention development and initial feasibility study. *Translational Behavioral Medicine, 1–8, 5*(3), 277–284.

Bachkirova, T. (2015). Foreward. In L. Hall (Ed.), *Coaching in Times of Crisis and Transformation: How to Help Individuals and Organizations Flourish* (pp. xi–xii). London: Kogan Page.

Bachkirova, T., & Cox, E. (2005). A bridge over troubled water. *Counselling at Work* (Spring), 2–9.

Bluckert, P. (2005). The similarities and differences between coaching and therapy. *Industrial and Commercial Training, 37*(2), 91–96.

Bonanno, G. A. (2008). Loss, trauma, and human resilience: Have we underestimated the human capacity to thrive after extremely aversive events? *Psychological Trauma: Theory, Research, Practice, and Policy, S*(1), 101–113.

Bonanno, G. A., Brewin, C. R., Kaniasty, K., & La Greca, A. M. (2010). Weighing the costs of disaster consequences, risks, and resilience in individuals, families, and communities. *Psychological Science in the Public Interest, 11*(1), 1–49.

Bonanno, G. A., & Mancini, A. D. (2012). Beyond resilience and PTSD: Mapping the heterogeneity of responses to potential trauma. *Psychological Trauma: Theory, Research, Practice, and Policy, 4*(1), 74–83.

Bradley, R., Greene, J., Russ, E., Dutra, L., & Westen, D. (2005). A multidimensional meta-analysis of psychotherapy for PTSD. *American Journal of Psychiatry, 162*(2), 214–227.

Briere, J. (2002). Treating adult survivors of severe childhood abuse and neglect: Further development of an integrative model. In J. E. B. Myers, L. Berliner, J. Briere, C. T. Hendrix, T. Reid & C. Jenny (Eds.), *The APSAC Handbook of Child Maltreatement* (pp. 175–202). Newbury Park, CA: Sage.

Calhoun, L. G., & Tedeschi, R. G. (Eds.). (2014). *Handbook of Posttraumatic Growth: Research and Practice*. London: Routledge.

Campone, F. (2014). At the border: coaching a client with dissociative identity disorder. *International Journal of Evidence-Based Coaching and Mentoring, 12*(1), 1–13.

Carol, J. (2004). *Journeys of Courage: Remarkable Stories of the Healing Power of Community*. Dublin: Sorin Books.

Clarke, S. P., Crowe, T. P., Oades, L. G., & Deane, F. P. (2009). Do goal-setting interventions improve the quality of goals in mental health services? *Psychiatric Rehabilitation Journal*, *32*(4), 292–299.

Clarke, S. P., Oades, L. G., Crowe, T. P., Caputi, P., & Deane, F. P. (2009). The role of symptom distress and goal attainment in promoting aspects of psychological recovery for consumers with enduring mental illness. *Journal of Mental Health*, *18*(5), 389–397.

Cox, E., & Patrick, C. (2012). Managing emotions at work: How coaching affects retail support workers' performance and motivation. *International Journal of Evidence Based Coaching & Mentoring*, *10*(2), 34–51.

Crowe, T. P., Deane, F. P., Oades, L. G., Caputi, P., & Morland, K. G. (2006). Effectiveness of a collaborative recovery training program in Australia in promoting positive views about recovery. *Psychiatric Services*, *57*(10), 1497–1500.

Deane, F. P., Andresen, R., Crowe, T. P., Oades, L. G., Ciarrochi, J., & Williams, V. (2014). A comparison of two coaching approaches to enhance implementation of a recovery-oriented service model. *Administration and Policy in Mental Health and Mental Health Services Research*, *41*(5), 660–667.

Deci, E. L., & Ryan, R. M. (1985). *Intrinsic Motivation and Self-determination in Human Behavior*. New York: Plenum Press.

Deci, E. L., & Ryan, R. M. (2008). Self-determination theory: A macrotheory of human motivation, development, and health. *Canadian Psychology*, *49*(3), 182–185.

DiGrande, L., Neria, Y., Brackbill, R. M., Pulliam, P., & Galea, S. (2011). Long-term post-traumatic stress symptoms among 3,271 civilian survivors of the September 11, 2001, terrorist attacks on the World Trade Center. *American Journal of Epidemiology*, *173*(3), 271–281.

Drake, D. B. (2007). The art of thinking narratively: Implications for coaching psychology and practice. *Australian Psychologist*, *42*(4), 283–294.

Drake, D. B. (2015). *Narrative Coaching: Bringing Our New Stories to Life*. Petaluma, CA: CNC Press.

Ellis, B. H., & Alisic, E. (2013). Maternal emotion coaching: A protective factor for traumatized children's emotion regulation? *Journal of Child and Adolescent Trauma*, *6*, 118–125.

Foa, E. B., Keane, T. M., Friedman, M. J., & Cohen, J. A. (2008). *Effective Treatments for PTSD: Practice Guidelines from the International Society for Traumatic Stress Studies*. New York: Guilford Press.

Frankl, V. E. (1985). *Man's Search for Meaning*. New York: Simon and Schuster.

Garland, E. L. (2007). The meaning of mindfulness: A second-order cybernetics of stress, metacognition, and coping. *Journal of Evidence-Based Complementary & Alternative Medicine*, *12*(1), 15–30.

Garland, E. L., Gaylord, S. A., & Fredrickson, B. L. (2011). Positive reappraisal mediates the stress-reductive effects of mindfulness: An upward spiral process. *Mindfulness*, *2*(1), 59–67.

Grant, A. M. (2005). What is evidence-based executive, workplace and life coaching. In M. J. Cavanagh, A. M. Grant & T. Kemp (Eds.), *Evidence-Based Coaching: Theory, Research and Practice from the Behavioural Sciences* (Vol. 1, pp. 1–12). Bowen Hills, QLD: Australian Academic Press.

Grant, A. M. (2007). Enhancing coaching skills and emotional intelligence through training. *Industrial and Commercial Training*, *39*(5), 257–266.

Grant, A. M., & Greene, J. (2003). *Coach yourself: Make real changes in your life*. Cambridge, MA: Basic Books.

Hall, L. (2015a). No mud, no lotus? Crisis as a catalyst for transformation. In L. Hall (Ed.), *Coaching in Times of Crisis and Transformation: How to Help Individuals and Organizations Flourish* (pp. 50–69). London: Kogan Page.

Hall, L. (Ed.). (2015b). *Coaching in Times of Crisis and Transformation: How to Help Individuals and Organisations Flourish*. London: Kogan Page.

Hart, V., Blattner, J., & Leipsic, S. (2001). Coaching versus therapy: A perspective. *Consulting Psychology Journal: Practice and Research*, *53*(4), 229–237.

Havighurst, S. S., Wilson, K. R., Harley, A. E., Kehoe, C., Efron, D., & Prior, M. R. (2013). Reducing young children's behavior problems using an emotion coaching parenting program. *Child Psychiatry & Human Development*, *44*(2), 247–264.

Jayawickreme, E., & Blackie, L. E. (2014). Posttraumatic Growth as Positive Personality Change: Evidence, Controversies and Future Directions. *European Journal of Personality*, *28*(4), 312–331.

Jopling, A. (2007). *Exploring the experience of space between psychotherapy and executive coaching (MSC Dissertation)* New School of Psychotherapy and Counselling. London.

Joseph, S. (2006). Person-centred coaching psychology: a meta-theoretical perspective. *International Coaching Psychology Review*, *1*, 47–54.

Joseph, S. (2011). *What Doesn't Kill Us: The New Psychology of Posttraumatic Growth*. New York: Basic Books.

Joseph, S. (2015). *Positive Therapy: Building Bridges Between Positive Psychology and Person-Centred Psychotherapy* (2nd ed.). London: Routledge.

Joseph, S., & Linley, A. (2005). Positive adjustment to threatening events: An organismic valuing theory of growth through adversity. *Review of General Psychology*, 262–280.

Joseph, S., & Linley, P. A. (2008). Psychological assessment of growth following adversity: A review. In S. Joseph & P. A. Linley (Eds.), *Trauma, recovery, and growth: Positive psychological perspectives on posttraumatic stress* (pp. 21–38). Hoboken, NJ: Wiley & Sons.

Joseph, S., & Williams, R. (2005). Understanding posttraumatic stress: Theory, reflections, context and future. *Behavioural and Cognitive Psychotherapy*, *33*(4), 423–442.

Kauffman, C., Joseph, S., & Scoular, A. (2015). Leadership coaching and positive psychology. In S. Joseph (Ed.), *Positive Psychology in Practice: Promoting Human Flourishing in Work, Health, Education, and Everyday Life* (2nd ed., pp. 377–390). Hoboken: NJ: Wiley & Sons.

Konner, M. (2007). Trauma, adaptation and resilience: A cross-cultural and evolutionary perspective. In L. J. Kirmayer, R. Lemelson & M. Barad (Eds.), *Understanding Trauma: Integrating Biological, Clinical, and Cultural Perspectives* (pp. 300–338). Cambridge: Cambridge University Press.

Lawton Smith, C. (2015). How coaching helps leadership resilience: The leadership perspective. *International Coaching Psychology Review*, *10*(1), 6–19.

Lazarus, R. S., & Folkman, S. (1984). *Stress, Appraisal and Coping*. New York: Springer.

Levine, P. A. (2010) *In an unspoken voice: How the body releases trauma and restores goodness*. Berkeley, CA: North Atlantic Books.

Linley, P. A., & Joseph, S. (2004). Positive change following trauma and adversity: A review *Journal of Traumatic Stress*, *17*(1), 11–21.

Maxwell, A. (2009). How do business coaches experience the boundary between coaching and therapy/counselling? *Coaching: An International Journal of Theory, Research and Practice*, *2*(2), 149–162.

McFarlane, A. C., & Yehuda, R. A. (1996). Resilience, vulnerability, and the course of posttraumatic reactions. In B. A. van der Kolk, A. C. McFarlane & L. Weisaeth (Eds.), *Traumatic Stress: The Effects of Overwhelming Experience on Mind, Body and Society* (pp. 155–181). New York: Guilford Press.

McGonagle, A. K., Beatty, J. E., & Joffe, R. (2014). Coaching for workers with chronic illness: Evaluating an intervention. *Journal of Occupational Health Psychology*, *19*(3), 385–398.

McMillen, J. C. (1999). Better for it: How people benefit from adversity. *Social Work*, *44*(5), 455–468.

Oades, L. G., & Crowe, T. P. (2008). *Life Journey Enhancement Tools (Life JET)*: Illawarra Institute for Mental Health, University of Wollongong.

Oades, L. G., Crowe, T. P., & Nguyen, M. (2009). Leadership coaching transforming mental health systems from the inside out: The Collaborative Recovery Model as person-centred strengths based coaching psychology. *International Coaching Psychology Review*, *4*(1), 25–36.

Oades, L. G., Deane, F., Crowe, T., Lambert, W. G., Kavanagh, D., & Lloyd, C. (2005). Collaborative recovery: An integrative model for working with individuals who experience chronic and recurring mental illness. *Australasian Psychiatry*, *13*(3), 279–284.

Park, C. L. (1998). Stress-related growth and thriving through coping: The roles of personality and cognitive processes. *Journal of Social Issues*, *54*(2), 267–277.

Patterson, T., & Joseph, S. (2007). Person-centered personality theory: Support from self-determination theory and positive psychology. *Journal of Humanistic Psychology, 47,* 117–139.

Pomerantz, J. I., Toney, S. D., & Hill, Z. J. (2010). Care coaching: an alternative approach to managing comorbid depression. *Professional Case Management, 15*(3), 137–142.

Price, J. (2009). The coaching/therapy boundary in organizational coaching. *Coaching: An International Journal of Theory, Research and Practice, 2*(2), 135–148.

Ringel, S., & Brandell, J. (2012). *Trauma: Contemporary Directions in Theory, Practice, and Research.* London: SAGE.

Rogers, C. R. (1942). *Counseling and Psychotherapy: Newer Concepts in Practice.* New York: Houghton Mifflin Co.

Rogers, C. R. (1951). *Client-Centred Therapy: Its Current Practice, Implications and Theory.* London: Constable & Company.

Rothschild, B. (2003). *The Body Remembers Casebook: Unifying Methods and Models in the Treatment of Trauma and PTSD.* New York: W.W. Norton & Company.

Saakvitne, K. W., Tennen, H., & Affleck, G. (1998). Exploring thriving in the context of clinical trauma theory: Constructivist self development theory. *Journal of Social Issues, 54*(2), 279–299.

Sahlen, K. G., Johansson, H., Nyström, L., & Lindholm, L. (2013). Health coaching to promote healthier lifestyle among older people at moderate risk for cardiovascular diseases, diabetes and depression: a study protocol for a randomized controlled trial in Sweden. *BMC Public Health, 13*(1), 199.

Schank, R. C. (1990). *Tell Me a Story: A New Look at Real and Artificial Memory.* New York: Charles Scribner's Sons.

Slade, M. (2009). *Personal Recovery and Mental Illness: A Guide for Mental Health Professionals.* Cambridge: Cambridge University Press.

Slade, M., Amering, M., & Oades, L. (2008). Recovery: an international perspective. *Epidemiologia e Psichiatria Sociale, 17*(2), 128–137.

Spence, G. B., Cavanagh, M. J., & Grant, A. M. (2006). Duty of care in an unregulated industry: Initial findings on the diversity and practices of Australian coaches. *International Coaching Psychology Review, 1*(1), 71–85.

Spence, G. B., & Deci, E. L. (2013). Self-determination with coaching contexts: Supporting motives and goals that prmote optimal functioning and well-being. In S. David, D. Clutterbuck & D. Megginson (Eds.), *Beyond Goals: Effective Strategies for Coaching and Mentoring* (pp. 85–108). Padstow, UK: Gower.

Spinelli, E. (2010). Coaching and therapy: Similarities and divergences. *Psychotherapy in Australia, 17*(1), 52–58.

Stiell, I. G., Nesbitt, L. P., Pickett, W., Munkley, D., Spaite, D. W., Banek, J., & Lyver, M. (2008). The OPALS Major Trauma Study: impact of advanced life-support on survival and morbidity. *Canadian Medical Association Journal, 178*(9), 1141–1152.

Stober, D. R. (2006). Coaching from the humanistic perspective. In A. M. Grant & D. R. Stober (Eds.), *Evidence-Based Coaching Handbook: Putting Best Practices to Work for your Clients* (pp. 17–51). New York: Wiley & Sons.

Stober, D. R., & Grant, A. M. (Eds.). (2006). *Evidence-based coaching handbook: Putting best practices to work for your clients.* New York: Wiley & Sons.

Tedeschi, R. G., & Calhoun, L. G. (1996). Posttraumatic growth inventory: Measuring the positive legacy of trauma. *Journal of Traumatic Stress, 9,* 455–471.

Tedeschi, R. G., & Calhoun, L. G. (2004). Posttraumatic growth: Conceptual foundations and empirical evidence. *Psychological Inquiry, 15*(1), 1–18.

Tedeschi, R. G., Park, C. L., & Calhoun, L. G. (Eds.). (1998). *Posttraumatic growth: Positive Changes in the Aftermath of Crisis.* New Jersey: Routledge.

Thompson, N., & Walsh, M. (2010). The existential basis of trauma. *Journal of Social Work Practice, 24*(4), 377–389.

Uppal, S., Oades, L. G., Crowe, T. P., & Deane, F. P. (2010). Barriers to transfer of collaborative recovery training into Australian mental health services: implications for the development of evidence-based services. *Journal of Evaluation in Clinical Practice, 16*(3), 451–455.

Watters, E. (2010). *Carzy like us: The globalization of the American psyche*. New York: Free Press.

White, M., & Epston, D. (1990). *Narrative Means to Therapeutic Ends*. New York: W.W. Norton.

Whitfield, C. (2010). Psychiatric drugs as agents of trauma. *The International Journal of Risk and Safety in Medicine*, 22(4), 195–207.

Williams, P. (2003). The potential perils of personal issues in coaching the continuing debate: Therapy or coaching? What every coach must know. *International Journal of Coaching in Organizations*, 2(2), 21–30.

Wilson, K. R., Havighurst, S. S., & Harley, A. E. (2014). Dads tuning into kids: Piloting a new parenting program targeting fathers' emotion coaching skills. *Journal of Community Psychology*, 42(2), 162–168.

Coaching for Role Transitions/Career Change

Polly Parker

Environmental shifts in the global economy have led to irrevocable changes in the nature of careers and their development. The current environment marked by volatility, uncertainty, complexity and ambiguity (referred to as VUCA) provides a dynamic backdrop for new career forms and patterns that belie formal planning processes. Individual coaching is increasingly being sought by people who need to develop individual VUCA qualities, which include vision, understanding, clarity and agility. Coaching provides support to adjust to the frequent yet often unexpected role transitions and career changes. In a VUCA environment, career decision-making, historically seen as an objective, rational and linear process is now more likely to be personal, values-oriented, connected to other lives and linked to society.

Careers comprise non-linear transitions that connect one employment episode to another, often driven by circumstances over which little control can be exerted. Such changes emphasise the need for continuous learning to identify goals, navigate pathways, develop or enhance employability, and manage work, relationships, aspirational goals, change and transitions throughout career journeys (Stringer, Kerpelman, & Skorikov, 2011). The increasing attention to career transitions in practice is reflected in the marked increase in published research. As Sampson and colleagues recently noted, career transition is 'a concept that continues to be important ... intermittently mentioned in the past' (Sampson Jr. et al., 2013: 294). Similarly there has been an exponential growth in coaching literature (Hagen, 2012) but a parallel increase specifically on coaching for transition has yet to emerge and presents as an opportunity for future research.

Coaching provides a range of personal development benefits including self-development (Aboalshamat, Hou, & Strodl, 2015), an increased ability to self-reflect leading to increased awareness (Hall, 2004) and support for sustained behavioural change (Bachkirova, 2011). Career coaching explores 'work-related issues – leading to effective action – in which the coach acts as both a catalyst and facilitator of individual and in turn, organisation development and transformation' (Bench, 2003 p. 9).

This chapter integrates recent and relevant outcomes from both the coaching and careers literature to focus on managing successful career transitions. The discussion commences with an introduction to coaching and the positioning of career coaching as a specialised form of coaching. Next, the changing world of work and its impact on career is explored. Relevant career theories that identify change, mobility, and uncertainty are then outlined as frameworks for coaches and clients alike to assist sense-making through transition experiences. This is followed by a discussion of the theoretical underpinnings of change and transition, in order to highlight the particular dynamics that are expected at different stages of the transition process. The chapter concludes by presenting recent approaches to career coaching that address key issues of managing career transition and identifying a possible agenda for future research.

AN INTRODUCTION TO COACHING

There is no clear definition or understanding of coaching, or of when, how and by whom it can be delivered to benefit individuals, teams and organisations. Like all the 'helping' professions (e.g. counselling), coaching focuses on promoting growth, development and improved functioning (Rogers, 1973) and most coaching definitions share important characteristics (Bennett & Bush, 2014). Specifically the descriptions of coaching reinforce a helping and facilitative process (Hamlin, Ellinger, & Beattie, 2009), and make learning, growth and adaptation possible (Hunt & Weintraub, 2002). They also connect critical reflection and emotion (Campone, 2015), a 'developmental process that builds a leader's capabilities' (Maltbia, Marsick, & Ghosh, 2014: 165) and 'a focussed dialogue ... where the facilitator uses open questions, active listening, summaries and reflections which are aimed at stimulating the self-awareness and personal responsibility of the participant' (Passmore & Fillery-Travis, 2011: 74).

A plethora of coaching types have been described, which are directed towards different audiences, used for different purposes and can be relatively formal and or relatively informal (Hamlin, Ellinger, & Beattie, 2006). According to Maltiba et al (2014), coaching can be distinguished across five dimensions: definition of work; focus; relationship; approach to emotions; and process. However, the dearth of empirical work distinguishing different forms of coaching in this increasingly popular field confounds the move toward and desire for conceptual clarity (Campone, 2015; Ciporen, 2015; Gilley, Gilley J., & Kouider, 2010). Currently, a substantial amount of career transition research is embedded in the leadership development literature and is often focused on transitions to more strategic leadership roles that involve different competencies (Campone, 2015; Passarelli, 2015; Simpson, 2010). The explicit reference to career transition is largely absent in other fields including intra-role transitions in which coaching focuses on career progression through improving performance (Kim, 2014; Pousa & Mathieu, 2015), or studies situated within disciplinary boundaries such as careers of scientists (Kamens, 2015) or academics (Collins, Lewis, Stracke, & Vanderheide, 2014), higher education (McDowall & Butterworth, 2014) or coaching minority groups (Williams, Thakore, & McGee, 2015).

At its core, coaching is a relational activity, a form of support that is central to making-meaning (Hamlin et al., 2009; Ladegard & Gjerde, 2014; Motulsky, 2010). Career coaching is similarly relational and supports the learning and development of people facing a career issue (such as transition). Its primary focus is the integration of work roles into a whole of life perspective, which emerges through engaging in a complex process of analysing lifespan experiences and events and synthesising emergent themes to increase self-direction in the learning process and career journey (Cox, 2015). Coaching differs markedly from other forms of helping, such as counselling, mentoring and therapy although these terms are often (mistakenly) used interchangeably (Cowan, 2013). Confusion can arise from role overlap as leaders and mentors engage in coaching activity to guide career progress and assist with transitions that are professional in nature (Cleary & Horsfall, 2015). Career coaching can be differentiated based on 'the focus of the work, who sets the agenda, the nature of the process itself, the education required, the time perspective, use of instruments, and who owns the results' (Bench, 2003:19).

Career coaching is typically short-term and focussed on a specific issue or event (Joo, Sushko, & McLean, 2012). Pertinent questioning draws upon relevant theoretical career frameworks and coaching practice to develop the client's insight, invites action to realise career goals and aspirations. Furthermore, coping with shifting identities inherent in moving through change and transition is essential (Ibarra & Despande, 2007) and, interestingly, empirical research on the changing identity of practicing coaches (Evans & Lines, 2014) could usefully be applied to clients in career transition.

The terminology surrounding career coaching is important for two reasons. First, its association to related fields of counselling (Amundson, 2015) and guidance (McMahon, Watson, & Bimrose, 2012) come with negative connotations. Whilst coaching is more acceptable than more 'remedial' types of support (especially in business settings), there is also a strong sporting connotation that can be unappealing to some. Second, increased coaching as an integral aspect of the role of human resource and organisational development professionals focusses on retaining talent in organisations (Hagen, 2012). Coaching has gained increased attention internally in organisations as companies compete for greater impact on employee satisfaction, career commitment and job performance (Kim, Egan, Kim, & Kim, 2013). To gain competitive advantage in a VUCA environment coaching must be perceived as being an intervention that is both positive and rigorous.

CHANGING MODELS OF CAREER

A widely accepted definition of career is 'the unfolding sequence of a person's work experiences over time' (Arthur, Hall, & Lawrence, 1989: 8). This definition is highly inclusive as it allows for everyone to have a career, not only those in selected occupations or professions. Furthermore the explicit reference to time highlights career as a process that incorporates a wide range of paid and unpaid experiences into a single overall lifetime experience (rather than a product that is changed at times). As such, one might experience multiple transitions and directional changes within a career, rather than simply change careers.

Coaching individuals according to traditional models of career assumed a steady linear progression usually within a single context of organisation, occupation or industry. Achieving and demonstrating mastery in work was a precursor to promotion, often focussed on task, competence and performance (Guest & Sturges, 2007). Whilst these assumptions about career have largely been implicit, they have also been widespread and have shaped the forms of support provided by coaches. Career transitions were marked at particular points within career trajectories such as entry to work from school, intra-role changes or into retirement.

Globalisation, technology and shifting demographics have brought changes to the previously stable working environment in which traditional careers were contextualised.

In a VUCA environment, *volatility* refers to instability and indicates a need to respond to rapid and unexpected changes. The pace of change also leads to *uncertainty* and a lack of clarity. *Complexity* positions threats and opportunities as two sides of the same coin and highlights non-linearity, which may be as overwhelming to the career actor as it is relentless. Furthermore, *ambiguity* presents the potential to misread situations accurately giving rise to misunderstanding and confusion (Lawrence, 2013).

In the increasingly confusing VUCA context flexible ways of working and new career patterns have emerged. Job shifts are more frequent (Peake & McDowell, 2012); increased mobility creates cross-boundary transitions; frequent intra-role and position changes generate mini-transitions; lateral as well as vertical moves influence career patterns; and movement between full time and part time work and alternate modes of employment grow (Culié, Khapova, & Arthur, 2014; Hess, Jepsen, & Dries, 2012). These variations have rendered career as a 'slippery' concept (Inkson, 2015), as the meaning of the concept has changed in almost all its aspects, other than its name. Coaching in multiple forms is in greater demand to support career crafting to improve performance, maintain employability, develop resilience and support learning (Evans & Lines, 2014).

CAREER TRANSITIONS

Transitions occur throughout careers and involve bridging the gap between where an individual is now, and where they will be in the future (Anderson, Goodman, & Schlossberg, 2011). A career transition marks a process of disengagement from one situation and engagement into a new situation (Fernandez, Fouquereau, & Heppner, 2008), with each transition affecting a person's identity, experience and attitude (Kunnen, 2013).

Increased emphasis on personal career agency places a lot of responsibility, obligation and often concern on career actors to be resilient, adaptable and ready for the unexpected (Tams & Arthur, 2010). Building career success through a wider range of career patterns has focussed on examining boundaries between work and the rest of life, including paid and unpaid work (Chudzikowski, 2012).

Career transitions incorporate attention to work, along with subjective criteria that include personal and social issues arising from change and its impact on living and working in the modern world (Spurk, Kauffeld, Barthauer, & Heinemann, 2015; Talbot, 2013). Such transitions involve decision making, identifying success criteria, option generation, strategy formulation, sense-making of new experiences, managing general expectations and/or specific issues of identity transformation. Not surprisingly, empirical evidence has shown that a wide range of feelings are associated with career transition including excitement, anticipation and challenge but also disappointment, disillusionment, fear, and betrayal (Haynie & Shepherd, 2011). As such, the process of coaching for transition involves helping the career actor to manage a range of challenging reactions, whilst seeking to align their career with a satisfying life.

While small, incremental changes (such as intra-role adjustments, inter-company shifts and minor variations in focus or approach) may be so gradual that they are barely discernible, others create jolts that may be quite affirming but be accompanied by fear, low self-efficacy, and insecurity about the future. Some transition points are more challenging than others, as they create more pain, disruption and, thus, require extra attention. These potential markers of growth and development may be voluntary or imposed, welcomed or not, and oftentimes will demand resilience, self-belief and an ability to adapt to change (Zacher, 2015). High profile transitions include the move from school to university/work (Cutts, Hooley, & Yates,

2015), mid-career adult transitions (Brown, Bimrose, Barnes, & Hughes, 2012; Peake & McDowell, 2012), and movements in and out of the workforce (Forret, Sullivan, & Maniero, 2010) and in and out of retirement (Wang, Hall, & Waters, 2014). Most importantly perhaps, all transitions are opportunities to learn and multiple mini-cycles of learning have now replaced a single trajectory, with career learning superseding mastery (Hall & Chandler, 2007; Hall & Las Heras, 2010).

The Emergence of Transition Models

As individual responses to career transitions can differ markedly, the value of coaching becomes clearer as it allows for different starting positions (Ladegard & Gjerde, 2014). Fortunately, typologies and models that incorporate the physical and emotional components inherent in the change process provide coaches with explanatory power to support individual capability development. The first typology of career transition was created by Louis (1980), who generalised across multiple types of career transition to identify common elements. Notably the typology included both physiological and psychological effects and recognised that individual responses to transition could 'contain elements from several types [of transition]' (Louis, 1980 p. 336). In addition, the role of sense-making in transition processes was included to modify cognitive maps used to interpret and understand experiences.

Of the other models that have been developed, Adams, Hayes and Hopson (1976) published some early work on the emotional stages of the transition, and Heppner (1998) presented a categorisation of the magnitude, task, position and occupation of career changes. More recent work has identified the criticality of readiness to change (Passmore, 2007) and the profound influence that cognitions have on resilience and the ability to adjust to external aspects of change, as well as internal transition processes (Dweck, 2008; Garvey-Berger, 2013; Yeager & Dweck, 2012).

Finally, personal and professional identity is central to career change and role transition (Ashforth, Schinoff, & Rogers, 2016; Ibarra, 2003). Described as the 'culmination of an individual's attributes, values, knowledge, experience and self-perceptions' (Day, Harrison, & Halpin, 2009: 57), identity is most poignant during periods of transition. Assuming a new role identity requires connecting past and present through a process of revision and reconstruction of narrative in which multiple life roles are integrated into a new self-definition (Ibarra & Barbaulescu, 2010). The impact of shifts in identity is a key area to address in career coaching, and best incorporated into a model of transition and change.

CHANGE AND TRANSITION THEORY AND IT USE IN COACHING

Managing internal transitions is an important factor in successful change (Bennett & Bush, 2014). Whilst the terms 'change' and 'transition' are frequently used as synonyms, they refer to processes that may oftentimes occur simultaneously. That is, an external change will often involve a situational shift, whilst an internal transition is a psychological 'process of letting go of the way things used to be and then taking hold of the way they subsequently become' (Bridges, 2001: 2). Transition requires coming to terms with external change and incorporates cognition, affect (including fear, anxiety, insecurity, happiness, etc.), along with various behavioural manifestations (e.g. avoidance).

Theoretical models of change and transition often emphasise career transition as sequences of stages that people move through and are useful for helping coaches to understand the overall process. Commonalities exist across models and highlight phases of letting go, a transitory or neutral period followed by an acceptance of a new juncture. Table 23.1 summarises some key models that are used in coaching.

Career coaching can be supported by the use of career theories that help people to make sense of their experience. Responding to the changing world, career theories have moved well beyond traditional models that matched a person's personality to a particular role (e.g., Holland, 1978), towards more contemporary theories that focus on learning, meaning and integration of work and non-work aspects of life as a whole (see Mainiero & Sullivan, 2006; Parker, 2002). A more holistic perspective of career positions transition coaching as professional support that may extend beyond aspects of the objective career (that denotes position, status and role) to encompass deeply held aspects of a person's subjective career (which can comprise self-belief, image and identity) that are affected by externally visible changes. The cognitive mental models that clients hold in respect of both career and change will influence the approach a career coach will select for clients.

Boundaryless Careers

Arthur and Rousseau (1996) proposed a theory of boundaryless careers in which careers unfold in more than one setting as people move across organisational, occupational or geographic boundaries. The mobility inherent in this model promotes possibility of boundary crossing transitions that are physical, such as shifts across departments and inter-organisational moves, and also psychological, such as a new role requiring mental adjustments (Sullivan & Arthur, 2006). The theory is broader than traditional schema of job changes within a single organisation or work unit and therefore most relevant for coaching clients who welcome

Table 23.1 Key theoretical models of change and transition that are commonly used in coaching

Model or theory	Authors	Key features
Force Field	Lewin (1951)	Proposes that change is marked by unfreezing, then movement, followed by refreezing.
Psychosocial Transition	Bridges (1986, 2001)	Three phase model that includes letting go of old situation or identity, a neutral zone and a new beginning.
Human Adaption to Transition (or the 4-S model)	Schlossberg (Schlossberg, 1981, 1995, 2005)	Three factors interact during a transition: individual characteristics; perceptions of the transition; characteristics of pre- and post-transition environments. The course of a transition is determined by: situation, self, support and strategies.
Transtheoretical	Prochaska & colleagues (James O. Prochaska, 2006; 1994)	Multi-stage model that identifies change over time occurring through stages of pre-contemplation, contemplation, preparation, action and maintenance (and lapse).
Work Role Transition	Nicholson (1984)	Four possible outcomes in new work roles: absorption; determination, exploration or replication, which is consistent with life cycle models (e.g., Super,1953).
Role Transitions	Ashforth (2001)	Developmental changes imply transition elements based on age; effect of past experience (i.e. success or failure) affecting future understanding; and transition bridges preserving continuity between changing roles.

change and respond well to different environments. There is little empirical support for boundaryless career theory and none linking coaching outcomes and boundaryless careers.

Protean Careers

Named after the Greek God (Proteus) who could change at will (Hall, 1976), a protean career is an orientation in which the person organises their career based on their values. The centrality of values provides core stability amidst other changes and a reference point to make decisions against which to assess career success. Herb Shepard's (1984) dictum of a 'path with a heart' spotlights what really matters within a holistic perspective, who one aspires to be rather than the work one aims to do. Empirical studies have shown the mediating role of self-management in the protean career which provides a practical approach for coaching (De Vos & Soens, 2008) and levels of organisational commitment are not less among those with protean or boundaryless attitudes (Briscoe & Finkelstein, 2009).

Intelligent Careers

DeFillippi and Arthur (1994) identified three career competencies that provide an holistic approach to career. The model can act as an umbrella concept that includes the three 'ways of knowing', along with data from other sources that provides coherence among many factors that contribute to work, career satisfaction and successful transitions. *Knowing-why* identifies personal motivation to work, values, interests, balance of work and family and resonance between 'who I am' and 'what I do', reinforcing the personal congruence within a life one creates. *Knowing-how* encompasses a person's job related skills and knowledge and ascertains job related expertise. *Knowing-whom* recognises a person's web of relationships that provide access to information, transmission of reputation and support. The model has highlighted the importance of context in career (Dickmann & Mills, 2009). The Intelligent Career Card Sort® based on the theory has been useful as a framework to guide career coaching for transition (Parker, 2002, 2006; Parker & Arthur, 2004).

Kaleidoscope Careers

Maniero and Sullivan's (2005, 2006) career theory is particularly useful for women to understand how career aligns with broader life commitments and foci that change in priority between *challenge*, *balance* and *authenticity* at different career and life stages. In early career, challenge, provides a driving force to grow and develop careers. Life changes such as having children may complicate career trajectories and trigger a focus on achieving balance. Later, authenticity becomes central and a need to be true to self is highlighted. As such, Kaleidoscope theory offers a potentially useful perspective that coaches can use when these shifts in focus are detected. Of the research reported to date, studies have shown no cross-generational differences in challenge needs although Gen X needed more balance and authenticity than baby boomers (Sullivan, Forret, Carraher, & Mainiero, 2009). Whilst it has been argued that HRD approaches need modification to better align themselves with women's career patterns (Sullivan & Maniero, 2008), no research has explicitly linked the model and coaching approaches.

It should be noted that a number of other theories and models exist that focus on complexity, uncertainty and the salience of chance events. These include Planned Happenstance (Mitchell, Levin, & Krumboltz, 1999) and Chaos Theory (Pryor, Amundson, & Bright, 2008; Pryor & Bright, 2011), along with work focused on the role of uncertainty in careers (Trevor-Roberts, 2006) and links between serendipity and chaos theory (Stone, 2007).

Whilst all offer promise as guiding frameworks for coaching, explicit links to coaching for transitions have yet to be presented.

CAREER COACHING AS A RELATIONAL PROCESS FOR CHANGE

Fundamental to successful career coaching is a relational approach that is predicated on the notion that relational aspects of self are central to human behaviour in daily interpersonal life (Chen, Boucher, & Tapias, 2006; Grote & Hall, 2013). The relational approach to careers was first introduced by Hall and Associates (1996) and emphasises affiliative behaviour, interdependence and social processes that enable co-learning processes to integrate the person and their interpersonal interactions (Hall & Associates, 1996; Kram, 1996). Since the dynamics associated with helping others was deemed under-theorised (Fletcher, 1996) there has been an upsurge in attention to the influence of significant others and both theory and data pertaining to the relational self. The relational career draws attention to interdependence, relationality and cooperation, which stands in marked contrast to notions of the independent self that have prevailed for much of the past century (Chen et al., 2006; Gelfand, Smith Major, Raver, Nishii, & O'Brien, 2006; Gergen, 2009).

The capacity to build high quality relationships has attracted much attention in recent years by scholars whose research has demonstrated they are conducive to active learning with less risk, increased satisfaction, growth and positive performance (Cameron, Dutton, Quinn, & Wrezesniewski, 2003; Carmeli & Gittell, 2009; Dutton & Heaphy, 2003; Dutton & Ragins, 2007). The essence of relational support within a high quality connection is marked by interdependence, mutuality and reciprocity (Fletcher, 2010; Stephens, Heaphy, Carmeli, Spreitzer, & Dutton, 2013). While the link between coaching and high quality relationships has been noted within the coaching process (Western, 2012) empirical studies that focus explicitly would make a valuable contribution to coaching literature and practice.

Effective coaching requires the creation of 'an open, trusting, non-judgmental, and supportive environment' (Carey, Philippon, & Cummings, 2011 p. 62). Trust, confidentiality and a commitment to change are essential aspects of all coaching relationships and reported elsewhere in this volume in detail. A relational approach in coaching begins with the fit between coach and client and the ability to adapt to others' styles and preferences. Indeed, it would appear that all approaches to coaching could be applied to careers and role changes. Relational approaches are increasingly reported in a wide range of fields including work design (Grant & Parker, 2009), negotiation (Gelfand et al., 2006), HR (Mossholder, Richardson, & Settoon, 2011), work engagement and job design (Freeney & Fellenz, 2013; Grant, 2007), yet there is surprisingly little empirical research focussed on results (Hazen & Stechler, 2014). Whilst coaching research is extremely limited in this area one study has shown that women's connections across a range of relationships were supportive of mid-career transitions (Motulsky, 2010). Given that a relational perspective on leadership coaching has been proposed (Ladegard & Gjerde, 2014), future research could seek to establish broader connections to other forms of coaching, including career and transition coaching.

Peer Coaching as a Relational Approach

Peer coaching is a focused relationship between individuals of equal status who support each other's personal and professional development goals (Parker, Hall, & Kram, 2008). Often confused with peer mentoring, although distinct from it (Ladyshewsky, 2014), peer coaching creates an internal dynamic that differs from professional coaching because of its lateral nature, which has the effect of neutralising power dynamics. However, building such connections can be more complex than it might initially appear (Parker, Kram, & Hall, 2012). As with other forms of coaching, peer coaching is most effective when the characteristics of high quality connections are established and can be used as a foundation to promote growth and learning, such as that evidenced through a career community (Kotlyar, Richardson, & Karakowsky, 2015). This permits strong emotional connections and provides a powerful influence for change (Parker, Wasserman, Kram, & Hall, 2015). As such, peers can be very effective in supporting the change and transition challenges of career actors today.

COACHING FOR TRANSITION

Coaching for transition is about managing both the *external* career change which is evident in a different role, status or position, whilst simultaneously managing the *internal* impact of a career transition, which challenges motivation, identity, and emotional management. The emphasis on personal responsibility in career behaviour compels career actors to build resilience (Pousa & Mathieu, 2015), adapt and change. Career adaptability focusses on readiness to manage predictable tasks and unpredictable role adjustments (Savickas, 1997). Empirical research has focussed on the development and validity of the career adaptabilities scale in several countries (Maggiori, Rossier, & Savickas, 2015; Savickas & Porfeli, 2012; Soresi, Nota, & Ferrari, 2012; Tolentino et al., 2013). Adaptability has been shown to be moderately correlated with an internal locus of control in adolescents (Hirschi, 2009), whilst readiness for change has been correlated with career adaptability but not confidence to change (Ghosh & Fouad, 2015).

Highly individualised coaching is essential as the psychological impact of career transition is not necessarily aligned to the magnitude of the change. Openness to explore and engage in new learning may depend on the trigger event for transition. Involuntary transitions caused by redundancy, job loss, and forced exits engender markedly different responses from those instigated by choice such as a new role or perhaps a welcomed move into retirement (Wang et al., 2014). Responses to shifts in work, identity and self-concept require attention to be directed towards the associated feelings such as anger, loss, disillusionment, despair, and anxiety (Peake & McDowell, 2012). In this respect, strength-based coaching approaches may be potentially beneficial as they support the development of a coherent sense of self (McDowall & Butterworth, 2014; Spreitzer, 2006; Zackery, 2014) and have been reported to reduce turnover, and increase productivity and customer loyalty in organisations (Damle, 2015). Such approaches align well with contemporary 'positive' approaches to coaching (Boniwell, Kauffman, & Silberman, 2014).

Distinctive features in career coaching exist at the intersection of work and identity, inextricably linked at points of transition where both self-worth and identity can be disturbed. Identity is about meaning and mattering, and often gauged through the reactions of family and friends and colleagues. In this respect, work reported on the construct of possible selves seems highly relevant for career coaches (Ibarra, 2002, 2003; Ibarra & Petriglieri, 2007; Ibarra, Snook, & Guillen Ramo, 2010). This has included the idea that transition management can include the low-risk process of 'trying on' possible identities, which enable crafting experiments of possible selves (Ibarra, 2003). Possible selves position the self as 'dynamic, contextually interactive, and evolving, rather than fixed' (Rossiter, 2009: 61) and, indeed, the identity of career coaches themselves provides a model and guide for further research into the impact of transition on identity (Evans & Lines, 2014).

Successful career counselling applications are also applicable to career coaching, particularly the motivational effect of concrete future possibilities, and the feelings associated with future states and schema that enable positive action (Meara, Day, Chalk, & Phelps, 1995). Conceptualising multiple identities that shape behaviours in many life spheres is well recognised, yet the empirical base for examination is in its infancy (Ramarajan, 2014). Experimenting with new identities may occur in transition spaces such as education programs (Petriglieri, Wood, & Petriglieri, 2011).

The ability to coach for career transition and change draws attention to antecedents factors such as self-efficacy and personal mindsets, which frame not only the immediate situation but also the underlying belief systems that inform fundamental aspects of transitions. Understanding the mental models of clients may be critical to achieving effective outcomes. A particular marker of successful adaptation is the differential impact of growth versus performance mindsets (Dweck, 2008). According to Dweck (2008), growth mindsets are grounded in a belief that abilities can be developed and enhanced through education and learning which positively influences motivation. In contrast the underlying belief in a performance mindset is that basic qualities are set (or fixed). However, performance mindsets can be identified and changed, leading to the development of resilience and enhanced performance (Yeager & Dweck, 2012).

Career coaches recognise how beliefs and feelings may reveal orders of mind that reflect a person's meaning-making system. According to Kegan (1994), there are five orders of mind that can be identified to explain whether or not people are 'in over their heads' or capable of cognitively managing the complexity of modern life (Kegan, 1994). Deep issues of beliefs and habits of mind manifest in behaviours, relationships and change (Garvey-Berger, 2013; Garvey-Berger & Johnston, 2015). Whilst the theory is complex it offers potentially valuable insights to career coaches for ensuring their practices are responsive to the psychological, behavioural and practical factors that impact on individuals experiencing transition or career change (Pinkavova, 2010).

Finally, working with narratives (see Drake this volume) can also assist clients to connect past with current circumstances and construct a view of the future. Career stories have long been used to elucidate the unfolding series of experiences over time as a sense-making process (Cochran, 1997). However, narrative coaching represents a new wave of practice (Stelter, 2013), as stories give clients 'openings for new narratives about who they are and how they want to be in the world' (Drake, 2007: 284). The narrative content facilitates sense-making about transitions providing insight into reasons for actions and choices. Empirical evidence supports links with adaptability that emerges through stories (McMahon et al., 2012).

DIRECTIONS FOR FUTURE RESEARCH

Empirical studies in both coaching and career transitions exist although are rarely explored together. Integrating both fields of study would deepen the theoretical underpinnings of coaching for role transitions and career change, by improving conceptual quality and supporting practice development. A first step is to clearly identify the composition of the extant research literature, which are currently embedded in areas such as leadership development, mentoring or organisationally situated HRD (where both coaching and specific types of career transition occur). A second step is to build a critical mass of empirical work, that might include some or all of the recommendations set out below:

- As mentioned earlier, theories of change are particularly relevant to coaching for transition. Yet few theories have been explicitly linked to career, particularly models that include aspects of

mobility, adaptability, resilience, decision-making amid uncertainty, dealing with complexity and ongoing learning. As such, future research could focus on understanding the impact of explicitly linking career and transition models to such elements and potentially lead to the development of a coaching-specific theory of career change and transition.
- The application of relational approaches to career and transition coaching is another area for future research. Relational approaches are gaining momentum in a wide range of disciplines and seem particularly aligned with coaching for career change, as identity formation can be facilitated through the renewal and development that occurs with others. As both major and minor transitions involve shifts in identity, a further area for future research is to evaluate the impact of coaching on identity transformation. The work of Evans and Lines (2014) on the changing identity of practicing coaches provides a useful template for advancing such work.
- Finally, there appear to be opportunities to explicitly connect newer models of career to transition coaching processes. An example of this would be the assessing Protean orientation (De Vos & Soens, 2008), for which measurement scales are already available, and may include investigating the extent to which its characteristic attitudes work to support successful career transition.

CONCLUSION

Careers are personal journeys marked increasingly by transitions of varying magnitude. As has been repeatedly argued in this chapter, coaching provides career actors with a valuable form of support that helps them develop flexible ways to respond to an increasingly volatile, uncertain, complex and ambiguous world. Whilst coaches have access to a variety of different change models to guide their work, the plethora of approaches can be as confronting as they are helpful. The most appropriate will depend on the client, the change or transition they face and their response to it – cognitive, emotional and behavioural. However, the professionalism and integrity of the coaching process demands that the coach have personal clarity about his or her own underlying assumptions and beliefs about careers, and the theories used to assist the client in the process. As such, if career and transition coaching is to support people successfully traverse Herb Shepherd's 'path with a heart', then the field will be well served by theoretical and empirical work capable of generating an evidence-base that is specific to this context.

REFERENCES

Aboalshamat, K., Hou, X.-Y., & Strodl, E. (2015). The impact of self-development coaching programme on medical and dental students' psychological health and academic performance. *BMC Medical Education*, 15(1), 134–146.

Adams, J. D., Hayes, J., & Hopson, B. (1976). *Transition: Understanding and managing personal change*. London: Martin Robertson.

Amundson, N. (2015). Using metaphor in carer intervention. In P. J. Hartung, M. L. Savickas, & W. B. Walsh (Eds.), *APA Handbook of Career Intervention* (Vol. Two, pp. 293–304). Washington DC: American Psychological Association.

Anderson, M. L., Goodman, J., & Schlossberg, N. K. (2011). *Counseling Adults in Transition: Linking Schlossberg's Theory with practice in a diverse world*. New York, NY: Springer.

Arthur, M. B., Hall, D. T., & Lawrence, B. S. (Eds.). (1989). *Handbook of Career Theory*. Cambridge: Cambridge University Press.

Arthur, M. B., & Rousseau, D. M. (Eds.). (1996). *The Boundaryless Career: A new employment principle for a new organizational era*. New York: Oxford University Press.

Ashforth, B. E. (2001). *Role Transitions in Organizational Life: An identity-based perspective*. Mahwah, NJ: Lawrence Erlbaum.

Ashforth, B. E., Schinoff, B. S., & Rogers, K. M. (2016). 'I Identify with Her,' 'I Identify with Him': Unpacking the dynamics of personal identification in organizations. *Academy of Management Review*, 41(1), 28–60.

Bachkirova, T. (2011). *Developmental Coaching: Working With The Self: Working with the Self*. New York: Open University Press.

Bench, M. (2003). *Career Coaching: An insider's guide*. Palo Alto, CA: Davies-Black Publishing.

Bennett, J. L., & Bush, W. M. (2014). *Coaching for Change*. London: Routledge.

Boniwell, I., Kauffman, C., & Silberman, J. (2014). The positive psychogical approach to coaching. In E. Cox, T. Bachkirova, & D. Clutterbuck (Eds.), *The Complete Handbook of Coaching* (pp. 157–169). London, UK: Sage.

Bridges, W. (1986). Managing organizational transitions. *Organizational Dynamics*, *15*(1), 24–33.

Bridges, W. (2001). *The Way of Transition*. Perseus.

Briscoe, J. P., & Finkelstein, L. M. (2009). The 'new career' and organizational commitment: Do boundaryless and protean attitudes make a difference? *Career Development International*, *14*(3), 242–260.

Brown, A., Bimrose, J., Barnes, S.-A., & Hughes, D. (2012). The role of career adaptabilities for mid-career changers. *Journal of Vocational Behavior*, *80*, 754–761.

Cameron, K. S., Dutton, J. E., Quinn, R. E., & Wrezesniewski, A. (2003). Developing a discpline of positive organizational scholarship. In K. S. Cameron, J. E. Dutton, & R. E. Quinn (Eds.), *Positive Organizational Scholarship* (pp. 361–370). San Francisco: Berrett-Koehler Publishers Inc.

Campone, F. (2015). Executive Coaching Practices in the Adult Workplace. In J. P. Pappas & J. Jerman (Eds.), *New Directions for Adult and Continuing Education* (pp. 59–67). Wileyonline.

Carey, W., Philippon, D. J., & Cummings, G. G. (2011). Coaching models for leadership development: An integrative review. *Journal of Leadership Studies*, *5*(1), 51–69.

Carmeli, A., & Gittell, J. H. (2009). High quality relationships, psychological safety, and learning from failures in work organizations. *Journal of Organizational Behavior*, *30*, 709–729.

Chen, S., Boucher, H. C., & Tapias, M. P. (2006). The relational self revealed: Integrative conceptualizations and implications for inter-personal life. *Psychological Bulletin*, *132*(2), 151–179.

Chudzikowski, K. (2012). Career transitions and career success in the 'new' career era. *Journal of Vocational Behavior*, *81*(2), 298–306.

Ciporen, R. (2015). The emerging field of executive and organizational coaching: An Overview. In J. P. Pappas & J. Jerman (Eds.), *Transforming Adults Through Coaching: New Directions for Adult and Continuing Education, Number 148* (pp. 5–15): Wiley.

Cleary, M., & Horsfall, J. (2015). Coaching: comparisons with mentoring. *Issues in Mental Health Nursing*, *36*(3), 243–245.

Cochran, L. (1997). *Career Counseling: A narrative approach*. Thousand Oaks, CA: Sage.

Collins, J., Lewis, I., Stracke, E., & Vanderheide, R. (2014). Talking career across disciplines: Peer group mentoring for women academics. *International Journal of Evidence Based Coaching and Mentoring*, *12*(1), 92–108.

Cowan, K. (2013). What are the experiences of external executive coaches working with coaches' assigned goals? *International Journal of Evidence Based Coaching and Mentoring*, Special Issue (7), 1–14.

Cox, E. (2015). Coaching and adult learning: Theory and practice. *New Directions for Adult and Continuing Education*, *148*, 27–38.

Culié, J.-D., Khapova, S. N., & Arthur, M. B. (2014). Careers, clusters and employment mobility: the influences of psychological mobility and organizational support. *Journal of Vocational Behavior*, *84*, 164–176.

Cutts, B., Hooley, T., & Yates, J. (2015). *Industry and Higher Education*, *29*(4), 271–282.

Damle. (2015). Managing multiple career transitions sustained over a long period. *Indian Journal of Science and Technology*, *8*(S6), 61–70.

Day, D. V., Harrison, M. M., & Halpin, S. M. (2009). *An Integrative Approach to Leader Development*. New York: Routledge.

De Vos, A., & Soens, N. (2008). Protean attitude and career success: The mediating role of self-management. *Journal of Vocational Behavior*, *73*(3), 449–456.

DeFillippi, R. J., & Arthur, M. B. (1994). The boundaryless career: a competency-based perspective. *Journal of Organizational Behaviour*, *15*, 307–324.

Dickmann, M., & Mills, T. (2009). The importance of intelligent career and location considerations. *Personnel Review*, *39*(1), 116–134.

Drake, D. B. (2007). The art of thinking narratively: Implications for coaching psychology and practice *Australian Psychologist*, *42*(2), 283–294.

Dutton, J. E., & Heaphy, E. D. (2003). The power of high quality connections. In K. S. Cameron, J. E. Dutton, & R. E. Quinn (Eds.), *Positive Organizational Scholarship* (pp. 263–278). San Francisco, CA: Berrett-Koehler.

Dutton, J. E., & Ragins, B. (Eds.). (2007). *Exploring Positive Relationships at Work: Building a theoretical and research foundation*. Mahwah, NJ: Lawrence Erlbaum Associates.

Dweck, C. S. (2008). *Mindset: The new psychology of success*. New York: Ballantine Books.

Evans, C., & Lines, D. (2014). 'Which hat do I say I'm wearing?': identity work of independent coaching practitioners. *European Journal of Training and Development*, *38*(8), 764–779.

Fernandez, A., Fouquereau, E., & Heppner, M. J. (2008). The career transition inventory: A psychometric evaluation of a French version. *Journal of Career Assessment*, *16*, 384–398.

Fletcher, J. (1996). A relational approach to the protean worker. In D. T. H. Associates (Ed.), *The Career is Dead: Long live the career*. San Francisco, CA: Jossey-Bass.

Fletcher, J. (2010). Leadership as Relational Practice. In K. Bunker, D. T. Hall, & K. E. Kram (Eds.), *Extraordinary Leadership: Addressing the gaps in senior executive development* (pp. 121–136). San Francisco, CA: Jossey-Bass.

Forret, M. L., Sullivan, S. E., & Mainiero, L. A. (2010). Gender role differences in reactions to unemployment: Exploring psychological mobility and boundaryless careers. *Journal of Organizational Behavior*, *31*, 647–666.

Freeney, Y., & Fellenz, M. R. (2013). Work engagement, job design and the role of the social context at work: Exploring antecedents from a relational perspective. *Human Relations*, *66*(11), 1472–1445.

Garvey-Berger, J. (2013). *Changing on the Job: Developing leaders in a complex world*. Stanford, CA: Stanford Business Books.

Garvey-Berger, J., & Johnston, K. (2015). *Simple Habits for Complex Times*. Stanford, CA: Stanford University Press.

Gelfand, M. J., Smith Major, V., Raver, J. L., Nishii, L. H., & O'Brien, K. (2006). Negotiating relationally: the dynamics of the relational self in negotiations. *Academy of Management Review*, *31*(2), 427–451.

Gergen, K. J. (2009). *Relational Being: Beyond self and community*. Oxford: Oxford University Press.

Ghosh, A., & Fouad, N. A. (2015). Career transitions of student veterans. *Journal of Career Assessment*, *24*(1), 99–111.

Gilley, A., Gilley, J., & Kouider, E. (2010). Characteristics of managerial coaching. *Performance Improvement Quarterly*, *23*(1), 53–70.

Grant, A. M. (2007). Relational job design and the motivation to make a prosocial difference. *Academy of Management Review*, *32*(2), 393–417.

Grant, A. M., & Parker, S. K. (2009). 7 Redesigning work design theories: The rise of relational and proactive perspectives. *The Academy of Management Annals*, *3*(1), 317–375.

Grote, G., & Hall, D. T. (2013). Reference groups: A missing link in career studies. *Journal of Vocational Behavior*, *83*(3), 265–279.

Guest, D., & Sturges, J. (2007). Living to work – working to live. In H. Gunz & M. Peiperl (Eds.), *Handbook of Career Studies* (pp. 310–326). Thousand Oaks, CA: Sage.

Hagen, M. (2012). Managerial coaching: A review of the literature. *Performance Improvement Quarterly*, *24*(4), 17–39.

Hall, D. T. (1976). *Careers in Organizations*. Pacific Palisades, CA: Goodyear.

Hall, D. T. (2004). Self-awareness, identity, and leader development. In S. J. Z. David, V. Day, & Stanley M. Halpin (Eds.), *Leader Development for Transforming Organizations: Growing Leaders for Tomorrow* (pp. 153–176). New York: Lawrence Erlbaum Associates, Inc.

Hall, D. T., & Associates. (1996). *The Career is Dead: Long live the career*. San Francisco, CA: Jossey-Bass.

Hall, D. T., & Chandler, D. E. (2007). Career cycles and mentoring. In B. R. Ragins, & K. E. Kram (Eds.), *The Handbook of Mentoring at Work. Theory, research and practice.* (pp. 471–497). Thousand Oaks, CA.: Sage.

Hall, D. T., & Las Heras, M. (2010). Reintegrating job design and career theory: Creating not just jobs but *smart* jobs. *Journal of Organizational Behavior, 31*, 448–462.

Hamlin, R. G., Ellinger, A. D., & Beattie, R. S. (2006). Coaching at the heart of managerial effectiveness: A cross-cultural study of managerial behaviours. *Human Resource Development International, 9*(3), 305–331.

Hamlin, R. G., Ellinger, A. D., & Beattie, R. (2009). Toward a process of coaching? A definitional examination of 'coaching', 'Organizational Development,' and 'Human Resource Development'. *International Journal of Evidence Based Coaching and Mentoring, 7*, 13–38.

Haynie, J. M., & Shepherd, D. (2011). Toward a theory of discontinuous career transition: Investigating career transitions necessitated by traumatic life events. *Journal of Applied Psychology, 96*(3), 501–524. doi: http://dx.doi.org/10.1037/a0021450

Hazen, B., & Stechler, N. (2014). Career coaching. In E. Cox, T. Bachkirova, & D. Clutterbuck (Eds.), *The Complete Handbook of Coaching* (2nd ed., pp. 329–341). London, UK: Sage.

Heppner, M. J. (1998). The career transition inventory: measuring internal resources in adulthood. *Journal of Career Assessment, 6*, 135–145.

Hess, N., Jepsen, D. M., & Dries, N. (2012). Career and employer change in the age of the 'boundaryless' career. *Journal of Vocational Behavior, 81*, 280–288.

Hirschi, A. (2009). Career adaptability development in adolescence: Multiple predictors and effect on sense of power and life satisfaction. *Journal of Vocational Behavior, 74*(2), 144–155.

Holland, J. L. (1978). *The Ooccupations Finder*. Palo Alto, CA: Consulting Psychologists Press.

Hunt, J. M., & Weintraub, J. R. (2002). *The Coaching Manager: Developing top talent in business*. Thousand Oaks, CA: Sage.

Ibarra, H. (2002). How to stay stuck in the wrong career. *Harvard Business Review*, December, 40–47.

Ibarra, H. (2003). *Working Identity*. Boston, MA: Harvard Business School Press.

Ibarra, H., & Barbaulescu, R. (2010). Identity as narrative: Prevalence, effectiveness, and consequences of narrative identity work in macro work role transitions. *Academy of Management Review, 35*(1), 135–154.

Ibarra, H., & Despande, P. H. (2007). Networks and identities. In H. Gunz & M. Peiperl (Eds.), *Handbook of Career Studies*. Thousand Oaks, CA.: Sage.

Ibarra, H., & Petriglieri, J. (2007). *Impossible Selves: Image strategies and identity threat in professional women's career transitions*. Working Paper Series. INSEAD Fontainebleau, France.

Ibarra, H., Snook, S., & Guillen Ramo, L. (2010). Identity-based leader development. *Leadership: Advancing an intellectual discipline*, 657–678.

Inkson, K. I. (2015). Contemporary conceptualizations of career. In P. J. Hartung, M. L. Savickas, & W. B. Walsh (Eds.), *APA Handbook of Career Intervention: Vol 1 Foundations* (pp. 21–42). Washington, DC, USA: American Psychological Association.

Joo, B.-K., Sushko, J. S., & McLean, G. N. (2012). Multiple faces of coaching: Manager-as-coach, executive coaching, and formal mentoring. *Organization Development Journal, 30*(1), 19–38.

Kamens, J. (2015). Career coaching for scientists. *Nature Biotechnology, 33*(6), 668–669.

Kegan, R. (1994). *In Over Our Heads: The mental demands of modern life*. Cambridge, MA: Harvard University Press.

Kim, S. (2014). Assessing the influence of managerial coaching on employee outcomes. *Human Resource Development Quarterly, 25*(1), 59–85.

Kim, S., Egan, T., Kim, W., & Kim, J. (2013). The impact of managerial coaching behavior on employee work-related reactions. *Journal of Business Psychology, 28*, 315–330.

Kotlyar, I., Richardson, J., & Karakowsky, L. (2015). Learning to lead from outsiders: The value of career communities as a source of external peer coaching. *Journal of Management Development, 34*(10), 1262–1271.

Kram, K. E. (1996). A relational approach to career development. In D. T. Hall & Associates (Eds.), *The Career is Dead: Long live the career*. San Francisco, CA: Jossey-Bass.

Kunnen, E. S. (2013). The effects of career choice guidance on identity development. *Education Research International*, 2013, 1–9.

Ladegard, G., & Gjerde, S. (2014). Leadership coaching, leader role-efficacy, and trust in subordinates. A mixed methods study assessing leadership coaching as a leadership development tool. *The Leadership Quarterly*, 25, 631–646.

Ladyshewsky, R. K. (2014). Peer coaching. In E. Cox, T. Bachkirova, & D. Clutterbuck (Eds.), *The Complete Handbook of Coaching* (2nd ed., pp. 285–297). London, UK: Sage.

Lawrence, K. (2013). *Developing Leaders in a VUCA Environment*. Retrieved from https://www.td.org/Publications/Blogs/ATD-Blog/2013/02/Developing-Leaders-in-a-VUCA-Environment

Lewin, K. (1951). *Field Theory in Social Science*. New York: Harper & Row.

Louis, M. R. (1980). Career transitions: varieties and commonalities. *Academy of Management Review*, 5(3), 329–340.

Maggiori, C., Rossier, J., & Savickas, M. L. (2015). Career Adapt-Abilities Scale–Short Form (CAAS-SF): Construction and Validation. *Journal of Career Assessment*, 1–14.

Mainiero, L. A., & Sullivan, S. E. (2005). Kaleidoscope careers: An alternate explanation for the 'opt-out' revolution. *The Academy of Management Executive*, 19(1), 106–123.

Mainiero, L. A., & Sullivan, S. E. (2006). *The Opt-out Revolution: Why people are leaving companies to create kaleidoscope careers*. Mountain View, CA: Davies-Black.

Maltbia, T. E., Marsick, V. J., & Ghosh, R. (2014). Executive and organizational coaching: A review of insights drawn from literature to inform HRD practice. *Advances in Developing Human Resources*, 16(2), 161–182.

McDowall, A., & Butterworth, L. (2014). How does a brief strengths-based group coaching intervention work? *Coaching: An International Journal of Theory, Research and Practice*, 7(2), 152–163.

McMahon, M., Watson, M., & Bimrose, J. (2012). Career adpatability: A qualitative understanding from stories of older women. *Journal of Vocational Behavior*, 80, 762–768.

Meara, N. M., Day, J. D., Chalk, L. M., & Phelps, R. E. (1995). Possible selves: Applications for career counseling. *Journal of Employment Counseling*, 3, 259–277.

Mitchell, K. E., Levin, A. S., & Krumboltz, J. D. (1999). Planned happenstance: Constructing unexpected career opportunities. *Journal of Counseling and Development*, 77(2), 115–124.

Mossholder, K. W., Richardson, H. A., & Settoon, R. P. (2011). Human resource systems and helping in organizations: A relational perspective. *Academy of Management Review*, 36(1), 33–52.

Motulsky, S. L. (2010). Relational processes in career transition: extending theory, research, and practice. *The Counselong Psychologist*, 38(8), 1078–1114.

Nicholson, N. (1984). A theory of work role transitions. *Administrative Science Quarterly*, 29(2), 172–191.

Parker, P. (2002). Working with the Intelligent Career Model. *Journal of Employment Counseling*, 39(2), 83–96.

Parker, P. (2006). Card sorts: constructivist assessment tools. In M. McMahon & W. Patton (Eds.), *Career Counselling: Constructivist approaches* (pp. 176–186). Abingdon, Oxford: Routledge.

Parker, P., & Arthur, M. B. (2004). Coaching for career development and leadership development: an intelligent career approach. *Australian Journal of Career Development*, 13(3), 56–60.

Parker, P., Hall, D. T., & Kram, K. E. (2008). Peer coaching: a relational process for accelerating career learning. *Academy of Management Learning and Education*, 7(4), 487–503.

Parker, P., Kram, K. E., & Hall, D. T. (2012). Exploring risk factors in peer coaching: a multilevel approach. *Journal of Applied Behavioral Science*, 49(3), 361–387.

Parker, P., Wasserman, I., Kram, K. E., & Hall, D. T. (2015). A relational communication approach to peer coaching. *The Journal of Applied Behavioral Science*, 51(2), 231–252.

Passarelli, A. M. (2015). Vision-based coaching: optimizing resources for leader development. *Frontiers in Psychology*, 6, 412–426.

Passmore, J. (2007). An integrative model for executive coaching. *Consulting Psychology Journal: Practice and Research*, 59(1), 68–78.

Passmore, J., & Fillery-Travis, A. (2011). A critical review of executive coaching research: a decade of progress and what's to come.

Coaching: An Internaitonal Journal of Theory, Research and Practice, 4(2), 70–88.

Peake, S., & McDowell, A. (2012). Chaotic careers: a narrative analysis of career transition themes and outcomes using chaos theory as a guiding metaphor. *British Journal of Guidance and Counselling*, 40(4), 395–410.

Petriglieri, G., Wood, J. D., & Petriglieri, J. L. (2011). Up close and personal: Building foundations for leaders'development through the personalization of management learning. *Academy of Management Learning and Education*, 10(3), 430–450.

Pinkavova, E. (2010). Keeping our heads above water: applying Kegan's 'orders of consciousness' theory in coaching. *International Journal of Evidence Based Coaching and Mentoring*, 8(1), 14–21.

Pousa, C., & Mathieu, A. (2015). Is managerial coaching a source of competitive advantage? Promoting employee self-regulation through coaching. *Coaching: An International Journal of Theory, Research and Practice*, 8(1), 20–35.

Prochaska, J. O. (2006). Is social cognitive theory becoming a transtheoretical model? A comment on Dijkstra et al. (2006) *Addiction*, 101(7), 916–917. doi:10.1111/j.1360–0443.2006.01500.x

Prochaska, J. O., Velicier, W. F., Rossi, J. S., Goldstein, M. G., Marcus, B. H., Rakowski, W., & Rossi, S. R. (1994). Stages of change and decisional balance for 12 problem behaviours. *Health Psychology*, 13(1), 39–46.

Pryor, R. G. L., Amundson, N., & Bright, J. E. H. (2008). Probabilities and possibilities: The strategic counselling implications of the chaos theory of careers. *The Career Development Quarterly*, 56, 309–318.

Pryor, R. G. L., & Bright, D. (2011). *The Chaos Theory of Careers*. New York: Routledge.

Ramarajan, L. (2014). Past, present and future research on multiple identities: Toward an intrapersonal network approach. *The Academy of Management Annals*, 8(1), 589–659.

Rogers, C. (1973). Characteristics of a helping relationship. In W. G. Bennis, D. E. Berlew, E. H. Schein, & F. I. Steele (Eds.), *Interpersonal Dynamics* (3rd Edition, pp. 223–236). Homewood, IL: Irwin-Dorsey.

Rossiter, M. (2009). Possible selves and career transition: implications for serving non-traditional students. *The Journal of Continuing Higher Education*, 57, 61–71.

Sampson Jr., J. P., Pei-Chun Hou, Kronholz, J. F., Dozier, V. C., McClain, M., Buzzetta, M., & Kennell, E. L. (2013). A content analysis of career development theory, research, and practice. *The Career Development Quarterly*, 62, 290–326.

Savickas, M. L. (1997). The spirit in career counseling: fostering self-completion through work. In D. P. Bloch & J. R. Lee (Eds.), *Connections Between Spirit and Work in Career Development* (pp. 3–25). Palo Alto, CA: Davis-Black.

Savickas, M. L., & Porfeli, E. J. (2012). Career Adapt-Abilities Scale: Construction, reliability, and measurement equivalence across 13 countries. *Journal of Vocational Behavior*, 80, 661–673.

Schlossberg, N. K. (1981). A model for analyzing human adaptation to transition. *The Counseling Psychologist*, 9(2), 2–18.

Schlossberg, N. K. (1995). Adult development theories: ways to illuminate the adult experience. In N. K. Schlossberg, E. Waters, & J. Goodman (Eds.), *Counselling Adults in Transition: Linking Practice with Theory* (2nd ed.). New York: Springer.

Schlossberg, N. K. (2005). Help consultants to deal with transitions: the particular case of non-events. *The Educational and Vocational Guidance*, 34(1), 85–101.

Shepard, H. A. (1984). On the realization of human potential: A path with a heart. In M. B. Arthur, L. Bailyn, D. J. Levenson, & H. A. Shepard (Eds.), *Working with Careers* (pp. 25–46). New York: Columbia University School of Business.

Simpson, J. (2010). In what ways does coaching contribute to effective leadership development? *International Journal of Evidence Based Coaching and Mentoring*, 4 (Special Issue), 114–133.

Soresi, S., Nota, L., & Ferrari, L. (2012). Career Adapt-Abilities Scale–Italian Form: Psychometric properties and relationships to breadth of interests, quality of life, and perceived barriers. *Journal of Vocational Behavior* (80), 705–711.

Spreitzer, G. (2006). Leadership development lessons from positive organizational studies. *Organizational Dynamics*, 35(4), 305–315.

Spurk, D., Kauffeld, S., Barthauer, B., & Heinemann, N. S.R. (2015). Fostering networking behavior, career planning and optimism, and subjective career success: An intervention study. *Journal of Vocational Behavior*, 87, 134–144.

Stelter, R. (2013). Narrative approaches. In J. Passmore, D. B. Peterson, & T. Freire (Eds.), *The Wiley-Blackwell Handbook of the Psychology of Coaching and Mentoring* (First ed., pp. 407–425). New York: John Wiley and Sons.

Stephens, J. P., Heaphy, E. D., Carmeli, A., Spreitzer, G. M., & Dutton, J. (2013). Relationship quality and virtuousness: emotional carrying capacity as a source of individual and team resilience. *The Journal of Applied Behavioral Science*, 49(1), 13–41.

Stone, W. (2007). Organizing serendipity: four tasks for mastering chaos. *Career Planning and Adult Development*, 23, 73–81.

Stringer, K., Kerpelman, J., & Skorikov, V. (2011). Career preparation: A longitudinal, process-oriented examination. *Journal of Vocational Behavior*, 79, 158–169.

Sullivan, S. E., & Arthur, M. B. (2006). The evolution of the boundaryless career: examining physical and psychological passages. *Journal of Vocational Behavior*, 69(1), 19–29.

Sullivan, S. E., Forret, M. L., Carraher, S. M., & Mainiero, L. A. (2009). Using the kaleidoscope career model to examine generational differences in work attitudes. *Career Development International*, 14(3), 284–302.

Sullivan, S. E., & Maniero, L. A. (2008). Using the Kaleidoscope Career model to understand the changing patterns of women's careers: designing HRD programs that attract and retain women. *Advances in Developing Human Resources*, 10(1), 32–49.

Super, D. E. (1953). A theory of vocational development. *American Psychologist*, 8, 185–190.

Talbot, C. (2013). *Essential Career Transition Coaching Skills*. London: Routledge.

Tams, S., & Arthur, M. B. (2010). New directions for boundaryless careers: agency and interdependence in a changing world. *Journal of Organizational Behavior*, 31(5), 629–646.

Tolentino, L., Garcia, P. R. J. M., Lu, V. N., Lloyd, S., Restubog, D., Bordia, P., & Plewa, C. (2013). Career adaptation: the relation of adaptability to goal orientation, proactive personality, and career optimism. *Journal of Vocational Behavior*, 84, 39–48.

Trevor-Roberts, E. (2006). Are you sure? The role of uncertainty in careers. *Journal of Employment Counseling*, 43(3), 98–116.

Wang, L., Hall, D. T., & Waters, L. (2014). Finding Meaning During the Retirement Process: Identity development in later career years. In *Oxford Handbooks Online*. New York: Oxford University Press. DOI 10.1093/oxfordhb/9780199935291.013.25

Western, S. (2012). *Coaching and Mentoring: A critical text*. Thousand Oaks, CA: Sage.

Williams, S. N., Thakore, B. K., & McGee, R. (2015). Coaching to augment mentoring to achieve faculty diversity. *Academic Medicine*, 91(2), 1–8.

Yeager, D. S., & Dweck, C. (2012). Mindsets that promote resilience: when students believe that personal characteristics can be developed. *Educational Psychologist*, 47(4), 302–314.

Zacher, H. (2015). Daily manifestations of career adaptability: relationships with job and career outcomes. *Journal of Vocational Behavior*, 91, 76–86.

Zackery, A. (2014). How strengths-focussed coaching can help military personnel in their transition to 'civvy street'. *International Journal of Evidence Based Coaching and Mentoring*, (8), 54–64.

PART IV
Coaching in Contexts

24

Interculturally-Sensitive Coaching

Christian van Nieuwerburgh

INTRODUCTION

This chapter is written for coaches who work with people from different cultures. In today's multicultural world, that probably includes the vast majority of professionals who undertake coaching in organisational settings. Coaching also now takes place in a wide variety of professional contexts (van Nieuwerburgh, 2016) and therefore the question of coaching 'across cultures' has become an important topic. According to Abbott (2014), 'coaching – particularly executive and business coaching – has become a necessarily cross-cultural practice' (p. 343). The growing influence of globalisation has increased interest in and debate about the need for coaching people from different cultures. Although the chapter takes a pragmatic approach, it is not a guide about how to coach *clients* to work across different cultures. Instead, attention is focused on the role of culture in the interplay *between* coach and coachee.

This chapter starts by considering definitions of the word 'culture'. It then discusses theories relating to cultural 'difference' before surveying a number of cultural frameworks based on 'dimensions'. The main section explores the concepts of intercultural sensitivity and cultural proficiency. The chapter concludes with some practical ideas for how to engage in intercultural coaching conversations. At the outset, it may be helpful to note that this chapter is likely to raise complex questions rather than provide simple answers. As we will discover below, we are exploring a complex concept and its application to meaningful interpersonal relationships.

WHAT IS CULTURE?

Why start with a definition of 'culture'? In many ways, it can seem to be a familiar concept. We are all born into a 'culture' whether we like it or not. We are all being influenced by 'culture', even now, as we interact as writer and reader. So many of us might argue that we know what is meant by the term. However, a clear, agreed and unambiguous definition remains elusive.

So what is 'culture'? Edgar Schein, a renowned and well-respected professor of management, defined culture as the 'pattern of shared, basic taken-for-granted assumptions ... that manifests itself at the level of observable artifacts and shared espoused values, norms, and rules of behavior' (2010, p. 32). The 'taken-for-granted' nature of the assumptions is an important consideration. Often, these shared assumptions are not questioned. Intercultural scholars Nuri Robins, Lindsey, Lindsey and Terrell define culture as the beliefs and practices shared by a group (2006). So 'culture' can be understood as the beliefs and values held in common by a group of people. These beliefs and values often underpin the behaviours and practices of group members.

People *demonstrate* their membership of a group by behaving in ways that are consistent with the group's shared beliefs and values. As Lindsey, Martinez and Lindsey elaborate, 'these beliefs and practices enable an individual to identify as a member of a group as well as for other members of a group to recognize fellow members' (2007, p. 22). By having these characteristics, people are able to identify themselves as group members, recognise other members of the group and distinguish themselves from members of *other* groups. Rosinski, a leading thinker in this field, proposes that, 'a group's culture is the set of unique characteristics that distinguishes its members from another group' (2003, p. 20).

The discussion above, however, is complicated by three factors that should be raised here. Firstly, the type and size of a 'group' can vary. The term could refer to people living in a geographic area (e.g. Africa). At the same time, people who share a house could be considered to be a group with its own unique characteristics. Furthermore, groups often contain groups within them (often called subgroups). For example, 'people from Africa' is a group, but so are 'people living in Egypt', 'residents of Cape Town' or 'the villagers of Ogidi-Ijumu'. Secondly, as becomes apparent from the point above, people may be members of a number of groups, each with its own cultural characteristics. For example, a person could be European, a national of Belgium, from the region of Flanders and a resident of Ghent. In another example, students easily adopt the lifestyle and culture of their universities while maintaining their membership of national, regional and other groups. If this is not complicated enough, people can be considered to be part of a group but choose not to adhere to the values and principles of that group. For example, a Japanese person could intentionally reject Japanese culture, instead adopting the traditions and values of another.

Leading cultural scholars Trompenaars and Hampden-Turner propose that culture is 'layered'. At the centre of their model are the 'implicit basic assumptions' of a culture. The next layer is comprised of the 'norms and values' of the culture. The final, explicit outer layer is made up of the 'artifacts and products' of that culture (2012). In superficial interactions, only the outer layer (artifacts and products) is visible. However, Trompenaars and Hampden-Turner's theory suggests that the artifacts and products have been informed by the norms and values of that culture. This theory is of interest to coaches because coachees' implicit basic assumptions may emerge as relevant during coaching conversations. These assumptions that could hold the keys to unlocking people's potential are invisible to outside observers and sometimes even obscure to the coachees themselves. In other words, coaching can afford clients an opportunity to become aware of these assumptions in order to evaluate their relevance and usefulness.

An alternative perspective on culture is presented by Hofstede, Hofstede and Minkov (2010). They argue that every person has a 'mental programme' that is influenced by the social environments in which they were raised. Mental programming is understood as having three levels. At the foundational level, all people share what is known as 'human nature'. This is universal and inherited through our genes. Beyond this, people are part of a 'culture' that is specific to certain groups of people. Culture is developed within the family, the neighbourhood, at school, at work and in the community. It is therefore argued that 'culture is learned, not innate' (p. 6). At the top level is 'personality', and this is specific to each person. Their theory allows coaches to believe that there is a common factor that connects all of us (human nature). Any differences are understood as being informed by the two other levels: firstly, the programming that occurs in particular contexts (known as culture) and secondly, individual differences between people (known as personality).

Taking these theories into account and allowing for some ambiguity and complexity in our understanding of the term, the word 'culture' in this chapter will refer to the generally accepted beliefs, conventions, customs, social norms and behaviours associated with people who self-identify as members of a particular group. This is not proposed as a generic definition of 'culture' but as a specific form of wording that will guide a pragmatic discussion about 'culture' in the rest of this chapter. Our focus will be on working with coachees who self-identify as members of a particular group or subgroups. In this way, it is possible for coaches to raise their own awareness of how they understand culture and work with it in their coaching interactions. We are interested in the dynamics of one person coaching another person in which one or both parties believe that culture is relevant. Because of the context of this book, we will limit our discussion to 'national' and 'organisational' cultures.

CULTURAL 'DIFFERENCES'

In their attempts to understand culture, leading theorists have proposed a number of frameworks. The purpose of these has been to provide practitioners in organisations with a 'terminology' (Abbott, 2014; p. 348) with which to discuss culture. It is notable, but perhaps unsurprising, that these frameworks have focused on *differences*. Contemporary discussions about coaching across national cultures have also highlighted *difference* as a starting point (e.g. Passmore, 2013). Below, we will consider traditional approaches to engaging with these differences.

DIMENSIONS

Hofstede (1991) is the author of one of the best-known cultural frameworks. Based on his theory, cultures can be evaluated by assessing them across five dimensions. According to Hofstede's thinking, cultures can be better understood by discovering where they feature on each of the five dimensions. The dimensions are listed below, with a brief explanation of each.

- *Power distance*: This dimension relates to the extent to which cultures find imbalances of power acceptable. Power imbalance is considered acceptable at one end of the scale while those at the other end would insist that everyone should be treated equally.
- *Uncertainty avoidance*: At one end of this scale is a distaste for uncertainty. Uncertainty is avoided and its chances are minimised through the creation of rules and laws. At the other end, cultures are relatively more at ease with some uncertainty.
- *Individualism vs. collectivism*: This is a commonly discussed scale. On the one hand, this relates to the tendency of cultures to celebrate individualism (sometimes understood, disparagingly, as the pursuit of self-interest). On the other end of the scale is collectivism (often presented as the pursuit of the 'collective good').
- *Masculinity vs. femininity:* Some cultures are more 'masculine' in nature, favouring competitiveness, bravery and success (measured through material means) while other cultures are more 'feminine'. According to Hofstede, feminine cultures value cooperation, caring for others and

the seeking of consensus. In a feminine culture, success is measured by quality of life rather than material means.
- *Long-term vs. short-term*: This dimension is about the different perspectives of cultures. In some cultures, short-term gains are prioritized while in others there is more of a focus on anticipating longer-term benefits.

According to Hofstede, it is possible to gain a broad understanding of a culture by using these five dimensions. His framework has been used as the basis of training programmes in many global organisations. As a result, his work is particularly relevant and influential in intercultural and business contexts. The framework provides a way of identifying key differentiators between cultures and of understanding the behaviours and attitudes of groups of people based on their underlying beliefs. It should be recognised that some may consider the attempt to understand cultural differences by evaluating only five factors to be simplistic. However, each of the factors is considered along a *spectrum*, allowing for a degree of differentiation. Even more importantly, while acknowledging that culture is more complex than can be captured in such a framework, there is little doubt that Hofstede's work can provide us with a way to start noticing and discussing cultural dimensions.

In a related piece of work, Trompenaars and Hampden-Turner (2012) undertook research on cultural preferences, proposing the existence of *seven* cultural dimensions that could be studied in order to understand cultural differences. These are presented below.

Universalism vs. Particularism

- From a universalist point of view, everyone should be treated equally and should follow the same rules and laws.
- From a particularist point of view, every case is different and people should be treated differently based on their particular circumstances.

Individualism vs. Communitarianism

- Individualism values personal freedom and decision-making. As a result, it is believed that people should take care of themselves.
- Communitarianism relies on the group to provide protection to its members. In return for this, individuals are expected to show loyalty to the group. As a result, the group always comes first.

Specific vs. Diffuse

- In specific cultures, there is a belief that work and personal relationships can be kept separate. There is an implicit belief that people can work together even if they do not enjoy a good personal relationship.
- In diffuse cultures, social relationships are highly prized. There is less distinction between work and personal life. Colleagues tend to spend time together at work as well as socially.

Neutral vs. Emotional

- In a neutral culture, people do not openly display their emotions. In fact, emotions are not welcome in the workplace. It is felt that 'feelings' are not relevant when making professional decisions.
- In emotional cultures, emotions are expected at work. People look for opportunities to display their emotions. Emotional responses can be the basis of decision-making.

Achievement vs. Ascription

- In an achievement culture, a person's worth is evaluated based on their performance and achievements. Such cultures could be considered meritocratic.
- In an ascription culture, status is more important than performance. Titles and hierarchies matter deeply in such cultures.

Sequential Time vs. Synchronous Time

- In cultures with a sequential view of time, schedules are highly rated. In such cultures, it

is important that things happen in a particular sequence. Being punctual is considered very important.
- In cultures with a synchronous view of time, people often work on multiple projects simultaneously. Sequence is not that important, and time commitments are viewed more flexibly.

Internal Direction vs. Outer Direction

- In cultures with internal direction, people believe that they have control over their environments. This means that people are encouraged to take responsibility and make things happen for themselves.
- In cultures with outer direction, people believe that nature is powerful and ultimately in control. This means that it is important for people to work in accordance with the environment in order to get good outcomes.

While some of the differentiating factors vary, this framework is based on the same assumption as Hofstede's – namely, that it is helpful to understand differences between cultures in order to be able to work more effectively across them. While both provide a language and a structure for exploring cultural factors, the risks of over-simplifying and generalising are significant. However, these frameworks are valuable in that they challenge the notion of a 'best' culture, allowing coaches to adopt a more open, curious approach.

WHAT IS CULTURAL PROFICIENCY?

While the theorists discussed in the section above have presented frameworks relating to key features of cultures, others have considered ways that individuals can improve their ability to work across cultures. These theories are less about the difference between cultures and more about the ability of individuals to work in diverse settings. As such, they are particularly relevant to coaches wishing to work in a range of cultural contexts. Below we will consider some of these theories.

A leading intercultural scholar, Bennett (1993) proposed six stages of development in 'intercultural sensitivity'. The first stage (**denial of difference**) is characterised by people believing that their own culture is the only 'real' culture. Other cultures are ignored or suppressed. The second stage (**defence against difference**) is one in which people recognise the existence of other cultures but believe that theirs is the most advanced (and therefore the best). People at this stage tend to be protective about their own culture and belittle other people's cultures. The third stage (**minimisation of difference**) involves the belief that people are essentially similar and all adhere to a set of universal values. While well-meaning, differences are minimised because of an unintentional privileging of one's own culture. People in the fourth stage (**acceptance of difference**) understand their own culture as one of a number of advanced worldviews. They accept that there are different ways of understanding the world and are open to this. However, they are not able or willing to accept some aspects of the other cultures. In the fifth stage (**adaptation to difference**), people are able to broaden their worldviews in order to understand other cultures. They are able to adapt their behaviours in different cultural contexts. The final, sixth stage (**integration of difference**) allows people to shift between different cultural worldviews. At this stage, a person's definition of their 'self' is not too rigid to move between cultures.

The benefits of Bennett's theories may be immediately obvious to readers who may already have automatically assessed themselves against the stages outlined above. For many of us, this may have been a discomforting experience, especially if we have realised that we may be at a stage that is not most appropriate for intercultural coaching. If we were to adopt Bennett's theory, it could be argued that it would be necessary for coaches to develop their 'intercultural sensitivity' so that they operate at levels five and six. Some

Table 24.1 Bennett's stages of intercultural sensitivity for coaches

Denial of differences	Coach is unaware of the need to consider culture when coaching
Defence against difference	Coach is aware of cultural differences but believes that their own culture is 'right'
Minimisation of difference	Coach is aware of cultural differences but thinks that these are not important
Acceptance of difference	Coach recognises and accepts other cultures (but with some reservations)
Adaptation to difference	Coach is able to adapt to different cultures and is empathetic
Integration of difference	Coach appreciates other cultures and is able to move freely between them

strategies for doing so have been suggested by Drake (2009) who offered an intrapersonal view of these stages as seen through a case study. Below, we consider the six stages with reference to coaching (see Table 24.1).

Philippe Rosinski has developed the ideas of Bennett further, specifically thinking about coaching across cultures. As Rosinski (2003) explains, the first three stages of Bennett's model can be considered 'ethnocentric'. These, he argues, are unhelpful when coaching across cultures. He suggests that 'ethnocentricism occurs in three forms: ignoring differences, evaluating them negatively, and downplaying their importance' (p. 31). According to him, stages 4–6 could be considered 'ethnorelative'. This means that people recognise that cultural differences are inevitable and accept that their worldview is not shared by everyone. Importantly, people adopting an ethnorelative approach are not threatened by other cultures. Instead, they are 'curious and eager to learn about differences' (p. 34).

Rosinski then proposes an additional (seventh) level entitled 'Leverage Differences'. This stage is presented as proactive and involves 'looking for gems in your own culture(s) and mine for treasures in other culture(s)' (p. 40). These 'gems' consist of 'useful insights' and 'alternative perspectives on issues' (p. 40). The additional stage is characterised as 'Ethnointegrative'. Out of this work, Rosinski developed a 'Cultural Orientations Framework' (2007) assessment questionnaire that provides a useful tool for use in cross-cultural settings.

Some US scholars (Lindsey, Martinez and Lindsey, 2007) have taken a related but slightly different approach to the intercultural sensitivity of coaches. They see 'cultural proficiency' as a continuum (rather than stages). This means that coaches can be at any point between 'cultural destructiveness' to 'cultural proficiency' (see Table 24.2).

By considering these factors along a continuum, it becomes possible to evaluate the intercultural sensitivity of coaches and their practice. This model allows for the possibility that a coach might work in a 'culturally competent' way with one coachee while being at a different point in the continuum with another. Further, the aspiration of 'cultural proficiency' at the positive end of the continuum recognises the need for ongoing learning and development for coaches who wish to work in interculturally sensitive ways. In summary, we have reviewed a number of frameworks used to discuss culture. These can be helpful when exploring cultural differences at an organisational or national level. We have also considered the notions of cultural proficiency and intercultural sensitivity. These concepts allow coaches to evaluate their own level of development or proficiency, raising their self-awareness and identifying ways of improving their practice.

COACHING 'OTHERS'

While there has been much thought given in the West about intercultural issues, we should

Table 24.2 Cultural proficiency

Cultural destructiveness	Seeking to destroy the cultures of others (artifacts, traditions etc.)
Cultural incapacity	Belittling other cultures and seeking to show that they are wrong
Cultural blindness	Refusing to acknowledge the cultures of other people
Cultural precompetence	Having an awareness of cultural difference and recognising that they need to learn more about working with diversity
Cultural competence	Understanding the interactive nature of coaching and working in ways that support cultures that are different from the coach's own culture
Cultural proficiency	Committing to lifelong learning in order to better work with people from cultures that are different from the coach's own culture

Source: Adapted from Lindsey, Martinez and Lindsey (2007)

heed Rosinski who warns of the 'trap of adopting an enthnocentric view' (2003, p. 31) in our response. In fact, even the enthnorelative and ethnointegrative approaches suggested by Bennett and Rosinski could be questioned. While Bennett's stages of 'adapt to differences' and 'integrate differences' and Rosinski's additional stage of 'leverage differences' are all positive in their intentions, there is nonetheless a focus on 'difference'. All these interactions position the coachee as being from a 'different' culture from the coach and therefore 'other'.

Indeed, there has been a tendency in the field of coaching to focus on difference when considering ways of undertaking 'cross-cultural coaching'. Much of the literature about coaching and diversity to date has presented culture as problematic. Both Rosinski and Abbott note that there is often an underlying assumption that culture is an obstacle to be overcome. For example, the book *Diversity in Coaching* (Passmore, 2013) is advertised as exploring 'the impact and implication of difference in coaching' (back cover). Alongside chapters on 'coaching in Europe', 'coaching in North America' and 'coaching in Australasia' are chapters on 'coaching with men: alpha males' and 'coaching gay and lesbian clients'. In many cases, the starting point seems to be that the coachees are from a 'different' culture. Put differently, in discussions about cross-cultural coaching, the coachee is often placed in the position of 'other' and the coach in the position of 'not other'.

As Abbott (2014) argues, there is a curious paradox at the heart of cross-cultural coaching. On the one hand, it may be necessary to 'deal explicitly and primarily with culture as a variable and influence in coaching' and on the other, the idea of undertaking cross-cultural coaching is 'theoretically dubious and can be highly perilous' (p. 345). A discussion about the concept of 'otherness' is beyond the scope of this chapter. However, it has been addressed critically by leading 20th century thinkers including Edward Said, Michel Foucault and Simone de Beauvoir who discuss the relationship between the concepts of 'identity' and the position of the 'other'. In every case, the position of 'other' is presented as negative or inferior. As coaches, we must avoid positioning ourselves or our coachees as 'other'. An approach that responds to this challenge is presented below.

BEING EQUAL

Arguing that we must not position our coachees as 'other' does not deny that differences do exist between cultures. That is what makes travel so interesting, working across organisations stimulating and diversity so important. But we are proposing that, in coaching, it is not helpful to become preoccupied with these differences. There is no doubt that effective coaching should take culture into account. Cultural factors, more than ever, feature in *every* coaching conversation. Cultural 'differences' are only one set of variables in a very complex set of factors. Rather than focus on the potential for misunderstanding based on perceived cultural differences, we believe that it is preferable to attend to the nature of the coaching relationship. To use Kemp's (2011) phrase, the coach should invest in 'the experiential, emergent, and iterative nature of the coaching engagement' (p. 153).

Therefore, it becomes incumbent on coaches to be sensitive to culture in *all* conversations while simultaneously attending to the creation of a one-to-one relationship based on mutual respect, openness and trust. Building such relationships requires skill and humility on the part of the coach. Trusting, mutually respectful relationships in coaching should be characterised by a sense of equality (Knight, 2011). According to Knight, equality is one of the principles underpinning successful coaching relationships. A conversation between two people in which one person is characterised as 'other' cannot be considered to be a dialogue between equals. Both persons must feel that they are of equal value as human beings.

I have argued elsewhere (van Nieuwerburgh, 2014, p. 158) that effective coaches should be humble. Interculturally-sensitive coaches will necessarily have to develop their capacity to practise humility. This means that a coach would not presume that their cultural beliefs and values are in any way superior to those of their coachees. This is not to suggest that coaches should abandon their own convictions. On the contrary, 'humility applied to convictions does not mean believing things any less; it means treating those who hold contrary beliefs with respect and friendship' (Dickson, 2011, p. 167). By demonstrating humility and creating mutually-respectful relationships between two human beings of equal value, interculturally-sensitive coaches are best placed to support their coachees to flourish.

THE COMPETENCIES OF INTERCULTURALLY-SENSITIVE COACHES

We must now address the thorny issue of the competencies needed for *interculturally-sensitive* coaching. Building on Sue and Sue's (1990) seminal work on counselling across cultures, Baron and Azizollah (2007) propose that coaches working with people of different cultures should develop self-awareness, knowledge and skills. They argue that coaches 'must continuously reflect on their own cultural assumptions and biases' (p. 372), acquire 'the basic knowledge needed to have a good chance of initiating a positive coaching relationship' (p. 373) and develop a 'broad range of strategies and approaches' for working in diverse environments (p. 376). This tripartite understanding (self-awareness, knowledge and skills) is a helpful way of thinking about the necessary development of an interculturally-sensitive coach. Plum (2008), for example, has argued that coaches should develop their 'cultural intelligence'. This is defined as 'the ability to make oneself understood and the ability to create a fruitful collaboration in situations where cultural differences play a role' (p. 1).

In addition to cultural intelligence, Abbott, Stening, Atkins and Grant (2006) have proposed that coaches working in cross-cultural contexts need to have

'Sound appreciation of the cultures of the client and the host country'

'Self-awareness of the coach's own cultural background'

'Personal experience in cultural adaptation and acculturation'

'Familiarity with cross-disciplinary theory and research'

(2006, cited in Abbott, 2014, p. 354)

In other words, it is suggested that coaches require self-awareness (about their own stage of cultural proficiency, cultural beliefs and assumptions), knowledge (about the cultures of the client and the host country; personal experience of cultural adaptation; and an understanding of cross-disciplinary theory and research about cultures) and skills (the ability to build relationships; strategies and approaches for working in multicultural settings). This seems like the job specification for an interculturally-sensitive coach!

This specification may be too demanding, limiting the number of people able to apply for the role. In addition, coaches would still need to perform a delicate balancing act: on the one hand, referring to theories and frameworks to help to reflect on the dimensions of their coachees' cultural context and, on the other, avoiding the trap of making unhelpful assumptions about their coachee and their cultural group. As Abbott suggests, coaches should always 'be mindful of the potential for culture to be a major influence but to be very open-minded as to how it may be playing a part in the client's situation' (2014, p. 358). Furthermore, Bossons, Kourdi and Sartain suggest that 'when dealing with culture, it's important to maintain a balance between paying too much attention to it or not enough' (2012, p. 74). In real terms, such advice may add to a coach's uncertainty about how to respond to culture within coaching conversations. It becomes an essential skill to be aware of our own approach to culture, so that we can determine the right balance.

We therefore concur with Baron and Azizollah's (2007) idea that interculturally-sensitive coaches require self-awareness, knowledge and skills. The self-awareness relates to one's own culture and one's level of cultural proficiency. We would argue, however, that there may be an overemphasis on the 'knowledge' needed. Apart from some knowledge of the theories about cultural dimensions, we are not convinced that personal experience of cultural adaptation is needed. Furthermore, an in-depth understanding of a person's cultural context may be unnecessary, and in some cases unhelpful. Any relevant information needed about a coachee's cultural identity can come from conversations with the coachee. Finally, the skills needed are those necessary for any effective coaching (discussed further below).

THE PRACTICE OF INTERCULTURALLY-SENSITIVE COACHING

According to Passmore and Law (2013), intercultural coaching 'journeys' occur over four stages. During the assimilation stage, the coach should listen to and validate the coachee's experiences. In the following consolidation stage, the coach and coachee strengthen their relationship by developing 'trust and mutual respect'. During the exploration stage, the coach works with the coachee to 'open up new insights from the coachee's assimilated experience'. Finally, in the maturation stage, the coach uses a range of methods and approaches to support the coachee to find culturally-appropriate strategies to move towards their goals (p. 7). This process is suitable for coaching in these situations. However, other well-known coaching processes would also be appropriate if used with intercultural sensitivity.

BEST PRACTICE

The process itself seems less important than the way in which the coach behaves in order to build a trusting and mutually respectful relationship. While recognising that every coaching conversation will be different, we tentatively propose below some ideas about how to coach in an interculturally-sensitive way (see Table 24.3). Some of these are applicable in *all* coaching interactions and

Table 24.3 Suggested ideas for best practice in intercultural coaching

Best practice in all coaching interactions
Be clear about the purpose of coaching
Follow a clear process that is shared with the coachee
Commit explicitly to the principle of non-directivity
Respect the role of the coachee as a decision-maker
Regularly check the health of the coaching relationship

Behaviours that may demonstrate intercultural sensitivity
Demonstrate appropriate curiosity about the coachee
Take an interest in the coachee's cultural milieu
Maintain a respectful attitude to the coachee's self-identified cultural group
Maintain a non-judgemental attitude to the coachee's self-identified cultural group
Invite feedback about your coaching practice from the coachee

Behaviours to avoid when there is a risk of cultural misunderstanding
Avoid making assumptions about the coachee's cultural group or groups
Do not allow stereotypes to influence your perception of the coachee
Avoid discriminatory language
Do not belittle or make humorous comments about the coachee's cultural group
Avoid ethnocentric tendencies to impose your cultural values onto others

others may be used specifically to demonstrate intercultural sensitivity. We also suggest some behaviours to avoid when there is a risk of cultural misunderstanding. As may have become apparent in this chapter, some of these best practices should apply to all coaching that is delivered in a supportive and mutually-supportive way.

- Firstly, coaches should be clear about the purpose of the coaching interaction – in other words that the conversation aims to support the coachee to set their own goals and identify a range of options for working towards them.
- Secondly, the coach should share the conversational framework (e.g. GROW) with the coachee. It is helpful for both parties to be clear about the outline structure of the conversation.
- Thirdly, the power of coaching comes from the non-directive nature of the interaction (van Nieuwerburgh, 2014). An explicit acknowledgement of this at the start of the coaching relationship can help to build rapport and encourage the coachee to take responsibility for working towards their goals.
- Fourthly, wherever possible the coach should support the coachee to explore choices and make decisions for themselves. Not only is this a respectful way of interacting with others, it also ensures that the coachee is making decisions that are in line with their own cultural contexts.
- Finally, it is good practice to actively check on the health of the coaching relationship. This can be done at the start and end of every coaching session. Doing this will show that the coach cares about the relationship, while also allowing for open and honest conversations about how it may be improved.

In some cases, it may be deemed necessary for the coach to *demonstrate* intercultural sensitivity. This may be due to some concern on the part of the coachee about a coach's lack of knowledge about the coachee's context. In such scenarios, it may be appropriate for the coach to show an *appropriate* level of curiosity about the coachee and her cultural milieu. Perhaps questions about cultural practices that the coach has noticed or general questions about unique aspects of the coachee's self-identified cultural group could be asked by way of small talk at the start of the coaching conversation. In every circumstance, the self-identified cultural group should be afforded respect and appreciation. Finally, we recommend that the coach should seek feedback about the appropriateness of their coaching style and questions at the end of the first conversation.

In addition to the best practice suggestions above, there are also some behaviours that should definitely be avoided in situations where there may be a risk of cultural misunderstanding. Firstly, the most dangerous of these is to make assumptions about the coachee's self-identified cultural group. Stereotyping is unhelpful in most situations, and certainly in coaching conversations when the focus is so clearly on an individual coachee. Secondly, care should be used to avoid discriminatory language. For example, using one gender (he or she) to refer to people in general is discriminatory. Thirdly, humorous comments about the coachee's self-identified cultural groups, perhaps shared in an attempt to lighten the mood, should be avoided at all costs. This applies even if such jokes are initiated by the coachee. Any such remarks by the coach could be perceived as belittling or disrespectful. Finally, and perhaps most challenging of all, is the need to resist any tendency in the coach to adopt an ethnocentric view by attempting to promote or impose their own value judgements on the coachee.

SOME CHALLENGES

As we have suggested in this chapter, interculturally-sensitive coaching is complex. While it has been possible to propose some best practice suggestions for consideration, there are some challenges that require further reflection. Each coach will need to find a way of navigating the challenges below:

Being Non-Judgemental but Ethical

While being non-judgemental is essential to the creation of mutually respectful relationships, it should be remembered that every executive coach must work within a set of professional and ethical guidelines. The stance of 'non-judgement' cannot override the Code of Ethics of a professional coach. So, for example, if your coachee tells you of something that is *illegal* in the jurisdiction in which they live or work, this must be addressed accordingly. Equally, any information that indicates that the coachee is at risk of harm must also be dealt with, regardless of cultural milieu. Obviously, there will be some grey areas that are not as clearcut at the examples above. This highlights the added importance of having good-quality supervision. It is recommended that coaching supervision be sought from an interculturally-sensitive coach supervisor.

Offering Coaching, not Mentoring or Consultancy

The real challenge for practitioners as they work in various cultural contexts could well be more about remaining true to the principles of coaching than the question of interacting with people from diverse cultures. In attempts to ensure a 'cultural fit', coaches may be at risk of adapting coaching to such an extent that it starts to lose its focus or power. In being flexible and open to different views and cultures, coaches may inadvertently deliver less-than-optimal coaching experiences. In some cases, it may be more appropriate to introduce alternative conversational interventions.

For example, in a context where hierarchies are important, mentoring may be a more appropriate intervention (rather than adapting our understanding of coaching to include direct instruction). In others, where the dissemination of expertise is needed, training or consultancy might be better suited to supporting improvement. In our well-intentioned attempts to demonstrate the value of coaching (in all circumstances) we are at risk of increasing confusion about coaching itself. Simply calling an intervention 'coaching' when it is in fact group facilitation, training, consultancy or mentoring can be counterproductive. Therefore, clear and honest contracting with the client at the outset of any coaching-related work takes on added importance in intercultural contexts.

CONCLUSION

As we reach the close of this chapter, it may be helpful to review what has been discussed. Initially, we explored the term 'culture' with reference to leading scholars in the field. While acknowledging the complexity of the concept, we proposed a working definition for this chapter: 'generally accepted beliefs, conventions, customs, social norms and behaviours associated with people who self-identify as members of a particular group'. We then surveyed a number of theoretical frameworks used to explore and understand cultural differences. This was followed by a consideration of the notions of 'cultural proficiency' and 'intercultural sensitivity'. We then raised questions about the idea of 'otherness', proposing that the principle of equality is at the heart of coaching relationships. Finally, we considered some practical ideas and concerns relating to intercultural sensitivity.

It is tempting to conclude that there is nothing unique about intercultural coaching. One could easily argue that all coaching is intercultural. However, in doing so, might we be at risk of reverting to an ethnocentric view that minimises cultural differences? Or does the highlighting of 'intercultural coaching' as unique bring the focus back to 'differences' and 'others' in an unhelpful way? Abbott highlights the conundrum when he says that 'all coaching is cross-cultural – and none.' (Abbott, 2014, p. 342)

There can be no doubt that every coachee is entitled to the highest level of respect. It therefore should go without saying that their culture should be accepted completely and without judgement. The fact that this may be easier said than done should give us reason for careful self-reflection. We live in a world where discrimination is sadly pervasive. Even in the 21st century, many people hold racist, sexist and homophobic views (among a variety of others discriminatory beliefs). Whether explicitly or implicitly, people in the West often suggest that their culture is superior. The phrase 'third world' is an obvious example of this. The more politically correct 'developing world' falls into the same trap. While pragmatism would suggest that we must accept that things will not change as rapidly as we might like, it is right to insist that discriminatory views are not acceptable when coaching.

Building a strong relationship is paramount in every coaching assignment. Demonstrating respect is the minimum responsibility of every coach. The ability to maintain a non-judgemental stance and adopt a broad range of perspectives therefore become essential competencies. We must remember that our coachees must generate solutions and ideas that are *aligned with their own principles* and *workable within their own cultures*.

In closing, let us remind ourselves of the primary role of a coach. It is to facilitate a conducive and effective thinking environment for learning and development to take place for the coachee. It is not to instruct, tell or educate. Our purpose is not the make the world a better place, or impose our belief systems on others. We must remember that there should be no 'other' in the coaching relationship. It is a relationship of equals. Intercultural-sensitivity is an essential part of the 'coaching way of being'.

RELEVANT TERMINOLOGY

Cross-cultural	Across cultures, involving two or more different cultures
Cultural diversity	Refers positively to the variety of human cultures
Cultural imperialism	When a powerful culture imposes its views and beliefs onto other, less powerful, cultures
Cultural intelligence	The ability to work successfully in diverse cultures – a development of the concept of emotional intelligence
Cultural milieu	A cultural setting or a cultural context
Cultural proficiency	Having the self-awareness, knowledge and skills to work with and support people from diverse cultural backgrounds
Culture	The generally accepted beliefs, conventions, customs, social norms and behaviours associated with people who self-identify as members of a particular group
Ethnocentric	The tendency to judge people and situations in other cultures based on a person's own cultural beliefs and values
Ethnointegrative	The tendency to be open to the integration of cultures
Ethnorelative	The tendency to appreciate different cultures, recognising that there are different, valid sets of beliefs and values about the world
Interculturally-sensitive coaching	Coaching undertaken by a culturally intelligent coach who is alert to the possible role of culture in every coaching conversation
Multicultural	Relating to or including more than one culture
National culture	The culture that exists within populations of countries
Organisational culture	The culture that exists within organisations

REFERENCES

Abbott, G. N. (2014). Cross-cultural Coaching: A Paradoxical Perspective. In E. Cox, T. Bachkirova and D. Clutterbuck (eds), *The Complete Handbook of Coaching* (2nd edition). London: Sage.

Abbott, G. N., Stening, B. W., Atkins, P.W. B. and Grant, A. J. (2006). Coaching expatriate managers for success: Adding value beyond training and mentoring. *Asia Pacific Journal of Human Resources*, 44(3): 295–317.

Baron, H. and Azizollah, H. (2007). Coaching and diversity. In S. Palmer and A. Whybrow (eds), *Handbook of Coaching Psychology: A Guide for Practitioners*. Hove: Routledge. (pp. 367–384).

Bennett, M. J. (1993). Towards ethnorelativism: A developmental model of intercultural sensitivity. In R. M. Paige (ed.), *Education for the Intercultural Experience* (2nd edition). Yarmouth, ME: Intercultural Press. (pp. 21–71).

Bossons, P., Kourdi, J. and Sartain, D. (2012). *Coaching Essentials: Practical, Proven Techniques for World-Class Executive Coaching* (2nd edition). London: Bloomsbury.

Dickson, J. (2011). *Humilitas: A Lost Key to Life, Love, and Leadership*. Grand Rapids, MI: Zondervan.

Drake, D. B. (2009). Identity, liminality, and development through coaching: An intrapersonal view of intercultural sensitivity. In M. Moral and G. Abbott (eds), *The Routledge Companion to International Business Coaching*. London, UK: Routledge. (pp. 61–74).

Hofstede, G. H. (1991). *Cultures and Organizations: Software of the Mind*. London: McGraw-Hill.

Hofstede, G. H., Hofstede G. J. and Minkov, M. (2010). *Cultures and Organizations: Software of the Mind* (3rd edition). New York: McGraw-Hill.

Kemp, T. (2011). Building the coaching alliance: Illuminating the phenomenon of relationship in coaching. In G. Hernez-Broome and L. A. Boyce (eds), *Advancing Executive Coaching: Setting the Course for Successful Leadership Coaching*. San Francisco, CA: Jossey-Bass. (pp.151–176).

Knight, J. (2011). *Unmistakable Impact: A Partnership Approach for Dramatically Improving Instruction*. Thousand Oaks, CA: Corwin.

Lindsey, D. B., Martinez, R. S. and Lindsey, R. B. (2007). *Culturally Proficient Coaching: Supporting Educators to Create Equitable Schools*. Thousand Oaks, CA: Corwin.

Nuri Robins, K., Lindsey, R. B., Lindsey, D. B. and Terrell, R. D. (2006). *Culturally Proficient Instruction: A Guide for People who Teach* (2nd edition). Thousand Oaks, CA: Corwin Press.

Passmore, J. (ed.) (2013). *Diversity in Coaching: Working with Gender, Culture, Race and Age* (2nd edition). London: Kogan Page.

Passmore, J. and Law, H. (2013). Cross-cultural and diversity coaching. In J. Passmore (ed.), *Diversity in Coaching: Working with Gender, Culture, Race and Age* (2nd edition). London: Kogan Page. (pp. 1–11).

Plum, E. (2008). *Cultural Intelligence: The Art of Leading Cultural Complexity*. Middlesex: Middlesex University Press.

Rosinski, P. (2003). *Coaching Across Cultures*. London: Nicholas Brealey Publishing.

Rosinski, P. (2007). The Cultural Orientations Framework (COF) assessment questionnaire. Rhode-St-Genèse (Belgium): Rosinski & Company. Retrieved 6/9/2015, http://www.philrosinski.com/cof/

Schein, E. H. (2010). *Organizational Culture and Leadership* (4th edition). San Francisco, CA: Jossey-Bass.

Sue, D. W. and Sue, D. (1990). *Counselling the Culturally Diverse: Theory and Practice* (2nd edition). New York: Wiley.

Trompenaars, F. and Hampden-Turner, C. H. (2012). *Riding the Waves of Culture: Understanding Diversity in Global Business* (3rd edition). London: Nicholas Brealey.

van Nieuwerburgh, C. (2014). *An Introduction to Coaching Skills: A Practical Guide*. London: Sage.

van Nieuwerburgh, C. (ed.) (2016). *Coaching in Professional Contexts*. London: Sage.

25

Cross-Cultural Coaching: An Emerging Practice

Geoffrey N. Abbott and Raija Salomaa

INTRODUCTION

The world is highly and increasingly interconnected economically, socially and technologically; and, as a result, coaching assignments are invariably and increasingly 'cross-cultural' in some way. This interconnectedness is coupled with turbulence. We live and work in a global environment of volatility, uncertainty, complexity and ambiguity (VUCA) characterised by constant change, including dangerous ruptures and positive innovation (Johansen, 2007; Bernstein, 2014). The practice of cross-cultural coaching is emerging and shaped by this heightened interconnectedness and complexity.

This developing field of interest has gained growing attention among coaching practitioners and scholars (Abbott et al., 2013) since Rosinski (2003) introduced his book *Coaching across Cultures*, where he combined coaching with cultural theories. Cross-cultural coaching is descriptive of coaching practice that occurs when 'the context is somehow "cross-", "multi-" or "inter-" cultural, with an aim to promote desirable and sustainable change for the benefit of the coachee and potentially for other stakeholders' (modified from Bachkirova et al., 2010: 1). 'Global coaching' is a term that is increasingly used to describe the practices of coaches who are globally mobile and who often have international networks that can provide coaching services to multinational companies and in multiple countries.

In this chapter, we consider global coaching under the umbrella of cross-cultural coaching. We refer readers to a related Chapter 24 of this Handbook on 'Interculturally-Sensitive Coaching' as it includes more discussion of the key definitions and distinctions. The underlying premise of cross-cultural coaching is a commitment to the sensitive treatment of relevant cultural beliefs, dimensions, preferences, orientations and practices. As a theme, we have noted that most cross-cultural coaching continues to utilise mainstream coaching methodologies, but that adaptation of such approaches is critical. We have also noted that recent developments in management and leadership that draw on complexity theory and systems thinking have particular resonance in the cross-cultural coaching landscape where one salient variable – culture – is increasingly interrelated with other shifting and volatile variables in the global environment.

The focus in this chapter is primarily on emerging directions and practices in cross-cultural coaching. There are some challenges in surveying the field of cross-cultural coaching because it can be conducted in any genre or tradition of coaching where culture emerges in some way as a significant variable – whether in executive coaching, group and team coaching, managerial coaching, sports coaching, and so on. We have mainly examined executive coaching and managerial coaching practices in organisations with cross-cultural and cross-border contexts, primarily because this is where the bulk of the literature and research is focused. The application of coaching as a practice largely rooted in Western culture in other cultures with different traditions and orientations is also addressed. The chapter is offered in five parts: (1) the context of cross-cultural coaching, (2) current instruments, models and approaches for cross-cultural coaching, (3) complexity systems, complexity of mind: relevance to emerging cross-cultural coaching practice, (4) recent empirical studies, and (5) future research and concluding comments.

THE CONTEXT OF CROSS-CULTURAL COACHING

Technological advances in information and communication technologies and globalisation in general have resulted in most executives in developed and developing economies being drawn into the international arena in some way. The early iterations of cross-cultural coaching were often around the need to bring in a specialist to work with a traditional expatriate manager from one country who was embedded in another. Now, we are seeing much more complex scenarios of multicultural and virtual teams, and global companies that don't have an identifiable national culture. There is also growing diversity in demographics with third culture kids (TCKs) moving into management roles – even as high as President of the United States of America.

There is now a generation of young professionals and potential leaders who have spent all their formative years in a globalised environment – 'third culture kids' (Fail, Thompson and Walker, 2004) – the children of expatriates, who have grown up in cultures different from their parents, often living nomadic lives as their parents moved, or were moved, around the globe. International activity generally is growing. Research by PWC (2012) found that the number of people on international assignments increased by 25 percent in the last decade, with the number of international assignments expected to further grow by 50 percent in 2020. The trends in these assignments included greater virtual work, shorter assignments, and a greater diversity in demographics and assignment type. With this background and direction, executives need to develop new skills to address the challenges. Executive coaching seems to be finding a place in developing these skills and abilities (Awal and Stumpf, 2009; Bernstein, 2014). Cross-cultural coaching is becoming increasingly relevant because of the greater cultural diversity of modalities and interactions.

Culture defines the context of cross-cultural coaching, and the fact that it surfaces as a significant variable for various stakeholders suggests a need for an approach which gives it some priority. Culture has been variously defined (see Chapter 24 for further discussion). In this context of the emergent practice of cross-cultural coaching a definition of culture from Hampden-Turner and Trompenaars (1998: 6) is of particular resonance. They define culture as, 'the way a group of people solve problems and reconcile dilemmas'. This definition is significant for cross-cultural coaching as it is geared towards engaging multiple approaches to the diverse challenges being faced by executives in a vast array of cross-cultural contexts.

Cross-cultural situations often require a sophisticated treatment of the coachee-in-context, which utilises knowledge about cultural differences, intercultural effectiveness, systems thinking, and human flourishing. Existing knowledge and previous understandings of both the coach and the coachee are significant in positioning a coaching process for success (Cox, 2003). The role of the coach includes teasing out the cognitive, behavioural and affective interactions and patterns that are present in the context. This helps coachees understand how they are operating and how they can make a constructive impact for themselves, their organisations and their society.

Consideration of the concept and practice of 'cross-cultural coaching' raises the question of the cultural essence of contemporary executive coaching as a whole. At face value, it can be classified as a Western management practice. Rosinski (2003, p. 20–21) writes that, 'traditional coaching has implicitly reflected particular norms, values, and basic assumptions that reflect the originating culture of the field of coaching, the United States, and do not necessarily hold true universally.' Brock (2008, p. 174) concluded from a literature review that the major influences on the current coaching discipline are from psychology (primarily humanistic and clinical), business (organisation development, management, and consulting), philosophy (both Eastern and Western), adult learning and development, sports, performing arts, biology, and systems theory. It is reasonable to conclude that, other than Eastern philosophy, its roots are mostly from contemporary Western societies. However, the Eastern influence is perhaps significant in explaining why executive coaching and coaching methodologies have gained a strong presence around the globe.

Eastern influences have entered coaching, particularly through the humanist movement which draws on Buddhist teaching (Skiffington and Zeus, 2003). Jung's work on the unconscious informs many coaching approaches and his ideas are closely connected to Eastern philosophies. Fritjof Capra's work *The Tao of Physics* (1975) is sometimes used in coaching training (e.g. Institute of Executive Coaching and Leadership, Sydney). Western philosophies give primacy to objective investigation based on reason and the role of the individual. Eastern philosophy is based more on an assumption that the individual is entwined in context and there is a continuity between nature and nurture. In Eastern philosophy there is accommodation for subjectivity in accepting that different ways and perspectives can exist together, and a concern with the 'big picture', harmony and unity (Brock, 2008:114).

CURRENT INSTRUMENTS, MODELS AND APPROACHES FOR CROSS-CULTURAL COACHING

The emerging field of cross-cultural coaching has created and utilised various instruments, models and approaches. It has also remained largely faithful to the fundamentals of executive coaching and managerial coaching practices that have become an accepted part of contemporary business practice. It is a matter of adaptation and evolution rather than one of radical departure in approach. Intercultural management theories and intercultural researchers have influenced the field of cross-cultural coaching and, as a result, the understanding of cultural dimensions and values as well as being aware of one's own cultural assumptions are commonly stated as requirements for coaches working in this field (e.g. Peterson, 2007; St Claire-Ostwald, 2007). At the core of much of the practice of cross-cultural coaching is a reliance on research and measurement of cultural dimension, most notably from Geert Hofsede's work (Hofstede, 1997, 2001, 2011).

People, organisations, and societies can be mapped onto a scale using these dimensions, with the underlying premise that the scores are relatively stable and can be used by executives as valuable data for understanding behaviour and making decisions in culturally diverse situations. Hofstede's model has evolved over time. His original four dimensions now number six, with 'indulgent versus restraint' being the most recent addition (Hofstede, 2011: 8). Hofstede has made a huge contribution in providing theory and language around culture to enable conversations and to validate culture as a major variable in executive and organisational life. As a caution, Osland et al. (2000) highlighted the risks of falling into cultural stereotyping when considering individuals in the light of the dimensions of their home culture.

Typically, cross-cultural coaching is discussed in coaching handbooks (e.g. Stober and Grant, 2006; Drake et al., 2008; Bachkirova et al., 2010), in handbooks devoted to coaching and mentoring psychology (Law et al., 2009; Law, 2013; Passmore, 2013a; Palmer and Whybrow, 2008), and in some books dedicated purely or partly to cross-cultural coaching or diversity issues (Rosinski, 2003, 2010; Moral and Abbott, 2009; Passmore, 2013b). Until recently, most of the chapters and articles have been conceptual with some individual case studies. They present, for example, coaching frameworks and approaches suitable for cross-cultural contexts (Handin and Steinwedel, 2006; Peterson, 2007; Abbott and Stening, 2009; Law et al., 2009; Coultas et al., 2011, 2009; Plaister-Ten, 2013). Some of the recent texts show how cross-cultural issues in coaching are expanding into various fields of coaching. For example, Curry (2015) discusses coaching as an intervention to develop global teams and global team leaders (see also Abbott and Stening, 2009). He proposes that increasing self-awareness and cultivating mindfulness relate back to the importance of self-regulation in global team effectiveness.

There have been a number of different but related approaches to coaching across cultures. Philippe Rosinski's work (2003) is prominent. Rosinski (2003, p. 21) takes the position that, 'The fact that our behaviors depend in part on the particular cultural context further justifies the need for coaches to integrate the cultural perspective into their practice.' He proposes that coaches build on Milton's Bennett's six stages for developing cultural sensitivity to include a stage for leveraging differences, striving for synergy, and looking for gems in different cultures. See Chapter 24 (this volume) for a more detailed analysis of the importance of this intercultural sensitivity. Rosinski (2003) argues that this requires more than an intellectual commitment. It requires a deep belief that there is value in leveraging diversity. He says, 'You need to become convinced in your heart and in your guts that a different truth or ideal is legitimate' (p. 36).

Passmore and Law (2013) survey existing models for cross-cultural coaching, including Rosinski (2003) and Trompennars and Hampden Turner (2012). They propose a 'pragmatic implementation model' – the Universal Integrated Framework – which embeds five factors:

- Continuous professional development
- Appreciation of the cultural environment
- Coach fluidity and capacity for integration
- Cross-cultural emotional intelligence; and
- Communication methods and feedback mechanisms.

Rosinski's work and the model proposed by Passmore and Law are consistent with the notion that cross-cultural coaching is a field that requires continuous learning, heighted sensitivity to cultural influences, and adaptability. Further, most cross-cultural approaches aim to individualise cultural influences and help coachees to make sense of what is going in their unique contexts. David Peterson (2007, p. 262), makes the observation that, 'Because coaches work one-on-one, they can discover and work with each person as a unique human being rather than forming opinions based on generalisations and stereotypes about the person's cultural background.' His advice includes (1) searching for hidden layers, (2) personalising the approach, and (3) orchestrating change in a way that suits the individual. Trust building is given strong attention in his approach. He recommends the use of the Development Pipeline, which is his standard executive coaching model. An example of how 'mainstream' coaching approaches continue to be operational in different contexts is in the chapter on the Middle East (Palmer and Arnold, 2013) where Peterson's (2007) Developmental Pipeline is used to guide coaches in adapting practice for cultural variation.

Plaister-Ten (2013) takes a systems view of cross-cultural coaching in presenting a 'kaleidoscope' that calls for the consideration of a variety of contextual factors that have cultural implications (across history, economics, geography, legal frameworks, religion, and family). The centre of the model includes values and self-awareness. Her focus is mainly on executive coaches working across cultures. From a psychological perspective, Coultas et al. (2011) present a values-sensitive cross-cultural approach to coaching that is designed for culturally diverse executives. They describe it as 'DELTA' and base it in an assumption that coaches may move away from established Western coaching practices. The model includes: Determining cultural values, Employing typical coaching techniques, Listening for motivational needs, Tailoring coaching techniques to motivation needs and cultural values, and Assessing effectiveness. They argue that while it has been demonstrated that many of the foundational principles behind goal-setting and feedback theory are fairly universal, using these techniques within a cross-cultural coaching relationship may not always look the same (Coultas et al., 2011: 157).

Companies are emerging that are specialising in global and cross-cultural coaching. The Global Coaches Network (Zucal, 2016) specialises in training and connecting coaches for global and cross-cultural work. Their model views coaching as a way of working that integrates three competencies (personal, leadership and cultural). In the field of expatriate coaching, the Global Coaching Center (Gokun Silver, 2016) proposes a four step approach of: calculating your cultural preferences and gaps, choosing what is negotiable and what is not, changing your cultural habits within negotiable variables, and creating cultural alliances from non-negotiable variables. The role of the coach is to assist coachees to work through these steps within their contexts.

Alongside the emergence of cross-cultural coaching has been the development of instruments and models that aim to measure a person's capacity for cross-cultural effectiveness, with Cultural Intelligence (CQ) and Global Mindset (GM) being the most prominent. Coaches have embraced these instruments as they move beyond measuring individual cultural dimensions to a focus on the factors for success in working across cultures. In turn, the designers and distributors of the instruments have developed training and manuals for coaching with the instruments.

One example is Cultural Intelligence, which is defined as the capability for consciousness and awareness during intercultural situations (Earley and Ang, 2003, Ng et al., 2009). CQ requires knowledge about cultural differences, a capacity to change behaviour to fit context, and a willingness to engage with cultural change. More recent conceptualisations give prominence to the role of meta-cognition (thinking about thinking). For example, Global Mindset is a construct consisting of psychological, social and intercultural capital (Javidan et al., 2010), with psychological capital including cognitive complexity. Global Dexterity (Molinsky, 2013) is a recent approach that is grounded on academic foundations but written for a practitioner audience. GD is the ability to adapt your behaviour smoothly and successfully to the demands of a foreign culture, without losing yourself in the process. The model proffers three challenges: an authenticity challenge, a competence challenge and a resentment challenge. The authenticity challenge is to remain faithful to one's own values and culture, while adapting to the new culture. The competency challenge is to master the skills required to be effective in a new cultural environment. The resentment challenge is the challenge to effectively answer such questions as, 'Why should I change?' and, 'Why don't others change to accommodate me?'

Common across these three approaches is a requirement for coaches to go beyond teasing out differences between cultures in order to holistically work in-situ across cognitive, emotional and behavioural domains. These approaches take cross-cultural practice to a higher level in encouraging coachees not only to look at the way different cultural influences are at play, but also how they are looking at the situation. CQ, GM and GD provide models for approaching cross-cultural challenges in any situation, rather than giving attention to the details of how specific cultures operate. That said, a well-thought-out investigation may go down that path in the course of the coaching engagement.

COMPLEX SYSTEMS, COMPLEXITY OF MIND: RELEVANCE TO EMERGING CROSS-CULTURAL PRACTICE

The context for cross-cultural coaching is the VUCA world described earlier. Some recent leadership and coaching texts have adopted the language of complexity to assist executives to work in ways that depart from traditional management approaches that have an underlying focus on control, hierarchy and hard systems approaches to data analysis. For example, Garvey-Berger and Johnston (2015) propose a leadership approach that is embedded in the language of systems thinking and complexity theory. It includes sections on polarity and paradoxical thinking which are consistent with the idea of leveraging advantage from different cultural frames as proposed by Rosinski (2003, 2010) and Abbott (2014) in the cross-cultural coaching literature.

Complexity theory and systems thinking (Holland, 2006; Snowden and Boone, 2007), and adult development (Kegan, 1982; Kegan and Lahey, 2009), provide some principles for coaches to apply in cross-cultural engagements, particularly in VUCA conditions. Culture is only one variable in the assessment, yet it is significant because of the interrelationships between cultural influences and other complexity variables as noted above (e.g., social upheaval, technological shifts, economic influences, demographic shifts). Snowden and Boone's (2007) Cynefin Framework provides a heuristic for managers and their coaches to help them assess the nature of problem situations they are facing. They delineate 'simple', 'complicated', 'complex' and 'chaotic' categories – each with an accompanying set of strategies for managers to adopt. They give emphasis to the growing number of problem situations that can be termed 'complex' – meaning that the challenges cannot necessarily be 'solved' by controlling variables and using expert analysis. The proposed first-line strategy in such situations is to 'probe' and to find opportunities to influence interrelated systems so that improvements can be achieved.

If the 'diagnosis' is complex, then the pathway for coaching is going to have certain characteristics consistent with complexity theory. Snowdon and Boone (2007) make reference to the characteristics of complex adaptive systems (CAS) in explaining how complex organisational situations behave and what features to look for when probing in complex challenge situations. CAS are common in the natural world (e.g. a weather system, the human immune system, and even organisations). CAS are systems that have a large number of elements or so called agents in human systems that interact and adapt to learn (Holland, 2006). They are complex in that there are many different parts that are dynamically interrelating. They are adaptive in that each piece of a system can adapt itself or change in relation to its environment.

CAS have the following features:

- the dynamic interrelationship of issues, events and elements; emergence (the unexpected is expected);
- phase changes where the whole nature of the industry and organisational environment shifts;
- open boundaries where the organisational system is influenced by a variety of external systems and forces;
- recurring patterns at different levels of the system;
- strange attractors where patterns emerge that seem to attract energy; and
- non-linearity where cause and effect relationships are not clearly apparent.

Viewed through Cynefin lens, many cross-cultural coaching assignments seem to fit in the complex quadrant. The empirical studies that we cite in a later section provide some insight into the variety and fluidity of cross-cultural coaching engagements. Many require a probing methodology that can identify the nature of problems and delve into situations to discover patterns and subtleties, with particular attention to the salient variable of culture. If there is a categorisation of a complex coaching challenge as 'complicated', there is a risk that the coach and coachee will collude to seek a perfect solution by the non-reflective application of data from cultural dimension measurement, or scores from GM and CQ. Early and accurate assessment of the situation is part of the cross-cultural coaching repertoire. In assessing the situation, there is also significance in the consideration of culture as a variable that is both influencing and influenced by the coachee's and coach's systems in ways that are not always apparent. Curiosity about what is known and not known, and what might be emerging are critical ingredients.

With the context moving towards greater complexity, there is a challenge for executives and coaches to understand and be functional in new kinds of ever-changing environments where approaches from the past may not (or may) serve them. Thomas (2010, p. 172) suggests that the future of leadership and management will require an enhanced cognitive element, describing a 'cognitive revolution' in international management. Advanced coaching approaches that are effective in the VUCA world will need to be applied at a high level of cognitive complexity. The coaching literature and practice (Cavanagh, 2006, 2013) has drawn from complexity theory, for example through identifying characteristics of Complex Adaptive Systems (CAS) in coaching engagements, and calling the attention of coaches to the systemic nature of organisational life in which there is always the element of the emergent and unknown. Curiosity is critical when operating in such systems – of valuing what one does know, while wondering about what one doesn't. As noted, effective cross-cultural coaching is likely be particularly demanding in this regard as cultural nuances are explored within an already turbulent situation.

In response, advanced coaching approaches (e.g. Berger, 2006) are drawing on the adult development framework of Kegan (1982, 1994) to conceptualise and structure executive coaching. Kegan's work is significant in exploring how experiential learning can enhance learning and movement through stages of consciousness, the outcome being a greater capacity to deal with the complexities and stress of contemporary organisational life. This is important for coaches in working with executives to navigate adaptive challenges that prompt shifts in their developmental stage. These concepts are even more significant in cross-cultural coaching in helping coachees face the challenges of integrating new cultural frames and advancing their capacity to work with multiple perspectives.

As cross-cultural coaching has evolved, the need for coaches to be able to engage their coachees and the interrelatedness and dynamic nature of the challenges they face has concurrently grown. Working from the cultural development frame of Bennett (1993), Rosinski (2003) proposes that coaches help people to move to a more integrative view of the world and to not only synergise but also develop new worldviews through deep coaching conversations and associated experiential learning. Drake (2009) applies a narrative coaching approach to Bennett's work to explore the way that cross-cultural coaching can help a coachee to navigate the 'in-between' space and liminal tension as they move toward more mature intercultural sensitivity. Abbott (2014) surfaces the paradoxical nature of cross-cultural assignments where coaches and coachees have to find ways of allowing worldviews, orientations and perspectives that are apparently in conflict to exist together in creative tension.

In complexity theory and systems thinking, interconnections and interrelations are seen as important – emphasising the position that the whole is greater than the sum of its parts. Emergence and interrelatedness are fundamental in systems thinking, and phenomena can be understood to be emergent property of an interrelated whole (Flood, 2001, p. 133). From a systems thinking perspective, a change process starts when people see the bigger picture of the setting they are in. Coaching from a complex systems view is embedded in a social constructivist view of the world where executive coachees are seen as both 'influencers of' and 'influenced by' organisations.

The use of imagery and metaphorical thinking are two methods that can encourage people to holistically engage with these reciprocal influences and the interrelationship of multiple variables and perspectives. Checkland's Soft Systems Methodology (Checkland and Scholes, 1990) promotes a holistic view of any situation where multiple perspectives are involved and cultural viewpoints and worldviews are given particular prominence. In the cross-cultural coaching literature, Rosinski's (2003) technique of using postcards from different countries to trigger new thinking about challenges in cross-cultural situations is consistent with concepts from Soft Systems Methodology.

In summary, complex systems theory is an area that has significant application for cross-cultural coaching in leading coaches and coachees towards an understanding of how culture as a variable is interacting in situ. However, it is of equal importance for cross-cultural coaches to give attention to how advanced they are in their own thinking in relation to complex challenges. The position of a coach as an objective and somehow separated player doesn't make sense when viewed in a systemic way. These challenges are all part of engaging with the complexity of coaching relationship in cross-cultural environments.

RECENT EMPIRICAL STUDIES

In this section, we present a sample of empirical studies and theoretical approaches that represent the wide variety of contexts and perspectives in cross-cultural coaching, each of which contains some insights on how the field is emerging. Overall, the literature focuses on cross-cultural coaching and diversity issues from the perspectives of multinational organisations, expatriates, global virtual teams, global nomads, gender issues, and coaching approaches suitable for different regions and countries. Across studies, there is increasing evidence that coaching is an effective means of assisting coachees and client-organisations to achieve objectives, though practices need to be adapted to take account of contextual issues and cultural orientations.

In reviewing literature specifically relating to the intersection of coaching with expatriate management, Salomaa (2011) found three empirical studies on expatriate coaching (Abbott, 2006; Herbolzheimer, 2009; and McGill, 2010), which all support the idea that coaching seems to be an efficient intervention in the expatriate context. Abbott (2011) explored evidence-based executive coaching as a means of supporting and developing expatriate executives through the facilitation of cognitive complexity and meta-cognition. He provided evidence of three coaching case studies conducted in Central America, interpreted in the light of knowledge from international management research. Coaching seemed to operate to enhance Global Mindset (GM) and Cultural Intelligence (CQ) through promoting higher order thinking. Coaching appeared to provide opportunities for expatriates to unravel and navigate the interrelationship of situational, cognitive, emotional and behavioural factors in new and volatile situations.

Gentry et al. (2013) conducted a qualitative study on coaches in Asia and Europe and concluded that coaches must be aware and have appreciation of the coachee's culture and background. They must also be able to use different cultural frameworks in coaching because cultural awareness can greatly increase the effectiveness of coaching engagements with highly diversified clientele. Wilson (2013) explored the Global Mindset (GM) construct of coaches who work across cultures, and concluded that the development of GM is a transformative and developmental experience that coaches will increasingly need in order to understand and work with the increasing complexities of a globally interconnected world.

Studies are emerging that look at the nature of coaching as a practice and how different cultural frames can be used to increase coaching effectiveness. Chatwani (2015) applied the ancient Indian Guru–Sishya (teacher–disciple) paradigm to coaching to offer an additional dimension that is in tension with the Western assumptions and practices of coaching. The cross-cultural coach, on the one hand, needs an acute level self-awareness and cultural sensitivity, and on the other hand, needs to avoid a perspective that all coaching issues are culturally imbued. She extends this paradoxical thinking when applying concepts from Indian philosophy, taking the view that the Western individualism and Eastern collectivism can co-exist, as can the position of coach as a wise advisor and a partner in reflective collaboration.

In contemplating the nature of coaching through the Guru–Sishya paradigm Chatwani presents cross-cultural coaching as a flexible practice that avoids universal truths. Consistent with the paradoxical thinking in the approach she then presents three principles for effective cross-cultural coaching: trust building, methodological flexibility, and sensitivity to context. While observing how coaching can work effectively in Indian society, Chatwani (2015, p. 71) reinforces the limitation of applying cultural measurement without due care in commenting that, 'Sociocultural anthropological frameworks in which characteristics of ethnic-based social interactions are mapped along defined dimensions to explain behaviors of the coach and coachee offer limited opportunities to culturally adapt the learning process entailed in coaching'.

Sood (2013) cites two case studies from India that are illustrative of how cross-cultural coaching is applied in globally active companies. In one case, coaching assisted an Indian country manager in negotiating challenges with a newly appointed CEO from Scotland. The other case was the application of coaching to assist an American expatriate working for an Indian subsidiary of a US multinational. The challenge involved bringing together two camps in an extended team – one with a traditional local mindset, and the other with a focus on pace-of-work and results. Nangalia and Nangalia's (2010) study illustrates how coaching needs to be adapted to local cultural values in the Asian context. They interviewed coaches based in seven Asian countries in a case study aimed at exploring the impact of social hierarchy on the coaching relationship. They found that coaching practices and expectations varied from conventional coaching practices to accommodate for social context. In particular, the coach was more likely to be considered as a respected elder or teacher rather than an equal. This has implications for how the coach is selected, how the coach presents and how expectations are set for coaching. The acceptance of coaching – even in adapted form – is consistent with the idea that coaching is itself a fusion of Western management principles and Eastern philosophy (Brock, 2008: 456)

Gan and Chong (2015) examined the executive coaching relationship in a collectivist and hierarchical Malaysian context. This study is relevant in exploring the impact of a Western-based management practice, delivered by local coaches to local managers. This study reinforced the view that an executive coach in an Asian context has a role more as a respected leader or teacher than an equal. The quality of the coaching relationship emerged as significant in predicting a positive outcome, a finding which spans across cultures. Lam (2016) provides a contrasting view of cross-cultural coaching in Asia. In another small scale study, she explored how coaching is received and conducted in Hong Kong, noting the unique and mixed cultural characteristics of Hong Kong Chinese people and the Western roots and techniques of coaching. Her sample was a group of Chinese coaches who received coach training in English from local coaching schools. She considered Hofstede's dimensions for cultural framing – noting in particular Hong Kong's relatively high scores on Power Distance and low scores on Individualism – which on face value would be counter to Western cultural underpinnings of coaching. Lam concluded that Hong Kong Chinese are greatly affected by Western ways of thinking and this has resulted in the acceptance of coaching as a practice without major shifts away from what might be termed standard approaches.

A different take on cross-cultural coaching is from Winum (2005) who detailed a case study from the USA of his role in coaching an African American executive (Tom) who was derailing. The coach (who was not African-American) engaged the support of an African-American clinical psychologist with expertise in diversity issues. The psychologist provided insights and knowledge to the coach to inform him about potential issues in the assignment, as well as being offered as a potential coach for Tom. Winum continued as coach and the case study report contained very little reference to cultural issues. This case study suggests that a careful handling of cultural context upfront can sometimes allow culture to be appropriately placed in the background during what might be viewed as a conventional coaching assignment.

Outside the field of executive coaching, McDonald (2016) takes a critical theory view to examine how a sensitivity to issues and narratives around race are critical for sports coaches. His context is coaching Pacific Islanders in elite private schools in Australia where he observes that 'whitestream' narrative is dominant. McDonald draws attention to what he terms 'Pacifica exotica' of the hangi, Cook Island dancing, cool names and tattoos. Hassanin and Light (2014) also discuss the power of underlying cultural narratives and influences in sports coaching, noting that coaches are often unaware of the influence of culture on behaviour in context. Such studies are informative in providing parallel contexts to the situation in companies where the dominant narrative is constructed by managers and their coaches, while significant elements of the workforce are of different cultural backgrounds and may be narrated into inferior roles or excluded altogether. This also raises questions about how coaches in cross-cultural contexts can easily be swept up in and reinforce dominant cultural narratives (of various kinds). Peterson's (2007) advice to coaches to search for hidden layers is salient in considering this issue.

Another challenge in cross-cultural coaching can be seen in a study by Rosha and Lace (2016) in Latvia and Lithuania in which they explored the scope of coaching in the context of organisational change. Their interest is a common one in the emerging field of global coaching, that is, how might coaching assist organisations to thrive in the face of the VUCA global business environment. In developed economies, it has led to an increasing interest in the construct of a 'coaching culture' (e.g. Lawrence, 2015). The unique feature of the study is that it was conducted in Latvia and Lithuania where coaching has had relatively limited penetration. Their study was of a survey of experts in the provision of coaching services. Their context was that many managers do not fully understand the essence of coaching and tended to confuse coaching with consulting. This study highlights the challenge for coaches working in relatively new coaching markets where they are attempting to bring in concepts and practices that are literally foreign to managers – not necessarily because of issues related to national culture – but simply because they are new. This is an example of how the cross-cultural element is increasingly a factor in the study of management culture.

Also from the field of managerial coaching in a cross-cultural context, Al-Nasser and Behery (2015) used a multivariate analysis of questionnaire responses from a random sample of 656 employees of varying levels from fourteen sectors to examine the relationship between organisational coaching and workplace counterproductive behaviours (workplace bullying and job alienation) and found that coaching had a positive effect. He noted that for this study, a meta-analysis of coaching evaluation research was not feasible because of the absence of comparative and cross-culture studies. For measuring organisational climate, the author adapted the SCARF model (Rock, 2008), which has a foundation in emotional intelligence, positive psychology and arguably neuroscience. Counter-intuitively, results from the study indicated a negative correlation between coaching and organisational climate via the 'certainty' dimension. It would be reasonable to expect that coaching would result in greater clarity about what is going on, therefore supporting the degree of certainty that people feel about their situation. However, it could be that the questioning nature of coaching had an unsettling affect, which flowed on to negatively influence organisational climate. Again, this indicates the role of context in determining the impact and conduct of coaching in its various forms. However, the findings provide empirical support for the soundness and validity of the effect of organisational coaching on the counterproductive behaviours of bullying and alienation within a non-Western context (the UAE).

One of the emerging areas in cross-cultural coaching is the research on expatriate coaching (coaching with managers who are on assignments in foreign countries). Empirical studies support the idea that coaching seems to be an efficient support and development intervention in the expatriate context (Abbott, 2006, 2011; Herbolzheimer, 2009; McGill, 2010; Salomaa, 2015). Expatriate studies indicate that assignees confront various challenges, including work–family conflicts, challenges related to stress and adjustment, career transition concerns and physical, emotional, and intellectual stress related to global travel, identity transformations, and non-work demands (Takeuchi, 2010; Shaffer et al., 2012). Therefore, expatriate coaches need to holistically understand the coaching context and be savvy in international business.

Expatriate coaches can utilise knowledge from the Global Mindset (GM) and Cultural Intelligence (CQ) literature to develop their own capabilities to work across cultures (Salomaa, 2015). Abbott (2011) has provided evidence that coaching of expatriates enhances CQ and GM through developing their cognitive complexity and meta-cognition. Executive coaching provided opportunities for assignees to navigate the interrelationship of situational, cognitive, emotional and behavioural domains of the coached expatriates. Furthermore, Salomaa and Mäkelä (2015) conducted a narrative analysis on expatriate stories in order to understand if and how coaching enhances the career capital development of expatriates. The career capital framework consists of three elements; knowing-how (e.g. technical skills), knowing-whom (e.g. social networks) and knowing-why (e.g. motivation). The complex and challenging expatriate environment was described in every analysed story, and the coaching processes were seen as helpful interventions that enhanced the development of their career capital.

Many organisations have begun to embrace a management paradigm that calls for facilitative behaviours that focus on employee empowerment, learning and development; in other words, coaching (Hamlin et al., 2006: 307). There is increasing interest in the use of coaching methodologies in leadership and management practice (Zenger and Stinnett, 2010). This has a flow on into cross-cultural coaching. Consequently, there is more focus on research on managerial coaching, including in a cross-cultural context. In addition, coaching is becoming an integral part of global leadership and talent development programs (CIPD 2013 Survey Report), and a few empirical studies focusing on coaching from an organisational perspective in a cross-cultural context have emerged. For example, Hamlin et al. (2006) conducted a cross-cultural study focusing on managerial coaching behaviours in the USA, Scotland and England. They found similar coaching behaviours across the three cultural groups of managers and concluded that truly effective managers and managerial leaders are those who embed effective coaching into the heart of their management practice (Hamlin et al., 2006: 326).

Phillips (2014) examines how Microsoft created a coaching culture across a global sales force. The case study illustrates how a coaching program was delivered that allowed for the complexity within the business as well as being flexible enough to meet the needs of different cultures. The training program gave attention to building mental toughness and was rolled out in five continents with 22 nationalities. A unique feature of this program was the use of action-learning groups of people from different cultures to build capability. Those who were familiar with coaching and were already skilled were able to assist those who were less familiar with and less skilled in coaching approaches (such as Brazil and Argentina). The study noted dramatic and far-reaching results in the form of positive behaviours and improved coaching skills. This study opens up consideration of three emerging fields relevant to coaching – manager-as-coach, virtual team coaching, and group coaching. The cross-cultural dimension in each of these provides another layer of complexity that coaches need to be able to navigate and leverage in order to add value.

Ye et al. (2015) provided another dimension by examining gender variation in the use of managerial coaching behaviours across cultures. Survey data were obtained from more than 600,000 employees, assessing coaching behaviour of more than 130,000 practicing managers from 51 countries/areas. Female managers displayed more coaching behaviour than their male counterparts worldwide, suggesting that coaching is not a gender-neutral phenomenon. The study also found that managers in collectivistic cultures are reported to exhibit more coaching behaviour than those in individualistic cultures. A counterintuitive finding was that male managers in high gender egalitarian (GE) cultures coach less than male managers in low GE cultures. One possible explanation (Ye et al., 2015: 14) was that subordinates in low GE cultures interpret male coaching behaviour differently than subordinates in high GE cultures.

Noer et al. (2005; 2007) reported on US and Saudi-Arabian managerial coaching behaviours. A significant feature of this study was that all of the Saudi managers were fluent in English and most educated 'out of Kingdom', again illustrating that cross-cultural coaching will often have layers of complexity of which coaches need to be mindful. The study used four Hofstede dimensions to compare the manager sample groups, with marked Saudi-US differences on all. The Saudi managers tended to exhibit less variance in coaching behaviours than their US counterparts, and were more relationship-based, consistent with cultural variances on uncertainty avoidance and masculinity. The study concluded that Islamic values as well as Bedouin tribal and family factors seemed to have influenced Saudi preferences in coaching. At the same time, the authors observed no inherent conflict between coaching as a practice in Saudi Arabian business culture.

Other empirical studies have focused on the characteristics and perspectives of coaches working in cross-cultural contexts. Plaister-Ten (2009) examined how 25 coaches conceptualised culture in coaching. She suggests that there are key qualities that a cross-cultural coach draws on: challenging assumptions, remaining open, cultural self-awareness, and coping with ambiguity. Milner, Ostmeier and Franke (2013) studied critical incidents experienced by German coaches in cross-cultural coaching settings, and found that communication, coach–coachee relationship, coaching setting, and role understanding were perceived as critical variables in predicting outcomes.

In the light of the above, cross-cultural coaching is becoming an integral part of coaching practice and research. Understanding the complexity of the coaching context is critical, and systemic approaches are gaining more attention. So far, there is a limited number of empirical studies on the various aspects of cross-cultural coaching and these are threaded through different traditions, genres and practices of coaching. Many questions remain open. What is evident is that the contexts of cross-cultural coaching are becoming increasingly complex – as is the task of constructing suitable high value research projects in the field.

FUTURE RESEARCH AND CONCLUDING COMMENTS

Cross-cultural coaching will continue to utilise the evolving knowledge about how cultures differ and are the same. However, the emerging practice and theory that we have discussed suggests that increasing weight might well be given to approaches that focus on the complex nature of the situations within which cross-cultural coaching occurs and the complexity of mind required by the executives being coached and their coaches. There are now instruments and models available that can assist coaches in deepening the impact and resonance of their coaching engagements. Cultural Intelligence and Global Mindset are two such approaches that are becoming increasingly connected to the practice of coaching.

Some approaches to coaching have embedded complexity theory and systems thinking in them now. Research into how these practices are making an impact will add to the depth and breadth of knowledge about how cross-cultural coaching might be enhanced. What seems apparent is that leadership and executive functioning does require a high level of cognitive functioning and a capacity to deal with massive complexity of context. Where culture surfaces as a significant variable in a situation that already has many characteristics that would place it in Snowden and Boone's (2007) 'complex quadrant', then clearly the coach and coachee will need to be extremely astute as they map a way forward. Research into how executives manage cognitive complexity and how this might be enhanced is a potentially rich source of knowledge for the cross-cultural coaching field.

We have looked across a variety of sources of knowledge that can inform coaches who are working across cultures and across borders, including some specific studies from the field. Our conclusion is that coaching across cultures is a highly contextual and emergent field that requires practitioners to be across multiple disciples and practices. Coaches need to be experts in adapting their approaches to the individual and unique challenges of their coaching clients. They also need to consider how effective they are in challenging their own assumptions and the assumptions of the coaching practices they are using. We have noted the growth of managerial coaching in many different cultural settings. While this practice seems to be well received, complexity theory would suggest that there are likely to be some 'emergent properties' – positive, neutral or negative – from the interaction of coaching methodologies with diverse organisational and cultural contexts. This is an area to which future research may give attention.

REFERENCES

Abbott, G. N. (2006). *Exploring Evidence-Based Executive Coaching as an Intervention to Facilitate Expatriate Acculturation: Fifteen Case Studies*. Unpublished dissertation, Faculty of Economics and Commerce, Canberra: Australian National University.

Abbott, G. N. (2011). *Executive Coaching with Expatriate Executives: Facilitating Cognitive Complexity to Enhance Cultural Intelligence and Global Mindset*. Conference paper, European Academy of Management, Tallinn, Estonia.

Abbott, G. N. (2014). Cross-cultural coaching: A paradoxical perspective. In E. Cox, T. Bachkirova and D. Clutterbuck (eds), *The Complete Handbook of Coaching* (2nd ed.). London: Sage.

Abbott, G., Gilbert, K., and Rosinski, P. (2013). Cross-cultural working in coaching and mentoring. In J. Passmore, D. Peterson, and T. Freire (eds.), *The Wiley-Blackwell Handbook of the Psychology of Coaching and Mentoring*. Chichester: John Wiley & Sons.

Abbott, G. N. and Stening, B. W. (2009). Coaching expatriate executives: Working in context across the affective, behavioral and cognitive domains. In M. Moral and G. N. Abbott (eds), *The Routledge Companion to International Business Coaching*. Milton Park: Routledge, pp. 181–202.

Al-Nasser, A. and Behery, M. (2015). Examining the relationship between organizational coaching and workplace counterproductive behaviors in the United Arab Emirates. *International Journal of Organizational Analysis*, 23(3): 378–403.

Awal, D., and Stumpf, S. A. (2009). *New Leadership Skills for Success in a Global Business Environment: Lessons from Executive Coaching*. Berlin: Springer.

Bachkirova, T., Cox, E. and Clutterbuck, D. (2010). Introduction. In Cox, E., Bachkirova, T., & Clutterbuck, D. A. (eds.), *The Complete Handbook of Coaching*, London: Sage.

Bachkirova, T., Cox, E. and Clutterbuck D. (2014). Introduction. In Cox, E., Bachkirova, T., & Clutterbuck, D. A. (eds.), *The Complete Handbook of Coaching*. London: Sage.

Bennett, M. J. (1993). Towards ethno-relativism: A developmental model of intercultural sensitivity. In R. M. Paige (ed.), *Education for the Intercultural Experience* (2nd ed.). Yarmouth, ME: Intercultural Press.

Berger, J. G. (2006). Adult development theory and executive coaching practice. In D. R. Stober and A. M. Grant (eds.), *Evidence Based Coaching Handbook: Putting Best Practices to Work for Your Clients*. New York, John Wiley & Sons.

Bernstein, L. E. (2014). *The Perceived Importance of VUCA-Driven Skills for 21st Century Leader Success and the Extent of Integration of those Skills into Leadership Development Programs*. (Doctoral dissertation, Drake University).

Brock, V. (2008). *Grounded Theory of the Roots and Emergence of Coaching. Unpublished Dissertation*. Maui: International University of Professional Studies.

Capra, F. (1975). *The Tao of Physics*. Boston, Shambhala.

Cavanagh, M. J. (2006). Coaching from a systemic perspective: A complex adaptive conversation. In D. R. Stober and A. M. Grant (eds.), *Evidence Based Coaching Handbook: Putting Best Practices to Work for Your Clients*. Hoboken: John Wiley & Sons.

Cavanagh, M. (2013). The coaching engagement in the twenty-first century: New paradigms for complex times. In S. David, D. Clutterbuck and D. Megginson (eds.), *Beyond Goals: Effective Strategies for Coaching and Mentoring*. Surrey: Gower.

Chatwani, N. (2015). *A Cross-Cultural Approach in Coaching as Viewed Through the Guru–Śiṣya Paramparā*. In V. Pereira, and A. Malik (eds.), *Investigating Cultural Aspects in Indian Organizations*. New York: Springer International Publishing.

Checkland, P. and J. Scholes (1990). *Soft Systems Methodology in Action*. New York: John Wiley & Sons.

Coultas, C. W., Bedwell, W. L., Burke, C. S. and Salas, E. (2011). Values sensitive coaching: The DELTA approach to coaching culturally diverse executives. *Consulting Psychology Journal: Practice and Research*, 63(3): 149–161.

Cox, E. (2003). The contextual imperative: Implications for coaching and mentoring. *International Journal of Evidence Based Coaching and Mentoring*, 1(1): 9–22.

Cox, E., Bachkirova, T., & Clutterbuck, D. A. (eds.). (2014). *The Complete Handbook of Coaching*. London: Sage.

Curry, C. D.(2015). Coaching global teams and global team leaders. In J. L. Williamson, R. Griffith (eds), *Leading Global Teams: Translating Multidisciplinary Science to Practice*. New York: Springer.

Drake, D. (2009). Identity, liminality and development: An interpersonal view of intercultural sensitivity. In M. Moral and G. Abbott. (eds.), *The Routledge Companion to International Business Coaching*. London: Routledge, pp. 61–74.

Drake, D. B, Brennan, D., & Gortz, K. (eds). (2008). The philosophy and practice of coaching. Insights and issues for a new era. Chichester: Jossey Bass.

Earley, P. C., & Ang, S. (2003). *Cultural intelligence: Individual interactions across cultures*. Stanford University Press.

Fail, H., Thompson, J. and Walker, G. (2004). Belonging, identity and Third Culture Kids: Life histories of former international school students. *Journal of Research in International Education*, 3: 319–338.

Flood, R. L. (2001). The relationship of systems thinking to action research. In H. Bradbury, and P. Reason (eds.), *The Handbook of Action Research*. London. Sage.

Gan, G. C. and Chong, C. W. (2015). Coaching relationship in executive coaching: A Malaysian study. *Journal of Management Development*, 34(4): 476–493.

Garvey-Berger, J. and Johnston, K. (2015). *Simple Habits for Complex Times: Powerful Practices for Leaders*. Stanford, CA: Stanford Business Books.

Gentry, W. A., Manning, L., Wolf, A. K., Hernez-Broome, G., and Allen, L. W. (2013). What coaches believe are best practices for coaching: A qualitative study of interviews from coaches residing in Asia and Europe. *Journal of Leadership Studies*, 7(2): 18–31.

Gokun Silver, M. (2016). *The 4's Process to Cultural Intelligence*. Available at: http://www.globalcoachcenter.com/ Accessed 20 January 2016.

Hamlin, R. G., Ellinger, A. D., and Beattie, R. S. (2006). Coaching at the heart of managerial effectiveness: A cross-cultural study of managerial behaviors. *Human Resource Development International*, 9(3): 305–331.

Hampden-Turner, C., and Trompenaars, F. (1998). *Building Cross-Cultural Competence: How to Create Wealth from Conflicting Values*. Chichester: John Wiley & Sons.

Handin, K. and Steinwedel, J. S. (2006). Developing global leaders: Executive coaching targets cross-cultural competencies. *Global Business and Organizational Excellence*, 26(1): 18–28.

Hassanin, R. and Light, R. (2014). The influence of cultural context on rugby coaches' beliefs about coaching. *Sports Coaching Review*, 3(2): 132–144.

Herbolzheimer, A. (2009) *Coaching Expatriates: The Practice and Potential of Expatriate Coaching for European Executives in China*. Kassel University Press.

Hofstede, G. (1997). *Cultures and Organizations: Software of the Mind*. New York: McGraw-Hill.

Hofstede, G. (2001). *Culture's Consequences: Comparing Values, Behaviors, Institutions and Organizations across Nations* (2nd ed.). Thousand Oaks, CA: Sage.

Hofstede, G. (2011). Dimensionalizing cultures: The Hofstede model in context. *Online Readings in Psychology and Culture*, 2(1). http://dx.doi.org/10.9707/2307–0919.1014

Holland, J. H. (2006). Studying complex adaptive systems. *Journal of Systems Science and Complexity*, 19(1), 1–8.

Javidan, M., Hough, L. and Bullough, A. (2010). *Conceptualizing and Measuring Global Mindset: Development of the Global*

Mindset Inventory. Glendale: Thunderbird School of Global Management.

Johansen, B. (2007). *Get There Early: Sensing the Future to Compete in the Present*. San Francisco: Berrett-Koehler.

Kegan, R. (1982). *The Evolving Self: Problem and Process in Human Development*. Cambridge: Harvard University Press.

Kegan, R. (1994). *In Over Our Heads: The Mental Demands of Modern Life*. Cambridge: Harvard University Press.

Kegan, R. and Lahey. L. (2009). *Immunity to Change: How to Overcome It and Unlock the Potential in Yourself and Your Organization*. Boston: Harvard Business School Publishing Corporation.

Lam, P. (2016). Chinese culture and coaching in Hong Kong. *International Journal of Evidence-Based Coaching and Mentoring*, *14*(1): 57–73.

Law, H. (2013). *The Psychology of Coaching, Mentoring and Learning* (2nd ed.). John Wiley & Sons.

Law, H., Laulusa, L., and Cheng, G. (2009). Where Far East meets West: Seeking cultural synthesis through coaching. In M. Moral and G. N. Abbott (eds.), *The Routledge Companion to International Business Coaching*. Milton Park: Routledge, pp. 241–255.

Lawrence, P. (2015). Building a coaching culture in a small Australian multinational organisation. *Coaching: An International Journal of Theory, Research and Practice*, *8*(1): 53–60.

McDonald, B. (2016). Coaching whiteness: stories of 'Pacifica exotica' in Australian high school rugby, *Sport, Education and Society*, *21*(3): 465–482.

McGill, J.O. (2010). The impact of executive coaching on the performance management of international managers in China. A thesis submitted in partial fulfillment of the requirements for the degree of doctor of philosophy. *Work and Organizational Studies*, University of Sydney.

Milner, J., Ostmeier, E. and Franke, R. (2013). Critical incidents in cross-cultural coaching: The view from German coaches. *International Journal of Evidence Based Coaching and Mentoring*, *11*(2): 19–32.

Molinksy, A. L. (2013). *Global Dexterity: How to Adapt Your Behavior Across Cultures without Losing Yourself in the Process*. Boston: Harvard Business School Publishing.

Moral, M., & Abbott, G. (eds.). (2008). The Routledge companion to international business coaching. Milton Park: Routledge.

Moral, M. and Abbott, G. (2009). *The Routledge Companion to International Business Coaching*. Milton Park: Routledge.

Nangalia, L. and Nangalia, A. (2010). The coach in Asian society: Impact of social hierarchy on the coaching relationship. *International Journal of Evidence Based Coaching and Mentoring*, *8*(1): 51–77.

Ng, K.-Y., Van Dyne, L., and Ang, S. (2009). From experience to experiential learning: Cultural intelligence as a learning capability for global leader development. *Academy of Management Learning & Education*, 8(4): 511–526.

Noer, D. M., Leupold, C. R., & Valle, M. (2005). Behaviorally based coaching: A cross-cultural case study. *International Journal of Coaching in organizations*, *3*(1), 14–23.

Noer, D. M., Leupold, C. R. & Valle, M. (2007). An analysis of Saudi Arabian and US managerial coaching behaviors. *Journal of Managerial Issues*, *19*(2): 271–287.

Osland, J. S., A. Bird, et al. (2000). Beyond sophisticated stereotyping: Cultural sensemaking in context. *Academy of Management Executive*, *14*(1): 65–79.

Palmer, S. and Whybrow, A. (2008). *Handbook of Coaching Psychology: A Guide for Practitioners*. Hove: Routledge.

Palmer, T. and Arnold, V. J. (2013). Coaching in the Middle East. In J. Passmore (ed.), *Diversity in Coaching: Working with Gender, Culture, Race and Age* (2nd ed.). London: Kogan Page

Passmore, J. (2013a). *Excellence in Coaching: The Industry Guide* (2nd Edition). London: Kogan Page.

Passmore (2013b). *Diversity in Coaching: Working with Gender, Culture, Race and Age* (2nd Edition). London: Kogan Page.

Passmore, J. and Law, H. (2013). Cross cultural and diversity coaching. In J. Passmore (ed.). *Diversity in Coaching: Working with Gender, Culture, Race and Age* (2nd ed.). London: Kogan Page.

Peterson, D. (2007). Executive coaching in a cross-cultural context. *Consulting Psychology Journal: Practice and Research*, *59*(4): 261–271.

Phillips, T. (2014) Creating a coaching culture across a global sales force. *Strategic HR Review*, *10*(4): 5–11.

Plaister-Ten, J. (2009). Towards greater cultural understanding in coaching. *International Journal of Evidence-Based Coaching and Mentoring, Special*, (3), 64–81.

Plaister-Ten, J. (2013). Raising culturally-derived awareness and building culturally-appropriate responsibility: The development of the Cross-Cultural Kaleidoscope. *International Journal of Evidence Based Coaching and Mentoring*, *11*(2), 54–69.

PWC (2012). Talent Mobility 2020. http://www.pwc.com/gx/en/managing-tomorrows-people/future-of-work/pdf/pwc-talent-mobility-2020.pdf/ Accessed 10 February 2016.

Rock, D. (2008). SCARF: A brain-based model for collaborating with and influencing others. *NeuroLeadership Journal*, *1*(1): 1–9.

Rosha, A. and Lace, N. (2016). The scope of coaching in the context of organizational change. *Journal of Open Innovation: Technology, Market and Complexity*, *2*(2): 1–14.

Rosinski, P. (2003). *Coaching Across Cultures: New Tools for Leveraging National, Corporate & Professional Differences*. London: Nicholas Brealey Publishing.

Rosinski, P. (2010). *Global Coaching: An Integrated Approach for Long-lasting Results*. London: Nicholas Brealey Publishing.

St Claire-Ostwald, B. (2007) Carrying Cultural Baggage: the contribution of socio-cultural anthropology to cross-cultural coaching in *International Journal of Evidence Based Coaching and Mentoring, 5*(2), 45–52

Salomaa, R. (2011). *Expatriate Coaching*, Conference Paper, European Academy of Management, Tallinn, Estonia.

Salomaa, R. (2015). Expatriate coaching: factors impacting coaching success. *Journal of Global Mobility*, *3*(3), 216–243.

Salomaa, R. and Mäkelä, L. (2015). Expatriates' experiences concerning coaching as a part of their career capital development. *Conference Proceedings of Academy of Management's UFHRD 2015 Conference*, Cork, Ireland.

Shaffer, M. A., Kraimer, M. L., Chen, Y. P., & Bolino, M. C. (2012). Choices, challenges, and career consequences of global work experiences a review and future agenda. *Journal of Management*, *38*(4), 1282–1327.

Skiffington, S. M. and Zeus, P. (2003). *Behavioral Coaching: How to Build Sustainable Personal and Organizational Strength*. Sydney: McGraw-Hill Australia.

Snowden, D. J. and Boone, M. (2007). A leader's framework for decision making. *Harvard Business Review, November*: 69–76.

Sood, Y. (2013). Coaching in India. In J. Passmore (ed.), *Diversity in Coaching: Working with Gender, Culture, Race and Age*. London: Kogan Page.

Stober, D. R., & Grant, A. M. (Eds.). (2006). *Evidence Based Coaching Handbook: Putting Best Practices to Work for Your Clients*. Hoboken, NJ: John Wiley & Sons.

Takeuchi, R. (2010). A critical review of expatriate adjustment research through a multiple stakeholder view: Progress, emerging trends, and prospects. *Journal of Management*, *36*(4), 1040–1064.

Thomas, D. C. (2010). Cultural intelligence and all that jazz: A cognitive revolution in international management research? In T. Devinney, T. Pederson and L. Tihanyi. (Eds.) *The Past, Present and Future of International Business and Management*. Bradford, Emerald Group Publishing, 169–187.

Trompenaars, F. and Hampden-Turner, C. (2012). *Riding the Waves of Culture: Understanding Diversity in Global Business* (3rd Edition). New York: McGraw-Hill Education.

Wilson, W. (2013). Coaching with a global mindset. *International Journal of Evidence Based Coaching and Mentoring*, *11*(2): 33–52.

Winum, P. C. (2005). Effectiveness of a high-potential African American executive: The anatomy of a coaching engagement. *Consulting Psychology Journal: Practice and Research*, *57*(1): 71–89.

Ye, R., Wang, X., Hein Wendt, J., Wu, J. and Euwema, M.C. (2015). Gender and managerial coaching across cultures: female managers are coaching more, *The International Journal of Human Resource Management*, http://dx.doi.org/10.1080/09585192.2015.1075570/Last accessed 15 December 2015.

Zenger, J. and Stinnett, K. (2010). *The Extraordinary Coach: How the Best Leaders Help Others Grow*. New York: McGraw Hill.

Zucal, B. (2016). http://www.globalcoaches.com Accessed 20 January 2016.

Coaching in the HRD Context

Andrea D. Ellinger, Robert G. Hamlin and Rona S. Beattie

INTRODUCTION

Coaching has emerged as a significant service industry with the growing investments in coaching reaching over 2 billion dollars worldwide and the increasing numbers of self-identified professional coaches at over 47,500 according to the 2012 and 2013 International Coach Federation reports (Egan and Hamlin, 2014). It is anticipated that the demands for coaching will continue to increase along with expectations about its effectiveness as a developmental intervention and the quality associated with its provision (Bennett and Bush, 2009; Grant and Cavanagh, 2004). Coaching has been described as 'a human development process that involves structured, focused interaction and the use of appropriate strategies, tools and techniques to promote desirable and sustainable change for the benefit of the coachee and potentially for other stakeholders' (Bachkirova, Cox, and Clutterbuck, 2014, p. 1). Coaching is considered to be a relatively new field of study and an applied field of practice that has gained tremendous popularity and growth in recent years (Cox, Bachkirova, and Clutterbuck, 2014a, 2014b; Gray and Goregaokar, 2010). Bachkirova et al. (2014) acknowledged that coaching has intellectual roots that draw upon many disciplines and that it is used in many different contexts.

Human Resource Development (HRD) is one such context given that coaching has been used to develop employees, managers, and leaders within organizations. Yet, coaching is not a new phenomenon in HRD. It has consistently been featured in ASTD's (formerly American Society of Training and Development, now Association for Talent Development) competency studies over the years. McLagan (1989) conceived of HRD as being comprised of three domains: training and development (which included coaching), career development, and organization development. In ASTD's 2004 follow-up study, coaching featured as an area of expertise within the HRD domain (Davis, 2004). A subsequent model was presented with coaching still featuring as an important area of practice for human resource development and workplace learning professionals (Arneson et al., 2013; Rothwell et al., 2013; Werner, 2014, 2015). The Chartered Institute of Personnel and Development (CIPD) in the UK also recognizes coaching as an important domain within HRD and the role of HR professionals.

Therefore, it is necessary to further define and describe HRD so that an understanding of how 'coaching can be a powerful ally' can be achieved (Cox, Bachkirova, and Clutterbuck, 2014b, p. 141). The chapter begins with an overview of HRD and then looks at how coaching may occur and be deployed in organizational settings by internal and external professionals (from within HRD and not). In particular, it will synthesize the literature on the domains of coaching that may be more prevalent in the HRD context such as the provision of internal coaching, the use of external coaching such as executive coaching, and the use of action learning coaches in management and leadership development. It will then explore the changing roles of managers who are assuming HRD roles and responsibilities for coaching, and will conclude with recommendations for future research directions.

DEFINING AND CONCEPTUALIZING HRD

Lee (2015) acknowledged that, 'We talk about HRD and we work with it day in and day out – but what do we mean by it?' (p. 3). Human Resource Development (HRD) is considered to be a well-established area of practice with a long and rich history in many countries, particularly in the United States and the United Kingdom (Lee, 2015; Swanson and Holton, 2009), but a relatively young academic area of study. The definitions and conceptualizations of HRD by scholars have evolved over the course of the past three decades, with more than 20 published definitions of HRD in the scholarly literature (Hamlin et al., 2008a, 2009). While there is no universal agreement on a unitary definition of HRD, most definitions 'include the notions of performance improvement, individual and organizational effectiveness, behavior change, enhancing individual and organizational learning, developing knowledge, skills and competencies, and enhancing human potential and personal growth' (Hamlin et al., 2008a, p. 297). Therefore, based upon such definitions it would be reasonable to suggest that HRD includes enhancing learning and development, improving performance, and facilitating change in organizational contexts at multiple levels including individuals, groups and teams, organizations, and the broader society (McLean & McLean, 2001; Swanson & Holton, 2009).

In terms of conceptualizing HRD, some scholars consider it to be a process, while others suggest that it is either a distinct function comprised of specific components or a subsystem within organizations. Additionally, HRD 'can take on a variety of names and roles' (Swanson and Holton, 2009, p. 12), including: training; training and development; learning and development; management, leadership and executive development; performance improvement; organization development; change management; organizational change and development; and coaching. With regard to those who may identify themselves as HRD professionals and be a part of the HRD field, Watkins (1998) indicated that internal HRD practitioners, internal trainers, graphic and curriculum designers, non-trainers who train (such as line managers), training managers, training coordinators, internal performance and organization development (OD) consultants, and professional coaches would be considered primary providers. She further described support infrastructures and tertiary providers as including

Federally-funded workforce development, HRD academic programs, training/media production companies, professional associations, union training, consulting firms, performance support designers, training supplies vendors, academic institutions who train, training publications, and training course vendors. External organization development (OD) consultants and professional coaches could also consider themselves to be a part of the HRD field.

DEMARCATING THE BOUNDARIES OF HRD AS THEY RELATE TO COACHING

Egan (2015) acknowledged that demarcating the boundaries of HRD is challenging for both research and practice. HRD is often placed under a broader human resources (HR) umbrella, may be subsumed by human resource management (HRM), and may subjugate OD under it. Ruona and Gibson (2004) acknowledged that while HRD, HRM, and OD are multidisciplinary fields that have distinctively evolved, there are similarities and interdependencies among them such that they may no longer be perceived as truly distinct from each other given that 'knowledge, learning and development have emerged as essential for organizational success' (Egan, 2015, p. 55).

In terms of distinguishing HRM from HRD, Werner (2014) suggested that, 'topics such as staffing, compensation, and employee relations/communications are generally viewed as HRM topics that do not directly overlap with HRD' (p. 133). Werner draws upon Mankin (2001) who developed a framework to depict how HRM and HRD might work together to address people issues at work. This framework incorporates the need to connect organizational strategy/structure, culture with HRM with the central overlap being HRD and its focus on learning and knowledge given the importance of people in achieving organizational success. Within the HRM field, HRD would be considered a topical area in which coaching could be seen as an intervention to bring about learning and performance improvement.

Similarly, some scholars position OD as a separate field of research and practice, while others such as McLagan (1989) place OD within the HRD framework. OD is defined as 'a process that applies a broad range of behavioral science knowledge and practices to help organizations build their capability to change and to achieve greater effectiveness' (Cummings and Worley, 2015, p. 1). With regard to coaching, a recent survey of OD practitioners identified coaching as 'an integral part of OD today' (Shull, Church, and Burke, 2013, p. 19).

Within the HRD field, coaching is often conceived of as a powerful developmental intervention, among an array of others, that can be used to promote personal and professional learning, development and growth, performance improvement and change; and it has been linked to a number of individual and organizational work-related outcomes (Hamlin et al., 2008a; Ellinger et al., 2014). In terms of the OD field, scholars have depicted coaching as an individually focused intervention (Anderson, 2015). For Cummings and Worley (2015), coaching 'can be seen as a specialized form of OD … to increase the capacity and effectiveness of individuals as opposed to groups or organizations' (p. 474) and is typically concerned with talent management and is often categorized as an HRM intervention.

Coaching can be embedded as an HRD, HRM or OD intervention in ways that are contingent upon the frames of reference, knowledge and skills of the professionals involved. It is important to acknowledge that there are other developmental and change-focused interventions beyond coaching that can be used within organizations – such as training, mentoring, and those focused on improving human functioning, job and organizational design, and organizational strategies. Ultimately, coaching can be positioned as an integral aspect of the HRD and OD fields of study and practice as seen in the contention by Vaartjes' (2005) that 'coaching is rapidly emerging as a widely applied means of human resource development (HRD) in business' (p. 1).

COACHING WITHIN THE HRD CONTEXT

Despite the prevalence and growth of coaching and the recognition that coaching is a central aspect of HRD practice and holds much in common with the coaching industry, 'coaching is generally an under-explored and under-researched HRD-related practice' (Ellinger and Kim, 2014, p. 128). HRD professionals play a myriad of roles in the coaching space (Hamlin et al., 2008a; Joo, 2012), which warrants further attention. For example, they may serve as:

- internal coaches to internal clients;
- resources for developing coaching strategies and coaching capabilities among supervisors, line managers, and leaders;
- brokers who secure, deploy and assess external coaching specialists (Dagley, 2010);
- managerial coaches within their own functions;
- executive coaches or action learning coaches as part of management and leadership development initiatives in their organization; and
- resources for cultivating a 'coaching friendly' culture so organizational investments in coaching are effective.

Fillery-Travis and Lane (2006) have categorized these varied roles within the HRD context into internal, external, and manager modes as outlined below.

Internal Coaching

Consistent with the ASTD/ATD studies that have recognized coaching as an area of expertise among HRD professionals, Bachkirova, Cox and Clutterbuck (2010) point out that an internal professional coach 'is typically someone from human resources' (p. 4). Frisch (2001) indicated that internal coaches within organizations are a growing presence and he defined an internal coach as 'a fellow employee of the same organization as those he or she coaches' (p. 242). Frisch recommended that the internal coach is outside of the chain of command of the person being coached and this type of coach is distinguished from the manager who may provide job coaching. Building upon Frisch's definition of an internal coach, the coach could also be a peer colleague or a subject matter expert who has coaching expertise.

The benefits that have been attributed to the use of internal coaching include the cost savings over engaging external coaches, familiarity with the organization and its members, the ability to apply coaching more broadly to other organizational members, and opportunities for observing the outcomes of coaching. Internal coaches may also provide coach training to managers who coach and may serve as specialist coaches for senior managers (Fillery-Travis and Lane, 2006). Megginson and Clutterbuck (2006) suggested that the maturity of a coaching culture may influence who serves as coaches and the prevalence of coaching. Internal coaches and managerial coaches may be less prevalent in organizations that are in the early stages of developing a coaching culture. However, when coaching becomes a more established and accepted practice in an organization, internal and managerial coaches may become more prevalent (Segers, Vloehberghs, Henderickx, and Inceoglu, 2011). HRD professionals with recognized and established coaching capabilities may well be positioned to serve as internal coaches, along with others in the organization, like peers and SMEs who may possess formal and/or informal coaching expertise.

The 2013 International Coach Federation (ICF) Organizational Coaching Study found that the organizations participating in their study used both internal and external coaches, and those organizations more advanced in the implementation of coaching within the organization tended to use internal coaches. The 2015 Chartered Institute of Personnel and Development (CIPD) Learning and Development Survey reported that just over 75% of organizations in the United Kingdom (UK) were offering coaching and mentoring to their employees. Furthermore, nearly 40% were using in-house coaches/trainers, peers and line managers, an additional 33% were using a combination of in-house and external coaches, and only 6% were relying solely upon external providers. Of the other 21% organizations not offering coaching, 12% were looking to do so in 2016 and beyond, whereas the other 9% had no plans to do so (CIPD, 2015).

Key challenges for HRD professionals in implementing and leveraging internal coaching

In addition to the many benefits associated with using internal coaches cited in the 2013 ICF Coaching Study, a number of drawbacks have been identified, including: internal politics; the potential for bias; and issues associated with confidentiality. While familiarity with the organizational culture and members is often a strength associated with using internal coaches, such familiarity may breed contempt. It may be possible that the internal coach has specific knowledge and insights about the coachee that may detract from an unbiased perspective when engaged in coaching. It is also possible that breaches of confidentiality can inadvertently occur given the personal and professional relationships that may exist. Lastly, but equally importantly, is the question regarding the perceived level of coaching capability possessed by internal coaches. Concerns were cited as to the training and preparation for those serving as an internal coach relative to external professional coaches who may be expected to have specific training, education, qualifications, and accreditations.

LINE MANAGER COACHING/ MANAGERIAL COACHING

McGuire and Kissack (2015) acknowledged that the role and responsibilities of the line manager have changed considerably in the past decade as a consequence of environmental and organizational issues that have resulted in the devolution of some human resource functions to line managers. They presented a model that describes six specific HRD roles line managers are increasingly asked to play: working with HR business partners, workforce planning and talent pipelining, coaching and mentoring of subordinates, fostering a learning climate, career planning and development, and designing, delivery and evaluation of training programs. Previous research on managerial behavior has resulted in various taxonomies that suggest that managers are involved in instructing, training, providing growth and development, mentoring and coaching (Ellinger et al., 2010, 2014). In particular, Evered and Selman (1989) established coaching as a central component of managerial activity and it has been considered to be at the heart of managerial effectiveness (Hamlin et al., 2008b).

Managerial coaching has grown rapidly over the past decade (Beattie et al., 2014) as supervisors and line managers become increasingly held more accountable for helping employees to improve their performance through learning and development, in part to influence their engagement and retention (Ellinger & Kim, 2014). Managerial coaching is defined as 'a manager or supervisor serving as a coach or facilitator of learning in the workplace setting, in which he or she enacts specific behaviors that enable his/her employee (coachee) to learn and develop' (Ellinger et al., 2010, p. 257). This type of coaching represents an informal learning strategy used by managers to help an employee improve his/her performance, as well as grow and develop through learning. While managerial coaching may be structured, Hunt and Weintraub, 2002, 2011 suggest that such coaching should be 'slipped into' the manager's daily routines through the interactions that occur between frontline supervisors, managers, and their respective employees. This is supported by more recent research by Dixey (2015) that suggests a preference for an informal, conversational style of managerial coaching.

In 2006, a CIPD Learning and Development Survey suggested that 47% of line managers were using coaching in their work with growth trajectories anticipated. A 2011 CIPD survey 'found coaching by line managers to be the second most effective form of learning and that there had been incremental increases over the previous two years' (Beattie et al., 2014, p. 187). According to a more recent CIPD (2011) study, of the 600 organizations sampled in the United Kingdom, more than two thirds reported that line managers were mainly responsible for delivering coaching, with only 1% indicating that managers had no responsibility for coaching. These trends clearly support the integration and growth of this form of coaching.

Although still considered somewhat in its infancy, the research base on managerial coaching has been expanding (Hagen, 2012; Kim, 2014). There have been several predominant streams of research on managerial coaching. Early studies focused on the skills and behaviours required of managers to coach (see for example, Graham et al., 1993–1994; Orth et al., 1987). Several behavioural taxonomies have been developed that depict managerial coaching behaviours (see for example, Ellinger and Bostrom, 1999; Beattie, 2002, Longenecker and Neubert, 2005, Amy, 2005, and Noer et al, 2007). Comparative analyses among the Ellinger and Beattie taxonomies have revealed considerable congruency among behaviours and other studies have offered additional support for the behaviours that have been identified.

Additionally, McLean, Yang, Kuo, Tolbert and Larkin (2005) developed a managerial coaching skills self-assessment, which has subsequently been revised. The beliefs of managerial coaches have also been examined (Ellinger and Bostrom, 2002; Hunt and Weintraub, 2011; Hagen, 2012; Misuikonis, 2011), along with the outcomes associated with the provision of managerial coaching. Employees' perceptions of their managers' coaching has been linked to employee job satisfaction and job performance (Ellinger, Ellinger, and Keller, 2003); commitment to service quality (Elmadag, Ellinger, and Franke, 2008); the achievement of organizational goals (Wheeler, 2011); and role clarity among other work-related outcomes and organization citizenship behaviors (Kim, 2014; Kim, Egan, Kim, & Kim, 2013; Kim, Egan, and Moon, 2013; Kim and Kuo, 2015).

Key challenges for managerial coaches in implementing and leveraging coaching

Based on an exploratory study in Australia involving a focus group of accredited Australian and UK coaches and middle managers, Bond and Seneque (2013) noted that managerial coaching is perceived to be a form of management practice intended to assess and improve individual and team performance through behavior change and thus to enhance organizational efficiency and effectiveness. However, unlike some coaches whose roles and responsibilities are devoted full time to coaching, most front line supervisors and managers have other roles and responsibilities in addition to those of developing their employees. Therefore, despite the positive benefits associated with managerial coaching, Ellinger (2013) contended that the managerial coach is often a rare species. Some of the issues most often cited for supervisors' and managers' lack of or infrequent coaching are a lack of time, other work pressures, insufficient rewards, lack of encouragement and training in preparation for the coaching role (Ellinger et al., 2010, 2014; Hutchinson and Purcell, 2007).

More recently, Dixey (2015) acknowledged that the reasons why managerial coaching may be infrequent could be attributed to variations in approach and questionable quality, along with how such coaching may be measured. Ultimately, she contended that managers may actually be coaching, but not in the manner that their organizations may be expecting or assessing. In addition to these challenges, it is quite possible that at some point, the coachee may require coaching that may be beyond the skill level of the coaching manager. According to Bond and Seneque (2013), coaching interventions need to be conceived systemically from the beginning rather than focus primarily on impacting individual effectiveness if coaching as a managerial practice is to effectively integrate individual, team and organizational learning and behavior change. They claimed that developing the individual/team's capacity to identify and find solutions to their own problem situations in line with the organization's strategic intent and broader goals should be at the heart of the coaching process. This will enable them to better promote sustainable learning processes and improved individual, team and organizational performance.

This view is supported by case study research conducted within a UK building society (financial institution) by Turner (2010) who explored the efficacy of an organization wide program of managerial coaching that he instigated as functional head of HR with the full support of his CEO. This doctoral study extended over a seven-year period to enable contextualization of the research activity within a realistic corporate planning cycle. By the end of the program, Turner was able to demonstrate empirically that managerial coaching in the workplace, supported by a 'strategic coaching approach', was an effective means of enhancing employee engagement and performance.

A critical insight gained from Turner's study was the importance of a holistic approach encompassing a range of organizationally driven interventions focused on leadership development at all levels of management. For example, support for emotional intelligence, HR systems alignment, evaluation and a drive for continuous improvement were all needed to achieve a sustainable coaching culture and the related performance benefits. Turner claimed that to align organizational [managerial] coaching with leadership behavior throughout the organization requires not just coaching skills development, but also the benefit of other supportive strategies to encourage ongoing coaching skills development and the linking of coaching practices to business outcomes. This means embedding coaching into the organization's overall leadership culture.

The coaching program had a significant impact on the organization through the changes in management behavior, but there was deemed to be a lack of consistency across the organization due to several functional areas not embracing coaching, e.g., senior managers/leaders not role modeling managerial coaching behavior. Furthermore, the significant improvements in employee engagement and individual, team and organizational performance achieved during the first 5 years of the program were not sustained during its final years after Turner, and subsequently his CEO, had left the organization. Therefore, embedding HRD and a high order of 'change agency' capability, cognition and competence into the 'fabric of management' and the 'bloodstream of the organization' (Hamlin, 2007) is a key precondition for achieving sustainable high performance through managerial coaching.

EXTERNAL AND EXECUTIVE COACHING

In addition to coaching that may be provided by internal coaches and managers who serve as managerial coaches, coaches external to the organization may be contracted for their expertise in coaching. Executive coaching will be explored here because HRD professionals may serve as executive coaches and/or may be required to purchase services from executive coaches from outside their organizations. Executive coaching emerged in the 1990s as an intervention largely designed to improve the behavior of middle- and senior-level leaders (Feldman and Lankau, 2005), often in terms of addressing what came to be known as 'derailers'. Conceptualized as a distinctive dyadic relationship between an executive and consultant, executive coaching is often focused on helping executives to improve their current performance by focusing on their work-related skills and abilities with the intent of changing behavior (Feldman and Lankau, 2005). According to Stokes and Jolly (2014), executive coaching is often distinguished from other forms of coaching because the organization is the primary client along with the coachee, the focus of the coaching is often to create alignment between the coachee's capabilities and the goals of the organization, and coaching fees are typically paid by the organization, suggesting that the coach is external to the organization.

Executive coaching has grown considerably in the past ten years and continues to be a predominantly used intervention for enhancing management and leadership development (Gray, Ekinci, and Goregaokar, 2011). Maltbia, Marsick, and Ghosh (2014) contended that executive coaching is now one of the top five leadership-development best practices. They also suggested that, 'executive and organizational coaching is a development process that builds a leader's capabilities to achieve professional and organizational goals' (p. 165). In this way, they acknowledged that their description is 'compatible with the role of HRD professionals who often partner with leaders in an organizational context' (p. 165). Similarly, Hamlin (2010) contended that management development and leadership development are core components of HRD that emphasize people and organization development.

Plunkett and Egan (2004) suggested that executive coaching is a 'fast growing human resource development role' (pp. 558–560) but that it is also an understudied HRD-related practice (Egan, 2013).

Much like coaching in general, there are various definitions of executive coaching that have been advanced over the years (Joo, 2005; Kilburg, 1996; Maltbia et al., 2014). Stokes and Jolly (2010) suggested that executive coaching is a form of 'personal learning and development consultation' (p. 245) but, that it is provided by 'someone external to the organization' (p. 245) with the intention of helping to improve an individual's performance and functioning within an executive role. Plunkett and Egan (2004) suggested that 'a trained HRD specialist who utilizes knowledge, skills and techniques from psychology and HRD-related fields in the design, development, and implementation of individually focused change efforts aimed at improving executives' effectiveness, learning and performance' (pp. 558–560) can serve as an executive coach. While executive coaching is primarily provided by external coaches, suitable internal coaches such as HRD professionals can also provide such coaching. Within the literature, there is also some disagreement on the requirements for executive coaching. For example, some suggest that, given the nature of the coaching that may be required, executive coaches should be trained psychologists, while others recognize that non-psychologists such as former executives and others with business expertise also serve as executive coaches.

The research base on executive coaching has been growing over the years but it has been suggested that academic research on executive coaching has lagged behind the practitioner literature (Bono et al., 2009; Feldman and Lankau, 2005; Joo, 2005). Bono et al. (2009) have also acknowledged that, 'much of the process and practice of executive coaching remains shrouded in mystery' (p. 362). They further contend that 'rigorous peer-reviewed empirical research on executive coaching is hard to find' (p. 362) and that 'systematic empirical examination of executive coaching is in its infancy' (p. 392). The research related to executive coaching, while under-developed and under-explored, have included: who serves as executive coaches and their backgrounds, the clients of executive coaches, the outcomes of executive coaching, the phases of the executive coaching relationship, the approaches to the executive coaching process, and the coach–coachee relationship (Feldman and Lankau, 2005; Joo, 2005).

Studies that have explored the backgrounds and demographic characteristics of executive coaches have demonstrated variability in terms of age, educational background, work experience, and organizational affiliation. In Judge and Cowell's (1997) study, the majority of executive coaches were employed by consulting services or self-employed as opposed to serving as internal coaches. More recently, Bono et al.'s (2009) study comparing psychologists and non-psychologist executive coaches suggested that relying upon educational background may be insufficient and a more relevant question might be focused on what knowledge, skills, and abilities are needed by coaches to help their clients. The literature suggests that executive coaching is most often used with leaders who are in transition, faced with performance problems, or are targeted as high potentials (London, 2002; Stokes and Jolly, 2014).

In terms of outcomes, a limited number of studies have examined the efficacy of executive coaching in organizations. Despite limitations in many of the studies, executive coaching has been linked to individual performance, self-efficacy, organizational commitment, leadership, self-awareness and learning (Baron and Morin, 2009, 2011; Feldman and Lankau, 2005; Joo, 2005). Executive coaching is typically a more formal approach consisting of the following activities: establishing the goals of the relationship; data gathering/assessment; feedback; action planning; implementation; and assessment (Cummings and Worley, 2015; Feldman and Lankau, 2005). Baron and Morin (2009) have indicated that the coach–coachee relationship is a prerequisite for coaching effectiveness. While HRD professionals, both internal and external to organizations, may be involved in providing executive coaching to executives, they may also be involved in identifying, selecting, and evaluating executive coaching services if they personally lack the specific expertise to deliver such coaching.

Key challenges for HRD professionals in implementing and leveraging external and executive coaching

As noted in the 2013 ICF Organizational Coaching Study, the benefits associated with using external professional coaches, include the specialized nature of expertise, training, qualifications, and accreditation that an executive coach may possess. The executive coach is often solely focused on the needs of the client and client organization, is independent and likely does not have preconceived notions that might bias the coaching work performed within a specific organization. Certainly the perceptions of credibility and confidentiality appear to be stronger for external coaches versus internal coaches. However, an important task for the HRD professional charged with identifying executive coaches when such expertise is not available in-house is assessing the merit and qualifications of the executive coach relative to the type of coaching that may be required, the expense of such services, and the match with the client and the broader needs in the organization. It is also important to determine if executive coaching is the most appropriate intervention. It is equally important to be clear on the nature and purposes of the coaching that is being contracted, consider if the coach possesses the requisite knowledge and skills given the situation, and ensure that an open and trusting working relationship is cultivated with the organization and the executive.

ACTION LEARNING AND ACTION LEARNING COACHES

Much like executive coaching, action learning (AL) represents another approach that can be used for management and leadership development (Cho and Egan, 2013; O'Neil and Marsick, 2007, 2014). Action learning has a rich history and is widely practiced. However, much of what is known about it is based upon experiences of practitioners and this points to a significant need for more empirical research (Cho and Egan, 2013; O'Neil and Marsick, 2014). Action learning, like coaching in general, is also defined and conceptualized in a number of ways. Scholars have identified four schools of action learning: tacit, scientific, experiential, and critical reflection. They range from a focus on the action itself and project results to a focus on critical reflection.

Action learning is differentiated from other 'learning by doing' approaches because it involves a 'focus on a real work problem in real time' (O'Neil and Marsick, 2014, p. 203). O'Neil and Marsick (2014) defined action learning as 'an approach to working with and developing people that uses work on an actual project or problem as the way to learn. Participants work in small groups to take action to solve their problem and learning how to learn from that action. Often [an action] learning coach works with the group in order to help the members learn how to balance their work with the learning from that work' (p. 203).

AL coaches are typically used in the experiential and critical reflection schools of AL where the focus is on fostering reflection to enhance learning, particularly in the critical school, where the basic premises that underlie thinking can be challenged. In the critical reflection school, the intent is to 'explicitly develop leaders' ability to learn-how-to-learn' (p. 206). However, O'Neil and Marsick acknowledged that the focus on learning and reflection may not be held in common with other forms of coaching that are intended to focus on performance improvement or behavioral change. Further, AL coaching is both similar to and different from team coaching. For example, the composition of the participants within AL sets may be different from teams that have been pre-established to work together; the type of team and its goals may not reflect all those of the AL program and AL sets; teams may or may not be established for durations longer than AL sets; and the goals of AL may extend well beyond problem-solving, conflict management, and team performance.

When organizational leaders determine that AL is an intervention that should be considered, the co-design process begins which includes an AL consultant, internal or external to the organization, the HR/OD client, and the organization itself comprised of executives and participants. O'Neil and Marsick (2007) outlined an extensive co-design process which involves making AL program decisions ranging from the strategic focus of the program, specific projects and their respective sponsors, learning needs and goals, and the duration of the program, along with considerations about the use of an AL coach. An AL coach typically 'comes from outside the culture' (p. 206) but may also be an experienced HRD professional, and the role may range from supporting the team's learning as in the case of the experiential school, to creating 'opportunities for learning from critical reflection' (p. 206) as in the critical reflection school. Some of the important roles of the AL coach include creating an environment for learning, using specific interventions for learning, and transferring the skills of the coach to the AL participants. AL coaches may also be involved in the personal development of participants.

Key challenges for HRD professionals in implementing and leveraging action learning coaching

The same challenges often exist in obtaining a qualified action learning coach as they do with identifying potential executive coaches.

For example, the critical tasks of the HRD professional to identify, select, and evaluate their merits can be challenging given the different schools of action learning and the range and depth of experience and expertise that may be desired. Additionally, Cho and Egan's (2013) acknowledged that organizational support for action learning programs are necessary and suggested that organizational sponsorship is crucial and that practitioners, like HRD professionals, need to educate sponsors about the benefits of action learning programs. They also suggested that: communication with program participants throughout the action learning process is critical, time is allocated for participation, personnel and physical resources are provided, and appropriate feedback on solutions is offered.

CONCLUSIONS AND RECOMMENDATIONS FOR FUTURE RESEARCH

This chapter began by acknowledging the growth and demand for coaching and the emergence of the coaching field. It introduced HRD as a context for coaching given the increasing use of coaching in organizational settings for employees, managers, and leaders; and it articulated how coaching has long been considered an important domain in HRD. It defined and described HRD and considered it relative to the HRM and OD fields with regard to coaching. It introduced coaching in the context of HRD by acknowledging the various roles that HRD professionals may play with regard to coaching: serving as internal or external coaches, being purveyors and purchasers of coaching, and how devolving some of the HRD roles to line managers has resulted in the importance of managerial coaches.

What becomes evident is that there are considerable opportunities for advancing the knowledge base about coaching given the various definitions and types of coaching that currently exist across varied disciplines. Grant, Passmore, Cavanagh and Parker (2010) acknowledged that clarification is needed – conceptually, empirically and pragmatically – regarding the boundaries between coaching and other forms of organizational and psychological intervention. They suggested a rich research agenda that examines several issues associated with coaching: At what level is it being deployed, by whom, for whom, and for what purposes? Other questions for which we need further scholarship and research include: What types of learning and development is coaching best suited for as compared to other methods or interventions? When and how does learning and development occur in the coaching cycle? Do the coach and coachee learn from each other? How can the organization learn as well? Ultimately, what is happening in the 'black box' of the coaching process?

While there appears to be a growing use of internal coaches, more research is needed to identify who are these internal coaches (HRD professionals, SMEs and/or peer colleagues), what are their characteristics, what coaching approaches are they using, and what are the consequences of this type of coaching for the internal coach, coachee, and organization? For example, under what conditions should internal coaching be used in conjunction with or instead of external coaching and managerial coaching? With regard to executive coaching, research that continues to examine the effectiveness of this type of coaching is needed, along with the factors that influence the coach–coachee relationship. More research is also needed on the quality and effectiveness of executive coaching relative to other methods in terms of outcomes, phases of the relationship, and approaches to the process (Bono et al., 2009). In particular, the role of HRD professionals with regard to serving as executive coaches or being purveyors of executive coaching services requires considerably more research.

More research is also needed on AL coaching as provided by external professional coaches or internal HRD professionals to further distinguish this type of coaching from other forms of coaching, such as team coaching. With regard to managerial coaching, there is a need for more comprehensive research on the antecedents or factors that may influence managers' willingness and propensity for coaching, the moderating and mediating influences of variables that may affect the coaching process, the exploring of the benefits to the manager and managers' development, and what enables the managerial coach and coachee relationship to be effective (Beattie, Kim, Hagen, Egan, Ellinger, and Hamlin, 2014; Ellinger, Beattie, and Hamlin, 2014; Hagen 2012). Furthermore, the potential drawbacks to managerial coaching, and its potential limitations within the workplace need to be examined, along with the use of technology to facilitate such coaching. Lastly, longitudinal research on the efficacy of managerial coaching, along with cross-cultural perspectives, is needed. To extend a sentiment from Bennett and Bush (2009), it seems that coaches and HRD and OD professionals – and all those with vested interests in the future of coaching – need to work together leveraging the best of all of these fields in terms of their research and practice for the good of organizations and human systems.

REFERENCES

Amy, A. H. (2005). *'Leaders as facilitators of organizational learning.'* Unpublished Doctoral Dissertation, Regent University at Virginia Beach, VA.

Anderson, D. L. (2015). *Organization development: The process of leading organizational change*. 3rd edn. Thousand Oaks, CA: Sage

Arneson, J., Rothwell, W., & Naughton, J. (2013). 'Training and development competencies redefined to create competitive advantage', *T & D*, *67*(1): 42–47.

Bachkirova, T., Cox, E., & Clutterbuck, D. (2010). 'Introduction,' In E. Cox, T. Bachkirova, & D. Clutterbuck (eds.), *The Complete Handbook of Coaching* (pp. 1–20). London, England: Sage Publications.

Bachkirova, T., Cox, E., & Clutterbuck, D. (2014). 'Introduction,' In E. Cox, T. Bachkirova, & D. Clutterbuck (eds.), *The Complete Handbook of Coaching*, 2nd edn (pp. 1–18). London, England: Sage Publications.

Baron, L., & Morin, L. (2009). 'The coach-coachee relationship in executive coaching: A field study,' *Human Resource Development Quarterly*, *20*(1), 85–106.

Baron, L., & Morin, L. (2011). 'The impact of executive coaching on self-efficacy related to management soft-skills,' *Leadership and Organization Development Journal*, *31*(1): 18–38.

Beattie, R. S. (2002). 'Line managers as facilitators of learning: Empirical evidence from voluntary sector.' *Proceedings of 2002 Human Resource Development Research and Practice Across Europe Conference*. Edinburgh, Scotland: Napier University.

Beattie, R. S., Kim, S., Hagen, M. S., Egan, T. M., Ellinger, A. D., & Hamlin, R. G. (2014). 'Managerial coaching: A review of the empirical literature and development of a model to guide future practice,' *Advances in Developing Human Resources*, *16*(2): 184–201.

Bennett, J., & Bush, M. W. (2009). 'Coaching in organizations: Current trends and future opportunities,' *OD Practitioner*, *41*(1): 2–7.

Bond, C., & Seneque, M. (2013). 'Conceptualizing coaching as an approach to management and organization development,' *Journal of Management Development*, *32*(1): 57–72.

Bono, J. E., Purvanova, R. K., Towler, A. J., & Peterson, D. B. (2009). 'A survey of executive coaching practices,' *Personnel Psychology*, *62*: 361–404.

Chartered Institute of Personnel and Development (CIPD). (2006). *Learning and development survey*. London: CIPD.

Chartered Institute of Personnel and Development (CIPD). (2011). *Learning and talent development annual survey report*. London: CIPD.

Chartered Institute of Personnel and Development (CIPD). (2015). *Learning and development survey*. London: CIPD.

Cho, Y., & Egan, T. (2013). 'Organizational support for action learning in South Korean

Organizations,' *Human Resource Development Quarterly*, 24(2): 185–213.

Cox, E., Bachkirova, T., & Clutterbuck, D. (2010). *The Complete Handbook of Coaching*. London: Sage.

Cox, E., Bachkirova, T., & Clutterbuck, D. (2014a). *The Complete Handbook of Coaching*. 2nd edn. London: Sage (1st edn., 2010).

Cox, E., Bachkirova, T., & Clutterbuck, D. (2014b). 'Theoretical traditions and coaching genres: Mapping the territory,' *Advances in Developing Human Resources*, 16(2): 139–160.

Cummings, T. G., & Worley, C. G. (2015). *Organization development and change*. 10th edn. Stamford, CT: Cengage Learning.

Dagley, G. R. (2010). 'Exceptional executive coaches: Practices and attributes,' *International Coaching Psychology Review*, 5(1), 63–80.

Davis, P. (2004). 'New roles and new competencies for the profession: Are you ready for the next generation?', *TD*, April: 27–36.

Dixey, A. (2015). 'Managerial coaching: A formal process or a daily conversation?', *International Journal of Evidence Based Coaching and Mentoring*, Special Issue No. 9.

Egan, T. (2013). 'Response to Nieminen et al.'s feature article on executive coaching and facilitated multisource feedback: Toward better understanding of a growing HRD practice,' *Human Resource Development Quarterly*, 24(2): 177–183.

Egan, T. (2015). 'Organization development in the context of HRD: From diagnosis to dialogic-perspectives,' In R. F. Poell, T. S. Rocco, & G. L. Roth (Eds.), *The Routledge Companion to Human Resource Development* (pp.53–66). Abingdon, Oxon: Routledge.

Egan, T., & Hamlin, R. G. (2014). 'Coaching, HRD, and relational richness: Putting the pieces together. *Advances in Developing Human Resources*, 16(2): 242–257.

Ellinger, A. D. (2013). 'Supportive supervisors and managerial coaching: Exploring their intersections,' *Journal of Occupational and Organizational Psychology*, 86: 310–316.

Ellinger, A. D., Beattie, R. S. & Hamlin, R. G. (2010). 'The manager as coach,' in E. Cox, T. Bachkirova, & D. Clutterbuck (eds.), *The Complete Handbook of Coaching* (pp. 257–270). London: Sage.

Ellinger, A. D., Beattie, R. S., & Hamlin, R. G. (2014). 'The manager as coach,' in E. Cox, T. Bachkirova, & D. Clutterbuck (eds.), *The Complete Handbook of Coaching* (2nd edn.) (pp. 256–270). London: Sage (1st edn., 2010).

Ellinger, A. D., & Bostrom, R. P. (1999). 'Managerial coaching behaviors in learning organizations,' *Journal of Management Development*, 18(9): 752–771.

Ellinger, A. D., & Bostrom, R. P. (2002). 'An examination of managers' beliefs about their roles as facilitators of learning,' *Management Learning*, 33(2), 147–179.

Ellinger, A. D., Ellinger, A. E., & Keller, S. B. (2003). 'Supervisory coaching behavior, employee satisfaction, and warehouse employee performance: A dyadic perspective in the distribution industry,' *Human Resource Development Quarterly*, 14(4), 435–458.

Ellinger, A. D., & Kim, S. (2014). 'Coaching and human resource development: Examining relevant theories, coaching genres, and scales to advance research and practice,' *Advances in Developing Human Resources*, 16(2): 127–138.

Elmadag, A. B., Ellinger, A. E., & Franke, G. R. (2008). 'Antecedents and consequences of frontline service employee commitment to service quality,' *Journal of Marketing Theory and Practice*, 16(2): 95–110.

Evered, R. D., & Selman, J. C. (1989). 'Coaching and the art of management,' *Organizational Dynamics*, 18: 16–32.

Feldman, D. C., & Lankau, M. J. (2005). 'Executive coaching: A review and agenda for future research,' *Journal of Management*, 31(6): 829–848.

Fillery-Travis, A., & Lane, D. (2006). 'Does coaching work or are we asking the wrong question?', *International Coaching Psychology Review*, 1(1): 23–36.

Frisch, M. H. (2001). 'The emerging role of the internal coach,' *Consulting Psychology Journal: Practice and Research*, 53(4): 240–250.

Graham, S., Wedman, J. F., & Garvin-Kester, B. (1993)). 'Manager coaching skills: Development and application,' *Performance Improvement Quarterly*, 6(1):2–13.

Graham, S., Wedman, J. F., & Garvin-Kester, B. (1994). 'Manager coaching skills: What makes a good coach ?,' *Performance Improvement Quarterly*, 7(2):81–94.

Grant, A. M., & Cavanagh, M. J. (2004). 'Toward a profession of coaching: Sixty-five years of progress and challenges for the future,' *International Journal of Evidence-based Coaching and Mentoring*, 2(1): 1–16.

Grant, A. M., Passmore, J., Cavanagh, M., J., & Parker, H. (2010). 'The state of play in coaching today: A comprehensive review of the field,' *International Review of Industrial and Organizational Psychology*, 25: 125–167.

Gray, D. E., & Goregaokar, H. (2010). 'Choosing an executive coach: The influence of gender on the coach–coachee matching process,' *Management Learning*, 41:525–544.

Gray, D. E., Ekinci, Y., & Goregaokar, H. (2011). 'Coaching SME managers: Business development or personal therapy? A mixed methods study,' *The International Journal of Human Resource Management*, 22(4): 863–882.

Hagen, M. S. (2012). 'Managerial coaching: A review of the literature,' *Performance Improvement Quarterly*, 24(4): 17–39.

Hamlin, R. G. (2007). 'An evidence-based perspective on HRD,' *Advances in Developing Human Resources*, 9(1): 42–57.

Hamlin, B. (2010). 'Evidence-based Leadership and Management Development,' In J. Gold, R. Thorpe & A. Mumford (Eds.), *The Gower Handbook of Leadership and Management Development*. Gower Publishing: England.

Hamlin, R. G., Ellinger, A. E., & Beattie, R. S. (2008a). 'The emergent "coaching industry": A wake-up call for HRD professionals,' *Human Resource Development International*, 11(3): 287–305.

Hamlin, R. G., Ellinger, A. D., & Beattie, R. S. (2008b). 'Coaching at the heart of managerial effectiveness: A cross-cultural study of managerial behaviours,' *Human Resource Development International*, 9(3): 305–331.

Hamlin, R. G., Ellinger, A. D., & Beattie, R. S. (2009). 'Toward a process of coaching? A definitional examination of "Coaching," "Organization Development", and "Human Resource Development",' *International Journal of Evidence Based Coaching and Mentoring*, 7(1): 13–38.

Hunt, J. M., & Weintraub, J. R. (2002). *The coaching manager: Developing top talent in business*. Thousand Oaks, CA: Sage.

Hunt, J. M., & Weintraub, J. R. (2011). *The coaching manager: Developing top talent in business* (2nd edn.). Thousand Oaks, CA: Sage.

Hutchinson, S., & Purcell, J. (2007). *Learning and the line: The role of line managers in training, learning and development*. London: CIPD.

International Coach Federation (2013). *Executive Summary: 2013 ICF Organizational Coaching Study*. PricewaterhouseCoopers.

Joo., B.-K. (2005). 'Executive Coaching: A conceptual framework from an integrative review of practice and research,' *Human Resource Development Review*, 4(4): 462–288.

Joo, B.-K. (2012). 'Multiple faces of coaching: Manager-as-coach, executive coaching, and formal mentoring,' *Organization Development Journal*, 30(1): 19–38.

Judge, W. Q., & Cowell, J. (1997). 'The brave new world of executive coaching,' *Business Horizons*, 40:71–77.

Kilburg, R. R. (1996). 'Toward a conceptual understanding and definition of executive coaching,' *Consulting Psychology Journal: Practice and Research*, 48: 134–144.

Kim, S. (2014). 'Assessing the influence of managerial coaching on employee outcomes,' *Human Resource Development Quarterly*, 25(1): 59–85.

Kim, S., Egan, T., Kim, W., & Kim, J. (2013). 'The impact of managerial coaching behaviour on employee work-related reactions,' *Journal of Business and Psychology*, 28(3): 315–330.

Kim, S., Egan, T. M., & Moon, M. J. (2013). 'Managerial coaching efficacy, work-related attitudes, and performance in public organizations: A comparative international study,' *Review of Public Personnel Administration*, 34(3): 237–262.

Kim, S., & Kuo, M. (2015). 'Examining the relationships among coaching, trustworthiness, and role behaviors: A social exchange perspective,' *The Journal of Applied Behavioral Science*, 51(2): 152–176.

Lee, M. (2015). 'The History, Status and Future of HRD,' In R. F. Poell, T. S. Rocco, & G. L. Roth (Eds.), *The Routledge Companion to Human Resource Development* (pp. 3–12). Abingdon, Oxon: Routledge

London, M. (2002). *Leadership development: Paths to self-insight and professional growth*. Mahwah, NJ: Lawrence Erlbaum.

Longenecker, C. O., & Neubert, M. J. (2005). 'The practices of effective managerial coaches.' *Business Horizons, 48*(6): 493–500.

Maltbia, T. E., Marsick, V. J., & Ghosh, R. (2014). 'Executive and organizational coaching: A review of insights drawn from literature to inform HRD practice,' *Advances in Developing Human Resources*, 16(2): 161–183.

Mankin, D. P. (2001). 'A model for human resource development,' *Human Resource Development International*, 4(1), 65–85.

McGuire, D., & Kissack, H. C. (2015). 'Line Managers and HRD,' In R. F. Poell, T. S. Rocco, & G. L. Roth (Eds.), *The Routledge Companion to Human Resource Development*, (pp. 521–530). Abingdon, Oxon: Routledge.

McLagan, P. A. (1989). 'Models for HRD Practice,' *Training and Development Journal*, 41(9): 49–59.

McLean, G. N., & L. McLean, (2001). 'If we can't define HRD in one country, how can we define it in an international context?,' *Human Resource Development International*, 4(3): 313–326.

McLean, G. N., Yang, B., Kuo, M. C., Tolbert, A. S., & Larkin (2005). 'Development and initial validation of an instrument measuring managerial coaching skill,' *Human Resource Development Quarterly*, 16(2): 157–178.

Megginson, D., & Clutterbuck, D. (2006). 'Creating a coaching culture,' *Industrial and commercial training*, 38(5): 232–237.

Misuikonis, T. (2011). 'The conclusions middle managers draw from their beliefs about organisational coaching and their coaching practices,' *International Journal of Evidence Based Coaching and Mentoring*, Special Issue No. 5.

Noer, D. M., Leupold, C. R., & Valle, M. (2007). 'An analysis of Saudi Arabian and US managerial coaching behaviors,' *Journal of Managerial Issues*, 19(2): 271–287

O'Neil, J., & Marsick, V. J. (2007). *Understanding Action Learning*. New York: American Management Association.

O'Neil, J., & Marsick, V. J. (2014). 'Action learning coaching,' *Advances in Developing Human Resources*, 16(2): 202–221.

Orth, C. D., Wilkinson, H. E., & Benfari, R. C. (1987). 'The manager's role as coach and mentor,' *Organizational Dynamics*, 15(4): 66–74.

Plunkett, B. L., & Egan, T. M. (2004). 'Application of Psychology-based Theoretical Approaches to Executive Coaching: A Summary and Exploration of Potential Utility,' In T. M. Egan & L. M. Morris (Eds.), *AHRD Conference Proceedings* (pp. 558–565). Bowling Green, OH: AHRD.

Rothwell, W. J., Arneson, J., & Naughton, J. (2013). *ASTD Competency Study: The Training and Development Professional Redefined*. Alexandria, VA: ASTD Press.

Ruona, W. E. A., & Gibson, S. K. (2004). 'The Making of Twenty-first Century HR: An Analysis of the Convergence of HRM, HRD, and OD,' *Human Resource Management*, 43(1): 49–66.

Segers, J., Vloeberghs, D., Henderickx, E., & Inceoglu, I. (2011). 'Structuring and understanding the coaching industry: The coaching cube,' *Academy of Management Learning & Education*, 10(2): 204–221.

Shull, A. C., Church, A. H., & Burke, W. W. (2013). 'Attitudes about the field of organization development 20 years later: The more things change, the more they stay the same,' *Research in Organizational Change and Development*, 21: 1–28.

Stokes, J., & Jolly, R. (2010). 'Executive and Leadership Coaching,' In E. Cox, T. Bachkirova, & D. Clutterbuck (Eds.), *The Complete Handbook of Coaching* (pp. 245–256). London: Sage.

Stokes, J., & Jolly, R. (2014). 'Executive and Leadership Coaching,' in E. Cox, T. Bachkirova, & D. Clutterbuck (eds.), *The Complete Handbook of Coaching* (2nd edn.) (pp. 244–255). London: Sage.

Swanson, R. A., & Holton, E. F, III (2009). *Foundations of Human Resource Development*. 2nd edn. San Francisco, CA: Berrett-Koehler, Inc. (1st edn., 2001).

Turner, P. S. (2010). *Aligning Organizational Coaching with Leadership Behaviour*. Published PhD Thesis. Birmingham City University, UK.

Vaartjes, V. (2005). 'Integrating action learning practice into executive coaching to enhance business results,' *International Journal of Evidence-Based Coaching and Mentoring*, 3(1): 1–17.

Watkins, K. E. (1998). 'Foundations for HRD in a knowledge era,' In B. R. Stewart & H. C. Hall (Eds.), *Beyond Tradition: Preparing HRD Educators for Tomorrow's Workforce* (pp. 1–32). Columbia, MO: UCWHRE.

Werner, J. M. (2014). 'Human resource development does not equal human resource management: So what is it?,' *Human Resource Development Quarterly*, 25(2): 127–139.

Werner, J. M. (2015). 'Human Resource Management and HRD: Connecting the Dots or Ships Passing in the Night?', In R. F. Poell, T. S. Rocco, & G. L. Roth (Eds.), *The Routledge Companion to Human Resource Development* (pp.89–98). Abingdon, Oxon: Routledge.

Wheeler, L. (2011). 'How does the adoption of coaching behaviours by line managers contribute to the achievement of organizational goals?', *International Journal of Evidence Based Coaching and Mentoring*, 9(1): 1–15.

Group and Team Coaching

Sean O'Connor and Michael Cavanagh

INTRODUCTION

It has become almost a cliché to say that the pace of change is accelerating and that the world of work, for an ever-growing number of people, is increasing in competitiveness, volatility, complexity and uncertainty. Nevertheless these challenges are real and have important consequences for individuals, teams, organizations and the planet. In order to meet them, organizations across most industries have been seeking out new and efficient ways to support leaders and teams. While business has been busy seeking answers to this complexity, coaching has grown in popularity as a methodology for developing and supporting individuals, teams and organizations alike (Cavanagh and Lane, 2012; Passmore and Fillery-Travis, 2011; Peterson, 2011; Theeboom, Beersman, and van Vianen, 2014). The rise of coaching as a developmental intervention at this time is no accident. Coaching, when done well, is an intervention that is able to draw from knowledge bases across a wide range of disciplines and contexts, to collaboratively develop bespoke solutions to novel problems on a just in time basis.

Despite this flexibility, the research base for coaching to date has focused primarily on one-to-one coaching (Brown and Grant, 2010). This type of coaching has been shown to be effective in enhancing individual performance (Grant, et al., 2010). However, when it comes to group or team coaching, we have relatively few theory driven models of practice, and almost no empirical evidence as to the efficacy of these approaches. Anecdotally, experience in the field suggests that a growing number of organizations are seeking group or team coaching, and coaches are adapting approaches to meet this demand, with mixed success. This chapter will review the current empirical evidence base and seek to define the differences between group, team and other forms of coaching, and to explore the key dimensions and criteria that might be useful for developing models of group and team coaching.

THE PROBLEM WITH GROUP COACHING

The literature on group and team coaching is bedeviled by a foundational lack of clarity. Most of the authors who attempt to publish in this area seek to reduce this lack of clarity, and do so by providing specific definitions of what is a team and what is a group, and how this difference has implications for coaching. However the lack of definitional clarity remains. This lack of clarity may have its roots, not in definitions of what constitutes a team or a group (though this definitional difference is important), but as a consequence of a failure to examine a more fundamental or foundational issue: Where does change take place? In other words, what is the fundamental unit of analysis that is relevant to group coaching?

The neglect of this question is neither deliberate nor malign. It simply demonstrates that the roots of coaching (and, indeed, most psychological models) are to be found in Western philosophical traditions that are centered on the individual as the fundamental unit of analysis. This has meant that the individual is typically seen as the key locus of change and therefore the fundamental target of both psychological and coaching interventions. Hence, most coaching approaches find it difficult to articulate a model of group or team coaching that extends beyond individual coaching conducted in organizations. A failure to address this question has meant that much of what is put forward as group coaching is really a modified version of group facilitation or team building. We will begin this chapter by questioning this root assumption, and noticing how it plays out in the extant models of group and team coaching.

The second key issue that arises is what is the typical pathway or trajectory of change. Most models of group and team coaching assume a cybernetic model of change. In other words, they see change as a rather linear affair that begins with assessing where one is, deciding on an appropriate goal or endpoint, charting a course to that endpoint, and measuring progress along the way, adapting as one departs from the charted course (e.g., Peters and Carr, 2013). Again, this belies the rational linearity of our philosophical traditions. In this chapter, we will seek to articulate a non-linear approach to group and team coaching that is more in keeping with a scientific model of experimentation than with a linear predictable approach to change.

The third issue of what we mean by 'group' and 'team' will also be addressed. As many authors have rightly found, the answer to this question revolves around the degree of shared goal focus and interdependence within a group. As mentioned above, this distinction is important and will enable us to distinguish different coaching interventions. When combined with our understanding of the locus of change and non-linearity, this final dimension will enable us to create a decision matrix for which issues are most amenable to group or team coaching and which issues are better dealt with at an individual or dyadic level.

UNDERSTANDING THE LOCUS OF CHANGE IN TEAM COACHING

As mentioned above, the individual is seen as the unit of analysis in most Western approaches to coaching (and psychological change more generally). In other words, coaching seeks to create change in the individual person, and this change is assumed to have an impact on the functioning of the relationships and groups in which the individual interacts. However, one of the key tenets of systems theories is that all systems are comprised of smaller systems nested

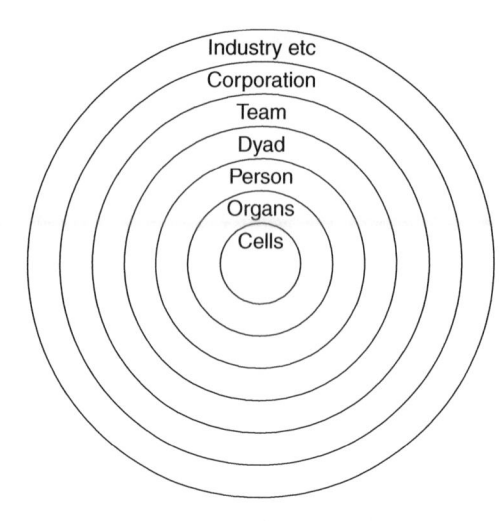

Figure 27.1 The hierarchical nature of systems

within larger systems (see Figure 27.1). Importantly, each new level of the system is not reducible to the sum of its parts – it is unique and whole in its own right. This leads to two critically important and practical implications. Firstly, each level of the system represents a valid point of practical focus for coaching. From a systems theory perspective, the individual is only one possible level of analysis among many, and may not necessarily deserve to be the privileged focus. Secondly, focusing on lower levels of a system does not provide an unproblematic insight into the dynamics of higher system levels, because these higher levels have their own dynamics. In other words, a focus on the individual (or even on relationships between individuals) is unlikely to meet the need for developing high performing groups and teams.

Margaret Thatcher's (1987) famous statement, '… there is no such thing [as society]. There are individual men and women, and there are families …' is flatly incorrect from a systems perspective. Society is not just the sum of its individuals, any more than the human person is simply the sum of their organ systems. All systems levels are entities in their own right, with unique internal and external dynamics, and importantly, unique goals and processes. It is this systems insight that makes team and group coaching possible, and which differentiate it from one-on-one or dyadic coaching. If we explore the dynamics of coaching from a systems perspective it soon becomes obvious that there is a fractal pattern to be found in coaching. Fractals can be defined as displaying self-similarity at different scales. In other words, similar but not identical forms appear at each new scale (Mandelbrot, 1983).

Coaching can be thought to display a fractal like pattern. In coaching the focus is on the relationship between the coachee and the coachee's challenge (and consequent goal). Typically that challenge is one that originates in the coachee's environment due to some change in external circumstances (a new work role, new relationship, new demand, etc.). Or the challenge may be precipitated by a change in the coachee's internal world (their beliefs, goals, desires, meanings, values, etc.). In either case, the coachee's 'internal organization' and dynamics of their current location in the system, means the coachee is unable to optimally meet and address the challenge before him or her. In order to meet this challenge, a coach might work with the client to explore their inner organization (beliefs, thoughts, decision making rules), their external actions (habits and patterns of behavior), and the pattern of relationships that establishes the coachee in their context and the relationship between this context and the wider environment.

In other words, coaching typically focuses on three sets of relationship across at least 3 systems levels:

1. The pattern of internal dynamics which shape what is possible for the coachee in their world. Focusing on these internal patterns is really a form of skills coaching. It seeks to develop the basic patterns required to think, behave and respond effectively.

2. The relationship between the coachee and the immediate context. In this coaching the coachee is supported to focus their skills and understanding on meeting the specific challenge facing them in the immediate environment (e.g., organizational targets, market challenges etc.). This focus is the heart of performance coaching.

3. *The relationship between the coachee and the wider systemic environment.* In this coaching focus, the immediate environment is not simply taken as a given, but is considered in the context of other competing environments and wider systems levels (e.g., other teams, the organization, family, society, the natural environment etc.). Here the emphasis is on exploring the relationship between the coachee, the coaching challenge and wider system dynamics. This exploration is at the heart of developmental coaching.

Figure 27.2 graphically demonstrates this pattern of focus for individual coaching. However a similar, but not identical pattern exists for coaching at different levels of the system.

Figure 27.3 shows the same sort of pattern for team coaching. Note that the internal dynamics of individuals is not a key focal point of team coaching. Team coaching, when it is focused internally (at a skills level), is only interested in the internal dynamics of the team as they relate to goal attainment externally. The individual (and even particular relationships between team members) are of minimal interest. From a coaching perspective, the conversation between team members may be considered similar to the internal

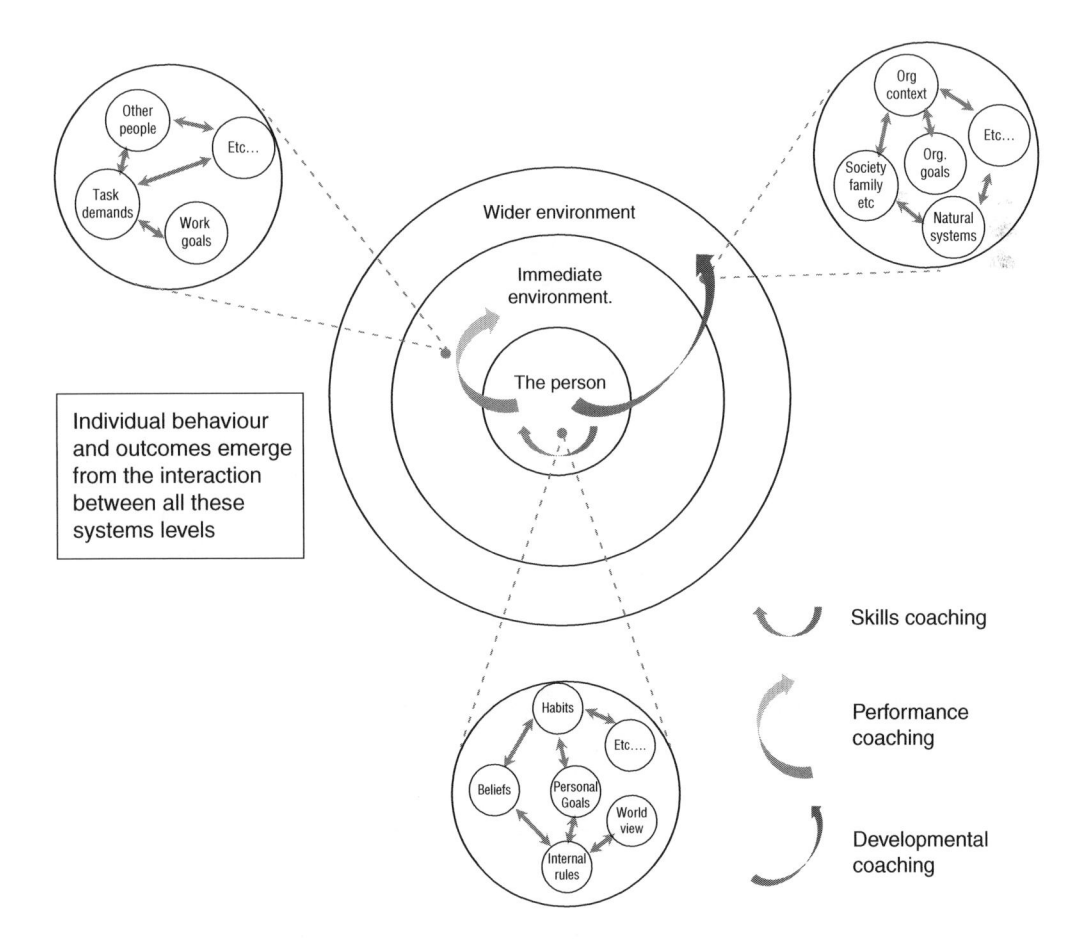

Figure 27.2 Three coaching foci for individual coaching

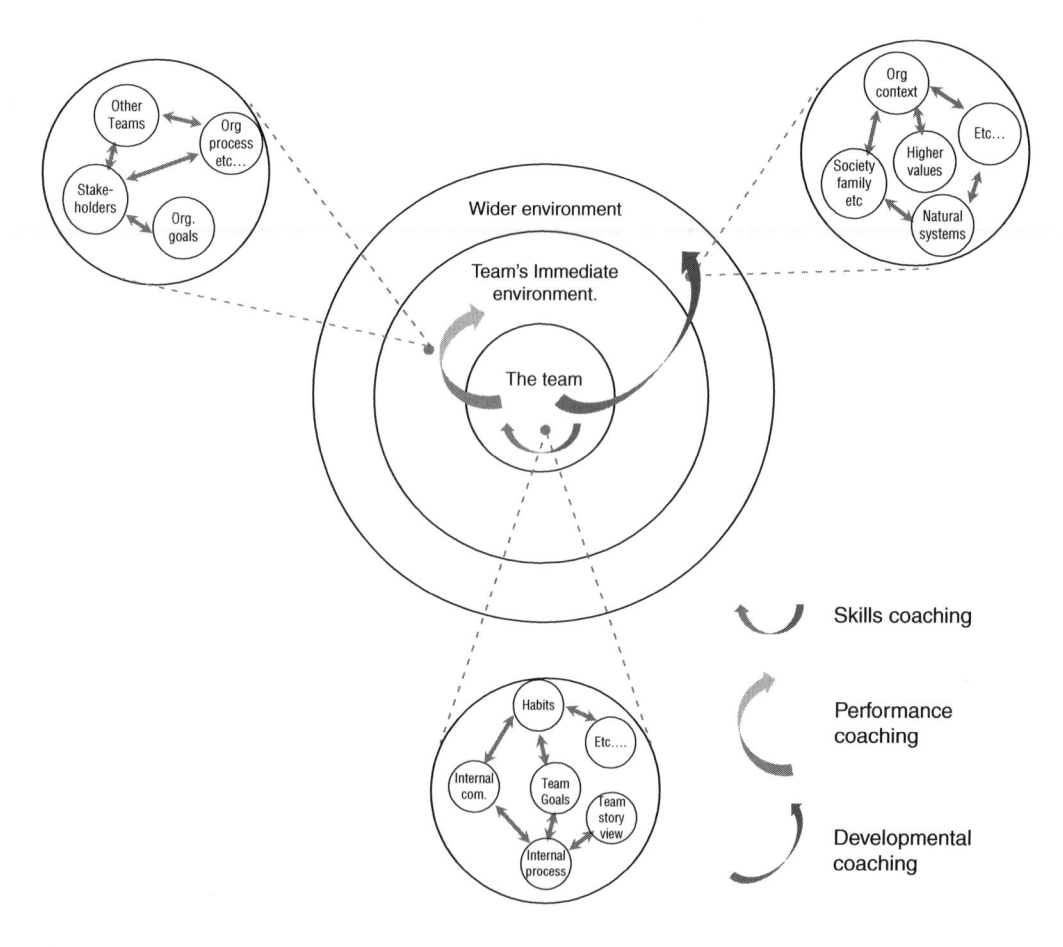

Figure 27.3 Three coaching foci for team coaching

conversation of the individual. In individual coaching, the coach's role is to support the quality of that internal conversation, and the behavior that flows from it. This means helping the individual notice, organize and resolve or address competing issues, assumptions faulty thinking and other tensions in that internal conversation, but only in as much as this is relevant to the person's goal.

At a team level, the internal conversation is the conversation (in its broadest sense) between team members and team behavior flows from it. Any focus on the team's internal conversation is only relevant to the extent that it is important for team goal attainment. In the context of team or group coaching, the quality of a particular team member's experience, or of particular relationships between team members is irrelevant except when that experience or those relationships get in the way of effective performance. The goal is not to make the team members comfortable, but to create an effective team, and that means focusing not on the members, but on the space between them: the processes and patterns of communication that are critical for task achievement. A good analogy can be made with sporting teams here. It matters little whether two players like each other, or whether an individual player is enjoying the game. Provided their task related behavior is functional for the team's goal, how individual team members manage their own internal processes is a matter for them.

Nevertheless, when considering the failure of particular team members to behave in a way that is functional for the team, it is tempting to resort to an individual level explanation. From a team coaching perspective, this risks missing much of the learning that may be available. Every system is designed to create the outcomes it achieves. In other words, from a systems perspective, individual performance is typically a function of team dynamics, rather than vice versa. Here we are reminded of the old adage that a team of champions does not always make a champion team. The individual is a part of the system, but outcomes are created by the whole system. A competent team coach will ask questions such as: How is the team (and wider system) organized to enable this outcome? What team processes and dynamics have tilted the balance toward this outcome rather than another?

For example, we are all familiar with the process of scapegoating in teams. One common example of seeking individual scapegoats for team performance occurs when the leader is accused of being over-controlling. Such behavior is usually a sign of anxiety, often driven by a more general failure of the team to properly select, agree, commit to, monitor, or enact goal directed behavior. As feedback and progress fail, the leader seeks to drive the team toward the goal more forcefully. The team, feeling this pressure, may push back or step back even further, leaving the leader holding the goal, and giving rise to a dysfunctional behavior cycle.

A systems team coach will see the team as a whole coherent unit. At the level of performance coaching, he/she will seek to help the team notice and improve how it organizes its activity, what emerges from team activity, the habitual patterns of relating and communication that bear on the teams capacity to meet the goals the organization has set for it, and will seek to develop new, more useful patterns of behavior, decision making and interaction. This will include goal and process selection and deployment, managing relationships with stakeholders and others in the immediate environment etc.

At the level of developmental coaching, the coach will seek to assist the team to reflect on their relationship to the wider environment. In other words, the coach will help the team to reflect on more than that they work together, but why they do what they do, and how the team activity relates to important aspects of the wider world. This sort of reflection may give rise to significant changes in understanding, direction and activity. Developmental team coaching is most easily understood at higher levels within the organization (e.g., senior leadership team), as these are the groups most empowered to make organizational level shifts in direction and emphasis. Nevertheless, even relatively low level teams may benefit from developmental coaching. Addressing the tensions between one's immediate goals and important wider system issues and pressures can give rise to new and innovative solutions.

GROUP VS TEAM COACHING

Thus far, we have considered team coaching as if the notion of team or group is clear and generally unproblematic. As noted in our introduction, the distinction between group and team is important and has implications for coaching practice. A range of taxonomies of groups and teams has been put forward by many authors over the years. It is not the place of this chapter to explore all the current definitions. Suffice it to say that across the literature there exists a broad consensus concerning the major differences between groups and teams. For example, Anderson and West (1998) define a work group as 'either the permanent or semi-permanent team to which individuals are assigned, whom they identify with, and whom they interact with regularly in order to perform work-related tasks' (Anderson and West, 1998, p. 236). In order for a team level climate to evolve, Anderson and West (1998) argue that three conditions are necessary:

1 There needs to be at least some interaction between members.
2 There is some sort of common goal or attainable outcome.
3 A degree of task interdependence requiring shared understanding exists.

Similarly, Katzenbach and Smith (1993), as well as Hawkins (2011), differentiate groups and teams on the basis of their interdependence (see Table 27.1)

In terms of differentiating team coaching from group coaching, team coaching is typically described as engagements with intact teams in which the members work together and share responsibilities for the output of the team (Hackman and Wageman, 2005; Hawkins, 2011). However, when looking at this position more carefully it can easily be seen that such a broad description hides multiple important distinctions. For example, the level of shared responsibility can vary greatly and may depend on the team structure, coaching purpose and the coaching approach used. Similarly, teams may be required to act in a more group like fashion regarding some aspects of their work, and in more interdependent team roles in others. Similarly, in today's organizations, people are typically members of multiple teams, some ongoing and some project based and of varying lifespans. A person's relationship to each of these teams may differ widely, adding further complexity to the set of possible dynamics associated with team membership. Access to and exercise of power similarly varies across team types and time frames. One issue common in team coaching engagements is how the coach helps the team notice and manage the power relationships between the team leader, team members and the coach in order to effectively support the purpose of the coaching engagement.

The most widely used definition of team coaching is that provided by Hackman and Wageman (2005) who define team coaching as a form of leadership which is enacted through: 'A direct interaction with a team intended to help members make coordinated and task-appropriate use of their collective resources in accomplishing the team's work' (p. 269). One of the issues with this definition is that almost any team level intervention could then be thought of as team coaching. This would include facilitated strategic planning, collaborative consultation approaches or team software training workshops to name just a few.

Clutterbuck (2010) provides a more specific approach to defining team coaching as a learning intervention, aimed at increasing team effectiveness through coaching principles like assisted reflection, analysis and motivation to change. This definition has a great deal of utility and effectively includes some of our understanding of known effective processes within dyadic coaching. However, by focusing on effectiveness there is a limitation set on the purpose that team coaching could fulfill, seemingly quite task focused. While there is much room for interpretation here, a more specific definition that expanded the utility of team coaching beyond task and effectiveness could be beneficial.

Hawkins and Smith (2007) take the definition one step further in specifically defining leadership team coaching as: 'Enabling a team to function at more than the sum of its parts, by clarifying its mission and improving its external and internal relationships' (p.82). This definition has many strong points, and is closest to our conception of systemic team

Table 27.1 Characteristics of working groups and teams

Working group	Team
Strong focused leader	Shared leadership roles
Individual accountability	Individual and mutual accountability
Individual work product	Collective work product
Efficient meetings	Time spent in open ended discussion

Source: Adapted from Katzenbach and Smith (2004)

coaching. It moves very specifically away from the development of individual skills and performance and embeds the team within the organizational systemic context.

One of the issues with over specifying the definition of group or team coaching is that it can often exclude special cases and structures of groups and teams that could be usefully assisted through coaching approaches. Despite this, it is important to be clear as to when and how the coach moves from a group or higher system level of coaching to an individual level of coaching, and why this transition is being made. For example, it is sometimes the case that individuals are coached in a group format with others who have similar individual level goals. A typical example might be a group of senior executive from different organizations who receive coaching together in a group, with the aim of each improving their leadership within their organizational context. This is analogous to counseling support groups in which individuals share their experiences and support each other in achieving their personal goals.

The benefit of conducting this type of coaching in a group is that the coach can help individuals draw from the challenges, progress, learning, experience and knowledge of all group members in order to support the development and change of each of the members in the group. Further to this, a coach may require a specific set of skills to translate the different experience of the individuals across the context of all those involved in order to best support an individual's development. Even though on the surface this may seem like individual coaching done together in a group format, a group dynamic does form that can be useful in assisting the group to achieve its common goal of improvement for all.

As the group evolves new relationships and understandings emerge that link them across their multiple contexts and may be adapted for individual growth. These emergent relational components would not be available for the coach and coachees to leverage in the usual dyadic approach. Additionally, if skilled enough, the coach can use many of the techniques used within dyadic approaches to support the development of multiple group members simultaneously. For example, immediacy can be used to reflect on the impact of behavior in the session, enabling members to identify important individual shifts. Similarly, understanding the motivations and perspectives of others may support needed changes in an individual. Through identifying similarities among group members, any positive change and growth for one individual can be leveraged for change in the other individuals via social learning processes. Of critical importance is that the coach recognizes that the group goal is actually held at an individual level, and therefore, coaching should focus on enabling the group to best organize to meet those individual level goals.

RESEARCH INTO GROUP AND TEAM COACHING

The sophistication and volume of coaching research is increasing (Grant, 2009), and the importance of coaching for groups and teams has been asserted previously (Arakawa and Greenberg, 2007). Despite this, the published research tends to focus heavily on individual level outcomes while the impact of coaching at the level of the group, team, organization or system has largely been ignored. The limited research that does exist in this area has focused mostly on return for investment (Feggetter, 2007; McGovern et al., 2001; Palmer, 2003). Focusing the literature toward higher system level outcomes may stimulate a new set of tools and approaches which may dramatically shift our understanding of coaching and leadership development interventions, particularly within the organizational context. Additionally there exists the potential for positive impact within multiple group types, including families, societies and communities.

RESEARCH ON GROUP COACHING

Considering group coaching specifically, Rauen (2005) describes group coaching as a process where individuals who do not necessarily work together engage simultaneously in a coaching process. While this perspective identifies one type of group clearly enough it does not identify the specifics of the coaching process used. Group coaching has been used to describe interventions that consist of facilitation and training mixed with peer-to-peer coaching across three day long sessions conducted monthly (Fusco, O'Roidan and Palmer, 2015). Group coaching has been used to describe a process within a leadership development programme were executives from different organizations experience psychodynamic development in which they are coached through a number of modules alongside facilitated peer-to-peer coaching (Florent-Treacy, 2009). In this last example the group coaching component seems to refer to a day of shared leadership 360 degree feedback (Florent-Treacy, 2009) and is shaped largely around group therapy practices. However, not enough detail is provided to inform practical application or comparisons across the research literature.

Another piece of research on assisting individuals through gender transition using a solution focused group coaching approach (Grajfoner, 2009) applied a mixed methodology of peer-to-peer coaching and group facilitation. While a very considered and specifically detailed structure was presented, there is still difficulty in assessing the impact of the coaching component within a seemingly mixed intervention. In action research on the application of group coaching in supporting lifestyle change experiences of individuals diagnosed with long-term medical conditions (Whitley, 2013), a very specific approach was taken. Whitley (2013) clearly identifies a number of coaching process particulars including the session length (two hours) and number of sessions (five). Whitley (2013) articulates her practice and approach to facilitating group interaction, SMART goal setting and individual level action planning through the group process. While this research presents a qualitative case study on one group of six individuals alone, it does provide a good example of articulating the relationship between individual and group coaching approaches that allow for a considered assessment in relation to both theory and practice. Whitley concludes that the group members felt that this approach to group coaching can be effective in supporting people through this specific life transition within a healthcare setting (Whitley, 2013).

Another pilot study compared four one-hour sessions of cognitive behavioral group coaching with a matched control on improvements in student procrastination (Torbrand and Ellam-Dyson, 2015). While the researchers identify the effectiveness of an articulated task oriented group coaching approach based on the individual level RE-GROW model (Grant, 2011), the sample size was small (N=7) with the coaching group consisting of only 3 individuals. This suggests an important consideration of the group size in relation to the time available for each group coaching session and while one hour may have been sufficient for a session with only three group members, others have found that longer is required for larger groups (Whitley, 2013).

In yet another mixed qualitative quantitative design Stelter, Nielsen and Wikman (2011) have applied what they define as a narrative collaborative group coaching approach to develop social capital in a randomized control trial (RCT) of elite sport students. In this design, group coaching consisted of eight 90-minute sessions with 4–6 group members in each coaching group. Stelter and colleagues (2011) clearly outline the theoretical underpinning to their narrative collaborative group coaching approach, while also outlining important assumption and guidelines. Concluding that a narrative collaborative group coaching approach has a positive impact on social recovery and well-being of elite student athletes (Stelter et al, 2011), this research provides a level of clarity and articulated process that is supportive of research in group coaching and practice moving into the future.

Barr and van Nieuwerburgh (2015) use the term group coaching to define a process of training and facilitation in which coaching one-to-one was demonstrated and then practiced between the novice group members in peer-to-peer coaching dyads. While Barr and van Nieuwerburgh (2015) reference Stelter et al (2011), the group coaching approach they employ bears little resemblance to that employed by Stelter and his colleagues (2011). From the description provided by Barr and van Nieuwerburgh (2015) their process resembles more closely a workshop based experiential learning exercise.

The first piece of research to date specifically comparing group and dyadic coaching approaches is that conducted by Mühlberger and Traut-Mattausch (2015). In this research Mühlberger and Traut-Mattausch (2015) compared dyadic coaching, group coaching, and a control group looking specifically at reducing procrastination and the impact of transformational leadership behaviors of the actual coaches. Applying a very specific definition of group coaching initially put forward by Rauen (2005) which suggests group coaching occurs when a group of people that do not necessarily work together, participate in a coaching process together. Mühlberger and Traut-Mattausch outline their SMART goal setting procedure quite clearly and have conducted a well-constructed randomized controlled comparison of dyadic and group coaching. However the dyadic coaching only consisted of one one-hour session, as did the group coaching approach with groups ranging from 10–16 members. Improvements in individual procrastination goals were found for both the group and dyadic conditions, yet there were higher increases in goal commitment, goal reflection and intrinsic goal motivation in the dyadic condition.

While Mühlberger and Traut-Mattausch conclude that the impact of the specific coaches transformational leadership behaviors may not translate to the group coaching approach, one session with 10–16 people on procrastination goals does not represent accurately the usual occurrences of group coaching in the industry. The additional positive outcome for the dyadic coaching may be easily explained by the large difference in time allotment for each coachee on an individual basis. If there is less time for interaction with the coach there is less opportunity for the coaching leadership behaviors to be experienced. Future research could benefit from taking this design and expanding it to include multiple sessions over time, as is usually the case for dyadic and group coaching. This may let some of the emergent benefits of the group coaching approach take hold while also providing a more analogous case to that of usual practice.

Other research has used the term group coaching to describe aspects of mixed intervention approaches. Often these include executive coaching, 360 degree feedback, peer-to-peer coaching, and group coaching sessions of varying lengths ranging from a day-long session to hourly engagements with little if any explanation on the specific group process that took place (Coates, 2013; Vesso, 2015). While mixed intervention approaches are important consideration with some using the term integrated leadership development programmes (Coates, 2013), more detail and specificity on the interventions and design can be helpful in informing practice and research. This brief review identifies a large range of approaches and some clear disparities in definitions within the literature on group coaching specifically. While the research on team coaching suffers from some similar issues there is a degree of specificity around different types of teams, which require particular attention.

RESEARCH ON TEAM COACHING

In research specifically looking at team coaching Godfrey and colleagues (2014) applied a mixed-methods design to assess the impact a team coaching programme had on two interprofessional health care improvement collaboratives consisting of 61 teams coached by 31–39 coaches. In this research the term collaborative referred to groups consisting of a mix of interprofessional health care teams, patients and family members. Through their quantitative analysis of qualitative focused group data they were able to identify a number of coaching actions that were perceived by the coaches, coachees and leaders to support improvement. Four categories emerged which included context, relationship, helping and technical support.

In this example it is easy to see how complex the relatedness or interdependence between team members becomes once a team definition is extended beyond the usual leadership or work team. While these findings for interprofessional collaboration are interesting and useful, more details concerning the specificity of the coaching processes would help considerably with replication and interpretation for practice. Further to this the finding concerning the usefulness of technical support suggests a level of consultation and expert advice that may have been provided by the coaches that seems beyond the usual expectations of a coach. In particular, the structure and frequency of the coaching engagement was left largely undefined with only limited description of the process provided. Furthermore two coaches were used per group for one of them with no clear articulation of the group session or session length. Additionally the level of experience of the coaches was mixed. If a minimal level of coaching skill requirements were defined specifically, more could be done to integrate these findings into the field.

Suggestions have been made for a cognitive behavioral team coaching model for increasing well-being (Hultgren, Palmer and O'Riordan, 2013). The design in general outlines a clearly goal-oriented task-based coaching approach. Intervention factors of coaching a team through collaborative goal setting which included issue identification, option generation, SMART goal setting, solution generation and implementation were similar to those outlined in the GROUP model by Brown and Grant (2010). The intervention proposed by Hultgren and colleagues (2013), presents a considered solution focused approach to team coaching however it is difficult to identify the cognitive component they refer to in the title. It is unclear in what way cognitions are being utilized and adapted for the benefit of the team.

Other models put forward include a salutogenic coaching approach (Gray, Burls and Kogan, 2014), focused on factors that promote human health and wellbeing. While it could be argued that supporting wellbeing is a general tenet of all coaching approaches (O'Connor and Cavanagh, 2013; Spence and Grant, 2012), this qualitative case study approach provides a model they suggest for both team and one-to-one coaching. What was required was a more careful consideration of adapting their approach specifically for a team coaching context and more clarity on what was meant by a team from their perspective.

Hauser (2014) argues that the historical definition of team coaching as generally conducted by managers, put forward by Hackman and Wageman (2005), and used broadly to define teams across the team coaching literature, does not represent the majority of team coaching approaches occurring in practice. Hauser (2014) suggests, as supported by many others (Brown and Grant, 2010; ICF, 2012; O'Connor and Cavanagh, 2013), that external coaches are providing these types of interventions for groups and organizations alike. Outlined in Hauser's (2014) model are a number of important considerations for behavioral based team coaching identified through qualitative interviews conducted with experienced external team coaches. These considerations include clarity concerning:

1. Outcomes of coaching: including multiple potential goal levels of personal, interpersonal, team and organizational
2. The coach's approach: identifying directive task-oriented vs. relational process-oriented approaches
3. Timing of interventions: referring to the interventions that tend to be used during the start middle and end phases of a coaching engagement
4. Roles enacted through behavior: the four roles enacted by team coaches over an engagement included were Advisory, Educational, Catalytic and Transitional
5. Influence on the coach's approach: including personal attributes, background and experiences.

While only eight team coaches were interviewed this outline provides a strong starting point for careful considerations required when coaching groups or teams. Additionally it provides a strong starting point for much needed further research.

RESEARCH ON SENIOR LEADERSHIP TEAMS

There are a number of empirical papers looking specifically at senior leadership teams. Kralj (2001) suggest that development programmes at executive levels usually include a range of approaches such as individual, team and organizational interventions. They provide a case study taking a more consultative than coaching approach, which they readily identify. While the systems level perspective they employ is very useful when working at this level, further detail is required on the team level coaching approach that was utilized.

Another case study approach by Carr and Peters (2013) proposed a high performance team coaching model. Using external coaches/researchers they reviewed the experience of two leadership teams. They found common coaching elements of importance including: the team's character and working agreement; level of participation, coach manner and actions; a team launch; as well as the coaching structure and follow-up process. Based on feedback from the coachees, potential improvements were identified in the areas of collaboration and productivity, relationships, personal learning, communication and participation, impact beyond the team and peer coaching. While Carr and Peters (2013) identify a range of coaching related processes, including an agreement process, team diagnostic and assessment, facilitated vision setting, mission creation and setting of stakeholder expectations as part of coaching engagement, more could have been done to explicate the coaching process and describe specific coaching activities.

Woodhead (2011) takes a considered case study approach to coaching a team of cross disciplinary healthcare leaders. The structure and process applied does reflect quite strongly a number of the key aspects of coaching in general. These included regular sessions, once per month for 2.5 hours over an 8-month period allowing for considered application of interventions and a reflective cycle of self-regulation. However, the definition used by Woodhead (2011) describes the coaching programme as 'a symbiotic intervention of team coaching and facilitation' (Woodhead, 2011, p.103).

While it is unclear what this intervention actually entails. Woodhead's findings seem to indicate a broadly developmental focus to the coaching intervention. Post session reflections used as part of the qualitative data for analysis required coachees to engage in written reflection exploring their experience as they move through the coaching process. The reflections gathered from the three leaders and the qualitative interviews subsequently conducted, identify a transition of understanding over time. The sharing of experience and letting go of assumptions stimulated the development of new perspectives. The causal themes identified through the analysis included having the time and forum for discussions, the focus and clarity of shared goals, the independence of the coach, a safe space for opening up, seeing beyond the professional image, understanding and appreciating others disciplines, cascading information to their own teams, collaborative decision making, improved communication and relationships, commitment and stability.

The context of the health care system requires a high degree of interactive work between the team members of the disciplines represented by the three leaders involved in the coaching. The small size of the team, the intimacy of the process, the willingness to be authentic and opportunity to see the person behind the professional position, seemed to help with the success of the developmental team coaching process. However it is hard to say if this process would translate to leadership teams in differing contexts, or of differing sizes. Another factor, which is noted by Woodhead (2011), may also be the degree of common responsibility emphasized through the shared goal process that supported the developmental transformation that they seemed to experience through the coaching engagement.

TEAM COACHING: LEADER AS COACH

There are a number of authors using team coaching under the definition of Hackman and Wageman (2005) to describe coaching like behavior performed by the leader of the team. The majority of research conducted under this paradigm is survey based (Liu et al., 2009; Rouseau et al., 2013; Hagen and Aguilar, 2012) and reflects many of the findings of the transformational leadership literature. Theories of transformational leadership suggest that leaders higher in transformational leadership are, better able to build trust, act with integrity, inspire others, encourage innovative thinking, and help others to develop for themselves (Avolio, Bass and Jung, 1999). This last factor concerning developing others is often referred to as individualized consideration or coaches others. Managerial coaching research has defined a number of specific behaviors including open communication, team approach, acceptance of ambiguity, and facilitation of development (Park, McLean, and Yang, 2008).

Others have considered team coaching as a specific style of leadership that focuses on developing team members towards higher levels of achievement through behaviors reflective of the general coaching behavioral methodology (Rousseau et al., 2013). Key findings include, leader coaching like behaviors, fostering team innovation (Rousseau et al., 2013), impacting team learning (Hagen and Aguilar, 2012) and having a positive influence on team effort and effectiveness (Liu et al., 2009). All of these results have similar counterpart findings in the transformational leadership literature (Barling et al., 1996; Gumusluoglu and Ilsev, 2009; Özaralli 2003; Garcia-Morales et al., 2012). The use of the term team coaching is somewhat confusing when applied to so many different processes. It should also be noted that the locus of change in all these activities is the individual not the team. Leadership is likewise seen as an individual characteristic rather than a quality distributed throughout the team and enacted at a team level.

GROUP AND TEAM COACHING MOVING FORWARD

Given the wide variety and disparity across the definitions identified for group and team coaching, it would seem almost impossible to have one definition to cover all of these cases. When considering group and team coaching as it currently stands, there seems to be a number of key considerations for supporting group and team coaching research and practice into the future. These considerations seem to fall into two categories, those that relate to the group and team and those that relate to the coaching process. While these two categories are likely to be interdependent, they may serve as a useful guide for developing research and intervention design.

IMPLICATIONS FOR COACHING PRACTICE

Given the lack of definitional and theoretical coherence in the coaching literature outlined above, we would suggest that a systemic perspective may be useful for coaching in deciding when, and how, to enter into group coaching. Specifically, we would suggest that coaches focus on four key questions:

1. What is the desired outcome of the coaching engagement? What type of outcome is sought?
2. What system level is best able to work toward this outcome?
3. What degree of interdependency is required to achieve this outcome?
4. What pattern of relationship will best serve goal attainment?

1. A Clear Focus on the Desired Outcome of the Coaching Intervention

As in individual coaching, clarity as to the purpose of the intervention is critical. Understanding the goal will enable the coach and client to decide what type of intervention might be useful, and at what system level the intervention should be enacted. It is likely that most coaching engagements may contain more than one aim, and these will be a mix of skills, performance and developmental coaching. Clarity regarding the purpose and level of goals in group or team coaching would also be extremely useful for extending our research and understanding. Furthermore, it would help to shape intervention design and identify common approaches and factors for effective intervention across the different areas.

A systemic understanding such as the one outlined in this chapter, enables a reasonably user-friendly way of categorization coaching aims. The development of skill consists of all those aims that specifically focus on the learning and creation of new forms of internal organization at the same system level. The use, testing, adaptation and skills (both new and old) to achieve goals within the groups immediate system level or context are performance goals, while those goals that seek to change the group's relationship with its immediate and wider environment are developmental aims.

2. Matching Coaching Aim to System Level

Categorizing coaching aims in this way helps us to see clearly what level of intervention may be most useful. From a practical standpoint one of the potential difficulties managing group or team coaching is that there may be a mix of individual and group level goals needed across one intervention. It is not hard to call to mind situations in which one (or many) group member may need to increase their personal skills in order for them to contribute toward attainment of a shared goal, while the group itself may need to work on its group level processes and communication in order to be successful. At the same time, the group may find more options for action through developing their perspective taking (requiring a more developmental approach). Understanding the coaching need in this way enables the coach to develop a more nuanced and sophisticated case conceptualization for both the team and the individual.

While spending time developing a case conceptualization of the specific coaching needs of an individual in a dyadic approach is relatively standard, it should be noted that the added degree of complexity across group and team contexts is likely to require greater amounts of time. The standard session length of an hour or hour and half are unlikely to be adequate in the context of team coaching. Time is needed to identify and work with the complex dynamics that emerge among groups and teams.

3. Understanding Group Member Interdependency of the Coaching Goal(s)

While there may be different requirements for change for each member of a given group, it is also important to consider the level of interdependency in their coaching goals. That is, to what degree does the goal or aim of the coaching require contribution between each of the group members? Another way to think about this is the degree to which a group or team shares responsibility for the outcome and purpose of the coaching process.

Interdependency across a group for a coaching outcome is likely to be high in project based situations in which the focus of the coaching is to support some form of effective project completion. However, the primary aim of the actual coaching will depend on the skill, performance, and developmental gap assessment across the group or team and the change requirements identified. For example, extending this project based focus, it is feasible that a disconnected team may have a large degree of shared responsibility but are fractured due the dynamics of the team interaction that have emerged over time. From this perspective a dysfunctional team might need coaching to increase their connectedness and quality of their interaction in order to progress in a given organization toward a particular agreed goal or outcome. If their perspectives and world views are incompatible then a developmental approach is most suitable, If they are exhibiting dysfunctional behavior that is self-defeating and negatively impacting the environment then a remedial aim may be well placed, If they do not have appropriate communication skills in order to provide effective feedback and to hold difficult conversations productively then a skills or performance approach might be best suited.

An example of group or team coaching in which the interdependence is lower might include a situation in which a leadership team has engaged a coach in order to assist them through shifting the culture of an organization in some way. While the broad definition of the goal would seem shared across the leaders, the level of the interdependency in relation to the actions to be taken could vary greatly. The individual leaders may need different skill, development, performance and even remedial approaches for their specific challenges in their teams. However, the shared experience may assist in learning and advancement with much of what they do remaining, to at least some degree, separate from the responsibilities of the other leaders within their team. This type of situation may allow for more frank conversations, sharing of difficulties and issues due to the minimization of risk related to the low interdependency of the goal attainment process. This experience would seem similar to that identified by Woodhead (2011) in working with the interdisciplinary health care leadership team.

4. The Relatedness of the Group or Team

One of the important considerations for both group and team coaching is that of membership. There are a number of variables related to team membership that are important consideration for how a coaching intervention is reported and may function. These include the relatedness of the group members as well as the frequency and quality of their interactions. It might seem easier to define the group relatedness based on the type of group for example leadership team group, neighborhood group, sporting team or social group. However, as we have seen in the research reviewed earlier the title of the group may have little bearing on the process through which they interact and work together. It may be much more advantageous to identify the connectivity or relatedness of the group in order to determine what coaching process and approach might work best for a given group dynamic and situation. While relatedness is likely to be connected to the interdependency of goals outlined earlier, a team or group could have highly positive and strong interrelatedness with little or no interdependence with respect to the goals on which they are working. The key difference is that relatedness is about the degree of ease with which group members are able to enact the interactions needed for goal attainment.

For example, senior leadership teams may vary greatly in the frequency of their interaction. This might have a significant bearing on the degree to which they feel safe exploring some of their insecurities and exposing themselves in order to have a developmental experience similar to that identified by Woodhead (2011). If as a coach we have some idea on the frequency and quality of their interaction we are in a better place to determine how we might work with the group or team. Extending this further, relatedness has a very specific meaning within social network analysis and aspects of systems theory, which is measurable. Relatedness or connectivity in social network analysis (Scott, 2012) refers to the number and, in some cases, the quality of the connection between members of a given group. This specific measurement approach has some important implications.

The first research conducted using social network analysis and coaching identified the coaching ripple effect (O'Connor and Cavanagh, 2013). This research found that when leaders were coached in an organization the wellbeing of others connected to those leaders also improved. Further to this it was the connectivity or relatedness (quality and frequency of interaction) that an individual had with the leaders coached that determined the degree to which their wellbeing improved. In brief the more connected you are to leaders who are coached the more likely you are to gain improvement in your wellbeing without even attending a coaching session. This research identified the impact of coaching beyond the individual coached and that relatedness or connectivity was the key to the impact spreading (O'Connor and Cavanagh, 2013). This would suggest that this type of relatedness might also be important for the impact of group and team coaching approaches. Given that this is relatively easy to measure, particularly with small groups, a leadership network measure of relatedness could be used as a variable in group and team research. Furthermore identifying and working with the connectedness of a coached group specifically may be an important process for extending the effective impact of coaching through the individuals coached to others in the system.

CONCLUSION

The above literature review has highlighted a lack of specificity and coherence in the coaching research regarding group and team coaching. However, coaching seems to be thriving and developing all the same. The disparate nature of the coaching literature can be thought of as, paradoxically, emerging from the very strength that has made coaching so popular over the past 20 years. Coaching is not limited to a single knowledge base, but rather draws from many (Standards Australia, 2011). This enables it to be a good partner for the complex, ambiguous and uncertain issues that are emerging in today's volatile world. The collaborative and personalized, just-in time nature of coaching interventions, are key to the success of coaching in today's complex contexts (Cavanagh and Lane, 2012).

The danger we face if we unreflectively assume change is primarily an individual accomplishment is that we assume that much of this personalization, flexibility and individual attention must be relinquished in group and team coaching. At the same time, if we fail to notice the difference between individual and group level interventions, we may erroneously expect group interventions to deliver the same as is delivered in one-to-one coaching – but for many individuals at once and with no additional time commitment or variation in approach. However, as we have seen, this may be a distorted perspective driven by an overly developed focus on the individual.

In this chapter we have suggested that more utility may come from thinking about the very core of what coaching is about and reinterpreting this within the context of group behavior. What does intervention personalization, goal progression and development look like at the group or team level? Just as with individual coaching, the breadth of potential clients at the level of group or team, the huge range of potential goals and the wide variety of contexts in which they work, means that it may seem impossible to provide specific answers to these types of questions.

Nevertheless, a similarity of pattern exists across coaching at different system levels and group and team coaching structures. That similarity is to be found in the specificity of coaching focus across system levels for the specific coaching engagement. Identifying the required coaching outcome, the systemic level best able to work towards that outcome, the level of interdependency required, and the pattern of relationship to support successful goal attainment can help to establish an appropriate group and team coaching intervention design. However this approach requires a carefully considered case conceptualization from a systemic perspective. While much is still unknown about the specific utility of group and team coaching approaches, through further investigation and careful consideration of the range of nuances, there is a great deal of potential for the utility of coaching for a wide range of important group and team contexts. If approaches to group and team coaching, both in practice and research, begin to embrace the complex nature of the context within which coaches hope to support change and development, a more utilitarian and dynamically effective field of intervention and support may emerge.

REFERENCES

Anderson, N.R. and West, M.A., 1998. Measuring climate for work group innovation: development and validation of the team climate inventory. *Journal of Organizational Behavior*, 19(3), pp. 235–258.

Arakawa, D. and Greenberg, M., 2007. Optimistic managers and their influence on productivity and employee engagement in a technology organisation: Implications for coaching psychologists. *International Coaching Psychology Review*, 2(1), pp. 78–89.

Avolio, B. J., Bass, B. M., and Jung, D. I., 1999. Re-examining the components of transformational and transactional leadership using the Multifactor Leadership. *Journal of occupational and organizational psychology*, 72(4), 441–462.

Barling, J., Weber, T. and Kelloway, E.K., 1996. Effects of transformational leadership training on attitudinal and financial outcomes: A field experiment. *Journal of Applied Psychology*, 81(6), p. 827.

Barr, M., and van Niewerburgh, C., 2015. Teachers' experiences of an introductory coaching training workshop in Scotland: An interpretative phenomenological analysis. *International Coaching Psychology Review*. 10(2), pp. 190–204.

Brown, S.W. and Grant, A.M., 2010. From GROW to GROUP: theoretical issues and a practical model for group coaching in organisations. *Coaching: An International Journal of Theory, Research and Practice*, 3(1), pp. 30–45.

Carr, C. and Peters, J., 2013. The experience and impact of team coaching: a dual case study. *International Coaching Psychology Review*, 8(1). pp. 80–98.

Cavanagh, M. and Lane, D., 2012. Coaching psychology coming of age: The challenges we face in the messy world of complexity. *International Coaching Psychology Review*, 7(1), pp. 75–90.

Clutterbuck, D., 2010. *Team coaching* (pp. 271–283). London: Sage.

Coates, D., 2013. Integrated leadership development programmes: Are they effective and what role does coaching play? *International Journal of Evidence Based Coaching and Mentoring*, 7(6), pp. 39–55.

Feggetter, A.J., 2007. A preliminary evaluation of executive coaching: Does executive coaching work for candidates on a high potential development scheme? *International Coaching Psychology Review*, 2(2), pp. 129–142.

Florent-Treacy, E., 2009. Behind the scenes in the identity laboratory. *International Coaching Psychology Review*, 1(9), 71–85.

Fusco, T., O'Riordan, S. and Palmer, S., 2015. Authentic leaders are … Conscious, Competent, Confident, and Congruent: a grounded theory of group coaching and authentic leadership development. *International Coaching Psychology Review*, 10(2), pp. 131–138.

García-Morales, V.J., Jiménez-Barrionuevo, M.M. and Gutiérrez-Gutiérrez, L., 2012. Transformational leadership influence on organizational performance through organizational learning and innovation. *Journal of Business Research*, 65(7), pp. 1040–1050.

Godfrey, M.M., Andersson-Gare, B., Nelson, E.C., Nilsson, M. and Ahlstrom, G., 2014. Coaching interprofessional health care improvement teams: the coachee, the coach and the leader perspectives. *Journal of Nursing Management*, 22(4), pp. 452–464.

Grajfoner, D., 2009. Managing change: role of coaching psychology in gender transition. *The Coaching Psychologist*, 5(2), p. 69.

Grant, A.M., 2009. Workplace, executive and life coaching: an annotated bibliography from the behavioural science and business literature. Coaching Psychology Unit, University of Sydney, Australia.

Grant, A.M., 2011. Developing an agenda for teaching coaching psychology. *International Coaching Psychology Review*, 6(1), pp. 84–99.

Grant, A.M., Passmore, J., Cavanagh, M.J. and Parker, H.M., 2010. The state of play in coaching today: a comprehensive review of the field. *International Review of Industrial and Organizational Psychology*, 25(1), pp. 125–167.

Gray, D., Burls, A., and Kogan, M., 2014. Salutogenisis and coaching: Testing a proof of concept to develop a model for practitioners. *International Journal of Evidence Based Coaching and Mentoring*, 12(2), 41.

Gumusluoglu, L. and Ilsev, A., 2009. Transformational leadership, creativity, and organizational innovation. *Journal of Business Research*, 62(4), pp. 461–473.

Hackman, J.R. and Wageman, R., 2005. A theory of team coaching. *Academy of Management Review*, 30(2), pp. 269–287.

Hagen, M. and Gavrilova Aguilar, M., 2012. The impact of managerial coaching on learning outcomes within the team context: An analysis. *Human Resource Development Quarterly*, 23(3), pp. 363–388.

Hauser, L.L., 2014. Shape-shifting: a behavioral team coaching model for coach education, research, and practice. *Journal of Psychological Issues in Organizational Culture*, 5(2), pp. 48–71.

Hawkins, P., 2011. *Leadership team coaching*. London: Kogan Page.

Hawkins, P. and Smith, N., 2007. *Coaching, Mentoring and Organizational Consultancy: Supervision and Development*. McGraw-Hill International.

Hultgren, U., Palmer, S., and O'Riordan, S. 2013. Can cognitive behavioural team coaching increase well-being? *The Coaching Psychologist*, 9(2), pp 100–110.

International Coach Federation, 2012. Retrieved September, 16, 2012 from, http://www.coachfederation.org/about-icf/overview/

Katzenbach, J. R., and Smith, D. K., 1993. The discipline of teams. *Harvard Business Review*, 71, 111–111.

Kralj, M.M., 2001. Coaching at the top: assisting a chief executive and his team. *Consulting Psychology Journal: Practice and Research*, 53(2), pp. 108–116.

Liu, C.Y., Pirola-Merlo, A., Yang, C.A. and Huang, C., 2009. Disseminating the functions of team coaching regarding research and development team effectiveness: evidence from high-tech industries in Taiwan.

Social Behavior and Personality: an International Journal, 37(1), pp. 41–57.

Mandelbrot, B.B., 1983. *The Fractal Geometry of Nature* (Revised and enlarged edition). New York, WH Freeman and Co.

McGovern, J., Lindemann, M., Vergara, M., Murphy, S., Barker, L. and Warrenfeltz, R., 2001. Maximizing the impact of executive coaching. *Manchester Review*, 6(1), p. 2001.

Mühlberger, M.D. and Traut-Mattausch, E., 2015. Leading to effectiveness comparing dyadic coaching and group coaching. *The Journal of Applied Behavioral Science, 51*(2), pp. 198–230.

O'Connor, S. and Cavanagh, M., 2013. The coaching ripple effect: The effects of developmental coaching on wellbeing across organisational networks. *Psychology of Well-Being, 3*(1), pp. 1–23.

Özaralli, N., 2003. Effects of transformational leadership on empowerment and team effectiveness. *Leadership & Organization Development Journal, 24*(6), pp. 335–344.

Palmer, B., 2003. Maximizing value from executive coaching. *Strategic HR Review, 2*(6), pp. 26–29.

Park, S., McLean, G. N., and Yang, B., 2008. Revision and Validation of an Instrument Measuring Managerial Coaching Skills in Organizations. *Online Submission*.

Passmore, J. and Fillery-Travis, A., 2011. A critical review of executive coaching research: a decade of progress and what's to come. *Coaching: An International Journal of Theory, Research and Practice, 4*(2), pp. 70–88.

Peters, J. and Carr, C., 2013. *High Performance Team Coaching: A comprehensive system for leaders and Coaches*. Victoria B.C. Canada: Friesen Press.

Peterson, D.B., 2011. Executive coaching: A critical review and recommendations for advancing the practice. In S. Zedeck (Ed.), *Handbook of Industrial and Organizational Psychology*. Washington, DC: American Psychological Association.

Rauen, C. ed., 2005. *Handbuch Coaching*. Hogrefe Verlag.

Rousseau, V., Aubé, C., and Tremblay, S., 2013. Team coaching and innovation in work teams: An examination of the motivational and behavioral intervening mechanisms. *Leadership & Organization Development Journal, 34*(4), 344–364.

Scott, J., 2012. *Social Network Analysis*. London: Sage.

Spence, G.B. and Grant, A.M., 2012. Coaching and well-being: A brief review of existing evidence, relevant theory and implications for practitioners. In S. David, I. Boniwell and A. Conley Ayers (Eds.), *The Oxford Handbook of Happiness* (pp. 1009–1025). Oxford: Oxford University Press.

Standards Australia, 2011. HB 332–2011: Coaching in organizations. Sydney: Standards Australia.

Stelter, R., Nielsen, G. and Wikman, J.M., 2011. Narrative-collaborative group coaching develops social capital – a randomised control trial and further implications of the social impact of the intervention. *Coaching: An International Journal of Theory, Research and Practice, 4*(2), pp. 123–137.

Thatcher, M., 1987. Quote taken from http://www.margaretthatcher.org/document/106689. 26/3/2015).

Theeboom, T., Beersman, B. and van Vianen, A.E., 2014. Does coaching work? A meta-analysis on the effects of coaching on individual level outcomes in an organizational context. *The Journal of Positive Psychology, 9*(1), pp. 1–18.

Torbrand, P. and Ellam-Dyson, V., 2015. The experience of cognitive behavioural group coaching with college students: an IPA study exploring its effectiveness. *International Coaching Psychology Review, 10*(1), p. 77.

Vesso, S., 2015. Strengthening Leader's Impact and Ability to Manage Change Through Group Coaching. In P.F.E. Dievernich, O.K. Tokarski & J. Gong (Eds.), *Change Management and the Human Factor* (pp. 91–107). Cham: Springer International Publishing.

Whitley, S., 2013. Group coaching as support for changing lifestyle for those diagnosed with long-term condition. *International Journal of Evidence Based Coaching and Mentoring*, Special Issue 7, pp. 82–89.

Woodhead, V., 2011. How does coaching help to support team working? A case study in the NHS. *International Journal of Evidence Based Coaching and Mentoring*, Special Issue 5, pp. 102–119.

Coaching in Education

Christian van Nieuwerburgh and Margaret Barr

INTRODUCTION

Coaching in education has seen a period of sustained growth over the last decade. Schools, colleges and universities in Australia, the United Kingdom and the USA have been introducing coaching interventions to get better results for learners (Knight, 2007; Kee et al., 2010; van Nieuwerburgh, 2012). The term 'coaching in education' covers a broad range of interventions that have the aim of improving outcomes for learners and within educational settings. Coaching is being used directly with educators, with students and with members of the educational community (Campbell, 2015). In this chapter, we will discuss the term 'coaching in education' before presenting an overview of the various ways in which coaching is having a positive impact within educational settings. The chapter will focus on evidence-based interventions, summarising relevant research where appropriate. We will conclude with some thoughts about the practice of coaching in education and the creation of coaching cultures.

As the term 'coaching' is sometimes used loosely within educational settings, it is important at the outset to clarify our terminology. Indeed one of the challenges facing the education sector is the lack of definitional agreement. The term 'coaching' is sometimes used interchangeably with words such as 'mentoring', 'teaching' or 'tutoring'. The type of coaching that will be discussed in this chapter is captured most powerfully in the definition of Whitmore: 'unlocking people's potential to maximise their own performance' (2009: 10). Coaching is understood as a facilitative intervention, aimed at supporting a coachee to take responsibility for adapting their behaviour or ways of thinking in order to achieve better results. Whitmore explicitly states that coaching is about 'helping [people] to learn, rather than teaching them' (2009, p. 10), thus setting 'coaching' apart from 'teaching'. In this sense, coaching can broaden the repertoire of educators by providing a non-directive approach to supporting others to learn for themselves.

So, coaching is different from teaching, but how does it relate to mentoring? This is another source of continued exploration (Megginson & Clutterbuck, 2005; Connor & Pokora, 2012; Fletcher & Mullen, 2012; Garvey, Stokes & Megginson, 2014). Both interventions are one-to-one conversations with the explicit intention of supporting the growth and development of another. The key difference relates to the relevance of 'knowledge transfer'. If the purpose of the relationship is to transfer knowledge and expertise from one (more experienced) person to a (less experienced) learner, then this is usually called 'mentoring'. If the purpose of the relationship is self-discovery, then this is usually called 'coaching'. Having set out the differences, it is worth noting that both interventions are helpful and can support the development of learners when employed in the right situations. In this chapter, we would like to define 'coaching in education' and 'mentoring in education' in the following ways:

Coaching in Education

A one-to-one conversation that focuses on the enhancement of learning and development through increasing self-awareness and a sense of personal responsibility, where the coach facilitates the self-directed learning of the coachee through questioning, active listening, and appropriate challenge in a supportive and encouraging climate. (van Nieuwerburgh, 2012, p. 17)

Mentoring in Education

A series of one-to-one conversations in which a more experienced person asks questions, provides guidance, shares knowledge and gives advice to support a learner to improve their performance and achieve success within a nurturing relationship. In addition to being experienced in the area of interest, the mentor should be effective at building relationships and skilled at supporting others to learn.[1]

While it is recognised that both coaching and mentoring can have positive impacts, the rest of this chapter will focus on 'coaching in education'.

THE GLOBAL FRAMEWORK FOR COACHING IN EDUCATION

An on-going challenge in coaching research is identifying explicitly the coaching methodology or approach in the studies that are found. While some studies provide clear descriptions, others do not define the actual intervention, making comparisons difficult. There are also noticeably few published longitudinal quantitative studies of coaching in educational settings, thus limiting our knowledge about the longer-term impact of introducing coaching to schools.

In a bid to celebrate and learn from successful coaching initiatives taking place across the world, a 'global framework for coaching in education' was developed (van Nieuwerburgh & Campbell 2015) (see Figure 28.1). The framework 'provides a coherent way of describing the various conversational contexts where coaching (and coaching approaches) can be explored' (Campbell, 2015).

It is currently represented as a 'playing field' of four quadrants. We use the term 'playing field' to capture a sense of positive excitement about what is happening in schools. The field is meant to be inclusive and the framework is open to change and adaptation in order to accommodate as many initiatives and practices as possible. Each quadrant represents an entry point, or 'portal', through which coaching can be helpfully introduced within educational settings. There is no prescribed order for 'opening' the portals and organisations may choose to work on more than one portal at a time. However, it will be suggested in this chapter that undertaking

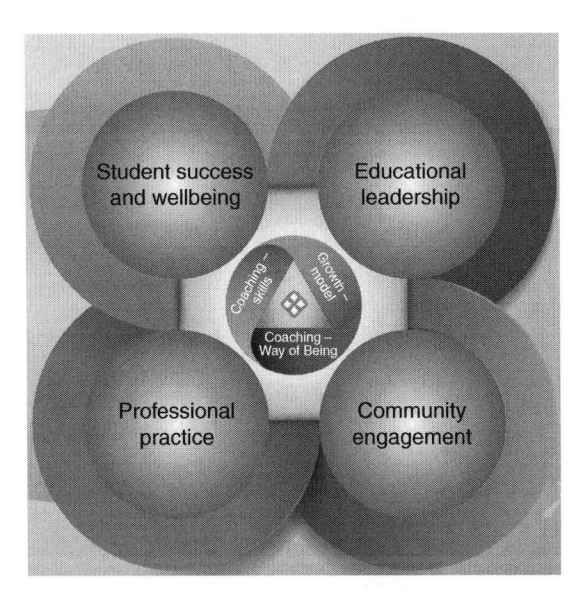

Figure 28.1 Global Framework for Coaching in Education

coaching activities across a number of portals may contribute to the creation of coaching cultures. Below, each of the portals will be considered in turn.

Coaching in the Educational Context

Coaching for Educational Leadership

The OECD publication *Preparing Teachers and Developing School Leaders for the 21st Century* highlights the pivotal role of school leaders in improving school and student performance, at a time when more countries are granting increasing autonomy to schools (Schleicher, 2012, p. 13). The most successful educational leaders spend time coaching and developing their teaching staff, and interacting with pupils (Donaldson, 2010). This section looks at some of the contexts where coaching is used to develop educational leadership.

- Educational leaders being coached
- Educational leaders learning to coach, then coaching others

Leaders being coached: Aspiring and current educational leaders

Coaching is a key component of many educational leadership programmes. Participants typically have one-to-one sessions with a coach, and may also undertake some (usually limited) coaching skills training. Some examples from the literature are: Denmark's Leadership Diploma of Education for aspiring school leaders, which includes coaching; England's Teaching Leaders (2015) programme where experienced senior leaders work as development coaches to support

Table 28.1 Characteristics of working groups and team (adapted from Katzenbach and Smith, 2004)

Working group	Team
Strong focused leader	Shared leadership roles
Individual accountability	Individual and mutual accountability
Individual work product	Collective work product
Efficient meetings	Time spent in open ended discussion

aspiring middle leaders working in the most challenging contexts; and Scotland's Flexible Route to Headship (FRH) programme in which the core learning process is through coaching from a head teacher of a different school (Scottish Executive Education Department, 2006). Although FRH participants valued the coaching, Forde et al. (2013) expressed caution about the ever-widening role of the coach (including roles as tutor, mentor and assessor). As we have argued above, the lack of clarity around definitions and roles can negatively affect the relationship between coach and coachee, which affected their role as a coach. As a result, the Scottish College for Educational Leadership (SCEL) has separated these roles in the new 'Into Headship' programme, where the coach, the headteacher mentor and the field assessor are separate people with distinctive roles.

The educational system perspective becomes more important when change is needed at the local, regional, national or international level. It would appear that coaching may have a role in supporting school leaders to become actively engaged in system leadership. In a qualitative study following 4 novice principals through one or two years of their leadership coaching experience in California, James-Ward (2013) claims that the success of the coaching experience was due (in part) to the coach's local and contextual knowledge, and their ability to collaborate and shape the thinking of the principals without being authoritative or intrusive. The principals in this study eventually advanced to system leadership roles.

In another United States study, fifty-two principals in elementary and middle schools took part in a year-long feedback and coaching study that measured changes in their behaviours (Goff et al., 2014). The study found that principals who received feedback *and* coaching were more likely to change their professional behaviour than those who were given feedback alone. Although further research is needed, this is a very promising outcome that may encourage system leaders to provide educational leaders with access to coaching support.

Another point to bear in mind is that educational leadership is no longer entirely positional, residing with a particular office. Everyone can develop leadership attributes and exercise leadership. Robertson (2008) puts it like this: 'Educational leaders are leaders who, no matter at what level in the institution, focus on improving learning opportunities as their main function, *and* work to develop their own educational leadership capacity and that of their institution.' An Australian study looked at the role of coaching in developing the leadership skills of teachers who were not designated 'school leaders'. In the study, Grant et al. (2010) sought to find out whether high school teachers might benefit from developmental coaching that draws on theories of leadership. The teachers were coached by executive coaches using cognitive behavioural coaching and solution-focused coaching methods. Compared with randomly allocated controls, the coached teachers experienced increased goal attainment, reduced stress and enhanced workplace wellbeing and resilience.

Leaders learning to coach, then coaching others

In their seminal work *Leading Coaching in Schools*, Creasy and Paterson (2005, p. 23) advised school leaders in the UK to 'first develop yourself'. In recent years, there has been a gradual movement towards a growing expectation that educational leaders should be able to adopt a coaching approach. In fact, this expectation has been made explicit is some nationally determined professional standards (e.g. Australian Institute for Teaching and School Leadership, 2015; General Teaching Council for Scotland, 2012). We believe that these are positive steps that should be encouraged and supported. Through the setting of professional standards that reference coaching, professional bodies are clearly endorsing the use of coaching within educational organisations.

Having experienced the benefit of coaching themselves, educators are undertaking coaching development programmes to extend their own leadership coaching skills and knowledge. In this way, educators are able to coach formally or use a coaching approach. In turn, educators can support their colleagues to do the same. These programmes can be in-person, online or blended. The process of learning about coaching skills can in itself be developmental; in one study, participants reported that the process of participating in a workshop to learn coaching skills led to insights about their own behaviours and relationships (Barr & van Nieuwerburgh, 2015).

Using the PRACTICE coaching model (Palmer, 2008), a school's educational psychologist worked with teachers in the early years section of a primary school in Bristol, UK (Adams, 2012). He led and coached them through the process as they planned for the arrival of a new intake – a number of children with significant special educational needs. The model, although not followed exactly, was deemed successful, with the participants especially learning the importance of goal-setting.

In London, UK where a school had been placed in 'special measures' because of underachievement, a whole-staff World Café style event (Brown & Isaacs, 2005) using coaching-style questions was held to plan for school improvement, and to begin to develop a coaching culture in the school (Cantore & Hick, 2013). The questions were influenced by Appreciative Inquiry (Orem et al., 2007) (e.g., 'Using the proforma as a guide, tell the story of when you felt you made a great personal contribution to the life and learning of the school') and ended in clear actions (e.g., 'Say to colleagues in one sentence what you plan to do on Monday morning to start putting the plan into action'). Coaching-style conversational practice became an ongoing part of staff training, with many staff choosing to undertake coaching training. The head teacher reported that staff were becoming more reflective and had space to discuss their ideas, and that the energy of the staff group had become more focused. This had a transformational effect, and the school moved from being in 'special measures' to 'outstanding' within a period of 18 months.

Above, we have considered the use of coaching to support the development of educational leadership capacity and capability. From educational leaders adopting a coaching approach to the use of coaching to support school improvement, there are a number of ways that coaching can be used within this quadrant of the playing field.

Coaching for Professional Practice

Another key area of focus for many educational organisations is the improvement of professional practice, particularly pedagogy. It has been argued that the best way of improving the experience of learners is to improve the skill and pedagogy of their educators (Knight, 2012: 94). One of the features of high performing schools aiming to improve both teaching and learning is that they provide opportunities for teachers to learn from one another (Barber & Mourshed, 2007). Coaching can provide a vehicle for these opportunities, and it enriches the development of professional practice.

Joyce and Showers (1995) illustrated how only 5% of teachers develop new skills if learning a theory. When the theory is supported by a demonstration, the amount grows to 10%. If practising the skills, 20% will develop the new skills. Formative feedback extends this to 25%. However, when job-embedded coaching is integrated in the process, 90% of teachers develop the new skills. Coached teachers are more likely than non-coached teachers to transfer newly acquired teaching practices into classroom use (Bradley et al., 2013; Cornett & Knight, 2008; Reinke et al., 2014; Showers, 1982). Furthermore, coaching teachers on specific educational content and teaching methods can have a positive impact on student achievement (Shidler, 2008).

Coaching for professional practice takes place in the following contexts:

- Instructional coaching
- Peer coaching

Instructional coaching

First, let us clarify the terminology. Educators in the UK refer to 'teaching practice', while educators in the USA refer to 'instructional practice'. Knight (2007) describes instructional coaches as onsite professional developers who work collaboratively with teachers, empowering them to incorporate research-based instructional methods into their classrooms. Instructional coaches can specialise in certain curricular areas, for example literacy (Hanson, 2011; Lowenhaupt et al., 2014; Matsumura et al., 2013; Moxley & Taylor, 2006; Stephens et al., 2011; Strahan et al., 2010; Taylor et al., 2012; Vanderburgh & Stephens, 2010), or mathematics (Morse, 2009; Mudzimiri et al., 2014; West & Staub, 2003).

Instructional coaching differs from other coaching models in that the process includes one component where the coach actually *teaches* the collaborating teacher how to learn very specific evidence-based practices (Knight & van Nieuwerburgh, 2012). The instructional coach is expected to be an expert in the evidence-based practices and can offer checklists or even role model a lesson to their coachee. Several studies have been very helpful in developing, validating and refining this approach to improving instruction (Knight & van Nieuwerburgh, 2012). Instructional coaching is widely used throughout the USA, and Schleicher (2012) also provides examples from Victoria (Australia), Shanghai (China) and Ontario (Canada).

Shrinking budgets in schools affect decisions about employing an instructional coach. Some would argue that the school leader should be the main instructional coach. However it can be difficult for leaders to find the time (Danielson, 2007), and there can be tensions with their role as line manager (Hobson & Malderez, 2013; Hoy & Miskel, 2013). Therefore developing teachers' capacities to help one another improve may be a more cost-effective investment. We now look at how teachers can help one another through peer coaching.

Peer coaching

Another similar intervention often used between educators is referred to as 'peer coaching'. According to Robertson, these are reciprocal relationships to set professional goals and achieve them through dialogue. The purpose is to facilitate the learning, development and wellbeing of both partners (2008). In a synthesis of the literature about 'peer coaching', Wong and Nicotera (2003) suggest that schools use peer coaching for four reasons:

- To establish a culture of standards and expectations
- To improve instructional capacity
- To support ongoing evaluation
- To connect what happens in the classroom with the policy context.

Peer coaching has been found to improve teaching practice and promote the idea that 'teachers are learners too' (Kidd, 2009). Lofthouse et al. (2010) observe that there is significant scope for teachers who have received coaching to take more responsibility for analysing their practice. At the same time, they also note that there is considerable evidence about the practical and logistical difficulties of bringing two teachers together for pre- and post-coaching sessions. It should be noted that Timperley and Parr argue that coaches are more effective when they are trained (2008). This view is supported by a peer coaching study in New Zealand. A group of student teachers in a field-based initial teacher education programme for Early Childhood Education found that training was important for successful peer coaching partnerships (Hooker, 2014). The student teachers valued being taught the skills of active listening, holding reflective conversations, goal-setting and planning.

The same study found the way in which student teachers were paired had an impact on outcomes. Hooker (2014) noted that no consensus could be found in the peer coaching literature as to whether it is better if peer coaches are paired by someone who knows them well, they are selected randomly or they choose their partner. However, the student teachers highlighted the importance of the relationship, and particularly valued having a peer of whom they could ask what they called 'the silly questions'. The benefits of peer coaching as identified by the student teachers included being able to give something back, provide encouragement and support, and learn from each other.

When designing peer coaching programmes focused on instructional practice, it may be helpful to consider ways of recording the observation of teaching, for example low-inference transcripts (Rivera-McCutchen and Sharff Panero, 2014) or the use of technology through audio or video recording. In their study in two New York City schools, Rivera-McCutchen and Sharff-Panero found that teachers experienced 'Aha!' moments (Kounios & Beeman, 2009; van Nieuwerburgh, 2014: 60) when their peer coaching interactions included the use of low-inference transcripts (highly detailed transcripts of the lesson and subsequent coaching conversation that are factual records with no assumptions or personal commentary). Factual records to support coaching conversations can also be provided through the use of video or audio recording. According to Knight, 'video-enhanced professional development' will make a significant impact on the professional practice of teachers in the coming years (2014).

The Centre for the Use of Research and Evidence in Education (CUREE) stated that *learning to be a* coach or mentor is one of the most effective ways of enabling teachers or leaders to become good and excellent practitioners (2005). Evidence from studies of peer coaching generally does not separate the positive outcomes derived by the coach from those derived by the coachee. The implication is that the 'peer' nature of the intervention means that both parties benefit equally. However, a key study by Showers and Joyce (1996) found that the benefits for the teacher observing were often *greater* than for those being observed. Therefore the programme was revised and the learning process became the act of observing another teacher, then reflecting. The omission of feedback did not depress implementation or growth. These are interesting findings that should also be considered when creating peer coaching programmes in educational organisations.

Coaching with Parents and the Wider School Community

As the use of coaching in schools, colleges and universities continues to grow and develop, a new area of focus is emerging. Building links with parents and other members of the wider educational community is now considered a portal in the Global Framework for Coaching in Education.

- Parent coaching by teachers and others
- Parents trained as coaches
- Coaching from the community

The interventions in this area are relatively under-researched and require further study (van Nieuwerburgh & Campbell, 2015). Below, we will survey the scant existing literature and suggest some possible areas for further exploration.

Parent coaching by teachers and others

Teachers may learn how to use coaching skills with parents, so that they can build relationships and engage parents in their children's education. Meetings with parents may be scheduled, for example to discuss student progress, or they may happen at short notice, perhaps when a concern has arisen unexpectedly. Teachers may find that if they use solution-focused, cognitive behavioural or goal-setting coaching approaches with parents, solutions can be found and relationships maintained. Research into the impact of teachers using a coaching approach during meetings with parents is needed.

Other members of the community could be trained to coach parents to support their children's learning and development. Parents may also be coached by other professionals in the wider school community, for example educational psychologists. Shapiro et al. (2010) observe that schools are one of the best places to reach large numbers of parents with evidence-based parenting interventions that are acceptable, practical and feasible. Parents in a London research project (Graham, 2013) were coached to address anxieties about their child's transition to primary school. The coach also shared techniques such as GROW or Appreciative Inquiry, which the parent could use between sessions. After two sessions, parents reported reduced stress, increased empowerment and improved confidence about the transition.

Parents trained as coaches

Bamford, Mackew and Golawski (2012) have found that coaching for parents can have a significant positive impact on the relationship between parents and children, so that children may enjoy learning more both at home and at school. Schools and educational psychologists may be able to offer coaching skills courses to parents, or recommend self-coaching parent workbooks (Golawski, Bamford & Gersch, 2013). Some schools have used formal 'parent as coach' programmes (Sterling, 2008) to provide parents with coaching skills, support their learners 'beyond the school gates' and build positive relationship with their communities.

Coaching from the community

In a current study in South West England, volunteer members of the local community have been trained in coaching and mentoring skills, then matched to a student beginning their secondary school (van Nieuwerburgh & Pawson, in preparation). The long-term project aims to study whether those students matched with a community coach or mentor will perform better at school. The study is also interested in the relationship between having access to a coach or mentor and student aspirations. According to staff, relationships between the school and its immediate community have been strengthened as a result of this programme. In informal education, coaching methodologies have not yet been widely promoted within the youth service (Leach et al., 2011), and there has been no specific examination of how interventions such as solution-focused cognitive-behavioural coaching, goal training and goal setting may be applied in the youth curriculum. Leach et al. (2011) posit that training youth workers in such interventions offers the potential to enhance young people's wellbeing.

Coaching for Student Success and Wellbeing

The coaching in education interventions already described – for educational leadership, professional practice and with parents and the wider community – should ultimately impact on the success and wellbeing of students. However, coaching is also being applied directly with students, with promising results (Devine et al., 2013), and the effects can last long after the coaching intervention ends (Franklin & Franklin, 2012). Schools are extending their focus on academic performance to recognise their role in nurturing the emotional, social, psychological and physical wellbeing of the learner (Waters, 2011), which itself has an impact on performance. Coaching has been used directly for improved attainment; it can also be used indirectly as a methodology to apply positive psychology research in education (Green et al., 2007) and to promote motivation and goal striving. The published research studies relate to a range of arrangements for coaching students:

- External coaches
- Internal coaches who are teachers or other staff in the institution
- Internal coaches who are students, with coaching being reciprocal (peer coaching) or one-way (e.g. students coaching younger students)

External coaches for students

In a study in the West Midlands, UK, a pool of newly-qualified graduates interested in teaching but with no teaching qualification, were trained as academic coaches, learning coaching skills, problem-solving, learning and group behaviour (Passmore & Brown, 2009). Over a three-year period, they coached 16-year-old students using a behavioural goal-focused model. Outcomes for the participating students included enhanced examination performance and increased hope. In addition, the school's performance improved above local and national trends.

Two UK studies report on coaching programmes led by external support agencies working with young people at risk of developing mental health problems, where the young people experienced increased wellbeing and positive emotions (Fredrickson, 2001). In the first study (Robson-Kelly & van Nieuwerburgh, 2016), young people in Leicestershire participated in group coaching and positive education programmes (Green et al., 2012) and individual coaching programmes. The programmes were held in community venues outside of the school environment and timetable. The young people found that coaching offered a place where they could develop a range of helpful tools and techniques, and could experience them through the group or with a coach. They also experienced positive emotions, fun, awe, hope, passion, pride and interest. The study has resulted in a theoretical model that suggests the experience of coaching creates three things – a process, a positive relationship, and a set of skills – where the young person, through growing accountability, awareness and responsibility, develops choice and control over their thoughts, feelings and behaviour. In London (Pritchard & van Nieuwerburgh, 2016), young inner-city girls participated in a similar appreciative coaching and positive psychology interventions programme. Three key themes emerged from the analysis: first, the ability to control emotions and reactions; second, increased experience of positive emotions and thoughts; and third, the identification of purpose and meaning to life, leading to an improved perception of quality of life.

Internal coaches who are staff

Several studies have been written about coaching programmes led by staff in Australian schools.

- Solution-focused cognitive behavioural life coaching for senior high school students was delivered by school counsellors (Campbell & Gardner, 2005), and by teachers trained in coaching techniques (Green et al., 2007). Compared to the wait-list control group, the coached students experienced improved coping skills and resilience, increased wellbeing, improved cognitive hardiness and hope, and decreased levels of depression. They believed that the improvements in their academic performance resulted from their improved study skills and their use of personal learning goals.
- After being trained in the use of evidence-based coaching (Grant, 2003) models and techniques (cognitive behavioural and solution-focused), teachers coached Year 11 high school students (Green et al., 2013). The students experienced increases in academic goal-striving. They also welcomed their new skills in changing Automatic Negative Thoughts (ANTs) into Performance Enhancing Thoughts (PETs).
- Increases in self-reported levels of engagement and hope were reported (Madden et al., 2011) when a teacher-coach (qualified at Masters level in coaching psychology) coached male primary school students using the strengths assessment Youth Values in Action survey (Park & Peterson, 2006).

Internal coaches who are students

The studies include reciprocal coaching where peers coach one another, and non-reciprocal coaching, for example where an older student coaches a younger student. Students in secondary school and at university are under considerable stress (Green et al, 2007; Roussis & Wells, 2008), and peer coaching has been shown to reduce stress that could impact on performance. Short et al. (2010) describe a reciprocal peer coaching study where university undergraduates coached one another before an examination period, after being trained in the key principles and models of coaching including TGROW (Downey, 2003). The students experienced a greater reduction in stress than those in the control group. Peer coaching has also been shown to work in groups. For example Stelter et al. (2011) describe narrative-collaborative group coaching where young sports talents engage in group dialogue for meaning-making. Results show a significant increase in the level of social recovery (Stelter et al., 2011, p. 133) and an effect on general wellbeing.

Coaching is also being used in primary or elementary schools (Briggs & van Nieuwerburgh, 2012). Primary-aged children can learn to give and receive feedback, a key skill in encouraging the coaching skill of reflection. Briggs and van Nieuwerburgh (2010) found that primary school aged children in years 5 and 6 (9–11 year olds) could learn peer coaching skills and could give and receive feedback. When the study was repeated in another primary school (Dorrington & van Nieuwerburgh, 2015) the children spoke about the factors that made them more likely to accept feedback, including the need to feel valued by the person giving feedback.

Peer coaching has increased the incidence of positive behaviour in social settings in children with attention deficit hyperactivity disorder (ADHD). In Plumer and Stoner's (2005) study set in the USA, children with ADHD who had difficulty with peer social relationships took part in a peer tutoring programme to improve their spelling. During the peer tutoring programme the children were actively and positive engaged with their peers in the classroom only, but not in the playground. However, improved peer relationships were observed in social settings during recess and lunch when the programme was complemented by peer coaching to remind the children of their goals and give feedback.

Several studies help us learn more about the benefits of educational coaching for the student coach, and two examples are given next. First, Year 12 students who coached Year 11 students after being trained in coaching skills and GROW by the school's educational psychologist, reported that the experience had developed their skills in communication, problem-solving and independent learning, and had improved their confidence in their ability to think and find solutions (van Nieuwerburgh et al., 2012). In a second study (van Nieuwerburgh & Tong, 2013), A-Level students were trained in behavioural coaching techniques, cognitive behavioural techniques and GROW by an occupational psychologist and an educational coach. After coaching GCSE-level students, the student coaches reported improvements in their own study skills, self-confidence, communication skills, relationships and emotional intelligence.

USING EVIDENCE-BASED COACHING APPROACHES

Having surveyed the ways in which coaching can be used in educational settings, it is encouraging to note that there are varied and innovative coaching-related interventions taking place across a wide range of institutions in different parts of the world. It seems that 'coaching in education' is seen as increasingly relevant for learners and educators. To support the field to grow and have an impact on larger numbers of people, we believe that it is important to:

1. Encourage further academic study of the impact and experience of coaching in educational settings. Longitudinal studies are needed within this field, considering the longer term benefits of introducing coaching, coaching-related skills and coaching approaches in educational settings. The studies should explicitly identify the coaching methodology or approach that was used and the intention of the coaching.
2. Celebrate what *is* already happening in schools, colleges and universities. One of the best pieces of 'evidence' about the difference that coaching is making in these institutions will be the stories of learners, educators, educational leaders and the organisations through which they flourish. Blogs, videos of good practice, written case studies, conference presentations and magazine articles will help to share good practice, raise the profile of the field and spread enthusiasm.
3. Harness the support of strategic local, regional, national and international partners. Organisations such as the National College for School Leadership (NCSL) in England and Learn Forward in the USA have been champions for coaching in educational settings. More recently, the Australian Institute for Teaching and School Leadership (AITSL), the General Teaching Council for Scotland (2012), have integrated coaching within their leadership development and teacher standards. Pioneering programmes in England such as Teaching Leaders and Future Leaders incorporate coaching as a key leadership skill. It seems to us that for the long-term success of coaching initiatives, both a 'top-down' (coaching promoted and encouraged at local, regional and national level) and a 'bottom-up' (individual schools, colleges and universities using coaching to respond to their own areas of interest) are needed.
4. Make time for coaching. With the various coaching interventions discussed in this chapter, logistical and practical difficulties were often mentioned. The most common challenge is the availability of time. Often educational leaders, educators and support staff feel overstretched. This makes it important to invest time and effort in a purposeful and considered manner. Furthermore, it would be helpful if learners, educators and educational leaders were confident of the 'dividends' of such an investment. It is hoped that this chapter will be supportive in this regard.
5. Work towards coaching cultures in our educational organisations. It has been argued that places of learning are 'the ideal context in which to grow coaching cultures' (van Nieuwerburgh & Passmore, 2012: 153). While a number of staged processes for 'creating a coaching culture' have been proposed (Gormley & van Nieuwerburgh, 2014), we believe that the process for working towards a coaching culture is necessarily more organic and will vary depending on the educational institution. We propose that starting to use coaching through any of the portals of the Global Framework for Coaching in Education will start to generate movement towards a coaching culture. The Global Framework recognises that every educational organisation is different. Therefore there is no suggestion of a 'correct order' of portals.

However, it seems to be important that the coaching interventions are used to address the priorities of the organisation. In other words, coaching should not be introduced as a 'new approach', but rather as a way of enhancing existing processes, supporting learners or educators to improve their performance or as a strategy of implementing important initiatives. It is critically important to note that a coaching culture is *not* a destination – rather the sense of a 'coaching culture' emerges as an organisation and its people work towards it. So, in a sense, it is an ongoing endeavour – part of the 'way we do things' in our educational institutions.

Three key questions can be helpful when setting off on this journey:

- What is the case for a coaching culture? (In other words, what makes it important to work towards such a culture?)
- How can we transfer what is most powerful about coaching conversations into our educational institution?
- What will be different in our organisation as we work towards a coaching culture? (van Nieuwerburgh, 2015)

The journey *must* start with the involvement of as many members of the organisation (and its stakeholders) as possible. In other words, everyone should engage with the questions above.

CONCLUSION

In this chapter, we have surveyed a number of ways in which educational organisations can use coaching to get better results for their learners and educators. We have concluded with some ideas to support the ongoing development of coaching in education. Ultimately, coaching initiatives in educational settings are about ensuring positive experiences for both learners and educators. We are primarily interested in the success and wellbeing of learners, while recognising that the success and wellbeing of educators is essential if we are to deliver the right type of learning environments.

NOTE

1 We are grateful to students on the Coaching in Education module at the University of East London for developing this definition of mentoring in education.

REFERENCES

Adams, M. (2012). Problem-focused coaching in a mainstream primary school: Reflections on PRACTICE. *The Coaching Psychologist*, 8(1), 27–37.

Australian Institute for Teaching and School Leadership. (2015). *Australian Professional Standard for Principals*. Retrieved from www.aitsl.edu.au/australian-professional-standard-for-principals

Bamford, A., Mackew, N. & Golawski, A. (2012). Coaching for parents: Empowering parents to create positive relationships with their children. In C. van Nieuwerburgh (Ed.), *Coaching in education: Getting better results for students, educators, and parents* (pp. 133–152). London: Karnac.

Barber, M. & Mourshed, M. (2007). *How the world's best performing school systems come out on top*. McKinsey & Company. Retrieved from www.smhc-cpre.org/wp-content/uploads/2008/07/how-the-worlds-best-performing-school-systems-come-out-on-top-sept-072.pdf.

Barr, M. & van Nieuwerburgh, C. (2015). Teachers' experiences of an introductory coaching training workshop in Scotland: An interpretative phenomenological analysis. *International Coaching Psychology Review*, 10(2), 190–204.

Bradley, B., Knight, J., Harvey, S., Hock, M., Knight, D., Skrtic, T., Brasseur-Hock, I. & Deshler, D. (2013). Improving instructional coaching to support middle school teachers in the United States. In T. Plomp & N. Nieveen (Eds.), *Educational design research – Part B: Illustrative cases* (pp. 299–318). Enschede, the Netherlands: SLO.

Briggs, M. & van Nieuwerburgh, C. (2010). The development of peer coaching skills in primary school children in years 5 and 6. *Procedia – Social and Behavioral Sciences*, 9, 1415–1422.

Briggs, M. & van Nieuwerburgh, C. (2012). Coaching in primary or elementary schools. In C. van Nieuwerburgh (Ed.), *Coaching in education: Getting better results for students, educators and parents* (pp. 47–61). London: Karnac.

Brown, J. & Isaacs, D., (2005). *The World Café: Shaping our futures through conversations that matter*. San Francisco, CA: Berrett-Koehler.

Campbell, J. (2015). Coaching in schools. In C. van Nieuwerburgh (Ed.), *Coaching in Professional Contexts*. London: Sage.

Campbell, M. A. & Gardner, S. (2005). A pilot study to assess the effects of life coaching with Year 12 students. In M. Cavanagh, A. M Grant & T. Kemp (Eds.), *Evidence based coaching: Volume 1. Theory, research and practice from the behavioural sciences* (pp. 159–169). Bowen Hills, Queensland: Australian Academic Press.

Cantore, S. & Hick, W. (2013). Dialogic OD in practice: Conversational approaches to change in a UK primary school. *OD Practitioner*, 45(1), 5–10.

Centre for the Use of Research and Evidence in Education. (2005). *National framework for coaching*. London: CUREE.

Connor, M. & Pokora, J. (2012). *Coaching and mentoring at work: Developing effective practice*. 2nd edition. Maidenhead: Open University Press.

Cornett, J. & Knight, J. (2008). Research on coaching. In J. Knight (Ed.), *Coaching:

Approaches and perspectives (pp. 192–216). Thousand Oaks, CA: Corwin.

Creasy, J. & Paterson, F. (2005). *Leading coaching in schools.* Nottingham: NSCL.

Danielson, C. (2007). The many faces of leadership. *Educational Leadership*, *65*(1), 14–19.

Devine, M., Meyers, R. & Houssemand, C. (2013). How can coaching make a positive impact within educational settings? *Procedia – Social and Behavioral Sciences*, *93*, 1382–1389.

Donaldson, G. (2010). *Teaching Scotland's future: Report of a review of teacher education in Scotland.* Edinburgh: The Scottish Government.

Dorrington, L. & van Nieuwerburgh, C. (2015). The development of peer coaching skills in primary school children: An exploration of how children respond to feedback. *International Journal of Information and Education Technology*, *5*(1), 50–54.

Downey, M. (2003). *Effective coaching: Lessons from the coach's coach.* Boston: Cengage.

Fletcher, S. J. & Mullen, C. A. (2012). *SAGE handbook of mentoring and coaching in education.* London: Sage.

Forde, C., McMahon, M., Gronn, P. & Martin, M. (2013). Being a leadership development coach: A multi-faceted role. *Educational Management Administration & Leadership*, *41*(1), 105–119.

Franklin, J., & Franklin, A. (2012). The long-term independently assessed benefits of coaching: A controlled 18-month study of two methods. *International Coaching Psychology Review*, *7*(1), 33–38.

Fredrickson, B. L. (2001). The role of positive emotions in positive psychology: The broaden-and-build theory of positive emotions. *American Psychologist*, *56*, 218–226.

Garvey, B., Stokes, P., & Megginson, D. (2014). *Coaching and mentoring: Theory and practice.* 2nd edition. London: Sage.

General Teaching Council for Scotland. (2012). Professional Standards for Leadership and Management. Retrieved July 2015 from gtcs.org.uk/standards/standards-for-leadership-and-management.aspx

Goff, P., Goldring, E., Guthrie, J. E. & Bickman, L. (2014). Changing principals' leadership through feedback and coaching. *Journal of Educational Administration*, *52*(5), 682–704.

Golawski, A., Bamford, A. & Gersch, I. (2013). *Swings and roundabouts: A self-coaching workbook for parents and those considering becoming parents.* London: Karnac.

Gormley, H. & van Nieuwerburgh, C. (2014). Developing coaching cultures: A review of the literature. *Coaching: An International Journal of Theory, Research and Practice*, *7*(2), 90–101.

Graham, G. (2013). A coach-therapy journey: Destination ICT with parents. *Association of Integrative Coach-Therapist Professionals*, *6*, 16–20.

Grant, A. M. (2003). The impact of life coaching on goal attainment, metacognition and mental health. *Social Behavior and Personality: An International Journal*, *31*(3), 253–264.

Grant, A. M., Green, L. S., & Rynsaardt, J. (2010). Developmental coaching for high school teachers: Executive coaching goes to school. *Consulting Psychology Journal: Practice and Research*, *62*(3), 151–168.

Green, L. S., Grant, A. M. & Rynsaardt, J. (2007). Evidence-based life coaching for senior high school students: Building hardiness and hope. *International Coaching Psychology Review*, *2*(1), 24–32.

Green, L. S., Norrish, J. M., Vella-Brodrick, D. A. & Grant, A. M. (2013). Enhancing well-being and goal striving in senior high school students: Comparing evidence-based coaching and positive psychology interventions. *Institute of Coaching, Breaking Research, Scientific Findings from Harnisch Grant Recipients.*

Green, L. S., Oades, L. G. & Robinson, P. L. (2012). Positive education programmes: Integrating coaching and positive psychology in schools, in C. J. van Nieuwerburgh (Ed.), *Coaching in education: Getting better results for students, educators and parents* (pp. 115–132). London: Karnac.

Hanson, L. (2011). The life of a literacy coach. *Educational Leadership*, *69*(2), 78–81.

Hobson, A. J. & Malderez, A. (2013). Judgementoring and other threats to realizing the potential of school-based mentoring in teacher education. *International Journal of Mentoring and Coaching in Education*, *2*(2), 89–108.

Hooker, T. (2014). The benefits of peer coaching as a support system for early childhood education students. *International Journal of Evidence Based Coaching and Mentoring*, *12*(1), 109–122.

Hoy, W. K. & Miskel, C. G. (2013). *Educational administration: Theory, research and practice*, 9th ed. New York, NY: McGraw-Hill.

James-Ward, C. (2013). The coaching experience of four novice principals. *International Journal of Mentoring and Coaching in Education*, 2(1), 21–33.

Joyce, B. & Showers, B. (1995). *Student achievement through staff development: Fundamentals of school renewal*, 2nd e). White Plains, NY: Longman.

Kee, K. M., Anderson, K. A., Dearning, V. S., Harris, E. & Shuster, F. A. (2010). *Results coaching: The new essentials for school leaders*. Thousand Oaks, CA: Corwin.

Kidd, W. (2009). Peer coaching and mentoring to improve teaching and learning. *Practical Research for Education*, 42, 50–55.

Kounios, J. & Beeman, M. (2009). The aha! moment: The cognitive neuroscience of insight. *Current Directions in Psychological Science*, 18(4), 210–216.

Knight, J. (2007). *Instructional coaching: A partnership approach to improving instruction*. Thousand Oaks, CA: Corwin.

Knight, J. (2012). Coaching to improve teaching: Using the instructional coaching model. In C. van Nieuwerburgh (Ed.), *Coaching in education: Getting better results for students, educators, and parents* (pp. 93–113). London: Karnac.

Knight, J. (2014). *Focus on teaching: Using video for high-impact instruction*. Thousand Oaks, CA: Corwin.

Knight, J. & van Nieuwerburgh, C. (2012). Instructional coaching: A focus on practice. *Coaching: An International Journal of Theory, Research and Practice*, 5(2), 100–112.

Leach, C. J. C., Green, L. S. & Grant, A. M. (2011). Flourishing youth provision: The potential role of positive psychology and coaching in enhancing youth services. *International Journal of Evidence Based Coaching and Mentoring*, 9(1), 44–58.

Lofthouse, R., Leat, D., Towler, C., Hall, E. & Cummings, C. (2010). *Improving coaching: Evolution not revolution*. Nottingham: National College for Leadership of Schools and Children's Services.

Lowenhaupt, R., McKinney, S. & Reeves, T. (2014). Coaching in context: The role of relationships in the work of three literacy coaches. *Professional Development in Education*, 40(5), 740–757.

Madden, W., Green, S. & Grant, A. M. (2011). A pilot study evaluating strengths-based coaching for primary school students: Enhancing engagement and hope. *International Coaching Psychology Review*, 6(1), 71–83.

Matsumura, C., Garnier, H. & Spybrook, J. (2013). Literacy coaching to improve student reading achievement: A multi-level mediation model. *Learning and Instruction*, 25(1), 35–48.

Megginson, D. & Clutterbuck, D. (2005). *Techniques for coaching and mentoring*. London: Elsevier.

Morse, A. (2009). *Cultivating a math coaching practice: A guide for K-8 math educators*. Thousand Oaks, CA: Corwin.

Moxley, D. E. & Taylor, R. T. (2006). *Literacy coaching: A handbook for school leaders*. Thousand Oaks, CA: Corwin Press.

Mudzimiri, R., Burroughs, E., Luebeck, J., Sutton, J. & Yopp, D. (2014). A look inside mathematics coaching: Roles, content, and dynamics. *Education Policy Analysis Archives*, 22(53), 1–28.

Orem, S. L., Binkert, J. & Clancy, A. L. (2007). *Appreciative coaching – A positive process for change*. San Francisco, CA: Wiley.

Palmer, S. (2008). The PRACTICE model of coaching: Towards a solution-focused approach. *Coaching Psychology International*, 1(1), 4–8.

Park, N. & Peterson, C. (2006). Moral competence and character strengths among adolescents: The development and validation of the Values in Action Inventory of Strengths for Youth. *Journal of Adolescence*, 29(6), 891–909.

Passmore, J. & Brown, A. (2009). Coaching non-adult students for enhanced examination performance: A longitudinal study. *Coaching: An International Journal of Theory, Practice and Research*, 2(1), 54–64.

Plumer, P. J. & Stoner, G. (2005). The relative effects of classroom peer tutoring and peer coaching on the positive social behaviours of children with ADHD. *Journal of Attention Disorders*, 9(1), 290–300.

Pritchard, M. & van Nieuwerburgh, C. (2016). The perceptual changes in life experience of at-risk young girls subsequent to an appreciative coaching and positive psychology interventions group programme: An interpretative phenomenological analysis. *International Coaching Psychology Review*, *11*(1), 57–74.

Reinke, W., Stormont, M., Herman, K. & Newcomer, L. (2014). Using coaching to support teacher implementation of classroom-based interventions. *Journal of Behavioral Education*, *23*(1), 150–167.

Rivera-McCutchen, R. L. & Sharff Panero, N. (2014). Low-inference transcripts in peer coaching: A promising tool for school improvement. *International Journal of Mentoring and Coaching in Education*, *3*(1), 86–101.

Robertson, J. (2008). *Coaching educational leadership: Building leadership capacity through partnership.* London: Sage.

Robson-Kelly, L. & van Nieuwerburgh, C. (2016). What does coaching have to offer to young people at risk of developing mental health problems? A grounded theory study. *International Coaching Psychology Review*, *11*(1), 75–92.

Roussis, P. & Wells, A. (2008). Psychological factors predicting stress symptoms: Metacognition, thought control, and varieties of worry. *Anxiety, Stress & Coping*, *21*, 12–44.

Schleicher, A. (Ed.) (2012). *Preparing teachers and developing school leaders for the 21st century: Lessons from around the world.* OECD Publishing.

Scottish Executive Education Department. (2006). *Achieving the Standard for Headship – Providing choice and alternatives: A consultation document.* Edinburgh: Scottish Executive.

Shapiro, C. J., Smith, B. H. & Tankersley, M. (2010). Taking a public health approach to school-based parenting interventions: The Triple P – Positive Parenting Program. *Advances in School Mental Health Promotion*, *3*(4), 63–74.

Shidler, L. (2008). The impact of time spent coaching for teacher efficacy on student achievement. *Early Childhood Educational Journal*, *36*(5), 453–460.

Short, E., Kinman, G. & Baker, S. (2010). Evaluating the impact of a peer coaching intervention on well-being amongst psychology undergraduate students. *International Coaching Psychology Review*, *5*(1), 27–35.

Showers, B. (1982). *Transfer of training: The contribution of coaching.* Eugene, OR: Centre for Educational Policy and Management.

Showers, B. & Joyce, B. (1996). The evolution of peer coaching. *Educational Leadership*, *53*(6), 12–16.

Stelter, R., Nielsen, G. & Wikman, J. (2011). Narrative-collaborative group coaching develops social capital – a randomised control trial and further implications of the social impact of the intervention. *Coaching: An International Journal of Theory, Research and Practice*, *42*(2), 123–137.

Stephens, D., Morgan, D. N., DeFord, D. E., Donnelly, A., Hamel, E., Keith, K. J., Brink, D. A., Johnson, R., Seaman, M., Young, J., Gallant, D. J., Hao, S. & Leigh, S. R. (2011). The impact of literacy coaches on teachers' beliefs and practices. *Journal of Literacy Research*, *43*(3), 215–249.

Sterling, D. (2008). *The parent as coach approach: The 7 ways to coach your teen in the game of life.* Albequerque, NM: White Oak.

Strahan, D., Geitner, M. & Lodico, M. (2010). Collaborative professional development toward literacy learning in a high school through Connected Coaching. *Teacher Development: An International Journal of Teachers' Professional Development*, *14*(4), 519–532.

Taylor, R. T., Zugelder, B. S., & Bowman, P. (2012). Literacy coach effectiveness: The need for measurement. *International Journal of Mentoring and Coaching in Education*, *2*(1), 34–46.

Teaching Leaders – Programmes (2015). Retrieved from www.teachingleaders.org.uk/wp-content/uploads/2015/05/Our-programmes-overview_May-2015.pdf

Timperley, H. & Parr, J. (2008). *Coaching as a process of knowledge building and self-regulatory inquiry.* Paper presented at the British Educational Research Association Conference, Edinburgh, September 2008.

Vanderburgh, M. & Stephens, D. (2010). The impact of literacy coaches: What teachers value and how teachers change. *The Elementary School Journal*, *111*(1), 141–163.

van Nieuwerburgh, C. (Ed.) (2012). *Coaching in education: Getting better results for students, educators and parents.* London: Karnac.

van Nieuwerburgh, C. (2014). *An introduction to coaching skills: A practical guide.* London: Sage.

van Nieuwerburgh, C. (2015). Towards a coaching culture. In. C. van Nieuwerburgh (Ed.), *Coaching in professional contexts.* London: Sage.

van Nieuwerburgh, C. & Campbell, J. (2015). A global framework for coaching in education. *CoachEd: The Teaching Leaders Coaching Journal*, February, 2–5.

van Nieuwerburgh, C. & Passmore, J. (2012). Creating coaching cultures for learning. In C van Nieuwerburgh (Ed.), *Coaching in education: Getting better results for students, educators, and parents.* London: Karnac.

van Nieuwerburgh, C. & Pawson, C. (in preparation). Perceptions of school-based coaching and mentoring provided by adult volunteers from the community.

van Nieuwerburgh, C. & Tong, C. (2013). Exploring the benefits of being a student coach in educational settings: a mixed-method study. *Coaching: An International Journal of Theory, Practice and Research*, 6(1), 5–24.

van Nieuwerburgh, C., Zacharia, C., Luckham, E., Prebble, G. & Browne, L. (2012). Coaching students in a secondary school: A case study. In C. van Nieuwerburgh (Ed.) *Coaching in education: Getting better results for students, educators, and parents.* London: Karnac.

Waters, L. (2011). A review of school-based positive psychology interventions. *Australian Educational and Developmental Psychologist*, 2,8 75–90.

West, L. & Staub, F. C. (2003). *Content-focused coaching: Transforming mathematics lessons.* Portsmouth, NH: Heinemann.

Whitmore, J. (2009). *Coaching for performance: GROWing human potential and purpose: The principles and practice of coaching and leadership*, 4th ed. London: Nicholas Brealey.

Wong, K. & Nicotera, A. (2003). *Enhancing teacher quality: Peer coaching as a professional development strategy: A preliminary synthesis of the literature.* Washington, DC: Institute of Education Sciences (ED).

Coaching in Healthcare

Ruth Q. Wolever, Margaret A. Moore and Meg Jordan

INTRODUCTION

The timely arrival of coaching in healthcare brings germinal seeds of hope to a landscape in dire need. The global healthcare industry is under siege by many forces: overuse of expensive medical procedures, dated volume-based reimbursement systems, and outdated, siloed models of care. Add the global epidemic of preventable chronic disease associated with unhealthy behaviors and you find healthcare systems facing massively disruptive change, and global economies enduring significant financial strain (Bloom et al., 2011; Marrero et al., 2012; Meeto, 2008). In this context, there is both enthusiasm and confusion regarding coaching.

There is enthusiasm for coaching because it aligns with the need to upgrade leadership competencies and provider well-being, reduce healthcare costs, redesign financial and care delivery models, and reverse negative behavior-driven public health trends. In particular, the epidemic of chronic illness has brought attention and research funding to enable much-needed, rigorous studies of coaching as an innovative and patient-centric process that may bring about sustainable behavior change in patients (Wolever, et al., 2013). However, the promise of coaching in healthcare has also brought confusion. For example, the burgeoning research on patient coaching includes confounds that lead many providers, patients and the public to misunderstand coaching as synonymous with educating and advising.

This chapter offers a map of the status and potential of coaching in the healthcare industry in an attempt to address both the enthusiasm and the confusion. We draw from coaching in other contexts to note potential solutions to healthcare challenges, overview the rapidly developing evidence base for patient coaching, and discuss distinctions of coaching in the healthcare context. We address the three primary applications of coaching in healthcare: 1) leadership coaching to address the unique challenges faced by the healthcare sector; 2) healthcare provider coaching for both well-being and performance; and 3) patient coaching to improve health and outcomes. Of these three applications, patient coaching is the most heavily researched in the academic literature; hence more attention is focused on patient coaching, including a discussion of coaching dimensions in healthcare that are not found in other domains.

THE STATE OF THE HEALTHCARE INDUSTRY

Also referred to as the medical industry, the healthcare industry denotes 'the aggregation and integration of sectors within the economic system that provide goods and services to treat patients with curative, preventive, rehabilitative, and palliative care. It includes the generation and commercialization of goods and services lending themselves to maintaining and re-establishing health' (Healthcare industry, 2015). Providers of healthcare include both institutions (e.g., hospitals or clinics) and people (e.g., physicians, nurses, allied health professionals) that provide these goods and services.

The healthcare industry is undergoing fundamental, structural shifts. While costly innovations for acute medical situations grow unabated (Skinner, 2013), the US and global healthcare industry is amidst a perfect storm of formidable challenges: structural fragmentation, unaffordable costs, deterioration in the well-being of the front line provider workforce, and suboptimal health outcomes for those with chronic disease. Additional healthcare challenges include vast new government regulations and initiatives (e.g., America's Affordable Care Act, Accountable Care Organizations, and patient-centered medical homes) as well as horizontal and vertical industry consolidation (Mattioli et al., 2015). These challenges are driving much-needed disruption through new models of organization, care delivery, payments, and insurance. Industry disruption and uncertainty promise to be immense, complex, and overwhelming.

Fortunately, coaching in healthcare may offer some mechanisms to support the reinvention of this critical industry by bolstering healthcare leaders, providers and patients.

> Coaching presupposes sufficient inner resources and the necessary expertise to tackle life challenges, and provides the guidance to harness these internal mechanisms … [to] amplify a client's internal locus of control, defined as the belief that one's actions have as much or more impact on life outcomes than external forces or individuals. In addition, coaching increases self-efficacy and self-determination. (Gazelle et al., 2015, page 509)

In essence, coaches in healthcare ask, 'how can people – healthcare leaders, providers, and the patients – be well-equipped to navigate the rough waters while also upgrading their own performance, health and well-being to master the huge demands?' In contrast to the siloed reality of healthcare, coaching takes a 'whole person' perspective in considering the full context of a person's life, including the external environment as well as social, political, and economic constraints and resources. Of critical importance will be the continued search for ways in which coaching can have systemic, not just personal, impact.

This chapter explores the status and emerging research of coaching in healthcare from four perspectives: 1) how coaching can help healthcare leaders develop healthy cultures that more handily meet current demands; 2) how coaching can help providers improve their well-being, resilience, and performance to be healthier themselves as well as better providers; 3) an overview of the expanding research on health coaching to help patients mobilize their own resources for improved health, along with the inherent conflicts in standardizing that process; and 4) a brief description of differences between coaching within healthcare and other contexts. Of the first three areas, patient coaching within healthcare has accumulated the most data and will be explored in more detail.

In short, coaching can support the widely disseminated Triple Aim (Berwick et al., 2008) that is guiding healthcare industry reinvention: applying integrated approaches to simultaneously improve population health, improve patient care, and reduce per capita costs. Because it is also clear that 'the care of the patient requires the care of the provider' (Bodenheimer & Sinksy, 2014, p. 573), provider well-being and that of healthcare leadership must also be included. This chapter discusses how coaching can offer one source of support to the healthcare industry to iteratively reinvent itself through coaching interventions targeting leadership, providers, and patients while simultaneously expanding the evidence base for coaching.

LEADERSHIP COACHING

The healthcare sector is ripe for leadership coaching to enable resilience and innovation during a time of massive disruption, while also cultivating healthier cultures. To improve population health in an entire system requires a wide spectrum of interventions from occupational health, to restructuring the environments, to outreach and education for those at-risk, to excellent access to primary care with referrals as needed, all the way to catastrophic care, disability management and complex care management (Nash et al., 2015). While the development of population health is beyond the scope of this chapter, there may be benefits to coaching the leaders in healthcare as a step to bringing about a healthier culture. However, the penetration of executive or leadership coaching in healthcare lags behind that observed in other industries.

This lag is partly due to a dearth in research supporting healthcare leadership training and practices, partly due to the industry's demand for rigorous studies and peer-reviewed evidence (historically lacking in the coaching industry), and partly due to the specialized knowledge required of the rapidly shifting operations of the complex healthcare sector, a knowledge that is not widespread among executive coaches. Nonetheless, the skillsets of executive coaches with this specialized knowledge are needed to support healthcare leaders in a tumultuous time.

Unfortunately, healthcare innovation is not supported by the culture of healthcare: 'While businesses in other sectors have become adept at bringing in ideas from outside their walls, healthcare has lagged behind' (Wagner, 2013). As healthcare leaders are forced to reinvent their organizations, the model for healthcare is being flipped upside down — from decades of focusing on acute care episodes and encouraging utilization to a future where successful organizations are able to reduce utilization, manage population health, and activate patients in the consumption (and delivery) of their own care. The only organizations that will prosper in this environment of disruptive and massive change are those that build a resilient and adaptive culture in which staff members:

- Welcome and seek change, rather than resist it;
- Experiment and innovate, rather than maintain the status quo; and
- Make hard decisions without relying on approval from senior leaders (Wagner, 2013).

As one of the largest sectors of developed economies, healthcare prides itself on being driven by rigorously collected data and peer-reviewed evidence. Surprisingly, however, there is paltry peer-reviewed literature on the study of healthcare leadership, leadership training, and executive coaching for healthcare leaders. Especially notable is the absence of a thorough discussion of leadership competencies needed in healthcare to deal with today's realities. Research is needed to elucidate the leadership competencies needed to support personal and workforce health, well-being and performance in these turbulent times.

Over the past decade, few peer-reviewed papers have evaluated the potential value of coaching for healthcare leaders (Henochowicz & Hetherington, 2006; Thompson et al., 2012). One randomized controlled trial (RCT) of executive coaching in an Australian public health agency demonstrated improved goal attainment, resilience and well-being in its leaders (Grant et al., 2009). Similarly, a case study in Malta showed that a coaching program for nurse ward leaders was effective in improving their leadership skills and performance (Law & Aquilinia, 2013). In sum, there is promising data, but it is quite limited. Perhaps the minimal empirical findings explain why a survey of 583 healthcare CEOs perceived only a moderate value for coaching, with many CEOs remaining neutral or reporting little worth in coaching (Walston, 2014).

Despite the dearth of evidence and apparently low value held by CEOs for coaching, enormous disruption in the industry is causing leaders to look for innovative solutions. Executive coaching is being recognized as one potential resource for healthcare leadership. 'Vanguard institutions have pioneered programs to identify, develop, and equip physician leaders; However, such programs are not widespread' (Shanafelt et al., 2015, p. 437). Within healthcare, leadership programs are often specialized for one group, reflecting some of the system siloes in healthcare – physicians, nurses, and administrators. Nonetheless, the separate silos are recognizing the importance of integrating executive coaching into their leadership curricula.

Physician-focused programs that integrate executive coaching include the American Association of Physician Executives, the American Association for Physician Leadership and the United Kingdoms's National Health Service Leadership Academy (NHS Leadership Academy, 2015). Similarly, leadership programs for nurses that integrate executive coaching include the Duke-Johnson & Johnson Nurse Leadership program, and the National League of Nursing's Executive Leadership in Nursing Education and Practice.

In addition to deploying executive coaches to support healthcare leadership, peer coaching is also being explored; for example, the University of Massachusetts Medical School is teaching peer coaching skills to physicians (Ziedonis, 2015).

At this point, an estimated 92% of surveyed hospital-based or healthcare system physician leadership programs 'always' or 'sometimes' offer an executive coach (US National Center for Healthcare Leadership, 2014). This growth has led to the emergence of a US coach training school that specializes in training coaches who work with healthcare leaders and physicians (Physician Coaching Institute, 2015). There are also many university and hospital healthcare and physician leadership programs (e.g., Cleveland Clinic, Duke Integrative Medicine, and Harvard-affiliated programs), but more studies of the impact of coaching healthcare leaders are warranted. Such studies are needed along with clear descriptions of validated competency models that are suited to industries experiencing immense disruption. Since 'the leadership competency models in widespread use today were developed prior to the passage of the Affordable Care Act; evolving into a new era ... will likely require new competencies of our leaders' (Garman & Lemak, 2011, p. 4).

Leadership competencies have been identified in industrial organizational fields, but limited work has been done in this arena in healthcare (Stoller, 2013), a rapidly changing sector where both administrative and physician leaders must increase innovation and improve managerial competencies (Walston, 2014). Some assert that leadership competencies in healthcare would ideally include coaching skills and self-management skills that foster optimal performance and well-being of the workforce:

'Integrating the principles and practices of professional coaching across the continuum and within the entire academic medicine community could gradually, but inexorably, shift the culture to be dynamic and relational: one in which talented individuals can and do apply their peak performance to all aspects of their work' (Thorn & Raj, 2012, p. 1482).

While new healthcare leadership competency models are evolving, executive coaches can support this evolution by helping to obtain data to clarify the competencies, and advocating for the integration of coaching into leadership models. Effectiveness and cost-effectiveness studies of specific healthcare leadership competencies are needed to analyze and validate the potential contribution of both leadership coaching and related programs (Stoller, 2013).

Since negative leadership qualities of physician supervisors significantly reduce both the well-being and job satisfaction of their physician staff (Shanafelt et al., 2015), it is important to develop leaders who can foster well-being and co-create a healthy and productive culture. In fact, such a culture is vital not just to support the marathon reinvention phase ahead, but as a key contributor to the health of the front-line providers and subsequently, of the patient population.

PROVIDER WORKFORCE COACHING

Extensive research indicates that physician well-being and professional satisfaction have a profound effect on the quality of their patient care as well as patient satisfaction and adherence. Unfortunately, the latest news is not good on the state of physician well-being (Shanafelt et al., 2012); in fact,

> 'the doctor–patient relationship … is in tatters … Being a caring doctor has become practically cost-prohibitive. Insurance companies don't pay enough for spending time with patients. But they do for CT scans and stress tests – whether they're warranted or not' (Meadows, 2014).

The emergence of electronic health records and other administrative work also compromise physician–patient relationships: 'The principal driver of physician satisfaction is the ability to provide quality care. Physician dissatisfaction, therefore, is an early warning sign of a healthcare system creating barriers to high-quality practice' (Bodenheimer & Sinsky, 2014, p. 574).

A growing burden of government regulation further compromises physician satisfaction and well-being along with the financial viability of physician practices (Friedberg et al., 2013). The restructuring and rapid corporatization of physician practices (CareCloud & QuantiaMD, 2014) adds dual sources of stress – the physician's skills gap in teamwork and leadership plus a decline in autonomy for physicians who collectively have high needs for independence and self-determination. In one survey, positive morale was reported by only 6% of physicians (Physicians' Foundation, 2008). Burnout has worsened from 2011 to 2014, with more than half of US physicians now reporting professional burnout (Shanafelt et al., 2015). In fact, 68% of family medicine physicians and 73% of general internists reported that they would not choose the same specialty if they started their careers over (Physicians' Foundation, 2008).

Burnout and dissatisfaction also affect nurses and other members of the healthcare workforce. Roughly one-third of hospital and nursing home nurses report burnout; in other settings, 22% of nurses report burnout (Bodenheimer & Sinsky, 2014). Similarly, 60% of healthcare employees in general reported job burnout and 34% were planning to look for another job (CareerBuilder, 2013). Not surprisingly, job satisfaction is strongly related to job burnout (Alacacioglu et al., 2009; McGowan, 2001; McHugh et al., 2011), as is lower patient satisfaction (McHugh et al., 2011; Vahey et al., 2004). Hence, financial investment in healthcare employee wellness and coaching has never been more important.

Coaching offers one path toward enhanced physician and nurse well-being. (Gazelle et al., 2015). As with leadership coaching in healthcare though, provider coaching in healthcare has limited empirical work to support its effectiveness. This is another area where coaching may offer support, yet is in great need of well-designed research studies that track both provider well-being and the impact of coaching on their medical work. One nicely designed coaching pilot did just this. A cohort of 25 physicians who received coaching demonstrated improved resilience and also better work boundaries and priorities, augmented mindfulness and self-awareness, as well as increased self-compassion and self-care (Schneider et al., 2014).

Qualitative analyses further revealed indirect improvement in patient care, reportedly as a function of increased physician energy and resilience, and because the physicians modeled their coach's presence and focus during patient visits (Schneider et al., 2014). Such findings support the efforts of groups like the Massachusetts Medical Society's Physician Health Services program, which provides a network of specialized physician coaches to address physician well-being and performance. In addition, multiple health coach training programs are targeting healthcare workers and including self-care as a major component of their training. Such programs include the nurse coach training program sponsored by the International Nurse Coach Association (2015), and health coach training programs at the University of Arizona, the University of Delaware, and the Vanderbilt Health Coaching Certificate Program.

PATIENT COACHING

The Need for Patient Coaching

Leadership competencies and workforce well-being are two of the cornerstones of a healthier healthcare system. A third is comprised of patient activation and sustainable behavior change, both for population health and for patients with chronic conditions. This domain is the most advanced of the three cornerstones with respect to describing the coaches and their necessary training and education. It is also the most developed cornerstone in terms of the rapidly accumulating evidence that can inform all fields of coaching. Coaching interventions are being explored and implemented across the spectrum of healthcare delivery including pediatrics, primary care, cardiac and other forms of rehabilitation, chronic disease treatment and prevention, complex care coordination, and hospice, as well as corporate/organizational health promotion and consumer wellness.

The rising burden of lifestyle-related chronic diseases, including type 2 diabetes, heart disease, stroke, and obesity, is a massive and growing challenge for healthcare systems. In the US, half of all adults have a chronic disease (Center for Disease Control and Prevention, Chronic Disease Overview, 2015). Furthermore, up to 86% of healthcare expenditures in the US are devoted to treating these lifestyle-driven chronic diseases (Center for Disease Control and Prevention, Chronic Disease Overview, 2015; Yach et al., 2004). 'Our current healthcare spending is unsustainable and could eventually bankrupt the country absent dramatic changes in our current healthcare programs and system' (Bouchard, 2012).

Fewer than 10% of US adults consistently engage in the top lifestyle behaviors (Berrigan et al., 2003) including consumption of fruits and vegetables and healthy dietary fat, regular exercise, moderate (if any) drinking, and not smoking. By two measures, only 20% of US adults are thriving mentally (Keyes, 2002; Kobau et al., 2010), revealing inadequate resources to sustainably adopt healthy lifestyles in our obesogenic environments. Clinicians, allied health professionals, and researchers struggle with how to best help patients become more engaged in sustaining healthy lifestyles to delay onset of, or reduce morbidity and mortality caused by, chronic diseases.

The clinical and economic case for interventions that target health-promoting behaviors as safe and effective primary and secondary interventions has led to a number of US federal directives. These include the Patient Protection and Affordable Care

Act (2010) and the formation of the Patient-Centered Outcomes Research Institute (2015). Population health aims also emphasize greater patient-centricity and patient engagement as seminal to enabling healthy lifestyles that are sustainable (Simmons et al., 2014). In the domain of public health, efforts such as coaching that improve individual well-being are being recognized as strong predictors of lower near-term healthcare utilization and costs (Harrison et al., 2012). In the domain of chronic illness, greater patient-centricity and patient engagement in care is finally seen as necessary to improve health outcomes (Bodenheimer et al., 2002; Simmons et al., 2014).

Both patients and providers need to have adequate knowledge of healthy lifestyles and clear methodologies to support behavioral change in order to improve health outcomes. These recognized needs have led to new specialties in medicine, including lifestyle medicine (e.g., www.lifestylemedicine.org and www.instituteoflifestylemedicine.org) and integrative medicine (www.imconsortium.org and https://nccih.nih.gov). Not surprisingly, both specialties have noted a clear place for health and wellness coaching as central to their implementation (Frates & Moore, 2013; Wolever et al., 2010). Yet much larger implementation efforts for health and wellness coaching are needed since most health professionals are not trained nor paid to support patient engagement and health behavior change as a means of treating and preventing chronic disease.

The Emergence of Patient Coaching

Professional health and wellness coaches, along with allied health professionals trained to use basic coaching skills, offer promise to help fill this gap. Health and wellness coaches are those that provide coaching services to patients, employees, or consumers, typically in an effort to prevent or treat chronic illness by supporting sustainable change in health behaviors as well as adherence to complex medical regimens. Our explorer's map requires a legend to understand the coach titles deployed in the clinical, corporate, and consumer sectors. The use of distinct titles (health coach, wellness coach or health & wellness coach) has emerged from debates concerning the depth and breadth of background knowledge required for coaches in healthcare, corporate and consumer wellness. In fact, it has been vigorously argued and remains largely unresolved depending on which sector addresses the question. For example, at the original 2010 Summit of the National Consortium for Credentialing Health and Wellness Coaches (NCCHWC), clinicians, educators, and other clinical, public health, corporate and consumer sector stakeholders held a lively discussion about the potential for drafting national standards for education, training and a possible certification (Jordan et al., 2015).

While many medical doctors and licensed healthcare professionals (e.g., medical doctors, registered nurses, psychologists, social workers, dieticians) recognized the need for a behavioral expert or coach to help patients adopt healthful habits, several also suggested that two levels of coaching competency should be recognized – one for licensed healthcare professionals due to their advanced clinical knowledge, and a lower tier for non-clinical coaches who work with 'healthy individuals' on exercise, nutrition, and weight. For example, they suggested that an exercise goal for a healthy person may be best supported by a wellness coach while exercise goals for those with heart disease require health coaches with greater knowledge. This reasoning is to be expected of an industry that emphasizes expert knowledge within the licensed biomedical professions. To stem the rising tide of the chronic disease epidemic or conquer unhealthful behaviors, it is assumed that one must have expert knowledge and clinical judgment. The deeply embedded stakes held by some licensed healthcare practitioners regarding the superiority of their education and training may continue to hold sway over where and how health and wellness coaches penetrate the long-established medical hierarchy.

Not only are coaching title descriptions at issue in healthcare, but so too is the very definition of 'coaching.' The definition is confounded because the scope of practice of most, if not all, health professionals includes educating and advising patients. When coaching is defined as educating and advising, most healthcare professionals do 'coach' patients. In the world of healthcare, for example, a medical assistant calling patients to remind them to take their medications has been considered 'coaching.' Whether or not this approach is helpful, in the world of professional coaching, this would not even approximate 'coaching.' Hence, changing the way the term 'coaching' is defined in healthcare is a massive undertaking. Nonetheless, inroads are being made in several healthcare professions to add a defined 'coach approach' to their clinical practice. Leaders at a 2009 Institute of Medicine Summit on Integrative Health called for a new profession of health and wellness coaches to assist the medical and public health professions in addressing this need for lifestyle turnaround.

Recognition of a 'nurse coach role' within nursing's scope of practice by the American Nurses Association was a significant step for nurses to embrace an evidence-based strategy for supporting lifestyle change and enhancing the health and well-being of patients (Dossey et al., 2014). Nurses, psychologists, clinical social workers, pharmacists, dieticians and other licensed health professionals who ascribe to a relationship-centered, holistic approach pursue coaching skills at the US Veterans Administration and the Osher Center for Integrative Medicine at Vanderbilt. Similarly, medical doctors who practice similar models add coaching skills at Duke Integrative Medicine and the University of Arizona. Chiropractors adopt coaching skills, based on training from the National Wellness Institute. Acupuncture students in traditional Chinese medicine programs at California Institute of Integral Studies are introduced to coaching knowledge and skills practice. The growing acceptance among the ranks of the licensed healthcare professions to adopt coaching methodology and skills aligns with current initiatives outlined in the Patient Protection and Affordable Care Act (2010). Health-enhancing behaviors must be addressed, and coaching appears to be an excellent way to do it.

Many argue that 'a coach is a coach is a coach' and the content of the coaching is less relevant. This argument suggests that coaches are process experts rather than content experts and can apply the process in any context. Moreover, when trying to help patients and other stakeholders in the healthcare system adopt a new perspective that is distinct from the conventional, expert-driven paradigm, coaches who are not trained in that very paradigm can be more open and objective on the limitations of existing paradigms. In healthcare, however, coaches who are *not* licensed healthcare practitioners raise the issue of the content and amount of specific knowledge bases needed to effectively coach medical patients. To understand this, it is helpful to review the collaborative input gathered by the NCCHWC.

To begin with, after six years of debate (2010–2015), the NCCHWC advisors and board members concluded that a single foundational level of certification was urgently needed for a broad transformation of health promotion, and dropped the two-tier notion (a higher certification for licensed healthcare professionals, a lower level for non-clinical coaches). A single national certification will encompass a basic, foundation level of knowledge and skills that assures competencies within the health and wellness coaching process, based upon a validated survey of job task analysis findings (Wolever et al., 2016). In other words, medical practitioners will not dictate how health coaches function; the emerging profession itself will chart that territory. In partnership with the NCCHWC, the National Board of Medical Examiners (NBME) will implement the first national exam in 2017. Hence, despite a great deal of ongoing debate and the strong possibility that a tiered system will be implemented at some future time, the terms 'health coach' 'wellness coach' and 'health and wellness coach' are currently used synonymously by the NCCHWC, the NBME, and in this chapter.

In North America, over the past 15 years more than 53 academic and private sector programs have emerged to educate and train approximately 20,000 health professionals to either coach professionally or to deploy coaching skills in their current scope of practice [personal communication, NCCHWC Executive Committee of the Board, 8/23/16]. Health and wellness coaches have diverse backgrounds including nurses, exercise professionals, dietitians, physical and occupational therapists, psychologists, social workers, other mental health professionals, and physicians (Wolever et al., 2013). A similar diversity exists in the settings in which health and wellness coaches work, including outpatient clinics, healthcare systems, health plans, employee wellness programs, government programs, health clubs, and private practice (Wolever et al., 2016). Coaching models include one-on-one coaching, group coaching (e.g., Armstrong et al., 2013), and a growing exploration of peer coaching (e.g., Botelho, 2015; Goldman et al., 2013; Rogers et al., 2014).

Coaching delivery includes in-person, phone, videoconference, and secure email and text. Coaching interventions are often supported by technology such as web coaching platforms (Appel et al., 2011) and mobile apps (Spring et al., 2010). Multiple books and papers support the training and education of health and wellness coaches, drawing from sources such as motivational interviewing, self-determination theory, the transtheoretical model, positive psychology, cognitive behavioral tools, social cognitive theory, emotional intelligence, mindfulness, empathy, and neuroscience (e.g., Dossey et al., 2014; Jordan, 2013; Moore et al., 2015). The Institute of Coaching (2015) at McLean Hospital, a Harvard Medical School affiliate, has supported the field since 2008 through education in the translation of science into coaching practice and coaching research grants.

The Evidence Base for Patient Coaching

While the peer-reviewed literature on health and wellness coaching is still in its infancy, both the theoretical and outcomes research is burgeoning, although constrained by heterogeneity in coach definitions, background, training, and study protocols. In terms of study protocols, not only do different studies define coaching in distinct ways, but each investigation differs in the choice of research participants (i.e. type of patient), the inclusion criteria for these participants, the selection of outcomes, the frequency and duration of the coaching (aka 'dose'), the timeline to measurement of the outcomes, and whether or not the coaching is combined with other interventions. In sum, the literature is challenging to digest because of this variability. So, what can be said at this point?

In 2009, the first review of coaching for improved health outcomes included articles from 14 literature databases and identified 72 studies (Newnham-Kanas et al., 2009). This useful overview highlighted concerns with lack of rigor. For example, only 34 studies were RCTs, 20 studies were educational interventions rather than professional coaching, and 12 studies did not define the 'coaching' intervention used. The overview makes clear that the operationalization of health and wellness coaching described in the medical literature is without a consistent standard. However, confusion about the definition of 'coaching' for patients is beginning to clear.

By the end of 2012, 284 peer-reviewed articles on health and wellness coaching were observed in the medical literature, with 76% being empirical (Wolever et al., 2013). A rigorous PRISMA-guided systematic review sought to shed light on the definitional confusion, and demonstrated that a consensus around the parameters for a definition of patient coaching in healthcare was beginning to show across the literature. The review specifically noted the following intervention components as key to the practice of health and wellness coaching: 1) the coaching process is fully or at least partially patient-centered (observed in 86% of the articles); 2) coaching centers around patient-determined goals (71%); 3) the coach elicits self-discovery and active learning processes rather than more passive patient roles where patients are solely 'advised' or 'educated' (63%); 4) the coaching process utilizes methods to encourage accountability for behaviors (86%); and 5) provides some type of education to patients along with using coaching processes (91%). Importantly, 78% of the articles indicated that coaching interventions occur in the context of a consistent, ongoing relationship with a human coach who has received specific training in behavior change, communication and motivational skills. This emerging consensus is a positive indication of improving consistency in the operationalization of health and wellness coaching.

Nonetheless, the state of this literature is far from the standards typically acceptable in medicine. For example, the systematic review included all relevant peer-reviewed articles on health and wellness coaching, but descriptions of the pertinent domains necessary to code the intervention were not adequate in 11% to 78% of the articles, depending on the research question (Wolever et al., 2013). As an example, 75% of the peer-reviewed articles did not specify the average length of coaching sessions, 52% did not specify the number of sessions provided and 64% did not specify the duration of the coaching process. It is impossible to understand the impact of coaching interventions without these intervention details. In other words, findings from this systematic review also concur with multiple calls in the literature for a clear definition of health and wellness coaching, supported by uniform standards for training and scope of practice (Ammentorp et al. 2013; Kivelä et al., 2014; Olsen & Nesbitt, 2010; Wolever & Eisenberg, 2011). In order to make more sense of the literature, and in particular, to ferret out equivocal results, greater transparency is needed in studies that claim to evaluate 'coaching.'

Despite definitional confusion about coaching as an intervention in healthcare, potential benefits of health and wellness coaching can be culled from five reviews that systematically and clearly define the inclusion criteria for the coaching studies they included. The total number of studies covered in these reviews is small (ranging from 5 to 25) and the need for further description of the interventions is apparent. For example, in one review, nine of the 15 assessed studies still did not define health coaching (Hill et al., 2015). Nonetheless, the reviews strongly suggest the effectiveness of health and wellness coaching in improving motivational processes, psychosocial outcomes, behavioral outcomes and to a lesser degree, immediate biological indices of chronic illness (Ammentorp et al., 2013; Hill et al, 2015; Kivelä et al., 2014; Lindner et al., 2003; Olsen & Nesbitt, 2010).

Sample of Studies of Patient Coaching

Impact of patient coaching on motivation, patient engagement, self-efficacy, and other psychosocial outcomes

While there are negative findings as well, the preponderance of studies that clearly describe their coaching interventions document that coaching increases patient engagement and the health-related self-efficacy necessary to enhance patient outcomes. These include prospective, observational trials (Galantino et al., 2009), quasi-experimental trials

(Linden et al., 2010) and RCTs2011). Even a large scale review of 275 studies that included those without clear coaching definitions concluded that 75% of the RCTs found that health coaching can support individuals' motivation to change health behaviors and their self-confidence to do so (National Health Service Evidence Centre, 2014). In terms of other psychosocial outcomes, RCTs of health coaching with patients with type 2 diabetes have shown improved depressive symptoms (Sacco et al., 2009), lowered perceived stress, and improved perception of health status (Sacco et al., 2009; Wolever et al., 2010). Similarly, RCTs of health coaching with cancer patients have shown greater vitality and improved mental health (Thomas et al., 2012).

Impact of patient coaching on adoption of health behaviors

When systematic reviews cast the net more widely to include studies that do not define health coaching clearly, the evidence is more muddled, but still suggests positive results in the domain of lifestyle behaviors. For example, 59% of 32 RCTs reviewed reported that health coaching can support people to adopt healthy behaviors and lifestyle choices such as lowered use of alcohol and tobacco, eating more fruits and vegetables, and exercising more regularly (National Health Service Evidence Centre, 2014). The nuances of the literature, however, point to the need of more consistent and rigorous definitions in the methodology. As an example, a well-designed and conducted RCT tested the use of coaching by physical therapists to help rheumatoid arthritis patients achieve standardized exercise goals. At the end of both the one-year coaching intervention, and a second year follow-up, the coaching intervention, in comparison to usual care, failed to demonstrate an improvement in physical activity at recommended levels (Sjöquist et al., 2011). Since multiple trials in other patient groups have demonstrated improvements in physical activity, it is unclear why this trial did not capture such.

Possible explanations include the background and coach training of the interventionists, how the outcomes were measured, and the very definition of 'coaches' and the 'coaching intervention.' More specifically, the intervention was described as physical therapists who 'informed [patients] about the benefits of physical activity' and discussed 'their thoughts about their body function and possibilities for physical activity' (Brodin et al., 2008). Description of the intervention states that goals for physical activity 'were formulated and documented according to a structured manual based on the principles of graded activity training' but the relative roles of self-determination in goal setting and active learning in problem solving are unclear (Brodin et al., 2008). The point is that the coaching intervention trials that have emerged in healthcare assess a wide range of disparate outcomes and reflect a variety of interventions delivered by a highly heterogeneous group of professionals and paraprofessionals, to quite variable patient groups.

At this point, most reviews suggest that the behavioral change evidence from coaching interventions provides at least a strong signal that merits further exploration. When considering only those trials with well-defined health coaching interventions, RCTs typically demonstrate improvement in lifestyle behavior. While conflicting reports with strong methodologies exist (e.g., Sjöquist et al., 2011), the majority of the more rigorous trials show improvement in physical activity (Hersey et al., 2012; Rimmer et al., 2009), dietary intake (Sacco et al., 2009), medication adherence (Wolever et al., 2010) and specific self-care procedures such as foot care for patients with diabetes (Sacco et al., 2009).

As an example of the impact observed when adding a health coach, consider that typical workplace tobacco cessations programs and smoke-free policies have generally resulted in meager reductions in smoking prevalence of 3.8% (Fichtenberg & Glantz, 2002). One telephone-based tobacco cessation program, which included health coaches as part of an employee wellness program, however, achieved a quit rate of 32% compared to 18% among nonparticipants (Terry, 2011). Another health coaching program delivered by a hospital to local employers noted that the quit rate at one year for 161 participants was 63% (Sforzo et al., 2014).

Impact of patient coaching on biological risk factors

In terms of a positive impact on biological outcomes, the evidence is more mixed. Only 2 of the 6 published reviews, 37% of the 60 RCTs and 84% of the non-RCT studies found largely positive results on biological outcomes (National Health Service Evidence Centre, 2014). The potential role of definitional confusion can be clearly seen in the biological results as well. In general, the strongest findings with the most highly defined coaching interventions that are provided by professionals well-trained in coaching, have been in cardiovascular and metabolic health. Coaching, whether provided alone or as part of a larger program, has been shown to improve biomarkers including total cholesterol, body mass index, fasting blood sugar, hemoglobin A1C, and risk of subsequent coronary events (Allen et al., 2011; Appel et al., 2011; Edelman et al., 2006; Kumanyika et al., 2012; Leahey & Wing, 2013; Rimmer et al., 2009; Sacco et al., 2004; Vale et al., 2003; Whittemore et al., 2004; Wolever et al., 2010).

Impact of patient coaching on cost and utilization

Finally, there is insufficient evidence to draw conclusions about the impact of health coaching on utilization or costs (National Health Service Evidence Centre, 2014). Several studies revealed promising findings, but this work is in its infancy. In an early study, 229 participants in a Duke employee health program received health coaching as part of a larger intervention that also involved case management and physician incentives. In year 1 (2003–2004), high-risk participants with heart disease, diabetes and history of expensive claims received nine 60-minute group coaching sessions and demonstrated a decline in inpatient admissions by 25.4%. Simultaneously, admissions increased 6.4% for similar participants who did not participate in the coaching program (Hignite, 2008). While one could argue that positive human contact of any kind could elicit a therapeutic effect for health issues, quality health coaching employs specific processes and also covers self-care and self-management that can impact the making of wise, cost-effective choices in terms of urgent care. Hence, it is reasonable to assume that health coaching is more likely to lower inappropriate emergency room usage and medical utilization than would a strictly supportive alliance that had no additional coaching elements.

In a more recent and much larger cost-effectiveness trial, 174,120 subjects were studied who had high healthcare costs and selected chronic and 'preference-sensitive' conditions such as those in need of hip-replacement or back surgery. Total medical costs and utilization metrics were compared for the subsequent 12 months between those participants randomized to health coaching versus a support condition. Average per member, per month (pmpm) medical and pharmacy costs were 3.6% lower in the coaching group, averaging $7.96 pmpm. The majority of the cost savings were generated by a 10.1% reduction in annual hospital admissions and some savings from decreased use of emergency rooms. Given that the cost to run the health coaching program was less than $2.00 pmpm, an estimated return on investment was documented of almost 4:1 (Wennberg et al., 2010).

ISSUES IN HEALTH AND WELLNESS COACHING

As the rigor of the research improves and definitional issues are addressed, this rapidly growing body of work on health and wellness coaching is likely to support other areas of coaching research. In addition to providing both efficacy and effectiveness data, the most powerful mechanisms of action in coaching will become more clearly delineated through empirical work. Moreover, as mechanisms are clarified, the use of particular skills can be assessed both when used by professional health and wellness coaches, and when used by other healthcare professionals in combination with their different roles. The healthcare context provides a particularly rich environment in which to study the use of coaching skills by non-coach professionals.

Compared to other coaching fields, however, there are also four main differences in health and wellness coaching which must be considered. One early health coaching review noted that health coaching interventions generally covered at least one of three domains: behavior change strategies, psychosocial support, or disease-related education (Lindner et al., 2003). Interestingly, the last of these domains represents a clear departure from other fields of coaching and reflects the historical context of medicine wherein providers educate patients. A related area of difference between health coaching and other coaching arenas include the knowledge base needed by coaches in the health and wellness arena, particularly when coaching medical patients. The third area of difference centers on the fact that patients as clients are likely to be more vulnerable than other coaching clients. Finally, the payment models for coaching in healthcare are quite distinct.

Content Education in Health and Wellness Coaching

Provision of content education is a significant point of debate in health and wellness coaching. Coaches are often asked by their employers to provide content education – information from expert credible sources, with the intention of helping patients to better understand a specific health condition or related factors (e.g., disease or condition information, typically tracked clinical markers) or well-established consensus guidelines for health behaviors. In fact, expert information is what patients expect from their healthcare providers. Here is the first place where where health coaching departs from health education in patient care. There is evidence that imparting knowledge is not the most useful approach to inspire sustainable change. Education is necessary but far from sufficient to self-manage chronic illness (Caldwell et al., 2013; Huffman, 2009; Lindner et al., 2003; Newnham-Kanas et al., 2009; Whittaker et al., 2012; Whittemore et al., 2004). Moreover, providing information prescriptively or with an expert attitude is counterproductive to involving patients in their own care (Joseph-Williams et al., 2014).

Keys to a helpful approach to education include optimal timing so that patients are open to take it in, offering the right dose of information to avoid overwhelm, and ensuring that clients get the knowledge immediately relevant for their next steps. Various evidence-based interventions that have an optimal approach to health education include relationship-centered methods that support autonomy (Williams et al., 2006) such as shared decision making (e.g., Durand et al., 2015), maintenance care interventions (e.g., Friedmann, 2006), and motivational interviewing (e.g., Rollnick et al., 2007). Theoretical models that go beyond health education and support coaching are often cited in health coaching research, including the application of Social Cognitive Theory (Bandura, 1997) to help build a patient's motivation, self-efficacy, and engagement. A well-researched change model, the Transtheoretical Model, assists health coaches to help their patients or clients appreciate the stages that they will cycle through as they contemplate, prepare, act and sustain change, and then match strategies to stages of readiness to change (Norcross et al., 2011).

For the most part, effective health coaches avoid teaching, advising, or telling clients what to do (Jordan, et al., 2015; Wolever et al., 2016). The most effective means of applying their health/disease lifestyle knowledge is to facilitate learning and discovery on the client's part through the cycle of health coaching itself by:

- establishing the alliance with trust, rapport and empathy;
- holding the client's agenda foremost;
- evoking client values and strengths;
- evoking the client's broader vision to support desired health outcomes;
- supporting the patient in seeking clarity and self-assessing readiness;
- identifying the patient-determined goals;
- supporting movement into action;
- tracking progress in ways the patient has identified to increase their own accountability;
- helping the client to articulate learning and insights; and
- continuing to plan for sustained changes (Jordan, 2013; Smith et al., 2013).

Application of a coach's health/disease knowledge may be required at any of these stages. The difficult balancing act for a health coach is to hold the health/disease knowledge, without acting like a content expert or interrupting the flow and dynamic process of clients gaining insight for themselves.

Here is the second place where health coaching departs from health education in patient care. In health and wellness coaching, the provision of information should be titrated to the needs of the coaching client. Specifically, coaches help clients determine the type and amount of information needed 'just in time,' find reliable information sources, and select an optimal learning mode (e.g., lecture vs. reading vs. video, or expert consultation). The coach should follow an evidence-based practice for supporting clients in gaining new knowledge and skills. Stober, Wildflower and Drake (2006), for example, suggest that the three primary ingredients make up the concept of an evidence-based practice. They include: 1) the preferences or interests held by the client; 2) the most credible and current information; and 3) the practitioner's expertise (p.8). This tension in how to best provide education is well articulated in narrative medicine; Haidet and Paterniti (2003) note that the provider's

> perspective may exclude crucial patient-oriented data necessary to achieve therapeutic effectiveness. The patient's perspective may miss critical biomedical facts needed for accurate diagnosis. [Providers] need a method of fostering efficient sharing of critical biomedical and patient-specific information necessary for both [the] biomedical management of disease and [the] therapeutic healing of illness. (as cited in Drake, 2015, pp.133–134)

Another hotly debated topic in health and wellness coaching is the appropriate and necessary knowledge base for a health and wellness coach. Most would agree that a coach must have sufficient health/disease knowledge to know when to interrupt a counterproductive or potentially dangerous action on the client's part. If a patient or client expresses an interest in pursuing a seemingly unsafe exercise routine after a heart attack, or wants to begin a nutritionally-deficient diet fad, then a health coach needs to switch roles, dropping the coach role and adopting a health educator stance while encouraging the patient to review their goals with a licensed healthcare provider. In those moments, the backdrop of quietly held health/disease knowledge moves to the forefront. Most health coach training curricula recommend that the coach asks permission to switch roles (e.g., Caldwell et al., 2013) explains the reasons, and reminds the client of a prior agreement that clarified that the coaching alliance would most likely contain a portion of health education along with the health coaching. After disabusing the patient of erroneous or potentially harmful information, the coach then returns to coaching methodology as soon as possible (e.g., Jordan, 2013; Moore et al., 2015).

Uniform Standards for a Knowledge Base for Coaches in Healthcare

The formation of the non-profit NCCHWC in 2010 is moving the field of health coaching forward in the United States (Jordan et al., 2015; Wolever et al., 2016). The NCCHWC sponsored a professionally-led job task analysis (JTA) to define the role of health and wellness coaches, clarify scope of practice, and determine training and education standards that would produce competent health and wellness coaches. The national standards further allow for a collaborative research agenda including broad compilation of evidence on the effectiveness of coaching in healthcare across diverse settings, as well as more specific findings on best practices within coaching that lead to optimal outcomes. The NCCHWC has launched national training and education standards to accredit programs, and individual certification for health and wellness coaches will become effective in 2017 with the joint support of the NCCHWC and the NBME.

With respect to the education of coaches in the domains of health sciences and lifestyle medicine, NCCHWC has set an initial standard of at least 15 hours of education in evidence-based healthy lifestyle information to acquire foundational knowledge of the factors that promote health and well-being. Health and wellness coaches should have knowledge of basic, evidence-based healthy lifestyle recommendations by credible sources, including the Centers for Disease Control and Prevention (CDC, Healthy Living, 2015), the National Institutes of Health, the American College of Sports Medicine (2015), and the American College of Lifestyle Medicine (2015). The required health knowledge will continue to evolve; for example, some health professionals also believe that health coaches should have foundational knowledge of the common chronic conditions that affect the majority of the US population: obesity, hypertension, diabetes, cardiovascular disease, other inflammatory diseases (e.g., degenerative brain disease and degenerative joint diseases), cancer, and chronic pain.

Patient Vulnerability

Unique to coaching in healthcare is the fact that many clients in need of health and wellness coaching are simultaneously struggling with medical conditions that threaten their self-definition, if not their lives. In addition, financial and familial pressures may add to this vulnerability. Patients may feel exposed discussing the types of behaviors and lifestyle that led to poor states of health. Health coaching clients may thus be more vulnerable than those coached in the executive or life coaching arena (Wolever et al., 2011). When patients face troubling chronic health conditions, limitations or illness, often co-morbid with mental health conditions, their vulnerabilities surface, presenting health coaches with an added challenge of being present and supportive, as patients face their fears. Vulnerability is often a reciprocated exchange. When patients deal with physical and mental health problems, health coaches may, in turn, face their own fears of insecurity (role and financial), disability, and mortality. Hence, vulnerability inherent in working with the physical body and the full gamut of mental and physical health issues may push buttons in health coaches – leading them to be more protective of their clients, or more judgmental. Either can lead to transference, over-identification and coach burnout.

Case reports on credentialed nurse coaches find that addressing holistic self-care for the coach herself is a critical keystone to ongoing professional development and prevention of burnout (Dossey et al., 2014). The nurse coach board certification was created in 2013 for registered nurses and advanced practice nurses who wish to add patient coaching skills to their practices (International Nurse Coach Association, 2015). Holistic self-care is particularly important, given the interpersonal and intrapsychic issues that arise in the coach when working with chronically ill patients. Furthermore, the interpersonal dynamic presented when coaching those who are ill, injured or traumatized requires clear skills in emotional self-regulation, and a well-developed awareness of the coach's own internal processes (Livingstone & Gaffney, 2013).

Payment Models

The final distinction between coaching in healthcare and coaching in other contexts is related to payment models. While in executive and life coaching, individuals or their corporations typically pay for coaching services, the use of health and wellness coaching will not flourish without capitalizing on multiple modes of payment. Indeed, 'who should pay for health coaching?' is more than a philosophical question. If coaching leads to improved health, which lowers the burden of chronic illness for healthcare institutions, federal and state budgets, and indeed society, then all parties ideally would support the use of health and wellness coaching. Self-insured companies and health insurance companies are already recognizing the promise of health and wellness coaching. Use of 'health coaching' is written into the US Accountable Care Act regulations (2010), although it is not defined and third-party reimbursement is primarily occurring through pilots and demonstration projects.

As the healthcare system moves from fee-for-service models, or volume models, into value-based models and accountable care organizations (ACOs), there is greater likelihood that coaching will be deemed cost effective and more widely disseminated in coming years in both clinical and community settings. While the promise of greater dissemination may increase access to coaching, the result of coaching being dictated by ACOs may put undue pressure on the need for immediate positive biological outcomes. If coaches are pressured to produce a priori-defined outcomes rather than self-determined goals, there is risk of undermining the learning process itself that is seminal to coaching.

One payment-related concern is third party requirements for reimbursement and the myriad questions they raise. If a third party (private insurance, government or employer) covers the cost of health and wellness coaching, what authority do they maintain in designing patient-determined goals? Where are coaching interventions best delivered – in clinical offices, corporations, or through communities and consumer channels? What coach training and expert background are needed for reimbursement? Should coaching clients be required to contribute a co-pay? Should payers be able to approve or deny target areas for coaching? To a payer, coaching to lower blood glucose seems quite different from coaching to lower distress, particularly if the distress is driven by personal or professional relationships and other life and work issues. Yet, improving the latter may be the germinal mechanism to lowering blood glucose.

Until the evidence base clearly demonstrates that patient-defined goals (versus externally-defined targets) produce stronger and more sustainable change, we may be left with policy driven by confounds rather than a clear evidence-base. On the positive side, however, the push to clarify the effectiveness of health and wellness coaching (as well as specific mechanisms of change) will propel the research agenda forward in a way that may also inform other fields of coaching.

Health Coaching Competencies Contribute to Healthcare Culture

Last we want to briefly touch on how coaching skills can be taught to non-coach health providers as a strategy to improve patient outcomes. For example, when physicians were trained in motivational interviewing techniques (collaboration, empathy, open inquiry, reflections), their patients lost an average of 1.6 kilograms three months later after a single patient visit. The patients whose physicians were not using motivational interviewing techniques maintained or even gained weight (Pollack et al., 2010). In a few moments, healthcare providers can make a difference by using a collaborative rather than a prescriptive dynamic. Similarly, physicians who employ another key competence of coaches – empathy - appear to produce better outcomes in their patients. Compared to patients whose physicians had low empathy scores, patients whose physicians had high empathy scores were significantly more likely to have good control of blood sugar and cholesterol levels (Hojat et al., 2011).

Finally, the training of providers in two other coach competencies may also be helpful: self-awareness and non-judgmental presence. An ongoing criticism in healthcare is that the 'unconscious bias by healthcare professionals' contributes to racial health disparities and deficits in the quality of care, and this deplorable situation continues to persist long after the 2003 report of the Institute of Medicine (Williams & Wyatt, 2015, p. 555). Training providers to recognize their own biases and to adopt a deeply non-judgmental presence may be helpful to all of healthcare.

CONCLUSION

The dissemination of coaches and coaching principles across the healthcare spectrum – to leaders, the provider workforce, and the entire population in clinical, corporate, community and consumer settings – is positioned to make a vital contribution to the reinvention of healthcare systems globally. Collectively we need healthcare systems that are led by highly competent leaders who foster organizational cultures that promote innovation and well-being of the healthcare workforce. All of that is in service of slowing the tide of chronic diseases and fostering optimal health for all. A key to progress is the development of a more coordinated and strategic research agenda on coaching in its many forms across the healthcare ecosystem.

REFERENCES

Alacacioglu, A., Yavuzsen, T., Dirioz, M., Oztop, I., & Yilmaz, U. (2009). Burnout in nurses and physicians working at an oncology department. *Psycho-oncology*, *18*(5), 543–548.

Allen, J. K., Dennison-Himmelfarb, C. R., Szanton, S. L., Bone, L., Hill, M. N., Levine, D. M., ... Anderson, K. (2011). Community outreach and cardiovascular health (COACH) trial: A randomized, controlled trial of nurse practitioner/community health worker cardiovascular disease risk reduction in urban community health centers. *Circ Cardiovasc Qual Outcomes*, *4*(6), 595–602. doi: 10.1161/CIRCOUTCOMES.111.961573

Ammentorp, J., Uhrenfeldt, L., Angel, F., Ehrensvard, M., Carlsen, E. B., & Kofoed, P. (2013). Can life coaching improve outcomes? – A systematic review of intervention studies. *BMC Health Services Research*, 13, 428.

American College of Lifestyle Medicine (2015). Retrieved 11/30/15 from http://www.lifestylemedicine.org/

American College of Sports Medicine (2015). Retrieved 11/30/15 from http://www.acsm.org/

Appel, L. J., Clark, J. M., Yeh, H. C., Wang, N. Y., Coughlin, J. W., Daumit, G., ... Brancati, F. L. (2011). Comparative effectiveness of weight-loss interventions in clinical practice. *New England Journal of Medicine*, *365*(21), 1959–1968.

Armstrong, C., Wolever, R. Q., Manning, L., Elam, R., Moore, M., Frates, E. P., ... Lawson, K. (2013). Group health coaching: strengths, challenges and next steps. *Global Advances in Health and Medicine*, *2*(3), 95–102. doi:10.7453/gahmj.2013.019.

Bandura, A. (1997). Self-efficacy: Toward a unifying theory of behavioral change. *Psychological Review*, *84*(2), 191–215.

Berrigan, D., Dodd, K., Troiano, R. P., Krebs-Smith, S., & Barbash, R. B. (2003).

Patterns of health behavior in U.S. adults. *Preventive Medicine, 36*(5), 615–623.

Berwick, D. M., Nolan, T. W., & Whittington, J. (2008). The Triple Aim: Care, health, and cost. *Health Affairs, 27*(3), 759–769.

Bloom, D. E., Cafiero, E. T., Jané-Llopis, E., Abrahams-Gessel, S., Bloom, L. R., Fathima, S., … & Weinstein, C. (2011). *The Global Economic Burden of Noncommunicable Diseases*. Geneva: World Economic Forum. Retrieved 11/24/15 from http://www3.weforum.org/docs/WEF_Harvard_HE_GlobalEconomicBurdenNonCommunicableDiseases_2011.pdf

Bodenheimer, T., Lorig, K., Holman, H., & Grumbach, K. (2002). Patient self-management of chronic disease in primary care. *Journal of the American Medical Association, 288*, 2469–2475.

Bodenheimer, T. & Sinsky, C. (2014). From triple to quadruple aim: Care of the patient requires care of the provider. *Annals of Family Medicine, 12*(6), 573–576.

Bouchard, S. (2012, June 13). *Gambling with the future of healthcare.* Healthcare Finance News. [Interview with David Walker, former U.S. Comptroller General.] Retrieved 11/27/15 from http://www.healthcarefinancenews.com/news/gambling-future-healthcare

Botelho, R. (2015). Health coaching buddies. Retrieved from www.healthcoaching-buddies.com

Brodin, N., Eurenius, E., Jensen, I., Nisell, R., & Opava, C. H. (2008). Coaching patients with early rheumatoid arthritis to healthy physical activity: A multicenter, randomized, controlled study. *Arthritis and Rheumatism, 59*(3), 325–331. doi:10.1002/art.23327

Caldwell, K. L., Grey, J., & Wolever, R. Q. (2013). The process of patient empowerment in integrative health coaching: how does it happen? *Global Advances in Health and Medicine, 2*(3), 48–57. doi:10.7453/gahmj.2013.026.

CareCloud & QuantiaMD. (2014). *The second annual practice profitability index. Tracking operational and financial health of US physician practices.* Retrieved 11/27/15 from http://on.carecloud.com/ppi-report-2014.html?lead_source=web&lead_source_detail=carecloud.com&ls_description=ppi-report-2014-resource-page

CareerBuilder. (2013). *More than one third of employed health care workers plan to look for a new job this year, CareerBuilder health care study reveals.* CareerBuilder. [Press Release.] Retrieved 11/27/15 from http://www.careerbuilder.com/share/aboutus/pressreleasesdetail.aspx?sd=4/30/2013&id=pr754&ed=12/31/2013

Center for Disease Control and Prevention. (2015). *Chronic Disease Overview*. Retrieved 11/27/15 from http://www.cdc.gov/chronicdisease/overview/index.htm

Center for Disease Control and Prevention. (2015). *Healthy Living*. Retrieved 8/14/15 from http://www.cdc.gov/healthyliving

Dossey, B. M., Luck, S., & Schaub, B. G. (2014). *Nurse coaching: Integrative approaches for health and wellbeing*. North Miami, FL: International Nurse Coach Association.

Drake, D. B. (2015). *Narrative coaching: Bringing our new stories to life*. Petaluma, CA: CNC Press.

Durand, M. A., Moulton, B., Cockle, E., Mann, M., & Elwyn, G. (2015). Can shared decision-making reduce medical malpractice litigation? A systematic review. *BMC Health Services Research, 15*, 167. doi:10.1186/s12913–015-0823–2

Edelman, D., Oddone, E. Z., Liebowitz, R. S., Yancy, W. S., Olsen, M. K., Jeffreys, A. S., … Gaudet, T. (2006). A multidimensional integrative medicine intervention to improve cardiovascular risk. *Journal of General Internal Medicine, 21*(7), 728–734. doi:10.1111/j.1525–1497.2006.00495.x

Fichtenberg, C. M., & Glantz, S. A. (2002). Effect of smoke-free workplaces on smoking behavior: Systematic review. *British Medical Journal, 325*, 188–194.

Frates, B., & Moore, M. (2013). Health and wellness coaching: Skills for lasting change. In J. Rippe (Ed), *Lifestyle medicine* (2nd ed., pp. 343–62). New York: CRC Press.

Friedberg, M. W., Chen, P. G., Van Busum, K. R., Aunon, F., Pham, C., Caloyeras, J., … & Tutty, M. (2013). *Factors affecting physician professional satisfaction and their implications for patient care, health systems, and health policy*. [Research Report.] Santa Monica, CA: RAND Corporation. Retrieved 11/27/15 from http://www.rand.org/pubs/research_reports/RR439.html

Friedmann, P., Rose, J., Hayaki, J., Ramsey, S., Charuvastra, A., Dube, C., ... Stein, M.D. (2006). Training primary care clinicians in maintenance care for moderated alcohol use. *Journal of General Internal Medicine*, *21*, 1269–1275.

Galantino, M. L., Schmid, P., Milos, A., Leonard, S., Botis, S., Dagan, C., ... Mao, J. (2009). Longitudinal benefits of wellness coaching interventions for cancer survivors. *International Journal of Interdisciplinary Social Sciences*, *4*(10), 41–58.

Garman, A.N. & Lemak, C.H. (2011). Developing healthcare leaders: What we have learned, and what is next. *National Center for Healthcare Leadership*. [White Paper]. Chicago, IL. Retrieved 11/27/15 from http://www.nchl.org/Documents/Ctrl_Hyperlink/doccopy6816_uid2202015927061.pdf

Gazelle, G., Liebschutz, J., & Riess, H. (2015). Physician burnout: Coaching a way out. *Journal of General Internal Medicine*, *30*(4), 508–513.

Goldman, M. L., Ghorob, A., Eyre, S. L., & Bodenheimer, T. (2013). How do peer coaches improve diabetes care for low-income patients? A qualitative analysis. *The Diabetes Educator*, *39*(6), 800–810. doi:10.1177/0145721713505779

Grant, A. M., Curtayne, L., & Burton, G. (2009). Executive coaching enhances goal attainment, resilience and workplace well-being: A randomised controlled study. *The Journal of Positive Psychology*, *4*(5), 396–407.

Haidet, P., & Paterniti, D.A. (2003). Building a history rather than taking one a perspective on information sharing during the medical interview. *Archives of Internal Medicine*, *163*(10),1134–1140.

Harrison, P. L., Pope, J. E., Coberley, C. R., & Rula, E. Y. (2012). Evaluation of the relationship is between individual well-being and future health care utilization and cost. *Population Health Management*, *15*, 325–330.

Healthcare industry (2015). Retrieved 12/28/15 from https://en.wikipedia.org/wiki/Healthcare_industry

Henochowicz, S., & Hetherington, D. (2006). Leadership coaching in health care. *Leadership & Organization Development Journal*, *27*(3), 183–189.

Hersey, J. C., Khavjou, O., Strange, L. B., Atkinson, R. L., Blair, S. N., Campbell, S, ..., Britt, M. (2012). The efficacy and cost-effectiveness of a community weight management intervention: A randomized controlled trial of the health weight management demonstration. *Preventive Medicine*, *54*(1), 42–49. doi:http://dx.doi.org.proxy.lib.duke.edu/10.1016/j.ypmed.2011.09.018

Hignite, K. (2008). STRATEGY: Segmenting risk. *NACUBO HR Horizons*, *3*(2), June 2010.

Hill, B., Richardson, B., & Skouteris, H. (2015). Do we know how to design effective health coaching interventions: A systematic review of the state of the literature. *American Journal of Health Promotion*, *29*(5), e158-e168. doi:http://dx.doi.org/10.4278/ajhp.130510-LIT-238

Hojat, M., Louis, D. Z., Markham, F. W., Wender, R., Rabinowitz, C., & Gonnella, J. S. (2011). Physicians' empathy and clinical outcomes for diabetic patients. *Academic Medicine*, *86*(3), 359–364.

Huffman, M. H. (2009). Health coaching: a fresh, new approach to improve quality outcomes and compliance for patients with chronic conditions. *Home Healthcare Nurse*, *27*(8), 490–496.

Institute of Coaching (2015). Retrieved 11/30/15 from http://www.instituteofcoaching.org/

International Nurse Coach Association (2015). Retrieved 11/24/15 from http://inursecoach.com/certificate-program/

Izumi, S., Ando, K., Ono, M., Suzukamo, Y., Michimata, A., & Fukuhara, S. (2007). Effect of coaching on psychological adjustment in patients with spinocerebellar degeneration: A pilot study. *Clinical Rehabilitation*, *21*(11), 987–996.

Jordan, M. (2013). *How to be a Health Coach: An Integrative Wellness Approach*. San Rafael, CA: Global Medicine Enterprises, Inc.

Jordan, M., Wolever, R. Q., Lawson, K. L. & Moore, M. (2015). National training and education standards for health and wellness coaching: The path to national certification. *Global Advances in Health and Medicine*, *4*(3), 46–56. doi: 10.7453/gahmj.2015.039

Joseph-Williams, N., Elwyn, G., & Edwards, A. (2014). Knowledge is not power for patients: A systematic review and thematic synthesis of patient-reported barriers and facilitators to shared decision making. *Patient Education and Counseling*, *94*(3), 291–309. doi:http://dx.doi.org.proxy.lib.duke.edu/10.1016/j.pec.2013.10.031

Keyes, C. (2002). The mental health continuum: From languishing to flourishing in life. *Journal of Health and Social Behavior*, *43*(2), 207–222.

Kivelä, K., Elo, S., Kyngäs, H., & Kääriäinen, M. (2014). The effects of health coaching on adult patients with chronic diseases: A systematic review. *Patient Education and Counseling*, *97*(2), 147–157.

Kobau, R., Sniezek, J., Zack, M. M., Lucas, R. E., & Burns, A. (2010). Well-being assessment: An evaluation of well-being scales for public health and population estimates of well-being among US adults. *Applied Psychology: Health and Well-Being*, *2*(3), 272–297.

Kumanyika, S. K., Fassbender, J. E., Sarwer, D. B., Phipps, E., Allison, K. C., Localio, R., … Wadden, T. A. (2012). One-year results of the think health! study of weight management in primary care practices. *Obesity*, *20*(6), 1249–1257. doi:10.1038/oby.2011.329

Law, H., & Aquilina, R. (2013). Developing a healthcare leadership coaching model using action research and systems approaches – a case study: Implementing an executive coaching programme to support nurse managers in achieving organisational objectives in Malta. *International Coaching Psychology Review*, *8*(1), 54–71.

Leahey, T. M., & Wing, R. R. (2013). A randomized controlled pilot study testing three types of health coaches for obesity treatment: Professional, peer, and mentor. *Obesity*, *21*(5), 928–934. doi:http://dx.doi.org/10.1038/oby.2012.179

Linden, A., Butterworth, S. W., & Prochaska, J.O. (2010). Motivational interviewing-based health coaching as a chronic care intervention. *Journal of Evaluation in Clinical Practice*, *16*(1), 166–174.

Lindner, H., Menzies, D., Kelly, J., Taylor, S., & Shearer, M. (2003). Coaching for behaviour change in chronic disease: A review of the literature and the implications for coaching as a self-management intervention. *Australian Journal of Primary Health*, *9*(2/3), 177–185.

Livingstone, J. & Gaffney, J. (2013). IFS and health coaching: A new model of behavior change and medical decision making. In M. Sweezy & E.L. Siskind (Eds.), *Internal family systems therapy: New dimensions* (pp. 143–158). NewYork: Routledge.

Marrero, S. L., Bloom, D. E., & Adashi, E. Y. (2012). Noncommunicable diseases: A global health crisis in a new world order. *Journal of the American Medical Association*, *307*(19), 2037–2038.

Mattioli, D., Siconolfi, M., & Cimilluca, D. (2015, October 27). Walgreens, Rite Aid unite to create drugstore giant: Merger deal with $9.4 billion price tag comes as companies across health-care industry seek to bulk up. *The Wall Street Journal*. Retrieved 11/25/2015 from http://www.wsj.com/articles/walgreens-boots-alliance-nears-deal-to-buy-rite-aid-1445964090

McGowan, B. (2001). Self-reported stress and its effects on nurses. *Nursing Standard (Royal College of Nursing)*, *15*(42), 33–38. doi: 10.7748/ns2001.07.15.42.33.c3050.

McHugh, M. D., Kutney-Lee, A., Cimiotti, J. P., Sloane, D. M., & Aiken, L. H. (2011). Nurses' widespread job dissatisfaction, burnout, and frustration with health benefits signal problems for patient care. *Health Affairs*, *30*(2), 202–210.

Meadows, S. (2014, August 19). A physician with a troubled conscience puts himself on the couch: In 'Doctored,' Sandeep Jauhar examines a broken system. *The New York Times*. [Book Review of DOCTORED: The Disillusionment of an American Physician.]. Retrieved 11/22/15 from http://www.nytimes.com/2014/08/20/books/in-doctored-sandeep-jauhar-examines-a-broken-system.html

Meeto D. (2008). Chronic diseases: The silent global epidemic. *British Journal of Nursing*, *17*(21), 1320–5.

Moore, M., Jackson, E., & Tschannen-Moran. (2015) *Coaching Psychology Manual* (2nd ed). Baltimore, MD: Wolters Kluwer.

Nash, D. B., Fabius, R. J., Skoufalos, A., & Clarke, J. L. (2015). *Population health: Creating a culture of wellnesss* (2nd ed). Burlington, MA: Jones & Bartlett.

National Center for Healthcare Leadership (2014). Physicians leadership development programs: Best practices in healthcare organizations. Retrieved 11/27/15 from http://www.nchl.org/Documents/Ctrl_Hyperlink/NCHL_Physician_Leadership_Development_White_Paper_Final_05.14_uid9142015803251.pdf

National Consortium for Credentialing Health and Wellness Coaches (2015). Retrieved 11/27/15 from http://www.ncchwc.org/

National Health Service Evidence Centre (2014). *Does health coaching work? Summary of key themes from a rapid review of empirical evidence.* East of England: The Evidence Center for Health Education East of England (HEEoE). Retrieved 2/2/16 from https://eoeleadership.hee.nhs.uk/sites/default/files/Does%20health%20coaching%20work%20-%20a%20review%20of%20empirical%20evidence_0.pdf

National Health Service Leadership Academy. (2015). *Coaching register.* Retrieved 11/27/15 from http://www.leadershipacademy.nhs.uk/resources/coaching-register/

Newnham-Kanas, C., Gorczynski, P., Morrow, D., & Irwin, J. D. (2009). Annotated bibliography of life coaching and health research. *International Journal of Evidence Based Coaching and Mentoring, 7*(1), 39–103.

Norcross, J. C., Krebs, P. M., & Prochaska, J. O. (2011). Stages of Change. In J.C. Norcross, (Ed.), *Psychotherapy relationships that work: Evidence-based responsiveness.* Oxford, UK: Oxford University Press.

Olsen, J. M., & Nesbitt, B. J. (2010). Health coaching to improve healthy lifestyle behaviors: An integrative review. *American Journal of Health Promotion, 25*(1), e1–e12.

Patient-Centered Outcomes Research Institute (2015). Retrieved 11/30/15 from http://www.pcori.org/

The Patient Protection and Affordable Care Act (PPACA). (2010). 124 Stat. 119 through 124 Stat. 1025 (906 pages).

Physician Coaching Institute. (2015). Retrieved 11/23/15 from http://physiciancoachinginstitute.com

The Physicians' Foundation. (2008). *The physicians' perspective: Medical practice in 2008.* Retrieved 11/27/15 from http://www.physiciansfoundation.org/uploads/default/PF_Medical_PracticeSurvey_Report_2008.pdf

Pollack, K. I., Alexander, S. C., Coffman, C. J., Tulsky, J. A., Lyna, P., Dolor, R. J., ...Ostbye, T. (2010). Physician communication techniques and weight loss in adults: Project CHAT. *American Journal of Preventive Medicine, 39*(4), 321–328.

Rimmer, J. H., Rauworth, A., Wang, E., Heckerling, P. S., & Gerber, B. S. (2009). A randomized controlled trial to increase physical activity and reduce obesity in a predominantly African American group of women with mobility disabilities and severe obesity. *Preventive Medicine, 48*(5), 473–479.

Rogers, E. A., Hessler, D. M., Bodenheimer, T. S., Ghorob, A., Vittinghoff, E., & Thom, D. H. (2014). Diabetes peer coaching: Do 'Better patients' make better coaches? *The Diabetes Educator, 40*(1), 107–115. doi:10.1177/0145721713513178

Rollnick, S., Miller, W.R., & Butler, C.C. (2007). *Motivational interviewing in healthcare: Helping patient change behavior.* New York: Guilford Press.

Sacco, W. P., Morrison, A. D., & Malone, J. I. (2004). A brief, regular, proactive telephone 'coaching' intervention for diabetes rationale, description, and preliminary results. *Journal of Diabetes and its Complications, 18*(2), 113–118.

Sacco, W., Malone, J., Morrison, A., Friedman, A., & Wells, K. (2009). Effect of a brief, regular telephone intervention by paraprofessionals for type 2 diabetes. *Journal of Behavioral Medicine, 32*(4), 349–359. doi:10.1007/s10865-009-9209-4

Schneider, S., Kingsolver, K., & Rosdahl, J. (2014). Physician coaching to enhance well-being: A qualitative analysis of a pilot intervention. *Explore: The Journal of Science and Healing, 10*(6), 372–379.

Sforzo, G. A., Kaye, M., Ayers, G. D., Talbert, B., & Hill, M. (2014). Effective tobacco cessation via health coaching: An institutional case report. *Global Advances in Health and Medicine, 3*(5), 37–44.

Shanafelt, T. D., Boone, S., Tan, L., Dyrbye, L. N., Sotile, W., Satele, D., ... Oreskovich, M.R. (2012). Burnout and satisfaction with work-life balance among US physicians relative to the general US population. *Archives of Internal Medicine, 172*(18), 1377–1385.

Shanafelt, T. D., Gorringe, G., Menaker, R., Storz, K. A., Reeves, D., Buskirk, S. J., ... Swensen, S.J. (2015). Impact of organizational leadership on physician burnout and satisfaction. *Mayo Clinic Proceedings*, 90(4), 432–440.

Simmons, L. A., Wolever, R. Q., Bechard, E. M., & Snyderman, R. (2014). Patient engagement as a risk factor in personalized health care: A systematic review of the literature on chronic disease. *Genome Medicine*, 6(2), 16. doi:10.1186/gm533 [doi]

Sjöquist, E. S., Brodin, N., Lampa, J., Jensen, I., & Opava, C. H. (2011). Physical activity coaching of patients with rheumatoid arthritis in everyday practice: A long-term follow-up. *Musculoskeletal Care*, 9(2), 75–85.

Skinner, J. (2013). The costly paradox of healthcare technology. *MIT Technology Review*, 116(6), 69.

Smith, L. L., Lake, N. H., Simmons, L. A., Perlman, A. I., Wroth, S. & Wolever, R. Q. (2013). Integrative health coach training: A model for shifting the paradigm toward patient-centricity and meeting new national prevention goals. *Global Advances in Health and Medicine*, 2(3), 66–74. doi:10.7453/gahmj.2013.034

Spring, B., Schneider, K., McFadden, H. G., Vaughn, J., Kozak, A., Smith, M., ... Hedeker, D. (2010). Make better choices (MBC): Study design of a randomized controlled trial testing optimal technology-supported change in multiple diet and physical activity risk behaviors. *BMC Public Health*, 10(1), 586. doi:10.1186/1471-2458-10-586

Stober, D.R., Wildflower, L., & Drake, D. (2006). Evidence-based practice: A potential approach for effective coaching. *International Journal of Evidence Based Coaching and Mentoring*, 4(1), 1–8.

Stoller, K. J. (2013). Commentary: Recommendations and remaining questions for health care leadership training programs. *Academic Medicine*, 88(1), 12–15. doi: 10.1097/ACM.0b013e318276bff1

Terry, P.E., J. B., Xi, M. & Harvey, L. (2011). The ACTIVATE Study: Results from a group-randomized controlled trial comparing a traditional worksite health promotion program with an activated consumer program. *American Journal of Health Promotion*, 26(2), e64-e73. doi: http://dx.doi.org/10.4278/ajhp.091029-QUAN-348ADDTERRY

Thomas, M. L., Elliott, J. E., & Rao, S. M. (2012). A randomized, clinical trial of education or motivational-interviewing-based coaching compared to usual care to improve cancer pain management. *Oncology Nursing Forum*, 39(1), 39–49.

Thompson, M. R., Wolf, M. D., & Sabatine, M. J. (2012). Mentoring and coaching: A model guiding professional nurses to executive success. *JONA: The Journal of Nursing Administration*, 42(11), 536–541.

Thorn, M. P., & Raj, M. J. (2012). A culture of coaching: Achieving peak performance of individuals and teams in academic health centers. *Academic Medicine*, 87(11), 1482–1483.

Vahey, C. D., Aiken, H. L., Sloane, M. D., Clarke, P. S., & Vargas, P. D. (2004). Nurse burnout and patient satisfaction. *Medical Care*, 42(2: suppl), II-57–II-66.

Vale, M. J., Jelinek, M. V., Best, J. D., Dart, A. M., Grigg, L. E., Hare, D. L., ... McNeil, J. J. (2003). Health Coaching patients On Achieving Cardiovascular Health (COACH): a multicenter randomized trial in patients with coronary heart disease. *Archives of Internal Medicine*, 163(22), 2775–2783.

Wagner, M. (2013). Bringing outside innovations into health care. *Harvard Business Review. October 28, 2013.* Retrieved on 11/25/2015 from https://hbr.org/2013/10/bringing-outside-innovations-into-health-care/

Walston, S. L. (2014). Chief executive officers' perceived value of coaching: Individual and organisational influences. *Coaching: An International Journal of Theory, Research and Practice*, 7(2), 115–131.

Wennberg, D. E., Marr, A., Lang, L., O'Malley, S., & Bennett, G. (2010). A randomized trial of a telephone care-management strategy. *New England Journal of Medicine*, 363(13), 1245–1255.

Whittaker, K. S., Krantz, D. S., Rutledge, T., Johnson, B. D., Wawrzyniak, A. J., Bittner, V., ... Merz, C. N. (2012). Combining psychosocial data to improve prediction of cardiovascular disease risk factors and events: The national heart, lung, and blood institute–sponsored women's ischemia syndrome evaluation study.

Whittemore, R., Melkus, G.D., Sullivan, A., & Grey, M. (2004). A nurse-coaching intervention for women with type 2 diabetes. *Diabetes Educator, 30*(5), 795–804.

Williams, D. R., & Wyatt, R. (2015). Racial bias in healthcare and health: Challenges and opportunities. *Journal of the American Medical Association, 314*(6), 555–556. doi:10.1001/jama.2015.9260.

Williams, E. C., Kivlahan, D. R., Saitz, R., Merrill, J. O., Achtmeyer, C. E., McCormick, K.A., & Bradley, K. A. (2006). Readiness to change in primary care patients who screened positive for alcohol misuse. *Annals of Family Medicine, 4*, 213–220. doi:10.1370/afm.542

Wolever, R. Q., Caldwell, K. L., Wakefield, J. P., Little, K. J., Gresko, J., Shaw, A., ... Gaudet, T. (2011). Integrative health coaching: An organizational case study. *EXPLORE: The Journal of Science and Healing, 7*(1), 30–36. doi:10.1016/j.explore.2010.10.003.

Wolever, R. Q., Dreusicke, M., Fikkan, J., Hawkins, T. V., Yeung, S., Wakefield, J., ... Skinner, E. (2010). Integrative health coaching for patients with type 2 diabetes: A randomized clinical trial. *The Diabetes Educator, 36*(4), 629–639. doi:10.1177/0145721710371523

Wolever, R. Q. & Eisenberg, D. M. (2011, Oct 10). What is Health Coaching anyway? Standards needed to enable rigorous research. Invited Commentary, *Archives of Internal Medicine, 171*(22), 2017–8. doi:10.1001/archinternmed.2011.508.

Wolever, R.Q., Jordan, M., Lawson, K.L., & Moore, M. (2016). Advancing a new evidence-based professional in health care: Job task analysis for health and wellness coaches. *BMC Health Services Research., 16*, 205. doi:10.1186/s12913-016-1465-8

Wolever, R. Q., Simmons, L.A., Sforzo, G. A., Dill, D., Kaye, M., Bechard, E. M., ... Yang, N. A. (2013). A systematic review of the literature on health and wellness coaching thru 2012: Defining a key behavioral intervention in health care. *Global Advances in Health and Medicine, 2*(4), 38–57. DOI:10.7453/gahmj.2013.042

Yach, D., Hawkes, C., Gould, C.L., & Hofman, K. J. (2004). The global burden of chronic diseases. *Journal of the American Medical Association, 291*(21), 2616–2622.

Ziedonis, D. (2015, September 10). *Transforming mentorship through coaching.* Paper presented at Psychiatry Grand Rounds for University of Massachusetts Medical School, Worcester, MA. Retrieved on 11/27/15 from http://www.umassmed.edu/globalassets/psychiatry/grand-rounds/grand-rounds-092005–102015.pdf

Coaching in Relationships: Working with Singles, Couples and Parents

Yossi Ives

Whilst close personal relationships are recognized as having a significant bearing on a person's wellbeing (Baumeister & Leary, 1995; Cramer, 1998), little serious attention has been paid to the role of coaching in supporting the flourishing of relationships. While many coaches include relationship coaching among their repertoire of services, it lacks an underpinning theory and a structured practice. As an aspirational discipline fostering human flourishing, coaching is equipped to support people in pursuance of relationship fulfilment and success. This chapter seeks to promote further investigation into the psychology and practice of relationship coaching.

Coaching as applied to relationship contexts can be approached from various angles. Nelson-Jones (2006, p. 20) views the role of coaching as helping to 'improve and maintain their mind skills and communication/action skills,' whereas Allen (2013, p. 77) advocates a view of 'coach as expert' where the coach has valuable understanding on the psychology of family relations. However, Ives and Cox (2014) propose a more holistic view arguing that relationship coaching should combine the client's self-management skills, together with adjusting attitudes and perceptions, whilst acknowledging the interplay of certain psychodynamic factors.

The concept of relationship coaching has not been well-defined. The Relationship Coaching Institute (2016) simply says 'Relationship Coaching is the application of coaching to personal and business relationships.' Another definition: 'Relationship coaching is a life coaching specialization that helps people find greater fulfillment in their personal relationships' (Noomii, 2016). Neither provide an indication as to the substance of relationship coaching. Other more popular definitions focus on the role of the coach, but likewise provide limited indication of the nature of the discipline. Although no formal definition of relationship coaching has been previously established in the literature, based on Ives and Cox (2014), the following definition is proposed:

> Relationship coaching is a pragmatic, evidence- and theory-based intervention that integrates goal-focused and developmental coaching and draws on therapeutic insights to help clients transform their relationship competencies thereby enhancing their prospects of relationship success, whether in establishing a new relationship or improving an existing one for individuals, couples and parents.

Accordingly, relationship coaching would typically involve a fusion of 1) personal development activity, 2) goal focused work, accompanied by 3) an understanding of therapeutic concerns.

The chapter consists of three main sections: (1) It begins with a brief review of the limited related coaching literature and an exploration of how aspects of personal development, goal-focused and therapeutic approaches to coaching feature in relationship coaching. The chapter then (2) addresses the application of coaching to three main relationship contexts: coaching with single people seeking to form a relationship, coaching with couples who want to enhance their relationship, and coaching for parents desiring to create better a relationship with their children and teenagers. The chapter concludes with (3) a discussion about the boundaries between coaching and therapy.

LITERATURE THAT UNDERPINS RELATIONSHIP COACHING

Research suggests that the desire for close personal relationships is regarded as a basic human motive and need (Deci & Ryan, 2002). Baumeister and Leary (1995, p. 497) state that 'human beings have a pervasive drive to form and maintain at least a minimum quantity of lasting, positive and significant interpersonal relationships.' Relationship success or failure impacts significantly on life satisfaction (Myers & Deiner, 1995), as well as psychological and physical wellbeing (Schwartzer & Leppin, 1992). Romantic relationships are the cause of the greatest joys, such as a deep sense of connection and fulfilment (Hatfield & Rapson, 2002), but can also be the cause of much sorrow, even depression and homicide (Cupach & Spitzberg, 2011). Yet, despite the central importance of relationships to our lives, relationship coaching is an area that has not attracted significant attention in the coaching literature.

Relationship Coaching Literature

There is little evidence or research-based literature about coaching in relationship contexts. However, the general coaching literature suggests that relationship coaches would benefit greatly from knowledge of relationship issues and concerns. Bachkirova, Cox and Clutterbuck (2014) argue that each context brings its own issues and challenges. Drake (2011, p. 149) suggests that coaches require what he terms 'foundational knowledge', which extends to 'the requirements of specific applications' – including 'knowledge how', 'knowledge that' and 'knowledge why'. Therefore, Ives and Cox (2014) argue that an understanding of relationship issues is critical to provide a useful coaching experience.

The relationship coaching literature appears to be dominated by self-help texts that provide relatively little theoretical or empirical basis. When addressing single people, the focus is often on dating advice rather than on relationship dynamics. Some texts present useful structures for understanding the challenges of forming relationship, such as (Steele, 2008) 'Conscious Dating', which adopts a cognitive-behavioural approach and presents ten principles of successful dating, such as being 'the chooser' and a 'successful single'. Gunther (2010) also presents ten types of problematic practices that stymie successful forming of relationships, what she terms 'relationship saboteurs', to help people identify how they may be persistently undermining their own relationship success.

When it comes to addressing couples, there is even less literature from a coaching perspective, as the preferred paradigm is therapy. Some authors adopt the term coaching within a therapeutic framework, such as Greenberg's (2002) *Emotion-focused therapy: Coaching clients to work through their feelings*. A notable exception is the study by Miser and Miser (2008, p. 207) that discusses coaching with expatriate couples as 'a paradigm of possibility in which the coach is a collaborator with the couple in designing and creating the life the couple wants to achieve.' The challenges they describe, such as 'problem-solving, negotiating roles and responsibilities, resolving conflict, planning and taking action together' (p. 206), seem relevant to most couples. Another relevant study was conducted by Bolstad (n.d.), who approached working with couples from a Neurolinguistic Programming stance, suggesting that coaching couples requires transforming the way they communicate. Bolstad identifies how when couples come to coaching they are 'either experiencing serious, unpleasant, unresolved conflict or at least one partner feels lonely and has major unmet needs for love and closeness' and the coach is 'an ally who helps identify and extend existing relationship strengths and supports clients in reaching for their own best dreams.'

A review of the literature relating to coaching with parents reveals that coaching in this context is generally skills focused rather than developmental, and frequently focuses on children with a disability. For example, Graham, Rodger and Ziviani (2009) propose a process of 'Occupational Performance Coaching,' whereby parents are 'guided in solving problems related to achieving self-identified goals'. Another approach is set out by Shanley and Niec (2010), who discuss coaching techniques in their behavioural parent training based on modelling skills. They provided parents with phrases to repeat verbatim to their children and then praise their use of modelled phrases. From an emotions perspective, McGoldrick and Carter (2001, p. 281) view the goal of coaching as helping to strike a balance with their children 'without emotionally cutting off or giving in.' They advised parents to become observers of their role and behaviour within the family, and to affect change in themselves that can trigger change in the family through 'reciprocity of emotional functioning.'

Several studies see coaching as aimed at empowering parents. For example, Bamford, Mackew and Golawski (2012, p. 134) insist that parenting coaching is not about telling parents they are 'doing something wrong or that they must follow a certain script,' but rather about posing 'powerful questions to enable parents to understand themselves and their children better'. Similarly, Haslett (2013) found that coaching provided new mothers with a sense of perspective and the freedom to trust their own judgement. Haslett likened coaching to having a 'focusing partner' who listens 'without judgement but seeks to clarify what is said as a means of facilitating a deeper understanding of experience' (Haslett, 2013, p. 43).

Key Dimensions: A Literature Review

This section will now address key literature relevant to the three main components of relationship coaching highlighted in the introduction: personal development, goal-focused, and therapeutic aspects. While set out below as discrete elements, in reality coaching is a holistic and integrated framework that interweaves all aspects. For example, while forming a future-focused goal it may become apparent that the client is deeply hurt by a past relationship, or when addressing a client's attachment difficulties it may be helpful or necessary to explore new developmental perspectives.

Personal Developmental Dimensions

Whilst relationship coaching aims to help people to improve their abilities to successfully relate to another, the adult development literature recognizes that this capacity is enhanced or hindered by our perspectives. Ives (2011) suggests that relationship coaching is primarily developmental – insofar as it aims for significant new awareness and growth opportunities – and it is based on a belief in human capability and potential (Spence, 2007) and provides opportunities to develop that capability and potential. According to Cox and Jackson (2014), personal development involves learning from the past and using previous experiences as a platform for growth. It aims to foster personal development and attitude change aimed at a sustained impact, rather than achieving a 'quick fix'.

Similarly, Ives and Cox (2014) explain that relationship coaching is focused on enhancing perspectives and changing attitudes through expansion of horizons and fostering of different ways of forming judgements, enlarging what Mezirow (2000) calls our 'habits of mind'. The relationship coach uses such developmental paradigms to help clients to discard or modify a habit of mind, to see possible alternatives, and as a consequence to act differently in the world. Cox and Jackson (2014) explain how our mind expands as it becomes able genuinely to see more points of view, to gain a better understanding of aspects of ourselves. Ives and Cox (2014) add that during relationship coaching clients are encouraged and supported to challenge and expand perspective on themselves and their partner viewpoints, which enables clients to better understand the impact of their own behaviour on others, and other's behaviour on them.

Palmer and Panchal (2011) discuss two broad theoretical approaches towards human development, both of which are relevant to coaching about relationship issues. Whereas ego-development and life-stage theories of development are concerned with psychological development of the individual, life events and transitions theories of adult development encompass sociological triggers for growth, development and change. Ego development and life stage theories of development, such as those developed by Erikson (1959), Levinson (1978) and Kegan (1994), present life as a series of major stages marked by particular dilemmas and responsibilities. In Erikson's theory, people go through a series of age-correlated conflicts and the outcome of each stage depends on how they handle these challenges. The literature shows that developmental issues can impact greatly on relationships: Teenagers may engage in unconventional behaviours in order to fit in with their peers. Couples who marry young sometimes have a higher risk of growing apart and relationship breakdown, what Oppenheimer (1988) describes as a 'maturity effect'. As adults gradually become more autonomous they attain a more universal perspective or increased wisdom, which should contribute to improve relationships but can also be disruptive if one partner matures at a different rate than the other.

Donaldson-Feilder and Panchal (2011) cite Levinson's view that a mid-life transition occurs when dreams formed in early adulthood are reappraised and modified. If the dream forged in early life is not followed or is thwarted for whatever reason, the mid-life period can be traumatic, triggering a 'mid-life crisis' (Jacques, 1965) and can result in people growing apart from their partners. For relationship coaching, the work by Kegan (1994) into cognitive development is most relevant, as it focuses explicitly on how personal development affects our ability to foster effective relationships. Bachkirova and Cox (2007 p. 331) argue that Kegan offers 'the most comprehensive description of underlying structures that give rise to the natural emergence of the self in relation to others.'

Kegan (1982, 1994) explains that as people mature they find it possible to interrelate in a more complex manner. They display enhanced autonomy and 'separation' so that the pursuit of a relationship is not burdened by a high level of dependence, yet sustain relatedness and 'inclusion' to foster intimacy. Kegan shows how people's perceptions of relationships are determined by what they perceive as 'self' and 'other' and their interrelations – what he terms 'subject–object relations'. As Bachkirova and Cox (2007 p. 331) explain: 'Things that are 'subject' in this theory are by definition experienced as unquestioned, simply a part of the self. Things that are 'subject' cannot be observed because they are a part of the individual, they cannot be reflected upon – that would require the ability to stand back and take a look at them. While things that are 'subject' *have* us, we *have* things that are 'object'. Sharma and Cook-Greuter (2010) propose that for successful relationships individuals should be supported to move towards being more inclusive, using 'both-and' rather than black and white thinking. According to Ives and Cox (2014), relationship coaching aims to help the client to approach relationships as 'object', in order to be able to act upon influences on relationships instead of being under their spell.

Ives and Cox (2014) highlight another aspect of personal development vital to relationship coaching: helping the client to become critically reflective of their assumptions, habitual responses and 'taken-for-granted beliefs' (Mezirow, 2000). Through transformative learning we reconstruct the stories – the 'dominant narratives' – we tell ourselves. As people confront relationship challenges, for example, the break-up of a relationship, critical reflection is needed to facilitate transformative learning, 'weighing the supporting evidence and arguments' and 'examining alternative perspectives,' which is enabled by 'an active dialogue with others to better understand the meaning of an experience' (Mezirow, 2000, p. 14). This may be facilitated by what Mezirow terms 'transformative learning', bringing to the fore 'the values that lead us to our perspectives' (2000 p. 8). The crucial part of transformative learning is 'becoming critically aware of one's own tacit assumptions and expectations and those of others, and assessing their relevance for making an interpretation' (2000, p. 4). The coach helps clients through critical discourse to assess their assumptions about themselves and their relationships and so lead towards a better understanding of both. The transformation may be 'epochal' involving a sudden shift in perspective, as in Hawkins and Smith's (2010) model of transformational coaching, but may also be a more transitional process, a gradual reorientation (Bridges, 1986).

Goal-Focused Dimensions

While relationship coaching seeks to understand the lessons from past experiences to generate insight and expand horizons, it remains forward-focused and goal-oriented. According to Ives (2011), it is helpful to view relationship coaching as goal-oriented, as a central component involves supporting the client to clarify his or her goal, to take effective action to pursue it, and to stay motivated throughout this process. Relationship issues often have a practical component that can be addressed through changes in behaviour. People with a possessive relationship orientation, for example, can be helped to set realistic levels of interaction with their partner, seek clarification from partners about their needs instead of anticipating them, and maintain friendships outside the relationships. However, even non-behavioural changes can also be set as goals, such as making tough choices, setting learning targets, and setting time limits for making decisions. Ives (2008) highlights three main aspects of goal construction: (1) goal setting ('what?'), (2) action planning ('when and how?'), and (3) motivation ('why?'). These aspects are briefly explored below in relation to relationship coaching.

Goal setting is a graduated process, in which setting the goal contributes to its achievement (Skiffington and Zeus, 2008).

Some clients will not have a clear goal in mind (Dembkowski & Eldridge, 2008) – for example whether they actually want a relationship. Carver and Scheier (1998) call these 'meta goals'; Whitmore (2003) calls them 'dream goals'; and Jackson and McKergow (2008) refer to them as the 'future perfect'. The second level defines the goal in operational terms, what the client wants to *do*, such as what kind of partner one should seek. However, the client is not always able to articulate a clear relationship goal. Therefore, as Stelter (2009, p. 207) advises, 'It is not always beneficial to define a goal at the beginning of the coaching session, but to allow narratives to unfold.' For this reason, Pemberton (2006, p. 67) advocates beginning with 'fuzzy vision', which 'validates people for not knowing precisely what they want.' In forming a practical relationship goal, as in all goal setting, there are three main factors for which it is essential to strike the right balance: goal proximity, goal specificity and goal difficulty, but for which there is no set formula (Locke & Latham, 1990).

Goal proximity involves setting relationship goals at suitable distances in time. Locke and Latham (1990) present goal setting and action planning as two separate stages in goal activity, each involving goals of different proximity: goal setting involves distal (long-term) goals, whereas action planning requires setting of proximal (short-term) goals. The goal of improving the relationship with a teenage daughter is a long-term objective that provides the basis for more practical goals for parents, such as setting individual time with each child. Distal goals need to be in concordance with the client's values and aspirations, and typically remain fixed unless there is a significant change in circumstances, whereas action planning are tactical and instrumental and focus on more immediate objectives (Latham, 2007).

Goal specificity enables a clear standard against which to measure attainment towards an improved relationship. 'Doing-your-best' or an unclear goal allows a person to settle for the lowest standard (Latham, 2007), as they 'are too indefinite and non-committing to serve as guides and incentives' (Bandura, 2001 p. 8). Flaherty (2005 p. 119) suggests that outcomes should be, 'stated in sufficient clarity that both parties [coach and client] will be able to recognize them as occurring or not, and also be able to discern what progress has been made toward them.' Thus, Alexander (2006) describes coaching as a precision tool to define words more precisely. A single person may say, 'I need to be more focused on choosing the right person' or a couple may say, 'we need to learn to communicate better,' but a specific goal would address specific issues, such as 'We will make a point of interrupting each other less' or 'I shall always give a compliment to my child when she is helpful.'

Goal difficulty refers to encouraging clients to set appropriately challenging relationship goals. Goal theory (Locke & Latham, 1990) posits that progress is primarily made when clients set challenging goals but which they consider attainable and realistic. In this conception, 'difficulty' is not an objective measure against a universal standard, but refers to the judgement of the individual, whether they are at the limit or close to the limit of the person's capabilities (Bandura, 1986). Relationship coaching needs to encourage the client to maintain goal difficulty at an optimal discrepancy level such that it sufficiently stretches them as a motivation to take action, but sufficiently narrows their focus to be considered attainable. Setting a goal such as 'Keep looking for a partner' is too easy of a goal, typically involving little new effort. Conversely, 'Go on a date every night' is probably too difficult a goal and may be abandoned as unrealistic.

Action planning is the stage that follows goal setting and, according to Grant (2006, p. 159), is 'the process of developing a systematic means of attaining goals.' 'Learning to put my past relationship behind me' is a fine goal, but planning is required to explore the various options and decide on a single action plan, as 'planning the when, where, and how of initiating goal-directed behaviours' (Gollwitzer & Schaal, 1998, p. 124). As relationship goals can be relatively long-term, it is particularly relevant to consider the advice of McDowall and Millward (2009, p. 74) that the goal should be 'unpacked into a hierarchy of concrete criterion-based sub-goals against which shorter timescales could be mapped.' Relationship coaching is best viewed as developing an ongoing engagement with the client, for as self-regulation theory (Carver & Scheier, 1998 p. 256) suggests, 'it makes sense to plan in general terms, chart a few steps, get there, reassess, and plan the next bits.' Detailed planning long into the future is not possible, as it 'would require omniscience to anticipate every situational detail' (Carver & Scheier, 1998, p. 256). An action plan must therefore be flexible (de Haan, 2008) as new issues arise on an ongoing basis, and would thus need to be continually reviewed during coaching. Action planning, Dembkowski and Eldridge (2008, p. 202) argue, often requires brainstorming options to 'develop a wider range of ways of achieving the goal,' as well as identifying strategies for achieving tasks (Kanfer & Ackerman, 1989).

Motivation is what drives a person toward their goal. According to self-determination theory (Deci & Ryan, 2002) fulfilling relationships are regarded as intrinsically motivated, so long as the person does not feel externally pressurized into entering them. Even where a relationship may be desired because of external reasons, such as financial stability, if the goal is well internalized (finds personal meaning in it) it may still be intrinsically congruent (Deci & Ryan, 1985). However, while pursuing relationship fulfilment can be very intrinsically motivational, it can at times also be profoundly challenging or dispiriting. Spence and Grant (2007, p. 185) argue that 'having a goal and owning a goal are not the same thing.' Coaching texts (Passmore, 2007; Pemberton, 2006) therefore advocate for the client to engage in activities that reinforce motivation and commitment. Ives and Cox (2012, 2014) highlight two particularly goal-focused motivational strategies: (a) Asking the client to identify and verbalize the benefits of achieving their relationship goal, a motivational interviewing approach which reinforces the goal (Passmore & Whybrow, 2007); and (b) Ensuring commitment by asking the client to rate from 1 to 10 their intention to carry out the steps planned to improve their relationships (see Whitmore, 2003), as articulating commitment is thought to increase the likelihood of actual implementation (Dunbar, 2009).

Therapeutic Dimensions

There are multiple psychological theories and approaches that are relevant to relationship coaching, but they are far too great to cover exhaustively or in detail. Some therapeutic models that have particular usefulness are summarized below. The suitability and application of Cognitive Behavioural Theory to coaching is well documented (e.g. Auerbach, 2006), highlighting how cognitions influence emotions and behaviour, which can influence relationship problems (Williams, Edgerton & Palmer, 2014). Ives and Cox (2014) show how Ellis' Rational Emotive Behaviour Therapy (Ellis, 1985; Dryden & Branch, 2008) and the ABCDEF model is well suited to Relationship coaching: An Activating event (e.g. relationship ends) arouses negative Beliefs ('I can't succeed at relationships') which has Consequences that hinder the client (the client avoids dating). The client needs to Dispute the presumed causal link between the A and B, thereby Effecting behaviour change and enabling creation of a more positive Future. The coach can help clients to be aware of how they perceive reality through such attribution schemas and perceptions of reality, which can hold them back from making things better.

A solution-focused approach (Grant, 2006) may also aid relationship improvement by averting attention from problems towards constructing solutions, as Steele (2008) highlighted. In this approach, clients focus only on the desired outcome and what it would feel like to achieve that outcome and therefore, Ives and Cox (2014) note, it is particularly suitable where couples are often 'at odds' with each other. Cavanagh and Grant (2014, p. 52) explain that 'a focus on solution talk, strengths and resources, rather than problem talk, was very effective for a large range of clients' and is effective when applied to coaching (Green, Oades & Grant, 2006). Coaches' texts (Jackson & McKergow, 2008; Szabo & Meier, 2009) explain that the solution-focused approach is underpinned by the assumption that a small adjustment can lead to a bigger change, because once we know what works we can do more of it and because small change can have a ripple effect. This is highly important in couple coaching, where often a sense of despair has already crept in. To affect positive change, solution-focused coaching leverages the client's own expertise and resources based upon their existing skills and prior success (Grant, 2006), such as identifying the attractive qualities in a partner or the moments when the couple are in harmony.

Attachment theory sheds light on the struggles that people face in relationships, and, in particular, offers valuable insights into the difficulties many single people face in forming and securing lasting relationships. Bowlby (1958, 1973) argued that children develop established relationship expectations from their interactions with primary caregivers. According to Hazan and Shaver (1987) these early attachments provide the template for future relationships and often carry over into adult romantic and parenting relationships. Bartholomew and Horowitz (1991) added further clarification, distinguishing between differing forms of avoidance. According to this view, there are broadly four styles of attachment orientation, as explained in detail in several excellent texts (Feeney & Noller, 1996; Rholes & Simpson, 2006).

Secure people find it relatively easy to get close to, trust, and depend on their romantic partners. They establish a long-term commitment, are responsive to their partner's needs, express feelings, articulate needs, and are willing to reveal their vulnerabilities. People with an *Avoidant* style tend to maintain emotional distance, struggle to articulate emotional feelings, and are reluctant to acknowledge their need for others. They become anxious with closeness, and find trust challenging. People with an *Anxious* style tend to be filled with worry and uncertainty about their romantic relationships. They suspect that they will not be loved and supported such that they often demand reassurance, becoming jealous and blaming, sometimes scaring their partner away. Those with a *Fearful* style tend to be ambivalent, desperately wanting yet afraid of closeness. They perceive themselves as unworthy of love and are afraid that they will be rejected. Thus, they vacillate between attachment and hostility.

While these mental models are generally stable, Ives and Cox (2014) explain that relationship coaching aims to change the attitudes and behaviour that arise from less than optimal relationship orientations through raising the client's awareness to their existence and impact. As Drake (2009, p. 57) suggests in relation to the workplace, encouraging adults 'to reflect on how their working models and their subsequent interpersonal patterns' interrelate can enable them to transition to more productive perspectives and behaviours. The relationship coach will benefit hugely from a thorough understanding of how attachment issues play themselves out in relationships.

Relationships are also at risk of boredom, what Bao and Lyubomirsky (2013) term 'hedonic adaptation' (becoming accustomed to pleasure), which is responsible for the waning of passion in couple relationship. Against this they propose a prevention model to reduce or stop the hedonic adaptation, such as increasing the number of positive events and emotions experienced together. Browne (2009) examined the potential of forgiveness therapy to resolve a personal conflict.

Ives and Cox (2014, p. 103) suggest that this would be 'useful in couples coaching, where acceptance of the faults of the partner are key to moving forward with the coaching task.' Hill (2010, p. 178) argues that for estranged couples forgiveness leads to a deep healing process, and is 'one of the most critical processes for facilitating restored relational and emotional well-being.'

CONTEXTS FOR RELATIONSHIP COACHING

This chapter addresses three contexts for applying relationship coaching: to help single people to form and secure sustainable relationships, to assist couples seeking to enhance their relationship, and to support parents looking to improve their relationship with their children. Before exploring this in greater detail, it is important to note evolving patterns in modern families and relationships and that formations of personal relationships are fluid and evolving (Allan & Crow, 2001). Strong and Cohen (2013, p. 22) describe the 'diversity of family lifestyles that people choose or experience.' Similarly, Long (2004) discusses the changing nature of parenting, such as the 'trend for families to live increasingly isolated and disconnected lives.' Mann (2009) shows how new complexities have entered into the picture of personal relationships, with changes in gender and racial identity, as well as a marked shift towards fewer marriages, more cohabitation and births outside of marriage, increased divorce, remarriage and reconstituted families as well as singles parents and smaller families. Walsh (2011 p. 3) also addresses the strengths and challenges of modern family configuration, such as adoptive, step and same sex families, in what she terms 'the new normal'. Helpful texts (e.g. Jordan and Carlson, 2014) address how to adopt a relational-cultural approach to support relationships through these complexities.

Singles Context

Singles is not a unitary category. The Relationship Coaching Institute (2015) identifies seven types of singles, including passively single, frustratingly single, and recently widowed or divorced. However, some major themes can be identified. When working with singles, the most important priority needs to be helping the client to gain clarity. Steele (2008, p. 68) states: 'If you're single and would prefer to be in a fulfilling relationship, I believe that the most important question for you to ask yourself is, "Why are you single?"' By 'Why?' he means 'What is getting in the way of your relationship?' Hence, Ives and Cox (2014) explain the purpose of coaching with singles is to help clients to identify what is getting in the way of a relationship and what needs to be addressed to maximize the chances of relationship success. Gunther (2010, p. 1) sets out a range of attitudes and practices that undermine relationship. She notes: 'Much of the time, relationship saboteurs are left confused, not knowing what they have done to cause their partners to pull away. Because the saboteurs don't understand what happened, they are likely to repeat the same undermining behaviours upon entering a new relationship.' Relationship coaching is premised on the principle that a person's thoughts and actions play a decisive role in relationships and that to change them we first need to be aware of them.

According to Ives and Cox (2014), many people are struggling to form lasting relationships, and coaching can help them to gain increased understanding of their situation and how to improve it. Some flit from relationship to relationship with little understanding of why they keep coming to an abrupt end. Others invest heavily in longer-term relationships that fail to result in lasting commitment. Some find they repeatedly reject their partners, whilst others find that they are often rejected. Parties to this continuous struggle end up frustrated, despondent and confused. To address this, Ives and Cox (2014) proposed the GREAT coaching model that emphasises exploring relationship perspectives, attitudes and strategies, with a view to expanding horizons and challenging assumptions. Ives (2011) describes how modest adjustments can significantly impact people's chances of success. Often, simple awareness of what is tripping them up is sufficient to radically improve their ability to navigate around the problem. Once the issue is revealed, clients are able to capitalize on their newfound insight.

Another key role for relationship coaching with singles is helping the client to observe patterns in their relationship experiences, as it enables the client to identify where along the relationship pathway issues normally arise. In keeping with Peterson's (2006) constraint model of coaching, relationship coaching is intended to help the client identify where there is a bottleneck in their 'pipeline' towards relationship success and to unblock those constraints. For example, Johnson (2004) explains that people with an anxious attachment orientation are strong at fostering a sense of closeness and intimacy, but they struggle to allow appropriate autonomy and self-sufficiency. Feeling insecure in relationships, they manifest obsessive or clingy behaviour (Feeney & Noller, 1996). A barrage of text messages, phone calls and emails may appear loving and caring, but to the recipient such attentions can feel suffocating. Demands for explanation about a partner's every move may have sincere motives, but can be experienced as highly intrusive.

> Kevin, a 31-year-old accountant, came to coaching both hurt and perplexed, as yet again a seemingly promising relationship had crumbled. Kevin started dating comparatively late in life, having struggled to emerge from the domination of overbearing parents. He would throw himself into any relationship that held some promise. While initially his partners would bask in the attention showered upon them, Kevin began to realize that they soon withdrew. Kevin did not realize, as Gunther (2010) explains, that flooding a partner with affections ceases to be endearing and can feel exhausting.

> Relationship coaching helped Kevin to set appropriate limits on the number of interactions he might have with a future partner, to be more cautious about asking intrusive questions and create a support mechanism for controlling anxiety-driven impulses.

Relationship coaching can also help singles to enter a relationship with the right kind of person for the right reasons. As Steele (2008) suggested, some people rush into almost any relationship, believing that this is their surest route to happiness. Some people start believing that there is a shortage of 'decent people' and that they should take whatever is on offer. Others are motivated by a sense of vulnerability and are searching for someone to rescue them. Conversely, some people think that their best chance of being in a relationship is to search for someone else to rescue, believing that their kindness will be repaid with love (Gunther, 2010).

For some single clients, coaching will help them to make sense of their conflicted relationship aspirations. Several theories contend that people consist of several parts that have differing preferences and needs (Schwartz, 1997) – what Ryan and Deci (2003) term multiple selves and Bachkirova (2011) describes as mini-selves – resulting in people seeking conflicting features in a partner. These various mini-selves operate mostly unconsciously, and therefore are typically unaware of each other's existence. The coach may need to help a client to recognize that when seeking a partner it may not be possible to please all parts of their persona (Bachkirova, 2011), and that one 'self' may need to be given overriding priority in the relationship context.

Problematic dating practices is another area that may need to be addressed in relationship coaching. Seeking to accentuate qualities judged to be attractive to another is common in relationship initiation (Bredow, Cate & Huston, 2011), leading some people to skew their image beyond reason. Rosen (2008) discusses changing courting behaviours, with a particular focus on how online dating leads to practices that are distinct from dating in person. Coaching can help transfer the cognitive insight into changes in behaviour. Pemberton (2006) refers to this as 'support for *thought*' and 'challenge for *action*', and Grant (2006, p. 157) terms it 'change his viewing' and 'change his doing'.

> Mandy, a 32-year-old lawyer experienced several dramatic but brief relationships. She was unaware that she had developed a hyper-dynamic persona to mask her internal fears stemming from a troubled upbringing. Through coaching, she was able to discern that behind the macho externality was insecurity resulting from rejection early in her life and resolved to present herself as more real and to look for the same in a partner.

Ives and Cox (2014) described the 'rollercoaster model of dating', whereby a relationship takes a steady but rather steep climb until it reaches the summit, before plunging down a precipitous drop, triggering an alarmed withdrawal from the relationship.

> Jenny, a vivacious 28-year-old advertising executive, came to coaching after her relationship ended with what she considered to be 'the man of her dreams'. She was initially swept away by this amazingly attractive and impressive man, but it became apparent that he had difficulty being open and had avoidant tendencies. Jenny was crushed when it dawned upon her that this picture of perfection was illusionary. This, it turned out, was a cycle that kept repeating itself. With this awareness it was possible to develop an effective strategy to break this cycle.

As the relationship becomes serious and turns towards commitment, some singles can enter into a state of panic and withdraw from the relationship. Such reactions are normally indicative of avoidance, ambivalence or even hostility to attachment (Feeney & Noller, 1996), 'attempting to avoid failure by avoiding commitment' (Steele, 2008, p. 71). People with an avoidant attachment style may sabotage their relationship efforts, often unconsciously. The coach can help the client to identify when and how this is happening and work on behaviour and attitude modification to make their avoidance tactics less pronounced.

> Jonathan, a 39-year-old graphic designer, had a history of entering into relationships and breaking off when things started to get 'too' serious. He was dating Debbie, whom everyone insisted was ideal for him, but Jonathan was experiencing his usual misgivings: 'There are some things about her that bother me; I can't go through with this'. The reasons were flimsy and by Jonathan's own estimation she met his key requirements. Debbie was ready to quit, having put up with Jonathan's endless prevarications. Jonathan was helped to understand that he had an avoidance issue and that his misgivings were based on his avoidant tendencies. With assistance and support, Dan was able to gain the perspective and the courage to propose.

While virtually no research has been conducted into the impact of relationship coaching on singles, a great deal of relevant quality literature is available. In particular, mention should be made of the *Handbook of Relationship Initiation* (Sprecher et al., 2008), which brings together a range of excellent chapters covering a vast array of issues relating to the formation of romantic relationships. Future research would do well to focus on any of the major areas just highlighted, but perhaps most important to study the value of coaching in addressing attachment issues – an area that is very well established from a therapeutic perspective. This section has addressed the role of coaching in addressing singles, where the focus is on forming or securing a relationship. The next section focuses on coaching couples, where there is often the added emotional entanglement that typically accompanies a long established relationship.

Couples Context

Numerous issues can introduce tension to an established relationship. A couple could disagree about whether or not to get married or whether or not to have a big wedding, which could raise doubts about commitment. If one partner wants children whilst the other does not, difficult choices will have to be made. These matters can become more sensitive and urgent, for example, if a partner is already pregnant and one of them is insisting on an abortion. Couples can also find themselves unable to resolve disagreements about where to live, whether to emigrate, gender roles, and many similar issues. Couples sometimes come to coaching accepting that their relationship has dissolved but unsure how to unravel it. Most often, the couple of have invested hugely in the relationship and are deeply distressed and worried about the way it has deteriorated.

Moreover, the challenges facing couples in our fast changing society are manifold. Women who were once expected to stay at home and raise their children are now expected to return to work several months following childbirth. Men, who once shunned domestic chores, are now increasingly expected to share in housekeeping responsibilities. In addition, both sexes are expected to be fully committed to their employer, often working at home in the evenings and at weekends. Many couples feel that their relationship has been neglected, or that the quality of their relationship has deteriorated – and this in a context in which people have greater expectations for a fulfilling relationship and are more ready to leave an unsatisfying one. Relationship coaching provides a framework for focused reflection for couples to improve their relationship.

Whenever possible, coaching for couples adopts a distinctive preventative approach, seeking to strengthen relationship capacities before issues reach a crisis point. Ives and Cox (2014) suggested the COUPLE model of coaching focused on strengthening relationships through encouraging examination of values, beliefs and assumptions and openness in communication. The model incorporates Commitment, Openness, Understanding, Performance, Learning and Evolution. At the heart of coaching for couples is an effort to identify what brings the parties together as a couple and focus on enhancing that, rather than overemphasizing that which is tearing them apart or on ensuring their individual needs are met. Ives and Cox (2014) argue that relationship coaching should not concentrate on what is perceived to be wrong in the relationship, but on strengthening the shared commitment to the relationship. Enhancing the insight of the couple both as individuals and as a unit are key to attaining those new capabilities, and this may include gaining fresh perspectives on the situation. As Cox (2013, p. 92) noted, 'We are more tolerant as we begin to see ourselves through the eyes of others.'

Helping the couple to compare and contrast their experiences, without blame or anger, they can be encouraged to take different perspectives and to develop alternative ways of looking at things. The coach's role is to create the space that will enable constructive conversation for the couple to examine together how they make meaning from their experience and from there go on to explore new possibilities. Ives and Cox (2014) argue that the key feature of coaching couples is the required presence of both partners. Leone (2013, p. 324) questions the validity of conclusions regarding the future of a relationship based on 'impressions of an unseen spouse' that 'based on only partial or limited information – not veridical truths.' Bolstad (n.d.) confirms that when just one partner has hired the coach, the coach is working only on an individual client basis rather than being responsible to the relationship. It is a dual encounter; in couples coaching the relationship is the client. Other authors adopt a similar orientation, with Kurtz and Ketcham (1992) advocating a 'relationship first' approach, and Browne (2009) highlighting the importance of forgiveness for healing a relationship.

Effective communication is thought to play a vital role in fostering the couples approach to a relationship sought in relationship coaching. Miser (2008, p. 1) argues that relationships are based on sets of shared values that guide 'choices and actions in life together' and explains how the values that a couple share and co-create could be seen as intrinsic to their 'couple-ness' and are a vital part of a successful relationship: 'Some couples value mutual understanding, validation, openness, compromise, and friendship. Other couples value individuality, expressiveness and passion. Still other couples value harmony, common ground and autonomy.' Ives and Cox (2014) suggest that fostering effective communication between partners depends on how the 'ownership' of issues are conceptualized.

Poor relationships are characterized by inadequate listening and constant interrupting, as Gottman et al. (1998) have demonstrated. So coaching endeavours to foster a happy relationship in which the partners seek clarification from one another, rather than a troubled one in which they tend to make assumptions. To foster more harmonious interactions, the coach may wish to highlight Rosenberg's (2003) Nonviolent Communication skills, an empathetic approach that acknowledges the other's feelings and needs. According to this model, people communicate a need, feeling, perception and request. Ives and Cox (2014) argue that this enables the couple to make decisions and solve problems effectively and to deal with disagreements without damaging the relationship.

This section dealt with the application of coaching to couples in a romantic relationship. While complicated in so many ways, it is still a relationship between two adults. The next section addresses coaching parents to more effectively approach their relationship with their children, with poses a range of new challenges.

Parenting Context

Bamford, Mackew & Golawski (2012, p. 134) note that, 'rapid social change has intensified pressure on the family.' Additionally, Berk (2006) highlights how the culture of long working hours and multiple pressures from housework, financial strains, the daily struggle of juggling childcare, homework, and ferrying kids around are among the many demands that put added pressures on parents. Added to this are the demands that children are under, which can make them difficult to manage, especially as they enter the teenage years. These demands include academic pressures to excel, peer pressures to conform, as well as social pressures emanating from the media and internet. Many parents feel overwhelmed by the demands of parenting and find themselves responding to immediate events rather than working to a longer-term parenting goal. This leaves some parents wracked with feelings of guilt and failure, as they worry that they are not raising their children effectively, as Ives and Cox (2014) explain. Coaching can help by creating a safe platform to discuss and plan parenting strategies, consider and determine priorities, and ensure their parenting values and practices are aligned.

Speaking about parenting as a single construct is simplistic (Eagle, 1995), since the role of the parent of an infant can be very different from the role of the parent of a teenager, and this is likewise very different from parenting a fully-grown adult. Added in are the cultures or backgrounds of the parents and of the society in which the children are raised, which shape the expectations of parents and their children and influence the relationships between them. Coaching provides support for functioning families where the parents recognize that their approach may not be working and are seeking to develop as parents and become better communicators and role models for their children. O'Brien and Mosco (2013, p. 93) point out how 'parenting styles are often not questioned until something goes awry' and that only then might parents look for help and 'discover they need to change how they are parenting.' While it is not the coach's role to provide answers to particular issues, he or she can help parents develop perspectives and strategies that enable them to feel more confident and competent (Ives & Cox 2014).

Parents coming to coaching may well be facing a problem and could be looking to find ways to 'fix' or 'cope' with their children. At the heart of coaching is the view that the parents need to invest in their own capabilities to identify new perspectives and approaches to create an effective parenting context. Accordingly, parenting coaching is not primarily about better ways to manipulate children to do the things that adults want them to do, but should involve creating an environment that supports and nurtures valued behaviours (Ives & Cox, 2014). Coaching can support parents in perceiving the home as an ecosphere; the key is to identify where changes could have the maximum impact and benefit. How the parents interact with one another and modelling adaptive behaviour are central to parenting (Grusec, 2002), as is adopting a 'co-parenting stance' (McHale & Fivaz-Depeursinge, 2010) in which both parents support a consistent line. Below is a sample of theories and approaches for coaches helpful when coaching parents:

Parenting Styles

Coaching itself is a relevant paradigm for parents to use in interacting with their children. In fact, Alegre (2011) found that children of parents who use a 'coaching style' of parenting are better behaved and have better physical health. A foundational and enduring conception for parenting is the well-established notion of 'authoritative parenting', eschewing an overly democratic or permissive approach that makes few demands or imposes few restrictions on children, whilst also critiquing an overly dictatorial style of parenting that allows for no negotiation and brooks little independence (Baumrind, 1967). O'Brien and Mosco (2013, p. 102) suggest that 'authoritative' parenting, as a parenting style, 'maintains its effectiveness across the developmental journey and is particularly valuable during the adolescent stage in its more democratic nature.' Authoritative parents are warm and responsive and have 'high age appropriate expectations and limits for their children and the provision of support to meet these' (p. 92). As noted, most research-based work on coaching in the parenting context focuses on skills, such a literacy, or disabilities, such as autism. It is suggested that through the coaching encounter coaches could role model and parents can role play effective communication styles, an idea that while touched upon (e.g. Hudson, 1999; Peltier, 2009) would benefit from further research.

Values-Based Parenting

To gain compliance from a child, parents are prone to use the metaphoric carrot or stick, promise of reward or threat of punishment (see Kohn, 2006). An alternative method is to inspire expected behaviour from children by putting moral values at the heart of the family's and the child's choice-making. In this approach parents help children to associate behaviours with values that are well understood and embraced by the entire family (Ives & Cyprys, 2016). Ives and Cox (2014) present a five-part approach to imparting values and good behaviour to children based on the notion that character building in young children needs to combine ideas and action. Their approach involves establishing common understanding of values through simplified concepts, stories and slogans.

Individuation

As noted earlier, attachment is a central issue in relationships, and parents can optimize their relationship with their child to benefit them in childhood and adulthood. As children grow up they need greater individuation, so parents need to moderate their attachment accordingly (Eagle, 1995). Lapsley and Stey (2012) highlight how as young people mature through a process of separation-individuation, they become increasingly differentiated from relational attachments, such as the mother, and come to see themselves as separate and distinct from the familial context. Saarni (2011) notes that changing demands for separateness and connectedness or intimacy during childhood necessitate an evolving attachment, involving ever increasing autonomy. For children this process involves a growing sense of empowerment and confidence that emerges from developing greater self-responsibility. Furthermore, as Byng-Hall (2008) argues, parents may need to consider how their own attachment strategies interact. Parenting coaching can support parents to establish a healthy balance of separation and closeness, autonomy and attachment. In well-differentiated families individuality is expressed while remaining intimately connected to others, whereas families in which this balance is lacking may experience extreme clinginess or detachment (Bowen, 1978). The coach can help a family restore balance of separateness and connectedness, striking the appropriate level of differentiation.

Emotion Coaching

Parenting adolescent children can be particularly challenging, in part because children in this age group struggle to regulate their own emotions (Larson & Sheeber 2008). Shortt, Stoolmiller, Smith-Shine, Eddy and Sheeber (2010, p. 3) explained how adolescence is a period of increased vulnerability because neural regulatory structures are still developing whilst the child is coping with increased emotionality and independence, thereby increasing the potential for externalizing behaviours such as 'academic failure, school drop-out, substance use, and delinquent peer affiliation' (p. 2). They found that 'maternal emotion coaching', which they describe as a 'socialisation process wherein parents provide guidance in understanding and coping with emotions' was effective in managing such relationships.

Emotion coaching includes parents increasing awareness and acknowledgement of emotion, showing respect for the child's emotional experience through offering comfort, advising on appropriate ways to express emotions and discussing strategies for dealing with emotional situations. Havighurst, Wilson, Harley and Prior (2010) confirmed that emotionally unsupportive approaches impact negatively on a child's socio-emotional functioning, whereas mothers who used an 'emotion coaching' approach showed 'more validating and affectionate behaviour and less contemptuous and belligerent behaviour' (Shortt et al., 2010, p. 8). Parenting coaching focused on enhancing emotional literacy and building emotional self-understanding and management is a particularly fruitful and valuable strand of further research.

CONCLUSION

'Relationships' is an extremely broad area, including siblings and friends, grandparents and co-workers, and this chapter has been unable to address all these areas. This leaves a huge amount of room for future work to explore the application of coaching to the full gamut of relationships. The extensive writing about the coaching relationship itself (e.g., de Haan & Sills, 2012; Palmer & McDowall, 2010) offers a great starting point for this continued work. As for the contexts of singles, couples and parenting addressed in this chapter, it should by now be apparent that coaching offers a non-clinical, and asset-focused framework to support people to greater success in these vital relationships.

As relationship issues are typically addressed in a therapeutic framework, it is valuable to explore in conclusion the place of coaching and how it differs from therapy, whilst remaining mindful that both coaching and therapy are fluid terms about whose characteristics and parameters there is still much debate. Ives and Cox (2014) argued that while relationship coaching incorporates therapeutic elements, it is fundamentally different to therapy. It has often been acknowledged (Hart et al., 2001; Peltier, 2009) that coaching is not a substitute for family therapy or counselling, which might focus more tightly on problems and problematic transactions within the family. Coaching benefits from having less of a stigma attached to it and from it being positively oriented, and may be preferred in some cases where both therapy and coaching are suitable options.

According to Bachkirova (2007, p. 357) whereas therapy focuses primarily on 'eliminating psychological problems and dysfunctions,' coaching has an overriding focus on 'enhancing life, improving performance.' Ives and Cox (2014) suggest that the main difference between coaching and therapy is about the kind of change that it seeks to affect: for coaching it is primarily around awareness and learning, whereas in therapy it is often on emotions and healing. However, theorists of both coaching and therapy may disagree, amplified by a recent trend towards integrative coaching-therapy (Popovic & Jinks, 2014; Lee, 2014). However, to be effective coaches do need a good grasp of psychological dimensions. Bachkirova (2007, p. 360) posits that to deliver developmental coaching the coach needs to understand theories and the processes that underpin adult development, including the dynamics of the coaching relationship, so as to 'notice and interpret developmental phenomena and blocks to development'. Where theories are used to facilitate development, the coach will always share such knowledge with the client.

Relationship coaching addresses attachment and similar psychological issues by raising awareness about the client's attitudes and behaviours, rather than a therapeutic approach focused on changing emotions (see Greenberg & Goldman, 2008). Coaching works primarily with cognition and the resultant behaviours, whilst therapy works primarily with emotion and the experiences that gave rise to them. Coaching texts (Starr, 2007; Rogers, 2008) note that coaching focuses on the regulation of attitudes and behaviours, rather than adjustment to the person's deep psychological processes. While coaching is less suited for enabling what Greenberg (2010, p. 37) terms 'enduring emotional change', coaching helps people 'learn to understand that certain emotional or somatic reactions are erroneous interpretations of what is occurring or belong to the past and are now irrelevant' (Greenberg, 2004, p. 6). Coaching and therapy exist along a spectrum and individual coaches or schools of coaching each have their own perspective, but it is argued here that coaching is primarily about helping the client to identify and understand their negative emotions and discover ways of handling them, and would not focus on accessing, venting or re-experiencing those emotions as is quite common in many therapies. Thus, arguably, if a client is experiencing particularly strong emotions, a therapeutic approach is more suitable.

For the same reason, it could be argued that whereas therapy often has as its central activity addressing unfinished business, such as addressing traumas from previous relationships, coaching concentrates on dealing with the current or future relationships. Coaching aims to enable the person to gain clarity around issues and it can help to map out likely consequences so they can be aware of their behaviour and why it is happening. Through this, clients can also recognize the triggers of the behaviour and take action to avoid reacting in a maladaptive manner; coaching is not designed to address the unfinished business itself. Ives and Cox (2014) argue that while therapy would tend more towards reducing the unpleasant affect to mitigate its impact on people's reactions, coaching looks to help people understand that their negative affect may not be a reason to avoid something. People can often override their instinct to avoid pain if they understand that either it will subside or it is unavoidable.

Another key difference between coaching and therapy lies in the role of the professional helper and the helping interaction. Davila and Cobb (2004, p. 151) suggest that the benefits of therapy are most often attributed to the impact of the therapeutic experience itself, including the values of the relationship with the therapist. By contrast, the benefit of coaching lies mostly in the coach's impact on the client's growth and personal development. Writing from a psychotherapeutic perspective, Purnell (2004) argues that the provider of help acts as a secure base from which it is possible for the client to embark on self-exploration, whereas in coaching the relationship between the coach and client is not viewed as a key mechanism for change (Ives & Cox, 2012).

Although little has been written about coaching in the relationship context, it is suggested that coaching is highly suited for helping people in many relationship situations. This chapter surveys the application of coaching to singles, couples and parents, but the relationship field is much wider than that. There is a growing awareness of the intergenerational aspects of relationships, varying family configurations and evolving relationship formations, all of which require careful research and thought into how coaching may be best able to provide relevant support. Virtually all people are in a relationship of one sort or another, and the potential for relationship coaching is vast. For it to realize this potential, there is a pressing need for evidence-based studies into the effectiveness of relationship coaching, as well as the specific approaches used by coaches.

REFERENCES

Alegre, A. (2011). Parenting styles and children's emotional intelligence: What do we know?. *The Family Journal*, 19(1), 56–62.

Alexander, G. (2006). Behavioural coaching: The GROW model. In J. Passmore (Ed.), *Excellence in Coaching* (pp. 83–93). London, England: Kogan Page.

Allan, G. & Crow, G. (2001). *Families, Households and Society*. Southampton, UK: Palgrave.

Allen, K. (2013). A framework for family life coaching. *International Coaching Psychology Review*, 8(1), 72–79.

Auerbach, E. A. (2006). Cognitive coaching. In D. Stober & A. M. Grant (Eds), *Evidence-Based Coaching Handbook*. New York: Wiley & Sons.

Bachkirova, T. (2007). Role of coaching psychology in defining boundaries between counselling and coaching. In S. Palmer & A. Whybrow (Eds), *Handbook of Coaching Psychology* (pp. 351–366). London, England: Routledge.

Bachkirova, T. (2011). *Developmental Coaching: Working With the Self*. Maidenhead, England: Open University Press.

Bachkirova, T., & Cox E. (2007). A cognitive-developmental approach for coach development. In Palmer, S. & Whybrow, A. (Eds.), *Handbook of Coaching Psychology: A Guide for Practitioners* (pp. 325–350). London: Routledge.

Bachkirova, T., Cox, E. & Clutterbuck, D. (2014). Introduction. In E. Cox, T. Bachkirova & Clutterbuck, D. (Eds.), *The Complete Handbook of Coaching* (pp. 1–18). London, England: Sage.

Bamford, A., Mackew, N. & Golawski, A. (2012). Coaching for parents: Empowering parents to create positive relationship with their children. In C. van Nieuwerburgh (Ed.), *Coaching in Education*. London, England: Karnac.

Bandura, A. (1986). *Social Foundations of Thought and Action: A Social Cognitive Model*. Englewood Cliffs: Prentice-Hall.

Bandura, A. (2001). Social cognitive theory: An agentic perspective. *Annual Review of Psychology*, 52, 1–26.

Bao, K. J. & Lyubomirsky, S. (2013). Making it last: Combating hedonic adaptation in romantic relationships. *The Journal of Positive Psychology*, 8(3), 196–206.

Bartholomew, K. & Horowitz, L.M. (1991). Attachment styles among young adults: a test of a four-category model. *Journal of Personal and Social Psychology*, 61(2): 226–244.

Baumeister, R. F. & Leary, M.R. (1995). The need to belong: Desire for interpersonal attachments as a fundamental human motivation. *Psychological Bulletin*, 117, 497–529.

Baumrind, D. (1967). Child care practices anteceding three patterns of preschool behavior. *Genetic Psychology Monographs*, 21, 43–48.

Berk, L. (2006). *Child Development*. London, England: Pearson/Allyn and Bacon.

Bolstad, R. (n.d.). *Couples Coaching: A 21st century NLP approach to working with couples*. Retrieved 16 December 2013 from: http://www.transformations.net.nz/trancescript/couples.html

Bowen, M. (1978). *Family Therapy in Clinical Practice*. New York: Jason Aronson.

Bowlby, J. (1958). The nature of the child's tie to his mother. *International Journal of Psycho-Analysis*, 39, 350–373.

Bowlby, J. (1973). *Attachment and Loss: Vol. 2. Separation: Anxiety and Anger*. New York: Basic Books.

Bredow, C. A., Cate, R. M. & Huston, T. L. (2008). Have we met before? A conceptual model of first romantic encounters. In S. Sprecher, A. Wenzel & J. Harvey, (Eds.), *Handbook of Relationship Initiation*. New York: Psychology Press.

Bridges, W. (1986) Managing organizational transitions. *Organizational Dynamics*, 15(1), 24–33.

Browne, P. E. (2009). *Forgiveness as a Counseling Intervention*, PhD Dissertation, Capella University. Retrieved 17 February 2014 from: http://media.proquest.com/media/pq/classic/doc/1711359521/fmt/ai/rep/NPDF?_s=HOGthK4LRx9pM9UWugymRL%2F84Bk%3D

Byng-Hall, J. (2008). The crucial roles of attachment in family therapy. *Journal of Family Therapy*, 30, 129–146.

Carver, C. S. & Scheier, M. F. (1998). *On the Self-regulation of Behaviour*. New York: Cambridge University Press.

Cavanagh, M. and Grant, A. M. (2014). Solution focused coaching. In E. Cox, T. Bachkirova & D. Clutterbuck (Eds.), *The Complete Handbook of Coaching* (pp. 51–64), 2nd Edn. London, England: Sage.

Cox, E. (2013). *Coaching Understood: A Pragmatic Inquiry into the Coaching Process*, London, England: Sage.

Cox, E., Bachkirova, T. & Clutterbuck, D. A. (Eds.) (2010). *The Complete Handbook of Coaching*. London: Sage.

Cox, E. & Jackson (2014). Developmental coaching. In E. Cox, T. Bachkirova & D. Clutterbuck (Eds.), *The Complete Handbook of Coaching* (pp. 215–227). London, England: Sage.

Cramer, D. (1998). *Close Relationships: The Study of Love and Friendship*. London: Oxford University Press.

Cupach, W. R. & Spitzberg, B. H. (Eds.) (2011). *The Dark Side of Close Relationships – II*. New York: Routledge.

Davila, J. & Cobb, R. J. (2004). Predictors of change in attachment security during adulthood. *Adult Attachment: Theory, Research, and Clinical Implications*, 133–156.

de Haan, E. (2008). *Relational coaching: Journeys towards mastering one-to-one learning*. Chichester: John Wiley & Sons.

de Haan, E. & Sills, C. (Eds.) (2012). *Coaching Relationships: The Relational Coaching Field Book*. Faringdon: Libri Publishing.

Deci, E. L. & Ryan, R. M. (1985). *Intrinsic Motivation and Self-determination in Human Behavior*. New York, NY: Plenum.

Deci, E. L. & Ryan, R. M. (2002) *Handbook of Self-determination Research*. Rochester: University of Rochester.

Dembkowski, S. & Eldridge, F. (2008). Achieving tangible results: The development of a coaching model. In D. Drake, D. Brennan & K. Gortz (Eds.), *The philosophy and practice of coaching: Insights and Issues for a New Era* (pp. 195–211). London, England: Wiley.

Donaldson-Feilder, E. & Panchal, S. (2011). In S. Palmer & S. Panchal (Eds.), *Developmental Coaching: Life Transitions and Generational Perspectives*. New York: Routledge.

Drake, D. B. (2009). Using attachment theory in coaching leaders: The search for a coherent narrative. *International Coaching Psychology Review*, 4(1), 49–58.

Drake, D. (2011). What do coaches need to know? Using the Mastery Window to assess and develop expertise. *Coaching: An International Journal of Theory, Research and Practice*, 4(2), 138–155.

Dryden, W. & Branch, R. (2008). *The Fundamentals of Rational Emotive Behaviour Therapy: A Training Handbook*, 2nd edn. Chichester: Wiley.

Dunbar, R. I. (2009). The social brain hypothesis and its implications for social evolution. *Annual Journal of Human Biology*, 36, 562–572.

Eagle, M. (1995). The developmental perspectives of attachment and psychoanalytic theory. In S. Goldberg, R. Muir & J. Kerr (Eds.), *Attachment Theory: Social, Developmental, and Clinical Theory* (pp. 123–150). Hillsdale, NJ: The Analytic Press.

Ellis, A. (1985). Expanding the ABCs concept of rational-emotive therapy. In M. Mahoney & A. Freeman (Eds.), *Cognition and Psychotherapy* (pp. 313–323). New York: Plenum.

Erikson, E. H. (1959). *Identity and the Life Cycle*. New York: Norton.

Feeney. J. & Noller, P. (1996). *Adult Attachment*. London, England: Sage.

Flaherty, J. (2005). *Coaching: Evoking excellence in others*. Oxford, England: Elsevier.

Gollwitzer, P. M. & Schaal, B. (1998). Metacognition in action: The importance of implementation intentions. *Personality and Social Psychology Review*, 2, 124–136.

Gottman, J. M., Coan, J., Carrere, S. & Swanson, C. (1998). Predicting marital happiness and stability from newlywed interactions. *Journal of Marriage and the Family*, 60(1), 5–22.

Graham, F., Rodger, S. & Ziviani, J. (2009). Coaching parents to enable children's participation: an approach to working with parents and their children. *Australian Occupational Therapy Journal*, 56(1), 16–23.

Grant, A. M. (2006). An integrative goal-focused approach to executive coaching. In D. Stober & A. M. Grant (Eds.), *Evidence-based Coaching Handbook* (pp. 153–192). New York, NY: Wiley.

Grant, A. M. & Cavanagh, M. (2014). Life coaching. In E. Cox, T Bachkirova & D. Clutterbuck (Eds.), *The Complete Handbook of Coaching* (pp. 298–312). London, England: Sage.

Green, L., Oades, L. & Grant, A. (2006). Cognitive-behavioral, solution-focused life coaching: Enhancing goal striving, well-being and hope. *The Journal of Positive Psychology*, 1(3): 142–9.

Greenberg, L. S. (2002). *Emotion-focused Therapy: Coaching Clients to Work Through Their Feelings*. Washington, DC: American Psychological Association.

Greenberg, L. S. (2004). Emotion-focused therapy. *Clinical Psychology & Psychotherapy*, 11(1), 3–16.

Greenberg, L. S. (2010). Emotion-focused therapy: A clinical synthesis. *The Journal of Lifelong Learning in Psychiatry*, 3(1), 32–42.

Greenberg, L. S. & Goldman, R. (2008). *Emotion-focused Couples Therapy: The Dynamics of Emotion, Love and Power*. Washington, DC: American Psychological Association.

Grusec, J. E. (2002). Parental socialization and children's acquisition of values. *Handbook of Parenting*, 5, 143–167.

Gunther, R. (2010). *Relationship Saboteurs*. Oakland, CA: New Harbinger Publications Inc.

Hart, V., Blattner, J. & Leipsic, S. (2001). Coaching versus therapy: A perspective. *Consulting Psychology Journal: Practice and Research*, 53(4), 229.

Haslett, S. G. (2013). How do parents experience coaching? A case study of 'Babies-Know'. Unpublished MA dissertation, Oxford Brookes University, Oxford, UK.

Hatfield, E. & Rapson, R. L. (2002). Passionate love and sexual desire: Cross-cultural and historical perspectives. In A. Vangelisti, H. T. Reis & M. A. Fitzpatrick (Eds.), *Stability and Change in Relationships* (pp. 306–324). Cambridge, England: Cambridge University Press.

Havighurst, S. S., Wilson, K. R., Harley, A. E. & Prior, M. R. (2010). Tuning in to kids: An emotion-focused parenting program – initial findings from a community trial. *Journal of Community Psychology*, 37(8), 1008–1023.

Hawkins, P. & Smith, N. (2010) Transformational coaching. In E. Cox, T. Bachkirova & D. Clutterbuck (Eds.), *The Complete Handbook of Coaching* (pp. 231–244). London, England: Sage.

Hazan, C. & Shaver, P. R. (1987). Romantic love conceptualized as an attachment process. *Journal of Personality and Social Psychology*, 52(3), 511–524.

Hill, E.W. (2010). Discovering forgiveness through empathy: implications for couple and family therapy. *Journal of Family Therapy*, 32, 169–185.

Hudson, F. M. (1999) *The Handbook of Coaching: A Comprehensive Resource Guide for Managers, Executives, Consultants and Human Resource Professionals*. San Francisco: Jossey-Bass.

Ives, Y. (2008). What is 'coaching'? An exploration of conflicting paradigms. *International Journal of Evidence Based Coaching and Mentoring*, 6(2) 100–113.

Ives, Y. (2011). What is relationship coaching? *International Journal of Evidence Based Coaching & Mentoring*, 10(2), 88–99.

Ives, Y. & Cox, E. (2012). *Goal-focused Coaching: Theory and Practice*. New York: Routledge.

Ives, Y. & Cox, E. (2014). *Relationship Coaching: The Theory and Practice of Coaching with Singles, Couples and Parents*. New York: Routledge.

Ives, Y. & Cyprys, N. (2016). Values-based parenting: a methodology for the internalisation of values in young children. In Ben-Avie, M., Ives, Y., & Loewenthal, K. (Eds.), *Applied Jewish Values in Social Sciences and Psychology*. (pp. 111–130). New York: Springer International Publishing.

Jackson, P. Z. & McKergow, M. (2008). *The Solutions Focus: Making Coaching and Change Simple*. London, England: Nicholas Brealey.

Jaques, E. (1965). Death and the mid-life crisis. *The International Journal of Psycho-analysis*, 46, 502.

Johnson, S. M. (2004). *The Practice of Emotionally Focused Marital Therapy. Creating Connections* (2nd ed.). New York: Brunner/Mazel.

Jordan, J. V. & Carlson, J. (2014). *Creating Connection: A Relational–Cultural Approach with Couples*. New York: Routledge.

Kanfer, R. & Ackerman, P. L. (1989). Motivation and cognitive abilities: An integrative/aptitude treatment interaction approach to skill acquisition. *Journal of Applied Psychology*, 74, 657–690.

Kegan, R. (1982). *The Evolving Self: Problem and Process in Human Development*. London: Harvard University Press.

Kegan, R (1994). *In Over Our Heads*. London, England: Harvard University Press.

Kohn, A. (2006). *Beyond Discipline: From Compliance to Community*. Alexandria, VA: ASCD.

Kurtz, E. & Ketcham, K. (1992). *The Spirituality of Imperfection: Storytelling and the Search for Meaning*. Nashville, TN, Abingdon.

Lapsley, D. & Stey, P. (2012). Dysfunctional individuation in early and late adolescence, Paper presented at the *14th Biennial Meeting of the Society for Research on Adolescence*, Vancouver, 10 March.

Larson, R. W. & Sheeber, L. B. (2008). The daily emotional experience of adolescents: Are adolescents more emotional, why, and how is that related to depression? In N. B. Allen & L. B. Sheeber (Eds.), *Adolescent Emotional Development and the Emergence of Depressive Disorders* (pp. 11–32). Cambridge, UK: Cambridge University Press.

Latham, G. P. (2007) *Work Motivation: History, Theory, Research, and Practice*. London: Sage.

Lee, G. (2014). The psychodynamic approach to coaching. In E. Cox, T. Bachkirova & D. Clutterbuck (Eds), *The Complete Handbook of Coaching* (2nd ed.; pp. 21–33). London, England: Sage

Leone, C. (2013). The unseen spouse: Pitfalls and possibilities for the individual therapist. *Psychoanalytic Dialogues*, 23(3), 324–339.

Levinson, D. (1978). *The Seasons of a Man's Life*, New York: Ballantine Books.

Locke, E. A. & Latham, G. P. (1990). *A Theory of Goal Setting and Task Performance*. Englewood Cliffs, NJ: Prentice-Hall.

Long, N. (2004). The changing nature of parenting in America. *Pediatric dentistry*, 26(2), 121–124.

Mann, R. (2009). Evolving family structures, roles and relationships in light of ethnic and social change. *Review for the Beyond Current Horizons Programme*. Bristol: Futurelab. www.beyondcurrenthorizons.org.uk/evidence/generations-and-life-course.

McDowall, A. & Millward, L (2009). Feeding back, feeding forward and setting goals. In S. Palmer & A. McDowall (Eds.) *The Coaching Relationship: Putting People First* (pp. 55–78). Hove, England: Routledge.

McGoldrick, M. & Carter, B. (2001). Advances in coaching: Family therapy with one person. *Journal of Marital and Family Therapy*, 27(3), 281–300.

McHale, J. P. & Fivaz-Depeursinge, E. (2010). Principles of effective co-parenting and its assessment in infancy and early childhood. In S. Tyano, M. Keren, M. Herrman & J. Cox (Eds.), *Parenthood and Mental Mealth* (pp. 357–373). Chichester: John Wiley.

Mezirow, J. (2000). Learning to think like an adult: Core concepts of adult learning theory. In J. Mezirow (Ed.), *Learning as Transformation: Critical Perspectives on a Theory in Progress*. San Francisco, CA: Jossey-Bass.

Miser, A. L. (2008). Connecting with your 'coupleness'. Retrieved 18 February 2014 from http://www.elysianenterprises.net/wp-content/

uploads/2011/09/Connecting-with-your-Couple-ness.pdf
Miser, A.L. & Miser, M.F. (2008) Couples coaching for expatriate couples. In M. Moral & G. Abbott (Eds.), *The Routledge Companion to International Business Coaching* (pp. 203–217). Abingdon, UK: Routledge.
Myers, D. G. & Diener, E. (1995). Who is happy? *Psychological Science, 6*, 10–19.
Nelson-Jones, R. (2006). *Human Relationship Skills: Coaching and Self-coaching*. London, England: Routledge.
Noomii (2016). http://www.noomii.com/relationship-coaching. Last accessed 06 June 2016.
O'Brien, K. & Mosco, J. (2013). Positive parent–child relationships. In S. Roffey (Ed.), *Positive Relationships* (pp. 91–107). London: Springer.
Oppenheimer, V. K. (1988). A theory of marriage timing. *American Journal of Sociology, 94*, 563–591.
Palmer, S. & McDowall, A. (Eds.) (2010). *The Coaching Relationship: Putting People First*. New York: Routledge.
Palmer, S. & Panchal, S. (Eds.) (2011). *Developmental Coaching: Life Transitions and Generational Perspectives*. New York: Routledge.
Passmore, J. (2007) An integrative model for executive coaching. *Consulting Psychology Journal: Practice and Research, 59*(1), 68–78.
Passmore, J. & Whybrow, A. (2007). Motivational interviewing: a specific approach for coaching psychologists. In S. Palmer & A. Whybrow (Eds.), *Handbook of Coaching Psychology: A Guide for Practitioners* (pp. 160–173). London, England: Routledge.
Peltier, B. (2009). *The Psychology of Executive Coaching: Theory and Application*. New York: Brunner-Routledge.
Pemberton, C. (2006). *Coaching to Solutions: A Manager's Toolkit for Performance Delivery*. Oxford: Butterworth-Heinemann.
Peterson, D.B. (2006). People are complex and the world is messy: A behavior-based approach to executive coaching. In D. Stober & A. M. Grant (Eds.), *Evidence-based Coaching Handbook* (pp. 51–76). New York: Wiley & Sons.
Popovic, N. & Jinks, D. (2014) *Personal Consultancy: A Model for Integrating Counselling and Coaching*, Hove, UK: Routledge.
Purnell, C. (2004). *Attachment Theory and Attachment-based Therapy*. Karnac Books.
Relationship Coaching Institute (2016). http://www.relationshipcoachinginstitute.com/what-is-relationship-coaching/. Last accessed 11 January 2016.
Rholes, W. S. & Simpson, J. A. (Eds.) (2006). *Adult Attachment: Theory, Research, and Clinical Implications*. New York: Guilford Press.
Rogers, J. (2008). *Coaching Skills: A Handbook*. New York: Open University Press.
Rosen, C. (2008). New technologies and our feelings: Romance on the Internet. In L. G. Whitaker (Ed.), *Getting Started in Sociology* (pp. 147–156). New York: McGraw Hill.
Rosenberg, M. (2003). *Nonviolent Communication: A Language of Life* (2nd ed.). Encinitas, CA: Puddle Dancer Press.
Ryan, R. M. & Deci, E. L. (2003). On assimilating identities to the self: A self-determination theory perspective on internalization and integrity within cultures. In M. R. Leary & J. P. Tangney (Eds.), *Handbook of Self and Identity* (pp. 253–272). New York: Guilford Press.
Saarni, C. (2011). Emotional development in childhood. In R. E. Tremblay, M. Boivin, & RDeV. Peters (Eds.), Encyclopedia on early childhood development (pp. 1-7). Montreal, Quebec: Centre of excellence for early childhood development and strategic knowledge cluster on early child development.
Schwartz, R. C. (1997). *Internal Family Systems Therapy*. New York: Guilford Press.
Schwarzer, R. & Leppin, A. (1992). Social support and mental health: a conceptual and empirical overview. *Life Crises and Experiences of Loss in Adulthood*, 435.
Shanley, J. R. and Niec, L.N. (2010). Coaching parents to change: The impact of in vivo feedback on parents' acquisition of skills. *Journal of Clinical Child & Adolescent Psychology, 39*(2), 282–287.
Sharma, B. & Cook-Greuter, S. (2010). Polarities and ego development: Polarity thinking in ego development theory and developmental coaching. Integral Theory Conference, August 2010, Pleasant Hill, CA. Retrieved 22 March 2014 from: http://integraltheory-conference.org/sites/default/files/itc-2010-papers/Cook-Greuter%20&%20Sharma_ITC%202010.pdf

Shortt, J. W., Stoolmiller, M., Smith-Shine, J. N., Eddy, J. M. & Sheeber, L. (2010) Maternal emotion coaching, adolescent anger regulation, and siblings' externalizing symptoms. *Journal of Child Psychology and Psychiatry, 51*(7), 799–808.

Skiffington, S. & Zeus, P. (2008). *Behavioral Coaching: How to Build Sustainable Personal and Organizational Strength*. Sydney: McGraw-Hill Australia.

Spence, G. B. (2007). GAS powered coaching: goal attainment scaling and its use in coaching research and practice. *Coaching Psychology Review, 2*, 155–167.

Spence, G. B. & Grant, A. M. (2007). Professional and peer life coaching and the enhancement of goal striving and well-being: An exploratory study. *The Journal of Positive Psychology, 2*(3), 185–194.

Sprecher, S., Wenzel, A., & Harvey, J. (Eds.). (2008).*Handbook of relationship initiation*. New York: Taylor & Francis.

Starr, J. (2007) *The Coaching Manual: The Definitive Guide to the Process, Principles and Skills of Personal Coaching*. Upper Saddle River, NJ: Prentice Hall.

Steele, D. (2008). *Conscious Dating: Finding the Love of Your Life in Today's World*. RC Institute.

Stelter, R. (2009). Coaching as a reflective space in a society of growing diversity – towards a narrative, postmodern paradigm. *International Coaching Psychology Review, 4*(2), 207–217.

Strong, B. & Cohen, T. (2013). *The Marriage and Family Experience: Intimate Relationships in a Changing Society*. Cengage Learning.

Szabo, P. & Meier, D. (2009) *Coaching: Plain and Simple*. New York: W. W. Norton & Co.

Walsh, F. (Ed.) (2011). *Normal Family Processes: Growing Diversity and Complexity*. New York: Guilford Press.

Whitmore, J. (2003). *Coaching for Performance*. London, England: Nicholas Brealey.

Williams, H., Edgerton, N. & Palmer, S. (2014). Cognitive behavioural coaching. In E. Cox, T. Bachkirova & D. Clutterbuck (Eds), *The Complete Handbook of Coaching* (2nd ed.; pp. 34–50). London, England: Sage.

PART V
Researching Coaching

31

Researching Outcomes of Coaching

Siegfried Greif

INTRODUCTION

The outcomes of coaching are manifold. They differ depending on the client and on the subject of the coaching. For example, a manager changes her management behavior as a result of coaching and gives her employees encouraging feedback more frequently. A project manager manages resistance to change and conflicts more constructively. An employee works more efficiently and remains calmer in stressful situations. Other clients reflect intensively on their professional and private life goals and draw important conclusions for themselves from this. In his review on coaching outcome studies, Grant (2013, p.32) names a sample of indicators of coaching efficacy, e.g. leadership style, reductions in wastage, psychological well-being, employees' absence due to sickness, personal resilience, well-being in the workplace, sales performance, safety behaviors, Return on Investment (ROI), and goal attainment.

As this list shows, the results of coaching are extremely heterogeneous raising a question as to whether coaching outcomes can be studied in a scientific manner. In order to be able to answer this question, the following chapter will begin with an analysis of the particular characteristics of coaching that must be taken into account when researching its manifold outcomes. Some specific issues following the above characteristics of coaching will be discussed with a review of approaches that can be used to address them. This chapter will deal with the various options for qualitatively or quantitatively recording and measuring complex and heterogeneous coaching outcomes, as well as considering the results found in existing studies.

THE PARTICULAR CHARACTERISTICS OF COACHING AND ITS OUTCOMES

The following section analyzes those characteristics of coaching that make the evaluation of outcomes difficult. An important lens by means of which these difficulties can be understood is to regard coaching as a complex and co-created service and to refer to the general literature on the features and outcome evaluations of such type of service.

The Intangibility of Coaching

The individual results achieved by coaching services are not things or material products that can be picked up and passed on physically to the client. Many outcomes are intangible. Examples are changes in the thoughts, feelings, intentions or actions of clients that are set in motion by coaching. Similar to other services, intangibility is a basic characteristic of coaching services. Schneider and Bowen (1995, p. 19) describe this particularity of services: 'Services tend to be acts and processes more than products; services yield psychological experiences more than they yield physical possessions.' Consequently, 'manage the intangible' is the key conclusion that Schneider and Bowen (1995, p. 20) draw for practice with regard to services. 'Capture the intangible' would be an analogous conclusion for the assessment of coaching outcomes.

Inseparability of Production and Consumption

For many services, the outcome is often realized before the end of the service provision. Visitors at a concert listen to the musicians while they are making music and enjoy the music while the service provided is in the process of being created. This points to a further general characteristic of many services: inseparability of production and consumption (Schneider & White, 2004, p. 6 f.). The service is at least partly delivered and at the same time consumed during the process of it being produced. This applies in part to coaching too. Coaching is co-created within the interactions between client and coach, but also subsequent to the coaching process through the self-directed action of the clients within their particular context. A short question posed by the coach may stimulate a self-reflective thought on the part of the client. In the course of the dialogue, supported by the coach through empathetic encouragement, this can then result in new plans. It is difficult to separate the process of value creation and consumption here. Substantial outcomes can be generated even in the first coaching session.

Heterogeneity

Services are often more heterogeneous than produced and retailed products both in their production and their delivery (Schneider & White, 2004). Differences between clients need to be taken into consideration in the interaction. This can lead to no two clients ever having taken advantage of exactly the same service. Coaches must not only take into account the demands, expectations and desires of the client but also explore and activate both their potential and their available resources. This heterogeneity makes researching the common outcomes of coaching more difficult and legitimizes the use of individual case studies that analyze the particular features of individual cases of interest.

In summary, coaching can be regarded as a prototypical service that fulfills to a great extent the three fundamental service characteristics of *intangibility*, *inseparability* and *heterogeneity*. Coaching outcomes embrace all tangible and, more importantly, intangible effects that occur in the moment of interaction between coach and client and between coaching sessions, as well as in the short and long term after the coaching has been formally ended.

ISSUES WITH EVALUATING THE OUTCOMES OF COACHING

It is difficult for customers to evaluate the quality of complex services: the process triggers uncertainty with regard to evaluation (Meffert & Bruhn, 2012). In order to reduce this uncertainty, customers resort to confidence-inspiring information such as relationship quality (that is, the perceived quality of the relationship between customer and service provider, and in particular the customer's subjective trust, as well as the level of familiarity between customer and service provider). Another information that customers use is the reputation of the provider or brand quality, both of which are known as 'surrogates' of quality criteria in service research (Meffert & Bruhn, 2012). An investigation into how coaching is marketed (Stephan & Gross, 2011) found that 58 percent of personnel managers who seek coaches, largely and by far most frequently rely on informal mouth-to-mouth recommendations within their networks.

Alvesson (2001) points out that problem-solving knowledge, which is sold by consultancies, is ambiguous and difficult to define and evaluate. The value of what is offered by consultancies is a matter of beliefs and of impressions. Reputation and image become therefore vital as a substitute for the ambiguities of the content, skills and knowledge of the professionals (Alvesson, 2001). Von Nordenflycht (2010, p. 161 f.), for example, analyzes services 'where the quality of an expert's output is hard for non-experts (i.e., customers) to evaluate, even after the output is produced and delivered.' He describes this kind of quality as 'opaque quality' and illustrates it with examples of various professional services: 'Was the ad agency's campaign responsible for a sales increase? Was the lawyer's argument responsible for the client's acquittal? Was the consultant's report responsible for the company's bankruptcy?' Coaching could be listed here as a further example, with such questions as: 'To what extent was the input from a coach responsible for the successful change?' In order to evaluate output of complex services, Von Nordenflycht (2010) considers it necessary to take into consideration such indirect influencing mechanisms as bonding, reputation, appearance, and ethical codes.

Consequently, it could be argued that scientific research and outcome studies can increase credibility and are of particular value for the reputation of the coaching profession due to the difficulties involved in assessing the effectiveness of coaching. The finding might be helpful in order to reduce the client's informational deficit when evaluating services. Schneider and Bowen (1995) argued that when the client has learned how to evaluate the outcomes as well as what active part they play in their co-creation, this can lead to an improvement of the outcomes. With evidence of such an effect in some complex services, they advocated that companies should reward training of this nature. The content of this chapter could serve as a potential basis for such training.

Coaching is not only difficult to evaluate on the basis of its intangibility, opacity and complexity, but also because of the confidential nature of the conversations. Outcome evaluation using scientific methods is thus more important for coaching than for other services. Leading professional bodies of coaching (for example the International Coach Federation) emphasize that the effectiveness of coaching methods must be scientifically grounded. Outcome research is thus essential for the reputation of the coaching profession and the continuous improvement of coaching methodologies.

METHODS AND RESEARCH DESIGNS FOR EVALUATION OF COACHING OUTCOMES

Many diverse scientific disciplines, traditions, and research perspectives are represented in the varying approaches to coaching research (Bachkirova & Kauffman, 2008). The research embraces case studies that use qualitative methods, within-subject studies that compare measures before and after the coaching intervention, and between-subject studies that assess the efficacy of coaching in comparison with control groups or alternative interventions (e.g. training). From 2000 to January 2011, Grant (2013) found 234 published outcome studies, among them 131 case studies, 77 within-subject studies and 25 between-subject studies. He emphasizes that case studies provide valuable insights when exploring the efficacy of coaching. However, within-subject studies with Randomized Controlled Trials (RCT), in which the effects of coaching are compared with control groups and allocation to the groups is randomized, deliver more meaningful evidence. They are rated as the 'gold standard' of evaluation.

One of the best ways in which to summarize RCT-studies and studies that compare improvements within treatment groups are meta-analyses. The central parameters estimated by meta-analyses in addition to the statistical significance are so called effect sizes. They show whether the effects of the interventions are small, medium or strong according to common standards.

So far, few such meta-analyses have been published in the field of business coaching. A first small meta-analysis concerning the effectiveness of executive coaching conducted by external coaches was published by De Meuse, Dai and Lee (2009). They found only six empirical studies, which all followed a within-subjects design (individual sample sizes were not specified). Theebom et al. (2014) performed a second meta-analysis of business coaching in organizations by external coaches. They identified 18 investigations in total: 8 RCT-studies with randomized control groups, 6 with non-randomized comparison groups, and 4 with one study sample each with before and after measurements; sample sizes were from N=14 to 103, and one exceptionally large sample of N=1,243). The third meta-analysis was presented by Jones, Woods and Guillaume (2015), evaluating executive coaching. It includes 17 investigations (14 RCT or comparison groups and three with before and after measurements; sample sizes were from N=14 to 127, with one exceptionally large sample of N=1,361). The fourth meta-analysis by Sonesh et al. (2015) investigates the outcome of coaching (undergraduates, MBA students, executive and non-executive clients) and explores different moderators of the effects (24 studies and 26 independent samples, within- and between-subjects design; sample sizes not specified).

According to the analysis by Jones et al. (2015), the medium effect sizes for the average effectiveness of coaching are small (d= 0.33), and according to Theebom et al. (2014) they are of a medium size (g=0.66). Kotte, Hinn, Oellerich and Möller (2016) summarize the overall effects found in these four meta-analyses (estimated by Cohen's d index or Hodges' g index, which is corrected for small samples). 40 Studies (overall N=3,756) show very small effect sizes, 17 studies low to medium (N=2,267), and 22 more than medium and up to high effect sizes (N=2,263). They conclude that coaching interventions do not always work as expected. The size of the effects of coaching varies depending on the criteria applied in the studies and possibly on the type of coaching.

There are limitations to meta-analyses. Since only quantitative and typical outcome criteria can be used, the number of representative studies is limited; effects are neglected that have been found using infrequently applied criteria, even when these effects are strong. Randomization of the groups in no way guarantees that the interventions are of a high quality. This suggests the need to conduct studies which research the effects achieved by well-trained coaches and to evaluate the quality of the coaching performance as a predictor of coaching effectiveness. Summaries of studies based on qualitative methods or case studies are needed as well in order to record what specific changes are to be observed in the course of the coaching process.

COACHING EVALUATION FRAMEWORK

In many coaching evaluation studies, the choice of criteria for evaluation appears to be at least partly arbitrary. Often, a small number of measurable output criteria are selected. The formulation of scientifically founded hypotheses about relationships between the criteria and assumptions about important prerequisites of a positive outcome is often neglected. In addition, the research evidence available about relevant criteria that have shown effects in several coaching evaluation studies are not taken into consideration. We can therefore assume that the chances of finding such effects are small. An evaluation model would provide a better opportunity for the systematic selection of relevant criteria. This model can be defined as a scientifically-informed framework that describes and explains the results of an intervention in terms of the criteria to be expected from the intervention as well as hypothetically relevant preconditions, contextual conditions, processes, factors for success, and the assumed relations between the criteria.

The structure of the coaching evaluation framework shown in Table 31.1 has been adapted from a mentoring evaluation model by Wanberg, Welsh, Hezlett, Martocchio and Ferris (2003). These authors differentiate between participant/relationship-antecedents and program antecedents, characteristics of the mentoring received, organizational context, and proximal and distal outcomes. Transferred to the field of coaching, antecedents are all those characteristics that are assumed to be present before the start of the first coaching session. Context conditions can be differentiated from antecedents. Their hypothetical influence exists solely during the performance of the coaching. As explained at the beginning, the results of the coaching are co-created by coach and client during the coaching process. The framework must therefore take into account both the characteristics and behavior of the client and coach as well as the coaching relationship.

The final outcomes after the coaching are divided into short-term (proximal) and long-term (distal) outcomes. In the majority of studies, outcomes are only described in summary. It would however be more accurate to name the period of time during which and under which conditions the results are to be expected (that is, during the coaching process, or in the short- or long-term after the coaching process has been ended).

In ideal case scenario all elements of this framework would be valuable. However, since it would appear to be impossible to include all the criteria of the evaluation framework in a single evaluation study, it is recommended to select those criteria that are assumed to be the most relevant.

TAXONOMIES OF OUTCOME CRITERIA

In his classic taxonomy, Kirkpatrick (1977) differentiates between four different types of assessment criteria for evaluating educational programs as well as other kinds of human resource development programs: (1) *Reaction* (e.g. customer satisfaction), (2) *Learning* (e.g. knowledge tests), (3) *Behavior* (e.g. behavior observation), and (4) *Results* (e.g. profit, return on investment, sales, production quality and quantity, costs, absenteeism or turnover). Kraiger, Ford and Salas (1993) have proposed a modification that takes into account the usual means of differentiating that are employed in the field of psychology and classify all of the striven-for effects as

Table 31.1 Framework of the general evaluation of coaching

Antecedents	Coaching process and effects	Proximal outcomes	Distal outcomes
Client characteristics	Client	Client	Client
Coach characteristics	Coach	Coach	Coach
Program antecedents	Coaching relationship		
Organizational context	Organization	Organization	

learning (Table 31.2). Ely et al. (2010), in their summary of leadership coaching outcomes, refer to this taxonomy, and differentiate between cognitive and affective learning outcomes. Jones et al. (2015) also make reference to this differentiation in their meta-analysis. They supplement it by adding Kirkpatrick's results category.

Table 31.2 also shows two other taxonomies: by Theebom, Beersma and Vianen (2014) in their meta-analysis of coaching studies and by Sonesh et al. (2015) who develop their taxonomy more inductively. In the subgroup of coachee outcomes, goals attainment and overall satisfaction are measures that are not subsumed jointly in a superordinate category. An advantage for the meta-analysis is that the effects can be interpreted less ambiguously.

The criteria that have been developed in coaching research are based in all subgroups almost exclusively on self-report data (Grant, Passmore, Cavanagh & Parker, 2010; Greif, 2013). This is the case for both qualitative and quantitative research methods in the form of written questionnaires (paper-pencil and online) or interviews with open or closed questions (multiple choice and ratings). Self-report data can be influenced by self-serving biases and unrealistic positive self-evaluations (Taylor & Brown, 1988). Theebom et al. (2014), for example, criticize the lack of investigations using objective achievement data. In their opinion, outcome studies should not be based on self-report questionnaires or qualitative interviews alone. Nevertheless, it is hardly possible to do without these methods. Self-serving illusions may even be partly protective for individuals in threatening situations und therefore correlate positively with well-being (Alicke & Govorun, 2005).

If the self-report questionnaires have been developed strictly according to the rules of test development (Lane, Raymond & Haladyna, 2015) and when their reliability and validity have been proven in several investigations, then it can be assumed that they deliver robust practical evaluation data. It could also be recommended that in future evaluation research,

Table 31.2 Comparison between different taxonomies of outcomes

Kraiger, Ford and Salas (1993)	Theebom, Beersma and Vianen (2014)	Sonesh et al. (2015)
Cognitive outcomes (verbal knowledge, knowledge organization and cognitive strategies), tested by recognition and recall tests	*Performance/skills:* Subjective and objective measures related to behavior (e.g. number of sales, ratings of job performance, questionnaire scales for leadership behavior).	*Relationship outcomes* Generic coach–coachee relationship Working alliance
Skills-based outcomes (skill compilation and automaticity), assessed through behavior observation methods and multi-source feedback ratings	*Well-being:* Subjective and objective measures of health (e.g. absence rates, Depression, Anxiety, Stress and Burnout scales).	*Coachee outcomes* • Goal attainment • Behavioral change • Work-related attitude change • Personal attitude change • Improved relations with others • Overall satisfaction with coaching • Cognitive change • Task performance
	Coping: Measures related to coping with present and future job demands and stressors (e.g. self-efficacy and mindfulness scales).	
	Work attitudes: Measures of cognitive, affective, and behavioral responses towards work and career (e.g. job satisfaction, organizational commitment, and career satisfaction).	
Affective outcomes (attitudinal and motivational outcomes), measured by self-report questionnaires	*Goal-directed self-regulation:* Outcome measures related to goal-setting, goal-attainment, and goal-evaluation (especially goal-attainment scales).	*Organization outcomes*

other methods are included: behavior observation, transcripts and linguistic analyses, achievement data, Key Performance Indices (KPI), or further types of data such as physiological measurements in stress management and health coaching.

MIXED QUANTITATIVE AND QUALITATIVE METHODS

Qualitative methods employ so-called triangulation in order to improve the quality of the analyses. Triangulation refers to the collection of data from multiple sources for the same event, for example, interviews, observation, documents, and video recordings or interviews with various people (Barusch, Gringeri & Molly, 2011, p. 12). Similarly, mixed methods studies, combining both qualitative and quantitative methods 'provide a fruitful approach for researchers seeking to capture more fully the complexity of the objects under study' (Hantrais, 2014, p. 133). In coaching outcome research in particular, the combination of both is seen as an adequate approach (Greif, 2011b).

A study by Bachkirova, Linet and Reading (2015) on a coaching and mentoring program at a London Deanery might serve as a recent example. They employed well-validated measures of standard questionnaires on Employee Engagement, Self-Efficacy and Self-Compassion in order to measure the outcomes quantitatively. Statistical comparisons of the scale values before and after the program showed highly significant improvements in all of the constructs measured (n=120, p<0.01) as well as effect sizes that vary between small and medium. In their qualitative analysis, Bachkirova et al. (2015) asked participants to describe in a word or phrase what difference the coaching and mentoring program had made to them. The authors performed a qualitative content analysis of the themes of the answers provided (Bachkirova, et al., 2015). Nearly all showed positive changes with examples of improved self-efficacy and confidence to make changes in the workplace. Only 4.96 percent mentioned effects that were not positive, showing that not all problems can be solved through coaching. This and similar studies can serve as a model for future evaluations that combine quantitative measures and qualitative assessments.

FREQUENTLY USED CRITERIA FOR EVALUATION OF COACHING OUTCOMES

In this section, constructs and criteria for outcome evaluation are discussed in terms of their use in coaching research. They can be employed for all elements of the outcome framework described in Table 31.1. The description of the criteria begins with outcomes that are assessed after the end of the coaching. The majority of studies use criteria from this group, and therefore we find here the greatest variation of these criteria.

Frequently Measured Proximal and Distal Post-Coaching Outcomes

In the evaluation framework in Table 31.1, a difference is made between proximal (short-term) and distal (long-term) outcomes after the coaching process has ended. The majority of evaluation studies refer to proximal outcomes and more studies applying distal outcomes are needed.

A further distinction is made between general and specific measures of outcomes in relation to proximal outcomes. General measures refer to measures that are used for evaluation without distinction in the field of training and other human resource development interventions. As suggested by Greif (2007) and Grant et al. (2010) in their reviews of the current state of coaching research, measures for more specific effects in coaching, such as an increase in self-reflection, need to be taken into account.

The taxonomy in Table 31.2 is similar to Sonesh et al. (2015), who developed an inductive taxonomy of frequently applied outcome measures. It does not, however, sum up typical measures such as goal attainment or self-efficacy into superordinate categories. In Table 31.3 only those criteria are included which, according to available evidence, are sensitive enough to record changes resulting from coaching, i.e. have consistently shown at least significant changes in different evaluation studies. More studies using identical measures are needed before we can identify those, which are to be particularly recommended because they tend to detect strong effects. Meanwhile this table provides an overview of possible measures for researchers who are looking for criteria for their evaluation studies.

General Post-Coaching Proximal Client Outcomes

In Table 31.3, ratings for satisfaction, success, or degree of goal achievement are classified within the category of proximal *general measures*. They are used in different fields of human resources development and beyond. For example, Blackman and Carter (2014b) questioned 644 coaching clients from 34 countries. 89 percent rated the coaching as successful. According to the meta-analysis performed by Theebom et al. (2014), goal attainment ratings belong to the subgroup of outcome measures related to goal-directed self-regulation and show strong positive effects (g=0.74; 11 studies, N=789). However, it is not clear whether the strength of these effects is caused solely by goal attainment ratings, since they are summed up with other goal-oriented self-regulation measures. Before-after-studies without control groups, which show very strong effects, are included in these results. In the meta-analysis by Sonesh et al. (2015) goal attainment ratings alone show only small effects (g=0.21; six studies, N=216). The effects on overall satisfaction with coaching are moderate (g=0.39; two studies, N=173). The coaching profession cannot be content with such low levels of improvement of perceived goal-attainment and satisfaction in comparison with control groups.

Table 31.3 Classification of post-coaching outcomes

	Proximal outcomes		Distal outcomes
	General measures	*Specific to coaching*	
Client	• Satisfaction • Success • Goal attainment • Affect • Self-esteem • Anxiety • Depression • General well-being	• Self-reflection • Self-efficacy • Specific improvements of performance and skills	• Job satisfaction • Career development • Work-life balance • Life satisfaction
Coach	• Satisfaction • General well-being • Self-esteem	• Self-reflection and continuous improvement • Professional skills	• Occupational success • Reputation • Income
Organization	• Satisfaction • Attainment of organizational goals • Commitment	• Specific leadership behavior • Team performance • Conflict management	• Organizational climate and culture • Organizational leadership behavior • Productivity • Efficiency • Cost reductions • Economic return

General measures for this group that frequently produce significant positive effects in evaluation studies are the robust and reliable PANAS-scales for measuring positive and negative affect or proven self-esteem scales, anxiety and depression questionnaires, and well-being questionnaires (see in Greif, 2007). Theebom et al. (2014) categorize them in their meta-analysis in the group of *Well-being-Measures*, and found significant middle-sized effects here (g= 0.46; ten studies; N=564). Jones et al (2015) detected strong effects in the group of affective outcome measures (δ=0.51, corrected population d statistic; ten studies, N= 592). The effects found in this group of measures are encouraging. Instruments measuring affect or well-being are normally short: it is advisable to consider them in future evaluation studies.

In addition, ratings of goal attainment may also be recommended as general measures of coaching outcome. The number of studies in the meta-analysis by Sonesh et al. (2015) where goal attainment resulted only in small effects, was small. The larger subgroup in the meta-analysis by Theebom et al. (2014), which included goal attainment, has however shown strong effects.

Specific Post-Coaching Client Outcomes

Measures that are more typical or specific to coaching and hopefully show stronger effects, are categorized in the second group of post-coaching outcomes. One characteristic effect after coaching is an increase in result-oriented self-reflection (Greif & Berg, 2011). In a RCT study by Röhrs (2011) on the coaching of students to improve their presentation behavior, middle-sized significant interaction effects were found for result-oriented self-reflection concerning the person's own presentation behavior. Improved self-efficacy can also be seen as a result that is typical for coaching (Grant et al., 2010). Theebom et al. (2014) combine them together with mindfulness scales in their rather heterogeneous Coping group, with their relatively small effect size (g=0.43; ten studies, N=1,703).

Coaching is frequently employed in order to bring about specific improvements of performance and skills. In their small meta-analysis, De Meuse et al. (2009) summarized the effects of the performance self-ratings of clients (six studies, N= 173) and ratings of the coaches or client's managers (four studies, N= 591). All of the studies are based on a within-subjects design. The effect sizes are very high for the studies with self-ratings (δ=1.27) and high for the other group (δ=0.50). However, they themselves acknowledge that the results from this small number of studies should only be generalized with caution.

In their meta-analysis, Theebom et al. (2014) take into account both subjective and objective outcome measures (e.g. number of sales, job performance rated by self, supervisors and peers) or scales, which assess behaviors needed for organizational effectiveness (e.g. transformational leadership behaviors). The effect sizes that are found by Theebom et al. (2014) for this admittedly relatively small group are large (g=0.60; six studies, N=2.007).

An example for the academic performance of university students measured by the average grades of the subjects that they had completed is to be found in a study by Franklin and Franklin (2012). They found highly significant and large long-term effects after coaching in comparison to a control and a group with a self-regulated treatment (12 months: d=0.60/0.76, 18 months: d=0.66/0.81; N=27/25, control N>2,000). We need more studies, testing the effects of coaching on measures of performance and skills, before we can derive reliable conclusions. However, the strong effects found in these existing studies seem remarkable.

Multisource Feedback methods (self-evaluation as well as parallel evaluations by line managers, colleagues and staff) are often used for evaluation when coaching is provided for managers with the goal of improving their leadership behavior. Atwater, Waldman and Brett (2002) point out in their general review of the research into Multisource Feedback that the hope that the evaluations from various sources would be consistent with the self-evaluations was not fulfilled. This creates various difficulties in terms of quality of evaluation and willingness of managers to change.

Multisource-Feedback has already been used in a large classic study with 1,202 senior managers conducted by Smither, London, Flautt, Vargas and Kucine (2003). In contrast to the comparison group, however, they did not find any significant improvement in the ratings of leadership behavior. After coaching, they more frequently found specific (rather than vague) goals and solicited ideas for improvement from their supervisors. The effect sizes were, however, small. In a RCT study by Röhrs (2011) on the coaching of students to improve their presentation behavior, no significant effects could be found either using multisource feedback. It is possible to explain such missing effects by inconsistencies of the multisource ratings over time.

The study by Smither et al. (2003) (above) involved a large number of participants and found only a low effect size. As this study was included in both the meta-analysis of Theebom et al. (2014) and separately in Jones et al. (2015), this one study had a major effect in reducing the overall effect sizes found in these meta-analyses. A closer look at the study shows that, besides possible inconsistencies in the ratings, there are additional reasons to doubt whether the quality of the study justifies its inclusion in the analyses. The participants in the coaching were not selected by random. Participation of the senior managers in the coaching program was very different in the units of the firm: often it was optional, some business units declined, and some required that all participate. It is possible that, by self-selection, self-confident managers did not choose coaching. The in-person-meetings with the coaches comprised only two or three hours. The goal was to help the senior manager interpret their multisource feedback results, and to create a development plan as well as ideas for improvement. It is therefore questionable whether such a complex goal can be achieved in such a short time.

In using coaching specific outcomes it is also important to acknowledge that coaching can have negative side effects for the client. In their study Schermuly et al. (2014) asked the participants to enumerate 'all harmful or unwanted results for coaches directly caused by coaching'. Sixty percent of the coaches reported results that fall for the authors into the category of 'negative effects' for their clients. The most frequent were 'problems of a deeper nature' that were touched upon and could not be dealt with (26%), modification of the original goals of the clients without the client's wishes (17%), and experiencing their work as being less meaningful (17%).

Distal Client Outcome

Some coaching effects need more time in order to unfold or may be seen as an indirect result of self-reflection or other changes. One example is general life satisfaction. This is not something that will be likely to improve after only a few coaching sessions but is possible through a process of regular self-reflection or conscious daily attention to positive experiences.

Green, Oades and Grant (2006) found significant long-term increases of up to 30 weeks in goal striving, well-being and hope in comparison to a wait-list control group. Franklin and Franklin (2012) conducted a study on long-term performance improvements after coaching of students after 12 and 18 months. When compared to a control group without treatment, significant improvements were found for both time points. In independently assessed academic performance, some 10 percent improved in comparison with the control group. There are a few more longitudinal studies with very specific coaching programs. Altogether, however, the existing studies deliver only very scattered results. By means of larger longitudinal studies with different panels and modern statistical models (Singer & Willett, 2003) it would be possible to derive more reliable insights into the short- and long-term effects of coaching.

Coach Outcome

Coaches are important partners in the co-creation of the coaching service. Evaluation research should not take into account the results of coaching for the clients alone. It can be useful for the professional development of coaches as well as for preparing them for the possible negative effects of their job. In Table 31.3 self-reflection and continuous improvement as well as professional skills are included as possible positive proximal results as well as the distal results occupational success, reputation and last but not least, income. There is however a general lack of investigations that focus on these outcomes.

In a recent study, Schermuly (2014) inquired into effects for the coaches that he calls 'negative'. Over 90 percent of coaches listed such effects. The most frequently named effects were disappointment that the coach could not observe the long-term influences of the coaching (45%), being personally affected by the subject (44%), and fear that they did not do justice to the coaching role (40%). In terms of long-term outcomes regarding income, it is interesting to find that 36 percent of coaches have the impression that they are underpaid.

Outcome for the Entire Organization

Criteria regarding this outcome group have received little research attention. General short-term criteria that should be named here include satisfaction of the organization representatives that has commissioned the coaching as well as that of stakeholders, and the attainment of short-term organizational goals that can generally be achieved through the coaching program. More specific outcomes would be individual improvements as required by the line manager of the coachee, for example with regard to leadership behavior or the reduction of conflict between individual leaders within the team. Long-term positive effects on the improvement of organizational climate and culture are not to be expected immediately after coaching. This and other changes may have an indirect long-term influence on Key Performance Indicators (KPIs) and economic return.

In terms of the use of ROI, Anderson and Anderson (2005) asked managers to deliver estimations by means of which they attempted to calculate individual *monetary benefit* and the *Return on Investment* (ROI) resulting from coaching for the entire organization. According to their calculations, the result was an amazing individual benefit in monetary terms of up to $240,625. When several managers and workers received coaching they claimed to observe large increases in the ROI of the entire company. Their numbers are however by no means based on real economic profits. They asked their clients for a subjective estimation of the proportion of individual increases in the revenue or the entire ROI of the company. This can lead to huge overestimations and is not suitable for use as a method for proving the objective benefits of coaching (Grant, 2012; Greif, 2013).

Economic return is classified as a distal outcome, since it takes time and often results from a combination of interventions and additional supportive processes. One example of a combined intervention is a change project in a major bank (Greif & Benning-Rohnke, 2015). Here, a new tool for customer advisory services was introduced, combined with training, individual goal definition in teams, individual implementation intentions, support by line managers, and special transfer coaching methods for bringing about consistent changes in behavior. Long-term profitability improved from a previous 92 to 118%, and customer numbers even increased by 105% from 38% to 78%. Participants and stakeholder attributed these results, to a large extent to the support provided by coaching, and in particular the changes in individual behavior towards customers brought about through coaching. This may indicate that coaching has an influence on the KPIs. It would not however be possible with this evaluation design to estimate the proportion that is to be attributed to coaching alone. The impressive results are evidently only made possible by the interaction of the various interventions.

ANTECEDENTS

Ely et al. (2010) emphasize the great importance of antecedents for evaluation of the effectiveness of coaching: they criticize the fact that antecedents have so far not received enough attention. In Table 31.4, characteristics of the clients and coaches as well as organizational preconditions are listed as hypothetically beneficial antecedents.

Only a few examples of studies can be listed in this category. In the largest international investigation into coaching so far, with 1,100 coaches and 1,800 coaching-clients, De Haan and Page (2013) have shown that there is a relationship between the client's conviction regarding his or her self-efficacy pre-coaching and the success of the coaching and self-efficacy as rated by the coach. A concept of *'coaching culture'* (Clutterbuck and Megginson, 2012) could also be seen as an organizational precondition of the effectiveness of coaching. Unfavorable preconditions are also reported: Blackman and Carter (2014a) found in their international survey of coaching clients that the clients regarded the personality or behavior of the coach as the greatest barrier to success.

ORGANIZATIONAL CONTEXT

Differently to antecedents, which influence the outcome *before* coaching engagements started, context conditions may affect the process *after* it has started. Coaching culture is a construct that refers to both. Beneficial organizational contextual conditions are useful when supporting and maintaining the coaching processes as well as the changes aimed at in the coaching. So far, there is very little empirical research on the subject. In a small study (N=21) with three different measuring time points, Hentrich, Müller, Zimber and Künzli (2015) have found that the level of goal attainment in coaching depends positively on the work decision latitude as well as on positive social climate (mutual interest, trust, openness, and humor).

Only two broad constructs can be identified, which are both very comprehensive and integrate a number of factors. The first, *coaching culture*, received particular attention in the general coaching literature. The second, *transfer climate*, can be found in the empirical research. They refer to a set of detrimental or beneficial organizational preconditions for the transfer and employment of what is learned in a particular application. Stewart, Palmer, Wilkin and Kerrin (2008)

Table 31.4   Antecedents of coaching outcome

Client
- Advance knowledge about coaching
- Realistic expectations
- Change motivation
- Self-reflection (trait)
- Persistency

Coach
- Social competencies
- Professional knowledge
- Self-efficacy
- Credit
- Advance clarification of expectations

Organization
- Enough time and money
- Coaching program announcement
- Acceptance of coaching in the organization
- Coaching culture

make reference to learning transfer research and explore individual and organizational facilitators and barriers to transferal in the field of coaching. In their first study, they sought to operationalize perceived transfer factors and interviewed 25 coaching clients, nine coaches and five organizational stakeholders. In the second study, an online self-report questionnaire assessing the factors was completed by 110 coaching clients. Results show a moderate correlation ($r=.319$, $p<.005$) between the client's perceived psychosocial transfer support from their managers and the application of the developments brought about by coaching ($r=.319$, $p<.005$).

Holton, Bates and Ruona (2000) have constructed a comprehensive Learning Transfer System Inventory (LTSI) whose factor structure could be confirmed repeatedly in the training field. The inventory measures eleven training-specific factors (e.g. learner readiness, motivation to transfer, positive personal outcomes) as well as five generic factors (e.g. transfer effort-performance expectations, openness to change and feedback). Schnieders (2016) has adapted the LTSI for the field of coaching. Using confirmatory factor analyses, she was able to validate the factor structures with good fit values in both a coaching and a training sample. However, several factors from the LTSI and the model by Stewart et al. (2008) refer to individual attributes of the learner (e.g. motivation or self-efficacy) and overlap with antecedents in our evaluation model in Table 31.3. Again, the predictive value for transfer of the transfer by supervisors is much lower than that of the individual motivation. Systematic transfer support by line managers is perhaps inconsistent in practice and therefore does not allow for high correlations.

COACHING PROCESS

As portrayed at the start, coaching is a service that is co-created by the coach and the client in the course of interactional processes. 'Process' can be defined as the course of interactions between coach and client, or common workflow that creates the service. Comparable to other types of services (Schneider & White, 2004), production and consumption of the service are, at least partially, not separable. In analogy to the insight that the 'route is the goal', we can assume that *the interaction process between coach and client is a substantial part of the outcome.*

One example for this is the '*relationship outcomes*', which are identified in the meta-analysis by Sonesh et al. (2015). They assume them to depend on the input of client and coach (attitudes, motivation and behavior) and to predict goal attainment and insight. In their model they differentiate between (1) '*emotional components of the coach-coachee relationship*' and (2) the '*working alliance*', which refers to the informational components, quality and strength of the collaborative relationship and mutual commitment to shared goals. In their meta-analysis, these two *relationship outcomes* are amongst the outcomes with the strongest effects (g=0.33, 3 studies, N=385; g=0.391, 3 studies, N=195). In other words, they could be classified as intervening outcome variables and resources for the client, which support proximal and distal goal attainment as listed in Table 31.3 above.

When summarizing research on interaction processes between coach and client, five methodologically distinguishable process research approaches can be discerned:

1 Self-reports of coaches and clients
2 Micro-analysis by Q-Methodology
3 Methods of behavior observation and interactional process analyses
4 Analyses of transcripts
5 Reconstruction of the coaches' and clients' subjective theories

Self-Reports

As previously mentioned, De Haan and Page (2013) reported data that showed that the supportive coaching relationship shows the strongest connections with coaching outcomes. Seen together, an appreciative and respectful relationship is certainly beneficial according to the correlations with the coaching results found in the study; however stronger relationships are found when coach and client work together in tandem on tasks or with regard to goal-orientation.

Micro-Analysis by Q-Methodology

Bachkirova, Sibley and Myers (2015) apply a different approach, a micro-analysis of coaching processes as viewed by 41 coaches from different countries and from a variety of coaching backgrounds. They performed an inverted factor analysis and correlated the rank orders of the coaches by their items describing typical coaching sessions. The method is unique in how it identifies the attributions of coaches about characteristics of the coaching process. It was possible to explain the correlations between coaches by a strong common factor, characterizing the coach as 'collaborative explorer' rather than 'informed expert'.

Behavior Observation and Interaction Process Analyses

The behavior of the coach within the interaction with the client is expected to be of crucial importance for the outcome of coaching. Models and behavior observation studies on hypothetical success factors of coach behavior that predict outcome have been inspired by research on the behavior and training of psychotherapists (Behrendt & Greif, 2016). An example model has been published by Greif (2010) that embraces seven *success factors of coach behavior*: (1) Appreciation and emotional support of the client, (2) result-oriented problem reflection, (3) result-oriented self-reflection, (4) reflection and calibration of affects, (5) clarification of goals, (6) resource activation, and (7) support of transfer into practice. Observers are trained to rate video or tape recordings of coach behavior consistently on the basis of an observation manual. First exploratory studies show that the ratings observed correlate with outcome criteria. For example, coach behavior that facilitates self-reflection correlates with a reduction of helplessness ($r= 0.56$) and resource activation with goal satisfaction ($r= 0.49$), measured after the coaching. It therefore seems possible to use these factors for coach training.

The limitation is that the observation focuses on the coach behavior and neglects the interaction with the clients. As an alternative, Ianiro, Schermuly and Kauffeld (2013) analyzed the videotaped interactions of coach-client dyads in their first coaching session. As expected, affiliative and self-assured behavior of the coach seemed to function as a model for similar client behavior and a positive coaching relationship. The behavior in the first session predicts coaching success, measured by ratings of the clients after the end of coaching.

Analyses of Transcripts

Geißler (2009) is one of the first to transcribe and analyze complete coaching conversations (9 coaching session with 3 dyads) using content analysis. Approximately 30 to 60% of the most frequently used communication on the part of the coach consists of asking the client questions. On the other hand, there are coaches who use other typical means of communication such as explaining (30%) or reflection (20%).

Graf (2015) developed a basic activities model of coaching and analyzed transcripts from business coaching using an exact linguistic method. She differentiates between four basic activities, namely *Defining the Situation*, *Building the Relationship*, *Co-constructing Change* and *Evaluating the*

Coaching. Each activity is subdivided into different communicative tasks. 'Defining the Situation' includes, for example, *Establishing the Coaching Realm, Methodological and Procedural Framing of Coaching* and *Temporal Framing of Coaching*. All of the activities are described using examples from her transcriptions.

A further methodological approach for the individual analysis of interaction transcripts consists of contrasting in the end successful and unsuccessful coaching sessions in the client's view using interpretative methods (Hempel & Schubert, 2013). When comparing a very successful course of coaching with an unsuccessful course of coaching, both of which having been conducted by the same coach, differences can be observed in result-oriented self-reflection and the planning of behavior modifications (Greif & Schubert, 2015).

Reconstruction of the Clients' and Coaches' Subjective Theories

The subjective theories of the coach and the client on concrete coaching experiences can be explored using a method called the *Coaching Explorer* (Greif, 2008; 2013). This method is generally used by the coach at the end of coaching in order to reconstruct and reflect on the results, subjective causes, and processes together with the client and to evaluate the completed coaching. It consists of a self-interview by the coach and an interview conducted by him with the client in the last coaching session. The method uses a simplified structure mapping technique with presentation cards (Scheele & Groeben, 1988) for visualization purposes. In contrast to the usual feedback methods, here the client and coach compare their visualized structure maps and reconstruct together the processes that made them possible. For a detailed description of the method, its social constructivist theoretical background and the research, see Johanning (2014).

Summary of Process Characteristics Beneficial to the Outcome

Table 31.5 lists constructs as well as process characteristics that potentially make the outcome of coaching possible. As has been shown, these characteristics can be examined either qualitatively or quantitatively, by means of self-reports as well as by observation and the analysis of transcripts or the reconstruction of the subjective theories of the persons involved. Since the research into connections of coaching process with coaching outcomes is still in its early days the list is still very provisional. Future challenges for theory development and research include questions as to how to study outcomes that are intangible and opaque, and where process and outcome are inseparable.

CONCLUSION

At the beginning of this chapter, coaching was characterized as an intangible co-created service that is hard to evaluate for both customer and client. The effectiveness of coaching can therefore easily be cast into doubt by sceptics. Methodologically sound scientific

Table 31.5 Coaching process

Coaching relationship
• Mutual respect and trust
• Working relationship
Coach behavior supporting the client
• Appreciation and emotional support
• Friendly and confident behavior
• Problem- and self-reflections with the client
• Goal clarification with the client
• Resource activation with the client
• Support of the client's transfer into practice
Client
• Problem- and self-reflection
• Goal commitment
• Determined implementation intention
• Self-efficacy

examinations therefore have a particularly important role to play in the evaluation of coaching outcomes. In this chapter a general framework for the evaluation of coaching was presented that exemplifes a systemic approach to coaching outcomes. The following conclusions indicate relevant implications for further research:

(1) Coaching Works, but Stronger Effects and More Evidence Based on Performance Criteria and Long-Term Outcome are Needed

Randomized control studies and meta-analyses show that coaching works. The effect sizes however vary greatly between studies. Outcome criteria which show strong effects are rare and can often only be found in subgroups of meta-analyses with small numbers of studies. Improvement of the effects of coaching is a challenge for the profession. Most outcome studies so far are based largely on self-report with standardized questionnaires or qualitative surveys. It would be desirable in future to have more outcome studies with performance criteria which focus on the long-term organizational effects, in particular Key Performance Indices. Their inclusion in meta-analyses shows encouraging results, but the number of studies is still too small to draw any general conclusions.

(2) Possible Negative Side-Effects of Coaching Need Attention

Does coaching only ever have positive side-effects for all concerned? Negative side-effects appear to be rare and not strong. It would be important to understand more about the negative side-effects of coaching for both clients and coaches, and maybe also for the organizations, in order to reduce them by means of suitable measures.

(3) Antecedents and Context Conditions Need to be Studied

Client, coach and Organizational characteristics, which could have a positive influence on the outcome in the form of antecedents, has thus far not been paid enough attention. A favorable transfer climate can be measured in coaching by the same means with which it is measured for training. It can be recommended that it does not remain forgotten in future outcome studies.

(4) Multidisciplinary Studies of the Coaching Processes have to be Encouraged

Studies into the coaching process have been lacking because they are not easy to be organized for pragmatic reasons. Recently, small studies have been published that apply qualitative as well as quantitative analyses and criteria, transcripts, behavior observation or subjective perceptions based on methods taken from different scientific disciplines such as psychology, communication studies and linguistics with behavior observation. More of this type of research would be desirable. What has so far been investigated is the non-verbal and verbal behavior of the coach and their hypothetical effects on outcomes. Insight gained in this way could be useful for the future training of coaches. What appear to be particularly interesting however are the theories and analyses concerning the interactions of coaches and clients as well as micro-processes through which the outcome of coaching is co-created. More attention could be paid to outcomes when analyzing transcripts or behavior observation that are already visible directly during the process. Comparisons of the interaction processes between different coaching approaches would furthermore be of interest (Bachkirova, 2013).

(5) Future Measures are Necessary that make the Intangibles Visible

Coaching research today focuses on measures of constructs, which are assessed by means of self report or overt interactive behavior and performance. Future research might use more indirect and sophisticated outcome measures, e.g. projective tests of implicit motives (Baumann, Kazén & Kuhl, 2010) or of subconscious implicit memories of intentions (Goschke & Kuhl, 1996). In the field of stress management and health coaching today, physiological measures are already in use (Greif, 2011a; Newnham-Kanas, Gorczynski, Morrow & Irwin, 2009).

Coaching outcome research is fascinating not only for scientists. It is hoped that the various multi-layered questions and studies discussed in this chapter will stimulate the curiosity of professional coaches, clients and customers, and ideally their interest in taking an active part in future coaching research. The field of coaching research is still very young and there is a great deal still to be discovered.

REFERENCES

Alicke, M. D. & Govorun, O. (2005). The Better-Than-Average Effect. In M. D. Alicke, D. A. Dunning & J. I. Krueger (eds.), *The Self in Social Judgment* (pp. 85–106). New York, NY, US: Psychology Press.

Alvesson, M. (2001). Knowledge work: Ambiguity, image and identity. *Human Relations*, 54(7), 863–886.

Anderson, D. L. & Anderson, M. C. (2005). *Coaching that Counts: Harnessing the Power of Leadership Coaching to Deliver Strategic Value*. Amsterdam: Elsevier Butterworth-Heinemann.

Atwater, L. E., Waldman, D. A. & Brett, J. F. (2002). Understanding and optimizing multisource feedback. *Human Resource Management*, 41(2), 193–208.

Bachkirova, T. (2013). Developmental Coaching – Developing the Self. In J. Passmore, D. B. Peterson, T. Freire (eds.), *The Wiley-Blackwell Handbook of the Psychology of Coaching and Mentoring* (pp. 135–154). New York: Wiley-Blackwell.

Bachkirova, T. & Kauffman, C. (2008). Many ways of knowing: How to make sense of different research perspectives in studies of coaching. *Coaching: An International Journal of Theory, Research and Practice*, 1(2), 107–113.

Bachkirova, T., Linet, A. & Reading, E. (2015). Evaluating a coaching and mentoring program: Challenges and solutions. *International Coaching Psychology Review*, 10(2), 175–189.

Bachkirova, T., Sibley, J. & Myers, A. C. (2015). Developing and applying a new instrument for microanalysis of the coaching process: The coaching process q-set. Human Resource Development Quarterly. Published online in Wiley Online Library (wileyonlinelibrary.com). DOI: 10.1002/hrdq.21215, pp. 1–32.

Barusch, A., Gringeri, C. & Molly, G. (2011). Rigor in qualitative social work research: A review of strategies used in published articles. *Social Work Research*, 35(1), 11–19.

Baumann, N., Kazén, M. & Kuhl, J. (2010). Implicit motives: A look from personality systems interaction theory. In O. C. Schultheiss & J. C. Brunstein (eds.), *Implicit Motives* (pp. 375–403). Oxford: Oxford University Press.

Behrendt, P. & Greif, S. (2016). Erfolgsfaktoren im Coachingprozess. In S. Greif, H. Möller & W. Scholl (eds.), *Handbuch Schlüsselbegriffe im Coaching*. Heidelberg: Springer (in print).

Blackman, A. & Carter, A. (2014a). Barriers to successful outcomes from coaching, *4th Annual European Mentoring and Coaching Research Conference, June 26th–27th 2014*, http://research2014.emccconference.org/speakers/alison-carter-anna-blackman-2 (retrieved 14.10.2014). Cergy Pontoise University. Paris, France.

Blackman, A. & Carter, A. (2014b). Initial findings from the Coaching for Effectiveness Survey, *4th Annual European Mentoring and Coaching Research Conference, June 26th–27th, 2014*, http://research2014.emccconference.org/speakers/alison-carter-anna-blackman (retrieved 14.10.2014). Cergy Pontoise University. Paris, France.

Clutterbuck, D. A. & Megginson, D. (2012). *Making Coaching Work*. London: CIPD.

De Haan, E. & Page, N. (2013). Outcome report: Conversations are key to results. *Coaching at Work*, *8*(4), 10–13.

De Meuse, K. P., Dai, G. & Lee, R. J. (2009). Evaluating the effectiveness of executive coaching: Beyond ROI? *Coaching: An International Journal of Theory, Research and Practice*, *2*(2), 117–134.

Ely, K., Boyce, L. A., Nelson, J. K., Zaccaro, S. J., Hernez-Broome, G. & Whyman, W. (2010). Evaluating leadership coaching: A review and integrated framework. *Leadership Quarterly*, *21*(4), 585–599.

Franklin, J. & Franklin, A. (2012). The long-term independently assessed benefits of coaching: A controlled 18-month follow-up study of two methods. *International Coaching Psychology Review*, *7*(1), 33–38.

Geißler, H. (2009). Die inhaltsanalytische 'Vermessung' von Coachingprozessen. In B. Birgmeier (eds.), *Coachingwissen - Denn sie wissen nicht, was sie tun?* (pp. 93–128). Wiesbaden: Verlag für Sozialwissenschaften.

Goschke, T. & Kuhl, J. (1996). Remembering what to do: Explicit and implicit memory for intentions. In M. Brandimonte, G. O. Einstein & M. A. McDaniel (eds.), *Prospective Memory: Theory and Applications* (pp. 53–91). Mahwah, NJ: Erlbaum.

Graf, E.-M. (2015). *The Discourses of Executive Coaching – Linguistic Insights into Emotionally Intelligent Coaching*. Universität Klagenfurt, Habilitationsschrift.

Grant, A. M. (2012). ROI is a poor measure of coaching success: Towards a more holistic approach using a well-being and engagement framework. *Coaching: An International Journal of Theory, Research and Practice*, *5*(2), 74–85.

Grant, A. M. (2013). The efficacy of coaching. In J. Passmore, D. B. Peterson & T. Freire (Eds.), *The Wiley-Blackwell Handbook of the Psychology of Coaching and Mentoring* (pp. 15–49). Oxford: Wiley Blackwell.

Grant, A. M., Passmore, J., Cavanagh, M. J. & Parker, H. M. (2010). The state of play in coaching today: A comprehensive review of the field. *International Review of Industrial and Organizational Psychology*, *25*, 125–167.

Green, L. S., Oades, L. G. & Grant, A. M. (2006). Cognitive-behavioral, solution-focused life coaching: enhancing goal striving, well-being, and hope. *The Journal of Positive Psychology*, *1*(3), 142–149.

Greif, S. (2007). Advances in research on coaching outcomes. *International Coaching Psychology Review*, *23*, 220–247.

Greif, S. (2008). *Coaching und ergebnisorientierte Selbstreflexion*. Göttingen: Hogrefe.

Greif, S. (2010). A new frontier of research and practice: Observation of coaching behaviour. *The Coaching Psychologist*, *6*(2), 97–105.

Greif, S. (2011a). Gesundheits- und Stressmanagementcoaching. In E. Bamberg, A. Ducki & A.-M. Metz (eds.), *Handbuch Gesundheitsförderung und Gesundheitsmanagement in der Arbeitswelt - Ein Handbuch* (pp. 341–369). Göttingen: Hogrefe.

Greif, S. (2011b). Qualitative oder quantitative Methoden in der Coachingforschung – Methodenstreit zwischen unversöhnlichen Wissenschaftsauffassungen? In E.-M. Graf, Y. Aksu, I. Pick & S. Rettinger (eds.), *Coaching, Beratung und Supervision - Multidisziplinäre Perspektiven vernetzt* (pp. 37–52). Wiesbaden: VS Verlag für Sozialwissenschaften.

Greif, S. (2013). Conducting Organizational based Evaluations of Coaching and Mentoring Programs. In J. Passmore, D. B. Peterson & T. Freire (eds.), *The Wiley-Blackwell Handbook of the Psychology of Coaching and Mentoring* (pp. 445–470). Oxford: Wiley Blackwell.

Greif, S. & Benning-Rohnke, E. (2015). Konsequente Umsetzung von Zielen durch Coaching. *Coaching | Theorie & Praxis*, *1*(1), 25–35.

Greif, S. & Berg, C. (2011). *Result-oriented Self-reflection – Report on the Construct Validation of Theory-based Scales*. Osnabrück: University of Osnabrück, http://www.home.uni-osnabrueck.de/sgreif/english/downloads.html (retrieved 28.3.2013).

Greif, S. & Schubert, H. (2015). Ergebnisorientiertes Reflektieren im Coaching. In A. Ryba, D. Pauw, D. Ginati & S. Rietmann (eds.), *Professionell coachen – Das Methodenbuch: Erfahrungswissen und Interventionstechniken von 50 Coachingexperten* (pp. 54–80). Weinheim: Beltz.

Hantrais, L. (2014). Methodological pluralism in international comparative research. *Inter-*

national Journal of Social Research Methodology: Theory & Practice, 17(2), 133–145.

Hempel, K. & Schubert, H. (2013). Reflexionen zum Prozessbeginn im Coaching. Was begünstigt den Erfolg? Universität Osnabrück, Osnabrück.

Hentrich, S., Müller, A., Zimber, A. & Künzli, H. (2015). Zielerreichung im Coaching und die Rolle von Kontextfaktoren. Coaching | Theorie & Praxis, 1(1), 43–50.

Holton, E. F., III, Bates, R. A. & Ruona, W. E. A. (2000). Development of a generalized learning transfer system inventory. Human Resource Development Quarterly, 11(4), 333–360.

Ianiro, P. M., Schermuly, C. C. & Kauffeld, S. (2013). Why interpersonal dominance and affiliation matter: An interaction analysis of the coach–client relationship. Coaching: An International Journal of Theory, Research and Practice, 6(1), 25–46.

Johanning, M. (2014). Testing the Coaching Explorer as a Standard Instrument of Evaluation in Coaching. Dilploma Thesis, University of Osnabrück, Institute of Psychology.

Jones, R. J., Woods, S. A. & Guillaume, Y. R. F. (2015). The effectiveness of workplace coaching: A meta-analysis of learning and performance outcomes from coaching. Journal of Occupational and Organizational Psychology, doi:10.1111/joop.12119.

Kirkpatrick, D. L. (1977). Evaluating training programs: Evidence vs. proof. Training & Development Journal, 31(11), 9–12.

Kotte, S., Hinn, D., Oellerich, K. & Möller, H. (2016). Der Stand der Coachingforschung: Kernergebnisse der vorliegenden Metaanalysen. Organisationsberatung Supervision Coaching, 23 (in print).

Kraiger, K., Ford, J. K. & Salas, E. (1993). Application of cognitive, skill-based, and affective theories of learning outcomes to new methods of training evaluation. Journal of Applied Psychology, 78(2), 311–328.

Lane, S., Raymond, M. R. & Haladyna, T. M. (eds.). (2015). Handbook of Test Development (2nd ed.). New York: Taylor & Francis.

Meffert, H. & Bruhn, M. (2012). Dienstleistungsmarketing: Grundlagen - Konzepte - Methoden: Grundlagen - Konzepte - Methoden. Mit Fallstudien (7th ed.. Stuttgart: Gabler (Kindle Edition).

Newnham-Kanas, C., Gorczynski, P., Morrow, D. & Irwin, J. (2009). Annotated bibliography of life coaching and health research. International Journal of Evidence Based Coaching and Mentoring, 7(1), 39–103.

Röhrs, B. (2011). Selbstkonzept und Selbstreflexion im Multidirektionalen Feedback. Hannover: ibidem.

Scheele, B. & Groeben, N. (1988). Dialog-Konsens-Methoden zur Rekonstruktion Subjektiver Theorien: Die Heidelberger Struktur-Lege-Technik (SLT), konsensuale Ziel-Mittel-Argumentation und kommunikative Flußdiagramm-Beschreibung von Handlungen. Tübingen: Francke.

Schermuly, C. C. (2014). Negative effects of coaching for coaches: An explorative study. International Coaching Psychology Review, 9(2), 165–180.

Schermuly, C. C., Schermuly-Haupt, M.-L., Schölmerich, F. & Rauterberg, H. (2014). Zu Risiken und Nebenwirkungen lesen Sie ... – Negative Effekte von Coaching. = For risks and side-effects read ... Negative effects of coaching. Zeitschrift für Arbeits- und Organisationspsychologie, 58(1), 17–33.

Schneider, B. & Bowen, D. E. (1995). Winning the Service Game. Boston: Harvard Business School Press.

Schneider, B. & White, S. S. (2004). Service Quality - Research Perspectives. Thousand Oaks, CA: Sage.

Schnieders, T. (2016). Einflussfaktoren auf den Transfererfolg von Coaching im Vergleich zum Training. Eine vergleichende Analyse anhand des deutschen Lerntransfer-System-Inventars (in print). Dissertation (DPhil), University of Osnabrück, Institute of Psychology.

Singer, J. D., & Willett, J. B. (2003). Applied Longitudinal Data Analysis: Modeling Change and Event Occurrence. Oxford: Oxford University Press.

Smither, J. W., London, M., Flautt, R., Vargas, Y. & Kucine, I. (2003). Can working with an executive coach improve multisource feedback ratings over time? A quasi-experimental field study. Personnel Psychology, 56(1), 23–44.

Sonesh, S. C., Coultas, C. W., Lacerenza, C. N., Marlow, S. L., Benishek, L. E. & Salas, E. (2015). The power of coaching: A meta-analytic investigation. Coaching: An

International Journal of Theory, Research and Practice, 8(2), 73–95.

Stephan, M. & Gross, P.-P. (Eds.). (2011). *Organisation und Marketing von Coaching: Beiträge des Marburger Coaching Symposiums 2010*. Wiesbaden: VS Verlag für Sozialwissenschaften.

Stewart, L. J., Palmer, S., Wilkin, H. & Kerrin, M. (2008). Towards a model of coaching transfer: Operationalising coaching success and the facilitators and barriers to transfer. *International Coaching Psychology Review, 3*(2), 87–109.

Taylor, S. E. & Brown, J. D. (1988). Illusion and well-being: A social psychological perspective on mental health. *Psychological Bulletin, 103*(2), 193–210.

Theebom, T., Beersma, B. & Vianen, A. E. M. v. (2014). Does coaching work? A meta-analysis on the effects of coaching on individual level outcomes in an organizational context. *The Journal of Positive Psychology, 9*(1), 1–18.

Von Nordenflycht, A. (2010). What is a professional service firm? Toward a theory and taxonomy of knowledge-intensive firms. *The Academy of Management Review, 35*(1), 155–174.

Wanberg, C. R., Welsh, E. T., Hezlett, S. A., Martocchio, J. J. & Ferris, G. R. (2003). Mentoring research: A review and dynamic process model. In *Research in personnel and human resources management, Vol 22.* (pp. 39–124). Oxford, England: Elsevier Science.

Researching the Coaching Process

Adrian Myers

There are two 'hot topics' in coaching research. The first is whether coaching works and the second is how coaching might work. The second topic addresses questions such as 'What is helpful in coaching sessions?' and 'What do coach and/or client need to do in order to achieve the goals of a coaching session?' This chapter discusses how coaching researchers might address these and similar questions. The chapter begins by suggesting that there are sufficient grounds for addressing the second question. Definitions of coaching process and coaching process research are provided. Important lessons from psychotherapy process research are then considered. Finally, a breadth of empirical literature exploring coaching process will be reviewed. The focus of this chapter is on one-to-one coaching in organizations (e.g., executive coaching, leadership coaching) although is of general relevance to all one-to-one formal coaching interventions.

DOES COACHING WORK?

De Haan et al. (2013) have argued that: a) there is convincing evidence that psychotherapy works; b) coaching and psychotherapy are sufficiently similar processes for the assumption to be made that if psychotherapy is effective then coaching will also be effective; c) there is unlikely to be any serious funding in the foreseeable future to evaluate rigorously the effectiveness of coaching; d) initial research in coaching has already provided tentative evidence that coaching is effective. On the basis of these arguments, de Haan et al. (2013) argue that coaching researchers should focus their attention on exploring how coaching works. These arguments are considered sufficient to justify addressing the second 'hot topic' about how coaching works which is currently under-researched, has remained theoretical or is based on the 'reflections of practicing coaches'

(Smith and Brummel, 2013, p. 58). Given the much reported growth in coaching (Lai and McDowall, 2014), it is important that educators, professional bodies, sponsors of coaching and coaches understand the processes underpinning coaching effectiveness so that practice can be improved and coaching as a body of knowledge can be progressed.

DEFINING COACHING PROCESS RESEARCH

The coaching process might be defined very simply as *the interaction between the coach and client within a single session of coaching and/or across a series of coaching sessions*. It follows from this definition that coaching process researchers are tasked with describing and analysing that interaction. Defining the content and boundaries of 'interaction' is nonetheless problematic. Boyce and Hernez-Broome (2011, p. liv) for example suggest that the coaching process consists of 'mechanics' (e.g., number of sessions, duration, session preparation and documentation of the meeting); content (e.g., contracting, action planning and evaluating progress); relationship; tools and techniques (e.g., active listening, questioning and feedback). One might question however whether 'mechanics' relate more to the structuring of the engagement and 'content' more to the issues and goals the client brings to coaching rather than the interaction itself. The notion of 'relationship' might well be considered integral to the coaching process (because the relationship is developed through interaction or might be instrumental in enabling other processes to occur) but might equally well be considered as something separate to and occurring alongside the coaching process (Sale, 2016). It also seems reasonable to suggest that it is the application of tools and techniques (behaviours) rather than the tools and techniques themselves that might be conceptualized as the coaching process. There also seems to be a need to consider the phenomenological experience of the client in any description of the coaching process (Cox, 2013). The point being made in this brief discussion is that while a simple definition or description of coaching process might be readily provided, actually trying to define the appropriate parameters of that definition is evasive. Similar difficulties have been discussed elsewhere in the literature in trying to establish a definition of coaching (Bachkirova and Kauffman, 2009). It is nonetheless important to construct a working definition of process because otherwise, it would not be clear from a research perspective what to include and exclude from the focus of a research investigation. It is therefore suggested that researchers should consider as *coaching process* any aspect of the coaching engagement occurring within and across coaching sessions including the development of the relationship and which can in principle be explored and conceptualized. This could include the observable behaviours occurring between coach and client, the tasks and activities which are conducted and the broader phenomenological and meaning-making process occurring between coach and client. This is a micro-analytically focused yet broad conceptualization of the coaching process which serves to encourage researchers to explore a breadth of perspectives on the moment to moment interaction occurring between coach and client. However, this attempt to place a boundary on the immediacy of the coaching process should not pre-empt other researchers from exploring coaching as a process occurring over time in and between coaching sessions (Cox, 2013, p. 2) as well as the broader context (e.g. organizational context) which might still be considered important in understanding how coaching works.

It might however be useful to draw a distinction between inputs and outputs of a micro-analytically informed definition of coaching process. All processes start with inputs and produce outputs (European

Foundation for Quality Management, 2015). We might therefore conceptualize inputs into the coaching process as for example the personal characteristics (e.g. personality, self-esteem, motivation, expertise and experience) of the coach and client. The outputs would refer to the changes we might see primarily in the client (e.g. achievement of goals and other benefits). However, we might well observe or assume that coach and client characteristics are being expressed in some way during the interaction which means that we should not be dismissive of any study which considers personal characteristics (traits or states) as integral to the exploration of the coaching process. In psychotherapy research, there is also considerable literature on the notion of *suboutcomes* in studies of the psychotherapeutic process (Rice and Greenberg, 1984) which suggests that specific outputs are actually achieved within the boundaries of a single session or across a series of sessions; for example the accomplishment of particular in-session tasks and activities (e.g. goal setting) or specific moments of client learning and the events that give rise to this learning. There are in fact specific research methodologies which explore how particular tasks are achieved in psychotherapy (e.g., 'task analysis', Greenberg, 1986) so while a definition of coaching process might consider the achievement of the goals of coaching as outputs rather than as integral to the coaching interaction, the notion of *suboutcomes* and how those *suboutcomes* are achieved within coaching sessions do seem to be integral to *process* research.

LESSONS FROM PROCESS RESEARCH IN PSYCHOTHERAPY

The brief reference to *suboutcome* research provided above points to the wider lessons that might be taken from psychotherapy process research. While it is recognized that there are important differences between psychotherapy and coaching (Peltier, 2001), it could be argued that there are sufficient similarities between coaching and psychotherapy for the relevance of the huge volume of literature in psychotherapy process research to be considered (McKenna and Davis, 2009).

In the review which follows, three areas of psychotherapy process research will be considered owing to their potential relevance for understanding and exploring coaching process. The first relates to the way psychotherapy process has been conceptualized and researched as well as overall findings. The second area will consider the literature relating to 'common factors' and which will lead in turn to a broader discussion of a 'contextual model' and other meta-models. Implications for coaching process researchers will be considered throughout.

A Review of the Psychotherapy Process Literature

Llewellyn and Hardy (2001) and Hardy and Llewelyn (2015) classify the change process literature in psychotherapy in terms of three broad areas of investigation: *hypothesis testing, descriptive studies* and *theory building studies. Hypothesis testing* studies 'attempt to predict outcome from a number of variables, which are assumed to be critical in determining whether or not a therapy is effective' (Hardy and Llewelyn, 2015, p. 187). There are four groups of variables: specific techniques; patient/therapist characteristics; timing and context of interventions; and finally, events associated with potentially negative outcomes. *Descriptive studies* 'aim to provide a clear account of behaviours and processes which can be observed to occur during therapy, or in the accounts, beliefs, feelings and behaviours of participants, and which do not yet have a theoretical base' (Hardy and Llewelyn, 2015, p. 186). The authors cite a number of examples including Rennie's (1994) session transcript analyses, showing how clients influence therapists.

Theory building studies aim to examine how psychological change itself occurs, often from a multi-theoretical perspective and assume that change is multi-dimensional; for example in the sense of being influenced by internal and external events (Hardy and Llewelyn, 2015, p. 188). The authors cite an example of the assimilation model (Stiles et al.,1990) which stresses that change takes place in therapy when information and experiences are fully assimilated into a client's schemata (Llewelyn and Hardy, 2001, p. 12).

In their summary of these three approaches, Hardy and Llewellyn (2015) are generally uncritical about the contribution of descriptive studies. This may be because their accounts seem to acknowledge that descriptive studies are less ambitious in their aspirations to identify causality. The authors state for example that descriptive studies 'do not propose causality, but suggest that a full understanding of the process needs to be mindful of its complexity' (p. 187). In their summary of hypothesis-testing studies however, Hardy and Llewelyn (2015) argue that in spite of much research, the variables hypothesized to be associated with effective outcomes have not been identified: 'What is striking about this approach is that despite many thousands of studies, few variables have been found to consistently predict outcome across most therapies' and how the 'most robust finding [from hypothesis testing studies] has been the contribution of the quality of the therapeutic relationship and the quality of client participation' (p. 187). This evaluation is in turn qualified by their suggestion that 'measures of therapeutic relationship, which consistently predict outcome, in fact constitute an early measure of outcome, thus conflating the measure of process, with outcome, thereby arguably rendering the reported link theoretically uninformative' (p. 187). In reference to the limitation of theory building studies, Hardy and Llewellyn (2015) argue that theory building studies have 'systematically attended to therapist-driven features of the therapeutic encounter whereas it is in fact essentially the client who does the changing' (p. 188). In their overall review of the process literature, Hardy and Llewelyn (2015) refer to a range of methodological challenges including small unrepresentative samples, differing definitions of the same constructs and an over-reliance on correlational data (p. 190).

The views expressed by Llewellyn and Hardy (2001) and Hardy and Llewelyn (2015) are supported elsewhere in reviews of the psychotherapy process literature. Elliott (2010, p. 124) for example suggests that a major limitation of process-outcome studies is that the 'change process is treated as a black box where only input and output are looked at.' Elliott (2010, p. 125) refers to the 'generally disappointing results of process-outcome research' and also outlines a range of methodological difficulties (e.g., measurement problems and internal validity) associated with the approach. He suggests optimistically that these issues may be addressed in future by the use of relatively sophisticated research designs and the application of more advanced statistical analyses made possible by having large sample sizes (he cites an exemplary study by Anderson et al., 2009 which included 1,140 clients of psychotherapy). Elliott (2010) refers to the time consuming nature of in depth exploratory research which he suggests might have limited research in this area but suggests that some difficulties could be addressed by building knowledge cumulatively over a series of research studies. Elliott (2010, p. 131) concludes his paper presenting a case for 'systematic methodological pluralism' in which he suggests that advances in psychotherapy process research are likely to reside in the use of a range of approaches. This brief review of the psychotherapy process research suggests some useful lessons for coaching process researchers:

1 Be cautious about trying to demonstrate causality between events occurring in sessions and

post-session outcomes. Address these issues by conducting research with large sample sizes and sophisticated designs.
2 Studies which focus more on exploring the interaction while less ambitious might provide useful ways of conceptualizing coaching process but are likely to prove time-consuming and technically challenging.
3 Researchers should be open to exploring a breadth of approaches and to take account of the role of the client.

The approaches outlined by Llewelyn and Hardy (2001), Hardy and Llewelyn (2015) and Elliott (2010) in addition to the broader research generally in psychotherapy process research provide a rich resource of methods, tools and techniques as well as a range of possible research topics/variables which coaching process researchers could draw upon in designing their own investigations. Research methods could also include methods such as conversational analysis which are not included in the reviews of the authors provided in this sub-section (see for example Gale and Newfield, 1992).

Common Factors

There is a great deal of support in the literature for the relative importance of 'common factors' (components common to each and every psychotherapy) compared to 'specific factors' (the specific techniques or characteristics of a particular method or psychotherapeutic tradition) impacting on the effectiveness of psychotherapy. Arguably, the most convincing argument for this has been put forward by Wampold (2001) in a review of a series of meta-analyses which compared different forms of psychotherapy. The study by and large failed to demonstrate the differential effect of any one form of psychotherapy but did demonstrate the relative importance of a range of factors common to all forms of psychotherapy or 'common factors'.

The literature on common factors is somewhat confusing with different authors providing different classifications of common factors and/or distinguishing between common factors and other variables impacting on outcomes. Grencavage and Norcross (1990) identified 89 'commonalities' which they divided into 5 categories: client characteristics; therapist qualities; change processes (e.g., provision of a rationale, catharsis); treatment structure (e.g., exploration of client's inner world) and therapeutic relationship. Lambert (1992, p. 97 cited in Wampold, 2001, p. 208) refers to common factors as a sub-set of overall processes impacting on outcomes and suggests that the impact of techniques accounts for as little as 15% of the effectiveness of psychotherapy. As much as 40% of the variance is accounted for by extra-therapeutic change (e.g., client capacities/individual characteristics and support available in the environment). An additional 15% of the variance in outcomes can be attributed to expectancy effects (placebo effects). Finally, another 30% of the variance can be accounted for by 'common factors' including for example, therapist empathy and encouragement of risk taking. If Lambert's (1992) suggested percentage contributions of differing factors hold equally true for coaching process as they have been argued to hold for psychotherapy process, then the implications for coaching process researchers are far reaching. Coaching process researchers would be advised to focus their research efforts primarily toward exploring generic influences on the coaching process rather than specific techniques associated with any particular method. This includes in particular the coaching relationship and coach/client characteristics. Coaching process researchers should not look at the effect of specific techniques or approaches associated with any one tradition. There would be further benefit in exploring the client's wider support structures/extra-therapeutic factors (e.g. organizational context) although these would arguably rest beyond the immediacy of a micro-analytically informed exploration of the coaching process (what happens within one or more sessions).

A Contextual Model of Psychotherapy and Other Meta-Models

Wampold (2001) argues that a common factors conceptualization of psychotherapy process should be contrasted with a 'contextual model' of psychotherapy process, the latter emphasizing that it is the overall context of therapy that brings about change rather than individual factors acting independently. However, a contextual model is derived from common factor models (p. 20):

> The first important point to make is the distinction between the common factor model and the contextual model. Common factor models contain a set of common factors, each of which makes an independent contribution to outcome ... In a contextual conceptualization of common factors, specific therapeutic actions ... cannot be isolated and studied independently. (p. 26)

Braakmann (2015, p. 56) attributes the first notion of a contextual model to Frank and Frank (1991) which 'stresses contextual factors of psychotherapy like the relationship with a helping person, the healing setting, and the conceptual scheme or rationale that is provided as the causal influence on clinical change.'

A contextual model of the psychotherapy process seems to raise important questions from a research perspective. If common factors cannot be isolated and studied independently (Wampold, 2001, p. 26), it is not clear how researchers can actually research them. However, Wampold (2001, p. 211) still recommends that 'research on the common factors should be supported'. The point that Wampold (2001) is making is that all psychotherapeutic approaches contain aspects of the relationship, issues of practitioner credibility, client expectations, practitioner skills and the therapist's belief in his/her own practice. It is very difficult to conduct studies which isolate any one of these factors because they may act interdependently (p. 128). This suggests perhaps the importance of a holistic understanding of the change process and a research programme that would conceptualize process in this manner.

Both a 'common factors' and a 'contextual' understanding of process represent alternative 'meta-models' in the sense that each provides a way of theorizing at a higher level, a breadth of theoretical models (Wampold, 2001). A common factors and separately, a contextual meta-model of psychotherapy, stand in opposition to a medical (meta-) model of psychotherapy (Wampold, 2001). Wampold (2001, pp. 13–14) suggests that a medical model assumes that there is a definable problem, that the problem has a particular aetiology and that specific mechanisms of change can be clearly identified and applied to 'treat' the problem. The notion of 'specific factors' is integral to a medical model of process. Even a Rogerian person-centred approach fits the description of a medical model because it still 'contains a clear theory of the person and therapeutic change as well as techniques for facilitating such change' (p. 27).

Constructing coaching in the context of a medical model would seem alien to the current cultural climate in coaching which generally considers coaching to be a shared endeavour (Bachkirova and Kauffman, 2009), rather than something 'done to the client'. However the argued failure of a medical model in psychotherapy to explain and treat assumed pathology (Wampold, 2001) serves to forewarn coaching process researchers to be cautious about embarking upon a journey of attempting to identify how specific types of intervention might be more or less appropriate for addressing particular types of problem or specific issues that coachees might take to coaching. For example, coaching process researchers might be tempted to identify which particular types of intervention might be more or less relevant for increasing a client's sense of self-efficacy. This would be to embrace implicitly a medical model of process which at least in psychotherapy has not largely proven to be successful in identifying specific mechanisms of change (Wampold, 2001).

In light of Wampold's (2001) conceptualization of different meta-models, coaching process researchers are encouraged to reflect on whether the aims of coaching process research might be to develop a common factors meta-model of coaching, a contextual meta-model or whether for that matter, there are in fact some grounds for progression towards developing a more medically oriented meta-model (coaching process might be different). Alternative to these models are integrationist or eclectic meta-models of process (Wampold, 2001). The trend towards integration in psychotherapy (combining two or more techniques or approaches to produce a more effective integrated model) is highlighted by Wampold (2001). He argues that the danger with integration (e.g., behaviourist approaches and psychodynamic approaches merged together) is that one risks producing a third and new method of psychotherapy when research has suggested that factors which are specific to any one tradition do not generally seem to provide a differential benefit compared to any other approach. Coaching process researchers are therefore minded to be cautious about the potential of integrative approaches. Wampold (2011) also argues that 'eclectic' psychotherapeutic approaches are technique driven when research suggests that most of the variance in psychotherapeutic outcomes has not been demonstrated to relate to technique. Again, coaching process researchers might pause to reflect in light of this finding before pursuing any temptation to contribute to the development of an eclectic model of coaching, if the purpose of that model is to identify specific mechanisms of change to address specific coaching challenges identified from a broad Church of existing coaching traditions. In principle, there seems to be a close relationship between a medical model of process and an eclectic one as both assume that specific techniques are more or less useful in specific situations. However much depends on the practitioner's conceptualization of how an eclectic model might work.

Summary

It is not possible in the space available to elaborate in depth on the breadth and complexity of the arguments currently discussed in the psychotherapy process literature. There are advocates of an integrated approach in psychotherapy (see for example Solomonov et al., 2015) and there are still debates in the literature about the relevance of specific factors relative to common factors (see Chwalisz, 2001 for example who highlights some of the debates and implications of Wampold, 2001). These issues are raised because of their theoretical relevance in formulating a research agenda for coaching process researchers. These arguments are not new. Stober and Grant (2006) for example have already considered the relevance of a contextual model in coaching; likewise Kemp (2008). McKenna and Davis (2009) have elaborated in detail how coaches might apply a common factors conceptualization of coaching process.

It is also important to stress that in spite of the possibility of coaching process research arriving at similar findings to those made in psychotherapy, it is possible that the construction of a body of knowledge relevant to coaching might encounter different challenges, address different topics and establish different findings to those in psychotherapy. However, and as suggested earlier, process researchers are at least encouraged to be aware of research that has been conducted in psychotherapy process and to consider lessons that they can take from it. It is in any case already happening, as will be illustrated in the next section. Interested readers may wish to consult Gelo, Pritz and Rieken (2015) which is a testimony to the extensive research being conducted in the field of psychotherapy process.

A REVIEW OF THE LITERATURE ON COACHING PROCESS RESEARCH

In the following section, a review of the empirical coaching process research literature will be provided. The overview is intended to be illustrative of the work that is being conducted around the world. Using the convenient taxonomy of Llewelyn and Hardy (2001) and Hardy and Llewelyn (2015), studies are classified as *hypothesis testing* or *descriptive studies*. No studies could be identified which followed the *theory building* design. However, much depends on how one conceptualizes *theory building*. The distinction which follows helps classify in particular between more quantitative (hypothesis-testing) and qualitative (descriptive) oriented approaches.

Hypothesis-Testing Studies

A summary of 25 coaching hypothesis testing studies identified in a review of the literature is presented in Table 32.1. Relevant studies identified were those which had conducted a statistical analysis of a range of variables hypothesized to impact on the effectiveness of coaching. While the review does not claim to be a systematic review (Lai and MacDowall, 2014), it is considered to include a large proportion of empirical studies recently conducted in coaching process. It is based on a search of relevant databases and well-known coaching journals. Relatively few studies could be identified which suggests a general limitation in the volume of studies conducted in hypothesis-testing relative to the 'thousands of studies' (Llewellyn and Hardy, 2001) highlighted in psychotherapy process research. It is interesting to note that only three of the studies listed (12%) pre-date 2010 which serves to indicate the recent increase in hypothesis-testing in coaching process research.

The variables tested included the coaching relationship, coachee-coach fit, client/coach characteristics and goal setting. A number of studies considered the importance of the relationship specifically as an influencing variable. Four of the studies considered the coachee–client match as a main focus of the research. Eight studies evaluated the influence of client characteristics including the coachee's readiness to engage in coaching. Five studies evaluated the effect of goal setting or goal/task agreement. Only four studies listed in Table 32.1 appeared to study the 'moment by moment' interaction (sequential process analysis) between client and coach using video-recordings (Ianiro, Lehmann-Willenbrock and Kauffeld, 2015; Ianiro and Kauffeld, 2014; Ianiro, Schermuly and Kauffeld, 2013; Gessnitzer & Kauffeld, 2015). This suggests that most researchers are identifying inputs into the process rather than the interaction itself. The research conducted to date provides both a picture of confusion and clarity. Confusion relates to mixed findings. For example, the finding of Scoular and Linley (2006) suggests that 'difference' in coach–client fit might matter while Boyce, Jackson and Neal (2010) suggests the opposite.

Part of the difficulty may relate to very different ways of operationalizing and measuring constructs, a problem that has been identified within the psychotherapy literature (Hardy and Llewelyn, 2015). Care also needs to be taken in comparing data in the table given that some authors conceptualize 'coaching' quite differently with at least one study (Sue-Chan, Wood and Latham, 2012) focusing on a type of *orientation*. One study (Grant, 2012b) presented a task to research participants rather than engaged participants in a formal one-to-one coaching intervention. Other studies used professional, internal coaches or recently 'trained coaches'. In evaluating findings in coaching studies, there is therefore a need for a detailed understanding of the definition and context of coaching.

With respect to clarity, research is beginning to emerge that might indicate the relative importance of agreement on tasks/goals relative to bonds (Bordin, 1979) within the coaching relationship (Gessnitzer and Kauffeld, 2015; Grant, 2012a) as well as the importance of the

Table 32.1 A review of hypothesis testing coaching process literature

Study/Location	Influencing variables	Main findings (relevant to coaching process)
Scoular and Linley (2006) UK	Goal setting Personality preferences (matching) (MBTI)	Goal setting did not impact on outcomes Coaching effectiveness higher when coach and client differ in personality type
Boyce, Jackson and Neal (2010) USA	Coach–coachee match Coaching relationship	Rapport, trust, and commitment predicted coaching outcomes; the client-coach relationship fully mediated two match criteria (compatibility, credibility) with coaching outcomes (p. 914)
Bozer, Joo and Santora (2015) Israel	Gender similarity and perceived similarity	'Overall, the coach–coachee match had little significant effect on coaching outcomes' (p. 218)
Bozer, Sarros and Santora (2013) Israel	Goal Orientation Pre-training motivation Developmental self-efficacy Feedback receptivity	'Significant interaction between learning goal orientation and pre-training motivation on improvement in job self-reported improvement' (p. 277) Developmental self-efficacy associated with coaching outcomes
Stewart et al. (2008) UK	Coachee personality and self-efficacy	Personality measures (openness, conscientiousness, emotional stability and self-efficacy) were associated with coachee self-reports of transfer of learning but magnitude of correlations was low
Sue-Chan, Wood and Latham (2012) Study 1: Canada Study 2: Malaysia	Regulatory fit: Prevention vs. Promotion focus	A 'prevention' coaching orientation (avoidance of mistakes) was more effective for coachees with implicit 'entity' beliefs (beliefs that ability and other personality characteristics are stable) than those with 'incremental' beliefs (beliefs than abilities can be improved)
Jarzebowski, Palermo and van de Berg (2012) Australia	Regulatory fit: Positive Feedback	'Motivation was significantly higher after positive feedback in the regulatory fit condition' (p. 14)
Gessnitzer and Kauffeld (2015) Germany	In session behaviours (working alliance): Agreement on goals and tasks Appraisal and bonding	No relationship identified between perceptions and observations of working alliance Client-initiated agreement on goals/tasks was positively related to coaching success; coach-initiated agreement had the opposite effect; bonding behaviours did not influence coaching success
de Haan et al. (2013) UK	Strength of coaching relationship Coach–client dissimilarity Client self-efficacy Use of techniques (common factor)	'… client perceptions of coaching outcome were significantly related to their perceptions of the working alliance, client self-efficacy, and to client perceptions of the range of techniques … client–coach relationship mediated the impact of self-efficacy and range of techniques on coaching outcomes, suggesting that the relationship is the key factor in determining how clients perceive the outcome of coaching' (p. 40)
Ianiro, Schermuly and Kauffeld (2013)	Verbal and non-verbal affiliation and dominance behaviours of coach and client	'Similarity of coach and client in terms of domination and affiliation predicts positive ratings by the client on relationship quality and goal attainment' (p. 25)

(Continued)

Table 32.1 Continued

Study/Location	Influencing variables	Main findings (relevant to coaching process)
Ianiro and Kauffeld (2014) Germany	Interpersonal behaviours of coach Coach mood Working alliance	Coach's mood impacts on expression of his/her dominant-friendly interpersonal behaviours Coach friendly-dominant interpersonal behaviours impact on client ratings of the working alliance
Ianiro, Lehmann-Willenbrock and Kauffeld (2015) Germany	Interpersonal behaviours of coach and client	'Reciprocal friendliness patterns were positively linked to working alliance. Coaches' dominance-friendly interaction behavior particularly activated clients … Clients' dominance was linked to their overall goal attainment' (p. 435)
MacKie (2015) Australia	Coachee developmental and change readiness Coachee Core Self-evaluations (CSEs)	Partial support for change readiness and CSEs as predictor variables of coaching outcomes
Grant (2012a) Australia	Goal focused versus person centred coaching style	Both goal setting and person-centred aspects of the relationship associated with positive coaching outcomes but a goal-focused coaching style remained significant even when statistically controlling for a 'common factors' person-centred coaching style
Grant (2012b) Australia	Solution-focused versus problem-focused questions	Solution-focused approach led to greater increases in goal approach Solutions-focused approach increased positive effect and increased self-efficacy
Gan and Chong (2014) Malaysia	Rapport Trust Commitment Coach–coachee match	Rapport and commitment impact on coaching effectiveness
McDowall, Freeman Marshall (2014) UK	Feedforward Interviewing (FFI) and Feedback coaching	FFI led to bigger increases in self-efficacy and greater likelihood of goal attainment
Jones, Woods and Hutchinson (2014) UK	Client personality: Five Factors Model (FFM)	Only extraversion was associated with self-reported benefits of coaching
Baron and Morin (2009) North America	Coach's relational and motivational skills and skills in promoting learning and development Coachee's motivation to transfer Coachee's perception of supervisor support No. of coaching sessions	Coach–coachee relationship plays a mediating role between coaching and coachee's self-efficacy Four significant correlates of coach–coachee relationship: coach's self-efficacy in facilitating learning and results; coachee's motivation to transfer learning; coachee's perception of supervisor support; number of coaching sessions received (p. 85)
Baron and Morin (2010) North America	Perceived utility of coaching Learning goal orientation Organizational commitment Work-environment support	'The number of coaching sessions has a positive and significant relationship with post-training self-efficacy Utility judgement, affective organizational commitment and, work-environment support … have each a positive and significant relationship with post-training self-efficacy' (p.18)
Baron, Morin and Morin (2011) North America	Coach perceptions of working alliance	'… coaches' underestimation of the working alliance is the best predictor of post-coaching self-efficacy in coachees' (p. 856)

Smith and Brummel (2013) USA	Coachee involvement Perceptions of 'developability' Individual development plans	All variables were related to greater gains in competency development
Sonesh et al. (2015a) USA	Possible influencing variables: Expertise of coach (time practising) Background of coach (psychology/ non psychology/ business) Number of sessions held Possible moderator: Coaching relationship	Experience of coach unrelated to coachee goal-attainment Coaches with a mixed background associated with better outcomes No. of sessions held associated with coach goal attainment (1–3 is better than 4–6 but not as effective as 7–9 sessions) Relationship correlates with overall coachee goal-attainment
Sonesh et al. (2015b) USA	Coachee Motivation Coach Psychological Mindedness Coach Behaviours (e.g., rapport building) Working Alliance Information Sharing	Coachee goal motivation was significantly positively related with coachee goal attainment and coachee insight in academic sample (Study 1) but not in a field sample (Study 2) Working alliance and information sharing partially mediated the relationship between a coach's psychological mindedness and coachee insight in academic but not a field sample (p. 189)
Lai and McDowall (2014) UK	Coach attributes	'Professional psychological training/background is necessary to understand and manage coachee's emotional reactions ... Coaches' attributes have a significant influence on the effectiveness of coaching process and results' (p. 117) 'Coaching relationship is the key factor for enhancing the effectiveness of coaching results' (p. 132)

coach acting to facilitate learning (Baron and Morin, 2009) and to encourage the client to set goals rather than the coach being active in this process (Gessitzner and Kauffeld, 2015). The relative importance of these process elements may be due to the distinct nature of coaching and the fact that coaching is not considered primarily a restorative process (Gessnitzer and Kauffeld, 2015. Gessnitzer and Kauffeld (2015, p.178) suggest that the coaching relationship is being perceived as 'the most important success factor in the coaching process' which seems to be corroborated in many of the findings listed in Table 32.1 and underpins the interest in the coaching relationship as a research topic relevant for understanding the coaching process.

The meta-analysis of Sonesh et al. (2015b) further provides some interesting findings in relation to the apparent importance of the coaching relationship as well as the background of the coach and the significance of number of sessions held. However, these findings are qualified given that very few studies were used to arrive at these conclusions. While no study listed in Table 32.1 has systematically evaluated organizational factors impacting on the effectiveness of coaching, their possible relevance is mentioned in a number of studies (e.g., Baron and Morin, 2009).

Overall, the limitations are quite common. Most studies highlighted sample size restrictions (e.g., Bozer, Sarros and Santora, 2013; Ianiro, Schermuly, and Kauffeld, 2013) and restricted range (e.g., Boyce, Jackson and Neal, 2010; Jarzebowski, Palermo and van de Berg, 2012). A number of studies reported the use of self-reports as limitations (e.g., Bozer et al., 2013; Stewart et al., 2008) which were considered to lead to a lack of objectivity and common methods bias (e.g., de Haan et al., 2013). The possibility of reverse causality (associated with correlational designs) was highlighted by a number of authors including Sue-Chan, Wood and Latham (2012) and Baron and Morin (2009) but might equally have applied in some of the other studies employing a non-experimental design. The possibility of confounding factors such as compensatory behaviours in control groups (Scoular and Linley, 2006), variations in coach attributes (Bozer, Joo and Santora, 2015) and self-selection bias (Stewart et al., 2008) were also highlighted as possible confounding effects.

While Smith and Brummel (2013) appear to be following the advice of Wampold (2001) in researching the relevance of common factors, they reported difficulties in collecting data on 'extra-therapeutic factors' (Lambert, 1992) and problems associated with collecting retrospective data. McDowall, Freeman and Marshall (2014) highlight the ethical difficulty of collecting time series data with clients participating in a voluntary capacity while Baron, Morin and Morin (2011) noted the difficulty in identifying large numbers of participants within a single organizational setting.

On the one hand, it would therefore seem that many of the methodological problems which have been encountered in psychotherapy process research (Llewellyn and Hardy, 2001; Hardy and Llewelyn, 2015; Elliott, 2010) are being experienced by researchers conducting quantitative studies in coaching process research. However, attempts are being made to address some of these issues. For example, Sue-Chan, Wood and Latham (2012) highlighted the specific challenge of generalizing findings beyond an experimental context but attempted to address this by conducting a parallel study in an organizational setting. The study by Gessnitzer and Kauffeld (2015) is also a good example of how researchers are beginning to use more objective data rather than relying solely on self-reports. Gessnitzer and Kauffeld (2015) conducted multiple measurements over time, addressing perhaps some of the concerns raised by McDowall, Freeman and Marshall (2014). Gessnitzer and Kauffeld (2015) argue that while sample size could have been larger and that more sophisticated statistical analyses could have been conducted with a larger data set, it was sufficient in their study (p. 194). The amount of data collected in the studies relating to sequential analysis is also impressive (96,512 'sequences' across 93 coaching sessions; Gessnitzer and Kauffeld, 2015, p. 189). Much of the research listed generally in Table 32.1 is also exploring issues of relevance if it is to be assumed that 'common factors' are likely to be important in coaching (e.g., focusing on the relationship and client characteristics). Many of the authors refer specifically to the need to identify 'common factors' (e.g., de Haan et al., 2013). This indicates how researchers are adopting approaches which appear to have been informed from findings in psychotherapy.

In summary, it would appear that while relatively few hypothesis-testing studies have been conducted to date, there is a growing number of studies which has been published in the last five years. Coaching process research is already providing some useful insights in particular into aspects of the coaching relationship as well as its overall importance in influencing effective coaching outcomes. There are many and varied methodological challenges that researchers are experiencing in hypothesis-testing studies however.

DESCRIPTIVE STUDIES

Various coaching studies have explored the coaching process from a more qualitatively oriented approach and are summarized in Table 32.2. This table is intended to be illustrative of the range of coaching process research from a qualitative perspective rather than an exhaustive literature review.

Table 32.2 Summary of descriptive studies

Study/Location	Focus of study	Main findings (relevant to coaching process)
Geißler (2009) Germany	Speech Acts	50–70% of all coach utterances related to asking questions and reflecting. For the client, the most frequently used communications were *self-disclosure* and *delivering case specific information*. Initial research has suggested that the most useful questions asked by coaches are those that encourage a coachee to reflect
de Haan, 2008a; de Haan, 2008b; Day et al., 2008; de Haan et al., 2010a; de Haan et al., 2010b; de Haan and Nieß, 2012; de Haan and Nieß, 2015 UK	Critical Moments	New realizations and insights are the most common type of moment identified by coach and client although moments of doubt and tension can also be significant if less frequent. The events identified by coach and client are often similar
Bachkirova, Sibley and Myers (2015) UK but based on research in UK, USA, Canada and worldwide survey	Q Methodology (rank-ordering of descriptors of the coaching process)	A typical coaching session is characterized by a warm and encouraging atmosphere in which the coach acts as a 'collaborative explorer'
Myers (2014) UK	As above	Coaching is a process of inter-subjective meaning-making
Greif, Schmidt and Thamm (2010) Germany	Coaching Success Factors	8 aspects of the coaching interaction are considered critical in coaching (e.g., emotional support; clarification of goals)
Wesson & Boniwell (2007) UK	Experience	A Rogerian (1990, p. 58) approach of practitioner congruence, unconditional positive regard and empathy were associated with feelings of 'flow' (Csikszentmihalyi, 1992)
Buckle (2012) UK	Experience	The usefulness of psychometrics in coaching
Gyllensten and Palmer (2007) UK /Sweden	Experience of the Coaching Relationship	The importance of 'Valuable coaching relationship', 'transparency' and 'trust' (p. 168). The study also identified the importance of 'working towards goals'
Cilliers (2005) South Africa	Coachee Experiences (psychodynamic perspective)	Importance of a range of psychodynamic processes in coaching
Day (2010) UK	Parallel Process	Importance of psychodynamic processes
Schulz (2013) Germany	Critical Perspective	The importance of power relations in coaching

Speech Acts

The findings of Geißler (2009) seem to complement those conducted by other researchers operating from a more quantitative paradigm. Geißler's (2009) observation that clients need to reflect seems quite similar to the analysis of Gessnitzer and Kauffeld (2015) who also arrived at the conclusion of the importance of an 'active client' (p. 177) and of the importance of 'especially open questions, [which] should be helpful in supporting clients in their ability to formulate goals, develop solutions and specify tasks'

(p. 194). There seems therefore to be scope for acknowledging how both quantitative and qualitative approaches can contribute to building an understanding of the nature of the coaching process. From a methodological perspective, Geißler's (2009) study also illustrates the challenge of conducting in-depth qualitative research, including the time consuming nature of the research (Elliott, 2010) which took several years to complete (Geißler, 2015).

Critical Moments

The research that has been carried out by Eric de Haan and colleagues at Ashridge is based on the critical incident technique (Flanagan, 1954 cited in de Haan, 2010b, p. 127) and the 'events paradigm' (Llewelyn and Hardy, 2001) which has been much used in psychotherapy research. The focus of the work, particularly in some of the earlier investigations included 'ruptures' in the relationship which has also been widely investigated in psychotherapy research (e.g., Safran et al.,1990).

One of the earlier investigations suggested that novice coaches often experienced moments of tension and doubt (de Haan, 2008a). These moments could provide the potential for a 'breakthrough' because 'they are moments in which deeper layers and ways of viewing things and assessing things differently are found' (p. 102). Similarly, Day et al. (2008) suggested that critical moments could represent 'turning points in the work' (p. 207). The research by the 'Ashridge Critical-Moment Study Group' (de Haan and Nieß, 2012) provides a valuable window into psychologically meaningful events occurring in coaching. Over the course of several studies, the research has also now collected a substantial dataset of 555 critical moments (de Haan and Nieß, 2015). The research demonstrates how knowledge can be built progressively through a series of individual research studies over time (Elliott, 2010) and the benefits of using a number of researchers sharing expertise and introducing a degree of objectivity in the coding of categories (e.g., de Haan et al., 2010b).

The research doesn't however consider whole sessions of coaching. This leads to a construction of the coaching process as a series of significant moments whereas it seems equally plausible that the coaching process 'works' holistically. For example, it could be the overall meaning and experience of a session or even programme of coaching which leads to valued client outcomes rather than specific events occurring in a session.

Q methodology and Analysis of Whole Coaching Sessions

Bachkirova, Sibley and Myers (2015) study involved the development of an instrument to explore whole sessions of coaching (the Coaching Process Q Set; CPQS). The tool was developed in consultation with focus groups of experienced coaches from a range of traditions in UK, USA and Canada. The instrument is a Q-set (Block, 2008) which provides short descriptors (Q-items) of coach, client and dyadic behaviours as well as overall session characteristics. This research tool is an adaptation of a methodological approach which has been widely used in psychotherapy (e.g., Ablon and Jones, 1999) which again illustrates the influence of psychotherapy in coaching process research. In testing the instrument, coaches from around the world were invited to use the descriptors to describe their own typical mid-engagement session. Myers (2014) has used the instrument to evaluate the subjective impressions of coaches and clients participating in coaching sessions as well as other coaches observing video-recordings of these sessions.

Coaching Critical Success Factors – an Integrationist Perspective

Greif, Schmidt and Thamm (2010) provide an observation manual of 'coaching success factors' which can be identified through behavioural indicators. The frequency of behavioural indicators can be measured and correlated alongside measures of coaching outcomes. The research enables the analysis of whole sessions or a series of coaching sessions. While this approach undoubtedly demonstrates how different behaviours can be broken down and measured in relation to coaching outcomes, the approach appears to represent a proposed integrative meta-model, the basis of which has been challenged in psychotherapy process (Wampold, 2001). Greif (2010) provides an overview of this approach.

Phenomenological Investigations

A number of studies has explored the in-session experience of participants (e.g., Wesson and Boniwell, 2007; Buckle, 2012; Gyllensten & Palmer, 2007). Gyllensten & Palmer (2007) suggested that 'working towards goals' was important, supporting findings from the more quantitative oriented coaching process literature (e.g., Gessnitzer and Kauffeld, 2015; Grant, 2012a). This study further demonstrates how quantitative and qualitative methods can contribute towards building an understanding of the coaching process.

Psychodynamic and Critical Perspectives

Cilliers' (2005) study asked coachees to describe their experience of executive coaching by writing essays which were subsequently analysed using content analysis. The research adopted a 'systems psychodynamic interpretive stance' (p. 26). One of the key findings from this research was that 'interdependency facilitates taking responsibility for the self' (p. 23).

The study also showed how 'executive coaching resembles the family dynamic of children acting towards parental figures and using them as objects for projections and projective identification' (p. 28). This is a very different sort of study to those focused purposefully on observable behaviours or on the conscious recollections of participants. Also from a psychodynamic perspective, Day (2010) considered the relevance of the 'parallel process' using a case study methodology which indicated the importance of unconscious process considered to be important generally in coaching (Hawkins, 2014). From a critical perspective, Schulz (2013) conducted empirical research using video recordings of coaching sessions which among other findings suggested that 'the coach consistently uses internalizing and emotionalizing problem constructions to frame the managers' [coachees'] experiences' (p. 4).

All of these studies mentioned in this sub-section (Cilliers, 2005; Day, 2010; Schulz, 2013) and in the previous sub-section (Wesson and Boniwell, 2007; Buckle, 2012; Gyllensten & Palmer, 2007) seem to be making important contributions to understanding coaching process. However, they approach the subject matter quite differently to hypothesis-testing studies or even to some of the more behaviourally oriented, descriptive research outlined earlier in this section. Coaching process researchers are encouraged to reflect on the value and relevance of a broad conceptualization of coaching process and coaching process research.

TOWARDS A FUTURE AGENDA FOR COACHING PROCESS RESEARCH

There is an enormous gap between the scope and scale of research conducted to date in psychotherapy process and that conducted in coaching. This seems to suggest a need for coaching process researchers to 'catch-up' and to conduct more empirical studies to understand the coaching process. While the field of psychotherapy research offers rich resources for coaching researchers to draw upon, as indicated earlier, researchers are nonetheless encouraged to explore empirically, theoretical differences such as the relative importance of goal/tasks in the context of the working alliance (Grant, 2012a) which might discourage researchers from simply assuming that the findings from psychotherapy might be readily transferred into knowledge of coaching process. Similarly, in coaching, particular processes may be considered of general significance (e.g., transference processes; Hawkins, 2014) but which tend to have been conceptualized as tradition specific in psychotherapy process research. However, psychotherapy research can still serve as a useful compass for beginning an exploration of coaching process.

Similar problems to those highlighted by de Haan (2013) in relation to the challenge of conducting large scale randomized trials to evaluate the overall efficacy of coaching are likely to present challenges to those researchers designing investigations to conduct hypothesis-testing studies. However, some examples were given earlier in this chapter about how coaching process researchers are designing multiple studies or are conducting well-designed investigations of the coaching process which will help address some of the challenges identified. It is possible that an accumulation of small scale studies may be necessary to enable more systematic reviews in due course and this is likely to constitute the route that coaching process researchers interested in conducting hypothesis-testing studies will adopt in the forthcoming years. Securing the participation of coaches and their clients for those researchers working from more qualitative traditions (or those researchers exploring behaviours quantitatively) will also depend on the goodwill of practising coaches and coaching clients who are encouraged to help wherever possible in providing access to video-recordings of actual coaching sessions. Given the recent interest in video-recorded material, this trend is likely to continue.

The review of the literature described in this chapter failed to identify any studies which might readily be classified as 'theory building studies'. This seems to be a missed opportunity. Cox (2013) and separately Kemp (2008) have proposed theories and models of learning which could in principle be explored empirically. Cox (2006) has also highlighted a range of theories of adult learning and development which could be usefully explored in coaching. This type of research would place the emphasis on the client. This is an area which is under-researched in psychotherapy (Elliott, 2010) and coaching alike and could help differentiate coaching process as a body of knowledge. Cox (2013, p. 1) for example defines coaching as a 'facilitated, dialogic, reflective learning process' which includes 'Pre-reflective Experience, Reflection on Experience and Post-reflective thinking' (p. 5). This is a very different conceptualization of coaching when compared to many definitions of psychotherapy which place greater emphasis on the restorative or therapeutic process of being in relationship (e.g., Butler and Strupp, 1986).

In future research investigations, it would seem important to take account of the broader context in which coaching takes place, an area of research which has been often signalled as important but not explored systematically to date. The theoretical literature has for example outlined the importance of organizational context and the importance of well-designed coaching programmes impacting on the effectiveness of coaching (Hunt and Weintraub, 2006; Clutterbuck and Megginson, 2005; Smith and Brummel, 2013). Organizational processes are considered to impact within the coaching process at an unconscious level (Day, 2010; Hawkins, 2014) and are arguably part of the 'extra-therapeutic' environment which research in psychotherapy has suggested to be of particular significance in understanding the overall effectiveness of coaching (McKenna and Davis, 2009, p. 248).

The 'elephant in the room' in this chapter however relates to the possibility of micro-analytically oriented process research not serving to identify the 'active ingredients' of change (McKenna and Davis, 2009) which is an explicit goal of much change process research. The possibility of identifying causal mechanisms has been challenged elsewhere in the literature (e.g., Western, 2012). Instead of this positivistic approach, Western (2012) suggests that coaching process researchers might usefully explore broader influences impacting on the practice of coaching:

> Developing coaching theory is to develop knowledge about what coaching is, what works, how it works and also what claims are false or exaggerated. Other questions, such as how coaching fits into wider social phenomena, the discursive nature of coaching and what power relations are at play, are also part of explaining how coaching works and why it is popular. (p. 239)

In a similar vein, Stelter (2014) has described coaching as a 'process of personal and social meaning making' (p. 191) which suggests that coaching is more than a process of interacting variables. The contextual model discussed by Wampold (2001) and in the coaching literature (Stober and Grant, 2006; Kemp, 2008) suggest different ways of conceptualizing process beyond the influence of interacting variables. However, these arguments for alternative ways of understanding the process of coaching should not discourage any particular avenue of coaching process research. Elliot's (2010) call for 'systematic methodological pluralism' and Wilber's (2007) 'integral methodological pluralism' both suggest that all perspectives have value. Examples of research studies were given earlier in this chapter which illustrate how both quantitative and qualitative approaches seem to be able to identify similar findings and which together build knowledge of the coaching process. They are testimony to the value of a multiple methodological approach.

CONCLUSION

This chapter started by justifying the need to explore coaching process and provided a definition of both coaching process and coaching process research. Important lessons were highlighted in psychotherapy process research from which coaching process researchers may be able to learn when designing their own studies. The empirical literature on existing coaching process research was explored. The overall conclusion is perhaps that coaching process research seems to be adopting many research methods, topics of interest and research paradigms from psychotherapy. In particular, there seems to be an interest in exploring, *de facto*, common factors such as coach and client characteristics and the relationship. Coaching studies conducted to date suggest the relative importance of these factors in influencing the effectiveness of coaching. However, some possible differences in findings between coaching and psychotherapy may already be emerging.

In designing future research projects, coaching process researchers need to decide whether to focus their research on inputs into the coaching process, the actual interaction, sub-outcomes in coaching/in-session task accomplishments or for that matter broader contextual issues impacting on the coaching process. They need to decide whether to focus their attention on experience or the study of specific process variables and whether to design their investigations for example as hypothesis-testing studies, descriptive studies or theory-building studies. Perhaps the intrinsic creativity of the research process will introduce new research approaches altogether. Researchers also need to reflect on the assumptions behind their research designs; whether for example they are assuming that their research might contribute to the identification of specific factors impacting on specific issues clients might bring to coaching or whether they are helping to develop a model of coaching more informed from common factors or a contextual conceptualization of coaching. Research choices might well be influenced by the values and beliefs about the nature of coaching held by the researcher as much as informed rationale.

The possibility of conceptualizing the immediacy of the coaching engagement as a learning process (Cox, 2013), as a discursive process (Western, 2012) and/or as a meaning making process (Stelter, 2014) are possible ways which could be explored in addition to exploring coaching as a process of influencing micro-variables. All of the approaches discussed have enormous contributions to provide collectively. It is hoped that this chapter will serve to encourage more research and an informed and diverse approach to researching the coaching process over forthcoming years.

REFERENCES

Ablon, J.S. and Jones, E.E. (1999) 'Psychotherapy process in the national institute of mental health treatment of depression collaborative research program', *Journal of Consulting and Clinical Psychology*, 67(1), pp. 64–75.

Anderson, T., Ogles, B.M., Patterson, C.L., Lambert, M.J. and Vermeersch, D.A. (2009) 'Therapist effects: Facilitative interpersonal skills as a predictor of therapist success', *Journal of Clinical Psychology*, 65(7), pp. 755–768.

Bachkirova, T. and Kauffman, C. (2009) 'The blind men and the elephant: using criteria of universality and uniqueness in evaluating our attempts to define coaching', *Coaching: An International Journal of Theory, Research and Practice*, 2(2), pp. 95–105.

Bachkirova, T., Sibley, J. and Myers, A.C. (2015) 'Developing and applying a new instrument for microanalysis of the coaching process: The Coaching Process Q-Set', *Human Resource Development Quarterly*, 26(4), pp. 431–462.

Baron, L. and Morin, L. (2009) 'The coach–coachee relationship in executive coaching: a field study', *Human Resource Development Quarterly*, 20(1), pp. 85–106.

Baron, L. and Morin, L. (2010) 'The impact of executive coaching on self-efficacy related to management soft-skills', *Leadership & Organization Development Journal*, 31(1), pp. 18–38.

Baron, L., Morin, L. and Morin, D. (2011) 'Executive coaching: the effect of the working alliance discrepancy on the development of coachees' self-efficacy', *Journal of Management Development*, 30(9), pp. 847–865.

Block, J. (2008) *The Q-sort in Character Appraisal: Encoding Subjective Impressions of Persons Quantitatively.* Washington DC: American Psychological Association.

Bordin, E.S. (1979) 'The generalizability of the psychoanalytic concept of the working alliance', *Psychotherapy: Theory, Research & Practice*, 16(3), pp. 252–260..

Boyce, L.A. and Hernez-Broome, G. (2011) 'Introduction: State of Executive Coaching – Framing Leadership Coaching Issues', in Hernez-Broome, G. and Boyce, L.A. (eds), *Advancing Executive Coaching: Setting the Course for Successful Leadership Coaching.* San Francisco: Jossey-Bass, pp. xliii–lxi.

Boyce, L., Jackson R. and Neal, L.J. (2010) 'Building successful leadership coaching relationships: examining impact of matching criteria in a leadership coaching program', *Journal of Management Development*, 29(10), pp. 914–931.

Bozer, G., Joo, B.-K. and Santora J.C. (2015) 'Executive coaching: Does coach–coachee matching based on similarity really matter?', *Consulting Psychology Journal: Practice and Research*, 67(3), p. 218 –233.

Bozer, G., Sarros, J.C. and Santora, J.C. (2013) 'The role of coachee characteristics in executive coaching for effective sustainability', *Journal of Management Development*, 32(3), pp. 277–294.

Braakmann, D. (2015) 'Historical Paths in Psychotherapy Research', in Gelo, O.C., Pritz, A. and Rieken, B. (eds), *Psychotherapy: Foundations, Process, and Outcome, Research.* London: Springer, pp. 39–65.

Buckle, T. (2012) 'It can be life-changing: an interpretative phenomenological analysis of the coach and coachee's experience of psychometrics in coaching', *International Journal of Evidence Based Coaching and Mentoring*, Spec. Issue (6), pp. 102–118.

Butler, S.F. and Strupp, H.H. (1986) 'Specific and nonspecific factors in psychotherapy: a problematic paradigm for psychotherapy research', *Psychotherapy*, 23(1), pp. 30–40.

Chwalisz, K. (2001) 'A common factors revolution: Let's not cut off our discipline's nose to spite its face', *Journal of Counseling Psychology*, 48(3), pp. 262–267.

Cilliers, F. (2005) 'Executive coaching experiences: a systems psychodynamic perspective', *SA Journal of Industrial Psychology*, 31(3), pp. 23–30.

Cox, E. (2006) 'An Adult Learning Approach to Coaching', in Stober, D.R. and Grant, A.M. (eds), *Evidence-Based Coaching Handbook. Putting Best Practices to Work for Your Clients*. New York: John Wiley & Sons, pp. 193–218.

Cox, E. (2013) *Coaching Understood: A Pragmatic Inquiry into the Coaching Process*. London: Sage.

Clutterbuck, D. and Megginson, D. (2005) *Making Coaching Work: Creating a Coaching Culture*. London: CIPD Publishing.

Csikszentmihalyi, M. (1992) *Flow: The Psychology of Happiness*. London: Rider.

Day, A. (2010) 'Coaching at relational depth: a case study', *Journal of Management Development*, 29(10), pp. 864–876.

Day, A., de Haan, E., Blass, E., Sills, C. and Bertie, C. (2008) 'Coaches' experience of critical moments in the coaching', *International Coaching Psychology Review*, 3(3), pp. 207–218.

de Haan, E. (2008a) 'I doubt therefore I coach: critical moments in coaching practice', *Consulting Psychology Journal: Practice and Research*, 60(1), pp. 91–105.

de Haan, E. (2008b) 'I struggle and emerge: critical moments of experienced coaches', *Consulting Psychology Journal: Practice and Research*, 60(1), pp. 106–131.

de Haan, E. (2011) *Relational Coaching: Journeys Towards Mastering One-to-One Learning*. Chichester: John Wiley & Sons.

de Haan, E. (2013) 'Critical moments of coaching: a comparison between clients, coaches and sponsors of coaching', *International Coaching Psychology Review*, 10(1), pp. 38–61.

de Haan, E., Bertie, C., Day, A. and Sills, C. (2010a) 'Clients' critical moments of coaching: Toward a "client model" of executive coaching', *Academy of Management Learning & Education*, 9(4), pp. 607–621.

de Haan, E., Bertie, C., Day, A. and Sills, C. (2010b) 'Critical moments of clients and coaches: A direct-comparison study', *International Coaching Psychology Review*, 5(2), pp. 109–128.

de Haan, E., Bertie, C., Day, A. and Sills, C. (2010) 'Critical moments of clients and coaches: a direct-comparison study', *International Coaching Psychology Review*, 5(2), pp. 109–128.

de Haan, E., Duckworth, A., Birch, A.D. and Jones, C. (2013) 'Executive coaching outcome research: the contribution of common factors such as relationship, personality match, and self-efficacy', *Consulting Psychology Journal: Practice and Research*, 65(1), pp. 40–57.

de Haan, E. and Nieß, C. (2012) 'Critical moments in a coaching case study: illustration of a process research model', *Consulting Psychology Journal: Practice and Research*, 64(3), pp. 198–224.

de Haan, E. and Nieß, C. (2015) 'Differences between critical moments for clients, coaches and sponsors of coaching', *International Coaching Psychology Review*, (10)1, pp. 38–61.

Elliott, R. (2010) 'Psychotherapy change process research: realizing the promise', *Psychotherapy Research*, 20(2), pp. 123–135.

European Foundation for Quality Management (2015) *What do we mean by Processes?* Available at: http://www.efqm.org/efqm-model/efqm-model-in-action/processes-products-services (accessed: 24th December 2015).

Flanagan, J. C. (1954) 'The critical incident technique', *Psychological Bulletin*, 51(4), pp. 327–358.

Frank, J.D. and Frank, J.B. (1991) *Persuasion and Healing* (3rd ed.). Baltimore: Johns Hopkins University Press.

Gale, J. and Newfield, N. (1992) 'A conversational analysis of a solution-focused marital therapy session', *Journal of Marital and Family Therapy*, 18(2), pp. 153–165.

Gan, G.C. and Chong, C.W. (2015) 'Coaching relationship in executive coaching: A Malaysian study', *Journal of Management Development*, 34(4), pp. 476–493.

Geißler, H. (2009) 'Die inhaltsanalytische "Vermessung" von Coachingprozessen', in Birgmeier, B. (ed.), *Coachingwissen – Denn sie wissen nicht, was sie tun?* Wiesbaden: VS Verlag, pp. 93–125.

Geißler, H. (2015) Skype Conversation with Harald Geißler, 23 June.

Gelo, O.C.G., Pritz, A. and Rieken, B. (2015) *Psychotherapy Research: Foundations, Process, and Outcome*. London: Springer, pp. 183–194.

Gessnitzer, S. and Kauffeld, S. (2015) 'The working alliance in coaching: why behavior is the key to success', *Journal of Applied Behavioral Science*, 51(2), pp. 177–197.

Grant, A.M. (2012a) 'An integrated model of goal-focused coaching: an evidence-based framework for teaching and practice', *International Coaching Psychology Review*, 7(2), pp. 146–165.

Grant, A.M. (2012b) 'Making positive change: a randomized study comparing solution-focused vs. problem-focused coaching questions', *Journal of Systemic Therapies*, 31(2), pp. 21–35.

Greenberg, L.S. (1986) 'Change process research', *Journal of Consulting and Clinical Psychology*, 54(1), pp. 4–9.

Greif, S. (2010) 'A new frontier of research and practice: observation of coaching behaviour', *The Coaching Psychologist*, 6(2), pp. 21–29.

Greif, S., Schmidt, F. and Thamm, A. (2010) *The Rating of Eight Coaching Success Factors: Observation Manual (Version 4)*. Available at: http://www.home.uni-osnabrueck.de/sgreif/downloads/Rating_of_Coaching_Success_Factors_Version4-May_2010.pdf (accessed: 15 December 2015).

Grencavage, L.M. and Norcross, J.C. (1990) 'Where are the commonalities among the therapeutic common factors?', *Professional Psychology: Research and Practice*, 21(5), pp. 372–378.

Gyllensten, K. and Palmer, S. (2007) 'The coaching relationship: an interpretative phenomenological analysis', *International Coaching Psychology Review*, 2(2), pp.168–177.

Hardy, G.E. and Llewelyn, S. (2015) 'Introduction to psychotherapy process research', in Gelo, O.C.G., Pritz, A. and Rieken, B. (eds) *Psychotherapy Research: Foundations, Process, and Outcome*. London: Springer, pp. 183–194.

Hawkins, P. (2014) 'Coaching Supervision', in Cox, E., Bachkirova, T. and Clutterbuck, D. (eds), *The Complete Handbook of Coaching*. London: Sage, pp. 391–404.

Hunt, J.M. and Weintraub, J.R. (2006) *The Coaching Organization: A strategy for Developing Leaders*. London: Sage.

Ianiro, P.M. and Kauffeld, S. (2014) 'Take care what you bring with you: how coaches' mood and interpersonal behavior affect coaching success', *Consulting Psychology Journal: Practice and Research*, 66(3), pp. 231–257.

Ianiro, P.M., Lehmann-Willenbrock, N. and Kauffeld, S. (2015) 'Coaches and clients in action: a sequential analysis of interpersonal coach and client behavior', *Journal of Business and Psychology*, 30(3), pp. 435–456.

Ianiro, P.M., Schermuly, C. C. and Kauffeld, S. (2013) 'Why interpersonal dominance and affiliation matter: an interaction analysis of the coach–client relationship', *Coaching: An International Journal of Theory, Research and Practice*, 6(1), pp. 25–46.

Jones, R.J., Woods, S.A. and Hutchinson, E. (2014) 'The influence of the Five Factor Model of personality on the perceived effectiveness of executive coaching', *International Journal of Evidence Based Coaching & Mentoring*, 12(2), pp. 109–118.

Jarzebowski, A., Palermo, J. and van de Berg, R. (2012) 'When feedback is not enough: the impact of regulatory fit on motivation after positive feedback', *International Coaching Psychology Review*, 7(1), pp. 14–32.

Kemp, T.J. (2008) 'Searching for the elusive model of coaching: could the "Holy Grail" be right in front of us?', *International Coaching Psychology Review*, 3(3), pp. 219–226.

Lai, Y. and McDowall, A. (2014) 'A systematic review of coaching psychology with focus on the coaching relationship', *International Coaching Psychology Review*, 9(2), pp. 135–146.

Lambert, M.J. (1992) 'Implications of Outcome Research for Psychotherapy Integration', in Norcross, J.C. and Goldfried, M.R. (eds), *Handbook of Psychotherapy Integration*. New York: Basic Books, pp. 94–129.

Llewelyn, S. and Hardy, G. (2001) 'Process research in understanding and applying psychological therapies', *The British Journal of Clinical Psychology*, 40(1), pp.1–21.

MacKie, D. (2015) 'The effects of coachee readiness and core self-evaluations on leadership coaching outcomes: a controlled trial', *Coaching: An International Journal of Theory, Research and Practice*, 8(2), pp. 120–136.

McDowall, A., Freeman, K. and Marshall, S. (2014) 'Is feedforward the way forward?', *International Coaching Psychology Review*, 9(2), pp.135–146.

McKenna, D.D. and Davis, S.L. (2009) 'Hidden in plain sight: rhe active ingredients of executive coaching', *Industrial and Organizational Psychology*, 2(3), pp. 244–260.

Myers, A.C. (2014) A Multiple Perspective Analysis of a Coaching Session. PhD thesis. Oxford Brookes University. Available at: https://radar.brookes.ac.uk/radar/items/7759944f-6ff4-4e91-9ae9-01e62f2217b6/1/ (Accessed 4 March 2016).

Peltier, B. (2001) 'The Psychology of Executive Coaching: Theory and Application. New York: Routledge.

Rennie, D.L. (1994) 'Clients' deference in psychotherapy', *Journal of Counseling Psychology*, 41(4), pp. 427–437.

Rice, L., N. and Greenberg, L., S. (eds.) (1984) *Patterns of Change: Intensive Analysis of Psychotherapy*. New York: Guilford.

Safran, J.D., Crocker, P., McMain, S. and Murray, P. (1990) 'Therapeutic alliance rupture as a therapy event for empirical investigation', *Psychotherapy: Theory, Research, Practice, Training*, 27(2), pp. 154–165.

Sale, R. (2016) *The Coaching Relationship* (Unpublished doctoral thesis). Oxford Brookes University, Oxford, UK.

Schulz, F. (2013) *The Psycho-Managerial Complex at Work: A Study of the Discursive Practices of Management Coaching*. PhD thesis. University of St Gallen, Germany. Available at: http://www1.unisg.ch/www/edis.nsf/SysLkpByIdentifier/4111/$FILE/dis4111.pdf (accessed 22 December 2015).

Scoular, A. and Linley, P.A. (2006) 'Coaching, goal-setting and personality type: what matters?', *The Coaching Psychologist*, 2(1), pp. 9–11.

Smith, I.M. and Brummel, B.J. (2013) 'Investigating the role of the active ingredients in executive coaching', *Coaching: An International Journal of Theory, Research and Practice*, 6(1), pp. 57–71.

Solomonov, N., Kuprian, N., Zilcha-Mano, S., Gorman, B.S. and Barber J.P. (2015) 'What do psychotherapy experts actually do in their sessions? An analysis of psychotherapy integration in prototypical demonstrations', *Journal of Psychotherapy Integration*, 25(4), pp. 1–15.

Sonesh, S.C., Coultas, C.W., Lacerenza, C.N., Marlow, S.L., Benishek, L.E. and Salas, E. (2015a) 'The power of coaching: a meta-analytic investigation', *Coaching: An International Journal of Theory, Research and Practice*, 8(2), pp. 73–95.

Sonesh, S.C., Coultas, C.W., Marlow, S.L., Lacerenza, C.N., Reyes, D. and Salas, E. (2015b) 'Coaching in the wild: Identifying factors that lead to success', *Consulting Psychology Journal: Practice and Research*, 67(3), pp. 189–217.

Stelter, R. (2014) 'Third-generation coaching: reconstructing dialogues through collaborative practice and a focus on values', *International Coaching Psychology Review*, 9(1), pp. 51–66.

Stewart, L.J., Palmer, S., Wilkin, H. and Kerrin, M. (2008) 'The influence of character: does personality impact coaching success?', *International Journal of Evidence Based Coaching and Mentoring*, 6(1), pp. 32–42.

Stiles, W.B., Elliott, R., Llewelyn, S.P., Firth-Cozens, J.A., Margison, F.R., Shapiro, D.A. and Hardy, G. (1990) 'Assimilation of problematic experiences by clients in psychotherapy', *Psychotherapy: Theory, Research, Practice, Training*, 27(3), pp. 411–420.

Stober, D.R. and Grant, A.M., (2006) 'Toward a contextual approach to coaching models', in Stober, D.R. and Grant, A.M. (eds), *Evidence-Based Coaching Handbook. Putting Best Practices to Work for Your Clients*. New York: John Wiley & Sons, pp. 355–365.

Sue-Chan, C., Wood, R.E. and Latham, G.P. (2012) 'Effect of a coach's regulatory focus and an individual's implicit person theory on individual performance', *Journal of Management*, 38(3), pp. 809–835.

Wampold, B. (2001) *The Great Psychotherapy Debate: Models, Methods, and Findings*. Abingdon: Routledge.

Wesson, K. and Boniwell, I. (2007) 'Flow theory – Its application to coaching psychology', International Coaching Psychology Review, 2(1), pp. 33–43..

Western, S. (2012) *Coaching and Mentoring: A Critical Text*. London: Sage.

Wilber, K. (2007) *Integral Spirituality: A Startling New Role for Religion in the Modern and Postmodern World*. Boston: Shambhala Publications.

Neuroscience in Coaching Research and Practice

Angela M. Passarelli, Ellen B. Van Oosten and Mark A. Eckert

Coaching is fundamentally about change. As stated by Bennett and Bush (2014), 'every coaching engagement holds the promise of moving the client in a better direction or to a more desired state' (p. 3). In keeping with psychological and sociological traditions, coaching research and practice has largely focused on psychosocial factors related to change in individuals and groups. However, recent advances in neuroimaging technology and neurobiological research have stimulated fervent interest in a new domain, the role of neuroscience in coaching.

As neuroscience is an emerging domain in the field of coaching psychology, its fate is yet unclear. Advocates have embraced the potential of neuroscience to guide the coaching process (Brown & Brown, 2012; Habermacher, Ghadiri, & Peters, 2014), even going so far as to coin a new label. *Neurocoaching* has been defined by Dias et al. (2015) as the 'application of neuroscientific knowledge to the understanding and improvement of the coaching process' (p. 11). On the other hand, neuroscience has also been the source of speculation from researchers who argue that current applications of neuroscience are fraught with misconceptions (Grant, 2015; Lindebaum, 2012; Lindebaum & Zundel, 2013).

The aim of the chapter is to present a balanced view of the state of the science at the nexus of coaching and neuroscience. We first provide a primer on brain structure and function for those who are new to neuroscience. We then discuss ways in which neuroscience can be used to advance coaching research and practice with attention to potential pitfalls. We conclude with an illustrative example of Intentional Change Theory as a coaching framework that effectively draws on neuroscience to inform research and practice.

WHAT IS NEUROSCIENCE?

Neuroscience is the study of the structure and function of the nervous system and brain (Cacioppo & Decety, 2011). Many specializations have emerged in the broad discipline of neuroscience. Of particular interest to coaching scholars and practitioners are neuropsychology, cognitive neuroscience, social neuroscience, and decision neuroscience. Although these specializations vary in their target interests, they share a common interest in understanding the neurobiological mechanisms of behavior and behavioral effects on brain structure and function. Research in these areas draws both on measures of brain activity derived from neuroimaging as well as from hormonal, cellular, and electrophysiological processes elsewhere in the body (Cacioppo & Decety, 2011). It can be difficult to read this research because it is highly technical. Here we attempt to provide a simple explanation of the brain and how its activity is measured.

Organization of the Brain

Despite tremendous variation, human brains have quite similar structural and functional organization (Glickstein, 2014). This organization can be described in terms of three levels: (1) neurons and supporting cells, (2) nuclei and cortical regions that support a common function (e.g., speech perception), and (3) neural pathways comprised of interconnected regions that form a functional network (e.g. a frontal-parietal orienting network; Becker, Cropanzano, & Sanfey, 2011). At the most basic level, the brain is comprised of billions of neurons. Neurons are specialized cells comprised of a cell body (soma) connected to branching receivers (dendrites) and a terminal (axon) that sends information to other neurons. Neurons receive and transmit information through electrical and chemical signals. These signals are communicated from one neuron to another across a synapse, the junction between the axon of one neuron and the dendrites of another (Kandel, Schwartz, Jessell, Siegelbaum, & Hudspeth, 2013). The signal creates an electro-chemical reaction in the receiving neuron. If this reaction reaches a certain threshold, often due to the input from multiple neurons, an action potential in the receiving neuron will cause it to 'fire' a message to downstream neurons. Chemical messengers called neurotransmitters carry the information across the synapse to the other neuron. The axons of some neurons have a myelin sheath that allows them to transmit information more rapidly. In essence, this 'firing' is how different parts of the brain interact.

At the second level, neurons that work together to perform specific functions are bundled in specific regions of the brain. Of particular interest to social cognitive neuroscientists are regions in the cerebral cortex, the deeply folded surface of the brain responsible for cognitive functions. The major folds and valleys of the brain, called gyri and sulci, are present in most people and provide landmarks to grossly define the functional roles of different brain regions (Figure 33.1). Familiarity with key landmarks in the brain aids in understanding the basic orientation of these structures. Neuroscientists often describe the position of these landmarks using directional terms that include anterior–posterior (front–back), medial–lateral (interior–exterior), and dorsal–ventral (top–bottom; note that these directions change to signify back–belly in the spinal column; Glickstein, 2014). These directional terms also apply to sub-cortical (deeper) regions of the brain such as the limbic system, which supports a number of processes including emotional processing (Figure 33.1).

The cerebral cortex is comprised of left and right hemispheres that are connected by large bundles of axons that collectively are called the corpus callosum. Each hemisphere contains maps for the opposite side of the sensory space (e.g., left somatosensory cortex maps fine touch sensations on the right hand). These maps appear to be established in posterior brain regions that are important for perception. The maps are maintained through connections in frontal (anterior) regions that

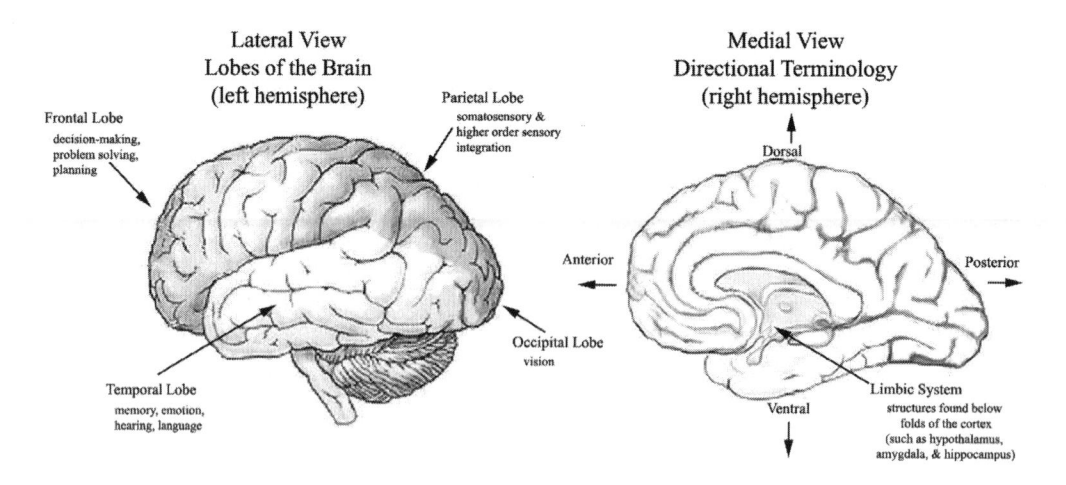

Figure 33.1 Basic brain anatomy

are important for monitoring and producing behavior.

Finally, the third organizational level of the brain is the neural pathway or network, a set of brain regions that are commonly activated for a given function. Neural networks have three organizing principles that allow them to be extremely flexible – interconnectivity, bidirectionality, and competition (Becker & Cropanzano, 2010). Research has moved toward a focus on functional connectivity rather than functional specificity. That is, neuroimaging scientists examine the pattern of activation across brain regions or networks of brain regions involved in psychological processes. Finally, perceptual representations in specific regions and the organization of brain networks can be modified through neuromodulatory systems. For example, a prominent hypothesis states that we redirect our attention to new stimuli or goals when poor performance leads to a release of the neuromodulator norepinephrine (Aston-Jones and Cohen, 2005).

Imaging Techniques

Brain imaging techniques are used to 'evaluate metabolic activity of discrete regions of the brain while people are engaged in specific tasks under controlled conditions' (Kandel & Hudspeth, 2013, p. 9). Two of the most common include electroencephalography (EEG) and magnetic resonance imaging (MRI). Participants involved in EEG studies are typically seated upright and wear a cap containing electrodes that align to certain parts of the head. (EEG data can also be acquired while the participant is lying down as in the case of sleep studies.) The electrodes, small disks placed on the scalp, measure electrical activity of neurons on the outer layer of the cortex (Glickstein, 2014). Event-related potentials (ERPs) are often examined in EEG studies and reflect the response of large numbers of neurons to a time-locked stimulus or behavior. The spectral power for specific frequency domains is also commonly measured for task and non-task experiments. For example, the alpha range (~7.5–12.5 Hz) can provide an estimate of the degree to which cortical regions are inhibited or attention is diminished to a stimulus that is represented by the sensory cortex (Händel, Haarmeier, & Jenson, 2011).

MRI data are gathered using a high magnetic field to measure changes in deoxygenated to oxygenated blood (BOLD – blood oxygen level dependent response) when brain regions are engaged in a task (Clay, 2007). Data are gathered while a participant lies down with his head immobilized and covered by a coil. Experimental tasks are presented via audio or video channels, and behavioral responses are recorded with a button press. These types of experiments require a baseline condition that is important to consider when interpreting reports of brain activity. Functional MRI (fMRI) is also used in non-task experiments where correlated patterns of activity across the brain are measured to characterize network structure. We describe below examples of networks such as a default mode network that is particularly engaged when thinking about the self.

Both EEG and fMRI have pros and cons. EEG allows for precise measurement of neural activity over time, but the spatial resolution is weak. fMRI, on the other hand, provides relatively more precise localization of neural activity, but has less temporal resolution (Lieberman, 2010). For a more detailed account of these and other physiological techniques, see Lee and Chamberlain (2007).

Physiological Measures

The constraints of current imaging techniques, such as the expense and being confined to the laboratory, suggest that coaching researchers interested in measuring bodily processes should consider alternative measures of brain activity. Because the brain innervates peripheral organs and controls chemical processes in the body, measures obtained from the cardiovascular, dermal, muscular, and/or hormonal systems can be considered indirect measures of neural activity. The techniques used to acquire such data (e.g. electrocardiography/ECG, electrodermal activity/EDA, electromyography/EMG, hormonal assays – salivary cortisol, etc.) are generally non-invasive, less expensive to administer, and can be collected in both the field and lab settings.

USING NEUROSCIENCE TO ADVANCE COACHING RESEARCH

Coaching is not the first field to look to neuroscience for findings and methodologies relevant to human behavior. Psychology has long embraced neuroscience and physiology as sub-disciplines. More recently neighboring fields such as economics, marketing, and education have also adopted a neurobiological perspective. Advocates of a neurobiological perspective in these fields argue that it provides a basis by which to extend current theories and models, endeavor in new research directions, and resolve longstanding debates (Becker et al., 2011; Lee & Chamberlain, 2007). We contend that a neurobiological perspective provides an additional window into the dynamics of coaching via a new level of analysis. This new window allows access to biological processes that shape and are shaped by individual and social factors, often outside one's conscious awareness (Becker & Menges, 2013). In addition to circumventing issues associated with self-report and subjective observational measures, neurobiological methods have the potential to explain when and why coaching approaches are effective. This is not to say that a neurobiological approach alone is a sufficient way forward for coaching research. Rather, we suggest neuroscience should play a complementary role to current coaching research by providing added insight at the biological level of analysis.

With regard to levels of analysis, the issue of reductionism is of particular concern for the social sciences, coaching included. Namely, critics of the neurobiological perspective hold that complex social behavior cannot be reduced to cellular processes in the brain (Grant, 2015; Lindebaum & Zundel, 2013). Although these concerns have been largely overstated (Marshall, 2009), we see warrant in this concern. Drawing on arguments in social neuroscience (Ochsner & Lieberman, 2001) and organizational

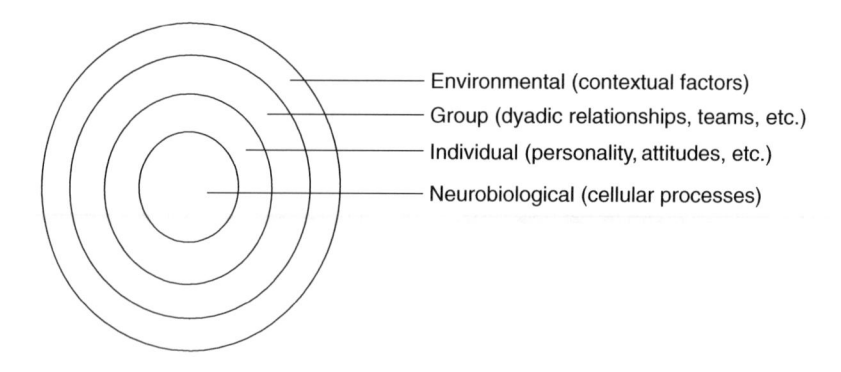

Figure 33.2 Levels of analysis in coaching research

- Environmental (contextual factors)
- Group (dyadic relationships, teams, etc.)
- Individual (personality, attitudes, etc.)
- Neurobiological (cellular processes)

neuroscience (Ashkanasky, Becker, & Waldman, 2014), we advocate the adoption of a multilevel approach to connecting neuroscience and coaching research. Acknowledging bi-directional influence between factors at the biological, individual, and socio-environmental levels, a multilevel approach integrates findings across these levels of analysis and, thus, can yield more complete and robust accounts of the phenomena of interest than a single level can provide (Figure 33.2; Becker et al., 2011; Cacioppo, Berntson, Sheridon, & McClintock, 2000). A multilevel approach requires that well established theories of cognition (e.g. working memory), affect (e.g. positive emotions) and/or social behavior (e.g. attachment) related to coaching are brought to bear on theorizing about the functioning of the brain and body (Lee & Chamberlain, 2007). Research integrating coaching and neuroscience in this multilevel model has the potential for mutual benefit (Ashkanasky et al., 2014; Grant, 2015). Coaching research and methods can modify and expand neurobiological interpretations, while neuroscience can inform more precise measures and models in coaching psychology.

Two examples from the field of management are illustrative of the benefits of a multilevel approach to leveraging neurobiological measures. First, it has been a long-held belief that work-related stress increases as leaders climb the organizational hierarchy and gain additional responsibility. However, a study by Sherman et al. (2012) found that individuals in senior leadership roles actually have less stress than non-leaders, especially when they have a sense of control over their work situation. The hypotheses in this study were tested with a multilevel approach, using both self-reported anxiety and cortisol, which is a hormone responsible for the human stress response. These results could guide future multilevel experiments in which leaders are presented with cognitive, affective, and/or social stressors to determine the extent to which and when their stress responses are relatively limited compared to a control group. Germane to coaching, such studies could also explore the extent to which a coaching intervention attenuates an identified stress response.

A second benefit relates to resolving theoretical debates. For example, there has been disagreement on whether the concept of 'justice' (perceived fairness) can be factored into subtypes of justice that stand as distinct constructs. Specifically, one issue is whether individuals discern between the fairness of outcomes or resources received (distributive justice) and the process by which those resources were allocated (procedural justice; Greenberg & Colquitt, 2005). Using fMRI, Dulebohn et al., (2009) found that different brain regions were involved in perceptions of distributive and procedural justice. The authors assert that the results are indicative of two distinct constructs. The authors also show overlapping effects related to these constructs in a neural system involved in performance monitoring. Together, these results provide important supplemental evidence to advance the justice debate.

As the field of coaching moves forward, Grant (2015) posed an important and provocative question with regard to the application of neuroscience to coaching research. To paraphrase, he asked '*what can we learn from neuroscience that we cannot learn from behavioral science?*' This is an important question to ask before undertaking expensive and time-consuming research projects. At risk of sounding facetious, our answer is quite simple – we cannot learn what is happening physiologically from behavioral science alone. Neurobiological measures offer not only a window into health and well-being factors in coaching, but also uniquely capture mechanisms that neither coaches nor coachees can accurately self-report because they are beyond conscious awareness or may not be socially desirable to admit (Becker & Menges, 2013). Furthermore, neuroscience has already begun to explore topics germane to coaching such as creativity, emotion regulation, decision-making, attention, mindfulness, empathy, social rejection, and motivation (Bowman, Ayers, King, & Page, 2013). This science brought to bear on coaching-related research questions may produce a more complete understanding of the phenomena. Such questions may include: How do racial biases or stereotypes impact the development of coaching relationships? When are coachees most likely to repeat self-defeating behaviors? How does the coach's level of stress or ease transfer (or not) to the coachee and vice versa? How does the language used by a coach affect the coachee's ability to self reflect during the coaching conversation? For example, we might address this latter question by examining the extent to which frontal regions of the brain that monitor performance and adjust behavior to optimize performance are engaged with a default mode network set of regions that are engaged during self-referential thinking. Moreover, this approach could characterize individual differences in benefits from coaching style and/or language use. The questions above could be answered using a behavioral approach, but neuroscience offers an additional avenue for replication and extension of previous findings via the biological level of analysis.

PROMISING NEUROBIOLOGICAL FINDINGS FOR PRACTICE

Advances in neuroscience are rapidly changing what we know about the brain. Research by Dweck demonstrated that an elementary understanding of how the brain functions fosters a growth-oriented mindset associated with increased motivation and performance (Blackwell, Trzesniewski, & Dweck, 2007). As an extension of this work, it stands to reason that both coaches and coachees will benefit from familiarity with basic neurobiological processes. Although neurobiological research should not be over-simplified, below we summarize a few well-supported findings and theories that can inform coaching. Specific neural regions of interest (ROIs) associated with these areas can be found in Table 33.1.

Neuroplasticity

There is now compelling evidence of the brain's ability to generate new neurons and neuronal connections across the lifespan (Doidge, 2007). Even after brain development is complete, experience modifies brain structure by enhancing synaptic connectivity. Albeit most evidence comes from animal studies, there is evidence that stimulating environments and skill training alter the organization of neural connections in the brain, and these changes are associated with changes in behavior (Kolb & Whishaw, 1998; Pascual-Leon, Amedi, Fregni, & Merabet,

Table 33.1 Regions of interest involved in coaching-relevant neural systems

Theory	Regions of interest	Application to coaching	Reference
Neuroplasticity	Synaptic connections throughout brain; neurogenesis in hippocampus and cerebellum	Learning and development; necessity for deliberate practice	
Social Detection System	*Reward* ventromedial prefrontal cortex[1,2] ventral striatum[1] posterior cingulate cortex[1,2] septal area[1]	Reward: coaching relationship; caregiving; attenuation of pain; pleasure, safety, cooperation	[1]Eisenberger & Cole, 2012 [2]Delgado, Ollson, & Phelps, 2006; Phelps, Delgado, Nearing, &LeDoux, 2004 [3]Baumgartner, et al., 2009
	Threat amygdala[1,2] dorsal anterior cingulate cortex[1,3] anterior insula[1] periaqueductal grey[1]	Threat: disconnection; threats to self worth; social evaluation	
Opposing Domains	*Social* *(Default Mode Network)*[1] dorsal and ventral midline structures[2] right temporo-parietal junction[2]	Self awareness processes; empathy; evaluation; task versus relationship leader demands	[1]Jack et al., 2013b [2]Boyatzis, Rochford, & Jack, 2014
	Analytical *(Task Positive Network*[1] dorsal attention system[2] fronto-parietal control network[2] ventral attention network[2]		
Automaticity v. Control Networks	*Automatic*[1] Amygdala Basal ganglia Ventromedial prefrontal cortex Dorsal anterior cingulate cortex Lateral temporal cortex	Automaticity: unconscious biases, reactions, and impulses Control: effortful regulation, intentional action	[1]Satpute & Lieberman, 2006
	Controlled[1] Lateral prefrontal cortex Posterior parietal cortex Rostral anterior cingulate cortex Medial temporal lobe Medial prefrontal cortex		

Note: References supporting 'regions of interest' in the second column are indicated by corresponding superscripted numbers in the final column.

2005). Accordingly, neuroplasticity may be the primary reason neuroscience matters for learning, development, and change in adulthood. The popular phrase 'neurons that fire together, wire together' describes the way in which neurons adapt in the learning process (Hebb, 1949; Schatz, 1992). That is, repeated and persistent stimulation of a neural network can rewire the brain. Relatedly, a second rule of thumb applied to neuroplasticity is 'if you don't use it, you lose it.' Neural connections in the brain can be lost when they are not used. In coaching this underscores the importance of deliberate practice in which one continuously practices a desired behavior until it becomes a natural and consistent response (Zull, 2002). For example, Dias et al. (2015) argued that neuroplasticity provides evidence for the importance of coaching techniques like cognitive reappraisal for fostering change in coachees' patterns of thinking and behaving.

Social Reward and Threat Detection

Given the importance of social relationships to human survival and flourishing, it is no surprise that sophisticated systems exist in the human brain to detect reward and threat in our relationships with others. The social reward system is sensitive to human bonding, safety and caregiving. In a review article documenting the neurological links between social support and health, Eisenberger and Cole (2012) provide evidence that cues signifying a positive social connection – that one is cared for, valued by, and connected to others – activate the reward centers in the brain (Table 33.1). Evidence suggests that activity in the social reward system is associated with reduced fear responding (Delgado, Ollson, & Phelps, 2006; Phelps, Delgado, Nearing, & LeDoux, 2004), attenuation of physical and social pain responses (Eisenberger, 2012) and a buffer against the effects of social disconnection (Onoda, et al., 2009). More relevant to the coach, these neural areas are associated with caregiving activity and promote one's ability to reciprocate care (Eisenberger & Cole, 2012).

On the other hand, social disconnection may be processed as a threat to survival, which triggers a neural alarm system that elicits adaptive emotional, behavioral, and physiological responses (Table 33.1; Eisenberger & Cole, 2012). Perceived rejection, negative social evaluation, and/or threats to one's intellectual competence (sense of self-worth and potential for connection) can activate this neural alarm system, producing a stress response that can limit the effectiveness of coaching (Boyatzis, Smith, & Blaize, 2006). Broken promises also trigger the neural alarm system (Baumgartner, Fischbacher, Feierbend, Lutz, & Fehr, 2009). It is unknown but likely that even anticipated social disconnection (e.g. through social evaluation) would trigger the alarm system (Eisenberger & Cole, 2012). The sensitivity of social reward and threat detection in the brain underscores the importance of a high quality coaching relationship and the challenges coaches may face dealing with coachees who have experienced social disconnection.

Opposing Domains Theory

The relationship between two large-scale networks in the brain, the task positive network (TPN) and the default mode network (DMN), has been heavily contested in the academic literature. As our knowledge of the functions of these networks has become more sophisticated, it has been argued that the labels task-positive and task-negative (the latter referring to the DMN) no longer offer sufficient precision (Spreng, 2012). However, we use these labels for the sake of parsimoniously explaining opposing domains theory.

Generally, the TPN is activated during tasks that require goal directed attention whereas the DMN is activated when the mind is at rest (e.g. awake but not engaged in a task; Raichle et al., 2001). More recently, it has also been determined that the DMN is activated when individuals are engaged in tasks involving social cognition (e.g. empathizing with others; Mars et al., 2012; Van Overwalle, 2009). Based on this more recent characterization of the function of the DMN, opposing domains theory holds that the TPN and DMN are associated with broad cognitive domains that represent incompatible modes of information processing – non-social versus social, respectively – and are negatively correlated (Jack et al., 2013b). Using tasks designed to isolate non-social reasoning and social reasoning (e.g. solving a physics problem versus empathizing with characters in a social scenario), this research found that the TPN was engaged during non-social or analytical reasoning, and the DMN was suppressed. In contrast, the DMN was engaged during social tasks and the TPN was suppressed.

This work presents the notion that we are neurobiologically constrained from being able to engage in both analytic and empathetic activities simultaneously. In a coaching setting, this work suggests that to the extent that certain practical techniques such as presenting data from 360-degree feedback trigger an analytic response, they can actually impair one's ability to regulate emotions or engage in creative thought, other correlates of DMN activity (Takeuchi et al., 2012). Furthermore, this theory has particular relevance for coaches working with leaders on self-awareness and overall strategies for success because the findings challenge the long-held assumption that an individual can effectively engage in both task- and relationship-related aspects of leadership simultaneously (Boyatzis, Rochford, & Jack, 2014). Instead, coaches may be better inclined to help leaders cycle efficiently between task and relationship demands. As more is learned about opposing domains theory, it may point to strategies for coaches to effectively manage the analytical versus social demands of coaching conversations.

Automaticity v. Control

Like opposing domains theory, automaticity and control is a dual-process model of brain function. Unlike opposing social and analytic domains, automatic and controlled processes are not antagonistic. Rather, they are often both involved in complex social behavior. Controlled processes refer to those functions that require awareness, intention, and effort whereas automatic processes occur outside conscious awareness and are unintentional or effortless (Satpute & Lieberman, 2006). A common example of these processes is driving home from work (automatic processing) while thinking about events that occurred earlier that day or what is for dinner (controlled processing).

Challenging tasks recruit frontal 'control' regions of the brain for compensatory support. For example, Vaden et al. (2013) showed that elevated activity in frontal brain regions involved in performance monitoring were predictive of one's ability to accurately identify words on a difficult word recognition task. Engaging in controlled processing may contribute to fatigue or a desire to reduce effort toward a goal. For example, young adults are more likely to report that they want to avoid challenging trials (McGuire & Botvinik 2010) and report that a creative task is difficult (Saggar et al., 2015) when a task engages inferior frontal sulcus brain regions that support working memory and the ability to inhibit or suppress potentially distracting information. In this way, automatic processes free up resources for other activities. The influence of automatic and control processes on social perception and attribution is also an ongoing area of inquiry that can inform coaching in the future (Mason & Morris, 2010; Spunt & Lieberman, 2013). Familiarity with automatic and controlled processes can help coaches not only understand coachee behaviors, but also assist them in being more aware and present in coaching interactions themselves.

PITFALLS IN 'COACHING NEUROSCIENCE'

Several leading consultants and trainers in coaching and leadership, such as David Rock and Paul Brown, have turned to neuroscience as the basis of their coaching models. Few of these individuals actually conduct neurobiological research themselves. In fact, most do not conduct any kind of research that would meet the standards for rigorous scientific study. Grant (2015) raised a concern about the allure of neuroscience creating a 'pop-science' in which 'neuroscientific jargon and brain images [are used] as pseudo-explanatory frameworks for atheoretical proprietary coaching systems' (p. 21). Thus, it is important that consumers of such literature are educated about the potential pitfalls of commercializing neuroscience for coaching applications. Below we discuss three such pitfalls – over-simplification, jargonizing, and overreaching our expertise.

Over-Simplification and Jargonizing

The inherent appeal of neuroscience has caused an explosion in the commercial market place. Unfortunately, efforts to capitalize on neuroscience findings and techniques often extend beyond the science (Ashkanasky, Becker & Waldman, 2014). Accordingly, many coaching models packaged as 'neurocoaching' use neuroscience to support their claims, but are not neurobiological models per se. For example, Habermacher, Ghadiri, and Peters (2014) claim that fulfilling the basic human needs in their SCOAP model 'will create a healthy chemical environment in the brain and promote positive learning and wiring in the brain' (p. 14). Yet they do not specify the details or constraints of their proposition, nor do they address the interrelations between SCOAP needs (self-esteem, control, orientation, attachment and pleasure). For example, given that testosterone has links to status-seeking behavior and aggression (Eisenegger, Haushofer, & Fehr, 2011), how might the testosterone-enhancing fulfilment of the need for 'control' impact one's ability to fulfil 'attachment' needs? Grant (2015) warns that the popular press creates misconceptions by overstating the conclusions that can be drawn from the scientific literature.

Furthermore, commercialized neuroscience is saturated with jargon. On one hand jargon might foster adoption of a neurobiological perspective by providing us with a new language and mechanism for sense-making or translation. On the other hand, excessive use of jargon runs the risk of further separating the world of coaching and the world of neuroscience due to a lack of shared terminology. In the worst-case scenario, jargon could undermine the status of coaching as a scientific discipline. As Grant (2015) suggests '… coaches, trainers, and consultants that use neuroscientific jargon as a means of gaining credibility and developing an aura of scientific respectability in order to sell their products and services run the very real risk of having their own professional standing diminished, as well as doing their clients and broader coaching industry a disservice' (p. 24).

Going Beyond our Expertise

Dias et al. (2015) claim that 'the application of neuroimaging techniques to the coaching context could not only contribute to the development and optimization of coaching techniques that could be considered more effective for enhancing certain identified brain areas, but could also become a tool to predict coaching effectiveness to a given individual' (p. 13). This assertion suggests that coaches have the requisite knowledge and tools to assess neural activity, which is a lofty aim. Understanding neuroscience is a complex task that requires years of intensive study in a specialized domain. Dias et al. (2015) provides the example of making choices for treatment of depression based on activation in the right anterior insula in a PET scan (McGrath et al., 2013). However, there are practical issues to consider. Today, access to such technology is still very expensive, rendering it an unviable option. Even if the technology were readily available, it is unlikely that the majority of coaching practitioners would be prepared to assess brain images and draw from them conclusions about coaching techniques. Furthermore, it may be unethical to do so (Shams, 2015). Lindebaum (2012) cautions that once neurobiological methods and theories move from the laboratory environment into the non-medical commercial domain, they are no longer governed by a set of ethical principles and protocols that guide scientific research. In the absence of such constraints, Lindebaum argues, the risk increases that neuroscience data could be manipulated in ways that dehumanize or marginalize the individuals who are providing access to the brain data to move the science forward.

As such, both research and practice must be careful to not overstate claims from a still quite nascent science.

INTEGRATING NEUROSCIENCE AND COACHING: AN ILLUSTRATION USING INTENTIONAL CHANGE THEORY

As previously stated, neuroscience and coaching have not evolved to the point at which an evidence base exists for 'neurocoaching' per se. However, neuroscience can currently inform coaching in at least two ways. First, from a practice perspective, familiarity with the basics in psychophysiology and neuroscience helps coaches more fully understand what is happening in coaching contexts. It is common to augment training for therapists, psychologists, and educators with foundational courses in psychophysiology and neuroscience. Along with training that prepares coaches to understand individual and interpersonal psychological dynamics, neuroscience provides another dimension to the holistic nature of coach training. Second, as previously stated, neuroscience can open new lines of scholarly inquiry, provide measures otherwise unobtainable, and serve as a source of triangulation for findings from more mainstream techniques, such as qualitative and survey research.

To provide an example of how neuroscience is currently being used for both research and practice in coaching, we highlight Intentional Change Theory (ICT; Boyatzis, 2006). With origins in self-directed learning theory (Kolb & Boyatzis, 1970) and self-discrepancy theory (Higgins, 1987), ICT has been refined through empirical research using both traditional approaches and neurobiological approaches.

Overview of ICT

Intentional Change Theory presents a useful framework to examine how sustained change occurs in coaching research and practice. The process of personal change is discontinuous, often provoked by personal discoveries or epiphanies from which a new way of seeing, thinking or acting emerges. ICT identifies five such discoveries: the ideal self, the real self, learning plan, experimentation and practice, and supportive relationships (Table 33.2; Boyatzis, 2006). Experiences within each discovery promote a person's desire and ability to change in sustainable ways.

Table 33.2 Personal discoveries in intentional change theory

Discovery	Description
1. Ideal Self	Considers question of 'what do I wish to do and who do I wish to be in my work and life?' and manifests into personal vision; Emerges from our ego ideal, dreams and aspirations; includes (1) An image of a desired future; (2) Hope that one can attain it; and (3) Inclusion of one's core identity
2. Real Self	Considers question of 'who am I today?'; the person that others see and with whom they interact; includes assessment of strengths and weaknesses
3. Learning Agenda	Considers question of 'what do I want to or need to do to make my vision a reality?'; framework for translating vision into learning goals, actions and milestones; embodies a learning orientation rather than a performance orientation
4. Experimentation and Practice	Considers question of 'what am I learning from practicing new behaviors?'; includes implementing goals and practicing new habits
5. Supportive, Trusting Relationships	Considers question of 'who can help me?'; recognizes that support is needed for the change process from a variety of sources

The Ideal Self

One of the distinctive aspects of ICT is its emphasis on the ideal self. A considerable amount of research has been dedicated to examining the unique role of the ideal self in the developmental process. The ideal self is a version of the self that includes (1) an image of a desired future, (2) hope that one can attain it and (3) one's core identity (Boyatzis & Akrivou, 2006). In an ICT-based coaching process, coaches encourage coachees to consider deeply meaningful topics like core values and future dreams and aspirations before any feedback or goal setting process occurs. The process of discovering the ideal self is especially powerful in launching a path of change, and subsequently sustaining effort toward it. A 25-year program of outcome assessment demonstrated that coaching with an early emphasis on the ideal self was linked to development of emotional and social competencies among graduate students in a two-year business program (Boyatzis & Saatcioglu, 2008; Boyatzis, Lingham, & Passarelli, 2010; Boyatzis, Stubbs, & Taylor, 2002). Similarly, ICT-based coaching relationships were found to amplify work engagement and career satisfaction in a field study of financial service executives (Van Oosten, 2013).

Emotional Attractors

The process of imagining a future linked to one's passion, purpose and values evokes a psychophysiological state that provides motivation to move to action. This state, referred to as the Positive Emotional Attractor (PEA), is characterized by varying degrees of positive emotions. Positive emotion here refers to discrete feelings experienced in response to a pleasant experience or object. Examples include but are not limited to joy, gratitude, hope, serenity and love. Positive emotion alone does not characterize a PEA state. A person's positive emotion is also likely accompanied by the relatively greater arousal of the parasympathetic nervous system (PNS) compared to the sympathetic nervous system (SNS). The PNS is a subset of the autonomic nervous system that supports our 'rest and digest' functions and bolsters immune, cardiovascular, and neuroendocrine system functioning (Uchino, Cacioppo, & Kiecolt-Glaser, 1996). The PNS also supports social engagement (Porges, 2003). Arousal of positive emotions and the PNS over periods of time is associated with health benefits and increased well-being (Boyatzis, Smith, & Blaize, 2006).

In stark contrast to the PEA, the Negative Emotional Attractor (NEA) state is characterized by negative emotions such as fear, anxiety, sadness, anger, disgust, and despair. It is also characterized by the arousal of the sympathetic nervous system (SNS). The SNS is associated with the human stress response and is aroused when we feel that we are in physical danger, something is uncertain, or we are being evaluated. What is especially notable is that these events do not actually need to occur to arouse the SNS; the SNS can be aroused merely by thinking about one of these conditions, such as anticipating the possibility of being evaluated by someone else. With this in mind, a situation in which a coachee is faced with a performance imperative or one who envisions a future based in someone else's vision, referred to as the ought self, almost certainly arouses the SNS (Howard, 2006). Unlike the health benefits associated with positive emotions and PNS arousal, prolonged periods of negative emotion and SNS arousal can be harmful to our health and wellbeing. NEA states narrow our vision, deplete our energy and shut us down emotionally, cognitively and psychologically (Boyatzis, Smith, & Blaize, 2006).

NEUROBIOLOGICAL EMPIRICAL RESEARCH

Because emotional attractors have a neurobiological dimension, measures of brain activity have been used in empirical research on ICT. The first in this series of studies was a quasi-experimental study in which participants were randomly assigned to PEA and NEA conditions for one-time coaching sessions in which they received multirater (360-degree) feedback. (The coaching session in the PEA condition began with a discussion of one's personal vision/ideal self whereas the session in the NEA condition did not.) The results of this study showed that PEA-framing of coaching sessions was associated with less expressed negative emotion upon discussing the feedback results. Contrary to what was predicted, no difference was found in the level of stress as measured by salivary cortisol following the coaching sessions (Howard, 2015). This was a curious result and spawned a series of additional studies.

To increase the level of control and address the constraints of neurobiological methods, an experimental protocol was developed for subsequent studies. The protocol was comprised of a set of standardized coaching questions that were validated to evoke PEA and NEA states. Experienced coaches were trained to deliver these protocols in 'laboratory' settings designed to represent real-life coaching settings. Two fMRI studies and one multilevel psychophysiological study have since been conducted. The first fMRI study elucidated several neural regions of interest differentially evoked by PEA and NEA coaching interactions (Jack et al., 2013a). These relate to activation of brain regions associated with autonomic arousal (PNS/PEA and SNS/NEA), as well as unexpected differences visual processing between the two conditions. A second fMRI study was conducted to replicate and extend these results. Importantly, this study confirmed evidence from Jack et al., (2013a) that coaching interactions characterized by the PEA and NEA differently impact a coachee's perception. After face-to-face coaching sessions, participants completed scanner tasks in which they responded to (1) their coaches asking questions in the PEA and NEA conditions and (2) cues instructing them to identify global or local features of an image. Extensive neural overlap was found linking PEA coaching to global attention or the overall shape of the figures and NEA coaching to local attention or the smaller shape that were used to compose the overall shape of the figures (Passarelli et al., 2013). This suggests that coaching conversations based on the ideal self can help coachees understand the big picture, whereas NEA conversations focus the coachee on smaller details. Utilizing the same experimental protocol with indirect measures of brain activity (ECG and EDA) and individual-level self-report data, the third study found that PEA interactions evoked more positive affect, fostered a more positive coaching relationship, and evoked a more promotion-oriented approach to goal setting than the NEA interactions (Passarelli, 2014). Similar to Howard's results of cortisol levels, no differences in sympathetic or parasympathetic nervous system arousal were found between the two conditions. However, post hoc analyses showed that coachees were less internally distracted, based on measures of vagal withdrawal and spelling/grammatical errors, following the PEA condition than the NEA condition when engaging in goal setting. Taken together, Howard (2015) and Passarelli (2014) point to two possible interpretations that require further research. First, it could be that discussing one's personal vision or ideal self is stressful and arouses the NEA – especially for the first time, if unexpected, and/or in the context of a new coaching relationship. A second interpretation could be that the NEA-effects of goal setting override any previous PEA effects. Thus, more research is needed to understand the sequencing and temporal orientation of PEA and NEA interactions within a coaching engagement. Neuroimaging studies could help test these competing interpretations.

In summary, ICT-based coaching is not neurocoaching (Dias et al., 2015). Rather, it uses neuroscience to explicate and test the theory, which is primarily rooted in behavior change. As a multilevel model, ICT has been tested in numerous ways – not only from a biological approach, but also a behavioral approach (survey and qualitative research). We offer this as an illustration of how coaching research might proceed with integrating a neurobiological perspective. Future research in the area will examine the effect of 'dose dependence' or number of coaching sessions on predicted patterns of brain activity, as well as the role of opposing domains in various coaching scenarios.

CONCLUSION

The aims of coaching and neuroscience are well aligned. Ultimately, both fields seek to improve the human condition. Neuroscience provides a window into the biological level of behavior operating in coaching interactions, which broadens and deepens our comprehension of the interplay between the coach and coachee. In turn, coaching offers to neuroscience a context of rich human relationships, development and behavior change. As technology continues to advance, a partnership between neuroscience and coaching offers provocative possibilities for research that informs practice. As this new domain evolves, it is prudent for coaching researchers and practitioners to be educated consumers of 'neurocoaching' literature. It was our aim in this chapter to begin that work.

REFERENCES

Ashkanasy, N. M., Becker, W. J., & Waldman, D. A. (2014). Neuroscience and organizational behavior: Avoiding both neuro-euphoria and neuro-phobia. *Journal of Organizational Behavior*, 35, 909–919.

Aston-Jones, G., & Cohen, J. D. (2005). An integrative theory of locus coeruleus-norepinephrine function: Adaptive gain and optimal performance. *Annual Review of Neuroscience*, 28, 403–450.

Baumgartner, T., Fischbacher, U., Feierabend, A., Lutz, K., & Fehr, E. (2009). The neural circuitry of a broken promise. *Neuron*, 64(5), 756–770.

Becker, W. J., & Cropanzano, R. (2010). Organizational neuroscience: The promise and prospects of an emerging discipline. *Journal of Organizational Behavior*, 31, 1055–1059.

Becker, W. J., Cropanzano, R., & Sanfey, A. G. (2011). Organizational neuroscience: Taking organizational theory inside the neural black box. *Journal of Management*, 37(4), 933–961.

Becker, W. J., & Menges, J. I. (2013). Biological implicit measures in HRM and OB: A question of how not if. *Human Resource Management Review*, 23(3), 219–228.

Bennett, J. L. & Bush, M. W. (2014). *Coaching for Change*. New York: Routledge.

Blackwell, L., Trzesniewski, K. H., & Dweck, C. S. (2007). Implicit theories of intelligence predict achievement across an adolescent transition: A longitudinal study and an intervention. *Child Development*, 78(1), 246–263.

Bowman, M., Ayers, K. M., King, J. C., & Page, L. J. (2013). The neuroscience of coaching. In J. Passmore, D. Peterson, and T. Freire (Eds.), *The Wiley-Blackwell Handbook of the Psychology of Coaching and Mentoring* (pp. 89–111). West Sussex, UK: John Wiley & Sons, Ltd.

Boyatzis, R. E. (2006). Intentional change theory from a complexity perspective. *Journal of Management Development*, 25(7), 607–623.

Boyatzis, R. E. & Akrivou, K. (2006). The ideal self as a driver of change. *Journal of Management Development*, 25(7), 624–642.

Boyatzis, R. E., Lingham, A., & Passarelli, A. (2010). Inspiring the development of emotional, social, and cognitive intelligence competencies in managers. In M. Rothstein & R. Burke (Eds.), *Self-Management and Leadership Development*: 62–90. Edward Elgar Publishing.

Boyatzis, R., Rochford, K., & Jack, A. (2014). Antagonistic neural networks underlying differentiated leadership roles. *Frontiers in Human Neuroscience*, 8, 1–15 doi: 10.3389/fnhum.2014.00114.

Boyatzis, R. E., & Saatcioglu, A. (2008). A twenty year view of trying to develop emotional, social and cognitive intelligence competencies in graduate management education. *Journal of Management Development*, *27*(3), 92–108.

Boyatzis, R. E., Smith, M. L., & Blaize, N. (2006). Developing sustainable leaders through coaching and compassion. *Academy of Management Learning & Education*, *5*(1), 8–24.

Boyatzis, R. E., Stubbs, E. C., & Taylor, S. N. (2002). Learning cognitive and emotional intelligence competencies through graduate management education. *Academy of Management Journal on Learning and Education*, *1*(2), 150–162.

Brown, P., & Brown, V. (2012). *Neuropsychology for Coaches: Understanding the Basics*. New York: McGraw-Hill.

Cacioppo, J. T., & Decety, J. (2011). Challenges and opportunities in social neuroscience. *Annals of New York Academy of Sciences*, *1224*(1), 162–173.

Cacioppo, J. T., Bernston, G. G., Sheridan, J. F., & McClintock, M. K. (2000). Multilevel integrative analysis of human behaviour: Social neuroscience and the complementing nature of social and biological perspectives. *Psychological Bulletin*, *126*(6), 829–843.

Clay, R. A. (2007). *Functional Magnetic Resonance Imaging: A New Research Tool*. Washington DC: American Psychological Association – Science Directorate.

Delgado, M. R., Olsson, A., & Phelps, E. A. (2006). Extending animal models of fear conditioning to humans. *Biological Psychology*, *73*(1), 39–48.

Dias, G. P., Palmer, S., O'Riordan, S., Bastos de Freitas, S., Habib, L. R., Mário Cesar do Nascimento Bevilaqua, & Nardi, A. E. (2015). Perspectives and challenges for the study of brain responses to coaching: Enhancing the dialogue between the fields of neuroscience and coaching psychology, *The Coaching Psychologist*, *11*(1), 11–19.

Doidge, N. (2007). *The Brain that Changes Itself: Stories of Personal Triumph from the Frontiers of Brain Science*. New York: Penguin.

Dulebohn, J. H., Conlon, D. E., Sarinopoulos, I., Davison, R. B., & McNamara, G. (2009). The biological bases of unfairness: Neuroimaging evidence for the distinctiveness of procedural and distributive justice. *Organizational Behavior and Human Decision Processes*, *110*(2),140–151.

Eisenberger, N. I. (2012). The pain of social disconnection: Examining the shared neural underpinnings of physical and social pain. *Nature Reviews Neuroscience*, *13*(6), 421–434.

Eisenberger, N. I., & Cole, S. W. (2012). Social neuroscience and health: Neurophysiological mechanisms linking social ties with physical health. *Nature Neuroscience*, *15*(5), 669–674.

Eissenegger, C., Haushofer, J. & Fehr, E. (2011). The role of testosterone in social interaction. *Trends in Cognitive Sciences*, *15*(6), 263–271.

Glickstein, M. (2014). *Neuroscience: A Historical Introduction*. Cambridge, MA: MIT Press.

Grant, A. (2015). Coaching neuro-science or neuro-nonsense. *The Coaching Psychologist*, *11*(1), 21–27.

Greenberg, J., & Colquitt, J. A. (2005). *Handbook of Organizational Justice*. Mahwah, NJ: Lawrence Erlbaum Associates.

Habermacher, A., Ghadiri, A., & Peters, T. (2014). The case for basic human needs in coaching: A neuroscientific perspective – the SCOAP coach theory. *The Coaching Psychologist*, *10*(1), 7–16.

Händel, B.F., Haarmeier T., & Jensen, O. (2011). Alpha oscillations correlate with the successful inhibition of unattended stimuli. *Journal of Cognitive Neuroscience*, *23*(9), 2494–2502.

Hebb, D. O. (1949). *The Organization of Behavior: A Neuropsychological Theory*. New York: Wiley.

Higgins, E. T. (1987). Self-discrepancy: A theory relating self and affect. *Psychological Review*, *94*(3), 319–340.

Howard, A. (2006). Positive and negative emotional attractors and intentional change. *Journal of Management Development*, *25*(7), 657–670.

Howard, A. (2015). Coaching to vision versus coaching to improvement needs: A preliminary investigation on the differential impacts of fostering positive and negative emotion during real time executive coaching sessions.

Frontiers in Psychology, 6, 455. doi:10.3389/fpsyg.2015.00455.

Jack, A. I., Boyatzis, R. E., Khawaja, M. S., Passarelli, A. M., & Leckie, R. L. (2013a). Visioning in the brain: An fMRI study of inspirational coaching and mentoring. *Social Neuroscience, 8*(4), 369–384.

Jack, A. I., Dawson, A. J., Begany, K. L., Leckie, R. L., Barry, K. P., Ciccia, A. H., & Snyder, A. Z. (2013b). fMRI reveals reciprocal inhibition between social and physical cognitive domains. *NeuroImage, 66*(1), 385–401.

Kandel, E. R., & Hudspeth, A. J. (2013). The brain and behavior. In E. R. Kandel, J. H. Schwartz, T. M. Jessell, S. A. Siegelbaum, & A. J. Hudspeth (Eds.), *Principles of Neural Science* (5th ed., pp. 5–20). New York: McGraw-Hill.

Kandel, E. R., Schwartz, J. H., Jessell, T. M., Siegelbaum, S. A., & Hudspeth, A. J. (2013). *Principles of Neural Science* (5th ed.). New York: McGraw-Hill.

Kolb, B., & Whishaw, I. Q. (1998). Brain plasticity and behavior. *Annual Review of Psychology, 49*, 43–64.

Kolb, D. A., & Boyatzis, R. E. (1970). Goal-setting and self-directed behavior change. *Human Relations, 23*(5), 439–457.

Lee, N., & Chamberlain, L. (2007). Neuroimaging and psychophysiological measurement in organizational research: An agenda for research in organizational cognitive neuroscience. *Ann. New York Academy of Sciences, 1118*, 18–42.

Lieberman, M. (2010). Social Cognitive Neuroscience. In S. T. Fiske, D. T. Gilbert, & G. Lindzey (Eds.), *Handbook of Social Psychology* (Vol. 2). (pp. 143–193). Hoboken, NJ: John Wiley & Sons.

Lindebaum, D. (2012). Pathologizing the healthy but ineffective: Some ethical reflections on using neuroscience in leadership research. *Journal of Management Inquiry, 22*(3), 295–305.

Lindebaum, D., & Zundel, M. (2013). Not quite a revolution: Scrutinizing organizational neuroscience in leadership studies. *Human Relations, 66*(6), 857–877.

Mars, R. B., Neubert, F. X., Noonan, M. P., Sallet, J., Toni, I., & Rushworth, M. F. (2012). On the relationship between the 'default mode network' and the 'social brain'. *Frontiers in Human Neuroscience, 6*, 189.

Marshall, P. J. (2009). Relating psychology and neuroscience: Taking up the challenges. *Perspectives on Psychological Science, 4*, 113–125.

Mason, M. F., & Morris, M. W. (2010). Culture, attribution and automaticity: A social cognitive neuroscience view. *Social Cognitive and Affective Neuroscience, 5*(2–3), 292–306.

McGrath, C. L., Kelley, M. E., Holtzheimer, P. E., Dunlop, B. W., Craighead, W. E., Franco, A. R., Craddock, R. C. & Mayberg, H. S. (2013). Toward a neuroimaging treatment selection biomarker for major depressive disorder. *JAMA Psychiatry, 70*(8), 821–829.

McGuire, J. T., & Botvinick, M. M. (2010). Prefrontal cortex, cognitive control, and the registration of decision costs. *Proceedings of the National Academy of Sciences, 107*(17), 7922–7926.

Ochsner, K. N., & Lieberman, M. D. (2001). The emergence of social cognitive neuroscience. *American Psychologist, 56*(9), 717–734.

Onoda, K., Okamoto, Y., Nakashima, K. I., Nittono, H., Ura, M., & Yamawaki, S. (2009). Decreased ventral anterior cingulate cortex activity is associated with reduced social pain during emotional support. *Social Neuroscience, 4*(5), 443–454.

Pascual-Leon, A., Amedi, A., Fregni, F., & Merabet, L. B. (2005). The plastic human cortex. *Annual Review of Neuroscience, 28*, 377–401.

Passarelli, A. M. (2014). The Heart of Helping: Psychological and Physiological Effects of Contrasting Coaching Interactions. Unpublished doctoral dissertation, Case Western Reserve University.

Passarelli, A. M., Abou Zeki, D., Boyatzis, R. E., Dawson, A. J., & Jack, A. I. (2013). *Coaching with compassion helps you see the big picture: fMRI reveals neural overlap between different styles of coaching and visual attention*. Poster presented at Coaching in Leadership and Healthcare conference, Harvard Medical School. Boston, MA.

Phelps, E. A., Delgado, M. R., Nearing, K. I., & LeDoux, J. E. (2004). Extinction learning in humans: Role of the amygdala and vmPFC. *Neuron, 43*(6), 897–905.

Porges, S. W. (2003). The polyvagal theory: Phylogenetic contributions to social behavior. *Physiology & Behavior, 79*(3), 503–513.

Raichle, M. E., MacLeod, A. M., Snyder, A. Z., Powers, W. J., Gusnard, D. A., & Shulman, G. L. (2001). A default mode of brain function. *Proceedings of the National Academy of Sciences, 98*(2), 676–682.

Saggar, M., Quintin, E. M., Kienitz, E., Bott, N. T., Sun, Z., Hong, W. C., Chien, Y., Liu, N. Dougherty, R.F., Royalty, A., Hawthorne, G. & Reiss, A.L. (2015). Pictionary-based fMRI paradigm to study the neural correlates of spontaneous improvisation and figural creativity. *Scientific reports, 5*, 10894.

Satpute, A. B., & Lieberman, M. D. (2006). Integrating automatic and controlled processes into neurocognitive models of social cognition. *Brain Research, 1079*(1), 86–97.

Schatz, C. J. (1992). The developing brain. *Scientific American, 267*(3), 60–67.

Shams, M. (2015). Why is it important to understand the neurological basis of coaching intervention? *The Coaching Psychologist, 11*(1), 28–29.

Sherman, G. D., Lee, J. J., Cuddy, A. J. C., Renshon, J., Oveis, C., Gross, J. J., & Lerner, J. S. (2012). Leadership is associated with lower levels of stress. *Proceedings of the National Academy of Sciences, 109*(44), 17903–17907.

Spreng, R. N. (2012). The fallacy of a 'task-negative' network. *Frontiers in Psychology,* 3, 145.

Spunt, R. P., & Lieberman, M. D. (2013). The busy social brain evidence for automaticity and control in the neural systems supporting social cognition and action understanding. *Psychological Science, 24*(1), 80–86.

Takeuchi, H., Taki, Y., Hashizume, H., Sassa, Y., Nagase, T., Nouchi, R., & Kawashima, R. (2012). The association between resting functional connectivity and creativity. *Cerebral Cortex, 22*(12), 2921–2929.

Uchino, B. N., Cacioppo, J. T., & Kiecolt-Glaser, J. K. (1996). The relationship between social support and physiological processes: a review with emphasis on underlying mechanisms and implications for health. *Psychological Bulletin, 119*(3), 488–531.

Vaden, K. I., Kuchinsky, S. E., Cute, S. L., Ahlstrom, J. B., Dubno, J. R., & Eckert, M. A. (2013). The cingulo-opercular network provides word-recognition benefit. *The Journal of Neuroscience, 33*(48), 18979–18986.

Van Oosten, E. (2013). The impact of emotional intelligence and executive coaching on leader effectiveness. Unpublished doctoral dissertation, Case Western Reserve University, Cleveland, Ohio.

Van Overwalle, F. (2009). Social cognition and the brain: A meta-analysis. *Human Brain Mapping, 30*(3), 829–858.

Zull, J. E. (2002). *The Art of Changing the Brain: Enriching Teaching by Exploring the Biology of Learning*. Sterling, VA: Stylus Publishing, LLC.

The Use of Psychological Assessments in Coaching and Coaching Research

Almuth McDowall

INTRODUCTION

This chapter outlines the nature, value and use of psychological assessments in coaching with particular reference to how such assessments can be used in coaching research. The content extends beyond existing material on this topic (Bourne, 2007; Smewing & McDowall, 2010; Passmore, 2012) to include conceptual issues, such as the nature of psychological constructs being examined, the rationale for their respective measurement, but also the gaps in our understanding. In particular, the chapter argues that trained coaches should use psychometrics appropriately by checking and corroborating outputs and reports with the coachee. This constitutes good and appropriate practice but is rarely done in research, where profiles are usually taken at face value, without further exploration of the accuracy of the results.

Specifically, this chapter commences with an overview of a range of psychological assessments available to coaches and their application, building on Smewing and McDowall (2010) to include contemporary developments. The next section will outline some of the conceptual debates in the field with particular reference to person- rather than task- or performance-focused constructs through examination of key meta-analytic literature and other reviews. As much of the literature has been written with a general audience in mind, rather than for coaching specifically, it draws the link back to a coaching context as appropriate to include a discussion of relevant, but usually smaller scale, studies in a coaching context. The last section of this chapter leaves the reader with an agenda to improve the use of psychological assessments in research and practice, referencing the need for professional development in the area. Future directions for the use of psychological assessment in coaching include that research could learn much from practice to utilise psychological assessments as part of a process, rather than relying on numbers and scores alone.

WHAT ARE PSYCHOLOGICAL ASSESSMENTS?

Although it is anticipated that many of the features of psychological assessments detailed should not be a surprise to many readers, it is vital that coaching practitioners understand and can accurately explain these key elements to a coachee. Psychometrics, as they are also referred to, are standardised and quantitative methods of observing and summarising human behaviour and have firmly taken hold in educational, clinical and occupational practice around the globe. Each psychological assessment should be marked by the following four core features: (a) they should be reliable across situations and time, (b) measure validly what they set out to measure, (c) have appropriate reference points of comparison (standardisation against population norms, or against a priori agreed standards), and (d) be free from bias (not disadvantaging particular groups of people). These features are outlined in Table 34.1, which links these elementary features to general implications and more specific implications for coaching.

The summary offered in Table 34.1 shows that all psychological assessments have to be considered in the light of their technical properties, as these need to be adequate to justify their choice and use. Whilst coaches would not normally make selection decisions, where predictive validity (how is the construct related to performance outcomes?) is of crucial importance, psychological assessments nevertheless need to be consistent and measure appropriate content so that coaching can be structured around a meaningful conversation. Psychometrics have been widely criticised for their potential adverse impact which refers to a situation where minority groups score lower on assessments than majority groups (e.g. Rust & Golombok, 2014). However, the actual impact varies and is affected by a large range of factors which include the specificity of the test, but also how well test takers understand the test and instructions and their reactions to the assessment as such (Hough, Oswald & Ployhart, 2001). The latter aspect is particularly relevant in a coaching context which encompasses far more discussion and corroboration of results than a typical selection process. Coaches need to become attuned to how candidates react to assessments, and where necessary explain instructions or processes with further tailored instructions, so that all coachees can benefit from an assessment process. In this context, it is also necessary to bear in mind that whilst any assessments can help to estimate an individuals' performance, they cannot ever be 100% certain, but rather that error terms need to be remediated as much as possible in test construction and use in practice (Schmidt and Hunter (1996) outline measurement error in psychological research very lucidly).

What do Psychological Assessments Measure?

Aside from technical properties, arguably the most important differentiator between different types of assessment is their underlying construct – what do they actually measure? Smewing and McDowall (2010) set out some of the basic features. Assessments may measure a range of attributes, including knowledge and skill, specific performance, attitudes, personal preference and values, interests or decision making. One way of illustrating the range of assessments available is to plot these along a person–task continuum, depicting the range or breadth of measures as illustrated by the indicative bars (see Figure 34.1).

Naturally, the diagram is an oversimplification, as in practice, many of the assessments overlap, and may be understood broader or

Table 34.1 Psychometric features

Psychometric feature	Definition	General implication	Implications to consider in coaching
Reliability	Test–re-test: consistency over repeated administration Internal consistency: do the items measure the same thing? Inter-rater reliability: do different raters agree?	What does the test manual say about reliability, how was this measured? As a benchmark, professional guidelines recommend a minimum of .7 for a reliability coefficient	If reliability statistics appear insufficient, should the instrument be used?
Validity	Construct: does the measure assess what it set out to measure, does it correlate with measures of a similar kind, and differ from tests which measure separate constructs? Criterion related validity: the extent to which the measure correlates with, or predicts measures you are interested in, such as work performance, educational outcomes or well-being?	What is the underlying construct? How has this been operationalised? Is the content of the scales and items adequate to measure the construct? What is the relationship between scores on this assessment and other outcome measures? Absolute guidelines are slightly more complex to provide than for reliability, but a minimum solid evidence should exist on at least two features of validity	If validity statistics appear insufficient, should the instrument be used? What is the underlying construct? How can the discussion of the content measured best feed into a coaching context (e.g. are some dimensions more relevant than others?)
Standardisation	Norm-referenced assessment: this is when a test score is compared to a benchmark group of people who have also taken the test Criterion-referenced assessment: here the test score is benchmarked against an absolute standard (e.g. a test taker has to get say 80% of test items right to pass)	Do the norm groups adequately reflect the coachee or group of coachee's characteristics? Is the norm group large enough to allow reliable estimates? Professional guidelines suggest at least 150 people as a minimum	Are there any specific aspects about the norm group and/or the standardisation process which need to be explained to the coachee?
Freedom from bias	This refers to a situation where a test systematically over- or underestimates test performance; this can manifest itself for instance as difference between different ethnic groups, or by gender. If any discrepancy represents a true difference, then the test is not biased, but if the difference is due to errors in estimation, then the test is biased. Bias can result from a number of factors including how the test is constructed and put together, how the items are worded	Is there any evidence on group differences? If so, are these likely to be due to genuine differences?	If the coach is working with a diverse portfolio of coachees, is a particular test or assessment the right choice? What is coacheee's feedback on the assessment used, such as the language and instructions?

narrower than shown here (and there are many more types of specific assessments available not included here). To illustrate, whilst traditional personality assessments, such as the NEO PI-R® are based on personality theory, modern generation assessments encompass both the aspect of personal preference, but also work-based competence and situational questions. However, it should serve to illustrate that the reach of psychometric tools

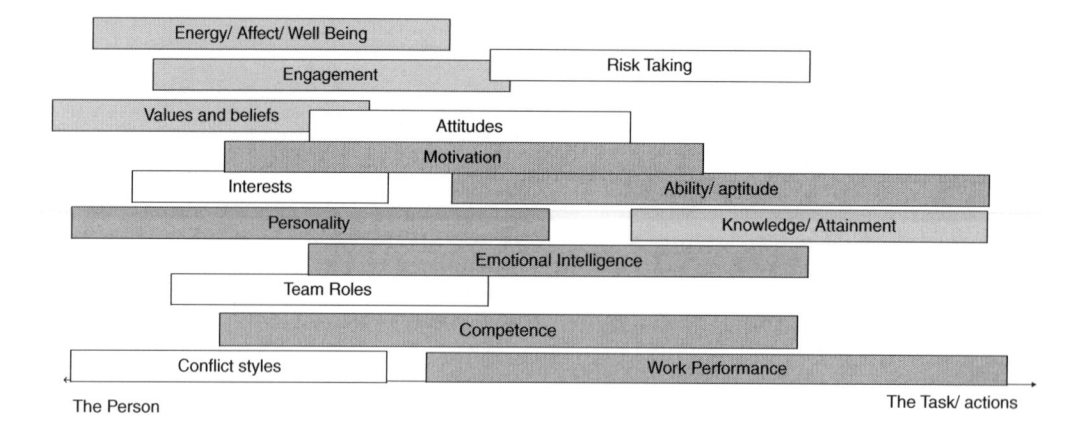

Figure 34.1 The content and reach of psychometric assessments
Source: After Smewing and McDowall (2010)

differs. Another differentiation between psychological assessments is how they are delivered. Some psychological assessments rely on face-to-face interpretation, whereas the reality these days is that they are administered online, controlled through a username and password. This has many advantages for coaching processes, as coachees can complete them readily before any coaching session and the coach will have time to prepare beforehand, without using face-to-face time. However, there is value in the coach being present during assessments, particularly where test takers might be struggling with the instructions or wording of particular items. This might be a particular issue when coachees are not taking an assessment in their native language.

The above illustration is also reflective of the use of psychometrics in coaching and developmental contexts, as coaches are more likely to use assessments that are based on person-based characteristics than assessments based solely on tasks or actions. Given that the aims of coaching are broadly to facilitate personal change and growth (e.g. Grant & Cavanagh, 2004), but also to consider potentially maladaptive behaviour patterns, for instance in health and obesity coaching (e.g. van Zandvoort, Irwin & Morrow, 2008), any assessments which consider personal-centred characteristics are probably most valuable. That said, task oriented measures can also have their value in executive coaching in the context of a leadership development programme, to target performance areas which provide a particularly useful starting point.

AN EXAMPLE FOR SCORING AND INTERPRETING A PSYCHOLOGICAL ASSESSMENT

All psychological assessments are based on a number of items, which can be questions, statements, or tasks such as puzzles, which are then evaluated against a set of agreed criteria, and calculated to arrive at one or several scores, measured either against a population of people similar to the test taker (known as a norm group) or against an agreed standard (through criterion referencing with an example being of a driving test). Some assessments, such as the Wechsler Adult Intelligence Scale (WAIS), are complex in administration and scoring, requiring detailed face-to-face or online administration, providing the test user with a wealth of information. The Wechsler Adult Intelligence Scale (WAIS) is one of the most frequently used psychological assessments around the globe for assessment of cognitive abilities. The current version is the WAIS-IV which was published in 2008. The test provides four major scores (or sub tests):

(i) Verbal comprehension
(ii) Perceptual reasoning
(iii) Working memory
(iv) Processing speed.

WAIS assessment is used to determine individual levels of ability for a whole range of purposes, including the assessment of cognitive factors such as working memory. As an example, one of the applications in coaching might be to use the assessment to determine dyslexic difficulties in adults. In common parlance and understanding, dyslexia is often thought to present as spelling difficulties, but current psychological research shows that the underlying issues are more complex, and encompass a range of symptoms including memory and organisation (Doyle & McDowall, 2015). The following section illustrates how results from an assessment using the WAIS or a similar diagnostic tool plotted across a graph might show levels of neurotypicality; in other words to which extent an individual shows abilities commensurate with a typical ability profile. Figure 34.2 shows a typical profile; the numbers on the vertical axis stand for standardised test scores on an ability test, the numbers along the horizontal axis denote different tests. Here it can be seen that whilst there are strengths and weaknesses, the profile looks overall relatively evenly distributed.

However, when someone's scores deviate from the norm, there are typically large variations between the scores on each sub test, statistical analysis can be applied to assess how significant those differences are. A profile which might indicate dyslexia would look similar to the illustration in Figure 34.3.

When a coach works with a neuro-diverse client (e.g. someone with dyslexic difficulties), part of the coaching process would be to discuss the profile and then identify and agree strategies for managing any difficulties linked to the assessment which typically encompass a range of topics including managing workload and working memory (Doyle & McDowall, 2015). This example shows that it is not the psychological assessment in itself which contributes to the coaching process, but rather the analysis, corroboration and discussion of the results in the light of future action planning. The reader is referred to Lichtenberger and Kaufman (2013, 2nd edition) for further reading on the WAIS assessment as such.

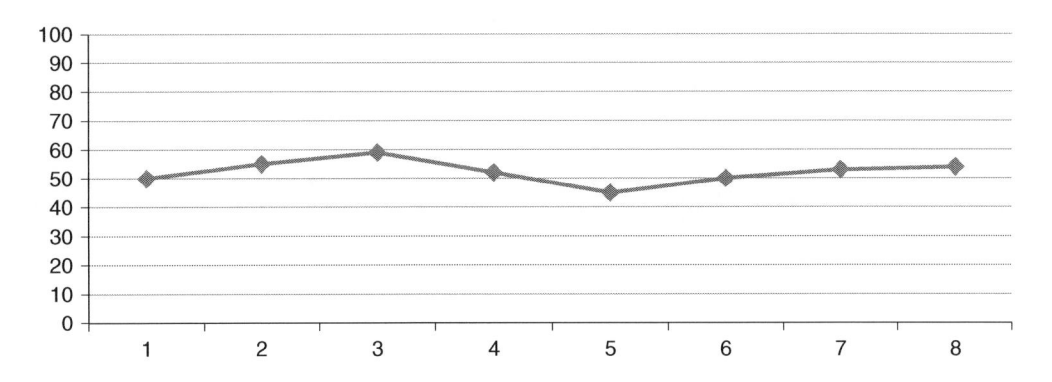

Figure 34.2 (Imaginary) neuro-typical profile across a range of ability measures

Source: Reproduced with kind permission from Genius Within

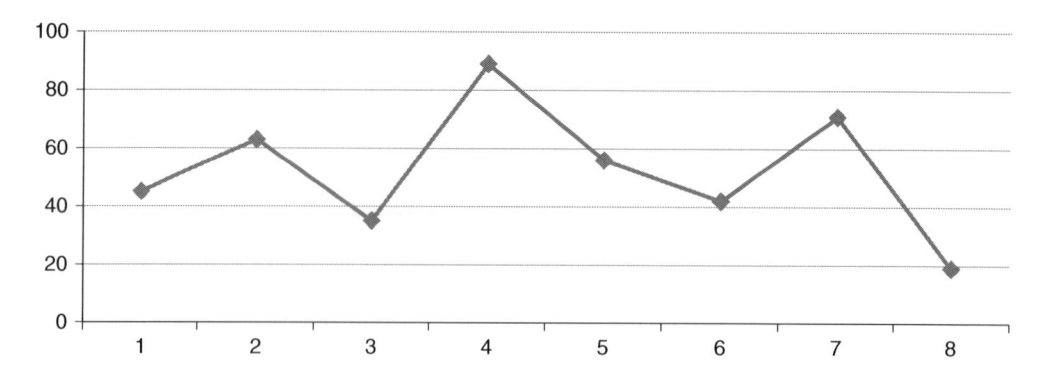

Figure 34.3 Neuro-diversive profile: across a range of ability measures
Source: Reproduced with kind permission from Genius Within

When to Use Assessments in Coaching

This section considers the different purposes for using assessments in coaching. Usually, one of the key aims is to raise coachee self-awareness, and to provide structure for a coaching conversation. It might be useful at the beginning of a coaching process to 'fast track' coach and coachee mutual understanding and report, sometime during a coaching process to introduce new source of data for stimulation and discussion or indeed at the end to measure and evaluate change, for instance through a 360 degree feedback questionnaire as a measure of behaviour change. This is illustrated in Figure 34.4, which outlines at what stages of coaching process assessments might be used in coaching. The reader should note that this is not meant to depict a linear process, but to illustrate that assessment may take on different purposes depending on when they are deployed in coaching.

As can be seen above, the nature and purpose of psychological assessments varies

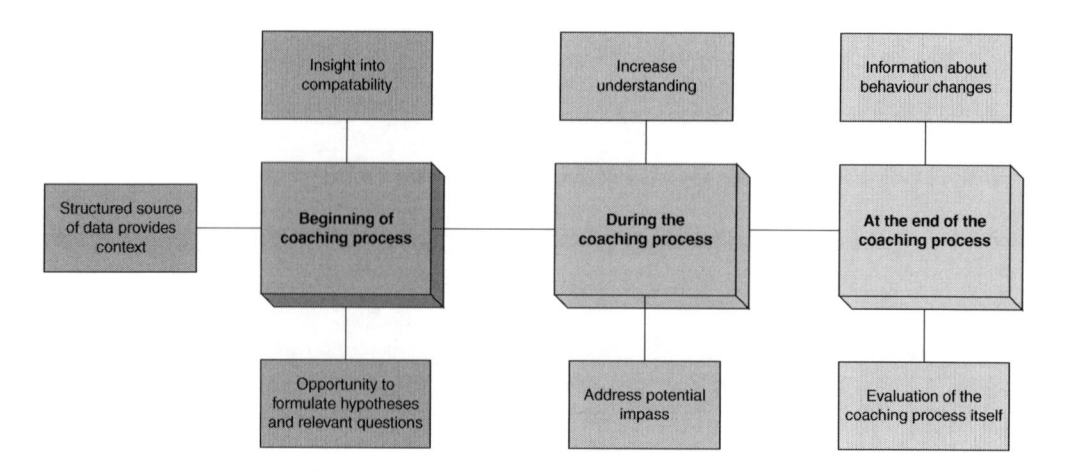

Figure 34.4 Application of assessments during coaching
Source: Adapted from Smewing and McDowall (2010)

by when they are used during the coaching process. One caveat is that more assessment might not be necessarily better – psychometrics have greater add on value for the coaching process if they are used sparingly rather than in abundance. But there is little research on the utility of multiple psychometric assessments in a development context, so this is a clear gap which needs to be addressed.

Normative and Idiographic Assessment

Last but not least, the chapter should also turn to the difference between normative and idiographic psychological assessment. Most of the measures we discussed above take a normative approach, in that the overall purpose is to compare a test takers' results to a referent point of comparison. As outlined above, these vary in their reach and extensiveness. Full personality questionnaires will take a good half an hour or so to administer (other measures much longer still), whereas very specific measures such as the Work-life Indicator© (Centre for Creative Leadership) can be completed in as little as a few minutes. Idiographic approaches, such as repertory grids (e.g. Jankowicz, 2005), are primarily focused on the individual and typically use questioning or stimuli to elicit relevant information. One issue to be mindful of for coaching practice (and indeed research) is that there are many assessments which 'look and feel' like a validated psychometric assessment, but should really be interpreted with an idiographic stance in mind and as a 'question aid' rather than a robust assessment.

RESEARCH ON PERSON FOCUSED PSYCHOLOGICAL CONSTRUCTS

Research on psychological assessment is continuously advancing. In this section of the chapter, we will therefore turn to some of the recent developments in psychological theory, and point the reader to particularly informative review articles to further their understanding.

Personality

A comprehensive and thought provoking paper in the *Annual Review of Psychology* cogently sets out an issue which is often absent from more assessment focused literature on personality, namely the question of *why* personality characteristics might predict any outcomes, rather than *what* it is they predict. Over the years, the Big Five model of personality (also known as the acronym OCEAN; which stands for openness to experience, conscientiousness, extraversion, agreeableness and neuroticism (Goldberg, 1990) has become well accepted in research and practice as one of the most powerful predictive models. However, as the model itself was based on data generation, it describes personality well, but does not explain why people behave in the way that they do; an issue to which the chapter returns in the concluding section. Other aspects which need to be considered therefore are temperament and emotionality, as well as social-cognitive perspectives which explain how individuals categorise the world around them.

Does Personality have a Direct Influence on Individual Outcomes?

Another consideration is whether personality directly or indirectly (through mediation or moderation) predicts the relationship between predictors and outcomes, which are illustrated through three diagrams drawing on Hampson's (2012) chapter. Figure 34.5 outlines a direct relationship. In this instance, a person's level of neuroticism is directly linked to their confidence at work. The more worried and stressed they are the more this impacts on their confidence.

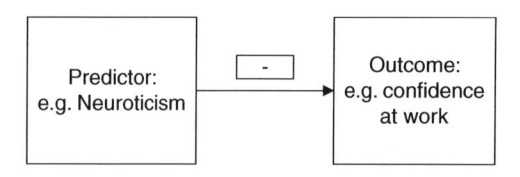

Figure 34.5 Direct relationship between personality and outcomes

It is equally tenable that personality factors could have a less direct effect. Figure 34.6 shows a moderated relationship. Here, the predictor is a coachee's reactions to stressful organisational change and the impact on their confidence when going about day-to-day tasks at work in such an uncertain environment. It is a likely hypothesis that this relationship would be stronger for those who are high in neuroticism as shown in Figure 34.6 which indicates a moderated relationship.

Figure 34.7 illustrates a potential mediated relationship. The illustration simplifies the association between personality and health outcomes where it might be argued that individuals who are more conscientious will engage more fully in a health coaching programme, and hence have better treatment outcomes as a result, a reduced body mass index.

Whilst some of the manuals for existing psychological measures purport the view that traits are rarely good or bad, but context dependent, Hampson's review (2012) sets out persuasively that personality processes are

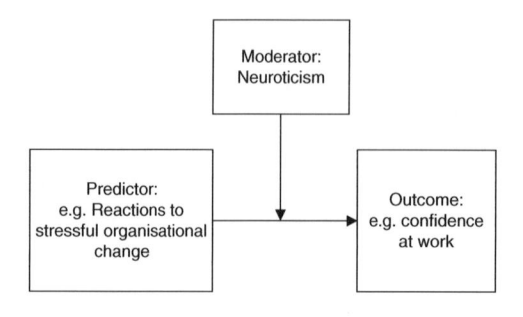

Figure 34.6 Moderated relationship between personality and outcomes

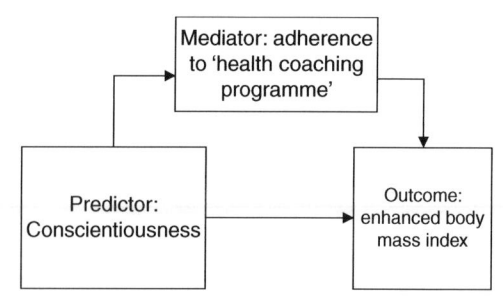

Figure 34.7 Mediated relationship between personality and outcomes

bound up with emotion. Research on negative emotionality, namely neuroticism and anger, shows that individuals with these characteristics experience more pronounced emotional reactions and are more likely to experience adverse outcomes. The author also notes that these aspects of personality are not valence free, as they are seen as negative in practice and research. Positive emotionality, extraversion, is linked to positive outcomes, such as 'happiness', but existing research does not yet quite capture the link between characteristics and experiences; for instance, to what extent personality might change long term through cumulative positive experiences. The third category discussed in Hampson's review are avoidance tendencies, here in particular conscientiousness, which may directly and indirectly influence outcomes through a range of behavioural strategies such as conscious control of efforts and impulses. The reader is referred back to this review for additional food for thought and detail. The implications for personality and coaching are clear though. Personality will influence how people behave in complex and manifest ways, both directly and indirectly, only longitudinal research can bring these to light in their complexity. Coaches are hence cautioned to a) advance their knowledge not only of personality instruments but also advances in current theory to inform interpretation, and b) in particular consider hypotheses around indirect effects on behaviour in coaching conversations.

Emotional Intelligence

The assessment of Emotional Intelligence (EI or EQ) has been critiqued extensively (for an overview see Murphy, 2014) and gone through phases of increasing and then declining popularity. Different conceptualisations of EI are one of the reasons for the controversy about its use in assessment. In the US, the ability model of EI is predominant which measures EI as the capacity to think about and use emotions accurately (Mayer, Roberts & Barsade, 2008). Mixed method approaches for EI have much broader conceptualisations, focusing on competence and skill (Bar-On, 1997) or dispositions and trait like characteristics (Petrides & Furnham, 2003). Recent research would suggest that EI can inform our understanding of human behaviour beyond measures of personality and ability. Joseph and Newman (2010) undertook a conceptually challenging meta-analysis where they tested ability based and mixed model EI studies against each other in terms of their predictive validity drawing coefficients from existing meta analyses, as well as conducting original meta-analyses of primary studies (118 usable studies). The results are revealing and sobering in equal measure. Whilst ability measures of EI are theoretically less grounded, they predict performance only for those jobs where emotion is an integral aspect of the work (emotional labour). Mixed model measures predict on the whole better, but also show gender and race differences. The implications for the coaching context are that practitioners need to choose their measures very carefully and interpret with caution. The chapter returns to the concept of EI in the later section detailing research in coaching.

Motivational Theories

Motivation is one of the most important, but one of the most difficult to measure constructs in psychological assessments. It is important, as individuals can be very able, or very predisposed to something but not actually chose to enact the behaviour; the levels and nature of personal motivation will influence what people chose to do, how much effort they invest and for how long they keep doing it (Pinder, 2008). Motivation can be facilitated through extrinsic factors, such as rewards, or through intrinsic factors, such as one's own sense of satisfaction. A now classic contribution to the *Annual Review in Psychology* (Latham & Pinder, 2005) sets out many of the core theoretical propositions around (work) motivation, but also highlights some of the aspects which deserve further attention. Latham and Locke (2012) expand on what is perhaps one of the most promising and exciting areas in motivational research, which is the role of the subconscious in motivation. Experimental approaches have shown that goals can be subconsciously primed, as argued for instance by Stajkovic et al. (2006). Ganegoda, Latham and Folger (2015) showed that both conscious and primed (not conscious) goals result in fairer behaviour during a negotiation task in an experimental study. Results in this research domain are still relatively preliminary, and need further replication, but the interesting implication for psychometric assessment of motivation in coaching is that questionnaire measures may not be enough to measure relevant constructs fully.

Another important aspect is the link between personality and motivation, in other words to what extent individuals' preferences influence what they do, as measured by performance outcomes. Judge and Ilies (2002) undertook a comprehensive meta-analysis of over 65 studies where they linked the big five model to performance measures and three theories of motivation, namely goal-setting, expectancy and self-efficacy. They found that three of the big five traits (extraversion, conscientiousness and neuroticism) have a link to performance outcomes, and therefore are a source of motivation for individuals.

Strengths-Based Paradigms

Perhaps one of the most fervent developments in assessment practice has been the recent development and proliferation of strengths-based assessments. The work of scholars focused on individual (e.g. Judge & Bono, 2001) and group level characteristics (Luthans, Youssef & Avolio, 2007) provide evidence that a positive self concept is linked to a range of performance and well-being outcomes although positive psychology is not without criticism (e.g. Miller, 2008). Judge and Bono (2001) put forward self-core evaluations, which are (a) self-esteem (to what extent people 'like' themselves), (b) generalised self-efficacy (belief in ones' capabilities), (c) locus of control (the degree of owning one's actions) and (d) emotional stability. These self-core evaluations also have a strong link to motivational aspects (Erez & Judge, 2002).

Luthans and colleagues refer to the concept of psychological capital which like self-core evaluations is made up of four established psychological constructs. These are (a) hope, (b) optimisim, (c) resilience and (d) efficacy. The authors have put forward a measure and published a number of intervention studies measuring the construct, and showing that psychological capital can be affected positively through even very short interventions (Luthans et al., 2006). These are built around the PsyCap model, and use a combination of goal-setting, visualisation and anticipation of potential adversity, as well as how to overcome these, to enhance resilience and performance.

With regards to coaching undertaken with groups, a recent paper outlines a very brief focused group coaching intervention to determine whether this was an effective means of facilitating people's goal confidence and strengths knowledge, compared to a control group which undertook a brief self-led goal review, but did not take part in coaching. Interestingly, both groups improved somewhat, both on self-efficacy and strengths knowledge (McDowall and Butterworth, 2014).

A second example compared how a strengths-focused 'feedforward interview' (FFI) compared to a more traditional coaching-based session using feedback based on a psychometric career profile (McDowall et al., 2014) in terms of affecting participants' self-efficacy, goal attainment and strengths-confidence, as well as mood. The FFI intervention had positive effects on self-efficacy and goal attainment, but we also observed results we had not quite expected, as self-efficacy and also strengths-confidence dropped in the feedback condition. Feedback from participants showed that they reacted much more positively to FFI. One of the limitations highlighted in the write up of this research was that it measured knowledge of strengths, but not how individuals deploy and *use* their strengths, as there might be difference between knowing and doing (Govindji & Linley, 2007). This is an aspect to bear in mind when using strengths-based measures in coaching, which are about focused identification, hence the discussion around any profile may need to give particular reference to what people actually do.

Coaching-Specific Assessments: Culture

In practice, coaches may use a number of other assessments, including pre-coaching questionnaires or reflective tools such as life 'audits' (see Smewing & McDowall, 2010). To date, there seem to be relatively few psychometric measures designed specifically for a development and coaching context. One exception is the Cultural Orientations Framework (COF, Rosinski, 2010) which is a questionnaire written to assess individual cultural profiles as a basis for further discussion. A cross-validation study (where two or more psychometric instruments are compared on a range of scales or scores) compared the COF against the Wave Focus®, a preference-based personality questionnaire to consider cultural differences between German and UK participants (Rojon & McDowall, 2010). In this context, differences by gender were more marked than by national origin, but clearly more research is needed on a wider scale to compare other national backgrounds, too.

360-DEGREE FEEDBACK

It is remiss to offer a chapter on psychological assessment without discussing 360-degree feedback or multi-rater assessments. As described in McDowall and Kurz (2007) such tools allow the direct comparison of feedback from multiple sources, the underlying notion being that especially discrepant feedback, and the discussion thereof, will prompt behaviour change. It is disappointing that research using such instruments has somewhat ground to a halt. Whilst there was considerable research in the early 2000s, in all likelihood reflecting their popularity in organisational practice at the time, far fewer studies have emerged over the last few years. Luthans and Peterson (2003) and Smither and colleagues (2003) found that 360-degree feedback works more effectively if followed up by coaching to embed behavioural change. Bracken and Rose (2011) offer the most recent review of 360-degree feedback. Based on the literature, they identify four characteristics to enable organisational change which need to be considered when designing 360-degree feedback processes. The four principles outlined are (1) relevant content,

Table 34.2 Principles for 360-degree feedback in coaching

Characteristic	This refers to ...	Questions to ask for use in coaching
Relevant Content (Bracken & Rose, 2011)	... the features to do with the instrument itself, such as the reliability and acceptance by users, and also the evidence for construct validity across cultures; as well as specific features such as verbal comments.	What is my client group like? Does the instrument sample relevant behaviours?
Credible Data (Bracken & Rose, 2011)	... the kind of items and questions used in the instrument, the nature of the rating scale, as well as who and how many provide ratings, and whether they are trained; as well as time intervals between ratings.	Who can provide meaningful ratings, or are the ratings provided already from relevant people? Are the response scales appropriate? At what point in the coaching process do I want to use 360-degree feedback?
Accountability	... how the results are used, including the role of a coach and the line manager, as well as the integration with other HR systems.	How can I help the coachee to embed behaviour change? Is it necessary to act on all of the information provided (is it reliable), what needs to be prioritised?
Organization-wide participation	... where participation is mandatory or voluntary; and how can raters be supported.	What is the rationale for using 360-degree feedback, particularly if commissioned by the client?
Ownership of the feedback (McDowall & Mabey, 2008)	... with whom the data is shared.	Who should have access to data or profiles? What needs to be put in place if feedback is particularly discrepant, or negative?
Focus, frequency and timing (extended from McDowall & Mabey, 2008)	... how often feedback is repeated, and to what extent the focus is on past, present or future.	At what point in a coaching programme is 360-degree feedback utilised, is there a case for repeating a feedback profile?

Source: Based on Bracken and Rose (2011) and McDowall and Mabey (2008)

(2) credible data, (3) accountability, and (4) organisation-wide participation. These are adapted here in Table 34.2 and modified, building on McDowall and Mabey (2008) and Bracken and Rose (2011), setting out principles for evaluating four different development activities including coaching.

Clearly, 360-degree feedback offers a unique opportunity to compare direct feedback from various sources. This can be a powerful form of assessment, particularly where the feedback format also allows raters to convey direct comments. However, these can be bruising to individuals concerned, even where well meant, where feedback is unexpected (McDowall & Millward, 2010). For this reason, it is particularly important that those who help the focal individual put the feedback into context, are appropriately trained, as shown in the example relating to 360-degree feedback in the subsequent section on best practice.

SOME BEST PRACTICE GUIDELINES FOR USING PSYCHOLOGICAL ASSESSMENTS IN RESEARCH AND IN COACHING

There is no doubt that the range of psychological assessments has mushroomed, both in terms of their content, but also the various outputs (reports) that can be produced. These differ in the sophistication and the format of the data presented as well as at whom such reports are aimed. Some reports are designed in such a way that they can be given to the test taker (coachee, or another individual who was assessed using the measure) directly without the need for interpretation or feedback by another use. Such reports are usually relatively short and simple, and avoid technical detail such as standardised scores.

For good reason, many publishers stipulate that their assessments should only be used by appropriately trained practitioners who can explain and explore the reports with the test taker. For many reasons, there is considerable benefit from such mutual discussion of psychological assessments. In a coaching context, it firstly provides the coach with an opportunity to obtain additional data about the coachee, and to prepare very specific questions and discussion topics for subsequent meetings. A psychological assessment thus provides a potential structure for a coaching conversation. One of the key benefits of having this personal discussion is the opportunity to ask questions around how 'true' the assessment profile is, as individuals can adopt behavioural strategies which counter or remediate personal preferences.

As an example, someone's Personality Profile as mapped onto the Big Five model might indicate them as on the far 'left hand side' of conscientiousness (so with a low standard score – although in practice one would usually avoid the language of 'high' and 'low' as this would imply ability rather than preference), therefore a strong preference not to concern themselves with detail. However, this does not mean that a coachee is not able to do things which are indicative of conscientiousness, such as very diligent checking of relevant procedures. Nevertheless, such checking of work may not come naturally to them. For this reason, they may have adopted compensatory strategies to remind themselves of what needs to be done, for instance by referring to regular check lists or other prompts, which means that they would work to someone who has a strong natural preference for conscientiousness. Such nuances and compensation strategies cannot be gleaned from the automated profile on its own, so rely on questioning and exploration as part of a mutual discussion. Such discussion also provides the coachee with the opportunity to query any of the results, to check mutual understanding and contextualise the results to the particular situation of the coachee, and identify strategies and plans for future action.

To this extent, it is important that the coach has an in depth understanding of the instrument, and how the scales measure relevant behaviours; in particular where the instrument is focused on the person, rather than task or knowledge, the latter being based on an arguably more objective assessment, which is less open to interpretation.

As alluded to in the introduction to this chapter, it is a great shame that such in depth discussions of profiles are very rarely considered in research. At the time of writing this chapter, there is little if any robust research which investigates the process for psychological assessment in coaching practice, as opposed to the outcomes. The bulk of research evidence on personality for instance (see the discussion of relevant research outlined above) uses standardised scores from any instrument, without any corroboration or interpretation. This is also referred to as an 'actuarial' approach, so taking the data at face value, whereas discussion and corroboration is more in line with a clinical approach, which relies more heavily on interpretation. With regards to the latter, there are three main ways in which a coach can feedback the results of an assessment:

1. Base the discussion on prior planning and 'tell' the coachee about the results of particular aspects. For instance, the coach might explain some or all aspects of the assessment in turn, and then ask for feedback from the coachee.
2. Consider the assessment in advance and identify broad themes for discussion, with particular reference to how different dimensions or scales of the assessment link with each other.
3. Identify a broader topic for discussion to situate the assessment, for instance working with the coachee on utilising their strengths, or planning career options and then bringing in the assessment results as appropriate.

Each of these approaches has advantages and disadvantages, experienced test users would probably highlight that it is best to adapt the style of discussion as necessary. Another issue which deserves mention here is how to share the actual profile with the coachee or test taker. Again, this is an issue rarely sufficiently addressed in research, since at best participants tend to get 'told' of their results, but rarely have the chance to discuss these further. Whilst relevant professional guidelines issued by bodies such as the International Test Commission (ITC) and British Psychological Society (BPS) are clear about the necessity to corroborate and feedback results, the use of online testing and the availability of user reports has made this less common practice than would be desirable. Psychological assessment results are essentially data information, it's the discussion and utilisation of this information, and translation into concrete action, that makes them valuable.

Thus the format and delivery, as well as the type of feedback used, have a bearing on how useful psychological assessments are. It is equally important to consider the role of assessments and their purpose: for example, are they used for profiling purposes, to better understand individuals or groups of individuals? Are they used as 'predictors', so to explain why individuals may behave or present in a certain way? Are they used as an evaluation of a process and activity, or to make decisions about people? These are questions which need to be considered upfront, before using any psychological assessments, to ensure that ethical and professional considerations are duly addressed.

There is also the issue of data ownership. This is particularly pertinent where the assessment information may be potentially sensitive or controversial, a 360-degree feedback profile detailing very diverse ratings, and also potentially including raw data (comments from others in the work place) is a case in point.

The following abbreviated case study example of using a 360-degree profile in an executive leadership coaching context illustrates relevant points. A series of coaching sessions was commissioned by a large organisation to coach one of their senior leaders. It was part of the remit to use a number of psychological assessments including a 360-degree feedback profile; the data would be gathered before the coaching sessions and fed into relevant discussions to pinpoint areas where coaching conversations might want to be focused. Prior to the first coaching meeting, it was contracted in advance and in writing that only the coachee, the coach and one other person would have access to the data; any relevant outputs such as a personal development plan would however be shared. Nevertheless, the coach received repeated requests from other members of the organisation to share psychological assessment data, which was not appropriate in this instance for a number of reasons including particularly sensitive interpersonal dynamics in the organisation which were addressed in coaching. This example highlights the value of the 'safeguard' of the prior agreement illustrating that psychological assessments need to consider factors beyond the actual nature of the profile, to also address data ownership.

FUTURE DIRECTIONS

Psychological assessment is here to stay and likely to play a role in both coaching practice and coaching research. However, in order to obtain best value from such data much more synergy is needed between these two applications. On the one hand, practitioners need to engage with the evolving research particularly on personality and personal characteristics, but also other constructs such as situational awareness, to inform their own understanding, choice and interpretation of psychological assessments to ensure informed decisions. On the other hand, research can also learn a lot from practice. Given that no psychological assessment can ever be 100% accurate and purely objective, assessments rely on interpretation. This is not necessarily a disadvantage, but on the contrary, can lead to more meaningful and individualised discussion of profiles. This is notably absent in the relevant evidence base as researchers tend to rely on assessment results at face value. There is a real need to conduct more research on how psychological assessments are best communicated, including when and where they add most value in coaching practice, whether there is a 'best way' to discuss results, or whether it is better to adopt a contingency approach appropriate to the respective coaching context every time. Can psychometrics 'fast track' coaching outcomes for instance, allowing a coaching process to gain momentum and traction more quickly? Given the 'marketing spiel' for many psychometrics this is a valid question to pose, but one to which the available evidence does not yet offer an answer.

Psychological assessments also need to be more considerate of increasingly global and international test takers and test users. Some, but not all, psychometrics have been designed with an international audience in mind, for instance using idiom- and jargon-free language. We also need more instruments which cater for indigenous needs, so are suitable for a particular cultural context. As research on personality has shown (e.g. Cheung, van de Vijver & Leong, 2011) even established personality models such as the 'Big Five' do not necessarily hold up around the globe as a sixth factor of personality emerges in other cultures for instance. The implication is that coaches using psychological assessments also need to be trained in the consideration of the cultural context. Whilst existing guidelines address this to some extent, for instance in the choice of appropriate norm groups, not enough emphasis and consideration is given to the interpretation of psychological profiles.

CONCLUDING REMARKS

Psychological assessments have much to offer, as they can provide insight, stimulus and structure to coaching conversations, as well as offer a source of data in coaching research. Their effective deployment in coaching however depends on one overriding factor – the people who use and interpret them. It is hoped that this chapter has highlighted some of the complexities in psychological interpretation. This includes how personality may have indirect, rather than direct, effects on behaviour, the value of in depth discussions of relevant issues in a coaching context and how the value of multi-source assessments depends on their design, as well as principles for use. Still, there are many areas where more research underpins best practice, such as more context specific research on how profiles are used and interpreted in the context of coaching. It is hoped that an increasing number of coaches will conduct their own research and contribute to further specific understanding of how and for whom psychological assessments make a contribution to coaching.

REFERENCES

Bar-On, R. (1997). Development of the BarOn EQ-i: A measure of emotional and social intelligence. In 105th Annual Convention of the American Psychological Association in Chicago.

Bourne, A. (2007). Using Psychometrics in Coaching. In Palmer, S. & Whybrow, A. (eds.), *Handbook of Coaching Psychology*. Routledge, London

Bracken, D. W., & Rose, D. S. (2011). When does 360-degree feedback create behavior change? And how would we know it when it does? *Journal of Business and Psychology*, 26(2), 183–192.

Cheung, F. M., van de Vijver, F. J., & Leong, F. T. (2011). Toward a new approach to the study of personality in culture. *American Psychologist*, 66(7), 593.

Doyle, N. & McDowall, A. (2015). Is coaching an effective adjustment for dyslexic adults? *Coaching: An International Journal of Theory, Research and Practice*. Online First. DOI: 10.1080/17521882.2015.1065894

Erez, A., & Judge, T. A. (2001). Relationship of core self-evaluations to goal setting, motivation, and performance. *Journal of Applied Psychology*, 86(6), 1270.

Ganegoda, D. B., Latham, G. P., & Folger, R. (2015). The effect of a consciously set and a primed goal on fair behavior. *Human Resource Management*. Online First. DOI: 10.1002/hrm.21743

Goldberg, L. R. (1990). An alternative 'description of personality': a big-five factor structure. *Journal of Personality and Social Psychology*, 59, 1216–1229

Govindji, R., & Linley, P. A. (2007). Strengths use, self-concordance and well-being: Implications for strengths coaching and coaching psychologists. *International Coaching Psychology Review*, 2, 143–153.

Grant, A. M., & Cavanagh, M. J. (2004). Toward a profession of coaching: Sixty-five years of progress and challenges for the future. *International Journal of Evidence Based Coaching and Mentoring*, 2(1), 1–16.

Hampson, S. (2012). Personality processes: Mechanisms by which personality traits 'get outside the skin'. *Annual Review of Psychology*, 63, 315–339

Hough, L. M., Oswald, F. L., & Ployhart, R. E. (2001). Determinants, detection and amelioration of adverse impact in personnel selection procedures: Issues, evidence and lessons learned. *International Journal of Selection and Assessment*, 9(1–2), 152–194.

Jankowicz, D. (2004). *The Easy Guide to Repertory Grids*. Chichester, UK: John Wiley & Sons.

Joseph, D. L., & Newman, D. A. (2010). Emotional intelligence: An integrative meta-analysis and cascading model. *Journal of Applied Psychology*, 95(1), 54.

Judge, T. A., & Ilies, R. (2002). Relationship of personality to performance motivation: A meta-analytic review. *Journal of Applied Psychology*, 87(4), 797.

Judge, T. A., & Bono, J. E. (2001). Relationship of core self-evaluations traits – self-esteem, generalized self-efficacy, locus of control, and emotional stability – with job satisfaction and job performance: A meta-analysis. *Journal of Applied Psychology*, 86(1), 80.

Latham, G. P., & Locke, E. A. (2012). The effect of subconscious goals on organizational behavior. *International Review of Industrial and Organizational Psychology*, 27, 39–63.

Latham, G. P., & Pinder, C. C. (2005). Work motivation theory and research at the dawn of the twenty-first century. *Annual Review of Psychology*, 56, 485–516.

Lichtenberger, E. O. & Kaufman, A. S., & (2013). *Essentials of WAIS-VI assessment* (2nd Ed.) Hoboken, New Jersey: John Wiley & Sons Inc.

Luthans, F., Avey, J. B., Avolio, B. J., Norman, S. M., & Combs, G. M. (2006). Psychological capital development: Toward a micro-intervention. *Journal of Organizational Behavior, 27*(3), 387–393.

Luthans, F., & Peterson, S. J. (2003). 360-degree feedback with systematic coaching: Empirical analysis suggests a winning combination. *Human Resource Management, 42*(3), 243–256.

Luthans, F., Youssef, C. M., & Avolio, B. J. (2006). *Psychological Capital: Developing the Human Competitive Edge*. Oxford, UK: Oxford University Press.

Mayer, J. D., Roberts, R. D., & Barsade, S. G. (2008). Human abilities: Emotional intelligence. *Annul Review of Psychology, 59*, 507–536.

McDowall, A., & Butterworth, L. (2014). How does a brief strengths-based group coaching intervention work? *Coaching: An International Journal of Theory, Research and Practice, 7*(2), 152–163.

McDowall, A., Freemann, K. & Marshall, S. (2014). Is Feedforward the way forward? A Comparison of the effects of FeedForward Coaching and Feedback. *International Coaching Psychology Review. 9*(2), 135–146.

McDowall, A & Kurz, R. (2007). Making the most of psychometric profiles – effective integration into the coaching process. *International Coaching Psychology Review, 2*(3), 299-309.

McDowall, A., & Mabey, C. (2008). Developing a framework for assessing effective development activities. *Personnel Review, 37*(6), 629–646.

McDowall, A., & Millward, L. (2010). Feeding back, feeding forward and setting goals. In Palmer, S. and McDowall, A. (eds) *The Coaching Relationship. Putting People First*. Hove, East Sussex: Taylor & Francis.

Miller, A. (2008). A critique of positive psychology – or 'the new science of happiness'. *Journal of Philosophy of Education, 42*(3–4), 591–608.

Murphy, K. R. (2014). *A Critique of Emotional Intelligence: What are the Problems and How can they be Fixed?* Hove, England: Psychology Press.

Passmore, J. (2012). *Psychometrics in Coaching: Using Psychological and Psychometric Tools for Development*. London: Kogan Page.

Petrides, K. V., & Furnham, A. (2003). Trait emotional intelligence: Behavioural validation in two studies of emotion recognition and reactivity to mood induction. *European Journal of Personality, 17*(1), 39–57.

Pinder, C. C. (2008). *Work Motivation in Organizational Behaviour*. New York, NY: Psychology Press.

Rojon, C., & McDowall, A. (2010). Cultural Orientations Framework (COF) Assessment Questionnaire in Cross-Cultural Coaching: A Cross-Validation with Wave Focus® Styles. *International Journal of Evidence Based Coaching and Mentoring, 8*(2), 1–26.

Rosinski, P. (2010). *Coaching Across Cultures: New Tools for Leveraging National, Corporate & Professional Differences*. London, UK: Nicholas Brealey Publishing.

Rust, J., & Golombok, S. (2014). *Modern Psychometrics: The Science of Psychological Assessment*. London: Routledge.

Schmidt, F. L., & Hunter, J. E. (1996). Measurement error in psychological research: Lessons from 26 research scenarios. *Psychological Methods, 1*(2), 199–223.

Smewing, C., & McDowall, A. (2010). Assessments in Coaching. In Palmer, S. & McDowall, A. (Eds.), *Putting People First. Understanding Interpersonal Relationships in Coaching*. London: Routledge

Smither, J. W., London, M., Flautt, R., Vargas, Y., & Kucine, I. (2003). Can working with an executive coach improve multisource feedback ratings over time? A quasi-experimental field study. *Personnel Psychology, 56*(1), 23–44.

Stajkovic, A. D., Locke, E. A. B., & Blair E. S. (2006). A first examination of the relationship between primed subconscious goals, assigned conscious goals, and task performance. *Journal of Applied Psychology, 91*, 1172–1180.

van Zandvoort, M., Irwin, J. D., & Morrow, D. (2008). Co-active coaching as an intervention for obesity among female university students. *International Coaching Psychology Review, 3*(3), 191–206.

WEB LINKS

Information on test user qualifications as validated by the British Psychological Society, also other publications and guidance sheets relevant to psychometric assessment, as well as test reviews: www.psychtesting.org.uk

The Buros Centre for Testing Test Reviews: http://buros.org/test-reviews-information

International Test Comission: https://www.intestcom.org/

European Association of Psychological Assessment: http://www.eapa-homepage.org/

PART VI
Development of Coaches

Trends in Development of Coaches (Education and Training): Is it Valid, Is it Rigorous and Is it Relevant?

David A. Lane

INTRODUCTION

A core discourse in the education and training of coaches has centred on the role of competence led approaches to accreditation. Many programmes worldwide are driven by the need to satisfy these approaches and their implicit and explicit requirements, which is highly contentious. Alternatives to this approach, primarily from university led programmes, focus instead on a knowledge base for coaching and finding meaning. This chapter will look at this discourse and explore the basis for competence led models, the implications for practice and the limitations. Alternative approaches will also be explored in light of the emerging study of professional practices.

In a review based on twelve coaching programmes that responded to a request for information about their underlying philosophy (Gray, Garvey and Lane, 2016) it is clear that a very wide range of approaches are in play. Many courses use a theoretical knowledge base to inform the way candidates are trained and concern themselves with how learning can emerge as coaches develop their sense of self as well as their sense of being a practitioner. Multiple approaches are taught within courses and while some programmes favour certain approaches, most require the student to develop their own model of practice. Thus, although most of the psychological theory used in coaching originated in counselling or therapy contexts, students of coaching are not trained within one preferred frame as they are in these fields.

Coaching, therefore, is in some important ways unlike the fields from which it is drawn. Most programmes are asking candidates to understand and critically reflect on the ideas and build a personally relevant model of practice. Some explicitly use the theory itself to ask the student to look at themselves and create an integrative model of practice, which fits with their own sense of self. The directions for that exploration vary between courses, with some placed within certain linked theories and others adopting a wider range of exploration. One common element tends to be the significant use of adult learning theory, particularly the theories put forward by Kegan, Kolb, and Meizrow (see Lane, Kahn and Chapman, 2016).

Nevertheless, there are two features which Gray, Garvey and Lane (2016) identify that seem to mitigate against the exploratory principles which courses want to adopt:

1   The first is the use of competence to underpin training as required by professional bodies in the field. The difficulty with this is that while courses are all adopting different frameworks for development of students they are measured against a set but limited framework.
2   The second is the tendency of courses to require students to build their own personal model of practice usually from a limited range of psychological models. This raises the question of the role of the evidence base in the field. If each practitioner is building their own model how can we claim that we train students from an evidence base of practice?

The chapter will conclude by arguing that we can take a reformed approach to argue for multiple ways to validate knowledge. It is in this reformed concept that the chapter seeks to make a contribution. The two themes above, (1) the role of competence and (2) the requirement to build a personal model of practice, will feature strongly in the chapter.

THE ROLE OF COMPETENCE AND CAPABILITY IN COACH TRAINING AND EDUCATION

In common with many occupations, the field of coaching as represented by professional bodies and training organisations, has adopted the idea of competence as a core component of training and assessment. Alternatives to competence models include the more holistic concept of capabilities and theories of knowledge and expertise. There are long standing literatures in these areas. We will explore some of these literatures to consider the implications for coaching as a field of practice and an area of study. Many in the field have argued for broader approaches. Following work by Bachkirova and Lawton Smith (2015), Drake, (2015), Cavanagh, Stern and Lane, (2016) and Gray, Garvey and Lane (2016) it seems we can adopt a more broadly based approach that ensures criticality. This could be achieved by adopting one of a number of positions, discussed below, which are concerned with how we ensure we use appropriate knowledge in our practice.

The Debate on Competence

In recent decades professions have increasingly looked to competencies as a way to define and develop standards for practice. As Stasz (2011) points out this set the UK on a particular path. Critics of this approach argue that this undermines practitioners' ability to develop a meaningful knowledge base for practice. We need to address the critique and shift from competencies as a foundational basis for our practice to models that work when dealing with a world of uncertainty? Some bodies in the field (European Mentoring and Coaching Council is one example) have attempted to build frameworks that define competence from foundational to mastery levels. This only partially addresses the concerns of critics on how to address issues of competence and performance in foundational (simple) or complex situations.

As argued elsewhere (Lane, 2014; Gray, Garvey and Lane, 2016), when we engage in any art, craft or occupation we have to develop the necessary skills to carry out the activity. Delivering on the competence requires a set of underpinning knowledge bases and directs us to engage with a specified set of assumptions that others judge as indicative of competent performance. As a profession it is important to assess the person's skilled practice and confirm that they are competent to perform the skills and, more than that, they are fit to practise in that discipline. (Lane, 2014). Thus, in making that judgement we should do a number of things:

- We can set up a codified, cross-disciplinary knowledge base, in the form of single or multiple models for coaching, which we say provides an underpinning to our practice.
- We require coaches to be sufficiently familiar with the knowledge base, and know how to act, when to act and why to act.
- We determine what it means for coaches to have an ethical basis to their work and know why a particular act demonstrates a value base acceptable to the profession.

The concept of competence therefore goes beyond the demonstration of skill – it implies a judgement as to whether or not they should be admitted into our ranks. However, some within the competence movement focus just on skills and this has been a core issue for the critics of the field. The competence movement has become all encompassing in the UK, USA, Australia, South Africa to mention just a few. Groups from all occupations and professions are finding themselves subject to national vocational standards (Grant, 1979).

A key feature of the competence movement has been to establish generic competencies across occupational groups. Thus in the USA the Office of Personnel Management has promoted generic competence models (Rodriguez, Patel, Bright, Gregory and Gowing, 2002) and in the UK the Health and Care Professions Council has created cross-occupational competencies shared by its many different professional members. Competence-based education tends to be a form of education that derives a curriculum from an analysis of prospective or actual roles in modern society and that attempts to certify student progress on the basis of demonstrated performance in some or all aspects of that role. Theoretically, such demonstrations of competence are independent of time-served in formal educational settings.

There are three key features that are highlighted in competence based approaches to training:

1 the derivation of the goals of training from the analysis of occupational roles (this is currently happening in coaching),
2 the translation of these goals into training 'outputs' in the form of performance criteria rather than the more traditional teaching parameters of training 'inputs' such as syllabi (this is currently happening in coaching), and
3 the freeing up of possibilities for individuals to progress at their own speed on the basis of readily available opportunities for performance assessment rather than coverage of course content (this is not currently happening in coaching).

These practices – prior 'functional analysis' of occupations, the specification of what is to be learned in terms of performance criteria and self-paced learning – have come to be regarded as the defining characteristics of Competence Based Education and training (CBET).

Coaching and Coaching Psychology have followed other occupational groups in adopting competence models. We have models from American Psychological Association, Association for Coaching, European Mentoring and Coaching Council, International Coach Federation, International Society of Coaching Psychology, among many others. Each body builds its model (sometimes with reference to others or not), calls for collaboration by groups such as the Global Coaching Community (Mooney, Dublin Declaration, 2008) notwithstanding.

While such measures have value, as Passmore (2014) argues, once we move beyond core competence towards mastery other measures are needed. He argues that if other professions (such as medical consultants) can do it, why not coaching? Bates (1996) goes further and argues that the development of competence models outstrips the understanding of its effectiveness and social significance. Some argue that competence models are depriving students of access to the ability to define the meanings underpinning the knowledge base necessary for professional practice (Wheelahan, 2007). Competence models promoted by all coaching bodies have therefore been endorsed without reference to the serious debate on the consequences of adopting this approach to selecting, training and assessing fitness to practise.

What Alternatives to Competence Exist?

There are alternative models for defining competence which focus on defining conditions for excellence (Ericsson, 2006), for example, comparing top practitioners with average ones, or asking practitioners to look at factors underpinning their best work.

In coaching there are attempts to do this – as an example Vicki Vandaveer's (2014) work has looked at this. The model used by European Federation of Psychologists' Associations for psychotherapy was based on aspirational standards which recognised that for many they would be currently beyond reach (Lane and Althaus, 2011). Much of the debate has also ignored the difference between competence to practise and conditions related to actual performance in the work context. Developments in areas such as practice theory present frameworks for exploring this through consideration of activity in context (Nicolini, 2012).

During the last few decades, the concept of the profession has itself become fragile. The main reason for this process of disintegration is that professionals have been losing their monopoly of knowledge. This loss, in fact, is one of the fundamental reasons for the rapid development of the coaching industry: knowledge has become something that evolves in specific communities of practice. Knowledge is not a list of facts that is stable, but it is contextualised and relational – that is, it depends upon how and where it is being used, by whom and for what purpose. Furthermore, knowledge is democratised by being made accessible through channels open to everybody, mainly through the internet. In that sense there is no profession that has exclusive ownership over the knowledge base in specific areas of expertise. Even within traditional fields such as medicine there is growing competition from alternative practitioners such as herbalists and homeopaths. This development in recent decades has shown that, because of fast and diversified knowledge production and dissemination, traditional professions no longer enjoy automatic respect from clients based on their superior access to information.

Thus the complexity of professional practice is not recognised in oversimplified and reductionist accreditation systems for coaching (Gray, 2011). Consequently, it is crucial to think about an alternative understanding of the concept of profession. Drake (2007), for example, has argued that we have moved beyond the traditional profession towards a craftsperson's view of professional practice, blending science and art in what he terms the 'pursuit of conscious mastery'. This has clear implications for the professionalism of coaching. Drake (2009) has argued further that coaches need to move beyond their biases for their specialised, professional knowledge to make sufficient room for other forms of knowledge and toward an engagement in a mutual and co-creative process to formulate what is happening in the coaching conversation. He makes the distinction between novice and master coaches.

> [A]s novices they learn the rules, as intermediates they break the rules, as masters they change the rules and as artisans they transcend the rules. (Drake, 2011:143)

Bachkirova and Lawton Smith (2014) also take a different stance and compare competence with capability. The latter they see as more holistic in approach and include within it:

- the diversity of coaching styles rather than predictability of the coaching process,
- the development of the coach congruent with the individual's values and identities, and
- a more contextual and multidimensional view on quality of practice.

Thus mastery can be seen to transcends rules and recognise complexity in ways of thinking about self, client and context. They identify four areas for the assessment of coaches:

- quality of skills and responsiveness, reflecting the skills and behaviours required;
- quality of awareness and flexibility, the ability to apply psychological mindedness;
- quality of professional commitment, the motivation to develop coaching capability; and
- quality of conceptual thinking, holding the knowledge and understanding of coaching.

Where else might we look for alternatives to competence models? Given that the focus of this chapter is on education and training, perhaps an important source can be found in ideas on professional development (Eraut, 1994) and the development of expertise (Ericsson, 2006). These fields are largely absent from much of the debate on the development of coaches, although it is touched upon in approaches such as Cognitive-Developmental Coaching (see Bachkirova, 2010).

Developmental Theories

There is an interesting literature looking at the development of practitioners in various fields as they move from novice to expert (Eraut, 1994). Some of these see a gradual progression from rule following to pattern recognition and increasing confidence to step outside protocol to meet perceived client need. The idea of a developmental approach to coaching is well established (Cox and Jackson, 2014). Within such approaches we see the discussion on progression from skills coaching through performance coaching and onto developmental coaching. The work of Stoltenberg and McNeill (2010) and their Integrative Development Model is a widely known example. It is proposed as a way to supervise counsellors and therapists at various stages of their development. It identifies specific levels of progression as experience is gained and the particular supervisory needs at each level. Cavanagh, Stern and Lane (2016) similarly proposed a developmental frame for supervision in coaching. Early on, Carkhuff and Berenson (1967) proposed developmental levels for counsellors through which they could potentially progress. However, they made the point that not all practitioners progress through the levels and, for some, their practice remains at lower levels.

Dreyfus and Dreyfus (2008) extend these ideas more widely by positing five stages of skill acquisition through which professionals may pass. These include:

- Novice – essentially rule learning and following
- Advanced Beginner – using more sophisticated rules and able to recognise contextual elements but tending to treat all aspects of a task equally
- Competent – able to set plans conceptually and within context and use standardised procedures within a decision hierarchy
- Proficient – sees client's issues holistically and can combine analytical decision making with intuition
- Expert – no longer rule dependent and able to use novel decision making processes.

How professionals develop these capabilities is important – to the extent that we can see such progression – and to adopt a routinised model to develop novel capabilities seems jarring.

Excellence Theories

There is a large literature on the development of expertise across a wide range of activities and professions. For example, medicine and surgery, transportation, software design, sports, maths, history (see Ericsson, 2006), as well as in emerging theories of expertise (Cianciolo et al., 2006; Endsley, 2006; Horn and Masunaga, 2006). Ericsson (2006) points out that those who excel place a strong emphasis on the role of the coach. Yet as coaches, with the possible exception of sports coaches, the knowledge base in the field of excellence is essentially absent from the coaching literature and apparently from many training programmes in coaching. What can we learn from this field to assist us in developing coaches? To the extent that developing expertise is much aided by having a good coach we could point to the role of coaching for coaches. Working with a great coach, seeing him/her coach, being coached and being supervised while coaching would seem to enable us to benefit from what coaching offers in support of expert performance. Certainly this idea is present in some coach education programmes (Gray, Garvey and Lane, 2016).

However, unlike many of the areas researched by Ericsson where what counts as superior performance can be measured (that is, experts consistently outperform novice or average performers) it might be difficult to get agreement within the coaching community on the definition of superior performance. At the same time, what we do know from research in other fields is that experts (defined by their reputation) are not always able to exhibit superior performance. Indeed at times they are no better than beginners (Camerer and Johnson, 1991). The pattern seems to be, according to Ericsson (2006), that most increase performance over time until they reach an acceptable level. Beyond that experience is a poor predictor of performance, yet in many professions time served is seen as necessary for progression to advanced membership categories. Those who do progress have in common that they seek out specific experiences with good teachers and engage in deliberate practice. It is accumulated amounts of that deliberate practice which leads to higher performance levels.

So it is not just about doing more CPD but having a clear plan to enhance expertise guided by a great coach. Ericsson also agues that a feature of a great coach is helping the practitioner to become their own self-coach. The later also seems to be a feature of enhanced expertise. However, as Hunt (2006) has pointed out, different types of expertise make different cognitive demands, it is not just practice but the specific forms that matter. Even this depends on igniting personal interests and the availability of social support. Similarly, Feltovich, Prietula and Ericsson (2006) have concluded that it is not just that experts know more but that they know differently and they restructure, reorganise and refine their knowledge to apply it to work day environments.

If developmental theory and expertise research gives us a possible alternative to competences we can then address the second area, the idea that courses teach practitioners to build their own model of practice. While it is clear from the study in Gray, Garvey and Lane (2016) that courses largely (but not exclusively) ask students to build their own model of practice, the field of scholarship primarily concerned with the nature of practices (Nicolini, 2012) is essentially absent from coaching texts.

THE REQUIREMENT TO BUILD A PERSONAL MODEL OF PRACTICE

There is increasing interest in the idea that phenomena that concern us such as knowledge, activity, construction of meaning, language, social institutions and human transformations are aspects of the field of practices (Schatzki, 2002). This leads us to the possible use of this literature from related fields. In particular, the fields known as 'practice theory' and 'professional learning' are helpful.

Practice Theories

These theories are primarily concerned with enabling us to describe features of our world (and in this case our work as coaches) as something that is made, remade, continually in flux and interconnected (Nicolini, 2012). As Nicolini argues, this radically changes the focus of our interest from concern with individual competence to one in which knowledge is a form of mastery expressed in our capacity to operate within both social and material worlds. It is always shared with others. 'Becoming part of an existing practice thus involves learning how to act, how to speak (and what to say), but also how to feel, what to expect, and what things mean' (Nicolini, 2012: 5).

In a practice-based approach (adapted from Nicolini):

- The basic units of analysis are practices not practitioners.
- Practices are meaning making, identity forming and order producing activities.
- Cognition and sense making emerge from the practice itself rather than from the brains of individuals.
- Organisations and institutions are made and remade through the material and discursive work that is undertaken.
- Discursive processes are central but not sufficient since the material world itself can resist our discourses about it. We need theories to encompass all aspects of organisational life.
- The world is depicted in relational terms and composed of a network of practices. Thus, how practices are performed and connected make a difference.

Hence, building a model of practice primarily from a personal philosophy gives way to building an understanding of practice from the study of how practices emerge. In this view, learning involves engaging in inquiry in the world in the form of an intervention that gives it a chance to bite back and challenge our presuppositions. Our practice as a coach has to be made and remade – or in narrative terms be re-storied (Corrie, Drake and Lane, 2010). One possibility for building a model of practice can be found in generating a narrative based on practices in contrast to the current requirement of courses where the emphasis is on practitioners to build a personal account. Thus, consideration of the points above would lead us to craft different stories about practice. We would not need to emphasise particular psychological theories which could be used to inform our personal model of practice. The study of the network of practices that encompass the field of coaching would enable us to remake those narratives to fully represent the social and material worlds in which coaching happens, not just the individual worlds. As Fenwick and Nerland (2014) have illustrated across a range of professions' material (including technological), changes have transformed our practice and we have to incorporate the role of the material world in our understanding of practice. An additional area to explore further is the study of professional learning as the basis for building a model.

Professional Learning

To face the challenges of the 21st century Lane and Corrie (2006) argue that we need skills in creativity and an ability to improvise because there are many ways in which we can come to know the world. This requires us to move beyond the constraints of competence led standards. This is even more the case in coaching given the broader knowledge base upon which we draw than those working in more constrained areas of practice. This means that our approach to learning within our field needs to reflect this position. As Schön (1987) posed the question, can prevailing concepts of professional education ever create the type of curriculum that is going to be capable of meeting the needs of the complex, unstable, uncertain and conflictual worlds of practice? To do so means that different development plans are needed, which can challenge our core perspectives and open them to deconstruction and possible reconstruction. Coaches are no different and, therefore, our personal models of practice are always open to deconstruction and reconstruction (Cavanagh and Lane, 2012).

In seeking to reconceptualise professional learning, Fenwick and Nerland (2014) celebrate the innovative research that has burgeoned in the last decade, but despair of the policy and curricula for professional learning that continue to be based on models which they argue have long ago been debunked. They make the point, echoing a similar position of Miller and Lane (1993), that public policy will often respond to a crisis by calling for more training of professionals. This ignores the web of relations within which practice happens. Fenwick cites an example of this pattern in which the enquiry into the crash of flight 447 in June 2009 identified the causation as inadequate competency of the flight crew – which was interpreted as calling for a requirement for more training. While this was the conclusion of the enquiry she points to the complex web of the material and human factors which actually contributed to the crash. She argued that there was an interwoven assemblage of factors – some human and some material – that were part of and contributed to the unfolding event.

Similarly, Lane and Corrie (2012) quote examples from various disasters to look at the complex nature of our decision making and Miller and Lane (1993) trace various scandals in education and care pointing to the limited response from enquiries calling for better training and communication rather than seeing the complex web of assemblage (in Fenwick's phrase). There is, in her view, an entanglement of all of the human and material factors that needs to be understood as effects of connections and activities. Things are performed into existence through these interrelations. This idea of a performative perspective moves our focus on producing knowledge and learning from mapping what is out there (what pre-exists) to a view that the world is doing things (and therefore a focus on how this is 'enacted'). We thus become concerned with 'enactments' and all the factors which produce them. Hence, building a model of practice has to be similarly concerned with enactments and the factors that produce them. A traditional approach in which students are asked to build a personal model of practice from a limited range of psychological perspectives does not address the human and material assemblages that are present in practices.

How are We Training Coaches Now?

In considering this issue in relation to current training in the UK, existing programmes provided by universities or training companies were approached to provide information (Gray, Garvey and Lane 2016). Information on twenty programmes was available and twelve agreed to provide responses to specific questions. A pattern emerged which pointed to three main approaches to student development. Training in coaching tends to operate in a number of ways, for example:

1. You learn a model (within a specific primarily psychological perspective).
2. You integrate models (from a family of perspectives).
3. You build your own model (based on your own experience, reading, beliefs).

Core within all programmes reviewed was the concept of reflective practice, however much less in evidence was a considered approach to how coaches can become evidence-based practitioners. For example, Cavanagh and Grant (2006) called for us to adopt a scientist-practitioner framework. This leaves open a whole set of issues (and possible research questions) when it comes to the competence debate:

- Do the same set of competencies apply to all three approaches?
- The professional body competencies exist independently of the course content – how does that shape the way coaching is taught/learned?
- If each course is subject for accreditation to a generic competence model how is diversity managed?
- Can the same set of competencies apply across all industries or professional skills? (Can competency models apply that generically?)
- If we adopt an excellence approach what competencies are relevant to excellence in specific contexts?
- How do we actually choose which models to use with the client in front of us?
- Given that coaches often work across professional disciplines and in diverse contexts how well are coaches prepared for inter-professional working?

While many courses share with psychology a commitment to reflective practice, the concept of evidence-based approaches is less clear.

Given that most trainees are asked to build their own model of practice what is the evidence base that supports a personal model of practice? This is an important debate and we have to ask – what scientific discourse and what discourse of the practitioner underpins the way we train coaches How are those discourses related? Are they complementary or contradictory and how do they emerge in practitioner accounts? What might a practitioner say they use to inform their work? What are the responsibilities of education providers for promoting such an approach to professional practice? If we are to recognise the role of the broader debate on the nature of 'practices' and professional learning, development and excellence, especially in the inter-professional contexts in which most coaches practice, then we perhaps need to rethink our approach to professional learning.

Guile (2014) proposes four elements for reconceptualising professional learning in inter-professional contexts (adapted for this chapter):

- Re-contextualisation of content – so that there is an opportunity to understand different forms of expertise in their own and other professions using case study or work placement.
- Re-contextualisation of pedagogy – to understand the relationship between different concepts and practice so that they can make inferences when working in inter-professional contexts.
- Re-conceptualisation of the workplace – to create opportunities to co-mingle the respective expertise they encounter in practice so that the resolution to shared problems in the workplace can be developed.
- Re-conceptualisation for the learner – in order to develop the capabilities required to work within the inter-professional context typical of the workplace we encounter as coaches. This needs to include opportunities to co-mingle theoretical and practical reasoning with others and for those others (in organisations using coaching) to learn to understand what coaching can and cannot offer to joint problem solving.

As Lane and Corrie (2006) argue we are seeing a new approach to professional learning across the lifespan as an activity that is tailored to the individual but is organisationally embedded and culturally and politically aware. We could reconceptualise professional learning for coaching in a way that generates engagement with these areas. The following three areas of discussion from parallel fields of practice may need to be more fully considered in coach education.

1. Decision Sciences

Much of what we do as coaches is help others to make decisions. We facilitate their finding goals that take them forward, make plans, review and make judgements on progress. The decision sciences are an area of research, which has influenced many fields, and we have decision sciences in economics, psychology, consumer behaviour and marketing and behavioural finance (Corrie and Lane, 2013). In recent years the interest has also extended to neuroscience and exploration of fast and slow decision making based in different parts of our brains (Kahneman, 2011). Issues such as the way we make judgements also feature in this field (Hardman, 2009) and the accuracy and utility of professional decision making and bias (Arkes, 1981; Sterman, 1994). The way we make decisions under conditions of certainty or uncertainty (Lane and Corrie, 2012) and for complex times (Corrie, Drake and Lane, 2010) is also developing as a field of study.

2. Formulation and Case Conceptualisation

A case was made by Corrie and Lane (2009), echoed by Grant (2011) and Drake, (2014, 2015) for the introduction of formulation and case conceptualisation into coach education (Bruch and Bond, 1998). Drake (2010: 247) in particular has explored this area and identified four core elements of a narrative approach to formulation in coaching:

1 *Person:* An emphasis on (a) self-knowledge for both coach and coachee; (b) creating an empathic container for awareness; (c) multiple sources of expertise and knowledge; and (d) attention to what they think is going on.

2 *Story:* An emphasis on (a) foundation knowledge about narrative structure and psychology; (b) searching for openings for change; (c) the impact of the past, present and future; and (d) attribution of what they think caused it.
3 *Elements:* An emphasis on (a) professional knowledge about work with the narrative material; (b) new opportunities that emerge from the interplay of the elements; (c) insights gained from assessing various streams of causality; and (d) action based on what they think they should do about it and why.
4 *Field:* An emphasis on (a) contextual knowledge as found in the space between and around the coach and coachee; (b) a structure for new stories and behaviours; (c) a holistic view on what is possible now; and (d) anticipation of what they think will happen as a result.

Teaching this and other approaches to formulation – as well as inviting greater use of case conceptualization methods – would increase the capability of coaches to engage with the complexity of operating in inter-professional contexts.

3. The Scientist-Practitioner Model

Originally conceived in the post war era as a way to bring the scientific study of psychology together with concerns to intervene successfully in clinical settings the scientist-practitioner model was proposed as a framework (Boulder Conference, 1949; see Lane and Corrie, 2006 for a review). In discussing its application to coaching by Corrie and Lane (2009) Grant (2011, p 86.) states:

> … we need to harness the strengths of the scientist-practitioner model; rigorous thinking; the ability to weave data from different sources into a coherent case conceptualisation; the ability to devise and implement specific interventions strategies on a case by case basis; and the skills to evaluate and critique our work – whilst discarding its weakness. These include the over-reliance on previously conducted research and the rigid application of such, which may not be appropriate for the emergent, iterative nature of coaching, particularly at this point in time when there is still somewhat limited coaching-specific research.

What the model brings to coaching is a way to apply rigour to our work with clients in emergent contexts. It enables evidence informed practice even when the coaching-specific research base is limited.

CONCLUSION

Given the diverse contexts for our work and the need for a relevant, rigorous and valid approach to meet them, some ideas for possible future directions for coach training and education will be explored. There are a number of reformulations already appearing in the literature. The work emerging from Bachkirova and Lawton Smith (2015) points to a more holistic perspective for viewing the capabilities we need to practise as coaches. Drake (2008) and Wheelahan (2007) address how we are immersed in a culture of pragmatism. One potential consequence of this is a climate in which coaches' thinking may divorce the content (such as deciding which intervention to use) from the context (such as the systems of meaning from which the selected intervention originated). Drake (2014) has offered three new perspectives (aimed at supervising coaches but which also have clear implications for training coaches) that reflect embodied practices yet address the increased complexities of our postprofessional era. He presents an Artistry Window through which choices are made, the Identity Window covering the roles and functions provided, and the Mastery Window representing the domains of knowledge and evidence needed. This provides a rich picture of the developmental demands of working as a coach (or coach supervisor). The arguments presented in this chapter are in line with the views taken by these authors.

A revised approach to coach education and training is in essence about how we make the choices in our practice. It can be considered from three perspectives: that of advocates of the scientist-practitioner model, from philosophy and from practice theory. From their account of the development of the scientist-practitioner model in psychology (applied to multiple areas including coaching) Lane and Corrie (2006) conclude that the model is essentially concerned with multiple forms of knowing that can be recruited to enrich our understanding with the client of the world they inhabit. It is as Abrahamson and Pearlman (1993) observed, the model is less concerned with distinct activities or roles and more with an inner professional compass which provides a moral injunction to distinguish between the sources of knowledge we use on the basis of their origins. All knowledge is not equal to the task at hand.

Lane and Corrie (2006) propose that the scientist-practitioner cannot be defined by any particular model. Instead, it provides a narrative framework in which the disciplines (forms of knowledge) upon which we rely are paramount but individualised and self reflective. More recently, Lane, Kahn and Chapman, (2016) argued that they should also be both reflexively and relationally narrated. So this means that we must pay close attention to the contextual factors that impact on the construction of our practice and be willing to entertain a range of ways of knowing. Our practice is socially constructed in conversations with our clients, not predetermined by us or by the dictates of a specific approach. If we choose to use a scientist-practitioner model to inform our work as coaches we have a responsibility to hold in our mind explicit frameworks by which we can differentiate ways of knowing and a set of principles for creating a systemic approach to decision making. Hence, we will be better able to evaluate the limits of our practice, our chosen models and the purposes they can fulfil.

The philosopher Stengers (1997) suggests the adjective 'scientific' defines the extent to which some propositions about the world make us more articulate. Articulate means to be able to appreciate differences that matter. It means we can make new and even enlightening connections between things of the world. This opens up possibilities for informed acting or not acting. Hence good science, as Stengers conceptualises it, is generative not eliminativist and increases our capacity to make connections. In considering her work Nicolini (2012) draws out key implications of her approach to professional practice. As coaches adopting good science, we do not close down the possible connections in order to operate within a limited psychological or personal model that pre-defines what is and is not worthy of exploration.

From the perspective of practice theory, Nicolini (2012) proposes a package of theory/method (which he sees as inseparable) we can bring to bear to improve the extent to which we are articulate. He argues that all science is performative and constructivist. Learning requires engaging with the world in an enquiry that gives it a chance to bite us. Thus if we are to understand any practice (coaching in this case) we must, in his view, get close to the activity at hand and build – or slice – the world in terms of the practices. We must find a way to re-present the practice as text, and our theory/method must be articulate and offer resources for building narratives and plotting the world.

We need to include in our education and training of coaches processes by which they can become rigorous and more articulate and develop explicit frameworks to understand the ways of knowing that permeate their practices. Key questions we can use in the process include:

- How do we justify the choices we make? What have we learned from the practices of coaching?
- What is the evidence base upon which we rely to inform our practice? Which ways of knowing are opened up and which are closed down in practice?
- How do we constantly challenge and refine our practice in the light of the literature and the experience of the world biting us back?
- How is our learning developing through our performance and informing the way it is constructed?

Whereas in the past the universities and professional bodies jointly sought to define the field, more recently there has been a separation of ways with each pursuing different ideas about what constitutes a valid basis for developing both our understanding of practice and the education of practitioners (see Bachkirova and Lawton Smith, 2015, for this debate). That few universities now seek accreditation of their programmes with the bodies that represent practitioners (some preferring to maintain their own registers) is a worrying trend. It is to be hoped that a wakeup call has been heard and we will see a re-emergence of a shared concern for our field. However, this cannot be achieved by a compromised position (an accreditation fudge) that lacks validity. Similarly the professional bodies cannot seem to bring their competence models together through discussion or take a serious look at practices – and perhaps if they did they may abandon that approach altogether.

We need to include in our education and training of coaches and their accreditation by the professional bodies representing practitioners opportunities to question the validity of what is currently offered. Key questions we can use in the process include:

- How can it be that we have either drifted apart through ignorance or deliberately split universities from representative bodies?
- What can we now do to create a valid framework for educating and training coaches in the practice of coaching?
- What does the world need from us and how best can we offer it?

I believe that coaching has much to offer the world if we open up to the possibility that it is more than the provision of narrowly defined services. As the Dublin Declaration (2008) contended, we face a world beset by challenges that demand our attention. We cannot only look inward to our own matters but need to also look outward to what does matter. I believe we are doing this and we can do this more. Unfortunately, at times we become distracted by narrow parochial concerns. In Dublin many coaches from across the globe called on the profession to make a difference. We can do so in ways that are relevant, rigorous and valid.

REFERENCES

Abrahamson, D. J. and Pearlman, L. A. (1993) The need for scientist-practitioner employment settings. *American Psychologist*, 48: 59–60.

Arkes, H. R., (1981) Impediments to accurate clinical judgment and possible ways to minimize their impact. *Journal of Consulting and Clinical Psychology*, 49(3): 323–330.

Bachkirova, T. (2010) The Cognitive-Developmental Approach to Coaching. In E. Cox, T. Bachkirova, and D. Clutterbuck, (eds), *The Complete Handbook of Coaching*. London: Sage.

Bachkirova, T. and Lawton Smith, C. M. (2015) From competencies to capabilities in the assessment and accreditation of coaches. *International Journal of Evidence Based Coaching and Mentoring*, 13(2): 123–138.

Bates, I. (1996) *The Competence and Outcomes Movement: The Landscape of Research, 1986–1996*. Leeds: School of Education University of Leeds.

Bruch, M. and Bond, F. W. (1998) *Beyond Diagnosis, Case Formulation Approaches in CBT*. Chichester: Wiley.

Camerer, C. F. and Johnson, E. J. (1991) The process–performance paradox in expert judgment: How can experts know so much and predict so badly? In K. A. Ericsson and J. Smith (eds), *Towards and General Theory of Expertise: Prospects and Limits*. Cambridge: Cambridge University Press, pp. 195–127.

Carkhuff, R. R. and Berenson, B. G. (1967) *Beyond Counselling and Therapy*. New York: Holt, Rinehart and Winston.

Cavanagh, M. and Grant, A. M. (2006) Coaching psychology and the scientist-practitioner model. In D. A. Lane, and S. Corrie (eds), *The Modern Scientist-Practitioner: A Guide to Practice in Psychology*. Hove: Routledge, pp. 146–157.

Cavanagh, M. and Lane, D. (2012) Coaching psychology coming of age: the challenges we face in the messy world of complexity?

International Coaching Psychology Review, 7(1): 75–90.

Cavanagh, M., Stern, L. and Lane, D. A., (2016) Coaching supervision: A systemic developmental psychological perspective. In D. A. Lane, M. H. Watts and S. Corrie (eds), *Supervision in the Psychological Professions Building your Own Personalised Model*. Maidenhead: Open University Press.

Cianciolo, A.T., Matthew, C., Sternberg, R. J. and Wagner, R. K. (2006) Tacit knowledge, practical intelligence and expertise. In K. A. Ericsson, N. Charness, P. J Feltovich and R. R. Hoffman (eds), *The Cambridge Handbook of Expertise and Expert Performance*. New York: Cambridge University Press.

Corrie, S., Drake, D. B. and Lane, D. A. (2010) Creating stories for complex times. In S. Corrie and D. A. Lane (eds), *Constructing Stories Telling Tales, A Guide to Formulation in Applied Psychology*. London: Karnac.

Corrie, S. and Lane, D.A. (2009). The scientist-practitioner model as a framework for coaching psychology. *The Coaching Psychologist*, 5(2): 61–67.

Corrie, S, and Lane, D. A. (2013) Decision-making and the coaching context. *International Coaching Psychology Review*, 8(2): 70–79.

Cox, E. and Jackson, P. (2014) Developmental coaching. In E. Cox, T. Bachkirova, D. Clutterbuck, (eds), *The Complete Handbook of Coaching*. London: Sage.

Drake, D. B. (2007) The art of thinking narratively: Implications for coaching psychology and practice. *Australian Psychologist*, 42(2): 283–294.

Drake, D. B. (2008) Finding our way home: coaching's search for identity in a new era. *Coaching: An International Journal of Theory, Research and Practice*, 1(1): 15–26.

Drake, D. B. (2009) Evidence is a verb: a relational approach to knowledge and mastery in coaching. *International Journal of Evidence Based Coaching and Mentoring*, 7(1): 1–12.

Drake, D. B. (2010) What story are you in? Four elements of a narrative approach to formulation in coaching. In S. Corrie, and D. A. Lane (eds), *Constructing Stories Telling Tales, A Guide to Formulation in Applied Psychology*. London: Karnac.

Drake, D. B. (2011) What do coaches need to know? Using the Mastery Window to assess and develop expertise. *Coaching: An International Journal of Theory, Research and Practice*, 4(2): 138–155.

Drake, D. B. (2014) Three windows of development: A post-professional perspective on supervision. *International Coaching Psychology Review*, 9(1): 38–50.

Drake, D. B. (2015) Improving your AIM: Using the Three Windows to develop yourself as a supervisor, 5th International Conference on Coaching Supervision Oxford-Brookes University, UK, 10 July.

Dreyfus, H. and Dreyfus, S. E. (2008). Beyond Expertise: Some Preliminary Thoughts on Mastery. *A Qualitative Stance: Essays in Honor of Steiner Kvale*. Arhus University Press. Retrieved 1 March, 2015, from www.ieor.berkeley.edu/People/Faculty/dreyfus-pubs/mastery.doc.

Endsley, M. R. (2006) Expertise and Situation Awareness. In K. A. Ericsson, N. Charness, P. J. Feltovich and R. R. Hoffman (eds), *The Cambridge Handbook of Expertise and Expert Performance*. New York: Cambridge University Press.

Eraut, M. (1994). *Developing Professional Knowledge and Competence*. London: Routledge.

Ericsson, K. A. (2006) An Introduction to the Cambridge Handbook of Expertise and Expert Performance: Its Development, Organization and Content. In K. A. Ericsson, N. Charness, P. J. Feltovich and R. R. Hoffman (eds), *The Cambridge Handbook of Expertise and Expert Performance*. New York: Cambridge University Press.

Feltovich, P. J., Prietula, M. J. and Ericsson, A. (2006) Studies of Expertise from Psychological Perspectives. In K. A. Ericsson, N. Charness, P. J. Feltovich and R. R. Hoffman (eds), *The Cambridge Handbook of Expertise and Expert Performance*. New York: Cambridge University Press.

Fenwick, T. and Nerland, M. (2014) Introduction: Sociomaterial professional knowing, work arrangements and responsibility: new times, new concepts. In T. Fenwick and M. Nerland (eds), *Reconceptualising Professional Learning: Sociomaterial Knowledges, Practices and Responsibilities*. Abingdon: Routledge, pp. 1–8.

Grant, G. (1979) *On Competence: A Critical Analysis of Competence-Based Reforms in Higher Education*. San Francisco, CA: Jossey-Bass.

Grant, A. M. (2011) Developing an agenda for teaching coaching psychology. *International Coaching Psychology Review*, 6(1): 84–99.

Gray, D. (2011). Journeys towards the professionalisation of coaching: Dilemmas, dialogues and decisions along the global pathway. *Coaching: An International Journal of Theory, Research and Practice*, 4(1): 4–19.

Gray, D, E., Garvey, R. and Lane, D. A. (2016) *An Introduction to Coaching and Mentoring: Thinking Critically about Theory, Practice & Context*. London: Sage.

Guile, D. (2014) Interprofessional working and learning: A conceptualisation of their relationship and its implications for education. In T. Fenwick and M. Nerland, (eds), *Reconceptualising Professional Learning: Sociomaterial Knowledges, Practices and Responsibilities*. Abingdon: Routledge, pp. 125–139.

Hardman, D. (2009) *Judgement and Decision Making: Psychological Perspectives*. Oxford: BPS Blackwell.

Horn, J. and Masunaga, H. (2006) A Merging Theory of Expertise and Intelligence. In K. A. Ericsson, N. Charness, P. J. Feltovich and R. R. Hoffman (eds), *The Cambridge Handbook of Expertise and Expert Performance*. New York: Cambridge University Press.

Hunt, E. (2006) Expertise, Talent and Social Encouragement. In K. A. Ericsson, N. Charness, P. J. Feltovich and R. R. Hoffman (eds), *The Cambridge Handbook of Expertise and Expert Performance*. New York: Cambridge University Press.

Kahneman, D. L. (2011) *Thinking Fast and Slow*. New York: Macmillian.

Lane, D. A. (2014) Understanding client needs in a world of uncertainty – why competencies and why not, 4th International Conference on Coaching Psychology, Melbourne, Novebmer 13-15 2014.

Lane, D. A. and Althaus, K. (2011) The development of psychotherapy as a specialism for psychologists. *European Psychologist*, 16(2): 132–140.

Lane, D. A. and Corrie, S. (2006) *The Modern Scientist-Practitioner: A Guide to Practice in Psychology*. Hove: Routledge.

Lane, D.A. and Corrie, S. (2012) *Making Successful Decisions in Counselling and Psychotherapy: A Practical Guide*. Maidenhead: Open University Press.

Lane, D., Kahn, M. S. and Chapman, L. (2016) Understanding Adult Learning as Part of an Approach to Coaching. In S. Palmer and A. Whybrow (eds), *Handbook of Coaching Psychology: A Guide for Practitioners* (2nd edn). Hove: Routledge.

Miller, A. and Lane, D. (eds.) (1993) *Silent Conspiracies: Successes and Scandals in the Care and Education of Vulnerable Young People*. Stoke-on-Trent: Trentham Press.

Mooney, P. (2008) The Dublin Declaration on Coaching, Version 1.3, Global Community of Coaches, Dublin. Available at: gccweb.ning.com/forum/topics/2328492:Topic:47 (accessed 12 October 2015).

Nicolini, D. (2012) *Practice Theory, Work and Organization: An Introduction*. Oxford: Oxford University Press.

Passmore, J. (2014) *Mastery in Coaching: A Complete Psychological Toolkit for Advanced Coaching*. London: Kogan Page.

Rodriguez, D., Patel, R., Bright, A., Gregory, D. and Gowing, M. K. (2002) Developing competency models to promote integrated human resource practices. *Human Resource Management Special Issue: Human Resources Management in the Public Sector*, 41(3): 309–324.

Schatzki, T. R. (2002) *The Site of the Social: A Philosophical Exploration of the Constitution of Social Life and Change*. University Park, PA: Pennsylvania State University Press.

Schön, D. A. (1987). *The Reflective Practitioner: How Professionals Think In Action*. New York: Basic Books, Inc.

Stasz, C. (2011) *The Purposes and Validity of Vocational Qualifications*, Cardiff: SKOPE Research Paper No. 105, November.

Stengers, I. (1997) *Power and Invention: Situating Science*. Minneapolis: University of Minneapolis Press.

Sterman, J. D. (1994) Learning in and about complex systems. *Systems Dynamics Review*, 10(2–3): 291–330.

Stoltenberg, C. D. and McNeill, B. (2010) *IDM Supervision: An Integrative Developmental Model for Supervising Counsellors and Therapists*. New York: Routledge.

Vandaveer, V. V. (2014) Excellence in Professional Practice of Coaching Psychology: Competency Models, Reductionism and Emergence. Melbourne: Australian Psychological Society Conference, 13–15 November.

Wheelahan, L. (2007) How competency-based training locks the working class out of powerful knowledge: A modified Bernsteinian analysis, *British Journal of Sociology of Education*, *28*(5): 637–51.

Towards a Systemic Model of Coaching Supervision

David E. Gray

INTRODUCTION

Like a commitment to virtue, ask most coaches whether they engage with supervision and most will reply in the affirmative. Scratch the surface, however, and the real picture is more complex. How often do they undertake a supervision session? Are such sessions regular or only triggered by, say, critical incidents faced by the coach? How trained and accredited is the supervisor to fulfil their role? What functions does the supervisor serve and what models of supervision (or combinations of models) does the supervisor use? As Moyes (2009) points out, despite some research into supervision in the therapeutic disciplines of social work, psychology, counselling and psychotherapy, there is virtually no research into what happens during coaching supervision.

Many coaching supervisors use models of supervision they emanate from counselling and psychotherapeutic traditions. As Hay (2011) suggests, this means that a key consideration is maintaining the boundary between supervision and therapy when using an approach that has its origins in psychotherapy. However, as Carroll (2006) makes clear, the focus of supervision has widened since its inception. In the early days, counselling supervision concentrated on the individual, but in the 1990s the organizational dimension came of age with the growth of workplace counselling and the upsurge of counselling in workplace settings (medical, educational, industrial and religious). But, as Carroll (2006) concedes, there is still wariness and suspicion in counselling supervision as to whether companies, organizations and institutes are legitimate foci for supervision since most supervisors have little training, experience or knowledge about the dynamics of working in organizational settings.

As yet, however, there is no specific theoretical model for effective coaching supervision (Bluckert, 2004; Butwell, 2006), in part because coaching itself suffers from a proliferation of different theoretical models and standards. This lack of coherence in the profession makes it harder to develop a common approach to coaching supervision (Moyes, 2009). This problem is exacerbated by coaches working in a highly diverse set of environments, organizations and settings, bringing the issues and complexities of their clients back into their supervision sessions. If they are trained as therapists, how equipped are supervisors to assist with and address issues that extend beyond individual therapy and into themes that include organizational behaviour, culture and change? Towler (2005: 309) calls the organization the 'invisible client', a factor that imposes unconscious influences in the supervision room. Indeed, in executive coaching, for instance, it is the organization that often sets the coaching agenda, keeping an evaluative eye on the outcome (Carroll, 2006). Hence, coaching supervision has to be systemic – and hold the tensions among a number of subsystems (Gray, 2007).

This chapter will therefore ask: how appropriate are psychological models to coaching supervision? It will also explore the growth of supervision in coaching and critically evaluate the kinds of models of supervision currently used, arguing that, particularly when coaching takes place within a business or organizational context, both coaches and their supervisors must engage at both the individual and *systemic* level. However, there are challenges here. As Hawkins (2011) points out, some coaches struggle to engage with a systemic perspective because of the levels of complexity it brings even to individual coaching. With this caution in mind, a systemic model of coach supervision will be presented towards the end of this chapter.

WHAT'S IN A NAME?

There is currently no widely agreed definition of coaching supervision (Moyes, 2009). Discussing supervision within the context of coaching and consultancy, de Haan (2012: 2) refers to it as: 'disciplined reflection-in-relation wherein case history and principles are transformed into new potential for action and skills.' For Carroll (2007) it is a forum where supervisees review and reflect on their work in order to do better. These definitions focus largely on supervision as a one-to-one process with the influence of external factors at best implicit. Hawkins and Smith (2006: 147), however, introduce systemic elements, defining supervision as: 'The process by which a coach/mentor/consultant with the help of a supervisor, who is not working directly with the client, can attend to understand better both the client system and themselves as part of the client–coach/mentor system, and transform their work'. In the second edition of their book they take contextual factors further: 'Supervision also does this by attending to the transformation of the relationship between the supervisor and coach and *to the wider contexts in which the work is happening*' (Hawkins and Smith, 2013: 169 – my emphasis).

One of the problems embedded within the word 'supervision' is 'super' (from the Latin *super* (over) and *videre* (to watch, see), a term that implies that supervisors monitor supervisees from a superior position. Most coaches and their supervisors would agree with Carroll (1996) that in practice this should not be the case. One attempt to avoid pejorative suggestions of power has been to change the word to 'extra-vision', that is, the provision of support that is outside the line management relationship (Inskipp and Proctor, 1995). Other suggestions have included 'practice developer', 'coaching advisor', 'thinking partner' and 'co-explorer'. These terms, however, have not caught on. It seems that, at least for the moment, we are stuck with 'supervision'.

This lack of an agreed definition of coaching supervision should come as no surprise given the proliferation of models and standards in coaching itself. Gray (2011) comments that coaching is currently, at best, a helping intervention that seeks rather than has attained, professional status. Certainly, there are a number of coaching associations, ICF, EMCC, AC, APECS, to name but four, that offer professional training and accreditation in coaching, and there have been several collaborative discussions about the issues facing coaching (including supervision). One of these was the Global Coaching Convention that met in Dublin in 2008 and emerged with a call for the creation of an International Best Practice Competency Framework for coaching as well as a statement of shared values. Crucially, the convention also explicitly stated that supervision is an important element of the 'coaching journey', and sees supervision as an effective element of education and development of coaches.

It posed two important questions for further research:

- What is the role of supervision in the education of coaches?
- What are the essential elements of effective supervision?

Also in 2008 the International Coaching Research Forum (ICRF) was convened of 40 internationally recognized researchers, coaching professionals and other stakeholders to start to define an evidence-based research agenda for coaching. The result was 100 research proposals organized into 16 main areas, one of which was on supervision. The questions covered in this subject area included:

- Does supervision work?
- What aspects of supervision work?
- Who can supervise others?
- What is the model of supervision?
- What is the purpose of supervision?

However, Stern and Stout-Rostron (2013) reviewed the extent to which the research subjects of the 100 ICRF proposals have been addressed by substantive, primary and evidence-based research. Their analysis of peer-reviewed journal articles published between 2008 and 2012, found that there were only five articles on supervision practices (12th out of the list of 16 themes), while for coaching processes (1st out of the 16 themes) there were 88. Supervision, then, is on the agenda, but the attention given to it by researchers is still limited. Furthermore, while supervision is mandatory in some helping professions, notably social work, and counselling and psychotherapy (Grant, 2012), while growing in coaching it is not, currently, mandatory. Even when used, as we show next, the models used are varied and far from consistent.

MODELS OF SUPERVISION AND THEIR RELEVANCE TO COACHING

Currently, coaching lacks its own, distinctive and purpose-built model of coaching supervision, although, as we shall see, some models have been adapted to a coaching perspective. It is for this reason that it has been forced to adopt models from other helping interventions such as counselling and psychotherapy where supervision is mandatory (Passmore, 2011). Early models were based on psychoanalytic theory and were largely informal, whereas in the 1950s new models gave an emphasis to the supervisee's skills development through a somewhat didactic, 'teaching' approach adopted by the supervisor (Carroll, 1996). Beginning in the 1970s, more recent models have been more developmental, emphasizing the roles and tasks of the supervisor and the learning stages of the supervisee. Before exploring some of these it is worth noting Hess' (1986) somewhat phlegmatic comment that supervision probably gets done irrespective of the model or model used by the supervisor.

DEVELOPMENTAL AND PSYCHOTHERAPEUTIC MODELS

Early and Developmental Models

Developmental approaches to supervision have focused mainly on a *stages* model of development (Ronnestad and Skovholt, 1993). Some models offer three development stages and others four, but all, essentially, demonstrate how the trainee (supervisee) develops from a state of dependency on the supervisor, to more of a peer or equal status, as the trainee becomes more skilled, knowledgeable and confident in their own abilities. Stoltenberg and Delworth (1987), for example, present a three-stage Integrated Developmental Model (IDM) through which trainees progress in relation to three primary structures:

- *Level 1: Self-awareness.* Trainees focus primarily on themselves, especially in terms of fears and uncertainties, often failing to acknowledge the needs of their clients. Although trainees tend to be highly motivated, this is characterized by uncertainty and a desire to follow the 'correct' approach to counselling.
- *Level 2: Other-awareness.* The trainee begins to focus more on the emotional and cognitive needs of the client. However, in doing this, the trainee may become pulled into their problems and as confused and pessimistic as the client themselves.
- *Level 3: Motivation and autonomy.* Trainees are able to identify the impact of a client's problems on themselves and can move backwards and forwards between a focus on his/her own emotional responses to the client and what the client is experiencing. Motivation becomes more consistent as the trainee begins to gain greater self-knowledge and understand and accept his/her own strengths and weaknesses.

The IDM model is dynamic in that a trainee may be at Level 2 in some domains (such as theoretical orientation or assessment techniques) but at Level 1 in others. Stoltenberg and Delworth (1987) also suggest a Level 4 stage that can occur when the therapist has integrated Level 3 skills and knowledge across all domains. This stage is not attained by most therapists and can be regarded as a 'master level'.

Some, however, have questioned the somewhat mechanical framework presented by developmental models. Hence, Chagnon and Russell (1995) argue that trainees may ebb and flow from one developmental level to the next. In addition, a meta-analysis of numerous empirical studies, finds that differences between levels appear most pronounced largely at a very beginning-level when novice trainees need more support, while interns demonstrate a sense of increasing independence (Holloway, 1987). It is the recognized weaknesses in developmental models that led researchers to explore other alternatives such as social role models (next).

Psychotherapeutic Models

Psychotherapeutic models of coach supervision include Gestalt, person-centred transactional analysis and cognitive-behavioural therapy, each of which we will look at in turn.

Gestalt

Gestalt is a *process* methodology that focuses on psychological patterns or forces that influence the ways in which people interact with each other and their environment (Congram, 2011). Gestalt supervision, then, has as its core model: dialogic process, phenomenological method and the holistic field. Hence, the holistic nature of the human being is key to the work, and body responses seen as important to providing clues as to how the coach perceives the world; emotions emerging between the supervisor and coach help inform the supervision process itself (Congram, 2011). So, the content of what the coach reveals is less important than *how* they present the case material, *how* they coach and *how* the coach and supervisor relate to each other in the here-and-now.

Central to the Gestalt model is field theory developed by Lewin (1946, 1947) who described a field as the totality of coexisting facts which are conceived as mutually interdependent. Hence, in order to understand peoples' behaviour, it becomes necessary to explore the psychological, emotional and experiential field within which they act.

People both are influenced by and are also influencers of the field. According to Parlett (1991) in Gestalt, there is a willingness to investigate the organized, interconnected, interdependent and interactive nature of complex human phenomena. Hence, what a person does is a function of sets of forces relative to one another and all interacting together (Parlett, 1997). So, distinctions such as 'person' and 'situation', for example, are both contained with the field and are also provisional and relativistic. Field theory invites the Gestalt practitioner into avoiding simplistic notions of cause and effect (Parlett, 1997).

For Gestalt supervision, fields are both multiple and interconnecting (see Figure 36.1). Not only is there the field of the supervisor–coach relationship, but there is the 'absent presence' in the room of the client. Beyond this is the client-context field, not directly present in supervision, but a point of focus from time to time. As Congram (2011) discusses, the Gestalt model is similar to the seven-eyed model (discussed below) in that it attends to not just the supervisor–coach relationship but wider processes. However, according to Congram (2011: 126) while the seven-eyed model 'helicopters over the different fields, dropping into each mode to gain understanding', the Gestalt holistic field perspective assumes an interconnectedness between them. Hence, a change in one field will have an effect on the other fields.

A tree, for example, does not exist independently. According to Parlett (1997: 20) 'A tree forms part of a landscape – affected by other vegetation, predators, soil chemistry – and provides shelter and nourishment for other plant and animal life. If one uproots a tree, the landscape is changed, the ecosystem disrupted. Unless replanted, the tree dies – still undergoing further transformation as part of a wider system, natural or artificial.' In an organizational context, managers often talk in dualist lines in terms of 'the organization' and 'we managers', as though the latter were not an integral part of the organization (Parlett, 1997). But we cannot talk in simplistic terms about the 'interdependence of everything'. Work must be done on analysing the structure of the field, the layers of meaning, the circular patterns of mutual influence and changes in different organizing needs. In supervision, this means attending to the field dynamics that take place between the supervisor and coach, the coach and client and between the client and the system or organization they interact with.

Person-Centred

Like many coaching supervision methods, person-centred supervision has its origins in therapeutic practices. The fundamental assumption that underlies person-centred therapy is that people are intrinsically motivated to self-actualize, that is, to grow and develop into their optimal form. Originally developed by Carl Rogers (1961), self-actualization can only occur in situations where people feel understood, valued and accepted for who they are. However, if people self-actualize in a way

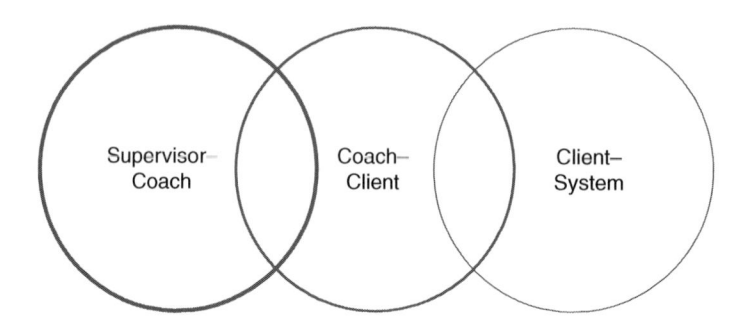

Figure 36.1 Interconnected Gestalt fields

that is not congruent with their natural actualizing tendency, say, due to the pressure of others, then their self-concept may produce dysfunction and distress.

As Cook (2011) makes clear, the influence of Rogerian theory on person-centred coaching supervision, will depend on the extent to which 'pure' or modified versions of the theory are adopted. So, while purists maintain that all six conditions of Rogers' model and the non-directive stance of the therapist are essential, experimentalists hold that a more directive approach between the therapist and client is permissible. As Cook (2011) points out, it could be argued that the psychoanalytic school would place the expertise with the therapist, whilst a person-centred approach would view it as residing purely with the client. In contrast, experimentalists in the person-centred school would see the client's 'reality' as co-created between the therapist and the client. Hence, it is important that the supervisor and coach contract clearly at the start as to what model the supervisor offers and what the coach needs. For example, if the coach was seeking supervision to deal with transference issues, or had concerns about the mental health of their coachee, then psychodynamic rather than person-centred supervision would be more appropriate.

Transactional Analysis

Transactional analysis (TA) examines the interactions or transactions between a person and other people and is based on Berne's (1961) concept of ego-states. Ego-states refer to three major parts of a person's personality and reflect an entire system of thought, feeling and behaviour, determining how individuals express themselves, interact with each other and form relationships. The three ego-states comprise:

- The parent ego-state, a set of thoughts, feelings and behaviours learnt from the individual's parents.
- The adult ego-state, a mostly rational set of responses based on the 'here and now'.
- The child ego-state, a set of thoughts, feelings and behaviours learnt from the individual's childhood.

Script theory helps the supervisor to identify unconscious scripts in the supervisee, often repetitive patterns of thoughts, feelings and behaviours, suggesting that the child ego-state is dominating and seeping into other parts of the individual's personality. Transactions occur when individuals communicate and their ego-states interact and can include 'strokes', a transaction that provides a person with either recognition or stimulation. Sometimes, however, ego-states can contaminate each other to produce distorted views, and psychological games can occur when individuals fail to achieve closeness or the intimacy they seek. According to Hay (2011) supervisors can analyse ego-states to identify and avoid potential parent–child co-dependent relationships between supervisor and supervisee, or recognizing when supervisors exhibit a need for 'admiration strokes' from supervisees.

Hay (2011) points out that TA encourages supervisors to be aware of unconscious processes and the need to be aware of the psychological distance between themselves and the supervisee and also the organization they are coaching in. Micholt (1992) suggests that the supervisee might be asked to think of a triangle (the three-cornered contact) and whether all sides are equal (the optimal shape), or whether they are closer to the client than to the supervisor. In Figure 36.2 (A), the supervisor and supervisee are psychologically close but both are psychologically distant from the organization the supervisee is coaching in. Towler (2009) for example describes a supervisor as feeling she was colluding with the negative feelings of her supervisee towards the organization. Hay (2011) argues that the triangle may be multi-dimensional and include, for example, professional associations. If, say, both supervisor and supervisee are members of the same association, the supervisor may be seen as a kind of police officer, enforcing the norms of the association, making them psychologically distant as in Figure 36.2(B). Here the supervisor is also psychologically closer to the organization than they are to their supervisee – maybe they also work in the same organization as their supervisee, are paid by that organization and feel they owe loyalty to it.

Another important element is contracting since it is through this that the supervisor invites the supervisee to be autonomous. Autonomy is a key element in TA encouraging supervisees to engage in the here and now instead of engaging in regression, projection and/or transference or being stuck in unhelpful patterns (Hay, 2011). Contracting occurs at three levels: the psychological (as above), administrative (fees, timing of payments, cancellation arrangements, etc.) and professional elements (what coaching style will be used, the boundaries between therapy and consulting, etc.) According to Towler (2009) many of the supervisees' anxieties of feeling unsafe and misunderstood result from supervisors not being clear about their roles and responsibilities in the contracting process.

Finally, another important element of TA is discounting, which is defined as minimizing or ignoring some aspects of ourselves, others or the situation. While we can successfully discount background noise, we can also discount to maintain limiting beliefs or our failure to address a problem. As Hay (2011) makes clear, discounting is why supervision is necessary because supervisors can get the supervisee to address what is being ignored.

Cognitive-Behavioural Therapy (CBT)

The effective CBT supervisor conveys warmth, interest and curiosity towards the supervisee to enhance safety and trust. Above all, they are committed to the development of the supervisee, providing a reliable and consistent presence during the supervisee's learning experience offering both support and challenge (Storrie and Lane, 2015). Pretorius (2006: 414) argues that both CBT and its supervision are: 'systematic, goal-directed, structured, time-limited, collaborative, person-focused, confidential and active, with clear boundaries and a power-imbalance that requires to be managed ethically'. Perris (1993) argues that CBT supervision tends to adopt a relatively didactic approach, with the supervisor's focus often being on the theoretical and technical and practical aspects of therapy. However, what represents optimal supervision and the range of competencies and skills needed to make supervision effective still remains limited (Storrie and Lane, 2015).

SOCIAL ROLE SUPERVISION MODELS

Social role models place an emphasis on the roles and tasks of the supervisor as well as

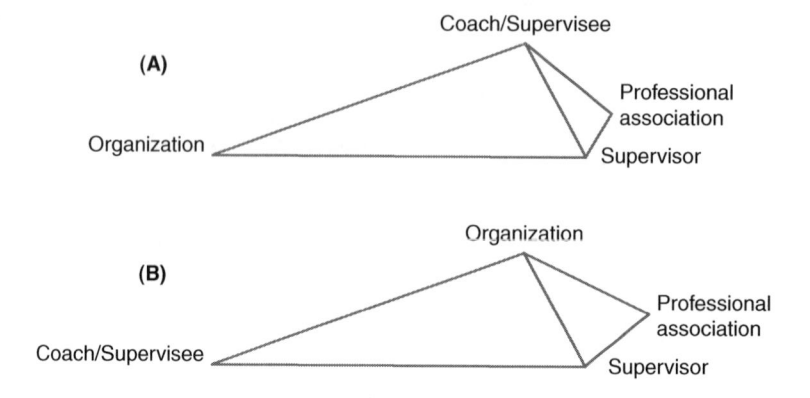

Figure 36.2   TA models: contracts and unconscious processes

the stages of development of the supervisee, the most popular of which has been the six focused model (Hawkins and Shohet, 2000) which was followed by the seven-eyed model of supervision (Hawkins and Smith, 2006), the latter adding Mode 7 (systems and context) to the original model.

The Seven-Eyed Model

In their original six focused model, in contrast to stages models, Hawkins and Shohet (2000) place emphasis on the *process* of supervision within an organizational context and within accompanying constraints and norms. Supervision operates at many different levels and involves four elements: the supervisor, the therapist (supervisee), the client and the work context. While usually only the supervisor and supervisee will be present at the supervision session, nevertheless, both the client and the work context will be present during the session at both a conscious and unconscious level. Hence, the supervision process involves two interlocking matrices:

- A therapy/coaching system connecting the supervisee and the client
- A supervision system connecting the supervisor and supervisee

The seven foci (as in the name of the model) comprise:

Mode 1 The Client and their Context

Here the supervisor gets the coach to focus on the client and the choices the client is making, or as Hawkins and Schwenk put it, 'getting the client(s) into the room' (2011: 30). The first stage here might be to get the coach to describe the client in some detail, including their physical appearance, their verbal and non-verbal behaviours and how they came to engage with therapy.

Mode 2 The Coach's Interventions

This mode looks at how the coach works with the client. In this mode the aim is to improve the coach's choices and skills in intervention, by exploring the strategies they used and what alternative strategies might be considered. New options are generated through discussion,

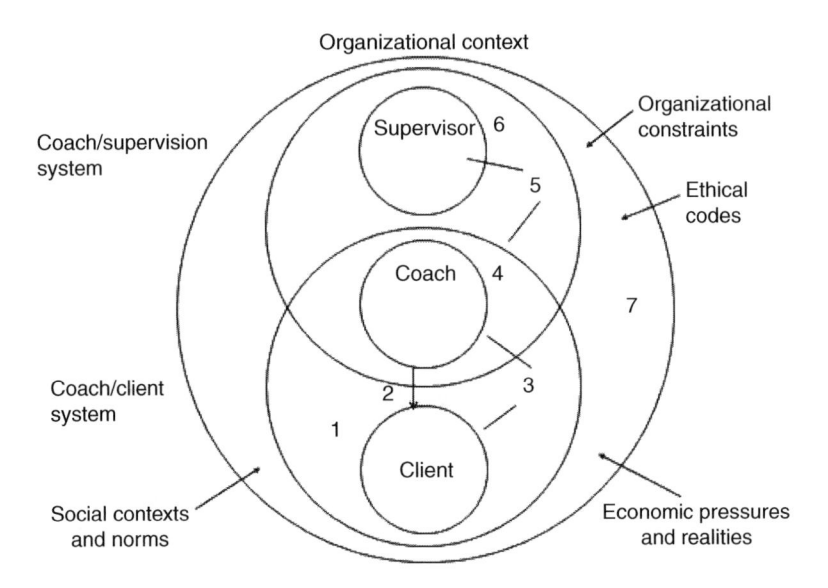

Figure 36.3 The seven foci of supervision

Source: Adapted from Hawkins and Schwenk (2011)

with the supervisor taking care not to impose their own strategies on the coach.

Mode 3 The Relationship Between the Coach and Coachee

The focus here is the relationship that the coach and client are co-creating. Here, the supervisor focuses on what is happening at the conscious but also the unconscious level in the coaching session. It includes looking for clues to the transference that is happening from the client to the coach (and the coach's counter transference – see next section).

Mode 4 The Coach's Awareness

Here the focus is on the coach's own internal processes and how these are affecting the coaching process. These include the coach's counter-transference, a predominantly unconscious reaction by the coach to the client's transference.

Mode 5 The Supervisory Relationship (Supervision Process)

At this level, the processes at work between the coach and client are explored through how they are reflected in the relationship between the coach and the supervisor. So, a coach who is experiencing challenging behaviour from a client, may exhibit challenging behaviour towards the supervisor. The task of the supervisor is to identify this process so that learning can emerge from it.

Mode 6 The Supervisor's Own Process (Supervisor's Experience/ Self-Reflection)

The emphasis here is on the supervisor's 'here and now' experience while with the coach and what can be learned about the coach/coachee from the supervisor's response to the coach and what they are presenting about the client. For example, does the supervisor feel threatened, challenged or merely bored? In this mode, the supervisor pays attention to his/her own shifting feelings and sensations towards the coach, while at the same time attending to the content and process of the session.

Mode 7 The Wider Context in Which the Coaching Happens

This focus acknowledges the organizational, social, cultural, ethical and contractual context in which the coaching takes place. This includes a wider group of stakeholders, that includes the client organization and its stakeholders, the coach's organization and its stakeholders, and the organization and professional affiliations of the supervisor. It includes the power and cultural dynamics that underlie these various relationships, 'to understand how the culture of the systemic context might be creating illusions, delusions and collusions in the coach and in oneself' (Hawkins and Schwenk, 2011), and in the relationship between the coach and the supervisor. As Hawkins (2011) points out, supervisors need to be trained not only in individual psychology but also to understand the wider, organizational context and to see patterns between issues over time.

The role of the supervisor, then, focuses on handling the tensions and sometimes different interests between the coach, the coachee and their organization (Paisley, cited in Carroll, 2006). Here, a high level skill involves coping with the complex dynamics such as maintaining professional boundaries, and being aware of the needs and responsibilities of each stakeholder (Carroll, 2006). Hence, while a coach and coachee may negotiate a set of objectives as part of a contracting process, the needs and requirements of the coachee's sponsoring organization are never far away. As noted above, Towler calls the organization the 'invisible client' (2005: 309). Supervisors of coaches, therefore, need to understand the systemic and cultural aspects of organizations and be sensitive to the fact that they are always present during the supervision conversation (Towler, 2005).

Cook (2011) argues that the seven-eyed model, poses problems for those who adopt a person-centred approach to supervision. In mode 2, for example, the focus is on the coach's own interventions. From a person-centred perspective, this poses the danger of encouraging the coach to adopt a mind-set of *doing things* for the client, as opposed to facilitating the resourceful coach to find their own approach. In mode 3 the focus is on the relationship between the coach and the client and, as we saw above issues of transference. In mode 4 counter-transference is explored. However, as Cook (2011) points out, Rogers would view dealing with transference as a great mistake, since the creation of the therapeutic relationship based on unconditional positive regard, empathy and congruence are far more important than therapeutic techniques. For person-centred approaches, while the use of psychodynamic theory in supervision is not a problem per se, the danger is that it places too much emphasis on the individual technique of the supervisor at the expense of the relationship between the supervisor and supervisee (Cook, 2011). As Moyes (2009) points out, the seven-eyed model was developed for social work and psychotherapy supervision not for coaching. Butwell (2006) is critical of this, arguing that a model developed for one function cannot be blithely transposed across to another arena.

Clutterbuck (2010) offers a seven conversations process which, he argues, enhances the seven-eyed model through exploring conversations the client is not having, or conversations that are antecedents to those occurring in the coaching session. This framework helps to identify where the dialogue between a coach and coachee is most effective and least effective, and helps to raise the coach's awareness of what was going on in their own mind and that of the client. The seven conversations comprise:

1. The coach's reflection before dialogue (their prepatory thinking before the coaching conversation).
2. The client's reflection/prepatory thinking before the dialogue.
3. The coach's internal, unspoken reflections during the dialogue.
4. The spoken dialogue.
5. The client's internal, unspoken reflections during the dialogue.
6. The coach's reflections after the conversation.
7. The client's reflections after the dialogue.

The seven conversations model can be used by supervisor and supervisee to deconstruct their own conversations. For example, the supervisor reflects back to the coach their feelings and observations about what is being said and how it is being said.

The Discrimination Model

Another social role supervision model is the discrimination model proposed by Bernard and Goodyear (1998). It is called a discrimination model because it requires the supervisor to tailor their responses to the supervisee based upon their individual needs. It is a social role model because the intervention is tailored, depending on the situation the supervisee faces. The discrimination model focuses on the three roles of the supervisor: teacher, counsellor and consultant. Within each of these roles the supervisor can adopt three different types of supervision, namely:

- Intervention, where the supervisor concentrates on the supervisee's intervention skills
- Conceptualization, and how the supervisee understands what is happening in the session
- Personalization, and how the supervisee adopts an approach which is uncontaminated by personal issues and counter-transference.

In the role of teacher the supervisor might adopt an intervention approach and didactically teach the supervisee a therapeutic technique. Again in the role of teacher, but adopting a conceptualization approach, the supervisor might use transcripts from the supervisee's coaching sessions to help him/her identify themes within the client's statements. In the role of counsellor, and adopting an intervention focus, the supervisor might help the supervisee to identify how the client is undermining their ability to use their skills in the therapy sessions. As in other models there is an acknowledgement that for novice supervisees there may be more focus on the teaching role of the supervisor, while for more advanced supervisees the role adopted might be one of consultant. This recognizes that supervisees pass through developmental stages.

MODES OF SUPERVISION

Although one-to-one supervision is traditionally the norm, in recent years we have seen the growth of other modes including peer-to-peer and group supervision, partly, as we shall see, because they offer potential benefits.

One-to-One Supervision

In this format, a supervisor provides supervision for one coach in a one-to-one relationship. Mead, Campbell and Milan (1999) assert that one-to-one supervision is the classic form, providing a confidential space for undiluted attention and in-depth inquiry, with a typical session lasting between 60 and 90 minutes. Sessions take place between 4 and 6 weeks as a minimum, although this can be increased for novice practitioners or where experienced coaches run into trouble. This might be the format favoured by inexperienced coaches, since it is more personal and private, allowing the supervisee to show vulnerability (for example, concern about a lack of skills, whether imagined or real). The Association for Coaching (2005) maintains that inexperienced coaches need to choose a supervisor who has been a practising coach for a number of years.

Peer Supervision

Many coaches engage with fellow coaches in peer supervision where each takes on the role of supervisor and supervisee alternately. For peer supervision to be effective, both participants need to be experienced as coaches and possess supervision skills. A potential drawback of this approach is that both participants may have weaknesses or blind spots in the same area. As an approach peer supervision may have grown because it has the potential for the development of deep mutual understanding and relationships. However, another reason for its popularity is that it comes at zero cost! Peer supervision can take place on a one-to-one basis (reciprocal supervision) or within a group. In forming a group, Hawkins and Smith (2013) recommend that the group should, ideally, have shared values but a range of approaches, otherwise the group can become too collusive.

Group Supervision

Group supervision is described by Holloway and Johnston (1985: 333) as a process 'in which supervisors oversee a trainee's professional development in a group of peers'. One way of organizing this is that the supervisor allocates time amongst the group of coaches they are supervising individually. Another approach is that the coaches allocate supervision time amongst themselves (peer-to-peer coaching) drawing on the supervisor as an expert when and if needed. Yet another model is peer group supervision where three or more coaches share responsibility for each other's supervision within the group. In this format, there is no supervisor who acts as the expert. Hence, peer group supervision is a form of group supervision, in which it is assumed that the group members have the resources to help themselves and to make sense of their practice (Lakeman and Glasgow, 2009). This approach is most effective where all the coaches are of broadly equal experience and training.

A version of peer group supervision is the use of Action Learning sets, developed around the ideas of Revans (1982). Here, a group of between 5 and 8 coaches meet on a scheduled basis (typically every 4 to 6 weeks for half a day), to learn from and support each other. After 'checking in' and reconnecting with the group, members are given 'air time', to raise problems and concerns. Other members of the group listen without interruption; once the member has told their story, other members ask challenging and supportive questions. The supervisor's role here is to facilitate the processes of the group and to act as an expert (when needed). Childs, Woods, Willcock and Man (2011) recommend the use of action learning sets for supervision, not in place of traditional approaches but as running alongside.

THE GROWTH OF SUPERVISION

Although supervision is a requirement within the professional training (and on-going professional development) in helping professions such as counselling and psychotherapy, its status in coaching is often less formalized. While the EMCC's code of ethics makes supervision a requirement, most of the professional coaching associations recommend and encourage supervision, rather than making it compulsory. This is, perhaps, one reason why supervision is not undertaken by all coaches, even though the majority feel it is important. Hence, while some studies suggest that 86 per cent of coaches believe that they should have regular supervision, only 44 per cent of respondents were currently receiving supervision and only 23 per cent of the 120 organizations contacted provided regular on-going supervision (Hawkins and Schwenk, 2006). Reasons for not engaging with supervision included that it is not required by organizations (but this position is changing), is too expensive or it is difficult to find a suitable supervisor.

The picture is also varied internationally. One global study, for example, found that supervision was used in only 15 per cent of the countries surveyed, with most of these being countries with only a small coaching presence. In contrast, in South Africa which boasts the presence of 1,600 coaches, supervision is hardly used at all (Global Coaching Survey, 2009). A study by Grant (2012), however, found that amongst an experienced sample of 179 coaches, 17 per cent had no supervision, 18 per cent had an informal supervisor, 26 per cent a formal supervisor and 39 per cent used peer supervision. Of those who did engage with supervision, 42 per cent of respondents had been using supervision for less than two years. Overall, the future may see supervision becoming more widespread, not least because many of the commissioners of coaching programmes such as large corporates, are demanding it. Hence in the AC's first survey in 2005, only 48 per cent of respondents had supervision in place. In 2008, this had increased to 71 per cent of respondents. In the last few years, in the UK and other parts of the world the number of training courses for supervisors, conferences, workshops and books on the subject of supervision have grown rapidly (Hawkins and Smith, 2013).

One, perhaps significant, emerging trend is the growth of internal rather than external coaching, and the implications this has for supervision. The Ridler Report (2013) suggests that nearly 80 per cent of its survey respondents expect a growth in internal coaching over the next three years, largely because internal coaching is seen as less expensive. External coaches tend to be used in situations where the coachee is a board member, where there may be conflicts of interest between an internal coach and the coachee, and where there are tensions between the coachee and the organization. The latter, of course, relates to the coachee and wider, organizational systems. Whether organizations that sponsor coaching (internal, external or both) make use of internal or external supervisors remains under-researched and under-discussed.

TOWARDS AND INTEGRATED *SYSTEMIC* MODEL OF COACH SUPERVISION

Although, as we observed in the previous section, Hawkins' (2011) seven-eyed model has been criticized for being too rooted in social work, he remains one of the few authors to link coaching supervision with wider systems thinking that include the individual, and a wider system of stakeholders. Systems thinking is fundamentally different to traditional forms of analysis which focus on separating what is being studied into individual constituent parts. In contrast, systems thinking focuses on how the elements being studied interact with other constituent parts of the system, and is often effective in the analysis of dynamically complex systems. Senge (1990: 68) argues that systems thinking is a discipline for recognizing the whole. 'It is a framework for seeing interrelationships rather than things, for seeing patterns of change rather than static "snapshots"'.

According to Hawkins (2011) systematic coaching supervision involves the supervision of an individual coach or team of coaches and what he terms the four pillars. This systemic supervision:

- Is informed by a systemic perspective. Many organizational problems relate to a wide system of stakeholders which include the organization's customers, suppliers, partner organizations, employees, investors, communities within which the organization operates and the ecological environment. This means that supervisors need to be trained not only in individual psychology, but in systems thinking so they are able to see issues in their wider context, over time.
- Performs in the service of all parts of the system of learning and development. Hence, the supervisor must contract with the coach as a joint enterprise in the service of the individual and the organizational clients, the relationship between them, the wider stakeholder system and the coaching profession.
- Attends to the client in relation to their systemic context(s). So even at the contracting stage, the focus is on the needs of the supervisee, but also the organizations their clients work for and the wider system they serve.
- Includes and reflects upon the coach and the supervisor as part of the systemic field.

In a similar vein, Carroll (2006) refers to four subsystems that the supervisor must keep in mind: the coach, the executive coachee, the coachee's employing organization and the coaching organization to which the coach belongs (since the latter may often have contracted the organization for the work in the first place). The effective supervisor holds these four subsystems in mind in terms of their needs and interactions in a creative tension. Sometimes all five subsystems are involved but at other times only three: the executive, the coach and the supervisor. The challenges the supervisor faces include maintaining professional boundaries, managing contracts (particularly the psychological contract) and being aware of the needs and responsibilities of all parties. Drake (2014) notes other subsystems. For example, supervision takes place at both a formal, vertical level when both coaches and supervisors may be accountable to professional associations and their ethical and accreditation frameworks. There are also less formal, horizontal systems such as social networks and communities of coaches that exert an influence on the values, behaviours and norms that coaches adhere to.

These systemic principles can be viewed in the conceptual framework for coach supervision (see Figure 36.4) which integrates the ideas of Passmore and McGoldrick (2009) and Carroll (2006). Carroll (2006) notes two initial subsystems that include the organization and the coaching organization it contracts with for the coaching work. Clearly what is contracted drives much of what happens next. Passmore and McGoldrick (2009) discuss the *context* of the coaching which includes the needs and expectations of the coach (for example, that the supervisor will be trained and experienced). To these can be

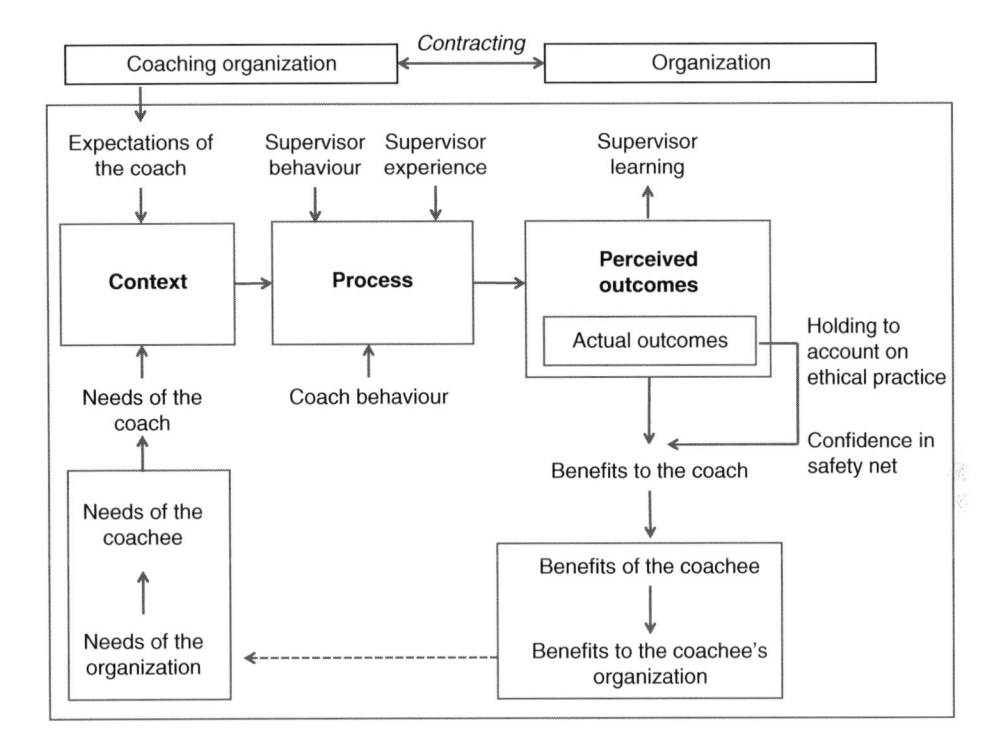

Figure 36.4 Conceptual framework for coaching supervision
Source: Adapted from Passmore and McGoldrick (2009) and Carroll (2006)

added the needs of the coachee and, in turn, systemic elements (his/her organization), particularly if the coachee is being sponsored or asked to undertake coaching. Supervisors also need to have knowledge of the context in which they are supervising.

For executive coaches this means knowledge and/or experience of the dynamics present in the top tiers of organizations and the pressures senior executives experience in their daily roles. Simply drawing on counselling and transferring these to the coaching role is inadequate (Passmore and McGoldrick, 2009). While counselling and psychotherapy practice serves the client in front of them, the coach has always got at least the client and the organization and the client's performance in view.

Processes comprise dynamic interactions between supervisor and coachee or group of coachees in which the supervisor acts as a facilitator to open up a critical reflective space. The supervisor is both supportive but also challenging in order to assist the coach in their reflective process, helping towards both individual and wider organizational change (Passmore and McGoldrick, 2009). *Perceived outcomes* include learning for the supervisor as well as the coachee (and their organization). For example, the outcome of multiple supervisory conversations (within clear confidentiality boundaries) may help to identify systemic patterns, through the sharing of high-level themes within the organization. As one supervisor commented: '... what are the systemic patterns, what does that tell us about the current state of the culture, and how that matches the vision and strategy, and work out what the organization can do to shift these patterns' (Respondent, Passmore and McGoldrick, 2009: 19).

As the coaching supervision model shows, supervision needs to take into account the context in which the coach is working (influenced by the initial contract between the organization and the coaching organization), a context that is shaped by the expectations of the coach but also his/her needs and, critically, by the needs of the coachee and their organization. As Drake (2011) proposes, this contextual knowledge is a way of thinking and acting strategically, based on an awareness of needs, motives and contextual constraints. Nor is the process linear. As the dotted line in Figure 36.4 suggests, at the end of the coaching supervision process (and its outcomes), individual and organizational change may result in new needs.

CONCLUSION

A number of core themes have emerged in this chapter: (1) that 'supervision' is a broad term that has a multiplicity of interpretations, models, types and contexts; (2) that it is performed in a variety of forms from individual, to peer and group; (3) that supervision takes place at both an individual level but also systemically within a complex interaction of subsystems.

As we have seen, the term 'supervision' itself is loaded with unhelpful associations of power (watching over) whereas in most (but not all) contexts it is a collaborative and supportive process. However, definitions of the supervision process are wide and varied, reflecting, in part, the fact that coaching itself is an intervention that lacks a standardized format. The situation is further complicated by the fact that much of the current practice of supervision is based on therapeutic models, many of which are antipathetic to each other. As Carroll (2006) asserts, while it is certainly appropriate to 'borrow' elements and models used by supervision as applied in other professions, coaching supervision needs to develop its own framework and theoretical underpinning.

We have noted the importance of systems thinking and how subsystems include the supervisor, the supervisee (coach), the coachee and his/her organization dynamically interacting. The development of a coaching supervision framework is therefore becoming more urgent because many of the most significant sponsors of coaching programmes (large corporations and public service organizations) are demanding it. They see that supervision is an important contributor to the quality of coaching processes and outcomes. The role and influence of the coaching associations should also be factored in as another subsystem.

When hiring supervisors, coaching sponsors may wish to take into account their professional qualifications, for example. When supervising, supervisors may wish to pay adherence to the ethical codes and norms represented by the professional association they have joined. Currently, however, supervision is the Cinderella of the piece – talked about but rarely going to the ball. In other words, most coaching associations focus on the training and accreditation of coaches rather than of supervisors. This is slowly changing in coaching, but supervisors remain under-represented in terms of coach supervisor-specific accreditation.

Alongside the development of a systemic approach to coaching, we also need to make supervision an evidence-based intervention. Hence, as the 2008 International Coaching Research Forum (ICRF) demanded, we need a research agenda that addresses key issues that include:

- What is the purpose of supervision?
- Does supervision work?
- What aspects of supervision work?

Above all, we need to ask: What models of supervision work? What modes of supervision are effective? How, when and why are they effective? How does supervision balance the needs of all stakeholders including the coach, his or her coaching organization, the coachee, the client organization and the wider coaching profession?

What of the future? As coaching expands globally so, in all probability, will supervision – but there the predictability ends. As Gray, Garvey and Lane (2016) comment, coaching exists in many forms and, as we have attempted to show in this chapter, so does supervision. However, if coaching does grow, where will we find the cadre of supervisors in terms of both numbers and expertise? Furthermore, what kind of expertise or competency do we need? Currently many coach supervisors are steeped in therapeutic traditions that may encourage them to serve the client in front of them rather than the organization in which the person works. A key question that is not often addressed is, 'what is the responsibility of a supervisor to the organization?' This chapter calls for a systemic model of supervision based in a blend of therapeutic thinking and systems thinking and it suggests a putative framework as a place to start.

REFERENCES

Association for Coaching (2005) 'Association for Coaching Supervision Report' at: www.associationforcoaching.com (Accessed 28 April, 2013).

Bernard, J.M and Goodyear, R.K. (1998) *Fundamentals of Clinical Supervision* 2nd edn. Needham Heights, MA: Allyn & Bacon.

Berne, E. (1961) *Transactional Analysis in Psychotherapy*. New York: Grove Press.

Bluckert, P. (2004) 'The state of play in corporate coaching: Current and future trends'. *Industrial and Commercial Training*, 36(2): 53–56.

Butwell, J. (2006) 'Group supervision for coaches: Is it worthwhile?' *International Journal of Evidence-Based Coaching and Mentoring*, 4(2): 1–11.

Carroll, M. (1996) *Counselling Supervision: Theory, Skills and Practice*. London: Cassell.

Carroll, M. (2006) 'Supervising executive coaches', *Therapy Today*, 17(5): 47.

Carroll, M. (2007) 'One More Time: What is Supervision? *Psychotherapy in Australia*, 13(3): 34–40.

Chagnon, J. and Russell, R.K. (1995) 'Assessment of Supervisee Developmental Level and Supervision Environment Across Supervisor Experience'. *Journal of Counseling & Development*, 73(May/June): 553–558.

Childs, R., Woods, M., Willcock, D. and Man, A. (2011) 'Action learning supervision for coaches'. In J. Passmore (ed.), *Supervision in Coaching* (pp. 31–43). London: Kogan Page.

Clutterbuck, D. (2010) Using the seven conversations in supervision. Retrieved 11 February 2016 from http://www.davidclutterbuck-partnership.com/wp-content/uploads/Using-the-seven-conversations-in-supervision.pdf.

Congram, S. (2011) 'The use of Gestalt approach in supervision'. In T. Bachkirova, P. Jackson and D. Clutterbuck (eds), *Coaching and Mentoring Supervision: Theory and Practice* (pp. 87–88). Maidenhead: Open University Press.

Cook, B. (2011) 'The person-centred approach in coaching supervision'. In T. Bachkirova, P. Jackson and D. Clutterbuck (eds), *Coaching and Mentoring Supervision: Theory and Practice*. Maidenhead: Open University Press.

De Haan, E. (2012) *Supervision in Action: A Relational Approach to Coaching and Consulting Supervision*. Maidenhead: Open University Press.

Drake, D.B. (2011) 'What do coaches need to know? Using the Mastery Window to assess and develop expertise'. *Coaching: An International Journal of Theory, Research and Practice*, 4(2): 138–155.

Drake, D.B. (2014) 'Three windows of development: a postprofessional perspective on supervision'. International Coaching Psychology Review, 9(1): 38–48.

Grant (2012) 'Australian coaches' views on coaching supervision: A study with implications for Australian coach education, training and practice'. *International Journal of Evidence Based Coaching and Mentoring*, 10(2), 17–33.

Gray, D.E. (2007) 'Towards a systemic model of coaching supervision – some lessons from psychotherapeutic and counselling models'. *Australian Psychologist*, 42(4): 300–309.

Gray, D.E. (2011) 'Journeys towards the professionalisation of coaching: Dilemmas, dialogues and decisions along the global pathway'. *Coaching: An International Journal of Theory, Research and Practice*, 4(1): 4–19.

Gray, D.E., Garvey, R. and Lane, D. (2016) *A Critical Introduction to Coaching and Mentoring:* Debates, Dialogues and Discourses. London: Sage.

Hawkins, P. (2011) 'Systemic approaches to supervision'. In T. Bachkirova, P. Jackson and D. Clutterbuck (eds), *Coaching and Mentoring Supervision: Theory and Practice.* Maidenhead: Open University Press.

Hawkins, P. and Schwenk, G. (2006) *Coaching Supervision: A Paper prepared for the CIPD Coaching Conference.* London: CIPD.

Hawkins, P. and Schwenk, G. (2011) 'The seven-eye model of coaching supervision'. In T. Bachkirova, P. Jackson and D. Clutterbuck, *Coaching and Mentoring Supervision: Theory and Practice.* Maidenhead: OUP.

Hawkins, P. and Shohet, R. (2000) *Supervision in the Helping Professions.* 2nd edn. Buckingham: Open University Press.

Hawkins, P. and Smith, N. (2006[2000]) *Coaching, Mentoring and Organizational Consultancy: Supervision and Development.* 2nd edn. Maidenhead: Open University Press.

Hawkins, P. and Smith, N. (2013) *Coaching, Mentoring and Organizational Consultancy: Supervision, Skills & Development.* 2nd edn. Maidenhead: Open University Press.

Hay, J. (2011) 'Using transactional analysis in coaching supervision'. In T. Bachkirova, P. Jackson and D. Clutterbuck (eds), *Coaching and Mentoring Supervision: Theory and Practice.* Maidenhead: Open University Press.

Hess, A.K. (1986) 'Growth of supervision: stages of supervisee and supervisor development', *The Clinical Supervisor,* 4: 51–67.

Holloway, E.L. (1987) 'Developmental models of supervision: is it development?', *Professional Psychology: Research and Practice,* 18(3): 209–216.

Holloway, E.L. and Johnston, R. (1985) 'Group supervision: Widely practiced but poorly understood'. *Counselor Education and Supervision,* 24(4): 332–40.

Inskipp, F. and Proctor, B. (1995) *Art, Craft and Tasks of Counselling Supervision.* Oregon: Cascade Publications.

International Coach Federation 'Global Coaching Survey (2009) at: www.http://coachfederation.org/ (Accessed 15 June, 2016).

Lakeman, R. and Glasgow, C. (2009). 'Introducing peer-group clinical supervision: An action research project'. *International Journal of Mental Health Nursing,* 18(3): 204–210.

Lewin, K. (1946) 'Behaviour and development as a function of the total situation', in D. Cartright (ed.) *Kurt Lewin: Field Theory in the Social Sciences, Selected Theoretical Papers.* New York, Evanston and London: Harper Torchbooks, pp. 238–297.

Lewin, K. (1947) 'Frontiers in group dynamics'. In D. Cartright (ed.), *Kurt Lewin: Field Theory in the Social Sciences, Selected Theoretical Papers.* New York, Evanston and London: Harper Torchbooks, pp. 188–237.

Mead, G., Campbell, J. and Milan, M. (1999) 'Mentor and Athene: supervising professional coaches and mentors', *Career Development International,* 4(5): 283–290.

Micholt, N. (1992) 'The concept of psychological distance'. *Transactional Analysis Journal,* 22(4): 228–33.

Moyes, B. (2009) 'Literature review of coaching supervision'. *International Coaching Psychology Review,* 4(2): 162–173.

Paisley, P. 'Towards a theory of supervision for coaching – an integrated approach', cited in Carroll, M. (2006), 'Supervising executive coaches', *Therapy Today,* 17(5).

Parlett, M. (1991) 'Reflections on field theory'. *British Gestalt Journal,* 1(2): 63–81.

Parlett, M. (1997) 'The unified field in practice'. *Gestalt Review,* 1(1): 16–33.

Passmore, J. (2011) 'Supervision and continuous professional development in coaching'. In J. Passmore (ed.), *Supervision in Coaching.* London: Kogan Page, pp. 3–9.

Passmore, J. and McGoldrick, S. (2009) 'Supervision, extra-vision or blind faith? A grounded theory study of the efficacy of coaching supervision'. *International Coaching Psychology Review,* 4(2): 145–161.

Perris, C. (1993) 'Stumbling blocks in the supervision of cognitive psychotherapy'. *Journal of Clinical Psychology and Psychotherapy,* 1, 29–43.

Pretorius, W.M. (2006) 'Cognitive-behavioural therapy supervision: Recommended practice'. *Behavioural & Cognitive Psychotherapy,* 34, 413–420.

Revans, R. (1982) *The Origin and Growth of Action Learning.* Brickley: Chartwell-Bratt.

Ronnestad, M.H. and Skovholt, T.M. (1993) 'Supervision of beginning and advanced graduate students of counseling and psychotherapy'. *Journal of Counseling and Development*, 71: 396–405.

Ridler Report (2013) *Trends in the Use of Executive Coaching*. London: Ridler & Co.

Rogers, C. (1961) *On Becoming a Person*. Boston, MA: Houghton Mifflin.

Senge, P. (1990) *The Fifth Discipline: The Art and Practice of the learning Organization*. Doubleday, NewYork.

Stern, L. and Stout-Rostron, S. (2013). 'What progress has been made in coaching research in relation to 16 ICRF Focus Areas from 2008 to 2012?' *Coaching: An International Journal of Theory, Research and Practice*, 6(1): 1–25.

Stoltenberg, C.D and Delworth, U. (1987) *Supervising Counselors and Therapists*. San Francisco: Jossey-Bass.

Storrie, S. and Lane, D. (2015) *CBT Supervision*. London: Sage.

Towler, J. (2005) 'A grounded theory study of organizational supervision of counselors: The influence of the invisible client'. PhD thesis. University of Surrey, Guildford.

Towler, J. (2009) 'Friend of foe? The influence of the invisible client'. *Counselling at Work* (Spring) 2–7.

Issues of Assessment and Accreditation of Coaches

Bob Garvey

INTRODUCTION

This chapter critically explores the issues of assessment and accreditation of coaches through the lens of 'discourses'. Discourses reflect and shape social contexts. It is argued that coaching, located primarily within a business context, is influenced by two main discourses. The psychological discourse and the managerialist discourse. This means that certain ways of thinking and behaving are valued and others are not. For example, the managerialist discourse values a reductionist perspective and is concerned with the simplification of the complex and the celebration of the practical (*techne*, in Aristotelian terms) and the psychological discourse is influenced by scientific thinking and methods (*episteme*, in Aristotelian terms). These discourses shape both theory and practice in coaching. It is argued here that the professionalisation agenda has also adopted these discourses, and this is reflected in the approaches taken to coach education and the resultant assessment and accreditation of coaches. Additionally, it can be argued that certain theories of adult learning inform the design of coach education and the discourses of professional coaching bodies and associations. Ultimately, this creates approaches to coach education and systems of training, assessment and accreditation which may not adequately reflect the complexities of the coach's role and practice.

The chapter starts with a brief explanation of the meaning of discourses and then goes on to explore some of the discourses found in coaching associations and professional bodies. These act as a backdrop to the rest of the chapter and are explored in terms of both academic and practitioner coaching literature. From the beginning, coaching has been linked with learning. At Oxford University in the 19th century, for example, coaching was used to assist students in their academic performance (Garvey et al., 2014). It is therefore appropriate to consider the discourses found in learning theories in relation to assessment and accreditation approaches found in coach education and training.

It could also be argued that the discourses associated with some providers of coach education and training are 'power' discourses (see Garvey, 2011). This makes some sense given that some discourses of learning theory are based in a 'power and control' discourse (Coopey, 1995; Contu & Willmott, 2003). However, many others are rooted in emancipatory and humanistic philosophies (Dewey, 2012; Vygotsky, 1978) which often seem absent from the discourse in use in coaching (as compared to the espoused discourse). It could also be argued that the 'inclusive', person centred humanist philosophies that often inform the coaching literature (Rosinski, 2003; Whitmore, 2009; Starr, 2008) are also at odds with the discourses of professionalisation. This creates a paradox between the espoused 'inclusive' philosophy of coaching and the lived experience of the 'exclusive' behaviours of the professional associations and bodies.

It will be demonstrated that there is a broad mismatch between the common coaching discourses and adult learning theory and the discourses of the coaching bodies and also that these mismatches get played out in the professionalisation agenda through accreditation and assessment processes. The chapter concludes by offering an alternative to the competency discourse that is so commonly found in coach education and training as well as assessment and accreditation. The alternative to these discourses is influenced by the idea of humanism, the journey learning theory and the Aristotelian concept of *phronesis*.

WHAT ARE DISCOURSES?

This section explores the nature of discourses within social settings and the ways in which human behaviour is shaped, influenced or controlled by and through them. A discourse (Kroger & Wood, 1998) is a way of talking about something that shapes how meaning is made and how people organise around shared meanings. As Wood & Kroger, (2000: 4) state: 'language is taken to be not simply a tool for description and a medium of communication (the conventional view), but as a social practice, as a way of doing things.'

Webster (1980) emphasises the importance of language as a cultural driver when he states: 'Language is the primary motor of a culture ... Language is culture in action, but just as we are led to believe that our culture is "natural" so too do we come to overlook the intricacies of our language.' (206). However, Layder (1994) warns us that '... language is never "innocent"; it is not a neutral medium of expression. Discourses are expressions of power relation and reflect the practices and the positions that are tied to them' (97). Finally, Hatch and Cunliffe (2013) argue that power 'is exercised through practices that arise in discourse to regulate what will be perceived as normal' (43) and what actions are sanctioned as a result.

So, discourses may contain 'truths' but they may also contain 'lies' and deceptions (Gabriel, 2004). This observation is important. For discourses to be effective in shaping cultural behaviour they are dependent on interpretation and the powerful reinforcement of meanings through the symbols and rituals of a society (Bruner, 1996); hence why 'walking the talk' is so important in organisations. Therefore discourses need to be understood within the social context in which they are employed. In this chapter, this is mainly within the context of professional bodies and associations, e.g., European Mentoring and Coaching Council (EMCC); International Coach Federation (ICF); Association of Professional Executive Coaching and Supervision (APECS) and Association for Coaching (AoC). The next section explores some of the discourses commonly found in the coaching literature.

DISCOURSES OF PROFESSIONAL BODIES AND ASSOCIATIONS

Coaching could be viewed as a social phenomenon (Garvey, 2011) and, as such, it becomes subject to the power of the discourses that shape it in particular contexts. Therefore, coaching for performance on a sports field will have a different discourse than in a business or in a health context – although it could be argued that there are some overlaps between the different modes of practice. For example, the concept of goals is associated with the sports context and it is also found in business settings. This chapter focuses mainly on the contexts of business and of professional coaching associations and bodies. The burgeoning professional bodies and associations in coaching are calling for a professionalisation agenda and, arguably at least, this may be in response to what can be described as the 'Wild West of Coaching' discourse.

This phrase first appeared in Morris and Tarpley (2000) and was later developed by Sherman and Freas (2004) in their article in the *Harvard Business Review*. This article exploits the 'Wild West' metaphor and uses graphic language from within that discourse to support its claim that coaching is problematic and uncontrolled and that the solution can only be found in a professionalised body. However, little consideration is given to the potential benefits of the 'Wild West' nature of coaching. For example, it brings with it a pioneering and creative energy, a desire to do things differently and willingness to engage in a different form of conversation that makes a positive difference to people and society. It would appear that reactions to this discourse may have contributed to shaping the frameworks we now find in the ever expanding numbers of professional bodies and associations. The result is that these frameworks are, in part, born of protectionism and a desire to exclude those who do not meet the protectionist agenda. They are power discourses, which often are in contradiction to the nature of the coaching ethos itself.

Discourses Found in Coaching Literature

Western (2012) argues that the 'Psy Expert' discourse is one of four dominating discourses found in coaching. Palmer and Whybrow, (2007: 3) suggest that, 'the key difference between definitions of coaching and coaching psychology is that the latter include the application of psychological theory.' So what is 'psychological theory'? This is a complex question because there appears to be a variety of psychological theoretical 'homes'. Whilst some of these overlap, for example, the psychoanalytical and the psychodynamic, they also seem to hold their own discourses.

These may include:

- *Biological* – discourses of human behaviour and mental processes associated with the effects of evolution and genetics
- *Evolutionary* – discourses of survival and reproductive instincts
- *Psychoanalytical* – discourses of unconscious mental processes, developed in early childhood and emerging in adulthood as impulses, desires and demands
- *Psychodynamic* – discourses of the forces behind human behaviour and interaction (similar to the psychoanalytical)
- *Behaviourism* – discourses of the role of learning processes in shaping behaviour
- *Cognitive* – discourses of the mental processes such as reasoning, problem solving memory and how mental plans and thoughts shape behaviour
- *Humanistic existential* – a discourse about the uniqueness of individuals and their ability to exercise free choice
- *Sociocultural* – discourses of social and cultural factors which shape behaviour.
- *Feminism* – discourses about the rights of women and the influences of these on both men and women's behaviour
- *Developmental* – discourses of development for human growth and learning

- *Personality* – discourses around patterns of thought, feelings and behaviour
- *Postmodernism* – a challenging discourse which goes to the very substance of psychological sciences by arguing that these are versions of power discourses aimed at maintaining power positions

This would suggest that, despite the idea that coaching psychology has some kind of coherence to it, there are more likely to be different discourses within these different factions of psychology (see Dafermos & Marvakis, 2006 for a full critique of psychology) as they relate to coaching. For example, Stelter (2014) states, 'I use the terms coach and coaching psychologist, respectively coaching and coaching psychology, as more or less parallel concepts' (1).

It is possible to speculate on the reasons for the dominance overall of psychology in coaching. One explanation is the dominance of the thinking and discourse of coaching psychology in professional bodies. This can be seen in the adaptation of psychologically informed models of practice found in competence frameworks, like those from solution focused approaches and models of supervision. Another explanation is related to the increasing pressures on people in the workplace to perform in particular ways. In this respect, Arnaud (2003) links the discourses of sport to the business sector, arguing that sporting discourses are often employed to support the notion of competitiveness in business. However, he states that this is 'more bitter, individualistic and prevalent in the workplace now than ever before'. He goes on to argue that the increased pressure to perform and develop individual employability in a context of poor job security leads to the need for 'personalized counselling, both on the part of those most directly concerned ... and on the part of the heads of organizations and top executives' (1132).

It is clear that living, working and functioning in the modern capitalist world places people under considerable psychological strain (Sennett, 1998) and that coaching could be viewed as a socially acceptable form of therapy (Grant, 2007). Western (2012) argues that another dominating discourse in coaching is the managerialist discourse. Bauman (1989) argues that the managerialist discourse positions people in particular ways: 'Reduced, like all other objects of bureaucratic management, to pure, quality-free measurements, human objects lose their distinctiveness. They are already dehumanized ... It is difficult to perceive and remember the human behind ... technical terms' (103). The risk therefore of the managerialist discourse finding its way into the coaching discourse is that coachees become dehumanised as the organisation seeks to extract a little more performance out of its employees in the 'bitter competition' suggested by Arnaud (2003).

It is probable that much coaching takes place in organisations where there is often a strong alignment with the managerialist discourse. This discourse favours hierarchy, measurement and accountability; it is concerned with objectivity, practicality and the simplification of the complex. Garvey and Williamson (2002) refer to this discourse as the 'rational pragmatic' and Johnson and Duberley (2000) argue that the dominant management discourse is rooted in pragmatic positivism and it could be argued therefore that the managerialist discourse is a derivative of the scientific discourse.

The scientific discourse of psychology resonates well with the rational pragmatic managerialist frames in organisations. In practical terms it leads to a supposedly 'objective' measurement management culture where numbers dominate and any kind of social interaction tends to become devalued or treated sceptically as 'subjective'. With its weighting on rationality and objectivity, this discourse also underpins a great deal of coaching psychology. This can be seen, for example, in the call from coaching psychologists for more research based on scientific positivist methods into coaching (Page and de Haan, 2014; Grant and Cavanagh, 2011). The combination of the managerialist discourse and the scientific, it could be argued, is also played out in the dominance of return on investment research found in some coaching evaluation research (Carter, 2006; Garvey et al., 2014).

However, while this way of thinking has contributed much to human progress, it could also have limited it as well. This can be seen in the double-edged sword of the bias for scientific measures. For example, Porter (1995) states: 'Numbers create and can be compared with norms, which are among the gentlest and yet most pervasive forms of power in modern democracies' (Porter, 1995: 45). Porter argues that the supposed links between 'objectivity' and numbers are problematic and are generally more prevalent in social contexts where there is a lack of trust, weak leadership and private, individual negotiation is morally suspect. Measurement and the supposed objectivity of numbers then become a substitute for poor leadership and management as human qualities are dismissed and measurement dominates, leading to Sennett's (1998) 'corrosion of character' and Bauman's (1989) 'dehumanizing' effect of the managerialist discourse. Further, Amabile (1997) argues that measurement driven management is a form of social coercion that constrains creativity and innovation. It 'ranks' people and can lead to people feeling excluded. This may also be true of assessment by numbers, which will be discussed later.

A further discourse also found in coaching is the philosophical position of humanism (Cox et al., 2014; Garvey et al., 2014; du Toit, 2014; Rogers, 2012; Connor & Pokora, 2012; Western, 2012; Garvey, 2011; Parsloe & Leedham, 2009; Whitmore, 2009; Rosinski, 2003). Humanism is about an ethical and democratic way of being. It is about individuals having the right and responsibility to give meaning and shape to their own lives. It recognises the human potential to act in an ethical way to build a more humane society through a sense of free inquiry and the infinite capacity for people to learn and develop. It is an inclusive philosophy. Ultimately, humanism is all about the challenge of diversity and this challenge is a huge one for humankind. However, the struggle remains as to how to bring this discourse more fully to the fore in the approaches to assessment and accreditation by coaching associations and professional bodies.

Related to humanism is the way in which coaching writers position the coach. Many, (Downey, 2014; Gallwey, 1974; Whitmore, 2009; Rogers, 2012; Starr, 2008; Hayes, 2008; Berg & Szabo, 2005; Kimsey-House et al., 2011; Passmore et al., 2013) position the coach as providing a humanistic activity to facilitate another person's learning and development. Stelter (2014), for example, positions the coach as a particular kind of expert practitioner promoting agency and facilitating the self-building process. Other literature (Whitmore, 2009; Starr, 2008; Downey, 2014) argues that the coach acts as a facilitator, listens, ask questions, and enables coachees to discover for themselves what is right for them (Rosinski, 2003: 5) thus implying that the coach performs a non-directive and facilitating role. There is also clearly expertise in the person of the coach and therefore he or she must need some form of development to perform the role. The implications of this for the assessment and accreditation of coaches are considerable. It therefore becomes appropriate to explore adult learning theories as they relate to the process by which learners reach a position to be assessed or accredited.

ADULT LEARNING THEORIES

First, what is learning? Vygotsky (1978) suggested that learning happens in the 'zone of proximal development'. He described this as:

> the distance between the actual development level as determined by independent problem solving and the level of potential development as determined through problem solving under adult guidance or in collaboration with more capable peers. (86)

Bruner (1985) interprets this position as 'passing on knowledge is like passing on language – his [Vygotsky's] basic belief that social transaction is the fundamental vehicle of education and not, so to speak, solo performance' (25). The implication here is that a greater potential for enhanced understanding and learning is unlocked if there is guidance from or collaboration with others. Whereas development is an individual activity, as Vygotsky noted, learning is a social activity. People learn with, from and by others. This notion, first formulated by Vygotsky around 1930, has major implications for how we organise for learning. Given the influence and power of the social context in the learning process it is important to consider the social contexts of coaching and the associated discourses which impact on the approach taken by providers of coach training and education.

Within the discourses of coaching as outlined above, the psychological and the managerialist discourses bring with them a particular model of learning and a resultant assessment of that learning. A critical factor for both is the distinction between 'what' is learned and 'how' it is learned. The 'what' can be construed in many ways depending on the context and the background and experience of the individual learner. The rational pragmatic discourse specifies what should be learned in advance and often positions this as learning outcomes or objectives. This approach is similar to goal setting in coaching. Learners are taught to the learning outcomes and tested to see if they have achieved them. This is a 'technicist's' approach to learning. We have become so used to this approach that we no longer notice it; it has become a dominating discourse with an overwhelming rationality and practicality and is therefore difficult to challenge.

The 'how' of learning offers a different potential. It is related to process of learning and is associated with the idea of 'practical judgement' (Harrison & Smith, 2001) or 'reflective skills learning' (Jarvis, 1992; Schön, 1983). Practical judgement has its roots in Aristotle's ideas. Aristotle presents three notions (see Frank, 2004; Drake, 2011):

- *episteme* (knowledge that), which emphasises scientific theories and analysis and is seen to be favoured in psychological discourse;
- *techne* (knowledge how), which is associated with production-orientated craft and a focus on mastery and is seen to be favored in managerialist discourse; and
- *phronesis* (knowledge why), which is defined as a practical wisdom related to dealing ethically with context, practice and experience (Flyvbjerg, 2001) and is seen to be largely absent from the institutional professional discourse.

Phronesis is linked to the idea of 'noticing' or attentiveness to a specific situation. It involves flexibility of thought, sensitivity of context, an orientation to the subject and critical interpretation. It refers to

> a reflective analysis on personal-value judgements in relation to future actions. In this respect, it involves a shift from instrumentality to a deliberation over what constitutes ethical praxis. ... Phronetic thinking then is concerned with deliberation about values and interests, as a precursor for action (Flyvbjerg, 2001). (Hemmestad, 2010: 450)

Operating from the *techne* and *episteme* frames often results in pre-planned learning whereas a *phronetic* frame is designed to be exercised in the course of what might be called 'hot action'. It happens in the moment as an activity, rather like when a coach is working with an executive. The idea of 'hot action' in the moment or 'practical judgement' (Harrison & Smith, 2001) has an ethical dimension. For example, it is not ethical to pursue an 'end' with people while being indifferent to 'means'. Learning is such an ethical activity. As Jarvis (1992: 7) states: 'learning, and perhaps knowledge itself, has significant moral connotations'. His argument is rooted in the narrative of Adam and

Eve. Before eating the apple both were innocent and morality was not an issue. Afterwards, they had knowledge and with it came morality – an awareness of good and evil and the power of choice. As Jarvis (1992) noted:

> Archbishop William Temple once commented that if this was a fall, it was a fall upwards! Perhaps this is the greatest paradox of all human learning – the fact that something generally regarded as good has been intimately associated with a myth of the origin evil in the world ... learning, and perhaps knowledge itself, has significant moral connotations. (7)

Within coaching there are potential ethical issues of manipulation, control and the abuse or uses of power as central elements within practice. These dynamics cannot be ignored as part of coach education or assessment.

'Practical judgement' (Harrison & Smith, 2001) also has an emotional dimension. It combines many elements of what might be characteristics of ethical behaviour, e.g., integrity, honesty and positive regard and it therefore contributes greatly to building learning relationships and enhancing the learning process. The dominant approach to coach training is expressed through competence frameworks, which emphasise *episteme* (and *techne*) at the expense of *phronesis*. This is discussed in relation to assessment later but, in the mean time, it is important to understand something about the discourse on learning within psychology and how it arguably has informed the curriculum design in coach education.

Daloz (1999) helpfully classifies the various learning theories that have been developed in psychology into three main categories:

- Phase theory (e.g., Levinson, Jung, Buhler, Neugarten)
- Stage Theory (e.g., Kegan, Piaget, Gilligan)
- Journey Theory (e.g., Perry, Daloz)

These categories have within them certain discourse assumptions about the nature and form of adult learning. These are first presented and then discussed in relation to *episteme*, *phronesis* and the curriculum for coach education and the training, assessment and accreditation of coaches.

Phase Theories

Phase theory is influenced by the psychological discourse on how people change psychologically *as they age*. Phase theories often draw on cultural factors at work in the ageing process in that different cultures have different views on ageing and the treatment of older people. Levinson et al.'s (1978) work on the age-related development of men, for example, is viewed as seminal in the mentoring literature. Jung (1958) contributed the concept of individuation to phase theories. It is an age-related concept, where an individual reassesses his or her life such that previously neglected or underdeveloped aspects are often re-examined. He suggested that the process involves a psychological separation from one's cultural foundations in order to move forward in one's life or develop a stronger and deeper association with one's sense of self.

As a phase theorist, Buhler (1972) defined four basic human tendencies that can be tracked across the phases of a person's life:

- The tendency to strive for personal satisfactions in sex, love, and ego recognition
- The tendency toward self-limiting adaptation for the purpose of fitting in, belonging, and gaining security
- The tendency toward self-expression and creative accomplishments
- The tendency toward integration or order-upholding (Buhler, 1972: 48).

Neugarten, another example of a phase theorist, presented the 'Social Clock Theory'. Here she posited the idea that adults could be 'on time' or 'off time' in terms of their life's experiences and events and people adjust their behaviour accordingly. These 'time events' are often socially constructed, but the adjustments are made psychologically.

Phase theory tells us that not all people go through the same phases at the same age and, therefore, there are variations. It is not a given that at age 40 or 50, people will behave in certain ways and have certain crises. Still, using an age-related discourse may be helpful in supporting an age transition (Garvey, 2013) through coaching. Phase theories also may influence the curriculum design so that there might be, for example, minimum age requirements for entry into a coach education or training programme. The assumption being that a coach needs certain life experiences, often acquired through age, to perform the function. It may also be that the curriculum is designed in phases with the assumption that certain things must be learned first and others later once the trainee coaches mature and develop in their experience and understanding.

Another aspect of Phase Theory discourse is found in the idea that a coach must 'put in the flying hours' in order to be properly accredited and that time runs out so renewal becomes necessary (see ICF, 2015). The argument being that only spending time doing something enables skill development. Whist it is clear that there is a certain logic to this justification, it says very little about the 'quality' of those hours, the critical reflection on these hours or the internalisation of these reflections in order to be more reflexive on and effective in the development of reflexivity in one's practice. Assessments may also be phased in relation to the level of competence and the number of hours completed at each level. This leads to a graded set of phases e.g., a novice coach, practitioner coach and master coach. This tends to favour a *techne* approach in training and assessment and results in an assessment based in the passing of time. This also leads to a reductionist approach to competencies, which favors an *episteme* approach and results in assessment by the ticking of boxes. A focus on phronesis is often missing from these phase-based discourses.

Stage Theories

Stage theories are based on the idea that people go through stages of development that are more clearly demarcated than phases. Stage theories are mainly identified in educational settings (see Kegan, 1982, 1994). In the former he argues that educators should identify which stage the learner is at in order to provide appropriate opportunities for problem solving and growth to the next stage. In the latter he suggests that it is very easy for a practitioner to misconceive the nature of the transformation a person may need or seek to make. He believed that no one should expect people to master higher order stages unless they are ready and have appropriate help, e.g., through coaching (see Bachkirova, 2009) and this adds a high degree of complexity to the process.

Piaget is probably the best-known stage theorist. Despite the criticism that his stages of development are not rigidly defined and, from a positivistic point of view, his research methodology was unrepresentative and therefore not generalisable, his stages of development model still dominates the discourse within education systems around the world. Gilligan's (1982) 'Stages of the ethic of care' offers the following as another perspective on the stages, particularly as they relate to moral development:

- Preconventional stage in which one's own survival is important with a transitional stage from selfishness to responsibility *to*
- Conventional stage in which we wish to fit and belong through self-sacrifice *to*
- Post conventional stage in which broader issues than survival or fit are considered, such as 'do not hurt self or others'.

The relationship between this set of theories and coaching is similar to the Phase theories. A coach may enable a shift from the plateau affect implied by Stage theory to enable progression to the next stage.

Stage theory discourse can be found in educational settings in the design of the curriculum. An assumption within the discourse of Stage theory is that there are levels of attainment. When this is applied to coach training it manifests in similar models as those derived from phase theories. For example, the European Mentoring and Coaching Council has four levels or stages: Foundation; Practitioner; Senior Practitioner and Master Practitioner. Similarly the International Coaching Federation has three levels or stages: Associate Coach; Professional Certified Coach; Master Certified Coach. The assessment process is based on simple description of each competence within a specific level. The assessor observes this and exercises a judgement about the descriptor being met and the individual may move to the next stage on the ladder of attainment, in Kegan's terms of when they are ready. This also favours an approach to assessment and accreditation more rooted in *techne* and *episteme* than *phronesis*.

Journey Theories

In journey theory, learning and development do not follow phases or stages. Learning is positioned as a journey in which choices are made, interests are followed and adventures happen whether they are experienced as positive or negative. The idea of a journey of learning is the basis of the ancient Greek poem, 'The Odyssey' and the metaphor of a 'journey' is often used in practice in relation to coaching activity (Stelter 2014, for example). A coach could be positioned as a guide or a catalyst for the journey or as one who enables choice at particular milestones along the way. There are many variations and different interpretations of Perry's (1970) work in this area. In essence, he presents four elements for learners to travel through and these are broken down into nine smaller elements. The first is 'dualism'. This is where there is a belief in right or wrong answers and with this is accompanied obedience to power. The second is multiplicity. Here, the fallibility of authority, ambiguity or a sense that there might be multiple truths emerges. The third element is relativism. Here the learner escapes from the ambiguity of multiple truth and recognises that there may not be one truth. The fourth is commitment within contextual relativism. Here the learner appreciates and delights in ambiguity, commitment to learning and critical thought within a particular context.

Whilst many refer to these as 'stages', Perry argued that his theory was fundamentally about having a brain and learning how to use it irrespective of a stage or a phase. He suggested that learning is not just about facts and figures (*episteme*) or practical applications (*techne*) but about developing higher thinking abilities (*phronesis*). People make choices about how, when or even if they move. These are like the choices made on a journey. Perry argued that the learning journey does not necessarily follow a particular route and that travellers may be in a different position in the journey for different areas of their learning. He also considered the developmental journey as one that moved erratically and with varying directions. Perry also argued that some learners can enable or disable their progress by delaying or denying a pluralistic position which they may find threatening or unattractive. It could be argued that this thinking adds subtlety to both phase and stage theories and therefore it offers a more journey oriented perspective.

What then, are the implications for coach education? Coach education based on a journey theory perspective will focus on who the person is and how they think and relate to ideas and experiences. This kind of development will be seen as continuous. Like Stage or Phase theories, the learner may have resting places where he or she may say, 'that will do for now, let me reflect a little before moving on'. It will be seen as an ongoing dialectic based on critical debate, critical reflection and reflexivity and it could be argued that this is a central role for the coach as a facilitator of this type of learning. Reflexivity here is seen as a capacity or potential to identify and critique the dominance of certain discourses and their power to socialise and as a result make changes and choices to influence that discourse. A reflexive coach would be aware, sensitive, and empathetic and would shape his or her own norms and standards reflexively as an ongoing practice. Contextual relativism would therefore play its part in developing higher thinking abilities. The reflexive coach would celebrate the 'Wild West', engage with its excitement and pioneer new thoughts and new ways and not seek to 'tame' it for his/her own ends. This favours a more *phronesis* approach.

Another way to consider these issues is through the principles of adult learning (andragogy) as expounded by Knowles (1984) and experiential learning, as put forward by Kolb (1984). The standard approach in education is generally to 'teach' theory and then test the 'learners' on what they have been taught. In the experiential and andragogic approach theory is derived from practice. Therefore, participants need to engage in practice and critically reflect on that practice, generate theory and compare that with the literature. This leads to the development of embedded and deeply learned skills and behaviours, which in themselves become subject to further critical reflection and self-reflection, which leads to advanced, sophisticated and original development (critical reflexivity) – and the loop continues. This can be seen, for example, in the moral dilemmas around the concepts of 'power', 'manipulation' and 'dependency' in coaching activity. Ethics are highly situational, complex and enacted in the moment and, as argued above, inherent in knowledge. By highlighting these dilemmas through practice, participants in a learning programme become aware of what constitutes ethical conduct in coaching activity. They are not 'taught' it; they come to discover it through critical reflection.

Therefore, learning in this approach is:

- based on the adult's need to know,
- experience-based,
- involving, shared and participative,
- relevant and applied,
- problem-centred rather than content-oriented, and
- driven by the individual's internal motivations rather than external motivators (after Knowles, 1984).

The above section has briefly outlined three discourses within adult learning theories and linked these to the Aristotelian ideas of *episteme*, *techne* and *phronesis* and the curriculum for coach education. In the next section these underpinnings will be explored in relation to the resultant assessment and accreditation policies.

ASSESSMENT AND ACCREDITATION

The educational world is very familiar with assessment and accreditation. These are like a rite of passage. There are two main sorts of assessment: formative and summative. Formative assessment is ongoing and is there as an aide to learning. Feedback is sought over a period of time from which development is mapped. It is often thought of as preparatory for the main summative assessment. Sometimes it is diagnostic in nature and employs both self-assessment and forward-looking assessment, which aims to be predictive. This might include scenario-based assessment or case study work. This type of assessment is more likely to be associated with journey theory and more likely to relate to a developmental philosophy.

Summative assessment mostly happens at the end of a learning programme and a grade or mark is issued. Its general purpose is to assess what has been taught or learned. Summative assessment is evaluative and often judgemental. It can also relate to a performance orientation based on pre-specified learning outcomes or objectives. It is generally standards-based and supposedly objective. This type of assessment is more akin to the phase and stage theories of learning and more associated with the rational pragmatic discourse. It is a very commonly adopted approach to assessment. Accreditation might involve assessment of some kind but is essentially different. It is often about third parties certifying or 'credentialising' against 'official standards'. These processes are supposed to ensure that competence is assured, that accredited individuals will behave ethically and are suitably quality-controlled.

To explore the learning and development issues raised by these approaches to assessment and accreditation, it is helpful to consider a short vignette (Box 33.1). The consequences of the various discourses underpinning learning and development as well as assessment and accreditation are made clear by this vignette. In relation to coaching, the professionalisation, standards, quality assurance and rational pragmatic discourses have become so loud and so dominant that any alternative is squeezed out, marginalised or simply ignored. This is a very big problem for coaching practice where many authors in the literature make big claims for coaching in terms of its ability to develop individualism, creative and innovative thought, change and the tolerance of complexity, for example – to mention a few commonly cited benefits. There is a prima facie case at least to claim that the discourse of coaching, as outlined above, is at odds with the discourse of the professional bodies and associations in terms of coach education.

Thinking about the animal story, one issue, as raised previously, which comes to mind is 'ranking' e.g., novice coach, master coach, supervisor coach. Is this appropriate for a practice like coaching? Clearly there is a very conventional logic to ranking, however, like the animals in the vignette, some will drop out or be damaged by this approach. Of course, if one subscribes to the rational pragmatic discourse, this may not be such a bad thing because this is the assumption of performance that some will fail. In a Darwinian survival of the fittest world this would be an acceptable loss. However, as raised earlier in the chapter, an often cited coaching discourse favours a person centred humanistic approach, which is clearly at odds with the 'ranking' and excluding philosophy

---

Box 33.1   Animal School: A parable (Gupta and Pandhee, 2006)

Once upon a time the animals decided to do something decisive to meet the increasing complexity of their society. They held a meeting and finally decided to organise a school. The curriculum consisted of running, climbing, swimming and flying. Since these were the basic behaviours of most animals, they decided that all the students should take all the subjects.

The duck was excellent at swimming, better in fact, than his teacher. He also did well in flying. But he was very poor in running and he was made to stay after school to practise. He had to drop swimming in order to get more time in which to practise running. This continued until his webbed feet were so badly damaged that he became only average at swimming. But average was an acceptable grade in the school, so nobody worried about that except the duck.

The rabbit started at the top of her class in running, but finally had a nervous breakdown because of so much time spent in practising swimming.

The squirrel was excellent at climbing until he developed a psychological block in flying class, when the teacher insisted he start from the ground instead of from the tops of trees. He was forced to practise flying until he became muscle-bound and received a 'C' in climbing and a 'D' in running.

The eagle was the school's worst discipline problem; in climbing class, she beat all of the others to the top of the tree but she insisted on using her own method to get there.

The dogs, of course, stayed out of school and fought the tax levied for education because digging was not included in the curriculum. They apprenticed their children to the badger and later joined the groundhogs, and eventually started a private school offering alternative education.

employed in the *techne* discourse of the professional bodies and coaching associations.

Another problem illustrated by the animal vignette is that the education system is instructor led. This may seem an odd criticism, perhaps because we are so used to this model that we no longer notice or question it. However, it assumes that the instructor has the knowledge and the experience and the learner learns it. The learner is 'taught' and the instructor teaches to the 'standards' set by the assessment or accreditation process. Again this is at odds with the discourse found in coaching itself, which is dominated by the idea of the 'learner's agenda' (Cox et al., 2014; Garvey et al., 2014; du Toit, 2014; Rogers, 2012; Connor & Pokora, 2012; Western, 2012; Garvey, 2011; Parsloe & Leedham, 2009; Whitmore, 2009; Rosinski, 2003). It is also at odds with the fundamental principles of adult learning as outlined above (Knowles, 1984).

The vignette raises the issue of standards to be pursued versus the recognition of special abilities which may lie outside of the scope of the prescribed standards. Prescribed standards, in the case of coach education offer a 'blanket' approach to development where specific talents or contexts of practice are ignored. This limits the scope of a list of standards, unless, of course, the standards are particularly comprehensive. However, within the rational pragmatic discourse, so favoured by professional associations, comprehensiveness gives way to reductionism and simplicity where special abilities are generally ignored.

Barnett (1994: 73) comments that: 'the notion of competence is concerned with predictable behaviours in predicable situations'. This is a seriously concerning observation for those involved in coaching. How often is a coaching conversation predictable? The competence qualified coach who subscribes to the rational pragmatic discourse might think – 'mostly'. Competency frameworks, developed out of rational pragmatic discourses assume stability. This is a problem when most coaching situations are fluid, based on change and transition, and complex (Lane, 2014). The competence models for coach development that are based in a rational pragmatic discourse (techne) are weak because they rarely allow for complexity.

Further criticisms of competence frameworks are offered by Bolden and Gosling's (2006: 148) analysis of the literature on the subject. They present five arguments as to why competencies are inadequate as follows:

- Ecclestone (1997), Grugulis, (1998) and Lester (1994) all state that the reductionist nature of competencies make them inadequate to deal with the complexities of a job role;
- Grugulis, (2000), Loan-Clarke (1996) and Swailes and Roodhouse (2003) argue that the generic nature of competencies mean that they are not sensitive to specific situations, tasks or individuals;
- Cullen (1992) and Lester (1994) argue that competence frameworks represent a view of past performance rather than act as a predictor of future behaviour;
- Bell et al. (2002) suggest that competence frameworks exclude subtle qualities, interactions and situational factors; and
- Brundrett (2000) argues that they create a limited and mechanistic approach to learning.

It is argued that competencies generally reflect the *techne* and episteme discourse and the critical comments above raise the need to shift the discourse to approaches more based on *phronesis*. Schön (1987) provides some help here in the following quote:

> On the high ground, management problems lend themselves to solution through the application of research-based theory and technique. In the swampy lowland, messy confusing problems defy technical solution. The irony of this situation is that the problems of the high ground tend to be relatively unimportant to individuals or society at large, however, great their technical interest may be, while in the swamp lie the problems of greatest human concern. (3)

As previously argued coaching is dynamic, complex and situational, it is varied in its application and is employed in a variety of contexts and is of great human concern. Its potential for doing 'good' and making a positive difference to people is huge. It is therefore, quite firmly in the 'swampy lowlands' as a complex activity.

Barnett (1994: 37) sheds light on this rise and rise of the rational pragmatic in society at large: 'Society is more rational; but it is a rationality of a limited kind.' 'Limited rationality' is a rational pragmatism devoid of ethical or environmental justification. The limited rationality is a pragmatic response to pragmatic issues – 'techne' issues, the issues of professionalisation raised by the 'Wild West' discourse. It is argued here that this has become so engrained as a dominant discourse that we simply accept it as 'normal'. This 'techne' mode is the foundation of current competence-based learning and it is the main agenda in coaching assessment and accreditation. Whilst this approach makes it easier to judge if these outcomes or objectives are met, it also treats learning as a 'linear' activity (Garvey et al., 2014) where the learner moves in a straight line through the phases or stages rather like moving along a road or up a staircase. This discourse is attractive; if we know the precise route then the logic dictates that the most helpful thing we can do is accelerate the journey and get a pre-specified destination as quickly as possible.

Progress does happen in this way but it represents only a fraction of human capability. Yes, this approach enhances accountability and quality control (the arguments of professional bodies in coaching) but it is also 'limited' in the Barnett sense. It may get us to where we want to go by the fastest and most direct route but it 'cannot develop our awareness of the different kinds of destination available, the speed of travel or the choice of route, nor does it hold out any promise that we will be enriched simply by the travelling' (Garvey et al., 2014:113).

Another issue with the *techne* and episteme approaches is that we simply learn what is pre-specified and then feel that we have 'arrived', often as an expert. This excludes the possibility of further learning as it inhibits the concept of the ongoing development associated with all learning theories outlined above. *Techne* does not develop the essential quality of *phronesis* so needed by a coach operating in 'hot action'. The holders of the *techne* competence frameworks have power over the assessment and accreditation system. In this case, the professional bodies and their agents who accredit and assess coach development. This probably means that *phronesis* is reduced in importance in these *techne* based models. As Barnett (1994: 37) states 'genuinely interactive and collaborative forms of reasoning' or *phronesis* are being driven out by *techne* and as a result, we may not be developing coaches capable of the very qualities we hope that coaching will help develop in others.

TOWARDS INCLUSIVITY

Much of the critique of coach education, training, assessment and accreditation in this chapter is a challenge to the scientific, rational pragmatic discourse and their dominance in the coaching world, particularly in professional bodies. There are hints at an alternative perspective throughout this chapter. Examples include the underpinning humanistic philosophy of coaching, the complex skills and abilities needed to act as a coach and the notions of journey theory and *phronesis*. However, offering a critique without providing an alternative is unhelpful, and so the concept of 'inclusivity' seems appropriate to bring these alternatives together. As raised earlier in this chapter, many argue that coaching has its roots in a person-centred humanistic philosophy. It is an inclusive philosophy and deeply challenging to operationalise. Exclusivity is easier. In relation to assessment and accreditation, power discourses are pertinent. It is the 'credentialisers' who have the power to include or exclude. So what is an alternative to assessment and accreditation as positioned by the current power holders?

One way forward is to return to the underpinning values of humanism, consider journey theory as a viable and realistic alternative and recognise that, whilst *techne* and episteme hold much promise, they do not hold all the answers and *phronesis* needs to be involved. This would mean that assessment and accreditation become dynamic, situational and peer led. Clearly this would also require changes in the way coaches are developed and supported in their development. Here, critical reflection would be necessary and critical reflexivity essential. A coach would not 'arrive' when 'passing', in fact, the concept of 'passing' may need to change as coaches would be developing a way of life and a way of relating. Assessment would therefore be continuous, embedded in practice and peer supported. A true examination of Knowles'(1984) andragogy in the context of coach education could be considered as an approach to the delivery of a curriculum which develops critical reflection and reflexivity. Are we ready for that or are the dominant voices just too dominant? Time will tell.

REFERENCES

Amabile, T. (1997) Motivating creativity in organizations: On doing what you love and loving what you do, *California Management Review*, 40, 39–58.

Arnaud, G. (2003) A coach or a couch? A Lacanian perspective on executive coaching and consulting, *Human Relations*, 56(9), 1131–1154.

Bachkirova, T. (2009) Cognitive-developmental approach to coaching: an interview with Robert Kegan, *Coaching: An International Journal of Theory, Research and Practice*, 2(1), 10–22.

Barnett, R. (1994) *The Limits of Competence*, London: Open University Press & Society for Research into Higher Education.

Bauman, Z. (1989) *Modernity and the Holocaust*, Cambridge: Polity.

Bell, E., Taylor, S. & Thorpe, R. (2002) A step in the right direction? Investors in People and the learning organisation, *British Journal of Management*, 13, 161–171.

Berg, I.K. & Szabo, P. (2005) *Brief Coaching for Lasting Solutions*, New York: Norton

Bolden, R. & Gosling, J. (2006) Leadership competencies: time to change tune? *Leadership*, 2(2), 147–163.

Brundrett, M. (2000) The question of competence: the origins, strengths and inadequacies of a leadership training paradigm, *School Leadership and Management*, 20(3), 353–369.

Bruner, J. (1985) Vygotsky: a historical and conceptual perspective, In: J.V. Wertsch (ed.), *Culture, Communication and Cognition: Vygotskian perspectives*, Cambridge, London and New York: Cambridge University Press, pp. 21–34.

Bruner, J. (1996) *The Culture of Education*, Cambridge, MA: Harvard University Press.

Buhler, C. (1972) *Introduction to Humanistic Psychology*, Bellmont, CA: Wadsworth Publishing Co., Inc.

Carter, A. (2006) *Practical Methods for Evaluating Coaching*, Institute for Employment Studies, report 430. Available at: http://www.employment-studies.co.uk/system/files/resources/files/430.pdf

Connor, M. & Pokora, J. (2012) *Coaching and Mentoring at Work: Developing effective practice*, Maidenhead, UK: McGraw-Hill.

Contu, A. & Willmott, H. (2003) Re-embedding situatedness: the importance of power relations in learning theory. *Organization Science*, 14(3), 283–296.

Coopey, J. (1995) The learning organization: power, politics and ideology introduction, *Management Learning*, 26(2), 193–213.

Cox, E., Bachkirova, T. & Clutterbuck, D. (eds) (2014) *The Complete Handbook of Coaching* (2nd Edition), London: Sage.

Cullen, E. (1992) A vital way to manage change, *Education*, November 13, 3–17.

Dafermos, M. & Marvakis, A. (2006) Critiques in psychology – critical psychology, *Annual Review of Critical Psychology*, 5, 1–20.

Daloz, L.A. (1999) *Mentor: Guiding the Journey of Adult Learners*, San Francisco: Jossey-Bass.

Dewey, J. (2012) *How we Think*, USA, ReadaClassic.com (reprint form the 1910 original).

Downey, M. (2014) *Effective Modern Coaching: The Principles and Art of Successful Business Coaching*, London: LID publishing Ltd.

Drake, D.B. (2011) What do coaches need to know? Using the Mastery Window to assess and develop expertise, *Coaching: An International Journal of Theory, Research & Practice*, 4(2), 138–155.

du Toit, A. (2014) *Making Sense of Coaching*, London: Sage.

Ecclestone, K. (1997) Energising or enervating: implications of National Vocational Qualifications in professional development, *Journal of Vocational Education and Training*, 49, 65–79.

Flyvberg, B. (2001) *Make Social Science Matter: Why social inquiry fails and how it can succeed again*, Cambridge, UK: Cambridge University Press.

Frank, A.W. (2004) Asking the right question about pain: narrative and phronesis, *Literature and medicine*, 23(2), 209–225.

Gabriel, Y. (2004) *Myths, Stories and Organizations: Premodern Narratives for Our Times*, Oxford, UK: Oxford University Press.

Gallwey, T. (1974) *The Inner Game of Tennis*, London: Pan Books.

Garvey, B. (2011) *A Very Short, Slightly Interesting and Reasonably Cheap Book on Coaching and Mentoring*, London: Sage

Garvey, B. (2013) Coaching people through life transitions, in J. Passmore (ed.), *Diversity in Coaching*, London: Kogan Page.

Garvey, B. & Williamson, B. (2002) *Beyond Knowledge Management: Dialogue, creativity and the corporate curriculum*, Harlow, UK: Pearson Education.

Garvey, B., Stokes, P. & Megginson, D. (2014) *Coaching and Mentoring: Theory and practice* (2nd Edition). London: Sage.

Gilligan, C. (1982) *In a Different Voice: Psychological Theory and Women's Development*, Cambridge, MA and London: Harvard University Press.

Grugulis, I. (1998) 'Real' managers don't do NVQs: a review of the new management 'standards', *Employee Relations*, 20, 383–403.

Grugulis, I. (2000) The Management NVQ: a critique of the myth of relevance, *Journal of Vocational Education and Training*, 52(1), 79–99.

Grant, A.M. (2007) Past, present and future: the evolution of professional coaching and coaching psychology, In A. Palmer & A. Whybrow (eds), *Handbook of Coaching Psychology: A Guide for Practitioners*, Hove: Routledge, pp. 23–39.

Grant, A.M. & Cavanagh, M.J. (2011) Coaching and positive psychology, in K.M. Sheldon, T.B. Kashdan & M.F. Steger (eds), *Designing Positive Psychology: Taking stock and moving forward*, Oxford: Oxford University Press, pp. 293–309.

Gupta, A. & Pandhee, S. (2006) The Animal School: A Parable. Retrieved from: http://www.arvindguptatoys.com/arvindgupta/springdales.htm

Harrison, R. & Smith, R. (2001) Practical judgement: its implications for knowledge development and strategic capability, in B. Hellgren & J. Lowstedt (eds), *Management in the Thought-Full Enterprise – European Ideas on Organizing*, Poland, OZGraf SA: Fagbokforlaget.

Hatch, M.J. & Cunliffe, A.N., (2013) *Organization Theory: Modern, Symbolic and Postmodern Perspectives* (3rd Edition), Oxford: Oxford University Press.

Hayes, P. (2008) *NLP Coaching*, Maidenhead: Open University Press.

Hemmestad, L.B., Jones, R.L., & Standal, Ø.F. (2010) Phronetic social science: a means of better researching and analysing coaching? *Sport, Education and Society*, 15(4), 447–459.

ICF (2015) Member eligibility requirements. Retrieved from http://coachfederation.org/join/landing.cfm?ItemNumber=984&navItemNumber=563%20and%20http://www.emccouncil.org/eu/en/accreditation

Jarvis, P. (1992) *Paradoxes of Learning – on becoming an individual in society*, San Francisco: Jossey Bass Higher Education Series.

Johnson, P. and Duberley, J. (2000) *Understanding Management Research*, London: Sage.

Jung, C. J. (1958) *Psyche and Symbol*, New York, USA: Doubleday.

Kegan, R. (1982) *The Evolving Self: Problem and process in human development*, Cambridge, MA: Harvard University Press.

Kegan, R. (1994) In Over Our Heads: The Mental Demands of Moderrn Life,

Cambridge, Massachusetts: Harvard University Press

Knowles, M. (1984) *Andragogy in Action*, San Francisco: Jossey-Bass.

Kimsey-House, H., Kimsey-House, K., Sandahl, P. & Whitworth, L. (2011) *Co-Active Coaching: Changing Business, Transforming Lives*, London, Nicholas Brealey.

Kolb, D.A, (1984) *Experiential Learning*, Englewood Cliffs, NJ: Prentice Hall.

Kroger, R.O. & Wood, L.A. (1998) The turn to discourse in social psychology, *Canadian Psychology*, 39(4), 266–279.

Lane, D.A. (2014) Series Editor Foreword, in M.S. Kahn, *Coaching on the Axis: Working with complexity in business and executive coaching*, London: Karnac.

Layder, D. (1994) *Understanding Social Theory*, London: Sage.

Lester, S. (1994) Management standards: a critical approach, *Competency*, 2(1), 28–31.

Levinson, D.J., Darrow, C.N., Klein, E.B., Levinson, M.H. & McKee, B. (1978) *The Seasons of a Man's Life*, New York: Knopf.

Loan-Clarke, J. (1996) The Management Charter Initiative: a critique of management standards/NVQs, *Journal of Management Development*, 15, 4–17.

Morris, B. & Tarpley, N.A. (2000) So You're a Player, Do You Need a Coach? *Fortune*, 141(4), 144–150.

Page, N. & de Haan, E. (2014) Does executive coaching work? *The Psychologist*, 27 (August), 582–587.

Palmer. S. & Whybrow, A. (2007) *Handbook of Coaching Psychology: A guide for Practitioners*, Hove, Routledge.

Parsloe, E. & Leedham, M. (2009) *Coaching and Mentoring: Practical conversations to improve learning*, London: Kogan Page.

Passmore, J., Peterson, D.B. and Freire, P. (eds) (2013) *The Psychology of Coaching & Mentoring*, Chichester: John Wiley and Sons.

Perry, W.G. (1970) *Forms of Intellectual and Ethical Development in the College Years: A Scheme*, New York, Holt: Rinehart and Winston.

Porter, T.M. (1995) *Trust in Numbers*, Princeton, Princeton University Press.

Rogers, J. (2012) *Coaching Skills: A Handbook* (3rd Edition), Maidenhead: Open University Press.

Rosinski, P. (2003) *Coaching Across Cultures*, London: Nicholas Brealey.

Schön, D.A. (1983) *The Reflective Practitioner*, New York: Basic Books.

Schön, D.A. (1987) *Educating the Reflective Practitioner: Towards a New Design for Teaching and Learning in the Profession*, San Francisco, CA: Jossey-Bass.

Sennett, R. (1998) *The Corrosion of Character: The Personal Consequences of Work in the New Capitalism*, New York; Norton.

Sherman, S. and Freas, A. (2004) The Wild West of executive coaching, *Harvard Business Review*, 82(11), November: 82–90.

Starr, J. (2008) *The Coaching Manual: The definitive guide to the process, principles and skills of personal coaching*, London: Pearson Edition Limited.

Stelter, R. (2014) *A Guide to Third Generation Coaching: Narrative-Collaborative Theory and Practice*, Dordrecht, Heidelberg, New York, London: Springer.

Swailes, S. & Roodhouse, S. (2003) Structural barriers to the take-up of Higher Level NVQs, *Journal of Vocational Education and Training*, 55(1), 85–110.

Vygotsky, L.S. (1978) *Mind in Society: The Development of Higher Psychological Processes* (Ed. M. Cole et.al.), Cambridge, MA: Harvard University Press.

Webster, F. (1980) *The New Photography: Responsibility in Visual Communication*, London: John Calder.

Western, S. (2012) *Coaching and Mentoring: A critical text*, London, UK: Sage.

Whitmore, J. (2009) *Coaching for Performance: Growing human potential and purpose* (4th Edition), London: Nicholas Brealey.

Wood, L.A. & Kroger, R.O. (2000) *Doing Discourse Analysis: Methods for studying action in talk and text*, California, USA: Sage.

Developing Ethical Capabilities of Coaches

Ioanna Iordanou and Patrick Williams

INTRODUCTION

Over the last two decades, the use of coaching as a developmental tool has increased in vast proportions. This exponential growth has taken place primarily in the Anglosphere and increasingly in Asia and Africa. In a survey conducted in 2012, the International Coach Federation found that coaching is a $2 billion per year industry with a global workforce of 47,500 professionals that is constantly on the rise; so is the quantity of coaching programmes that enter the training market (PricewaterhouseCoopers, 2012). This rapid proliferation of coaching comes with great responsibility and, simultaneously, a certain degree of notoriety (Brennan and Wildflower, 2014). This is because coaching, unlike other relevant 'helping professions' like medicine, nursing, social work or counselling and psychotherapy, continues to remain unregulated, despite its burgeoning popularity.

As a result, coaching professionals operate autonomously and with no obligation to comply with any regulatory body's code of ethics or code of conduct. Before we explore this issue further, it is significant to distinguish between the two terms. The *Collins English Dictionary* (http://www.collinsdictionary.com) defines a code of ethics as 'an agreement on ethical standards for a profession or business' and a code of conduct as 'an agreement on rules of behaviour for a group or organization'. For the purposes of this chapter, we adopt these definitions and we refer to conduct as the actual behaviour and ethics as the general guides that influence that behaviour.

The lack of regulatory imposition of ethical standards has been deemed one of the key determinants of the inability of coaching to be recognized as a legitimate, stand-alone profession (Brennan and Wildflower, 2014). This is partly because this regulatory absence has offered fertile ground for the development of independent professional activity and, in consequence, idiosyncratic and self-imposed ethical standards in the coaching practice. But how viable is ethical pluralism or, put better by Soltis (1986: 3), ethical *subjectivism*? This brings us to the topical issue of whether coaching is or can be a stand-alone profession. Echoing Soltis (1986: 3), we see a profession as a 'community of practice with a telos, a general purpose that one must be committed to in order to be a professional.' Being part of such a community entails subjecting one's professional freedom to the ethical principles and standards of that professional community of practice (Soltis, 1986). In this respect, the very lack of regulatory imposition of ethical standards in coaching has jeopardized its advancement into a stand-alone profession.

In response to this issue, a number of professional coaching associations have initiated self-regulation mechanisms by producing in-house codes of ethics. While these types of separate initiatives have been embraced by the coaching community, their lack of systematic coordination has spawned a variety of individualized ethical codes that reflect each association's individual priorities. Of course, coaches are only asked to espouse such ethical principles when they opt for professional membership and even then, ethical conduct is contingent upon the coach's conscience rather than systematic monitoring by the affiliated professional body. The landscape of ethical standards in coaching, therefore, is muddled, leaving coaches to rely on their own devices regarding the development and maturity of their ethical capabilities. As Jonathan Passmore (2009: 8) put it graphically:

> Most coaches are in most cases ethical pluralists, who hold to a few solid principles, but for most of what they do they consider the circumstances of the situation and consider the motives and situations of the characters involved to help them reach a decision about the course of action to follow.

Against this backdrop, practitioners, scholars and even critics of coaching have accentuated the need for a commonly driven code of ethics with clearly defined guidelines that coaches and clients can refer to as a benchmark for ethical conduct in coaching (Brennan and Wildflower, 2014). Several proponents of coaching have embraced this prospect, as it could help the profession move away from what Grant and Cavanagh (2004: 2) have termed 'pseudo-credentialising mills' and move closer to the aim of professional legitimization. Other voices, however, have warned against the dangers of such pursuit. This is because the mere existence of normative and prescriptive codes of ethics that attempt some degree of pervasiveness are likely to compromise the very existence of genuine ethical dilemmas that naturally arise during the coaching practice (Garvey et al., 2014: 226–227). The big question for coaching is: Is a unified code of ethics sufficient to undergird the pluralistic range of individual, cultural, and professional values that coaches around the world bring into the coaching practice on a daily basis?

While answering this question is not the primary purpose of this chapter, an effort to examine it further brings to the fore the topical issue of developing ethical capabilities in coaches. This chapter, therefore, will explore the instrumentality of how this might be done. It will particularly discuss the different ways in which coaches can fine-tune their ethical capabilities in order to advance not only their practice, but also the coaching profession as a whole. The chapter will start with a review of the literature on the subject of ethics in coaching. It will then proceed to a brisk historical overview of the development of professional ethics in order to conclude by offering suggestions as to how coaches can develop and enhance their ethical capabilities.

Moreover, the chapter will briefly survey the attempts of major professional coaching associations to produce codes of ethics in an effort to uphold ethical practice for their members and the coaching profession. Two case studies from practice at the end of the chapter will help contextualize seminal ethical issues that novice and seasoned coaches face in their coaching journey: coaching one's first client, in the case of the former;

and working within the triadic relationship of coach, client and the sponsoring organization, in the case of the latter. Overall, this chapter will argue that the development of ethical capabilities is the professional responsibility of the coach and an auspicious opportunity for personal and professional maturity.

ETHICS IN COACHING: THE BACKGROUND

According to the *Oxford Dictionary* (www.oxforddictionaries.com) ethics are 'moral principles that govern a person's behaviour or the conducting of an activity'. Ethics, therefore, determine a person's decisions and actions, as dictated by their beliefs and values. Put more simply, ethics is the practice through which people determine what is good or bad, right or wrong, just or unjust. Indeed, people usually think and act according to their values; that is, they attempt to act ethically in ways that are consistent with their value system. In coaching, ethical principles determine the virtue of helping clients to develop and progress, focusing on their needs and interests, honouring trust and confidentiality, and promoting individual autonomy (de Jong, 2010).

In 2008, the Global Convention of Coaching (GCC) – a symposium of coaching scholars and practitioners from around 40 countries – prioritized the issue of ethics in coaching as of paramount significance for the legitimization and preservation of the coaching profession (GCC, 2008). Yet, despite this cruciality, the burgeoning coaching literature has been sluggish in systematically exploring this issue. The first methodical attempt to collate some scholarly views on this subject was made by Patrick Williams and Sharon Anderson (2006). In their *Law and Ethics in Coaching*, several scholars and practitioners of coaching offered their personal insights on the practical application of values and ethical standards in the coaching practice. This work, however, is overwhelmingly grounded on North-American case studies and, as such, may not be fully applicable in other parts of the world.

Brennan and Wildflower (2014) offered a more generic overview of the current landscape of ethics in coaching by attempting a comparison of the various associations' ethical codes and a typology of the key ethical issues a coach may encounter. Passmore and Mortimer (2011) made a similar attempt, extracting parallels from the sphere of nursing and postulating a framework for ethical decision-making (see also, Duffy and Passmore, 2010). Finally, Ives and Cox (2014) offered balanced suggestions for ethical considerations, particularly within the sphere of relationship coaching, while Hawkins and Shohet (2012: 131–151) explored the subject of ethics in coaching supervision.

All these texts have most certainly brought to the fore key issues surrounding the intricate matter of ethics in coaching. Yet, they are either conceptual in nature (Brennan and Wildflower, 2014; Ives and Cox, 2014; Hawkins and Shohet, 2012; Passmore, 2009; Passmore and Mortimer 2011) or they are based on small-scale empirical research (Duffy and Passmore, 2010). Due to the gravity of the issue, however, the subject of ethics in coaching is in great need of a more systematic empirical grounding in such a way that is commensurate with the recent proliferation of coaching practices and scholarship. Given the significance of ethical conduct in any profession, such empirical pursuits will enable coaching practitioners and scholars to move beyond the 'face value' existence of ethics in practice and systematically explore and promote the development of ethical capabilities. This needs to be addressed within a global context and in a way that takes into consideration the nuances of diverse individual, cultural, and professional values. This is a great challenge, indeed, but one that awakens us to the significance of being vigilant about our idiosyncratic way of thinking about ethics. A brisk historical overview of ethics may help us understand how the latter can be viewed from a variety of perspectives.

THE DEVELOPMENT OF ETHICS: A BRIEF HISTORICAL OVERVIEW

The Western history of ethics can be traced back to the work of ancient Greek philosophers such as Socrates (c. 470–399 BC), Plato (c. 428–c. 348 BC), and Aristotle (384–322 BC), who laid the foundations for the development of moral philosophy. Moral philosophy is primarily concerned with the question of what is morally 'right' and 'wrong' behaviour and has produced a variety of ethical models to answer this question. In the Western world, primarily in Europe and North America, the two historically prevailing models have been *deontological* ethics and *utilitarian* ethics. The former is grounded on the doctrines of Immanuel Kant (1724–1804) and places reason at the core of morality. In essence, *deontological* ethics determines one's sense of duty and is premised on a set of universal beliefs about the nature of reality. *Utilitarian* ethics derives from the writings of David Hume (1711–1776), Jeremy Bentham (1748–1832) and John Stuart Mill (1806–1873). Contrary to *deontological* ethics, *utilitarian* ethics focuses on the maximization of utility for the benefit of society. Whether an action is right or wrong is judged by an evaluation of its positive and negative consequences. In essence, the deontological approach sees human beings as ends in themselves, while the utilitarian approach considers them as a means to an end (Bond, 2015: 47).

The competition between – and at times the restriction of – these two prevalent approaches to ethics has spawned other ethical positions. The revival of Aristotle's ethics, for instance, generated *virtue* ethics. Virtue ethics dictates that the 'rightness' or 'wrongness' of an action is not determined by duty, obligation or consequence, but by the virtues that enable an individual's growth (see, for instance, Hursthouse, 1999). *Ethics of care* is a feminist approach to ethics that was premised in women's experience of acting as carers for others, for instance, children (Gilligan, 1993). In particular, Gilligan suggested that women's tendency to define themselves in terms of their connection to other people explained their propensity to assuming caring responsibilities. This 'overriding concern with relationships and responsibilities' was part of a woman's 'moral strength' (Gilligan, 1993: 16). Of course, where there is more than one person involved, the question of power will inevitably arise. This takes us back to Karl Marx's (1818–1883) views on morals being dictated by the most powerful in a society. When we think in this way, we attempt to establish whose interest would be served better by a specific action. This approach has been termed *ethics of power and structure* (Becket and Maynard, 2013: 23).

It becomes apparent that different approaches to ethics depend on a variety of factors and cannot easily converge into one coherent and pervasive ethical line of action that everyone can follow. This realization has led to *discourse* and *narrative ethics* (see, for instance, Habermas, 1990; and Newton, 1997). This approach is grounded on a postmodern assertion that a universally distinct ethical system may not be possible. In essence, it may be wiser, if not more practical, to explore what kind of ethics is more appropriate for a particular context, rather than to attempt to impose a universal code that everyone must adhere to. This issue is particularly pertinent in professional contexts, where a morally 'right' or 'wrong' action is dependent on a variety of conflicting factors, including knowledge, culture, and pluralistic values, amongst others.

This issue naturally leads us to *professional* ethics, a rapidly growing discipline that is informed by several strands of social sciences and the law. Professional ethics comprises a set of values that dictate an ethical professional conduct and constitute 'an integral part of professional identity' (Bond,

2015: 47). The most elaborately developed type of professional ethics is medical ethics. This is probably due to the long history and ethos of the discipline of medicine that necessitates the combination of ethical and technical matters in the training and practice of physicians. The first modern code of medical ethics was crafted by the English physician Thomas Percival (1740–1804), who in 1794 published them in the form of a pamphlet entitled *Medical Ethics, or a Code of Institutes and Precepts, Adapted to the Professional Conduct of Physicians and Surgeons* (Waddington, 1975).

Professional codes of ethics like Percival's code have had a direct influence on the development of other relevant professions' ethical standards of practice, such us counselling and psychotherapy (Bond, 2015). As Brennan and Wildflower (2014: 432) appositely argued, these codes have gradually created a consensus of morally acceptable behaviour that transcends professional activities and encompasses all aspects of human interactions. 'It is', they maintained, 'in the nature of being a professional that one functions with a particular level of consciousness of the effect of one's behaviour' (Brennan and Wildflower, 2014: 432).

Practical guidance on ethical professionalism has come a long way since Percival's work. Professionals nowadays have access to a plethora of sources that can assist them in the development of their ethical capabilities. One of these sources is the Merkkula Center for Applied Ethics at Santa Clara University (USA). For the past 25 years, the Center has been a pioneer in the research and dissemination of practical tools that facilitate and enhance ethical conduct. As stated on the Center's website (www.scu.edu/ethics), some of the ethical approaches that the Center postulates for ethical behaviour are the following:

The Utilitarian Approach[1]

Influenced by the writings of David Hume, Jeremy Bentham, and John Stuart Mill, some ethicists emphasize that the ethical action is the one that provides the most good or does the least harm, or, to put it another way, produces the greatest balance of good over harm. The ethical corporate action, then, is the one that produces the greatest good and does the least harm for all who are affected, e.g., customers, employees, shareholders, the community and the environment. Ethical warfare balances the good achieved in ending terrorism with the harm done to all parties through death, injuries, and destruction. The utilitarian approach deals with consequences; it tries both to increase the good done and to reduce the harm done.

The Rights Approach

Other philosophers and ethicists suggest that the ethical action is the one that best protects and respects the moral rights of those affected. This approach, premised on the work of the German philosopher Immanuel Kant, starts from the belief that humans have a dignity based on their human nature and their ability to choose freely what they do with their lives. On the basis of such dignity, they have a right to be treated as ends and not merely as means to other ends. The list of moral rights – including the rights to make one's own choices about what kind of life to lead, to be told the truth, not to be injured, to a degree of privacy, and so on – is widely debated; some now argue that non-humans have rights, too. Also, it is often said that rights imply duties – in particular, the duty to respect others' rights.

The Fairness or Justice Approach

Aristotle and other Greek philosophers have contributed the idea that all humans should be treated equally. Today we use this idea to say that ethical actions treat all human beings equally – or if unequally, then fairly based on some standard that is defensible. We believe that it is fair to claim a salary that is commensurate with one's hard work and how much one contributes to an organization. But there is a debate over CEO salaries that are multiple times larger than the pay of others; in which many ask whether the huge disparity is based on a defensible standard or whether it is the result of an imbalance of power and hence is unfair.

The Common Good Approach

The Greek philosophers have also contributed the notion that life in a community is a good in itself and our actions should contribute to that life. This approach suggests that the interlocking relationships of society are the basis of ethical reasoning and that respect and compassion for all others – especially the vulnerable – are requirements of such reasoning. This approach also calls attention to the common conditions that are important to the welfare of everyone. This may be a system of laws, effective police and fire departments, health care, a public educational system, or even public recreational areas.

The Virtue Approach

One of the earliest approaches to ethics is that ethical actions ought to be consistent with certain ideal virtues that provide for the full development of our humanity. These virtues are dispositions and habits that enable us to act according to the highest potential of our character and on behalf of values like truth and beauty. Honesty, courage, compassion, generosity, tolerance, love, fidelity, integrity, fairness, self-control, and prudence are all examples of virtues. Virtue ethics asks of any action, 'What kind of person will I become if I do this?' or 'Is this action consistent with my acting at my best?'

Each of these approaches can help us determine what standards of behaviour can be considered ethical. Still, several issues present themselves as obstacles. The first one is that there may not be common approval of these specific approaches. For example, there may not be a consensus on the same set of human and civil rights. Similarly, there may not be mutual agreement on what constitutes 'common good'. People may naturally disagree on what is a good and what is bad. Another problem is that the different approaches may not answer the question 'What is ethical?' in the same way. These discrepancies on what constitutes ethical behaviour are not to be considered detrimental to the coaching practice. Instead, they should be seen as an incentive to both scholars and practitioners of coaching, to be critically reflexive about the personal, social, and cultural context in which their ethical practice is situated. Ultimately, the fact that each approach enables critical consideration of what is ethical in a particular circumstance can be greatly beneficial for the coach and the coaching researcher.

ETHICS IN COACHING: THE CURRENT STATE OF PLAY

Over the past two decades coaching has seen exponential growth on a global level. Yet, it is still not recognized as a legitimate, stand-alone profession, and more recently some scholars have even suggested that a unified field of coaching may not even be possible (see, for instance, Drake, 2008). There are several reasons for this and one is most certainly the lack of regulation of coaching by an independent – or even endogenous – authority. This means that anyone can embark on the coaching practice even without relevant competences, academic and professional credentials or formal guidelines for ethical behaviour. The title of the coach, therefore, just like that of speaker, consultant or trainer, remains unprotected. This can be detrimental to the credibility of the profession and its professionals. The progression from a service industry to a legitimate profession must be charted through the development of a coherent body of knowledge grounded on evidence-based competencies and ethical standards (Grant and Cavanagh, 2004; Kauffman, 2005). These are some of the prerequisites for any professional service to be accepted and achieve the status of a true profession (Bennett, 2006). In order to place these important claims into context, let us explore a real and practical example of what may happen if coaching is not backed by regulatory mechanisms or a robust evidence base for its existence.

Case Study: The Colorado Case

In June 2001, an opinion piece entitled 'Coaching: Is this Psychotherapy?' appeared in the Newsletter of the Colorado Mental Health Board. The author of the piece, who was the administrator of the Board at the time, argued that, for the state of Colorado, coaching fell within the broad category of psychotherapy. As a result, word began to spread that Colorado-based coaches had to register as unlicensed psychotherapists and observe the regulation of the state's Mental Health Act. Fearful of the potential consequences of this confusion, Dr Lloyd Thomas and Dr Patrick Williams strove to elucidate the Board regarding this misinterpretation, albeit to no avail.

This issue came to the fore two years later when a Colorado-based ICF Master Certified Coach was accused by the Department of Regulatory Agencies in Colorado of practising psychotherapy without a license. Although the charge was eventually dropped as frivolous, the coach was still forced to register as an unlicensed therapist. Opposing this demand and unable to meet the legal cost of defending her position, the coach was forced to close her practice. This event provided the catalyst for the Colorado Coalition of Coaches to initiate a process for challenging and changing the relevant regulation. The initiative lasted for nearly 18 months and with the prodigious support of individual coaches and formal professional coaching associations like the International Coach Federation, the International Association of Coaching, and the Worldwide Association of Business Coaches, an amendment of the Colorado Mental Health Act exempted coaching from the legislature's oversight (Williams and Anderson, 2006).

PROFESSIONAL COACHING ASSOCIATIONS AND THEIR CODES OF ETHICS

This case study brings to the fore a very important issue: the lack of systematic regulation of coaching by a state agency or any relevant regulatory board. To be sure, this limitation does not imply that the coaching profession is premised on superficial incentives with no regard for ethical standards for professional conduct. On the contrary, several coaching associations, recognizing the significance of self-regulation, have striven to delineate professional norms through producing their own codes of ethics. These are approved standards of ethical practice that members are expected to adhere to. Some of the most prominent professional associations that have produced their own codes of ethics are the following:

- The International Coach Federation (ICF)
- The European Mentoring and Coaching Council (EMCC)
- The Association for Coaching (AC)
- The International Association of Coaching (IAC)
- The International Coaching Community (ICC)
- The Association for Professional Executive Coaching and Supervision (APECS)
- The Worldwide Association of Business Coaches (WABC)
- The Africa Board for Coaching, Consulting and Coaching Psychology (ABCCC)
- The Center for Credentialing and Education (CCE)

Several professional associations of Psychology have also established special interest groups in coaching psychology. This is in recognition of the relevance of coaching in the realm of Counselling and Psychotherapy. Some of these associations are:

- The American Psychological Association (APA)
- The Australian Psychological Society (APS)
- The British Psychological Society (BPS)
- The British Association for Counselling and Psychotherapy (BACP)

The debate over who, if anyone, ought to regulate coaching is one that still awaits serious consideration and is beyond the scope of this chapter. While all these professional bodies operate independently from each other and set different priorities, if one carefully examines their codes of ethical practice (frequently termed 'code of ethics' or 'code of conduct'), one will most certainly notice some similarities in their ethical standards. Brennan and Wildflower (2014: 431–432) conducted a survey of several professional bodies' codes of ethics across various related professions and found that there is a degree of consistency in the ethical principles that underpin professional practice, the most common of which are:

- Do no harm: Do not cause needless injury or harm to others.
- Duty of care: Act in ways that promote the welfare of other people.
- Know you limits: Practise within your scope of competence.
- Respect the interests of the client.
- Respect the law.

To comprehend the provenance of these directives, it is important to have clear understanding of the common ethical issues that may arise in coaching. Brennan and Wildflower (2014) enumerate seven topical categories: contracting, confidentiality, misrepresentation, conflict of interest, dual and multiple relationships, competence, and self-management. Based on the principles of counselling and psychotherapy, de Jong (2010: 208) produced a taxonomy of six primary issues: beneficence, non-malfeasance (that is, doing no harm), fidelity, promoting autonomy, justice, self-care and respect. In a similar vein, Law (2011: 53) introduced the 'six R's' of ethical practice (rights, respect, recognition, relationship, representation, and responsibility), which were adapted as the Code of Ethics and Practice for the Society for Coaching Psychology.

The codes of ethics of the professional coaching associations cover all these ethical issues. A more nuanced examination, however, reveals the different ethical priorities they set for their membership. The ICF, for instance, particularly frowns upon sexual relationships between clients and coaches. It also condemns potential monetary benefits coaches may incur by a third party in order to establish or prolong a coaching relationship. The AC places strong emphasis on indemnity insurance and issues of diversity and equality that are only implicit in the codes of ethics of the EMCC. The latter seems to be the only coaching body that clearly expresses the significance of respecting the different approaches to coaching.

Table 38.1 The key ethical responsibilities of three professional coaching associations

International Coach Federation (ICF)	European Mentoring and Coaching Council (EMCC)	Association for Coaching (AC)
Professional conduct at large	Competence	Fitness to practice
Professional conduct with clients	Context	Contracting
Confidentiality/privacy	Boundary management	Statutory and legal duties
Conflicts of interest	Integrity	Maintaining good practice
	Professionalism	

Source: Ives and Cox (2014, p. 139)

All these institutional similarities and divergences are bound to cause a certain degree of perplexity (Brennan and Wildflower, 2014). If coaches opt for membership in more than one of these organizations, conflicting ethical guidelines may cause further confusion (Passmore and Mortimer, 2011). To mitigate this risk, in 2008 a conglomeration of these bodies (ICF, AC, APECS and the EMCC) embarked on an initiative to produce the First UK Statement of Shared Professional Values (Association for Coaching, 2008). A few years later, in 2012, the ICF, the EMCC and the AC joined forces in an attempt to create a globally shared and accepted code of conduct as a benchmark for ethical practice in coaching and mentoring. This endeavour was termed Global Coaching and Mentoring Alliance (GCMA) and was formed with the purpose of advancing the emerging professions of coaching and mentoring (Brennan and Wildflower, 2014: 433).

At the time of writing this chapter, two members of the Alliance, the AC and the EMCC, announced the creation of the Global Code of Ethics (GCoE). Premised on four distinct sections (terminology; working with clients; professional conduct; and excellent practice) the GCoE was primarily produced to provide 'appropriate guidelines, accountability and enforceable standards of conduct for all our members' (www.emccouncil.org). This is an extremely positive step forward but begs the following question: 'Is a commonly shared code of ethics a panacea for the lack of regulation of coaching, when the criticality of ethical behaviour is implicit not explicit in the realm of coaching practice?' Let us not forget that membership in any of these established institutions is purely optional and may be driven by a coach's personal and/or professional interests rather than the imperative to safeguard the client or the contracting organization. If a coach does not opt for membership, there is no recourse for providing any discipline or recommendation for further training and, as a result, the public may be confused as to who is a qualified coach and who is not. In fact, with professional coaching associations also linking certification to membership, the service becomes monetized in a revenue stream, constructing its own potential conflict of interest.

To be sure, by joining a professional coaching body, a coach concedes to entering a community of practice with mutual obligations towards the profession (Khurana and Nohria, 2008). This entails accountability for ethical conduct and, by proxy, consent to be subjected to the organization's ethical review procedure, in case of breech of its code of ethics. Indeed, most organizations mentioned in this chapter have an Independent Ethical Review Board and an Ethical Conduct Review process, lest one of their members has a complaint filed by another coach or someone from the public domain (a client or client organization). Being reviewed or interviewed does not necessarily imply an ethical breach. Instead, this can be a process for educating, clarifying, and informing both the coach and the complainant. In this respect, a coaching association's code of ethics can be one of the tools a coach can use to develop ethical capabilities. Ethical decision-making, however, is a process that is enhanced in a variety of different ways.

DEVELOPING ETHICAL CAPABILITIES OF COACHES

Professional associations' codes of ethics are one resource a coach can turn to for enhancing his or her ethical capabilities. Still, such codes are not necessarily the recipe for best practice, as they cannot guarantee a solution to every ethical problem a coach is faced with in practice (Bailey and Schwartzberg, 1995). Instead, ethical codes that aim to create frameworks for ethical decision-making can only function as a moral map or, as Duffy and Passmore (2010) pertinently put it, the scaffolding that can undergird professional practice. While frameworks can provide a self-contained manual for ethical decision-making, their very labelling as *framework* can imply intellectual and practical complication that can be off-putting to practitioners. On the other hand, the very nature of a legitimate profession entails terms and conditions that can, at times, be complex. However, such intellectual and practical complexities are paramount for the sustainability and advancement of a profession.

Aside from formalized ethical frameworks, other avenues exist for the development of coaches' ethical capabilities. One starting point can be the wilful cultivation of ethical maturity. A person's individual maturity determines their ability to understand others and can be developed through practical experience (Cross and Wood, 2005; Laske, 2006). The latter can be achieved through the conscious understanding and appreciation of one's principles and values, continuous professional development, and, importantly, consistent reflection on one's practice through a 'virtuous cycle of ethical maturity' (van Nieuwerburgh, 2014: 178). This involves being consciously aware of one's principles and values, embracing ethical dilemmas, making courageous ethical choices, and reflecting on them, in order to enhance one's ethical maturity.

According to van Nieuwerburgh (2014: 179), a coach's conscious awareness and reflection on her principles and values can inspire confidence and competence in her ability to address any ethical issues that may arise in the coaching process. Coaching supervision can, of course, provide the workspace for such reflexive activity that can enhance and sharpen one's ethical maturity (Duffy and Passmore, 2010). While utilizing supervision is not yet a mandatory requirement, it can provide an excellent means for building ethical maturity. This is because it affords the space for learning and even celebrating one's constantly evolving professional and, in consequence, ethical maturity.

Another vehicle for the development of ethical capabilities is the cultivation of a stance of critical enquiry. A stance of critical enquiry enables critical reflexivity, that is, the 'questioning of taken-for-granted assumptions, frames, and mental models' (Yanow and Tsoukas, 2009: 1341). Critical reflexivity is a powerful tool that a coach can use to facilitate a coachee's critical reflection. We concur that critical reflexivity enables the evaluation of one's actions within a political, social, even historical context and, in consequence, generates and solidifies learning (Cunliffe, 2002). The coach, therefore, can wield this tool as a means of critical enquiry towards his or her practice, in an effort to explore doubts, contradictions, dilemmas, even possibilities, and to periodically evaluate his or her values and their effect on others (Cunliffe, 2004: 38). The use of critical reflexivity, then, has the potential of enhancing a coach's ability to critically and subjectively evaluate one's own values and beliefs (Gray, 2007), and by extension, ethical principles.

Aside from the above, Caroll and Shaw (2013: 60) have postulated several strategies that can help professionals act ethically and fine-tune their ethical capabilities. Some of these are:

- Do not think, *I*; think *we*.
- Consider issues of power, domination, privilege, and how they can easily move into abuse and harm of others who are less privileged.
- Ask yourself if you would recommend what you are about to do to someone else.
- Try to look at your behavior, not your intention – what am I actually doing? Too often we use our intention (which is almost always good) to evaluate our behaviour (which is often not as good).
- Use empathy and ask yourself how this might be perceived from the other's point of view. It can bring about a radical change in what you do.
- Look for the truth in the opposite position to the one you hold; this can expose limitations in your point of view.
- Ask yourself: 'What are my habitual ways and points of denial?'
- Identify your Achilles heel.
- Beware of the extremity of any of your ideals (fundamentalism).

These strategies are designed to help one consciously reflect on the principles and values that drive one's actions. Van Nieuwerburgh (2014: 179) argues that fine-tuning one's ability to consciously reflect on personal and professional principles can render the coach more open-minded and confident in making ethical decisions and actions. This can be achieved in a variety of ways. Coaching supervision, for instance, is an ideal setting for the 'hypothetical testing of dilemmas', as it offers fertile ground for 'recurrent ethical thinking' (Duffy and Passmore, 2010). It is significant that coaches discuss and reflect on dilemmas and ethical issues in the supervision process, as they provide an opportunity for learning and further development of one's ethical capabilities. Such pursuits will benefit not only the coach and the client, but also the collective efforts to see coaching achieve full professional status (Brennan and Wildflower, 2014).

A FRAMEWORK FOR MAKING ETHICAL DECISIONS

Making good ethical decisions requires a fine-tuned sensitivity to ethical issues. It also necessitates an expert method for exploring the ethical aspects of a decision and weighing the considerations that determine our choice of a course of action. Having a method for ethical decision-making is, therefore, necessary. When practised regularly, the method becomes so familiar that we work through it automatically without consulting the specific steps. This is where codes of ethics may become useful.

Codes have been designed to promote moral thinking and function as a quality assurance mechanism (Bailey and Schwartzberg, 1995). As we have seen, they can provide a roadmap for ethical professional practice but cannot offer a solution to every ethical problem faced by a coach. Yet, in a professional service that is still unregulated, developing potential ethical decision-making frameworks has been deemed a possible route towards effective professional practice (see, for instance, Duffy and Passmore, 2010; Passmore and Mortimer, 2011). The Markkula Center for Applied Ethics at Santa Clara University (www.scu.edu/ethics) has created an easy-to-follow framework that practitioners can use when faced with ethical questions:[2]

Recognize an Ethical Issue

1. Could this decision or situation be damaging to someone or to some group? Does this decision involve a choice between a good and bad alternative, or perhaps between two 'goods' or between two 'bads'?
2. Is this issue about more than what is legal or what is most efficient? If so, how?

Get the Facts

3. What are the relevant facts of the case? What facts are not known? Can I learn more about the situation? Do I know enough to make a decision?
4. What individuals and groups have an important stake in the outcome? Are some concerns more important? Why?
5. What are the options for acting? Have all the relevant persons and groups been consulted? Have I identified creative options?

Evaluate Alternative Actions

6. Evaluate the options by asking the following questions:
    - Which option will produce the most good and do the least harm? (The Utilitarian Approach)
    - Which option best respects the rights of all who have a stake? (The Rights Approach)
    - Which option treats people equally or proportionately? (The Justice Approach)
    - Which option best serves the community as a whole not just some members? (The Common Good Approach)
    - Which option leads me to act as the sort of person I want to be? (The Virtue Approach)

Make a Decision and Test it

7. Considering all these approaches, which option best addresses the situation?
8. If I told someone I respect – or told a television audience – which option I have chosen, what would they say?

Act and Reflect on the Outcome

9. How can my decision be implemented with the greatest care and attention to the concerns of all stakeholders?
10. How did my decision turn out and what have I learned from this specific situation?

To be sure, the Merkkula Center's framework for ethical decision-making is not the only tool available to coaches and relevant professionals. Several such frameworks have been proposed by coaches and coaching psychologists (see, for instance, Duffy and Passmore, 2010). A brisk internet search will provide the interested reader with several such frameworks postulated by academic institutions and training providers within the realm of helping professions and beyond. What we wish to emphasize here is that ethical decision-making can never be completely objective, as it is dependent on the coach's personal beliefs, values, even ethical bias. For this reason, it is important that ethical decision-making is regularly practised and reflected upon.

CASE STUDIES FROM PRACTICE[3]

In our effort to support coaches who wish to reflect on the significance of making ethical decisions, we would like to offer two case studies that demonstrate the key ethical issues that may arise in coaching and ways in which a coach can think in order to make an ethically grounded decision. The first case study is targeted at the novice coach, while the second will be more useful to the seasoned coach. Both case studies showcase common ethical dilemmas coaches might face in practice. These relate to confidence in one's ability to coach; and the triadic relationship between a coach, a coaching client, and the sponsoring organization.

Case Study: The Novice Coach

Judie is a freshly qualified coach who has just completed a program with a reputable coach-training provider. While she holds a certificate from the latter, she has not pursued accreditation from professional coaching association. She also has no practical experience in coaching, as her previous employment did not offer her the opportunity to support individuals in their personal or professional development. Anxious to start practising her newly certified skills, she is excited when a former colleague refers Mike to her, Judie's first paying client. In anticipation of her first meeting with Mike, Judie's excitement turns into mild nervousness, as she feels somewhat insecure about her competence and ability as a novice coach. As such, she begins to experience the mounting intensity of her ethical dilemma: should she reveal or conceal her lack of practical experience to Mike? Moreover, she asks herself what steps she should take to ensure that she delivers good quality coaching.

This scenario is not unfamiliar to novice coaches. Indeed, the prospect of the first paying client can be exciting and daunting at the same time. The intense excitement these types of experiences often spawn can, more often than not, camouflage the ethical concerns involved in it. Indeed, revealing one's lack of practical experience to a paying client is a substantial ethical consideration that is related to the issue of readiness. When is a novice coach ready to coach? Recent research has shown that focusing on the key attributes of coaching, that include the ability to demonstrate empathy, non-judgemental acceptance, and active listening, can help the novice coach build experience and confidence which, in consequence, can help enhance the coaching process and strengthen the coaching relationship (Machin, 2010). These attributes can complement the lack of default knowledge on setting focus and parameters and selecting course of action (Turner, 1993). Of course, the coach's readiness to coach comes hand in hand with the coachee's eagerness to be coached – their willingness to embrace change, challenge, and the ensuing transformation that the coaching process may bring (Machin, 2010). Reflecting on some of these attributes might help Judie manage her ethical apprehensions.

Overall, the fact that Judie is concerned about her coaching competence is encouraging, as it shows that she cares about her work and her service to her client. There are several options Judie can consider in her effort to offer a good and ethical service to Mike. Finding a supervisor, especially at the initial stage of her coaching practice, could be immensely beneficial. Reflecting on her work with Mike, either in writing or during her supervision, is another way in which she can evaluate her practice. Consciously exploring and adopting a code of ethics will provide her with a 'moral map' for her practice. While the 'moral map' cannot cover all ethical issues that can arise in coaching, it can provide the moral platform on which to build her practice and help her develop what Elaine Cox (2003) has called a *contextual imperative*. A contextual imperative is the relevant experience that a variety of contexts might offer in order to act ethically and effectively for the benefit of the client, the coach, and the profession as a whole. These are some of the options that will help Judie understand that coaching is not solely a product of training but an outcome of constant learning, practice, and conscious reflection. In other words, these types of ethical issues facing novice coaches provide excellent developmental opportunities that, if reflected upon carefully and pursued methodically, can only enhance the coach's ethical maturity.

Case Study: Layers of the Onion

Ian is an experienced executive coach with over twenty years' coaching experience under his belt. He was recently invited by the chief executive officer (CEO) of a large international corporation to support Fiona, one of his senior vice presidents. Fiona joined the organization with an impressively successful professional background and, as predicted, in a short period of time she rose meteorically through the ranks of the organization. Lately, however, Fiona's excellent professional reputation has started to be tarnished by accusations of an authoritative management style, lack of empathy for other colleagues, and overall poor work performance. These developments have caused uproar within the senior management team of the organization, who urged for the sponsoring of executive coaching. In consequence, Ian was called in to support Fiona. As part of the process, Ian has been informed by the CEO that he is expecting regular updates on the coaching, as well as periodic assessments of Fiona's progress.

During the first coaching session, Fiona reveals to Ian that, as a result of her over-demanding job, her marriage is foundering and she feels an enormous sense of guilt that she spends very little time with her two young children. In essence, she concedes, the nanny knows her children better than she does. Ian also begins to sense that Fiona is showing signs of depression and anxiety that seem to be caused by her personal circumstances and accentuated by the unrealistic sales targets she has to achieve. In fact, Fiona openly reveals to Ian that, in order to be able to cope with the work pressure, she has begun to consume excessive quantities of alcohol even during lunches and behind closed doors in her office.

This case, indeed, demonstrates the many 'layers of the onion' in which the coaching practice can, more often than not, get enmeshed. Firstly, Fiona is showing signs of a mental condition that is most probably beyond Ian's capability as a coach. Secondly, Ian is torn as to whose agenda the coaching serves – the sponsoring organization's or Fiona's. Importantly, Ian needs to address the principal ethical issue of the confidentiality of coaching sessions and the coaching relationship. So, how can Ian go about approaching these ethical issues?

The surfacing of mental health problems during the coaching process is not uncommon. While the coach's task is to support the development of the client, it is important to understand the fine line between coaching and therapy and, in consequence, to be aware of the boundaries of the coaching practice. In Ian's case, unless he has a background in psychotherapy, he needs to explicitly delineate his professional boundaries and refer Fiona to an appropriate mental health professional. This does not mean that he ought to terminate the coaching process. Ian and Fiona might agree that while she will seek a therapist to explore her personal life issues, she can continue working with Ian on work-related concerns (Thomson, 2014: 49, 64). On the other hand, if Ian had a background in psychotherapy, he would still need to explicate from the outset of the coaching relationship what the boundaries of his role as a coach are in this particular context. Boundary awareness, therefore, is of primary ethical significance in coaching.

This brings us to the second ethical issue that has arisen in this case. Who is the client, the organization that is paying for the coaching or Fiona? Opinions on this matter vary. Coaching practitioners and scholars agree that the client is the coachee (Brennan and Wildflower, 2014; Thomson, 2014). Other voices, especially from the realm of counselling and psychotherapy, claim that the paying organization is the client because the contract is between the organization and the coach (Peltier, 2010; Scoular, 2011). Ultimately, the identification of the primary client may affect ethical considerations, such as providing progress reports on coaching or psychometric testing results to the organization. These are some of the reasons why the contracting process is crucial and can offer a solid backdrop for ethical behaviour. A clear contract from the outset of the coaching process will allow all three parties involved – the coach, the client, and the sponsor – to be clear as to the expectations and anticipated outcomes of coaching. In our case, if the sponsor has an agenda for the coaching, Ian might request that this be clearly communicated to Fiona.

And what about confidentiality? Let us suppose, for instance, that Fiona has agreed to regular progress reports – as is very common in the sphere of executive coaching (Kauffman and Coutu, 2009). What aspects of the coaching should be revealed in those? Is it ethical that any aspect of coaching is included in such reports? Brennan and Wildflower (2014: 435–436) argued that, to avoid any unintentional breach of confidentiality, 'the coach should not be in a position to prepare or present a report on the client's progress', as it is the client that should communicate such information. Peltier (2010: 363), on the other hand, maintained that such progress reports, especially delivered on a regular basis, can enhance the coaching if done in collaboration with the client. In fact, Peltier (2010: 363) went on to argue that such reports can protect confidentiality, because both coach and client can anticipate any questions about progress, on the pretext that a written report will be imminently produced. Ultimately, a clear contract can help any coach, including Ian, to state exactly what the coach's responsibility and obligation is to the sponsoring organization and to the client. The contract, of course, needs to be accepted by both the client and the sponsor. Finally, Ian can reflect on these ethical issues during his supervision. Such ethical moments, while challenging, offer auspicious opportunities for personal and professional learning, development, and maturity.

CONCLUSION

Our ethical behaviour is invariably influenced by political, social, and even institutional imperatives. This does not mean, however, that we should not be conscious of how our personal values and ethics can affect our coaching practice. Ultimately, we are responsible for our own ethical behaviour as coaches. Ethical dilemmas – what van Nieuwerburgh (2014: 172) calls 'ethical moments of choice' – will inevitably arise in all aspects of our personal and professional lives. If treated appropriately, ethical dilemmas can enhance our personal and professional development. This is because they alert us to what is morally right or wrong. The feeling of worry or unease that ensues from such occurrences need not be alarming. On the contrary, a healthy dose of worry is indicative of the coach's commitment to offering a good and ethical service to his or her clients. It also enables a coach to be critically reflexive of his or her coaching practice which, in consequence, contributes towards the development of professional maturity.

It is important to understand that ethical decisions are driven by moral principles and, as such, they are not always easy to make. This is because doing the right thing may not always feel right. This feeling of 'wrong-ness' – what Passmore and Mortimer (2011: 212) call *cognitive dissonance*, echoing Festinger's (1957) seminal theory – can spawn further reflection, learning and development. The key to making ethical decisions is to continuously reflect on one's values and their impact on the coaching practice. In other words, making ethical decisions is contingent upon cultivating ethical mindfulness. Ultimately, making ethical decisions is a primary ethical responsibility of coaches towards themselves, their clients, and the coaching profession as a whole.

We close with this final note for coaches and coaching researchers. In this *postprofessional* era that has seen enormous evidence-based advances in related disciplines such as medicine and psychotherapy, coaching has started to embrace the use of evidence-based research and practice in its pursuit for establishment as a valid discipline (Drake, 2008). The increasing emphasis on evidence in this era is partly responsible for the development of widely accepted codes of ethics in other disciplines, as governments, institutions, and health care organizations are seeking more objective and standardized principles to guide practice and policy (Drake, 2008). In order for the coaching profession to produce more unified and widely accepted ethical standards, there needs to be a solid consensus not only on the significance of evidence, but, as Drake (2008: 20) appositely put it, on the discipline's 'desired relationship to evidence and to the EBP [Evidence Based Practice] paradigm itself.' The focus could be cast on how we bridge differences of opinion on what constitutes 'evidence' and its contribution to practice. It is our systematic espousal of inclusive and generative evidence that will contribute to the development, advancement, and dissemination of ethical coaching practices and, in consequence, the reliability of coaching.

NOTES

1. The following summaries derive from the Merkkula's Center for Applied Ethics website. The interested reader can be informed about the framework for ethical decision making proposed by the Merkkula Center for Applied ethics on this web-page: http://www.scu.edu/ethics/practicing/decision/
2. This framework for ethical decision making derives from the Merkkula Center's website and is the product of dialogue and debate at the Markkula Center for Applied Ethics at Santa Clara University. Primary contributors include Manuel Velasquez, Dennis Moberg, Michael J. Meyer, Thomas Shanks, Margaret R. McLean, David DeCosse, Claire André, and Kirk O. Hanson. It was last revised in May 2009.
3. These case studies are adapted from Williams, P., and Anderson, K. S. (2006), *Law and Ethics in Coaching: How to Solve – and Avoid – Difficult Problems in Your Practice*. Hoboken, NJ: John Wiley & Sons.

REFERENCES

Association for Coaching (2008). 'Statement of Shared Professional Values'. Retrieved 28 April 2015 from http://www.associationforcoaching.

com/media/uploads/press_releases/M80221.pdf

Bailey, D. M. and Schwartzberg, S. L. (1995). *Ethical and Legal Dilemmas in Occupational Therapy*. Philadelphia, PA: F. A. Davis.

Beckett, C. and Maynard, A. (2013). *Values and Ethics in Social Work*, 2nd edn. London: Sage.

Bennett, J.L. (2006). An agenda for coaching-related research: A challenge for researches, *Coaching Psychology Journal: Practice and Research*, 58(4), 240–49.

Bond, T. (2015). *Standards and Ethics for Counselling in Action*, 4th edn. London: Sage.

Brennan, D. and Wildflower, L. (2014). Ethics in Coaching. In E. Cox, T. Bachkirova and D. Clutterbuck (eds), *The Complete Handbook of Coaching*, 2nd edn (pp. 430–44). London: Sage.

Carroll, M. and Shaw, E. (2013). *Ethical Maturity in the Helping Professions: Making Difficult Life and Work Decisions*. London: Jessica Kingsley.

Cox, E. (2003). The contextual imperative: implications for coaching and mentoring. *International Journal of Evidence Based Coaching and Mentoring*, 1(1): 9–22.

Cross, M. and Wood, J. (2005). The Person in Ethical Decision Making: Living with Choices. In R. Tribe and J. Morrissey (eds), *Handbook of Professional and Ethical Practice for Psychologists, Counsellors and Psychotherapists*. Hove: Brunner-Routledge.

Cunliffe, A. L. (2002). Reflexive dialogical practice in management learning. *Management Learning*, 33(1): 35–61.

Cunliffe, A. L. (2004). On becoming a critically reflective practitioner. *Journal of Management Education*, 28(4): 407–426.

de Jong, A. (2010). Coaching Ethics: Integrity in the Moment of Choice. In J. Passmore (ed.), *Excellence in Coaching*. 2nd edn. (pp. 204–14). London: Association for Coaching.

Drake, D. B. (2008). Finding our way home: coaching's search for identity in a new era. *Coaching: An International Journal of Theory, Research and Practice*, 1(1): 15–26.

Duffy, M. and Passmore J. (2010). Ethics in coaching: an ethical decision making framework for coaching psychologists. *International Coaching Psychology Review*, 5(2): 140–151.

Festinger, L. (1957). *A Theory of Cognitive Dissonance*. Stanford, CA: Stanford University Press.

Garvey, B., Stokes, P. and Megginson, D. (2014). *Coaching and Mentoring: Theory and Practice*, 2nd edn. London: Sage.

Gilligan, C. (1993) *In a Different Voice*. Cambridge, MA: Harvard University Press.

Global Convention of Coaching (2008). White Paper of the Working Group on a Research Agenda of the Development of the Field. Global Convention of Coaching. Available from http://www.instituteofcoaching.org/images/pdfs/State-of-Coaching-Research.pdf Accessed on 16 July 2015.

Grant, A. M. and Cavanagh, M. J. (2004). Toward a profession of coaching: sixty-five years of progress and challenges for the future. *International Journal of Evidence Based Coaching and Mentoring*, 2(1): 1–16.

Gray, D. E. (2007). Facilitating management learning: developing critical reflection through reflective tools. *Management Learning*, 38(5): 495–517.

Habermas, J. (1990). *Moral Consciousness and Communicative Action*. Cambridge, MA: MIT Press.

Hawkins, P. and Shohet. (2012). R. *Supervision in the Helping Professions*, 4th edn. Maidenhead: Open University Press.

Hursthouse, R. (1999). *On Virtue Ethics*. Oxford: Oxford University Press.

Ives, Y. and Cox, E. (2014). *Relationship Coaching: The Theory and Practice of Coaching with Singles, Couples and Parents*. London: Routledge.

Kauffman, C. (2005). De-mystifying research: an introduction for coaches. In I.F. Stein, F. Campone, and L.J. Page, (eds), *Proceedings of the Second ICF Coaching Research Symposium* (pp. 161–168). Washington, D.C.: International Coach Federation.

Kauffman, C. and Coutu. D. (2009). Harvard Business Review research report: The realities of executive coaching. Available online at http://www.carolkauffman.com/images/pdfs/kauffman_coutu_hrb_survey_report.pdf Accessed on 20 August 2015.

Khurana, R. and Nohria, N. (2008). It's time to make management a true profession. *Harvard Business Review*, 86(10; October): 70–77.

Laske, O. (2006). Why does your maturity matter? *Choice*, 4(3): 10–12.

Law, H. (2011). Intellectual coaching approach for Asian family businesses. In M. Shams, and D. Lane (eds), *Coaching in the Family Owned Business: A Path to Growth*. London: Karnac.

Machin, S. (2010). The nature of the internal coaching relationship. *International Journal of Evidence Based Coaching and Mentoring*, Special Issue 4, 37–52.

Newton, A. Z. (1997) *Narrative Ethics*. Cambridge, MA: Harvard University Press.

Passmore, J. (2009). Coaching ethics: making ethical decisions – novices and experts. *Coaching Psychologist*, 5(1): 6–10.

Passmore, J., and Mortimer, L. (2011). Ethics in coaching. In L. Boyce and G. Hernez-Broome (eds), *Advancing Executive Coaching: Setting the Course for Successful Leadership Coaching* (pp. 205–28). San Francisco, CA: Jossey-Bass.

Peltier, B. (2010). *The Psychology of Executive Coaching: Theory and Application*, 2nd edn. New York: Routledge.

PricewaterhouseCoopers (PwC). (2012). *International Coach Federation Global Coaching Study*. Lexington, KY: International Coach Federation.

Scoular, A. (2011). *The Financial Times Guide to Business Coaching*. Harlow: Prentice Hall.

Soltis, J. (1986). Teaching professional ethics. *Journal of Teacher Education*, 37(3): 2–4.

Thomson, B. (2014). *First Steps in Coaching*. London: Sage.

Turner, R. M. (1993). Context-sensitive Reasoning for Autonomous Agents and Co-operative Distributed Problem Solving, In *Proceedings of the IJCAI Workshop on Using Knowledge in its Context*. http://citeseerx.ist.psu.edu/viewdoc/summary?doi=10.1.1.34.993 Accessed 14 February 2016.

Van Nieuwerburgh, C. (2014). *An Introduction to Coaching Skills: A Practical Guide*. London: Sage.

Waddington, I. (1975) The Development of Medical Ethics: A Sociological Analysis. *Medical History* 19(1): 36–51.

Williams, P. and Anderson, K. S. (2006). *Law and Ethics in Coaching: How to Solve – and Avoid – Difficult Problems in Your Practice*. Hoboken, NJ: John Wiley & Sons.

Yanow, D. and Tsoukas, H. (2009). What is reflection-in-action? A phenomenological account. *Journal of Management Studies*, 46(8): 1339–1364.

Adapting to Working with New Technologies

Stella Kanatouri and Harald Geißler

INTRODUCTION

Since the 1990s the number of coaching methods and target groups has multiplied. Once offered only to top management, coaching is now also used with middle and lower levels of management and offered to individuals and groups with various life and work-related coaching issues. In addition to these developments, the coaching market has also diversified in terms of delivering coaching through technological media (Geißler, 2010).

As demonstrated by industry-led reports (Grant & Zackon, 2004; PwC & ICF, 2007; Sherpa, 2012), technology-assisted coaching is becoming an increasingly popular coaching modality. The PricewaterhouseCoopers and International Coaching Federation's (ICF) survey in 2007 for instance, indicated that 50% of a sample of 7,000 coaches delivered coaching mainly over distance, particularly via telephone (PwC & ICF, 2007, In: McLaughlin, 2012, p.10). As evidenced by the results of the Sherpa Executive Coaching Survey (2012), only 41% of coaching was delivered exclusively face-to-face, whereas the remaining 59% was delivered via distance through various technologies (31% telephone, 14% webcam, 11% e-mail and text, and 3% HD video). In comparison, the Sherpa Executive Coaching Survey in 2015 found an even higher trend for distance coaching, and in particular coaching via webcam (40% delivered coaching via webcam at least sometimes) and HD video (6% of coaches used HD video). It is clear that coaching delivery is no longer limited to face-to-face or even telephone coaching, but has expanded to the use of newer, more sophisticated technological media.

The growing popularity of technology-assisted coaching is no surprise, as this mode of coaching corresponds to current socio-economic and technological developments as well as to the need for flexible coaching formats. More specifically, as technology advances rapidly and becomes increasingly sophisticated, it infiltrates more and more aspects of our lives. Through its frequent use, individuals are becoming increasingly comfortable with using technology in their professional and personal environments. In addition, working remotely is becoming progressively common in our globalized society. These developments also affect coaching practice, as technology provides the option to coach at a distance and independent of geographic location.

Moreover, living in the knowledge society induces the need for continuous development and learning in a self-directed way. The need for self-direction is met by technology-assisted coaching, which offers individuals the opportunity to receive coaching as and when the need for it arises. Added to this, technology also supports applications for self-coaching, without direct facilitation by a coach. Whether it is with or without a coach, technology-assisted coaching is delivered in a time-flexible way, whilst also reducing travel time and cost. Technology-assisted coaching offers a cost-efficient solution at a time when coaching has expanded to include target groups other than top management and organizations have an interest in keeping costs down for coaching. The increased use of technology in coaching is, therefore, justified by the need for time savings, cost efficiency and flexibility in coaching delivery.

Despite the growing popularity of technology-assisted coaching however, there is an apparent conceptual confusion around its meaning (Boyce & Clutterbuck, 2011, p. 286). A plethora of terms appear in literature, such as 'distance coaching' (Ghods, 2009), 'e-coaching' (Geißler, 2008; Geißler & Metz, 2012; Geißler et al., 2014; Ribbers & Warringa, 2015), 'online coaching' (Koch, 2012), 'web-based coaching' (Poepsel, 2011), and 'virtual coaching' (Ghods & Boyce, 2013; Clutterbuck & Hussein, 2010). However, this leads to potential confusion in the interpretation of the concept of coaching through technology, as it is unclear precisely how these terms differ from one another.

Understanding the meaning of technology-assisted coaching is useful, as it has implications for grasping the breadth of its value for coaching practice.

In this chapter, the term 'technology-assisted coaching' is used to refer to five different coaching formats: First, distance coaching, in which face-to-face communication is replaced with modern media (Geißler, 2015b, 2015c, 2015d). Second, blended coaching, where face-to-face communication and technology-assisted communication are alternated. Third, distance coaching enhanced with technological coaching tools (Geißler, 2015e, 2015f, 2015g, 2015h, 2016a, 2016 b). Fourth, face-to-face coaching enhanced with technological coaching tools; and fifth, self-coaching, which is supported by technological coaching tools (Geißler et al., 2007).

This chapter sets out to explore the breadth of technological media that are available for coaching purposes and their implications for coaching practice. While empirical research has mainly focused on telephone coaching, the technological landscape of coaching is proliferating and is waiting to be explored.

MAPPING THE TECHNOLOGICAL LANDSCAPE OF COACHING

Whilst empirical research in technology-assisted coaching focused mainly on telephone coaching, a whole new range of possibilities for technological use in coaching practice has recently unfolded. Technology offers various alternatives for communicating remotely, as well as an increasing spectrum of tools to augment the coaching process. Technological media can be used in coaching practice in different ways: firstly, they can be used to support coaching that is partly or entirely delivered at a distance; secondly, they can be used to facilitate coach-supported dialogue; and thirdly, they can be used to enable self-guided coaching interventions. These different applications of technological media have direct implications for how technology-assisted coaching is conceptualized.

More specifically, technology can be used in two distinct coaching modes, distance coaching and blended coaching. In the distance coaching mode, technology is used to entirely replace face-to-face communication with technology-mediated dialogue. Distance coaching offers several advantages, such as reduced cost and travel, and alleviation of geographic boundaries (Clutterbuck, 2010), thereby making coaching more accessible. On the other hand, working with technology exclusively at a distance is potentially challenging for both coaches and clients, particularly for rapport building between coach and client and for coping with sensitive issues (Charbonneau, 2002). In the blended coaching mode, distance coaching sessions are alternated with face-to-face sessions or they are used as a follow-up to face-to-face coaching. This mode of working with technology implies that coaching can be sustained for a longer period of time, while keeping costs down. Alternatively, technological tools can also be used during face-to-face coaching, to enhance the process.

Aside from coach-supported interventions, technology can also be used in mobile and web-based applications for self-coaching, without direct facilitation by a coach. Self-guided coaching interventions are offered at a significantly lower cost than coach-supported programs (Geißler et al., 2007). As content structure is critical for their efficacy (Geißler et al., 2007), self-coaching programs typically consist of structured written questions, which guide clients through a problem-solving process and enhance their self-reflection. As technology-assisted coaching includes both, distance coaching and blended coaching (Geißler & Kanatouri, 2015), and coach-supported interventions as well as self-guided coaching programs, the spectrum of technologies that can be used for coaching purposes widens. It includes standalone communication media or otherwise called basic communication media (Geißler, 2015a; Geißler & Kanatouri, 2015), such as telephone, video calls or email, which replace face-to-face dialogue in a distance coaching mode, and secondly, it includes problem-solving tools that enhance the coaching process in a distance or a blended mode, such as for instance, drawing tools or simulations.

Among basic media, the telephone has been one of the first technologies to be used for coaching purposes (Boyce & Clutterbuck, 2011) and perhaps the predominant technology for delivering coaching at a distance for over twenty years. Coaching seems to have followed the path of its sister discipline, counselling, for example in crisis hotlines such as the Samaritans who used the telephone for over sixty years to deliver psychological support and later added email and instant messaging (Pollock et al., 2010). Asynchronous text-based communication media have also been incorporated into coaching practice (Ribbers & Warringa, 2015), although to a lesser extent than telephone (Geißler & Kanatouri, 2015). Technologies are becoming more sophisticated, user-friendly and offered at lower cost, for example the advances in video calling technologies, high definition video communication and synchronous text-messaging.

In addition to these basic media, various technological tools can be used for coaching, including online drawing and whiteboard tools, videos and online simulation tools. Aside from these general purpose tools, numerous technological tools and platforms have been developed specifically for coaching purposes. Table 39.1 provides a list of examples of purpose-built technologies.

The numerous examples of technologies available for coaching suggest that the field is growing to offer solutions for meeting different coaching needs. Coaching software applications provide ways to enhance coaching through virtual worlds and simulations, through written coaching resources for self-reflection and session follow-ups, documentation of the coaching conversation for referring back to it later, as well as through gamification approaches to sustain clients'

Table 39.1 Examples of purpose-built technologies

Technology name	Description
Text-based tools	
CAI® Coaching World www.cai-world.com	The CAI® Coaching World platform incorporates video and text-chat communication and offers a drawing tool, a pre-determined question framework and user-generated questions, a coaches' discussion forum and a space for storing contacts.
CoachAccountable www.coachaccountable.com	The CoachAccountable platform incorporates asynchronous communication through an in-built email system, and offers a shared repository for session plans, journaling tools and metrics to visualize progress.
CoachCampus www.coachcampus.nl/	The CoachCampus platform enables asynchronous and synchronous text-based communication and it offers tools that include a repository for file sharing, and an objectives function to graphically display goals.
CoachingCloud® www.coachingcloud.com	The CoachingCloud® platform offers mentors and coaches the option to book their sessions, add and save session notes, have coaching conversations online, view clients' goals and outcomes and create online coaching modules.
CoachMaster™ https://coachmaster.co.uk/	CoachMaster™ is a text-based tool based on the GROW model, which comprises of pre-determined question sets that can be used synchronously, or asynchronously.
Coach Simple http://www.coachsimple.net/	The Coach Simple platform for life and business coaching allows setting and tracking goals, uploading videos and links, keeping a history of coaching notes and discussions and following up on clients' progress.
JournalEngine™ http://www.journalengine.com/	JournalEngine™ is a tool for clients to write a journal, following the coach's prompt. The journal may be kept private, or shared with the coach when given read permission.
Lifecoachhub https://www.lifecoachhub.com	Lifecoachhub is a platform that enables clients to select a life or a business coach and book a free initial appointment. It provides a variety of tools, such as journaling, goal tracking and homework assignments.
My360 plus www.my360plus.com	My360 plus is a tool for individual, team and organizational development that allows clients to complete a survey to assess their strengths and to choose an online network of 'observers' (boss and peers) who provide feedback online.
Virtual coaching www.virtual-coaching.net	This online text-based tool consists of sets of pre-determined written questions for different coaching issues, which can be used in a synchronous mode, as a basis for a session, or in an asynchronous mode, between sessions.
Visual tools	
Coaching Spaces http://coachingspaces.com/de/	CoachingSpaces is a virtual systemic constellation platform of three-dimensional objects and avatars that can be given a posture and speech statements. Constellations are discussed via an integrated instant chat or video call with the coach.
LPS Cocoon® http://www.lpscocoon.de	LPS Cocoon® is an interactive virtual constellation business coaching tool, which consists of 13 symbolic, 3D virtual sculptures in different shapes, to support coaching clients in visualizing their thoughts and simulating their developmental process.
ProReal http://www.proreal.co.uk	ProReal, is a virtual world designed for coaches, consultants and therapists. It involves the use of plain, androgynous avatars, which can be given different postures and captions to express their emotional states, as well as a metaphoric landscape and a variety of tools, such as a clock, a key, a wall etc. in which, clients can visually represent their situation.

Virtual constellations™ http://www.virtualconstellationwork.com/	Virtual constellations™ is a free for a limited period, simple, online systemic tool for virtual constellations.
Mobile phone and iPad Apps	
Breeth App https://play.google.com/store/apps/details?id=com.thegoodcoach&hl=en	The Breeth App supports individuals who are in a charged emotional state to decide on the next appropriate action to take.
Beyond Expectations App https://play.google.com/store/apps/details?id=com.smallpackageapps.beyondexpectations&hl=en	The Beyond Expectations app is a four-month course of weekly narrative NLP exercises designed to help individuals release themselves from expectations that hold them back.
The Coaching App™ http://www.thecoachingapp.com/	The Coaching App™ is a free coaching app that can be used for individuals, or for inspiring a team and includes features such as, podcasts for learning, a leadership learning journal, a coaching journal for working with the coach, and a coaching log to track activity.
iPlan Success© http://www.iplansuccess.com/	iPlan Success© is an iPad application, which supports individuals to develop a plan for their personal or professional success.

motivation. On the other hand, potential ethical risks, particularly with regard to clients' data security when using these technologies should be avoided by ensuring that the online environment used for coaching is secured through firewalls, computer virus protection and data encryption (Anthony & Nagel, 2009).

The above mentioned technologies, as well as the general technological communication media used for coaching purposes can be distinguished based on six criteria:

i *Industry focus:* A differentiation can be made between purpose-built technologies, which have been specifically designed for coaching purposes – such as the technologies that were presented in Table 39.1– and technologies that are not specific to coaching, such as the telephone and email.

ii *Function:* Technologies may be distinguished based on their function, which is either to facilitate communication between coach–client (basic media), or to support the process between sessions or during a coaching session (supporting tools).

iii *Feature complexity:* Coaching technologies can be distinguished based on feature complexity. Point solutions are focused on one main feature – as for instance, a tool with written coaching questions – and they can be contrasted to platforms with multiple capabilities, which may involve for instance, visually tracking progress, enabling online communication between coach–client, coaching exercises, journal entries, private messaging or peer discussions.

iv *Synchronicity:* Another differentiation is made on the basis of synchronicity. Technologies enable communication in either synchronous or asynchronous modes.

v *Communication channel:* Technologies rely on different communication channels that range from text (email, text-based tools and online platforms), audio (telephone), to audio-visual media (video calls).

vi *Content creation:* Coaching technologies differ in terms of whether they contain pre-defined materials, particularly sets of questions for all practitioners using the software, or they are open content authoring tools for practitioners using the software to create their own coaching content. Some technologies include both pre-defined materials and the option to create one's own and save them in the system.

The characteristics of these coaching technologies have several implications for coaching practice. Firstly, many purpose-built technologies are not conceptually neutral, but are guided by particular theoretical approaches and coaching models (as opposed to technologies that are not specific to coaching). For instance, the CoachCampus platform uses the Accelerated Behavioral Change (ABC) model for coaching, which consists of three phases: The analysis phase is used to map coachees' current situation and to formulate clear coaching goals. The internalizing phase, during which, coachees work closely with their coach towards achieving their goal and towards internalizing new behaviors or skills. In the final phase, the focus lies on ensuring the sustainability of coaching outcomes.

Another tool that is linked with the behavioural approach to coaching is Virtual Coaching (VC), which places strong emphasis on formulating specific and achievable goals. This tool is also based on a solution-oriented approach to help clients focus positively on their strengths and resources, set goals and work out how to achieve them. It has a clear focus on the present and future and uses methods, such as the miracle question and scaling questions to facilitate clients' progress towards their goals. ProReal on the other hand, uses elements of the psychodynamic approach, as clients can add for instance, head-like figures behind their avatar to represent their inner voice. The client's sub-egos are given a speech caption, colour and size and can move behind the client's avatar.

Secondly, with regard to the functions of the different technologies, supporting tools add different elements to the coaching process. For instance, coaching tools might offer a visualization aid of the coaching issue from different perspectives through the use of symbolic objects (CoachingSpaces) or a virtual world where clients can use avatar representations of themselves, they can reflect on their issues and test potential solutions in a safe environment (ProReal).

Whilst communication media are essential, as they facilitate the coaching conversation through verbal or written language, tools play a significant role in the coaching process by supporting clients' meta-communication, analytical reflection of the coaching issue and solutions to it, as well as scenic imagination of events or experiences (Geißler & Kanatouri, 2015). As an example, the ProReal environment includes beaten tracks, mountains, a ravine, a river and a castle, and symbolic objects such as a key or a wall. Clients can create their own scene that represents their situation and they can imagine possible solution paths. Other examples include CoachingSpaces and LPScocoon, whereby clients can represent and position themselves and other stakeholders on a platform, reflect upon their coaching issue, and visualize possible solutions. The use of these tools allows clients to visualize their problem from different perspectives, and they help coaches to get insights into clients' visualized thoughts, which might have otherwise not come to surface during the coaching conversation.

In addition to the various visual or text-based reflection tools that are used to enhance the coaching process, coaching platforms involve a number of capabilities. For instance, they may incorporate basic communication media as well as supporting coaching tools, such as sets of written questions or virtual worlds, and they may use gamification to encourage or motivate the client. Coaching platforms offer an all-in-one solution, equipping coaches with a variety of tools to work with while keeping client data in one place, yet questions about their usability, technical quality and coach skill required for using these conglomerate solutions remain to be tested.

Moreover, the aspect of synchronicity and the different communication channels that various technologies support, affect the coaching conversation. Arguably, the quality of the coaching process depends, not only on the message, i.e. on what is said, but also on the form of the message, i.e. how it is said (Gsöllpointner, 2012). As different technological media rely on different senses and modes of communication, they affect communication in distinct ways. As an example, in telephone communication between coach and client, the communication message is transmitted by the medium – in this case the voice, but also by the volume, tone of voice, pitch and rhythm of speaking.

However, there is no one best way to deliver technology-assisted coaching. Whilst from a media richness theory point of view (Daft et al., 1987), technologies such as telephone, video communication, asynchronous and synchronous text can be seen along a continuum, with asynchronous text-based communication being the leanest medium and video communication the richest, there are advantages and disadvantages in each of these technological media (Boyce & Clutterbuck, 2011). Despite the resemblance of richer media – such as video communication – with face-to-face coaching, lean media are not necessarily less appropriate for coaching. For instance, even though telephone communication lacks visual cues, there is some evidence to suggest that the missing cues help to enhance focus on the coaching conversation and eliminate distractions and social prejudice (McLaughlin, 2013).

Similarly, despite the missing visual and verbal cues in asynchronous text-based communication, which could risk miscommunication between the coaching pair (Clutterbuck, 2010), this communication modality offers several advantages, including clients' reflection and documentation of coaching interactions (Hancock, 2014), and more openness and equality as the power dynamics embedded in face-to-face communication are reduced (Clutterbuck, 2010). Moreover, synchronous and asynchronous modes of communication have implications for coaching processes and outcomes. Whereas asynchronous communication enables clients and coaches to reflect before responding, synchronous communication offers immediacy. The advantages of asynchronous communication have been evidenced by several online therapy and counselling research studies, which reported that asynchronous online media afford anonymity (Richards, 2009), enhance reflection (Suler, 2000; Richards, 2009; Beattie et al., 2009), reduce social stigma towards seeking help (Efstathiou, 2009) and have a disinhibition effect (Suler, 2000). Research has also suggested the efficacy of synchronous text-based communication in building rapport, and in allowing directness and immediacy, whilst at the same time it provides emotional distance (Stephen et al., 2014).

Moreover, the challenge of lacking sensory cues can be overcome through coaches' skill development. To avoid the risk of miscommunication (Clutterbuck, 2010) in asynchronous text-based coaching requires coaches' skill adaptation to write and to interpret the clients' messages (Ribbers & Warringa, 2015). Particular attention to language is also necessary in verbal communication. For instance, when coaching via telephone, the lack of visual cues can be compensated for by developing coaching skills to ask powerful questions, to attend to the subtle parts of the coaching conversation (Charbonneau, 2002; Frazee, 2008), to use visual language that is rich in metaphors and analogies (Collett, 2008), and to pay attention to the clients' silences and verbal cues (McLaughlin, 2013).

Furthermore, the content creation aspect of technologies also has an effect on the coaching process. Authoring tools offer coaches the flexibility to create their own modules according to the clients' needs. On the other hand, pre-defined materials involve a didactic structure (Geißler, 2008), which guides clients throughout the coaching process. Didactically open tools, where coaches create their own materials possibly require more experience, whereas pre-defined materials can facilitate the work of less experienced practitioners.

Summarizing, practitioners have several choices for using technology in coaching. To facilitate the coaching conversation, they can select between media that support synchronous or asynchronous communication and different sensory cues, depending on their own and their clients' preferences. To enhance the process, practitioners can use one tool and/or a combination of coaching tools. Questions about the tools' functionality, data security, usability and purpose are decisive factors for making a choice. Cost is another important factor, as purpose-built tools offer more choice than generic tools, but come with a higher cost. In addition, practitioners can select between using software to create their own coaching content or using pre-configured materials to structure their coaching sessions, as well as choosing between coaching tools that are conceptually neutral or not. What all these options suggest is that the technological landscape of coaching has expanded to offer more solutions for different needs, preferences and levels of experience and to provide new alternatives for face-to-face coaching.

EMPIRICAL RESEARCH IN TECHNOLOGY-ASSISTED COACHING

Despite its growing popularity, empirical evidence to support the efficacy of technology-assisted coaching is limited. Past literature in the field has focused mainly on distance coaching and especially on telephone coaching and – with some exceptions (Geißler et al., 2007; Geißler et al., 2012; Geißler et al., 2014) – it has paid little attention to the other coaching formats that were mentioned in the introductory section. The available research on telephone coaching offers some encouraging insights, indicating client satisfaction (Berry, 2005) as well as coaches' positive experiences (McLaughlin, 2013). Moreover, it has been suggested that positive coaching outcomes can be achieved in a distance coaching mode (Ghods, 2009; Poepsel, 2011) and that coaching relationships can be developed and maintained over distance (Ghods, 2009). Contrasting these findings however, other studies indicated coaches' and clients' preferences for face-to-face coaching over distance coaching, particularly for dealing with personal and sensitive issues and for establishing initial rapport with the client (Charbonneau, 2002; Frazee, 2008).

Table 39.2 provides an overview of past empirical research studies in technology-assisted coaching, indicating their design, variables tested and technological media used.

As it can be seen from the above table, the variables that were used in these investigations ranged from clients' or coaches' experiences with coaching using a particular technological medium, satisfaction with the process and outcomes, to factors affecting technology use in coaching. This section reviews the above mentioned literature and also draws from relevant empirical mental health investigations, in order to compare findings on the efficacy of the technology-assisted mode of coaching.

The existing empirical evidence on technology-assisted coaching efficacy can be examined with regard to the role that specific technological media, such as telephone, text-based coaching and immersive virtual worlds play in coaching processes and outcomes. Five key studies examined distance coaching interventions that involved the use of telephone (Charbonneau, 2002; Berry, 2005; Frazee, 2008; Ghods, 2009; McLaughlin, 2012) and indicated mixed findings regarding the suitability of this medium for coaching. Berry's (2005) quantitative research study, which administered a web-based questionnaire to a sample of 102 coaches to compare their perceptions of face-to-face coaching with telephone coaching, suggested that telephone is an equal alternative to face-to-face coaching, in terms of rapport building and coaching outcomes. Unfortunately, Berry's research examined only the perspectives of coaches and it was based on participants' self-reports about their relationship to their clients and the coaching outcomes achieved.

Berry's (2005) findings contrasted the evidence provided by two further studies (Charbonneau, 2002; Frazee, 2008). Charbonneau's qualitative study (2002), which carried out semi-structured interviews with 10 executive coaches and 10 clients to examine the factors affecting participants' media choices in coaching, revealed that participants favoured face-to-face over telephone contact, particularly for establishing a trusting coaching relationship, and for providing sensitive feedback. However, although Charbonneau's

Table 39.2 Empirical research overview

Date	Researcher(s)	Design	Technologies investigated	Variables
2002	Charbonneau, M.A.	Qualitative	Phone	Factors influencing coaches' and clients' media choices
2005	Berry, R.M.	Quantitative	Phone	Clients' satisfaction with coaching relationship and coaching outcomes
2007	Geißler, H., Helm, M., Nolze, A.	Qualitative	Asynchronous text-based questions for self-coaching	Acceptance of technology-assisted self-coaching for different target groups and different coaching issues
2008	Frazee, R.V.	Mixed methods	Phone, Skype, email	Extent and factors affecting the use of technology-assisted coaching in organizations from the perspectives of coaches and learning professionals
2009	Ghods, N.	Quantitative	Phone	Coaching relationship and outcomes as perceived by clients and their observers
2011	Poepsel, M.	Quantitative	Asynchronous text-based coaching program	Clients' hope, subjective well-being, goal attainment
2012	McLaughlin, M.	Qualitative	Phone	Coaches' experiences with telephone coaching
2012	Geißler, H., Kurzmann, C., Metz M.,	Qualitative	Phone, text-based tools	Distance coaching enriched with text-based tools and online counselling, as compared to face-to-face processes
2013	Taranovich, Y.	Qualitative	WebCo@ch platform (text-based)	Requirements, design, implementation and evaluation of a web-based system for project management coaching
2014	Hancock, B.	Qualitative	Skype and CoachMaster™ (text-based)	Clients' experiences with the coaching program
2014	Andrews, A.	Qualitative	SecondLife® (virtual world)	Clients' experiences with Second Life coaching
2014	Geißler, H., Hasenbein, M., Kanatouri, S., Wegener, R.	Qualitative	Phone and Virtual Coaching (VC) (text-based)	Clients' satisfaction with the coaching program and goal attainment
2014	Ribbers, A., Warringa, A.	Mixed methods	CoachCampus (text-based)	Clients' evaluation of web-based coaching program effectiveness in improving their managerial skills

research offered valuable insights into distance coaching from the perspectives of both coaches and clients, the accuracy and transferability of her findings may have been affected by the fact that the data emanated from participants' retrospective reflections and the sample size of this study was small and mainly from a single geographic region.

A subsequent mixed methods research (Frazee, 2008) explored the extent and the factors influencing the use of technology-assisted coaching in organizations from the perspectives of coaching practitioners and learning professionals. Frazee administered an online survey to a sample of 200 workforce and learning professionals and carried out semi-structured telephone interviews with 20 coaching practitioners. Consistent with Charbonneau's (2002) findings, this study demonstrated that participants preferred using face-to-face coaching, particularly for providing sensitive feedback and for addressing deeper issues.

On the other hand, Frazee's (2008) and Charbonneau's (2002) studies highlighted the advantages of telephone coaching as perceived by participants, such as enabling coaching on-demand, allowing access to a wider audience of clients, serving geographically dispersed individuals, reducing costs and promoting follow-through and accountability. Moreover, both studies suggested that the barriers associated with telephone coaching, such as the lack of visual cues, can be overcome by verbalizing the process to the client – for instance, by asking powerful questions – and by paying attention to the subtle parts of the coaching conversation.

Further investigations revealed that telephone is a suitable medium for coaching, as it allows the development of strong relationships between coach and client and leads to positive and sustainable coaching outcomes (Ghods, 2009; McLaughlin, 2013). Ghods (2009) investigated the effectiveness of telephone coaching from clients' perspectives. Her study employed a sample of 152 leadership level coaching clients and their observers, which involved their boss, direct reports and peers, in order to examine client satisfaction with their coaching relationship and coaching outcomes. The findings of this study suggested that clients had developed strong rapport to their coach over the telephone and achieved positive coaching outcomes that were sustained six months after completion of the program, as perceived by clients and their observers.

Consistent with Ghods (2009) and Berry (2005), the efficacy of telephone coaching was also demonstrated by a qualitative study conducted by McLaughlin (2012), which carried out semi-structured interviews to explore the experiences of six executive coaches with telephone coaching. McLaughlin's findings revealed that telephone may even be a more powerful medium than face-to-face communication, as the missing visual cues enhance the focus and depth of the coaching conversation and help to eliminate judgements and visual distractions. McLaughlin's study also revealed that telephone coaching requires an adaptation of coaches' skills, such as paying close attention to the silences and verbal cues, thereby lending support to Charbonneau's (2002) and Frazee's (2008) conclusions that coaches can compensate for the lack of visual cues by paying attention to the subtle parts of the conversation and by asking powerful questions.

Unfortunately, the limited number of telephone coaching studies prevent any firm conclusions to be drawn. However, several empirical studies have demonstrated the effectiveness of telephone-based interventions for mental health issues and thereby supported Berry's (2005), Ghods' (2009) and McLaughlin's (2013) findings. These mental health studies indicated that telephone-based interventions led to client satisfaction in terms of the process and outcomes of the treatment and were equally effective as comparable face-to-face treatments (Reese et al., 2002; Simon et al., 2004; Lovell et al., 2006; Ludman et al., 2007; Mohr et al., 2012).

A very small number of investigations have been carried out to examine the efficacy of coaching through technological media other than the telephone. Three studies investigated online coaching via asynchronous text (Poepsel, 2011; Taranovich, 2013; Ribbers & Warringa, 2014), and four studies explored coaching formats that involved audio or video communication combined with text-based coaching tools (Geißler et al., 2007; Geißler et al., 2012; Geißler et al., 2014; Hancock, 2014), while only one study examined coaching through virtual worlds (Andrews, 2014). While these studies differed in focus, methodology and coaching medium, they all supported the effectiveness of online coaching.

Poepsel's (2011) experimental study adopted a control group approach to investigate the impact of an eight-week online coaching program that involved asynchronous online text-based dialogue and structured coaching exercises, on coachees' levels of hope, subjective well-being and goal attainment. Data was collected from a sample of 42 participants, who were randomly assigned to either a coaching group or a waitlist control group. The findings indicated that participation in the online coaching program increased participants' subjective goal attainment and well-being. Poepsel's study suggested positive findings regarding the efficacy of text-based coaching, which were consistent with later studies indicating that asynchronous text-based media effectively supported coaching for project management (Taranovich, 2013) and for managerial skills (Ribbers & Warringa, 2014). These studies were also consistent with therapy and counselling research, which demonstrated the feasibility of online interventions and agreed that text-based treatments are a viable mode of therapy and equally efficacious as face-to-face interventions (Cohen & Kerr, 1998; Day & Schneider, 2002; Cook & Doyle, 2002; Baraka et al., 2008; Murphy et al., 2009; Murphy et al., 2011).

Positive findings were also suggested by a qualitative case study research that explored coachees' experiences with coaching in a virtual world (Andrews, 2014). Andrews's research revealed that the virtual world Second Life permitted coachees to have a sense of presence and to immerse in the coaching experience, suggesting the feasibility of this online technology for coaching. In a small pilot study Geißler et al. (2012) compared the features of face-to-face coaching and therapy processes, as well as online counselling and distance coaching enriched with text-based tools. This study found that there were significantly more commonalities than differences; however, due to the very small study sample this result cannot be generalized.

Similarly, research in distance coaching combined with text-based supporting tools offered promising results. In Geißler et al.'s (2007) research, participants used pre-prepared coaching questions for self-coaching purposes and were interviewed afterwards. The most important finding was that there was high acceptance of this tool by the coachees, but also the request to get additional support via telephone conversation with a personal coach. This finding triggered a subsequent study (Geißler et al., 2014), in which 14 coachees participated in a program that consisted of 3 coaching sessions, delivered through telephone and pre-determined written coaching questions. Data was collected through a series of semi-structured interviews with each of the coachees and with their coach after each coaching session, as well as one, three, six and twelve months after completion of the program. The findings of this study indicated participants' satisfaction with this coaching format and demonstrated its effectiveness with regard to goal attainment.

Hancock (2014) also examined a coaching program, consisting of Skype video calls combined with pre-determined written coaching questions, which were used in synchronous communication mode. This study carried out semi-structured interviews with three coaches and administered an online qualitative questionnaire to six coaching clients after each of the three coaching sessions they had received. The findings indicated clients' positive evaluations of the coaching they had received, providing support to other coaching studies (Poepsel, 2011; Geißler et al., 2014) and to online therapy and counselling research (Suler, 2000; Beattie et al., 2009). Moreover, Hancock's research supported the findings suggested by Poepsel (2011) and Geißler et al. (2014), who highlighted the advantages of text-based coaching, particularly coachees' enhanced reflection and documentation of the process.

Overall, the coaching literature has mainly provided positive findings with regard to the efficacy of telephone and online tools for coaching delivery. Despite some contrasting results, which indicated practitioners' and clients' preferences for face-to-face communication, other research studies demonstrated that coaches' skills can be adapted for technology-assisted coaching in order to compensate for the loss of sensory cues in the coaching conversation. However, empirical investigations in technology-assisted coaching are scarce and contain several methodological limitations, which prevent us from drawing conclusions about the efficacy of this coaching mode.

Coaching practitioners would benefit from a greater understanding of how different communication media and supporting tools affect the coaching intervention. Future research should investigate the process and outcomes of coaching through specific technologies from both coaches' and clients' perspectives. Particularly, randomized controlled investigations would be useful to compare coaching through audio, video and text-based media with traditional coaching, in terms of the process and outcomes of the intervention. Such research would be useful to gain a deeper understanding of the possibilities and limitations of these communication media and how effective they are as compared to traditional coaching. In addition, further research should use pre-post approaches to compare coaches' and clients' experiences before and after receiving technology-assisted coaching. Robust research is necessary, not only as a source of evidence on the efficacy of technology-assisted coaching, but also to gain insight into the contributing factors of positive experiences and outcomes – be it coaching skills or familiarity with or openness to using technology in coaching.

Furthermore, as technology continues to advance, empirical research needs to catch up with the new technological modalities for delivering coaching. Particularly, online technologies, such as video calling technologies, and their implications for coaching practice require empirical investigation. Future research should also explore coachees' experiences with self-coaching, used as an adjunct to coach-guided intervention or as a standalone tool. In addition, very little is known about the impact of virtual worlds on the coaching process and there is no research available on the effectiveness of supportive coaching tools, such as virtual constellations for systemic work. Empirical investigations examining coaches' and clients' experiences with such technological tools would be useful to further understand their potential value for coaching and to inform coaching practitioners looking to incorporate them into their practice.

CONCLUSION

Technology is offering increasingly improved ways to support coaching. As communication technologies are rapidly advancing, we are likely to see increasingly sophisticated technologies used for coaching purposes that widen the scope and enhance the potential of delivering coaching via distance. Avatar worlds are already offering new dimensions for delivering coaching. Telepresence robotics have emerged into the market and are just starting to be discovered by coaches. As their cost reduces over time, they could have a positive impact on coaching via distance. Virtual reality solutions are also likely to become more affordable and they could offer suitable applications for immersive coaching experiences over the next few years. Moreover, purpose-built technologies incorporate coaching expertise and may thus, be valuable for enhancing the coaching process. As practitioners accumulate experiences with coaching tools and platforms, the capabilities of these technologies are likely to improve and to become increasingly useful.

Taking this into account, coaches could benefit from staying up to date with emerging and innovative technologies that may be suitable for coaching. In doing so, they would benefit from solid empirical research to guide their decisions about which technologies are appropriate, what coaching skills are required to effectively use the capabilities of these technologies in their practice and how to avoid ethical risks associated with these technologies. In addition, for coaching practitioners who work with technology it is vital to continuously refine their skills in order to work around challenges, such as the lack of presence and the missing sensory cues. Research has provided evidence that challenges can be overcome by adapting coaching skills to delivering coaching through technology.

The increased use of technology by coaching clients also has implications for technology-assisted coaching. Individuals are progressively developing their skills for using technology to perform their daily work virtually, and to create and sustain personal or working relationships online. Millennials will soon comprise the majority of the workforce. Given their technological competencies, coaching clients are likely to be open to and increasingly accepting of technology-assisted coaching.

The greater use and acceptance of technology-mediated communication also has implications for coaching practice, as it may be changing clients' expectations of technology-assisted coaching. Specifically, clients' stronger technological competencies create a need for coaches to have an understanding of how to effectively use technology in their practice, in order to build and sustain strong relationships with their clients. This also implies the need for coaches to evaluate the suitability of technological tools for different coaching needs and contexts.

Compared to the exciting developments in technology-assisted coaching however, empirical research is lacking behind. More research is necessary to further understand the potential that various technological media have in assisting the coaching process. Future investigations should examine the efficacy of coaching through different technological modalities, including telephone, video communication and text-based coaching, and should explore the effect of supporting tools in the coaching process. Coaching practitioners and stakeholders of technology-assisted coaching services would also benefit from research evidence about which technological media and tools are suitable for different coaching needs. It is expected that robust research will increase coaches' confidence and trust in working with technology and will contribute towards further developing effective coaching tools.

REFERENCES

Andrews, A.R. (2014). *Avatar coaching: A case study on the perceptions of virtual reality coaching interventions with an avatar coach.* Unpublished Doctoral Dissertation, Capella University, USA.

Anthony, K. & Nagel, D.M. (2009). *Therapy Online: A Practical Guide.* London: Sage Publishing.

Baraka, A., Hena, L. Boniel-Nissima, M. & Shapiraa, N. (2008). A comprehensive review and a meta-analysis of the effectiveness of internet-based psychotherapeutic interventions. *Journal of Technology in Human Services,* 26 (2–4), 109–160.

Beattie A., Shaw, A., Kaur, S. & Kessler, D. (2009). Primary-care patients' expectations and experiences of online cognitive behavioural therapy for depression: a qualitative study. *Health Expectations: An International Journal of Public Participation in Health Care and Health Policy,* 12 (1), 45–59.

Berry, R.M. (2005). *A comparison of face-to-face and distance coaching practices: The role of the working alliance in problem resolution.* Unpublished Doctoral Dissertation, Georgia State University, Atlanta, Georgia.

Boyce, L.A. & Clutterbuck, D. (2011). E-coaching: Accept it, it's here, and it's evolving! In G. Hernez Broome & L. Boyce (Eds.), *Advancing Executive Coaching: Setting the Course for Successful Leadership Coaching* (pp. 285–315). San Francisco: Jossey-Bass.

Charbonneau, M.A (2002). *Participant self-perception about the cause of behavior change from a program of executive coaching.* Unpublished Doctoral Dissertation, Alliant International University, Los Angeles, CA.

Clutterbuck, D. (2010). Welcome to the world of virtual coaching and mentoring. In D. Clutterbuck & Z. Hussain (Eds.), *Virtual Coach, Virtual Mentor* (pp. 31–52). Charlotte: Information Age Publishing.

Clutterbuck, D. & Hussain, Z. (Eds.) (2010). *Virtual Coach, Virtual Mentor.* Charlotte: Information Age Publishing.

Cohen, G.E. & Kerr, B.A. (1998). Computer-mediated counseling: An empirical study of a new mental health treatment. *Computers in Human Services,* 15 (4), 13–26.

Collett, K. (2008). *A case study on the effectiveness of telephone coaching*. Work-based research. I-Coach Academy and Middlessex University. Retrieved from: http://www.i-coachacademy.com/media/research/A%20case%20study%20on%20the%20effectiveness%20of%20telephone%20coaching.pdf

Cook, J.E. & Doyle, C. (2002). Working alliance in online therapy as compared to face-to-face therapy: preliminary results. *Cyber Psychology and Behavior*, 5 (2), 95–105.

Daft, R.L., Lengel, R.H. & Trevino, L.K. (1987). Media symbolism, media richness and media choice in organizations. *Communication Research*, 14 (5), 553–574.

Day, S.X. and Schneider, P.L. (2002). Psychotherapy using distance technology: A comparison of face-to-face, video, and audio treatment. *Journal of Counseling Psychology*, 49, 499–503.

Efstathiou, G. (2009). Students' psychological web consulting: Function and outcome evaluation. *British Journal of Guidance & Counselling*, 37 (3), 243–255.

Frazee, R.V. (2008). *E-coaching in organizations. A study of features, practices, and determinants of use*. Unpublished Doctoral Dissertation, San Diego University, USA.

Geißler, H. (2008). *E-Coaching – Eine Konzeptionelle Grundlegung*. Baltmannsweiler: Schneider Hohengehren.

Geißler, H. (2010). Produkt und Marktsegmenterung von Coaching. In Breitner, Voigtländer, Sohns (Eds.), *Perspektiven des Lebenslangen Lernens –dynamische Bildungsnetzwerke, Geschäftsmodelle, Trends* (pp. 223–236). GITO-Verlag: Berlin.

Geißler, H. (2015a). Coaching through modern media – lesson 3 – Introduction (3): What are media in coaching – A first approach. http://www.e-coaching-education.com

Geißler, H. (2015b). Coaching through modern media – lesson 8 – Coaching basic media (4): Synchronous & asynchronous audio communication. http://www.e-coaching-education.com

Geißler, H. (2015c). Coaching through modern media – lesson 9 – Coaching basic media (5): Synchronous & asynchronous text communication – part 1. http://www.e-coaching-education.com

Geißler, H. (2015d). Coaching through modern media – lesson 9 – Coaching basic media (6): Synchronous & asynchronous text communication – part 2. http://www.e-coaching-education.com

Geißler, H. (2015e). Coaching through modern media – lesson 12 – Problem solving tools (1): Freely documented phone and video coaching. http://www.e-coaching-education.com

Geißler, H. (2015f). Coaching through modern media – lesson 13 – Problem solving tools (2): pre-prepared optional coaching questions. http://www.e-coaching-education.com

Geißler, H. (2015g). Coaching through modern media – lesson 14 – Problem solving tools (3): pre-prepared obligatory coaching questions. http://www.e-coaching-education.com

Geißler, H. (2015h). Coaching through modern media – lesson 15 – Problem solving tools (4): 2D visual tools. http://www.e-coaching-education.com

Geißler, H. (2016a). Coaching through modern media – lesson 16 – Problem solving tools (5): 3D static visual tools. http://www.e-coaching-education.com

Geißler, H. (2016b). Coaching through modern media – lesson 17 – Problem solving tools (6): 3D dynamic visual tools (avatars). http://www.e-coaching-education.com

Geißler, H. Hasenbein, M., Kanatouri, S. & Wegener, R. (2014). E-coaching: Conceptual and empirical findings of a virtual coaching programme. *International Journal of Evidence Based Coaching and Mentoring*, 12 (2), 165–187.

Geißler, H., Helm, M. & Nolze, A. (2007). Virtuelles Selbstcoaching – Konzept und erste Erfahrungen. *Organisationsberatung Supervision Coaching (OSC)*, 14 (1), 81–93.

Geißler, H. & Kanatouri, S. (2015). Coaching mit modernen Medien. In A. Schreyögg & C. Schmidt-Lellek (Eds.), *Die Professionalisierung von Coaching: Ein Lesebuch für den Coach*. Wiesbaden: Springer Fachmedien.

Geißler, H., Kurzmann, C. & Metz. M. (2012). Coaching und Beratung mit und ohne moderne Medien – ein empirischer Vergleich. In H. Geißler & M. Metz (Eds.), *E-Coaching und Online-Beratung* (pp. 359–380). Wiesbaden: Springer VS.

Geißler, H. & Metz, M. (2012). *E-Coaching und Online-Beratung*. Wiesbaden: Springer VS.

Ghods, N. (2009). *Distance coaching: The relationship between coach–client relationship, client satisfaction, and coaching outcomes.* Unpublished Doctoral Dissertation, San Diego University, USA.

Ghods, N. & Boyce, C. (2013). Virtual coaching and mentoring. In J. Passmore, D.B. Peterson & T. Freire (Eds.), *The Wiley-Blackwell Handbook of Psychology of Coaching and Mentoring* (pp. 501–523). Oxford: Wiley-Blackwell.

Grant, A.M. & Zackon, R. (2004). Executive, workplace and life coaching: Findings from a largescale survey of International Federation members. *International Journal of Evidence Based Coaching and Mentoring*, 2 (2), 1–15.

Gsöllpointner, K. (2012). Medienästhetik – Wozu? In K. Gsöllpointner (Ed.), *Medien der Beratung: Ästhetik, Methoden, Praxis* (pp. 9–23). Vienna: Facultas Verlags- und Buchhandels.

Hancock, B. (2014). *The design of a framework and instrument for assessment of virtual coaching competence: An exploratory study*. Master's thesis, Stellenbosch University, S. Africa.

Koch, B. (2012). 'onlineCoaching': ein geschriebener Dialog unabhängig von Zeit und Raum. In H. Geißler & M. Metz (Eds.), *E-Coaching und Online-Beratung* (pp. 87–102). Wiesbaden: Springer VS.

Lovell, K., Cox, D., Haddock, G., Jones, C., Raines, D., Garvey, R., Roberts, C. & Hadley, S. (2006). Telephone administered cognitive behaviour therapy for treatment of obsessive compulsive disorder: Randomised controlled non-inferiority trial. *The British Medical Journal*, 333 (7574), 883.

Ludman, E.J., Simon, G.E., Tutty, S. & Von Korff, M. (2007). A randomized trial of telephone psychotherapy and pharmacotherapy for depression: Continuation and durability of effects. *Journal of Consulting and Clinical Psychology*, 75 (2), 257–266.

McLaughlin, M. (2012). *Less is more: The executive coach's experience of working on the telephone*. Unpublished Master's thesis, Oxford Brookes University, UK.

McLaughlin, M. (2013). Less is more: The executive coach's experience of working on the telephone. *International Journal of Evidence Based Coaching and Mentoring*, Special Issue No. 7, June 2013, pp. 1–13.

Mohr, D.C., Ho, J., Juffecy, J., Reifler, D., Sokol, L., Burns, M.N., Jin, L. & Siddique, J. (2012). Effect of telephone-administered versus face-to-face cognitive behavioural therapy on adherence to therapy and depression outcomes among primary care patients: A randomized trial. *The Journal of the American Therapy Association*, 307 (21), 2278–2285.

Murphy, L.J., Mitchell, D.L., Hallett, R.H. (2011). *A Comparison of Client Characteristics in Cyber and In-Person Counselling*. Retrieved from: http://therapyonline.ca/cybercounselling/_protected/resources/Readings/Client_Characteristics_in_Cyber_and_In-Person_Counselling.pdf

Murphy, L.J., Parnass, P., Mitchell, D.L., Hallett, R.H., Cayley, P. & Seagram, S. (2009). Client satisfaction and outcome comparisons of online and face-to-face counselling methods. *British Journal of Guidance and Counselling*, 39, 627–640.

Poepsel, M. (2011). *The impact of an online evidence-based coaching program on goal striving, subjective well-being, and level of hope*. Doctoral Dissertation, Capella University, USA.

Pollock, K. Amstrong, S., Coveney, C. & Moore, J. (2010). *An evaluation of Samaritans telephone and email emotional support service*. NHS National Institute for Health Research and University of Nottingham. Retrieved from: http://www.samaritans.org/sites/default/files/kcfinder/files/research/Samaritans_service_evaluation_Nottingham_Full_Report.pdf

PricewaterhouseCoopers & ICF Global Coaching Study (2007). In M. Mc Laughlin (Ed.), *Less is More: The Executive Coach's Experience of Working on the Telephone*. Unpublished Master's thesis, Oxford Brookes University, UK.

Reese, R.J., Conoley, C.W. & Brossart, D.F. (2002). Effectiveness of telephone counselling: A field-based investigation. *Journal of counselling Psychology*, 49 (2), 233–242.

Ribbers, A. & Warringa, A. (2014). E-coaching for leadership development. *E-coaching: A Knowledge Base*, January 15th, 2014: https://ecoachingbase.wordpress.com/2014/01/15/research-report-about-web-based-coaching-by-anne-ribbers-alexander-warringa

Ribbers, A. & Warringa, A. (2015). *E-Coaching: Theory and Practice for a New Online Approach to coaching*. London, New York: Routledge.

Richards, D. (2009). Features and benefits of online counselling: Trinity College online mental health community. *British Journal of Guidance & Counselling*, 37 (3), 231–242.

Sherpa Executive Coaching Survey: *Seventh Annual Report (2012)*. Retrieved from: http://www.associationforcoaching.com/media/uploads/publications/Survey-Executive-Coaching-2012.pdf

Sherpa Executive Coaching Survey: *Tenth Annual Coaching Survey, Public Report (2015)*. Retrieved from: http://www.sherpa-coaching.com/pdf%20files/2015_Executive_Coaching_Survey_Public-Report.pdf

Simon, G.E., Ludman, E.J., Tutty, S., Operskalski, B. & Von Korrf, M. (2004). Telephone psychotherapy and telephone care management for primary care patients starting antidepressant treatment: a randomized controlled trial. *The Journal of the American Therapy Association*, 292 (8), 935–942.

Stephen, J., Collie, K., McLeod, D., Rojubally, A., Fergus, K., Speca, M., Turner, J., Taylor-Brown, J., Sellick, S., Burrus, K. & Elramly, M. (2014). Talking with text: communication in therapist-led, live chat cancer support groups. *Social Science & Medicine*, 104, 178–186.

Suler, J. (2000). Psychotherapy in cyberspace: a 5-dimensional model of online and computer-mediated psychotherapy. *CyberPsychology and Behavior*, 3, 151–160.

Taranovich, Y. (2013). *Web Based Project Coaching: Requirements, Design, Implementation, and Evaluation of Online Coaching Services*. Doctoral Dissertation, TUM School of Management, Technische Universität München.'

Discipline, Profession and Industry: How our Choices Shape our Future

Annette Fillery-Travis and Ron Collins

INTRODUCTION

> The coach began as a technology used for transportation, evolved into an object that was associated with a type of status and then becomes a prominent character in sport, before ultimately becoming an influential management concept. (Stec 2012, p. 331)

This historian of coaching makes the rather tongue in cheek comment as he seeks to identify the tensions inherent in exploring the professional and scientific legitimacy of the occupation. Others have also explored potential antecedents to coaching, for example see Garvey, Stokes and Megginson (2014). At the time of writing the practice of coaching is definitely an industry, could be underpinned by a discipline but is yet to be a fully developed and distinct profession. Each of these concepts – industry (practice), trade or discipline, or profession, – carry with them the associated 'badges of varying professional or academic status' and with it the rights to authority, autonomy and high remuneration/resources for its practitioners or scholars. The stakes are perceived to be high in this debate and there are a number of perspectives on the issues which we will consider in this chapter.

Where the occupation of coaching will eventually be placed in the spectrum of occupational forms, from trade to profession, is not clear. There is no requirement or necessity for it to progress from trade or service industry to the perceived lofty heights of a profession. It may be that maintaining itself as a service underpinned by a growing discipline will be sufficient for the industry to flourish and develop. Indeed there is an opinion that the post war stampede by trades to become professions has been overplayed and in fact a number of trades have proudly stood by their status. There is also the issue of amateurism and professionalism where the cult of the amateur persisted (Crook 2008) and occupations like architects bemoaned the 'loss of art' (Gerstenblith 1994). Indeed there has been some identification of coaching as simply a sub-role or activity of other professions and therefore with no identity as a separate profession, for example Hamlin et al. (2008) suggest that coaching is a significant part of modern Human Resource Development practice and, as pointed out by Gray (2010), the American Society for Training and Development and the UK-based Chartered Institute of Personnel and Development both agree with the identification of coaching as being part of the role of the HRD 'professional'. Furthermore, surveys in the UK and globally have both identified the increasing use of coaching within the role of managers (CIPD 2015; ICF 2012).

A parallel debate is being enacted within the academy concerning the notion of whether coaching is a discipline. There are a number of reviews reflecting upon the growing body of knowledge and whether it is of sufficient coherence, unique perspective and maturity to delineate it as that of a 'discipline' (Kombarakaran et al. 2008; Grant et al. 2010). Can (or should) coaching be a full discipline in its own right or is it a sub-discipline of another more elite or established field of study? Is it a nascent discipline in the nursery space between more established disciplines? Although the whole concept of disciplinarity sits within the academic realm (with the specific role as an educational device) there is a common misconception that a discipline must have an associated profession and vice versa.

This is clearly not the case and a moment's reflection allows us to consider three potential types of pairing of discipline and profession: discipline exists before profession (for example history) and can exist separate from it; discipline and profession completely locked together (medicine); disciplines and profession are linked but NOT required by either (a spectrum exists here from accountancy to chemistry). We will consider these in due course. The determination of where the coaching body of knowledge sits in terms of disciplines has consequences for where it sits in terms of academic 'tribes' (Becher and Trowler 2001; Gibb and Hill 2006) and this is critical to how the practice evolves. This positioning will determine what knowledge is deemed legitimate and appropriate to the field, how it is created and by whom (Kuhn 1962). In effect, it determines what questions are deemed suitable for research and hence how coaching will evolve.

As authors we represent the two distinct communities involved in this debate – academia and high-level practice. This allows us to consider how these issues influence both communities as we explore how the labels of profession and/or discipline – with their respective responsibilities and advantages – will influence the evolution of coaching in the medium to long term. In this chapter we describe the current status of coaching within each realm, the possible routes for development, their advantages and dilemmas, and how this will impact upon both the coaching and the client (see Figure 40.1 for key considerations in each realm). We first consider the notions of trade and profession before moving to discuss what is a discipline. We then critique coaching's current position and armed with such reflections speculate on the development routes open to the coaching occupation.

COACHING AS AN INDUSTRY, TRADE OR CRAFT

Industries, trades and crafts have been recognised since the Middle Ages and their organisation has grown and developed continuously and organically from these roots. Crafts and trades in the Middle Ages were externally regulated not at the national level but locally by cities (Thrupp 1962). A good example is the City of London, which provided the status of Freeman to those practising a trade or craft allowing them to operate within the City free of any feudal lord (Hickson and Thompson 1991). These crafts and trades were organised by guilds or livery companies formed by experienced practitioners, governed by a Master and a Court and to which membership was gained by 'servitude' i.e. apprenticeship to a master craftsman (but also by patrimony or redemption i.e. inheritance or payment). They controlled both the supply of craftsmen and the standards to which they were trained. Thus they established a form of the 'bargain' between skilled suppliers, customers and the city authorities that still endures today. This was a degree of social and market closure (restriction of practice to those certified to undertake it) together with price protection, in return for guaranteed standards both of skill and honesty. In the extreme case where the state, rather than the city, viewed the provision and standard of these services as critical, they became formalised and regulated as the first professions, most famously Law, Medicine and the Church underpinned by university-level education, then a rarity unlike today (Carr-Saunders 1928).

A key distinction from the beginning between crafts and professions was this balance between academic learning and practical experience. For crafts the overwhelming emphasis was on experience and practical learning through apprenticeship, while in contrast for professions the mastery of a significant high-level body of knowledge (as measured by independent examination) was additionally required. Indeed it seemed to be the risk to the client and/or the state, either to wealth, health or reputation that normally forced the formalisation of a profession (Klegon 1978). High value activity with low risk to the client, such as gold or silver smithing remained crafts with only the independent certification of the precious metal itself controlled by the state (Joann and Netelkos 2006).

In the modern world surprisingly little has changed in the workers' motivation for forming such associations. Skilled practitioners, tradespeople and craftsmen and women still seek to be recognised by forming themselves into trade associations that represent their manufacturing, service or trading interest. These associations lobby, now at the national level or even international level, for regulations and market structures that favour their members in return for promoting standards and ethics. They set codes of conduct and standards for their members, provide training, guarantee work and champion best practice. A typical example of this is provided by the UK Electrical Contractors Association (ECA); it provides standards, training and regulation for its members and their customers.

The most striking change in the twentieth century was the explosion in the variety of these skilled occupations, particularly new services driven by expanding technological and managerial sophistication and underpinned by technical and occupational training (Ackroyd 1996). Furthermore this expansion has produced two new classes of occupation or practice that differ from the traditional 'blue collar' craft in a number of ways. Firstly there has been the emergence of specialised service based practices delivered by 'artisan' knowledge workers: trainers, facilitators, project managers, management consultants, quality assessors etc. In addition there has been the emergence of 'assistant professionals': paralegals, paramedics, scientific and engineering technicians (Evetts 2013a). The situation is made slightly more complex by the fact that existing professionals often choose to deliver the specialist practice themselves, i.e. Chartered Accountants often deliver management consultancy, or Chartered Engineers act as their own project managers. However this does not make such practices a profession in their own right.

Coaching as an industry clearly possesses all the attributes required for a modern service based managerial craft. It requires both the acquisition of technical knowledge and the use and development of practical interpersonal skills. Associations such as EMCC, WABC, ICF and the AC provide training accreditation and define ethics and codes of practice (EMCC, WABC 2015). Managers and leaders now often acquire the coaching skill set and act formally as coaches within their own organisations. As management becomes increasingly professionalised there is an increasing need for them to acquire formal certification and academic qualifications. This is illustrated by the increasing numbers of Masters programmes in this area and the extent of research being conducted by those undertaking Doctoral degrees. An interesting observation is the emergence of first/baccalaureate degrees in coaching – specifically in sports coaching, where the short span of a sporting career, the potentially high rewards at risk and the central role of the coach may well force full professionalisation earlier than for business and executive coaches.

Indeed, as a managerial craft, business and executive coaching still has room to develop. Coaching associations are not yet influential enough with national and international governmental organisations to achieve the regulation needed for a degree of market and social closure. The risk to business posed by poor coaches in the market may not be sufficient for government or regulators to take action. If it is, or becomes so, we would expect to see this first in the public sector where the need to demonstrate 'good value for money' in public procurement may produce a NOCNOC (no certification no contract) situation as it has in the past for quality certification.

A further interesting consideration is the development of the coaching craft's body of knowledge, its codification and qualification against standards. This is a challenge also faced by a number of similar management craft areas, indeed some are very closely related. For example, coaching, mentoring, facilitating and counseling share many underlying people related skills while having many differences in objectives and intent. Does this mean that these crafts span more than one academic discipline or just that we have not yet crystallised the relevant pedagogies sufficiently at this stage? We will return to a number of these issues during the consideration of professions and disciplines to which we now turn.

CONSIDERATION ON THE REQUIREMENTS FOR A COACHING PROFESSION

In this section we evaluate the occupation of coaching in terms of whether it can be considered a burgeoning profession or as a management craft used within other occupations. To do so we first consider what delineates a profession and how it evolves into being in effect the 'natural history' of professions within UK, Europe and US. This allows us to place coaching as a practice used by range of other professions.

What is a Profession?

The sociological analysis of professional work has differentiated professions and professionalism as a special means of organising work and controlling workers; in contrast to the hierarchical, bureaucratic and managerial controls of industrial and commercial organizations (Evetts 2013a). The first theorists of professions (e.g. Pearson 1939) laid down a description of the characteristics of professional work and the professions that persists today. The professional practitioner's work is held distinct from organisational employees and is organised or characterised as; the professional practitioner's work was: specific, required extensive training based on intellectual skill, involved apprenticeship socialisation into the community of practitioners who had a monopoly on the provision of the work (Goode 1969) and the work is of critical importance to the client (i.e. the client is 'at risk'). The education and training of a professional is generally highly regulated, requiring study at the level of higher education; but the road to full proficiency requires significant experience applying it to a variety of issues within a range of contexts. The development of sophisticated reflection capable of producing *phronesis* 'lies at the heart of professional mastery' and indeed is the basis of professional chartering, fellowships and similar certifications (Kinsella and Pitman 2012).

The attainment of professional status for an occupation provides considerable claim to social standing for members and the presumption of a degree of autonomy in exchange for self-regulation of training and ethical practice (Gilmore and Williams 2007). Practitioners can claim high fees for their services in relation to the rarity of their knowledge and skill. There is also a concept of 'service to community' in the provision of professional services which is identified as part of many professional associations' vision as identified by Gray (2011), 'There is a presumption that professional practice has an orientation towards the public good rather than narrow self-interest' (p. 11). However, this could be argued to be a self-seeking assertion by the professions to justify market closure.

There have been a number of studies of how professions keep their status both socially and in the market place (Abbott 1988). This mainly operates through social and market closure as we identified previously (Abbott 1988). In this process the boundaries are sustained around the occupation as in 'the way that the members of professional groups routinely disparage members of related or competing groups' (Neal and Morgan. 2000, p. 10). Not wholly thought of as positive there is a school of thought that identifies this as: 'The process to pursue, develop and maintain the closure of the occupational group in order to maintain practitioners' own occupational self-interests in terms of their salary, status and power as well as the monopoly protection of the occupational jurisdiction' (Evetts 2013b p. 35). A higher-level qualification is required for entry in all cases and this is perhaps the defining characteristic of a profession. Whether the gatekeeper regulating the qualification is a professional association or the state is of no import to its defining role. In addition the qualification cannot be by academic knowledge alone but requires some kind of monitored practical experience (e.g., articles).

The professional association mostly maintains the qualification requirements but in general there will be an academic pathway that fulfils this requirement wholly or partly. This market and social closure is accepted on the basis that the risks (financial, physical, reputational or psychological) associated with the practice are such that practitioners need to be 'safe' or 'fit to practice' and carry appropriate Professional Indemnity Insurance cover to protect their clients. Examples of new professions hitting this criteria are sports coaching where the financial and status risks can be very high and nursing where the redistribution of work between nurses and doctors has required nurses to perform higher risk and more complex tasks, i.e. to be fully professional.

The 'natural history of professions' was studied in detail by Neal et al. (2000) building upon the foundation of Morgan (1998) and Freidson (1983). Comparing the pattern of development of a range of professions in UK and Germany they identified a staged route to full professional status in the UK as 'bottom up' whereas in Germany the state played an active interventionist role in a 'top down' process. In the 'bottom up' case the occupation becomes full time and an articles system is established. Professional associations are then formed conferring certification for the better-qualified or more prestigious practitioners. In this stage there may be several competing associations but in due course one emerges as the lead. Qualifying examinations are then introduced often on a voluntary basis but this becomes mandatory for new members. There may be difficulties at this point as the experience-rich but lightly certificated seasoned practitioners start to compete with the well credentialed but less experienced newcomers to the occupation (Neal and Morgan 2000).

At this point there begins the political agitation for legal protection of specific work areas for example in the UK a Royal Charter. This is usually driven through the professional association with the aim of protecting the area of work for its members. A case is made for a decrease in potential risk to the public and/or client with the use of suitably qualified professionals to provide the service. Usually the regulation is delegated to the leading professional body but there are instances where the risk is too great and/or the emerging profession is not able to provide such regulation. In this case statutory regulation is introduced as is being seen within the health professions in the UK. At this point there can also be a separation between the governing body and the professional body as in the General Medical Council of the UK and the British Medical Association. Academic routes to qualification are also established in co-operation with higher education authorities combined with some kind of practicum. The attainment of the degree provides significant exemption from the professional certification route.

Negotiating such exemptions allows the professional association to control the curriculum content and the body of knowledge identified as being within the profession. This is non trivial and often used. The most famous example is the refusal of the Royal Society of Chemistry (RSC) in the UK to validate the Chemistry degree from Imperial College until relatively recently as Imperial failed to ensure all fields of chemistry were taught in the final degree year. A requirement for CPD is introduced to ensure professionals continually update their skills and knowledge. Thus in general professions are largely self-regulated and retain responsibility for professional education. Such responsibility is seen to operate most markedly by the new professions such as British Psychological Society who ruthlessly regulate the use of the term psychology in any degree title. Such tenacity has resulted in a very strong regulation of the curriculum and training regimes required to be completed before an individual is licensed to practise. This is at the core of maintaining market closure and specifically allows for direct self-regulation (BPS 2015).

The natural history identified above has resonance with the evolution of the older professions but has little to say concerning the work context for professionals or how their work patterns have evolved in line with changing economics and workplaces. Indeed the traditional view we have identified above presupposes professionals to have a degree of control on both the context and autonomy of their work (Leicht and Fennell, 2001). In the last decades there has been a 'shift of professional activity [to] within the confines of increasingly large and complex organisations' (Muzio, Brock and Suddaby 2013), e.g., lawyers and accountants. Indeed it is acknowledged that there is a sizable body of literature that now identifies the need for professions to adapt to organisational life. Reed (1996) notes the emergence of professional activities which 'unfold entirely within organisational boundaries and structures' (p. 574). The newly evolving professions and professionals 'structure themselves so as to accommodate corporate patterns' (Dacin et al. 2002, p. 49). These 'organisational' professions (equivalent perhaps to our management craft) include the emerging practices of HRM, management consultancy, health and safety officers and project managers as well as the traditional profession of law.

Originally it was argued that such incorporation into organisational life would erode professionalism through exposing professionals to managerial pressures and in the worst case 'factory like conditions' and thereby losing traditional qualities to the professional work pattern such as autonomy and discretion (Oppenheimer 1973, pp. 213–214). The current analysis identifies instead an ability of professions to control and impact upon organisational structure and functions through a process of dual closure – the occupational closure we considered earlier with the additional control of space, tasks and processes within their employing organisations (Ackroyd 1996). We argue below that both models have a contribution to the understanding of coaching professionalization.

Where is Coaching Positioned Now?

If we were to compare the current direct line of travel for coaching there would be agreement that full-time practitioners of coaching exist to some significant level (CIPD 2015). Even the most recent economic difficulties and the constriction of the economy have not stopped the use of coaching within the organisational context (Jarvis et al. 2006). It has however shifted its delivery to include the lower cost internal coach and manager as coach (McComb 2012) as well as the high cost external practitioner. This has split the emerging practice into independent practitioners operating a full-time practice and employed organisational staff.

There is also a range of coaching associations EMCC, WABC, ICF and others who are jostling for various sectors of the coaching market. These emerged in a bid to begin the social and market closure. Their early work concentrated upon delineating the unique forms of expertise required of their occupation (Eraut 1994) through the development of competency frameworks (EMCC). These were developed with varying degrees of robustness and have evolved into similar forms. All the associations offer some individual accreditation against these frameworks at what is identified as a 'professional' level. The market response to such credentialing has been predictable with companies starting to seek to employ coaches with such a 'license' to practise (Bono et al. 2009) but this is not universal as yet. The work of associations has also included accreditation of coach training and the majority run such programmes allowing training providers to claim external standards of rigour. At the moment the criteria against which the courses are assessed are light on the curriculum requirements but with a focus on a significant practicum. For a critique of this role and that of individual practitioner accreditation by coaching professional associations the reader is directed to Bachkirova and Smith (2015). Further development is on the agenda as we consider in the following section.

Professional associations will also generally seek to maintain the autonomy of their profession, justifying this through their custodianship of the standards and ethical codes of practice (Williams and Anderson 2006). Specifically they make the case that it is they who are best placed to make decisions on this practice over and above the claims from the state or from older and more established professions. We see some elements of this occurring with health and psychology professions (Williams et al. 2010) in regard to coaching. The literature contains a number of studies proposing a need for psychology training for coaching practice (Sherman and Freas 2004) and in the US there has been some move to identify coaching with forms of therapy thereby requiring practitioners to have psychology credentials to practice.

At the moment coaching associations are holding such incursions into their perceived territory at bay with the explicit identification that coaches work with clients who are psychologically well and who want to work with coaches to fulfil their potential in their professional or personal lives. However, this clearly does not take into account that organisational psychologists work with well populations. They argue that their work with their clients needs to go beyond a purely psychological intervention. This overlap with other professions has encouraged the coaching associations to try to be explicit in identifying the boundaries of their work and where their members should operate. Ethical codes are a specific example of such activity. Although common throughout the coaching associations there is no explicit procedure for their imposition in any forum. A coach undertakes to abide by their association's ethical code of conduct as part of their membership but there are no standing committees to receive complaints from clients or to investigate membership concerns.

This analysis identifies coaching as a practice that has developed in a similar manner to the 'organisational professions' identified before with a significant range of the qualities associated with a professional occupation. These are specialisation, codes of ethics (although voluntary), practitioner associations offering accreditation of training and practice and higher level training and development (Bennett 2006). As a practice, coaching is used by a range of associated professions and management crafts (HRD, psychology and education for example) to achieve individual and team learning objectives within their own practice contexts. It does however fail on one professional criteria in that it has not achieved market closure. The coaching associations have had their individual credentialing programmes for some time but cannot make them obligatory for practice in the field. It is clear that the risk perceived by the client in this situation is concerned with quality of the provision not the safety of provision or its effectiveness to mitigate against some risk for the client. Hence while the value to the organisation or individual may be high the risk level can be thought of a low.

Some traction towards professional status has also been lost through the ICF choosing ISO standards as a benchmark within their system of certification (Gray 2011). Their use for an emerging practice seems to be contrary to an avowed direction of travel to professionalisation. This could be argued to indicate a lack of commitment to progression to professional status for the ICF and as such leads to a number of dilemmas for their member coaches in identifying where they see their practice positioned most authentically (Lane 2010). The EMCC has taken the mantle of driving forward to professionalisation but it still falls short of requiring personal accreditation for membership. Which approach will dominate in the future remains to be seen.

Thus coaching could be identified as failing the professional test if the traditional criterion of closure is applied. But more recent sociological perspectives on professionalism have suggested these normative notions to be of limited value to the 'professional project' (Hanlon 1998) of 'organisational' professions that emerge from practice within an organisational context and if this is true it may not be in the best interests of coaching or its clients to pursue this traditional route to being a profession. This argument does conflate the concepts of a profession and a professional practice. Currently this is not common practice (see Directive on Recognition of Professional Qualifications (2005/36/EC) as we have identified previously. Notwithstanding this argument it is clear practitioners value an association with others that provides professional elements such as common standards so it may be time for the voluntary bodies (EMCC, ICF etc.) to define new models of association that would suit the development and purpose of coaching more closely (Lane, Stelter and Stout-Rostrum 2014).

Whatever form the occupation may take in the future, its development will be associated with coach education (initial and continuing) and specifically the development of an academic route to qualification. As mentioned previously professional associations maintain control of the content of training through the training course accreditation but it is the level of such training that is a critical point in the discourse around professionalisation. These factors are in the realm of the development of an academic discipline and it is to this notion that we now turn.

CONSIDERATIONS ON THE REQUIREMENTS FOR A COACHING DISCIPLINE

Within this section we consider whether coaching can be considered as a discipline. At first pass this may seem a more trivial question to that of professional status, but upon closer inspection the concept of discipline is ill defined and inconsistent in use. It is essentially operationally defined, i.e. it becomes one by common agreement. It is essentially a highly pragmatic classification of knowledge without a strongly theoretical basis, which allows curricula to be taught in a purposeful manner (Messer-Davidow and Shumway 1993). There are no established criteria beyond this. Below we consider the coaching body of knowledge as it currently stands and the current research trajectory in the field. Consideration of these elements strongly suggests the body of knowledge intersects significantly with at least three other practices (counselling, facilitation and mentoring) leading to the suggestion that this body of knowledge may not be wholly unique to coaching but is one that provides value to a range of other professions and as such is of specific merit.

What is a Discipline?

The concept of a discipline is one that people generally associate with an established and relatively stable body of knowledge that has been identified as robust and rigorous by a dedicated collection of academics trained to teach and research within this field of study. In reality disciplines are far more dynamic and as identified by Krishnan are 'themselves fragmented and heterogeneous' (2009, p. 5) and interact with other disciplines in complex ways. In fact the *Oxford English Dictionary* definition is 'a branch of learning or knowledge; a field of study and experience; a subject' and what constitutes a branch of learning or knowledge is clearly up for debate. Klein (1990) has pointed out that the academic discipline was an invention of the late Middle Ages and first applied to three academic areas for which universities had the responsibility of producing trained professionals: theology, law and medicine. She argues that this early 'disciplining' of knowledge was a response to external demands from the associated profession or vocation in contrast with the specialisation into disciplines that emerged in the 19th century that was due to internal drivers within academia i.e. the increase in size and discreet-ness of the field of study driving the desirability to segment it for effective teaching and research. In the time of Galileo and Newton natural philosophy was a single discipline (Shapin 1992).

Later, science and the pursuit of new knowledge had become an institutionalised and highly systematic endeavour and it became impossible to teach as a single subject. The response from the Universities was to divide it into the subject of chemistry, physics and biology: a process that was widely accepted and adopted (except for the University of Cambridge UK which persists in teaching a natural science tripos). This disciplining of knowledge helped in the recruiting and production of the specialists that were needed in the context of the industrialisation and the advance of technology. As society grew in complexity in the late 19th and early 20th century a whole range of new disciplines were institutionally established including the main social sciences: sociology, anthropology, psychology, political science and economics. Bourdieu and Bernstein (Singh 2015) remind us that 'the symbolic boundaries that define these disciplines are culturally arbitrary ... the array of academic disciplines is a matter of convention rather than a reflection of an inherent order' (p. 14).

In essence the purpose of disciplines is to package knowledge in a convenient format for teaching students. When questions or needs arise outside the realms of the established disciplines then multi- and inter-disciplinary work needs to be developed to address them (Collins and Fillery-Travis 2015). This type of work will be collaborative between the disciplines but with each maintaining their own disciplinary paradigm in response to the question. If such work provides viable and effective results in relation to this new type of question and such questions are complex and important to a significant number of practitioners then new disciplines will emerge. This 'push' from professions, vocation, industry or state can result in dramatic change and this is identified in a number of the newer disciplines e.g. nanochemistry. Some of the non-commercially oriented disciplines (such as philosophy) are exempt from such professional 'interference' and hence tend towards less discontinuity and haste in change (Krishnan 2009).

Hence new disciplines can form either:

a) in a process of fragmentation when their parent disciplines become too bulky to be taught as a whole. The new discipline can form if there is sufficiently discrete knowledge to 'stand alone', for example, biochemistry fragmenting off from chemistry; or
b) through synthesis and coalescence of knowledge from distinct disciplines brought together to address an interdisciplinary problem or issue usually driven from external practice. For example, food science emerged as 'a discipline in which the engineering, biological, and physical sciences are used to study the nature of foods, the causes of deterioration, the principles underlying food processing, and the improvement of foods for the consuming public' (Heldman 2006 p. 11).

Is Coaching a Discipline Presently?

The emergence of coaching within the work environment (and personal sphere) is well documented and reflects the clear formation of a practice ahead of any disciplinary construct. The practice itself has been identified as interdisciplinary in drawing upon a range of disciplines (Cox et al. 2014; Garvey et al. 2014). These include management, psychology, education and social sciences. An alternative view of this shared knowledge is that it is generic and held in common by these disciplines. Such a view has not been extensively critiqued as yet but if shown to be appropriate it would have significant impact to the design of education programmes in these fields and would pave the way for a core curriculum in people intensive interventions.

All of these disciplines are constructed through specific paradigms and they each hold separate perspectives and assumptions as to the development of human beings as well as holding different criteria for what constitutes knowledge. This provides an interesting challenge within interdisciplinary work in general: to provide an internally coherent output when the tools, methods or instruments are drawn from different paradigms (Collins and Fillery-Travis 2015). Within coaching one of the responses has been to categorise coaching models in terms of the paradigm that is privileged in its underpinning theoretical frame. Indeed Cox et al. (2014) have identified 13 specific theory-based approaches to coaching, mostly coming from the psychotherapeutic traditions whereas Garvey et al. (2014) considered five categories sufficient, with two coming from psychological disciplines.

Numerous reviews have been written on the development of the knowledge base to support and extend the practice of coaching. They have all been concerned with the overall development of the coaching research base, the type of studies reported and the quality of the evidence produced (for example Passmore and Fillery-Travis 2011; Passmore and Gibbes 2007; Grant and Cavanagh 2007). Specifically they lament the paucity of empirical studies and the small number of experimental studies that draw upon the 'gold standard' of research design – the randomised controlled trial (RCT). Such laments seem rather premature given the relative immaturity of the field of study and also offer a very limited view of research validity. As identified by Fillery-Travis and Cox (2014) coaching research is going through a similar development process to that experienced in counselling and HRM. The research focus is initially to establish a defined field of practice through the sharing of case studies but this widens to include ROI and evaluation to justify the investment by clients. This expansion of research continues as the questions develop and mature attracting investment by individuals, research groups and organisations.

The origin of the discontent with progress in achieving RCTs has been mainly from academics in psychology and related disciplines as they use their own discipline's criteria for what constitutes knowledge and its rigour. Psychologists have a rich tradition of quantitative studies seeking generalisable evidence whereas educationalists, for example, have a mixed tradition of both qualitative and quantitative studies, as do management science and HRM. This is a clear example of differing paradigms operating within one field of study and there are a number of papers calling for larger scale generalisable results that mimic the psychological elite research at the same time as others are calling for the development of new methodologies such as 'interspective research approaches' (inherently qualitative) to explore the coaching interaction itself (Cox 2015). There is a tension in the research field between the development of a research literature based in the established criteria and norms of psychology and a body of knowledge answering (probably) broader questions with a more eclectic mix of methods and criteria for rigour. This tension can impact upon what knowledge the field considers to be sufficiently rigorous for publication and hence what is included within the established body of knowledge and what is not. This in turn will determine the scope and form of the emerging discipline.

In terms of overall progress the research arena is evolving and has moved from purely case study reporting into more consistent attempts to structure a theoretical framework for the practice and a delineation of where coaching adds its unique contribution to the field of human performance. The aim of research and hence the discipline must be to enable practitioners to tailor their interventions more finely to their clients' needs and to enable practitioners to be trained to provide an effective service. Maintaining the dialogue between practice, teaching and research is critical to producing a robust body of evidence. Coaching journals such as the *International Journal of Evidence Based Practice*; *Coaching: An International Journal of Theory, Research and Practice*; *International Journal of Mentoring and Coaching*; *Mentoring and Tutoring* and the *International Coaching Psychology Review* all publish practitioner based research and are excellent sources of what practice the discipline must speak to as it evolves.

The training and development of coaches is the final role in the discipline and one that started for coaching, not in academia, but within the professional training and development arenas and off-shoots of counselling and consulting psychology courses. For a discussion on the implication of this for the future of coaching as a postprofessional practice please see Drake 2008. Now there are 84 postgraduate courses (PGC or above) in the UK covering coaching and mentoring as a single focus but noticeably also as subject specific variants specifically within education and health. A scoping project in the US during 2007 identified 49 academic institutions providing coaching courses at degree or postgraduate level with 65 offering it as a continuing education programme (Stein et al 2014). Outside the US there are over 200 masters level course with significant focus on coaching although there is still significant provision at lower levels by non-academic training schools as exemplified by the 111 training providers accredited with the EMCC to provide coach training of which only 7 are from academic institutions (EMCC). A critical point in this analysis is the paucity of undergraduate degrees in coaching – the authors know of only one in the UK and this one incorporates counselling and mentoring as well. So coaching is taught as part of the academic offers for other disciplines and at a predominantly postgraduate level in its own right. This is in marked contrast to the degrees available in social work – currently debating its professional standing – and nursing which is a profession newly formed from a very well established specialised trade or vocation where the growth in academic offerings is dominated by undergraduate provision (Findlow 2012).

One purpose of a discipline for the profession or practice of coaching would be the delineation of the curriculum that is the benchmark for professional training within the academic environment. This has progressed in a meaningful way in the US with the Graduate School Alliance for Executive Coaching (GSAEC), a body developed with the aim 'To establish and maintain the standards for education and training provided by academic institutions for the discipline and practice of executive and organizational coaching' (Stein et al. 2014). Within Europe such initiatives are in their infancy and driven by the professional associations through accreditation and provision of credentials.

Having reviewed the current perceptions of what a discipline is and how it links with the professional and research field we can now consider how coaching is currently placed. There is clearly a coaching body of knowledge that is large and drawn from a range of disciplines but applied within a specific context (cf. food science). There is also unique knowledge of sufficient depth within the current field to warrant postgraduate study. At the same time the core activity (and underpinning knowledge) is shared with other practices such mentoring, counselling and facilitation. Each practice requires exquisite skills and competencies to be effective but we need to ask the question as to whether they are sufficiently differentiated to be considered disciplines in their own right? As we identified previously there is no criteria for a discipline other than usefulness in an academic context of teaching. Coaching does not sit under one discipline but could be considered a specialisation within the range of people-intensive interventions and contributing to a number of other disciplines including education, health, sociology, philosophy, sport and finally psychology (Garvey et al. 2014). For example there is a rich literature on the development of coaching within other disciplinary contexts and developing models of practice of specific relevance to that context (see for example van Nieuwerburgh 2012 in regard to education or Hadikin 2004 in terms of health care).

There are a number of possible future routes for coaching in regard to its position as a discipline:

- it becomes established and fully recognised as a discipline in its own right;
- it is considered as part of a number of disciplines and practices such as education, psychology, sport and HRM;
- it becomes fully identified as a sub-discipline of one particular discipline e.g. psychology; and/or
- it emerges as a significant component of an entirely new (and as yet unnamed) discipline of people-intensive interventions including mentoring, facilitation and counselling.

Obviously some of these options are more possible then others and the outcome will be dependent upon a number of drivers, including internally from the practitioners themselves and externally from the demands of the market place and the choices of academia in how they research and teach the subject.

In part the outcome will also be determined by how we expect the body of knowledge to grow in future and even this is not straightforward. Each field of coaching practice (education, health etc.) will have their own criteria for evidence and coaching practitioners will require a sophisticated understanding of what constitutes evidence to allow them to consider what is appropriate knowledge to use within their practice e.g. does the evidence produced working with motivational interviewing in health apply to teachers working in secondary schools? There can be no simple retreat to large scale, generalisable research outcomes but a more pragmatic approach that allows the question being asked (itself a product of the paradigm being used) to drive the research design and hence dedicate the criteria for rigour. As Fillery-Travis and Cox (2014, p. 450) identify 'If we look at what could usefully be the focus of research in the future, as well as exploring elements of the interaction in order to understand what constitutes coaching, there appears to be a significant need to test the entire model of coaching.'

Specifically, coaching suffers from the same issue as therapy – our clients are not uniform. Addressing this 'uniformity myth' we might adjust the oft-cited comment by

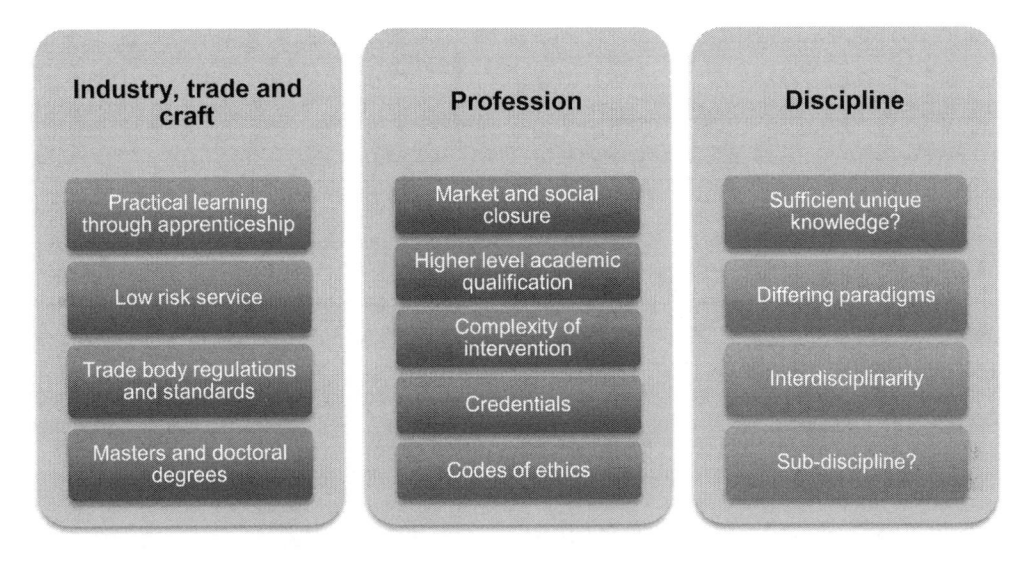

Figure 40.1 Discipline, profession and industry: key considerations for each concept

Industry, trade and craft
- Practical learning through apprenticeship
- Low risk service
- Trade body regulations and standards
- Masters and doctoral degrees

Profession
- Market and social closure
- Higher level academic qualification
- Complexity of intervention
- Credentials
- Codes of ethics

Discipline
- Sufficient unique knowledge?
- Differing paradigms
- Interdisciplinarity
- Sub-discipline?

Paul (1967, p. 111) from counseling to relate to the coaching context: '*what* coaching, delivered by *whom*, is most effective for *this* client with *that* specific issue and under *which* set of circumstances?' Each element of this question requires varying forms of evidence and the elucidation of these will require a further integration of practice and evidence. It would therefore seem highly appropriate for coaching to continue with its interdisciplinary research.

CONCLUSION

We suggest that currently coaching may be described as a management craft or organisational profession underpinned by a distinct body of knowledge, some of which is shared by related activities (facilitation, mentoring etc.). Whether it becomes a fully developed profession or emerges as a distinct academic discipline remains, as with any practice, in the hands of its practitioners. It will depend on the direction they collectively take and on the impact they have on their clients and their businesses as a result.

REFERENCES

Abbott, A. (1988) *The System of Professions: An Essay on the Division of Expert Labor*. Chicago: University of Chicago Press.

Ackroyd, S. (1996) Organization contra organizations: professions and organizational change in the United Kingdom. *Organization Studies* 17 (July): 599–621.

Bachkirova, T. and Smith, C. L. (2015) From competencies to capabilities in the assessment and accreditation of coaches. *International Journal of Evidence Based Coaching and Mentoring* 3(2): 123–140.

Becher, T. and Trowler, P. (2001) *Academic Tribes and Territories: Intellectual Enquiry and the Culture of Disciplines*. London: McGraw-Hill Education

Bennett, J.L. (2006) An agenda for coaching-related research: A challenge for researchers. *Consulting Psychology Journal: Practice and Research* 58: 240–249.

Bono, J. E., Purvanova, R. K., Towler, A. J., and Peterson, D. B. (2009) A survey of executive coaching practices. *Personnel Psychology* 62(2): 361–404.

BPS (2015) Accredited Courses and Training Programmes. Retrieved from http://www.bps.org.uk/careers-education-training/accredited-courses-training-programmes/accredited-courses-training-progra.

Carr-Saunders, A.M. (1928) *Professions: Their Organization and Place in Society.* Oxford (UK): Clarendon Press

CIPD (2015) Learnng and Development Survey Report. Retrieved from http://www.cipd.co.uk/hr-resources/survey-reports/learning-development-2015.aspx

Collins, R. and Fillery-Travis, A. (2015) Transdisciplinary problems: The teams addressing them and their support through team coaching in Gibbs, P. (ed) *Transdisciplinary Professional Learning and Practice*, pp. 41–52. London: Springer.

Cox, E. (2015) Coaching and adult learning: theory and practice. *New Directions for Adult and Continuing Education* 148: 27–38.

CIPD (2015) Learning and development. *Annual survey report.* London: CIPD.

Cox, E., Bachkirova, T. and Clutterbuck, D. (2014) Theoretical traditions and coaching genres: mapping the territory. *Advances in Developing Human Resources* 16: 139–160.

Crook, D. (2008). *Some Historical Perspectives on Professionalism.* London: Institute of Education.

Dacin, M.T., Goodstein, J. and Scott W.R. (2002) Institutional theory and institutional change: introduction to the special research forum. *Academy of Management Journal* 45: 45–56.

Drake, D. B. (2008) Finding our way home: Coaching's search for identity in a new era. *Coaching: An International Journal of Theory, Research and Practice*, 1(1), 16–27.

EMCC (2015) Global Code of Ethics. Retrieved from http://www.emccouncil.org/webimages/EMCC/Global_Code_of_Ethics.pdf

Eraut, M. (1994) Developing Professional Knowledge and Competence. London: Psychology Press.

Evetts, J. (2013a) Professionalism: Value and ideology. *Current Sociology* 61(5–6): 778–796.

Evetts, J. (2013b) The concept of professionalism: Professional, work, professional practice and learning in Billett, S., Harteis, C., & Gruber, H. (eds) *International Handbook of Research in Professional and Practice-based Learning*, pp. 29–56. London: Springer.

Fillery-Travis, A. and Cox, E. (2014) Researching coaching in E. Cox, T. Bachkirova and D. Clutterbuck (eds), *The Complete Handbook of Coaching*, pp. 445–459. 2nd ed. London: Sage.

Passmore, J, and Fillery-Travis, A. (2011) A critical review of executive coaching research: a decade of progress and what's to come. *Coaching: An International Journal of Theory, Research and Practice* 4(2): 70–88.

Findlow, S. (2012) Higher education change and professional-academic identity in newly 'academic'disciplines: the case of nurse education. *Higher Education* 63: 117–133.

Freidson, E. (1983) The reorganization of the professions by regulation. *Law and Human Behavior* 7: 279–289.

Garvey, B., Stokes, P. and Megginson, D. (2014) *Coaching and Mentoring: Theory and Practice.* London: Sage.

Gerstenblith, P. (1994) Architect as artist: artists' rights and historic preservation. *Cardozo Arts and Entertainment Law Journal 12*, 431–444.

Gibb, S. and Hill, P. (2006) From trail-blazing individualism to a social construction community; modelling knowledge construction in coaching. *International Journal of Mentoring and Coaching* 4 (2): 58–77.

Gilmore, S. and Williams, S. (2007) Conceptualising the 'personnel professional': a critical analysis of the Chartered Institute of Personnel and Development's professional qualification scheme. *Personnel Review* 36: 398–414.

Goode, W. J. (1969) The theoretical limits of professionalization. *The semi-professions and their organization*, pp. 266–313. New York: Free Press.

Grant, A. M., and Cavanagh, M. J. (2007) Evidence-based coaching: Flourishing or languishing? *Australian Psychologist* 42(4): 239–254.

Grant, A.M., Green, L. and Rynsaardt, J. (2010) Developmental coaching for high school teachers: executive coaching goes to school. *Consulting Psychology Journal: Practice and Research* 62: 151–168.

Gray, D. E. (2010) Towards the lifelong skills and business development of coaches: an integrated model of supervision and mentoring. *Coaching: An International Journal of Theory, Research and Practice* 3(1): 60–72.

Gray, D. E. (2011) Journeys towards the professionalisation of coaching: Dilemmas, dialogues and decisions along the global pathway. *Coaching: An International Journal of Theory, Research and Practice* 4(1): 4–19.

Hadikin, R. (2004) Effective Coaching in Health Care. London: Elsevier Science Limited.

Hamlin, R.G., Ellinger, A.D. and Beattie, R.S. (2008) The emergent 'coaching industry': a wake-up call for HRD professionals. *Human Resource Development International* 11(3): 287–305.

Hanlon, G. (1998) Professionalism as enterprise: service class politics and the redefinition of professionalism. *Sociology* 32(1): 43–63.

Hawkins, P. (2008) The coaching profession: some of the key challenges. *Coaching: An International Journal of Theory, Research and Practice* 1(1): 28–38.

Heldman, D.R. (2006) IFT and the food science profession. Food Technology October: 11.

Hickson, C.R. and Thompson, E.A. (1991) A new theory of guilds and European economic development. *Explorations in Economic History* 28(2): 127–168.

ICF (2012) Global Coaching Study Report. Retrieved from http://coachfederation.org/about/landing.cfm?ItemNumber=828 International Coach Federation.

Jarvis, J., Lane, D. and Fillery-Travis, A. (2006) *The Case for Coaching - Making Evidence-Based Decisions on Coaching*. London: CIPD.

Joann, J. and Netelkos, J. (2006). *The Crafts and Culture of a Medieval Guild*. New York: The Rosen Group.

Kinsella, E. A., and Pitman, A. (eds) (2012) *Phronesis as Professional Knowledge: Practical Wisdom in the Professions* (Vol. 1). London: Springer Science & Business Media.

Klegon, D. (1978) The sociology of professions: an emerging perspective. *Work and Occupations* August: 259–283.

Klein, J.T. (1990) *Interdisciplinarity/History, Theory, and Practice*. Detroit: Wayne State University Press.

Kombarakaran, F.A., Yang, J.A., Baker, M.N., et al. (2008) Executive coaching: It works! *Consulting Psychology Journal: Practice and Research* 60(1): 78–90.

Krishnan, A. (2009) What are academic disciplines? Some observations on the disciplinary and interdisciplinarity debate. NCRM Working Paper. Southampton: University of Southampton.

Kuhn, T. (1962.) *The Structure of Scientific Revolutions*. Chicago: University of Chicago Press.

Lane, D.A. (2010) Coaching in the UK – an introduction to some key debates. *Coaching: An International Journal of Theory, Research and Practice* 3: 155–166.

Lane, D., Stelter, R. and Stout-Rostrum, S. (2014) The future of coaching as a profession, in E. Cox, T. Bachkirova, and D.A. Clutterbuck (eds), *The Complete Handbook of Coaching*, pp. 377–390. London: Sage.

Leicht, K.T. and Fennell, M.L. (2001) *Professional Work: A Sociological Approach*. Malden, Mass., USA: Wiley-Blackwell.

McComb, C. (2012) Developing coaching culture: are your coaching relationships healthy? *Industrial and Commercial Training* 44(4): 232–235.

Messer-Davidow, E. and Shumway, D.R. (1993) *Knowledges: Historical and Critical Studies in Disciplinarity*. Virgina: University of Virginia Press.

Morgan, T.D. (1998) Impact of antitrust law on the legal profession. *The Fordham Law Review* 67: 415–441.

Muzio, D., Brock, D.M. and Suddaby, R. (2013) Professions and institutional change: towards an institutionalist sociology of the professions. *Journal of Management Studies* 50: 699–721.

Neal, M. and Morgan, J. (2000) The professionalization of everyone? A comparative study of the development of the professions in the United Kingdom and Germany. *European Sociological Review* 16: 9–26.

Newman, Russ. and Reed, Geoffrey M. (1996) Psychology as a health care profession: Its evolution and future directions in Resnick, Robert J. and Rozensky, Ronald H. (eds), Health Psychology Through the Life Span: Practice and Research Opportunities, pp. 11–26. Washington, DC, US: American Psychological Association.

Oppenheimer, M. (1973) Proletarianization of the professional in Halmos, P. (ed) Professionalization and Social Change, pp. 213–227. Keele: Keele University Press.

Passmore, J. and Gibbes, C. (2007) The state of executive coaching research: what does the current literature tell us and what's next for coaching research? *International Coaching Psychology Review* 2(2): 116–128.

Paul, G. L. (1967) Strategy of outcome research in psychotherapy. *Journal of Consulting Psychology*, 31(2): 109–118.

Pearsons, T. (1939) The professions and social structure. *Social Forces* 17: 457–67.

Reed, M.I. (1996) Expert power and control in late modernity: an empirical review and theoretical synthesis. *Organization Studies* 17(4): 573–97.

Shapin, S. (1992) Discipline and bounding: the history and sociology of science as seen through the externalism-internalism debate. *History of Science* 30: 333–369.

Sherman, S. and Freas, A. (2004) The wild west of executive coaching. *Harvard Business Review* 82: 82–90.

Singh, P. (2015) The knowledge paradox: Berstein, Bourdieu and beyond. *British Journal of sociology of Education 36*(3): 487–494.

Stec, D. (2012) The personification of an object and the emergence of coaching. *Journal of Management History* 18(3): 331–358.

Stein, I.F., Page, L.J. and Maltbia, T.E. (2014) Coaching education: coming of age. *Journal of Psychological Issues in Organizational Culture* 5: 7–15.

Thrupp, S.L. (1962) *The Merchant Class of Medieval London, 1300–1500*. (Vol. 72). Michigan, US: University of Michigan Press.

Turner, B. S. (2006) Discipline. *Theory, culture & Society 23*(2–3):183–186.

van Nieuwerburgh, C. (2012) *Coaching in Education: Getting Better Results for Students, Educators, and Parents*. London: Karnac Books.

WABC (2015) Codes of Business Coaching Ethics and Integrity Retrieved from http://www.wabccoaches.com/includes/popups/code_of_ethics_2nd_edition_december_17_2007.html

Williams, H., Edgerton, N. and Palmer, S. (2010) Cognitive behavioural coaching in E. Cox, T. Bachkirova and D. Clutterbuck (eds), The Complete Handbook of Coaching, pp. 34–50. 2nd ed. London: Sage.

Williams, P. and Anderson, S. K. (2006) *Law and Ethics in Coaching: How to Solve–and Avoid Difficult Problems in Your Practice*. London: John Wiley & Sons.

Index

Page numbers in **bold** indicate tables and in *italic* indicate figures.

3+1Cs model, 203–6, 208–9
360-degree assessments, 146, 313, 315, **315**, **316**, 637–38, **637**

Abbott, Geoffrey N., 439, 445, 446, 447, 450, 453–66
ABC model, 275, 717–18
ABCDE model, 275
ABCDEF model, 550
Abma, T. A., 302
Abrahamson, D. J., 657
Abrahamson, E., 225
AC *see* Association for Coaching (AC)
Accelerated Behavioral Change (ABC) model, 275, 717–18
Acceptance and Commitment Training (ACT), 354, **354**
accreditation, 31, 535, 658, 689–3
achievement cultures, 442
action learning (AL), 106, 111–12, 479–0, 672–3
action planning, relationship coaching, 549–0
Actor-Network theory, 54
actualising tendency, 410
Adams, J. D., 423
Adams, M., 177
ADHD (attention deficit hyperactivity disorder), 514
Adler, R. B., 282
adult developmental theories, 113–14, 121–36, 143–4, 223
　challenging contemporary practice, 129–30
　coach development, 134–5
　constructive-developmental theory, 113–14, 121, 122–6, **124–5**
　and cross-cultural coaching, 459
　ethical concerns, 129
　evidence and critique, 126–9, **128**
　and feedback, 321, **321**
　group/team coaching, 133–4
　individual coaching, 131–3, **131**, **133**
　judgmental nature of, 128
　measurement tools, 127, **127**
　and relationship coaching, 547–48
　and resilience, 351
　and transformative adult learning, 113–14
adult ego-state, 667
adult learning styles, 387–88, 389
adult learning theories, 684–89
　journey theories, 688–1, 693
　phase theories, 686–7
　stage theories, 687–88
　see also learning

advanced coaching approaches, 459
adventure programming, 266
Africa Board for Coaching, Consulting and Coaching Psychology (ABCCC), 702
age-related discourses, 686–7
agency, 392
　collective, 108, 110
　personal, 107–8, 116
　proxy, 108
agreement–certainty matrix, 228, *228*
AL *see* action learning (AL)
Al-Nasser, A., 463
Aldao, A., 276
Alegre, A., 557
Alexander, G., 549
Allen, K., 544
alpha males, 247, 279–0
Alvesson, M., 23, 571
Amabile, T., 684
American Association for Physician Leadership, 524
American Association of Physician Executives, 524
American Nurses Association, 528
American Psychological Association (APA), 649, 703
American Society for Training and Development, 730
amygdala, 401
Analytic-Network coaching process (A-NcP), 182
Anderson, D. L., 579
Anderson, Merrill C., 165, 170–1, 579
Anderson, N. R., 491–2
Anderson, Sharon, 698
Anderson, T., 301
andragogy, 101–2, 178–1, **178**, 387–88, 389, 689, 693
Andrews, A., **721**, 723
Androgogical Practices Inventory, 388
Angell, L. C., 241, 243
Anna, A., 146, 148
anthropological framework, 389–0, 391–4
anti-realism, **26**
anxious attachment style, 551, 553
Anzaldua, G., 294
APECS *see* Association for Professional Executive Coaching and Supervision (APECS)
Appreciative Inquiry, **371**, 372, 374, 509
Argyris, Chris, 105, 163
Aristotle, 293, 334, 335, 338, 685, 699, 700
Arnaud, G., 49, 683
ART *see* Attention Restoration Theory (ART)
Arthur, M. B., 424, 425

ascription cultures, 442
Ashforth, B. E., 279, **424**
Ashkanasy, N. M., 281
Ashridge Critical-Moment Study Group, **601**, 602
Ashworth, P., 28
Askeland, M. K., 88, 89
Askew, S., 182
assessment and accreditation, 31, 535, 658, 689–3
asset approaches to resilience, 348–0
assimilation stage, 447
Association for Coaching (AC), 649, 664, 672, 673, 702, 703, **703**, 704, 731
Association for Professional Executive Coaching and Supervision (APECS), 664, 702, 704
Association for Talent Development (ATD), 470–1, 473
asynchronous communication, 717, 719
Atkins, P. W. B., 113–14, 144, 147, 151
attachment theory, 295–6, 551
attention deficit hyperactivity disorder (ADHD), 514
Attention Restoration Theory (ART), 266–7
attentional control, and resilience, 349
Atwater, L. E., 315, 578
Austin, J. T., 219
Australian Institute for Teaching and School Leadership (AITSL), 515
Australian Psychological Society (APS), 703
Authier, J., 390
authoritative parenting, 557
Automatic Negative Thoughts (ANTs), 513
automaticity versus control networks, **616**, 618
Autonomist Leadership, 54
autonomous regulation, 222–3
autonomy
    of coaches, 665
    human need of, 392
    and learning, 109, 110
    and well-being, **347**, 353
autonomy-community paradox, 353
Avatar worlds, 724
avoidant attachment style, 551, 554
Azizollah, H., 446, 447

Bachkirova, Tatiana, 1–19, 23–38, 44, 46, 73, 75, 123, **125**, 128, 132, **133**, 134, 143, 147, 185, 212, 223, 273–4, 279, 280, 321, **321**, 322, 386, 405, 470, 473, 545, 547, 548, 553, 559, 575, 582, **601**, 602, 650–1
Badrinarayanan, V., 71
Bakan, D., 299
Baker, A. C., 105, *105*, 116, 117
Bamford, A., 512, 546, 556
Banas, J., 348
Bandler, R., 261, 263
Bandura, A., 107–8, 109, 110, 116, 549
Bao, K. J., 551
Bar-On, R., 281
Barak, M. E., 252
Barbuto, J. E., **128**

Barnett, R., 691, 692
Baron, H., 446, 447
Baron, L., 75, **199**, 209, 211, 478, **598**, **599**, 600
Barr, Margaret, 495, 505–16
Bartholomew, K., 551
Bartone, P. T., **128**
Bass, B. M., 151–2
Bauman, Z., 683, 684
Baumeister, R. F., 545
Bäuml, J., 390
Beattie, Rona S., 470–81
Beck, Aaron, 48
Beck, U., 332
Beckhard, Richard, 167
Behery, M., 463
behaviour observation studies, 582
behavioural diversity, 240
behaviourism, **319**
behaviourist discourses, 682
Bell, E., 691
Bem, S., 28
Bench, M., 421
Bennett, John L., 100–17, 481, 610
Bennett, Milton, 443–4, **444**, 445, 456, 460
Bentham, Jeremy, 699, 700
Beradi, F., 46, 49
Berenson, B. G., 651
Berger, J. G., 116, 128, 131, **131**, 132
Berger, P. L, 294
Berglas, S., 89
Berk, L., 556
Bernard, D., 353
Bernard, J. M., 671
Berne, E., 667
Bernstein, Basil, 737
Berry, R. M., 720, **721**, 722
Berto, R., 267
Bettleheim, B., 44
Bettridge, N., 181
Beyond Emancipation programme, 183
Beyond Expectations App, **717**
Bhabha, H., 300
Big Five model of personality, 633, 638, 640
Bilhuber Galli, E., 150
bioenergetics, 263
biological discourses, 682
Biswas-Diener, R., 364–5, 371, 372, 373
Black, C., 280
Blackie, L. E., 405
Blackman, A., 576, 580
Blackmore, J., 279
Blakey, I., 314
Blanc-Sahnoun, P., 302–3
blended coaching, 714, 715
Bligh, M. C., 73
Block, J., 349
Bluckert, P., 264
Bodenheimer, T., 523, 525

body–mind types, 263
Bolden, R., 691
Bolstad, R., 546, 555
Bolton, S., 283
Bonanno, G. A., 348, 402–3, 404
Bond, C., 475, 476
Bond, T., 699
bonds, in coaching relationship, 197–2
Boniwell, I., **601**
Bono, J. E., 283, 477–78, 636
Boone, M. E., 458, 465
Bordin, E. S., 210–11
Bossons, P., 284, 447
Bouchard, S., 526
Boud, D., 178
boundaryless careers theory, 424–5
Bourdieu, Pierre, 737
Bowen, D. E., 570, 571
Bowlby, J., 551
Bowles, S., 145, 147, 148–9
Box, G. E. P., 35
Boyatzis, R. E., 31, **36**, 74, 140, 143, 223–4, 277, 620–1, **620**
Boyce, L. A., 75, 197, 198, **199**, 203, 206, 590, 596, **597**
Bozer, G., 207, 208, **597**
BPS *see* British Psychological Society (BPS)
Braakmann, D., 594
Bracken, D. W., 637, **637**
brain
    automaticity versus control networks, **616**, 618
    default mode network (DMN), 617–18
    imaging techniques, 612–13, 622
    neuroplasticity, 615–16, **616**
    organisation of, 611–12, *612*
    reactions to trauma, 401
    social reward and threat detection, **616**, 617
    task positive network (TPN), 617–18
    see also neuroscience
Breeth App, **717**
Brennan, D., 698, 700, 703, 709
Brett, J. F., 315
Brewerton, P., 373
bricolage, 144
Bridges, W., 423, **424**
Briggs, M., 514
Bright, J. E. H., 224
Brim, J. B., 225
British Association for Counselling and Psychotherapy (BACP), 703
British Medical Association, 734
British Psychological Society (BPS), 639, 703, 734
broaden and build theory, 352, 368
Brock, V., 455
Brockbank, A., 180, 303
Brown, Andrew D., 167
Brown, Donald R., 165
Brown, Paul, 618

Brown, S. W., 150, 496
Browne, P. E., 551, 555
Brummel, B. J., 75, **599**, 600
Brundrett, M., 691
Bruner, J., 293, 294, 297–298, 685
Buckingham, M., 364
Buckle, T., **601**
Buckley, A., 88
Buddhism, 455
Buddhist meditation, 381, 382–3
buffering, 372
Bugenhagen, M. J., **128**
Buhler, C., 686
Burbules, N., 32
Burch, G. S. J., 146
Burke, K., 293
Burnes, B., 30
burnout and exhaustion, 89, 91, 333, 525
Buschor, C., 367
Bush, M. W., 481, 610
Butcher, J., 303
Butwell, J., 671
Byng-Hall, J., 558
Bynum, C. W., 303

Caffarella, R. S., 100
CAI Coaching World platform, **716**
Campbell, J., 293, 294, 506
Campbell, M. A., 87, 88
Campone, Francine, 100–17, 406
CAP *see* Coaching and Philanthropy project (CAP)
capabilities
    in coach training and education, 31, 650–1
    development of ethical, 704–6
    organisational, 164–6
capitalisation, 352–3
Capra, Fritjof, 455
Caramazza, A., 263, 265
career capital framework, 425, 464
career transitions, 419–29
    boundaryless careers theory, 424–5
    career coaching, 374, 420–1, 426–29
    change and transition theories, 423–4, **424**, 428–1
    changing career models, 421–2
    intelligent careers theory, 425, 464
    kaleidoscope careers theory, 425
    protean careers model, 425, 429
    relational approaches, 426–7, 429
    strengths-based coaching, 374, 427
    typologies and models of, 423
Carey, W., 144–6, 147, 148, 149, 426
Carkhuff, R. R., 651
Carmody, J., 384
Carnell, E., 182
Carney, D. R., 263
Carol, J., 399
Carr, C., 497
Carroll, M., 662, 663, 674, *675*, 676, 705

Carter, A., 576, 580
Carter, B., 546
Cartwright, S., 280
Carver, C. S., 549, 550
case conceptualisation, 655–6
case study research, and theory development, **34**
Casey, C., 49
Caspi, J., 183
categorical imperative, 336
Cavanagh, Michael, **36**, 69, 77, 93, 196, 350, 383, 385–6, 486–502, 551, 651, 654, 697
CCRW (Creative, Connected, Resourceful and Whole) approach, 183
CDF *see* Constructive Developmental Framework (CDF)
CDST *see* constructivist self-development theory (CDST)
Center for Creative Leadership, 143
Center for Credentialing and Education (CCE), 702
Centre for the Use of Research and Evidence in Education (CUREE), 511
cerebral cortex, 611–12, *612*
CFE *see* Coaching For Emancipation (CFE) framework
Chagnon, J., 665
change
    locus of change in coaching, 487–91, *488*, *489*, *490*
    narrative theory and process of, 299–2, *300*
    organisational, 166–7
    see also career transitions; coaching for social change
chaos theory, 425
Chappell, C., 178
character strengths *see* strengths
Charbonneau, M. A., 720–1, **721**, 722
Charcot, Jean Martin, 400
Charon, R., 299
Chartered Institute of Personnel and Development, 730
Chartered Institute of Personnel and Development (CIPD), 471, 474, 475
Chatwani, N., 461
Checkland, P., 460
child ego-state, 667
children
    coaching in education, 512–14
    individuation, 557–58
    maternal emotion coaching (MEC), 406–7, 558
    peer coaching, 514
    see also parents
Childs, R., 673
Chinn, A. T., 73
Cho, Y., 480
Chong, C. W., 197, 198, **202**, 203, 206–7, 209, 462, **598**
Christian, J., 238, 241, 252
chronic diseases, 526–7, 535
chronic dysfunction, after traumatic events, 402–3, **403**
CIAO *see* Coaching Inside and Out (CIAO) programme
Cilliers, F., 239, 249, **601**, 603
Cilliers, P., 30, 37

CIPD *see* Chartered Institute of Personnel and Development (CIPD)
Clandinin, D. J., 300–1
Clarke, J., 349
Clarkson, P., 211, 322
clients
    coaching and psychotherapy, 87–91
    see also coaching relationship
Clifton, D. O., 364
clinical recovery, 403, **403**
Clinton, Bill, 53
Clutterbuck, David Ashley, 218–32, 473, 492, 671
Co-Leadership Model, 250
co-parenting stance, 557
Coach–Athlete Relationship Questionnaire (CART-Q), 208–9
coach behaviour, and coaching outcomes, 582
coach development
    and adult developmental theories, 134–5
    see also coach training and education
coach matching, and gender, 248
Coach Simple platform, **716**
coach training and education, 647–58, 732, 739–0
    assessment and accreditation, 31, 535, 658, 689–3
    capability in, 31, 650–1
    coaching for social change, 186–3
    competence in, 31, 648–1, 654, 691
    decision sciences, 655
    developmental theories, 651, 664–5
    evidence-based coaching, 78, 654–5
    excellence theories, 651–2
    formulation and case conceptualisation, 655–6
    health and wellness coaching, 535
    inclusivity, 692–3
    and journey theory, 688–1, 693
    in mental health issues, 94–6
    personal models of practice, 652–6
    and phase theory, 687
    practice theories, 652–3, 657
    prescribed standards, 691
    professional learning, 653–4, 655
    scientist-practitioner model, 654, 656–7
    and stage theory, 688
    see also coaching supervision
CoachAccountable platform, **716**
CoachCampus platform, **716**, 717–18
coaching
    defining, 5–7, 257, 420–1
    as discipline, 730, 736–41, *741*
    as industry, trade or craft, 729, 730–2, *741*
    as profession, 729–0, 732–6, *741*
    situating, 2–4
Coaching and Philanthropy project (CAP), 182–3
Coaching App, **717**
coaching body politic, 57–8, *57*
coaching critical success factors, **601**, 603
Coaching Explorer, 583

Coaching For Emancipation (CFE) framework, 184
coaching for social change, 176–88
    contexts and models, 181–4
    critical analysis of, 179–1
    implications of, 184–87
    individual development and social change, 177–2
    locating, 178–1, **178**
    training programmes, 186–3
coaching in education, 505–16
    for educational leadership, 507–9
    evidence-based coaching, 513, 514–15
    global framework for, 506–7, **507**, *507*, 515
    for parents and wider school community, 511–12
    for professional practice, 509–11
    strengths-based, 374
    for student success and wellbeing, 374, 512–14
Coaching Inside and Out (CIAO) programme, 183–4
coaching models and goals, 227–1, *228*
coaching process research, 589–606
    critical moments studies, **601**, 602
    critical perspectives, **601**, 603
    critical success factors, **601**, 603
    defining, 590
    descriptive studies, 591, 592, 600–3, **601**
    hypothesis testing studies, 591, 592, 596–600, **597–599**
    lessons from psychotherapy process research, 591–5
    phenomenological investigations, **601**, 603
    psychodynamic perspectives, **601**, 603
    Q methodology, **601**, 602
    speech acts studies, 601–2, **601**
    theory building studies, 591–2, 604
coaching psychology, 682–3, 703
Coaching Psychology Unit, University of Sydney, 63
coaching relationship, 74–5, 195–213
    bonds and rapport, 197–2
    career coaching, 426–7
    coach and coachee attributes and compatibility, 74–5, 206–7
    coaching for social change, 185
    and coaching outcomes, 581–2
    commitment and collaboration, 203–6
    empirical studies, **199–2, 204–5**
    employee coaching, 209–10, 308
    executive coaching, 209
    interpersonal difficulties, 92, 93
    and multiple stakeholders, 161–2
    physicality of, 263–5
    and resilience, 353
    sports coaching, 208–9
    stages in, 196–3
    transference–countertransference, 92, 93, 264, 265
    transparency, 198
    trust, 198, 203
    working alliance, 198, 210–12, 581
coaching ripple effect, 77, 165, 350, 357, 501

coaching supervision, 662–77
    cognitive-behavioural therapy, 668
    and development of ethical capabilities, 705
    developmental models, 664–5
    discrimination model, 671–2
    Gestalt, 665–6, *666*
    group supervision, 672–3
    growth of, 673
    in mental illness recovery coaching, 91, 94–6
    one-to-one supervision, 672
    peer supervision, 672
    person-centred, 666–7
    psychotherapeutic models, 665–68
    seven-eyed model, 96, 264, 666, 669–1, *669*
    social role models, 668–2
    systemic model of, 674–6, *675*
    transactional analysis, 667–68, *668*
CoachingCloud platform, **716**
CoachingSpaces platform, **716**, 718
CoachMaster tool, **716**
Cobb, R. J., 559
Cockerill, I. M., **204**
codes of conduct, 696
codes of ethics, 449, 673, 696, 697, 700, 702–4, **703**, 735
COF *see* Cultural Orientations Framework (COF)
cognitive-behavioural coaching, 47, 48, 49, 220, 351–2, 513, 668
cognitive-developmental theories, 73, 122, 351
    feedback, **319**, 320–1, **321**
    relationship coaching, 547–48
cognitive discourses, 682
cognitive dissonance, 710
cognitive diversity, 241, 242
Cognitive Hardiness Scale, 348
Cohen, T., 552
Colby, A., 123
Cole, S. W., 617
collaboration, in coaching relationship, 203–6
collaborative learning, 110–12, **115**
Collaborative Recovery Model (CRM), 92–3, 353, 374, 407–9, **408**
Collard, P., 385
collective action, 244–5, *244*
collective agency, 108, 110
collective coaching influences, *57*, 58
collectivism, 441, 442, 461, 462, 464
Collins, D. B., 144
Collins, Ron, 729–41
Colorado Coalition of Coaches, 702
Colorado Mental Health Board, 702
commitment, in coaching relationship, 203–6
common factors, 210, 593, 594
common good approach to ethics, 701
communications, and relationships, 555–6
communitarianism, 442
compatibility, in coaching relationship, 74–5, 206–7

competence
    in coach training and education, 31, 648–1, 654, 691
    human need of, 392
    interculturally-sensitive coaching, 446–7
    and learning, 109
    training physicians in coaching competencies, 536–7
    and well-being, 353
complex adaptive systems (CAS) theory, 30, 350, 458–1
complex systems, goals in, 224, **224**, 228–1, *228*
complexity theories, 29–31, **30**, **36**, 37
    and cross-cultural coaching, 454, 458–0, 465
conflict and diversity, 241, 242–5, *244*
Congram, S., 665, 666
connectionism, **36**
Connelly, F. M., 300–1
conscientiousness, and coaching outcomes, 634, 635, 638
Conscious Dating, 545
consciousness, and emotions, 275
consequentialism, 336
conservation of resources model, 350
consolidation stage, 447
constellation method, 266
constraint model of coaching, 553
Constructive Developmental Framework (CDF), **127**
constructive-developmental theory, 113–14, 121, 122–6, **124–5**
constructivism
    feedback, **319**, 320, **320**
    see also social constructionism
constructivist self-development theory (CDST), 411
consulting approach, 145
content education, health and wellness coaching, 533–4
contextual imperative, 708
contextual model of psychotherapy, 594
contextual relativism, 688, 689
contextualism, **26**, **36**
contracting, 668
control theory, 310–11, 318, **319**
controlled regulation, 222
Cook, B., 667, 670–1
Cook-Greuter, S. R., 123, **125**, **127**, 134, 321, 548
Cooper, C., 349
Corazon, S., 266
Corey, G., 250
Corey, M. S., 250
Corporate Leadership Council, 366, 373
Corrie, S., 301–2, 653, 654, 655, 656, 657
Cotter, S., 263
Coultas, C. W., 249–0, 457
counseling approach, 145–6
countertransference, 92, 264, 265, 670, 671
COUPLE model, 555
Coutu, D., 227, 349
Cowell, J., 478
Cox, Elaine, **36**, 73, 100, 101, 104, 111, 128, 144, 181, 197, 207, 257, 272–86, 302, 317, 407, 544, 545,

547, 548, 550, 551, 552–3, 554, 555, 556, 557, 559, 604, 698, 708, 738, 740
CQ *see* Cultural Intelligence (CQ)
craft, coaching as, 729, 730–2, *741*
Crant, J. M., 389
Creasy, J., 508
Cremona, K., 264, 266, 285
critical enquiry, 705
critical moments studies, **601**, 602
critical pedagogical tradition, 178–1, **178**
critical postmodernism, 36, **36**
critical reflection, 181
critical reflective learning theory, 110–11, 114–15
critical reflexivity, 705
critical success factors, **601**, 603
critical theory, **26**, 28, **36**, 182
critical thinking skills, 187
CRM *see* Collaborative Recovery Model (CRM)
cross-cultural coaching, 453–66
    and complexity theory, 454, 458–0, 465
    context, 454–5
    empirical studies, 460–5
    instruments, models and approaches, 455–58
    and systems thinking, 454, 457, 458, 460, 465
    see also interculturally-sensitive coaching
Crowe, Trevor, 85–97
Cullen, E., 691
cultural bias in coaching, 180
cultural diversity, 249–0
Cultural Intelligence (CQ), 446, 457, 458, 461, 463, 465
Cultural Orientations Framework (COF), 636–7
cultural proficiency, 444, **445**
cultural sensitivity, 443–4, **444**, 456
culture
    defining, 439–1, 454–5
    dimensions of, 441–3
    organisational, 162–4, 580–1
    see also cross-cultural coaching; interculturally-sensitive coaching
Cummings, T. G., 472
Cunliffe, A. N., 681
Current Way of Being (CWOB), 265
Curry, C. D., 456
cybernetic systems, 219, 220
Cynefin Framework, 458, 459
Czarniawska, B., 292

Dagley, G. R., 73
Dalakoura, A., 141
Daloz, L. A., 686
Dalto, C. A., 33
Damasio, A. R., 258, 259, 275
Danzig, A., 303
David, S., 229
Davies, B., 301
Davila, J., 559
Davis, P. A., 277
Davis, S. L., 595

Davis, T. S., 385
Davison, M., 88–1
Day, A., **601**, 602, 603
Day, D. V., 140, 141, 150–1, 152–3, 423
Day, I., 314
de Beauvoir, Simone, 445
de Haan, Erik, 75, 195–213, 373, 580, 581–2, 589, **597**, 600, **601**, 602, 604, 663
de Jager, W., 183
de Jong, Allard, 703
De Jong, H., 28
De Meuse, K. P., 572, 577
Deane, F. P., 90
Deci, E. L., 109, 223, 323, **323**, 353, 392, 553
decision sciences, 655
deconstruction, **26**
Deep Democracy Model, 251
deep-level diversity, 241
default mode network (DMN), 617–18
DeFillippi, R. J., 425
deliberate judgement, 334
DELTA model, 250–1
Delworth, U., 665
demand and supply conceptualisation, 2
Dembkowski, S., 550
demographic diversity, 240, 241–2
DeNisi, A., 313, 314
Denzin, N., 144
deontological ethics, 336, 699
Depraz, N., 294
DeRue, D. S., 139–40, 141, 150, 151
Descartes, R., 257–58
descriptive studies, 591, 592, 600–3, **601**
developmental approaches
    to coach training and education, 651
    to coaching supervision, 664–5
    to relationship coaching, 547–48
    to resilience, 349, 351
developmental coaching, 143, 147
    group and team coaching, *490*, 491, 497–498, 499
developmental discourses, 682
Developmental Pipeline, 457
developmental relationships, 195–196
    see also coaching relationship
developmental structuralism, **36**
Dewey, J., 28, 387
Dias, G. P., 610, 616, 619
Dickson, J., 446
Dickson, M. W., 241
DID *see* dissociative identity disorder (DID)
diffuse cultures, 442
DiGrande, L., 402
Dirkx, J. M., 276
discipline, coaching as, 730, 736–41, *741*
discounting, 668
discourse ethics, 699
discourses of coaching, 42–59, *43*, 680–93
    episteme (knowledge that), 685, 686, 687, 688

humanistic, 682, 684, 690–1, 692–3
journey theory, 688–1, 693
managerial, **45**, 50–3, *57*, 680, 683–4
meta-theory of coaching, 56–8, *57*
Network, **45**, 53–5, 56, *57*
phase theory, 686–7
phronesis (knowledge why), 685, 686, 688, 689, 691, 692
Psy Expert, **45**, 47–50, *57*, 682–3
rational pragmatic, 683, 685, 690, 691, 692
Soul Guide, 44–6, **45**, 47, *57*
stage theory, 687–88
techne (knowledge how), 685, 686, 687, 688, 691, 692
discrimination supervision model, 671–2
discriminatory language, 449
disorienting dilemma concept, 110, 114
displacement, 277
dissociative identity disorder (DID), 406
distance coaching, 714, 715, 720–1, **721**, 723
distributed leadership, 52, 54
diversity, 238–53
    business case for, 239, 241–5, *242*, *244*
    cognitive, 241, 242
    and conflict, 241, 242–5, *244*
    cultural, 249–0
    definitions and dimensions, 239–0
    executive coaching, 246–49
    gender, 245–48, 249, 252
    inclusion vs exclusion, 240
    race and ethnicity, 248–1
    techniques for working with, 250–1
diversity legislation, 239
Divine, L., 259–0
Dixey, A., 475, 476
DMN *see* default mode network (DMN)
dominance, in coaching relationship, 203, 207
Donaldson-Feilder, E., 547
Donaldson, S. I., 365–6
Doran, G. T., 220
Doran, J., 348
double-loop learning, 105
Douglas, C. A., 195
Downey, M., 314
Drago-Severson, E., 133
Drake, David, 1–19, **36**, 159–71, 229, 291–304, 365, 372, 373, 428, 460, 545, 551, 650, 655–6, 674, 676, 710
dramatism, 293
Draper, N. R., 35
Drath, W., 133
Dreyfus, H., 651
Dreyfus, S. E., 651
Driver, M., 317
Dryden, W., 275
Du Toit, A., 176, 182
dualism, 257–58
Duberley, J., 683
Dubin, R., **34**

Dubin's theory building method, **34**
Dublin Declaration, 658, 664
Duffy, M., 704, 706
Dulebohn, J. H., 614–15
duty, 336
Dweck, C., 371, 428
Dyer, T. J., 181–2
dyslexia, 631

Eastern philosophies, 455, 461, 462
Ecclestone, K., 691
Eckert, Mark A., 610–23
Eco-leadership, 52, 53–4
economic benefits, 579–0
education
    critical approaches, 179
    pedagogical traditions, 178–1, **178**
    see also coach training and education; coaching in education; learning
EEG *see* electroencephalography (EEG)
Egan, T., 472, 477, 480
ego-development theories, 547
ego-resilience scale, 349
ego-states, 667
EI *see* emotional intelligence (EI)
Eigel, K. M., **128**
Eisenberger, N. I., 617
Eldridge, F., 550
electroencephalography (EEG), 612, 613
Ellam-Dyson, V., 494
Ellinger, Andrea D., 161, 470–81
Elliot, A. J., 229
Elliott, R., 592, 593, 604
Ellis, Albert, 130, 275, 550
Ely, K., 143, 148, 150, 151, 574, 580
emancipatory knowledge, 100
embodied coaching, 261
embodied cognition, 258, 263
embodied countertransference, 264, 265
embodied phenomenology, 259
embodiment *see* physicality
EMCC *see* European Mentoring and Coaching Council (EMCC)
Emmons, R. A., 220
emotion coaching, 406–7, 558
emotional attractors, 277, 621, 622
emotional climate inventory, 285–6, **285**
emotional cultures, 442
emotional intelligence (EI), 280–1, 313, 635
emotional labour, 283–4
emotions, 272–86
    in adolescence, 558
    in coaching process, 273–4, 284–5
    cognitive theories, 275–6
    and countertransference, 264
    emotional climate inventory, 285–6, **285**
    and empathy, 282–3
    enhancement of emotional capacities, 406–7

    evolutionary theories, 274–5
    and gender, 279–0
    and motivation, 277–78
    in organisations, 278–4
    and physicality, 262–3
    regulation of, 281–2
    and resilience, 352, 355
    social constructionist perspective, 276–7
    and transformational learning, 278
empathy, 282–3, 537
empirical evidence, 64–7, *64*, **65**, *66*
empiricism, **26**
employee coaching, coaching relationship, 206, 209–10
empowerment, 185–4, 187
enactment, 265–6
Engel, J., 2
Enlightenment, 257–58, 336
environmental mastery, and well-being, **347**
epigenetics, 31
episteme (knowledge that), 685, 686, 687, 688
epoché, 294
Ericsson, K. A., 651, 652
Eriksen, K., 131
Erikson, E. H., 547
Erlandson, E., 247, 279–0
ERPs *see* event-related potentials (ERPs)
ethical pluralism, 696–7
ethics, 335–7, 696–710
    of care, 687, 699
    case studies, 707–9
    in coach training and education, 689
    and coaching for social change, 185
    and coaching in mental illness recovery, 94
    codes of, 449, 673, 696, 697, 700, 702–4, **703**, 735
    Colorado Case, 702
    common good approach, 701
    deontological, 336, 699
    development of ethical capabilities, 704–6
    ethical decision-making framework, 706–7
    fairness approach, 700–1
    and goal setting, 226
    history of, 699–1
    and interculturally-sensitive coaching, 449
    lack of regulatory standards, 696–7, 701–2
    and learning, 685–6
    and managerial coaching, 50–1
    medical, 700
    and multiple stakeholders, 162
    narrative, 699
    and Network coaching, 55
    and neuroscience in coaching, 619
    of power and structure, 699
    professional, 699–0
    and Psy Expert coaching, 49
    rights approach, 700
    utilitarianism, 336, 699, 700
    virtue ethics, 699, 701
ethnicity and race, 248–1

ethnocentricism, 444, 445, 449
ethnointegrative approaches, 444, 445
ethnorelative approach, 444, 445
eudaimonia, 335, 336, 338
European Federation of Psychologists' Associations, 650
European Mentoring and Coaching Council (EMCC), 183, 649, 664, 673, 688, 702, 703, **703**, 704, 731, 735, 736, 739
evaluation of coaching outcomes, 569–85
    antecedents, 580, **580**
    challenges, 569–1
    coach outcomes, **576**, 579
    coaching evaluation framework, 572–3, **573**
    coaching process, 581–3, **583**
    distal client outcomes, **576**, 578–1
    leadership development coaching, 150–2
    meta-analyses, 572
    methods and research designs, 571–2
    mixed methods studies, 575
    organisational context, 580–1
    organisational outcomes, **576**, 579–0
    proximal client outcomes, 575–78, **576**
    taxonomies of outcome criteria, 573–5, **574**
Evans, C., 429
event-related potentials (ERPs), 612
Evered, R. D., 474
evidence-based coaching, 48, 62–78
    coach training and education, 78, 654–5
    coaching research trends, 67–69, *68*
    defining, 63–7, *64*, **65**, *66*
    in education, 513, 514–15
    empirical evidence, 64–7, *64*, **65**, *66*
    in healthcare sector, 533, 534
    multiple-perspective model of coaching research (MPM), 69–7, *70*
    practitioner research, 64, **65**
    professional wisdom, 64, *64*
    strong and weak evidence, 65–7, *66*
evocative approach, 48
evolutionary discourses, 682
excellence theories, 651–2
exclusion vs inclusion, 240
executive coaching
    coaching for social change, 181–2
    coaching relationship, 209
    cross-cultural context, 454, 455, 461–2, 463–4
    expatriate coaching, 454, 463–4
    and gender, 89, 246–48, 249
    in healthcare sector, 523–5
    and human resource development, 476–78
    race and ethnicity, 248–1
    strengths perspective, 374
    value-oriented, 342
    see also leadership development coaching; organisation development
exhaustion and burnout, 89, 91, 333, 525
existential coaching, 339–0
existential-experiential coaching, 261, 264–5

expatriate coaching, 454, 463–4
experiential learning, 104–6, *105*, **115**, 117, 387, 390, 459, 689
expertise theories, 651–2
explicit knowledge, 100
exploration stage, 447
external coaches
    and human resource development, 476–78
    leadership development coaching, 148–9
    student coaching, 513
    and supervision, 673
external social influences on coaching, *57*, 58
extraversion
    and coaching outcomes, 634, 635
    and resilience, 349
eye movements, 263
Eyre, E., 181

Fanon, F., 179
Farnham, J., 266
fearful attachment style, 551
feed forward, **317**, 318
feedback, 310–24
    360-degree/multi-rater assessments, 146, 313, 315, **315**, **316**, 637–38, **637**
    best practice guidelines, 639–0
    challenges to dominant discourse, 313–14
    cognitive-developmental theories, **319**, 320–1, **321**
    constructivism, **319**, 320, **320**
    defining, 310–11, *311*, *312*
    evaluative versus developmental, 311–12
    externally generated, *312*, 314–17, **315**, **316**
    extrinsic versus intrinsic motivation, 323, **323**
    feed forward, **317**, 318
    formative assessment, 689
    Gestalt psychology, **319**, 322–3, **322**
    immediacy, 316–17, **316**
    internally generated, *312*, 317–18, **317**
    leadership development coaching, 146
    mirroring and paraphrasing, 317, **317**
    objectivism, 318–0, **319**, **320**
    primary-aged children, 514
    psychometrics/personality assessments, 314, 315–16, **315**, **316**
    self-consistency versus self-enhancement theories, **319**, 321–2
    self-feedback, **317**, 318
feedback control systems, 219
feedback intervention theory, **319**
Feedforward, 352
feedforward interview (FFI), 636
Feldman, D. C., 148, 477
Felton, L., **205**
Feltovich, P. J., 652
feminine advantage perspective, 247
feminine cultures, 441–2
feminism, 245, 682
    ethics of care, 687, 699

feminist therapy, 179
Fenwick, T., 653, 654
Ferch, S. R., 353
Festinger, L., 710
Feyerabend, P., 33
field theory, 665–6
Fielden, S. L., 151
Fillery-Travis, Annette, 420, 473, 729–41
Fineman, S., 273, 274, 276, 278, 279, 280–1
Fitzgerald, C., 131, **131**
Flaherty, J., 73, 549
Flexible Route to Headship (FRH) programme, Scotland, 508
flourishing approach, 336
Flyvbjerg, B., 331, 685
fMRI *see* functional magnetic resonance imaging (fMRI)
focusing, 261
force field model, **424**
Ford, M. E., 277
Forde, C., 508
forethought, 107–8
forgiveness therapy, 551–2
formative assessment, 689
formulation and case conceptualisation, 655–6
Foucault, Michel, 42, 46, 188, 297, 445
four-quadrant flourishing model, 90, 94
fractals, 488
Francis, Sophie, 363–75
Frank, Jerome D., 594
Frank, Julia, 594
Frankl, V. E., 402
Franklin, A., 577, 578
Franklin, J., 348, 577, 578
Frankovelgia, C. C., 141
Frazee, R. V., 721–2, **721**
Freas, A., 682
Fredrickson, B., 277
Freedman, D. H., 225
Freidson, E., 733
Freire, Paulo, 179, 188
Freud, Sigmund, 2, 44
Friestad, J. M., 388
Frisch, M. H., 473
functional magnetic resonance imaging (fMRI), 612–13, 622
Furedi, F., 49
fuzzy goals, 224, 228

Gable, R., 352–3
Gable, S., 352
Gale, J., 89
Gan, G. C., 197, 198, **202**, 203, 206–7, 209, 462, **598**
Ganegoda, D. B., 635
Gannon, Judie, 195–213
Gardiner, G. S., 335
Garman, A.N., 524
Garrison, D., 106–7, *108*, 117
Garvey Berger, J., 113–14, 144, 147, 151, 228–1, 458

Garvey, Bob, 35–6, **36**, 51, 680–93, 738
Gasiorowski, F., 88–1
Gatrell, C., 245
Gazelle, G., 522
GD *see* Global Dexterity (GD)
Geertz, C., 294
Geißler, Herald, 582, 601–2, **601**, 713–25, **721**
Gelo, O. C. G., 595
gender
    coach matching, 248
    coaching relationship, 208
    diversity, 245–48, 249, 252
    emotions, 279–0
    executive coaching, 89, 246–48, 249
    managerial coaching across cultures, 464
    mental health help-seeking, 89–0
Gendlin, E. T., 261
General Medical Council, UK, 734
General Teaching Council for Scotland, 515
genetic epistemology, 122
Gentry, W. A., 461
George, M., 283–4
Gergen, K. J., 294, 303, 333
Gergen, M. M., 303
Gessnitzer, S., **202**, 203, 206, **597**, 600, 601–2
Gestalt psychology, 264, 266
    coaching supervision model, 665–6, *666*
    feedback, **319**, 322–3, **322**
GFC model *see* goal-focused coaching (GFC) model
Ghods, N., **721**, 722
Gibson, S. K., 472
Giddens, A., 333
Gilley, Ann, 165
Gilligan, C., 296, 687, 699
Gioia, D. A., 33
Gjerde, S., 69
Glenn, C. G., 293
Global Coaches Network, 457
global coaching *see* cross-cultural coaching
Global Coaching and Mentoring Alliance (GCMA), 704
Global Coaching Center, 457
Global Coaching Convention, 658, 664
Global Code of Ethics (GCoE), 704
Global Convention of Coaching (GCC), 698
Global Dexterity (GD), 457–58
Global Mindset (GM), 457, 458, 461, 463, 465
globalisation, 332
goal abstraction, 220
goal attainment scaling (GAS) methods, 228
goal difficulty, 220, 549
goal-focused coaching (GFC) model, 228
goal proximity, 549
goal-setting theory, 221–2, 225–27, **319**
goal specificity, 549
goals, 49, 51–2, 72–3, 218–32
    of coaches, 73–4
    in coaching models, 227–1, *228*
    critiques of goal-focused theories, 224–27

cultural differences, 229
definitions and dimensions, 219–1, **221**
practical considerations, 229–1, **230**
and relationship coaching, 548–0
and strengths, 366
theoretical influences, 221–4, **224**
Godfrey, M. M., 496
Goff, P., 145, 147, 148, 508
Goldie, P., 277
Goleman, D., 280, 281, 313
Gollwitzer, P. M., 550
Goodyear, R. K., 671
Goregaokar, H., 238–1, 248
Gosling, J., 691
Gottman, J. M., 556
governmentality, 188
Govindji, R., 368
Graduate School Alliance for Executive Coaching (GSAEC), US, 740
Graf, E.-M., 582–3
Graham, F., 546
Grajfoner, D., 494
Grant, Anthony M., 35–6, **36**, 62–78, 86, 87, 93, 150, 171, 196, 197, **202**, 221, 228, 277, 318, 346, 348, 352, 370, 407, 410, 480, 496, 508, 549, 550, 551, 554, 569, 572, 575, 595, **598**, 615, 618, 619, 654, 673, 697
Gray, David E., 116, 238–1, 248, 648, 652, 662–77, 730, 733
Gray, Dee, 496
Green, L. S., 578
Green, S., 88
Greenberg, L. S., 275, 276, 277, 282, 546, 559
Greenson, R. R., 210
Gregory, J. B., **199**, **200**, **201**, 206, 210, 313, 318
Greif, Siegfried, 569–85, **601**, 603
Grencavage, L.M., 593
Griffiths, K., 87, 88
Grinder, J., 261, 263
Gross, J. J., 281, 283
grounded theory, **34**
group and team coaching, 486–502
adult developmental theories, 133–4
defining, 491–3
group versus team coaching, 487, 491–3, **492**
key considerations for practice, 499–1
lack of definitional clarity, 487
leadership development coaching, 149–50
locus of change in, 487–91, *488*, *489*, *490*
research into, 493–498
senior leadership teams, 497–498, 501
team leaders as coaches, 498
group supervision, 672–3
GROW model, 150, 227, 371–2
growth mindset, 353, 371, 428
Grugulis, I., 691
Guba, E., 27, 33
Guerney, B., 390
Guile, D., 655

Gunther, R., 545–6, 552, 553
Guru–Sishya (teacher–disciple) paradigm, 461
Guzzo, R. A., 241
Gyllensten, K., 196, 198, **199**, 206, **601**

Habermacher, A., 619
Hackman, J. R., 492, 496
Hagmann, J., 183
Haidet, P., 534
Haidt, J., 352
Hall, D. T., 148, 426
Hall, L. M., 261–2
Hall, Liz, 385, 409, 412
Hamill, P., 265
Hamlin, Robert G., 464, 470–81, 730
Hampden-Turner, C. H., 440, 442, 454–5, 456
Hampson, S., 633, 634
Han, B.-C., 333, 334
Hancock, B., **721**, 723
Hanna, David P., 168–9
Hantrais, L., 575
happiness, 335–6
happiness imperative, 49
hardiness, 356
Harding, C., 266
Hardingham, A., 196
Hardy, G., 591–2, 593, 596
harmonious passion, 368
Harré, R., 301
Harrington, S., 363, 364
Harris, L. S., **128**
Hart, E. W., 148
Hart, V., 86–7
Hartel, C., 280, 283
Harvey, Don, 165
Harvey, M., 279
Haslett, S. G., 546
Hassanin, R., 462
Hatch, M. J., 681
Hauser, L. L., 496–7
Haver, A., 282, 284–5
Havighurst, S. S., 558
Hawkins, Peter, 35–6, **36**, 96, 143, 163, 164, 264, 265, 492, 548, 663, 669–0, *669*, 672, 674, 698
Hay, J., 662, 667, 668
Hazan, C., 551
Health and Care Professions Council, UK, 649
health and wellness coaching, 527–37
healthcare sector, 521–37
content education, 533–4
leadership development coaching, 523–5
patient coaching, 526–37
patient vulnerability, 535–6
payment models, 536
provider workforce coaching, 525–6
senior leadership team coaching, 497–498
training of providers in coaching competencies, 536–7

hedonic adaptation, 551
Hefferon, K., 272
Heffes, E. M., 335
Heidegger, Martin, 259, 333–4
Heldman, D. R., 738
Hemmestad, L. B., 685
Henning, P., 351
Hentrich, S., 580
Heppner, M. J., 423
hermeneutics, **26**, 31, 37
Hernez-Broome, G., 590
Herring, C., 245
Hess, A. K., 664
heterogeneity of coaching, 570
Hetzner, S., 109
Hewson, D., 302
Hezlett, Sarah A., 164
Hill, A. P., 277
Hill, E. W., 552
Hirschhorn, L., 142, 147
Ho, V. T., 366, 367–68
Hobfoll, S., 350
Hochschild, A., 283
Hodson, R., 280
Hofsede, Geert, 440–2, 456, 462
Holloway, E. L., 672
Holton, E. F., 144, 581
Hooker, T., 511
Horowitz, L. M., 551
Houle, C. O., 107
Howard, A., 622
HRD *see* human resource development (HRD)
HRM *see* human resource management (HRM)
Hultgren, U., 496
human adaption to transition model, **424**
human potential movement, 3, 180
human resource development (HRD), 159, 167, 470–81, 730
  action learning coaching, 479–0
  defining, 471–2
  demarcating boundaries of, 472–3
  executive coaching, 476–78
  internal coaching, 473–4
  managerial coaching, 474–6
human resource management (HRM), 472
humanistic discourses, 682, 684, 690–1, 692–3
humanistic pedagogical tradition, 178–1, **178**
humanities, and narrative turn, 293–5
Hume, David, 699, 700
humility, 446
humorous comments, 449
Humphrey, R., 279
Hunt, E., 652
Hunt, James M., 164, 165, 475
Hunt, Joanne, 259, 264, 265
hypercomplex society, 332–3
hypothalamus, 401

hypothesis testing studies, 591, 592, 596–600, **597–599**
Hyvärinen, M., 292

Ianiro, P. M., 196, 197, **201**, 206, 207, 582, **597**, **598**
Ibarra, H., 231, 297, 427
ICF *see* International Coach Federation (ICF)
ICRF *see* International Coaching Research Forum (ICRF)
ICT *see* intentional change theory (ICT)
ideal self, **620**, 621
identity
  and career transitions, 423, 427–28
  dissociative identity disorder, 406
  and narratives, 294, 296–7
  self-identity theory, 243
Ilies, R., 635
imaging, brain, 612–13, 622
immediacy, 316–17, **316**
Immunity to Change framework, 132
implicit knowledge, 100
implicit theories of self, **319**
inattentional blindness, 225–6
inclusion vs exclusion, 240
Independent Ethical Review Board processes, 704
Indian philosophy, 461
individual development
  and leadership development coaching, 148
  and social change, 177–2
individual learning, 106–10, *108*
individual strengths assessments (ISAs), 369
individualisation, 177, 180
individualism, 441, 442, 461, 462, 464
individuation, 557–58, 686
industry, coaching as, 729, 730–2, *741*
informational diversity, 240
instructional coaching, in education, 510
intangibility of coaching, 570
integral coaching, 259–0, 264
Integrated Developmental Model (IDM), 651, 665
integrative development, 168–70
integrative medicine, 527
integrative practice and somatic awareness, 259–2, 264–5
Intelligent Career Card Sort, 425
intelligent careers theory, 425, 464
intentional change theory (ICT), 31, 129, 223–4, **319**, 320, 620–3, **620**
intentionality, 337, **337**
interaction process analyses, 582
interculturally-sensitive coaching, 439–51
  best practice, 447–49, **448**
  challenges, 449–0
  competencies, 446–7
  cultural proficiency, 444, **445**
  definitions of culture, 439–1
  dimensions of culture, 441–3
  equality and humility, 445–6

intercultural sensitivity, 443–4, **444**, 456
terminology, 451
see also cross-cultural coaching
internal coaches
    HRD professionals, 473–4
    leadership development coaching, 148–9
    student coaching, 513–14
    and supervision, 673
internal direction of cultures, 443
internalisation of oppression, 177–2
International Association of Coaching (IAC), 702
International Best Practice Competency Framework, 664
International Coach Federation (ICF), 57–8, 78, 470, 473–4, 478, 649, 664, 688, 696, 702, 703, **703**, 704, 713, 731, 735, 736
International Coaching Community (ICC), 702
International Coaching Research Forum (ICRF), 664, 676
International Nurse Coach Association, 526
International Society of Coaching Psychology, 649
International Test Commission (ITC), 639
intuitive judgement, 334
Iordanou, Ioanna, 696–710
iPlan Success app, **717**
ISAs (individual strengths assessments), 369
ISO standards, 736
Ives, Yossi, 47, 544–60, 698

Jack, A. I., 25, 31, 277, 622
Jackson, B., **204**
Jackson, D., 350
Jackson, P. Z., 549
Jackson, Peter, 128, 256–68, 547
James-Ward, C., 508
James, William, 28, 129, 296
Jarvis, P., 100, 106, 107, 110–11, 115, 685–6
Jarzabkowski, P., 240, 243–5, *244*
Jarzebowski, A., **597**
Jayawickreme, E., 405
Johari window, 313
Johns, C., 111, 114
Johnson, P., 683
Johnson, S. M., 553
Johnston, K., 228–1, 458
Johnston, R., 672
joint meaning making, 26, 31
jokes, 449
Jolly, R., 477
Jones, R. J., 72, 572, 574, 577, 578, **598**
Jones, R. L., 303
Joplin, L., 387
Jordan, Meg, 521–37
Joseph, D. L., 635
Joseph, Stephen, 399–14
JournalEngine tool, **716**
journey theory discourses, 688–1, 693
Jowett, S., 195, **201**, **204**, **205**, 208, 209
Joyce, B., 509, 511

Judge, T. A., 635, 636
Judge, W. Q., 478
Jung, Carl, 129, 298, 455, 686

Kabat-Zinn, Jon, 354, 381, 382, 383, 384–5, 392
kaleidoscope careers theory, 425
Kanatouri, Stella, 713–25, **721**
Kant, Immanuel, 278–1, 336, 699, 700
Kaplan, S., 266–7
Karoly, P., 219
Kasozi, A., 373
Katzenbach, J. R., 492
Kauffeld, S., **202**, 203, 206, **597**, 600, 601–2
Kauffman, C., 5, 6, 212, 227
Kayes, D. C., 226
Keep, J. A., 284
Kegan, R., 112–13, 116, 122, 123, **124**, 127, 128, **128**, 129, 130, 132, 223, 296, 428, 459, 547–48, 688
Kemp, Travis J., 73, 266, 381–94, 446, 595, 604
Kennedy, D. L., 260, 265
Kerka, S., 388
Ketcham, K., 555
Kets de Vries, M. F. R., 149, 386
Key Performance Indicators (KPIs), 579, 580
Keyes, C. L., 90, 94
Kiken, L. G., 384
Kilburg, Richard R., 48, 147, 161, 227
Kim, Sewon, 161, 473
King, E. B., 239
King, P. M., 122, **127**
Kirkeby, O. F., 334, 337, 339
Kirkpatrick, D. L., 144, 573, 574
Kissack, H. C., 474
Kitchener, K. S., 122, **127**
Klein, J.T., 737
Kluger, A. N., 313, 314
Knight, J., 446, 510, 511
knowing-how, 425, 464
    see also techne (knowledge how)
knowing-whom, 425, 464
knowing-why, 425, 464
    see also phronesis (knowledge why)
knowledge, 23–38
    creating knowledge base of coaching, 32–5, **34**
    episteme (knowledge that), 685, 686, 687, 688
    explicit, implicit and emancipatory, 100
    modernism and postmodernism, 25–7, **26**, **27**, 28, 29–30, 31, 32–3, 37, **37**
    multidisciplinary context, 29–32, *29*, *30*
    phronesis (knowledge why), 334, 685, 686, 688, 689, 691, 692, 732
    pragmatism, 28, 31, **36**
    techne (knowledge how), 685, 686, 687, 688, 691, 692
    using, 35–7, **36**, **37**
Knowles, M. S., 101–2, 106, 121–2, 129, 386, 387–88, 689, 693

Kohlberg, L., 122, 123, **124**
Kolb, D. A., 105–6, *105*, 117, 386, 387
Kolb, D.A., 689
Kombarakaran, F., 143
Kong, D. T., 366, 367–68
Korotov, Konstantin, 139–53
Kotte, S., 572
Kouzes, J. M., 129
Kraiger, K., 573–4, **574**
Kraimer, M. L., 389
Kralj, M. M., 497
Kremen, A. M., 349
Krishnan, A., 737
Kristal, Z., 181
Kristiansen, E., **205**
Kroger, R.O., 681
Kuhnert, K. W., **128**
Kurtz, E., 555
Kurz, R., 637

Lace, N., 462–3
Ladegard, G., 69
Ladyshewsky, R., 314
Lafrenière, M. A. K., **205**
Lahey, L., 127, **127**, 132
Lai, Y., **599**
Lam, P., 462
Lambert, M. J., 593
Lane, David A., **36**, 301–2, 473, 647–58
Langdridge, D., 342
Langer, Ellen, 383–4
Lankau, M. J., 148, 478
Lapsley, D., 557
Larrick, R. P., 226
Laske, O. E., 122, **127**, 134
Lasley, M., 186–3
Latham, G. P., 221–2, 224, 549, 635
Launder, A.G., 392
LaVoi, N. M., **204**
Law, H., 447, 456, 703
Lawrence, Paul, 121–36
Lawton Smith, Carmelina, 31, 346–58, 650–1
Layder, D., 681
LDP *see* Leadership Development Profile (LDP)
Leach, C. J. C., 512
leadership development coaching, 139–53
    coachees, 147–8
    coaches, 148–9
    defining, 142–4
    educational leadership, 507–9
    evaluation, 150–2
    group, 149–50
    in healthcare sector, 523–5
    leader and leadership development, 139–42
    models and perspectives, 144
    senior leadership team coaching, 497–498, 501
    sessions, 144–7
Leadership Development Profile (LDP), **127**

Leadership Diploma of Education, Denmark, 507
Learn Forward, USA, 515
learning, 100–17, 684–89
    action, 106, 111–12, 479–0, 672–3
    andragogy, 101–2, 178–1, **178**, 387–88, 389, 689, 693
    anthropological framework, 389–0, 391–4
    coaching and mindfulness, 386–91
    collaborative, 110–12, **115**
    common elements in adult learning theories, 115–17, **115**
    constructive-developmental theory, 113–14
    experiential, 104–6, *105*, **115**, 117, 387, 390, 459, 689
    individual, 106–10, *108*
    integrative approach, 117, *118*
    pedagogical traditions, 178–1, **178**
    positive psychoeducation, 390–1
    problem-based, 106
    reflective, 110–11, 114–15
    and self-determination, 109–10
    self-directed, 106–7, **108**, 388
    and self-efficacy, 107–9, 116
    social cognitive theory, 109, 110, 116, 533
    transformative, 112–15, **115**, 116–17, 278, 548
learning cycle, 105–6, *105*, 109
learning goals, 224, 226
Learning Transfer System Inventory (LTSI), 581
Leary, M. R., 545
Lee, G., 284
Lee, M., 471
Lemak, C. H., 524
Leone, C., 555
Lerner, D., 88
Lerner, Richard M., 162, 177
Lester, S., 691
Leszcz, M., 133
Levine, M., 383
Levinson, D. J., 547, 686
Levy, P. E., **199**, **200**, **201**, 206, 210
Lewin, Kurt, 168, **424**, 665–6
Lewis-Duarte, M., 73
Lewis, P., 246
liberation psychology, 179
Liebnau, D., 225
Life Journey Enhancement Tools (LifeJET), 93, 408
life satisfaction, and strengths, 365–6
life stage theories of development, 547
Lifecoachhub platform, **716**
lifelong learning, 107
lifestyle medicine, 527, 535
Light, R., 462
Lincoln, Y., 27, 33, 144
Lindebaum, D., 619
Linder-Pelz, S., 261–2
Lindsey, D. B., 440, 444
line managers *see* managerial coaching
Lines, D., 429

lingering, art of, 333–4
Linley, A., 368
Linley, P. A., 74, 207, 227, 363, 364, 365, 368, 370–1, *370*, 372, 596, **597**
Lipchik, E., 285
literary theory, 292–3, **292**
Littman-Ovadia, H., 383
Llewelyn, S., 591–2, 593, 596
Loan-Clarke, J., 691
Locke, E. A., 221–2, 224, 549, 635
Loevinger, J., 123, **124**, **127**
Lofthouse, R., 510
Long, N., 552
long-term perspectives of culture, 442
Louis, M. R., 423
Lowen, Alexander, 263
LPS Cocoon tool, **716**, 718
Luckmann, T., 294
Ludeman, K., 247, 279–0
Luhmann, N., 332
Lukens, R., 149
Lupton, D., 276
Luthans, F., 636, 637
Lyubomirsky, S., 551

Mabey, C., **637**
McCauley, Cynthia D., 122, 123, 127, 164, 195
McCormick, I., 146
McDonald, B., 462
McDowall, Almuth, 314, 315, 316, 317, 550, **598**, **599**, 600, 627–41
McGill, I., 180, 303
McGoldrick, M., 546
McGoldrick, S., 674–5, *675*
McGregor, C., 183–4
McGuire, D., 474
Machin, S., **200**, 210
MacIntyre, A., 50, 51
McKee, A., 225
McKee, R., 293, 295
McKelley, R., 88, 89
McKenna, D.D., 595
McKergow, M., 549
MacKie, D., 144, 151, 152, 366–7, **598**
McLagan, P. A., 470, 472
McLaren, P., 294, 296
McLaughlin, M., **721**, 722
McLean, G. N., 475
McNally, K., 149
McNeill, B., 651
macro-social influences on coaching, 56–8, *57*
Maddi, S., 356
Madison, G., 261, 264–5
Mahon, B. Z., 263
Mahony, M. J., 296
Mainiero, L. A., 425
Mäkelä, L., 463–4
Malone, John W., 166

Maltbia, T. E., 420, 477
managerial coaching
    cross-cultural context, 462–3, 464–5
    human resource development, 474–6
    strengths perspective, 374
    team coaching, 498
managerial coaching discourse, **45**, 50–3, *57*, 680, 683–4
Mancini, A. D., 402, 403
Mankin, D. P., 472
Mann, R., 552
Marianetti, O., 385
Marquardt, M. J., 111
Marques, D., 248
Marsick, V. J., 111–12, 479
Martín-Baró, Ignacio, 179
Marx, Karl, 699
Mascolo, M. F., 33
masculine cultures, 441
Massachusetts Medical Society, 526
maternal emotion coaching (MEC), 406–7, 558
Mattingly, C., 302
Maurer, T. J., 315
Maxwell, Alison, 96, 310–24
Mayer, J. D., 278, 281
MBSR *see* Mindfulness-Based Stress Reduction (MBSR) programmes
Mead, Geoff, 672
Mead, George Herbert, 296
Meadows, S., 525
medical ethics, 700
medical model of psychotherapy, 594–5
meditation, Buddhist, 381, 382–3
Megginson, D., 473
memes, 58
mental health, 405–6
    coach training and education in, 94–6
    of coaching clients, 88–0
    gender and mental health help-seeking, 89–0
    strengths-based coaching, 92–3, 374
    see also psychotherapy
mental programming, 440–1
mental toughness, 356
Mental Toughness Questionnaire (MTQ48), 356
Merkkula Center for Applied Ethics, 700, 706–7
Merleau-Ponty, M., 258, 259
Merriam, S. B., 100–1
meta-analytic theory, **34**
meta-models of psychotherapy, 594–5
meta-theory of coaching, 56–8, *57*
metaphor, 266, 460
methodologies, 32–3
Mezirow, J., 110, 112, 114, 278, 293, 386, 547, 548
Micholt, N., 667
mid-life transitions, 547
Mill, John Stuart, 336, 699, 700
Millard, J. A., 147–8
Miller, C. C., 241

Miller, J.-A., 49
Millward, L., 317, 550
Milner, J., 465
mind–body interconnectedness, 262–3
Mindful Attention and Awareness Scale (MAAS), 382
mindfulness, 262, 381–94
    andragogy, 387–88, 389
    anthropological framework, 389–0, 391–4
    and Buddhist meditation, 381, 382–3
    and coaching, 385–91
    defining, 383–5
    experiential learning, 387, 390
    positive psychoeducation, 390–1
    proactivity, 388–1
    and resilience, 354–5
Mindfulness-Based Stress Reduction (MBSR) programmes, 354, 382, 384
mindfulness meditation practice (MMP), 391, 392
mindfulness training, 354–5
mindlessness, 226, 384
mini-selves, 553
Mintzberg, H., 48, 52
mirroring and paraphrasing, 317, **317**
Miser, A. L., 546, 555–6
Miser, M. F., 546
Mishler, E. G., 302
mixed intervention approaches, 495
MMP *see* mindfulness meditation practice (MMP)
mobile phone apps, **717**
modernism, 25–7, **26**, **27**, 28, 29, 31, 32–3, 37, **37**
Mohammed, S., 241, 243
monetary benefits, 579–0
Montgomery, M. J., 294
Moore, Margaret Ann, 521–37
moral neutrality, 51
moral philosophy, 699
    see also ethics
Moran, D., 354
Morgan, Gareth, 163
Morgan, J., 733
Morgan, T. D., 733
Morin, L., 75, **199**, 209, 211, 478, **598**, **599**, 600
Morris, B., 682
Mortimer, L., 698, 710
Mosco, J., 556, 557
motivation, 392
    of coaches, 73–4, 665
    extrinsic versus intrinsic, 323, **323**
    and learning, 107, 109, 110
    and personality, 635
    psychological assessments, 635
    and relationship coaching, 550
    role of emotions, 277–78
    role of subconscious in, 635
motivational interviewing techniques
    physicians, 537
    relationship coaching, 550
Motsoaledi, L., 239, 249

Moyes, B., 662, 671
MPM *see* multiple-perspective model of coaching research (MPM)
MRI *see* functional magnetic resonance imaging (fMRI)
Mühlberger, M. D., 495
Müller-Stewens, G., 150
multi-rater assessments, 146, 313, 315, **315**, **316**, 637–38, **637**
multiple-perspective model of coaching research (MPM), 69–7, *70*
multiple selves, 553
Multisource Feedback, 577–78
Muzio, D., 734
My360 plus tool, **716**
Myers, Adrian, 26, 589–606
Myers, C. G., 139–40, 141, 150, 151

Nangalia, A., 461–2
Nangalia, L., 461–2
narrative-collaborative practice, 334, 341–2
narrative ethics, 699
narratives, 291–304
    career coaching, 428
    cross-cultural coaching, 460
    and formulation in coaching, 655–6
    humanities, 293–5
    literary theory, 292–3, *292*
    psychology, 295–299
    and resilience, 355–6, *356*
    and strengths, 372
    theory and process of change, 299–2, *300*
National Board of Medical Examiners (NBME), US, 527
National College for School Leadership (NCSL), England, 515
National Consortium for Credentialing Health and Wellness Coaches (NCCHWC), US, 527, 528–1, 535
National Health Service Leadership Academy, UK, 524
natural environments, 266–7
Naughton, J., 2
Neal, M., 733
Neenan, M., 275, 351
Negative Emotional Attractor (NEA) state, 277, 621, 622
negativity bias, 363
Nelson-Jones, R., 544
Nerland, M., 653
Network coaching discourse, **45**, 53–5, 56, *57*
Neugarten, B., 686–7
neural networks, 612
Neuro-Linguistic Programming (NLP), 47, 48, 261–2, 263, 546
neurocoaching, 610
neurons, 611
neuroplasticity, 615–16, **616**
neuroscience, 31–2, 48, 67, 610–23

automaticity versus control networks, **616**, 618
brain organisation, 611–12, *612*
and coaching practice, 615–18, **616**
and coaching research, 613–15, *614*
concerns about use in coaching, 618–0
and emotions, 277
empirical research, 621–3
imaging techniques, 612–13, 622
intentional change theory (ICT), 620–3, **620**
neuroplasticity, 615–16, **616**
opposing domains theory, **616**, 617–18
physiological measures, 613
social reward and threat detection, **616**, 617
neuroticism
and coaching outcomes, 633, 634, 635
and resilience, 349
neurotransmitters, 611
neutral cultures, 442
New Way of Being (NWOB), 265
Newman, D. A., 635
Newnham-Kanas, C., 529
Nezlek, J., **204**
Ngwenya, H., 183
Nicholson, J., 349
Nicholson, N., **424**
Nicolini, D., 652–3, 657
Nicolopoulou, A., 303
Nicotera, A., 510
Niec, L. N., 546
Niederhoffer, K., 355
Niemiec, R. M., 371
NLP *see* Neuro-Linguistic Programming (NLP)
Noer, D. M., 464–5
non-directive stance and feedback, 314
non-judgemental approach
healthcare sector, 537
interculturally-sensitive coaching, 449
nonprofit sector, coaching for social change, 182–3
Norcross, J. C., 593
Nuri Robins, K., 440
nurses
as coaches, 528, 535–6
coaching for well-being and performance, 525–6
leadership development coaching, 524
Nussbaum Martha, C., 275

Oades, L. G., 110, 238, 407–8
Oakley, A., 245
objectivism, **26**
feedback, 318–0, **319**, **320**
O'Brien, K., 556, 557
O'Broin, A., 196, 197–2, **200**, 203, 206, 211–12
O'Connor, Sean, 69, 77, 350, 486–502
OD *see* organisation development
Office of Personnel Management, US, 649
O'Neil, J., 111–12, 479
O'Neill, M. B., 317
online coaching, **716–17**, 722–3

ontological coaching, 261
openness
in coaching relationship, 198
and resilience, 349
Oppenheimer, V. K., 547
opposing domains theory, **616**, 617–18
oppression, 177–2, 187
oppressive contexts, coaching in, 183–4
Ordóñez, L. D., 225, 226
Orenstein, R. L., 101, 264
organisation development, 159–71, *160*, **168**, 472–3
capabilities, 164–6
change, 166–7
culture, 162–4
integrative development, 168–70
strengths perspective, 374
see also human resource development (HRD)
organisational culture, 162–4, 580–1
organisational input-based approach, 145, 146
organismic valuing process (OVP), 368, 411, 412
Orzech, K., 348
Oshry, Barry, 167
Osland, J. S., 456
other-awareness, 665
outcomes of coaching *see* evaluation of coaching outcomes
outdoor therapy, 266
outer direction of cultures, 443
Outhwaite, A., 181
outsider witnessing, 341
OVP *see* organismic valuing process (OVP)

Page, N., 580, 581–2
Palmer, S., **36**, 196, 197–2, **199**, **200**, 203, 206, 211–12, 547, **601**, 682
Pals, J. L., 302
Palus, C., 133
Panchal, S., 547
Pappas, C., 280
paraphrasing and mirroring, 317, **317**
parasympathetic nervous system (PNS), 401, 621, 622
parent ego-state, 667
parents
authoritative parenting, 557
as coaches, 512
coaching in education, 511–12
emotion coaching, 558
relationship coaching, 546, 556–58
values-based parenting, 557
Parker, M., 50
Parker, Polly, 419–29
Parkes, R. C., 218
Parlett, M., 666
Parr, J., 510
particularism, 442
Passarelli, Angela M., 610–23
Passmore, Jonathan, 74–5, 143, 385, 420, 447, 456, 515, 649, 674–5, *675*, 697, 698, 704, 706, 710

Paterniti, D. A., 534
Paterson, F., 508
Patient-Centered Outcomes Research Institute, US, 527
patient coaching, 526–37
Patient Protection and Affordable Care Act (2010), US, 526–7, 528
Patrick, C., 274, 407
Paul, G. L., 740–1
PCT *see* person-centred therapy (PCT)
Pearlman, L. A., 657
pedagogical traditions, 178–1, **178**
peer coaching
    career transitions, 426–7
    in healthcare sector, 524
    students, 514
    teachers, 510–11
peer group supervision, 672–3
peer supervision, 672
Peirce, C., 28
Pelled, L. H., 242–3, *242*
Peltier, B., 246, 709
Pemberton, C., 227, 549, 554
Penn Resilience Programme (PRP), 352
Pennebaker, J., 355
perceived quality of the employee coaching relationship (PQECR) measure, 210, 213
Percival, Thomas, 700
Performance Enhancing Thoughts (PETs), 513
performance mindset, 428
Perls, Fritz, 130
PERMA framework, 352
Perreault, S., 243
Perris, C., 668
Perry, W. G., 122, 688
Person-Centred Practitioners for Social Change, 179
person-centred supervision, 666–7
person-centred therapy (PCT), 179
personal agency, 107–8, 116
personal attributes
    coachees, 72, 206–7
    coaches, 73, 206–7
    and coaching relationship, 74–5, 206–7
personal growth
    and strengths, 366
    and well-being, **347**
personal life systems
    coachees, 73
    coaches, 74
personal models of practice, 652–6
personal resilience *see* resilience and well-being
personal strivings, 220
personality
    and coaching outcomes, 633–4, *634*
    and coaching relationship, 74–5, 206–7
    diversity, 240, 241
    ego-states, 667
    and leadership development coaching, 146–7

    and motivation, 635
    trait theory of resilience, 349
    see also personal attributes; strengths
personality assessments, 314, 315–16, **315**, **316**, 633, 638, 640
    see also psychological assessments
personality discourses, 683
Peters, J., 497
Peterson, C., 364, 365
Peterson, David B., 265, 456–7, 462, 553
Peterson, S. J., 637
Pfeffer, J., 140
phase theory discourses, 686–7
phenomenological investigations, **601**, 603
phenomenology, 258, 259, 260, 294
Phillips, T., 464
philosophical foundation of values, 335–7
phronesis (knowledge why), 334, 685, 686, 688, 689, 691, 692, 732
physical environment, 266–7
physicality, 256–68
    coach–client relationship, 263–5
    conceptual framework, 257–9, **259**
    emotional and psychological state, 262–3
    physical environment, 266–7
    rehearsal and enactment, 265–6
    somatic awareness and integrative practice, 259–2, 264–5
physicians
    as coaches, 528
    coaching for well-being and performance, 525–6
    leadership development coaching, 524
    motivational interviewing techniques, 537
    training in coaching competencies, 536–7
Piaget, Jean, 122, 296, 687
Pinkavova, E., 113
Pitre, E., 33
Pizarro, D., 274, 281
Plaister-Ten, J., 457, 465
planned happenstance theory, 425
Plato, 278, 387, 699
Plum, E., 446
Plumer, P. J., 514
Plunkett, B. L., 477
PNS *see* parasympathetic nervous system (PNS)
Poepsel, M., **721**, 722–3
Pohlman, R. A., 335
Polanyi, M., 28
Porter, T. M., 684
positive education, 386
positive emotion
    and resilience, 352
    and strengths, 368
Positive Emotional Attractor (PEA) state, 277, 621, 622
positive psychoeducation, 390–1
positive psychology, 48, 49, 335, 352–3, 363, 381
positive psychology interventions (PPIs), 365–6

positivism, **26**, 28, 33
Posner, B. Z., 129
post-positivism, **26**, **36**
post-structuralism, **26**
postmodernism, 25–7, **26**, **27**, 28, 30, 31, 32–3, 37, **37**, 683
  critical, 36, **36**
posttraumatic growth (PTG), **403**, 404–5, 411–14
  constructivist self-development theory (CDST), 411
  organismic valuing theory (OVP), 411, 412
  re-authoring, 411–12, 413
  THRIVE model, 413
Posttraumatic Stress Disorder (PTSD), 400–1, 402–3
power discourse, 681
power discourses, 681
power distance, 441, 462
PPIs *see* positive psychology interventions (PPIs)
Practical Inquiry Model, 107, *108*, 117
practical judgement, 685–6
PRACTICE coaching model, 509
practice theories, 652–3, 657
practitioner research, 64, **65**, 739
pragmatism, 28, 31, **36**
preferred representational system (PRS), 263
prescribed standards, 691
presence based coaching, 262
Pretorius, W. M., 668
PricewaterhouseCoopers, 713
Pritchard, James, 159–71
proactivity, 388–1
problem-based learning, 106
process consulting, 165
process models of coaching and goals, 227–1, *228*
Prochaska, J. O., **424**
Proctor, G., 179, 185
profession, coaching as, 729–0, 732–6, *741*
professional coaching associations, 731, 732, 735–6
  codes of ethics, 449, 673, 696, 697, 700, 702–4, **703**, 735
  see also assessment and accreditation
professional ethics, 699–0
Professional Indemnity Insurance, 733
professional learning, 653–4, 655
professional wisdom, 64, *64*
professionalisation, 48, 682, 736
progressive sequencing, 393
ProReal virtual world, **716**, 718
prospect theory, 226
protean careers model, 425, 429
protreptic coaching, 340–1
proxy agency, 108
Proyer, R. T., 372
PRP *see* Penn Resilience Programme (PRP)
PRS *see* preferred representational system (PRS)
Pryor, R. G. L., 224
Psy Expert coaching discourse, **45**, 47–50, *57*, 682–3
psychoanalysis, 2, 44, 48

psychoanalytical discourses, 682
psychodynamic coaching, 48
psychodynamic discourses, 682
psychoeducation, positive, 390–1
psychological assessments, 314, 315–16, **315**, **316**, 627–41
  360-degree assessments, 146, 313, 315, **315**, **316**, 637–38, **637**
  best practice guidelines, 638–0
  culture, 636–7
  emotional intelligence, 635
  features and range of, 628–0, **629**, *630*
  leadership development coaching, 146
  motivational theories, 635
  normative and idiographic assessment, 633
  personality, 633–4, *634*, 638, 640
  scoring and interpretation example, 630–1, *631*, *632*
  strengths-based, 636
  when to use, 632–3, *632*
psychological capital, 636
Psychological Capital Questionnaire (PsyCap), 348, 636
psychological diversity, 240
psychological flexibility, 354
psychological theory, 682–3
psychological well-being *see* resilience and well-being
psychology and narratives, 295–299
psychometrics *see* psychological assessments
psychosocial transition model, **424**
psychotherapeutic supervision models, 665–68
psychotherapy, 2–3, 85–97
  client populations, 87–91
  Collaborative Recovery Model (CRM), 92–3, 353, 374, 407–9, **408**
  common factors, 210, 593, 594
  contextual model, 594
  critical approaches, 179
  embodied countertransference, 265
  emotion focused, 275, 276, 282, 283, 285
  integration with coaching, 91–7
  medical model, 594–5
  meta-models, 594–5
  overlap with coaching, 86–7
  and physicality, 258–1, 260
  process research, 591–5
  versus relationship coaching, 558–0
  training and development, 94–6
PTG *see* posttraumatic growth (PTG)
PTSD *see* Posttraumatic Stress Disorder (PTSD)
Purnell, C., 559–0
purpose in life, and well-being, **347**

Q methodology, 6, 75, 582, **601**, 602
Qin, J., 239

R2 Strength Profiler, 368, **369**
race and ethnicity, 248–1
Radjou, Navi, 171

Raj, M. J., 524
randomised controlled trials (RCTs), 738–1
Rappaport, J., 302
rapport, in coaching relationship, 197–2
rational emotive therapy model, 275, 550
rational pragmatic discourse, 683, 685, 690, 691, 692
rationality, and emotions, 274, 278–1
Rauen, C., 494, 495
re-authoring, 411–12, 413
realism, **26**
Reb, J., 382
recovery, 348
    after traumatic events, 403–4, **403**
    in mental illness, 90–1
    see also Collaborative Recovery Model (CRM)
reductionism, 613, 691
Reed, M. I., 734
reflected best-self exercise, 369
reflective conversations, 385–6
Reflective Judgment Interview (RJI), **127**
reflective learning, 110–11, 114–15
reflective-practitioner concept, 105
reflective skills learning, 685
reflexivity, 182, 333, 688–1
regulation of coaching, 48
rehearsal, 265–6
Reich, W., 258, 260
Reissner, S. C., 182
Reivich, K., 349
relatedness
    group and team coaching, 500–1
    human need of, 392
    and well-being, **347**, 353
relational approaches, career coaching, 426–7, 429
relationship coaching, 544–60
    action planning, 549–0
    with couples, 546, 554–6
    defining, 544–5
    goal-focused approaches, 548–0
    and motivation, 550
    with parents, 546, 556–58
    personal developmental approaches, 547–48
    versus psychotherapy, 558–0
    with single people, 545–6, 552–4
    therapeutic approaches, 550–2
Relationship Coaching Institute, 544, 552
relationship outcomes, 581
relationships
    and career transitions, 426–7
    and communications, 555–6
    developmental, 195–196
    and well-being, **347**, 353
    see also coaching relationship
relativism, 27
Renshall, K., 96
research, 32–3
    multiple-perspective model of, 69–7, *70*
    using neuroscience, 613–15, *614*

practitioner, 64, **65**, 739
trends in, 67–69, *68*, 738–1
see also coaching process research; evaluation of coaching outcomes
resilience and well-being, 346–58
    Acceptance and Commitment Training (ACT), 354, **354**
    after traumatic events, **403**, 404
    asset approaches, 348–0
    cognitive behavioural approaches, 351–2
    definitions and dimensions, 346–48, **347**
    developmental approaches, 349, 351
    hardiness, 356
    mental toughness, 356
    and mindfulness, 354–5
    narrative approach, 355–6, *356*
    positive psychology models, 352–3
    self-determination theory (SDT), 353
    systemic approaches, 349, 350–1
Resilience Enhancing Imagery, 351–2
Resilience Scale for Adults (RSA), 348
resistance to change, 167
Return on Investment (ROI), 579
Revans, R., 170, 673
Rexhaj, B., 296
Ribbers, A., **721**
Richards, J. M., 283
Richardson, G., 351
Riddle, D. D., 141
Ridler Report, 673
Riessman, C. K., 301
Riggio, R. E., 151–2
rights approach to ethics, 700
Rimé, B., 278
ripple effect, 77, 165, 350, 357, 501
risk taking, and goal setting, 226
rites of passage framework, 299–0, *300*
Rivera-McCutchen, R. L., 511
RJI *see* Reflective Judgment Interview (RJI)
Roberson, Q. M., 240
Roberts, R. D., 280
Robertson, J., 508, 510
Rochlen, A. B., 88, 89
Rock, David, 618
Rogers, Carl, 130, 198, 282–3, 410, 412, 666–7, 671
Rogers, J., 100, 101, 284, 314, 316, 339
Röhricht, F., 258
Röhrs, B., 577, 578
role transitions *see* career transitions
role transitions theory, **424**
Roodhouse, S., 691
Rooke, D., 123, 130
Rose, D. S., 637, **637**
Rosen, C., 553–4
Rosenberg, M., 556
Rosha, A., 462–3
Rosinski, Philippe, 250, 440, 444, 445, 453, 455, 456, 458, 460

Rossiter, M., 128, 129, 296, 427
Rousseau, D. M., 424
Rowan, J., 46, 265
Royston, V., 303
Ruona, W. E. A., 472
Russell, K., 266
Russell, R. K., 665
Ryan, R. M., 109, 110, 323, **323**, 392, 553
Ryff, C., 347, **347**

Saakvitne, K. W., 411
Saarni, C., 557
Sachs, J., 279
Said, Edward, 445
Salomaa, Raija, 453–66
Salovey, P, 281
Sampson, J. P., 419
Satir, Virginia, 263
scaffolding, 297–298
scapegoating, 491
SCARF model, 463
scepticism, 182
Schaal, B., 550
Schäfer, J., 349
Schallow, F., 336
Scheel, M. J., 374
Scheier, M. F., 549, 550
Schein, Edgar, 163, 165, 440
Schermuly, C. C., 578, 579
Schleicher, A., 510
Schlossberg, N. K., **424**
Schneider, B., 570, 571
Schnieders, T., 581
Schön, Donald A., 105, 163, 653, 691
schools *see* coaching in education
Schulz, F., **601**, 603
Schwartz, B., 370
Schwartz-Salant, N., 300
Schwenk, G., 96
scientist-practitioner model, 654, 656–7
SCOAP model, 619
Scott, Beverly, 170
Scottish College for Educational Leadership (SCEL), 508
Scoular, A., 74, 207, 227, 596, **597**
script theory, 667
SDT *see* self-determination theory (SDT)
Searle, R. H., 240, 243–5, *244*
Second Life virtual world, **721**, 723
secure attachment style, 551
Segal, Z. V., 385
Sekerka, L., 284
self-acceptance, and well-being, **347**
self-actualisation, 666–7
self-awareness
    of coaches, 206, 446–7, 665
    in healthcare sector, 537
    internally generated feedback, *312*, 317–18, **317**
self-care, 284, 535–6

self-categorisation theory, 243
self-coaching, 714, 715, 723
Self-Compassion Scale, 348
self-concordance theory, 368
self-consistency theory, **319**, 321–2
self-core evaluations, 636
self-determination theory (SDT), 222–3, 388–1, 392, 410–11, 412
    feedback, **319**, 323, **323**
    and goal setting, 72
    learning, 109–10
    resilience and well-being, 353
    strengths, 367–68
self-directed learning, 106–7, **108**, 388
self-efficacy, 107–9, 116
self-enhancement theory, **319**, 321–2
Self-Esteem Scale, 348
self-feedback, **317**, 318
self-help tradition, 180
self-identity theory, 243
self-management, 107
self-monitoring, 107
self-reactiveness, 108
self-reflectiveness, 108, 187
self-reflexivity, 333
self-regulation, 219, 222–3, 275, 550
Seligman, M. E. P., 48, 57, 352, 364, 365
Selman, J. C., 474
Seneque, M., 475, 476
Senge, Peter M., 163, 674
senior leadership team coaching, 497–498, 501
Sennett, R., 684
sequential view of time, 442–3
serotonin, 349
service to community concept, 733
seven conversations model, 671
seven-eyed coaching supervision model, 96, 264, 666, 669–1, *669*
sexual harassment, 248
Shadow, 298
shadow sides, 373
Shanafelt, T. D., 524
Shanley, J. R., 546
Shapiro, C. J., 512
Shapiro, S. L., 392
Sharff Panero, N., 511
Sharma, B., 548
Shatté, A., 349
Shaver, P. R., 551
Shaw, E., 705
Shaw, R., 264
Shepard, Herb, 425
Sherlock-Storey, M., 348, 350
Sherman, G. D., 614
Sherman, S., 682
Sherpa Executive Coaching Survey, 713
Shields, S. A., 279
Shohet, R., 669–0, *669*, 698

Short, E., 514
short-term perspectives of culture, 442
Shoukry, Hany, 176–88
Showers, B., 509, 511
Shull, A. C., 472
Siebert, S. E., 389
Sieler, A., 46, 261, 338
Sills, C., 210
Silsbee, D., 262, 264
Sim, S., 182
similarity–attraction theory, 243
Simpson, R., 246
Singer, J. A., 296
Singh, N.N., 382, 385
single-loop learning, 105
Sinsky, C., 523, 525
six step reframing, 261, 262
Skiffington, S., 48
skills coaching, 143, 212, 488, *489*
Skinner, S., 247
SMART goals, 220, 224, 225, 227, 229, **230**, 232
Smewing, C., 314, 627, 628
Smith, B. W., 348
Smith, D. K., 492
Smith, I. M., 75, **599**, 600
Smith, N., 35–6, **36**, 143, 264, 265, 492, 548, 663, 672
Smither, J. W., 314, 578, 637
SNA *see* Social Network Analysis (SNA)
Snowden, D. J., 458, 465
SNS *see* sympathetic nervous system (SNS)
social action, 186, 187
social change, 332–3
    see also coaching for social change
Social Clock Theory, 686–7
social cognitive theory, 109, 110, 116, 533
social constructionism, **26**, 28, **34**, **36**
    and adult learning, 110, 111
    emotions, 276–7
    feedback, **319**
    and narrative turn, 294
    values, 338–1
social cultural theory, **319**
Social Network Analysis (SNA), 77, 152, 501
social reward and threat detection, **616**, 617
social role supervision models, 668–2
social sector, coaching for social change, 182–3
sociocultural discourses, 682
Socrates, 387, 699
Soft Systems Methodology, 460
SOI *see* Subject–Object Interview (SOI)
Solidarity Coaching programme, 183
Soltis, J., 697
solution-focused coaching, 48, 220, 351–2, 513, 550–1
somatic awareness and integrative practice, 259–2, 264–5
somatic coaching, 260
Sonesh, S. C., 572, 574, **574**, 576, 577, 581, 599, **599**
Sood, Y., 461
Sorell, G. T., 294

Soth, M., 258–1
Soul Guide coaching discourse, 44–6, **45**, 47, *57*
specific cultures, 442
speech acts studies, 601–2, **601**
Speedy, S., 279, 280, 283
Spence, Gordon, 1–19, 73, 110, 218–32, 238, 323, 353, 354–5, 383, 385–6, 392, 399–14, 550
Spinelli, E., 340, 342
spirituality *see* Soul Guide coaching discourse
sponsors, 75–6
sports coaching relationship, 208–9
Stacey, R. D., 30, 228, *228*
stage theory discourses, 687–88
Stajkovic, A. D., 635
stakeholders, 76–7
    multiple, 161–2
Standards Australia, 76
Starkey, Ken, 167
Stasz, C., 648
Stec, D., 729
Steele, D., 551, 552, 553, 554
Stein, N. L., 293
Stelter, Reinhard, 291, 303, 331–43, 494–5, 514, 549, 604, 683, 684
Stengers, I., 657
stereotyping, 449, 456
Sterman, C. M., 262
Stern, L., 181, 664
Sternberg, R. J., 384
Stewart, L. J., 580–1
Stewart, L.J., **597**
Stey, P., 557
Stiles, W. B., 591
Stober, D. R., 87, 410, 534, 595
Stokes, J., 477
Stoltenberg, C. D., 651, 665
Stoneham, D., 260
Stoner, G., 514
stories, 292–3
    see also narratives
Stout-Rostron, Sunny, 238–53, 664
Strang, S. E., **128**
Strawson, G., 302
Strean, W. B., 260
strengths, 363–75
    balance, 372
    benefits and outcomes, 365–7, **367**
    blindness, 373
    coaching contexts, 374
    development models, 371–2, **371**
    identification models, 368–1, **369**
    nature of, 364–5
    positive emotion, 368
    regulation, 370–1, *370*
    self-determination theory (SDT), 367–68
    sensitivity, 373–4
    shadow sides, 373
    weaknesses, 372–3

strengths-based assessments, 636
strengths-based coaching
    career transitions, 374, 427
    education, 374
    mental health, 92–3, 374
Strengths Gym, 374
Strengthscope, 368, **369**
StrengthsFinder 2.0, 368, **369**
strengthspotting, 369, 374
stretch goals, 225
Strong, B., 552
Strozzi- Heckler, R., 257, 260, 265
students
    as coaches, 514
    coaching for success and wellbeing, 374, 512–14
subconscious, role in motivation, 635
Subject–Object Interview (SOI), 113–14, 127, **127**
subject–object relations, 116, 122–3
Sue-Chan, C., **597**, 600
Sue, D., 446
Sue, D. W., 446
Suh, E., 276
Suh, T., 71
Sullivan, N., 42
Sullivan, S. E., 425
summative assessment, 689–0
Sun, B. J., **201**, 212, 213
supervision *see* coaching supervision
surface-level diversity, 241
sustainability, personal, 348
Sutcliffe, K. M., 351
Swailes, S., 691
Swan, E., 245
Swart, C., 303
sympathetic nervous system (SNS), 401, 621, 622
synchronous communication, 717, 719
synchronous view of time, 443
systemic approaches to resilience, 349, 350–1
systemic coaching, 266
systemic model of coaching supervision, 674–6, *675*
systems theory, **36**, 487–91, *488*, *489*, *490*
systems thinking
    and coaching supervision, 674
    and cross-cultural coaching, 454, 457, 458, 460, 465

TA *see* transactional analysis (TA)
Taranovich, Y., **721**
targets, 51–2
    see also goals
Tarpley, N. A., 682
task motivation, 107
task positive network (TPN), 617–18
Taylorism, 50
teachers
    coaching for professional practice, 509–11
    parent coaching, 511–12
    student coaching, 513
Teaching Leaders programme, England, 507–8, 515

team coaching *see* group and team coaching
techne (knowledge how), 685, 686, 687, 688, 691, 692
technology-assisted coaching, 713–25
    blended coaching, 714, 715
    communication media, 714–15, 718–1
    distance coaching, 714, 715, 720–1, **721**, 723
    empirical research, 720–4, **721**, 725
    online coaching, **716–17**, 722–3
    purpose-built tools, 715–18, **716–17**, 719–0, 724
    self-coaching, 714, 715, 723
    synchronicity, 717, 719
    telephone coaching, 713, 715, 718–1, 720–2, **721**, 723
    virtual worlds, **716**, 718, **721**, 723, 724
telephone coaching, 713, 715, 718–1, 720–2, **721**, 723
telepresence robotics, 724
Terblanche, N., 77, 141
Thatcher, Margaret, 488
Theebom, T., 572, 574, **574**, 576, 577, 578
theories-in-use, 36, 105
theory building studies, 591–2, 604
theory of coaching, 35–7, **36**
    development of, 32, 33–5, **34**
therapy *see* psychotherapy
third culture kids (TCKs), 454
third-generation coaching, 341–2
Thomas, D. C., 459
Thomas, Lloyd, 702
Thorn, M. P., 524
Three Approaches to Psychotherapy, 130
THRIVE model, 413
thriving, 348
Tiedens, L. Z., 274
Tillich, P., 300
Timperley, H., 510
Timson, S., 355
Ting, S., 148
Tolle, Eckhart, 129
Torbert, W. R., 123, **124–5**, **127**, 130
Torbrand, P., 494
Torraco, R., 34
Totton, N., 265
Towler, J., 663, 667, 670
Towne, N., 282
TPN *see* task positive network (TPN)
trade, coaching as, 729, 730–2, *741*
training *see* coach training and education
training pedagogical tradition, 178–1, **178**
trait theory of resilience, 349
transactional analysis (TA), 667–68, *668*
transcript analyses, 582
transfer climate, 580–1
transference, 92, 93, 264, 265, 670, 671
transformational coaching, 143, 182, 212, 548
transformational leadership theory, 151–2, 498
transformative learning, 112–15, **115**, 116–17, 278, 548
transitions *see* career transitions
transparency, in coaching relationship, 198

transtheoretical model, **424**, 533
trauma and adversity, 400–2
    actualising tendency, 410
    acute and sub-acute forms of trauma, 401–2
    appropriateness of coaching for, 409–11, 412–13
    biological reactions, 401
    chronic dysfunction, 402–3, **403**
    Collaborative Recovery Model (CRM), 92–3, 353, 374, 407–9, **408**
    constructivist self-development theory (CDST), 411
    delayed reactions, 403, **403**
    enhancement of emotional capacities, 406–7
    mental illness and coaching, 405–6
    organismic valuing theory (OVP), 411, 412
    posttraumatic growth (PTG), **403**, 404–5, 411–14
    Posttraumatic Stress Disorder (PTSD), 400–1, 402–3
    re-authoring, 411–12, 413
    recovery, 403–4, **403**
    resilience, **403**, 404
    THRIVE model, 413
Traut-Mattausch, E., 495
Trenier, E., 374
triangulation, 575
Trompenaars, F., 440, 442, 454–5, 456
Truijen, K. J., 149
trust, in coaching relationship, 198, 203
Trzaskoma-Biscerdy, G., **204**
Tsoukas, H., 705
Tugade, M., 277
Turkle, S., 54
Turner, E., 264
Turner, J. C., 278
Turner, P. S., 476
Turner, V., 294

uncertainty avoidance, 441
unethical behaviour, and goal setting, 226
Universal Integrated Framework, 456
universalism, 442
Usher, R., 178, 188
utilitarianism, 336, 699, 700

Vaartjes, V., 473
Vaden, K. I., 618
Vallen, G., 280
value-based leadership, 337, 342
value-driven management, 335
values, 331–43
    coaching perspectives, 339
    cross-cultural coaching, 457
    existential coaching, 339–0
    and intentionality, 337, **337**
    philosophical foundation of, 335–7
    protreptic coaching, 340–1
    and social change, 332–3
    third-generation coaching, 341–2
    vita contemplativa concept, 333–4

values-based parenting, 557
Values-In-Action Inventory of Strengths (VIA-IS), 335, 368, **369**
van Deurzen, E., 340, 342
van Diemen van Thor, F., 129
van Gennep, A., 294
Van Knippenberg, D., 239
van Nieuwerburgh, Christian, 439–51, 495, 505–16, 705, 706, 710
Van Oosten, Ellen B., 610–23
van Woerkom, M., 149
Vancouver, J. B., 219
Vandaveer, Vicki, 650
Vannini, P., 258
Veage, S., 89
Vecchio, R. P., 246, 247
VIA-IS *see* Values-In-Action Inventory of Strengths (VIA-IS)
Vincent, N., 151
Virgili, M., 354, 385
Virtual Coaching tool, **716**, 718
Virtual constellations tool, **717**
virtual worlds, **716**, 718, **721**, 723, 724
virtue ethics, 699, 701
vita contemplativa concept, 333–4
Vogel, M., 303
Vogus, T., 351
Von Nordenflycht, A., 571
VUCA (volatility, uncertainty, complexity, ambiguity) environment, 419, 422, 453, 458, 459
vulnerability, and patient coaching, 535–6
Vygotsky, L. S., 297, 684, 685

WABC *see* Worldwide Association of Business Coaches (WABC)
Wacker, J., 33
Wageman, R., 492, 496
Wagner, M., 523
WAI *see* Working Alliance Inventory (WAI)
WAIS *see* Wechsler Adult Intelligence Scale (WAIS)
Walsh, F., 552
Walsh, J., 385
Walsh, R., 383
Wampold, B., 210, 593, 594–5, 600, 604
Wanberg, C. R., 348, 573
Warringa, A., **721**
Washington University Sentence Completion Test (WUSCT), **127**
Waskul, D., 258
Wasylyshyn, K. M., 76, 89
Watkins, K. E., 471–2
weaknesses, 372–3
Weber, Max, 279
Webster, F., 681
Wechsler Adult Intelligence Scale (WAIS), 630–1
Weick, Karl E., 167, 168, 170
Weintraub, Joseph R., 164, 165, 475

Welch, D., 374
well-being
    and flourishing approach, 336
    and strengths, 365–6
    see also resilience and well-being
wellness coaching, 527–37
Wells, G., 298
Welman, P., 185
Werner, J. M., 472
Wessler, R., **127**
West, M. A., 491–2
Western, Simon, **36**, 42–59, 176, 180, 181, 182, 188, 314, 604, 682, 683
Whitfield, C., 401–2
Whitley, S., 494
Whitmore, Sir John, 181, 318, 505–6, 549
Whittington, J., 266
Whitworth, L., 262, 263
Whybrow, A., 335, 682
Wilber, K., 260, 604
'Wild West' metaphor, 682
Wildflower, L., 180, 698, 700, 703, 709
willful blindness, 226
Williams, A., 335
Williams, Patrick, 696–710
Williamson, B., 683
Wilson, S. M., 353
Wilson, W., 461
Winnicott, D., 142, 147
Winter, D. A., **230**

Winum, P. C., 462
Witherspoon, Robert, 161
Wolever, Ruth, 521–37
Wong, K., 510
Wood, D, 297
Wood, L.A., 681
Woodcock, C., 303
Woodhead, V., 497–498, 500, 501
work role transitions theory, **424**
workgroup diversity, 241–5, *242*, *244*
working alliance, 198, 210–12, 581
Working Alliance Inventory (WAI), 211, 212
Worldwide Association of Business Coaches (WABC), 702, 731, 735
Worley, C. G., 472
WUSCT *see* Washington University Sentence Completion Test (WUSCT)
Wycherley, I. M., 207

Yalom, I. D., 130, 133, 134
Yanow, D., 705
Ye, R., 464
yoga practice, 382
Young, K. C., 372
Youth Values in Action survey, 513

Zarecky, Alison, 363–75
Zautra, A., 348
Zeus, P., 48
zones of proximal development, 297